THE DECLINE AND FALL OF
THE BRITISH ARISTOCRACY

David Cannadine was born in Birmingham in 1950, and educated at the Universities of Cambridge, Oxford and Princeton. From 1975 to 1988, he was a Fellow of Christ's College, Cambridge, and University Lecturer in history, since when he has taught at Columbia University, New York, where he is now Moore Collegiate Professor of History. He is the author of *Lords and Landlords: The Aristocracy and the Towns, 1774–1967*, *The Pleasures of the Past* and *G. M. Trevelyan: A Life in History*. He is the editor or co-editor of many other books, a member of the Editorial Board of *Past and Present*, a frequent reviewer in Britain and the United States, and a regular broadcaster on radio and television. He divides his time between New Haven, New York, and a summer cottage in Norfolk, and has been described by Sir John Plumb as 'the brightest and liveliest of our young historians, and also the most readable.'

1. *The Marlborough Family*, 1905 by John Singer Sargent.

£6·50

THE DECLINE AND FALL OF THE BRITISH ARISTOCRACY

'No praise can be too high for the skill with which he has stalked his quarry . . . The wealth of examples, the tireless pursuit down trails never previously explored, and the vitality of his writing make his book a major achievement'

Noel Annan, NEW YORK REVIEW OF BOOKS

'Endless anecdotes, facts, names, quotations and statistics are piled up, swept along by a fluent and often witty prose celebrating the demise of an elite world'

Roy Foster, INDEPENDENT ON SUNDAY

'Simon Schama's *Citizens*, Roy Foster's *Modern Ireland*, these mega-books of history have become best-sellers, and now here comes another one, which is virtually certain also to be a best-seller . . . What Cannadine has done is, for the first time, to survey and display the whole grand panorama . . . magnificent and comprehensive, Cannadine has produced a great book, one that is comprehensive in its scope, and of critical importance in understanding how Britain has changed from the era of Gladstone and Lord Salisbury to that of Mrs. Thatcher . . . This is history on the grand scale . . . nobody before has had the audacity, the erudition and the energy to describe, with scrupulous objectivity, every possible aspect of the destruction of an ancient ruling class . . . This is history at its very best. David Cannadine has recorded in one sweeping sequence the greater events and movements that have swayed the destinies of man'

Lawrence Stone, LONDON REVIEW OF BOOKS

'If L. B. Namier and Chips Channon could have mated they might have produced this book. Professor Cannadine's scholarship is deep . . . But there is enough association of noble names with trivial facts to satisfy the most avid reader of gossip columns . . . In general, Professor Cannadine's judgments are penetrating, his facts voluminous, his sense of what is interesting acute'

Roy Jenkins, THE OBSERVER

'Cannadine's forte is to be exhaustive without being exhausting. He is a talented writer who deploys literary stratagems with a staff officer's ingenuity, resource and thoroughness. We are simply not permitted to flag in our enthusiasm, or curiosity, or our appetite for the information which he has marshalled. Right from the first page he gets a button-hold, with one glittering eye cocked on the grand portent of his story and another constantly alert for the graphic detail with which to bring it alive . . . His anatomy of the aristocracy is brought alive through flesh-and-blood examples conveyed with a verve which sometimes

achieves a shock of recognition and sometimes just a shock. There is nothing anodyne about Cannadine'

Peter Clarke, NEW STATESMAN & SOCIETY

'Formidable, enjoyable . . . Professor Cannadine's book is splendid reading'

Michael Bentley, THE SPECTATOR

'How real history should be written: the mixture of dashing judgements and riveting detail'

Michael Foot, THE GUARDIAN

THE
DECLINE AND FALL OF THE
BRITISH ARISTOCRACY

DAVID CANNADINE

PAPERMAC

First published simultaneously in America and Great Britain 1990
by Yale University Press, New Haven, Connecticut

This revised edition first published 1992
by Macmillan General Books in Picador

This edition published 1996 by Papermac
an imprint of Macmillan General Books
25 Eccleston Place London SW1W 9NF
and Basingstoke

Associated companies throughout the world

ISBN 0 333 65218 5

1 3 5 7 9 8 6 4 2

A CIP catalogue record for this book is available
from the British Library

Printed and bound in Great Britain by Mackays of Chatham plc, Kent

In memory of
Harriet Fenella Saffron Cannadine

Born 3 February 1988
Died 19 March 1988

CONTENTS

PART TWO: THE LIGHT OF COMMON DAY

How can I live among this gentle
obsolescent breed of heroes and not weep?
Unicorns, almost,
for they are fading into two legends
in which their stupidity and chivalry
are celebrated. Each, fool and hero, will be an immortal.

The poem from which this stanza is taken, originally entitled
'Aristocrats', was written by Keith Douglas in Tunisia in 1943.
It was occasioned by the death, on active service, of Lt. Col. J.
D. Player, who left £3,000 to the Beaufort Hunt, and also
directed that the incumbent of the living in his gift should be 'a
man who approves of hunting, shooting, and all manly sports,
which are the backbone of the nation.'
(Desmond Graham (ed.), *Keith Douglas: Complete Poems* (1978),
p. 139.)

PREFACE

In 1905, John Singer Sargent, the most celebrated society painter of his time, completed a portrait of the ninth Duke of Marlborough and his family which still hangs in Blenheim Palace.[1] It is a magnificent canvas – vast, formal, splendid, majestic, brilliant, the largest family portrait that Sargent ever painted, the culmination of his great series of country-house commissions, consciously rivalling the master-pieces of Reynolds and Van Dyck. As befits the holder of one of the grandest and most illustrious titles in the land, the Duke appears in the mantle and collar of the Most Noble Order of the Garter. The Duchess wears a black dress, reminiscent of a Van Dyck portrait in the Blenheim collection, and their two sons are clad as if for a painting by Lawrence. The dogs are Blenheim Spaniels, which had been bred on the estate since the eighteenth century. The bust of the great first duke looks down on them, and the Blenheim standard, with its fleurs-de-lis, flies above. Commissioned to hang opposite Reynolds' huge portrait of *The Fourth Duke of Marlborough and His Family* in the Red Room at Blenheim, Sargent's overwhelming painting captures the British aristocracy in the full plenitude of its pomp and power.

Or does it? On closer inspection, the initial impression of splendour and greatness is belied by much of the detail. The ancestral trophies date back to the early eighteenth century: since then, the family history has been at best mundane, at worst notorious.[2] The Duke, for all his Gartered grandeur, looks detached, melancholy and disillusioned. And the Duchess dominates the picture in a way that would never have been permitted in the paintings of earlier centuries. How perceptively Sargent caught the disappointments, the tensions and the anxieties that lay behind this last, and rather implausible, display of patrician magnificence! The ninth duke inherited an estate in parlous financial condition, and recently denuded of many of its finest treasures. In an effort to recoup the family fortunes, he married Consuelo Vanderbilt, the American heiress. But the union was not a success, and they were divorced in 1921. The Duke himself lived the whole of his life in the 'depressing shadow' of aristocratic decline, and 'was always conscious that he belonged to a system which had been destroyed, to a society which had passed away.'[3] Only in the maverick career of his illustrious first cousin, Winston Churchill, was the family's much-diminished claim to greatness reasserted once more.

Thus described, the history of the Dukes of Marlborough during the last one hundred years is emblematic of the decay of the British aristocracy as a whole. As the last quarter of the nineteenth century opened, the traditional, titled, landowners were still the richest, the most powerful and the most well-born people in the country. Today, they retain but a fraction of their once unrivalled wealth, their once unchallenged power, and their once unassailable status; and the few exceptions to that generalization merely demonstrate its essential validity. The story of their decline and fall – one of the greatest, least recognized, and least understood changes in modern British history – forms the subject of this book. In fiction, this journey has often been traced: from Barset to Brideshead, from Wilde to Wodehouse. But the reality is at once more varied and more extraordinary: from death duties to the 'Getty Factor', Lord Rosebery to Lord Carrington, the Hotel Cecil to Happy Valley, the English shires to the trenches of the First World War, the *nouveaux riches* to the *nouveaux pauvres*, the country house to the stately home. It is a broad and arresting subject, at once moving and infuriating, poignant and comical, and this work attempts to deal with it on the scale, and in the manner, that it undoubtedly deserves, but has thus far never properly received.

Strictly speaking, the patrician group that forms the subject of this book encompasses the titular aristocracy, the territorial baronetage, and the landed gentry. But in the interests of variety, I have also used several other terms interchangeably: 'gentry and grandees', 'nobles and notables', 'the titled and genteel classes', 'the territorial élite', and 'the British landed establishment', this last being the phrase that best conveys the geographical spread, the political importance, and the social prestige of the aristocratic class in its soon-to-be ended heyday. There is a further difficulty, inseparable from this subject, which Harold Nicolson once described as 'the habit possessed by eminent Englishmen and Scotsmen of frequently altering their own names.' The young aristocrat who began his parliamentary career as MP for Lanarkshire was known as Lord Dunglass. On inheriting his father's titles and estates, he became the fourteenth Earl of Home. On disclaiming his peerage, he reappeared as Sir Alec Douglas-Home, KT. And after retiring from public life, he returned to the House of Lords as Lord Home of the Hirsel. In general, I have followed Nicolson's practice, 'calling people by the names they possessed at the date of which I am writing' – except in those cases where it would be unnecessarily pedantic to do so, or merely create more confusion.[4]

Although it has taken ten long and eventful years to write this book, I am only too well aware that in many places it merely skims the surface of this vast and varied subject. Each chapter could easily be turned into a volume in its own right, and there are certain topics that are scarcely touched upon at all. But in all conscience, this work is already long enough: other ideas are demanding attention, other books are clamouring to be written, and there is also life to be lived. Meanwhile, it is a great pleasure to acknowledge the many debts I have incurred in the course of writing it. Much of the early work was done while I was a Visiting Member at the Institute for Advanced Study at Princeton in 1980–1, and I am especially grateful to Professor John Elliott for his unstinted kindness and support. An early draft was virtually completed while I was a Visiting Fellow of Berkeley College, Yale University, in 1984–5, and I owe a particular debt of gratitude to the Master, Professor Robin Winks, for so generously placing an office at my disposal. But my greatest institutional debt is to the Master and Fellows of Christ's College, Cambridge, in whose stimulating and civilized surroundings most of the work on this book was undertaken between 1980 and 1988.

My individual and scholarly obligations are no less great. During my years at Christ's, I learned much about the nature and diversity of history from my colleagues, Joachim Whaley, David Lieberman, Barry Supple, Quentin Skinner, David Reynolds and Susan Bayly. Lawrence Stone and Michael Thompson first stimulated my interest in the English (*sic*) aristocracy, and this volume owes much to the inspiration of their pioneering and seminal work. To the extent that this book is informed by a love of life, a desire to reach a broad and non-professional audience, and a determination to re-create the teeming diversity of a vanished world in all its exuberant abundance, I am deeply indebted to the example and the inspiration of Sir John Plumb. Mike Shaw of Curtis Brown has, once again, been the most admirable and excellent of agents. Betty Muirden and the staff of the British Art Center at Yale University were unfailingly helpful when it came to choosing the appropriate illustrations. As both copy editor and picture researcher, Isobel Willetts has provided the sort of expert assistance and unfailing professionalism that most authors only dream of encountering. Colin Hynson has laboured heroically to compile and complete the index. And in his endless forbearance, his imaginative encouragement, and his untiring resourcefulness, John Nicoll has time and again demonstrated why Yale University Press is, quite simply, the best academic publishing house in the world.

My last, and greatest debt, is of a very similar, but also of a very different kind. My wife, Linda Colley, has lived with this monstrous and overbearing enterprise for as long as she has lived with me, and she has contributed more to the making of this book than any other individual. She has neither typed successive drafts of the manuscript, nor made the index. But she has endured uncomplainingly the self-absorption and generally anti-social behaviour inseparable from the creative process. She has improved the content, the argument, the documentation, and the style of the book at many points. And she has never wavered in her belief that it would one day be completed. Nor is that the full extent of my debt to her. The final version of this book was begun amidst circumstances of scarcely believable joy, but was completed at a time of the most terrible grief. Without her life and her love, I should never have known the one, and could not possibly have borne the other.

DNC,
New Haven,
3 February 1990.

The appearance of this book in paperback has given me the opportunity to correct some factual and typographical errors. I am most grateful to reviewers, colleagues and friends for pointing them out.

DNC,
New Haven,
7 September 1991.

LIST OF ABBREVIATIONS

The following abbreviations have been used throughout the notes and occasionally in the text:

A.H.R.	*American Historical Review*
Bateman	John Bateman, *The Great Landowners of Great Britain and Ireland* (4th edn., 1883)
D.N.B.	*Dictionary of National Biography*
Ec.H.R.	*Economic History Review*
Eng. Hist. Rev.	*English Historical Review*
E.G.	*Estates Gazette*
H.C.	House of Commons
H.J.	*Historical Journal*
H.L.	House of Lords
19C	*Nineteenth Century*
P.P.	Parliamentary Papers
P. & P.	*Past & Present*
R.C.	Royal Commission
V.C.H.	*Victoria County History*

A NOTE ON SOURCES

Since the references to each chapter constitute what is in effect a running bibliography, I have dispensed with a separate list of further reading. In each chapter, references are given in full with every first citation, and are abbreviated thereafter. The place of publication is the United Kingdom, unless otherwise stated.

In order to avoid encumbering the text with a excess of citations, I have followed the convention outlined in F. M. L. Thompson, *English Landed Society in the Nineteenth Century* (1963), and have not given specific references to such standard works of reference as *Who Was Who*, *Burke's Peerage*, and G. E. Cokayne, *The Complete Peerage*.

For the same reason, I have not provided explicit citations to John Bateman, *The Great Landowners of Great Britain and Ireland* (4th edn., 1883), when giving figures for the acreage and/or rental of landed estates.

1

PROLOGUE: PRESUPPOSITIONS AND PROBLEMS

A more discriminating 'history from above' [is trying] to catch up with 'history from below'.
(T. Nairn, 'The Glamour of Backwardness', *Times Higher Education Supplement*, 11 January 1985, p. 13.)

The notion that societies are stratified into three separate 'dimensions', of 'class', 'status' and 'power' is thoroughly familiar in the academic literature. But . . . only occasionally is it explicitly adopted as the framework for empirical research.
(W. G. Runciman, *Sociology in its Place* (1970), p. 102.)

In the 1880s, aristocracies everywhere were in decline . . . The nobility were going gradually, and not so gradually, to the wall. In most countries, the expression 'the decline of the notables' fits the decade well enough.
(N. Stone, *Europe Transformed, 1878–1919* (1983), pp. 20, 21, 42.)

Ever since the French Revolution, the shadow of catastrophe had on occasion flitted through English aristocratic minds. About the 1880s, the shadow deepened, and something like the mood of a beleaguered noblesse began to take shape.
(D. Spring, 'Land and Politics in Edwardian England', *Agricultural History*, LVIII (1984), p. 18.)

When seeking for a partner worthy of the delectable Zuleika Dobson, Max Beerbohm created the Duke of Dorset, an aristocratic paragon, endowed with Olympian wealth, rank, and intellect. His inherited possessions were stupendous, his riches were incalculable, his British titles were innumerable, and he was in addition a prince of the Holy Roman Empire and a duke in the peerage of France. As an Oxford undergraduate, he took a First in Mods. and carried off a clutch of university prizes, he was awarded the Garter by the government in instant recognition of a dazzling speech he delivered impromptu in the House of Lords, and he excelled at any human activity to which he turned his hand or his head. Yet for all his youth, his great position, his brilliant attainments, and the splendid prospects that lay before him, the Duke of Dorset was a fallen idol, who drowned himself in a gesture at once utterly magnificent yet totally futile.[1] And, appropriately enough, the novel that related his fictional and fanciful plunge into the River Cherwell was first

2. 'The fullness of his glory and his might', The Duke of Dorset by Max Beerbohm.

published in 1911, the very year that, in reality, witnessed the most successful assault in recent history on the House of Lords – and thus on the hereditary, titled, landowning classes of the British Isles.

This volume may seem to have almost nothing in common with Max Beerbohm's frothy, light-hearted Edwardian fantasy: it is a history book conceived in Cambridge rather than a love story set in Oxford, and it is about a social class rather than a courting couple. Nevertheless, in his fortune and in his fate, the Duke of Dorset may be taken as a larger-than-life exemplar of the people with whom it is concerned: the gentry and grandees, the notables and nobles of the British Isles, as they have lived out their individual and collective lives during the last one hundred years. As late as the 1870s, these patricians were still the most wealthy, the most powerful, and the most glamorous people in the country, corporately – and understandably – conscious of themselves as God's elect. But during the hundred years that followed, their wealth withered, their power faded, their glamour tarnished, and their collective sense of identity and purpose gradually but inexorably weakened. This book seeks to recover and re-create, to evoke and explain, the decline and fall of this once pre-eminent élite, one of the greatest changes to have occurred in modern British history. How, when, and why did this pride of lions decay into a fable of unicorns?

i.   Bias and Intention

E. H. Carr's oft-quoted injunction that you cannot understand works of history without first understanding the historian who writes them is of especial force in the case of this particular book.[2] Anyone who writes at length on such a controversial and contemporary subject as the eclipse the British patrician élite is bound to be both negatively constrained and positively influenced by the prejudices of his outlook and the circumstances of his life. The fact that we historians make a profession of studying past people in past societies does not thereby render us miraculously immune from those same traps of time and temperament, however much we may be trained to recognize them and to correct for them. Moreover, I have written this book with a definite view of modern British history and of modern British historians held firmly in mind. And these, as well as my own background, need some brief exposition.

As a lower-middle-class product of the Welfare State, educated at grammar school and Oxbridge, I come from a social group generally renowned for its conservatism, its deference, its loyalty to hierarchy, and its acquiescence in the status quo. That I should choose to write of those much higher up the social scale than myself is no more (but also no less?) remarkable or significant than the fact that upper-middle-class historians should be among the foremost writers of the lives of the labouring masses.[3] Like them, I can claim no first-hand acquaintance with much of what I write: in this case the management (or sale) of a landed estate, the enjoyment (or loss) of an unearned income, the day-to-day experience (or termination) of country-house life, the wielding (or weakening) of political power. And I must also declare my belief that some of the most attractive and abiding features of life in Britain today are the legacy of those who form the subject of this book – a view that some may find intrinsically distasteful and implausible, and that others may feel makes the general tone far too indulgent and uncritical.

But I have also been described by a prominent historian of political theory as a 'left-wing intellectual.'[4] This may merely imply an excessive range of political sympathies, or a regrettable lack of firm ideological commitment, and if so, it will no doubt be reflected in the pages that follow. More positively, it suggests a determination not to accept individuals and institutions at their own self-evaluation, a refusal that some members of the right ('I have no politics, but I vote

Conservative for the good of the country') may find disconcertingly unattractive. And, at least in part, this book is written very much from such a sceptical standpoint. It is not merely trying to discover what members of the patrician élite thought about themselves in their silver age of vanishing supremacies: it also seeks to understand them better than they could ever possibly have understood themselves. It is concerned to explore the gap between what they thought was happening and what was actually happening; and it tries to lay bare the reality behind the myths that they invented or believed about themselves, rather than merely provide yet further historical validation for them.

In these ways, the subject and content of this work is influenced by me; in other ways, much more important, it is influenced by the prevailing sense of the past that rules in Britain today, and by the current state of the historical art and of the historical profession. To begin with, it is written in dissent from, and in protest against, the present craze for national heritage, which so often misrepresents the substance and seriousness of aristocratic existence.[5] All too frequently, the contemporary cult of the country house depicts the old landowning classes as elegant, exquisite patrons of the arts, living lives of tasteful ease in beautiful surroundings. Of course, there is some truth in this. But as a representation of the totality of patrician existence, it misleads and distorts, by failing to recognize them for what they really were: a tough, tenacious, and resourceful élite, who loved money, loved power, and loved the good life, and who surrendered their once pre-eminent position with feelings compounded of ignorance and awareness, resentment and regret, folly and fortitude, anger and resignation. In their declining years, as in their heyday, they were very interesting, very important, very complex, not always very refined, and not always very agreeable. By thus treating them seriously rather than sentimentally, this book seeks to rescue the British upper classes from the endless (and mindless) veneration of posterity.

In the same way, this work is written in protest against the current fashion in British history writing that stresses continuity at the expense of change.[6] Of course, it is never easy to get the balance right between what is old and what is new in any past age, and it cannot be denied that during the 1960s, 'crisis' and 'revolution' were among the two most over-used words in the historian's vocabulary. But now the fashion has gone too far the other way, and it has become all too common for scholars to claim that nothing important ever actually happened, that there are no great landmarks in our national story. The account unfolded in this book gives only very limited support to such a constipated view of the past. Undeniably, there were elements of continuity and survival in the history of the British patrician classes from the 1880s, and they are given full and substantial treatment here. But taking the period as a whole, the changes overwhelmingly outweigh the continuities, as five centuries of aristocratic history and hegemony were irrevocably reversed in less than one hundred years.

This book is also written in opposition to the increasing fragmentation of Clio's raiment, to what Professor Hexter rightly and disparagingly described as 'tunnel' history, a weakness to which the study of the recent British past is particularly prone.[7] Political history, economic history, constitutional history, and diplomatic history have, during the last thirty years, been joined by social history, urban history, family history, women's history, the history of childhood, the new economic history, and a host of others. Undeniably, these burgeoning and proliferating sub-specialisms have greatly enriched our understanding of the past by drawing attention to sources and subjects hitherto and otherwise neglected. But such sub-disciplinary chauvinism has its dangers, too. Sometimes, it leads to sterile demarcation disputes, inflated claims, and excessive introversion. Even worse, it means that the totality, complexity, and diversity of the unfolding historical process is often completely lost sight of. However imperfectly, I have sought in this book to poke my head above the many specialist molehills, to describe the eclipse of the British patrician classes in its many and manifold guises.

These rather panoramic ambitions are geographical as well as methodological. For this is emphatically a work of *British*, not just of English history.[8] It is the study of the interlocking, interrelated, and interacting élites of England, Ireland, Scotland, and Wales, which had come into being as a supra-national territorial entity during the period from the 1780s to the 1830s, which had survived and prospered during the half-century that followed, but which then gradually fragmented and decayed, and ceased to be what it had once been: a truly British territorial class. In addition, this book also encompasses, where necessary, the British Empire, something that is now lamented even more absent-mindedly than it was created, but that was an integral part of the patricians' world vision from the 1880s to the 1930s. Whether there was a distinctive 'British history' for the middle or for the working classes remains unclear and unproven. But there certainly was for the people at the top.

The history of this extended, supra-national élite, which even in decline encompassed and transcended the confines of the four constituent nations, is a large enough subject, in all conscience. But to obtain a proper perspective, there must also be some broader, external viewpoint. 'Fog in Channel: Continent cut off', has been the prevailing weather condition in which most of us have recently been doing British history. Yet to write of these British gentry and magnificoes without some comparative, continental perspective is both misleading and unwise. Most members of the patrician class also thought of themselves as part of a broader, continental aristocracy, into which they married, and with whom they were at ease in the courts, chancelleries, and country houses of Europe. Moreover, many claims have been made for the 'uniqueness' of the British territorial classes: but all of them implicitly assume continental comparisons that are rarely, if ever, actually made.[9] However speculatively, this book is intended to rectify that omission.

To that extent, the decline and fall of the old order can be understood, analyzed, and explained only by looking beyond it, and by evaluating it with at least some reference to the parallel experiences of similar élite groups in other countries. But in addition, because class formation, class consciousness, and class disintegration do not occur in a vacuum, the eclipse of these notables must also be seen – and in large part explained – in terms of its interaction with other classes and social groups within Britain. In this sense, the history and experience of the British landed establishment can neither be evoked nor explained simply or entirely in terms of itself. Ultimately, the limits to patrician survival were set, not so much by what they themselves were willing and able to do on their own initiative, but rather by what people from other classes allowed them to do. And in the century from the 1880s, they were allowed much less freedom than ever before. To that extent, the social history of this one class must encompass, however sketchily, the societal history of all classes.[10]

Given the scope and ambition of this work, it should now be clear that it is not, and could not be, based primarily on archival sources that have been individually researched. It took Lawrence Stone fourteen years to collect material from the much thinner archives of the much smaller landed élite of Tudor and Stuart England.[11] For one scholar to undertake such an enterprise for the much larger landed élite of nineteenth- and twentieth-century Britain, whose more voluminous papers have survived in far greater abundance, would be quite impossible. Put more positively, it is important to remember that many of these archives have already been plundered by historians, usually looking at single families or counties or individuals or estates. The result has been a massive proliferation, during the last quarter-century, of dissertations, monographs, and articles on different aspects of the decline and fall of the British landed establishment during the last one hundred years.[12] And it is these that provide the essential scholarly base for this present work, as they must for any serious piece of historical writing.

But while this book is dependent on – and appreciative of – the mass of learned literature on the subject, it is also concerned to transcend the very real limitations of such material. Although there is still a great deal more detailed information to be gleaned by this method, it is already clear in some areas that the law of diminishing returns is setting in. But more importantly, the narrow approach that is embodied in such monographic work virtually precludes any appreciation of the broader ebb and flow of the historical process. Studies of individual estates, of the politics of one specific county, or of a particular aristocratic profession, often seem completely un-aware of the diverse totality of patrician life. The purpose of this book is to stand back, and to survey the broader historical landscape, to re-create the greater historical drama of which these detailed case studies are but a small constituent part. As such, the perspective that it offers on the aristocracy is unapologetically that of the parachutist, not the truffle hunter.

The result is that this is essentially a public rather than a private history of the gentry and the grandees. It is not much concerned with the realm of aristocratic emotions, with states of feeling, with sex, marriage, and child-rearing, upper-class style. This is in no sense to belittle the importance of this large and amorphous subject: some very good books have been written on these topics, and more are badly needed. But here these matters are largely left aside. And this means that there is a second realm of patrician life about which this volume has almost nothing to say. There are not many women in this book, and those few who do appear in its pages are usually either adjuncts to men or surrogate men. I fear that this will give the greatest offence to many feminist historians, and for that I can only apologize. There is an urgent need for more women's history of upper-class women.[13] By definition, this book does not provide it. It is concerned with wealth, status, power, and class consciousness, which in this period were preponderantly masculine assets and attributes. And that must be the justification for the seemingly chauvinistic approach I have adopted here.

These are the personal and scholarly biases of which I myself have been aware while I have been working on this book. Like all professional historians, I have sought to make it both as accurate and as objective as possible, viewing my material with (I hope) sympathy and detachment.[14] And, like all works of history, I believe that it says much more about the time *of* which I write than the time *in* which I write, and far more about the people of whom I write than about the person who has actually written it.[15] Nevertheless, in

putting this book together, some degree of personal bias is unavoidable and, to the extent that I am aware of this, I have tried to lay it
bare at the outset.

ii.   Wealth, Status, and Power

So much for the author: but who, exactly, is the book about? To
state the obvious, it is about a large number of people with various
things in common: the grandees and gentry of the British Isles
during the century from the 1880s to our own time. Therein lies the
substance and the significance of the subject; but therein lies the
practical difficulty in dealing with it. Inevitably, some collective
vocabulary must be employed to describe and summarize this mass of
individuals, and some abstract, organizing concepts must be used to
sort the voluminous material that relates to them into some intelligi-
ble order.[16] As such, this book is, of necessity, a monstrous over-
simplification of the richness and variety of the patrician condition.
But that is unavoidable: like any work of history, it summarizes key
features, but does not exhaust realities.[17] More precisely, it seeks to
recover, over time, both the objective circumstances and the subjective consciousness of the British grandees and gentry in their century
of decline and decay, disintegration and disarray.

The best way to recover the objective circumstances of this – or
any – élite is to employ the three approaches to social analysis
devised by Max Weber, and recently reformulated by W. G.
Runciman.[18] The first is to consider the patricians' financial resources: how rich were these people in the days of their economic
pre-eminence, and how, when, and why did their wealth diminish
over time? The second is to look at their social position: in what
ways were they the most high-ranking and illustrious group in the
years of their social supremacy, and how, when, and why was their
unchallenged status subsequently eroded? And the third line of
inquiry is to consider their political activities: how powerful were the
gentry and grandees when they formed the only governing class in
the British Isles, and how, when, and why did they cease to fulfil
these functions? Before explaining how this unrivalled wealth,
supreme prestige, and undisturbed power was undermined, it is
necessary to describe the substance of it during the 1870s, the last
decade of apparently undisputed patrician pre-eminence.

In terms of its objective economic circumstances, the British
landed establishment still formed the country's wealth élite during
the third quarter of Queen Victoria's reign. Individually, most of
them owned estates of at least 1,000 acres, and collectively this meant
that they possessed the overwhelming majority of the land of the
British Isles:

Table 1.1: Land of the British Isles Held in Estates of 1,000+ Acres, c.1880

Country	Number of owners	Total acres owned	% of total land area owned
England	4,736	12,825,643	56.1
Wales	672	1,490,915	60.78
Ireland	3,745	15,802,737	78.4
Scotland	1,758	17,584,828	92.82
Total	10,911	47,704,123	66.14

Source: Calculated from: P.P., H.C., 1876 (335), *Summary of the Returns of Owners of Land in England and Wales . . . And Similar Return for Scotland*, pp. 21, 33; P.P., H.C., 1876 (422), *Summary of the Return of Owners of Land in Ireland*, p. 25.

Here was the statistical support for those who asserted that landownership was highly concentrated in the hands of a few. Indeed, the imperfections and inadequacies of this data are such that they probably overestimate the number of individuals and underestimate the true extent of their dominance. A more accurate figure is probably 4,200 owners for England and Wales, 2,500 for Ireland, and 800 for Scotland, which together comes comfortingly close to those 7,000 families that A. Arnold, reworking these same statistics, claimed owned between them four-fifths of the land of the British Isles in the late 1870s.[19]

Within this relatively homogeneous and monolithic group, it is helpful to provide three sub-divisions. The first, numbering about 6,000 families in the late 1870s, were the small landowners, whose estates were between 1,000 and 10,000 acres, and whose gross rental incomes were between £1,000 and £10,000 a year. They encompassed the local village squire and the commanding county personage, the full-time landowner who lived on his estate and the full-time *rentier* who lived there merely for recreation, a family locally established for centuries, and a newly arrived self-made man. It was at this level that the landed classes shaded most frequently and least perceptibly into other economic groups, and drawing the line is not always easy. Some just below would count in; some just above would not. Towards the lower end of the scale, landowners would possess only one estate and mansion; they would rarely visit London; and they would have only their rents to live off. At the top end of the scale, there might be more than one house and estate, some non-agricultural income, and even a London town house. But overriding these variations was the fundamental fact that the majority owned at least 1,000 acres.

The second group, numbering perhaps 750 families, were the middling proprietors, with estates ranging from 10,000 to 30,000 acres, and with corresponding incomes from £10,000 to £30,000 a year. Again, there were many variations. Some, like the Earl of Hardwicke, had almost all of their holdings consolidated in one county: in this case, 18,900 out of the total of 19,300 acres were located in Cambridgeshire. Others owned estates in several counties, like the Earl of Macclesfield, whose 14,500 acres were divided between Oxfordshire, Staffordshire, and Devon. Some, like Ralph Sneyd, enjoyed extensive non-agricultural income; while others, like Earl Beauchamp, were entirely dependent on their rentals. Many were exclusively English or Irish or Welsh or Scottish owners; others like Sir George Tapps-Gervis-Meyrick owned lands that straddled national boundaries. But whatever the particular circumstances and distribution of their holdings, all these middling proprietors were, economically, great men, rarely tied down to one estate, and all able (though not all willing) to maintain a London house as well. As Bence Jones explained, 'a man who only wanted all the conveniences and comforts that London and the country could give, could have got them for £10,000 a year.'[20]

At the very top of the pyramid were 250 territorial magnates, each with more than 30,000 acres and £30,000 a year to their name. Assuming their land to be worth thirty-three years' purchase, they were all, by definition, millionaires. The majority held estates in many counties (although a few like the Derbys and the Northumberlands maintained very compact holdings), owned at least two great mansions in the country, and boasted a grand London house, in Grosvenor or Belgrave Squares, in Park Lane or Piccadilly. Many were extensively involved in non-agricultural forms of estate exploitation, like mines and docks, markets and building estates, and some, like the Dukes of Sutherland, also maintained massive investments in the Funds and in railway shares. At the very pinnacle of this group were the Dukes of Dorset and of Omnium as they really existed – the twenty-nine prodigiously wealthy super-rich with incomes in excess of £75,000 a year (see Appendix A). These were families like the Buccleuchs, the Derbys, the Devonshires, and the Bedfords, who owned lands in several counties, who sometimes had more country houses than they knew what to do with, and who possessed private art collections almost without rival in the world.

Viewed as an economic class, the gentry and grandees were thus both the wealth élite in that they encompassed most of the richest men in the country, and the territorial élite in that they owned most of the land of Britain. At the very apex, the super-rich among them were undoubtedly worth more than any other group, even the most opulent bankers or financiers. And they were very much a *British* landowning élite, whose supra-national territorial agglomerations transcended the limits of the four constituent nations. Taking the small landowners, the middling proprietors, and the territorial magnates together, it seems clear that, collectively, they owned a greater proportion of the land of the British Isles than had their forebears at any time since the Reformation.[21] Moreover, many of them had benefited very greatly from the Industrial Revolution, while agriculture itself had been very prosperous during the period from the 1840s to the mid-1870s. Not surprisingly, then, land remained the securest way in which to hold wealth. In more senses than one, the patricians who held it so tightly and so monopolistically in mid-Victorian Britain were truly the lords of the earth.

Seen from another perspective, these same people were, in addition, the status élite. In objective terms, they were virtually the sole recipients of those highly esteemed titles of honour that defined and preserved the gradations of society, and their own position at the very top. At the summit of this system came the five ranks of the peerage, recognized by law as the hereditary nobility, and holding privileges denied to commoners. After the extensions, conflations, and rationalizations of the late eighteenth and early nineteenth century, this had indeed become a truly British nobility, as if to parallel a truly British territorial class.[22] In 1880, there were 580 peers, of whom 431 were hereditary members of the House of Lords by virtue of possessing United Kingdom peerages. In addition, there were 7 peeresses in their own right, and 41 Scottish and 101 Irish peers, who were unable to sit in the Lords because they lacked UK titles.[23] Compared with their continental counterparts, their judicial privileges were substantial but their fiscal exemptions nil. But this did not matter: there was no rival to their position at the top of an objective hierarchy of British ranks. As Edmund Burke put it, 'Nobility is a graceful ornament to the civil order. It is the Corinthian capital of polished society.'[24] As the last quarter of the nineteenth century opened, that remained essentially correct: the peerage was still peerless.

Between the peers and the commoners came the baronets, of whom there were 856 in 1880.[25] This, again, was a legally established title, a hereditary knighthood, the holders of which ranked next to the peers in order of precedence. Indeed, many baronets ultimately became peers, and some rose very high into the ranks of the nobility, as with the Dukes of Devonshire and of Marlborough. Originally, as with the peerage, there were separate orders for each kingdom: baronets of England, then Ireland, and finally Scotland were established in the first quarter of the seventeenth century, as a way of raising money for royal coffers. The subsequent union of England and Scotland, and then of Great Britain and Ireland, meant that these separate orders of baronets were superseded – in the manner of the peerage – by one order of baronets of the UK. In law, their privileges were even fewer than those of the nobility. 'It seems a pity,' lamented *Burke's Landed Gentry* in 1883, 'that so important an hereditary order should possess no designating mark of distinction.' But for any ambitious commoner, the title was highly prized.

The third layer of the status rankings of titles of honour were the landed gentry of Great Britain and Ireland. In 1883, there were 4,250 families listed in *Burke*, to which another 250 should be added for cadet branches spawned by other families from the landed gentry, the baronetage, or the peerage. Unlike the peers and the baronets, the landed gentry possessed neither hereditary titles nor legal privileges. But that did not matter: for it was obvious to contemporaries that the landed gentry were for all practical purposes the equivalent of continental nobles, with their hereditary estates, their leisured lifestyle, their social pre-eminence, and their armorial bearings. Even if they did not constitute an order legally speaking, they certainly behaved like one, and were viewed as one by outsiders. The preface to the 1886 edition of *Burke* caught this exactly:

> The landed gentry, the untitled aristocracy of England, Ireland and Scotland, is a class unexampled and unrivalled in Europe, invested with no hereditary generation . . . this class has had, and continues to hold, the foremost place in each county. A right to arms, sometimes of remote antiquity, sometimes of modern acquisition, serves to supply the want of an hereditary dignity, and is the rallying point, around which are collected various members of the family.[26]

Whereas small landowner, middling proprietor, and territorial magnate are class designations, signifying particular gradations of wealth, landed gentleman, baronet, and peer are status designations, signifying precise degrees of rank. But there were other ways in which the high status of the territorial patricians was recognized and expressed. In law, their affairs were ordered by, and were subject to, a variety of arrangements and rules exclusive to themselves, and practised by no other group. They used strict settlement and entail, partly to keep their estates, houses, heirlooms, and titles (if any) together, and partly to ensure that they descended intact in the direct male line. Middle-class people, by contrast, tended to divide their money equally, and had no sense of the elder son's importance in carrying on the line. But for the grandees and gentry, primogeniture ruled: and entail and strict settlement were the means of giving effect to it. As G. C. Brodrick explained, 'it has been a most powerful agent in moulding the sentiment of the class by which the custom of primogeniture is maintained.'[27]

More subjectively, their lives were lived in certain ways, and in accordance with certain attitudes, which also served to mark them off from the rest of the population. They were educated in public schools and sometimes at Oxbridge; they lived in country mansions and town houses. They were of gentle status in that they did not have to work for a living; they were a leisured class in that they had no occupation; and they were usually endogamous in their choice of marriage partners.[28] In the localities, they made up county society, and in London they were the foundation of high society. Gentlemen, by definition, had a safe seat in the saddle, and were very sensitive to matters of honour, precedence, and protocol. In terms of the amount of time and effort they devoted to it, most members of the patrician élite were more interested in spending money than in making it. They possessed a strongly developed sense of liberality and hospitality – of keeping up their position. They were concerned with voluntary service to the state, both locally and nationally, as civilians and as military men. And they accepted, implicitly and absolutely, an unequal and hierarchical society, in which their place was undisputedly at the top.[29]

This was the formal and informal system of status and rank, title and honour, as it existed among the élite in Britain during the early 1870s. Two points stand out most markedly. Once again, as if to parallel the pattern of landholding, this was an essentially *British* status stratum, into which earlier, separate systems from England, Scotland, and Ireland had been integrated and absorbed. Moreover, even by the mid-Victorian period, nearly a century after the beginning of the Industrial Revolution, no new economic or social group had yet come into being that had mounted any significant or sustained challenge to their social hegemony. The members of the titled and genteel classes were not merely the lords of the earth, they were also the stars of the firmament. They boasted unrivalled and unquestioned glamour and prestige. Put another way, almost anybody who was anybody in the British Isles before the 1880s was to be found in one or other of *Burke's* consolidated and systematic guides to the titled and the leisured classes: the *Peerage and Baronetage*, and the *Landed Gentry*.

These notables not only formed the wealth and the status élites of Britain in the 1870s: they were also still very much the governing élite of the nation. Not all of them held important power positions, because the number of notables far exceeded the number of available posts, both nationally and locally. Nevertheless, the majority of

these jobs were indeed held by men of patrician background. Until
the 1880s, the lower house of Parliament was essentially a landowners' club: the majority of MPs were recruited from the British
landed establishment – Irish peers, sons of UK peers, baronets, or
country gentlemen. As late as the 1860s, it was claimed that one-
third of the Commons was filled by no more than sixty families, all
landed, and that three-quarters of all MPs were patricians.[30] The
upper house was even more the monopoly of landowners, and
during the nineteenth century, these hereditary, aristocratic legislators remained at the apex of the power élite. They could throw out
any Commons measure, with the exception of money bills; they
dominated every cabinet directly or through their relatives; they
virtually monopolized important offices like the Foreign Secretary-
ship; and Prime Ministers sat in the Lords for a longer span of time
than in the Commons.

In the same way, national administration and local government
were still dominated by the landed classes in the third quarter of the
nineteenth century. The judiciary, the army, the church, the law,
and the civil service were the favourite occupations of younger sons
who wanted a high status job that perpetuated their patrician position. Most of those who made their way to the top in these
professions were either recruited from, or subsequently drawn into,
the landed-establishment world. In the case of the army and the
church, this link was reinforced by purchase and by property; and in
the case of the home and overseas civil service, by the exercise of
patrician patronage. The ethos of all these great professions was
leisured and amateur, and most of them were rurally-based and
hierarchically organized. In the countryside, too, these grandees and
gentry were still the unchallenged authorities, responsible to no one
but themselves. As owners of great estates, they wielded substantial
private influence, which merely reinforced their public power. The
Lord-Lieutenant was invariably a peer, while the administration and
enforcement of justice was in the hands of the JPs, a self-perpetuating
oligarchy rightly – and significantly – known as the 'rural House of
Lords'.

Until the 1880s, the patricians provided most of the personnel in
most of these power positions. But their political dominance was
more complex and complete than that. In part, this was because of
their success in restricting the agenda of political discussion, largely to
their own advantage.[31] Popular pressure, and demands for major
reforming measures, made little real impact during the first three-
quarters of the nineteenth century. For most of the time, the governing class were able to confine the substance of politics to a limited
number of issues, largely concerned with finance, religion, adminis-

tration, and foreign affairs. But the structure of politics, and especially the personnel of politics, were rarely discussed. Throughout the years from the 1820s to the 1860s, the aristocracy might have liked to believe (or to regret) that they had made many concessions to the forces of change; and no doubt to some extent they had.[32] But in practical terms, these did not amount to much. Their position of dominance was so entrenched, so complete, that their generosity (or cowardice, or foolishness, or self-deception) in making concessions mattered far less than it was commonplace to suppose.

Moreover, this position as the power élite also rested on popular sanction. For the first three-quarters of the nineteenth century, the majority of the population unquestioningly accepted the patricians' right to rule. Landowners had leisure, confidence, experience, expertise: they had time to govern; they were expected to govern. The business of businessmen was business; the business of landowners was government.[33] For generations, and in some cases for centuries, the same gentry and noble families had sent representatives into Parliament. Dynasties like the Derbys, the Bedfords, the Devonshires, and the Salisburys were generally recognized to constitute the great governing families of the realm. To most people, this was the natural order of things: it had been ever thus. As such, these gentry and grandees possessed that most indispensable of all characteristics in a dominant group – the sense shared, not only by themselves but by the populace, that their claim to govern was legitimate.[34] They were not only the lords of the earth and the stars of the firmament: they were also the makers of history.

Such was the British landed establishment as it existed, apparently secure, serene, and unchallenged in the early 1870s, a formidable agglomeration of territory and titles, of power and influence. In terms of its resources, its prestige, and its dominance, it was a truly supra-national class, embracing the whole of the British Isles with its patrician tentacles. In terms of wealth, it probably owned more of the land of the British Isles than ever before. In terms of status, it had largely and successfully preserved its aristocratic exclusiveness, and remained unsullied by the advent of the Industrial Revolution. And in terms of power, it possessed a very unusual degree of influence over both the centre and the periphery and, despite genuine beliefs to the contrary, had in fact made remarkably few concessions to the forces of demos during the previous half-century. To the extent that the gentry and the grandees formed what Tocqueville had celebrated as a liberal élite, it prompts the comment that with such wealth, such status, and such power, they could well afford to be.[35] It was, as Disraeli truly remarked, a time when the world was for the few – and especially for the very few who have been described here.

iii.   Correlation, Comparisons, and Consciousness

The objective circumstances of the British grandees and gentry in
their heyday up to the 1870s, and in their years of decline thereafter,
are most appropriately analyzed in these terms of wealth, status, and
power. Of course, as W. H. Mallock long ago foresaw, there are
genuine difficulties in applying these essentially abstract and water-
tight categories to the messy reality of patrician life:

> The relation that prevails, and indeed has always prevailed in
> England, between birth and riches, between rank, power and
> talent, may not, perhaps, be the most important problem in the
> world; but, excepting Chinese grammar, I doubt if anything is
> more complicated; and judgement on it that even approaches truth
> is as nice a thing as the most delicate chemical compound.[36]

Put more positively, this means that until the 1870s, there was an
exceptionally high correlation between wealth, status, and power,
for the simple reason that they were all territorially determined and
defined. Land was wealth: the most secure, reliable, and permanent
asset. Land was status: its ownership conferred unique and unrivalled
celebrity. And land was power: over the locality, the county, and the
nation. As Trollope made Archdeacon Grantly say: 'Land gives so
much more than the rent. It gives position and influence and political
power, to say nothing about the game.'[37]

Indeed, wealth, status, and power were so closely intertwined in
the case of the British patrician classes that it is virtually impossible
to write of one without mentioning the others. So, until the 1870s,
there was a broad and general correspondence between the hierarchy
of wealth and the hierarchy of status.[38] Of course, there was no exact
fit between small landowners and landed gentry, between middling
proprietors and baronets, or between territorial magnates and the
House of Lords. Some dukes, like St Albans, Leeds, Manchester, and
Somerset, were nowhere nearly as great in wealth as in status.
Among earls, some like Derby, Lonsdale, and Sefton were very rich;
while others like Clarendon, Granville, and Beaconsfield were relatively poor. And some untitled landowners, although mere gentry or
baronets, held acres sufficiently broad to place them among the
territorial magnates in terms of wealth. In England, for example, in
the 1870s, one-quarter of those with incomes from land in excess of
£30,000 a year were commoners: they counted relatively low in
terms of status but relatively high in terms of wealth.[39]

Nevertheless, the system as a whole was sufficiently close to the
ideal type of high correlation between wealth and status to be
credible. In 1880, there were 580 peers. Of these, 450 (over 75 per

cent) owned at least 2,000 acres, and 525 (over 90 per cent) held some land. Only 60 peers (10 per cent) were landless, and between 1832 and 1883, only 9 new landless peers were created.[40] In 1883, there were also 848 baronets, of whom 413 (49 per cent) owned at least 2,000 acres, and it seems reasonable to suppose that between two-thirds and three-quarters owned at least some land. As for the landed gentry, they too were, by definition, territorially based. As *Burke* explained in 1886, 'the tenure of land was, in the olden time, the test of rank and position, and even now . . . it remains the same.' Only one-third of the 4,250 landed gentry held estates of over 2,000 acres. But approximately 90 per cent of those listed in *Burke* owned country seats with smaller estates attached. Altogether, this makes a total of roughly 5,500 landed families who were members of both the status and the economic élites.

Within this group, the hierarchies of wealth and rank corresponded closely enough for the exceptions not to matter, at least before 1880. There may have been some poor dukes; but the majority were very rich indeed. Of the twenty-nine wealthiest landowners in Britain in 1883, twelve were dukes, a majority of their order, including the top five. Indeed, the richest of them all, Westminster, was promoted from his marquessate purely on the grounds of his Olympian wealth. Conversely, but again in accordance with the system, Disraeli, Salisbury, and Lansdowne refused dukedoms on the grounds that they lacked the resources to support the dignity. In general, it was widely accepted that the richer the members of the landed establishment were, the higher their status and titles were supposed to be. In 1873, there were 363 owners of 10,000 acres in England, of whom exactly one-half were peers. But of those who owned 30,000 acres, three-quarters were members of the House of Lords.[41] However the matter is approached, it was land that was the key to riches and status.

What of the connection between wealth and power? Again, it is very close, though not of quite the same kind. Essentially, the landed establishment was an economic élite, from whose ranks the power élite, both nationally and locally, was recruited. The likelihood of office is the most significant index of the relative power of any group and, in Britain before the 1880s, it was much more likely that grandees and gentry would hold office than any other group. They did not *have* to hold office, and many did not do so; but by virtue of their ownership of broad acres, members of the titled and genteel classes boasted an inherited right to compete for access to offices involving administrative duties and public service. Peers were part of the wealth élite because they were great landowners: they were also part of the power élite as hereditary legislators. In the same way, most country gentlemen could, if they wanted to, become both JPs and MPs with a fair degree of ease and assurance. From land to power the line ran, and only very occasionally in the opposite direction, as with Disraeli who, having nearly got to the top of the greasy pole, was obliged to set himself up as a country gentleman. He was a member of the power élite drawn into the wealth élite; but in most cases, the former was recruited from the latter, and not the other way round.

The last fit, between status and power, follows both logically and evidentially from what has just been said. The status élite and the wealth élite were essentially the same people. In the main, the power élite was recruited from the wealth élite. Therefore it was also recruited from the status élite. Again, there was only very rarely an exact fit between dukes as Prime Ministers, peers as cabinet members, and baronets and gentry as MPs. But as a leisured class of high status, it was expected that members of the landed establishment would govern. That was part of the job of having no job. So, although Wellington was the only ducal Prime Minister after 1815, the majority of them came from the Lords rather than the Commons. Trollope's Duke of Omnium was not so much the exception that proves the rule as the ideal type. Most members of the Commons were in fact recruited from gentry, baronets, and relatives of peers. Being a peer was both a power and a status position. From land to status to power the line ran, and rarely the other way.

Until the 1870s, power, prestige, and property were thus exceptionally highly correlated in the patrician élite of the British Isles. The United Kingdom may have been the first industrial nation, but even in the third quarter of the nineteenth century, when Britain was the workshop of the world, it was the country house not the counting house that was still emphatically in charge. Yet if the British landed establishment remained so undisputedly in the ascendant domestically, how did its position compare with that of equivalent continental notabilities? Set beside the titled and landed élites of Europe, were the British patricians rich or poor, glamorous or shoddy, powerful or puny? These are questions that it is easy and necessary to pose; but formidably difficult to answer. For while every country in Europe possessed its own titled–cum–territorial élite, they differed so markedly in their patterns of wealth holding, their systems of status, their exercise of power, and their overall position, that exact comparison is virtually impossible. Nevertheless, to set the British landowning classes in proper perspective on the eve of their decline and fall, the effort must be made.

In terms of territory, it seems likely that the notables owned a greater proportion of the British Isles than almost any other élite owned of almost any other country. At the very bottom of the scale, in European Russia, the holdings of the old territorial establishment, although they amounted to a massive 177 million acres, made up only 14 per cent of the total land area of the nation. In France, there was by the nineteenth century no such entity as a landed interest, less than 20 per cent of the country was actually owned by the old élite, and in 1885, there were fewer than 1,000 estates of 1,000 acres.[42] In Prussia, the *Junkers* owned perhaps 40 per cent of the land, but a large amount of this was in very small holdings of less then 1,000 acres. Likewise, in Spain, while 52 per cent of the country was covered by estates, much of it was made up of insubstantial plots. Compared with the landowning élites of these four countries, the British aristocracy was clearly pre-eminent. Indeed, it seems possible – but not certain – that it was the landowning classes only of Austria, Hungary, and Roumania that could rival the territorial dominance of the British patrician classes in their heyday.[43]

It also seems likely that the British gentry and grandees were, collectively speaking, the wealthiest of the European territorial élites. In part, this was because they came to the most profitable terms with the Industrial Revolution. Britain was, after all, the first nation to industrialize; the patricians themselves owned so much of the land surface; and they were more advantageously placed to exploit the minerals beneath than many continental owners.[44] As a result, there were also more very wealthy grandees. In France, there were hardly any estates in excess of 10,000 acres: a magnate like the Duc de La Rochefoucauld-Doudeauville simply could not compete with the super-rich magnificoes of Britain.[45] In Prussia, most holdings were less than 10,000 acres, and there were a mere five, after the emperor's own, that amounted to 100,000 acres each. Only in Eastern Europe were there to be found those vast accumulations, held by families like Sheremetev and Yusupov in Russia, and Esterhazy, Schwarzenberg, and Lichtenstein in Austria-Hungary, that rivalled, and occasionally surpassed in acreage, the massive empires of the Sutherlands, the Breadalbanes, and the Buccleuchs.[46]

But many of these great European agglomerations included land that was worthless, or was bearing exceptionally heavy debts. Continental agriculture was, in general, much less efficient than British farming, and in addition, many European landowners were far more severely encumbered than were the territorial classes across the Channel. Most *Junker* estates were very heavily mortgaged, and in Russia, chronic indebtedness was endemic.[47] But above all, the British patricians were more efficient and more ruthless in keeping their estates together. The combination of primogeniture and entail meant that family holdings usually passed intact from one generation to another, and were not sub-divided each time there was a succession, as was the case in most of Europe.[48] In France, entail and primogeniture had been abolished at the time of the Revolution, and they disappeared in Spain in 1836. In Russia and Prussia, they were not outlawed, but were very rarely used, and even in Austria-Hungary, the practice was probably less widespread than in Britain.

As a status group, the British patricians were equally pre-eminent in continental terms. In France, titles had been abolished at the time of the Revolution, and were restored in the nineteenth century only for as long as the monarchy itself was restored: thereafter, they had no legal existence, and lacked the legitimating influence of a hereditary sovereign.[49] Elsewhere, by contrast, titles of nobility were so numerous that their prestige was never so great as in Britain. In Prussia, there were already 20,000 titled families in 1800. In Russia, some 20,000 ennoblements took place between 1825 and 1845, and in 1858 there were altogether 600,000 hereditary nobles.[50] In Austria-Hungary, there were 9,000 ennoblements between 1800 and 1914, which brought the total patrician population of the empire to 250,000. And in Italy, there was a massive usurpation and misuse of titles, with the result that there were some 12,000 aristocrats by 1906.[51] Compared with such numerous nobilities, the British peerage was a very small and very exclusive caste indeed, and, even if the baronetage and the landed gentry were also included, it remained an astonishingly tight and tiny status élite.

Why was the British nobility so much smaller, and in consequence, so much more illustrious? In part it was because titles, like territory, were usually sub-divided on the Continent on succession, whereas in Britain, the heir inherited everything. The result was that most European titles proliferated exponentially, and so became correspondingly commonplace and debased. In part, it was also because the system of ranks was, in virtually every other country, much more complex and elaborate than was the case in Britain, which was an added incentive to proliferation. And it was also because most European nations – with the significant exception of Britain – boasted a service nobility, which meant that honours were widely distributed to bureaucrats and military men of humble, non-landed background. As a result, most continental nobilities lacked the territorial base and thus the strict numerical constraints that were so characteristic of the British status stratum.[52] By comparison, the British titular élite was exceptionally difficult to get into, and landed resources were almost invariably necessary. It was thus probably the smallest and the most exclusive in Europe, and was certainly the most strongly based on territorial connection.

As a power élite, the British landed establishment was also un-

usually dominant, both at the centre and in the localities, in government and in administration.[53] In Belgium, the notables had ceased to
provide the governing class by the 1830s. In France, they did not
control the countryside, the national government, or the National
Assembly. In Russia, most of the hereditary nobles stayed away
from their estates, and spent their time in Moscow and St Petersburg. Apart from the army, they played little part in national or
regional administration, preferring to leave it to the parvenu service
nobility.[54] Only in Hungary and in Prussia were the grandees and
gentry powerful in ways that invited comparison with the British
governing class. There, too, they dominated the localities, monopolized the upper houses of both legislatures, and played a major part in
government, in the civil service, and in the army. But they did so in
collaboration with a non-patrician service élite of which there was no
British equivalent, and in each country, the notables were ultimately
the subordinate partners in conservative and essentially absolutist
regimes.[55]

These continental comparisons are necessarily vague, tentative,
and speculative. But some striking conclusions emerge nevertheless.
Compared with the titled and territorial classes of Belgium, France,
Spain, Italy, and Russia, the British landed élite was more wealthy,
more exclusive, and more powerful. And even compared with the
more robust notabilities of Prussia, Roumania, and Hungary, it was
probably richer, was certainly more exclusive, and exercised its
power in a significantly different way. Above all, it was the preponderance of land in the British case that most stands out. It gave them
so much wealth and such territorial pre-eminence. It was virtually
impossible for a non-landed person to obtain a peerage.[56] And it was
the landed élite, not a separate service élite, that was in control of
public affairs. In no other country in Europe were wealth, status, and
power so highly correlated or so territorially underpinned. In addition, the British landed establishment had survived the revolutions of
1789 and 1848 unscathed, while other nobilities had been abolished
and outlawed or had suffered an immense blow to their pride and
prestige. In European terms, the British patricians were almost
certainly the most illustrious and class conscious of them all.

But were they aware of this? Were they themselves conscious that
they belonged to what was, before the 1880s, an unrivalled élite, not
merely in domestic terms, but in comparative terms as well? How –
to pose the question in another way – do we move from the objective circumstances of highly correlated wealth, status, and power, to
the subjective feelings of class consciousness, most memorably described by E. P. Thompson as being when 'some men, as a result of
common experience (inherited or shared), feel and articulate the

identity of their interests as between themselves and as against other men whose interests are different from (and usually opposed to) theirs'?[57] For any social group, the notion of subjective consciousness is even more difficult to deal with than that of objective circumstances, and the British patrician élite is no exception. In terms of wealth, status, and power, the landed establishment may have existed objectively. But subjectively, what sense of themselves and of their order did these people actually share? And what, more negatively, were the limits to and constraints upon such feelings?

In the first place, there were very real limits to what they actually knew about themselves and their class. Even as individuals, many of them did not know how rich they were, how much land they owned, how many titles they possessed, or who all their ancestors were. Like all amateurs, they never knew as much as the experts – even about themselves. And so it inevitably followed that they knew even less in detail about the collective circumstances of their order. When Lord Derby pressed for a government inquiry into the ownership of the land of the British Isles in the 1870s, he was convinced that the notables did not hold much of it, and was much surprised to learn that they did.[58] In the same way, very few grandees actually knew just how many peers sat in the Lords, or precisely how many members of the Commons were part of the patrician élite. The danger, for the historian, in recovering objective circumstances with any real degree of precision, is that it gives the misleading impression that, because this is what we know about them now, this was also what they knew about themselves, then. But that is rarely if ever the case.

In addition, the range of circumstances that these broad categories of wealth, status, and power encompassed was quite astonishingly wide and varied, and this was bound to inhibit any sense of class solidarity and class consciousness. As W. L. Burn once rightly put it, 'the Duke of Omnium and the small squire were half a world apart', and this was something that even the most ignorant patrician could scarcely fail to know.[59] The marginal landowner, eking out his existence on £1,000 a year, was a very different person from the Duke of Westminster, jogging along on his income of nearly £1,000 a day. An untitled gentleman, even if recorded in *Burke*, was in no sense as glamorous as the Duke of Marlborough. And a country squire who did not sit on the bench, and entertained no parliamentary ambitions, was hardly in the same league as the Duke of Devonshire. In addition, there were great variations across the British Isles. In Ireland, Scotland, and Wales, there was a religious divide between owners and tenants that did not exist in England. There were more big estates in Scotland and in Ireland than in

England and Wales. And there were differences between those
owners who had access to non-economic resources and those who
did not, those who were indebted and those who were unencumbered.

Moreover, there were competing and conflicting reference groups
to which landowners might belong. Anglican or Catholic, Whig or
Tory, Irish or English, Free Trader or Protectionist: these were
divisions where aristocrats took different sides, so that sometimes,
over some issues, they had more in common with other people from
different social groups than they had with people from the same
background as themselves. Bernard Cracroft caught this well in his
account of patrician divisions in the House of Commons:

> A and B are cousins, landowners, country members. Both are
> Etonians, both Guardsmen, both have married daughters of peers.
> But one is a member of the Carlton, the other of Brooks's. One is
> a Protectionist, the other a Free Trader. One hugs primogeniture,
> the other thinks that land should be as saleable as a watch. One is
> an enthusiastic defender of the Protestant faith in Ireland, the other
> thinks that the Irish Church would be best swept off the face of the
> earth.[60]

With the British aristocracy, as with any such group, economic and
social categories cannot be effortlessly elided into political parties or
monolithic class consciousness. Over Home Rule or death duties or
any major issue that affected the future of the gentry and grandees,
they were invariably divided as to how to respond.

Even so, during their heyday, and also during their century of
decline, the most important reference group for most notables was
that they belonged – or had once belonged – to the British landed
establishment. For most of the time, they had much more in common with each other (whatever their occasional and sometimes
abiding differences) than with any other social group (whatever their
occasional and sometimes abiding similarities). The forces making
for unity of perception and of interest were very much stronger than
the forces making for diversity, and they were also much more
powerful than those moulding and unifying any other class. As a
result, the gentry and grandees almost invariably shared the same
cast of mind and unspoken assumptions; they looked at the rest of
the people and the rest of the world in a similar way; and they
boasted what Joseph Schumpeter rightly called a 'simplicity and
solidity of social and spiritual position', a simplicity and a solidity
that no other class in Britain could equal or rival.[61] Even when they
sold their estates, or when aristocratic rebels publicly rejected their
class, they almost invariably behaved in ways that made their ori-

gins, their status, and their view of themselves and the world abundantly plain.

But if the British patricians were indeed conscious of themselves as a class, even in decline and decay, what exactly did that class consciousness consist of? To begin with, most of them were roughly but rightly aware that they belonged – or that their forebears had belonged – to an élite of wealth, status, and power. This was rarely more than a general impression; but it was sufficiently plausible, powerful, and pervasive for them to know this meant that they were – or had once been – God's elect. In the words of M. L. Bush, 'landownership, a ruling function, shared ideals and a sense of being socially distinguished from the commonality, made [them] aware that they belonged to the same social order.'[62] They possessed, in short, a collective awareness of inherited and unworked-for superiority. In this very general sense, class consciousness brought together and articulated, subsumed and transcended, great wealth, high status, and supreme power. Hence the study of objective circumstances is also the best way into the rediscovery and evocation of subjective consciousness. For class consciousness was, essentially, the limited but real subjective awareness of the objective circumstances of wealth, status, and power.

In addition, the British patricians were highly conscious of themselves, their families, and their order *in time*. More than any other class, they knew where they had come from, they knew where they were, and they hoped and believed they were going somewhere. This was what Edmund Burke meant when he spoke of 'partnership not only between those who are living, but between those who are living, those who are dead, and those who are yet to be born.'[63] The walls of their houses were adorned with ancestral paintings; the pages of *Burke* and *Debrett* catalogued and chronicled their forebears; their homes were usually in the style of an earlier period. They planted trees that only their descendants would see in full splendour; they granted building leases for ninety-nine years in the confident hope that their grandchildren would enjoy the reversion; and they entailed their estates so as to safeguard them for as long as possible. It may not have mattered much in 1964 to Harold Wilson that he was the fourteenth Mr Wilson; but it no doubt mattered a great deal to Sir Alec Douglas-Home that he was the fourteenth earl.

But as well as being conscious of themselves over time, the British patricians were also the prisoners of time. Whether they liked it or not, whether they knew it or not, and whether they fully understood it or not, it is clear that from the 1880s onwards, their circumstances and consciousness changed and weakened. What is more, the rate of change varied: the very rich survived better and longer than the less well off; the exact chronology of the undermining of wealth, the erosion of status, and the attenuation of power was different in each case; and the dilution of class consciousness, a sense of collective identity, and corporate confidence was subject to a different time scale again. By investigating the decline and fall of the British notables and nobles over one hundred years, it is possible to see the process almost at full stretch. It is the story of the unmaking of the British upper classes, a story that most appropriately begins in the 1880s.

iv. The 1880s: A Troubled Decade

From an international, no less than from a domestic standpoint, it is clear that the members of the titled and genteel classes of Britain were still undeniably in charge and on top in the 1870s. In terms of preferment and prestige, power and property, pride and panache, their position was essentially unrivalled. Yet within the space of one hundred years, they were to be eclipsed as the economic élite, undermined as the most glamorous social group, and superseded as the governing class. Given the strength and resilience of their position during the first three-quarters of the nineteenth century, their subsequent decline and fall will by definition take some explaining – indeed it will take more explaining than is necessary in the case of other less robust élites.[64] It was no simple or straightforward matter. They took an unconscionable time a–dying. There was no single cause of death. But there was, at least, a turning point. For it is clear that the 1880s were the most troubled decade – for the nobles and notables of Britain, no less than for the titled and territorial classes of Europe – since the 1840s or the 1790s.

Across the entire Continent, and among the most illustrious names, there were unmistakable indications that all was not well with the old order. The Lieven mansion on Morskaya in St Petersburg, close to the Winter Palace, where the family had lived for centuries, was rented out to the Italian government. For the same reason, the Hotel de Talleyrand in the Rue Saint-Florentin in Paris was taken over by the Rothschilds. And the Stolberg Palace in Berlin, belonging to a high-ranking family of imperial counts, was sold up to pay gambling debts, and became the grandest hotel in the capital. In France, the Marquis Boni de Castellane married an American heiress, Anna Gould, who brought with her a fabulous, life-restoring dowry of three million pounds. And in Italy, the proliferation of hereditary titles had been so widespread, so corrupt, and so uncontrolled, that the Royal College of Arms was reconstituted in a vain attempt to authenticate and to restrict these cheapened claims to aristocracy and nobility.[65]

These examples are but the merest token of a much broader and deeper patrician malaise, which had appropriately broad and deep causes. The first was the sudden and dramatic collapse of the agricultural base of the European economy, partly because of the massive influx of cheap foreign goods from North and South America and the Antipodes, and partly because of the final and emphatic burgeoning of the fully fledged, large-scale, and highly concentrated industrial economy. The result was that the rural sector was simultaneously depressed and marginalized, and the consequences for the essentially agrarian élite of European landowners were inevitably severe. Across the Continent, agricultural prices and rentals collapsed. In France, the value of land fell by a quarter between 1880 and 1890. In Russia, a special land bank was established in 1885 to prop up the tottering estates of the nobility, but as Chekhov's plays so eloquently demonstrate, it did so with very limited success. And in Prussia, a fund was created by state legislation to take over bankrupt *Junker* holdings. By the end of the decade, many estates were dangerously over-mortgaged, and many *Junkers* were resorting to extraordinary measures of economy and retrenchment, including more rigorous family limitation and – in sheer desperation – sending their daughters into convents.[66]

For the titled and territorial classes, the political and social consequences were also severe. Agricultural depression spawned peasant revolts and nationalist movements in each of the four great polyglot countries: Germany, Russia, Austria-Hungary, and the British Isles. The increasingly prosperous and assertive middle class shaded imperceptibly into the new and fabulously rich international plutocracy. By the last quarter of the nineteenth century, these men were no longer satisfied with mere wealth: they craved both the political power and the social recognition to which they believed their fortunes entitled them.[67] At the same time, urban and industrial growth brought into being a new world of strikes and riots, socialists and anarchists, and working-class political parties. Throughout Europe, there were widespread demands for extensions of the franchise, which were to be conceded during the next two decades, and which fundamentally changed the nature of political life and the balance of political power. In future, it would be numbers and people and organization that would matter, rather than nobles and patricians and patronage. The age of the masses had superseded the age of the classes. At the same time that the economy became global, politics became democratized.

The result was the gradual eclipse of the old order as the dominant force in the legislature and in government. Many patricians could no longer afford a career in public life; many now found it impossible to

get themselves elected to public office. In Germany, the National
Liberal Party contained only a fraction of businessmen in 1878, but
many more ten years later. In France, the nobility had constituted
one-half of the Assembly in 1871, but only one-fifth by 1889.[68] At
the same time, the growth of collectivism meant a decline in individual freedom, and also that the nobles and the gentry could no
longer dominate the state in the way they once had. As Max Weber
rightly noted, bureaucracy was as much the enemy of aristocracy as
was democracy or depression.[69] Perhaps, too, as Joseph Schumpeter
saw later, the flowering of formal, belligerent, jingoistic imperialism
was connected with the need of the old titled and territorial classes to
indulge overseas their atavistic longings for plunder, for glory, and
for dominion, at a time when their wealth, their status, and their
power, and thus their sense of purpose and identity, were being so
massively undermined at home.

In retrospect, at least, it is clear that these major shifts in the
balance of economic, social, and political power portended the end of
the old aristocracies of nineteenth-century Europe. And what was
true for the Continent in general was equally true of the British Isles
in particular. There, too, the world-wide collapse in agricultural
prices meant that estate rentals fell dramatically, and that land values
plummeted correspondingly. As a result, the whole territorial basis
of patrician existence was undermined, and the easy confidences and
certainties of the mid-Victorian period vanished for ever. Land was
no longer the safest or securest form in which to hold wealth, and
this was to remain so for the next seventy years – a long time, even
for aristocrats conditioned to take the long view. Some, indeed,
found their financial position so precarious that they were forced to
begin selling their assets, and this, too, was very much the shape of
things to come during the next half-century and beyond. At the same
time, prodigious, unprecedented plutocratic fortunes were now
being made around the world in business, in industry, and in finance,
which equalled and soon surpassed the wealth of all but the greatest
of the super-rich magnates.

Such was the challenge to landed wealth that was gathering
momentum in Britain during the 1880s. Of course, in the heyday of
the gentry and grandees, land had not only meant wealth, it had also
meant power. But during this troublesome decade, it was people,
rather than property, who wrested the political initiative. The passing of the Third Reform Act in 1884–5 tilted the balance of the
constitution more markedly and more irrevocably than ever away
from notables to numbers, and patrician dominance of the lower
house soon vanished for ever as a result. In England, there were
unprecedented attacks on the great ground landlords, and wide-

spread demands for leasehold enfranchisement. In Wales, there was extensive rural unrest culminating in a tithe war. In Scotland, the crofters were in open rebellion against their landlords. In Ireland, there were demands for the extinction of landlordism and for Home Rule. Everywhere, the owners of land were on the defensive. Even in the counties, the reform of local government meant that the 'rural houses of lords' were swept away. And at the centre, the end of *laissez-faire*, and the rapid growth of government, portended the eclipse of patrician–dominated administration.

These challenges to landed power which became so forceful during the 1880s were accompanied by equally formidable threats to landed status. In the localities, county society was irrevocably weakened, many owners were forced to let or close their houses, and fox-hunting ceased to be a preponderantly patrician pastime. In London, high society was diluted (or, as some claimed, polluted) by the advent of vulgar international plutocrats, American multimillionaires, and Jewish adventurers, who brutally and brashly bought their way in. For the first time, peerages were now regularly bestowed on men of non-landed background, and the honours system ceased to be territorially based, as it had to accommodate and reward the massively expanded imperial and domestic non-patrician bureaucracy. Significantly, it was in that very decade that two new publications began, which between them sounded the death-knell of the old, tiny, concentrated élite of landed wealth, landed power, and landed status: the *Directory of Directors* and *Who's Who*. In the new and more complex world of the late nineteenth century, there was no longer only one undisputed, aristocratic élite.

Internationally and domestically, the writing seemed plainly on the wall for the noble and landowning classes during the 1880s. In Britain, there were three upper-class pessimists who most perceptively read the signs of the times. The first was Lord Salisbury, who in January 1883 published his last essay in the *Quarterly Review* entitled, significantly, 'Disintegration.'[70] It was an outspoken attack on the evils of unbridled democracy, which seemed poised to overwhelm the propertied, patrician polity in which he so ardently believed, and to the maintenance of which he had devoted his public life. Salisbury deeply distrusted the hasty clamour of the popular will, and feared that government in the interests of the working class was the inevitable prelude to anarchy and despoliation. The Whigs who remained in the Liberal party were now, he averred, quite ineffectual. The landowners in Ireland were at the mercy of a disloyal government and a rapacious tenantry. And the House of Lords was the object of almost unprecedented popular attack. The war of the classes, Salisbury concluded, could not be long delayed, and he was all too fearful as to who would be the victor.

" DISINTEGRATION ! "

3. 'Disintegration!' *Punch*, 27 Oct. 1883.

Three years later, Salisbury's gloom was echoed by another commentator, who was equally out of sympathy with what he regarded
as an increasingly radical and hostile world. Although he was never a
major landowner in his own right, Alfred Lord Tennyson spoke as
much as Salisbury with the authentic voice of the landed classes, and
especially for the squires and minor gentry.[71] His socially ambitious
grandfather had built up a modest accumulation in Lincolnshire, and
eventually became a fully-fledged country gentleman at Bayons
Manor. But his eldest son, Tennyson's father, was left only a small
amount of property, and the main estate passed instead to his
younger brother, the poet's uncle, and thence to his descendants, the
poet's cousins. Tennyson remained obsessed by this disinheritance
all his life, and was constantly torn between the competing claims of
revenge and emulation. He was proud to use the family coat of arms.
He set himself up, on his poet's earnings, as a country gentleman in
the Isle of Wight and in Surrey. He behaved very grandly when he
was awarded his peerage in 1884. And he regarded squirearchy and
hierarchy as the ideal form of social organization.

In late 1886, he poured out his feelings about the future fate of the
landowners in 'Locksley Hall Sixty Years After', an impassioned
lament for the gradual passing of the old social order to which he was
so attached, and an attack even more fervent than Salisbury's on the

general doctrine of progress and the democratic tendencies of the age.[72] He lamented the demise of patrician standards of morality and integrity, mourned the passing of the old paternalism, and took issue with the new politics of vulgar demagoguery. On the eve of the Queen's Jubilee, the strident tone of its anguished outrage caused a great stir, and Gladstone, who had actually given Tennyson his peerage, felt moved to reply, pointing out the very great and varied progress that had been made by mankind during the last sixty years.[73] But ironically, his riposte served merely to strengthen Tennyson's case: partly because it showed that it was the lower classes, rather than the patricians, who had benefited most; and partly because even Gladstone was forced to admit that, 'for a series of years', all had not been well for the landlords.

While 'Locksley Hall Sixty Years After' is, essentially, 'Disintegration' in verse, W. H. Mallock's *The Old Order Changes*, which also appeared in 1886, is 'Disintegration' as fiction. Like Tennyson, Mallock was the scion of a minor squirearchical family, which had been established in the West Country since the seventeenth century, and as a young boy, he had adored the intimate, paternal world of the Devonshire gentry.[74] But by the 1880s, he had become convinced that this entire way of life was on the brink of dissolution. In *The Old Order Changes*, he tried to explain why 'aristocracy, as a genuine power, as a visible fact in the world, may not yet be buried, perhaps; but it is dead.' As in his other books, Mallock assembled a country-house party of rather stock characters, who discuss contemporary problems in the manner of Plato's dialogues. The central figure, Carew, is clearly Mallock himself. He is heir to a decayed estate in the West Country, and believes passionately in 'our birthright of rule and leadership'. But, although he is only thirty-five, he feels he has outlived his time. 'If', he remarks at the outset, 'our landed aristocracy ever come to an end, my England will have come to an end also.'[75]

The remainder of the book suggests that the end is indeed not that far off. The general tone of the ensuing discussions is one of 'doubt and bewilderment.' Everywhere, it seems, the influence of the old aristocracy has declined. Their economic might has been eroded and their social standing has diminished. They are no longer the leaders of the nation or of the localities. The estates of many landowners are so heavily mortgaged that they have become, essentially, the hangers-on of the bourgeoisie. High society is now dominated by the vulgar wealth of the new plutocracy. In the Commons, it is the middle classes who have become the dominant voice. The streets of London are swamped by socialist agitators, inciting the workers to riots and revolution, who are motivated by no more than personal bitterness and social envy, and who seek to abolish the House of Lords and outlaw primogeniture. For the representatives of a class so strongly aware of its superior status, its past glories, and its historic functions, these are terrible circumstances to endure, and terrible prospects to face. 'Anger, contemptuous amusement and blank despair' seem the only possible responses.[76]

v. Conclusion: The End of the Beginning

Of course, these three pieces of writing may be easily dismissed as early examples of that carefully cultivated genre of panic, persecution, and paranoia that have characterized the public utterances of the British aristocracy for the last one hundred years. Despite their gloomy forebodings, there was, during the decades that followed, much vigour and resolution, much resourceful resistance, much outright defiance, much adroit adaptation. Nevertheless, in the broader context of continental developments and domestic difficulties, there can be no doubt that they were correct in their central perception that – as Salisbury himself put it – 'things that have been secure for centuries are secure no longer.'[77] They did not understand in detail the economic, social, and political forces that were responsible; and they misjudged the speed at which these developments would work themselves out. But in their hunch that this was the beginning of the end for the traditional territorial classes, they were not mistaken. In the course of the next one hundred years, the lords of the earth would become strangers in their own lands, the stars of the firmament would cease to shine with such unrivalled brilliance, and the makers of history would become, at last and at length, its victims.

Beyond any doubt, the 1880s were the decade when this outcome first became a real and foreseeable possibility, and it is not coincidence that this was the very time when the upper-class pessimists began to complain in earnest, and when even those more robust grandees began to experience nagging doubts and intimations of mortality. In the very middle of that decade, on 23 August 1885, the fifteenth Earl of Derby recorded this entry in his diary:

> This day is the four hundredth anniversary of Bosworth – the foundation of our family greatness. It has been well maintained so far, through many vicissitudes: indeed, we never played a more considerable part than in the last generation, and are still fairly prominent in public affairs. As to wealth, we have more of it than at any former time: but that is the result of chance rather than our work. Will either last?[78]

4. Lord Derby by Harry Furniss.

During that disturbed and anxious decade, there were many such patricians who were peering into the future, and wondering and worrying what it would bring. It is now time for us to follow them on their journey down the marble steps of history into the light of common day.

PART ONE:

INTIMATIONS OF MORTALITY

Great people lived and died in this house;
Magistrates, colonels, Members of Parliament.
Captains and Governors, and long ago
Men that had fought at Aughrim and the Boyne.
Some that had gone on Government work
To London or to India came home to die,
Or came from London every spring
To look at the may-blossom in the park . . .
But he killed the house; to kill a house
Where great men grew up, married, died,
I here declare a capital offence.
(W.B. Yeats, 'Purgatory', in S.F. Siegel (ed.), *Purgatory:
Manuscript Materials Including the Author's Final Text by W.B.
Yeats* (1986), pp. 78–9.)

2

THE EMBATTLED ELITE

The dawning of mass democracy [in 1884–5] brought into being a new sort of popular power which could, if it wished, make the possession of title, money and even land quite irrelevant.
(R. Lacey, *Aristocrats* (1984), p. 133.)

With the [House of] Lords' power of veto went all those claims to . . . leadership which had formerly belonged to the owners of great estates . . . . If Mr Asquith's Resolutions and his Parliament Bill meant anything, they meant that land's political power was on the wane . . . Away with it, and away with . . . aristocracy, too: it had become too old-fashioned to do its work.
(G. Dangerfield, *The Strange Death of Liberal England* (1970 edn.), pp. 40–1.)

From the early 1880s, landowners were attacked by politicians and land reformers in Parliament, in the press, and in a welter of literature on various aspects of 'the land question'.
(D. Reeder, 'The Politics of Urban Leaseholds in Late Victorian England', *International Review of Social History*, VI (1961), p. 413.)

Lloyd George began his political life attacking the landlords . . . His cause, the one programme he remained with throughout his life, was the destruction of the monopoly of land . . . The landlord – there was the enemy. Idle land in the hands of idle men.
(B. B. Gilbert, 'David Lloyd George: Land, the Budget, and Social Reform', *American Historical Review*, LXXXI (1976), pp. 1059, 1062, 1066.)

The [First World] War . . . changed the British aristocracy for ever . . . The belief . . . that proportionately more of their sons died than those of other classes was not just an arrogant illusion. It was true . . . Not since the Wars of the Roses had the English aristocracy suffered such losses as those which they endured during the Great War.
(A. Lambert, *Unquiet Souls: The Indian Summer of the British Aristocracy, 1880–1918* (1984), pp. 186, 188, 205.)

In 1880, the former Conservative Prime Minister, Benjamin Disraeli, predicted that 'the politics of this country will probably for the next few years mainly consist in an assault upon the constitutional position of the landed interest.' By this, he meant both an attack on 'the system of government that now prevails in this country', and also on 'the principles upon which the landed property of this country should continue to be established.'[1] Had he lived a little longer, he would have been the unhappy witness to the widespread fulfil-

ment of both of these prophecies. The passing of the Third Reform
Act in 1884–5, and the Liberal triumph over the House of Lords in
the aftermath of the People's Budget of 1909, meant that the traditional aristocratic constitution was definitely brought to an end. At
the same time, the grandees and gentry came under bitter attack
because of their monopolistic territorial holdings. In England, Scotland, and Wales, the revival of the 'land question' generated unprecedented animosities and anxieties. And in Ireland, the sustained
protests of the agrarian nationalists persuaded successive British
governments that it was the landlords who were the greatest single
cause of rural discontent, and that they should be investigated,
regulated, and encouraged to disappear.

During the last quarter of the nineteenth century, the patricians
were obliged to adjust themselves for the first time to the unfamiliar
and uneasy world of democratic politics and a mass electorate. The
Reform measures of 1832 and 1867 had simply altered and adapted
the old rural, oligarchic and proprietary system. But the Third
Reform Act created a new and very different representational structure for the whole of Great Britain and Ireland, in which the cities
and the suburbs were pre-eminent, and in which a working-class
electorate possessed the dominant voice.[2] Nor was this the only way
in which the Act undermined the old form of aristocratic politics. For
the more representative and democratic the Commons became, the
more anachronistic and unacceptable the House of Lords appeared by
comparison. From 1880 onwards, every Liberal government found
its legislative programme thwarted by the obstructive Conservative
majority in the upper house, and the Lords rejection of Lloyd
George's People's Budget precipitated a final confrontation between the elected and the hereditary chambers. The passing of the
Parliament Act, two years later, did more than curb the peers' legislative veto: it also signified the end of landed society's political
power.

As legislators the patricians were on the defensive: and as landowners they were no less embattled. A series of official inquiries,
undertaken during the 1870s and 1880s, revealed for the first time the
astonishing extent of their territorial monopoly and collective
wealth. This, in turn, led to widespread demands for changes in the
distribution and control of property, and for much heavier taxation
of unearned incomes. At the same time, there was also an unprecedented upsurge in agrarian agitation and protest – in Wales, Scotland, and especially in Ireland. In many parts of the country, tenants
turned against their landlords, frequently refused to pay their rents,
and stridently demanded an end to the system of great estates. In Ireland, successive governments responded by curbing the powers of

the landlords, and by encouraging them to sell their holdings to their
tenants. In the Scottish Highlands, the results were scarcely less
momentous, and in England and Wales, the landowners feared that
their turn would soon come. The culmination of this long drawn-out
struggle came with Lloyd George's 'Land Campaign' of 1912–14,
which briefly threatened to undermine the whole territorial basis of
traditional landed society.

Disraeli's gloomy predictions were thus amply borne out by subsequent events. But not even he foresaw an even greater catastrophe
lying over the twentieth-century horizon, by which so many members of the titled and genteel classes were to be consumed: the First
World War. Despite the unsympathetic and vindictive treatment that
they believed they had received at the hands of successive governments, the young patricians rushed to join the colours in the autumn
of 1914. But the war itself brought death and bereavement in unexpected and unprecedented abundance, as cohorts of young notables were slaughtered on the fields of Flanders and killed on the
beaches of Gallipoli. Not since the Wars of the Roses had so many
aristocrats suffered so much violent death, and thereafter the landed
classes were never the same again. Their self-confidence was permanently undermined by this military catastrophe, and they looked
to the future with grief, with gloom, and with apprehension. Between 1880 and 1914, the world that they had been brought up to
dominate and to control had emphatically turned against them. And
between 1914 and 1918, it was turned completely upside-down.

i.   The End of the Patrician Polity

For the first time in its modern history, the United Kingdom, in
common with most western states, entered the realm of mass politics
in the years from 1880 to 1914.[3] Reactionary aristocrats like Lord
Eustace Cecil and Lord Salisbury believed that 'the full tide of
democracy' had been flowing unabated since the passing of the
Second Reform Act in 1867. But as the last quarter of the nineteenth
century opened, Britain remained essentially a patrician polity. The
electorate was restricted to one-third of all adult males, the vote was
firmly attached to property, and the great territorial magnates still
wielded significant influence in many county and borough constituencies.[4] And as the supreme embodiment of institutionalized aristocratic power and hereditary political privilege, the House of Lords
retained the unchallenged right to veto virtually all legislation initi-
ated in the Commons. Yet within thirty years, the balance of political power was changed dramatically and irrevocably – away from
the patricians and towards the people. For the widening of the

THE OLD STORY.

Red Riding-Hood (*a Rising Power*). "WHAT LARGE EYES YOU'VE GOT!"
The Wolf. "ALL THE BETTER TO SEE WITH, MY DEAR!"
"R.R. "WHAT A WONDERFUL TONGUE YOU'VE GOT!"
W. "ALL THE BETTER TO *PERSUADE* YOU, MY DEAR!"
"R.R. "BUT—WHAT GREAT BIG TEETH YOU'VE GOT!"
W. "NYUM! NYUM!" *To himself*. "ALL THE BETTER TO *EAT* YOU, MY DEAR!"

5. 'The Old Story.' *Punch*,
26 Jan. 1884.

franchise in 1884–5, and the emasculation of the House of Lords in
1910–11, meant that the politics of deference had definitely ended,
and that the politics of demos had emphatically arrived.

The first inklings that the future would see an increasingly 'beleaguered noblesse', overwhelmed by sheer weight of numbers, and
driven on to the political defensive, came with the massive Liberal
victory in the general election of 1880. Like Disraeli, Lord Salisbury
rightly saw this dramatic 'swing of the pendulum' as portending 'a
serious war of [the] classes.' Gladstone's Midlothian Campaign had
plumbed new depths of sensational demagoguery, and in the general
election itself, he had promised (among other things) 'emancipation
and reform' to wild and delirious crowds. The number of votes cast
was greater than in any previous election, and more seats were contested than ever before.[5] Jittery grandees like Lord Brabourne feared
that 'the devouring spirit of democracy' had already arrived, and that

it could not be led or controlled by traditional means. 'We can', observed Lord Warwick apprehensively, 'neither flatter demos nor bribe him.' Earl Percy was even more gloomy, and worried that recent developments amounted to 'a real, though not as yet complete, revolution'. And in essence he was right: for there was much more to come. As Frederick Calvert warned in 1880, the Liberal victory meant that 'all our institutions are on trial' – and in a way that had not been true for nearly half a century.[6]

Inevitably, this put the restructuring of the oligarchic constitution high on the agenda of public discussion and radical demand. No one had seriously expected the Second Reform Act of 1867 to be final, and in 1880 it was widely believed that Gladstone would soon extend the householder franchise from the boroughs to the countryside. Since this would involve a general election soon after, he preferred to bide his time. But in 1883, he passed the Corrupt Practices Act, which significantly limited the power of local constituency notables by curbing the sums that they could spend at election times, by precisely defining irregular and illegal conduct, and by imposing stiff penalties for infringement.[7] As such, this measure also drew renewed attention to the electoral system itself, and as the fourth year of Gladstone's administration opened, the demand for more general parliamentary reform gathered momentum. Within the cabinet, it was strongly urged by the two most radical members, Sir Charles Dilke and Joseph Chamberlain. During the winter of 1883–4, public meetings were held up and down the country at which motions in favour of reform were passed. And in January 1884, a deputation representing 240,000 delegates from every trade union in the land waited upon Gladstone himself.[8]

The outcome was two complementary measures passed in 1884 and 1885, which together made up the Third Reform Act.[9] The first was concerned with the substantial enlargement of the electorate, and essentially extended the householder and lodger franchise from the boroughs to the countryside. As a result, the voting population of the United Kingdom of Great Britain and Ireland was increased from just above three million men in 1883 to nearly six million in 1885, the greatest numerical enlargement of any nineteenth-century reform act. The second measure was concerned with redistribution and with the redrawing of constituency boundaries. More than one hundred and fifty small borough seats were abolished throughout the British Isles, some were redistributed towards the counties, and even more in favour of large towns. The representation of Manchester, Birmingham, Edinburgh, Glasgow, Dublin, and Belfast was significantly increased, and Greater London obtained thirty-nine extra seats. The old county divisions, which had each returned two members, and the large boroughs, which had previously returned three, were done away with, and almost everywhere, single member constituencies were introduced instead.[10]

Of course, these measures did not bring – and were never intended to bring – universal adult suffrage for men, and they were constrained and compromised by many anomalies and anachronisms which were not fully swept away until the Fourth Reform Act of 1918.[11] But they did comprise 'the most substantial package of parliamentary reform in the nineteenth century'. And this 'pacific revolution' was dramatically and irreversibly in the direction of democracy. For the first time ever, the majority of men now enjoyed the vote – approximately 60 per cent. For the first time ever, the majority of the electorate was working class in its social background – certainly two-thirds, and perhaps as much as three-quarters by 1906. And for the first time ever, the landed interest was no longer acknowledged as being paramount – individuals were represented, rather than communities, and large towns at last received the number of MPs proportional to their populations. In short, the whole basis of the representational structure had been fundamentally changed: instead of being an essentially rural system, with urban modifications, it had became an overwhelmingly urban system, with limited rural exceptions.[12]

According to Lawrence Lowell, 'no considerable class in the country' was 'aggrieved' with the general outcome. But the solid gains for the middle and the working classes were very much at the expense of the traditional territorial order. In the countryside, the extension of the vote to agricultural labourers (and to small farmers in Ireland) meant that landed magnates had to work much harder than before to maintain their once dominant position.[13] The creation of many new suburban constituencies might be good for the Conservative party, but 'villa Toryism' was hardly a world in which most patricians felt at home or at ease. In terms of the number of seats and the number of voters, both Scotland and Wales were over-represented, something that did not bode at all well for their Anglo-centric landowners. And this was even more so in Ireland, which retained its 103 MPs when the number should have been reduced to 92, with the result that the native population could 'speak its mind' as never before.[14] By definition, a reform measure that benefited the agricultural labourers, the suburban bourgeoisie, the working-class residents of the inner cities, and the disenchanted inhabitants of the celtic fringe was bound to cause the landowners anxiety. It may not have been fully-fledged democracy; but as Neal Blewett rightly remarked, 'the post-1885 electoral order resembled that of 1960 more than that of 1832.' And as such, it spelt 'the end of the historic [i.e. patrician] House of Commons.'[15]

For all these reasons, Joseph Chamberlain was quite correct to welcome the Third Reform Act as 'a revolution which has been silently and peacefully accomplished.' As he went on to argue, it was not just that there was now 'government of the people, by the people', with 'the majority of the nation' represented 'by a majority in the House of Commons.' It was also that 'the centre of power has been shifted, and the old order is giving place to the new.' Lord Randolph Churchill took the same view, and tried to exploit these new developments by embracing something he defined as 'Tory Democracy'. But as a member of the old order himself, he could not share Chamberlain's confidence about the future. 'Are we', he asked, 'being swept along a turbulent and irresistible torrent which is bearing us towards some political Niagara, in which every mortal thing we know will be twisted and smashed beyond all recognition?'[16] No one knew. But it seemed clear that this 'frightfully democratic measure' boded ill for the grandees and gentry. As the Duke of Northumberland put it in 1908, 'Our ancestors kept the political power of the state in the hands of those who had property.' But their successors 'had destroyed that system, and placed political power in the hands of the multitude, and we must take the consequences.'[17]

Precisely what those consequences might be was made emphatically (and alarmingly) clear, even before the Third Reform Bill itself had become law. In July 1884, the House of Lords deliberately defied the majority in the freely elected Commons, and blocked the government's Franchise Bill (which dealt with the electorate) on its second reading, on the grounds that it was not accompanied by a Redistribution Bill (which would deal with the constituencies). Eventually, a compromise was reached, whereby the Franchise Bill was let through, and a Redistribution Bill soon followed.[18] But between May and October 1884 there was an outbreak of popular agitation against the Lords unprecedented in its scope and intensity since the 'days of May' in 1832. At least 1,500 public meetings were held to protest against the peers' action, including one monster gathering in Hyde Park. A People's League for the Abolition of the Hereditary Legislature was established in London, with over fifty branches. More pamphlets were produced on the subject than in any other year between 1880 and 1895. There were demands that three hundred peers should be created, to ensure the passage of the bill; and in the Commons in November, the radical MP, Henry Labouchere, obtained seventy-one votes in support of his motion that the relationship between the lower and the upper houses should be fundamentally altered.[19]

These attacks on the peers ranged from the constructively critical to the vituperatively hostile. The National Liberal Federation passed

THE GRADUATES OF THE SEVEN SLEEPERS

a resolution condemning 'the habitual disregard of the national will manifested by the House of Lords', and urged that there must be 'an end to the power of the House of Lords to thwart and deny the will of the people.'[20] John Bright proposed the substitution of powers of delay for powers of veto, so that the peers would no longer be a 'permanent obstacle to the will of the nation as represented and freely expressed in the House of Commons.' John Morley suggested that the Lords should be either 'mended or ended.' Joseph Chamberlain claimed that the upper house had obstructed reform for the last one hundred years, and that it was 'irresponsible without independence, obstinate without courage, arbitrary without judgement, and arrogant without knowledge.' One pamphleteer, J. M. Davidson, described the Lords as a 'chamber of robbers', a 'hospital for incurables.' But he was outdone by J. E. Thorold Rogers who, in phrases that anticipated Lloyd George, likened their lordships to 'Sodom and Gomorrah, and to the collective abominate of an Egyptian temple.'[21]

The successful passing of the Third Reform Act effectively brought this agitation to an end. But it had become abundantly clear that a substantial proportion of the Liberal party were bitterly opposed to a second chamber consisting of hereditary legislators of almost exclusively aristocratic background. As one pamphleteer had remarked in 1883, the passing of the First and Second Reform Acts had already called into being 'a power antagonistic to landed and hereditary pretensions', and the further widening of the Commons franchise should 'make the upper house tremble for its very existence.' Lord Rosebery agreed that with 'a strong, powerful and democratic assembly', the House of Lords 'could not remain as it was.'[22] In the general election of 1885, seventy Liberal MPs were returned who were pledged to abolish the upper house altogether. Between 1886 and 1890, Labouchere's annual motions attacking the power and the composition of the Lords regularly obtained more than one hundred and fifty supporters. And the National Liberal Federation made the 'mending or ending' of the upper house a permanent feature of its programme from 1888. As James Bryce perceptively observed, 'the question dealing with the second chamber has been so raised that it cannot again sleep.'[23]

For many Liberals, the passing of the Third Reform Act made the House of Lords seem even more anomalous in an increasingly democratic age. But the Conservative response was an ingeniously inventive attempt to justify the continued existence of the upper house in the new age of mass politics. To this end, Lord Salisbury developed what became known as the 'referendal theory', which sought to put the Lords on the side of democracy, rather than in opposition to it, by reworking traditional notions of feudal responsibility and paternal concern.[24] According to this argument, the House of Lords was not the bastion of exclusive, aristocratic privilege, which its enemies accused it of being: it was on the side of the people, not against them. For if the Commons passed legislation that was unusually contentious, or that had not been fully discussed at the previous general election, then it was the duty of the Lords to reject it, and to compel a dissolution of Parliament, so that the matter could be referred to the electorate as a whole, for public debate and final decision. Viewed from this perspective, the powers of veto possessed by the Lords were not exercised self-interestedly to thwart the people's wishes, but were deployed democratically to ensure that the national will was properly ascertained.

This argument had been first developed at the time of the debates over Irish church disestablishment during the late 1860s. But it was only after Salisbury became leader of the Conservative peers in 1881, that it was fully worked out and articulated. Ever since the days of Wellington, the conventional wisdom had been that the Lords was essentially a leisured and revising chamber. The peers did not seek to thwart the will of the Commons, and governments did not resign if they were defeated in the upper house.[25] But the new referendal theory greatly inflated the pretensions of the peers, with the result that they were far more vigorous and active in the 1880s than they had been for many decades. As landowning legislators, they used their privileged position to amend and to delay Gladstone's Irish Land Bill of 1881, and his Arrears Bill of the following year. And Salisbury opposed Gladstone's Franchise Bill of 1884 on the grounds that it had not been explicitly discussed during the last general election. As he put it in the Lords, 'We are bound as guardians of their interests, to call upon the government to appeal to the people, and by the results of that appeal we will abide.'[26]

But despite the claim that the Lords was 'an instrument for reserving on all great and vital questions a voice for the electors and the people', the referendal theory was a doctrine at once dubious, disingenuous, and dangerous. It implied that the hereditary and unrepresentative peers could challenge the lower house in the name of the nation as a whole, and that the Lords possessed the right to force a dissolution on the Commons – both conventions quite unknown to the British constitution.[27] Moreover, it soon emerged that the only measures the Tory-dominated upper house felt bound to refer to the people were the radical proposals of successive Liberal governments, which showed up their claim of non-partisan concern for the national will as ridiculous humbug. And the admission that the voters were ultimately sovereign meant that the upper house would appear even more vulnerable and unrepresentative, if the electorate

ever upheld the verdict of the Commons rather than the veto of the
Lords. The danger of proclaiming that the peers would never 'set
themselves against the clear and deliberate judgement of the country'
was that they might be forced to abide by that judgement, even
when they did not like it. And this would be even more unfortunate
if the country condemned the powers and the performance of the
Lords themselves – as, between 1909 and 1911, it was effectively to
do.[28]

The election of the last Gladstone government in 1892 meant that
conflict was inevitably renewed between the Liberal Commons and
the Tory Lords; and among the Prime Minister's more radical followers, there were hopes that the peers might now be 'mended or
ended.' But in the aftermath of Home Rule, the Liberals were scarcely in a condition to confront the Lords head on, and the massive
Whig defections meant that the traditional Conservative majority in
the upper house had been even further enlarged.[29] In the autumn of
1893, the peers threw out Gladstone's second Home Rule Bill by an
unprecedented majority of 419 to 41, and thereafter, they destroyed
the Employers Liability Bill, and drastically altered the Parish Councils Bill. By early 1894, Gladstone told the Queen that there was 'not
only a readiness, but even a thirst, for conflict with the House of
Lords' in certain quarters of the party, and the Prime Minister himself looked forward to dissolving Parliament, and to fighting a
general election on the issue of 'peers versus people'. But his years
and his cabinet were against him, and he was forced to resign instead.
Nevertheless, his very last speech in the Commons warned that the
situation in which the Lords defied 'a deliberative assembly, elected
by the votes of more than six million people', could 'not continue'
indefinitely.[30]

When Lord Rosebery took over from Gladstone, in March 1894,
he informed the Queen that at least half of his cabinet were definitely
in favour of unicameral government, and he himself believed that
'with the democratic suffrage we now enjoy, a chamber so constituted [as the Lords] is an anomaly and a danger.' Indeed, to
Rosebery, who had spent all his public life in the upper house,
the prospect of solving the problem of the peers was far more
appealing than vainly trying to give Home Rule to Ireland. But in
this matter as in most others, the new Prime Minister lacked the will
to act. The National Liberal Federation urged him to introduce
legislation for 'the abolition of the House of Lords veto'.[31] But he
showed no inclination to do so, and merely asked the Commons to
propose resolutions proclaiming the preponderant authority of the
lower house – something that they conspicuously failed to do. The
cabinet was divided between reforming or abolishing the Lords,

ministers were more interested in death duties and Home Rule, and by January 1895, the issue had been effectively dropped. In the upper house, the Duke of Devonshire taunted Rosebery with displaying 'so much hesitation, so much doubt, so much vacillation', and during the course of the general election held later that year, he was the only leading Liberal who mentioned the subject at all.[32]

In the short run, the Lords' successful rejection of Home Rule in 1893, which was overwhelmingly endorsed by the victory of the Conservatives and their Unionist allies at the polls in 1895, provided ample vindication for Salisbury's referendal theory.[33] The fact that Gladstone did not enjoy a parliamentary majority among English MPs meant the Lords could plausibly present themselves as the more accurate barometer of public opinion. And according to Salisbury, they were further justified in rejecting Home Rule because such a major alteration to the constitution should not become law without full national discussion and electoral assent:

> The second chamber ... exists ... for the purpose of insisting on delay, and on an appeal to the people whenever an accidental, temporary and unreal advantage is to be used for the purpose of permanently modifying the constitution ... We quite acknowledge that the House of Lords must submit to the will of the nation, but we must have the will of the nation clearly ascertained.

By the end of the decade, Salisbury had come to regard the Lords as the last line of defence against the radical tyranny of single chamber government. If future attempts were made to undermine 'the integrity of the Empire or ... any of our vital institutions', without 'the full and undoubted assent of the people', he felt confident that 'the resistance of the House of Lords' could safely be relied upon. Indeed, it was Salisbury's belief that 'no political force exists in the country which can overwhelm it.'[34]

Thus equipped, with a massive majority in the upper house, with the inflated pretensions of the referendal theory, and with the successful precedent of Home Rule rejection, the patrician leadership of the Conservative party regarded the sweeping Liberal victory at the polls in January 1906 with relative equanimity. As Balfour proudly boasted later that year, whether 'in office or out of office', the Unionists would 'continue to control the destinies of this great empire' from their lofty and impregnable citadel in the House of Lords.[35] And as in the 1880s and 1890s, they still claimed to do so *in the name of the people*. For the Unionists refused to acknowledge the massive Liberal majority in the Commons as an unambiguous expression of the national will. Following his uncle's referendal doctrine, Balfour insisted that the Lords existed, 'not to prevent the people of this country having the laws they wish to have', but to see that those laws were not 'the hasty and ill-considered offspring' of what he dismissed as 'one passionate election.' As he explained to Lord Lansdowne, the leader of the Unionist peers, it was the duty of the upper house to make 'serious modifications in important government measures.' And Balfour believed that the Lords 'may come out of the ordeal strengthened rather than weakened.'[36]

Put more bluntly, this meant that the peers set about sabotaging the Liberal government's legislative programme.[37] But they did so in a manner that was acutely (and self-interestedly) selective. They did not reject measures that directly benefited the working classes, such as the Trade Disputes Act of 1906 and the Factory and Workshops Act of the following year. Instead, they concentrated their opposition on measures that were not generally popular or of only marginal interest. In 1906, they threw out the Plural Voting Bill, and so modified the Education Bill that the government was forced to withdraw it. Thus directly but deviously defied, the Liberals were unsure what to do. The cabinet, like Rosebery's, was divided between those who wanted to end the Lords' veto, and those who wanted to reform its composition. It was too soon to call another general election, and in any case, neither the Education Bill nor the Plural Voting Bill were sufficiently emotive issues on which to base a 'peers versus people' campaign. In the end, the Prime Minister, Campbell-Bannerman, confined himself to warning the Lords and assuring the Commons that 'a way must be found, a way will be found, by which the will of the people, expressed through their elected representatives in this House, will be made to prevail.'[38]

But it was not at all clear how this should be brought about. Some Liberals favoured a drastic reform of the Lords' composition, which would eliminate its Conservative majority and hereditary structure. Others, including Campbell-Bannerman, thought it more politic to adopt John Bright's suggestion, and reduce its powers of veto. In June 1907, the Prime Minister proposed a resolution in the Commons, which urged that the power of the Lords 'should be so restricted by law as to secure that within the limits of a single parliament, the final decision of the Commons must prevail.'[39] The motion was passed by a majority of 432 to 147, but nothing substantial was accomplished, as the Lords subsequently rejected bills concerning evicted tenants in Ireland and smallholdings and land values in Scotland. The replacement of Campbell-Bannerman as Prime Minister by Asquith in the spring of 1908 did not ease the Liberals' plight. Later that year, the Lords threw out the Licensing Bill, and so modified a second Education Bill that once more the government was forced to withdraw it. By the autumn, the prospects seemed

bleak. 'The session is spoilt', recorded Lord Carrington, one of the
few great landowners still loyal to Liberalism. 'Balfour and the Lords
are masters of the situation.'[40]

It was in this context, of a government visibly losing ground in the
country, in large measure because of its inability to carry a substantial part of its legislative programme, that Lloyd George, the Chancellor of the Exchequer, devised his famous People's Budget of
1909.[41] There was no intention, at least initially, of provoking the
Lords into rejecting it. Faced with the need to raise unprecedented
sums to finance Old Age Pensions and to pay for the cost of eight
new Dreadnoughts, the Chancellor had no choice but to increase old
taxes, and devise new ones. Taxation on alcohol, tobacco, motors
and petrol was increased. Death duties were raised to unprecedented
levels, and supertax was introduced for the first time. And there
were a series of new exactions on land: a 20 per cent tax on the unearned increment of land values; an annual duty of one halfpenny in
the pound on the capital value of undeveloped land; a 10 per cent
reversion duty on the benefits to lessors at the termination of leases;
and a mineral rights duty of one shilling in the pound on mining
royalties. In addition, there was to be a complete survey and valuation of all land throughout the country. This was not just a budget
designed to raise money from the rich: it was the landed rich who
were its principal target and victim.[42]

By latter-day standards, these taxes were relatively mild, they
raised less money than they cost to collect, and they were repealed in
1920. But in the summer of 1909, most landowners reacted with self-
righteous indignation and outraged incredulity. Among patrician
politicians, Balfour condemned the budget as 'vindictive, inequitable, based on no principle', while Lansdowne described it as 'a
monument of reckless and improvident finance.' Lord Rosebery,
long since a Conservative in all but name, denounced it as 'not a
Budget but a Revolution, a social and political revolution of the first
magnitude.'[43] Great landowners publicly paraded their new-found
poverty, and made it plain that others would suffer, too. Lord Sherborne gave notice that he would be cutting his estate expenditure,
because 'super-taxation' necessitated 'super-economy.' Lord Onslow
told his tenants that he would have to dismiss all directly employed
labourers, and put work out to contract instead. And the dukes made
a series of speeches that were especially imprudent. Beaufort wanted
the Liberal politicians put in 'the middle of twenty couple of dog
hounds.' Rutland condemned them as 'piratical tatter-demalions.'
And Buccleuch announced that he would be cancelling his annual
subscription of one guinea to the Dumfreis-shire football club.[44]

Even by their supporters, these patrician interventions were widely regarded as unhelpful, unfortunate, and embarrassing. One junior Tory MP, William Joynson-Hicks, 'wished the dukes had held their tongues, every one of them.' But for Lloyd George, these landed laments were a heaven-sent opportunity for him to pillory the whole aristocratic order, and he did so with a bravura display of vituperative demagoguery and memorable phrase-making. He had already dismissed the House of Lords, not as 'the watchdog of the people', but as 'Mr Balfour's poodle.'[45] At Limehouse, in June 1909, he depicted the landowners as idle, greedy, parasitical, self-interested profiteers, as men who enjoyed wealth they did not create, while begrudging help to those less fortunate whose labours had helped to make them rich. 'Oh these dukes', he sighed, 'how they oppress us.' Three months later, in Newcastle, he was even more scathing. Who was governing this country, he asked, the people or the peers? How could 'five hundred... ordinary men, chosen accidentally from among the unemployed' override 'the judgement of millions of people who are engaged in the industry which makes the wealth of the country?' The Lords, he concluded, turning Rosebery's words on their head, 'may decree a revolution, but the people will direct it.'[46]

These speeches enraged the peers, upset the King, and dismayed many of Lloyd George's cabinet colleagues. To describe the House of Lords as five hundred men drawn randomly from the unemployed was as inaccurate as it was unfair: many of its members were both distinguished and hard-working. But there were enough peers who were idle and irresponsible for the label to stick. And at a time when unemployment was one of the great issues of the day, and when it was still widely believed that men were out of work because of their own faults of character, it was a brilliant touch to liken the noblest men in the land to the residuum of wastrels and loafers. By reacting as they did to his budget, the patricians played into Lloyd George's hands. They allowed him to capture the rhetorical initiative, and to depict them as greedy, effete, self-centred anachronisms, whose only concern was with the size of their own pockets, rather than with the national interest or the well-being of the people. More successfully even than Joseph Chamberlain, Lloyd George had toppled the peers from their lofty eminence of invulnerable superiority and effortless assurance. After Limehouse, the House of Lords was never quite the same again. At best, its inmates were emperors whose clothes seemed more than a little threadbare.[47]

Thus insulted and provoked, the Lords decided to reject the budget in November 1909. Although it was against all precedent for the peers to veto a money bill, they did so by 350 votes to 75. And when Lansdowne moved its rejection, he did so in explicitly referendal terms: 'That this House is not justified in giving its consent to the

Bill until it has been submitted to the judgement of the country.'[48] But the argument that the Lords was compelled to refer it to the people because it was a piece of punitive social legislation improperly masquerading as a budget failed to convince. As Asquith observed in the Commons, the peers had rejected the Finance Bill 'not because they love the people, but because they hate the Budget.' And it was an action as reckless as it was shortsighted. For the rejection of the budget made the destruction of the Lords' veto virtually inevitable. But very few Tory peers counselled moderation. One of them, Lord St Aldwyn, felt that 'for the Lords to reject a budget because it hits the "classes" unfairly would . . . give the government a really strong case against the Lords in the country.' And Balfour of Burleigh agreed. 'My Lords', he warned, with what turned out to be ominous prescience, 'if you win, the victory can at most be a temporary one. If you lose, you have altered the position, the power, the prestige, the usefulness of the House.'[49]

Since the government was unable to carry its financial legislation, there was no alternative but to dissolve Parliament, and in January 1910 a general election was fought, explicitly on the issue of the budget and the Lords.[50] The Liberals sought a mandate to pass their Finance Bill and smash the veto, and Asquith repeatedly insisted that the national will, as embodied in the democratically elected House of Commons, must be allowed to prevail within the lifetime of a single Parliament. In his best Limehouse form, Lloyd George denounced the House of Lords as 'broken bottles stuck on a park wall to keep off radical poachers from lordly preserves.' Patrician Tories like Walter Long, Alfred Lyttelton, and Henry Chaplin were regularly shouted down at the hustings, and the Hon. F. W. Lambton was actually stoned in South East Durham. Quite by coincidence, this was also the first general election in which the peers themselves took part in large numbers. But most of them were out of touch with electioneering, and they did their order little credit. Curzon did not endear the peers to the people by claiming that the Commons was dominated by 'passing gusts of popular passion', while the Lords represented the 'permanent sentiment and temper of the British people.' And it was decidedly ill-advised for him to inform the electors of Oldham in his most superior proconsular manner, that 'all civilisation has been the work of aristocracies.'[51]

The result of the election was that the Liberals lost 100 seats to the Unionists, and only retained their parliamentary majority with the support of the Irish Nationalists and the Labour party.[52] The government's position had clearly been weakened, and although it was widely recognized that the electorate had declared in support of the budget, it had not spoken so emphatically about the House of Lords.

THE OLD TROJAN.

LORD LANSDOWNE. "DON'T LUG THAT INFERNAL MACHINE INTO THE CITADEL. THE THING'S FULL OF ENEMIES."
LORD HALSBURY. "I KNOW. THAT'S WHERE MY HEROISM COMES IN."

7. 'The Old Trojan.'
Punch, 2 Aug. 1911.

After a lengthy period of doubt, indecision, and prevarication on the part of the government, the budget was reintroduced in April 1910, and rapidly reached the upper house, where it passed through all its stages in one day, as the peers rather sheepishly let through a measure they had so recently denounced so vehemently.[53] In the same month, Asquith carried three resolutions into the Commons, which were explicitly designed to limit the power of the peers. In future, the Lords could neither amend nor reject money bills, the certification of which was at the discretion of the Speaker. They could reject any other bill from the Commons in two successive sessions, but if it was presented a third time, then it must pass into law. And so as to make the Commons even more the embodiment of the people's will, the lifetime of a full Parliament was to be reduced from seven to five years.

These resolutions were duly embodied in the Parliament Bill, which passed its first reading in the Commons in April 1910, with the support of the Irish and Labour parties. But in the increasingly tense and intransigent atmosphere of what soon became one of the hottest summers on record, it seemed highly unlikely that the peers would be prepared to vote through a measure that would be the instrument of their own permanent emasculation. In the midst of this uncertainty, King Edward VII – who had watched these recent developments with growing anxiety and alarm – died on 6 May 1910.[54] In the hope of averting what threatened to be a major constitutional crisis in the very first year of his reign, his worried and untried successor, George V, called an inter-party conference. But by November, it was deadlocked, and the government was clear that there must now be another general election. Asquith accordingly asked for a second dissolution, but at the same time obtained from the King a secret (and very grudging) undertaking that if the government was returned with an adequate working majority, he would be prepared to create the requisite number of peers to ensure that the Parliament Bill could be passed.[55]

The second general election of the year took place in December 1910. The only significant issue was the House of Lords and the Parliament Bill, and it was generally reckoned that this time, the outcome would be decisive. Lloyd George coined one more memorable phrase, noting that aristocracy was like cheese: 'the older it is, the higher it becomes.' The contest as a whole was fought in an atmosphere of increasing exhaustion, and when the results were in, the position of the parties remained essentially unaltered. In February 1911, the Parliament Bill was reintroduced, and it passed the Commons a second time in May.[56] The Lords allowed it through both its first and its second readings, but wrecked it in committee, and sent it back to the Commons in July. The lower house decisively rejected the Lords amendments, and Asquith now revealed that the King had already agreed to a substantial creation of peers if this was necessary to force the measure through the Lords. Threatened with the swamping of their house by as many as five hundred Liberal peers, the Unionist leadership of Balfour, Lansdowne, and Curzon, which had so recently been so intransigently defiant, promptly capitulated and, with varying degrees of enthusiasm and decisiveness, urged their followers to abstain, so that the measure might be voted through by the existing Liberal peers.[57]

But it soon became clear that this would not be enough to ensure that the Parliament Bill would pass. For while eighty-odd Liberal lords would vote for the bill, and more than three hundred Unionists would abstain, that left one hundred and twenty Tory peers who

were determined to defy Lansdowne and Curzon, and who preferred
to die in the last ditch by voting against a measure they believed
would ruin their House. At Curzon's behest, Lord Newton thereupon set out to persuade forty Unionist peers to vote in favour of the
government's bill.[58] But even at the final debate, on 10 August 1911,
it was not at all clear what the outcome would be. Many so called
'Ditchers' were sceptical of the government's threat to create more
peers, and refused to accept the verdict of the people against the
upper house. But many more peers agreed with the Duke of Devonshire, who could not 'regard the opinions and feelings of a large
number of my fellow-citizens' with 'complete indifference', and
resolved to abstain. In the end, the measure passed the narrow but
definite majority of 131 votes to 114. But most of those in favour
were bishops and recently created peers, rather than authentic grandees, and seven dukes actually voted against. In the words of Roy
Jenkins, 'for the first time in the advance to political democracy
in this country, there was hardly a patrician who would aid the
process.'[59]

As Lloyd George had predicted, the peers had indeed decreed a
revolution, but it was the people who had carried it out. Lord Salisbury's proud claim that 'no political force exists in the country' that
could overwhelm the Lords had been exposed as a hollow boast.
Instead of enhancing the power and prestige of the peers, as Balfour
had confidently and complacently predicted in 1906, their House had
been 'smashed beyond all recognition', and they themselves were
'the victims of a revolution'. But if anything, they were even more
the victims of their own political incompetence and selfish arrogance. As representatives of the hereditary governing class, Balfour,
Curzon, and Lansdowne had not exactly distinguished themselves,
as shortsighted defiance had been followed by indecisive submission.
And in the final vote, the massive phalanx of Conservative and
Unionist peers had divided three ways, which left them defeated,
discredited, and disillusioned.[60] They might, in some cases, retain
great individual wealth, political influence, or personal prestige. But
the belief in their innate superiority, in their collective political
wisdom, in their unique position as the responsible and hereditary
custodians of the national interest, was gone for ever.

As with the passing of the Great Reform Act, the repeal of the
Corn Laws, and the thwarting of Home Rule, the debates in the
Lords on the Parliament Bill ranked as one of the great occasions in
recent British political history. But whereas the peers survived 1832,
prospered after 1846, and enjoyed unprecedented popularity in 1893,
there was no such gain or recovery from 1911. As Lord Balfour of
Burleigh had predicted, their position, their power, their prestige,

and their usefulness were greatly and irrevocably diminished. While the rest of the polity had became more democratic, the veto power of the Lords had seemed increasingly anomalous and indefensible, and all the artifice of Salisbury, Balfour, and Lansdowne, in claiming that it was responsibly and altruistically exercised on behalf of the people, had convinced no one. By the passing of the Parliament Act, the House of Lords was effectively emasculated, and the advent of Labour as the second party in the state only marginalized it still further in the inter-war years. But it was 1911 that had been the great turning point. At the behest of Lloyd George, the people's trumpet had sounded, and though the blast had been a little uncertain, the citadel of patrician pre-eminence had finally fallen. Symbolically, and substantively, the political power of traditional landed society had been broken for good.[61]

ii. The Assault on 'Landlordism'

The 'war of [the] classes', to which Salisbury so presciently drew attention in the spring of 1880, was not confined to the battles over the extension of the franchise and the ending of the Lords' powers of veto. It also concerned what Disraeli had described as the principles on which the holding and ownership of land would in future be based. During the 1840s, at the time of the Anti-Corn Law League, there had been widespread agitation, led by Cobden and Bright, against the excessive concentration of landed property in the hands of a few patrician owners, and against the law of primogeniture and the practice of strict settlement, which were held to be responsible.[62] But it was mainly confined to England, and the demand for 'Free Trade in Land' was far less popular than that for free trade in corn. But during the last quarter of the nineteenth century, 'the land question' assumed an altogether more central place in British politics. In England, Ireland, Scotland, and Wales, there were varied, widespread, and sustained demands for changes in the structure of landholding, and even for the extinction of 'landlordism' itself. And in an increasingly democratic polity, these were demands that no government, whatever its political hue, could ignore.[63]

One reason why 'the land question' became so much more prominent was that for the first time since Domesday, detailed information became publicly available about the inequitable distribution of property and the remarkable extent of patrician wealth.[64] In early 1871, Lord Derby moved for an official inquiry into the pattern of landownership throughout the British Isles, and during the next four years, the data was collected by local government officials on a parish-by-parish basis. It was then reworked into an alphabetical list of owners for each county, and the results were duly published as the *Return of the Owners of Land*, in 1876. The figures were then reworked again by John Bateman, an Essex squire, who produced a book entitled *The Acreocracy of England*, which listed alphabetically all landowners with more than 3,000 acres, and gave details of their holdings, county by county, as well as of their rentals. The second edition, retitled *The Great Landowners of Great Britain and Ireland*, extended the coverage to the British Isles as a whole. And a final revision added all landowners with 2,000 acres and £2,000 a year. The result was the first comprehensive account of landholding in Britain in nearly a millenium.[65]

But what, exactly, did it show? Lord Derby's motive in moving for such an inquiry was that he believed its findings would refute the accusations made by radicals that landownership was concentrated in very few hands. In 1861, on the basis of the recent census data, John Bright had rashly claimed that the whole of England was owned by less than 30,000 people, and that 'fewer than one hundred and fifty men' held half of it. The *Return of the Owners of Land* gave Derby some comfort, because it showed that there were nearly one million owners in England and Wales alone. And it was certainly not the case that half of the country was owned by a mere one hundred and fifty people. But while Bright's detailed figures were discredited, his general argument was amply vindicated. For the statistics demonstrated beyond any reasonable doubt that the pattern of landownership throughout the British Isles was quite exceptionally concentrated. One-quarter of the land of England and Wales was owned by 710 individuals, and nearly three-quarters of the British Isles was in the hands of less than five thousand people. Even more remarkably, it emerged that twelve men between them possessed more than four million acres, and that 421 men owned nearly twenty-three million acres.[66]

In short, these figures revealed a pattern of landownership throughout the British Isles widely believed to be more concentrated and monopolistic than in almost any other European country. And they also revealed the Himalayan scale of the incomes that the patricians drew from their estates in the form of rent – incomes which, in the case of the super-rich, were well in excess of £100,000 a year, and which, in virtually every case, were *unearned*.[67] Inevitably, the publication of such data placed the notables of late-nineteenth-century Britain in an exceptionally exposed position. As a Belgian economist explained, 'the concentration of land in large estates among a small number of families' was 'a sort of provocation of levelling legislative measures.' And the more democratic the British polity became, the greater the provocation seemed. But in addition, it caused many people to wonder precisely what the grandees and gentry were doing to justify their unearned incomes and their monopoly holdings, and it enabled a succession of radical politicians, from Joseph Chamberlain to Lloyd George, to pillory them unforgettably (and unanswerably) as an idle and parasitic class, 'who toil not, neither do they spin.'[68]

Moreover, in one very significant way, these figures were underestimates, for they gave no details about urban, as distinct from agricultural land. But this defect was partially made good by two further government inquiries, the Royal Commission on the Housing of the Working Classes, and the Select Committee on Town Holdings, both of which met during the 1880s.[69] They did not provide systematic details of the rentals and acreage of the great aristocratic building estates, in London or the provincial towns. But they did furnish abundant information about the extent of patrician urban holdings, the likely revenue that was being drawn from them, the patterns and problems of management, and the complaints voiced by many tenants. And they also showed the massive gains that might be expected from the 'unearned increment' – when, at the end of a ninety-nine year lease, both the land and the buildings reverted to the ground landlord, who could then re-let at a vast profit. Here was yet further evidence of the power, the opulence, and the negligence of the landed class – enjoying enormous incomes that were the fruits of other people's labour, while often allowing the houses in which they lived to degenerate into squalid and appalling slums.[70]

These detailed revelations were a godsend to radicals anxious to agitate the land question throughout the British Isles in the more democratic climate of the 1880s. In assailing patrician privilege and territorial monopoly, they had the facts on their side. But in addition, the relations between landlords and tenants themselves markedly deteriorated because of the 'great depression' in agriculture, which began in the closing years of the 1870s. The economic consequences for the landowners of this sustained and debilitating slump will be discussed in the next chapter. But its political consequences were no less traumatic – for they severely strained the relatively harmonious connections that had existed between landlords and tenants in the relatively heady days of mid-Victorian prosperity.[71] The dramatic fall in prices meant that the farmers' profits also plummeted, and that the landowners' incomes suffered correspondingly. Inevitably, there were disagreements about who was bearing the greater burden, and about who, exactly, was responsible. Naturally enough, the hard-pressed tenant farmers blamed their landlords. And from there, it was but a short step to collective hostility, to organized and orchestrated protest, and to more widespread criticism of the conduct and legitimacy of the whole landed order.

The leading sector in this new and determined assault on 'landlordism' was Ireland, where even in the mid-Victorian years, relations between landlords and tenants had often been strained – partly because of the bitter legacy of the Famine, partly because of the endless sub-division of peasant holdings, and partly because the owners were Anglophile Protestants while the tenants were Anglophobe Catholics. During the late 1870s, and throughout the 1880s, the agricultural economy was destabilized by a combination of bad harvests and bad weather, falling prices and falling output.[72] The result was misery and starvation unprecedented since the Famine, and an explosion of anti-landlord feeling, which began among the smallholders on the west coast in County Mayo, and gradually spread among the tenant farmers throughout the whole of the country. In every province, mass meetings were held, tenants refused to pay their rents, landlords and their agents were subjected to assault, intimidation, and social ostracism. And in the autumn of 1879, these localized protests were moulded and mobilized into a national protest movement, known as the Land League. Its President was Charles Stewart Parnell, its Secretary was Michael Davitt, and its self-proclaimed objective was to wage unremitting 'war against landlordism for a root settlement of the land question.'[73]

The resulting Land War lasted for three years, and although the landlords retaliated by evicting recalcitrant tenants in unprecedented numbers, they never fully recovered from this nationwide display of rejection and hostility. The Land Leaguers' aims were plain. In the short run, they wanted their rents drastically and dramatically reduced. More generally, they sought to strengthen their position by winning from the landlords what was known as 'Tenant Right': fair rents, fixity of tenure, and free sale, together called the 'three F's'. And in the long run, they looked forward to regaining the soil for themselves, and to the extinction of 'landlordism' altogether. By the end of 1882, the agrarian violence had diminished, but it flared up again four years later, in what was known as the 'Plan of Campaign', led by William O'Brien and John Dillon. This time, the rent strikes were more carefully organized, and estates were deliberately selected that were already on the brink of bankruptcy, like Lord Kenmare's in Killarney, and Charles Ponsonby's in County Cork. Indeed, it was only the support of a patrician syndicate, organized by Arthur Smith-Barry, himself a Tipperary owner, and financed by some of the richest grandees in Britain, that enabled some of these estates to survive at all.[74]

In the Highlands and Islands of Scotland, there were similar out-
bursts of anti-landlord agitation among the crofting communities.[75]
As in the west of Ireland, the land was poor, the climate inhospitable,
the holdings too small. And there was the powerful folk-memory of
the Highland Clearances, half a century before. The winter of 1881–2
was particularly severe, and many crofters were so destitute they
were no longer able to pay their rents. The factors of the great estates
tried to evict them, and the crofters retaliated by taking back grazing
rights of which they had been deprived, or by not paying rent when
they could still afford to do so. Inevitably, this escalated into violence, most famously at the 'Battle of the Braes' on Skye, in April
1882, when policemen from Glasgow clashed with crofters. For the
rest of the decade, there were disturbances on Skye and Tiree, in
Ross and Sutherland, and gunboats and marines were regularly sent
in to quell the unrest. Harcourt believed this agitation marked 'the
opening of a new land question, which will not be confined to the
Western Highlands.' And in 1886, Balfour claimed that 'the condition of lawlessness which has been permitted to run an unchecked
course for three or four years exceeds that in any part of Ireland'.[76]

The Crofters' War was the most severe crisis in the Highlands
since the heyday of Jacobitism, it received the very widest attention
in the Scottish and English press, and it was supported by a much
larger population of urban and lowland Scots. Foremost among
these was John Murdoch, proprietor of *The Highlander*, an Inverness
newspaper, which was consistently hostile to the landowners.
Equally influential was Professor John Stuart Blackie, a Classicist
with a romantic passion for all things Celtic, who mobilized the
recently-founded Gaelic societies of Scotland in support of the
crofters, and who helped to found the Highland Land Law Reform
Association in 1883.[77] The Association soon boasted branches in
London, Edinburgh, Inverness, and most Highland towns, and was
renamed the Highland Land League in 1887. Its aim was to force the
crofters' campaign to the forefront of British politics, to support
their demand for the 'three F's', and to 'restore to the Highland
people their inherent rights in their native soil.' Both the Irish
precedent, and the Irish connection, were plain. In 1882, and again in
1887, Michael Davitt toured the Highlands, and urged the crofters
to 'organise and agitate until they had overthrown the whole fabric
of the landlord system.'[78]

In Wales, the animosity felt towards the grandees and gentry by
the farmers was equally intense. As in Ireland, the landlords and
tenants were divided by religion, and although there had been
nothing as severe as the Famine or the Clearances, there was the
memory of large-scale evictions after the general elections of 1859

and 1868. The collapse in livestock prices during the mid-1880s greatly aggravated these rural tensions, and once again it was the 'land question' and the very legitimacy of 'landlordism' which was at the centre of the ensuing agitation.[79] In 1883 the Rev. Evan Pan Jones formed the Society of the Land for the People. In 1884 Michael Davitt met with Welsh land reformers, and two years later, he went on a speaking tour throughout the country. At the general election of 1885, every Liberal MP elected for Wales had included land reform in his manifesto, and in the following year, the Rev. Thomas Gee established the Welsh Land League, explicitly modelled on its Irish counterpart, with branches up and down the Principality, which aimed to press for the 'three F's'. Soon after, it merged with the Anti-Tithe League, to mount a concerted campaign against the alien landlords, with their alien church.[80]

With the exception of the anti-tithe riots of 1887–9, there was hardly any unlawful violence in Wales, and rent strikes on the Irish or Scottish pattern were quite exceptionally rare.[81] But in the press, and from the pulpit, there was a widespread and sustained attack on the landowners, who were universally vilified – for their high rents, for their evictions, for their absenteeism, for being the one great cause of all the ills in contemporary rural society. In *The Baner*, Thomas Gee denounced them as 'cruel, unreasonable, unfeeling and unpitying men', who were 'devourers of the marrow of their tenants' bones'. And T. J. Hughes claimed that the landlord 'dwarfs and blights everywhere our national growth.' By the 1890s, the sustained and savage onslaught of the Welsh nonconformist press engendered an 'all-pervading, ubiquitous anti-landlord sentiment'.[82] Once again, the landlords were forced on to the defensive: not so much because their rents were being withheld, but because they were losing the battle in the propaganda war. Even more ominously for the future, it was in this tense and bitter atmosphere, suffused with hatred of the 'alien aristocracy', that a young Welshman called Lloyd George grew up, and grew up hating landlords . . .

The social fabric of rural England was never subjected to the same degree of stress that characterized Ireland, Scotland, and Wales during the 1880s. But in a less violent manner, the traditional ties of deference and dependency were substantially undone. It was widely believed that the landlords themselves were primarily responsible for the depression in agriculture, because their rents were too high. There was a noticeable revival of the 'Free Trade in Land' campaign, and a string of books and pamphlets were published by middle-class reformers such as G. C. Brodrick, J. E. Thorold Rogers, and C. Wren Hoskyns.[83] In 1879, the Farmers' Alliance was established, a national organization of disenchanted tenants, which demanded the abolition of the Game Laws and for the establishment of the 'three F's' in England. Two years later, the American socialist Henry George made the first of a series of sensationally successful visits to Britain, proclaiming that landownership was the cause of all inequality, and that a single tax on rent should supersede all others. In a different radical tradition, Alfred Russell Wallace urged that all land should be nationalized. And in his 'Unauthorised Programme' of 1885, Joseph Chamberlain made the landlords his prime target, demanded the return of the land to the people, and insisted that each rural labourer should be given 'three acres and a cow'.[84]

But it was not just in the English countryside that the landlords were increasingly beleaguered: it was in the towns and cities as well. The 'single tax' doctrines of Henry George were easily adapted to an urban setting, and by the end of the 1880s, there were widespread demands among more radical members of the Liberal Party for direct taxes on ground rents and the 'unearned increment'. In 1884, the Leasehold Enfranchisement Society was established, to campaign for greater security of tenure for urban lessees, and for the gradual breakup of the great urban estates. It produced a constant flow of books and pamphlets, gave some of the most damning evidence to the Select Committee on Town Holdings, and spawned a host of provincial branches.[85] For the attack on the great ground landlords was not confined to London. As the resources and confidence of local authorities grew, so did their hostility to nearby notables. In Bury, where Lord Derby was the pre-eminent owner, the Town Council passed a unanimous resolution against the leasehold system. In Sheffield, where the Duke of Norfolk and Earl Fitzwilliam held massive estates, the opposition was led by the Mayor. And in the 1880 general election in Birmingham, Joseph Chamberlain defeated Augustus Calthorpe, brother of the owner of Edgbaston, after a singularly vituperative and vitriolic campaign.[86]

So, in the very same decade that the patricians were being attacked for their monopoly of political power in the Lords, they were also being attacked for their monopoly of territorial power on the land. The degree of violence varied, and so did the degree of support: but during the 1880s, the landlords of Britain – *as landlords* – were the object of unprecedented criticism, hostility, and abuse. There were widespread demands that the state should intervene on the side of the people: by regulating the hitherto sacrosanct relations between landlord and tenant, by imposing heavier taxation on rural and urban rentals, and even by abolishing 'landlordism' altogether, and returning the land to the people. On the Celtic fringe no less than in England, the agitations mounted were popular and well organized, and used all the sophisticated techniques of modern propaganda. There

were clear connections in policy and personnel between the different
Celtic Land Leagues, and Henry George campaigned, not just in
England, but also in Ireland, Scotland, and Wales. And the result was
that throughout the length and breadth of the British Isles, it was the
landlord, rather than the capitalist, who was depicted as the scape-
goat for the ills of contemporary society.[87]

In retrospect, it seems clear that some of these arguments were
mistaken or over-simplified. In Ireland, Scotland, and Wales, the
charges made concerning unfair rents, punitive evictions, and a lack
of interest in improvement were distinctly exaggerated. In all three
countries, the real problems lay with the thin soil, the adverse
climate, and the peasant mentality, about which owners themselves
could do nothing. To a considerable extent, the landlords were as
much victims of circumstances as their tenants. And in the same
way, the power of the great ground landlords in London and the
provincial towns was much less absolute than it was fashionable to
suppose.[88] But this only makes it the more surprising that the representatives of the old order made no concerted attempt to produce a
coherent and reasoned defence of their position and of their property.
The Duke of Bedford published a book to show how zealous he was
as an agricultural landlord, and the Duke of Argyll wrote prolifically
in denunciation of Henry George, the Irish Land League, and the
Scottish crofters. But this was a feeble response to a formidable foe.
Perhaps the aristocracy realized that in the democratic climate of late-
nineteenth-century Britain, it was impossible to justify their financial
privileges and territorial monopoly.[89]

And if the landlords did not feel able to defend themselves and
their estates, they certainly could not expect the governments of the
time to come to their aid, however patrician in personnel they might
still be. For as Britain moved inexorably in the direction of democracy, it invariably followed that political parties would be obliged to
woo the mass electorate, and that administrations would be increasingly compelled to take the side of the tenant rather than the landlord, the crofter rather than the laird, the poor rather than the rich,
the town rather than the country.[90] As Lord Dufferin explained to
the Duke of Argyll in April 1881, a full four years before the passing
of the Third Reform Act, 'The tendency of the extreme section of the
Liberal Party is to buy the support of the masses by distributing
among them the property of their own political opponents, and it is
towards a social rather than a political revolution that we are tending.' And in 1885, the radical Henry Labouchere made precisely the
same point, but with relish rather than regret: 'The tendency of legislation in future', he noted, 'must be to suppress landlords.' As Gladstone himself admitted, when it came to a battle between 'masses'

and the 'classes', it was the 'masses' who were ultimately going to win.[91]

But it was not only the Liberals who effectively abandoned the defence of great estates and the landed monopoly: so, too, did the Conservatives. For they also felt the power and the pressure of democracy. As Salisbury himself admitted, 'all legislation' was 'rather unwelcome' to the élite, 'as tending to disturb the state of things with which they are satisfied.'[92] But after 1885, legislation could not be avoided, and after 1886, there was often Unionist pressure for more reform than the Conservatives themselves would ideally have countenanced. Even that most superior of men, the young George Curzon, was forced to admit in 1887 that 'the statesman who attempts to rule a democracy by laws framed on aristocratic lines is doomed to failure.' And another patrician colleague made the same point even more emphatically. 'Under our present suffrage', he noted in the following year, 'the Conservative Party can never again be an aristocratic party or a party of privilege . . . It is forced to appeal to the prejudices and desires of the poor.' Put the other way, it could no longer protect the assets and the estates of the rich. The best it could do was to pass pre-emptive legislation in the hope of fending off radical demands for even more drastic reform.[93]

This is most vividly illustrated in the case of Ireland, where Conservative land legislation was at least as radical as that passed by the Liberals. Gladstone's government of 1880 was deeply impressed by the intensity and extent of the Land War, and the Bessborough Commission, which was appointed to look into the land question in 1880, strongly recommended that the tenants' demands be met. The result was the Land Act of 1881, which duly granted the 'three F's', set up a judicial tribunal to adjust (i.e. reduce) their rents, and made a small sum of money available to encourage tenants to purchase their holdings from the landlord.[94] From the standpoint of the landowners, this was a measure at once momentous and ominous. It interfered with freedom of contract, effectively took away their power to fix rents, and greatly reduced their control over their estates. More generally, it was the product of an uncritical and wholehearted acceptance of the tenants' case against the landlord, and it assumed that only by regulating and restricting the owner could Irish discontent be alleviated. And the minor clauses for land purchase, which enabled tenants to borrow money to buy out the owners, portended the demise of landlordism itself. As the Duke of Argyll complained, it spelt 'death to ownership of land in Ireland.'[95]

But the Tory peers were so distressed and demoralized by the Land War that they eventually let the measure through. And thereafter, Lord Salisbury and Arthur Balfour soon decided that the only

IN A MAZE.

MASTER LAND BILL. "OH, MR. BALFOUR, I'M *SO* TIRED!"
MR. B. "CHEER UP, LITTLE MAN! NEXT TURN TO THE RIGHT,—AND I HOPE WE SHALL BE OUT OF F

9. 'In a Maze.' *Punch*, 23 May 1891.

hope for the Irish landlords was to extend the provisions of land purchase so that they could sell their estates to their tenants on the best possible terms. In 1885, the Ashborne Act made £5 million available for this purpose, and three years later, the sum was doubled. Meanwhile, the Cowper Commission had reported in 1887 on the working of the Land Acts of 1881 and 1885, and this resulted in a further round of judicial reductions in rents.[96] In 1891, a much more extensive Land Purchase Act was passed, which increased the amount of money available to £33 million, and there were further minor adjustments made in 1896. But it was not until 1903, with the passing of Wyndham's Land Act, named after the Irish Secretary of the time, that the land purchase scheme was widely adopted. It successfully encouraged the sale of entire estates, by making more money available to tenants on more advantageous terms, and by providing an extra bonus for the landlords. And in 1909, the Liberal government passed another measure, known as Birrell's Land Act, which extended its provisions still further.[97]

In the aftermath of the Land War, it was widely believed, by Liberals and Conservatives alike, that land purchase was the only viable solution to the land question. As *The Times* observed in December 1885 'the leading Irish idea at the present time is to transfer the land from the landlords to the tenants.' Naturally, there were variations of opinion among leading politicians of the day, and Gladstone himself was never fully reconciled to the idea.[98] But advanced Liberals enthusiastically embraced the programme of the Land League, and uncritically accepted the arguments that the landlords were entirely to blame. As John Morley remarked, 'In my heart, I feel that the League has done downright good work in raising up the tenants against their truly detestable tyrants.' At the other extreme, Lord Hartington wearily recognized that in the circumstances of the time, there was no viable alternative. And he was comforted to know that the Conservatives fully shared his views. As he put it in April 1882, 'There is very little real difference between us and the opposition now on Irish land questions. They have accepted the Land Act . . . ; and there is very little difference in principle between us about the extension of the purchase clauses.'[99]

As so often, Hartington's analysis was exceptionally acute. Although the Conservative party was, *par excellence*, the party of the landed interest, Salisbury had concluded as early as 1882 that nothing could be done to save the Irish landlords in the long run, and that their only hope was to sell out on the best terms they could get, rather than run the risk of forcible appropriation at a later date at the hands of a more radical government.[100] To the extent that the object of the exercise was to ensure that the Irish landowners were adequately compensated for the loss of their estates, this was indeed a sympathetically motivated policy. But in fact, the Tory hierarchy thought no more of the Irish landlords themselves than did the Liberals or the Land League. 'How is it possible', W. H. Smith once asked, 'to keep the [Irish] landlords and – I sometimes think – is it worthwhile to try?' It was reported of Sir Michael Hicks Beach, Chief Secretary for Ireland in 1886, that he 'dislikes and despises the Irish landlords, and has no inclination to make much effort on their behalf.' And his successor, Arthur Balfour, was equally censorious. 'What fools the Irish landowners are', he complained to Salisbury on one occasion, 'some stupid, some criminal, many injudicious.'[101]

Predictably, the Irish landlords bitterly resented what they regarded as their 'betrayal' by a succession of British governments. Of Gladstone, nothing better could realistically have been expected: it was their 'abandonment' by the Conservatives that caused them so much anger and pain. In 1887, Lord Westmeath complained that he had 'never expected to be ruined by the party that my family had spent hundreds of thousands of pounds to support.'[102] To Lord Clonbrock, it now seemed as though policy and legislation was entirely determined 'by resistance to the law and by votes in the ballot box.' In the Commons, Colonel Saunderson denounced the Land Bill of 1896 as a sign of the overweening influence of Chamberlain, and Arthur Smith-Barry described it as a surrender to the tenants. And on behalf of the Irish Landowners' Convention, an organization that vainly tried to protect the interests of the patricians and their property, the Duke of Abercorn claimed that 'the proper name of this Bill should be the "Save us from our friends Bill".' 'Who', asked Lord Muskerry at the time of Wyndham's Land Act, 'are the present custodians of Conservative principles? . . . Past governments who claim to be Conservative have been anything but Conservative as regards their Irish policy.'[103]

But it was not just that many landowners regarded this essentially bipartisan solution to the Irish land question as being intrinsically pusillanimous. It was also that they feared that what was being done to Irish landlords today would be done to British landlords tomorrow. When brooding on the terms of the Irish Land Bill in 1880, Gladstone was fully aware of the precedents which it would establish. It would, he recognized, 'introduce fundamental changes in the nature of property, which might . . . next be found difficult to confine to one country of this kingdom.'[104] And since disaffected tenants in Scotland, Wales, and England were soon to demand for themselves the 'three F's', judicially adjusted rents, and some measure of land purchase, the pressure to extend the terms of Irish land legislation to other parts of the United Kingdom was bound to become very great. As R. E. Prothero put it in 1887, 'the situation is indisputably grave; revolutionary legislation is powerfully advocated, and the position of the landlord is completely isolated.' Once the legitimacy of landed property was successfully challenged in one part of the kingdom, it was bound to be threatened elsewhere.[105]

In Scotland, the unrest in the crofting communities was very much observed through Hibernian spectacles, by Liberals and Conservatives alike. In February 1883, Gladstone appointed a Royal Commission, under the chairmanship of Lord Napier, which spent twelve months taking evidence from landowners, their factors, and the crofters themselves. Its report, published a year later, painted a vivid picture of poverty, insecurity and deprivation. For Gladstone, the solution was clear: 'the substantial application of the Irish Land Act to the Highland Parishes.'[106] And the Conservative leadership tacitly agreed with him. In 1886, Gladstone's short-lived third administration duly passed the Crofters Act, which gave the Highlanders fair rent and security of tenure, and set up a Crofters Commission to adjust rentals and reduce arrears. By 1889, many crofters' rents had been compulsorily lowered by as much as 30 per cent, and in 1897 the Unionist government set up the Highland Congested Districts Board, so as to make more land available to them. In 1907 and 1908, the liberals unsuccessfully attempted to extend this crofting legislation to the whole of Scotland, and to give local authorities powers of compulsory purchase. But in 1911, they finally did so, with the passing of the Pentland Act.[107]

Of course, this was not revolutionary legislation by comparison with Irish Land Purchase. And no such scheme was ever seriously contemplated north of the border. But for the landowners, the changes wrought by the passing and the provisions of the Crofters Act were themselves momentous enough. The appointment of the Royal Commission, and the legislation of 1886, demonstrated beyond all doubt that the government's sympathies lay with the crofters rather than with the landlords. Indeed, it was Gladstone's opinion that the crofters had been forcibly deprived of lands to which they possessed an inalienable historical right.[108] And the Crofters Act itself severely limited the powers of the landowner over his property. The Duke of Sutherland regretted that it had 'greatly altered the legal relations between tenant and landlord'. *The Scotsman* described it as 'a great infringement of the rights of private property.' And Fraser of Kilmuir feared 'communism looming in the future.' In Eric Richards's more measured words, the Crofters Act was 'a decisive and unambiguous piece of class legislation on behalf of the common people', 'retribution . . . imposed by a democratic government on a landowning class which was judged to have misused its traditional authority.'[109]

In Wales, by contrast, the issue never went so far, although in the early 1890s, it briefly looked as though it might. In 1892, Tom Ellis, a Welsh MP who had long been an activist in the land campaign, introduced a Tenure of Land Bill, which would have given security of tenure, fair rents, and a land court, on the Irish model. This time, however, Gladstone was convinced it was 'not the Irish case all over again'. But he did appoint a Royal Commission, under the chairmanship of the Liberal landowner Lord Carrington, to look into the land and agriculture of Wales, and promised 'a thorough, searching, impartial and dispassionate' inquiry.[110] For three years, it collected evidence, and the farmers, led by Gee and Ellis, produced their familiar litany of complaints. But the landlords and their agents made a much better showing than they had in Ireland or Scotland,

and provided ample evidence to rebut these accusations. When the commission finally reported, in 1896, it split on party lines, with the Liberal majority recommending that rents should be fixed by a court, while the Conservative minority insisted this would be an intolerable interference in freedom of contract. Since by then there was a Tory government, nothing more was done, and by the general election of 1906, the issue seemed moribund: only seven Liberal MPs included land reform in their election manifestos.[111]

In England, the course of land reform followed a different path again. The Select Committee on Town Holdings delivered no clear verdict for or against leasehold enfranchisement, and annual bills sponsored by the radical MP Henry Broadhurst went down to defeat in the 1880s and early 1890s.[112] Gladstone's Ground Game Act of 1880 gave tenant farmers the right to kill hares and rabbits, which had previously been the sole prerogative of the landowner, and was generally regarded as a victory over the landlords by the Farmers' Alliance. As Sir William Harcourt explained, 'the squires ground their teeth over it dreadfully, . . . but they dare not bite at it for fear of their constituents', an analysis grudgingly endorsed by William Bromley-Davenport, a back-bench Tory gentleman.[113] Three years later, the Liberal government passed an Agricultural Holdings Act, which made it compulsory for the landlord to compensate tenants for any improvements at the end of their tenancy. Once again, the measure was denounced as interfering with freedom of contract: but once again, the Tory peers felt obliged to let it through. Although it would be going too far to say that as a result, 'the injunctions of the state superseded the paternalism of the squire', it was clear that the landowners' autonomy had been further eroded.[114]

But these were relatively minor measures. More important, in intention if not in realization, was the policy of creating a new class of yeoman owner-occupiers in the countryside, and to do so by acquiring land from the holders of great estates, either voluntarily or compulsorily. This was partly a response to the statistical inquiries of the 1870s, which showed that the traditional small freeholder had virtually disappeared. It was partly an attempt to promote – or to pre-empt – Chamberlain's 'Unauthorised Programme' of 'three acres and a cow'. And it was partly designed to establish a new breed of peasant proprietor, with Ireland being regularly cited as an appropriate precedent. In 1887, the Conservatives passed an Allotments Act, which they followed with a Small Holdings Act five years later.[115] But although they gave limited powers to local authorities, these were minor pieces of legislation, and their effect on the structure of rural landownership was minimal. In 1907, the Liberal government passed the more powerful Small Holdings Act, which

gave local authorities compulsory power to buy land. It was hailed as
a 'peasants' charter', which would usher in 'a peaceful agricultural
revolution'. But as with its predecessors, little was effectively
accomplished.[116]

Much more threatening to the grandees and gentry was the prospect of increased direct taxation of land. By 1891, the Liberal party
was publicly committed to levies on mining royalties, to taxation of
land values and ground rents, and to the imposition of death duties.
In 1894, the Chancellor of the Exchequer, Sir William Harcourt,
brought in the last of these proposals, at the relatively gentle level of
8 per cent. But it was the first deliberate attempt to tax landed
wealth, and even among his colleagues it caused the greatest consternation. Gladstone, who had just retired, was much put out, and so
was Rosebery, who regarded the scheme as an unworthy attempt to
'woo the masses'.[117] But Harcourt stood his ground, and for all their
dislike of this 'punitive taxation', the Lords let the proposal through,
and no Conservative government thereafter ever promised to repeal
it. When the Liberals returned to power again, it was widely expected (and widely feared) that land reform would be high on their list
of priorities. At the general election of 1906, two-thirds of the
Liberal candidates endorsed such a programme, and Campbell-
Bannerman himself spoke of the need to 'make the land less of a
treasure house for the rich and more of a treasure house for the
nation.' But apart from Asquith's budget of 1907, which imposed a
higher rate of taxation on unearned income, little was done.[118]

Then came Lloyd George, and the People's Budget.[119] All his
life, Lloyd George had believed in attacking landlords, and in breaking their monopoly of the soil as the necessary prelude to overthrow-
ing their social privileges and political power. Quite simply, and
quite sincerely, he hated the grandees and the gentry, and everything
they represented. He had served his political apprenticeship in the
Welsh land agitation of the 1880s, and although the land question had
subsequently simmered down, Lloyd George himself never forgot it.
In the 1906 election campaign, he promised that the 'next great legislative ideal' was the emancipation of ordinary people from 'the
oppression of the antiquated, sterilising and humiliating system of
land tenure'. Inevitably, in 1909, when looking for additional sources
of revenue, he turned to the landowners. But the prime purpose of
the land taxes which caused such a furore in the Lords was not to
raise revenue. For Lloyd George, their real importance was that they
enabled him to add on to his budget a provision for the surveying
and valuation of all the land in the country, which was clearly
intended as the necessary and ominous prelude to more far-reaching
land taxes in the future.[120]

Once the budget was passed and the Lords' wings were clipped, Lloyd George moved rapidly into the attack again. For his aim was nothing less than to 'break down the remnants of the feudal system', by launching an unprecedented attack on the rural and the urban landowner, which he intended to make the centrepiece of the Liberal programme in the general election which was anticipated in 1915.[121] In the summer of 1912, he set up a Land Inquiry Committee, which planned to produce two reports on rural and on urban land in England, and two further volumes on Scotland and Wales. The first report, on rural land in England, appeared in the autumn of 1913, and formed the basis of the 'Land Campaign' which Lloyd George immediately launched. Once again, he pilloried the patricians, this time as men who selfishly monopolized the land, while allowing the rural economy to decay. And he outlined an audaciously wide-ranging scheme for rural regeneration and reform, including heavier taxation for landowners, state supervision and adjustment of rentals, greatly improved tenants' rights, the much more generous provision of smallholdings and allotments, and substantially increased labourers' wages. All this was to be financed out of landlords' rents, rather than farmers' profits, and it was to be superintended by a newly established Ministry of Land.[122]

It is no exaggeration to say that this programme put the fear of God into the landowning classes – which was exactly what Lloyd George intended. It was prefaced by what Lord Malmesbury called 'violent, uncalled for and unjust attacks upon landlords', and its proposals seemed to realize all their worst fears: unprecedented state intervention, higher taxation, judicial rents, and even some form of land purchase. They drew on a long tradition of radical demands, and of public hostility to the landed classes and the landed monopoly, and they were predictably popular with both the farmers and the labourers. As one Conservative agent noted, they attracted 'unprecedented enthusiasm in the rural districts.'[123] And they were followed in the spring of 1914 by equally radical proposals concerning urban land, which included a commitment to move the burden of local taxation from the tenant to the landowner, and a possible measure of leasehold enfranchisement. But neither campaign came to fruition. The proposals were only vaguely worked out, they were effectively repudiated by a group of influential Liberal MPs, the 1914 budget was a parliamentary fiasco, and then came the war.[124]

So there was no triumphant climax to the land campaign in the way that there had been over the People's Budget and the Parliament Act. But while it was not another victory for Lloyd George, it was in reality another defeat for the landowners. By 1914, the system

10. Lloyd George by Max Beerbohm.

of great estates had effectively disappeared in Ireland, and it was widely recognized, even by the landowners themselves, that it was no longer acceptable, or justifiable, in Great Britain. By 1914, many landowners had already decided to sell off parts of their holdings, and the First World War only accelerated that process. In many ways, market forces brought about exactly the result that Lloyd George had wanted to achieve by using the power of the state. When Lord Northampton put some of his property on the market in 1919, he did so in part because he believed 'that landowning on a large scale is now generally felt to be a monopoly, and is consequently unpopular.' Although lagged by a generation, the radical attack had finally and forcefully hit home. The assault upon 'landlordism' had struck its target.[125]

iii. Armageddon and Afterwards

On the death of his sovereign in 1910, the young Billy Grenfell wrote to his mother, Lady Desborough, as follows: 'I am sad about King Edward, aren't you? It seems as if the glory has departed; and there will be lots of war, and mothers will have to worry considerably.' It was understandable that in the summer of 1910, the titled and genteel classes should be feeling uncertain and unsettled. Yet within four years, maternal anxiety would reach new levels of intensity, and Lady Desborough herself would experience the bitter grief of twice-bereaved motherhood. In May 1915, her eldest son, Julian, died of wounds in France, and less than two months later, his younger brother Billy was also killed, only one mile from the spot where Julian had been fatally wounded.[126] According to Lady Curzon, the Desboroughs 'stood the loss of their two brilliant sons as only such characters as theirs would.' But inwardly, their lives were darkened for ever, by 'such utter desolation, such extinction of joy, glamour, and hope.' For them, as for many of their class, the words spoken by Sir Edward Grey, on 3 August 1914, had turned out to be cruelly and personally prophetic: 'The lamps are going out all over Europe; we shall not see them lit again in our lifetime.'[127]

Nevertheless, when war was formally declared, it was greeted with rapturous enthusiasm, and the greatest anxiety of most young patricians was that they might not get to the front in time to enjoy the fun. Lord Castlereagh was 'afraid of missing seeing anything before the war was over.' Lord Tennyson remembered 'dressing and packing . . . in feverish haste, so anxious was I not to run any chance of missing the war.' 'Our one great fear', Oswald Mosley agreed, 'was that the war would be over before we got there.'[128] From South Africa, where he was stationed with his regiment, Julian Grenfell wrote home disconsolately to his parents: 'It is hateful being away in a corner here at this time . . . It must be wonderful in England now . . . I suppose the excitement is beyond all words.' And so, indeed, it was – for the women no less than for the men. When Lord Tullibardine was told by the War Office that he must mobilize and command the Scottish Horse, his wife 'nearly burst with pride.' And twenty years later, Viscountess Barrington could still recall 'the pride and exaltation of fond parents and wives, their willing offering of their sons and husbands, to fight in so great a cause in the early days of the war.'[129]

At the same time, the older generation of grandees did all they could to encourage recruiting in their localities. Magnates like the Duke of Bedford, Lord Leconfield, and Lord Ancaster outdid each other in the generous terms they offered their tenants and employees. They kept jobs open for the men who had joined up, they allowed the families of volunteers to live rent free in their cottages, and they continued to pay a part of their wages to their dependants at home. As county notables, Lord-Lieutenants, and Colonels of the Yeomanry, their work extended far beyond the boundaries of their own estates. Lord Lincolnshire raised four battalions of Volunteers in Buckinghamshire.[130] Lord Rosebery made rousing speeches in Linlithgow and Midlothian, Glasgow and Edinburgh. Lord Derby toured the County Palatine in his capacity as chairman of the West

Lancashire Territorial Association. 'If', he told one meeting, 'I had twenty sons, I should be ashamed if every one of them did not go to the front when his time came.' And Lord Lonsdale devised and distributed an inimitable recruiting poster that was printed in his racing colours of yellow, white, and red, and was widely distributed and displayed throughout the Lake District. 'Are you', it asked the inhabitants of Cumberland and Westmorland, 'a man, or are you a mouse?' Only one answer was possible.[131]

During these early days of war, the *grandes dames* were as much enthused and excited as the grandees. The Duchess of Westminster established a Red Cross hospital at Le Touquet, Lady Dudley set up an Australian Hospital nearby, and the dowager Duchess of Sutherland organized her own ambulance unit to serve in Belgium. She was obliged to retreat in the face of the German advance, and returned to England where she wrote an account of her experiences entitled *Six Weeks at the War*. In London, Lady Lowther organized the production of food and clothing parcels for Belgian prisoners in Germany, Mrs Alfred Lyttelton supervised the reception of Belgian refugees and made arrangements for their accommodation and employment, the future Lady Curzon helped run a night canteen at Waterloo Station, and Jennie Churchill prompted butlers to join up by publicly expressing her preference for housemaids.[132] Among the younger generation, Lady Diana Manners became a VAD probationer at Guy's, Monica Grenfell trained at Whitechapel Hospital, and Helen Manners qualified as an anaesthetist. North of the border, Lady Tullibardine staged a series of concerts in support of her husband's recruiting efforts in Perthshire, and later organized the knitting of 15,000 pairs of 'hose tops' to keep the legs of kilted Highland soldiers warm.[133]

To some degree, this patrician response was part of the general enthusiasm for war at the time; but there were also specific reasons why so many rushed so fervently to the colours in the autumn of 1914.[134] For more than thirty years, they had been the object of radical (and sometimes not so radical) attack: for their unjustifiable monopoly of the land, for their unearned incomes and their unearned increments, for their reactionary attitudes to social reform, for their anachronistic possession of hereditary political power, and for their leisured lifestyle and parasitic idleness. And in the aftermath of the Parliament Act, there were many grandees and gentry who genuinely believed that the best years for their kind and class were emphatically over. But then came the war, which gave them the supreme opportunity to prove themselves and to justify their existence. By tradition, by training, and by temperament, the aristocracy was the warrior class. They rode horses, hunted foxes, fired shot-guns. They knew how to lead, how to command, and how to look after the men in their charge. Here, then, was their chance – to demonstrate conclusively that they were not the redundant reactionaries of radical propaganda, but the patriotic class of knightly crusaders and chivalric heroes, who would defend the national honour and the national interest in the hour of its greatest trial.[135]

But it soon became clear that discharging this traditional obligation was going to prove to be unexpectedly costly. Before the year was out, the Ancaster, Cadogan, Durham, Hardinge, Leconfield, Tweeddale, and Wellington families were plunged into mourning. The eldest sons of Lord Aylesford, Lord Yarborough, and Lord O'Neill were killed, the Hon. Arthur O'Neill being the first MP to lose his life in the war. The heirs to three great Scottish houses were also among the earliest victims: the Master of Burleigh, the Master of Kinnaird, and the Master of Kinloss. The Duke of Atholl, the Duke of Abercorn, and Lord Lansdowne each lost a son. When Percy Wyndham was killed, having inherited Clouds from his father only the previous year, his batman remembered that he 'died a soldier's death', and was 'like a father to his men'.[136] And when the Hon. John Manners died, his mother declared – in words reminiscent of Lord Derby – that if she had six sons, she would willingly send and sacrifice them all. Such 'spartan and stoical bravery' on the part of patrician parents was as predictable as it was becoming commonplace. For by the end of 1914, the death toll included six peers, sixteen baronets, ninety-five sons of peers, and eighty-two sons of baronets.[137]

During the course of 1915, it gradually became clear that the war and the casualties were going to be on a far greater scale than anything that anyone had imagined. The earliest victims of the new year included George Wyndham, the third member of his family to die, William Gladstone of Hawarden, the grandson of the Prime Minister, and Lord Wendover, heir to Lord Lincolnshire. 'He is very brave', Lord Bertie wrote of Wendover's father, 'but how sore his heart must be.' In the summer, the two Grenfell brothers were killed, and their deaths occasioned another outpouring of chivalric sympathy: Julian embodied 'all the glory and romance of war', while Billy was 'one perfect gallant knight'.[138] The Gallipoli campaign added yet more fatalities, including Lord Longford, Lord Vernon, and Charles Lister, the heir and only son of Lord Ribblesdale. But the most poignant death was that of Ivo Charteris, younger son of Lord Wemyss, aged only nineteen, after a mere five weeks on the Western Front. His father's response was 'most piteous – heartbroken and just like a child – tears pouring down his cheeks and so *naively astonished.*' And his sister, Lady Cynthia Asquith, was no less distressed. 'Really', she confided in her wartime diary, 'one hardly knows who is alive and who is dead.'[139]

For the Charteris family, as for many others, 1916 only added more bitterness to their cup of sorrow. During the early months of that year, both Viscount Quenington, heir to Lord St Aldwyn, and Lord Weymouth, eldest son of the Marquess of Bath, were killed. In April, Hugo Charteris, Lord Elcho, the elder brother of Ivo, was fatally wounded in Egypt at the Battle of Katia. *The Times* commemorated him as one who best 'embodied the heroic spirit of the younger generation.' But this was of little comfort to his widow. 'How can I face the long years? . . . What does one do?' she tearfully asked Lady Diana Manners. In November 1916, Auberon Herbert, Lord Lucas, who was serving in the Royal Flying Corps, took off on a routine flight, but never returned.[140] He, too, was mourned as a latter-day 'knight of the round table.' And when Lord Feversham was killed on the Western Front, his cousin Lord Londonderry opined that 'those who fall in the war are the truly happy ones.' Such pious and platitudinous hopes could be neither proved nor falsified: but it was certain that those left behind were more than ever overwhelmed with grief. 'Speaking metaphorically', Lord Rosebery wrote in one letter of consolation, 'the fountain of tears is nearly dry. One loss follows another till one is dazed.'[141]

During 1917, the cascade of coroneted casualties continued unabated. One of the earliest victims was the son and heir of Walter Long, the Conservative cabinet minister and archetypal country gentleman. Among heads of families, the Earl of Suffolk and the Earl of Shannon were both killed. Lord Basil Blackwood, son of the Marquess of Dufferin, died in July, having already lost a brother during the Boer War. Later that year, the victims included the Hon. Henry Vane, heir to Lord Barnard, and Edward Horner, who died leading an attack on a village near Cambrai. Like Julian Grenfell, Horner embodied the grace and gifts of his generation to a quite exceptional degree, and he was the heir to an estate in Somerset which had been in his family for four hundred years.[142] In the same month, November, Lord Rosebery lost his younger son, Neil Primrose, and his remaining hopes for the future effectively died with him. By this time, neither the older nor the younger generation could come to terms with the scale of aristocratic slaughter. Cynthia Asquith feared that 'soon there will be nobody left with whom one can even talk of the beloved figures of one's youth.' And Lord Bertie felt that 'the war has made death so common that the disappearance of friends becomes almost an everyday occurrence.'[143]

This was not the gentlemanly, chivalric conflict that had been so euphorically anticipated by the young and old patricians in the autumn of 1914: on the contrary, it was total war and total hell. But it was also total war in another quite novel way. For as the casualties mounted, many of the greatest country houses were converted into makeshift hospitals to accommodate the wounded and the convalescent, from Burleigh to Belvoir, Woburn to Windlestone. At Longleat, the famous Bath bedroom became an operating theatre, and beds were put in the saloon. The Duchess of Rutland turned 21 Arlington Street, the family's London house, into a hospital, with ten patients in the golden drawing room, and twelve more in the ballroom. Even the greatest town palaces were given over to the care of the sick, including Londonderry House and Grosvenor House. And the chatelaines often took it upon themselves to superintend the nursing. On his return to London as a wounded officer, the Hon. Lionel Tennyson found himself in the tender and titled hands of Lady Carnarvon and Lady Ridley. Their hospital was, he recalled, 'the best in London . . . No attention was too much trouble, the nursing was wonderful, and the food given us exquisitely cooked and served.'[144]

Some aristocratic ladies resolved to make their contribution to the war effort in the battle zone, rather than in the country house. Lady Muriel Paget organized an Anglo-Russian hospital on the eastern front, and her namesake, Lady Lelia Paget, went off to nurse the sick in Serbia. Lady Angela Stewart-Forbes established a canteen on the Western Front, and on the morning that the Somme offensive began, fried eight hundred eggs in three hours. But she so enraged Sir Douglas Haig that in the following year, he ordered her deportation. Her sister, the dowager Duchess of Sutherland, fared rather better. After her unhappy experiences in the autumn of 1914, she returned to the Continent and set up a hospital in Calais, which eventually contained 160 beds and employed a staff of one hundred people.[145] Not everyone approved of these 'grand ladies who are running hospitals in France.' Lord Crawford thought the Duchess of Westminster and the Duchess of Sutherland were particularly troublesome. They overspent, and expected the Red Cross to help them out. They shamelessly exploited their contacts in high places, and importuned busy generals and over-worked politicians. And they were so eager to keep their hospitals filled that they carried off invalids 'willy-nilly', like latter-day 'body snatchers'.[146]

But it was not just as nursing entrepreneurs that titled women involved themselves in the war effort. The Marchioness of Londonderry established the Women's Legion, a quasi-military organization, designed to free men, engaged in home duties, for military service. She wrote letters to *The Times*, obtained the support of Walter Long and Henry Chaplin, disregarded the hostility of the civil

servants in the Board of Trade, and secured official recognition for
the Legion in February 1916.[147] At one training centre in Rutland,
women were taught to work on the land as agricultural labourers.
Another 40,000 qualified as cooks, and were despatched to army
camps. And a third group were taught to drive ambulances and
motor cars. Less happy was the story of Lady Violet Douglas-
Pennant, sixth daughter of Lord Penrhyn. In the spring of 1918, she
was made Commandant of the WRAF, where she found inefficiency,
obstruction, and immorality in what she regarded as unacceptable abundance. The authorities did not share her view, and she was
hurriedly and humiliatingly dismissed, despite the efforts of such
aristocratic friends as Lord Ampthill and Lord Henry Bentinck to
secure an official inquiry on her behalf.[148]

The younger generation of patrician women never got this close to
the corridors of power. Lady Diana Manners had initially wanted to
go to France as a nurse, but was discouraged by Lady Dudley on the
grounds that 'wounded soldiers, so long starved of women, inflamed
with wine and battle, ravish and leave half dead the nurses who wish
only to tend them.' Having trained at Guy's as a VAD, she reluctantly became a nurse in her mother's hospital in Arlington Street. But
for her, as for many of her generation, this harrowing work was by
no means the most dreadful part of her wartime experience. Much
harder to bear was the lengthening list of friends, lovers, and contemporaries who had been killed, and the unceasing anxiety as to
who among the dwindling remainder would be next. In these 'nightmare years of tragic hysteria', she took refuge in drink and dancing,
morphia and chloroform. By the end of 1917, 'her world was disintegrating': Billy Grenfell, George Vernon, Charles Lister, and
Edward Horner were all dead. One of the reasons why she eventually married Duff Cooper – who was distinctly her social inferior, and
had very little money of his own – was that he was the only one of
her pre-war friends who came back from the killing fields.[149]

It was in this context – of disintegration such as the great Lord
Salisbury could never have imagined – that on 29 November 1917,
Lord Lansdowne published his famous letter in the *Daily Telegraph*,
calling for an end to the war, and for a negotiated peace with
Germany. Lansdowne was a patrician to his fingertips: 'the very
model of the well-meaning representative of the aristocracy.'[150] He
owned large estates in England, Scotland, and Ireland. Both by
ancestry and by attainment, he belonged to one of the great governing families of the realm. In the course of an exceptionally long
public life, he had been successively Governor-General of Canada,
Viceroy of India, Secretary of State for War, and Foreign Secretary.
He began his career as a Whig, split with Gladstone over Home Rule,

became leader of the Unionist peers, and from May 1915 to December 1916, was Minister without Portfolio in Asquith's coalition government. His patriotism and his integrity were beyond question. But his younger son had been killed in Flanders in 1914, and Lansdowne soon became convinced that Britain could not win, that Germany could not be broken, and that the senseless prolongation of 'the most dreadful war the world has known', would merely 'spell the ruin of the civilized world.'

Inevitably, Lansdowne's proposal was greeted with widespread amazement and hostility. In the aftermath of the Russian Revolution, and the entry of the United States into the war, it seemed peculiarly ill-timed. It caused surprise and distress among members of his family, many of whom were on active service. Like many disapproving politicians, Lord Crawford thought it the action of a 'nerve-wrecked wobbler' who felt 'vexation and annoyance' at 'being out of office'.[151] At best, Lansdowne's letter seemed a regrettable aberration at the end of a long and distinguished career; at worst, it was yet one more sign that the Whigs were incorrigible appeasers. But there was also something to be said in Lansdowne's defence. His action was neither hasty nor ill-considered. Far from being the product of a sudden loss of nerve, his letter merely elaborated in public the contents of his cabinet memorandum of November 1916. True to his Whig upbringing, he was making a 'dignified but fruitless appeal for moderation.' He was convinced that unless the war was rapidly terminated, 'the traditional social order' would be destroyed. Like his friend Sir Edward Grey, he knew that the lamps were rapidly going out: his peace proposal was a vain attempt to prevent them being extinguished altogether.[152]

But Lansdowne's letter was soon overtaken by events. Neither the final German onslaught, nor the Allied counter-attack, were propitious moments for peace negotiations. Meanwhile, the aristocratic fatalities continued throughout most of 1918. There were more heads of families, like Lord Rosse and Lord Poulett. There were more elder sons, like the Master of Belhaven, and Viscount Ipswich, heir to the Duke of Grafton. And there were younger sons like Eric Cawdor and Richard Clanmorris. Not surprisingly, when victory finally came, there were few among the patrician survivors who felt any sense of exultation. At the front, Oliver Lyttelton 'had expected riotous excitement, but the reaction of everyone, officers and men, seemed the same – flat depression.' In London, Oswald Mosley 'stood aside from the delirious throng, silent and alone, ravaged by memory.'[153] Alan Brooke felt exactly the same: 'That wild evening jarred on my feelings . . . I was filled with gloom . . . and retired to

The young Percy Wyndham.

12. John Manners on horseback.

bed early.' Mary Wemyss agreed: 'No one', she observed, 'can feel light of heart.... We miss our shining victors in the hour of victory.' For as Winston Churchill later recalled, 'the ache for those who will never come home' made the thought of joyous, carefree celebration seem almost blasphemous.[154]

Only in the aftermath of victory did the full magnitude of these patrician losses become apparent.[155] Three Wyndhams, two Grenfells, and two Charterises had fallen. Lord Penrhyn lost his eldest son and two half-brothers. The fifth Lord de Freyne and one of his half-brothers were killed on the same day in May 1915, and another half-brother died two years later. Lord Kimberley, Lord Middleton, and Lord Denbigh each lost two sons, and so did Sir George Dashwood. The dowager Countess of Airlie had lost her husband in the Boer War, and now lost a son, Patrick, and a son-in-law, Clement Mitford. One of Anthony Eden's brothers was killed in France in October 1914, and another went down at Jutland in May 1916.[156] Of the great Lord Salisbury's ten grandsons, five were killed in action. But even these examples cannot convey the full sense of bereavement that

13. The Egerton Monument in Chester Cathedral.

most landed families experienced, the inevitable result of their extended cousinhoods and interlocking marriage alliances, which meant that anxiety, loss, and grief were experienced many times over. On the west wall of the south transept in Chester Cathedral is a memorial commemorating *thirteen* members of the Grey-Egerton family of Oulton Park, who had died on active service during the war.[157]

Inevitably, these losses meant that the pool of aristocratic talent was visibly reduced during the inter-war years. It is not necessary to join the clichéd cult of the Wyndhams, the Grenfells, and the Charterises, to recognize that they were uncommonly gifted and promising young men, whose greatness had been predicted before they died, and was not just invented afterwards. In the same way, Lord Basil Blackwood seemed set for a distinguished career in colonial administration. Charles Lister was widely recognized as a diplomat of outstanding promise. And Edward Horner had begun to make his reputation at the bar. The deaths of Lord Alexander Thynne, Lord Quenington, Lord Ninian Critchton-Stuart, and the Hon. Arthur

O'Neill seriously depleted the dwindling ranks of patrician MPs. Lord Feversham was mourned as a landowner, politician, and soldier of peculiar versatility and promise. 'Not one of his contemporaries', Sir Almeric Fitzroy recorded, 'among the class which he represented had played so well in every sphere of activity the parts he assumed.' And Neil Primrose and William Gladstone were more than just the bearers of famous names out of the past: they were recognized by friend and foe alike as men with golden futures ahead of them.[158]

In the shadow of these grievous losses of irreplaceable talent and unrealized potential, it was widely believed that an entire generation of notables had perished during the First World War. Throughout the country, there were requiems for squires' sons whose swords were laid upon altar steps. Mourning hatchments were hung over the front door of many a mansion. And flags flew at half-mast from towers and turrets. Lord Henry Bentinck believed that 'everything generous, self-sacrificing and noble' had 'shed blood on the fields of Flanders.'[159] 'Truly', Lady Curzon later recalled, 'England lost the flower of her young men in those terrible days . . . There was scarcely one of our friends who did not lose a son, a husband, or a brother.' In an editorial of May 1920, *The Times* waxed unusually eloquent on the same theme, picturing aged patrician parents, with their sons 'lying in far away graves', and their 'daughters secretly mourning someone dearer than a brother.' But it was Alan Lascelles who summed up this feeling most pithily and poignantly on Armistice Day itself: 'Even when you win a war', he noted, 'you cannot forget that you have lost your generation.'[160]

Ironically enough, this argument received its most effusive and elegiac articulation at the hands of C. F. G. Masterman, who in pre-war days had been a member of Asquith's cabinet, and an enthusiastic supporter of Lloyd George, land reform, and the Parliament Act. But he was so impressed, and so saddened, by the supreme sacrifices made by the titled and territorial classes, that he devoted an entire chapter of his book, *England After the War*, to describing and lamenting what he called 'The Passing of Feudalism.'[161] The purpose of aristocracy, he contended, was war. And between 1914 and 1918, the British aristocracy had discharged its hereditary task with 'shining splendour – courage, devotion, care for the men under its charge.' But in the process, it had paid a mortally high price:

> In the retreat from Mons, and the first battle of Ypres, perished the flower of the British aristocracy . . . In the useless slaughter of the Grenadiers on the Somme, or of the Rifle Brigade in Hooge Wood, half the great families of England, heirs of large estates and

wealth, perished . . . in courage and high effort, and an epic of heroic sacrifice, which will be remembered so long as England endures.

During the First World War, Masterman regretfully concluded, 'the Feudal System vanished in blood and fire, and the landed classes were consumed.'[162]

But this haunting image of doomed genteel youth, of an aristocratic holocaust, needs to be set in proper perspective. Many of those who were posthumously recruited into the so-called 'lost generation' were in fact drawn from the middle classes: Raymond Asquith, John Kipling, Vere Harmsworth, Patrick Shaw-Stewart, Rupert Brooke, to name but the most famous examples. And while the Wyndhams, the Grenfells, and the Charterises wrote exceptional letters, in which they expressed their sorrows with searing articulateness, there is no reason to suppose that the members of the more humble and less epistolary classes were any less grieved. As G. W. E. Russell rightly remarked, 'The burden of the war lies as heavily on the poor as on the rich, for neither poverty nor riches can mend a broken heart.'[163] Nor should it be forgotten that there were many patricians who were true to their martial traditions, and who actually *enjoyed* the war. It was not only Julian Grenfell who 'loved fighting', and found it 'the best fun one ever dreamed of.' Oliver Lyttelton thought 'winning in war is at all times a beautiful and exhilarating experience.' And Harold Alexander regarded the whole thing as a 'terrific adventure', and much regretted the Armistice, when 'all good things' came to an end.[164]

Above all, it must be stressed that the overwhelming majority of those notables who served *actually returned home.*[165] Four-fifths of all British and Irish peers and their sons who joined up came back. For every family that suffered multiple losses, there were many more that survived intact. Seven close relatives of the Earl of Derby served in the war: all came back. Six kinsmen of Lord Saye and Sele were equally lucky. Five members of the Buccleuch, Courtown, Lucan, and Ampthill families also survived the war. The Dukes of Somerset, Marlborough, Atholl, Roxburghe, Manchester, Northumberland, Leinster, Sutherland, Abercorn, and Westminster joined the colours: all returned. And even when heads of families or elder sons were killed, this had 'extraordinarily little effect' on the continuity of landed life. The titles and estates of Lords Barnard, Powis, Yarborough, and Bath passed to a surviving younger son. And although Lord Lincolnshire's marquessate died with him, the older Barony of Carrington, and the family estates, passed to his younger brother. Only in a very few exceptional cases – like Ribblesdale and Llangattock – did a title become extinct because of death in war.[166]

Thus described, the genteel warriors of the 1914–1918 War were essentially the lost and found generation. And the survivors duly made their mark in the years that followed. Among prominent inter-war politicians, Edward Wood, Oswald Mosley, and Winston Churchill had seen service in the trenches. By the late 1930s, the wartime generation was well represented in the National Governments. Lord Stanhope had served in the Grenadiers, and Lord Winterton was at Gallipoli. Lord Swinton and Lord Londonderry survived the Somme.[167] Lord Stanley and his younger brother Oliver both won the Military Cross. And Anthony Eden had ended the war as the youngest brigade major in the army. In the same way, the three great patrician commanders in the Second World War had all won their spurs in the First: Montgomery, Alexander, and Alanbrooke. And every aristocratic member of Churchill's peacetime administration of 1951–5 had fought in the trenches. In addition to the Prime Minister himself, Anthony Eden, Alexander, and Swinton, Lord Salisbury had served in the Grenadiers, the Hon. James Stuart had won the Military Cross (and bar), and Oliver Lyttelton had survived almost the entire war on the Western Front unscathed.[168]

But although the myth of the 'lost generation' does not survive detailed scrutiny in its most familiar form, the fact remains that the British aristocracy was irrevocably weakened by the impact of the First World War. Not since the Wars of the Roses had so many patricians died so suddenly and so violently. And their losses were, proportionately, far greater than those of any other social group.[169] A majority of those who served may in fact have returned: but it was a much smaller majority than for the middle or the working classes. Of the British and Irish peers and their sons who served during the war, one in five was killed. But the comparable figure for all members of the fighting services was one in eight. And the explanation is clear. The patricians were either professional soldiers or among the first men to volunteer. Most of them were junior officers below the rank of Lt. Colonel, who were rapidly posted to the front, where they shared the risks and dangers of trench life, and led their men over the top and into battle. During the first year of the war, one in seven of such officers were killed, compared with only one in seventeen of the rank and file. And at the Somme, Bernard Montgomery noted that 'we have been unlucky in losing rather a lot of officers in proportion to the men.' In terms of the *relative* numbers of lives lost, there is no doubt that the titled and territorial classes made the greatest sacrifices.[170]

At the same time, the war made them seem less distant, less Olympian, less remote. In the trenches, the owners of great estates and the bearers of illustrious names lived side by side with their men in novel circumstances of easy camaraderie and extraordinary squa-

lor. Many patricians owed their lives to ordinary soldiers who rescued them and carried them to safety, and came to feel closer to them
than to their relatives back home. Across the length and breadth of
Britain, country houses, which had previously been bastions of aristocratic exclusiveness, were thrown open to the sick and the convalescent of all social classes. And at home and overseas, titled nurses
abased themselves to perform menial tasks for their social inferiors
which they would never have dreamed of doing for themselves in
ordinary life. They emptied chamber pots, changed soiled sheets,
bandaged wounds, attended operations. They witnessed terrible
pain, pointless agony, nightmarish death. They exchanged their cosseted, leisured, privileged existence for iron discipline, regular criticism, long hours, hard work, 'dirt, suffering, smells and squalor.'[171]
After such sudden and unprecedented social mixing, the distancing
aura that was an essential aspect of aristocratic hegemony would
never be inviolate again.

But it was not just that the war made the notables seem less
remote: it also made them seem much more vulnerable. Part of the
mystique of aristocracy was (and is) an unshakeable self-confidence
that all will turn out well, and an almost serene indifference to the
slings and arrows of outrageous fortune. In August 1914, the patricians had eagerly anticipated a gentlemen's war, which would be
over by Christmas. Despite the decline of the Irish landed ascendancy, despite the insults hurled at them by Lloyd George, despite the
Parliament Act and the subsequent 'Land Campaign', they had rallied
to the defence of their country and empire. But although they had
fought like knights of old, they had been slaughtered like animals,
and had fallen like flies. Among both the younger and the older generation, many shared Lord Wemyss's 'naive astonishment' that such
a thing *could possibly happen to them*. Their collective self-confidence
and their serene faith in their ultimate invulnerability were irretrievably damaged. It was no longer possible to regard the country house
and landed estate as 'a little self-contained kingdom, . . . immune
from unheralded invasion from outside.'[172]

Nor did such loss of life and confidence bring with it any gainful
compensation. In November 1916, Lord Murray of Elibank predicted that in the future, 'the position of the Lords in this country will be
much stronger, generally on account of the gallantry and losses on
the battlefield of the peerage families.'[173] But this did not happen.
The Parliament Act had made the second chamber effectively redundant, and most people were too preoccupied with their own grief
to have any sympathy (or admiration) to spare for the titled and territorial classes. In so far as any group benefited from the war, it was
the profiteers and the businessmen, the cronies and followers of

Lloyd George. As Lord Willoughby de Broke remarked in 1915, with understandable bitterness: 'His own friends are not being killed, while yours and mine are being picked off every day.'[174] Beyond that, it was the common man (and woman) who were the chief beneficiaries. In Eastern Europe, thrones and aristocracies tottered. And in Britain, the Fourth Reform Act gave the vote to all adult men, and to women over thirty. By an ironic turn of fate, the war in which the grandees and gentry had given so much was dedicated to 'making the world safe for democracy'.

Inevitably most surviving patricians, both young and old, contemplated the future with gloom and despondency that sometimes bordered on alarm. 'It is not so much the war', Arthur Balfour remarked, 'as the peace that I have always dreaded.' Old men like Rosebery, Lansdowne, and Balfour of Burleigh never really recovered from the deaths of their sons.[175] Bereaved mothers like Lady Desborough and Lady Horner (and Evelyn Waugh's Lady Marchmain in *Brideshead Revisited*) devoted themselves to compiling memorial volumes of letters and photographs.[176] Some surviving aristocrats felt a genuine sense of guilt that they had not shared the ultimate fate of their comrades and companions. Others, more certain than ever that the best years for their kind and class were gone, abandoned themselves to irresponsible self-indulgence. And most of them struggled, like Lady Cynthia Asquith, to come to terms with the fact that 'the dead are not only dead for the duration of the war.' In many ways, the lot of those who had passed on seemed infinitely preferable to the lot of those who were compelled to stay behind. The patrician paragons who had died never knew the disillusionment of the inter-war years. There were many who agreed with Norman Leslie: 'it is better far to go out with honour than to survive with shame.'[177]

The full extent of genteel bitterness, disenchantment, and infirmity of purpose during the inter-war years can only be guessed at. Even in private correspondence, complaining was not their style, and when the war memoirs began to flow during the late 1920s and early 1930s, they kept stern and significant silence. But there can be no doubting their bewildered resentment that a conflict which had seemed to be their opportunity had turned out instead to be a conflagration which nearly brought about their destruction. As Mary Elcho remarked, it was not just that the war destroyed millions of lives. It changed the world, *their* world, for ever, 'shaking all things to their foundations, wasting the treasures of the past, and casting its sinister influence far into the future.'[178] In this, as in so much else, the opinions of the Sitwells were far more typical of their class and their generation than they would ever have believed or admitted. For them, as for most patricians, the Great War was truly the 'Great Catastrophe': and it lay 'across the years like a wound that never heals.'[179]

iv.   Conclusion: The World Turned Upside-down

'Aristocracy', Robert Lacey once remarked, 'does not stand up well to misfortune. It is a fair-weather way of life.'[180] And as such, it was not at all well suited to the storms and tempests that raged and blew between 1880 and 1918. By definition, democracy and aristocracy do not cohabit easily, and they certainly did not do so in Britain between the passing of the Third and the Fourth Reform Acts. For these were the years in which the gentry and grandees lost the historical initiative, and lost the control of events. Instead of being the 'paragons of legislation' that W. S. Gilbert affectionately mocked in 'Iolanthe', they now appeared as the selfish and redundant vested interest that Lloyd George excoriated so unforgettably (and so unanswerably) at Limehouse. And instead of being the proud and revered holders of great estates which they administered with paternal benevolence, they were increasingly regarded as territorial monopolists who needed to be regulated and restrained. Undeniably, the nobles and notables had changed. They had become more anxious, and as a result, more selfish. But the world outside had changed even more. In the end, numbers triumphed over nobility, the vote vanquished the veto, the Land League conquered the landowner.

Three individuals stand out as the men who embodied and promoted these powerful anti-aristocratic impulses. The first was Michael Davitt, creator of the Irish Land League. For this was not merely the vehicle by which the cause of agrarian populism was so successfully advanced in his own country: in its programme and in its organization, it was the inspiration for similar anti-landlord movements in Scotland and Wales. The second was Joseph Chamberlain, whose big-spending brand of municipal socialism threatened the landowners in the towns, whose 'Unauthorised Programme' destabilized and enflamed the countryside, and whose vituperative vocabulary anticipated the rhetoric of the third of these aristocratic daemons: Lloyd George himself. With Lloyd George, the democratic attack on the traditional titled and territorial classes reached its climax. Quite simply, he refused to accept them at their own comfortable and superior self-evaluation, and he persuaded a large number of his fellow countrymen to agree with him. Instead of touching his forelock, he blew them raspberries. He taunted them, threatened them, taxed them, tormented them. He took away their hereditary power, and seemed set fair to take away their hereditary acres as well. No wonder, by 1914, they hated him as much as he hated them.

From their own particular standpoint, at once so privileged and yet so vulnerable, the patricians saw themselves as the persecuted victims of a predatory democracy. Then in 1914, their luck changed – but for the worse. For they now became instead the sacrificial victims of patriotic endeavour. In January 1918, Sir Cecil Spring-Rice, whose time as British Ambassador to the United States was just drawing to a close, and whose elder brother had been killed in France two years before, composed a poem which developed this theme:

> I vow to thee, my country – all earthly things above –
> Entire and whole and perfect, the service of my love.
> The love that asks no questions: the love that stands the test,
> That lays upon the altar the dearest and the best:
> The love that never falters, the love that pays the price
> The love that makes undaunted the final sacrifice.[181]

But for Spring-Rice, as for most patricians, the First World War meant more than martial martyrdom and poetic patriotism. For it was not just that they made these supreme sacrifices selflessly, stoically, and uncomplainingly. The greater and far crueller irony was that they had been made in the defence of a country that was gradually but irrevocably ceasing to be theirs.

3

THE DECLINE AND DISPERSAL OF TERRITORIAL WEALTH

Whatever the professed reasons – agricultural depression, death duties, the campaign against landlordism – the estate system as it existed prior to 1914 did not survive the First World War.
(J. V. Beckett, *The Aristocracy in England, 1660–1914* (1986), p. 475.)

The break-up of Welsh estates was even more thorough than in England.
(D. W. Howell, *Land and People in Nineteenth-Century Wales* (1977), p. 25.)

In the two years after the armistice, four million acres of Scottish land – a fifth of the total – came on to the market as owners found the combination of increased taxes and higher costs squeezing income.
(I. G. C. Hutchison, *A Political History of Scotland, 1832–1924: Parties, Elections and Issues* (1986), p. 320.)

By the early 1920s, . . . nearly two thirds of Ireland's total area had ceased to be the property of landlords.
(S. Clark, *Social Origins of the Irish Land War* (Princeton, 1979), p. 349.)

The measures that were threatened and enacted by successive Liberal governments between 1880 and 1914 filled the British territorial classes with alarm. And the growing evidence, during the same period, and on into the inter-war years, that the Conservative party was no longer either willing or able to defend the land, only accentuated their well-justified apprehension. Instead of being politically valuable, the land of the British Isles was becoming politically vulnerable. To make matters worse, it was becoming economically vulnerable at the very same time – partly because a new and rival wealth élite was coming into being, partly because agriculture ceased to be as prosperous as it had been, and partly because one expression of the new political hostility to the land was that it was subject to quite unprecedented taxation. The combined result of these political and economic changes was that, between the 1880s and the 1930s, the financial condition and territorial circumstances of the British landowning classes were fundamentally and irrevocably transformed.

To begin with, they ceased to be the wealth élite as the rise of the great international and plutocratic fortunes, from the 1880s, signified new forms and new amounts of wealth, which were easily and rapidly accumulated, which carried fewer attendant burdens and obligations, and which gradually eclipsed the resources of all but a very few very rich landowners. But simultaneously, the economic position of landowners was further undermined from within, as this period saw an almost uninterrupted depression in British agriculture, which led to a marked and sustained decline in prices, rentals, values, and confidence. In addition, a succession of Liberal, Conservative, Labour, and National governments increased their financial demands on landowners, by taxing both their capital and their income more severely than ever before. During the very period when land was losing both its political importance and its social prestige, it was increasingly becoming an uncertain and uneconomic asset.

Accordingly, from the 1880s, the attitudes that had customarily underpinned patrician landownership were brutally undermined, and the policies that landowners had pursued concerning their estates and their families were irrevocably put into reverse. Hitherto, most landowners had regarded their broad acres as a trust, an inheritance, which must be preserved and, if possible, enhanced, before being passed on intact and augmented to the next generation. They sought to improve and enlarge their holdings, to rebuild their mansions and their London houses, to fill and adorn them with works of art, and to exploit by their own efforts whatever non-agricultural resources they possessed. But from the 1880s, all this changed. Few great houses were built, either in London or the country, and many were sold or demolished. Works of art were dispersed rather than collected. There was a definite withdrawal from direct involvement in non-agricultural enterprises. Above all, there was a massive dispersal of land, throughout the British Isles, as estates tumbled into the market in the years immediately before and after the First World War.

The scale of this territorial transfer was rivalled only by two other landed revolutions in Britain this millenium: the Norman Conquest and the Dissolution of the Monasteries.[1] Put another way, this meant that the British landed establishment was in the process of dissolving itself, as it lost its unifying sense of territorial identity, and relaxed its dominant grip on the land. Of course, this was not a uniform process: poor patricians succumbed more easily than rich; the indebted were more vulnerable than those with unencumbered estates. In Ireland and Wales, the landowners virtually disappeared; but in England and Scotland, they survived more tenaciously. Yet whatever the qualifications, the fact remains that the dominant trend was no longer accumulation but dissolution. It was not just, as in former times, that a few families were selling out for strictly personal reasons, to be replaced by other landed dynasties. Between the onset of the Great Depression and the outbreak of the Second World War, the British patricians, as the landowning class and as the wealth élite, were in decline, disarray, and dissolution.

i. Landed Riches Eroded and Overwhelmed

During the first three-quarters of the nineteenth century, the British landed establishment had been the wealth élite of the richest nation in the world. But during the seventy years that followed, it was noticeably disturbed and diminished by new and international developments that it could not control, and in some cases could not survive. As the world became smaller, more competitive, and more unified; as distances were shortened by the steamship, the wireless, the telegraph, and the aeroplane; and as the economic autonomy and self-sufficiency of nations was eroded and undermined, the landowners of Britain were exposed to the full and icy blast of the global economy. Their economic circumstances were much less determined by the state of the harvest in Barset or by the health of their bank account in London, than by the price of wheat in Chicago and by financial dealings on the New York stock exchange. As Charles George Milnes Gaskell put it in an acute, prophetic, and pessimistic article, 'the vast increase in the carrying power of ships, the facilities of intercourse with foreign countries, [and] the further cheapening of cereals and meat', meant that, economically as politically, the patricians were no longer lords of the earth.[2]

One ominous sign of this was the explosive growth of a new international plutocracy, especially in the United States. As W. H. Lecky explained, 'there has probably never been a period in the history of the world when the conditions of industry, assisted by great gold discoveries in several parts of the world, were so favourable to the formation of fortunes as at present, and when the race of millionaires was so large.'[3] From the late 1870s to the First World War, there was a sudden expansion of quite unprecedented American fortunes – billionaires like Henry Ford, Rockefeller, and Andrew Mellon, and centimillionaires such as the Vanderbilts, the Astors, and Andrew Carnegie. And where these giants led, the lesser wealthy – like J. P. Morgan, who died in 1914 worth a mere eighty million dollars, Henry Clay Frick, and Samual P. Huntington—soon followed. Not only on the east coast, but also in the Midwest and California, these 'Trans-Atlantic Midases' amassed their millions: in railways, mining, iron and steel, urban real estate, chemicals and automobiles – but not, significantly, in agricultural land.[4]

In Britain, too, the same developments were evident. Between 1809 and 1879, only eleven fortunes were left in excess of two million pounds; but between 1880 and 1939, there were eighty-three. In the years 1906–12 alone, four mammoth sums were left of more than five million pounds, by Charles Morrison, H. O. Wills, Alfred Beit, and Julius Wernher. Between 1920 and 1930, there were twelve wills proved at four million pounds and above, three of which were greater than ten million.[5] As C. F. G. Masterman had put it in 1909, these were the 'astonishing facts of super-wealth' in twentieth-century Britain. It was, of course, not riches on the American scale: tens of millions of pounds did not signify compared with hundreds of millions of dollars, whatever the rate of exchange. Yet many of the areas in which such wealth was accumulated were the same: gold and diamonds, newspapers, consumer goods, international contracting and finance, but not agricultural land.[6] And, even more importantly, this new wealth dwarfed all except the greatest patrician fortunes. Between 1809 and 1879, some 88 per cent of British millionaires had been landowners, but between 1880 and 1914, the figure dropped to only 33 per cent, and it fell still further thereafter.[7] In short, the real leviathans of wealth were no longer British; or, if they were, they were no longer preponderantly drawn from the old landowning classes.

As A. J. Balfour put it in 1909, 'the bulk of the great fortunes are now in a highly liquid state . . . They do not consist of huge landed estates, vast parks and castles, and all the rest of it.'[8] And the advent of such wealth – often Jewish, often foreign, often American – engendered a real and justified sense of patrician anxiety. Quite rightly, they saw their economic supremacy threatened by this new form of wealth, which was in greater amounts, was in more liquid form, was less vulnerable to political exactions, and carried with it fewer obligations. They feared competition and corruption. Trollope explored these themes very early and very presciently in *The Way We Live Now*, and in 1887, Gladstone warned of the need to be 'jealous of plutocracy, and of its tendency to infect aristocracy, its older and nobler sister.'[9] During the mid-Victorian period, even a small landowner could compete in wealth with most British manufacturers; but from the late nineteenth century onwards, it was only a very tiny minority of the greatest magnates who could rival these new and colossal British fortunes. And even they were out of their depth compared with the new American super-rich.

The second world-wide development that threatened the patricians' financial pre-eminence and security was the growth of the international trade in agricultural produce. The opening up, in the last quarter of the nineteenth century, of the prairies and grasslands of America, Canada, Argentina, Australia, and New Zealand, combined with cheaper rail transport and fast, purpose-built refrigerated ships, led to a global glut of grain products and chilled meat that lasted until the 1930s. And as the domestic market in Britain expanded, consumption of these foreign products rose dramatically. In 1870, Britain imported 30 million hundredweights of grain; by 1900 the figure was 70 million; and by the inter-war years, the country was heavily dependent on imported foodstuffs of all kinds.[10] Here was a revolution in agricultural production and domestic consumption of quite unprecedented magnitude. As a result, the country that had once been the first agricultural nation, a self-sufficient producer of its own foodstuffs, suffered a sustained depression about which little could be done for seventy years.[11]

From the late 1870s, the prices of all agricultural products plummeted and, although there were occasional, brief upturns, they stayed depressed until the Second World War. In the prosperous years of mid-Victorian 'High Farming', wheat had averaged between 50 and 55 shillings a quarter; but in the 1880s and 1890s, it fell to 27 shillings, reaching a low point of 22s. 10d. in 1894.[12] By 1914, it had rallied to 30 shillings a quarter, and during the unusual conditions of wartime output and government guarantees, the price doubled. But the repeal of the Corn Production Act in 1921 led to a further slump, so that by the 1930s prices were back to the low levels of the 1890s. Livestock and dairy produce fell less dramatically, but the overall contours were very much the same. Indeed, between 1928 and 1931 alone, the average price of all farm produce fell by one-third.[13] The magnitude of this collapse can hardly be over-emphasized. From 1846 onwards, the prosperity of British agriculture had been dependent on high prices and low imports. But a generation on, those opponents of repeal who had argued that free trade in corn would destroy British agriculture by letting in cheap foreign produce seemed to have been vindicated – and in the most unhappy way possible.[14]

It is clear that this world-wide fall in agricultural prices led to an unprecedentedly gloomy period for British landowners. Undeniably, some contemporaries over-reacted to the late-nineteenth-century depression, there were considerable local variations, and pastoral farming was less hard-hit than arable. But even so, it was impossible to see signs of recovery, there was a continuous contraction of cultivation, and rents collapsed almost everywhere. In England, between the mid-1870s and the mid-1890s, they fell on average by 26 per cent: only 12 per cent in the pastoral north-west but 41 per cent in the arable south-east.[15] In Scotland and Wales, where farming was predominantly pastoral rather than arable, the fall was slightly less: 18.5 and 21 per cent respectively.[16] But in Ireland, where these general developments were exacerbated by the Land League rent strike and judicially adjusted rents, the fall was even greater. Between 1881 and 1902, the Irish Land Commission compulsorily reduced rents by 41 per cent; and even on estates that were never brought before it, the fall over the same period was in the region of 30 per cent.[17]

In general, by the mid-1890s, rents were probably back to where they had been in the early ·1840s; by 1914, as prices gradually improved, they had risen again, but were by no means back to their High Farming level. During the First World War, despite the doubling and trebling of agricultural prices, and the consequent enhanced prosperity of the farmers, the landowners themselves were forbidden from putting up rents, and so did not profit from this brief and prosperous period, as their predecessors had done during the Napoleonic Wars.[18] And when rents were finally raised, after 1918, it was usually by only 15 per cent. But even this was merely a brief interlude: for after the repeal of the Corn Production Act in 1921, the slide in prices began again, and landowners were obliged to reduce their rents once more, by as much as 25 per cent. Throughout the 1920s and 1930s, remissions of rents were as common as they had been half a century before.[19] By 1933, agricultural rentals were again at the level of 1914, and by 1936 they were back where they had been in 1800: which meant the lowest point of all since 1870.

But in addition, many landowners now found themselves squeezed between what seemed to be inexorably declining income, and outgoings that could not be correspondingly reduced. Almost all estates were burdened with jointures and other such payments, those essential items of family provision and continuity that still had to be met, even when income was reduced. And many were also bearing heavy debts and mortgages, on which fixed interest payments had to be made. In the heady days of the 1850s and 1860s, these burdens had been relatively easily assumed, when landowners had believed that their rentals would at worst remain static and at best continue to rise, so that there would be no difficulties about the payment of interest. But now, with reduced income, such fixed outgoings became much more burdensome. As one authority put it in 1890: 'when times are good, this state of things does not matter much; but when rents fall, the shoe instantly begins to pinch.' And, during the First World War, when interest rates rose from 3.5 per cent to 6 per cent, it pinched even more.[20]

The result was that decline in rentals severely understated the decline in disposable income for many landowners. In 1880, *The Spectator* calculated that for an averagely burdened estate, a fall of 30 per cent in gross income might mean a drop in net revenue of 50 per cent.[21] Put the other way, this meant that fixed charges took up a larger and larger part of a smaller and smaller income. On a Cambridgeshire estate, in a part of the country where depression hit particularly hard, interest payments took 41 per cent of revenue between 1881 and 1885, but 75 per cent of a much smaller income between 1885 and 1894. The Duke of Devonshire was spending 17 per cent of his disposable income on interest payments in 1874, but 60 per cent by 1880.[22] For landowners in Ireland, the position was even worse. The Land Commissioners had powers to reduce rents compulsorily, but no power to reduce fixed charges correspondingly. In many cases, reductions of 20 to 40 per cent completely wiped out any disposable income. And in times of rent strike, with no income coming in at all, the landowner suffered even more. 'How', one witness asked the Bessborough Commission, 'can he meet his payments, interest, annuities, jointures, on his property, and his other outgoings, if the Land Leaguers induce the tenants to refuse to pay their rents?' How, indeed?[23]

From prices to rental to values, the line of depression ran inexorably. For as the income that land generated declined, its capital value fell by at least 30 per cent. In 1890, English land that had been selling at between thirty and forty years' purchase in the golden age was now fetching only twenty to twenty-five years'. In Wales, the price was higher, at thirty years'; but in Ireland, it was generally as low as fifteen years', and often even less. And, although there was a brief upsurge between 1910 and 1921, in response to the temporary recovery of prices, there was another sudden collapse, amounting to a further 20 per cent, between 1925 and 1931. By the mid-1930s, land was selling for barely one-third of the sum it had fetched in the mid-Victorian period. By then, indeed, it had been so depressed for so long that there were few alive who could remember when it had last prospered, and few who dared predict when it would ever do so again. 'No security', noted *The Economist* at the beginning of it all, 'was ever relied upon with more implicit faith, and few have lately been found more sadly wanting, than English land.'[24]

But the collapse of land values also undermined the whole structure of patrician borrowing. For a fall in the value of land of 30 per cent wiped out the margin left between the value of land as collateral and the amount of the mortgage that had been raised upon it in more prosperous times. As one observer summarized it, 'upon many properties which are heavily charged, the depression has carried away much more than the margin of security'. Under such circumstances, insurance companies like the Royal Exchange, which were among the biggest lenders on landed security, began to 'review their mortgages'.[25] And many attorneys, who were also heavily involved in the mortgage business, did the same. In 1885, the solicitor of the fifth Lord Calthorpe, who had arranged a mortgage on his Acle estate, gave him the choice of providing more security or of paying off at least £10,000 at once. And if old loans were less secure, new mortgages were virtually impossible to obtain. 'Lawyers', a Herefordshire attorney explained, 'have grown very careful about advancing money upon a mortgage of land, since such extreme caution had to be exercised that the investment is rarely worth the anxiety.'[26]

In Ireland, the picture was even more bleak, as the combination of bad harvests, rent strikes, rural unrest, and compulsory rent reductions only depressed the value of land still further, and so made it even less secure. From 1880 onwards, major British lenders – whether insurance companies or individual solicitors – virtually refused to consider any more advances. One such institution, the Representative Body of the Church of Ireland, had approved 120 such loans between 1871 and 1876, but made only 25 from 1877 to 1925. Between 1866 and 1880, the Scottish Widows Company lent £1.2 million across the Irish Sea. But it then decided to call in these loans, and by 1894, some £850,000 had been repaid.[27] One of their mortgagors was the seventh Duke of Devonshire. In 1890, he owed the company £80,000, secured on his Irish estates, and was asked to begin paying it back at the rate of £10,000 a year. But many landowners, confronted with such abrupt demands for repayment, simply lacked the resources to do so. Indeed, in 1888, the Irish Landowners' Convention unavailingly begged the government to provide state loans with which they might pay off their mortgages and family charges.[28]

What did all this add up to? As Gaskell had foreseen, the result was that the patricians' territorial wealth was made to seem less Himalayan and less secure. The rise of the new plutocracy meant that, with one or two exceptions, landowners were no longer the wealthiest men in the land. And, at the same time, the global glut in agricultural produce, which led to a fall in prices, rentals, and land values, lessened very considerably the room in which members of the landed establishment could conduct their own financial manœuvres. Disposable income, adequate before, shrank alarmingly; fixed charges and interest payments, bearable in normal times, became burdensome; mortgages and encumbrances, safe hitherto, became dangerously large in relation to the diminished value of the land on which they were secured; and additional loans, which had been easily available in times past, were now much more difficult to obtain.[29] In sum, their finances were being squeezed, and their fortunes were being surpassed: in the sixty years from the late 1870s, the grandees and gentry were living in a new and increasingly hostile financial world.

But at the very same time, they were also confronted by a new

DEPRESSED DUKES.

Duke of Devonshire. "If this Budget passes, I don't know how I'm going to keep up Chatsworth!"
Duke of Westminster. "If you come to that, we may consider ourselves lucky if we can keep a Tomb over our Heads!"

14. 'Depressed Dukes.'
Punch, 30 June 1894.

threat: that of an increasingly predatory state. The most famous example of this was death duties, first introduced by Harcourt in 1894, and levied at 8 per cent on estates of over one million pounds. In fact the rate was relatively low. But at once they were described as 'calamitous', 'terrible', 'disastrous': for in both psychological and financial terms, they made an impact out of all proportion to their size.[30] At a time when confidence in the land was already undermined, they served only to erode it still further. To many estates already burdened with heavy debts, fixed outgoings, and reduced income, the effect of these duties at the margin might be quite crippling. There would be no surplus income to put away in anticipation; there might be no scope for further mortgaging; and loans might be impossible to obtain. It is easy to see why Oscar Wilde put these words into Lady Bracknell's mouth in *The Importance of Being Earnest*, first performed in 1895:

What between the duties expected of one during one's lifetime, and the duties exacted from one after one's death, land has ceased to be either a profit or a pleasure. It gives one a position, and prevents one from keeping it up. That's all that can be said about land.

Put less wittily, this meant that from the 1890s, the traditional territorial classes found themselves caught between a world economy that operated to their disadvantage, and British governments that seemed equally ill-disposed. Indeed, they very soon became more so, as death duties were raised inexorably: to 15 per cent from 1909 to 1914, 40 per cent from 1919 to 1930, 50 per cent from 1930 to 1934, and 60 per cent by 1939. There were, it is true, some slight concessions: payment could be spread over eight years (but with interest charged), relief for quick succession was introduced during the First World War, and agricultural land was exempted from the increases of 1925 and 1931.[31] But these counted for little. From 1919, land was valued for death–duty purposes at the current selling price, not – as formerly – on the basis of existing rents: so that at a time when land was very much under-rented, this meant duties became even higher. And the selling value was of the farms individually, not of the estates as a whole, which led to an even greater valuation. Even worse, the Treasury would not accept the land itself in lieu of payment, which meant that in the late 1920s, when the land market was depressed, such grandees as the newly inherited Dukes of Richmond and Montrose were obliged to pay large amounts in interest because they could not find buyers for their estates.[32]

At the same time that successive governments taxed landed capital, they also attacked landed income and capital gains. The most famous instance of this was the Incremental Value Duty and the Undeveloped Land Duty introduced by Lloyd George in his People's Budget of 1909. In fact, they raised little money and were repealed in 1920. But while they lasted, they only heightened the sense of encircling gloom. And even more burdensome was the inexorable rise of income taxes. During the First World War, super-tax was introduced for the first time on incomes in excess of £10,000, and it was retained and increased thereafter. In addition, it was levied on gross rather than net income, which was especially disadvantageous to landowners, with their large outgoings on charities and maintenance.[33] The only concessions were that the rating of agricultural land was halved, halved again, and finally abolished in 1896, 1923, and 1929. But this was soon negated by the rising income taxes of the inter-war years. The result was that even the richest of the grandees felt the pinch. As the seventeenth Earl of Derby explained in 1923, 'taxation at the present moment is so high that I may call myself a tax collector for the government. At present I am not living on my income. I am living on my capital.'[34]

By the inter-war years, even the greatest agricultural properties had become as uneconomic as Derby's comment implied. In 1918, some details were published of the Harwarden estate, where the young squire had been killed during the First World War. On his death, duties were paid that were six times the old Succession Duties, last levied in 1891. And, since taxation had quadrupled during the same period, the net result was that the new owner spent four-fifths of his rental income on rates, taxes, and maintenance, leaving only a small portion for living and annuities.[35] Other, larger properties, were equally blighted. On the Buccleuch estates in Eskdale and Liddesdale, gross revenue was £42,496, but £19,229 of this went on repairs, maintenance, and management, and £22,800 on taxes, leaving a surplus of £467 – and this on an unencumbered property. Overall, Lord Clinton calculated in 1919 that, on a selected group of estates with an average gross rental of £20,300, expenditure on income tax, tithe, and rates took £15,800, leaving the owners with a free income (before fixed payments) of only 4s. 6d. in the pound, compared with 10s. in the pound on an equivalent income derived from the Funds.[36]

So eloquent were these figures that the matter was even discussed in the House of Commons, where one MP summarized the position well: 'It is beyond doubt that English and also Scottish landowners, although some of them may possess apparently enormous rentals, are in reality in a condition of real poverty, unless they have some other source of revenue than the land.'[37] By the inter-war years, many landed estates had ceased to be economically viable, whatever the size of the rent roll. And even non-agricultural incomes of a traditional kind were, in some cases, less extensive than they had once been. In 1918, the Duke of Northumberland's gross income from mineral royalties was £82,450: but of that, he received net only £23,890, the rest having been taken as 5 per cent Mineral Rights Duty, 80 per cent Excess Mineral Rights Duty, plus income tax at 6s. in the pound, and supertax at 4s. 6d. By 1924, he was receiving only 2s. 6d. in the pound from his royalties, to which could be added, in 1931, only 7s. 9d. in the pound from his Alnwick rents.[38]

The combination of reduced incomes, increased exactions, and eroded confidence meant that most patricians were obliged to economize and to retrench, compared with the earlier and more prosperous period when, in retrospect, money had always seemed to be easily available. In the first place, everyday expenditure on conspicuous consumption had to be reduced: the country house might be let, hunting might be curtailed, the London season might be given up, and residence abroad might be contemplated for a time. The Earls of Verulam were faced with an income that declined from £17,000 in the 1870s to £14,000 in the 1880s. Tradesmen's bills were reduced, some of the servants were dismissed, the London season was cut from five months to two, consumption of alcohol was moderated, and both the big house at Gorhambury and the shooting were let.[39] Well on into the inter-war years, many families followed suit. In 1928, *Country Life* advertised Ingestre Hall, Staffordshire, on lease for seven years, with the option of shooting over 7,880 acres; Kedleston Hall in Derbyshire, available with fishing and 6,000 acres of shooting; and Levens Hall in Westmorland, with 1,814 acres of shooting, one and a half miles of salmon fishing, and a grouse moor of 5,200 acres.[40]

Such measures of retrenchment might make it possible for land-owners to come to terms with a much-diminished disposable income. But it was equally important to curtail or reduce much larger items of debt-incurring capital expenditure. This was particularly difficult in the case of jointures and portions, for they were the very sinews of family life and continuity, which had to go on if the family was to go on. In 1890, the Earl of Radnor had to make provision for the marriage of his eldest son; but with reduced rents, £100,000 worth of mortgages already incurred, and an annual expenditure on Longford Castle of £13,000, the only way to raise the money was by selling some old masters to the National Gallery for £55,000.[41] By 1899, the Peels of Tamworth, long since decayed from the halcyon days of the Prime Minister, were so indebted that there was no surplus to pay the Dowager Lady Peel's jointure of £350, and the money could be raised only by selling the great Sir Robert's library. And in 1921, a family like the Pryses in Wales found the greatest part of their liabilities derived from family charges from re-settlements of 1880 and 1919.[42]

Other forms of large-scale estate expenditure were curtailed more easily and more completely, especially the purchase of agricultural land itself. Even though the period from the late 1870s to the 1930s saw remarkably low prices, few landowners were rich or rash enough to buy on a large scale, as their forebears might have done. There were occasional exceptions: patricians who had outlived their own world, but who were unaware of it, and continued as before; and those with such large incomes that they could still afford to do so. The fifteenth Earl of Derby spent £100,000 on land in Fylde between 1878 and 1888, and on his death left £700,000 for further purchases. The very rich Lord Cadogan bought the Culford estate and mansion in Suffolk for £175,000 in 1890. And in the following year, the Hon. W. H. Fitzwilliam acquired the Wiganthorpe estate near Malton.[43] But these were among the richest of the super-rich, in two cases they were rounding out family holdings, and even their expenditure came to a halt well before the First World War. For most patricians, the growth and consolidation of great estates had effectively ended by the last quarter of the nineteenth century.

Equally marked was the decline in spending on agricultural improvement. The massive outlays in the age of High Farming had presupposed the availability of funds, the buoyancy of income and of land values, and an ultimate return on the investment. But from the 1870s, the sustained depression in agriculture undermined all these assumptions and expectations, so that even routine spending was much cut back, while improvements all but came to an end. In July 1886, when advertising for a new agent, Lord Harrowby specified that 'the strictest economy is necessary, and the agent is expected to diminish the large annual outgoings in connection with the estate.'[44] On the Leicester estates at Holkham, and the Abergavenny and Chichester estates in Sussex, expenditure was markedly cut back from the 1880s. By the inter-war years, when income was further reduced, and taxation had risen, along with the cost of labour and repairs, landowners were economizing even more drastically. As the *Estates Gazette* explained in 1935, landowners were no longer in a position to revive agriculture, because they no longer possessed the capital or the confidence to do so.[45]

As the political position of the land became more vulnerable, as the resources of those who held it in large quantities became less secure, and as loans became harder to obtain, there was also much less incentive to dabble in non-agricultural forms of estate exploitation. Lord Scarbrough at Skegness, and Lord de la Warr at Bexhill, were very late and very exceptional, lavishing considerable fortunes on the creation of new seaside resorts. But by then such patrician entrepreneurship was largely a thing of the past: at Eastbourne, from the 1890s, the Devonshires decided that they would, in future, no longer commit so much money to the resort's development, and other landowners with mines, markets, docks, and urban estates seem to have reached the same conclusion.[46] Significantly, when the Dukeries coalfield in Nottinghamshire was most profitably and productively opened up in the inter-war years, the great landowners of the locality were happy to collect their royalties, but left the mining operations entirely to private enterprise: something they would probably not have done a century earlier.[47]

For the same reason, expenditure on country houses was also markedly reduced. Between 1835 and 1874, traditional landowners

15. Middleton Park, Oxfordshire.

had been responsible for well over half of the mansions that were built; but from 1875 to 1914, they commissioned fewer than one-fifth; and by the inter-war years, the figure was even lower. Only a very few very rich aristocrats kept going, and most of them had stopped by 1914: the third Marquess of Bute remodelled Cardiff, the fifteenth Duke of Norfolk restored Arundel, the Duke of Portland extended Welbeck, and Lord Cadogan enlarged Culford.[48] But already, completely new mansions were extremely rare: only Bryanston for the Portmans and Clouds for the Hon. Percy Wyndham stand out before 1914. And in the inter-war years, country-house architects like Lorimer and Lutyens drew their clients from the new international plutocracy rather than from the old landed élite. Ironically, Lutyens' only mansion for an authentic grandee – Middleton Park for the Earl of Jersey in 1935–8 – was positively the last of its kind. And that was the exception that proved the rule, since the Jerseys were closely connected with banking.[49]

In 1921, on the occasion of the sale of Stowe, the *Estates Gazette* remarked, quite without irony: 'It seems improbable that any family, however rich, will ever again built a house nearly a thousand feet long, surrounded by a garden of 4,000 acres.'[50] How right they were. And the same was true of other traditional forms of patrician expenditure, which now came to an abrupt halt. With very few

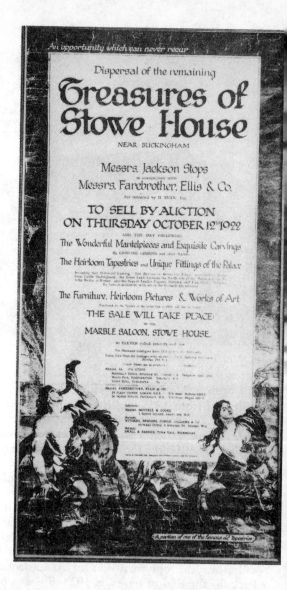

16. A poster for the 28-day auction of the contents of Stowe in Buckinghamshire in 1922.

exceptions, landowners ceased to be major figures in the sale rooms of the art world – at least as buyers. And their more general patronage of the arts, which had been steadily diminishing from the mid-nineteenth century, dwindled away almost to nothing. Country-house painters like Sargent and de Laszlo still thrived, though – like Lutyens – much of their work was for parvenus rather than patricians. The Beauchamps supported Elgar in his early, struggling years, as did the Sitwells with the young William Walton. And the

Marquess of Anglesey commissioned Whistler to paint the murals
that adorn Plas Newydd. But this was a very down-beat conclusion
to what had once been the flourishing realm of aristocratic
patronage.[51]

Compared with the easy certainties and unarticulated confidence
that most patricians had felt during the early and mid-nineteenth
century, it is clear that the economic environment between the Great
Depression and the Second World War was much less spacious and
far less optimistic. From the Reformation until the third quarter of
the nineteenth century, land had been seen as the most secure asset
economically, which also conferred appropriately real political influence, and unrivalled social status. But from the late 1870s onwards, all these assumptions were drastically eroded and irrevocably
reversed: the assurance of supreme, unchallenged wealth was lost;
the confidence in the stability and security of the land was undermined; the faith in a future like the past was much diminished; and
the demands of an increasingly hostile, predatory, and intrusive state
had to be met. Accordingly, economic decline had its effect, not only
on landowners' finances, but also on their minds, not just on their
wealth, but also on their self-esteem. Economically and psychologically, the grandees and gentry were under attack, on the defensive,
and in retreat.

ii.   The Breakup of Great Estates

The most impressive evidence of these changed conditions and
attitudes was the speed and determination with which many owners
sold all or part of their estates, abruptly putting into reverse the
centuries-long process of landed accumulation which had reached its
zenith during the third quarter of the nineteenth century. As Lord
Ailesbury put it in 1911, 'a man does not like to go down to posterity
as the alienator of old family possessions.'[52] Yet by that time, that
was exactly what he and many others of his class were doing. As land
ceased to be economically secure or politically important, and as it
seemed to be increasingly vulnerable to acquisitive government
measures, patricians no longer looked upon their holdings sentimentally and historically, as family heirlooms, but instead came to regard
them rationally and calculatingly as investments. As such, they
found that they did not pay, and that they should be disposed of.
And that, across the whole of the British Isles, is exactly what they
did.

It was in Ireland that the disappearance of the old territorial élite
was most complete and where, quite exceptionally, it was brought
about by state legislation and at the state's expense. The Land Acts of

1870, 1881, and 1891 began the process, but only very slowly.[53] Landowners wanted to obtain as good a price as possible for their estates, so as to pay off their debts and leave them with something for themselves. But the tenants, who were well aware of the massive fall in land values from the 1880s, were prepared to offer only very low prices which the owners would not accept. In 1881, Lord Fermoy's estate was put up for sale by the Norwich Union Assurance Company, the principal mortgagee: but when the tenants offered only eight years' purchase, it was withdrawn. Likewise, in 1889, the Earl of Bandon offered his lands at twenty-two years' purchase, but the tenants would pay only thirteen. 'There are', observed J. Fitzgerald, 'so many encumbered owners who are being forced by mortgagees and others to sell at ruinous rates that tenants don't understand being asked a fair price.'[54] As one witness put it before the Cairns Commission in 1882, 'To the heavily encumbered landlord, there was no alternative but to sell. But to whom?'[55]

Nevertheless, there were some quite spectacular individual transfers of property, especially in the late 1880s, when the pressure on the landowners from both their mortgagees and their tenants was especially severe. The Marquess of Bath sold 21,000 acres in County Monaghan for £290,054, the Duke of Abercorn 22,700 acres in Tyrone and Donegal for £267,604, Sir Victor Brooke 7,300 acres in County Fermanagh for £83,992, the Marquess of Waterford 9,500 acres in his titular county for £124,556, and the Duke of Leinster 19,000 acres in County Kildare for £240,000.[56] With the exception of Lord Bath, who was withdrawing almost completely, none of these sales was by a landlord who was selling the majority of his Irish acres. In every other case, the landowners were merely slimming down their estates, attracted by offers in the region of fifteen to twenty years' purchase, which were, in the circumstances, too good to refuse. But these sales also suggested that if such prices could be generally obtained in the future, the number of landowners tempted to sell would be much increased. To that extent, Michael Davitt was correct in predicting that the 1881 Land Act was indeed 'a legislative sentence of death by slow process against Irish landlordism.'[57]

But it was only in the 1900s that 'Irish landlordism' went into conspicuous and conclusive liquidation. For the terms of Wyndham's Land Act of 1903, and Birrell's Act passed six years later, were generous enough to both sides to encourage landowners to sell, and tenants to buy. The repayment period for the tenant's loan was extended to 68.5 years, the interest rate was reduced to 3.25 per cent, and a bonus of 12 per cent was given by the government to encourage landlords to sell.[58] The result was a 'rush to purchase' – and a rush to put up for sale – so great that the £5 million a year initially allocated was eagerly taken up. In late 1903, the Duke of Leinster was very quick off the mark, receiving £676,038 for the remainder of his Kildare estates. And, like him, many other landowners now resolved to liquidate their Irish holdings entirely: great Anglo-Irish grandees like Devonshire, Lansdowne, Fitzwilliam, and Leconfield; and also owners whose lands were exclusively Irish, like Kilmaine, Ranfurly, Wicklow, Fingall, and Meath.[59]

Within ten years of the passing of Wyndham's Act, the landowners of Ireland were in full territorial retreat. Under the legislation of 1870–96, only 2.5 million acres had been transferred; but between 1903 and 1909 alone, some 9 million acres were sold. In 1870, only 3 per cent of Irish holdings were owned by former tenants; by 1908 the figure was 46 per cent, and still rising rapidly. Indeed, by 1912, *Burke's Landed Gentry* felt moved to inquire whether 'there still remains a landed gentry at all in that country, so great has been the compulsory [sic] alienation of land in Ireland during the last decade.'[60] By 1914, many of the landed families were still actually resident in Ireland: they retained their houses and perhaps one hundred acres, but no longer a great estate. They were isolated and cut off: from their former tenantry in Ireland, and from the British government across the sea. On the eve of the setting up of the Irish Free State, over three-quarters of the land had been transferred from landlords to tenants. At a conservative estimate, some 11 million acres had changed hands under the UK Irish land legislation, at a cost – to the British taxpayer – of £100 million.[61]

Under the new Irish Free State, the process of territorial dismantlement was completed. The Hogan Act of 1923 put what had previously been the voluntary British system on a compulsory footing, by vesting the remaining land not yet tenant-owned in a reconstituted Land Commission, which paid the former owners a standard price, and then sold it off to the tenants. As a result, a further 3.1 million acres were vested in the Land Commission, at a cost of £21 million, which were gradually conveyed to the tenants. The combined effects of the British and Irish land legislation were that some 15 million out of 17 million acres were transferred from landlords to tenants, at a cost of £150 million in advances.[62] In scale, this was land reform on a par with Bolshevik Russia: the hereditary owners, who had held the land for centuries, now held it no more. It took three decades rather than three years, and the owners were bought out, not expropriated. To that extent, the nationalists were correct in describing the demise of the Irish landowners as a 'bloodless revolution'. But it was a revolution, none the less.

By the 1920s, there were virtually no great Irish estates left: at best, the patricians held on to their ancestral mansion and perhaps the park, but nothing more. 'Landlordism', the *Estates Gazette* announced towards the close of that decade, 'in the sense of ownership of the land tilled by others, is at an end in Ireland.' Or, as the sixth Marquess of Lansdowne – whose ancestors had owned nearly 120,000 acres – put it in 1937, 'there are, of course, today in Ireland no "landlords" in the old sense of the word.'[63] But the most vivid sense of Irish landowners at the end of the road was caught by Harold Nicolson who, in 1942, visited Lord Powerscourt at his great house in County Wicklow, where his family had once possessed 40,000 acres:

> A great ostentatious eighteenth-century mansion, with a most elaborate Italian garden, and a superb view of the Wicklow mountains . . . We leant upon a gilt balustrade, looking down over the fountains to the great pool between the statues. He said, 'Here I am marooned – the last of the Irish aristocracy, with nobody to speak to.'[64]

In Wales, by contrast, private enterprise accomplished unaided a similar transformation. Even in the 1880s and 1890s, the market for land was relatively buoyant, partly because, in a country where pastoral farming predominated, the price of land remained high, and partly because the tenantry were eager to buy. In 1887, it was claimed that thirty years' purchase was 'the rule rather than the exception'; and by 1890, prices as high as thirty-five to forty-five years' purchase were 'readily obtainable'.[65] In Cardiganshire alone, major owners like Pryse and Lisburne parted with 50,000 acres; and between 1894 and 1897, Lord Ancaster sold his Gwydir estate in North Wales. But the most spectacular sale was that of the 26,000-acre Monmouthshire estate of the Duke of Beaufort, which included eight castles as well as Tintern Abbey, and which was disposed of gradually between 1898 and 1901. And this was a portent of things to come: between 1901 and 1910, Lords Glanusk, Ashburnham, Denbigh, and Winchilsea sold land in Wales. Like the Beauforts, they were primarily English owners, who were as yet selling off only peripheral properties: the great Welsh heartland estates remained essentially intact.[66]

But from 1910 to 1914, there was a dramatic change, as almost every major Welsh owner whose territorial identity was mainly within the Principality began to dispose of parts of their estates. Among the foremost names in the market were Lord Powis in Montgomeryshire, Lord Harlech at Criccieth, Lord Wimborne in Glamorgan, the Duke of Westminster in Flint, the Rhug estate in Merioneth, and the Williams-Wynn holdings in Denbigh and Montgomery.[67] Such widespread selling by such illustrious and important

Welsh proprietors showed their real anxieties about the future of land-ownership in the immediate aftermath of Lloyd George. As one contemporary remarked, with only slight exaggeration, 'it has become very general to break up large estates.' Indeed, although the war slowed the market down, sales continued, as owners remained apprehensive about the future. In 1915, the Beauforts severed their connection with Wales completely by selling their 5,000-acre Brecon estate, and in the following year, the Marquess of Abergavenny followed suit, by disposing of his only Welsh property, 2,500 acres in Monmouth.[68]

With improved rentals and increased values in the immediate aftermath of the war, every major Welsh landlord placed at least part of his estate on the market, and some went a great deal further. Among the most famous were Major George Cornwallis-West, who sold Ruthin Castle and 11,000 acres in Denbigh for £76,000; the outlying parts of the Gladstone estate at Hawarden which went for £112,000; Lord Kensington's holdings in Pembrokeshire which fetched £100,000; the Raglan estates in Monmouthshire which realized £105,000; the Cofyn Maltby lands in Glamorgan which brought in £227,000; the Bute agricultural lands in the same county which sold for £124,000; and the Williams-Bulkeley estates, including Beaumaris Castle, which fetched £110,000.[69] There was a further, brief surge in 1924–5, when the remaining parts of the Penrhyn estate in Caernarfon, the Bute agricultural estates in Glamorgan, and the Pontypool estate in Monmouthshire were sold. But then the boom burst, and in 1927 Lord Bagot failed to sell his Denbighshire holdings.[70]

Thereafter, there were still occasional sales, as in 1930, when the Marquess of Londonderry disposed of 9,000 acres in Merioneth, and in 1938, when the recently succeeded Lord Harlech was obliged to part with 1,424 acres of his Brogyntn estate near Oswestry, and when the Tredegar settled estates came into the market. But by then, the major changes had taken place: the great transnational moguls had pulled out almost completely, and the largest Welsh proprietors were very much reduced. As the *Montgomery Express* had put it in 1919, in words that applied to the country as a whole, 'little short of an agrarian revolution is being witnessed in central Wales, where large tracts of territory are continually tumbling into the market.'[71] In 1909, only 10 per cent of Wales was owner-occupied; but by 1941, the figure was 39 per cent. Only in Ireland was the traditional territorial ascendancy vanquished more completely. As Kenneth Morgan correctly summarizes it: 'only a few great houses remained', while 'the gentry subsided as if they had never been.'[72]

In Scotland, as in Ireland, many of the estates were very large; and, as in Wales, the breakup was under the auspices of private initiative rather than that of the state. Once again, sales were sluggish in the period from the 1880s to the 1900s, although there was no shortage of landowners wanting to sell. In 1888–9, Lord Aberdeen sold his estates at Cromar, and in 1891 the Marquess of Tweeddale disposed of the outlying parts of his Roxburghshire lands. In 1897 the Marquess of Queensberry parted with 5,800 acres at Kinmount, Dumfriesshire, which had formed nearly half his holdings, for £130,000; and in the 1900s, the Eglinton estate was largely liquidated in Ayrshire.[73] But the most sustained seller in Scotland in this period was the Duke of Fife, who had originally owned very nearly 250,000 acres in Aberdeen, Banff, and Elgin, but who, between 1880 and 1899, sold off much of his land on the grounds that he preferred smallholdings. On the whole, though, the market was as slack as in Ireland: large, wild, and barren estates, often remotely situated and in an inhospitable climate, were easy to let for the game, but unattractive to sell.[74]

But as in Wales, the sales gathered pace between 1910 and 1914, sometimes limited to the outlying part of a vast highland agglomeration, but sometimes encompassing the whole estate itself. In June 1910, the Earl of Perth sold his Strathallan, Tullibardine, and Machany properties, amounting to 7,322 acres.[75] Other major sellers in these pre-war years included the Duke of Argyll, who put the Island of Tiree on the market; the Menzies family, who obtained £260,000 for their 70,000-acre estate and castle in Perthshire; Sir Frederick Johnstone, who sold his 14,462-acre Westerhall estate in Dumfries for £96,327; and the Earl of Kintore, who liquidated his entire holdings in Kincardine and Aberdeen – worth £22,000 a year – for £175,000. But the most astounding news of all in the Scottish property market broke in July 1914, when Knight, Frank, and Rutley announced that they were shortly going to put 330,000 acres of the Duke of Sutherland's massive northern latifundia on the market.[76]

The war led to postponement of this and other sales, although in 1916 the Earl of Erroll sold his Slains Castle estate of 4,200 acres, which severed his territorial connections with Scotland completely.[77] But as soon as peace was declared, the market boomed again, with the Duke of Sutherland taking the lead. In the autumn of 1918, he offered 238,000 acres, and in the next year added a further 114,000, including Dornoch Castle itself. By then, many of the greatest lairds were in the market: Lord Lovat sold 100,000 acres of deer forest and grouse moor in Inverness, and Lord Aberdeen sold 50,000 acres of the Haddo estate for £200,000, 'the largest break-up sale of high-class agricultural land that has ever taken place in the

United Kingdom.'[78] Between 1920 and 1922, the Duke of Portland sold in Ayrshire, Lord Carmichael in Peebles, the Earl of Airlie in Perth and Forfar, and the Earl of Strathmore in Teesside. And some of the greatest of the Scottish grandees began to follow the Sutherlands' lead: Sir Samuel Scott and Cameron of Lochiel sold, respectively, 60,000 and 110,000 acres in Inverness; the Duke of Argyll disposed of Tiree, Lismore, and Benmore, amounting to 50,000 acres; the Duke of Hamilton put 20,000 acres in Linlithgow and Stirling on the market; and the Breadalbanes parted with 40,000 acres in Perthshire, including Taymouth Castle itself.[79]

As in Wales and England, the market for Scottish land stagnated during the mid-1920s, which created great difficulties for the newly inherited Dukes of Richmond and Montrose, who were trying unavailingly to sell off parts of their vast inheritance so as to raise money for death duties.[80] But as the *Estates Gazette* predicted, 'when prices improve, it is probable that a good deal more Highland property will come on to the market.' And so it did – although in the main it was grouse moors and sporting estates, rather than prime agricultural land. In 1928, the Duke of Atholl made extensive sales in Perthshire, and the Duke of Montrose began to sell his Stirling, Lanark, and Dumbarton holdings, including Ben Lomond. Between 1934 and 1937, the Duke of Richmond finally succeeded in divesting himself of his extensive estates in Banff, Aberdeen, and Moray. The Breadalbanes, having already liquidated their 250,000 acres in Perth in the 1920s, sold off an equivalent amount in Argyll between 1934 and 1936. And where these giant proprietors led, such smaller owners as the Earl of Moray in Perth, and Macpherson of Cluny in Inverness, followed suit.[81]

Inevitably, such spectacular Scottish sales attracted much attention: 'on the sentimental side', noted the *Estates Gazette*, 'it is impossible not to regret the disappearance of some of the old northern families from their ancient moors and glens.'[82] The early disposal of entire estates before the First World War, the sheer size of many of the sales thereafter, and the dramatic recovery of the market in the 1930s were all quite remarkable. Between 1912 and 1920, Knight, Frank and Rutley alone claimed to have sold 1.6 million Scottish acres, equivalent to more than one-twelfth of the land area of the country.[83] Some ancient families, both great and small, disappeared almost completely, like the Errolls and the Breadalbanes. But others, like the Sutherlands, the Argylls, and the Atholls, were owners of such vast estates that, even after selling several hundred thousand acres, they remained substantial magnates. For this reason, and also because in many places estates were sold *en bloc* and not in lots, the demise of the landed establishment was less complete than in Wales: only about 30 per cent of Scottish land was now owner–occupied, compared with over 40 per cent in the Principality. But even so, the result was a dramatic and spectacular transformation.

In England, likewise, there was a strong desire to sell from the 1880s, and the passing of the Settled Lands Act made it possible for tenants for life to do so more easily. 'Were there any effective demand for the purchase of land', wrote the Duke of Marlborough in 1885, 'half the land of England would be in the market tomorrow.'[84] But as in Scotland and Ireland, the prevailing prices were so low – and the demand was so weak – that very few sales actually took place, as most landowners hung on, defiantly or desperately, in the hope of better times. In the late 1880s and early 1890s, the Duke of Newcastle and Lords Southampton, Ripon, Carlisle, Hardwicke, and Tollemache were all successful in selling part of their estates. But the list of those who tried and failed was at least as long: the Duke of Leeds, and Lords Rodney, Wilton, Cholmondeley, Westmorland, and Saye and Sele. As late as 1905, there were still almost insurmountable difficulties in disposing of estates 'in a block'.[85]

But in the years immediately before the First World War, the combination of slightly improved agricultural conditions and Lloyd George's anti-landlord campaigns meant that the market picked up. In 1909, the Duke of Bedford caused a sensation by putting his Thorney estate on the market, 'in deference to the social and legislative tendencies of the day.' Having failed to sell it in its entirety to the crown, it was bought piecemeal by the tenants for £566,000. 'We cannot doubt', noted one authority, 'that, as time goes on, the same sentiment will weigh with other landowners.'[86] And so, indeed, it did. In the very next year, Walter Long, the quintessential landed gentleman in politics, began to sell his Wiltshire estate, and he was only one of many. By June 1910, some 72,000 acres were on offer in thirty-six English counties, and the figures rose each year until 1913. In 1912, nineteen noblemen were listed as offering large estates, including the Duke of Sutherland, who sold all his Trentham and Lilleshall lands before the war for £400,000. By late 1914, some 800,000 acres of English land had changed hands for about £20 million. As the *Estates Gazette* noted, 'the unanimity of large English landlords in selling their estates clearly points to some great change in the condition of affairs in this country.'[87]

During the war, the market slowed down, but transactions still continued 'with a briskness which is astonishing in the present circumstances', as the Dukes of Beaufort, Westminster, St Albans, and Manchester, and Lords Somers, Normanton, Scarbrough, Londonderry, and Shrewsbury put land up for sale.[88] But it was the end of the war that really saw the market surge ahead. In the spring of 1919, Lords Aberdeen, Aylesford, Beauchamp, Cathcart, Middleton, Northampton, Petre, Tollemache, and Yarborough were among the leading vendors. There were in aggregate some half a million acres of English land up for sale, and in the year as a whole, twice that amount was actually sold. Then, in 1920, the records were broken again, as the sellers included the Dukes of Leeds, Beaufort, Marlborough, Grafton, and Northumberland. In addition, the Duke of Rutland sold a large part of his Belvoir holdings for £1.4 million; the Duke of Norfolk parted with 20,000 acres of his Yorkshire estate; and Lord Portman sold in Somerset and Dorset, as did Lord Dudley at Great Witley in Worcestershire.[89]

In 1921–2, with the beginning of a new depression in agriculture and in the aftermath of the repeal of the Corn Production Act, the boom broke, and the turnover was only half the previous year. But even so, there were some illustrious sellers: the Duke of Northumberland in Surrey and Yorkshire, Lord Ilchester in Somerset, and Lord Willoughby de Broke at Compton Verney. In 1923–5, the market picked up again briefly, and Lords Middleton, Howard, Portman, Eldon, Tankerville, and Brownlow all disposed of more property.[90] But by the late twenties, the market was so depressed that the Marquess of Ailesbury could sell only 25,000 acres of Savernake for £10 an acre. In 1930, the Duke of Leeds sold Hornby Castle and 6,000 acres in Yorkshire, and Lord Verulam parted with 5,000 acres of his Gorhambury estate adjacent to St Albans. In 1932, there were two major sales, of the Savile estates in Yorkshire and of Lord Ashburton's lands in Hampshire.[91] In 1934, the Portman trustees sold the Culford estate, which the family had purchased only forty years before. By the end of the decade, the market seemed to be picking up again, and major sellers included the Duke of Norfolk in Lincolnshire, the Duke of Portland in Northumberland, Lord Stanley of Alderley in Cheshire, and the Rufford Abbey estates of the Savile family in Nottinghamshire.[92]

Speaking in the House of Commons in December 1924, Edward Wood observed that there was 'a silent revolution in progress . . . We are, unless I mistake it, witnessing in England the gradual disappearance of the old landed classes.'[93] He was not at all mistaken. In the years immediately before and after the First World War, some six to eight million acres, one-quarter of the land of England, was sold by gentry and grandees. In Wales and Scotland, the figure was nearer one-third, and in Ireland it was even higher.[94] Across the whole of the British Isles, the change between the late 1870s and the late 1930s was remarkable, as five hundred years of patrician landownership had effectively been halted and reversed in seventy. The extent of

this transformation was well summarized by Bernard Shaw, who set
his play *Back to Methuselah* on the west coast of Ireland in the year
3000 AD, and included in it this piece of dialogue:

> Elderly gentleman: I am speaking the plainest English. Are you the
> landlord?
> The woman (shaking her head): There is a tradition in this part of
> the country of an animal with a name like that. It used to be
> hunted and shot in the barbarous ages. It is quite extinct
> now.[95]

iii.   The Disposal of Non-agricultural Assets

Psychologically and symbolically, as well as economically and financially, the sale of so much land so quickly by so many was the most
significant evidence of the transformation and decline of what had
once been the British landed establishment. But this was by no
means the only way in which landowners divested themselves of
their accumulated possessions during this period. When agricultural
acres were hard to sell (as they often were) and when sentiment
dictated that they should be retained at all cost (as it sometimes did),
many landowners preferred to realize alternative assets, which could
find more ready buyers and also realize a much better price: collieries
and minerals, docks and harbours, building estates and market halls,
country houses and London mansions, works of art and family
heirlooms. So, in the years from the 1880s until the Second World
War, many notables divested themselves of much more than just
their broad acres. In other ways, too, the great accumulators had
become the great dispersers.

The most well-publicized example of this was the progressive
disposal of patrician art collections. When they had been the richest
élite in the western world, the grandees (and gentry) of Britain had
bought from impoverished continental aristocrats. But now they in
turn had become relatively impoverished, and a new and even richer
élite had come into being across the Atlantic, appropriately dubbed
by Berenson the 'squillionaires'. And so the great works of art
moved west once more, to adorn the Fifth Avenue mansions and the
Newport 'cottages' of the new American plutocracy. Possessed of
the greatest wealth yet accumulated, determined to acquire the
trappings of cultural decency, and assisted by experts like Berenson
and dealers like Duveen, the wealthy men and women of America
effectively created the modern international art market between the
1880s and the 1930s.[96] For at the very time when they wanted to
buy, there were many British owners who wanted (and needed) to

sell, while the passing of the Settled Lands Act of 1882 made it much easier than before for such heirlooms to be disposed of.

Three particular landed families set the pattern for such dispersals. In 1875 and 1878, the Munros of Novar auctioned their collection of Turners and old masters for £100,000. (They were later to sell their Raphael Madonna for a great deal more.) On a much larger scale, the Duke of Hamilton sold the entire contents of Hamilton Palace in July 1882: 2,213 lots of paintings, glass, enamel, and furniture which realized the unprecedented sum of £397,562.[97] Not to be outdone, the much more impoverished Duke of Marlborough disposed of many of Blenheim's greatest treasures. In June 1875, he had already sold the Marlborough gems for 35,000 guineas, and had followed this in 1883 with the disposal of the Blenheim enamels and old master drawings. But the largest sale, between 1884 and 1886, was of the great collection of paintings. Initially, the Duke offered twenty-five of them to the National Gallery, for £400,000. The offer was refused, and instead, the Raphael Madonna and the Van Dyck *Charles I on Horseback* were bought by the nation for £87,500. But the rest, which included works by Breughel, Van Dyck, Rembrandt, Rubens, Claude, Holbein, Kneller, and Lely, along with porcelain and miniatures, were sold in July and August 1886.[98]

During the next thirty years, many landed families followed suit. Between 1886 and 1902, Lord Dudley parted with china, old masters, and jewels worth £240,000. In 1892, the Spencers sold their magnificent library to Mrs John Rylands for £250,000; the Earl of Orford's books went in two lots in 1895 and 1902; and the Crawfords disposed of their stamps and historical manuscripts in three sales between 1902 and 1914. In 1905, Lord Tweedmouth sold old masters worth £48,895; in 1907 the Duke of Fife auctioned 150 pictures from Duff House; and in 1913 J. P. Morgan bought the Knole tapestries, after the Sackvilles had impoverished themselves in a lawsuit, for $325,000.[99] Other sales were more bizarre. In 1899, Lord Francis Hope of Deepdene was prevented by the courts from selling the Hope Diamond for £18,000. But by then, he had already disposed of family pictures worth £120,000. And in 1904, the trustees of the Marquess of Anglesey sold the entire contents of Beaudesert and Anglesey Castle, which included jewelled walking sticks, paste diamonds, silken nightshirts, and 'an amazing collection of unnecessary gear.'[100]

But with works of art, as with broad acres, it was the anxiety engendered between 1909 and 1914 that really accelerated sales. In 1909 and 1910, the total value of works of art exported was over one million pounds, the highest ever figure. Among the foremost paintings were Raphael's *Three Graces* and Fra Angelico's *Last Judgement* –

Mr. Widener Pays More Than $500,000 for Raphael's "Madonna and Child"

Duveen Brothers End Most Important Single Art Transaction Ever Undertaken.

HINTED PHILADELPHIA COLLECTOR PAID $700,000

One of World's Greatest Pictures, Known as "Panshanger Madonna," To Be Exhibited Here.

17. Extract from *The New York Herald*, 7 Feb. 1914, on the acquisition of the Small Cowper Madonna by P. A. B. Widener.

formerly owned by Lord Dudley – the Marquess of Exeter's *Petrus Christus*, the Marquess of Lothian's *Virgin and Child* by Rubens, one Rembrandt each from Lord Ashburnham and Lord Ilchester, two Rubenses from Blenheim, and a Gainsborough from Knole.[101]

Other important sales at this time included a Holbein from the Duke of Norfolk's collection for £70,000, and Rembrandt's *The Mill*, which Lord Lansdowne sold to P. A. B. Widener for $500,000. Three years later, Widener scored an even bigger coup, when he obtained the 'small' Madonna by Raphael for $565,000, from Lady Desborough, who had inherited it from her aunt, the widow of the last Lord Cowper. Predictably, there were public outcries about the dispersal of the nation's artistic heritage, and of the financial pressure exerted by the government that was forcing landowners to respond in this way. 'The drain that is going on', one expert observed, 'may be expected to continue', thanks to 'the combined pressures of taxes and temptation.'[102]

After the war, that was precisely what happened, as the art market was re-established and prices soared higher than ever before. The Duke of Hamilton inaugurated this second phase by selling a further £242,000 worth of silver, furniture, and paintings; and he was soon followed by the Duke of Leeds, who disposed of the contents of Hornby Castle, including its Canalettos, for £85,000. But the most spectacular sale was that by the Duke of Westminster, who accepted a price rumoured to be between £200,000 and £750,000 from Samuel Huntington for *The Blue Boy* and *Mrs Siddons as the Tragic Muse*.[103] In the mid-1920s, when the land market stagnated, the sales of art went on: Lord Brownlow's pictures from Ashridge and Carlton House Terrace fetched £120,000; some of the Spencer art collection crossed the Atlantic; and Lady Desborough sold her second inherited Cowper Madonna, this time to Andrew Mellon for $875,000. Even in the depths of the depression, there were more major sales, including the paintings from Dorchester House, the marbles from Lansdowne House, and the pictures, furniture, and books from Lambton Castle. And in 1938, the contents of Norfolk House were auctioned by Christies, and the Savile treasures from Rufford Abbey, including sixty panels of tapestry, also went under the hammer.[104]

In an age used to the 'Getty Factor' and the National Heritage Fund, these events seem almost commonplace, and the prices rather on the low side. But the impact on contemporaries was very great, for they were well aware that it portended the breakup of many great patrician art collections, and their irrevocable dispersal across the Atlantic. To philistines like the second Duke of Westminster, who did not care about art and were happy to pocket the money, this did

not matter. But to a man like Lord Crawford, who regarded his
family collections at Haigh as a sacred trust, the prospect of losing
them was almost unendurable. 'They form', he recorded in 1932,
when it seemed he might have to sell extensively, 'the apanage of our
family, and their loss will cause us profound distress. Books and
pictures combine to make Haigh one of the great and famous houses
of England – stripped of these treasures, the place would be uninhabitable.' Yet this was the shape of things to come; as taxes rose,
houses were gradually denuded of their treasures, and pictures,
books, and precious objects passed to America, never to return. At
best, 'Victorian openhandedness' was replaced by 'elegant economy';
at worst, dispersal was sometimes total.[105]

Many of these famous art sales – of some or all of the Lansdowne,
Westminster, and Holford collections, for example – were occasioned by the disposal of the great family palaces in London that had
once housed them. As early as 1912, it was rumoured that the Duke
of Sutherland was about to sell Stafford House to Sir William Lever.
'It is rare indeed', the *Estates Gazette* rightly noted, 'that a family
voluntarily parts with its town palace.' And the same journal could
not help noticing the difference between the grandee who owned it,
and the rumoured purchaser – the son of a Bolton grocer, who had
started work in his father's shop at the age of sixteen.[106] In fact, it
was not until 1916 that Leverhulme (as he had by then become)
bought the palace, renamed it Lancaster House in honour of his
home county, and subsequently presented it to the government. In
the same year, the Duke of Westminster vacated Grosvenor House,
which became the headquarters of the Ministry of Food for the rest
of the war. Eventually, in 1924, Leverhulme purchased this palace as
well. On his death, it was demolished, and shops, flats, and a hotel
were constructed on the site.[107]

By then the gradual but inexorable disappearance of the great
London palaces was a well-recognized trend. 'The tendency of the
great territorial families', noted the *Estates Gazette* as it drew the
obvious parallel, 'to sell a considerable proportion of their land is
now extending to their expensive town houses.' Early in 1919, Lord
Salisbury sold his house in Arlington Street, which had been the
Cecils' London home for generations, for £120,000. In the same
year, Lord Dartmouth disposed of his great mansion in Mayfair, and
the Duke of Devonshire parted with Devonshire House, on the
north side of Piccadilly, for three-quarters of a million pounds. The
next to go, in 1928, was Dorchester House in Park Lane, which was
again demolished and replaced by a hotel.[108] Soon after, Lansdowne
House, built by Robert Adam, and occupying virtually the whole

18. The demolition of Devonshire House, Piccadilly.

southern side of Berkeley Square, disappeared as well. To a man with a strong and aesthetic sense of the past, like Lord Crawford, it was all very sad: 'Lansdowne House is about to fall into the hands of the housebreakers... Dorchester House is now level with the ground... I remember so many London palaces disappearing, in fact one can count on one hand those which survive, and soon they must be doomed before long.'[109]

He was quite correct, as sales and demolitions continued unabated during the 1930s. In 1931, Chesterfield House, the home of Lord Harewood, was put on the market, where it joined Sunderland, Curzon, and Brooke Houses. In the same year, Lord Derby decided to dispose of his family's grand mansion in Stratford Place, and soon afterwards his son Lord Stanley acquired a much more modest town residence in Belgrave Square. In 1934, the dowager Duchess of Rutland sold 16 Arlington Street for £70,000, the town house of the Manners family for over a century, which had been empty for nearly a decade. Three years later, Crewe House in Curzon Street was sold, and so was Norfolk House, St James's Square, which the young duke had been trying to sell since 1930, and which was now demolished to make way for flats and offices.[110] And these sump-

tuous palaces of the greatest grandees were soon followed by the
town houses of patrician politicians. In 1929, Lord Balfour's house at
4 Carlton Gardens was put up for sale, and in 1939 Lord Rosebery's
former home at 38 Berkeley Square fetched over £1 million. By the
time Lord Crawford attended a party at Londonderry House in 1937,
he reluctantly concluded that 'this is the last great house which can
conduct entertaining on this scale.'[111]

From the disposal of London palaces to the disposal of country
houses was but a step, often occasioned by the same pressure of
increased costs and the same allure of alternative investments. Before
the 1870s, it was very rare indeed for country houses to be sold or
demolished. Most families were extremely tenacious in retaining the
mansion and grounds, and devised elaborate methods of transference
if the male line died out. And houses that were pulled down had
usually been accidentally damaged beyond repair, or were being
demolished so that something more modern and more grandiose
might be put in its place. But gradually from the 1880s, and more
markedly from the First World War, these trends, too, were put into
reverse.[112] Many houses that had been extended during the high-
Victorian period to accommodate the unprecedented numbers of
servants, were substantially reduced in size by partial demolition.
Some families, who sold off subsidiary estates, decided to part with
their subsidiary houses as well. Others, who were selling out altogether, often disposed of the park and mansion at the sametime. And
in a growing number of instances, where no individual buyer could
be found, the house might be demolished completely.

As the pages of *Country Life* eloquently demonstrate, the sale of
patrician mansions, by such firms as Knight, Frank and Rutley,
became a flourishing business during the inter-war years. In Shropshire, for instance, 53 of the 173 principal seats changed hands
between 1922 and 1934, and this in an English county relatively
remote, conservative, and obscure. In the 1920s, such houses tended
to go to private purchasers: Lord Dudley sold Witley Court in
Worcestershire to Sir Herbert Smith, a Kidderminster carpet manufacturer; and Lord Willoughby de Broke disposed of Compton
Verney to a soap-boiler maker and racehorse owner.[113] But by the
1930s, this market was largely saturated, and country houses were
more likely to find institutional rather than individual purchasers. As
a result, Battle Abbey, Stowe, Culford, and Bryanston became
public schools; Taymouth Castle and Wickham Court in Kent
became hotels; and Escrick Park in Yorkshire was converted into
flats. Significantly, in 1930, when the Marquess of Londonderry put
his Welsh mansion, Plas Machynlleth, on the market separately from
its 9,000-acre estate, the advertisement noted that 'if not required,
the house is highly suitable for a hotel or school.'[114]

But neither private nor institutional purchasers could absorb all the country houses coming on to the market, especially those that were very large or very remote, and sooner or later, many were inevitably destroyed. 'When the war began', noted the *Estates Gazette*, 'no man would have ventured to prophecy that one of its consequences would be the demolition of many a stately building cherished for generations.'[115] Yet such was, indeed, the case. Among the most famous examples were Drayton Manor, the pathetic symbol of the decline and fall of the Peel family; Witley Court, which did not long survive the departure of the Dudleys; Frampton Court in Dorset, the home of Sheridan's descendants; Hornby Castle, once the seat of the Duke of Leeds; and Debden Hall in Essex, built by Henry Holland. And some houses experienced fates even more bizarre. Sutton Scarsdale, once the home of a branch of the Arkwright family, was sold to an American buyer, and three of its rooms were finally reconstituted in the Philadelphia Museum of Art. And it was reported that Sudbrooke Holme in Lincolnshire was 'likely to be purchased by a British film company, who proposed to burn it to the ground in order to produce a spectacular scene on the cinematograph.'[116]

There are no absolutely accurate figures available for the destruction of British country houses during this period; but those that do exist indicate an unmistakable trend. From 1870 to 1919, some 79 mansions were destroyed in England, Wales, and Scotland. But between 1920 and 1939, the figure was 221. 'It is', noted the *Estates Gazette*, 'melancholy to watch the disappearance of these stately places, and the concurrent decay of the class which once thought them necessary.'[117] But even this was as nothing compared with the much greater, and more malevolently motivated destruction of Irish country houses during the 'troubles' of 1919–24, when those patricians who had stayed on even after they had lost their estates now found themselves driven from their homes. In County Clare alone, some fifty or sixty houses were destroyed, being the majority of the élite's homes. In County Kerry, where once the Lansdownes had lorded it over a hundred thousand acres, Dereen was gutted in 1922, and the gardens were plundered. 'There is', the sixth marquess recalled sadly, 'probably not a gentleman's house in the district which has not been destroyed or threatened with destruction.'[118]

The real extent to which country houses became burdensome to their owners in the inter-war years is well illustrated in the case of Philip Kerr, who became Lord Lothian in 1930, and inherited 30,000 agricultural acres in Norfolk and the Scottish lowlands. The estate had paid nothing net since the war, so that his predecessor had survived only by living off mineral royalties and dividends from mining shares.[119] In addition, Lothian inherited death duties of £300,000, and four grand houses: Ferniehirst Castle, a border strong-

19. Lord Lothian.

hold on a cliff by the upper waters of the Jed; Newbattle Abbey, a
large seventeenth-century mansion by the Esk; Blickling Hall, an
exquisite Tudor house in Norfolk; and Monteviot, a Scottish baronial pile. As a bachelor, busy in Oxford and London, Lothian neither
needed nor could he afford such a clutch of mansions, and systematically divested himself of them. Ferniehirst was let to the Scottish
Youth Hostel Association; Newbattle was transferred to the Scottish
universities, and became an educational centre for summer schools
and residential courses; Monteviot was reserved as the one remaining
family home; and Blickling was left by Lothian to the National
Trust, to whom it passed on his death in 1940.

It was through Lothian's desire to hand over Blickling to the Trust
that the problem of country houses first became widely publicized.[120] In 1934, he offered the house to the Trust on his death,
together with 4,500 acres to provide an endowment. But although
the Trust already owned some houses, such as Barrington Court in
Somerset, it was not legally empowered to accept land or other gifts

20. Blickling Hall, Norfolk.

as an endowment. Accordingly, Lothian began to campaign for
legislation that would enable the Trust to accept country houses on
such conditions. 'Within a generation', he warned, 'hardly any of the
larger historic houses of Britain . . . would be lived in, certainly not
by the families that created them.' In 1937, an act was duly passed,
allowing former owners of country houses to remain as tenants,
while transferring the actual ownership to the Trust.[121] From the
latter's standpoint, it was a far-sighted and innovative development;
from the standpoint of the British landed classes, it was but further
indication that some patricians could no longer afford to live in the
homes that their ancestors had created.

Works of art, town palaces, and country mansions did not themselves generate revenue: they expressed status. On the other hand,
they were expensive to acquire, to create, and to maintain, and they
tied up capital that could be realized only by selling. But other non-
agricultural assets did indeed generate income, in many cases more
extensive than agricultural rental: urban estates in London or the
provinces, docks and harbours, markets and mines. Yet here, too,

there was during this period the same dramatic about-turn in policy: from acquisition to dispersal. The chronology of sales – bunching either side of the First World War, but with a buildup before and a continuing trickle thereafter – is by now familiar. And so, in essence, are the reasons: in the case of urban estates, there were fears for the future of real property; in the case of docks, harbours, and markets, the return on investment was often low; and in the case of minerals, it was because the mining industry was increasingly depressed, and the revenue was so severely taxed. In short, it was possible to make a safer investment, and obtain a greater return, elsewhere.

In London, the radical attacks on slum ground-landlords in the 1880s frightened many patrician owners, as did Lloyd George's onslaught in the era of Limehouse. And the chronology of early sales very much reflects this. In 1888, Lord Salisbury sold £200,000 worth of property in the Strand for commercial development, instead of creating new leases for himself, as would have been customary in earlier times.[122] In 1891, Lord Calthorpe disposed of his City Road building estate, when the leases were about to fall in, because the low quality of the houses meant he feared large-scale expenditure and widespread public criticism. And in 1902–3, Lord Kensington sold his London ground rents for £865,000, which established 'a record in the annals of the landmarket.'[123] But the most spectacular pre-war sale was still to come. As late as 1897, the Duke of Bedford's agent was advising against selling the Covent Garden estate, but to hold on and to augment it when possible. Yet by 1913, 'profound misgivings as to the future of real property, especially in towns', persuaded the Duke to part with it for £2 million. This sale, of an estate that had been in the Russell family since 1552, created a sensation similar to that resulting from the earlier decision to sell Thorney: 'a shock of surprise that a great London landlord should have parted with so great an inheritance.'[124]

The message was plain: 'the tendency to the breakup of large estates, which is now so familiar in the agricultural districts, is showing an increased inclination to become common in towns also.' As usual, the war slowed business down, although in 1915 the trustees of Lord Arundell of Wardour sold his Shaftesbury Avenue estate, which yielded £9,000 a year, for £250,000.[125] But thereafter, the great ground landlords of London rushed into the market. The 20-acre Berkeley estate, including both the square and its nightingale, went to a property company for £2 million. The Duke of Bedford sold part of Bloomsbury for a similar figure; Lord Portman disposed of 7 acres of St Marylebone for £95,000; Lord Southampton realized £200,000 from sales in Euston; and Lord Camden obtained nearly £150,000 for ground rents in St Pancras and Camden Town.[126] Two further sales in the late twenties were even more remarkable: Lord Howard de Walden, who had inherited the Duke of Portland's London lands, sold 40 acres, including Great Portland Street, to Sir John Ellerman; and even the tight-fisted Westminsters off-loaded their Millbank estate for £900,000.[127]

In the provinces, the trend of patrician dispersal was very similar. In 1885, the much-indebted Haldon family began to sell their build- ing estate in Torquay; in 1907, the Earl of Limerick disposed of his Limerick ground rents worth £6,000 a year for £113,000; in 1910 the Butes began to sell industrial land in the South Wales valleys; and during the war, Lord Tredegar sold ground rents in Monmouth and the Talbot estate and liquidated their holdings in Margham. After the war, the market surged forward again, and those who sold included the Calthorpe family at Edgbaston, the Butes at Aberdare, Lord Radnor at Folkestone, the Duke of Norfolk at Sheffield, and the Meyricks, Portmans, Levens, and Malmesburys at Bournemouth.[128] But the most remarkable sale was that of the Ramsden estate in Huddersfield, which included almost all of the land in the town. In 1894, the corporation had begun negotiations, with a view to pur- chasing; but they came to nothing. Now, in the changed post-war climate, the Ramsdens sold their lands to the town for £1.3 million. Like the Bedfords and Covent Garden, the reversal in attitudes and policy was sudden, definite – and irrevocable.[129]

As with works of art, the sales of provincial building estates continued throughout the inter-war years, and included some of the most renowned and valuable in the country. In 1925, Lord Derby sold land in Manchester, Salford, and Bury; in 1927 he disposed of his holdings in Bootle for £1.75 million; and in 1928 he realized some of his Liverpool ground rents for a similar sum. Between 1926 and 1944, the Earls of Dudley sold in Dudley itself, Sedgley, Tipton, and Brierley Hill.[130] In the late 1920s, the Scarisbrick family began to liquidate their share of the Southport building estate, and Charles Bibby Hesketh, the other main freeholder, sold 5,000 acres of undeveloped land, and 2,500 properties for £380,000. Other note- worthy sales included the Duke of Norfolk at Littlehampton, and the Duke of Newcastle, who disposed of the Park estate in Nottingham. But the greatest sale of all, which surpassed even the Ramsdens in Huddersfield, was made by the Marquess of Bute in 1938, when he liquidated the family holdings in Cardiff – amounting to two-thirds of the town, and containing 20,000 houses, 1,000 shops, and 250 pubs – for between four and five million pounds.[131]

From the dispersal of London and provincial building estates to the disposal of companies that had been set up by landowners to exploit their non-agricultural resources, was a natural progression. Here, again, there was a relatively rapid reversal of policy, well illustrated in the case of the Dukes of Devonshire.[132] During the lifetime of the seventh duke, the family undertook extensive investment in undertakings connected with Buxton, Eastbourne, and Barrow-in-Furness, as well as with their Irish estates. But between 1891 and 1936, under the eighth and ninth dukes, this expansive policy was abruptly reversed. The shares in the Waterford, Lismore, and Dungavron Railway were sold; the family holdings in the Buxton Baths Company were disposed of; at Eastbourne they withdrew from the pier company and vainly tried to persuade the corporation to take over the Parks and Baths Company; and at Barrow they liquidated their holdings in the Steel, Steamship, and Naval Construction Companies. The old policy of estate exploitation by family-financed companies was brought to an end. In future, they had to fend for themselves, while the Devonshires sought alternative, less vulnerable, and more profitable outlets for their investments.

Among the super-rich, the Devonshires were unusual in the diversity of their non-agricultural involvements, and in the suddenness with which they withdrew from them. But other families were behaving in essentially the same way. In 1886, the Earl of Eglinton sold Adrossan Harbour, and in 1924 closed down the family iron works. In 1888, Lord Lonsdale leased his Whitehaven coal-mines, and in 1896 the Earls of Durham sold off their collieries. In 1898, the Duke of Norfolk conveyed his Sheffield markets to the corporation for £530,000, and in 1922, the Marquess of Bute sold Cardiff docks to the Great Western Railway. More gradually, but with the same end in view, the Earls of Dudley withdrew from their direct involvement in Black Country mining and smelting.[133] But for Lord Crawford, no such dignified withdrawal was possible from the Wigan Coal and Iron Company. In the late 1920s, the company suffered big losses and paid no dividends, and in 1930–1, at the behest of the banks, it was taken over by the Lancashire Steel Corporation, and Crawford ceased to be chairman.[134]

By the late 1930s, therefore, the patricians' direct links with the industrial economy were very much reduced. And in 1938, their connection was further eroded by the nationalization of mineral royalties. The actual acquisition did not take place until 1942, but the earlier legislation vested the ownership of the royalties in the Coal Commissioners, and provided £66 million in compensation. Although the owners had unsuccessfully asked for £150 million, and although (like Irish land) this was a further example of the ill-disposed stance of an ostensibly Conservative government, the depressed state of the coal industry, and the weakened resolve of the landowners, may well explain why the measure was passed with little opposition.[135] And in any case, in individual terms, the compensation was not ungenerous. Among the foremost Scottish owners, the Earl of Wemyss received £500,000, the Duke of Hamilton £380,000, and the Duke of Buccleuch £125,000. Among great owners in the Nottinghamshire and Derbyshire coalfield, the Duke of Devonshire pocketed £404,939, and the Duke of Portland £1,976,775. And a multinational mogul like the Marquess of Bute received £187,000 for his Scottish minerals, and £1,222,425 for Glamorganshire.[136]

The very extensive withdrawal by so many patricians from these ancillary forms of non-agricultural estate exploitation received much less contemporary attention than the simultaneous 'revolution in landowning'. But it was an essential aspect of the same phenomenon, and it was in its way just as revolutionary. Once again, the traditions and assumptions of the past centuries were put into definite reverse, and once again, the motives were fear for the future of real property, and a belief that a bigger and safer return could be obtained by making investments elsewhere. The ownership of broad acres might have been the most important defining characteristic of the British territorial classes. But the whole additional paraphernalia of country houses, London palaces, art collections, and non-agricultural enterprises collectively counted for at least as much. And here, too, from the 1880s, the landowners were emphatically and conspicuously in retreat.

iv. The Diversity of Experience

The sale of broad acres and of non-agricultural assets by the grandees and gentry between the 1880s and the 1930s must rank as one of the most profound economic and psychological changes of the period. And for the landowners (or former landowners) themselves, it was an experience at once transforming and traumatic. The evidence is invariably impressionistic, but the message it conveys and the mood it expresses are both clear and unequivocal: from confidence to anxiety, buoyancy to pessimism, expansiveness to retrenchment, and acquisitiveness to dispersal. As generalizations, these antitheses may stand. But they need to be illustrated and qualified. For if these were the general patterns, how did they differingly affect the small landowners, the middling proprietors, and the super-rich? And there is also another side to this: having obtained so much money by selling so many things, what did the patricians actually do with the proceeds?

For the squirearchy and minor gentry – those with incomes between £1,000 and £10,000 a year – the chances of survival were by definition the least good. The pressure of debt was often at its greatest, the impact of depression and taxation was most marked, the alternative sources of non-agricultural income were least abundantly available, the room for financial manœuvre was accordingly the least generous, and decline and fall was in consequence the most poignant and the most complete.[137] How could mortgages be discharged or death duties be met by owners of estates so small that there were no outlying parts that could effectively and conveniently be lopped off for sale? Either the whole property must go under the hammer, or none. This is well illustrated in the case of the Bower family of Welham in Yorkshire, who in the 1870s possessed 2,000 acres valued at £4,000 a year. By 1891, income had plummeted to £2,400 a year, while taxation and interest payments amounted to £2,800. As a result, the land, the house, and the pictures were sold, and this impoverished patrician family completely disappeared.[138]

So, even before the Lloyd George budgets and the First World War, the position of many squires was greatly depressed. And these later developments, combined with the renewed depression in agriculture, drove many more small landowners to the wall during the inter-war years.[139] They were not off-loading surplus acres or outlying estates immediately before 1914 or after 1918: they were selling the entirety of their holdings, at almost any time, and in most cases simply because they were compelled to. In 1928, for instance, two such properties came into the market: the 3,175-acre Dering estate near Ashford in Kent, which had been held by the family in the male line since the reign of Henry VI; and the 950-acre Sandford estate near Whitchurch, which was for sale after an ownership of 850 years. Six years later, the Pusey estate came on the market: 1,400 acres near Farringdon in Berkshire worth £1,090 a year, which had been in the same family for nine centuries. And in 1939, the Burgoyne estate of Sutton Park at Sandy near Bedford was put up for sale: after holding the lands since the seventeenth century, the line had died out.[140]

In Wales, where the squirearchy was more widespread, there were constant examples of crippling debt and reduced income squeezing so hard that territorial abdication was almost the inevitable result.[141] The Royal Commission on Land in Wales and Monmouthshire summarized the squires' problem well when it observed, in its final report: 'we have reason to believe that the pressure of encumbrances is more severely felt by the owners of smaller rather than of larger estates.'[142] One such unfortunate was Sir Marteine Lloyd of Bronwydd, who possessed 8,000 acres worth £6,600 in 1883. His lands were bearing mortgages of £94,000, and only by extensive sales could such severe debts be reduced to £24,000 by 1922. Lloyd himself died in 1933, his wife four years later, and then the remnants of house and estate were sold off. The Powell family of Nanteos went exactly the same way. In the 1880s, their lands in Cardigan, Brecon, and Montgomery amounted to· 33,674 acres worth only £9,597 a year. In the 1890s and 1920s, sales under pressure of debts reduced the acreage to 4,300 and the net income to a mere £2,000 a year. But this, again, was an inadequate basis for survival: by 1930 the rest of the estate had been sold and the line was extinct.[143]

In Ireland, where the generally depressed circumstances of small British landowners were accentuated by rent strikes, even greater debts, and the drastic and downward rental revisions of the Land Commissioners, the plight of the gentry was much worse. One Kerry landlord drew a rental income of £1,200 a year, of which £1,050 went in head rents, tithes, jointures, taxes, management, and interest, leaving him with a mere £150 on which to live. The Land Commission thereupon reduced his rents by one-third! In County Carlow, Captain Newton's estate yielded £1,668 gross, of which outgoings (including interest payments of £800) absorbed £1,374. His rents were reduced by 30 per cent.[144] For such owners, the only hope was somehow to hold on until better times, and then to sell out under the Land Purchase Acts on the best terms available. With luck, it might just be possible for them to clear their debts, and to have a small sum left over.

Not surprisingly, the themes of the 'passing of the squires' and the 'ruin of the country gentry' were extensively treated in much contemporary fiction. The 'Irish RM' novels of Somerville and Ross well capture the circumstances of gentry landlords poignantly poised between survival and oblivion. In the Forsyte Saga, the declining fortunes of the Mont family are rescued by the marriage of Michael – the son and heir – to Fleur Forsyte, whose father, Soames, is a quintessential member of the Victorian middle classes. In Flora Major's story, *The Squire's Daughter*, she describes the decline and fall of the De Lacey family, as the heirlooms and mansion are sold, as the estate is broken up, and as the frail and shabby survivors end their days in exile abroad. Likewise, Francis Brett Young peopled his bestselling novels, set in the West Midlands, with a cast of declining gentry: families like the Abberleys, Pomfrets, Ombersleys, and d'Abitots, with their heavy mortgages, small estates, and burdensome death duties, almost all inexorably heading to extinction. Considering that the 1937 edition of *Burke's Landed Gentry* listed one-third of the families as completely landless (with many more only hanging on by the skin of their teeth), the accuracy of these portraits was hardly in doubt.

For these small landowners, their estates had ceased to be econo-

mically viable. But others, with lighter debts, smaller outgoings, less
depressed farms, or alternative sources of income, were able to carry
on. By the late nineteenth century, families like the Bests of Boxley
and the Brooks of Flintwick were drawing perhaps one-fifth of their
income from overseas investments. Alternatively, a squire like Reginald Bray, whose family had owned an estate at Shere in Surrey
since the fifteenth century, augmented his limited landed income by
working as a London lawyer, while his wife wrote children's
stories.[145] Indeed, as the Earl of Airlie pointed out in 1879, it was
possible – at least arithmetically – for a very small estate's finances
to be improved by judicious selling and investment. He gave an
example of a property yielding £3,000 a year, from which £400 went
on expenses and £600 on interest, and whose net rents were reduced
in the depression from £2,000 to £1,400 a year. If half the estate was
sold for £36,000, if £15,000 of that was earmarked for the repayment
of the debts, and if the remaining £21,000 was invested at 4 per cent,
the resulting income of rents and dividends combined would actually
be increased.[146]

Among landowners with greater but still relatively moderate
means – with incomes ranging from £10,000 to £30,000 a year – the
picture was fundamentally the same. Some did not survive, while
others carried on, but only in very changed and often reduced
circumstances. In Ireland, the picture was predictably gloomy. Lord
Belmore owned a 5,000-acre estate in Fermanagh, with a gross rent
of £3,500, of which he received only one-fifth net. When the Land
Commissioners compulsorily reduced his rents by 25 per cent, his
surplus vanished and he was left unable to meet even his fixed
outgoings. On a larger scale, Lord Dufferin, having spent £100,000
on estate improvements, found himself with an income of £21,180 in
the late 1870s, of which £13,700 went on interest, and £4,115 on
jointures and annuities. As a result, he sold off £370,042 worth of
land between 1874 and 1880, paid off his debts, and invested the
remainder, £54,580, in Canadian bonds.[147] Dufferin was very early
off the mark; but by the 1900s, most Irish landowners were selling
out, receiving their bonds and their bonus, paying off their debts,
and investing the surplus – if there was any left. Indeed, it was men
such as these – like Lords Bessborough and Fermoy – who were
among the most active buyers of small country houses in England
during the inter-war years.[148]

In Wales, the response was more varied. Some families sold early,
others late; some sold out completely, others only partially. The
Lisburnes were very early in the market, disposing of £68,000 worth
of land in Cardiganshire between 1876 and 1899. George Cornwallis-
West inherited a heavily encumbered estate at Ruthin Castle, and

sold the lot in 1922.[149] The decline and fall of the Pryses was more protracted. In 1876, they owned 32,000 acres, mainly in Cardiganshire, which produced £14,500 a year. From 1875 to 1895, they sold off some 10,000 acres for £186,000 to pay debts and portions, compelled to do so by the fact that interest payments were £13,500, giving them no effective margin on which to live. By 1896, they had met most of these liabilities, still had half of their estate intact, and had been able to invest some £26,800 in equities. But another round of portions, combined with death duties, meant that new encumbrances totalling £75,000 were accumulated by 1921, which inexorably led to a new series of sales. By 1934, a further £110,000 worth of lands had been sold, and by the time the Second World War broke out, the family was virtually landless and on the verge of complete extinction.[150]

In England, there were similar stories of disappearance, although other patricians survived more easily. Some who were only just within this category suffered the fate of the smaller squires, such as the Hart-Dyke family, who had held Lullingstone Castle in Kent for 500 years. In 1933, the trustees put the castle and 5,000 acres up for sale because of the pressure of heavy death duties. Miss Irene Lawley fared little better. In 1912, on the death of her father Lord Wenlock, she inherited (there being no son) the Escrick Park estate in Yorkshire. Death duties amounted to £60,000, of which she raised £20,000 at once by sales, paying the rest at the rate of £5,000 a year for eight years. But since her net income was only £4,000 a year, she had no choice but to let the house, and ultimately to sanction its conversion to flats.[151] Others were forced to similar if slightly less severe expedients. 'Oh!' wailed the third Lord Hatherton in 1891, 'what a dreadful thing it is to inherit a debt.' How right he was: on 15,000 acres producing £23,000 gross, his disposable income, once interest was paid, was a mere £1,000. Spending was curtailed, participation in politics abandoned, and land purchase terminated. Nearby at Keele Hall, Ralph Sneyd also found his burden of debt harder to bear than in more prosperous times, and let his house to a Russian grand duke.[152]

But for those so minded and so able, the easiest way to re-structure their finances was to follow Lord Airlie's advice, to sell part of their lands, to pay off their debts and encumbrances, and to reinvest the remainder in equities. Ironically, the trail blazer in this was the archetypal country gentleman, Walter Long, whose family estates in 1883 had amounted to 15,000 acres worth £23,000, mostly situated in Wiltshire. His decision to sell part of his holdings in 1910 was almost as momentous as the Duke of Bedford's sale of his Thorney estate. As he explained to Jesse Collings, 'I am selling a portion of my own estate now simply and solely because I feel that it is impossible for poor men like myself to keep up large estates in the face of the present burdens.'[153] Precisely what this meant was made clear in a subsequent exchange of letters in *The Times*. An estate of 10,000 acres produced £10,000 gross, from which was deducted £5,000 for maintenance and mortgages, leaving only £5,000 net for keeping up position. If half the estate was sold at twenty-seven years' purchase, that would realize £135,000, of which £62,000 could be put to paying off debts and charges, and the remaining £73,000 could be invested at 4 per cent. The result was an investment income of £2,900 a year, plus a net rental of £3,750 (being £5,000 gross minus £1,250 for expenses), totalling £6,650, or £1,650 more than before.[154]

As this correspondence makes plain, some middling landowners were able to increase their gross income, and to reduce their outgoings, even in such unpropitious times. They would be lesser men as landowners, and might find that the majority of their income was now coming from the stock exchange; but that was the price of survival. The Grahams of Netherby illustrate this well. They owned 26,000 acres in Cumberland, which were carrying debts of £275,000. Between 1882 and 1905, the gross rent fell by more than 25 per cent, from £26,718 to £20,000. In the years immediately before 1914, half the estate was sold, the debt was reduced by 40 per cent, and the remainder was invested in shares. The result was that the Grahams' net income actually rose from £14,000 to £16,000. The same strategy was adopted by the Stanhopes, who held their major estates in Kent. Under the sixth and seventh earls, they sold off their peripheral properties in Buckinghamshire, Devonshire, Derbyshire, and Ireland, paid off portions and mortgages, and consolidated their estates around Chevening itself.[155]

But whether the outcome was successful survival or decline and decay, the extent of the transformation, among the middling rich as among the small landowners, cannot be doubted. Evelyn Waugh caught it well in *Brideshead Revisited* with the Marchmain family, who were closely modelled on the Earls Beauchamp of Madresfield, who owned 17,000 acres, mainly in Worcestershire, which were worth £25,000 in 1883. In the early 1920s, the Marchmains maintained both Brideshead itself, and Marchmain House, their London palace. They still lived in great state; they kept their own pack of hounds; and they had not raised their rents since the war. But they were also overdrawn at the bank by £100,000, and they had other debts elsewhere, which compelled Lord Marchmain to take action. Eventually, the town house was sold and demolished, and the family finances were restored. 'Selling Marchers', Cordelia remarks of her father, 'has put him straight again, and saved I don't know how much a year in rates. But it seems such a shame to pull it down.'[156]

Even among the super-rich, the responses were more varied than might at first sight be expected. Again, there were some with very heavy debts, or with estates disadvantageously located, or with no non-agricultural assets. The Dukes of Manchester suffered in all these ways: very large accumulated encumbrances, no mines or urban estates or equities, and in total only 27,000 acres, yielding £40,000, equally divided between Ireland (the 'troubles') and Huntingdon (very depressed arable). The Irish estates disappeared under the Land Purchase Acts, and most of the Huntingdon property went in 1920, leaving the ninth duke with almost no income. The Duke of Leeds fared little better. He, too, was rich, but not broad-acred for a duke: 24,000 acres, mostly in Yorkshire, yielding £33,000. In 1920, he sold most of his outlying estates, in Cornwall and Buckinghamshire, and by 1930 had sold most of his land in Yorkshire, as well as Hornby Castle and its contents. Much richer, but again in sorry straits, were the Marquesses of Anglesey, who held lucrative mineral lands in Staffordshire and Derbyshire. They had accumulated vast debts by the close of the nineteenth century, which necessitated the sale of Beaudesert. For such families as these, with liabilities and assets so finely balanced, there was not much to emerge when the day of reckoning came.

Even patricians who might be expected to be more resilient sometimes found the going very difficult. The Earls of Crawford and Balcarres boasted an income of £39,252 in 1883, of which three-quarters was derived from a mere 1,931 precious coal-bearing acres near Wigan. With this income, they had amassed their fine art collection and an incomparable library, and had freed themselves entirely from the vicissitudes of agricultural rental. But in 1913 the twenty-sixth earl died, and his successor was faced with death duties, debts, and family portions of between £500,000 and £600,000. 'The financial situation', he concluded, 'gives me cause for anxiety . . . I can never look forward to becoming a collector, but I must strive to free the estates from debt, and to preserve the pictures and the books.' He at once instituted strict economy measures: the London house was let, the staff was much reduced, and he was forced to sell parts of the library.[157] The crisis was duly weathered, but in the late 1920s, the troubles in the coal industry meant that the mineral income was wiped out. Thereafter, Crawford could survive only by going into business or by living off his capital. In order to continue his varied public career, he chose the latter alternative. But the price was high: 'the dispersion at derisory prices of the treasures we have accumulated with so much pride.'[158]

But others among the rich, and especially among the super-rich, were much better placed, since they had far more room in which to conduct their financial manœuvres. Some, like the Bedfords and the Westminsters, were free from encumbrances altogether. And even those who were indebted usually found that the weight pressed much less heavily than on those who were poorer. Almost all of them enjoyed massive incomes that were uninfluenced by the vicissitudes of agriculture. At the time of the First World War, the Butes, the Northumberlands, and the Hamiltons were drawing £100,000 and more in mineral royalties; the income of the Dukes of Bedford and of Westminster from their London ground rents was considerably more than this; and men like Earl Fitzwilliam and Lord Derby were enjoying gross incomes of at least £250,000 a year.[159] Moreover, their assets and holdings were so diverse and varied that they could sell off a great deal, and still be very substantial figures. Many held estates in half a dozen counties, and could bear losing ten thousand acres with relative equanimity; some possessed so many country houses that the sale of one or two would be more a relief than a deprivation; and some owned such splendid collections of art that they would hardly notice the sale of a Rembrandt or two. Above all, they possessed assets that were more easily realizable at a good price than mere agricultural land.

Of course, they protested loudly, especially over death duties. There is a famous cartoon in *Punch* of 1894 that shows a disconsolate Duke of Devonshire saying to a worried Duke of Westminster, 'We may consider ourselves lucky if we can keep a tomb over our heads' (see p. 96). But as Loulou Harcourt pointed out, the Duke was merely 'posing as a pauper'.[160] For it quickly became clear that death duties could be avoided. All that was required, as one pundit early on remarked, was to devise a method 'by which property shall never pass on a death, but only upon some other event, to render the property altogether free from death duties.'[161] One option was for the owner to make the estates over to his successor in good time: in 1914, Lord Lansdowne dealt with his Scottish holdings in this way; and the Duke of Atholl, having held his lands for fifty years, handed over half his acres to his son. The alternative solution, which was even more widely adopted, was to set up a private estate company, which greatly reduced the value of dutiable property, while allowing the landowner to preserve full control. In the inter-war years, a variety of great grandees, like Buccleuch, Bute, Fitzwilliam, Rutland, Beaufort, Devonshire, and Salisbury set up such companies, and many small landowers followed suit.[162]

Even so, these great moguls could not and did not go on as before. Like the lesser rich among their friends, they were extremely worried by Lloyd George, who attacked the dukes with especial fervour:

if property was unsafe and threatened, then those who owned the most of it had the most to fear and the most to lose. In the same way, with agriculture so depressed, and with land no longer as important or as prized as an asset as it had once been, there was no point in holding on to tens of thousands of acres when there were alternative and more profitable assets to be held. And, at a time when the cost of living had gone up greatly, it made much less sense than before to spend on the upkeep of so many houses in town and country. There was thus, among the super-rich, a very strong incentive to restructure their assets in a more rational way. And, by sheer demographic chance, many of them had an unusually long period in which to do this, as a group of great grandees held their titles and estates for an unusually extended span of time, such as the sixth Duke of Portland (1879–1943), the eleventh Duke of Bedford (1893–1940), the second Duke of Westminster (1899–1953), the fourth Marquess of Bute (1900–47), the seventh Earl Fitzwilliam (1902–43), the seventeenth Earl of Derby (1909–48), the ninth Duke of Devonshire (1908–38), the fifth Duke of Sutherland (1913–63), and the sixteenth Duke of Norfolk (1917–75).

As the *Estates Gazette* had remarked in 1894, 'that family will flourish most which is most given to longevity'.[163] But how, exactly, did they restructure their financial affairs? In the first place, they sold a great deal: for them above all, the change from landed accumulation to landed disbursement was the most noteworthy. The Duke of Sutherland sold his Trentham and Lilleshall estates, his London town house, and half his massive highland empire. The Dukes of Westminster sold Cliveden, Grosvenor House, much of their unrivalled collection of paintings, and a large part of their Eaton estate. The Duke of Devonshire sold two great London houses, most of his Irish lands, some works of art from Chatsworth, and most of his holdings in most of his Buxton, Barrow, and Eastbourne companies. The Duke of Bedford sold the entire Thorney estate, the Covent Garden market, and parts of Bloomsbury. The Duke of Norfolk sold his Sheffield markets, parts of his building estate in the town, some agricultural lands in the West Riding, part of Little-hampton, and Norfolk House in London. The Marquess of Bute sold his Glamorgan agricultural estates, his docks and building estate in Cardiff, and his mineral rights. And Lord Dudley sold works of art, his estates in Wales and Scotland, the Whitley Court property, and most of his mineral-bearing lands in the Black Country.

What did the super-rich do with the very large sums of money – often running into several millions of pounds – thus realized? If necessary, the first call was to pay off debts, portions, and death duties. And the surplus that remained was invested, usually in a wide

range of equities, in accordance with the changed practices that had
been developing from the 1880s. From that decade onwards, most
landowners with money to spare preferred to put it in equities rather
than in land. As an investment, it was probably more secure; it was
certainly more liquid; and, if it was overseas, it avoided British
income tax or death duties. The Earls of Leicester had, until the
1870s, only invested, in the traditional mode, in local companies
usually connected with their estates. But thereafter, there was a
major change in their policy as, between 1876 and 1891, they
invested £320,000 in railway shares, of which £175,000 went into
British companies, while the remainder was dispersed overseas in
India, Canada, Argentina, and the United States. In addition, they
invested £30,000 in British banks and breweries, and a further
£40,000 in Australian, Canadian, South African, and Argentinian
bonds. And others did the same. In the 1880s, the Marquess of
Salisbury's trustees invested heavily in railway shares, and in the
1890s, such super-rich grandees as Durham, Fitzwilliam, Sutherland,
and Portland were putting their money into British and overseas
stocks and bonds.[164]

With the imposition of death duties, and the new Lloyd George
taxes, the temptation to pull out of land and out of Britain became
even greater; and among the richest of all, it even became fashionable
to buy lands as well as shares overseas. Before the First World War,
the second Duke of Westminster bought property in the Orange
River Colony, and afterwards extended his real-estate investments to
Rhodesia, Canada, and Australia. The Duke of Sutherland bought
land in Florida and Canada, while Earl Fitzwilliam acquired an estate
in California as well as putting a further £250,000 in shares.[165] The
Duke of Bedford, after his many sensational sales, invested the
proceeds, not as popular legend has it, in Russian government bonds
which became worthless in 1917, but in British War Bonds, and
Indian and Canadian stock. As one of his agents had explained in
1912, 'it is the security of their capital which landlords are frightened
about. They prefer the security they get in Canada to the security
they get in the British Isles.'[166] Indeed they did, and the trend among
the very rich was so marked that Lord Esher not only explained it to
George V, but suggested the King might follow suit:

> It has, perhaps, come to Your Majesty's notice that, of late years,
> some of the greatest landowners among Your Majesty's subjects
> have been acquiring large estates in the dominions overseas. No
> one who has watched the course of recent legislation in this
> country, both fiscal and social, can fail to understand and to see the
> wisdom of those who have capital to invest, taking advantage of

the fields still open in western Canada and certain parts of Africa.[167]

Two examples from among the very rich illustrate these developments in more detail. In the early 1880s, the income of the Duke of Devonshire was entirely derived from agricultural rentals, and from dividends in companies associated with his estates. There was also a debt of £2 million, the interest payments on which were taking some 60 per cent of his disposable income. Between 1891 and 1932, the eighth and ninth dukes mobilized £2.75 million by sales of land, of company shares, and of Devonshire House. They paid off most of the debt, and invested the remaining sum in equities, much of it in Canada. So, by the late 1920s, the ninth duke was enjoying a larger disposable income than his grandfather, the majority of which now came from stock-exchange dividends.[168] The same fundamental change took place in the finances of the Earls of Bridgewater. In the 1880s, the family estates consisted of 13,000 acres, yielding £71,000 a year, largely thanks to the family canal. On the death of the third earl, £480,000 was paid in death duties by mortgaging Bridgewater House, by selling the Bridgewater Library to Huntingdon in 1917, and by disposing of land between 1918 and 1922. By that time, it was calculated that the agricultural estates were yielding a return of only 2 per cent, so that the fourth earl sold all the remaining estates, except Bridgewater House itself, and invested the £3.3 million he obtained in equities.[169]

For the very richest landowners, transactions such as these were rarely impelled by immediate impoverishment, nor even by the pressure of death duties: they were, more often, rational decisions to restructure their assets more securely and more profitably, in the light of the prevailing and predicted political and economic conditions. So, despite Harcourt and Lloyd George, they survived. But only by changing. Compared with their forebears, they were emaciated grandees: with fewer houses, fewer works of art, less broad-acred, and no longer much involved in non-agricultural estate enterprises. And this was reflected in the marked change in their income structure. Before the 1880s, it was territorially generated: from agricultural or ground rents, from mineral royalties, or from dividends paid by companies on their estates. But by the 1920s, families like the Butes, the Devonshires, and the Ellesmeres were drawing the majority of their income from shareholdings in companies with which they had no such territorial link. Increasingly, the super-rich were becoming *rentiers*, while masquerading as grandees. Their style of life might have remained landed in its mode of expenditure; but it was increasingly plutocratic in terms of its source of income. And, while such men had once dominated the land, they certainly did not dominate the stock exchange.

v. Conclusion: A Balance Sheet

In strictly economic terms, there can be no doubt that the British patricians were a failing and fragmenting class in the years from the late 1870s to the late 1930s. Their position as an unchallenged wealth élite was undermined, their unifying sense of territorial identity was dissolved, and their financial circumstances became increasingly divergent. The most significant characteristic that landowners had in common in this period was that most of them were getting out of land. But it might be voluntary or because there was no choice, it might be done with relish or with regret, and it might be only in part or completely. And what happened thereafter was even more varied: some did not survive at all, while others remained quite prosperous; some just hung on, while others were better off than before; some remained primarily landowners, while others became predominantly *rentiers*; and some remained essentially British-based, while others became more international in their concerns. Even among the poorest landowners, there were some who survived; and even among the richest, there were some who succumbed. But on the whole, those who had been the most prosperous and the most landed before the 1880s remained so thereafter.

By the 1930s, it seems clear that the latter-day Duke of Omnium had less in common with the descendants of the small squire than his forebears had had a century before. But these were not the only variations. In different parts of Britain, the patricians disappeared with varying degrees of completeness. In Ireland, the demise of the landed establishment was almost total: the estates vanished, most of the houses were either destroyed or deserted, and many patricians fled the country. In Wales, too, there were only a few flourishing landowners left: some grandees buttressed by stock-exchange earnings; some tenacious squires, isolated and impover-ished. By contrast, the patricians survived rather better in England and in Scotland. North of the border, this was partly because there was by then less tenant hostility than in Wales and Ireland; partly because many holdings were so massive that even after selling two or three hundred thousand acres, families like the Sutherlands remained substantial owners; and partly because some of the estates were bought up intact by those who enjoyed their sporting rights, rather than sold off piecemeal to the tenantry.

In England, the picture was different again. This was to some ex-tent because most supra-national grandees were essentially English-based, so that as they sold off their peripheral lands on the Celtic fringe, they became less British but more English. The Devonshires and Fitzwilliams may have sold out in Ireland, but they remained important territorial powers in Derbyshire and Yorkshire. The Beauforts may have liquidated their Welsh holdings, but they retained massive estates in Gloucestershire. But even within England itself, there were variations. In counties like Worcestershire, where there were few great grandees, and where the gentry were emphatically in retreat, the turnover was relatively high; but in counties that boasted a large number of great estates heartlands, the change was much less dramatic. In West Sussex, the old order was much more stable, as the Norfolks, Richmonds, and Leconfields all survived as major territorial powers. But this was only because they were consolidating their holdings at Arundel, Goodwood, and Petworth, even as they sold extensively in Yorkshire, Scotland, and Ireland.

Whatever the qualifications and the variations, the *Estates Gazette* was not far wrong when it predicted in 1910, 'the ultimate consequence can only be that we shall find ourselves with a comparatively landless aristocracy.'[170] But while change was so great that it was the dominant feature of these years, there was also what sociologists call a lag, as inherited habits of patrician behaviour continued even when the circumstances that had given rise to them and justified them had disappeared. The ninth Duke of Devonshire was a much-diminished landowner compared with his grandfather, and obtained most of his income from the stock exchange rather than the land. But he kept up his great and grand progress from one stately home to another throughout the inter-war years, and the sumptuous life that he lived at Chatsworth, as evoked in the first volume of Harold Macmillan's memoirs, had more in common with that of his forebears than his descendants.[171] However ruthless and acute such patricians might be in disposing of family lands and heirlooms, and in moving into the new and alien world of international finance, they remained fundamentally landed in ethos and mentality.

So, even in retrenchment and in retreat, some landowners felt and behaved in a way that belied and even contradicted their own dramatically altered economic condition. In the mid-1880s, in the depths of the agricultural depression, Gladstone told his son that it was a 'high duty to labour for the conservation of estates, and the permanence of the families in possession of them', and even predicted that in one hundred years' time, the countryside would still be dominated by great territorial accumulations.[172] In the early 1920s, at the very moment when so much land was coming under the hammer, Lord Curzon could celebrate the fact that 'Son succeeds father for generation after generation; he retains or adds to, or diminishes the patrimony of his ancestors; he builds or rebuilds or alters the family mansion; he takes part in the public life of his country.'[173] And as late as 1929, in the midst of renewed agricultural depression, Lord Montagu chose these words as his epitaph: 'He loved Beaulieu, deeming his possession of it a sacred trust to be handed on to his successors in a like manner.'[174]

Yet when all due allowance is made for such lingering patrician hopes and sentiments, for the continuity that undoubtedly coexisted with the change, it is the facts of economic decline, the adjustment in territorial circumstances, the dispersal of hereditary possessions, the disappearance of so many families, that stand out most strongly. Gladstone may have cherished landed estates, but as a politician he did much to erode landowners' confidence, and the broad acres at Hawarden did not long survive inviolate after his death. Lord Curzon may have adored Kedleston, but he could maintain it only by depending on that very form of plutocratic American wealth that he so rightly feared. And even Lord Montagu could sustain his sacred, landed trust only by earning money as a motoring journalist. These ardent and adaptable patricians might weather the 'silent revolution' in landownership, but only on changed and increasingly non-landed terms. And even if such men had survived seventy years of bleak and bewildering agricultural depression, it was not at all clear that they could also survive another five years of world war.

4

THE EROSION OF LOCAL CONTROL

Landownership lost its perquisite of local political power in Britain, partly because of the democratisation of the national franchise in 1884–5 and of county administration in 1889, partly because administration became too complicated to be left to part-time and unqualified squires.
> (E. J. Hobsbawm, *Industry and Empire* (1969), p. 203.)

The new county councils created by the Local Government Act of 1888 showed more strikingly in Wales than in any other part of Britain the new transition to democracy. The landed gentry who had dominated the countryside for centuries as justices of the peace were routed in an immense social revolution.
> (K. O. Morgan, *Rebirth of a Nation: Wales, 1880–1980* (1981), p. 52.)

The necessity for Protestants to hang together in the face of Catholic and Nationalist pressures gave [the Ulster landowners] a larger political importance than any their southern brethren could aspire to . . . The gentry preserved a governing role there longer than in the rest of Ireland.
> (F. S. L. Lyons, *Culture and Anarchy in Ireland, 1890–1939* (1979), pp. 118, 121.)

From the 1880s, the sustained and successful political assault on the British landowning class coincided with – and further accentuated – its economic decline and territorial decay. But in addition, these developments necessarily weakened its local position as the élite that for centuries had represented and ruled the counties of the British Isles by hereditary right and unchallenged tradition. The extension of the franchise led to a widespread rejection of old-style rural politics and representation, while the creation of the new county councils brought a more gradual, but no less real, change in the personnel and nature of local government. At the same time, the financial anxieties of many landowners meant that they were less inclined to shoulder these traditional responsibilities or to assume new ones, while the great breakup of their estates before and after the First World War only accentuated this withdrawal from county politics and local leadership. And if this was the sad and sobering experience of many grandees and gentry in England, Scotland, and (especially) Wales, then how much more so was it their fate in large parts of Ireland?

Throughout the counties of Great Britain, the passing of the Third

Reform Act fundamentally weakened the position of the old territorial classes, ushering in a new political world in which the traditional methods of control no longer sufficed, and where the notables
and magnificœs were themselves decreasingly at home or at ease. Of
course, the change did not happen quite this abruptly: in many
industrialized counties, there had already been signs and portents in
the years since 1832, while in other parts of the country, old
structures of authority and patterns of behaviour lingered on into the
inter-war years. But the overall trend was unmistakable and irreversible. A much larger and independent electorate, combined with
patrician poverty and territorial decline, meant that fewer landowners were standing for Parliament and that even fewer were able to get
themselves elected. By the First World War, the majority of county
seats in England, Wales, and Scotland were no longer represented by
the once traditional landed class, and that very pronounced trend
was only further accentuated in the years after 1918.

In county government, the changes were of a similar kind and at a
similar time. By the 1880s, some heavily industrialized shires were
effectively governed by JPs of non-landed background, and the
Liberal reforms of the 1890s and 1900s changed fundamentally the
selection – and thus the composition – of the magistracy. The result
was that in most counties, the notables soon lost for good their
traditional dominance of the bench. But at the same time, the reform
of local government, undertaken by a Tory cabinet, robbed the 'rural
House of Lords' of most of its administrative functions, and finally
brought democracy to the countryside. In Wales, the more radical
regions of Scotland, and the more industrialized counties of England,
this did indeed bring about a rural revolution. Even in those remote
regions where the rule of the gentry and the magnates still persisted,
the social composition of the county councils gradually but inexorably moved towards the middle classes. And as local government
became more bureaucratic and more professionalized, the old style of
amateur, traditional, patrician administration seemed increasingly
inappropriate and anachronistic.

In Ireland, the position was, predictably, both more extreme and
more complex. Throughout most of the country, the aristocracy had
ceased to be the major governing or political presence before the
greatest sales of land actually began. Even by the early 1880s, the
new-style nationalist agitation had swept away most landowners as
Irish MPs, and had also removed them from their dominant position
on the local Poor Law Boards. The result was that the Conservative
reform of Irish local government in 1898 merely completed this
process of political overthrow: territorial abdication came in its
aftermath, rather than brought it about. Only in Ulster was the

picture markedly different, since the gentry and grandees retained some of their local influence in the most Protestant counties, both in terms of government and representation. But even there, such power was preserved only on the sufferance of the big bourgeoisie of Belfast, who by now were emphatically in charge of the Province's affairs. In the aftermath of partition, the patricians hung on in the north as the minority partners among the governing élite, but in the newly independent south, they effectively disappeared altogether.

i. County Representation: From Deference to Democracy

In his nostalgic reminiscences, *Some Memories*, Lord Percy of Newcastle noted that 'in the last quarter of the nineteenth century, the era of agricultural depression . . . , the great landowning families ceased to govern England.'[1] Despite its excessive simplicity and Anglocentrism, this statement is essentially correct. For the reaction against patrician control of county politics began even before the passing of the Third Reform Act, with the Liberal victory in the general election of 1880. Throughout Great Britain, landed families who had represented constituencies for decades, and who had controlled their politics for even longer, found themselves defeated in that contest: a Williams-Wynn in Montgomeryshire, Buccleuch nominees in Dumfries and Selkirk, and a son of the Earl of Ellesmere in Lancashire. The heirs of the Duke of Manchester, the Duke of Westminster, and the Marquess of Hertford failed to secure election, the latter in his local constituency of South Warwickshire.[2] As such, these results were not only a triumph for revived Gladstonian Liberalism: they were also the portent of patrician decline as the political arbiters and parliamentary representatives of the localities.

Accordingly, the tide of local feeling was already running strongly against the gentry and grandees when the passing of the Third Reform Act changed the structure of rural politics emphatically to their disadvantage. It gave a fair share of seats to metropolitan, urban, and industrial areas for the first time. It abolished many of those small boroughs where peers' sons and gentry had hitherto happily housed themselves: constituencies like Beaumaris and Pembroke in Wales, and Wenlock and Woodstock in England, which had been deliberately retained in 1867 to favour the landed interest. By merging these seats into the old county divisions, and by creating many new county constituencies that were highly urbanized or suburbanized, it markedly reduced the number of authentically rural seats for which patricians might hope to sit.[3] And it spectacularly extended the county franchise by giving the vote to the rural labourers: the Cheshire electorate grew from 20,800 to 100,000; in

Northamptonshire, it trebled; in Lincolnshire, the percentage of adult males with the vote increased from 34 to 85; and in Wales, the county vote went up from 75,000 to over 200,000.[4]

Despite the caveats that must be entered, these changes fundamentally transformed the nature and working of county elections. They removed rural politics from the direct and confident control of the landed interest, and made necessary a wholly new style of political management. The demise of the old two-member constituencies meant that the traditional pattern of gentry-arranged compromise between conservative and radical candidates was no longer possible. The massive extension of the electorate meant that old methods of control (and intimidation) would no longer work. The need to canvass more widely and to organize more thoroughly, combined with the intrusion of party agents from London, meant that politics became more professional. And the growth in the number of contested elections, the increased influx of non-landed and carpet-bagger candidates, and the greater stress on national issues eroded the local and intimate nature of county politics, which had been the essential precondition for patrician dominance.[5] In this sense, the reforms of 1884–5 were far more significant, and far more threatening, than the earlier measures of 1832 and 1867: for they emphatically spelt the end of the politics of Barset.

All this seemed confirmed in the general election of 1885, 'the great turning point', when the agricultural labourers – perhaps attracted by the radical Liberal slogans of 'three acres and a cow' – rejected their landed representatives in an ominous display of non-deferential voting. Throughout Great Britain, the aristocratic casualties were more numerous and even more spectacular than in the previous election. In England, Lord Henry Bentinck was beaten by Joseph Arch in Norfolk, a Lowther was defeated in Lincolnshire, and a Fitzwilliam in Yorkshire. In the lowlands of Scotland, Lord Haddo was turned out in Haddingtonshire, and in the Highlands, the crofter candidates vanquished their social superiors in Inverness, Argyll, Sutherland, and Caithness.[6] In Wales, the most symbolic defeat of all was that of Sir Watkin Williams-Wynn in Denbighshire, the county that his family had represented as of hereditary right for nearly two hundred years. And this humiliating rejection proved to be irrevocable: for although he stood again in 1886 and 1892, he failed to win the seat back, and thereafter, the family withdrew completely from parliamentary politics.[7]

But this dismal picture of landed rejection and patrician retreat must not be over-exaggerated. To begin with, the consequences of the Third Reform Act were not unrelievedly disastrous. By deliberately separating urban from rural communities in the shires, it

SIR WATKIN WILLIAMS-WYNN,

"THE PRINCE IN WALES."

"I am monarch of all I survey,
My right there is none to dispute."

21. Sir Watkin Williams-
Wynn, *Punch*, 28 Apr.
1883.

ensured that there were, in almost every county, at least some amenable constituencies where 'the "landed interest" was given a further lease of life.'[8] Moreover, the rural revolution that seemed to be threatening in 1885 did not in the end materialize: after their first flush of anti-landlord ardour, agricultural labourers became increasingly apathetic in attitude and reduced in numbers, while the Home Rule crisis tended to unite the rural communities around Conservative (and thus largely landed) leadership. Above all, it is important to remember that, whatever the difficulties and anxieties, the system of great estates endured in Great Britain largely unaltered until 1910. Provided they were still prepared to exert themselves as local political leaders, resident landowners remained potentially the most influential and significant element in the rural power structure.[9]

The result was that many patricians provided both the high
command and the essential financial support of the new constituency
organizations that sprang up in the shires in the aftermath of the
Third Reform Act, especially on the Conservative and Unionist side.
Great families like the Devonshires in Derbyshire, the Rutlands in
Leicestershire, the Norfolks in Sussex, and the Bedfords in their
titular county remained pre-eminent in terms of local leadership and
local subscriptions. The Stratford Division of Warwickshire was
dominated by the sixth Marquess of Hertford between 1885 and
1912, who personally appointed the committees of selection, and
effectively chose the candidates himself.[10] In southern Scotland, the
families of Stair and Buccleuch dominated the local associations in
Galloway and Dumfries. And even in Wales, the leaders of forlorn
Toryism were almost without exception the great landowners: Penrhyn in Caernarfon, Cawdor in Carmarthen, and Williams-Wynn in
Denbigh. They might no longer seek parliamentary honours themselves: but they still controlled the constituency machinery. Only in
counties like Cardigan, where there were no resident grandees, was
Conservative organization virtually non-existent.[11]

Likewise among the Liberals, some loyal patricians continued to
provide firm local leadership, which might still decisively influence
the outcome of an election. In the same Warwickshire constituency
where Lord Hertford dominated the Tory side, the fifth Marquess of
Northampton controlled the Liberal Association. He provided the
money, the initiative, and a Liberal imperialist tone: and in 1904 he
personally selected the candidate who actually won the division in
1906.[12] In Mid Northamptonshire, the unusual survival and success
of Liberalism in what should have become a staunchly Unionist
constituency owed much to the presence of the Spencer family: the
estate was the largest in the division; the fifth earl himself was a
Liberal, a cabinet minister, Master of Foxhounds, and chairman of
the quarter sessions and of the county council; and Althorp was the
centre of one of the few well-funded and well-run Liberal constituency organizations in the county.[13] Even in Wales, resident Liberal
landowners still counted for something. In Pembrokeshire, Lord
Kensington was a significant figure, and in Cardigan, the entire
association was effectively funded by a local squire, Matthew
Vaughan Davies.[14]

But in addition to controlling these new constituency organizations, landowners could also resort to the more traditional means of
influencing and intimidating voters. Predictably, the Conservatives
claimed that there was no such activity, but the Liberals naturally
took the opposite view. Beyond doubt, the 'secret' ballot was much
less confidential than was claimed: because the counting of votes was

22. Lord Spencer by
F. C.-Gould.

rather casual, it was still possible for candidates to find out how
entire villages had voted. Some landlords still made it clear that they
expected their tenants to vote for their candidate: as late as 1900 the
Marquess of Hastings allegedly evicted one who disobeyed his
instructions.[15] There were certainly instances of coercion when a
landed family changed sides, as with the Wimbornes, who switched
from Conservative to Liberal in 1904, and seem to have been very
heavy-handed in the contests of 1906 and 1910. And in the 1910
elections, there was general recognition that the landowners had
exerted themselves with more than usual vigour: Churchill's predictable denunciation of 'the feudal screw' was corroborated by Lord
Salisbury's admission that in the agricultural constituencies, the
leaders of opinion 'strove as they have never striven before to gain
the support of the electors'.[16]

Since it was still possible for the patricians to influence both the
selection of candidates and the decisions of some of the voters, it
automatically followed that traditional landed figures could also get
themselves elected for traditional landed constituencies. In Cheshire,
the two safe rural seats were both represented by scions of county
grandees: from 1885 to 1906, the Eddisbury Division returned the
Hon. H. J. Tollemache, and the Hon. Alan Egerton sat for

Knutsford.[17] In the Chichester Division of West Sussex, representation was provided, as before, by the Dukes of Norfolk and of Richmond. In 1894, on the resignation of Lord Walter Gordon-Lennox, the seat was taken over by Lord Edmund Talbot, who held it uninterruptedly until his appointment as Viceroy of Ireland in 1921. In Mid Northamptonshire, Lord Spencer's half-brother Robert held the seat from 1880 until 1895, a remarkable achievement against the national trend. And in West Derbyshire, the Devonshires' grip was virtually unbreakable: the first MP for the new constituency was Mr Victor Cavendish, who held the seat from 1885 until his succession to the dukedom in 1908; and he was followed by the Earl of Kerry, son of Lord Lansdowne and another very close relative.

But it was not only the grandees who survived: there were also country gentlemen who continued to represent their local constituencies. Henry Chaplin sat for the Sleaford Division of Lincolnshire for over twenty years. Walter Long was a Wiltshire MP from 1880 until 1892, and his younger brother represented another local constituency between 1895 and 1900. Nearby, in the Chippenham Division, John Dickson Poynder was elected in 1892 as a Conservative, changed to the Liberals over Free Trade in 1905, held his seat in the subsequent election, and retired only in 1910 on his appointment as Governor-General of New Zealand.[18] But it was in Shropshire that this pattern of gentry dominance was especially marked. The Ludlow, Newport, and Oswestry Divisions were dominated by traditional 'Tory squires' like R. J. More, W. S. Kenyon-Slaney, G. R. C. Ormsby-Gore, and W. C. Bridgeman. They came from families whose forebears had regularly represented the county, they were themselves closely related, and their right to be returned to Westminster remained virtually unchallenged. In 1892 it was observed that 'we have one common cause at heart, and that is to return Shropshire men to parliament'; and, for the next twenty years, that is precisely what happened.[19]

In many rural constituencies of Scotland, the dissolution of old patrician antagonisms in the aftermath of Home Rule, and the gradual weakening of the crofter agitation, meant that resident landowners and great magnates were able to reassert themselves in the south, and even recapture some of their influence in the northern, crofter counties. Roxburghshire returned the Hon. A. R. D. Elliot (a Minto), the Hon. M. F. N. Napier (a Napier), the Earl of Dalkieth (a Buccleuch), and Sir John Jardine. In the same period, Ayrshire was represented by Elliots and Cochranes, and Wigtown by Sir Herbert Maxwell and Viscount Dalrymple, son of the Earl of Stair.[20] Even in Sutherland, a kinsman of the county's titular duke, F. S. Leveson-Gower, won as a Unionist in the favourable circumstances of the

1900 election. And as late as 1910, one jaundiced contemporary felt moved to offer this analysis of constituency politics north of the border: 'In many Scottish counties, there is a . . . feeling of exclusiveness still somehow maintained, quite unsuited to these democratic days . . . The landed proprietors and "county families" are a class apart, and above the middle class . . . and the working classes generally.'[21]

Even in Wales, the landowners lingered less limply than is often supposed. Sometimes they survived as Liberal Unionists in Anglicized or border counties. In South Glamorgan, the influence of the Bute and Dunraven families remained considerable, and this enabled a member of the latter family to hold the seat as a Unionist from 1895 to 1906. Colonel Cornwallis-West was returned as Liberal MP for Denbighshire in 1880, but held on as a Liberal Unionist until 1892. Sometimes, as in England, they remained loyal to Liberalism. In Monmouth South, the Tory Tredegars were superseded by the Liberal Colonel Ivor Herbert in 1906, who was himself a local squire.[22] Arthur Humphreys-Owen, who owned 4,000 acres in Montgomeryshire, was Liberal MP for the county from 1895 until 1905. And Cardiganshire was represented by Matthew Vaughan Davies between 1892 and 1921. He was an unlettered, uncultured squire, who was Master of the local foxhounds; he had contested the same constituency unsuccessfully as a Conservative in 1885; and he ran the local Liberal constituency organization virtually as an extension of his own estate.[23]

But while patrician involvement in rural politics and representation did not disappear overnight in the aftermath of the Third Reform Act, it is important to keep it in proportion. For what had been the norm in the shires until the 1870s increasingly became the exception thereafter. Only in a very few Welsh constituencies, in the lowlands and on the east coast of Scotland, and in the rural heartlands of England, did the politics of Barset continue unaltered and unchallenged. And even where the landowners presided over the new constituency associations, real power had often passed elsewhere. The local branches of the Primrose League might be decorated with ornamental aristocrats: but the day-to-day work of management and fund-raising was undertaken by the increasingly bureaucratic Tory Central office.[24] In most Welsh and Scottish counties, it was the middle-class professionals – the solicitors, the clergymen, and the schoolteachers – who were increasingly dominant in all local affairs. And in England, it was Lord Salisbury himself who sought to purge the constituency associations of the solicitors and lawyers who were the clients of the landowners, and to put full-time professional party workers in their place.[25]

The real difficulty, as Lord Percy later remarked, was the coincidence of agricultural depression with the Third Reform Act. At the very time when politics required more money, many patricians had less of it to spend. A contested county election might cost £5,000, and there were also constant donations and expenses. As Lord Francis Hervey, MP for Bury St Edmunds from 1885 to 1892, explained, there was 'a mission hall to be erected, church repaired, organ provided, important alterations to hospital', as well as the ordinary contributions to the football and cricket clubs and the friendly societies.[26] The Herveys were reasonably well off. But many landowners, forced to economize, could no longer afford this expense. In 1894, Lord Warwick's son and heir refused to stand for a local constituency because he could not afford to. And Thomas Gibson-Carmichael felt compelled to resign as MP for Midlothian after only five years as part of a widespread programme of retrenchment and economy: the London flat was given up, the big house sold, and some of his paintings were sent to auction. As Lord Balcarres noted 'the average man with moderate income' could no longer afford to pay for politics.[27]

But it was not only the expense of being an MP that weighed heavily on many landowners in these years of depression: it was also that representing these large, sprawling, rural seats required more work than ever before. Nursing a constituency for a long period, and contesting the elections themselves, now meant the candidate had to reach out to the enfranchised labourers in every village community. A few set-piece speeches in town halls would no longer suffice: 'it is the visit to the village feasts, the chat in the village schoolroom, the likeness over the chimney corner, and the pleasant family musical evenings in the winter, which are the articles of war.'[28] With few motor cars, and as yet no wireless, the period from 1885 to 1914 was arguably the worst in which to be a county MP. As Lord Willoughby de Broke recalled, 'the comfortable evenings at home had to give way, with distressing frequency, to the village meeting.' And for many, like Bertram Freeman-Mitford, this was simply too much. After only three years as a Warwickshire MP, he gave up. As he later recalled, 'I was perfectly determined not to stand again . . . Primrose League meetings, bazaars, political gatherings in schoolrooms, attended perhaps by a dozen yokels, two or three women and a little boy . . . made life impossible.'[29]

As some patricians rushed to retire, and others refused to stand, many county constituencies were obliged to turn to candidates who were not only non-gentry, but increasingly non-resident as well. Even in such a rural enclave as Lincolnshire, 'candidates appeared' in the aftermath of the Third Reform Act, 'that the old farming

electorate would have scorned as foreigners and carpet baggers.'
In the West Country the same trend was so pronounced that as early
as 1895, one newspaper vainly lamented that 'it is quite time
that Cornwall ceased to import strangers as Parliamentary
representatives.'[30] In Cheshire, 70 per cent of its MPs who sat
between 1832 and 1885 had been born in the county, but the figure
dropped to 25 per cent for those returned from 1885 to 1918. And
when Freeman-Mitford gave up his Warwickshire constituency, he
was replaced, not by a resident landowner, but by one Victor
Milward, a Redditch needle-maker, who had lived in the division for
only seven years, who had no family or business links with it, and
who had been refused admission to the county bench in 1881 on the
grounds that he was too parvenu.[31]

This sudden, unprecedented influx of middle-class outsiders into
the county constituencies which had traditionally been the preserve
of the local aristocracy and resident gentry was much commented
upon at the time. Even in such sylvan and self-sufficient shires as
Shropshire, the same trend was in evidence in the more urbanized
constituencies. In 1906, the Wellington Division became vacant after
A. H. Brown, a local country gentlemen, retired on completing
thirty-eight years service. The Liberal candidate was C. S. Henry,
who was not only an outsider, but an Australian, and the Conservative was Hildebrand Harmsworth, an outsider and a plutocrat.
Henry won, and in 1910 actually held the seat, beating a much more
traditional Tory candidate, who was the son and heir of the last MP
for Wenlock borough, Captain the Hon. G. C. B. Weld-Forester.[32]
And in Wales, it was the new middle class and petty bourgeoisie who
were now firmly in command: the MPs for Anglesey, Glamorgan,
and Carmarthen tended to be radical, nonconformist, and Welsh-
speaking – journalists, solicitors, and clergymen.[33]

The 1906 general election wiped out another cohort of patricians
almost as completely as the last great radical triumph of 1885 had
done. In Glamorgan, the Talbots were vanquished after two hundred
years of county politics. The sitting MP for Sutherland, a member of
the Leveson-Gower family, went down to defeat, and after 1910 the
family never sought parliamentary honours there again. In Cheshire,
both Egerton and Tollemache were turned out, and they, too, withdrew from constituency politics for good.[34] The representation of
Huntingdonshire had been virtually monopolized by the Sandwich
and de Ramsay families, after the Third Reform Act as before. But both
their MPs were defeated in 1906, at which point the family names
disappear from the county's parliamentary history for ever. Even
more significant was the demise of the Manners family in Leicestershire. From 1885, three members of the family had represented the

Melton constituency, without a break, and often without a contest. In 1906, the last Manners MP stood down, and the family never contested the division thereafter. And Sir John Hazlerigg, a local squire, who came forward as the new Conservative candidate, was himself defeated and never stood for Parliament again.[35]

This trend towards patrician abdication in county politics may be seen most vividly in the case of Warwickshire, where landed leadership and landed representation virtually collapsed in the years just before and during the First World War.[36] The Marquess of Hertford retired as President of the Stratford Division Conservative Association in 1909, and his son, a divorced bankrupt, declined to follow him. Likewise, on the Liberal side, the Marquess of Northamptonshire died in 1913, and his son was no more willing or able to take over. Here, in the Stratford Division, landed leadership disappeared abruptly, and was never restored. And, within five years, there was an even more significant departure in a neighbouring constituency. F. A. Newdegate came from an ancient family of Warwickshire gentry, his forebears had regularly represented the county, and he himself was MP for the Nuneaton Division from 1892 to 1906, and for Tamworth from 1909 to 1917. But in that year, he resigned and became Governor of Tasmania, and his family, too, bowed out of Warwickshire's parliamentary affairs. Within less than a decade, the patricians had all but disappeared.

The end of the First World War brought with it two more drastic changes. The Fourth Reform Act undermined landed influence still further, by extending the franchise, by making the constituencies much more uniform, and by sweeping away most of the remaining vestiges of the old system.[37] And the simultaneous 'revolution in landholding' only accentuated this trend towards local political abdication. For as many small landowners sold out altogether, and as the great grandees trimmed down their holdings or sold off their peripheral estates entirely, the territorial connection, which had been the basis of the old-style county politics, was gradually but inexorably broken. As Walter Long explained to Bonar Law in 1919, 'we owe our position in the country, and always have done, much more to local personal influence than to the popularity of our own political party.' But, he went on, 'the bulwark of so much that stood for social respect and civic good has been removed'. And the effect was very real: when the Duke of Rutland sold much of his Haddon estate in the great post-war boom, the Bakewell area subsequently moved markedly to the left.[38]

By this time, therefore, the few old-world survivals were very much an anachronism. Where the great estates remained intact, deferential attitudes persisted, along with allegations of intimidation.

In West Derbyshire, in the Chatsworth constituency, Liberal canvassers claimed that local residents in the estate villages were afraid to open their doors to them. When Lord Willoughby d'Eresby won a hard-fought by-election for Rutland and Stamford in 1933, it was clear that the lustre of his name and the influence of his family was of positive, and perhaps decisive, benefit.[39] The Conservative Associations in such constituencies as West Derbyshire, Peterborough, Melton, and Newark were still presided over by the Duke of Devonshire, the Marquess of Exeter, the Marquess of Granby, and Earl Manvers. And their financial support was indispensable. At the Rutland and Stamford Conservative Association, the combined donations of Lords Ancaster and Willoughby d'Eresby in the 1930s amounted to £300 a year, which was nearly half of the total annual income. And in West Derbyshire, the Duke of Devonshire and his son provided 54 per cent of the Association's revenue.[40]

Under these circumstances, some great landed families still provided MPs for traditional county constituencies. The Marquess of Hartington was returned for West Derbyshire from 1923 until he became Duke of Devonshire in 1935. In Lancashire, Lord Stanley was MP for the Fylde Division from 1922 until his death in 1938, and Lord Balniel sat for the Lonsdale Division from 1924 until his succession to the peerage in 1940. Nearby, Oliver Stanley represented Westmoreland from 1924 until 1945, while the heirs of Lords Selborne and Salisbury represented county constituencies in Hampshire and Dorset. A smattering of local country gentlemen were also still in evidence: Ruggles-Brise in Essex. Courthope in Sussex, Acland Troyte and Dyke Acland in the West Country. And in Shropshire, the Oswestry and Ludlow Divisions continued their loyalty to home-grown patricians. When W. C. Bridgeman retired with a peerage in 1929, he was followed by Major B. E. P. Leighton, a country gentleman whose father had also been a Shropshire MP. And Ludlow's representation was both local and landed: Stanier, then Lord Clive, then George Windsor-Clive.[41]

In some Scottish constituencies, families that remained influential before the First World War continued to be so after, as their extensive sales of land still left them with acres to spare and influence to wield. The most conspicuous example of this was the Buccleuch family in Roxburgh, where the Earl of Dalkeith was MP from 1923 until his accession to the dukedom in 1935, when he was followed by his younger brother, Lord William Scott, who held the seat until the 1950s. In Caithness, Sir Archibald Sinclair was not only Lord-Lieutenant, but was MP from 1922 until 1945, and was returned unopposed in 1923, 1924, and 1931.[42] In Western Perth and Kinross, the Duchess of Atholl held the seat virtually unchallenged from 1923, until her disagreement with the government's policy towards the Spanish Civil War led to her defeat in 1938. Even into the 1930s, this tradition lingered, not yet quite extinct. The Marquess of Douglas held Eastern Renfrew from 1930 until he became Duke of Hamilton a decade later, and in 1931, the young Lord Dunglass, son of the Earl of Home, was returned for Lanarkshire. Thus began, in appropriately patrician style, the political career of the man who was to become the last authentically aristocratic Prime Minister of Britain thirty years later.

These few survivals from the pre-1885 world should not be ignored. But what was already an exception by the First World War had dwindled into a marginal minority by the 1930s: the examples given in the last two paragraphs are not exhaustive, but there are not many more. Some were still connected with traditional localities, but now sat only for a very short time: instead of representing a constituency for life, they were no more than stopgap candidates. Such were T. G. F. Paget for Leicestershire Bosworth, who sat in the Parliament of 1922–3 but not thereafter; the last member of the Long family, who represented the Westbury Division of Wiltshire, but only from 1927 to 1931; and the last Thynne in a Somerset seat from 1931 to 1935. Others sat for constituencies with which they had no territorial links. Lord Fermoy, an Irish peer who had relocated himself near Sandringham, represented the Kings Lynn Division of Norfolk. Viscount Elmley, son of the Earl Beauchamp, was returned for Norfolk East. And Earl Castle Stewart, another Irish peer and sometime schoolmaster at Rugby represented the Melton Division of Leicester.[44]

In Wales, by the inter-war years, the patricians were even more peripheral. Indeed, there are only two such MPs who immediately spring to mind, and both represented border constituencies in the most Anglicized part of the Principality: C. L. Forestier-Walker, who sat for Monmouthshire from 1918 to 1934, and the Hon. Ivor Guest, who was MP for Brecon and Radnor from 1935 until his accession to the Wimborne peerage four years later. But across most of Wales, the old territorial class was now quite irrelevant, as is shown by the electoral history of Cardiganshire. Throughout this period, the county was held by Liberals: a lawyer, a school teacher, and the son of a tenant farmer. The Tory cause was still led by the few surviving landowners, but was quite forlorn. In 1923, Sir Pryse Pryse considered intervening as an anti-waste Liberal, but was politely told not to bother; and Lord Lisburne (an Irish peerage) who stood as the Conservative against two Liberals, came bottom of the poll with only 25 per cent of the votes. He did not stand again.[45]

By the 1920s and 1930s, the patricians had effectively ceased to matter in the management and representation of most rural constituencies in England, Scotland, and Wales. In West Sussex, where once the Norfolks and Richmonds had ruled unchallenged, the new inter-war MP was a plutocratic carpet-bagger, Major John Courtauld. In the increasingly suburbanized county of Cheshire, the trend was overwhelmingly away from local landowners or entrepreneurs, towards outsiders, professionals, and trade-union leaders, men with no local links, or of limited standing in the community.[46] Even in some of the Shropshire constituencies, the tenacious tradition of local landowners was finally overturned: the inter-war MPs for the Wrekin Division included a London railwayman and a trade-union leader from the north of England, while those for the Shrewsbury Division included a Manchester architect of Russian-Jewish extraction. And in the rural central and eastern Midlands, the eclipse of the patricians was equally complete: the percentage of Conservative candidates with landed backgrounds declined from 46 in 1918 to 11.5 in 1929.[47]

Until the late 1870s, the British parliamentary system remained fundamentally rural, but with urban enclaves: the majority of the constituencies were either small boroughs or amenable counties, and the majority of their MPs came from the landowning élite. But by the 1930s, this had changed dramatically: rural constituencies were now a minority in the total representational structure, and even there the landowners were becoming increasingly marginal figures: at best, they were a dwindling band representing a declining part of Great Britain. The change may have been more protracted than the sudden territorial upheaval of 1910–22, but the overall result was the same: in political representation as in landownership, five hundred years of patrician history was reversed in fifty. County politics was no longer an essential outwork of country house life: it had been fully assimilated into the national organizations of the great political parties. Only in a few very rural constituencies, still dominated by a great heartland estate, or by a caucus of exceptionally tenacious gentry, did some vestiges of the world of Barset survive.

ii. County Government: From Oligarchy to Bureaucracy

Writing in 1882, Charles George Milnes Gaskell, a Yorkshire country gentleman worth £10,000 a year, offered these pessimistic remarks on the present and future prospects of landownership:

The privileges connected with the tenure of land are fast disappearing, if they have not already done so. The ranks of the magistracy

are recruited from all classes, and if any consideration attaches still
to the landowner from his official position, a county government
bill, making extensive changes, will impair if not destroy it.[48]

Considering that Milnes Gaskell sat as a Yorkshire county MP,
enjoying a comfortable majority, and was later to be chairman of the
West Riding County Council for more than ten years, it may seem
that his own experience belied his analysis and confounded his
predictions. Yet in essence he was correct in his belief – and in his
fear – that the patricians were soon to be superseded as the governing élite of England, Wales, and Scotland, partly because their
grip on the old system of local control was indeed weakening, and
partly because a new and ultimately very different structure of
county government was soon to come into being.

Nevertheless, in the early 1880s, the gentry and grandees, as JPs
and Lord-Lieutenants, seemed as fully in control of the British
countryside as ever. They dispensed justice at petty and quarter
sessions, and remained collectively responsible for the administration
of the county. And this 'rural House of Lords' was still overwhelmingly patrician in its composition. As late as 1887, some three-
quarters of the county magistrates of England and Wales came from
just this background. Indeed, many Lord-Lieutenants refused to
nominate magistrates from any other class. In Buckinghamshire, the
third Duke of Buckingham was careful to ensure that the majority of
his nominees were of authentic landed background or connection.[49]
In Shropshire, as late as 1905, there were 240 Tory JPs and only 10
Liberals, and this distribution was defended by the chairman of
quarter sessions, Sir Offley Wakeman, on the grounds that small
tradesmen would be inappropriate magistrates as they would be
unable to deal impartially with people who might be their cus-
tomers. And in Wales, the Anglicized, Tory gentry kept away
Liberal, nonconformist, nationalists even more completely: in Cardiganshire in 1893, there were 105 Tory JPs to 17 Liberals.[50]

But as new middle-class wealth inexorably accumulated, and as
the gentry's willingness and ability to discharge their traditional
functions was eroded, the take-over of the bench by non-landed
social groups could not be postponed indefinitely. Of the new
magistrates appointed in England and Wales between 1867 and 1877,
16 per cent were middle class; but of those appointed between 1877
and 1887, the proportion had increased to 30 per cent. Indeed, in
industrial areas like the North and West Ridings, self-made men had
been put on the bench since the middle of the century; by the 1890s
they were providing over half of the new appointments; and by
the 1900s, they constituted a majority of all JPs for the first time.[51]

Likewise in Cheshire, an increasingly suburbanized county, the majority of the bench by the 1880s came from the professional and business, rather than the landowning sectors: the first Duke of Westminster might preside over the county, but he could no longer govern it without the aid of these new and non-landed men. And even in some rural areas, the same problem occurred, if there were insufficient resident gentry. In the Lindsey Division of Lincolnshire, professionals and businessmen from Grimsby were already in the majority by the 1880s.[52]

In the early part of that decade, most Lord-Lieutenants were Liberals, and so were more likely to be sympathetic to non-landed magistrates. But the Home Rule split changed this dramatically. In part, this was because most county magnates went over to the Unionists. But it was also that between 1885 and 1905, the Conservatives systematically appointed young patrician Lord-Lieutenants, in the hope that they might entrench themselves in power for a long period. Between 1886 and 1906, 36 of the 42 English Lord-Lieutenancies fell vacant, as well as most of them in Wales and Scotland, and the majority of the new appointees served for over twenty-five years.[53] Some, indeed, seemed virtually immortal: the Marquess of Bath was Lord-Lieutenant of Somerset from 1899 to 1945; Sir John Williams-Bulkeley presided over Anglesey from 1896 to 1942; and the Earl of Powis held the office in Shropshire from 1896 to 1951. By placing these young grandees at the apex of county government, the Conservatives hoped to perpetuate patrician dominance in the shires, and to ward off middle-class encroachment on to the bench. And to some extent, they succeeded: even as late as 1941, Lord Powis considered the claims of one woman to be a JP simply on the grounds that she was the wife of the MFH.[54]

But during the 1890s and the 1900s, the Liberal party first circumvented and then overturned this Conservative policy. For by gradually changing the manner in which magistrates were appointed, they effectively ended the Lord-Lieutenant's power of socially exclusive selection. Between 1892 and 1894, James Bryce was Chancellor of the Duchy of Lancaster, and reassumed direct control of the nomination of magistrates for the County Palatine, which had previously been exercised by Tory Lord-Lieutenants. He personally appointed 257 new men, most of whom were either Liberals or members of the working class, or both.[55] And this deliberate policy, motivated by a mixture of party-political self-interest, and broader concerns of social justice and equity, was also followed by Lord Chancellor Herschell, who tried to put his own nominees on other county benches, in addition to the names forwarded to him by the Lord-Lieutenants. At the same time, the newly formed Welsh coun-

ty councils passed regular resolutions against the continued monopoly of Anglicans, Tories, and landowners on the bench.[56]

On their return to power with a great majority in 1906, the
Liberals sought to make more fundamental alterations to the system
of appointment. In that year, they abolished the £100 property
qualification for a county magistrate; in 1907, the Lord Chancellor
Loreburn encouraged the Lord-Lieutenant of Devon to appoint an
advisory committee to help him with the nomination of JPs; and in
1910 he set up a Royal Commission to consider the whole question
of appointments to the bench.[57] Its prime recommendation was that
it should not be barred to men because of their religious or political
views, and that magistrates should not be exclusively appointed
from the narrow social circles of the county community. Accordingly, Loreburn insisted that in future, the nomination of magistrates
should be in the hands of a committee, on which the Lord-Lieutenant
need not necessarily even sit, and which could bypass him and go
direct to the Lord Chancellor if he was a member and proved
obstructive. As a result, JPs were gradually recruited from a much
broader spectrum of society (which included women after 1918), and
even in Shropshire, Lord Powis notwithstanding, ten working-class
men were on the bench by 1940.[58]

These Liberal measures meant that the trend towards the broadening of the social background of the county magistracy, which was
already increasingly apparent by the 1880s, was only further intensified. The decline in the will and the numbers of the resident gentry,
the growth of a new rural middle class, and these changes in the
mode of appointment effectively ended the patrician monopoly on
the bench in England and Wales, and of the Commissionerships of
Supply in Scotland. Naturally, the precise rate and exact timing of
the change depended on the particular economic and social structure
of the county, but that was unmistakably the direction in which
developments were moving. In Wales, and in the industrialized
counties of England, the change was rapid and dramatic; in areas like
Wiltshire or Norfolk, it was naturally rather slower paced. But one
result was of more widespread significance: however broad his acres
might (or might not) remain, the Lord-Lieutenant ceased to be a
figure of real power and influence in the county, and increasingly
became little more than a dignified ornamental, wearing a grand
uniform to receive distinguished visitors.[59]

Even more important, a new system of county government was
also being constructed, which further undermined the old system of
resident landowner control. As Milnes Gaskell had predicted, it was
not just that the traditional patrician magistracy was being diluted, it
was also being superseded. By the mid-1880s, it was generally

accepted that the government of the counties by quarter sessions could not continue indefinitely. If the rural labourers were to be given a say in the choice of their parliamentary representatives, it was clearly both anomalous and indefensible that they should not be allowed to elect those responsible for their local government. In Gladstone's second ministry, Dilke and Chamberlain were much preoccupied with schemes for such reform, but the congestion of the parliamentary timetable meant that no measure was actually introduced.[60] And so, ironically, it was Lord Salisbury's Conservative government that introduced reform, for England and Wales in 1888, and for Scotland in the following year. According to Chamberlain, who had pressed for a measure both as a Liberal cabinet minister and as a Unionist, the result would be 'a peaceful revolution in the administration of our counties . . . second in importance only to the extension of the franchise.'[61]

Although Salisbury rightly feared that the squires would feel a sense of 'unutterable wrong' suffered at the hands of what was supposedly a government sympathetic to patrician concerns, the measure was conceived conservatively.[62] It was designed to pre-empt Liberal legislation, which would certainly have been more radical, and the scheme itself was in many ways far from revolutionary. In addition to an elected council, aldermen could be co-opted, thereby ensuring that landowners who did not stand or who failed to get elected could in fact be recruited. And the powers of these new bodies were very carefully restricted: the School Boards and Poor Law authorities were left undisturbed, and their own responsibilities were only vaguely defined. But there were two major changes. However falteringly and restrictedly, the democratic principle had indeed been introduced into rural administration, and the hereditary and oligarchic principle had been discarded. Moreover, by carving separate and autonomous county boroughs out of the shires, the integrity of the county community was undermined, and the resources of the new authority were correspondingly limited.

Inevitably, predictions varied as to what would be the results of the first elections. The Liberals feared that the landed interest would do well, the Conservatives that it would do badly. Lord Harrowby was worried that entrusting county administration to 'the untried and uncertain hands of those elected by popular vote must lead to confusion, bad management, suffering and expense.'[63] The *Quarterly Review* feared the rise of 'caucuses and wire pullers for distinctly party ends', and the departure of the 'devotion, sacrifice and high character of the English squires, who will no longer be at the helm.' Lord Powis thought that 'existing leading magistrates may get elected at first', but that power would soon pass to 'the farmer and

THE "GRAND TRANSFORMATION"!!

23. 'The "Grand
Transformation"!!' *Punch*,
19 Jan. 1889.

shopkeeper or tradesman, who will gradually elbow out the gentry.'
Lord Salisbury, by contrast, insisted that it was 'not a radical or
revolutionary measure', and *The Times* felt that 'it is tolerably certain
that the country gentry will secure sufficient representation upon the
new county councils.'[64] But F. W. Maitland caught most vividly the
sense that, regardless of the outcome, a major era in patrician history
was drawing to its close: 'As a governor he is doomed; but there has
been no accusation. He is cheap, he is pure, he is capable, but he is
doomed; he is to be sacrificed to a theory, on the altar of the spirit of
the age.'[65]

How, in practice, did the elections work out? In England, it is clear
that the worst forebodings were not realized, as the old ruling élite
remained the largest single element in the new county councils.
Throughout the country as a whole, slightly over one-half of all
newly elected county councillors were magistrates, and two-thirds
of the counties elected the chairman of quarter sessions or the Lord-

Lieutenant as the chairman of the new county council. Many of the seats were not contested; most gentry who stood were elected; those few defeated were usually co-opted as aldermen; and so were those who did not even deign to stand. The first act of the Shropshire County Council was to appoint the Lord-Lieutenant as an alderman. The Worcestershire County Council did exactly as Lord Beauchamp instructed it, even electing his complete slate of aldermen.[66] At Stafford, Lord Harrowby greeted his fellow councillors with positively patrician friendliness, including one man who turned out to be the porter. And in Devon, it was observed with surprise that 'the gathering looked much like quarter sessions . . . landlordism and squirearchy were in conspicuous force.'[67]

But this is not the whole of the picture, for if only one-half of the new county councillors were magistrates, the clear implication – given the growing infiltration of the county bench at that time by non-landowners – is that the territorial element was no longer in full control. And this was especially so in heavily builtup or industrialized counties, or in regions where the resident gentry were few and far between. In counties such as Kent and the West Riding, a peer or country gentleman was elected to the chair, but the majority of the councillors were already drawn from the business and professional classes.[68] In Durham, Lancashire, and Cheshire, the industrial and professional elements were so preponderant from the very beginning that they dispensed with aristocratic chairmen altogether.[69] And even in rural Lincolnshire, 'the gentry had been given notice that they should no longer expect to govern the county unchallenged'. Twelve magistrates were actually beaten at the polls, and in the Holland Division, the newly elected chairman was a Spalding wine merchant, not a JP.[70]

In Wales, the results were both less varied and less encouraging, as almost everywhere, the gentry and grandees were rebuffed and humiliated. For it was these local elections, even more than the parliamentary contests of 1880, 1885, and 1886, that emphatically marked the end of patrician ascendancy, as radicals, nationalists, and nonconformists triumphed almost everywhere. In the north, 175 of the 260 councillors were Liberals, and in the south, the figure was 215 out of 330.[71] Everywhere, the squires and grandees were rejected. In Caernarfon, the Lord-Lieutenant was defeated. In Montgomeryshire, Lord Powis' pre-eminent claim to the chair was passed over in favour of the Liberal squire Arthur Humphreys-Owen. And in Denbigh, Sir Watkin Williams-Wynn, still smarting from his electoral defeats in 1885 and 1886, was further humiliated when the council preferred Thomas Gee – a radical journalist, campaigner for church disestablishment, and President of the Welsh Land League –

as chairman.[72] Only in Brecon, with its highly Anglicized electorate, did the patricians survive in appreciable force. Elsewhere, they were almost totally wiped out by the nonconformist middle class.[73]

This is emphatically shown in the case of Cardiganshire, where the Liberals dominated the new council by a majority of 37 to 10.[74] Their backgrounds were exactly as expected: tenant farmers, small businessmen, shopkeepers, miners, and doctors. Only three major landowners were returned, Lord Lisburne, Colonel Davies-Evans, and Major Lewes. But others, such as Lloyd and Waddington, failed to secure election. Lisburne had hoped to be chairman, but was defeated by Peter Jones, a Methodist coal merchant from Aberystwyth. Almost at once, the council passed resolutions against the present method of appointing magistrates and in favour of church disestablishment. And the nationalists kept a firm hold on the appointment of committee chairmen and the co-option of aldermen. There was no obsequious or magnanimous recruitment of the vanquished gentry here. When speaking of the first elections, and arguing that 'the counties as a whole are not given to returning radical representatives', Lord Salisbury had been compelled to modify his remark by adding, 'I am afraid that in Wales I must speak with more caution.' How right he was.[75]

In Scotland, where the new county councils replaced the old Commissioners of Supply, the first elections were held in February 1889. Compared with England, fewer landowners stood; compared with Wales, more of them were successful. In Aberdeen, Lord Saltoun, Grant of Monymusk, and Farquharson of Haughton were defeated, and Lord Sempill withdrew before the poll. But these seem to have been unfortunate exceptions. In Ayr, the Hon. H. F. Elliot (who was also MP for the county) was elected; in Fife Sir Ralph Anstruther was successful; and in Kincardine the Hon. John Arbuthnott easily won his contest. Some patricians did not need to fight at all. Both Sir John Hay and Sir Graham Graham-Montgomery were returned unopposed in Peebles; and in Selkirk, the Earl of Dalkeith, heir to the Duke of Buccleuch, faced no contest.[76] But these few notables were decidedly atypical, as the overwhelming majority of the new county councillors came from the local middle classes: farmers, innkeepers, schoolteachers, clergymen, cattle salesmen, merchants, and businessmen. And in the Highlands, the crofting candidates put up by the Land League swept the board: in Sutherland they captured 14 out of the 16 contested seats.[77]

As in Wales, the patricians were thus in a minority in every Scottish county among the democratically chosen representatives: in electoral terms, there was a major transfer of power away from the traditional governing class. Nevertheless, in the lowlands and the north-east (but not in the Highlands), the grandees were soon co-opted, as had been the practice in England. In Midlothian and Ayrshire, the preliminary meetings were presided over by Lord Rosebery and the Earl of Stair. In Roxburgh, Lord Polwarth, the Earl of Minto, the Marquess of Lothian, and the Duke of Roxburghe himself attended the first session.[78] And in almost every county, the elected convenor was a local landowner: peers like Balfour of Burleigh in Clackmannan, Camperdown in Forfar, and Elgin in Fife; and gentry like Cameron of Lochiel in Inverness, Maitland in Stirling, and Grant in Banff. But this was often more the façade than the substance of power. The office of convenor never carried the weight associated with the county-council chairmanship in England; and from the outset, these notables were responsible to elected bodies that were overwhelmingly non-patrician in composition.

When looking at these elections, it has been customary to stress their fundamentally conservative consequences; to accept at face value the many contemporary claims that county councils were but the old quarter sessions under a new name; and even to argue that the landowners' position was consolidated because their supremacy was no longer oligarchic, but was strengthened with the sanction of popular election. Nevertheless, Joseph Chamberlain was surely correct in seeing the events of 1888–9 as being almost as revolutionary as those of 1884–5.[79] Throughout Wales, and in those parts of England where industry was strong or the landowners were weak, the grandees and gentry had been brutally and deliberately rejected by the agrarian nationalists, or overwhelmed by middle-class businessmen and professionals. And in Scotland, the Land Leaguers triumphed in the Highlands, while elsewhere the patricians were very much the junior partners, who largely participated on the sufferance of their social inferiors. When Salisbury expressed his fear that the squires would be cross, he had good grounds to do so. In county government as in county representation, the 1880s saw the notables and magnificœs in conspicuous retreat, and that trend became only more pronounced during the ensuing half-century.

But it was, nevertheless, a slow and dignified withdrawal. In Scotland, the pattern established in 1889 survived in recognizable form until the Second World War. In 1892, two-thirds of the convenors of Scottish county councils were local landowners, seven were peers, and five were also Lord-Lieutenants. As late as 1940, half of these offices were filled by bona fide patricians, seven were peers, and ten were also Lord-Lieutenants. In Inverness-shire, once a radical and crofting county, Cameron of Lochiel and the Mackintosh of Mackintosh were, successively, both Lord-Lieutenant and convenor throughout most of this period. And during the inter-war years, the

Duke of Roxburghe was both convenor and Lord-Lieutenant in his titular county; Lord Home held both these offices in Lanark, where his eldest son was also a county MP; and so did the Duke of Buccleuch in Selkirk, where his younger brother also sat for a local constituency. In these last two cases, at least, the patrician families remained a real force, not just in county representation, but in county government too.

Likewise, in England, there were some counties where landed power remained of real importance into the 1920s and 1930s. During the last decade of the nineteenth century, the eleventh Earl of Sandwich was Lord-Lieutenant of Huntingdonshire, first chairman of the county council, Mayor of Sandwich, and father of one of the county MPs. And his son followed him in many of these offices in the inter-war years.[80] The Duke of Bedford was the automatic first choice as chairman of Bedfordshire County Council, and he was succeeded by his relative, Lord Ampthill. In Wiltshire, power was divided between the Bath and Lansdowne families. The second chairman of the county council was Lord Fitzmaurice, who was also a local MP and chairman of quarter sessions, and whose brother, the Marquess of Lansdowne, was Lord-Lieutenant. And he was preceded by the fourth Marquess of Bath, and followed by the fifth, who was chairman of the county council from 1904 until 1945. In addition, Bath chaired the quarter sessions from 1890 until 1923, and was a long-serving Lord-Lieutenant of the neighbouring county of Somerset, for which his eldest son briefly sat as an MP in the 1930s.[81]

Elsewhere, the patricians survived through corporate rather than dynastic endeavour. In Shropshire, the council was chaired by a succession of local landowners, and seven members of the Powis family served as councillors or aldermen between 1889 and 1974. In Kent, there was a strong hereditary element provided by the Cornwallis family, who produced two chairmen in almost immediate succession.[82] And in Berkshire, a tightly-knit group of local gentry virtually monopolized the great county offices. Between 1889 and 1947, the chairmanship was held almost uninterruptedly by six successive members of the Mount, the Mowbray, and the Benyon families, all country gentry, who regularly provided Lord-Lieutenants of the county as well.[83] Even in Wales, the two most Anglicized counties conformed to this pattern. In Radnor, Charles Coltman Coltman Rogers was chairman of the county council from 1896 to 1929, and became Lord-Lieutenant in 1922; while in Brecon, Lord Glanusk held both positions before and after the First World War.

In localities such as these, it is clear that the nobles and notables

24. Lord Bath, chairman of
the Wiltshire County
Council, 1904–45.

survived more successfully as a major force in county government
than they did in county politics. And this is easily explained. For it
was largely a matter of deliberate choice and calculation, as many
landowners decided to withdraw from national politics and constituency affairs, and to redirect their public endeavours into this new
form of local administration. The work was less contentious, much
less demanding, much less expensive, and much less risky to reputation than the rough and tumble of parliamentary public life. In the
relative calm of the county council chamber, grandees like 'our much
loved Lord Bath' could still dominate with a patrician style no longer
acceptable in the Lords or the Commons or at the hustings.[84] They
were no longer powerful yet controversial political figures, but
presented themselves instead as loyal county men, and masters of
county business, who successfully justified their inherited broad
acres by disinterested, non-contentious public service. Aloof, Olympian, and detached, totally decent and totally incorruptible, they lent
a tone of aristocratic grandeur to the proceedings, and elevated the
whole level of county council business.

The evidence for this self-conscious shift of patrician priorities
seems clear. In Bedfordshire, the eleventh duke did not wish to play
any part in national politics, and saw his role on the county council as
essentially an extension of Woburn estate management. In Huntingdonshire, the Sandwich family withdrew from politics entirely after

their defeat of 1906, and concentrated their efforts in local government thereafter. In Leicestershire, it was only after Sir John Hazlerigg had been defeated for the Melton Division in 1906 that he chose to direct his energies towards the county council.[85] In Invernessshire, both Cameron of Lochiel and the Mackintosh of Mackintosh stood unsuccessfully for the county, and then withdrew into noncontentious local government. And in Radnor, Charles Coltman Coltman Rogers was MP for the borough constituency from 1884 to 1885, unsuccessfully contested the county in 1886, and thereupon withdrew from parliamentary politics and shifted his interests to local government. By contrast, those few aristocratic families who remained important in national affairs, like the Derbys, the Devonshires, and the Salisburys, had rather less time for day-to-day county council activity.[86]

But although this patrician persistence in local government provides some of the most emphatic evidence for the survival of the landed élite into the first half of the twentieth century, it must again be set in a broader perspective, and the façade and the substance must be distinguished. In Scotland, the number of county councils that were convened by grandees was markedly reduced by the 1930s, and in very few cases did real administrative dominance still coexist with local political influence. And in Wales, with the exception of Brecon and Radnor, the remaining gentry and grandees were little more than a marginal irrelevance. In 1892, the Liberals made more gains, and in 1904, they were in control of every Welsh county. By the inter-war years, Glamorgan, Carmarthen, and Monmouth were now dominated by the Labour party. 'Notable landowners still appeared as Lords Lieutenant, high sheriffs or JPs . . . They patronised local historical and antiquarian bodies . . . But their regime in real terms was dead.'[87]

In England, those county councils that had begun with middleclass businessmen and professionals in control continued as they had started. In Lancashire, the five successive chairmen between 1889 and 1937 were all drawn from the middle classes – a barrister, a colliery owner, a merchant, a *rentier*, and a retiree – and the chairmen of the most important committees were all of similar background. There were, indeed, representatives of the old county families to be found, but they were increasingly fobbed off with insignificant and unimportant jobs, and the Derbys were conspicuous by their absence.[88] In Cheshire, too, the professional and entrepreneurial middle classes had been in full control of the most important positions since 1889. Sir George Dixon was the only patrician chairman, but he never gained the personal ascendancy of a Bath or a Sandwich, and great county families like the Grosvenors had absented themselves completely by the inter-war years.[89] In shires such as these, with a vigorous and increasingly suburbanized middle class, they were in control throughout.

At the same time, many county councils, which had started out under patrician chairmanship, gradually began to move in the same direction. In the West Riding of Yorkshire, the first three chairman were Lord Ripon, John Dent, and Charles Milnes Gaskell himself. But by 1911, such men were thought to be increasingly unrepresentative of the council as a whole, and thereafter middle-class businessmen, on the model of those in Lancashire and Cheshire, were always preferred.[90] Even where landowners remained as chairmen, it was often the case that the council as a whole was ceasing to be dominated by the patricians. In the case of Kent, the middle-class business and professional element had been the majority from the very beginning, and by 1910 they had superseded the gentry as chairmen of the committees where most of the real business was decided. And even in rural, remote, and conservative Shropshire, the many members of the Powis family who served on the county council were never put in charge of any important committee. Very often, therefore, continued landed leadership was little more than a façade for increasing middle-class dominance.[91]

In fact, this was almost bound to happen. As Redlich and Hirst predicted in 1903, before the great sales of land had begun, the balance of administrative power in county government was certain to change if the balance of territorial influence altered. Just as the sale of estates effectively removed many patricians from constituency politics, so it also eliminated them from local government.[92] In some areas, on the Lincolnshire model, there were not enough resident gentry to retain power: in Devon by 1916, a middle-class businessman was in the chair because of the dearth of local notables. Moreover, not all landowners, even among those who stood in the 1889 elections, proved as interested or as tenacious as Lord Bath: in Cheshire, the Westminsters, Egertons, and Tollemaches occasionally deigned to turn up, but they were not prepared to do the real work. And so, as the middle-class element became more entrenched, they increasingly came to resent the airs and graces of such ornamental grandees, and after 1912 refused to co-opt them as aldermen, if they were not prepared to justify their places in terms of effort rather than status. Unlike the quarter sessions, the county council was not an extension of county society.[93]

Underlying this were major changes in the form and functioning of the county councils themselves. Initially, as Salisbury had intended, they were little more than quarter sessions under another name: their budgets were tiny, their responsibilities were limited,

and they employed only a small staff, with little professional expertise, who were often directly inherited from the earlier·regime. But
by the 1930s, the scale of their operations had been markedly expanded. In 1902, the county councils took over the functions of the
School Boards, and in 1929 they also assumed the duties hitherto discharged by the Poor Law Guardians. In between, they were loaded
with further responsibilities, for roads and hospitals, for planning
and for libraries. The signs of this expansion were well displayed in
the much-extended office accommodation, and in the greatly increased county council budgets: in Wiltshire, spending grew from
less than £100,000 a year in the 1890s to over £1.5 million by the
1930s, and this was the common pattern.[94]

Yet paradoxically, growing responsibility inevitably led to diminished autonomy. Legislation from Westminster and instructions
from Whitehall increasingly set the limits to county council freedom,
and the new and necessary exchequer grants (which were soon
providing more income than the rates) eroded fiscal independence as
well. As a result, the county councils (like the constituency associations) were ceasing to be an instrument of local self-government, and
were becoming instead the outworks of an intrusive centralized
bureaucracy. At the same time, the massive proliferation of responsibility necessarily changed the nature of business. The plenary sessions of the council, with the chairman in charge, ceased to be of
great significance, and the real work was increasingly done on the
sub-committees. And as the business grew in bulk and complexity, it
was the expert, full-time, local-government employees who acquired the dominant voice, not just in the implementation of policy,
but in its formulation as well. To this extent, the patrician element
on the county councils had not been undermined by the lower-class
democrats – as had been feared initially – so much as by the upstart
bureaucrats.[95]

Whether the chairman of the council was an authentic grandee, a
middle-class professional, or even a Labour party activist, these
developments were commonplace throughout Great Britain. And
so, by the 1930s, there were growing – and justified – complaints
that the aldermen and elected councillors were increasingly ineffectual in the face of Whitehall interference and the permanent officials.
When, in the 1930s, Lord Powis lamented that it would be 'an evil
day for England' if unpaid councillors found their duties beyond
them, he was effectively acknowledging that that day had already
arrived. As Captain Jebb, another Shropshire councillor, explained,
it was 'really difficult' for councillors to wield any influence, except
in matters of detail: 'the big questions were slipped through without
being properly investigated.'[96] And if that was true for a county

council like Shropshire – in a rural, conservative and agricultural region, with a tenacious gentry who remained well represented and often in the chair – then how much more so was this the case in those many British counties that were so much more urbanized and middle class?

By the 1930s, the county councils were no longer the old rural oligarchy under a new name, but a professional hierarchy and structured bureaucracy which might – or might not – be sheltering behind a façade of patrician authority. In England and much of Scotland (but not in Wales), it was not so much the democracy of the 1880s that undermined landed leadership in local government, but the bureaucracy of the twentieth century. Despite the deliberate diversion of effort in that direction by many patricians, their contribution to county government by the inter-war years was much less significant than it had been half a century before. During the long span of his Olympian chairmanship, even a grand seigneur like Lord Bath became less a chief executive, and more a constitutional monarch: no longer the driving force in administration and policy making, but a figure-head who leant a tone, and looked good in his Lord-Lieutenant's uniform on ceremonial occasions. As such, the aristocracy's part in the government of the countryside was increasingly moving towards that non-contentious and essentially ornamental role that, during the same period, they were perfecting and practising in the towns and in the empire.[97]

iii. *Ireland: Ruritania and Revolution*

Throughout Great Britain, patrician leadership in the shires had often declined well before the estates were actually sold, and it very rarely survived once they were actually disposed of. Yet in the case of Ireland, by contrast, it was a widely held belief that if only the landlords could be persuaded to part with their estates, popular hostility to them would then evaporate, and they would thus be able to play a renewed and enhanced role in the politics and government of the country. When introducing his Land Purchase scheme in 1890, Arthur Balfour claimed that if dual ownership was abolished, 'the influence of the landowners . . . will be greatly augmented.'[98] When sponsoring the Irish Local Government Bill of 1898, his brother Gerald made the same case: if the landlords would come forward to stand and serve, he predicted, 'their reward is certain.' And it was the same belief that underlay Horace Plunkett's policy of 'constructive unionism': 'the abolition of landlordism, so far from destroying the usefulness of the Irish gentry, really gives them their first opportunity, within the memory of living men, to fulfill the true function of

25. 'A Gift from the
Greeks.' *Punch*, 27 Feb.
1892.

A GIFT FROM THE GREEKS.

Right Hon. Arthur. "IF I CAN ONLY GET THIS THROUGH, IT OUGHT TO SETTLE 'EM!"

aristocracy.'[99] But in the event, it was an opportunity that most Irish patricians did not – and could not – take.

Until the late 1870s, in Ireland as in Great Britain, the landowning classes remained in control of local politics and national representation, and also of local government and the administration of justice. Even the success of Isaac Butt's Home Rule Party in the 1874 general election only slightly diminished the massive phalanx of landed MPs sent by Ireland to Westminster. Here, still more completely than in Wales, it was the contest of 1880 that saw the nobles and notables routed. The successful mobilization of anti-landlord sentiment by the Land League meant that patrician MPs were turned out, not only in the south, but also in Donegal, Tyrone, Fermanagh, and Cavan, those parts of Ulster that were seriously threatened by nationalist agitation.[100] A country gentleman like A. M. Kavanagh, who had represented Carlow, his local county constituency, for fourteen years, was devastated when rejected even by his own tenantry: 'The majority of my men broke their promise to me... That is the poisoned stab.' Indeed, the roll-call of patrician casualties reads like the pages of *Debrett*: 'Gone', lamented Frank Hugh O'Donnell, 'gone Lord Francis Conyngham, gone the O'Conor Don, gone the Hon. Charles ffrench.'[101]

So, in Ireland as in Wales and in parts of England and Scotland, the writing was on the wall for the gentry and grandees as parliamentary representatives, even before the Third Reform Act was passed: that measure, which massively increased the Irish electorate from 222,000 to 740,000, merely confirmed and accentuated developments already under way.[102] As in Great Britain, the 1885 election brought devastation in the wake of redistribution, and the 1886 election largely – if not entirely – confirmed these trends. For the net result was effectively to exclude the traditional territorial classes from any further participation in the constituency affairs and political representation of Ireland, except in some parts of Ulster. Here was a political revolution of the greatest magnitude, well displayed in the fact that, at the 1885 election, not one of the 52 candidates put up in the south by the newly established and landlord-controlled Irish Loyal and Patriotic Union was elected.[103] And even in Ulster, in 1885, the nationalist and tenant-right candidates did unexpectedly well, winning a majority of the seats in the province.[104] The result was a patrician rejection even more abrupt and complete than in Wales.

What happened thereafter? Did the nobles and notables claw something back from the débâcle, as in England, or did they abdicate through lack of choice, as in Wales? In most of Ireland, the landlords had vanished never to return, and parliamentary representation was taken over by small-town, middle-class nationalists as in Wales: doctors, solicitors, and merchants to begin with, but becoming inexorably more plebeian as the century drew on. Of the 86 Home Rule MPs elected in 1886, only 5 were landowners; of the 94 returned between 1906 and 1910, there were only 7, and the proportion in between was essentially the same.[105] And this was a deliberate policy on the part of the nationalists. The selection of candidates was now in the hands of middle class and petty bourgeois constituency organizers, with occasional interference from Dublin. And with rare exceptions, they were determined to keep the landowners out, even those few who were favourable to their cause. In 1893, at a by-election in West Mayo, there was some support in nationalist circles for Colonel Blake, a local landlord. But interference from John Dillon, and the power of the slogan 'No landlord from Mayo', prevented him from gaining the nomination.[106]

In terms of parliamentary representation, the patricians effectively disappeared as the governing class of Ireland in the 1880s. And, unlike some of their English cousins, they failed to retain (or regain) control of the constituency organizations. The few exceptions merely prove the rule. Very occasionally, a Unionist landowner might get elected for a short spell, like the Hon. M. H. F. Morris in Galway in 1900. Others might serve briefly as anti-Parnell nationalists, like the Hon. J. B. B. Roche for East Kerry from 1896 to 1900, and the Hon. Edward Blake for Longford South from 1892 to 1907. But throughout the period from the 1880s to the First World War, only three bona fide patricians were long-serving nationalist MPs. The most famous was Charles Stewart Parnell himself, who was elected for County Mayo in 1880, but preferred to represent Cork City until his death in 1891. And the others were a brace of nationalist, Catholic baronets: Sir Walter Richard Nugent, who sat for his local constituency, Westmeath South, from 1907 until 1918; and Sir Thomas Grattan Esmonde who represented County Dublin South, West Kerry, and North Wexford between 1885 and 1918.

But it was only in parts of Ulster that non-maverick notables were able to reassert themselves in a manner reminiscent of some English constituencies. The Home Rule issue effectively closed the rift that had been developing between the tenant farmers and their landlords, and allowed the patricians to place themselves at the head of both the revived Orange Order and the new constituency associations from 1886.[107] In East Antrim, the Unionist Association was formed by Colonel James MacCalmont of Maghnermorne, who was both a local landowner and a major figure in the Orange Order. He was the county MP from 1885 until his death in 1913; he had to face only one seriously contested election; and on his death, he was succeeded by his son, without a contest. In the same county, the O'Neills remained a formidable power, and one seat was filled by three successive members of the family. In County Down, the traditional rivalry of the Londonderry and Downshire families was transformed by Home Rule into Unionist collaboration, and one of the seats was usually held by a Hill or a Vane-Tempest. And in parts of Tyrone, the Abercorns still held sway, even providing a family MP for Londonderry city between 1901 and 1913.[108]

But however hard the Ulster patricians worked to adjust themselves to the new world of democratic politics, their control of county constituencies was – as in England – increasingly the exception rather than the rule. In the shires where the Catholic nationalists were in the majority – Cavan, Donegal, and Monaghan – the landowners were as powerless as their cousins in the south, and nationalist MPs were returned, uninterruptedly and unchallenged. In County Fermanagh, which had been dominated by the Archdales since the eighteenth century, the division of the constituency and the extension of the franchise meant the Protestant electors were now a minority, and in 1885 the nationalists captured both seats.[109] Although one seat returned to the Unionists in 1895, it was held by Richard Dane, an unorthodox MP, who was in favour of 'compulsory sale and purchase.' And in Tyrone, the Abercorns' grip was fading. T. W. R. Russell, who held one of the seats from 1886 to 1918, was leader of the Ulster Tenants Defence Association: hardly the platform of a landlord's candidate. And when Lord James Hamilton succeeded to the Abercorn dukedom in 1913, the Londonderry seat was lost.[110]

In short, the Ulster patricians' counter-attack on the forces of democratic nationalism in the aftermath of Home Rule was by no means everywhere successful. And there was a further challenge that was even harder to rebuff, since it came from within. From the 1880s, the province was dominated, both politically and economically, by the town of Belfast, and it was its burgeoning plutocracy that superseded the landowners as the leading Protestant influence in Ulster politics.[111] Of the twenty-odd Unionist MPs who were regularly returned for the province from the mid-1880s, the majority were middle-class businessmen and entrepreneurs like Harland and Wolf. The real driving forces in Ulster Unionism were not so much the traditional landowners like Colonel Saunderson, who was leader of the Ulster Unionist Parliamentary Party from 1886 to 1906, but Belfast businessmen like Craig and Bates. Significantly, when Saunderson tried to insinuate a patrician candidate into Belfast in 1886, he was firmly told that this was not his province. But conversely, from 1906, one of the MPs for County Down was James Craig himself, Ulsterman and businessman *par excellence*.[112]

So, despite the sales of estates that gathered force under the Land Acts during the 1890s and 1900s, the Irish gentry and aristocracy did not return to the public life of Ireland in the way that the Balfour brothers and Horace Plunkett had hoped they would. Even more than in Wales, the early 1880s were the great turning point. Throughout the south, and in parts of Ulster, where the forces of agrarian nationalism were irresistible, they had effectively disappeared from the political scene. And even where they reasserted themselves in the north, it was essentially on the sufferance of, and in collaboration with, the big bourgeoisie of Belfast. For while the landowners were in territorial retreat, the Belfast businessmen were at the peak of their prosperity and power in the years before the First World War. Under these circumstances, it was inevitable that the partnership should become increasingly unequal. Caught between a triumphant peasantry in the south, and an irresistible plutocracy in the north, there was little room left within which the patricians could recapture or exert the political initiative.

In the realm of local government, this pattern was almost exactly repeated. As the last quarter of the nineteenth century opened, the aristocracy and gentry were still emphatically in control: of the grand juries, of the Poor Law Boards, and of the magistracy. As late as 1886, over half the magistrates were landlords, and more than three-quarters were Protestants. But the attack on these local bases of patrician power was as sudden, and as successful, as the attack on parliamentary representation. In the late 1870s, one aspect of the 'Land League's campaign' was that Parnell determined to drive the landlords from their dominance of the Poor Law Boards. At that time, one-half of the seats were occupied ex officio by the JPs, and the elected representatives were usually their clients and retainers. Of the three major offices (chairman, vice chairman, and deputy chairman), 87 per cent were held in 1877 by landowners, including 161 of the 163 chairmanships. But in 1881, Parnell publicly urged that 'all exertions are to be made to secure the return of Land League candidates as Poor Law Guardians, and to drive from office the agents, bailiffs and landed nominees who have hitherto been allowed to fill these important posts.'[113]

This systematic attempt to capture these elected positions was astonishingly successful, not least because a majority of the elected posts usually brought with it power over the whole board, since many of the ex-officio Guardians were absentee. By 1886, the tenants had so completely overwhelmed the patricians and their clients that they had captured half the major offices throughout the country. More especially, this meant that they were in almost total control of the Boards in the south, the west, and central Ireland. Only in parts of Ulster, and in southern enclaves like Wicklow and Dublin, did the grandees and gentry hang on. The nationalist MP, William O'Brien, may have been overstating it when he later recalled that 'as if by one universal impulse the country rose . . . swept the landlords from the old ascendancy at the Poor Law Boards, and put the most advanced of suspects in their places'.[114] But he was essentially correct. At the very time that the landowners were decisively rejected in local politics, they were also emphatically rejected in local government. On the Poor Law Boards, as in the parliamentary constituencies, revolution had come before reform.[115]

Even before Irish local government was fundamentally re-structured on the British model, there had thus been two major developments in the localities: the balance of power had effectively passed from the patricians to the peasantry; and in most areas, there were already hundreds of experienced nationalist administrators.

And faced with the imminent prospect of local government reform, the landowners naturally feared that the nationalists would dominate the new county councils as they already controlled the Poor Law Boards. Not surprisingly, Balfour's first – and abortive – bill, introduced in 1892, contained many novel features, which were intended to protect the beleaguered landed minority. On the English model, the intention was to transfer the functions of the old grand juries to new county councils. But their powers were quite exceptionally limited. They could be dissolved for disobedience to the law, for corruption, for malversation, and for the suppression of minorities. The attempt to insert patrician safeguards was clear. But as a result, the bill seemed so anomalous compared with the British system that it did not pass.[116]

Accordingly, when Balfour's brother Gerald introduced a second and successful scheme in 1898, the checks and balances were removed, the franchise was made broader than that for parliamentary elections, and any claim to be making special provision for 'minority representation' was given up. With the Welsh precedent in mind, the outcome of the first elections – held in April 1899 – was thus a foregone conclusion: in Ernest Barker's words, 'the squirearchy was dethroned, and local self-government . . . took its place.'[117] Even in Ulster, the patricians fared no better than they did in parliamentary politics. Antrim, Armargh, and Down returned predictable Unionist majorities; Tyrone and Fermanagh were almost evenly divided; but Cavan, Donegal and Monaghan were overwhelmingly nationalist. In Antrim and Down (and even in Tyrone), the first chairman of the new county council was also the Lord-Lieutenant, on the model of the more conservative English and Scottish counties. But taking the nine counties as a whole, the nationalists were definitely in the majority with 95 seats to 86, and also possessed overall control of the Poor Law Boards.[118]

Elsewhere in Ireland, the grandees and gentry were almost totally rejected. Indeed, this was so obviously going to be the outcome that most ignored Gerald Balfour's exhortation to stand for election. Compared with England and Wales in 1888, the patrician candidates were decidedly thin on the ground. And those who were successful were very few and far between: Lord Powerscourt and Viscount Milton in Wicklow; Walter Kavanagh in Carlow; Lord Castlemaine in Westmeath; Lord Dunraven in Limerick; and the O'Conor Don in Roscommon. But there were also some famous casualties: Lord Rosse in Kings County; Lords Fitzgerald and Mayo in Kildare; and Lord Dunalley in Tipperary, where he obtained only four votes. In Leinster, Munster, and Connaught, every county was won by the nationalists, who obtained 456 seats to the Unionists' 39.[119] With this overwhelming majority, they soon passed resolutions in favour of Home Rule, and in one case even raised the nationalist flag. As the *Morning Post* rightly remarked, 'it would have been absurd to expect that in the first flush of their new powers, the democratic electorates of the Irish Counties should have returned the landed gentry, whom they had been taught to regard as hereditary enemies and oppressors.'[120]

Nor, in later elections, did the old territorial class succeed in clawing back any of the ground they had so decisively lost in 1899. When introducing his measure, Gerald Balfour had predicted that the patricians 'may meet with rebuffs at first, but let them persevere, and their reward is certain.' But events did not bear him out.[121] In the 1902 elections, the balance of power remained essentially unaltered: Lords Milton, Powerscourt, Monteagle, and the O'Conor Don retired; and Lords Greville, Nugent, and Emly were defeated. Three years later, the Unionists won a handful of extra seats in Ulster; but again, the overall position was unchanged.[122] In Ireland, as in Wales, most of the new county councils were from the outset a bastion of anti-landlord sentiment. With rare exceptions like Kavanagh in Carlow, and Esmonde in Wicklow, there was very little scope for patrician leadership in Munster, Leinster, or Connaught. In England and Scotland, some grandees happily and successfully diverted their local efforts from contentious constituency management to disinterested county government: but for most Irish notables, there was no such opportunity beyond the narrow and embattled confines of the Protestant heartlands of Ulster.

So, by the 1910s, there was virtually nothing left of the old ascendancy class as the governing and parliamentary élite of Ireland. As JPs, the patricians had effectively ceased to signify: the Liberal reforms of the 1900s led to a massive increase in the appointment of Catholic (and thus non-landed) magistrates; and in much of Ireland, the gentry had abandoned their judicial functions to the Resident Magistrates. All that remained was a faded pantomime of ornamental and anachronistic duties. The grand juries, shorn of their real power after 1898, continued to gather at the opening of the assizes, to receive the judge's address. The post of High Sheriff was still filled by the local gentry, but when Colonel O'Callaghan-Westropp was appointed in Clare in 1919, not even Dublin Castle knew what his duties were. The Lieutenants of each county were little more than figure-heads, while the lavish and glittering proconsular regime maintained at Dublin was very largely a charade. The Lord-Lieutenant was rarely a figure of real distinction, and in terms of his functions, he was by now essentially a 'constitutional monarch.'[123]

The parliamentary and local elections of 1918 and 1920 merely confirmed that the patricians had become all but totally irrelevant to Irish affairs. In 1918, 73 of the 105 Irish seats at Westminster were won by Sinn Fein, 26 by the Ulster Unionists, and only 6 by the old constitutionalist Home Rule Party. Even those two maverick baronets, Esmonde and Nugent, were defeated by this new form of revolutionary nationalism. At the most generous estimate, only a handful of these Irish MPs could be associated with the landed establishment, and they were a minority, even in Ulster. And after the local elections of 1920, Sinn Fein controlled 28 of the 33 county councils, and 138 of the 154 Poor Law Boards.[124] In Ulster, the nationalists captured Tyrone County Council, and increased their majority in Fermanagh, where they appointed Thomas Corrigan as Secretary, a man who had been a founder member of Sinn Fein in the county, and had been imprisoned in 1918 and 1919. And they at once passed a resolution pledging their loyalty, not to Belfast, but to the provisional nationalist government in Dublin.[125]

How, then, did these few embattled, beleaguered patrician remnants fare in the new system of government created for the north and south of Ireland in the aftermath of the rebellion, the partition, and the troubles? What hope remained for an élite whose estates were disappearing at an increasingly rapid rate, and whose houses were going up in smoke? What room would be left to them, by the triumphant middle-class Unionists in the north, and the rampant Catholic nationalists in the south? In Ulster, under the Government of Ireland Act, a separate constitution came into being for the six counties, providing for a governor, a cabinet, and a bicameral legislature with limited powers. In the south, this act never came into effective operation, and the constitution finally evolved for Eire was largely the creation of the Irish Treaty. This provided for two houses of parliament, the Dáil and the Senate, with the latter elected on a more narrow franchise, and with inbuilt safeguards for minorities. How, in this new world, did the remnants of the old order survive? And how far did their circumstances continue to diverge between north and south?

Beyond doubt, the new regime in Ulster provided some scope for continued patrician initiative and endeavour. Indeed, in many ways, it closely resembled a particularly traditional English county council. For most of this period, the Governor of Northern Ireland was the Duke of Abercorn, the foremost grandee in the province. He represented a great Ulster family, knew the six counties well, was personally liked and respected, and almost certainly 'exercised considerable indirect influence upon ministers.'[126] In the cabinet, the first Minister of Education was the Marquess of Londonderry, and on his resignation in 1926 he was replaced by Lord Charlemont. One of his colleagues, the Minister of Agriculture and Commerce, was E. M. Archdale of Fermanagh. And in 1933 he was followed by his near neighbour, Sir Basil Brooke. From 1921 until his death in 1930, the first Speaker of the Senate was Lord Dufferin, while the Speakers of the Lower House were, successively, the eldest surviving son of Lord O'Neill and the son of Lord Dunleath. To these should be added a smattering of authentically aristocratic MPs, one of whom was the wife of the Marquess of Donegall.[127]

At the same time, Ulster retained both its Westminster representation and its county government, and here, too, the patricians were still in evidence. Sir R. W. H. O'Neill was not only the Speaker of the lower house at Stormont: he also represented an Antrim County constituency at Westminster in the family tradition. And in the same way, in 1931, Viscount Castlereagh was elected unopposed in the Londonderry constituency of County Down. The Lord-Lieutenants of the six counties continued to be drawn from the ranks of the resident noblemen – like Londonderry himself – while gentry remnants still did duty as High Sheriff. County councils like Tyrone, Down, and Antrim remained well endowed with patrician chairmen. And even Fermanagh was won back to Unionist politics and ascendancy leadership in the aftermath of partition: a member of the Archdale family became chairman, while Lord Belmore served uninterruptedly from 1900 to 1946, and became chairman of the Education Committee.[128] In all these ways – both new and old – the grandees and gentry survived and governed in Ulster much as before: there was about the six counties more than just a touch of Ruritania.

Nevertheless, as its history from the 1880s inevitably implied, Ulster was neither created nor governed by the patricians, but by the Belfast business community. The most emphatic proof of this was the way in which the boundaries themselves were drawn for the province. In the 1918 election, the Unionists won no seats whatsoever in Cavan, Donegal, or Monaghan, and it seemed clear that, if these three counties were included in Ulster, the Unionist majority in the province would be precarious. Despite protests from resident landowners like Lord Farnham, who did not wish to be abandoned to the south, the Belfast businessmen had their way, and the smaller unit of six counties was chosen, while these three counties were abandoned to the south. By 1937, 63 per cent of Ulster's population lived within thirty miles of the city. And while Belfast thrived, the landowners were weakened still further: in 1925, the British Parliament rounded out the earlier land-purchase legislation, introducing an element of compulsion for Ulster, which brought the landed ascendancy finally to an end; and in 1935, lay JPs were no longer allowed to sit with RMs, who thus took over the administration of justice almost completely.[129]

Under these circumstances, the patricians were very much the minority partner in the government and administration of the province. The real power lay elsewhere. From 1921 until his death in 1940, the Prime Minister was James Craig, the most resourceful and intransigent Ulsterman, whose background was in business and finance. And he was succeeded by J. M. Andrews, another businessman, who had previously been Minister of Labour, and who was also chairman of the Belfast Chamber of Commerce. In the cabinet of 1921, Archdale and Londonderry were given the two least important posts: after Craig himself, and Andrews at Labour, the men who mattered were Pollock (another businessman) who was Minister of Finance, and Bates (a solicitor and former Secretary of the UDF) at Home Affairs.[130] And it was Bates and Craig who were responsible for the legislation of the early 1920s, which altered the franchise, led to the setting up of the Royal Ulster Constabulary, and the passing of the Special Powers Act. It was these measures, promoted by these men, that were the key to the making and management of Ulster: by comparison, the patrician contribution was dignified rather than efficient.[131]

If this was the most that the gentry and grandees could salvage in Ulster, their prospects in the newly independent south were bleak indeed. Their hopes were pinned on a second chamber that might safeguard their minority interests, and also give them a platform for playing a part in the public life of the new nation. Moreover, the Irish leaders, Griffiths and O'Higgins, seemed genuinely eager to offer them 'their full share of representation in the first chamber of the Irish parliament'.[132] There was to be a Senate; it was to be elected for a twelve-year term and on a narrow franchise; and half of the first house was to be nominated by the Prime Minister with special regard to minority interests. In the event, O'Higgins recruited many of his nominees from the old patrician class: Lords Dunraven, Wicklow, and Mayo, the Earl of Kerry (son of Lord Lansdowne), the dowager Countess of Desart, Sir Thomas Esmonde, Sir William Hutcheson Poe, Sir John Keane, Sir Horace Plunkett, General Sir Bryan Mahon and John Bagwell. As O'Higgins magnanimously explained, he had made 'a generous adjustment, to show that these people are regarded, not as alien enemies, not as planters, but that we regard them as part and parcel of this nation, and that we wish them to take their share of its responsibilities.'[133]

But in practice, these aristocratic Senators accomplished and contributed very little. In part, this was because they were forcibly and illegally prevented from doing so. De Valera and Sinn Fein had refused to recognize either the Irish Treaty or the Free State Constitution, and during 1922 and 1923, they conducted a sustained campaign of terror against O'Higgins's nominated notables. Sir William Hutcheson Poe was held up by the Irregulars in Queen's County; his watch and money were stolen and his car burned; and he retreated to England, although he did continue to attend some Senate meetings. The Earl of Mayo's home, Palmerstown, in County Kildare, was raided by armed men. The Earl and Countess were forced to leave; the house was burned down and only three paintings were saved; and they were obliged thereafter to live in the servants' quarters. John Bagwell fared even worse: his house in Tipperary was burned and its contents destroyed in January 1923, and later in the same month, he himself was kidnapped near Dublin. And Plunkett, Keane, Desart, and Esmonde suffered at least as much.[134]

These attacks eventually came to an end, but they did not make it easy for such figures to play any real part in Irish political life: they were worried about their property and their relatives; they were increasingly absentee in England; and they had little enthusiasm for leading a nation the majority of whose inhabitants seemed so implacably and aggressively hostile. And in any case, the Senate's powers of scrutiny and delay were minimal, and no member of the executive could sit there. The quality of the debates was often high, but had little bearing on events. Above all, the confidence, poise, and purpose of the old ascendancy class was broken.[135] Effectively, the notables had been out of power in Ireland for half a century, and they were quite incapable of responding to this new opportunity – minimal as it was. Increasingly, they withdrew into a ghetto-like mentality, sneering ineffectively at the education, the brogue, and the manners of the ministers, the men of power. They were not even willing or able to stand up for themselves. In 1923, when Sir John Keane tried to thwart the government's proposal to complete land purchase by compulsory means, his fellow patricians in the Senate would not even support him.[136]

Moreover, the death of O'Higgins in 1927, and the return of de Valera's party to the Dáil meant that the Senate's days were soon numbered. Because of its restricted powers and idiosyncratic composition, it was easily presented as irrelevant, anachronistic, and obstructionist. Between 1923 and 1934, Poe, Plunkett, Dunraven, and Kerry resigned; while Wicklow, Nugent, and Esmonde failed to secure re-election. After O'Higgins's initial nominations, there were few patrician recruits, apart from Sir Edward Bellingham in 1925 and the McGillicuddy of the Reeks three years later.[137] For de Valera, anxious to implement a new form of more extreme Catholic nationalism, the Senate stood as 'a remnant, a part of the defensive armour of the ascendancy class', which was 'in favour of vested interests and privilege', and against 'the march of the people and their rights.' In 1934, he introduced a bill to abolish the upper house, and two years later, it ceased to exist, and was replaced with a new body in the following year which was entirely the creature of the Dáil. As Lord Midleton had predicted in 1922, the Senate had failed to be either a safeguard for patrician interests or a springboard for patrician aspirations.[138]

In the lower house of the Free State legislature, the ascendancy's representation was totally insignificant. As if out of family tradition, several members of the Esmonde family were returned, and so was a Barton of Glendalough. But the only significant patrician was Bryan Cooper, whose family owned Markree Castle in County Sligo. In 1910, he had been elected Unionist MP for Dublin County South, but his service in the First World War caused him to take a more sympathetic view of nationalist aspirations. In 1923, he was elected to the Dáil as an independent member for the same constituency.[139] 'Regarding himself as a representative of a virtually unrepresented minority, he acted as one might have expected an ex-unionist brought up in the country gentleman's tradition to act.' He was a cosmopolitan figure, who believed that Ireland must become more internationalist and less introverted; his interests in peace, order, and tranquility, and in decency and economy in government, were classic signs of patrician disinterestedness. In the end, his loyalty to Cosgrave and hatred of de Valera drove him out of politics: and he was the last significant and self-conscious representative of the old order in the lower house.

Predictably, there was much less scope for the once pre-eminent territorial élite in de Valera's Eire than in Craig's Ulster. In the Gaelic, Catholic, nationalist, and proletarian south, there was no room, and still less enthusiasm, for the old landed ascendancy. Betrayed by the British and hated by the Irish, the surviving patricians turned in upon themselves. Their 'abdication of political responsibility at a national and local level was disappointing, but understandable.'[140] In effect, they had ceased to be the governing class of Ireland in the 1880s: only a romantic or a reactionary could have hoped they might be rehabilitated in inter-war Eire. In Ulster, the outcome was different, yet not as different as it seemed. They survived with greater ease: but increasingly on the sufferance – and essentially as the clients – of the bourgeoisie of Belfast. Either way, the fond hopes that the solution of the land problem would enable the old territorial ascendancy to recover its dominant part in Irish affairs had proved vain. Instead of giving them a new lease of life, their territorial demise merely made their political demise more easy and more certain.

iv. Conclusion: 'The End of the Notables'

When, during the inter-war years, King George V paid official visits to different parts of Great Britain, he was usually met – and sometimes accommodated – by the Lord-Lieutenant of the county. He might be a personal friend of his sovereign, he would almost invariably be a patrician, and in holding the position he did, was probably following in his forebears' footsteps. In the same way, when the King paid his memorable visit to Northern Ireland in 1922, opened the Ulster Parliament, and appealed to Irishmen to forgive and forget, he stayed in suitably splendid style with the Duke and Duchess of Abercorn. Such episodes were vivid reminders that during the 1920s and 1930s, the traditional territorial classes remained a visible presence in local affairs throughout the shires of the United Kingdom. And in some cases, these grandees combined ornamental splendour with real and significant influence – as the chairman of a county council or as the dominating force in a constituency association. Under these circumstances, the local power that they wielded was probably as much efficient as it was decorative.

But even allowing for this very real evidence of aristocratic survival as an ornamental (or influential) force in the government and politics of the shires, it is the challenges to their power, and the weakening of their position, that stand out as the major themes during the years from the 1880s to the 1930s. In Wales, most of Ireland, and parts of Scotland, the forces of anti-landlord agrarian nationalism were irresistible. In Ulster, and in the most heavily industrialized counties of England, the middle-class professionals, businessmen, and *rentiers* were no less inexorable in their advance. The agricultural depression of the late nineteenth century undoubtedly forced many notables to withdraw from county administration and constituency politics, and the great land sales of 1910–22 only intensified this development. At the same time, the extensions of the franchise in 1885 and 1918, and the reform of local government in 1888–9 and 1898, fundamentally weakened their position still further. And the remorseless professionalization of local government throughout the United Kingdom spelt the end of the amateur, patrician style in county administration. At the local level, no less than at the national, bureaucracy was the enemy of aristocracy.

In short, the attack on the aristocracy as the rulers and representatives of the localities was on a broad and varied front, and it occurred at a time, and in such a way, that most of them were not well equipped, or well disposed, to resist it. The timing and extent of their abdication necessarily varied from country to country, and region to region. But by the 1930s, there were very few shires left where the surviving landowners could accurately (or exclusively) be described as the local power élite. And if such men were no longer either governing or representing the localities, then what did this imply for them as the governors and representatives of the nation?

5
THE ECLIPSE OF A SENATORIAL ORDER

On a careful inquiry, it will be found that the coming in of American wheat has wrought a greater change in the composition of the British House of Commons than the first two Reform Acts.
(L. B. Namier, *Skyscrapers and Other Essays* (1931), p. 48.)

While the Reform Act of 1867 greatly increased middle-class power in the House of Commons, it was only after 1885 that the peerage creations marked this transfer of power in any considerable degree.
(R. E. Pumphrey, 'The Creation of Peerages in England, 1837–1911' (Yale University, Ph.D., 1934), p. 165.)

A century ago, a majority of all Cabinets consisted of great landowners and their close relatives; today, the presence of a single bona fide aristocrat even in a Tory Cabinet is a considerable and noteworthy oddity.
(W. D. Rubinstein, 'Education and the Social Origins of British Elites, 1880–1970', *Past & Present*, 122 (1986), p. 204.)

Though the Irish question in the 1880s brought virtually all important landed aristocrats into the Conservative fold, leaving the Liberals denuded of their traditional Whig nobles, even the Tory party was now a businessman's party. It was no longer led by a Bentinck, a Derby, a Cecil or a Balfour, but – after 1911 – by a Glasgow Canadian iron merchant, and two Midland industrialists.
(E. J. Hobsbawm, *Industry and Empire* (1969), p. 203.)

In landed-establishment Britain, broad-acred wealth had by definition spelt political power: the economic élite was *ipso facto* the governing élite, not only in the localities, but also in Westminster and Whitehall. Accordingly, as the new riches overwhelmed the old, it was not only the balance of economic power that shifted to the patricians' disadvantage, but the balance of political power as well. In 1909, the *Encyclopaedic Dictionary* had defined the plutocrat as 'one who has power or influence through his wealth', and in Britain, the half-century from the 1880s was the period when the plutocrats' riches were at their peak, when their political influence was at its most forceful. As E. T. Powell explained in 1915, the 'ceaseless and irresistible advance' of the new super-rich had been accompanied by 'the simultaneous weakening of those authorities which base their claims on political predominance, on tradition, custom, precedent, conventions, expediency.' In fearing the tendency of plutocracy to undermine its older and nobler neighbour, aristocracy, Gladstone had been entirely correct.[1]

But it was not just this *arriviste*, thrusting, vulgar wealth that successfully challenged the patricians' position as the power élite in the half-century from the 1880s: the attack was on a much broader front. It was also undermined by the new breed of full-time politicians like Asquith and Lloyd George, Simon and F. E. Smith, who proclaimed the arrival of self-made professional men in unprecedented numbers. And it was further threatened by the growth of mass politics in the aftermath of the Third and Fourth Reform Acts; by the development of a new and separate political party specifically devoted to advancing the rights and the welfare of the labouring classes; and by the appearance in Parliament of working men as its representatives. In the face of these new social and political forces, the once dominant landowners began their inexorable retreat – from politics, from power, and from government itself. In 1910, during the debates on the People's Budget in the House of Lords, Curzon had claimed that the hereditary principle had hitherto 'saved this country from the danger of plutocracy or an upper class of professional politicians.' But by then, it was no longer doing so.[2]

So, at the very same time that the grandees and gentry lost their overwhelming sense of territorial coherence and local dominance, they also began to lose their sense of identity as the national governing élite. In F. M. L. Thompson's felicitous phrase, the 'gentlemen' retired to the cricket pavilion, leaving the 'players' to dominate the field of affairs which the patricians had monopolized for so long.[3] As before, politics was still most easily espoused by the rich: but during this period, many landowners were no longer prosperous enough to participate, while those who had accumulated new wealth found it easy to force their way in. As before, politics also took time: but many patricians now had less leisure than before, some had to work for their living, and some had turned their backs on Britain altogether. As before, politics also required a belief in one's right and fitness to rule: but the radical attacks of the late nineteenth and early twentieth century meant that many nobles and notables had ceased to believe in their governing mission, found themselves increasingly ill at ease in a world of affairs that they no longer dominated, and in some cases became alienated from the whole political process.

The result was that the aristocracy and the gentry ceased to control either the legislature or the executive. It was a gradual and nuanced withdrawal, but that was undoubtedly the trend of the time, and not just the wisdom of hindsight. Indeed, in some ways, the patricians lessened their grip on the levers of national power more completely and more rapidly than they did upon the land. In the Commons, the peers' relatives and country gentlemen who had once been the majority interest gradually dwindled into a minor occupational group. The second chamber, too, was ceasing to be a territorial club: partly because many peers already there were getting out of land, and partly because the majority of the new recruits had never really got into it. At cabinet level, too, the great governing families ceased to be the dominant force, and survived in significant numbers only because of the Conservative successes of the inter-war years. But even among Tory Prime Ministers, the middle classes were by then triumphant. The past may have lain with the Duke of Omnium but, as Lord Curzon was to find, the future lay, if not with Mr Pooter, then at least with Mr Baldwin.

i.   The Commons: Country Gentlemen to 'Hard-nosed Men'

In the dark days of 1940, R. A. Butler wrote to Lord Templewood, then exiled by Churchill as Ambassador to Spain, implausibly claiming that the wartime coalition government 'depends upon the Tory squires for its majority.'[4] In the days of Liverpool, Peel, or Disraeli, when most MPs from both parties were drawn from landed backgrounds, such remarks were both commonplace and correct. Pace Walter Bagehot, the spirit and substance of the mid-Victorian Commons was aristocratic, not plutocratic. But by the 1930s, less than one-tenth of the massive phalanx of Conservative MPs could claim close landed connections, while of the remainder, one-third were from the professions, one-fifth from the services, another fifth from commerce, and the rest from industry.[5] Within half a century, the patricians' dominance of the House of Commons had been dramatically eclipsed. We have already traced this decline from the standpoint of the county constituencies. But how did it look, how did it happen, and what did it mean, from a parliamentary perspective?

Despite the great Liberal victory, and the many stunning patrician defeats, the House of Commons that was returned at the general election of 1880 was, like its predecessors, dominated by the landowning classes, who still formed the largest single category, just exceeding all other occupational groups combined. Of the 652 MPs, 394 were nobles, baronets, landed gentry, or their near relatives; and of these, 325 were primarily interested in land.[6] Some were the close relatives of great grandees, sitting for traditional family constituencies: Albert Grey headed the poll in South Northumberland; so did the second son of Earl Spencer in North Northamptonshire; and both the Devonshire and Fitzwilliam families returned three MPs apiece. And the country gentry were also out in force, traditional members in traditional seats: Williams-Wynn in Denbigh, Long in

26. *The Lobby of the House of Commons*, 1886, by Liberio Prosperi.

Wiltshire, Ridley in Northumberland, Buxton in Norfolk. Indeed, twenty-three MPs were directly descended from families who had sat in the Long Parliament, including such illustrious names as Percy, Clive, Northcote, Long, and Fitzwilliam.

Nor did this landed presence disappear overnight. For those inclined and able to exploit them, the advantages of a family tradition in public life, of territorial connections, of local political influence, and of independent income, meant that patricians could still enter Parliament at an earlier age and for a safer seat than most people drawn from other professions. In 1904, Lord Winterton – an Irish peer – was returned at a by-election in West Sussex when still an undergraduate at Oxford, largely at the behest of Lord Leconfield, the local grandee. The Hon. Edward Wood, son of Lord Halifax, was first elected for the Ripon Division of Yorkshire in January 1910 at the age of twenty-nine; and in 1922, 1923, and 1924, he was returned unopposed.[7] At the 1910 elections, the youngest candidates on both sides were the sons of peers: among the Conservatives the Marquess of Stafford was twenty-two, and Viscount Wolmer, the Hon. Jasper Ridley and the Hon. Charles Mills were twenty-three; while on the Liberal side, the Hon. Philip Wodehouse, a son of the Earl of Kimberley, was twenty-four.[8]

Even in 1914, the House of Commons included among its members the heirs to the Atholl, Lansdowne, Londonderry, Zetland,

Dartmouth, and Halifax titles; there were near relatives of Portland, Salisbury, and Derby; and there were younger sons of Norfolk, Bute, and Bath.[9] And this aristocratic presence was sustained into the inter-war years. In 1922, the Marquess of Titchfield, heir to the Duke of Portland, became MP for Newark when only twenty-nine. In the following year, the Earl of Dalkeith, son of the Duke of Buccleuch, was elected for Roxburgh and Selkirk at the same age. In 1929, Viscount Lymington, heir to the Earl of Portsmouth, became an MP at thirty-three for the local constituency of North-West Hampshire.[10] And in 1931, there was an even bigger influx of such well-connected youths: the future fifth Lord Brabourne for the Ashford Division of Kent at thirty-six; Lord Burleigh, son of the Marquess of Exeter, for the Peterborough Division of North-ampton, at twenty-six; Viscount Knebworth, son of Lord Lytton, for the Hitchin Division of Hertfordshire at twenty-eight; and Vis-count Castlereagh, heir to Lord Londonderry, for County Down at twenty-nine and unopposed.[11]

In some aristocratic families where the political tradition was especially strong, sons continued to follow fathers into the Com-mons in almost unbroken succession, and patrician cousinhoods persisted on what seemed an almost eighteenth-century pattern. Three sons of the sixteenth Earl of Derby, and both sons of the seventeenth earl, sat in the Commons, all – predictably – for Lan-cashire constituencies. So did three sons of the great Lord Salisbury, while Viscount Cranborne, heir to the fourth marquess, was elected for South Dorset in 1929. The tenth Duke of Devonshire, like his father, represented a Derbyshire constituency before succeeding to the title; and, during the inter-war years, three of his sisters, and three of his cousins, were married to MPs.[12] In the same way, both the seventh and eighth Marquesses of Londonderry were MPs before they inherited, as were the twenty-seventh and twenty-eighth Earls of Crawford and Balcarres. For aristocrats such as these, an apprentice-ship in the House of Commons was still seen as the best possible preparation for a lordly or ducal inheritance.

At the same time, there remained a recognizable phalanx of country gentlemen in the Commons, even if their numbers were by 1940 less significant than Butler's comments implied. There was still the occasional Liberal, like Ivor Herbert from Monmouth and Matthew Vaughan Davies from Cardigan. But the majority of them by this time were Unionists and Conservatives. Before 1914, there were famous figures like Henry Chaplin and Walter Long, both quin-tessential Tory squires and senior figures in the party. And, in a younger generation, there were men like Christopher Turnor, Wil-liam Bridgeman, and Charles Bathurst. In 1906, George Lane-Fox was returned for a Yorkshire rural constituency: he was landed, well born, and high-principled; he was a JP, an MFH, and a pillar of the Yeomanry; his second daughter married Bridgeman's eldest son; and he was devoted to his neighbour, brother-in-law, and fellow fox-hunter, the Hon. Edward Wood. When William Bridgeman died, he was described in his *Times* obituary as 'an admirable type of the English country gentleman who has for centuries played an important part in Church and State'.[13] It was an epitaph that all of these patricians aspired to earn; and, sooner or later, most of them did.

Even in the inter-war years, when men like Long and Chaplin had quit the Commons, the tradition lived on. At the 'coupon' election of 1918, some landed gentry were still returned for constituencies that their forebears had represented: Lloyd, Stanier, and Bridgeman in Shropshire, Lane-Fox and Sykes in Yorkshire, Courthope in Sussex, Williams in Dorset, and Carew in Devon. There were new recruits, including a Roundell for Yorkshire, a Burdon in Durham, a Child in Staffordshire, and a Lowther in Cumberland.[14] And there were others who were soon to make a name for themselves. There was Philip Lloyd-Greame, a major Yorkshire landowner in his own right, whose estates were soon to be augmented by those of his wife, inherited from Lord Masham. There was Archibald Sinclair, a descendant of the great agricultural improver, who was, appropriately, both MP and Lord-Lieutenant of Caithness. There was C. P. Trevelyan, heir to a baronetcy and the 13,000-acre Wallington estate, who eventually became Lord-Lieutenant of Northumberland. And there was Oswald Mosley, whose family had been Staffordshire landowners for three hundred years.

There is one additional element that must be recorded for the inter-war years: the advent of women MPs from the landed establishment. Once the Commons was open to the opposite sex, patrician ladies enjoyed special advantages.[15] They were born or married into political families; and they were often well placed to claim that they were essentially male substitutes. This was obviously so in the case of Lady Gwendolen Onslow, who followed her husband as MP for Southend when he inherited the earldom of Iveagh. And the same was true of Lady Davidson in Hertfordshire and Mrs Buxton in Norfolk: both were genteel women who took over their husband's constituencies. In a similar manner, Lady Cynthia Mosley, née Curzon, briefly represented Stoke-on-Trent essentially as an adjunct to her husband's career.[16] But this could not be said of the grandest of them all, the Duchess of Atholl. Admittedly, she was MP for the Kinross and West Division of Perthshire from 1923 to 1938, a constituency in which the family were great landowners. But she was first encouraged to stand for Parliament by Lloyd George, and the Duke helped to develop her confidence by hurling hecklers' hypothetical questions across the dinner table.[17]

It was the persistence (and intrusion) of these patrician figures in the House of Commons that led Simon Haxey to calculate, in 1938, that 145 Conservative MPs could be linked 'in a continuous chain of family relationship.' 'The "cousinhood" of today', he concluded, 'to a great extent governs the country.'[18] But as with great estates and constituency politics, this imaginative calculation needs to be set in a broader perspective of continuous and inexorable aristocratic decline. Ever since 1865, the landed element in the Commons had been in conspicuous retreat, and in the 1880 Parliament it was significantly weaker than it had been before. Inevitably, the massive rejection of landed candidates, on the Celtic fringe and in parts of England, greatly reduced the patrician element in the lower house. In 1865, the Wynn family boasted three representatives for three counties in the Welsh marches: but by 1880 there was only one left. In the previous House of Commons, three sons of the Duke of Abercorn were to be found; but in 1880 only one of the four family candidates was elected. And the representatives of the Hervey, Lowther, and Stanhope families were in each case reduced from two to one.[19]

Put the other way, the return of so many advanced Liberals in the 1880 election broadened the social background of the Commons considerably. In the 1865 Parliament, there had been 144 businessmen, 56 lawyers, and 20 other professionals; but by 1880, the numbers had increased to 194, 83, and 44.[20] To contemporaries, the moral was clear: 'the exclusive character of the House of Commons as a club for the rich, the fashionable and those who desire to be fashionable, is very slowly but very surely giving way, and the present election has marked the change.' *The Times* agreed. 'Members have been heard', it observed in 1883, 'during the last few weeks asking whether it was any longer an assembly of gentlemen.' Hitherto, it suggested, 'one class in its various sections supplied almost all of the members.' But, it concluded, 'a variety of social grades is now represented at Westminster, and the diversity is sure to multiply.'[21] And Lord Salisbury reached the same reluctant but unavoidable conclusion. 'Before this parliament is over', he told the Duke of Richmond in 1883, 'the country gentlemen will have as much to do with the government of the country as the rich people of America have.'[22]

Events were soon to bear him out. In the 1885 election, when the gentry were decimated in Ireland, Scotland, and Wales, and when the Conservative party did not obtain a majority even in the English counties, the titled and genteel contingent was reduced even more. By definition, the major turning point in the constituencies was also a major turning point in the Commons. Instead of providing just over half of the House, they now amounted to less than one-third. For the first time ever, the patricians had ceased to be a majority element in the lower house: their numerical supremacy was gone for good. Once more, there was a massive influx of new men: nearly half of the Liberal MPs had never sat in the House before, and the overwhelming majority were from non-landed backgrounds: businessmen, lawyers, journalists, tenant farmers, and even a few labourers. And contemporaries were clear as to the magnitude of the change. As Walter Long later and nostalgically recalled, the Commons of 1880 had been the last to contain the 'country gentleman's party' as it had existed for many decades.[23]

Thereafter, every time the Liberals won an election, the territorial element was further reduced, and even when the Conservatives returned to power, the old patrician phalanx was never fully restored. The landslide of 1906 saw an especially drastic decline, as the number of MPs with landed-establishment credentials fell to one-fifth or less, and such famous names as Arthur and Gerald Balfour, Alfred Lyttelton, St John Brodrick, Lord Hugh Cecil, and Henry Chaplin (after thirty-seven years in the House) lost their seats.[24] They were all subsequently re-elected, but many lesser landed luminaries never got back: their careers were permanently and prematurely ended. Even Balfour, normally detached and unflappable, admitted that 'the election of 1906 inaugurates a new era'; and Sir Henry Lucy, contemplating a House in which nearly half the members were sitting for the first time, felt that its tone and character was 'revolutionary'. And, although the Conservative party improved its position in the two elections of 1910, the number of landed candidates who stood was even smaller than in 1906, and the number of landed MPs was also correspondingly reduced.[25]

By the time of the 'coupon' election of 1918, the surviving patrician MPs were little more than a minority social group in the Commons. Of the 168 new Conservatives who took their seats early in 1919, only 25 could claim a landed background; and, although there were more Tories in this Parliament than in 1914, the number of peers' relatives declined from 38 to 22, of whom only 3 were newly elected.[26] This was the Parliament, dominated by elderly and opulent businessmen, memorably (and correctly) described by Baldwin (or Keynes) as being full of 'hard-faced men, who looked as if they had done well out of the war.' Asquith, who got back at a byelection in 1920, thought it the worst House he had ever known; and for once, Lloyd George agreed with him. As J. C. C. Davidson explained to George V, 'the old-fashioned country gentleman, and even the higher ranks of the learned professions, are scarcely represented at all.' 'A great pity', minuted George *RI*. Thereafter, the patricians never formed more than 10 per cent of the Commons: within less than fifty years, the once pre-eminent landowning class had dwindled into numerical insignificance.[27]

This dramatic decline is most eloquently shown in the case of the Conservative party itself. Even during the days of the third Lord Salisbury, the territorial contingent was already in retreat. Taking the whole period from 1885 to 1905, 39 per cent of Tory MPs were of landed background. But this conceals a sharp decrease: from well over 50 per cent of those returned in 1885 who had sat in the Commons before, to less than one-third of those newly elected in 1900.[28] Moreover, the new country gentlemen still getting in were not only appearing in reduced numbers: they also stayed for a much shorter period. Over half of those elected in 1885 who had sat before served for twenty-six years or more; but only one-tenth of those returned for the first time thereafter did so. By 1906, there were almost none of the pre-1885 squires left, and during the next fifteen years, there was little chance for recruiting any new landed blood. As a Tory party official rightly put it in 1907, 'forty or fifty years ago, it was all very well to manage things with a party of a few gentlemen, but those days are gone for ever.'[29]

During the inter-war years, the decline of the Tory patricians continued unabated.[30] Between 1914 and 1939, there were 1,195 Conservative and Unionist MPs, of whom 17 per cent were related by blood or marriage to the peerage, and just under 15 per cent possessed a male ancestor listed in Bateman. But again, even this low average conceals a much greater fall. In 1914, 23 per cent of Tory MPs boasted landed links (although even some of these were fairly remote); but by 1935 the figure was less than 10 per cent. On the eve of the First World War, 27 per cent were related by blood or marriage to the peerage (many of whom, by then, were non-landed themselves); but by the outbreak of the Second World War, it was only 18.5 per cent. At the most generous estimate, there were by 1939 only fifty MPs primarily interested in the land. In the Commons as in the countryside, five hundred years of aristocratic history had been reversed in fifty. Indeed, in numerical terms, the revolution in representation was even greater than the revolution in landowning. The Tory squires, of whom R. A. Butler wrote in 1940, were not the government's life support; they were little more than a rustic rump.

Why had the notables ceased to dominate the Commons so suddenly and so completely? Why had their numbers dropped, in less than half a century, from well over three hundred to no more than fifty? And why were those few remaining landed MPs serving for shorter terms than their predecessors? There are many explanations. The growing hostility of public opinion in the Celtic fringe meant that many seats that landowners had previously represented were effectively no longer available. The increasingly strident politics of class hatred genuinely deterred many patricians from carrying on a traditional interest in politics. The massive sales of land before and after the First World War meant that as the territorial links were weakened or broken, there was less incentive to stand for what had previously been the local constituency, and there was less power to wield over the local association. Some who kept their estates found their income much reduced by depression, and felt compelled to give up their political career as an economy measure. And even those who could still afford the time and the money often found the new political atmosphere – more demanding, time-consuming and acrimonious – decreasingly to their liking.

Significantly, many of the dwindling band of patrician MPs were no longer returned for a local constituency. The young George Curzon was defeated at South Derbyshire in 1885, and migrated to Southport. Lord Ronaldshay, son of the Marquess of Zetland, failed to win a nearby Yorkshire seat, and moved to Hornsey in Middlesex. The future Marquess of Londonderry was MP for Maidstone, Philip Cunliffe-Lister for Hendon, Lord Eustace Percy for Hastings, Evelyn Cecil for Aston, A. J. Balfour for East Manchester and then the City of London, and even Henry Chaplin, in the latter part of his Commons career, sat for Wimbledon. It was less demanding work to represent these suburban seats, close to London, than a sprawling, distant county constituency.[31] But the lack of a traditional territorial connection meant that many patricians, who might previously have been content to represent the same locality for a lifetime, were soon tempted away, often to proconsular offices: Carmichael, Pentland, Ronaldshay, Freeman-Thomas, Newdegate, and Stanley journeyed from the back-benches to Government House, never to return to the Commons.[32]

Indeed, they were usually happy to go: for most of them were clearly ill at ease in the world of mass politics in which they increasingly found themselves after the 1880s. Almost without exception, they were poor public performers; they tended to speak far over the heads of their audience; they lacked the demagogic skills of Chamberlain, Lloyd George, or even Baldwin; and they found the false heartiness of electioneering quite loathsome. In 1885, when Lord Cranborne and George Curzon were both standing, the former wrote in sympathy to the latter, regretting 'the disgusting character of the work in which we are engaged.' Edward Wood found the handshaking, the backslapping, and the baby-kissing equally dis-

27. The Hon. George Curzon
addressing the House of
Commons, by Harry Furniss.

tasteful, so it was perhaps as well for him that he fought so few
contests.[33] And in 1918, J. T. C. Moore-Brabazon summarized the
electoral process as 'one of the most ghastly nightmares that can
happen. You are not your own master, you are pushed about from
place to place, you have to make many speeches a day . . . and above
all, you must never lose your temper, but must continually present a
pleasant appearance.'[34]

Having successfully endured such indignities, most patricians
found the Commons itself both disillusioning and dispiriting. Lord
Ernest Hamilton was 'thrust an unwilling victim' into the Abercorn
family seat of North Tyrone. As an MP, he was 'a mere brick in a
buttress, whose sole purpose was to maintain a number of paid
officials in their billets . . . Nobody wanted me except as a voter in

divisions.' He sought consolation in racing with the youngest of his brothers along the Commons terrace on bicycles borrowed from the dining room attendants, and retired gratefully after one full Parliament.[35] Others stayed longer, but were no happier. Ronaldshay hated 'the strain and tedium of prolonged parliamentary sessions', and regarded the Commons in general as 'a sedentary and enervating life'. For Wood, it was too boisterous; for Curzon too trivial. The future seventh Marquess of Londonderry was so diffident as an MP that he failed to make an impact, even in the years 1906–15, when there were so few Tories in the House that it was easy to gain attention. He found it all rather boring. 'I sat', he wrote despondently to his mother, 'eight hours all but twenty minutes in the House yesterday, trying to take an interest.'[36]

During the inter-war years, this sense of aristocratic alienation from an institution they had so recently dominated became even more marked. Lord Eustace Percy was never 'a good House of Commons man': he pontificated too much. Nor was Lord Winterton: too honest, too outspoken, too independent. Philip Cunliffe-Lister fared no better: he hectored the House, and never hid his annoyance.[37] The future eighth Marquess of Londonderry was even less well disposed. 'I deplore the existence of politicians', he once explained, 'and regard it all as a rare waste of time.' So did Viscount Knebworth: 'I hate the thought of Parliament', he remarked, even before he stood for it; and when he got in, he found its dreariness hard to bear. Viscount Lymington was even more disenchanted: having been elected in 1929 and 1931, he found its inmates 'like a lot of schoolchildren', and in 1934 thankfully applied for the Chiltern Hundreds.[38]

These men, with their bored and bitter reactions, were clearly out of their depth in a democratic assembly which was no longer a gentleman's club where they might feel secure and at ease. Lord Eustace Percy hinted at this deeper sense of alienation when he deplored the demise of 'the older independence of inherited wealth' among MPs.[39] And the unfulfilled promise of Lord Hugh Cecil painfully corroborates this view. Son of the great marquess, an MP at twenty-six, a brilliant orator in the House, and talked of in his early years as a future Prime Minister, Cecil's parliamentary career was ultimately a disaster. He was arrogant, prejudiced, spoiled, and self-righteous; he was a bad party man and a poor platform speaker; he attacked both Joseph Chamberlain and Asquith with language too violent, bitter, and intransigent; and he never even held junior office. 'I am used to defeat', he once admitted. 'Everything I have tried to do has been a failure.'[40] Yet in a broader sense, his failure epitomized that of his class: genteel politicians who had lost their bearings in the new world of democracy.

As the patricians lost their grip on the Commons, they were superseded by those more vigorous occupational groups already in evidence by the late 1870s. In the Parliament of 1880, there were three working men; by 1918 there were fifty-seven Labour MPs, all lower class; and between the wars, the majority of the party came from this background, topped off by a few upper-class renegades and Hampstead intellectuals. Among the Liberals, professionals, financiers, and businessmen came to dominate, and the same was true among the Conservatives. The result was a Tory party increasingly 'rich, material and secular' in tone, which even began to use the language of the boardroom and the stock exchange.[41] Significantly, the merger between the Conservatives and the Liberal Unionists was described as a 'sound investment' promoted by 'a body of keen businessmen.' And when, in 1911, Arthur Steel-Maitland – a protégé of Joseph Chamberlain – was appointed first party chairman, Walter Long protested to Balfour that 'It will, of course, be said that you are handing the party over to Birmingham. This is really serious.'[42]

For the dwindling numbers of patricians, the general trend was as unmistakable as it was alarming – a massive influx of the new plutocracy into the Commons. Between 1809 and 1879, there were 13 non-landed millionaire MPs, and 33 half-millionaires. But between 1880 and 1939, the figures were 74 and 69 respectively. Many were entrepreneurs representing, as urban squires, the great constituencies in which their businesses were located and where their employees voted. Spencer Charrington sat for Mile End, Stepney, the home of his brewery; John Gretton, the Conservative MP for Burton on Trent, was chairman of Bass; Harland represented Belfast North while Wolff sat for Belfast South.[43] As Arthur Ponsonby disapprovingly and condescendingly explained, these new men represented 'a species of hardheaded genuine plutocrat untouched by moral scruple or old-fashioned gentlemanly refinement.' And it is easy to see what he meant. When Sir John Brunner sought adoption as a parliamentary candidate, he began by saying 'I am a rich man, and it is possibly because I am a rich man that I am standing here.' This was hardly the language of a Wood or a Bridgeman.[44]

Indeed, as if in plutocratic parody of the patricians themselves, some of these industrial magnates began to obtain an almost hereditary hold on their seats. In January 1910, Sir John Brunner retired as MP for the Northwich constituency of Cheshire, the home of his great chemical works, which he had represented almost uninterruptedly since 1885, and was replaced by his eldest son. In June of the same year, Stephen Noel Furness took over from his uncle as MP for Hartlepool, a town in which the family shipbuilding firm was one of the greatest employers of labour.[45] But the most famous example of an alien and plutocratic dynasty establishing itself, largely by the power of the purse, was the Astor family. From 1910 to 1919, Waldorf Astor was MP for Plymouth; when he inherited the family peerage, he was followed by his wife Nancy, the first woman MP, who held the seat until 1945; his brother John Jacob was MP for Dover from 1922 to 1945; and his son William was MP for Fulham East from 1935 to 1945. Plymouth and Dover in particular were treated very much as pocket boroughs: the Astors paid their own election expenses, bought large houses in their constituencies, gave regular treats, and made extensive donations.[46]

Writing in 1880, and analysing the new House of Commons, T. P. O'Connor observed that the British electorate had merely 'exchanged one oligarchy for another. The rule of the rich has simply been substituted for the rule of the noble.' As the evidence deployed here suggests, such a view was premature; but it was not, ultimately, incorrect. Haxey's elaborate cousinhoods of patrician MPs in the 1930s were not without their genealogical interest, but as John Ramsden has recently and rightly remarked, they 'missed the point that the proportion would probably [sic] have been higher in any previous generation.'[47] In 1914, the Commons could boast a Chaplin, a Hicks Beach, a Lowther, a Lyttelton, a Paget, a Newdegate, and a Sykes; but by 1939, all had vanished. Yet at the same time, some 44 per cent of all Conservative MPs were company directors, and that excluded members of the government like Chamberlain and Runciman who had resigned from similar posts. As Haxey himself admitted, in words that bore out the rightness of O'Connor's prediction, while undermining his own argument, 'the great industrial magnate has largely replaced the squire.'[48]

ii.   The Lords: Territorial Nobility to Plutocratic Peerage

When Archbishop Temple addressed their noble lordships in 1891, his colleague Edward Benson thought his 'accent a little provincial', and that he was 'not listened to at all by these cold, kindly, worldly wise, gallant landowning powers.'[49] This was hardly surprising, since until the fall of Gladstone's second ministry, the nobility had remained overwhelmingly the preserve of landed wealth and aristocratic connections, far more so than the House of Commons.[50] Indeed, in 1882, in *Iolanthe*, W. S. Gilbert celebrated, even as he ridiculed, the territorial nobility: 'paragons of legislation, pillars of the British nation.' But he also offered a brief glimpse of how the peerage might be altered in the future. At the close of the first act, the

fairy queen decrees how the House of Lords will be changed once
Strephon, her protégé, gets into Parliament:

> Titles shall ennoble then
> All the common councilmen.
> Peers shall teem in Christendom
> And a duke's exalted station
> Be obtainable by competitive examination!

In fact, a fundamental transformation was beginning to take place
at almost precisely this time. Dukedoms did not go to those who
performed well in examinations, but in the half-century from the
1880s, peerages were increasingly given out to those whose wealth
was not held in land, and even to those who were not wealthy at all.
And it is easy to see why. For the largest single field of recruitment to
the Lords remained, as it had always been, the Commons. Between
1885 and 1914, some two-thirds of all new peers had served in the
lower house before their elevation. And, as the field of recruitment
to the Commons was widened in accordance with the economic,
social, and political developments of the time, so within a generation, the composition of the Lords was correspondingly changed.[51]
As early as 1869, when vainly recommending a peerage for the
English head of the Rothschild family, Gladstone urged the Queen of
the need, 'in a few carefully selected cases', to 'connect the House
of Lords . . . with the great representatives of the commerce of
the country.' By the time of his death, this was precisely what was
happening.[52]

The statistical evidence is clear and emphatic. Between 1886 and
1914, some two hundred people entered the ranks of the hereditary
peerage for the first time.[53] Of these, only one-quarter were the
heads or scions of patrician families, the group that had previously
provided the overwhelming majority of the new recruits. Fully one-
third were professionals and state employees: lawyers who were
increasingly important in politics, as well as the diplomats, soldiers,
and civil servants required to maintain the nation and the empire.
And another third were the new, plutocratic rich, the men who had
stormed the Commons, and were now assailing the Lords in far
greater numbers than Gladstone's 'few carefully selected cases.' As
early as 1905, the *Saturday Review* had protested against 'this policy
of adulterating the peerage with mere wealth'; and it went on to
object to 'the principle that seems to have silently grown up and got
itself accepted in the last ten years that a man may be ennobled and
given the right to sit and vote among the hereditary aristocracy of
Great Britain merely because he is very rich.'[54] But by then, the

objection was no more than an ineffectual protest against current practice.

Of course, this did not change the overall character and composition of the Lords overnight. In 1880, it was so much more overwhelmingly landed than the Commons that it required a further generation before these new and different recruits made any appreciable impact. And in any case, the old qualifications of territorial influence and political service ensured that some authentic patricians continued to get in. In 1892, Gilbert Henry Heathcote-Drummond-Willoughby, who had recently succeeded his father as Lord Aveland and his mother as Lord Willoughby d'Eresby, was created Earl of Ancaster in his own right, for no other reason than that he had inherited estates amounting to 160,000 acres in seven counties.[55] And the same was true of the Allendale peerage, awarded to Wentworth Blackett Beaumont in 1906, and topped off with a viscountcy for his son five years later. Beaumont was a long serving but insignificant MP for Northumberland; but he also owned 24,000 acres in the north of England worth £34,670 and was reputedly 'one of the wealthiest, if not the wealthiest commoner, in the country.'[56]

By this time, however, there were few great territorial magnates left who had not already accepted or refused ennoblement, and as the breakup of estates began, there were even fewer such candidates for peerages. But other avenues of traditional recruitment to the Lords remained open. The most familiar of these were those long-serving politicians of landed background, whose careers were crowned (or terminated) with the grant of a peerage. Conservative ministers like Northcote, Ridley, and Hicks Beach were all broad-acred landowners, whose territory and public service well entitled them to this traditional reward.[57] And the same was true, at a slightly later date, of Walter Long, Henry Chaplin, Lewis Harcourt, and Edward Grey, as well as of Arthur Balfour, who was created an earl in 1922. Even in the 1930s, such ennoblements continued, based on a combination of landed background and political achievement: Jack Seely became Lord Mottistone, Evelyn Ashley was ennobled as Lord Mount Temple, George Lane-Fox reappeared as Lord Bingley, and Philip Cunliffe-Lister changed his name yet again, this time to Lord Swinton.

There were also country gentlemen, who had not held ministerial office, but whose claims to a peerage lay in the traditional combination of landownership, good works at the county level, and unostentatious service on the back-benches. They may already have been a dwindling band in the Commons, but those who survived were still able to get into the Lords. In the 1880s, the Haldon, Trevor, Lamington, Brabourne, and Ampthill peerages all came within this

familiar category. Thereafter, such titles as the Rolls barony of
Llangattock in 1892, the Heneage creation of 1896, and the ennoblement of Sir Charles Alfred Cripps as Lord Parmoor in 1914, were
further instances of landed gentry being transformed into peers. And
such creations continued throughout the First World War: in 1916,
Mr Tonman Mosley of Bangors Park became Lord Anslow; at the
same time Mr Charles Edward Colston of Roundway Park was
created Lord Roundway; and in 1917 Ivor John Caradoc Herbert of
Llanarth Court in Monmouthshire became Lord Treown. In each
case, there were the same qualifications: the bench, the county
council, the Yeomanry, or service as a county MP.

But while these traditional territorial routes to titles were still
trodden in the years before the First World War, they were no longer
the path of the majority. As with membership of the Commons,
patrician recruitment to the upper house must be set in a broader
perspective and kept in proper proportion. For it was not just
Gladstone who believed – or was forced to admit – that the Lords
must be opened to broader sections of the community: it was every
Prime Minister who came after him. In 1891, Lord Salisbury explained to the Queen that it was 'very desirable to give the feeling
that the House of Lords contained something besides rich men and
politicians.' What it needed, he felt, was 'eminence of a different
kind.' To this end, he obtained peerages for Sir Frederic Leighton,
the President of the Royal Academy; for the physicist William
Thompson, who became Lord Kelvin; and for Sir Joseph Lister,
'the first medical man to be made a peer.' As such, these cerebral
creations were very much in line with the peerage that Gladstone had
given to Tennyson in 1883 – although the Poet Laureate could also
boast close landed connections.[58]

A much more pronounced trend was the granting of peerages to
state servants, many of whom were now of more humble background than had previously been the case. Among Whitehall mandarins, this included men such as Sir Arthur Godley, Permanent
Under-Secretary at the India Office, who became Lord Kilbracken
on his retirement; and Sir Thomas Erskine May, Clerk of the House
of Commons, who enjoyed the title of Lord Farnborough for less
than a year. Great servants of the empire like Cromer and Milner
were also honoured: and although Cromer was from a landed-cum-
banking background, Milner was a self-made German émigré. And
when poor patrician soldiers like Wolseley, Roberts, and Kitchener
received their peerages and their promotions, they were also given
parliamentary grants ranging from £50,000 to £100,000 to enable
them to support their new dignity.[59]

But the greatest change was the increasing ennoblement of what

"GLAD, MY LORD, YOU HAVE BEEN TEMPTED TO CHANGE YOUR HAT!"

28. '"Glad, My Lord, You Have Been Tempted to Change Your Hat!"' *Punch*, 22 Dec. 1883.

was disparagingly (or enviously) described as 'mere wealth', the opening up of the peerage to many representatives of industrial, commercial, and financial riches. The starting point for this is correctly taken to be two of Disraeli's final creations: the Guest barony of Wimborne and the Guinness title of Ardilaun.[60] At the time, this was not particularly exceptional: both Sir Edward Guinness and Sir Ivor Guest had inherited baronetcies, owned extensive landed property, had made aristocratic marriages, and ardently desired total absorption into the landed establishment. But in retrospect, it was clearly the thin end of the plutocratic wedge. In his second ministry, Gladstone gave peerages to an unusually large number of bankers, albeit of landed background: Tweedmouth, Rothschild, and Revelstoke.[61] And in his short first ministry, Lord Salisbury followed the precedent set by Disraeli by creating Henry Allsopp Baron Hindlip. Like Guinness, he was essentially a brewer; but this time, he was self-made, came from Burton on Trent, and owned only a modest country seat at Hindlip Hall in Worcestershire.

Thereafter, the trend in new peerage creations moved strongly and permanently against the old territorial classes, whichever political party was in power. Gladstone, in his short first Home Rule ministry, created Michael Bass, a rival brewer, Baron Burton, and also ennobled Thomas Brassey, the son of the great contractor.[62] But it was the second, long Salisbury ministry, from 1886 to 1892, that really emphasized the change. John Hubbard, who was made Lord Addington, was a merchant and governor of the Bank of England: he might just have been given a peerage in the early 1880s. But other ennoblements were more varied: H. F. Eaton, the silk broker, became Lord Cheylesmore; Samuel Cunliffe-Lister, who had made his fortune in wool-combing, became Lord Masham; Lord Armstrong of Cragside was famous for his engineering and armament works; the peerage bestowed on the widow of W. H. Smith was as much in recognition of her late-husband's career as a railway-station bookseller as of his later political activities; and the second Guinness peerage, that of Iveagh, 'was plainly a case of having the other half.'[63]

The two decades between Gladstone's last ministry and the outbreak of the First World War saw the much-publicized proliferation of these plutocratic peers. In 1895, the first press baron was created, when Algernon Borthwick became Lord Glenesk. He was followed in 1903 by Edward Levy-Lawson, the proprietor of *The Daily Telegraph*, who became Lord Burnham. And in 1905, A. J. Balfour ennobled Alfred Harmsworth as Lord Northcliffe, who was only just forty years old, who had never sat in the Commons, and whose elevation occasioned the splenetic outburst from the *Saturday Review* at the adulteration of the peerage.[64] Other professions conspicuously rewarded included shipping, where the Inverclyde, Nunburnholm, Pirrie, Furness, and Inchcape titles were created between 1897 and 1911; more brewers such as Blyth and Marchamley; bankers like Wandsworth and Swaythling; chemical manufacturers such as Rotherham and Emcott; and such unclassifiable men as Weetman Pearson, the international contractor, who became Lord Cowdray. These were the 'representatives of great business interests and men of wide experience', whose entry into the Lords provoked the most adverse comment.[65]

Between 1905 and 1914, the Liberals ennobled more businessmen than had Salisbury and Balfour in seventeen years of Tory rule. Indeed, by 1913, 59 of the 104 Liberal peers had been created since 1892.[66] The list of government supporters for the final reading of the 1911 Parliament Bill looked more like the *Directory of Directors* or a Lloyd George honours list than a roll-call of the traditional titled élite. In a party where most of the landowners had left in the aftermath of Home Rule, this was not, perhaps, entirely surprising; in a way, it was even more significant that the Conservatives, the party of the land and of patrician premiers, were giving peerages

). Lord Astor.

30. Lord Iveagh.

1. Lord Cowdray.

32. Lord Northcliffe, by Edith Bell.

to men of almost identical background. Both parties honoured merchants, shipping magnates, and those from iron, steel, and engineering. The Tories preferred bankers of the gentlemanly type, newspaper men, and brewers; the Liberals showed a preference for merchant bankers from the City (often Jewish), and for shipping, shipbuilding, textiles, and coal. On the whole, too, the Liberal ennoblements were more self-made, less public school and Oxbridge educated, than those promoted by the Conservatives.

Either way, these new plutocratic peers were both more rich and less landed than those previously promoted to the Lords. Some, it is true, acquired considerable agricultural estates: Cowdray, Lever, and Guinness, bought in on a spectacular, if largely ornamental, scale; W. H. Smith created a substantial estate in East Anglia and the Home Counties; by 1900 Sir William Armstrong held 16,000 acres in Northumberland; and Samuel Cunliffe-Lister had laid out £750,000 on land purchases in the 1880s. Others, like Inverclyde, Furness, and Strathcona, put quite substantial parts of their fortunes into land, although probably retained the majority in more liquid assets. But most plutocratic peers seem to have made much more modest investments: a mansion, park, and home farm, the whole rarely amounting to more than 2,000 acres, as in the case of Lords Blyth, Burton, Cheylesmore, Mount Stephen, Nunburnholme, Overtoun, Swaythling, and Winterstoke.[67]

Here is the most emphatic proof of the way in which the new plutocracy overwhelmed the old territorial nobility. Those who bought big did so on an unprecedentedly massive scale, and no longer needed a probationary period among the landed gentry before their ennoblement: thanks to their plentiful millions, they got both their territory and their titles in a rush. Yet in a way, it was those new rich who did *not* buy in, who disregarded the old territorial foundations to the peerage, who most emphatically demonstrated the arrival of 'mere wealth', of a moneyed nobility, of men who did not have a stake in the country. Quite simply, a great estate was now no longer obligatory for those who aspired to nobility. Taking new peers not born into patrician families, only one-third held land extensively between 1885 and 1905, and only one-sixth between 1906 and 1916. Of course, some of these were lawyers, civil servants, and military men, who had only limited resources. But even among the bankers, brewers, manufacturers, and newspaper proprietors, only half bought significant landholdings between 1886 and 1914.[68]

So, in terms of *new* creations, the plutocrats and the professionals were already dominant by 1914. But in the Lords as a whole, this was not yet so, since the massive landed phalanx already there remained in the majority. On the eve of war, perhaps one-tenth of all

peers were from business backgrounds, and one-sixth were not substantially landed. But even allowing for the breakup of Irish estates
from the 1900s, and the beginning of sales in Great Britain from
1910, the Lords remained overwhelmingly landed a full generation
after the Commons had ceased to be so. Indeed, even after the First
World War, military commanders who were given peerages were
also given money with which to establish themselves as landed proprietors: Byng, Plummer, Rawlinson, and Horne obtained £40,000
and a barony; Allenby, Jellicoe, and French received £50,000 and a
viscountcy; and Haig and Beatty, deemed to be the heroes of the
contest, were given earldoms and £100,000, the former having told
Lloyd George that he would decline the peerage 'unless an adequate
grant was made to enable a suitable position to be maintained.'[69]

Even during the inter-war years, there were occasional ennoblements in the families of grandees and among the landed gentry that
were reminiscent of an earlier time. The Norfolks acquired two
subsidiary titles: Sir Edmund Bernard Fitzalan Howard, having
represented the Chichester Division of Sussex since 1894, was created Lord Fitzalan of Derwent in 1921 prior to becoming the last
Lord-Lieutenant of Ireland; and Sir Esme William Howard, who
retired in 1930 as British Ambassador to Washington, became Lord
Howard of Penrith. But the Cecil clan far surpassed this tally.
Balfour's earldom of 1922 has already been mentioned. Evelyn Cecil,
a grandson of the second marquess, became Lord Rockley in 1934;
Robert Cecil, a son of the third marquess, became Lord Cecil of
Chelwood in 1923; and in 1940 Winston Churchill ennobled Hugh
Cecil as Lord Quickswood. One year later, when Lord Cranborne,
the heir to the fourth marquess, was called up to the Lords prematurely in his father's barony of Essendon, no fewer than nine Cecils
or near relatives adorned the red benches. 'What a family the Cecils
are', exclaimed Harold Nicolson: and this in 1943.[70]

Among the country gentlemen, too, there were occasional ennoblements that apparently belied the 'social revolution' in landholding
which was going on around them. In 1921, Ailwyn Edward Fel-
lowes, second son of the first Lord de Ramsey, was created Baron
Ailwyn. His qualifications were highly traditional: he had been an
MP for North Huntingdonshire, and was also chairman of Norfolk
County Council. Six years later, Fiennes Stanley Wykeham Cornwallis became Lord Cornwallis, and his patrician credentials were
equally impeccable: MP for Maidstone from 1885 to 1895 and from
1898 to 1900, and chairman of Kent County Council from 1910 to
1930. In 1932, the third son of Mr Gladstone became the first Baron
Gladstone of Hawarden: he had inherited the family estate, was
Lord-Lieutenant of Flint, and an alderman of the county council.

And two years later, George Newton of Croxton Park St Neots was created Baron Eltisley, having been High Sheriff of Cambridgeshire in 1909, vice-chairman of the county council from 1911 to 1919, chairman from 1919 to 1920, and MP for the town from 1922.[71]

But by the inter-war years, these traditional patrician ennoblements were only a tiny fraction of the total: of the 280 new peers created between 1916 and 1945, only 9 were 'men of great eminence in local life, and generally possessed of inherited wealth and land.'[72] And, like many other surviving members of the inter-war landed establishment, they were much more involved in business than their predecessors. Rockley was a director of the Southern Railway and Chairman of the Foreign and Colonial Investment Trust. Eltisley had a host of business interests. Even Lord Gladstone was a director of P & O, and the senior partner in Ogilvy Gilland, East India merchants. At the same time, the upper house into which they were recruited had changed greatly in the aftermath of the People's Budget and the Parliament Act: its powers were so reduced that for many a peerage was now merely an honour to be won, not a hereditary legislatorship to be prized. And, from 1918, the territorial basis of the nobility was further undermined, as many established families joined the glut of post-war sales, and themselves became *rentiers* and businessmen. As early as 1922, it was calculated that of the 680 peers, only 242 were major landowners, but 272 were company directors.[73]

Under these changed circumstances, the continuing non-landed creations of the inter-war years merely accentuated the transformation of the Lords from a territorial nobility to a plutocratic peerage.[74] Between 1911 and 1940, some 312 people were newly ennobled, of whom, as before, between one-half and two-thirds were former MPs. Of this total, the largest single group, amounting to 108, were those in finance, industry, and commerce. The second largest category were the professionals, including lawyers, who contributed 55, followed by the home, armed, and colonial services, who numbered a further 50. Between them, big business, the professions, and service to the state made up over two-thirds of the new creations – an accurate reflection of the dominance of these groups in the country and in the lower house. The remainder of these creations were made up of the small number of landowners, the occasional academic, one member of the working class, and some whose backgrounds were not traced. But the overwhelming trend here is clear: the traditional patrician element in the new inter-war peerage was virtually non-existent.

This is so obviously an intensification of the trends discernible before the First World War that there seems little point in rehearsing it all again. But one or two developments – even further inimical to the position of the old territorial élite – merit attention. The first was the practice of giving peerages to men from overseas. This had already begun before 1914, with titles for Sir John Macdonald's widow, for the Strathcona and Mount Stephen cousins, and for de Villiers, the first native-born Chief Justice of South Africa.[75] But thereafter, it was the international plutocracy who received greater recognition: Astor in 1916, Beaverbrook and Atholstan in 1917, Ashfield in 1920, and Fairhaven in 1929. All these were North American plutocrats, to whom should be added a peerage for the Prime Minister of Newfoundland in 1909, and the first native-Indian ennoblement – Lord Sinha – in 1919. The divorce between British territory and British nobility could not have been more eloquently symbolized.

An upper house that also received in these years a New Zealand-born physicist (Lord Rutherford), the Chief Scout (Lord Baden-Powell), and two of the King's doctors (Lords Horder and Dawson of Penn) was clearly no longer the bastion of a territorial nobility, but was a body to which people from many walks of life might now realistically aspire. If they were wealthy, their chances were greater, but even that was not a necessary prerequisite. In 1930, Ramsay Macdonald offered hereditary peerages to Ernest Bevin and Walter Citrine, partly to buttress Labour's front-bench strength in the Lords, but also because he believed that working men should sit there as long as the chamber existed. Neither accepted, and throughout the 1930s, the Labour party itself remained hostile to the award of hereditary honours.[76] But in 1931, Macdonald did create a genuinely working-class peer: Lord Snell, who had begun life as a farm labourer, became a clerk in the Nottingham Blind Institution, was educated at Nottingham University College and the LSE, and ultimately became a member of the LCC and Labour MP for Woolwich. In its way, this proletarian promotion was as significant a portent as the plutocratic creations by Gladstone and Salisbury had been in the 1880s.

Nevertheless, it is the overwhelming preponderance of the big business battalions that most stands out: not only with the ennoblements of Lloyd George, but also with the titles given in the ensuing period of Conservative and National governments. Between 1931 and 1938, more than ninety peers were created or promoted, and of these sixty held directorships in 420 companies. And the list read like a roll-call of the business world: fifteen directors of the big five banks and of the Bank of England; Austin and Nuffield in motoring; Iliffe, Kemsley, and Southwood in newspapers; and the chairmen of ICI, GEC, and the Anglo-Iranian Oil Company. As Simon Haxey rightly remarked, 'the title of baron, earl or duke before the industrial revolution was . . . a reflex of landed property. The title of baron, viscount or earl is still . . . a reflex of property, but today mainly of industrial wealth.'[77]

In 1868, when refusing Mr Gladstone's request that she might ennoble Mr Rothschild, Queen Victoria had explained that 'she cannot think that one who owes his great wealth to contracts with foreign governments, or to successful speculations on the stock exchange, can fairly claim a British peerage . . . This seems to her not the less a species of gambling because it is on a gigantic scale.'[78] At the time, her objection prevailed, not least because it was consistent with contemporary custom. But during the last two decades of her reign, the power of such new, thrusting, plutocratic wealth proved to be irresistible. The Lords may have held out longer than the Commons as a bastion of territorial exclusiveness, but only by a little more than a generation. The fact that both new peers and old peers were decreasingly landed pointed inexorably to the same conclusion. By 1940, broad-acred nobles were no more the dominant force in the Lords than were authentic country gentlemen in the Commons. Most of W. S. Gilbert's predictions about the composition of the peerage had come true: but it was not the fairy queen from *Iolanthe* who had been responsible.

iii. The Cabinet: 'Governing Families' to Career Politicians

Nevertheless, it is clear that the territorial classes retained their dominance of the Lords for longer than they maintained their majority in the Commons. And, in the cabinet, the gentry and grandees survived as an important element even more tenaciously. Over a decade after the conspicuous creations of plutocratic peerages had begun, Lord Salisbury's cabinets remained so full of his relatives that Lord Rosebery felt moved to congratulate him on being the 'head of a family with the most remarkable genius for administration that has ever been known'. And even as late as the 1930s, Henry Channon claimed that 'it is the aristocracy that rules England, although no one seems to believe it.'[79] Of course, with cousinhoods in the cabinet, as with cousinhoods in the Commons, the long-term trend was inexorably downhill: but the period of inter-war Conservative dominance did ensure that the patricians remained numerically more important in the executive than in either branch of the legislature. As usual, Henry Channon's romantic fantasizing was somewhat wayward; but it contained a greater germ of truth than the remarks made by his friend R. A. Butler about the composition of the Commons.

The general social profile of British cabinets between Gladstone's second administration of 1880 and Chamberlain's government of 1937 is clear. There are, essentially, four different ways of showing their members' status and occupation (Appendix B). Three of these are derived from the work of W. L. Guttsman, and distinguish between landowners and the rest, aristocrats and the rest, and peers and the rest.[80] There are, of course, difficulties with any attempt to make such simple classifications. Guttsman's category of 'aristocrat' sometimes leaves out landed gentry, who for present purposes need to be included. On the other hand, his category of 'peers' becomes increasingly misleading after the 1880s, since it includes many non-landed figures who should be left out. Accordingly, a further attempt has been made to distinguish between those members of the cabinet who belonged to the British landed establishment, and those who did not. Even this has its difficulties. Some men, like R. A. Cross and W. H. Smith, became landowners, but were regarded by contemporaries as middle class. And no such head counting can ever precisely convey the real balance of power in an administration: a cabinet laden with peers might be dominated by a middle-class minority, or vice versa.

But despite these very real difficulties and ambiguities, the overall pattern seems clear. Until 1905, every British cabinet, whether Conservative or Liberal, was dominated by the traditional territorial classes, with the brief exceptions of the Liberal ministries of 1892–5. But a greater break came with Campbell-Bannerman's government, after which landowners were usually in a minority. The Asquith administration was slightly more patrician than its predecessor, but Lloyd George, as befitted the scourge of the peerage, gave much less space to them. So, predictably, did Macdonald, although in his case, it is the presence – rather than the absence – of a few notables that most merits attention. Predictably, the Conservative and National governments of the twenties and thirties were much more landed in membership: in 1924, at least half of Baldwin's cabinet could be so described, and in 1937 the aristocratic contingent in Chamberlain's administration was not much less. In both cases, this was a presence out of all proportion to their by now much-depleted ranks in the Commons and the Lords.

This general picture needs to be filled out more fully. Despite the gradual secession of the great Whig families, Gladstone's second administration of 1880 was still overwhelmingly landed and aristocratic in tone. There were one or two middle-class men like Bright, Chamberlain, and Forster, but they held relatively minor offices, such as the Board of Trade and the Duchy of Lancaster. Nearly half of the cabinet were in the upper house; Spencer, Granville, Kimberley, and Harcourt were the backbone of the government; in 1882

Lord Derby recorded that virtually the whole cabinet was composed
of 'large' or moderate landowners; and there were so many peers
that Gladstone had to wait until 1884 before he could bring in
Rosebery.[81] The subsequent secession of Whigs like Argyll, Lansdowne, and Hartington was reflected in the reduced numbers of
grandees in Gladstone's fourth ministry and in Rosebery's brief and
unhappy government. By then, the nobles and notables, although
still a real force in British politics, had ceased to dominate the upper
echelons of the Liberal party.

But on the Conservative front bench – now much augmented by
Whig defections – the picture was very different. Apart from W. H.
Smith and R. A. Cross, the Salisbury administrations of 1885 and
1886 were almost entirely filled by patricians. With considerable
justification, Barbara Tuchman has described the later Conservative
cabinet of 1895 as 'the last government in the western world to
possess all the attributes of aristocracy in working condition.'[82]
Apart from Joseph Chamberlain at the Colonial Office, almost all the
ministers were genteel: some were grandees like Lansdowne, Devonshire, and Cadogan; others were untitled gentlemen like Balfour,
Long, Ridley, and Hicks Beach; many were closely related to each
other. And peers in particular seemed to be exactly what was needed.
In 1885, Salisbury asked the Duke of Richmond and Gordon to be
the first Secretary for Scotland. 'You seem pointed out by nature', he
explained, 'to be the man . . . It really is a matter where the efful-
gence of two dukedoms and the best salmon river in Scotland will go
a long way.' Here, in all its *fin de siècle* glory, was a tight and
exclusive patrician cousinhood: the Hotel Cecil – unlimited.[83]

Indeed, its tone was as aristocratic as its composition. Lord Randolph Churchill dismissed Cross and W. H. Smith – both of whom
had bought estates – as 'Marshall and Snelgrove', and *The Times* and
the Queen also considered them to be middle class. In 1891, Balfour
described W. L. Jackson, a possible candidate for Postmaster-
General, as possessing 'great tact and judgement – middle-class tact
and judgement, I admit, but good of their kind . . . He is that *rara
avis*, a successful manufacturer who is fit for something besides
manufacturing.'[84] And Balfour carried this same view with him
when he followed his uncle as Prime Minister. His brother Gerald
and his brother-in-law Lord Selborne both held high office. His
cousin the new Marquess of Salisbury was soon promoted. And
Lansdowne (for whom Balfour had once been a fag at Eton),
Devonshire, and St John Brodrick were all more distantly connected.
As Lord Eustace Percy later recalled, Balfour's administration 'created, for the last time, the illusion of government by a group of
ruling families.'[85]

After this highly self-conscious aristocratic cabal, it was inevitable that Campbell-Bannerman's government should be seen as marking a great break with the past: in the cabinet as in the Commons, it seemed as though the old upper class had been thrust emphatically out, and the middle and lower classes thrust emphatically in. John Burns, the President of the Board of Trade, was the first authentic proletarian to enter the cabinet; A. G. Gardiner described Lloyd George as 'the portent of a new age – the man of the people in the seat of power'; and with other quintessentially middle-class men like Asquith, McKenna, Morley, and Haldane, it did indeed seem as if there had been a major change.[86] When Asquith succeeded, this trend was further consolidated, as Runciman, Samuel, McKenna, and Lloyd George were all promoted. 'Here we are', sighed Lord Esher, 'overwhelmed by the middle classes.' Lord Robert Cecil thought them a government of 'cardsharpers . . . no longer fit for the society of gentlemen.' And Lord Balcarres felt them to be 'divorced from every tradition which animated the old school' of patrician politicians.[87]

In fact, this clucking by some of the more snobbish and high-minded aristocrats was overdone. For Campbell-Bannerman's administration was no less grand than Gladstone's last, and contained an impressive weight of those with landed links. Despite the many Whig defections, the Liberals could still marshal a gaggle of gentry and grandees: Ripon and Elgin, Crewe and Carrington, Edward Grey and Herbert Gladstone, John Sinclair and Lord Tweedmouth. And although Asquith removed some of them, he brought in new men with similar backgrounds: Winston Churchill, the grandson of a duke, was the most obvious; but there was also Lewis Harcourt, Earl Beauchamp, and Lord Fitzmaurice, the brother of Lord Lansdowne. Appropriately enough, it was under Lloyd George that the patrician representation declined significantly again. His wartime government was essentially a Caesarist adventure of businessmen and tycoons, 'Great Britain limited'; and his peacetime administration of 1919 – appropriately coinciding with the great round of land sales – was the first in which the traditional territorial element amounted to less than one-third.[88]

By definition, the two brief Labour cabinets were emphatically middle- and working-class in tone, and to contemporaries, the advent of these socialist administrations seemed to portend 'a momentous transfer of political power, from the relatively small governing classes of the eighteenth and nineteenth centuries to a body of men and women representing between them, in birth, training and occupation, all classes of the community.'[89] Yet even here, the patricians did not go unrepresented. In Macdonald's first ministry, posts were given to Lords Parmoor and Chelmsford (the first an authentic country gentleman ennobled by the Liberals, the second a landless peer but of illustrious lineage), and also to Noel Buxton and C. P. Trevelyan (both scions of famous landed-gentry families). In 1929, Buxton, Parmoor, and Trevelyan returned to their old posts; and at a slightly lower level, there was a more conspicuous genteel presence, as Lords Russell, Ponsonby, and de la Warr, and the young Oswald Mosley, all held junior jobs.[90]

But it was in the post-war Conservative administrations that the patricians most stood out. The astonishingly aristocratic composition of Bonar Law's government seemed to belie the changes that had taken place in Britain since the days of the Hotel Cecil. There were seven peers in a cabinet of sixteen; the Foreign, Colonial, War, Indian, and Scottish Offices were held by Curzon, Devonshire, Derby, Peel, and Novar; and Lord Salisbury was both Lord President and Chancellor of the Duchy of Lancaster.[91] And among the commoners, W. C. Bridgeman, the Home Secretary, was a grandson of the Earl of Bradford and also a Shropshire squire; Lloyd-Greame at the Board of Trade was a country gentleman in his own right; and Edward Wood at Education was heir to Viscount Halifax. As one contemporary noted, with gentle but apt irony, 'the Duke of Devonshire must have thought that the world had turned back half a century to a time when both parties in turn, Liberal and Conservative, solicited his predecessor in the dukedom to become their leader.'[92]

While later Conservative and National cabinets did not repeat this top-heavy display of patrician personnel, they remained disproportionately recruited from that quarter. Indeed, as the authentically aristocratic element in the Lords and Commons diminished still further, this disparity between the Tory leadership and the rank and file became if anything even more marked. Initially, Baldwin took over Bonar Law's administration virtually unaltered; his ministry of 1924 contained more patricians than had Campbell-Bannerman's in 1906; and his National government, like that of Chamberlain which followed, showed only a slight diminution. In 1938, some nine cabinet ministers were related to each other, including Lords Zetland, de la Warr, Stanhope, Halifax, and Winterton, as well as Oliver Stanley and Sir Samuel Hoare. 'It is', Simon Haxey noted, 'a general opinion that the aristocracy plays little part in modern politics, but this is an illusion . . . Many of the most important positions in the state are held by aristocrats.' Here was some statistical corroboration for Henry Channon's more romantically impressionistic verdict.[93]

How are we to explain the stubborn persistence of gentry and aristocracy at this higher level, when at the lower echelons of politics, new groups had already gained ascendancy? In part, it was because many of the non-patricians who had stormed the Commons and swamped the Lords since the 1880s were not themselves serious candidates for government office. The businessmen MPs were usually the merest lobby fodder; Weetman Pearson attended the Commons so rarely that he was known as the 'Member for Mexico'; and most of the 'hard-nosed men' elected in 1918 were too old and too uninterested for office. And the plutocratic recruits to the Lords were usually full-time businessmen, who looked upon their title as a social honour, but not as a stepping-stone to government office; while those great servants of the state who were also thus rewarded were by definition rarely available for essentially political preferment. In short, while these new social groups had driven the landowners out of the Commons and on to the defensive in the Lords, they were much less interested in thrusting their way into the cabinet.[94]

Moreover, many gentry and grandees still enjoyed positive advantages in the race for office – should they choose to exploit them – which were even now denied to members of other and lower classes. At an age when most businessmen were active making their fortune, many patricians were already gaining valuable early experience through family connection in the service of a senior political figure.[95] Arthur Balfour began as private secretary to his uncle Lord Salisbury, when he was Foreign Secretary in Disraeli's second government. In 1880, Herbert Gladstone was elected unopposed to the Leeds seat vacated by his father, and was promptly appointed unpaid Junior Lord of the Treasury. Edward Grey began as private secretary to Erskine Childers, the Liberal Chancellor of the Exchequer, a position that had been found for him by his relative, Lord Northbrook, who was himself a member of the same cabinet. And the young C. P. Trevelyan launched himself into public life when he became private secretary to Lord Houghton when he was only twenty-two.[96]

From such a privileged apprenticeship to a seat in the Commons was but a step; and this most easily explains the sustained and disproportionate patrician importance even in these later cabinets. The sooner someone became an MP, the sooner he might become a minister: it was seniority, rather than age, that was the key to office. And, since aristocrats and country gentry reached the Commons on average ten years before those drawn from other classes, they were given a flying start. Between 1868 and 1955, two-thirds of aristocratic cabinet ministers were in Parliament by the time they were thirty, compared with less than one-fifth of those from the middle classes. And almost exactly the same proportion of these aristocratic ministers were in the cabinet by the time they were fifty, whereas less than half of the middle-class ministers were.[97] Men like Chamberlain or Mundella had to make their fortunes first, and then start at the bottom of the ladder in Parliament. But a Hartington or a Stanley could go direct from university to the Commons. And that gave them a life-long advantage in the race for office which those from other classes could rarely overcome.

These combined advantages of good connections and a youthful start meant that even in this later and more hostile political climate, patrician politicians could still enjoy government careers of unrivalled and quite elephantine length – if they so chose. Most of the cabinet ministers serving between 1886 to 1906 had entered Parliament in the days of Palmerston and Disraeli. Lord Kimberley began his ministerial career in 1852 as Under-Secretary of State for Foreign Affairs, and ended it in 1895 as Foreign Secretary. The Marquess of Ripon sat in every Liberal cabinet between 1863 and 1908. And most of the grandees who made up the Hotel Cecil were of equally impressive seniority. The eighth Duke of Devonshire's cabinet career lasted from 1866 to 1903, while the Marquess of Lansdowne began as Junior Lord of the Treasury in 1869, and retired as Minister without Portfolio in 1916. These were the natural government men: in Parliament very young, in power very early, and in office very regularly until old age disqualified them. However much the composition of the Commons and the Lords might be changing from the 1880s, these senior grandees were still there at the top.

It was careers such as these that underpinned the aristocratic governments of Salisbury and Balfour, and also provided the continuing landed element in successive Liberal administrations before 1914. And these long-serving and long-lasting notables remained a recognizable feature of the inter-war political scene. Walter Long's official career lasted from 1886 to 1921. Arthur Balfour first joined his uncle's cabinet in the same year, and was still holding senior office in Baldwin's second administration in 1929. Lord Curzon held his first minor post as Under-Secretary for India in 1891, and died in harness as Lord President in 1925. Lord Crewe was appointed Lord-Lieutenant of Ireland in 1892, and was briefly Secretary of State for War in 1931. Winston Churchill was in office almost continuously between 1905 and 1929, as was Edward Wood from 1922 to 1940. Even an unknown figure like Lord Stanhope looked back, in 1940, at a period of almost unbroken office since 1924. 'I had served', he recalled, 'in the Admiralty, War Office, Foreign Office, the Ministry of Works, Education, Admiralty again, and as Lord President of the Council.'[98]

Beyond any doubt, the patricians survived more tenaciously and more influentially in the British cabinet than in the Commons or the

Lords. Between 1898 and 1935, less than one-quarter of Conservative MPs came from landed backgrounds, yet in Tory cabinets, the proportion of landed ministers was never below one-third, and in the earlier period was well over one-half. But while this survival must be described and explained, the fact remains that the long-term trend – as in the Commons and the Lords – was inexorably downhill. Despite all the advantages enjoyed by such men in the race for office, fewer and fewer were actually competing, or staying the course, or triumphing at the finishing post. From the 1880s, excessively aristocratic cabinets were increasingly criticized for being alien to the spirit of the age; many landowning ministers were preoccupied with financial worries; and they were increasingly appointed to marginal and non-departmental offices. Even in those cabinets that they dominated numerically, their real contribution was often increasingly ornamental. In short, the 'great governing families' were ceasing to govern – and ceasing to be great.

By the late nineteenth century, cabinets that were top-heavy with aristocrats regularly incurred criticism, not only from extra-parliamentary radicals, but from the party rank and file in the Commons, on the grounds that this excessive patrician weight at the top blocked promotion, and no longer reflected the broader social spectrum in the lower house or seemed appropriate in the era of the Third Reform Act. Gladstone's administrations of 1880 and 1892 were sharply criticized in this regard, as was Rosebery's government of 1894, when both the Foreign Secretary and the Prime Minister were in the Lords.[99] Even the Hotel Cecil was not immune from the sniping of disgruntled Tory back-benchers, who saw in it an amalgam of nepotism and aristocracy which was quite unacceptable. In 1898, George Bartley complained to Salisbury that those who worked their hearts out for the party in opposition went unrewarded in government, since 'all honours, emoluments and places are reserved for the friends and relatives of the favourite few.' And in 1900, when Salisbury's last cabinet reshuffle brought in even more members of his own family, this criticism was redoubled.[100]

But in addition, these very men who were criticized for their aristocratic connections and patrician hauteur were often less robust than these attacks presupposed. In the 1880s, such Liberals as Carlingford, Spencer, Northbrook, and Lansdowne were deeply worried about their finances; Lord Granville's position was so parlous that he was kept going only by subsidies from Spencer, Devonshire, and Rosebery; and he died in 1891 with unsecured debts of £200,000.[101] Nor were the Tories and Liberal Unionists any happier. When the eighth Duke of Devonshire inherited in 1892, he found the family's financial position so desperate he thought of quitting public life altogether; Henry Chaplin overspent so much that he was bankrupt by 1897 and his estates passed to the mortgagees; and in 1911, Walter Long divested himself of half of his Wiltshire lands.[102] Such men were no longer secure in their unearned landed incomes. Barbara Tuchman may be correct in describing the last Salisbury cabinet as possessing 'all the attributes of aristocracy'; but in terms of finance, they were no longer in full 'working order'.

Moreover, even in the halcyon days of the Hotel Cecil, many of these patrician ministers were often decorative rather than efficient, whereas the middle-class minority was wielding disproportionate influence. W. H. Smith was the sheet anchor in the 1886 Parliament as Leader of the House; Goschen dominated finance; Ritchie was successively at the Local Government Board, the Board of Trade, Home Secretary, and then Chancellor; W. L. Jackson was equally important at the Treasury; and Joseph Chamberlain was the most charismatic figure in the last Salisbury government. Indeed, the Tory front bench in the Commons was decidedly middle class. In 1888, when Goschen proposed a tax on horses, he was attacked by Henry Chaplin, temporarily out of office, who looked at the Treasury bench, and concluded that 'there was not a single man amongst them who knows a horse from a cow.'[103] As J. P. Cornford rightly notes, 'that bankers, merchants, stationers, businessmen and manufacturers sat in such cabinets, occupied key positions, and took charge of important legislation suggests that aristocratic predominance may have been more numerical than influential.'[104]

Even these late-nineteenth-century cabinets, ostensibly groaning beneath the weight of aristocrats, were thus not quite what they seemed: politically and economically, the grandees were in retreat; in terms of the balance of power in government, the middle classes had already broken through and taken over. And by the early twentieth century, a whole generation of senior patricians had disappeared. Rosebery was sulking in his tent; Gladstone and Salisbury were both dead; so were Spencer and Devonshire. Sir William Harcourt gave up in 1898, telling Grey, 'I have had my full share of the nineteenth century, and the twentieth century belongs to you.'[105] On the Tory side, too, another cohort soon disappeared: Hicks Beach, Lord George Hamilton, Matthew Ridley, and Balfour of Burleigh retired; Chaplin and St John Brodrick were dropped; and Wyndham was forced to resign. And between 1909 and 1913, a succession of fortuitous deaths took off many of the next generation—Arnold Forster, Earl Percy, George Wyndham, and Alfred Lyttelton. As Lord Crawford explained to Lady Wantage, 'the grand old race of statesmen is passing away.' Less elegiacally, this meant the pool of patrician talent was drying up.[106]

33. Lewis Harcourt by Harry Furniss.

In the same way, most landed ministers in the last Liberal governments did nothing in particular, did not do it very well, and did not last very long. In 1908, Ripon retired, Elgin was sacked, and Tweedmouth departed insane. Between 1910 and 1914, Sinclair left for Madras, Elibank took up a business career, Gladstone and Buxton were shipped off to South Africa, Lincolnshire retired, and Fitzmaurice lasted only a year. Grey survived much longer, but was always thought by Campbell-Bannerman to be a lightweight: untravelled, lethargic, and preferring his birds and rods to the Foreign Office telegrams. And, after 1916, like Beauchamp, Lewis Harcourt, and Crewe, he never held serious office again.[107] At one level, the demise of the Liberal party may have destroyed their careers in their prime. But collectively, these conspicuous personal failures add up to something more: the decline in the staying power and ability of the old ruling class. Despite Sir William Harcourt's words, the twentieth century did not belong to men like Grey. As Grey explained in 1921, 'As to politics, I am not the sort of person that is wanted now . . . Lloyd George is the modern type, suited to an age of telephones and moving pictures and modern journalism.'[108]

From the mid-1900s to the early 1920s, there was a widespread sense that the patrician presence in politics was on the wane – and

34. Lord Lincolnshire by L. Ward.

35. Lord Crewe by Walter Frederick Osborne.

36. Lord Beauchamp.

37. Sir Edward Grey by Sir James Guthrie.

should be on the wane. In 1911, Lord Crawford attended a Tory shadow cabinet meeting, at which he found Henry Chaplin, and Lords Londonderry, Salisbury, and Derby. He thought them 'excellent though discredited politicians, whose inclusion in future Conservative Governments would create dismay and perhaps even resentment among the rank and file.'[109] Under Lloyd George, the landowners were even further pushed out. Some, like Grey, Selborne, and Salisbury, had virtually nothing to do with him. And those who held office were almost entirely ornamental. Lord Crawford was successively Lord Privy Seal, Chancellor of the Duchy of Lancaster, and First Commissioner of Works, but was quite unimportant. Balfour, as Foreign Secretary, swanned around the Paris peace conference in characteristically detached and lethargic fashion. Even the energetic Curzon achieved little. As Lord Privy Seal, he was described by Crewe as 'Like a Rolls Royce car, with a highly competent driver, kept to take an occasional parcel to the station.' And as Foreign Secretary, Curzon himself admitted that he was little more than 'a valet, almost a drudge.'[110]

So, by the early 1920s, it had been common practice for nearly two decades that landowners formed a minority in cabinet. Under these circumstances, the Bonar Law ministry was bound to seem anomalous, unacceptable, and inadequate – more like the peers' chorus from *Iolanthe* than a government seriously intent on coping with the pressing social and economic problems of the post-war era. In the first place, the number of nobles was thought to be quite unacceptable: even Lord Crawford admitted that there were 'too many peers in the Cabinet'. But in addition, there was a widespread belief that they were not very bright. Lord Derby, for all his influence and popularity in Lancashire, was so indecisive that he was known as 'Genial Judas'. 'A charming gentleman, sir', John Berry once explained to J. C. C. Davidson, 'a charming gentleman – but no brains, sir, no brains.'[111] Nor was the Duke of Devonshire any better: 'an apoplectic idol', thought Maurice Hankey, 'who adds little to council.'[112] These men may still have been first in the ranks of the aristocracy, but brought together in an administration, they composed what was generally known as the 'government of second class brains.'

Undeniably, some of the venom directed at this ministry by contemporaries like Birkenhead was merely personal frustration at loss of office. But it also possessed a deeper significance. For this was a ministry dominated by the most eminent and experienced patricians in the country, boasting many of the greatest and most illustrious names in the land. Yet it was widely thought to be both incompetent and anachronistic. Twenty years had elapsed since the

THE SPREAD OF DEMOCRACY.

CHORUS OF NOBLE SECRETARIES OF STATE. "WHERE'S YOUR CORONET?"
HOME SECRETARY. "SORRY I HAVEN'T GOT ONE. BUT I HAVE A KIND HEART."

38. 'The Spread of Democracy.' *Punch*, 1 Nov. 1922.

last stand of the Hotel Cecil, and what had incurred criticism then was now deemed to be totally unacceptable. This was an age of full adult suffrage; the power of the upper house had been clipped; the Labour party was barely represented in the Lords; the 'revolution in landholding' had just taken place. Seen in this context, these grandees were truly yesterday's men. And they were in power, not because they were still the ruling class, nor because of proven and recognized capacity, but essentially (and damningly) because the usual, middle-class government men were temporarily unavailable. In trying to govern almost alone, they showed they could no longer govern alone. Crawford's prediction of 'dismay and perhaps revolt' was well borne out.

The remaining inter-war governments provide only further evidence of the decline in the numbers and capacity of the patrician governing class. In the first place, many with genteel backgrounds were now longer bona fide landowners at all; they were often obliged to work for a living; and their time and thirst for office was correspondingly lessened. Lord Winterton's parliamentary prospects were not improved by the fact that he was often away on business in Rhodesia and Canada. J. T. C. Moore-Brabazon resigned as Parliamentary Secretary to the Minister of Transport in 1927 so he could make money, and ten years later refused to be lured back to the Under-Secretaryship for Air because he would have to resign from his directorates.[113] And throughout the 1920s, Cunliffe-Lister also seemed more interested in business than in office, and received many tempting offers, from public utilities in Argentina and banks in America. Indeed, between 1926 and 1929, he was little more than a passenger in Baldwin's ministry, and it was confidently predicted that he would soon return to business full time.[114]

Perhaps not surprisingly, many of the genteel ministers in this period did not do very well. Lord Eustace Percy was known to Churchill and Birkenhead as 'Lord Useless Percy', did not impress as Minister of Education, and later admitted that his period as Minister without Portfolio at the time of the Abyssinia crisis had been a 'disastrous mistake'. Both Buxton and Trevelyan resigned in a huff from Macdonald's second ministry, neither having achieved much. When Lord Crewe was briefly resurrected in 1931 to serve in Macdonald's first National Government, Walter Elliot refused to believe that he was still alive, and thought his corpse had been appointed as an economy measure.[115] The seventh Marquess of Londonderry was sacked by Baldwin in 1935 after four undistinguished years at the Air Ministry, a job he had obtained in the first place only thanks to Macdonald's favouritism. According to Davidson, he was 'not really equipped for thinking . . . not really fit for cabinet rank.' Although undoubtedly a better minister, Swinton ran into trouble there too; so did Winterton, his deputy; and Stanhope did no better at the Admiralty. On the whole, they were not very distinguished.[116]

As a result, most gentry and grandees who obtained cabinet office in this period were given relatively insignificant appointments, which provided a dignified façade, while the real power in the government lay elsewhere. This was most conspicuous in the two Labour administrations, where no patrician held a major portfolio; but it was almost as true of the Conservative and National governments that followed. Many of the offices given to landowners sounded grand, but conferred no real power, such as Lord President of the Council, Lord Privy Seal, or Chancellor of the Duchy of Lancaster. Or they were put in unglamorous or under-funded departments, such as the Colonies, the Dominions, India, Agriculture, or Education – appropriate billets for lightweight men who would soon be moved on and moved out. In 1852, when offering the post of Lord Privy Seal to the Duke of Argyll, Lord Aberdeen had described it as a job that 'would not impose any serious amount of official labour on you', and that remained the position even in the 1930s.[117]

Two ostensibly illustrious aristocratic careers vividly illustrate this essentially decorative marginality. Throughout the inter-war years, Lord Stanhope gave what has, with euphemistic correctness, been called 'a life of inconspicuous service.' Put more candidly, that means that he was moved around from ministry to ministry, that he never spent more than two years in any post, that he was quite unsuited to some of the jobs he was given (like Education), and that he was never in the 'inner ring' of policy makers.[118] But in a grander way, precisely the same may be said of Edward Wood, Lord Halifax. Like Stanhope, he was not interested in most of the jobs he held, and he kept them only briefly. Despite Christ Church and All Souls, he had no enthusiasm for Education, and although a landowner, regarded his time at Agriculture as one of 'complete futility and frustration'. He was at the War Office for only five months, had no departmental duties as Lord President and Lord Privy Seal, and was never a forceful Foreign Secretary. As with Curzon and Lloyd George, he was little more than a front man while foreign policy was made by the Prime Minister.[119]

The Cecil brothers, those gifted children of the great third marquess, were even more marginal. They shared the advantages of a great name, impeccable connections, and early entry into public life. Yet Hugh failed in the Commons, and Jim and Robert fared no better in the cabinet. From the 1900s to the 1920s, they held a succession of resounding offices, and sometimes even sat in the same administration. But while they obtained places and much honour, real power eluded them.[120] They preferred to denounce than to persuade, to resign than to compromise. They were no longer serious government men, and failed to leave an imprint on the course of events. By their day, Hatfield was more the home of lost causes than the centre of power. They were too concerned with the immortality of the soul, too preoccupied with unfashionable and trivial issues, to be men of affairs in the way that their father had been. They lacked the will to rule, the thirst for power, the flexibility and stamina for survival. As Lord Robert rightly admitted, 'I am quite unfitted for political life, because I have a resigning habit of mind.'[121]

By the inter-war years, whatever the statistics of patrician cabinet membership might suggest, the political initiative had emphatically passed elsewhere, to those bourgeois adventurers and professional

39. *The Cecils at Hatfield*, 1928, by F. H. S. Shepherd. (L. to r.) Lord Hugh Cecil; Viscount Cecil of Chelwood; James, Marquess of Salisbury; Lord William Cecil, Bishop of Exeter.

politicians against whom the Cecils railed so revealingly and ineffectually: *they* were now the men of government, who had effectively relegated the landowners to the margins of political life. Despite the large number of notables in Baldwin's second cabinet, Lord Robert Cecil had no doubt where the real power lay, with the 'middle class monsters' and 'pure party politicians.'[122] Significantly, the only people with whom he could talk 'with real freedom' were Salisbury and Halifax: men who were as marginal and as ornamental as he was. And, even more on the fringes by the 1930s, he found the National Governments exactly the same. 'Conspuez les bourgeois', he wrote in 1936, describing the attitude of Baldwin, Macdonald, Chamberlain, Runciman, and Simon to Mussolini. Halifax, on the other hand, he thought more culpable, since 'a poor old middle class monster could not be expected to know any better.'[123]

Although Channon's aristocracy and Haxey's patrician cousinhood had indeed survived into the 1930s, it was as an ornamental façade more than as a ruling class. They had ceased to constitute the governing élite, their right and capacity to rule *as a class* were no longer generally recognized, and they did not even dominate Conservative cabinets in the way that had been commonplace only fifty years before. Even in the days of the Hotel Cecil, there had been an element of the make-believe about it, and Lord Eustace Percy was

surely right when he described the Balfour administration as providing 'the *illusion* of government by a few great families.'[124]
In 1905, the illusion still convinced – just. But after Bonar Law's
government, it never did so again. Even the Cecils were forced to
recognize that the real power had passed elsewhere. After the 1945
general election, Lord Robert Cecil, who had by then taken the
Labour whip, looked disdainfully across at the Tory, opposition
bench in the House of Lords. 'Except for Bobbety and Munster', he
concluded, 'it was occupied by capitalists.'[125]

iv. Prime Ministers: Lord Salisbury to Mr Chamberlain

In any case, the tone of a government ultimately derives, not so
much from the corporate identity of the cabinet – assuming it to
have one – but from the style and personality of the Prime Minister
himself. And here, the transition from patrician premiers to men
from the business world, and even to a representative of the lower
middle classes and the proletariat, signified most conspicuously the
shift in political power away from the traditional titled and territorial
classes towards other social and economic groups. But again, there
was more to it than a simple change in occupational categories,
significant enough though that was. For even while Prime Ministers
continued to come from a landed background, they had already
ceased to rule in what might be called the interests of their class,
and were increasingly reacting to alien forces over which there
was no control. In this period, even the most patrician premiers
were something of an anomaly. And they soon became an anachronism.

It hardly needs saying that both Gladstone and Salisbury were
members of the old territorial élite. Some felt that in his earlier career
Gladstone's Liverpool and mercantile background had obtruded; but
by the 1880s, he was well established as the squire of Hawarden, a
devoted landowner and a firm believer in hierarchy based on agriculture as the best possible form of social and political organization. He
laboured mightily to free the Hawarden property from debt; he
subscribed generously to help rescue the encumbered acres of the
sixth Duke of Newcastle; and he believed that all landowners had 'a
very high duty to labour for the conservation of estates, and the
permanence of the families in possession of them, as the principal
source of our social strength.'[126] He was a self-confessed 'out and out
inequalitarian'; he strongly preferred aristocratic ministers in his
cabinets, even at the cost of criticism from his own radical colleagues; he hoped that in 1990, England would still be a land of great
estates; and he deeply regretted Harcourt's death duties, for fear that

landowners would be taxed out of existence, and forced to sell out to the vulgar 'neo-plutoi.'[127]

Robert Talbot Gascoyne-Cecil, third Marquess of Salisbury, could boast a lineage more illustrious and estates more broad-acred, than Mr Gladstone. As Lord Lytton put it, he represented 'a great name and a social position.' Two of his forebears had been the greatest statesmen of Elizabethan and early Stuart times; Hatfield was one of the grandest and most venerable houses in the country; the family were major landowners in Hertfordshire and Dorset; they held extensive urban properties in Liverpool and London; and Salisbury himself left a personal fortune of £300,000.[128] He became an MP for his cousin's pocket-borough of Stamford at twenty-three, when he was elected unopposed; he was chairman of Hertfordshire quarter sessions, and Chancellor of Oxford University. High office came through no apparent effort, and his ministerial career lasted from 1866 until 1902. He was an incorrigible and resourceful opponent of democracy, hostile to 'the bestowal on any class of a voting power disproportionate to their stake in the country.' 'Standing rock-like in the advancing tide of democracy, emblem of a vanishing world', he was the most patrician premier since Lord Derby.[129]

But while these two landowners were leading their respective parties for most of the 1880s and 1890s, and while their own careers illustrate many of the advantages that such a background might confer, they both showed that patrician government was already emphatically on the wane. For all his social conservatism, Gladstone was widely distrusted by most of the landed classes by the end of his life; the Ground Game Act, the Agricultural Holdings Acts, his Home Rule policy, and his wish to reform county government make it easy to see why; and the fact that he gave peerages to plutocrats and probably knew about the sale of two titles in 1892 hardly seemed the actions of a defender of the landed order.[130] In the 1880 election, he claimed that he could no longer 'reckon on the aristocracy. We cannot reckon on what is called the landed interest'. After the 1892 campaign, he told the Queen that the new government was 'against the sense of nearly the entire peerage and landed gentry'. And by 1894, he was in open conflict with the House of Lords. By the end of his life, Gladstone had lost faith in the aristocracy (just as they had lost faith in him): it no longer met up to his expectation that they would provide 'the rule of the best'.[131]

Nor, in practice, was Salisbury very different. As he admitted in 1889, 'We live no longer, alas, in Pitt's time; the aristocracy governed then . . . Now democracy is on top'. In policies, as in personnel, the patrician tone of the Hotel Cecil was something of an illusion. The number of peerages granted dramatically increased;

40. Lord Rosebery by G. F. Watts.

Exemplar
Photo by F. Hollyer

they went to plutocrats, brewers, and newspapermen; and the sale of honours came a stage nearer. Despite patrician pressure, Salisbury refused to contemplate the revival of protection for agriculture, and he neither reduced nor repealed the dreaded death duties. He may have resigned over the Second Reform Bill, but he compromised over the Third; and he created county councils, to the chagrin of the squires, on the grounds that 'representative bodies are the fashion of the day, and against a fashion it is almost impossible to argue.' Above all, his administrations took the first effective steps to dismantle the Irish landed ascendancy, with the Purchase Acts of 1891 and 1896. 'I do not in the least anticipate', Salisbury claimed, 'that it will put an end to the class of landlords.'[132] But the landlords felt betrayed; they knew different; and they were right.

In short, neither Gladstone nor Salisbury was able to sustain or support the patricians' class interests against the powerful adverse currents of their time. And nor were Balfour or Rosebery. Again, their careers show how easy it still was for those with the right background to get to the top. Rosebery's was particularly glittering. He was born in 1847 and inherited his titles and his estates from his grandfather when only twenty-one. He made a dazzling maiden

41. Arthur James Balfour by
Philip de Laszlo.

speech in the Lords in 1871; he married a Rothschild heiress and
£100,000 a year in 1879; and he was Gladstone's host during the
Midlothian campaign. He was a brilliant writer and orator, and a
discerning collector of books and letters; he boasted three princely
houses, a town palace in Belgrave Square, and a yacht; and he was
Lord-Lieutenant of two Scottish counties. His horses won the Derby
three times, he was much liked and patronized by the Queen, and he
left a personal and real fortune of £1.7 million.[133] He was given
minor office in Gladstone's second ministry, became Foreign Secretary in 1886 at the age of thirty-nine, held the same post again
from 1892 to 1894, and on Gladstone's resignation was personally
chosen by the Queen as Prime Minister.

Balfour, likewise, enjoyed all the advantages that birth (and
brains) could bestow. His father was a Scottish country gentleman,
owning 87,000 acres worth £19,800 a year. The great Lord Salisbury
was his uncle, the Duke of Wellington was his godfather, and one of
his brothers-in-law, Lord Rayleigh, won the Nobel prize for physics. He was clever, witty, urbane, detached; he was an amateur
philosopher of some distinction; and he was at the very centre of that
self-regarding coterie known as the Souls. He became an MP at

twenty-six through his Cecil connections, and was immediately appointed private secretary to his uncle. Despite a widespread belief that he was too languid and too limp, he established an outstanding reputation as a tough and determined Chief Secretary for Ireland; he dominated the Commons once Gladstone had departed; and he was clearly the obvious successor to his uncle. Even Joseph Chamberlain could not dispute the claims of 'Prince Arthur' to enter into his inheritance: the Hotel Cecil was still a family firm.

Yet these two men did much, by their inept handling of affairs, to discredit the whole notion of landed leadership at the very top. Neither Gladstone nor Salisbury governed with real patrician freedom; but on occasions, it seemed as if Rosebery and Balfour were not really governing at all. Rosebery has been rightly described by Lord Blake as 'palpably unfit for the job', completely devoid of Prime Ministerial temperament.[134] At all stages in his early career, he had hesitated before taking office; he told the Queen that being Foreign Secretary was 'too much'; and as Prime Minister he was insomniac and ineffectual. He was unable to conciliate Harcourt, who was annoyed at being passed over; he was too enthusiastic about the empire and House of Lords reform, and insufficiently interested in Home Rule; and he left behind no major legislative achievement. The radical press was hostile, he failed to unite the party, and the 1895 election was a fiasco. 'I never did have power', he once remarked. 'I was not intended or fitted for political life.'[135]

Nor was Balfour any better. He was tougher than Rosebery, and genuinely enjoyed power, but he did little with it as Prime Minister, and was a bad party leader. Like Rosebery, he was a patrician ultimately out of his depth in a democratic world. He was congenitally incapable of giving firm or decisive leadership, in government or in opposition, in the House or in the country. He was a bad platform speaker, was too often away in Scotland, and was inattentive to the party rank and file. He was unable to cope with Chamberlain and Tariff Reform; he could not keep the party together; and he was even less impressive as leader of the opposition. He lost three successive general elections, was driven from the leadership by his own supporters, and left his party divided, defeated and demoralized, and without any clear successor.[136] As Lloyd George cruelly but accurately observed, his place in history was no more than the scent of perfume on a pocket handkerchief. If Rosebery was the worst Liberal leader of the nineteenth century, there is a case for saying that Balfour was the worst Tory leader of the twentieth.

In the light of these unhappy experiences, it is hardly surprising that both parties soon rejected traditional landed leadership. After a brief and unhappy interlude with Harcourt, the Liberals selected

Henry Campbell-Bannerman, who was at best a marginal case. His father was a Glasgow draper and warehouseman, who bought a 4,000-acre estate in Forfar in 1847. The future Prime Minister was a younger son, but did inherit the Hunton Court estate in Kent from his maternal uncle, Henry Bannerman, in 1872: hence his hyphenated name.[137] To that extent, C-B's claims to be a patrician were sound. But his trading connections were undeniable; he had attended Glasgow University before Trinity College, Cambridge; he had worked as a partner in his father's business; and as Prime Minister, he was rightly seen as the portent of a new, less landed age. He was, essentially, 'an ordinary . . . run of the mill politician', and he never went out in society. When attending a dinner for colonial premiers at Marlborough House, Lady Derby asked her neighbour who the man was next to his wife. 'That', replied Sir Wilfrid Laurier, 'is your Prime Minister.'[138]

Campbell-Bannerman was no more than marginally patrician, and the advent of Asquith to the Premiership denoted an even greater change. Of course, there was what F. M. L. Thompson calls 'an aristocratic streak' to him – far more so than in the case of his predecessor.[139] He enjoyed the good things of life, was a regular country-house visitor, and was launched into high society by his second wife, Margot Tennant, whose family background was like Campbell-Bannerman's, but richer. And his children were married off quite astonishingly aristocratically: Raymond to Katherine Horner, the daughter of a Somerset landed gentleman; Herbert to Lady Cynthia, daughter of the eleventh Earl of Wemyss; Arthur to Betty, daughter of Lord Manners; Violet to Maurice Bonham Carter, another landed gentleman; and Elizabeth to a Roumanian prince. Only Cyril married into new wealth. Yet Asquith was in no sense a patrician (or even, in some men's eyes, a gentleman): he was a nonconformist provincial, a self-made lawyer, a resident of Hampstead, who never owned a landed estate, never established real roots in the country, and died leaving only £9,345.[140]

Thereafter, leadership on the left remained emphatically non-landed. Lloyd George never liked peers, and most peers never liked him. He was, after all, the man who had done most to inflame popular feeling against them in the 1900s; he had undermined their power by weakening the House of Lords; he had eroded their status by the blatant sale of peerages; he had attacked their wealth with his new and vindictive taxes; and in 1922 he abandoned the patricians in southern Ireland to their fate. Almost every landowner despised him as 'that damned Welsh attorney', an 'irresponsible demagogue', a 'dirty little rogue', whom they believed to be incompetent, dishonest, and immoral.[141] And Ramsay Macdonald was even more proletarian: he was poor and illegitimate; he took to high society (to his great political cost) with all the ardour of the outsider; and he was the first great beneficiary of Chequers, the mansion left to the nation by Lord Lee in the expectation – correct as it turned out – that future Prime Ministers would no longer possess country seats of their own.[142]

But the more abrupt and more significant change came in the Conservative party, where the rule of the Cecils ended when Balfour was hounded from the leadership in 1911. Who was to replace him? The choice seemed to lie between Austen Chamberlain, representing the new industrial element in the party, and Walter Long, a traditional Tory squire. But Chamberlain was too much of a Unionist outsider to command general support, and Long had 'few effective claims except squiredom and seniority.'[143] Eventually they both withdrew in favour of the relatively unknown Andrew Bonar Law, a man whom even Asquith described as 'a gilded tradesman with the mind of a Glasgow baillie.' A greater contrast to his predecessor could hardly be imagined. Law's father was a Presbyterian minister; he was raised in a Canadian manse; he attended Glasgow High School and became a partner in the family iron merchanting firm; and by the time of his elevation he was enjoying an income of £6,000 a year from profits and directors fees. He was also a morose widower and a teetotaller, who hated dinners and high society.[144]

Thus did the rule of the Cecils come to an abrupt end. 'One has to recognize', observed Lady Dawkins, 'that a new era in political life has dawned for England, the old aristocratic school is practically swept out of it, it is the dawn of a new regime.' As his 1922 ministry was to show, this was undoubtedly overstating it. But Law was in no sense rustic or landed, and unlike Disraeli, never felt the need to become so. 'I am concerned', one Tory told Lord Winterton, 'at dear Bonar's apparent ignorance of country life now that he is leader of the country gentleman's party', and went on to complain that Law could not even recognize a pheasant.[145] Lady Londonderry fulminated that he was not a country magnate, and Lord Balcarres disliked his food ('I kept the menu as a souvenir of discomfort') and his address ('a longish way beyond Cromwell Road'). But after Balfour's patrician detachment and ineffectual vacillation, middle-class firmness and aggressiveness was exactly what the party wanted, and such a leader was much more in tune with the background and feelings of the party rank and file in the Commons.[146]

The fact that Law was succeeded by another businessman who dealt in heavy metals effectively turned an innovation into a trend. Unlike Bonar, Baldwin talked a great deal about the countryside, and genuinely loved it. But it was in an essentially nostalgic, escapist, romantic way. For he was a member of the entrepreneurial middle classes: an ironmaster, whose family firm was established in Worcestershire and South Wales, and a director of the GWR and the Canadian Grand Trunk Railway. Although certainly not a 'hard-nosed man', he himself had done so well out of the war that he gave one-fifth of his fortune to the country as a thanks-offering.[147] He hated Bonar Law's top-heavy cabinet, ready-made with too many peers; when he returned triumphant in 1924, Derby, Devonshire, and Novar were not reappointed; Curzon was demoted from the Foreign Office; and Balfour, Salisbury, and Robert Cecil were kept in very subordinate positions. They felt marginal men because they had been deliberately marginalized. And when they re-emerged in the thirties as die-hards, Baldwin damningly described them as 'sitting in the smoking room of clubs, and never doing a hand's turn of work.'[148]

For all his spiritual communing with Halifax, Baldwin was certainly not the aristocrat's friend, and nor was Neville Chamberlain, whom Lord Londonderry once dismissed as 'a Birmingham tradesman'.[149] While his elder and more gifted brother had been groomed for stardom and statesmanship, Neville was chosen by his father to carry on the family business tradition. He had studied engineering and metallurgy at Mason College; he had tried to grow sisal in the Bahamas in the 1890s; before the First World War, he was in charge of a company that made ships berths; and he was also chairman of Elliotts Metal Company and a director of BSA. As such, he was a middle-class, Midlands industrialist, who lived entirely off his shares and his directors fees. 'I shall be interested', he wrote revealingly in 1922, 'to see how I get on with SB, but I fancy he will be alright. After all, he is a businessman himself.'[150] And when he became Prime Minister, he may have decorated his cabinet with peers and landowners, but the Cecils were correct in their belief that it was dominated by 'middle-class monsters', of whom Chamberlain himself was for them the supreme example.

Here, at the very summit of British politics and government, the patricians were in sustained and conspicuous retreat. The cabinets of Bonar Law, Baldwin, and Chamberlain may have been more aristocratic than those of Campbell-Bannerman, Asquith, and Lloyd George, but the most striking evidence for the shift in the balance of power is that they were no longer led by men drawn from the old territorial nobility. From Asquith to Chamberlain was an unbroken period of thirty years: five successive non-landed premiers were not so much aberrations from the old norm as a new and very different norm. For, unlike Disraeli, they no longer felt it necessary to *pretend* to be gentlemen, or to join the landed establishment to enhance their credibility, or even to take a title. Asquith, Lloyd George, and Baldwin took earldoms, but only after they had retired; Campbell-Bannerman, Bonar Law, Macdonald, and Chamberlain declined all valedictory honours. By the inter-war years, it was clearly establish-ed that the Prime Minister was neither landed nor a peer: the head of the government no longer came from the old governing class.

Of course, this must be kept in perspective. Although Salisbury would have found it difficult to govern without his nephew leading the Commons, no one really supposed at the time of his resignation that he would be the last Prime Minister who would ever sit in the Lords. There was constant talk, in the late 1890s and in the 1900s, that Rosebery might make a comeback. Had Lord Spencer not been ill in the autumn of 1905, he might have headed the new Liberal administration formed at the end of the year. And by then, Asquith, Grey, and Haldane had already been plotting to remove Campbell-Bannerman to the upper house if he became Prime Minister.[151] In 1911, when Balfour resigned, he was replaced, according to custom, with two Conservative leaders: Law in the Commons, and Lans-downe in the Lords. Had the Liberal government fallen before the First World War, the King might well have sent for Lansdowne as a replacement. Even as late as 1923, there was occasional talk of a Conservative-Liberal coalition under Derby or Balfour or Grey.[152]

The prospect of a patrician Premier in the Lords was thus not fully ruled out. But none of these schemes actually came to anything; and on the two occasions when peers *did* come close to the Premiership, they did not get it. The first was when a successor had to be found to Law, who resigned on the grounds of ill health in the autumn of 1923. The choice lay between the Marquess Curzon of Kedleston – the Foreign Secretary and Chancellor of Oxford University, a man with a lifetime of distinguished service to the state, a grandee with five houses and as many titles; and Stanley Baldwin – until recently an unknown quantity, with little cabinet experience, who was later described by Curzon as 'a man of the utmost insignificance.'[153] Here, perfectly encapsulated, was the contest for the dominion of the Tory party between the patrician and the businessman. And, as in 1911, it was the businessman who triumphed. Baldwin won, not because there was any conspiracy to mislead George V about Bonar Law's views, but because the consensus of opinion was that no peer, how-ever gifted or distinguished, could be Prime Minister of England in 1923.[154]

Balfour was strongly of this view, and told the King that even in the days of his uncle, with a more restricted franchise and as yet no Labour opposition, it had been virtually impossible for a peer to be Prime Minister, and that it had worked in Salisbury's case only

42. Stanley Baldwin and Lord Curzon outside 10 Downing Street, Jan. 1924.

because his nephew was leading the Commons. J. C. C. Davidson's famous memorandum was of the same opinion, noting that, whatever the constitutional theory might be, in practice, 'the time has passed when the direction of domestic policy cannot be placed outside the House of Commons.'[155] George V was much swayed by this argument, and it was the explanation that he later gave to Curzon himself. Since the Parliament Act, the balance of power had tilted more strongly away from the Lords to the Commons; with Labour so ill-represented in the upper house, government and debate would have been virtually impossible if the Prime Minister had been there; and in an administration already top-heavy with peers, there would have been even greater outrage if the Prime Minister had also sat in the Lords.

How circumstances had changed since the days of the Hotel Cecil. Had those grandees who dominated the Bonar Law ministry collectively insisted that Curzon be appointed, they would surely have prevailed: against so great a majority of ministerial opinion, the pragmatic arguments, however powerful, would not have counted, and an even more aristocratic regime would have been the result. But what is really significant is that no concerted attempt was made to achieve this. Even those patricians in cabinet recognized that theirs was no longer the class that could or should provide the man at the very top. Of the ministers who were consulted or who made their views known, only Lord Salisbury urged Curzon's claims upon the King. Derby and Halifax made it plain that they would not serve under him; and Balfour, consulted as an elder statesman, was equally damning: 'He had come to the definite conclusion that a peer as Prime Minister was impossible, and that in any case, Curzon was not the peer who could have done it.'[156]

But as these last words imply, there was in fact more to it: if Curzon was in some ways disqualified by being a peer, he was even more disqualified by being Curzon. As Lord Blake rightly summarizes it, 'there was no real reason why a peer should not have been Prime Minister in 1923, but there were cogent reasons why a person of Curzon's temperament, whether peer or commoner, should not have been at the head of affairs in the England of the 1920s.'[157] For all his gifts, he was a slightly ridiculous anachronism; he was out of touch with post-war Britain; his oratory was stately but inaccessible; he was overbearing, rude, and inconsiderate; and he was totally unsuited to dealing with such figures as trade-union leaders. As Davidson noted, Curzon was 'regarded in the public eye as representing that section of privileged conservatism which has its value, but which in this democratic age cannot be too assiduously exploited.'[158] The real point about the Curzon episode was that it merely confirmed, in an exaggerated and poignant way, the widespread belief that in the circumstances of the time, aristocrats were no longer suitable Prime Ministerial material.

This patrician inappropriateness for the highest office was shown again when Lord Halifax did not get the job in 1940. Though less of a superior person than Curzon, he, too, was a quintessential grandee: a former Viceroy, Foreign Secretary, Chancellor of Oxford, devoted to his hounds and his houses. Moreover, in May 1940, when it was clear that someone had to succeed Chamberlain, his claims were far more broadly supported than had been those of Curzon in 1923. The King wanted Halifax; Chamberlain wanted Halifax; most Conservatives wanted Halifax; and so did many in the Labour party.[159] But in the end, he did not kiss hands, and the disqualification of his peerage was the reason given then, which has often been repeated since. Indeed, it was Halifax himself who laid 'considerable emphasis on the difficult position of a Prime Minister unable to make contact with the centre of gravity in the House of Commons.' 'I should', he concluded, 'speedily have become a more or less honorary Prime

43. Winston Churchill
with Lord Halifax,
Whitehall, 29 Mar. 1938.

Minister, living in a kind of twilight, just outside the things that really matter.'[160]

But as with Curzon, Halifax's peerage was largely an excuse, a rationalization that concealed deeper explanations: for just as a titled landowner of Curzon's temperament had been unsuitable for the job in the circumstances of 1923, so a titled landowner of Halifax's characteristics was no more appropriate in the very different circumstances of 1940. He had spent most of his life as a decorative but essentially marginal figure in politics and in government, and the thought of real power, of great responsibility, of the grievous ordeal that lay before him and his nation, made him feel physically sick. He did not want the job, under these – or any ? – circumstances. Like Curzon, it was not so much his peerage, as his temperament, that was the decisive and deciding factor. In this case, it seems clear, Halifax could have had the job for the asking; but he did not want it; he did not push his claims; and he gave his peerage as his excuse.

If these two grandees, so decorated and so distinguished, who had spent their lives doing the state some service, were regarded by others as unfitted for supreme power, or effectively disqualified themselves, this merely reinforced the general view that the House of Lords was no longer a major forum of political life, and that the country house was no longer a relevant or reliable nursery of Prime Ministerial material. There might still be some notables in politics, but they conspicuously lacked the will, the temperament, the qualifications, the appetite, for the highest office. Indeed, it was only the extraordinary events of 1940, and the peculiar qualities of leadership then deemed desirable, that could bring to the Premiership the first patrician since Balfour: a man virtually as anachronistic as Curzon, an isolated outsider almost as marginal to the politics of the thirties as the Cecils – Winston Churchill himself.

v.   Conclusion: Vanishing Supremacies

When, as Prime Minister, Lord Palmerston considered giving junior office to the Marquess of Hartington, he wrote to his father, the Duke of Devonshire, to seek his advice and consent. 'Young men', Palmerston explained, 'in high aristocratic positions, should take part in the administration of public affairs, and should not leave the working of our political machine to classes whose pursuits and interests are of a different kind.'[161] For much of the nineteenth century, that was exactly what such young aristocrats did. Yet by the 1930s, such people had long since ceased to be able to govern either for or by themselves, and it was those very 'classes whose pursuits and interests are of a different kind' who had taken over. Although the rate of change varied, in the Commons, the Lords, the cabinet, and at Prime Ministerial level, that was the undeniable trend. At the same time that the patricians were ceasing to dominate the land, they were ceasing to dominate politics as well.

Of course, this general picture must be both qualified and set in perspective. For whatever idiosyncratic reasons, there were some families whose individual history and performance appears to belie and deny this overall trend. The grandees and gentry may have been in decline as the governing class, but between the 1880s and the 1930s, the Salisburys, the Devonshires, and the Churchills were more prominent in British politics than their forebears had been for several generations. This was not enough to disturb the general pattern, but it is a reminder that some particular families may not conform completely to the trajectory of the class to which they belong. Moreover, even in the days when the patricians *did* provide the governing élite of the country, the number of families from which they were recruited was always relatively small. In this later period, it simply became even smaller.

The result was that the British landed establishment failed to perpetuate and reproduce itself as the governing class. In the increasingly hostile world in which they found themselves from the 1880s, many patrician families simply abandoned their governing role, and wilfully withdrew into a much more private world. Evelyn Waugh captures this vividly in his picture of the Marchmains: absentee, Catholic, preoccupied with salvation in the next world and family quarrels in this. And so does Aldous Huxley in his account of the Tantamounts: the head of the family a crippled recluse, concerned only with the mathematical proof of the existence of God, and his younger brother completely uninterested in politics or the family estates, but obsessed with newts and tadpoles. And as such, these fictional evocations closely resemble the description given by the present Duke of Bedford of life at Woburn in the time of his grandfather: a man completely isolated from the world, who never used the telephone, was devoid of taste and culture, and was interested only in the birds and the bison in his park.[162] Whether out of choice, out of fear, or out of indifference, such people had effectively signed off from public and political life.

But this failure of will may well have occurred because they instinctively recognized that their particular abilities – the product of tradition, training, and temperament – were no longer those required to govern Britain in the massively changed conditions of the twentieth century. Arthur Ponsonby may have been hinting at this when he noted that in his day, the aristocracy seldom rose above the level of mediocrity; that they were in decline 'physically, morally and intellectually'; that 'in no way are they better suited than anyone else to govern the country'; and that 'there is every reason to believe they are conscious of it.'[163] In the inter-war years, Harold Laski put this view even more emphatically:

> The English aristocracy has long passed the zenith of its power. It no longer has a monopoly of those qualities which make for effective governance. It may even be said that the problems which confront civilization today are of a kind which call less for the qualities of the aristocrat than almost any others that can be imagined.

Or, as George Orwell summarized it in 1940, 'one of the dominant facts in English life during the past three quarters of a century has been the decay of the ability of the ruling class.'[164]

6

THE DEMISE OF PATRICIAN PROFESSIONALS

The downward mobility from above of younger sons . . . is one of the most important and obscure aspects of English history from the sixteenth to the twentieth centuries.

(L. Stone and J. C. Fawtier Stone, *An Open Elite? England 1540–1880* (1984), p. 6.)

The horizons of a nobleman's younger son in the late nineteenth century were hardly broader than those of his great grandfather. Unless the family happened to be exceptionally rich, the heir alone was found a seat in the House of Commons. His brothers were directed towards the army or the navy, the public service or the learned professions.

(K. Rose, *The Later Cecils* (1975), p. 112.)

Studies of the Church, army, navy and civil service indicate that the landed classes retained their traditional position in these professions during the first three quarters of the nineteenth century. Only after 1870, at which time competitive exams and other reforms were introduced, did a decline of the landed membership in these professions begin.

(D. Duman, 'A Social and Occupational Analysis of the English Judiciary: 1770–1790 and 1855–1875', *American Journal of Legal History*, xvii (1973), p. 354.)

The professions have changed from being an addendum to the nobility and gentry to being part of the occupational élite in modern society.

(P. Elliott, *The Sociology of the Professions* (1972), p. 143.)

The economic and political developments thus far outlined were by definition most damaging to the heads of aristocratic families. But there was also a broader penumbra of peripheral patricians who were beginning to feel the shades of the prison house closing in from the late 1870s. Even in the heyday of the old territorial élite, there were some landed gentry and inheritors of resounding titles who were so lacking in material resources that they were obliged to earn their living – either because of the accidents of inheritance, or because of the profligacy of their forebears. And in every generation, there were cohorts of younger sons who, having received their portion, were compelled to find their own means of life support.[1] From one perspective, the result was a constant and downward flow of patricians into the great professions to which they were so closely connected by property and patronage, by privilege and prestige.

44. The eight Lyttelton brothers.

From another, this meant that until the 1870s, the administrative apparatus of the British state was essentially a bastion of territorial power and control. The grandees and gentry dominated Whitehall as much as they dominated Westminster.

At the end of the nineteenth century, there were many titled and genteel dynasties in which younger sons still embraced these traditional career patterns. One such were the Lyttletons, whom Samuel Hynes has rightly – albeit anachronistically – described as 'an establishment family'.[2] George William, fourth Lord Lyttelton, produced eight sons. Of these, the eldest, Charles, inherited the titles and estates: they were adequate, but by no means extensive. Three of his younger brothers took Holy Orders: Albert spent his life as a parish clergyman; Arthur was Master of Selwyn College, Cambridge, and Bishop of Southampton; and Edward eventually became Headmaster of Eton. Two more brothers went into the law: Robert qualified as a solicitor, but spent most of his time writing a book on cricket, while Alfred became a barrister, was Recorder of Hereford and Oxford, and from this base launched his political career. Another brother, Neville, was a full-time soldier, who was eventually appointed first Chief of the General Staff and C.-in-C. Ireland. And George Lyttelton was private secretary to his uncle, Mr Gladstone, during his latter years as Prime Minister.

Here are classically exemplified all the great careers traditionally open to a patrician professional.[3] Yet such famous examples of

occupational continuities conceal major changes that began during
the last quarter of the nineteenth century. For many needy notables
discovered that these once exclusive professional preserves were
losing their traditional appeal, and were being successfully invaded
by intruders of a socially inferior status. As one contemporary
explained:

> In former times, a country gentleman could be almost certain of
> sending his son either into the army or the navy, or of educating
> him specially for the Church or Bar. Now, however, the avenues
> leading to these professions are crowded with applicants outbid-
> ding one another.[4]

During the 1880s, there was an extensive public discussion about the
plight of younger sons, who were revealingly described as 'supernumerary gentlemen', as 'gentlemanly failures.' And during the next
half-century, their prospects of preferment and promotion in the old
professions only diminished still further. By the 1930s, the civil
service, the law, the church, and the armed services were no longer
outworks of patrician power and propertied privilege, as they had
been only fifty years before.[5]

Why, exactly, was this? In part, they were squeezed out because of
the reforms in recruitment and selection that were begun in the
1870s, and which by the early years of the twentieth century were
making a significant impact: the abolition of purchase in the army,
the introduction of open competition into the civil service, the
innovations in the structure of ecclesiastical patronage, and the
changes in the format of legal training. And these reforms in recruitment coincided with major changes in the scope and extent of
government, in the resources and organization of the church, in the
structure and status of the legal profession, and in the technology and
ethos of warfare, which further diminished the appeal of these
careers to needy patricians in search of employment. In every profession, the old, amateur, traditional, gentlemanly ethos was in retreat.
The civil service was no longer an appropriate billet for literati and
dilettanti. The church was increasingly urban and professional in its
structure and orientation. The law was becoming precarious and
overcrowded. And in the aftermath of the Boer War, the army
needed educated experts rather than ornamental horsemen.

The result was that these great professions were swamped by the
ever increasing numbers of the upper middle classes, who were well
educated at public school, who excelled as Oxbridge undergraduates, and who were extremely good at taking and passing examinations. Continuity of style and tone may thereby have been preserved,

but this concealed a revolution in the corridors of power every bit as sudden and significant as that occurring on the land, in the shires, and at Westminster, namely the almost total eclipse of the old territorial order as the administrative élite. With recruitment increasingly based on competition rather than connection, on merit rather than money, on ability rather than on social position, the traditional patrician preponderance was bound to be broken. Instead of being an outwork of the landed establishment, the great professions had become the almost exclusive preserve of the middle classes.[6] Only at the court and in the Foreign Office – the two last bastions of recruitment by connection – did the grandees and gentry survive. And in the latter case, at least, the end of the road was already in sight.

i. The Civil Service and the Court

Nevertheless, the administrative élite that governed Britain as the last quarter of the nineteenth century opened remained in essence as genteel and as privileged as it had always been. The claim that 'by the 1870s, there seem to have been comparatively few members of aristocratic families in key positions in the higher civil service' is simply not borne out by the evidence.[7] At the Home Office, the senior mandarin was the Hon. Sir Adolphus Frederick Octavius Liddell, the sixth son of the first Lord Ravensworth. At the Colonial Office, the Permanent Secretary was Sir Robert George Wyndham Herbert, grandson of the first Earl of Carnarvon. At the Admiralty, Sir George Tryon, third son of Sir Thomas Tryon of Bulwick Park, Northamptonshire, was his opposite number. And the rationale for this state of affairs remained essentially unaltered. As Robert Lowe explained, when Chancellor of the Exchequer, it was necessary that Treasury officials be drawn from the upper classes. They must have daily contacts with 'gentlemen and noblemen from all parts of the country, and MPs', and under these circumstances, 'they should be of that class, in order that they may hold their own on behalf of the Government, and not be overcrowded by other people.'[8]

The result was a service that retained its essentially amateur and aristocratic ethos. The men in charge had usually been recruited several decades before, in the halcyon days of patronage, or under the system of limited competition, which was introduced in 1855, and had been expressly designed 'to strengthen and multiply the ties between the higher classes and the possession of administrative power.' Although the income no doubt came in useful, they did not think of themselves as professional, full-time, career civil servants: indeed it would have been anachronistic if they had. They spoke to politicians as social equals and in many cases as close relatives, and they went about as fully accepted members of high society. The great departments of state over which they presided were still so small in size (the Home Office boasted only thirty-six permanent officials in 1876) that their ambience was that of the club rather than the counting house.[9] The hours of work, even for the most senior officials, were short, and there were long holidays during the summer for country-house visiting. Each department was more like an old curiosity shop than a modern government bureaucracy.

Admittedly, open competition had finally been introduced by Order in Council in 1870. But this reform made much less immediate impact than it is usually fashionable to suppose.[10] There was a lag before specific departments accepted the scheme, and but a dribble of recruits by this means thereafter. The Home Office complied in 1873, but the first competitive entrant arrived only in 1880, and patronage appointments still continued nevertheless. A patrician like Edward Ruggles-Brise was given a junior position in the following year as the result of a direct request by his father to the Home Secretary himself. The Treasury followed suit in 1878, but for the next twenty years, direct entry by open competition was still the exception.[11] When the Department of Agriculture was set up in 1889, it recruited by patronage, and at the Board of Education, inspectors were appointed in the same way until 1914. A man such as E. M. Sneyd-Kynnersley – like Ruggles-Brise a well-connected but not well-off patrician – obtained a job as School Inspector by enlisting the help of his father's friends in the ministry of the day.[12]

So, despite the advent of open competition, the civil service retained both its genteel tone and its aristocratic personnel until the end of the nineteenth century and in some cases well beyond. At the Treasury, the two senior figures in the 1900s were Sir George Herbert Murray and Sir Edward Hamilton. Murray was a kinsman of the Duke of Atholl, and had briefly been heir presumptive to the dukedom. He joined the Foreign Office in 1873, moved to the Treasury seven years later, and between 1897 and 1903 was successively chairman of the Board of Inland Revenue and Secretary of the Post Office.[13] Hamilton was a relative of the tenth Earl of Belhaven, was a well-known figure in polite, aristocratic society, and during the early 1880s had been one of Gladstone's private secretaries. Among his many duties had been docketing and answering letters, choosing wine, finding the GOM's spectacles, and buying his railway tickets.[14] Between them, these two notables, who had been recruited long before open competition, dominated the Treasury for well over a quarter of a century.

In the Home Office, the picture was equally patrician. Liddell's period of dominance there lasted from 1867 to 1885, and he was followed as Permanent Secretary by Sir Godfrey Lushington, the fifth son of the second baronet. He, in turn, was superseded in 1895 by Sir Kenelm Digby, nephew of the ninth Baron Digby, who held the position until 1903 – exactly thirty years after the principle of open competition had been accepted. While these two men were in charge, the office retained its family and feudal atmosphere: the pace of life was unhurried, and the intellectual level was generally undistinguished.[15] Many of the crucial subordinate positions were also filled by patricians. Between 1885 and 1913, the Legal Assistant Under-Secretaryship was held by only two men. The first was Edward Leigh Pemberton, the scion of a Kentish gentry family. And the second was Sir Henry Cunynghame, who was the grandson of the fifth baronet, and himself married Lord Thurlow's illegitimate daughter. Meanwhile, the career of Sir Edward Ruggles-Brise (as he had now become) was prospering: in 1895 he was appointed Chief Prison Commissioner.[16]

Nor were these two ministries exceptional in either the extent or the longevity of notable preponderance. Between 1888 and 1892, the Permanent Under-Secretary at the Scottish Office was Robert Cochran-Patrick of Ladyland, a minor Scottish country gentleman. His almost exact contemporary at the Board of Trade was Sir Henry Calcraft, son of John Calcraft of Rempstone Hall, Wareham, who had entered the department as long ago as 1852. Calcraft was followed in turn by Sir Courtenay Boyle, the great grandson of the seventh Earl of Cork and Orrery.[17] In the same department, holding the job of Assistant Secretary from 1895 to 1913, was Thomas Pelham, third son of the third Earl of Chichester. Between 1884 and 1907, the Permanent Secretary at the Admiralty was Sir Evan MacGregor of MacGregor, the third son of the third baronet, and from 1902 to 1912, the same post at the Office of Works was held by Sir Schomberg McDonnell, the fifth son of the fifth Earl of Antrim.[18] Thirty years after the introduction of open competition, very little had yet changed at the very top.

There were also many parts of the government bureaucracy where patronage was not eliminated at all, and there the patricians thrived and flourished as before.[19] Between 1875 and 1898, the Clerk to the Privy Council was Sir Charles Peel, nephew of the great Sir Robert. From 1899 to 1903, the chairman of the Board of Customs was Sir George Ryder, great grandson of the first Lord Harrowby, and from 1894 to 1910, the Secretary and Comptroller-General of the National Debt was Sir George Hervey, a kinsman of the Marquess of Bristol. Sir Henry Primrose fared even better, no doubt helped by the fact that he was a cousin of Lord Rosebery, the Liberal Prime Minister.

Between 1886 and 1907, he was successively Permanent Secretary
to the Office of Works, chairman of the Board of Customs, and
chairman of the Board of the Inland Revenue. And Sir Spencer
Walpole's career was even more varied. He began as a clerk in the
War Office in 1857, but was soon transferred to the Home Office as
private secretary to his father. In 1867, his father appointed him
Inspector of Fisheries; in 1882 he was made Governor of the Isle of
Man; and in 1893 he became Secretary to the Post Office.[20]

Here, surviving well into the 1900s, was a closed, intimate,
aristocratic world – Cobbett's 'Old Corruption' a century on.[21] The
most vivid picture of this largely forgotten corner of landed-
establishment life is conveyed by the diaries of Sir Almeric Fitzroy.
He was the great grandson of the third Duke of Grafton, and his
mother was a daughter of Lord Feversham. He began his official life
as an Inspector of Schools in the Education Department of the Privy
Council. The appointment was arranged by family influence, and it
gave Fitzroy time to hunt three days in every fortnight.[22] In 1884,
Lord Carlingford transferred him to the Privy Council Office itself;
in 1895 the Duke of Devonshire (who had just become Lord President) made him his private secretary; and three years later, the
combination of family influence and the Duke's patronage brought
him the Clerkship of the Privy Council, which he held until his
retirement in 1923. Throughout this period, he was on the closest
terms with the leading politicians of the day, he moved easily in
royal and patrician society, he was a well-known figure in the clubs
of London, and he spent many a weekend at Chatsworth, Lissadell,
Osterley, Longleat, and Euston.[23]

Like Fitzroy, most of these genteel mandarins were very well
connected, but neither rich nor landed. They married appropriately:
Peel to a daughter of Lord Templemore, Boyle to a daughter of Lord
Cawdor, Digby to a daughter of Lord Belper, Ryder to a Harrowby
cousin. Many of them, like Lushington, Digby, and Hervey, began
life as lawyers, and they all moved easily between the professions,
government administration, and political life. They did not see
themselves as full-time civil servants, embracing an all-consuming
career. On the contrary, they had other things to do. Almeric Fitzroy
wrote books about his ancestors, and was a trustee of the Duke of
Grafton's settlement. Edward Hamilton was a man of letters and
confidant of Arthur Sullivan.[24] Cunynghame wrote books on the
law, electricity, and the fine arts, and was a friend of Holman Hunt,
Whistler, William Morris, and Oscar Wilde. And Spencer Walpole
wrote a biography of his ancestor, Spencer Perceval, and a six-
volume history of England.[25] In short, these men were aristocratic
dilettanti of a traditional, recognizable kind, and it was their civil

service employment that gave them both the leisure and the largess to pursue their amateur avocations.

Some vestiges of this cosy world of aristocratic connection lingered until well beyond the First World War. From 1909 to 1915, the private secretary to the Lord Chancellor was Adolphus Riddell, the son of the Permanent Secretary at the Home Office. At the same time, the private secretary to the Speaker was Edward Cadogan, the sixth son of the fourth earl. Between the wars, the successive chairmen of the Forestry Commission were the sixteenth Lord Lovat, the twenty-first Lord Clinton, and Sir John Stirling Maxwell, tenth baronet. During the same period, Sir George Evelyn Pemberton Murray, the son of Sir George Herbert Murray, clearly benefited from his father's influence.[26] Before 1914, he was successively private secretary to the Lord President and to the President of the Board of Education, and a Commissioner of Customs and Excise. Then from 1914 to 1941, he was Secretary of the GPO and chairman of the Board of Customs and Excise. And even as late as the 1930s, the Permanent Secretary at the Board of Education was Sir Edward Henry Pelham, great grandson of the second Earl of Chichester.

But by the inter-war years, this genteel presence in the civil service was very much a minority phenomenon. Albeit later, rather than sooner, the introduction of open competition did eventually spell the end of landed-establishment dominance. When the sons and scions of the aristocracy were forced to compete with a wider section of the population, educational success was far less certain a guarantee of continued patrician power than patronage and nepotism had been. As early as the 1890s, only 7 per cent of new civil service recruits came from a landed background, and by the 1930s, the figure was less than 3 per cent.[27] In every ministry, there is a clear break point where the old notability bowed out, and the new professionals took over: 1900 (very early) in the Colonial Office, 1908 in the Home Office, and 1911 in the Treasury. Here was a new world with a new ethos: of full-time work, of probity, loyalty, self-effacement, and secrecy, of detachment from high politics and high society, of rational promotion, and of rewards and honours. This new civil service was self-consciously a middle-class profession: the old aristocratic amateurs had gone for good.[28]

At the same time, there was unprecedented change in both the structure and the size of the civil service. The Liberal social reforms of 1905 to 1914 necessitated the complete reordering and massive expansion of the Home Office and Board of Trade. The First World War witnessed an even greater extension in the functions and size of the Treasury, and the Versailles Conference, the return to gold, and the slump only intensified this.[29] Moreover, these new rational and bureaucratic structures were presided over by a new breed of middle-class mandarins. The modern Home Office was the creation of Sir Charles Troup, Permanent Secretary from 1908 to 1922. At the Privy Council Office, Sir Almeric Fitzroy was followed by Sir Maurice Hankey, who was also Secretary to the Cabinet. At the Treasury, Sir Warren Fisher was in charge between 1919 and 1939, and he soon became Head of the Civil Service as well.[30] These were the new full-time professionals, the workaholic bureaucrats, who embraced the civil service as a lifetime's career. By comparison, Sir George Murray at the Post Office was widely regarded as an aristocratic anachronism.[31]

From the standpoint of the traditional territorial class, there can be no doubting or denying the magnitude of this change: it was emphatically the eclipse of the old aristocratic élite. But it has been masked by two apparent yet misleading continuities: the educational background and the amateur ethos of this new breed of civil servants. Of course, many of the new middle-class men had been to public schools: but they had rarely been to such aristocratic academies as Eton or Harrow.[32] And there was a real difference between the amateur ethos of the patrician and that of the mandarin. The aristocrats were amateurs because they regarded the civil service as providing the means whereby they might continue to live as genteel dilettanti. The new middle-class civil servants were amateurs in the very different sense that they were professional generalists. As the Chorley Committee noted in 1949, 'the days when senior civil servants of the administrative class had leisure to engage in literature or the arts as spare time occupations', in the manner of Walpole or Digby or Hamilton, had long since been a thing of the past.[33]

In less than fifty years, the patrician amateurs had been vanquished for good from the corridors of power: as Weber rightly opined, bureaucracy had proved to be the invincible enemy of aristocracy.[34] Indeed, this major administrative revolution is thrown into even sharper relief when compared with another noble profession where there was no such change, namely the court. At the very end of Victoria's period of unpopularity, during the late 1870s and early 1880s, it was still asserted that the monarch was surrounded by aristocratic hangers-on who were little more than drones and flunkeys, and that nepotism, extravagance, and peculation were rife.[35] But thereafter, as the monarchy became increasingly venerated and worshipped, the patrician personnel of the court also came to enjoy what might best be termed immunity by association. Criticism of the retinues of titled courtiers was effectively stilled, and the fact that recruitment remained entirely by patronage and connection went virtually unremarked. Unlike the civil service, there was no reform in procedure and no revolution in personnel. In the court, more than anywhere else, 'Old Corruption' did not merely linger: it positively thrived.

The positions in question were not the great offices of state such as Lord High Constable or Earl Marshal, which were held by grandees and were largely honorary. Nor were they political appointments such as Lord Chamberlain or Lord-in-Waiting, which changed with every government. Rather, they were the full-time court offices such as Private Secretary, Keeper of the Privy Purse, Master of the Ceremonies, and Comptroller of the Household, or the more humble positions of Equerry or Lady-in-Waiting. From the 1870s onwards, the nature and importance of these offices was transformed. Sir Henry Ponsonby effectively created the post of Private Secretary to the Sovereign in its modern guise.[36] The new imperial and ceremonial image of the monarchy required planning and organization on an unprecedented scale. The palaces, pictures, libraries, and archives of the sovereign needed extensive reform and restoration in the aftermath of late-Victorian neglect. The extended families of Victoria, Edward VII, and George V meant a proliferation of junior royal households which themselves needed to be staffed and administered. And the inevitable result, despite occasional attempts at economy, was an expanding royal bureaucracy.[37]

Almost invariably, such positions were filled by close relatives of peers. Lord Edward Pelham Clinton was brother of the sixth Duke of Newcastle, and was Master of the Household from 1894 to 1901. Lord Claud Hamilton was brother of the third Duke of Abercorn, was constantly at court between 1919 and 1953, and eventually became Comptroller and Treasurer to Queen Mary. Other patricians clearly benefited from family connection with the monarch. The Marquess of Lincolnshire was one of the greatest Liberal grandees of the land, personal friend of successive sovereigns, and joint hereditary Lord Great Chamberlain. His younger brother, Sir William Carington, enjoyed a courtly career that lasted from 1880 until his death in 1914, by which time he had been both Comptroller and Treasurer of the Prince of Wales's Household, and Keeper of the Privy Purse. In the same way, the sixth Earl of Dartmouth held the political office of Vice-Chamberlain of the Household from 1885 to 1891. His younger brother, Sir Harry Legge, was a courtier from 1889 until 1920, and eventually became Paymaster of the Household.

Many such patricians enjoyed full-time courtly careers of quite exceptional length. Sir Henry Stonor, brother of the fourth Lord Camoys, and Sir Derek Keppel, brother of the eighth Earl of Albemarle, served every sovereign from Queen Victoria to King George VI. And Sir George Crichton, son of the fourth Earl of Erne, held courtly offices from 1920 to 1952. There was even room for aristocrats with academic inclinations and aesthetic sensibilities, like Sir John Fortescue, who was the younger brother of Sir Seymour Fortescue, himself a courtier from 1893 to 1936. In 1906, the lobbying of 'kind friends' meant that Sir John was appointed Librarian at Windsor Castle, where he rearranged the royal books, prints, and archives, and also completed his monumental history of the British army in his spare time.[38] Likewise, Sir Lionel Cust, grandson of the first Lord Brownlow, could boast 'many friends and some relatives in court circles.' As a result, he became Surveyor and Keeper of the King's Pictures in 1901, and rearranged the royal collections in the royal palaces.[39] In both cases, it is clear that connection was of prime importance in securing their positions.

But all these younger sons were outclassed in the battle for the royal ear and courtly advantage by Sir Alec Hardinge, whose inexorable rise to the very top of the royal bureaucracy displays the characteristic combination of need and nepotism.[40] He was the second son of Lord Hardinge of Penshurst, and the family was very patrician, but without any great territorial resources. Like his forebears, Alec Hardinge was thus obliged to earn, and he was greatly assisted in this by his royal connections. Edward VII took the strongest interest in his father's diplomatic career; his mother was an Extra Lady of the Bedchamber to Queen Alexandra; the sovereign herself was one of Alec Hardinge's godparents; and King George V and Queen Mary attended his wedding in 1921. With connections such as these, a court job was effectively his for the asking. In 1920, he was appointed assistant private secretary to George V, and from 1936 to 1943 he was successively private secretary to Edward VIII and George VI. One of his sons was a page to George V, Edward VIII, and George VI, and his daughter married the Assistant Comptroller in the Lord Chamberlain's office.

Hardinge was followed by Sir Alan Lascelles, the grandson of the fourth Earl of Harewood.[41] He was educated at Marlborough and Trinity College Oxford, where he spent most of his time hunting, shooting and visiting country houses. The Indian Civil Service seemed too parochial and middle class, and he twice failed the entrance examination for the Foreign Office. In desperation, he took to stockbroking, which he hated, and from which he was rescued by the First World War. He was briefly ADC to his brother-in-law, the Governor of Bombay, and married a daughter of Lord Chelmsford, the Viceroy of India. From 1920 to 1925, he was private secretary to the Prince of Wales (whose manners and morals he came to detest); between 1931 and 1935 he was private secretary to the Governor-General of Canada; in 1936 he returned to Buckingham Palace as assistant private secretary; and from 1943 to 1953 he was Hardinge's successor. In 1922, his cousin, the future sixth Earl of Harewood, had married George V's only daughter, a connection that can hardly have done Lascelles's own career prospects any harm.

The most successful patrician courtiers established an abiding dynastic connection, so that generation after generation, their families enjoyed royal favour and preferment. From the late nineteenth century until the Second World War, the Ponsonbys were the pre-eminent courtly dynasty.[42] They were very aristocratic but not very rich, being a cadet branch of the Earls of Bessborough. Sir Henry Ponsonby, grandson of the third earl, became the Queen's private secretary in 1870, largely because his predecessor, General Grey, was his wife's uncle. He held the position until his death in 1895, by which time the Queen had already appointed his second son, Frederick, as an Equerry. By the reign of George V, Frederick had risen to be Treasurer of the Household and Keeper of the Privy Purse. Another branch of the family did equally well. Sir Spencer Ponsonby-Fane was the sixth son of the fourth Earl of Bessborough, was Comptroller to the Lord Chamberlain from 1857 to 1901, and continued to hold minor office until his death in 1915. And one of his grandsons, Sir George Arthur, served as Comptroller and private secretary to the Queen of Norway from 1919 to 1938.[43]

No other family managed to maintain courtly connections so successfully and so unbroken across the generations. But others did not lag far behind. Mabell Countess of Airlie was widowed when her husband, the sixth earl, was killed in the Boer War, and she was left far from comfortably off.[44] From 1902 to 1953, she was Lady-in-Waiting to Queen Mary, and during that period, her relatives also established close courtly connections. Her eldest son, the seventh earl, was Lord-in-Waiting to George V from 1926 to 1929, and Lord Chamberlain to Queen Elizabeth from 1937 to 1965; and her younger son was Equerry to the Prince of Wales between 1921 and 1930. In the next generation, the eighth earl was to become Lord Chamberlain, and his brother Angus married Princess Alexandra. Equally successful were the Colvilles, who were also patrician, Scottish, and not broad-acred.[45] Charles John Colville, tenth baron and first viscount, was Lord Chamberlain to Queen Alexandra from 1873 to 1903. His younger brother, Sir William, was Master of Ceremonies from 1894 to 1903. His daughter-in-law, Lady Cynthia, was a Woman of the Bedchamber to Queen Mary from 1923 to 1953. *Her* son, Sir John, was a Page of Honour to George V, and private secretary to Princess Elizabeth immediately after her marriage. And *his* cousin, Sir Richard, was Press Secretary at the Palace between 1948 and 1968.

45. Lord Ormathwaite.

Like most members of the titled and noble classes who were obliged to earn a living, the majority of these courtly patricians were relatively poor. Lady Airlie died in what might politely be called genteel poverty, and Sir Frederick Ponsonby constantly sought means of augmenting his income, either by becoming Governor of Bombay or by raising King John's Treasure from the Wash. (He did not succeed in either endeavour.)[46] And in strictly financial terms, the rewards of these offices were not great: rarely above £1,000 a year, and usually much less. But in every other way, they were exceptionally attractive. Life at court, though on occasions dull, was by definition comfortable and cosseted. There were sumptuous tours abroad, as when Sir John Fortescue accompanied King George V and Queen Mary to India for the Durbar. The grace and favour housing was also very generous. Lord Ormathwaite, who was Master of Ceremonies in the 1910s, enjoyed what he called 'a small house' in St James's Palace; but the picture in his autobiography hardly bears out the adjective. Sir Alec Hardinge had the use of a forty-five roomed residence in St James's, the Winchester Tower at Windsor, and a house on the Balmoral Estate.[47] And the honorary rewards were also considerable. Men like Hardinge and Lascelles were loaded with stars and ribbons, and Sir Frederick Ponsonby became a peer.

Partly because of their background, and partly because of their occupation, most of these courtiers were obscurantist and reactionary in the extreme. Sir Henry Ponsonby was a life-long Liberal, and Lady Airlie also seems to have been commendably unstuffy. But the remainder were far less open-minded. Sir John Fortescue thought the 1870 Education Act had merely produced 'a more accomplished type of criminal', and that democracy was 'the rule of the half educated and the wholly conceited.'[48] Lord Ormanthwaite began his autobiography with the candid admission that 'I must have been born a snob, for my earliest recollections are love of royalty and the best of everything.' Sir Alan Lascelles took what he called 'genuine pride in good lineage', which meant in practice that he was insufferably crusty. 'There is', he once observed, 'so much cant about snobbery.'[49] And Sir Alec Hardinge was described by Harold Macmillan as 'supercilious, without a spark of imagination.' Inevitably, such people were 'saturated in regal officialdom', besotted with hierarchy, order, and precedence, and obsessed with 'all the paraphernalia and etiquette of a court.'[50]

Viewed from one patrician perspective, the history of royal service appears totally at variance with the history of the civil service. For it is an account of successful survival rather than of inexorable decline. Despite the transformation in the position of the monarchy that took place between the late nineteenth century and the Silver Jubilee of George V, the court remained an essentially unreformed and aristocratic monopoly. Neither limited nor open competition was instituted. Recruitment remained as before, based essentially on personal contacts and patrician connections. And the rationale was clear. Being brought up 'on the steps of the throne' was the best recommendation, and the best training, for royal service. Those whose families were hereditary courtiers knew exactly what was required and expected. And good manners, decorum, discretion, a veneration for hierarchy, and a love of ceremonial were bound up with aristocratic life in a way that was not true of any other group, not even the public-school educated middle class. The result was that, by the 1930s, the court had become a caricature of the civil service as it had been fifty years before: it was the last bastion of 'Old Corruption'.

Seen from another perspective, however, the survival of this aristocratic royal bureaucracy was hardly a success story at all. To begin with, there were never that many jobs available: the individuals

who got (and kept) the best positions were relatively few in number.
In addition, the obsessive and excessive delight that many of them
took in order, hierarchy, rank, and title partly derived from their
resentful awareness that this world – which had once been *their*
world – now survived unchallenged and intact only within the hal-
lowed precincts of Windsor, Balmoral, Sandringham, and Buckingham Palace. But above all, the monarchy itself played a far less
influential part in British politics from the late nineteenth century
than it had done before. The courtly retinue of genteel bureaucrats
and armigerous ornamentals thus formed a hierarchy that no longer
corresponded to the ordering of the world outside, and provided
ceremonial spectaculars that were increasingly marginal to the
sinews and substance of British political life. The patricians might
still be central at court, but as such, they were no longer central to
the nation's affairs.

ii.   The Law and the Church

As late as the 1880s, the law was still widely regarded as the
profession that carried the greatest social prestige, and it was very
closely linked with the landed establishment itself.[51] For public men
such as Sir William Harcourt or Lord Tweedmouth or Lord Edmond
Petty-Fitzmaurice, it remained the best preparation for a needy
notable anxious to embrace a political career. To many an elder son,
the law was the obvious subject to study since, even if he never
actually practised, it was the best possible training for administering
estates and sitting on the bench. For many a younger son, it was also
the ideal career: a portion provided the necessary initial financing;
good connections were of inestimable value in obtaining briefs and in
securing promotion to the highest judicial office; and the style of life
was congenial and leisured in a quintessentially patrician way. As
The Times put it in 1884, choosing its metaphors with care, it was
still widely believed that 'the main object of the profession is to
furnish amusement for gentlemen, an agreeable change from field
sports and the pleasures of society. The clients . . . occupy very much
the same position as the foxes and the pheasants.'[52]

Almost without exception, the most successful lawyers came from
a titled and genteel background or, if from more humble beginnings,
were eventually assimilated into it. Indeed, this was virtually inevitable, since the House of Lords was not only the most patrician part
of the legislature: it was also the supreme court of appeal, which
meant that all the great law officers were peers. Outsiders, like
Lords Chelmsford, St Leonards, Denman, and Tenterden no longer
amassed the stupendous fortunes and vast estates of their eighteenth-

century predecessors like Eldon and Hardwicke, but they still became fully accepted members of the territorial and titled classes.[53] And insiders, like Lord O'Hagan, who was Lord Chancellor of Ireland, and made a peer in 1870, actually came from such a background before they went into the law. This two-way traffic continued thereafter. Roundell Palmer was another lawyer from a middle-class family; but he ended his career as Lord Chancellor and Earl of Selborne, and both he and his eldest son married into the heart of the peerage. On the other hand, Lord Halsbury was 'an authentic example of impoverished gentry of truly ancient lineage', and when he first became Lord Chancellor in 1885, he took his title from the family's historic country seat in Devon.[54]

This close connection between the law and the land continued in the lower echelons of the profession. Sir Edward Chandos Leigh was the second son of the first Lord Leigh of Stoneleigh Abbey in Warwickshire. He was educated at Harrow and Oriel and, after deciding against the army and the church (for which his younger brother seemed destined), decided to read for the bar. He was called in 1859, and in the following year joined the Midland Circuit, which also enabled him to hunt and stay with his family. Thereafter, his good connections worked greatly to his advantage: in the 1870s, he built up a flourishing practice at the Parliamentary Bar, and in 1884 he became Counsel to the Speaker.[55] A generation later, the career of Alfred Chichele Plowden conveys the same impression. He was one of the few members of his family who preferred a domestic profession to the ICS. After Westminster and Brasenose, he was called to the bar in 1870, and thereafter joined the Midland Circuit, which included Shropshire, where he was a welcome guest in many country houses. He joined the local Hunt, and was even invited to contest the Newport county division. Again, his connections helped him advance: in 1882 he was appointed Revising Barrister for Oxfordshire; and in 1888 he moved to London as a police magistrate.[56]

Leigh and Plowden were both younger sons. But there were also many instances among the lower echelons of the landed gentry where, generation after generation, the head of the family was obliged to augment an inadequate rental by taking up the law. The Harringtons held estates so limited that they did not appear in Bateman. As a result, both the eleventh baronet, who succeeded in 1877, and the twelfth, who followed in 1911, became practising lawyers: the former became a metropolitan police magistrate and county court judge, the latter one of the judges of the High Court of Calcutta. In the case of the Norths of Rougham the legal tradition was even stronger. They were a cadet branch of the Earls of Guilford, who owned 2,580 acres in Norfolk, and produced four

successive generations of lawyer-gentry between the 1880s and
1960s. But the most famous example were the Crippses of Parmoor
in Berkshire. Henry William Cripps was a Middle Temple lawyer
and ecclesiastical politician. His third son embraced the same profession, was a major figure in county affairs, and was eventually
ennobled as Lord Parmoor. And *his* fourth son was Sir Stafford
Cripps, another lawyer and Labour politician.

In the years before the First World War, some of these patrician
lawyers gained judicial preferment, through patronage and connection, if not always through merit. Some of Halsbury's appointments
to the bench were particularly criticized, such as Arthur Kekewich, a
country gentleman from Devon of no distinction except lineage and
loyalty. Even more unpopular was the elevation of the Hon. Edward
Ridley to be a High Court judge in 1897. He was the brother of the
Tory Home Secretary; he was a lawyer of very mediocre attainments; and the appointment was generally regarded as 'a political
job'.[57] Other patricians, who combined good connections with
genuine ability, still rose to the very apex of the profession. Sir
Edward Macnaghten was a fourth baronet, whose family held 8,000
acres in Northern Ireland. He trained as a lawyer, was an Ulster MP
between 1880 and 1887, and became a Lord of Appeal in Ordinary
and a life peer. Even more successful was Herbert Cozens-Hardy,
the second son of a Norfolk landowner who held 2,929 acres worth
£3,764. He was a practising barrister, chairman of the Bar Council,
and MP for North Norfolk from 1885. In 1899 he became a High
Court judge; two years later he was made a Lord Justice of Appeal;
in 1907 he was appointed Master of the Rolls; and in 1914 he became
a hereditary peer.[58]

But this traditional picture, of the law as a professional apanage to
the landed establishment, needs to be set in a broader context: for
these continuities belie major changes in structure and personnel,
which essentially parallel those in the civil service.[59] In the early
1870s, an Honour School of Jurisprudence was established at Oxford, and the Law Tripos set up at Cambridge, where academic
study underwent a great revival at the hands of scholars like Bryce,
Dicey, and Holdsworth. In 1877, the Law Society was empowered
to conduct professional exams, in 1903 it established a law school in
London, and it became increasingly important in setting up law
departments in provincial universities. In 1873 the Judicature Act
rationalized the structure of the superior courts by setting up a High
Court and a Court of Appeal, which were housed in suitably grand
buildings in the Strand completed in 1884.[60] The rise of local
provincial bars, and the decline of the old circuits, further undermined the traditional style and structure of the profession. In 1883,

the Bar Committee was set up to protect the interests of ordinary barristers, and evolved a decade later into the more representative and weighty Bar Council.[61]

Contemporaries had no doubt that these changes meant that the law was becoming much more professionalized and middle class than it had been previously, and thus much less attractive to the old amateur, leisured, patrician element. In 1872, when final exams were made compulsory for barristers who wished to be admitted to the bar, there were protests that this would deter country gentlemen who trained 'merely to acquire such status and so much professional knowledge as would be useful to them as magistrates, politicians, legislators and statesmen.'[62] At the same time, it was also being asserted – quite correctly – that the bar was no longer seen as 'as representing the higher status of society than solicitors', and that there was 'a much closer approximation in attainments and in social status than formerly.' In other words, the position of barristers was emphatically declining, whilst that of solicitors was correspondingly rising – so much so that they were increasingly seen as the classic symbol of professional, and thus of *middle-class*, respectability.[63]

At the same time that the profession was becoming more bourgeois and more bureaucratic in its lower echelons, the links at a higher level between the law and the Lords were also being progressively uncoupled. The Appellate Jurisdiction Act of 1876 effectively acknowledged that the upper house could no longer exercise its judicial functions unassisted. A new Court of Appeal was created, which was only nominally a part of the second chamber, and was dominated by Lords of Appeal in Ordinary, who were only peers for life. Despite such genteel appointments as Macnaghten and Cozens-Hardy, the overwhelming majority of these judges were middle-class professionals, like Dunedin, Sumner, and Macmillan.[64] And among Lord Chancellors, Selborne and Halsbury were the last patricians by ancestry or aspiration to sit on the Woolsack. Their twentieth-century successors were neither recruited from, nor did they join, the territorial élite: Buckmaster, Sankey, Hailsham, and Birkenhead were quintessentially middle class, as were most of the politicians who now took up the law, like Asquith, Simon, or Lloyd George.[65]

These new regulations, and these new recruits, spelt the end of the close connections between the law and the land. So professional, so middle class, and so overcrowded had the bar become, that it no longer provided a safe haven for patricians in search of a lucrative but undemanding profession. Between 1835 and 1885, the number of barristers tripled.[66] But there was no commensurate increase in the number of high offices, and average earnings were the lowest and the

most precarious of any of the great professions. By the last quarter of
the nineteenth century, it had become extremely difficult for a
lawyer to establish a secure and lucrative practice: less than two-fifths
of those who had qualified were able to earn their livings by
advocacy.[67] The result was that many patricians, who had looked to
the law as a traditional means of life support, were obliged to seek
employment elsewhere, and there was a marked exodus of the titled
and the genteel from the uncertainties and disappointments of the bar
at this time.

A few of them went into academe, like Sir William Anson, who
was Vinerian Reader in English Law, and Warden of All Souls, and
the ubiquitous Sir Kenelm Digby, who at this stage of his career
wrote the *History of Real Property*.[68] Others obtained secure positions
in local government. The office of Recorder – essentially a part-time
borough quarter-sessions judge – provided an assured income, while
also allowing the holder to continue to practise. Sir Edward Chandos
Leigh was Recorder of Nottingham for twenty-eight years, and
Alfred Chichele Plowden's Shropshire connections can have done
him no harm when he was appointed Recorder of Much Wenlock in
1878, a job that, on his own admission, involved very little work.[69]
Even more remarkable were a succession of Russell family appointments in Bedford. From 1912 to 1926, the Recordership was held by
Harold John Hastings Russell, a nephew of the ninth duke. And
from 1926 to 1948, he was succeeded by Victor Alexander Frederick
Villiers Russell, the third son of the second Lord Ampthill.

Many other lawyer-patricians decided that their best hope of
secure employment lay in moving into the civil service. Sir William
Alexander Baillie-Hamilton, a kinsman of Lord Haddington, was
Chief Clerk at the Colonial Office from 1896 to 1909. E. M. Sneyd-
Kynnersley, whom we have already met as a School Inspector,
deliberately gave up the bar because he was making no progress (and
no money) there. Likewise, Sir Kenelm Digby, after retiring from
his Oxford appointment, was a county court judge from 1892 to
1895 before going into the Home Office. In the same department,
patricians like Liddell, Leigh-Pemberton, and Lushington all joined
by that route. And one of Liddell's sons followed exactly in his
father's footsteps. He was called to the bar in 1872, and practised
very unsuccessfully on the northern circuit. But in 1886, he was
appointed Chief Clerk in the Crown Office, a post he held until
1920. His delight at abandoning the law for something more secure
was immense:

No one who has not followed the Bar and spent his time in
laborious idleness, with rare intervals of hard work done in terror

of failure, nor has not felt the degradation of a small attorney passing you by with contempt, and handing a guinea prosecution to the next man, or the apprehension of growing old in an unsuccessful life, can tell what a joy it is to me to quit the profession.[70]

But even this tenuous link between the land and the law did not last beyond the First World War. The cosy connections between the law and the civil service, which rescued many a frustrated and impoverished patrician barrister, broke down at the end of the nineteenth century, when the middle class professionals took over in Whitehall. In the same way, fewer aristocratic academics or Recorders were appointed in the inter-war years, and genteel judges were also much less in evidence. This in turn meant that the trend away from landed involvement in the law became self-reinforcing, since it no longer served even as an opening to other, non-legal careers. So, by the inter-war years, the law, like the civil service, was overwhelmingly in middle-class hands. To historians of the legal profession, it may be the *lack* of reform and professionalization that most stands out in these years.[71] But from the standpoint of the landed establishment, it is the changes in structure and in personnel that are the most significant – changes that were entirely to the disadvantage of needy patricians in search of a comfortable and secure career.

The same story unfolds in the case of the Church of England. But as the last quarter of the nineteenth century opened, the links that bound it to the landed interest were much stronger. For most parish clergymen held their public office essentially as the result of a private transaction with the owner of the right of presentation. In the late 1870s, over one-half of the 13,000 livings were in the gift of individuals, most of them, by definition, landowners.[72] Great magnates controlled appointments in abundance, like the Duke of Devonshire, who presented to thirty-eight parishes. And many lesser gentry nominated their relatives, or even themselves, to the one living they held: indeed, there were more than 1,000 parishes where the patron was also the incumbent, or boasted the identical family name. In the same way, the higher ecclesiastical appointments – to bishoprics and deaneries – were in the gift of the crown, which effectively meant that they were in the hands of the patrician political classes. As such, the Church of England was truly the landed establishment at prayer: rural, propertied, privileged, and suffused by a tone of aristocratic social authority. As one radical critic noted in 1873, it needed 'the help of divine grace to preserve it from an undue reverence for station and property.'[73]

Many younger sons of peers and gentry automatically went into the church – whether or not they had any great spiritual vocation or theological expertise – and were appointed to the local living which guaranteed a big house and an assured income for life.[74] The Revd Peter Leopold Dyke Acland was the fifth son of the tenth baronet. He became vicar of the family parish of Broadclyst in Devon at the age of twenty-six in 1845, and remained there for fifty-one years. The Hon. J. W. Leigh, younger brother of Sir Chandos Leigh, was appointed to the Parish of Stoneleigh in the late 1860s, and was thereafter Rector of Leamington Spa and of St Mary's Bryanston Square, until he returned to Severnside as Dean of Hereford in 1894. The Revd Sir Lovelace Tomlinson Stanmer was vicar of Stoke on Trent – where a relative owned the right of presentation – from 1858 until 1892.[75] The Hon. William Henry Lyttelton – younger son of the third Lord Lyttelton – was Rector of Hagley from 1847 to 1884. And Lord Curzon's father became Rector of Kedleston in 1855, the fourth successive member of the family to be presented to the living, and retained the position for sixty-one years.[76]

Inevitably, this meant that 'the leadership of the church was wealthy, aristocratic and oligarchical.' Dean Liddell of Christ Church (1855–91), Dean Stanley of Westminster (1864–81), and Dean Wellesley of Windsor (1854–82) were all relatives of peers, and when a replacement for Wellesley had to be found, it was argued that 'social position and superiority over others' was essential. During the first three-quarters of the nineteenth century, one-half of the bishops of England, Wales, and Ireland were of patrician background or connections, and in Ireland they were more aristocratic than in England.[77] In the mid-1880s, the fourth Lord Plunket was appointed Archbishop of Dublin, replacing Richard Chenevix-Trench, a member of the Ashtown family. He was welcomed by his brother primate, the Archbishop of Armagh, who was himself a great nephew of the first Marquis of Waterford, and who wrote Plunket a letter pointing out how comforting it was that the two Irish primates were distant relatives. Nor, in a world still dominated by the patrician élite, did this seem at all anomalous. As one contemporary explained, 'the bishop is a county magnate, and he associates with other county magnates, and his "light" and "sweetness", wines and dishes, are generally reserved for these.'[78]

At all levels in the church, this close patrician connection survived recognizably into the inter-war years. The Earls of Bradford presented to the parishes of Wigan, Blymhill, and Weston Under Lizard, and during the last quarter of the nineteenth century, all three were held by members of the family. The Revd Sir Francis Arthur Stanley ffoulkes was Rector of Hillington Norfolk, the family parish, from 1910 to 1936, and eventually inherited his brother's baronetcy. In reverse order, the Revd Sabine Baring Gould inherited the family estate of Lew Trenchard in Devon in 1872, and on the death of his uncle nine years later, appointed himself to the living, which he held until 1924. The Earls of Devon produced clergymen in successive generations: the fifteenth earl was Rector of Powderham from 1904 to 1927, and the sixteenth was Rector of Honiton from 1907 to 1925. Not surprisingly, one of the Lyttelton brothers was able to argue, as late as 1925, that 'it is easy to pick holes in the theory of squire, parson and tenants, but where you have the right people on the spot, it is found to be the best society of the kind yet devised by man.'[79]

Culturally, too, gentlemanly values lingered on in the parsonage. Like their cousins and contemporaries in the civil service, these patrician clergy were men of leisure, and played their full part in the social and public life of their class. Lord Curzon's father was a Justice of the Peace and a county alderman for Derbyshire. The Earl of Devon was not only Rector of Honiton, but was also mayor from 1929 to 1933. The Revd Thomas Mainwaring Bulkeley Bulkeley-Owen was a magistrate, a member of the Board of Guardians, and stood unsuccessfully for the first county council elections in Shropshire.[80] In another tradition, the Hon. and Revd George Thomas Orlando Bridgeman wrote a four volume history of Wigan Parish between 1888 and 1890, and the Revd Sir Henry Lyttelton Lyster Denning, seventh baronet, was editor of the *Genealogist's Magazine* between 1925 and 1931. But the most famous example of a squarson dilettante was Sabine Baring Gould. He fathered fifteen children, restored the parish church, and rebuilt the manor house. He wrote 'Onward Christian Soldiers', many novels, and several hundred articles. He produced fifteen volumes of the *Lives of the Saints*, edited a collection entitled *Songs of the West*, and was also a local archaeologist and antiquarian of note.[81]

Inevitably, this meant that in the higher echelons of the church, patrician bishops were also still to be found. There were survivors of an earlier era, like Lord Arthur Charles Hervey who was Bishop of Bath and Wells and the fourth son of the first Marquess of Bristol, and John Thomas Pelham at Norwich, who was the third son of the second Earl of Chichester.[82] Among a later generation, the Hon. Augustus Legge was the fourth son of the fourth Earl of Dartmouth, and was Bishop of Lichfield from 1891 to 1913. Edward Talbot, the grandson of the second Earl of Talbot, and himself married to a Lyttelton, was successively Bishop of Rochester, Southwark, and Winchester between 1895 and 1923. His near contemporary, Charles Gore, was a grandson of the second Earl of Arran, and was translated from Worcester to Birmingham and finally to Oxford. As his

46. Bishop Edward Talbot by L. Ward. 47. Bishop Charles Gore by John Mansbridge.

biographer put it, 'he had all the aristocrat's contempt for everything second rate or provincial or middle class'.[83] Lord William Cecil, a younger son of the great Lord Salisbury, moved from the family parsonage at Hatfield to be Bishop of Exeter. And Arthur Foley Winnington-Ingram, the scion of an ancient family of Worcestershire gentry, was Bishop of London from 1901 to 1939.[84]

These patrician prelates continued to live in a recognizably grand, superior, and dilettantish manner. Richard Chenevix-Trench wrote books of poetry, history, biblical exegesis, and patristics, and was one of the founders of the *Oxford English Dictionary*. When he was Dean of Westminster, Charles Gore took the greatest delight in pointing out his ancestor's tomb to visitors, and when he moved to Birmingham, the £10,000 he gave to endow the new bishopric had come to him under the terms of his mother's will.[85] Even more self-consciously grand was Bishop Talbot. He was related to both Salisbury and Gladstone, and was a frequent guest at Hatfield and Hawarden. While at Southwark, he played a full part in London society, and at Winchester, he lived like a grand seigneur. Nor did his aristocratic connections fail him when he went overseas. In 1912, he visited India, and was able to stay with his cousin, Sir Arthur Lawley, who was Governor of Madras.[86] As such, these baronial bishops had no sense of themselves as a separate, closed, professional

48. Bishop Lord William Cecil.

49. Bishop A. F. Winnington-Ingram by Sir Bernard Partridge.

caste: like their forebears, they saw themselves as part of a broader, patrician élite, in exactly the same way that Fitzroy and Walpole did in the civil service.

But as with the civil service and the law, these undeniable patrician continuities in the Church of England conceal fundamental changes that portended irrevocable decline. As Alan D. Gilbert has so rightly remarked 'the Church of England was involved inescapably in the slowly changing fortunes of Victorian landed society', and since these fortunes were now changing for the worse, the church was bound to suffer too.[87] To begin with, the abolition of purchase in the army and the implementation of open competition in the civil service meant that, by the last quarter of the nineteenth century, the system of irresponsible lay patronage seemed increasingly unacceptable. In 1874, there was a House of Lords Select Committee on Patronage, and four years later a Royal Commission on the Sale of Ecclesiastical Benefices. In 1898, a Benefices Act required the patron to give advanced public notice when exercising his right of presentation, and increased the power of bishops to prevent unsuitable appointments. In 1923, it became illegal for a clergyman patron to present himself to his own living, and in 1931 parish councils were given some influence in the choice of incumbent.[88]

These measures did much to erode the lay owner's virtual unfettered power of free choice; and the massive sales of estates before and after the First World War further undermined the old pattern of patrician domination. As a result, the number of private patrons fell dramatically in the fifty years from the 1880s, while the influence of the bishops in making appointments was greatly increased.[89] Gradually but inexorably, the balance of power in the church was shifting away from the old landed classes towards an increasingly centralized structure, dominated by the newly established Church Assembly, in which the bishops and the bureaucrats were becoming ever more influential. Accordingly, the diminishing number of remaining private patrons now had to consider broader and very different criteria of appointment from those that their forebears would have regarded as axiomatic. Property values and family connections were less likely to be treated as being of overriding significance: vocational training, professional experience and ideological compatibility were more important.[90] Taken together, these changes meant that the Church of England was no longer the landed establishment at prayer.

This decline in patrician powers of presentation was accompanied by the collapse of the church's economic position. The late-nineteenth-century agricultural depression has rightly been described by Geoffrey Best as 'the church's worst financial crisis since the middle of the sixteenth century.' Total revenue fell by between one-third and one-half, indigent clergy became a widespread phenomenon, and many could no longer even afford to marry. In 1837, the average clerical income had been £500; yet by 1901 it had slumped to £246.[91] Between 1885 and 1905, it became customary to give the Easter offering to the incumbent, and in 1897 the Queen's Clergy Sustentation Fund was set up. But this was to little avail. In the interwar years, clerical incomes remained as depressed as agriculture. In 1936, tithe was finally abolished, but on terms very disadvantageous to the church; and in 1939, nearly one-half of clerical incomes were still below £400, which meant that most clergy could no longer employ servants, and could not even afford a car or a phone.[92] In short, the church's close links to the landed establishment had not only made it politically vulnerable: they had also proved to be economically disastrous.

The result was a widespread collapse of ecclesiastical morale. In depressed and declining villages, where congregations dwindled inexorably, the parish priest seemed an isolated and anachronistic figure, a 'spiritually-minded vegetable'. Even Lord William Cecil admitted that his time in the family parish had been singularly unsuccessful: 'there is a terrible slackness and torpidity about religion in Hatfield; there is hardly any enthusiasm . . . Alas, what a confession of failure after twenty four years.'[93] In the towns, the church's hold was even weaker, and the decline in the numbers of new ordinands meant that there were now severe manpower shortages. Above all, there was a widespread anxiety at what Bishop Lord Hervey called 'the danger of growing infidelity'. By the end of the nineteenth century, it was chic – and it was middle class – to be an unbeliever, and for the first time, the best minds of a generation were outside the church rather than within.[94] In short, there was a general sense of discouragement and disillusionment and a feeling that, in the church in particular as among the patricians in general, the initiative and impetus had passed elsewhere.

But these were not the only developments that severely undermined the church's appeal to members of the landed establishment in search of employment. For at the same time, the clergy themselves were becoming more specialized in their conduct, more intense in their sense of mission, and more detached in their demeanour. From the mid-Victorian period, there were growing demands to raise and regularize the standards of knowledge at ordination.[95] They were increasingly expected to be competent theologians who could preach and teach, and capable bureaucrats who could administer parish affairs. By the late nineteenth century, many would-be ordinands were spending time at theological colleges like Ridley Hall, and in 1908, the Lambeth Conference called for a mandatory year of graduate training. At the same time, the financial arrangements were made more like those of a profession as a comprehensive and compulsory pension scheme was introduced between 1907 and 1926. The result, as one contemporary observed, was that 'the sacred ministry is a profession like any other, and . . . men "go into" Holy Orders as they go upon the Stock Exchange.'[96]

Thus professionalized, the clergy abandoned most of those secular functions that had been an integral part of their broader, patrician role in society.[97] From 1870 onwards, elementary education was gradually but inexorably taken out of the church's hands; among public school headmasters, genteel clergy like Lyttelton and Alington were increasingly unusual; and at Oxbridge, the position of Lyttelton at Selwyn and Talbot at Keble was quite exceptional. At the same time, the clergy abandoned their position as agents of law enforcement in the shires: in 1873 there were 1,043 clerical magistrates, but by 1906 the number had dwindled to a mere 32.[98] From the last quarter of the nineteenth century onwards, most newly ordained clergy either could not, or did not attend Oxbridge, they did not hunt and shoot, and they no longer played any active part in the politics or the administration of the county. Instead, they deliberately cut themselves off from the old, secular, landed élite, and

created for themselves a new, more intense and much narrower
rectory culture. 'The frock coated ally of the squire had been replaced
by a more narrowly professional, less pretentious figure.' And the
fact that *Crockford's Clerical Directory* began to appear annually from
1876 was a further sign of the new autonomy and self-consciousness
of the priestly profession.[99]

For younger sons in search of employment, the erosion in the
territorial connection, the fall in priestly incomes, the loss of secular
functions, the general decline in public standing, and the increased
professionalism meant that the appeal of Holy Orders was greatly
diminished during the fifty years from the 1880s, and that 'a family
living', had ceased to be 'a snug provision for a younger son.' When,
in 1898, Henry Jones published *An Entrance Guide to Professions and
Business*, he no longer put the church first, something that would
have been unthinkable only a generation before.[100] As A. C. Deane
explained:

> Many of those who a generation back would have taken Holy
> Orders in deference merely to their parents' wishes, and in order
> to succeed to the family living, now realise more clearly the claims
> and the responsibilities of the ministerial life, and refuse to enter a
> calling for which they feel they have no real fitness.

Instead, the average parish priest was 'drawn from a lower stratum
of society than used to be the case', which meant that the social
authority of the church was only further weakened.[101]

The inevitable result was 'an unbroken decline in landed and
peerage connections by birth and by marriage' among the bishops.
'In the old days', T. H. S. Escott noted, as early as 1885, 'the bench
of bishops was largely recruited from the sons of great families.' But,
he went on, 'this natural process of assent from the purple to the
prelacy has ceased to be the order of the day.'[102] Patricians like Gore,
Lyttelton, Talbot, and Cecil were superseded by such figures as
Bell, Benson, Davidson, Henson, and Temple, the members of a
new, professional élite, which was increasingly self-recruiting, self-
enclosed, and self-perpetuating. They were bureaucrats rather than
aristocrats, who sat on committees, wrote memoranda, and mastered intricate details of church policy and finance. Like the civil
service – but increasingly unlike the majority of newly recruited
clergy – there was continuity in terms of Oxbridge and public
school background. But like the civil service again, this disguised a
major change: the patrician prelates had emphatically retreated to the
margins.[103]

How did those dwindling numbers of genteel divines come to
terms with this very changed ecclesiastical world? One group re-

sponded by espousing a revived version of aristocratic paternalism, suitably redirected towards an urban environment. Such, in essence, was the Christian Socialist Movement, which gathered momentum during the 1890s, and which was dominated by such patricians as Gore, Lyttelton, Talbot, Scott Holland, and Winnington-Ingram.[104] They disapproved of profits, of *laissez-faire*, and of plutocracy. They supported trade unions, a minimum wage, and efforts to moderate unbridled competition. They disliked Joseph Chamberlain, imperialism, and the Boer War. When Winnington-Ingram became Bishop of London, he ordered a denunciation of slums to be read in every church in his diocese. And he and his colleagues chaired and dominated many important church committees, such as that on Christianity and Industrial Problems, and the Standing Committee on Social and Industrial Questions.[105]

They were not lacking in support in the lower echelons of the church. The Hon. and Revd 'Jimmy' Adderley was the younger son of Lord Norton, but was a strongly committed socialist. He spent the earliest years of his ministry in the East End, hated the plutocracy and 'the capitalist system of profiteering', and was a friend of Keir Hardie and Ben Tillett. But his memoirs were revealingly entitled *In Slums and Society*, and he ended his life in Saltley, a living that was in the gift of his brother.[106] Even more well known was Conrad Le Despenser Roden Noel, grandson of the Earl of Gainsborough, who was appointed to Thaxted by the socialist Countess of Warwick in 1910. He was a founder of the Christian Socialist League, and sought to turn Thaxted into a radical metropolis. He believed in collective ownership; he supported striking workers, both locally and nationally; he hung the red flag in the parish church; he opposed the celebration of Empire Day; and he even supported Sinn Fein.[107]

But this conspicuously aristocratic initiative accomplished very little. In one guise, it may best be seen as a vain attempt to regain lost social standing and moral authority. In another, it merely repeated in a religious and social setting the familiar arguments against the corrupting plutocracy which many patricians were making in Parliament at that time.[108] And the results were at best ineffectual, at worst ridiculous. The influence of men like Gore and Scott Holland was never as great as they thought it was; the church failed to win over the cities or the working classes in any appreciable numbers; the Christian Social Union had few plebeian members; and the Church Socialist League closed down in 1924. Men like Gore, for all their saintly aura, were regularly criticized for their ignorance of social conditions, for their exclusiveness, arrogance, and condescension. Asquith thought Winnington-Ingram 'an intensely silly bishop', and many others shared his views. Even Noel was more notorious than successful. Thaxted never became a socialist Mecca: it was the flags and the morris dancing that most people remembered.[109]

While these aristocratic crusaders were ultimately ineffectual, their few genteel critics in the church fared no better. Predictably, Lord William Cecil felt himself out of place in the early-twentieth-century church, because unlike many fellow bishops, he did not believe in socialism. But that was not the only reason he was an essentially peripheral prelate. Beyond question, he was a much-loved pastor: but he was quite unsuited to being a twentieth-century bishop. He greatly regretted leaving Hatfield (despite his own admission that he had not even been a success there), was hopeless at committees and administration, and was simultaneously both vague and authoritarian.[110] Equally out of touch was Dean Inge, the scion of a family of Staffordshire gentry, who was Dean of St Pauls from 1911 to 1934. Like the Christian Socialists, he too hated the vulgarity of industrial competition. But he also hated the working classes and the trade unions, thought that the servant problem was the most pressing issue of the day, and believed in eugenics as the best way to stop the working classes breeding.[111]

The degree to which the old territorial master-class had withdrawn from its control of the Church of England was well summed up in 1940 by a committee that had been appointed to investigate the church in country parishes. 'We regard', they concluded, 'the church's association with the land as out of date.'[112] Within half a century, the Church of England had ceased to be aristocratic and amateur, and had become lower middle class and professional. It was no longer primarily rural and rich, but was now urban and poor. The 'undue reverence for station and property', which had been the outward and visible expression of traditional territorial control, had indeed vanished. But as with the other professions from which the patricians had been driven, it was not 'divine grace' that was the explanation.

iii.   The Armed Forces

As the last quarter of the nineteenth century opened, it was still generally agreed that 'war is the occupation of the nobility and gentry.' Because they were the leisured class, they were also the fighting class, duty-bound and historically conditioned to protect civil society from invasion and disruption. Honour and glory, courage and chivalry, gallantry and loyalty, leadership and horsemanship were quintessential patrician attributes, inculcated in the country house and learned on the hunting field.[113] The majority of army officers were still recruited from the aristocracy and the gentry; their claims to command were based on character and social standing rather than expertise and professional training; they were at ease leading troops who were mostly from rural and humble backgrounds; and they regarded their occupation as the natural extension of familiar country pursuits. Moreover, the whole rationale of the purchase system of recruitment and promotion was that officers should be men 'of high social position, holding large possessions and attached to the Protestant succession', who would not form a separate 'military interest' that might threaten the patrician governing class. As the Duke of Cambridge explained, 'the British officer should be a gentleman first and an officer second.'[114]

Although it was the senior service, the navy was never quite so aristocratically appealing as the army: long spells at sea and in distant postings meant there was much 'hardship and separation from home life'; sailing and navigation were not skills that were an integral part of country living; there was no system of purchase to favour the landed rich; the prospects of prize money were extremely remote; and there were long periods on half pay.[115] Nevertheless, it did attract many patricians of less advantaged backgrounds, who turned to the sea as a lifelong career. Even if there was no purchase, good connections were indispensable both for initial entry and for subsequent promotion. In the age of fighting sail, technology was primitive, and discipline Draconian. During the mid-Victorian period, slightly less than half of all naval officers came from a titled or genteel background. And in the early 1870s, the majority of principal commands were held by notables: the Hon. Sir Henry Keppel at Devonport, the Hon. Charles Elliot at the Nore, the Hon. Sir James Drummond in the Mediterranean, George Greville Wellesley in North America, and so on.[116]

To a certain degree, these territorial traditions lingered in the armed services until the inter-war years.[117] As with the law, some heads of families continued to go into both the army and the navy, because their relatively impecunious circumstances obliged them to do so. The fourth Earl of Clanwilliam was an Irish peer, who owned a mere 3,500 acres in County Down worth only £4,305. He spent his whole life in the navy, eventually becoming C.-in-C. Portsmouth between 1891 and 1894. Two of the senior commanders in the Boer War were also the owners of relatively limited estates: Sir Redvers Buller was a classic red-faced squire, with 5,000 acres in Devon and Cornwall, and the third Lord Methuen owned almost precisely the same amount of land at Corsham Court in Wiltshire. The tenth Earl of Cavan, who was Chief of the Imperial General Staff between 1922

50. Lord Cavan.

and 1926, was descended from an Anglo-Irish family which held only 2,700 acres in 1883. Sir Philip Chetwode, who was C.-in-C. India in the early 1930s, was also the seventh baronet: but the family estates in Staffordshire and Cheshire scarcely exceeded 4,000 acres. And by the time Admiral the Earl of Cork and Orrery succeeded to his grand titles, the family's once great holdings in Cork and Kerry had been almost completely dissolved under successive Land Purchase Acts.[118]

But these impoverished notables were naturally outnumbered by the younger sons of peers and gentry. The Hon. Sir Henry Keppel, Queen Alexandra's 'beloved little Admiral', was the twelfth child of the fourth Earl of Albemarle. Lord Charles Beresford, who clashed so publicly and acrimoniously with Sir John Fisher, was the second son of the fourth Marquess of Waterford, and his autobiography began with a zestful evocation of his ancestors and of the Curraghmore estate. We have already met the Hon. Sir Neville Lyttelton, who became first Chief of the General Staff in 1904, albeit a pliant and ineffectual one.[119] His near contemporary, Admiral the Hon. Sir Hedworth Meux, was C.-in-C. Portsmouth between 1912 and 1916.

51. Lord Charles Beresford
by C. W. Furse.

In fact, he was a Lambton, the third son of the second Earl of Durham, but he was compelled to change his name in 1911 on inheriting through his wife the Theobalds estate in Wiltshire. Sir Henry Wilson, who was CIGS between 1918 and 1922, was the second son of James Wilson of Currygrane, County Longford, where the family owned 1,158 acres in 1878, worth a mere £835 a year. And one of his successors was Sir Archibald Montgomery-Massingberd, second son of Hugh de Fellenberg Montgomery, of Blessingbourne, County Tyrone, who acquired the second part of his Wodehousean surname in 1926, when his wife inherited Gunby Hall in Lincolnshire.[120]

Inevitably, there were many patrician officers whose territorial connections were much more remote. The most famous was the young Winston Churchill, who was commissioned into the Fourth Hussars in 1895. He was, of course, a direct descendant of the great Duke of Marlborough. But he himself was the elder son of a younger son, and had briefly toyed with the idea of going into the church. Two of the central figures in the Curragh 'Mutiny' were the brothers John Edmond and Hubert de la Poer Gough, both relatives of the Viscounts Gough, who owned 13,700 acres in Ireland worth only £7,900.[121] Admiral Sir Francis Bridgeman was a kinsman of the Earls of Bradford, and was First Sea Lord from 1911 to 1912, when he was

52. Sir Archibald
Montgomery-Massingberd.

unceremoniously bundled out of office by the former Lieutenant in
the Fourth Hussars, now First Lord of the Admiralty. Charles Vere
Townshend, the hero of Chitral and defender of Kut, was a distant
relative of the Marquess Townshend, to whose magnificent but
impoverished estates at Raynham he was briefly heir. And Admiral
'Rosey' Wemyss, who was First Sea Lord from 1917 to 1919, was
descended from a cadet branch of the Earls of Wemyss and March,
who had inherited Wemyss Castle and 7,000 acres in Fife during the
eighteenth century.[122]

In certain cases, this patrician involvement with the armed services
resulted in extensive dynastic connections, as son followed father
into uniform across the generations. Henry Keppel, 'Rosey'
Wemyss, and the Gough brothers were themselves sprung from
families with very strong military traditions. Even more impressive
were the Fremantles, cousins of Lord Cottesloe, who produced four
admirals in succession, spanning one hundred and fifty years service
in the Royal Navy, from the 1770s to the 1920s.[123] The last of the
line, Sir Sydney Robert, who was C.-in-C. Portsmouth from 1923
to 1926, waxed lyrical in his autobiography about his upbringing on
the Cottesloe estate, and aspired (in vain, as it turned out) to end his
own days 'as a country gentleman, taking a part in the political and
social activities of the neighbourhood, and enjoying such sport as I

53. Lord Wester Wemyss
by Sir William Orpen.

could afford.' But even the Fremantles were outdone by the Cochranes, Earls of Dundonald, where the military connection followed
the direct line of descent. The ninth, tenth, and eleventh earls were
famous sailors, but the twelfth earl chose the army instead since, as
he explained, his family 'had suffered in losses of property at home
from having been so much at sea.'[124]

Like the Cochranes, many of these military magnificoes were relatively poor. And many of them were Anglo-Irish – sailors like the
Earl of Clanwilliam, Lord Charles Beresford, and the Earl of Cork
and Orrery, and soldiers like Wilson, Cavan, and Montgomery-
Massingberd, to say nothing of those earlier men-at-arms such as
Wolseley and French. As Correlli Barnett has rightly noted, these
men were 'the nearest thing Britain ever possessed to the Prussian
Junker class', and even in the twilight of the ascendancy, a new
generation emerged.[125] The Hon. Harold Rupert Leofric Alexander
was the third son of the fourth Earl of Caledon. He was educated at
Harrow and Sandhurst, commissioned into the Irish Guards in 1911,
and but for the First World War, would probably have given up his
military career to become a painter. Emerging from slightly lower in
the landed hierarchy of Ulster was Alan Francis Brooke, sixth son of
Sir Victor Brooke, whose resources were so meagre that he went to
Woolwich rather than Sandhurst, and was obliged to postpone his

marriage for six years. And at the very boundary of the Irish landed ascendancy was the young Bernard Law Montgomery, whose father owned a mere 3,500 acres in Londonderry and Donegal, and who was generally reckoned to be the poorest Sandhurst cadet of his year.[126]

Why did these relatively unwealthy patricians continue to follow the drum? Paradoxically, it was partly because a private income was still the essential pre-condition for a military career. For as the examples of Brooke and Montgomery imply, it did not have to be enormous, but it certainly had to be there. As late as the 1900s, it cost £1,000 to buy the uniforms and the horses considered necessary in a glamorous cavalry regiment, and the cost of living was £600 or £700 a year in excess of the meagre salary.[127] As the son of an impoverished father, Winston Churchill survived in the army only by getting into debt, by taking up journalism, and by accepting gifts from more distant Marlborough relatives. Likewise, Charles Vere Townshend was paid an allowance by his cousin, the fifth marquess, until he was thirty-one.[128] And the navy was also a 'poor man's service.' The parents of Sydney Robert Fremantle were provided with a house on the Cottesloe estate, and Fremantle himself was given an allowance from his grandfather, which enabled him 'to enjoy a full social life free of serious pecuniary trouble.' And even during the inter-war years, the C.-in-C. Portsmouth was often an aristocrat, who was expected to enjoy the private income necessary to maintain the lavish hospitality customarily associated with the position.[129]

But it was not just that a military career needed private wealth. In the navy, it also required the support of what was termed 'social and family interest.' Admiral the Hon. Sir Henry Keppel vigorously promoted the career of his son, Colin, who ultimately rose to the peak of his profession. And Sydney Robert Fremantle owed his early advancement to the exertions of his father, who obtained a place for him on the flagship of the C.-in-C. Mediterranean in 1883 as a junior midshipman.[130] It was the same in the army. As his biographer explains, Charles Vere Townshend benefited from 'the incessant wire pulling of his influential friends', including Lord St Levan and Redvers Buller, to whom he was related by marriage. And the young, brash, ambitious, impoverished Winston Churchill was even more incorrigible. His mother lobbied the Duke of Cambridge to obtain his commission in the cavalry, and he himself approached Lord Salisbury requesting a posting to Egypt. Both Townshend and Churchill were eventually rebuked for their excessive and brazen importuning. But even in the inter-war years, connection still mattered. In 1930 there were two and a half times as many patricians holding the rank of major-general and above as there should have been on the basis of their numbers among more junior officers.[131]

Naturally, these men did not think of themselves as belonging to a separate caste, cut off from the broader aristocratic élite to which they belonged: on the contrary, they played their full part in the varied life of their class. This was especially so in the realm of politics and administration, where a younger son like Vice-Admiral Sir George Tryon moved with effortless ease from the civil service (where we have already met him) to sea-going command, to constituency politics. In 1882, he was Permanent Secretary at the Admiralty, in 1885 he was appointed C.-in-C. Australia, and two years later, he unsuccessfully contested the Spalding Division of Lincolnshire as a Unionist.[132] And throughout his public life, Lord Charles Beresford divided his time between the navy and the House. He began his Commons career as MP for Waterford (the family constituency) between 1874 and 1880, and ended it representing Portsmouth from 1910 to 1916, when he was followed by Admiral the Hon. Sir Hedworth Meux, who had just retired as the local C.-in-C.[133] Even more remarkable was Field Marshal Sir Henry Wilson, who retired as CIGS in 1922, became MP for North Down, and began to criticize in the Commons the very government he had recently been serving as a soldier.

Aside from their direct involvement in parliamentary life, many genteel officers were, by definition, closely related to patrician politicians. As a boy, Admiral Sydney Fremantle remembered being taken to the Lords to see his grandfather, Lord Cottesloe, in action. He was also first cousin to St John Brodrick, who was Secretary of State for War in Balfour's administration. Neville Lyttelton was an Eton contemporary of Balfour and Rosebery, and one of the reasons that he survived as Chief of the General Staff, despite widespread criticism, was that his brother Alfred was Colonial Secretary at the time.[134] Lord Charles Beresford and Winston Churchill were related by marriage, although this did not prevent them disagreeing violently in the Commons on naval policy on the eve of the First World War. In one generation, the Bridgeman family provided the professional head of the navy, when Sir Francis was First Sea Lord. In the next, it provided the political head, when William Bridgeman was First Lord of the Admiralty from 1924 to 1929. And one of the reasons why 'Rosey' Wemyss was appointed First Sea Lord in 1917 was because he was 'a naval statesman', 'a very sociable man . . . having from his youth been accustomed to mix in court, and high political and diplomatic circles.'[135]

Socially, as well as politically, these aristocratic officers were an integral part of the titled and territorial élite. The Earl of Cork and Orrery married the daughter of the Earl of Albemarle, and the Hon. Harold Alexander wed the daughter of Lord Lucan. Sydney Fremantle married his first cousin, and spent his honeymoon at Peper Harrow, a mansion owned by St John Brodrick's father. When Neville Lyttelton went to India in the 1890s, he fraternized effortlessly with the Viceroy, Lord Lansdowne ('an old Etonian Friend') and the Governor of Madras, Lord Wenlock ('my cousin').[136] Lord Charles Beresford was a member of the Marlborough House set, until his affair with Lady Warwick became the talk of London society, and led to a permanent estrangement from the Prince of Wales. He was also the man who dubbed Balfour's precious friends 'the Souls', and kept up a London establishment so splendid that Fisher claimed he could 'do more with his chef than by talking.' And Charles Vere Townshend was obsessed with his family's history and prospects. He wrote a military biography of the first marquess, did his utmost to rescue the estate from debt, bought back some of the ancestral pictures, and was himself buried at Raynham when he died in 1924.[137]

As gentlemen first and officers a long way second, these notable warriors could hardly be described as professional careerists. As Neville Lyttelton candidly admitted, 'to too many of us, soldiering was not a profession, . . . only an occupation', an opinion that the highly critical committees of inquiry in the aftermath of the Boer War did much to endorse. For most officers, soldiering in the 1900s was still primarily an endless round of polo, parties, and playtime. They were interested in 'exercise, companionship and enjoyment', but little else. Good breeding and good manners mattered much more than rigorous training or technical expertise. Hunting, shooting, and fishing took more time than routine regimental duties.[138] And in the inter-war years, after the horrors and irregularities of the trenches, there was an overwhelming desire to re-establish soldiering as a gentleman's occupation, which was once again primarily concerned with social and sporting activity. Above all, it was still dominated by the horse, the single most potent symbol for the traditional aristocratic fighting class. As Major-General Howard-Vyse explained, the 'constant association' with 'that comparatively swift animal, the horse, has resulted in quickness of thought and an elasticity of outlook which are almost second nature.'[139]

Even the navy, notorious for loneliness and isolation, provided ample scope for patrician style and indulgence. When the Hon. Sir Henry Keppel was C.-in-C. Devonport in the early 1870s, he naturally fraternized with the great county families of the West Country – the Mount Edgcumbes, the St Germans, and the Pole-

Carews. And he surrounded himself with a highly aristocratic entourage: Algernon Heneage was his Flag Captain and Lord Charles Beresford was his Flag Lieutenant. Keppel and Beresford regularly turned out with the Dartmoor Hunt, and many admirals like Fremantle, Dundas, Tryon and Wemyss found time and opportunity to indulge their love of hunting, shooting, and fishing.[140] The protocol of naval life afloat and overseas could also be exceptionally elaborate. When he was C.-in-C. China, Admiral the Hon. Sir Assheton Curzon-Howe regularly spent an entire afternoon setting out the dinner places, in a manner reminiscent of his viceregal namesake. And as C.-in-C. Channel Fleet, Lord Charles Beresford lived in what could only be described as 'the grand manner'. He brought his own retinue of liveried servants, gave majestic speeches to the ships companies, and was obsessed with ceremonial – 'endless pipings, callings to attention, and buglings.'[141]

Nevertheless, despite these undeniable continuities of patrician tone and personnel, the fact remains that by the inter-war years, the majority of officers were no longer being drawn from the old territorial classes. Inevitably, historians disagree over the precise figures; but there can be no doubt that from the 1870s onwards, the close connection between the landowning class and the warrior class was being inexorably uncoupled:

Table 6.1: Social Background of British Army Officers, 1870–1939

Date	Aristocracy	Landed Gentry	Middle Class	Date	Nobility	Middle Class
1875	18	32	50	1870	50	50
1912	9	32	59	1897	40	60
1930	5	6	89	1913	35	65
1939	< 8 >		92	1926	27	73
				1939	22	78

All figures are percentages.

Source: For 1875–1939, P. E. Razzell, 'Social Origins of Officers in the Indian and British Home Army', *British Journal of Sociology*, xiv (1963), p. 253. For 1870–1939, C. B. Otley, 'Militarism and the Social Affiliations of the British Army Elite', in J. van Doorn (ed.), *Armed Forces and Society: Sociological Essays* (The Hague, 1960), p. 100. Note: Razzell's figures relate to Major-Generals and above, while Otley's are restricted to the more exclusive group of Lieutenant-Generals and their superiors.

Of course, these figures must be treated with caution. The categories are not exactly identical, and the falling trajectory differs

significantly in detail. But they tell essentially the same story –
'a marked decline in the contribution of landed families.'[142] During
the early 1870s, the patricians were still the dominant element
in the officer corps. But by the inter-war years, that dominance
had long since vanished. In particular, there was a dramatic and
abrupt decline in the proportion of aristocratic officers at the end of
the 1870s, while after the First World War, contemporaries were
right to notice a sudden and 'marked shortage of young men from
the landed gentry' among new recruits.[143] The steeper decline revealed in the first set of figures shows that in the officer corps as a
whole, including a whole generation of new recruits, the patricians
were only a small minority by this time. But the more gentle falling
off revealed in the second table shows that, in the very top ranks, the
older generation of notables survived more tenaciously. And although
there are no equivalent figures for naval officers, the impressionistic
evidence suggests that the general trend was in markedly the same
direction.

How, exactly, had these changes come about? Undoubtedly, part
of the answer lies in the abolition of purchase in 1870. Instead of a
system based on property and patronage, entrance to Sandhurst and
Woolwich was based on a competitive examination, held under the
auspices of the Civil Service Commissioners. When introducing the
scheme, Cardwell tried to pre-empt patrician wrath by predicting
that competition would not harm their prospects. 'It is', he noted, 'a
libel upon the old aristocracy to say that they are ever behindhand in
any race which is run in an open arena, and in which ability and
industry are the only qualifications which can insure success.'[146] But

Among officers, as among bishops and civil servants, it was the
public-school middle class that superseded the country-house patricians as the dominant social group. In the 1870s, only 30 per cent of
officers had been educated at public school; by the Boer War, the
figure had doubled; and by 1939, the proportion was more than 80
per cent. Even the navy introduced a scheme of public-school entry
on the eve of the First World War.[144] In terms of their ethos, their
curriculum, their endowed scholarships, and their military governors and alumni, the very closest link between the public schools
and the armed services was established between 1870 and 1939. As in
other professions that had been simultaneously transformed, the
gentlemanly tone that survived was the product of education, not
ancestry. At the same time, there was also a conspicuous increase in
the number of middle-class military dynasties, famously exemplified in the case of Field Marshal Wavell, a Winchester-educated
son of the regiment. In 1870, 20 per cent of officers came from such
military backgrounds; by 1939 the figure was 34 per cent.[145]

as with the civil service, open competition did in fact spell the end of genteel hegemony. The aristocratic contingent among the officer corps dropped away sharply from the late 1870s, and the public schools soon became geared to training examination candidates for Sandhurst and Woolwich. In 1857, Charles Trevelyan had predicted that the abolition of purchase would 'draw the army to the middle classes', and subsequent events undoubtedly proved him right.[147]

In the navy, limited competition was introduced in 1870, but it was not until the time of 'Radical Jack' Fisher that more drastic reform was undertaken. As a middle-class, workaholic meritocrat, Fisher believed passionately that 'an exclusive system of nomination is distasteful, if not alien, to the democratic sentiment.' With pardonable exaggeration, he claimed that 'ninety nine per cent at least' of naval officers were 'drawn from the "Upper Ten"'. 'It is', he went on, 'amazing to me that anyone should persuade himself that an aristocratic service can be maintained in a democratic state.' The aim of his new common-entry scheme was that 'every fit boy' might 'have his chance . . . , irrespective of the depth of his parents' purse.'[148] By ensuring that executives, engineers, and marines were trained together for four years, first at Osborne and then at Dartmouth, Fisher sought to break down the social barriers that existed between them. Even after his departure from the Admiralty, some of his most cherished reforms were finally implemented. Just before the outbreak of the First World War, fees at Osborne and Dartmouth were reduced by 50 per cent, and the last shreds of the old system of entry by nomination were finally abolished.

Of course, as long as the cost of living remained high in the military services, this effectively limited the officer class to the well-to-do. But as landed resources declined, this 'social filter' increasingly came to work against the patricians, rather than in their favour.[149] By the 1900s, there were regular complaints that 'fewer country gentlemen can afford the requisite allowance for their sons. Expenditure all round has increased, whilst incomes – at any rate those derived from land – have shrunk.' Just as the new plutocracy were buying power and peerages, so it was feared that they were buying their way into the military élite. Even in the aftermath of the Boer War, Leopold Amery was prepared to defend 'an aristocratic class of officers.' But there was 'absolutely nothing to be said for a military plutocracy.' 'How many brainless sons of wealthy parvenus', he inquired, 'enter the cavalry simply and solely for the sake of the social connections they hope to acquire?'[150] And there can be no doubt that the sudden drop in gentry recruitment to the army after 1919 owed much to the breakup of estates at that time.

These changes explain why the armed services were becoming

more difficult for the patricians to get into. But they were also
becoming less attractive occupations, as war ceased to be a gentlemanly activity at all. Lord Cork and Orrery rightly described the
years 1886 to 1941 as 'a period during which the changes introduced
into the Navy far exceeded those of any other half century of its long
history.'[151] They saw the end of the age of fighting sail, and the
advent of the ironclad, the dreadnought, the submarine, the torpedo,
and the aircraft carrier. And in the army, the developments and
innovations were no less momentous. The Franco-Prussian War,
and the American Civil War, portended a new military era – of rifles
and machine guns, trains and telegrams, typewriters and telephones.
In the aftermath of the Boer War, the lance was abolished except for
ceremonial purposes, and khaki replaced red as standard peacetime
dress. The First World War spelt the obsolescence of the horse, and
the advent of barbed wire, poison gas, and mass, citizen armies.
From a patrician perspective, the pride, pomp, and circumstance of
glorious war was gone – and one of their traditional occupations
was gone along with it.[152]

Between them, these unprecedented technological changes meant
the end of the landed class as the warrior class. Instead of being the
natural extension of country pursuits, war had become a sophisticated, scientific, intellectual affair. As Cardwell had predicted in
1870, 'neither gallantry nor heroism will avail without professional
training.' And Lord Esher made the same point in describing the
amiable but ineffectual Lyttelton as CIGS: 'a strong character and the
most recent and wide theoretical experience are necessary. Amiabil-
ity and gentlemanly qualities take second place.'[153] Hence the new
courses in War Studies at Greenwich and Camberley. Hence the
stress on the properly trained professional soldier, rather than the
languid and dilettantish amateur. Hence the rise of middle-class
intellectuals, like J. F. C. Fuller and Basil Liddell Hart, with their
fanatical belief in mechanization. And hence a succession of middle-
class reformers, from Cardwell and Haldane, via Esher and Fisher, to
Hore Belisha. In all these ways, the initiative in military matters had
emphatically passed out of the patricians' hands: they were no longer
in charge.[154]

Most genteel soldiers regarded these developments with disapproval and dismay. As the officer corps became increasingly middle
class, they responded defensively by concentrating in the most
exclusive regiments, from which outsiders were still successfully
excluded. In 1800, patrician officers were widely distributed
throughout the army, but by 1900 they were crowded together into
'the regimental havens of social security' – the Life Guards, the
Grenadiers, and the Household Cavalry – which thus became the

most socially exclusive regiments ever. In 1914, 70 per cent of the officers in the First Life Guards were aristocratic, and another 18 per cent were from the landed gentry – far higher proportions than in 1830 and 1852.[155] And during the inter-war years, the remaining patrician officers became increasingly isolated and insulated from the nation as a whole, jealously guarding their regimental communities against the outside world. As Lord Dundonald—by no means the most reactionary soldier – once put it: 'I felt whenever I entered the barrack gate, no matter what people were outside, inside there were gentlemen, with the ideas of gentlemen.'[156]

Underlying these feelings of beleaguered introversion was a growing and snobbish hostility towards politicians and democracy. In the early 1870s, officers were very much divided – as were the landed classes as a whole – between Whig and Tory. But by the 1900s, the overwhelming majority were Conservative, and many were distinctly die-hard in sympathy.[157] In the 1880s, Lord Wolseley attacked 'the license of democracy and socialism', and 'the foolish public' who preferred 'believing the tradesman who has become a politician to the gentleman who wears Your Majesty's uniform.' To Lord Charles Beresford, the party system inevitably involved 'a sacrifice of principle.' And the Liberal governments of 1906–14 were viewed with hostility bordering on paranoia. At the height of the constitutional struggle in 1910, 'Rosey' Wemyss feared that 'if the radicals increase their majority, there will be no stopping the avalanche, and I think that Cannes or Rhodesia will be the places of the future.' And in 1914, the so-called 'Mutiny' at the Curragh was led by patricians like the Gough brothers, who despised 'these dirty swines of politicians', and were not prepared to assist in the coercion of Ulster.[158]

But it was the coalition government of Lloyd George that provoked their most bitter anger. 'Rosey' Wemyss contemplated the prospect of mass democracy with unconcealed disapproval: 'when every crossing-sweeper has a voice in matters, it is quite impossible for any government to rule.' And he regarded Bonar Law with withering scorn: 'what have we come to that we have to pick up our ministers from that class of men?' In the same way, Sir Henry Wilson despised 'the Frocks', for their ignorance, dishonesty, cowardice, and duplicity. He thought Asquith was in the pay of the Boche, and that Lloyd George was probably a Bolshevik. 'The Frocks', he once observed, 'have muddled everything, . . . everything. They seem incapable of governing.' By the time he entered the Commons, he had taken up with such Tory die-hards as Londonderry, Salisbury, and Northumberland. He was more than mildly anti-semitic, became increasingly authoritarian, and radiated a tone of disgruntled Blimpery which was widely shared during the inter-war years.[159]

But Lloyd George, at least, got his revenge. In his *War Memoirs*, his index contained this devastating entry: 'Military mind: narrowness of; stubbornness of . . . ; does not seem to understand arithmetic . . . ; impossibility of trusting; regards thinking as a form of mutiny.'[160]

Inevitably, most patrician officers were bitterly opposed to political reform of the armed services. As Lord Blake observed, the abolition of purchase was 'a semi-class issue, on which the vast majority of the upper ranks in the army were united with the territorial aristocracy against the reformers.' In the Commons, a group called 'the Colonels' opposed the measure with the most resourceful vehemency, displaying what John Morley later described as 'all the vigour peculiar to irritated caste.'[161] Col. Loyd-Lindsay argued that purchase ensured that officers were gentlemen, that 'the Queen's commission . . . was a passport to the best society, intellectual and social', and that officers needed inherited qualities that 'no examiner could ever bring to light'. Lord Elcho thought the scheme 'the most wicked, the most wanton, the most uncalled for waste of public money.' Lord Eustace Cecil canvassed opinion in the officer corps, and reported that virtually no one was in favour. And the Hon. Augustus Anson feared that the abolition of purchase would end the political subordination of the army. Eventually, the measure passed the Commons; but the Lords were so vehement in their opposition that abolition had to be carried by Royal Warrant.[162]

As reform accelerated during the 1900s, it was the patrician officers and their friends who took the lead in opposing it. Sir Redvers Buller was hostile to all technological change, claiming that in military matters, there was 'nothing new under the sun', and in 1909, the defenders of the lance actually secured its reinstatement as an offensive weapon.[163] When Arnold-Forster attempted to reform the almost moribund militia, in 1904, he was successfully thwarted by Lords Selborne and Cranborne, two 'good fellows and good militiamen', who 'naturally stuck up for a force they have worked so hard to save from decay.' They put pressure on Balfour and on Lyttelton, which effectively scotched his scheme. Two years later, R. B. Haldane was also obliged to face 'London society opposition', when he tried to transform the militia into the new Special Reserve. The county magnates, who regarded the militia as their exclusive preserve, refused to join the new Territorial Force or to let their men serve overseas, and carried their opposition to the Lords, where strong and stubborn speeches were made by the Duke of Bedford, Lord Wemyss, and Lord Raglan. But this time, it was in vain, and Haldane triumphed where Arnold-Forster had failed.[164]

Yet this was as nothing compared with the controversy surrounding Admiral Fisher's reforms. Undoubtedly, there were genuine issues at stake, concerning the disposition of the Fleet and the need for a Naval Staff. But as Lord Charles Beresford's biographer perceptively notes, there was also an 'ominous undertow': 'the latent contempt of the aristocrat for the bourgeois.' Fisher's background was as ungentlemanly as his methods. He was a poor, self-made man, who 'entered the Navy penniless, friendless and forlorn.'[165] He passionately believed in modernization and reform, and was idolized by the lower deck. He was unscrupulous and vindictive, and had no time for the old patrician guard, which he scornfully dismissed as 'the bow and arrow party'. Inevitably, he found himself opposed by 'all the armies of blue blood and society', including such aristocratic admirals as Wemyss, Meux, and Fremantle. But the leader of this 'syndicate of discontent' was Lord Charles Beresford. Dashing, brave, impetuous, well-connected, lacking in technical knowledge and strategic skill, he was the very antithesis of Fisher, whom he disparagingly dismissed as 'the Mulatto'.[166]

After the First World War, the same snobbish obscurantism re-emerged among senior patrician officers. On his appointment as CIGS, Lord Cavan disarmingly described himself as 'a poor common semi-educated soldier, who has . . . always hunted once a week and often more', an opinion which his predecessor, Sir Henry Wilson, fully endorsed ('ignorant, pompous, vain and narrow'). He had no experience of staff work, no discernible views on strategic issues, and was obsessed with the cavalry. He regarded Fuller's ideas as heretical, and tried to ban him from publishing them.[167] A decade later, Montgomery-Massingberd was even more incorrigible. He may not have been 'the almost criminally incompetent reactionary depicted by his bitterest critics.' But he did believe that hunting taught speed of thought, felt that 'character' was more important than 'brains', and regarded any evidence of independent or creative thought as 'disloyalty'. He hated Fuller, did his best to thwart his career, and roundly condemned his books – which he had never read. Nor was Lord Gort, CIGS from 1937 to 1939, much better. He did not want to 'upset people in Clubs', came to despise Hore-Belisha for his middle-class origins and Jewish background, and successfully intrigued to get him removed as Secretary of State for War.[168]

But however Blimpish their braying and bluster, these men could not stand against the tides of change indefinitely, nor conceal from themselves the fact that by the inter-war years, military service was no longer the patrician pastime it had once been. Among the dwindling number of new genteel recruits, men like Alan Brooke and Montgomery were professional soldiers rather than aristocratic *flâneurs*. In their single-minded dedication, they had more in com-

mon with the workaholic Fisher than the dilettantish Beresford.[169]
Meanwhile, for the older generation, there was nothing left to do but
to lament the world they had lost. In 1928, the dowager Countess of
Airlie accompanied the King and Queen to Aldershot, where she saw
for the first time 'the new, mechanised army.' 'There was', she
concluded, 'none of the élan and glory of a cavalry charge.' To Lady
Wester Wemyss, her late husband 'belonged to another world,
another age, an age of chivalry, of generosity, of . . . courage and
courtesy.' But it was Sir Neville Lyttelton who best summed up
these changes, in the closing pages of his autobiography. 'It is strange
to me today', he concluded, 'to scan the pages of the *Army List*, and
to find only a sprinkling of the old names. The old Army has
gone.'[170]

iv. The Foreign Service

Early in 1939, Sir Hughe Knatchbull-Hugessen, who was shortly to
be appointed British Ambassador to Turkey, wrote to Sir Alexander
Cadogan, Permanent Secretary at the Foreign Office, reaffirming the
traditional view that diplomats (and their wives) should be recruited
from only the very highest social circles. It was essential, he insisted,
that they should possess 'personality', 'address' and 'savoir-faire';
that they should be able to 'deal as an equal with foreign colleagues,
Cabinet Ministers, Prime Ministers and Heads of State'; that they
should hold their own 'with sovereigns and other royalties' in all the
nations of the world; and that the faintest suspicion 'of an inferiority
complex must be absent'.[171] In short, he believed that the conduct of
British foreign policy should remain where it had always been – in
patrician hands. For while the home civil service, the law, the
church, the army and the navy had been taken over by the middle
classes, the foreign service remained the one 'stronghold of privilege
and prerogative', which had 'again and again beaten off or baffled the
assaults of democracy.'[172]

In part, its uniquely genteel tone was set by the Foreign Secretaries themselves: Granville and Salisbury, Lansdowne and Grey,
Balfour and Curzon, Eden and Halifax. No other ministry was so
regularly headed by a member of the landed establishment. But the
full-time professionals – both in Whitehall and overseas – were
equally aristocratic (see Appendix C). Between 1873 and 1945,
eleven men held the post of Permanent Under-Secretary: nine were
peers, close relatives of peers, or bona fide landed gentry; only two
came from the middle classes.[173] And the department over which
they presided was unquestionably the most patrician part of the civil
service. Until the 1900s, the majority of new recruits came from

landed backgrounds: they were 'gentlemen by birth and habits and feelings.' In tone no less than in personnel, the Foreign Office retained the atmosphere of an exclusive club: there was ample time for society and the season, and in 1914 the total staff was only 176, of whom 40 were doorkeepers, cleaners, and porters. The Crowe-Hardinge reforms of 1905–6 undoubtedly made the place more efficient, but even in the inter-war years, it remained in many ways 'the last choice reserve of administration practised as a sport.'[174]

Compared with the rest of the civil service, the Foreign Office mandarins formed a small, separate, and exclusive enclave – detached, superior, understated, unflappable. And the career diplomats who spent their lives overseas were even more aristocratic.[175] In 1880, there were peers or relatives of peers representing the United Kingdom in Austria, France, Germany, Italy, Russia, Turkey, and the United States. Immediately before the First World War, virtually every major embassy was occupied by the head or junior member of a landed establishment family, and names like Lascelles, Lowther, Paget and Buchanan reappeared with monotonous regularity. Even in the 1930s, the picture was virtually unchanged: Chilston, Phipps, and Selby in Austria; Clerk and Phipps in France; Rumbold and Phipps in Germany; Perth and Loraine in Italy; Ovey and Chilston in Russia; Clerk, Loraine, and Knatchbull-Hugessen in Turkey; Lindsay and Lothian in Washington. Eighty years after John Bright had scornfully described the conduct of British foreign policy as 'neither more nor less than a gigantic system of outdoor relief for the aristocracy of Great Britain', it seemed as if little had altered. Only the court itself was a more noble profession.[176]

Why did this patrician preponderance continue for so long, in such conspicuous defiance of the prevailing trends of the time? In part, it was because recruitment was deliberately and successfully restricted to the highest social classes.[177] Before the First World War, it was essentially by 'limited', not open, competition. No one could sit the exam for the diplomatic service without a certificate from the Secretary of State saying that he was known to him personally, or had been recommended by someone whose judgement he trusted. In 1907, the power of nomination was transferred from the Foreign Secretary to a Board of Control, but this had very limited effect, since the members of the Board were themselves senior Foreign Office figures, who were equally concerned to preserve the social exclusiveness of their service. There were also significant financial constraints, since entry to the diplomatic service was restricted to those with an income of at least £400 a year. And there were stringent language requirements in French and German, which could only be met by prolonged – and costly – residence abroad and by a

54. Lord Hardinge by Sir
William Orpen.

stint with a crammer at home, usually at Scoones in Garrick Street.

But it was not just that entry to the foreign service required comfortable means and good connections: so did subsequent advancement. The best hope for any aspiring diplomat was to be placed in the entourage of one of the senior ambassadors. Lord Lytton began his career as an unpaid attaché to his uncle, Sir Henry Bulwer, who was Minister at Washington. Both Sir Horace Rumbold and Sir George Buchanan started out as unpaid attachés in their father's embassies at the Hague and in Vienna.[178] During the early stages of his career, Sir Cecil Spring-Rice benefited from the patronage of Lord Granville and Lord Rosebery. And for those who wished to obtain the very top appointments in the great embassies of Europe, the support of the monarch, the Prime Minister, and the Permanent Under-Secretary was essential. Thus, Charles Hardinge was greatly helped at the beginning of his extraordinary diplomatic career by the patronage and support of Lord Dufferin, and in the later stages by the active assistance of King Edward VII. And his own cousin, Sir

Arthur – who eventually became Ambassador to Madrid – no doubt benefited from the fact that he had a close relative so highly placed.[179] In such an exclusive and enclosed profession, aristocratic connection was by definition essential.

Like patrician politicians, these men were recruited very young, and they also lasted very long. Most diplomats came straight from public school or university, and embarked on careers that might last until they were seventy or even older. Inevitably, this meant that the very senior positions – both in the Foreign Office itself and also overseas – were usually held by people who had been recruited thirty or forty years before. The great ambassadors of the 1880s had come in during the 1850s, and those who reached the top on the eve of the First World War had begun their careers during the last quarter of the nineteenth century. And so it was the patricians recruited under the restrictive regime still in force in the 1900s who were just beginning to reach positions of real power and influence in the 1930s. Men like Lindsay, Perth, Cadogan, and Chilston – the notable high-flyers and high-flying notables of their generation – had passed their exams at the turn of the century, and thus maintained aristocratic style and genteel hegemony at the Foreign Office for almost two generations after it had vanished in the civil service, the law, the church, the armed forces – or even the cabinet itself.

For men like Sir Hughe Knatchbull-Hugessen, this was not so much anachronism as professional necessity, since it was widely believed that patricians possessed 'a certain advantage' in the conduct of international relations.[180] By definition, the gifts needed by the ideal diplomat – poise, elegance, refinement, *savoir-faire*, and easy confidence in dealing with ministers and monarchs overseas – were most likely to be found in those of authentically aristocratic background. Moreover, until the First World War, most western nations boasted crowned heads and elaborate courts at their apex, while European aristocracy was itself a continental caste. In these circumstances, it seemed both rational and necessary that diplomats themselves should be recruited from the same genteel backgrounds, that they could boast the appropriate number of quarterings (sixteen in the case of the Viennese court), and that they would be easily accepted into foreign high society. As Walter Bagehot once explained, 'the old world diplomacy of Europe was largely carried on in drawing rooms, and to a great extent still is.' And until the First World War, at least, the making of foreign policy remained the preserve of 'social oligarchies with an acute sense of class.'[181]

In terms of recruitment, promotion, and performance, the foreign service was thus strongly biased in favour of the titled and the genteel. But what, in return, was in it for them? After all, the junior posts, both at home and overseas, paid very little, if anything, while ambassadors regularly complained that the cost of living was higher abroad than in England, that the expenses of their job were such that they could not live within their official salary, and that they were out of pocket after a long spell in a great embassy.[182] But no patrician ever resigned from the foreign service on the grounds of impoverishment, and during the thirty years before the First World War, ambassadors' salaries ranged from £5,000 to £11,500, which meant they were among the most well-paid official jobs in the country. There was, admittedly, no additional entertainment subsidy, but there was a generous 'outfit' allowance which covered moving expenses. And during the inter-war years, salaries were reduced, but very substantial entertainment allowances (which were not taxable) were introduced instead.[183] For aristocrats of limited means, these were in fact very attractive financial rewards.

Nor were these the only benefits, since many of the residencies were very grand establishments indeed. The Paris embassy, in the Rue du Faubourg St. Honoré, was revealingly described as 'a perfect example of what a rich gentleman's house should be'.[184] When the Washington embassy was rebuilt in the 1920s, the architect commissioned was Sir Edwin Lutyens, the greatest country-house designer of the age. And these great mansions were maintained and furnished at the government's expense, there was often a separate summer residence, and a large staff was provided. The result was a scale of splendid and sumptuous living that none but the richest grandees could have afforded from their own resources. In addition, there was the allure of high society in the great capitals of Europe: many a diplomat's memoirs wax lyrical on the elaborate court ceremonial, the grand entertainments, the country-house visits, and the opportunities for travel, and for hunting, shooting, and fishing. As Bright had cynically – but correctly – remarked, aristocratic diplomats were always to be found 'where the society is most pleasant and the climate most agreeable.'[185]

But there was more to being an ambassador than subsidized socializing, however magnificent and enjoyable that might be. Before the days of international conferences and shuttle diplomacy, Prime Ministers and Foreign Secretaries left the negotiation of treaties and the conduct of international affairs to the diplomats on the spot, which meant that ambassadors possessed real power to make foreign policy and influence events. For twenty years, Lord Lyons was the most powerful foreigner in Paris; Lord Odo Russell was the most important ambassador in Berlin, the friend and confidante of the Emperor, the Crown Princess, and Bismarck; and Sir Julian Pauncefote was the doyen of the diplomatic corps in Washing-

55. Lord Lyons by C. Pellegrini.

ton, where he negotiated a remarkable series of Anglo–American agreements.[186] And in the 1900s, Bertie in Paris and Nicolson in St Petersburg were formidable and important figures, who refused to be constrained by their masters in London. Not for nothing was Bertie known as 'the Bull'. For men like these, the charms and scope of 'la haute politique' were very real and very great: arguably they had more freedom of action than any minister in Britain.[187]

Such work was also appropriately recognized and rewarded. Every diplomat who became a Minister Plenipotentiary and Envoy Extraordinary received a knighthood, usually the KCMG. Those who obtained a principal European embassy were invariably promoted to the GCMG. For those who captivated the monarch, there was the GCVO, which Edward VII gave out with especial lavishness. Those who held two of the great embassies were usually made

Privy Councillors and received the Grand Cross of the Bath. When they finally retired, Lowther and Monson were given baronetcies, while Horace Rumbold—who already had one—thought himself hard done by not to be given a peerage. Odo Russell, Pauncefote, Nicolson, and Esme Howard received baronies, Lord Lyons was created an earl, and Sir Francis Bertie was elevated to the peerage, and subsequently promoted to a viscount. For those who held the top European embassies, there were also foreign honours galore in the days before the First World War. The greatest garnerer of gongs among British diplomats was Charles Hardinge. His own country bestowed upon him a peerage, the Garter, the Royal Victorian Chain, and four grand crosses, and he also collected an unrivalled array of foreign orders.[188]

Without exception, these patrician diplomats were obliged to earn their living. As Sir Philip Currie explained (and as the younger son of minor gentry, he himself had good cause to know), it was only those of 'intermediate fortune' who sought recruitment.[189] By definition, it was extremely unusual for heads of aristocratic families to work, and those who made a career in the foreign service invariably did so because they could not afford a leisured life. Among those who rose high in the service, Lords Erroll, Vivian, and Perth were Celtic landowners of very limited acres, and Sir Arthur Nicolson was a Scottish baronet with distinctly meagre resources. There was also a significant contingent of poorish English patricians who were heads of families. Lord Lytton and Lord Sackville both became career diplomats because their estates were in precarious condition, and on Lytton's death, Queen Victoria helped out his widow by making her a Lady of the Bedchamber.[190] Sir Edward Malet's family held only 2,000 acres worth £2,700. And in a later generation, Lords Acton (Finland, 1919–20), Granville (Brussels, 1928–33), and Chilston were heads of families whose titles were distinctly grander than their means.

In the main, however, it was younger sons and more distant relatives who went into the foreign service. Perhaps the most bizarre instance was Sir John Savile-Lumley, an illegitimate offspring of the eighth Earl of Scarbrough, who became a diplomat, and served as Ambassador to Italy from the mid-1880s. But he then inherited the Rufford estates, whereupon he promptly resigned, and was ennobled as Lord Savile. Much more conventional was Sir Francis Bertie, the second son of the sixth Earl of Abingdon, who began as a Foreign Office clerk, but later exchanged into the diplomatic service, and was Ambassador to France for more than a decade. And Charles Hardinge was the younger son of a poor peer, who was able to satisfy the property requirement of the diplomatic service thanks only to a

56. Sir Frank Lascelles.

timely legacy from his godmother, Lady Lucan.[191] As with the army and the navy, there was also a strong Celtic contribution. Both Sir Henry George Elliot, second son of the second Earl of Minto, and Sir Francis Richard Plunkett, second son of the ninth Earl of Fingall, became ambassadors to Vienna. And between the wars, Sir Ronald Charles Lindsay, fifth son of the twenty-sixth Earl of Crawford and Balcarres, was Ambassador to Turkey, Germany, and the United States.

Some patrician ambassadors came from more distant branches of the family tree. Among the high flyers, Sir Frank Lascelles was the third son of the third son of the second Earl of Harewood, and Sir Gerald Augustus Lowther was the second son of the second son of

the first Earl of Lonsdale. Lord Odo Russell's father was the second
son of the sixth Duke of Bedford. When his elder brother inherited
the dukedom, he himself was granted the style and precedence of the
younger son of a duke. Even more distant, but still of 'Irish landlord
stock', was Sir Cecil Spring-Rice, the second son of the second son
of the eldest son of the first Baron Monteagle. On his death in 1918,
he left so little that American friends raised £15,000 for the benefit
of his widow.[192] Some were even more remote in their patrician
connections – and it is probably not coincidence that they attained
only those embassies that were correspondingly far away. Sir Arthur
Robert Peel, who was a distant descendant of the Prime Minister,
was Envoy to Bangkok, Rio, and Sofia between 1909 and 1931; and
Sir Charles Henry Bentinck, who was Ambassador to Chile between
1937 and 1940, was a kinsman of the Duke of Portland.

There were also diplomats who came from the gentry rather than
the nobility. Some were heads of such families, who achieved top
postings: O'Conor (poor Irish), Vansittart (poor English), and
Selby (disinherited English). In every case, their landed resources
were distinctly limited: all appeared in *Burke*, but none in Bateman.
Some were younger sons of gentry who could also claim noble
connections. Sir George Glyn Petre was the younger brother of
Henry Petre of Dunkenlaugh, and the grandson of the ninth Baron
Petre, and was Envoy to Portugal from 1884 to 1893. And in a later
generation, Sir William Esme Howard, the fourth son of Henry
Howard of Greystoke, and a kinsman of the Duke of Norfolk,
became Ambassador to Washington in 1924. Some were younger
sons of minor gentry families: Currie, Pauncefote, Ovey, and Scott.
And some were more remotely connected to the landed establishment. Sir Hughe Knatchbull-Hugessen was the grandson of the
ninth baronet, and also a kinsman of Lord Brabourne. As he explained in his autobiography, he had hoped to follow in the steps of
his forebears, and take up a political career, but the family resources
were inadequate and so he turned to the foreign service instead.[193]

So, despite the regular complaints that diplomacy was an expensive and self-sacrificing career, it actually appealed overwhelmingly
to those members of the titled and genteel classes who possessed
distinctly limited means. This is further borne out by the frequency
with which son followed father into the same profession. Like the
army and the navy, diplomacy was becoming a dynastic affair for
many needy patricians. Lord Odo Russell was – in Lord Clarendon's
words – 'not rich in worldly goods'.[194] Nevertheless, his second
son, Sir Odo William Theophilus Villiers Russell, joined the diplomatic service in 1892, and became Envoy to the Hague in 1928. In
the same way, Sir Augustus Paget, grandson of the Earl of Ux-

bridge, was Ambassador to Italy, and his second son, Sir Ralph, became Ambassador to Rio in 1918. And Sir Eric Phipps, who held three top European embassies between the wars, was the son of Sir Constantine Phipps, who had himself been Ambassador to Brussels in the 1900s. Sir Constantine, in turn, was the nephew of the Marquess of Normanby—who had been appointed Ambassador to France by Palmerston in 1846 when ill-health had obliged him to give up his cabinet post.[195]

Like the patrician civil servants in the years before the First World War, these genteel diplomats moved and married almost exclusively in high society – this time both at home and abroad. The sister of Lord Lyons was married to the Duke of Norfolk, and Lyons himself spent his summers at Arundel, Chatsworth, Knowsley, and Raby.[196] Lord Odo Russell could boast a duke for a grandfather and a brother, the daughter of a marquess for a mother, and the daughter of an earl for a wife. Lord Bertie included King Edward VII, the Duke of Devonshire, and Lords Salisbury, Rosebery, and Lincolnshire among his personal friends. Sir Cecil Spring-Rice was a contemporary of Curzon's at Eton and Balliol, and shared with Sir Esme Howard and Sir Edward Grey a love of the hills and dales of northern England. Spring-Rice actually wed the daughter of Sir Frank Lascelles, who was his Ambassador while he held a junior post in Berlin. And some diplomats married into the higher echelons of international society: Esme Howard's wife was an Italian princess, who converted him to Roman Catholicism; Sir Ronald Lindsay married twice, on each occasion to wealthy Americans; and Sir Augustus Paget's wife was the daughter of an Austrian count.[197]

Predictably, the public impact that such men made on the countries to which they were accredited was very limited indeed. As befitted their patrician background, they saw their task as unostentatious and gentlemanly statecraft, rather than vulgar public relations. They would deal with heads of state and foreign secretaries in person and by correspondence, but beyond that they would not go. Among French ambassadors, Lord Lyons was silent and shy, had nothing to do with the press, and never travelled even in France itself. Monson was diffident and bad tempered, Bertie never gave interviews or made statements to the press, and Hardinge was distant, taciturn, pompous, and dull.[198] Even in Washington, where social conventions were more relaxed, Pauncefote never gave interviews, and made few speeches. During the darkest days of the First World War, Spring-Rice made no effort to put the British case across to the American public. He refused to counter German propaganda, and was known as 'the silent Ambassador.' Esme Howard was an appalling public speaker, and Sir Ronald Lindsay gave his first press conference only a few months before his departure. At that time, it was still believed that propaganda and public relations were 'diplomatically dangerous, and anyhow quite unworthy of Great Britain.'[199]

In the same way, many diplomats looked down on the non-patrician politicians who were increasingly important from the 1880s onwards, and regarded democracy as 'government by the ignorant many [rather] than by the expert few.' They no longer viewed politicians as their social equals, and like the officer corps in the army, became increasingly conservative in their general outlook. In 1886, the young Arthur Hardinge thought of standing for Parliament as an anti-Home Rule candidate.[200] During the 1900s, his cousin Charles, and Arthur Nicolson, were both violently opposed to the 'wildcat legislation' of the Liberal Government, and especially to its Irish policies. Esme Howard was a bad party-man himself, and condemned party government as 'oscillating between two extremes.' And Francis Bertie thought 'politicians are everywhere a rotten gang. They think of party and place and power in preference to the good of their country.' But it was Lloyd George – who made no secret of his dislike for patricians and for diplomats – who roused their greatest fury. Charles Hardinge regretted 'his exceptional ignorance of foreign countries and foreign affairs', and his cousin Arthur dismissed him as 'the most dangerous and detestable of demagogues.'[201]

Predictably, most genteel diplomats knew little of trade, commerce, or big business. As *The Times* put it in 1886, they adopted a 'condescending, and even contemptuous attitude' to entrepreneurs; they regarded the consular service as a lower form of life; and many refused to soil their hands by lobbying on behalf of British business interests.[202] Even in a period of economic anxiety, they preferred the allure of high society and 'la haute politique' to grubbing for contracts and concessions. Like so many aristocrats, the majority regarded unbridled capitalism as dishonourable, corrupt, and immoral. Esme Howard was an admirer of Charles Booth, and hated 'the capitalist spirit which rates dividends as of more importance than flesh and blood.' Cecil Spring-Rice had no time for 'the Jews and the newspapers', or for Joseph Chamberlain and Tariff Reform, and regarded Newport society as 'the vulgarest in the world.' During the First World War, Francis Bertie vented his anger against 'financiers, mostly Jews or of Hebrew origin, and others who think only of money making.' And even in the depths of the depression, Sir Ronald Lindsay criticized the big business battalions of the American Republican party for their 'rapacity, blind egoism and moral insensitiveness.'[203]

57. Sir Cecil Spring-Rice.

Thus described, the foreign service as it existed between the 1880s and the 1930s seems fully to have deserved the strictures that Bright had levelled at it in the 1850s: it continued to provide 'outdoor relief' for the most needy notables; and it was exclusive in its personnel, aristocratic in its tone, and cut off from ordinary opinion both at home and abroad. From a patrician perspective, this was successful resistance to the tides of democracy. But this must be set in a broader context. For one inevitable result was that the foreign service seemed increasingly – and indefensibly – anachronistic. As the nobles and gentry ceased to be the dominant force in the government and administration of the country, the social distance between the diplomats, the politicians, and the mandarins inevitably widened. In the era of the common man, democratic government, and open diplomacy, the patrician exclusiveness of the foreign service was regularly and publicly attacked. And all the time, the middle classes were gradually but inexorably undermining this last exclusive enclave. Decline might be less rapid and less visible than in the other great aristocratic professions, but it was happening, nevertheless.

In part, this was because the original justification for appointing patrician ambassadors – that they were the only appropriate envoys

in an international polity that was everywhere courtly and aristocratic – abruptly vanished in the aftermath of the First World War.
In Germany, Austria, and Russia, the imperial dynasties were overturned, and with them went the hierarchical world of which pre-war
diplomacy had been an integral part. To the limited extent that
'society' survived in these countries, it was – as in Britain itself –
increasingly divorced from politics, government, and administration. And instead of a handful of embassies to the great powers of
Europe, there was, in the aftermath of Versailles, a proliferation
of minor legations to minor republics. The result, as Vansittart admitted, was the demise of 'a whole world of quarterings, sword-
play, mustachios and tight pants.'[204] Lord Bertie was the last British
ambassador in Paris to possess a state coach. International relations,
like domestic government, became more democratic, routine, and
humdrum. As Algernon Cecil put it, 'Diplomacy, once a question
between court and court, had now become a question between
people and people, and might thus be said to mark the conclusion
of one period of Foreign Office history, and the initiation of
another.'[205]

In this new and commonplace world, it was 'no longer enough
to know, as Lord Lyons always knew, what were the views held at
Chatsworth, Knowsley, Hatfield and Bowood; the whole nation
counts.' Instead of patrician reserve, ambassadors now needed to be
adept at public relations, and able to fraternize with people from all
classes and backgrounds. When Sir Hughe Knatchbull-Hugessen
was considered as a possible replacement for Sir Ronald Lindsay in
Washington, Roosevelt was distinctly unenthusiastic. 'How', he
asked, 'can a man with a name like that ever get his personality across
this country?'[206] And aristocratic amateurism seemed as out of place
as patrician exclusiveness. During the First World War, the Foreign
Office was compelled to take responsibility for overseas trade,
blockade, and contraband. 'Few of us', Knatchbull-Hugessen breezily recalled, 'knew anything about the normal workings of international trade.' But thereafter, with complex negotiations about
post-war loans and reparations, and with more general anxieties
about protection and Britain's own lacklustre economic performance, there were calls for diplomats to show 'a wider grasp of
commercial questions and of the importance of promoting trade in
unison with British political interests abroad.'[207]

In other ways too, diplomacy was becoming less attractive to
patrician practitioners. By the turn of the century, the advent of the
telegraph had robbed all but the most forceful ambassadors of much
of their autonomy: men like Bertie in Paris, who deferred to no one,

were already an exception. During the First World War, diplomacy was subordinated to military strategy, and Lloyd George further eroded the authority and influence of the foreign service. He believed that 'diplomatists were invented simply to waste time', and bypassed the official hierarchy by putting his own nominees in the most important embassies – Derby in Paris, Geddes and Reading in Washington, and D'Abernon in Berlin.[208] He took over the direct management of foreign policy himself, ignored and humiliated Lord Curzon, the Foreign Secretary, and inaugurated the first era of shuttle diplomacy, as he progressed around Europe from Versailles to Lausanne to Genoa to San Remo, meeting other heads of state, and negotiating directly and publicly with them. Inevitably, this 'travelling circus technique' was anathema to seasoned diplomats. It was vulgar, it was indiscreet, and it meant that the autonomy and importance of ambassadors was only further diminished: in his last years in Paris, even Lord Bertie admitted he was now little more than a 'damned marionette'. Instead of being practitioners of 'la haute politique', diplomats had been reduced to 'the delivery of messages and to [making] the preparations for ministerial visits.' And from this loss of prestige, they never recovered.[209]

At the same time that the politicians turned against the diplomats, public opinion did so too. There had been radical criticism of the foreign service in the years immediately before 1914, and for many people, the First World War itself was most plausibly explained as the outcome of secret and irresponsible diplomacy – an elaborate conspiracy conducted by the patrician diplomats behind the backs of ordinary citizens. Thereafter, post-war radicals denounced 'the whole of that industry of protocolling, diplomatising, remonstrating, admonishing and having the honour to be', which was 'in the hands of the British *Junkers*.'[210] In the era of Woodrow Wilson and so-called 'open diplomacy', there were widespread demands on the left to reform the 'whole corrupting system', to 'bring the diplomatic service into touch with democratic currents at home and abroad.' The problem with the 'old diplomacy' was that it was 'a conscious aristocratic instrument', which paid heed neither to people nor to Parliament, but was 'the last barrier interposed by providence between the English governing classes and the rising tide of world democracy.' What was needed, these critics insisted, was 'open' diplomacy: and the only way to have open diplomacy was to have open recruitment to the diplomatic service.[211]

Yet in fact, the pattern of recruitment had already begun to change by then. Even in the 1880s, a handful of middle-class men with public-school backgrounds were already getting in, like Eyre Crowe and William Tyrrell. But it was only after the reforms of 1906–7 that the social background of new entrants was noticeably widened to encompass the professional upper middle classes. Among the recruits of this period who were later to achieve distinction were Robert Craigie, whose father was a naval officer; Maurice Peterson, whose father was Principal of McGill University; Duff Cooper, whose father was a surgeon; and David Kelly, whose father was Professor of Classics at Adelaide.[212] The result was a significant broadening in the social mix of junior personnel. Admittedly, it did not extend far beyond the upper middle class, and it would be another thirty years before these men became really influential. But taking the long view, it is clear that, on the eve of the First World War, the patricians had already yielded their grip on the foreign service. At the very time when the radicals were beginning to protest against its continued aristocratic exclusiveness, the last bastion had already been effectively breached.

This was the position when the Macdonnel Commission reported on the eve of the First World War. Even allowing for the reforms of 1906, it insisted that the effect of recruitment procedures was 'to limit candidature to a narrow circle of society' – albeit a circle that was now upper middle class as well as aristocratic.[213] Accordingly, it recommended that the social background of new recruits should be further widened; that the system of nomination should be done away with and that the Board of Selection should be reconstituted; that the property qualification for the diplomatic service should be abolished; that the entrance examination should be assimilated to the rest of the civil service; that the foreign and diplomatic services should be amalgamated; and that adequate allowances should be given to those who were representing the country overseas. Between 1919 and 1922, all of these proposals were implemented, along with a further restructuring of the Foreign Office itself, which, combined with the increased pressure of business, made it less of a club, and more of a public institution.[214] Albeit two generations later, these reforms were as important for the foreign service as the abolition of purchase had been for the army, and the introduction of open competition had been for the home civil service.

The result was that by the inter-war years, the Foreign Office was more middle class than it had ever been before. At the very top, as the governing élite changed, there was a new order of non-patrician Foreign Secretaries: Ramsay Macdonald, Austen Chamberlain, Reading, Simon, and Henderson. Among Permanent Secretaries, too, middle-class men like Tyrrell and Crowe were now coming through. In 1939, there were non-patrician ambassadors in France, Germany, and Russia, which moved Victor Wellesley to lament –

quite correctly – that 'the grand seigneur type of diplomatist is a thing of the past.' Even Robert Nightingale, who had analysed the social backgrounds of ambassadors in 1930, admitted that there had been 'a well defined movement towards democratisation in the diplomatic service.' And it was this pronounced change in personnel that led many to argue, in the 1930s – like C. P. Snow's character Lord Boscastle – that the policy of appeasement was the inevitable result of letting the middle classes take over the management of the Foreign Office and the making of foreign policy.[215] As political analysis, this was at best a flawed interpretation; but as social observation, there was much more to it.

So, in the end, the story is familiar – but lagged.[216] On the one hand, as with the home civil service, the church, and the armed forces, foreign affairs became less attractive as a patrician career. On the other, it became more appealing for those many children of the professional and business classes who were public-school educated, and who were socially and occupationally ambitious. As the ruling élite in general became less landed and more diverse, even the Foreign Office was ultimately forced to recognize that aristocratic dominance could not last indefinitely. At the lower levels, if not yet at the higher, the poor gentry and the younger sons were being squeezed out, and it would only be a matter of time before the new middle class recruits worked their way through to the top. By the late 1930s, there were renewed demands for the further 'demo-cratization' of the service, and the Foreign Office set up a its own working party in the hope that it might forestall more drastic parliamentary reform. Despite the protests of Sir Hughe Knatchbull-Hugessen, the end of the road for the old guard was emphatically in sight.

v.   Conclusion: A Disguised Revolution

In 1856, Edward Stuart Talbot, the future patrician prelate, was sent to Charterhouse, where he enjoyed 'the companionship of a some-what unaristocratic class.' But his mother insisted that for someone of his background, this was, in fact, 'an advantage', and she pro-ceeded to set out for him the classic upper-class view of the pro-fessions. It was, she went on, 'the greatest mistake to consider the descendants in the second degree from the peerage as being only rightly placed among the aristocracy.' On the contrary, they formed 'a link with the working class of gentry', who carried down with them 'whatever is really good and highminded in the aristocracy', while at the same time 'looking upon those who are working their way in the professions as their real equals and natural companions.'[217] In short, there was the very closest link between younger sons and more distant relatives of the aristocracy, and those few select occupations that were deemed appropriate for gentlemen. And fourteen years later, Trollope's Mrs Marrable still had no doubt as to which those patrician professions were: the church, the bar, the army, the navy, and the civil service.[218]

Yet as Mrs Marrable reluctantly admitted, the world was going astray, and people were beginning to lose their landmarks. By the First World War, the patricians had yielded their pre-eminence in every profession except the court and the foreign service, and in the latter case, too, their days of dominance were numbered. Indeed, by the 1920s, the very idea that these once exclusive professions should exist primarily to provide safe and undemanding havens for younger sons and their more distant relatives was widely regarded as 'an injustice and an imposition.'[219] Here was yet another measure of landed-establishment decline. Of course, the fact that the younger sons of the country house had been superseded by the middle-class products of the public school was for many observers a 'gradual modification' rather than the 'radical transformation' they desired.[220] And there can be no doubt that in the civil service, the Church of England, the law, and the armed forces, the social background of the post-patrician professional élite was still very narrow. But from the standpoint of the landed establishment, there can be no disguising the magnitude of the change: in the professions, as in government, their bright day was done, and they were heading for the dark.

For it was not just agricultural depression and democratic politics that were the enemies of aristocracy: so, too, were bureaucracy, specialization and expertise. As society became more complicated, and knowledge more detailed, the old amateur attitudes and attributes no longer sufficed. As Harold Laski noted in a famous essay, they were 'a public danger in all matters when quantitative knowledge, unremitting effort, vivid imagination [and] organised planning are concerned.'[221] How, he went on, could Sir George Buchanan measure Russian military strength in 1914, when he did not 'even think it necessary to learn the language of the people to which he is accredited?' And how could the aristocracy be left to produce soldiers in this new era of mechanized warfare, when they still spent their time 'not in professional study but in the fulfillment of traditional social obligations?'[222] How, indeed? From a patrician perspective, the professional expert was as dangerous and as invincible as the common man himself.

7

THE 'CORRUPTION' OF PUBLIC LIFE

There is the danger of elevating too many persons, of too humble social origins [to the peerage], a process which, if accompanied by scandal, exposes the artificiality of the contrivance, and makes it the subject of public comment and ridicule.
(L. Stone, *The Crisis of the Aristocracy, 1558–1641* (1965), p. 66.)

History has yet to reveal – perhaps it never will fully reveal – the measure of corruption which Lloyd George permitted to enter politics during his six years as Prime Minister. There was another side to that brilliant sparkle . . . The world of Maundy Gregory was never far away.
(R. Blake, 'Baldwin and the Right', in J. Raymond (ed.), *The Baldwin Age* (1960), pp. 42–3.)

The fourth Marquess of Salisbury, and the latter's younger brothers, Lord Robert and Lord Hugh Cecil, seldom lost an opportunity of reminding the general public how standards were liable to slip once high offices of state were allowed to pass into the hands of men from outside the traditional ruling class . . . Underlying all these anxieties was a desire to return to an earlier period of aristocratic politics, when a handful of great families easily dominated public life.
(G. R. Searle, *Corruption in British Politics, 1895–1930* (1987), pp. 114–5.)

To some degree, the rise of 'independent conservatism' in opposition to the coalition government in 1921–2 was an aristocratic reaction, the response of the Salisburys, the Selbornes and the Devonshires to the passing of ancient patterns of deference, control and stability . . . Older landed proprietors, infused with a High Anglican sense of Christian obligation, abused the Coalition, and arriviste vulgar leaders such as Lloyd George, Horne or Birkenhead, for the sake of the deferential world they thought they had lost.
(K. O. Morgan, *Consensus and Disunity: The Lloyd George Coalition Government, 1918–1922* (1979), p. 160.)

As long as wealth and power in the United Kingdom were territorially based, it invariably followed that the status system was directly linked with the land. Titles of honour were virtually monopolized by the rich and the powerful, who were usually broad-acred; and the disinterested tone of public life was set by the same people, those men of affairs whose land, lineage, and leisure underpinned both their right to rule and their style of government. But inevitably, once one part of this interlocking élite structure of wealth, power, and status was challenged, the whole system was effectively at risk. And so, from the 1880s, as the patricians ceased to be either the richest or the ruling group, the status system that they had evolved, and the style of government that they had practised, were in turn fundamentally challenged and changed. New forms of wealth, and new people in power, demanded (and received) status recognition, and profoundly affected the whole ethos of public life. And, despite protests and laments, the gentry and grandees were unable to resist. As Gladstone had rightly foreseen, aristocracy was not only being undermined, it was also being corrupted.

One aspect of this major change was that the honours system ceased to be exclusively linked to the British landed establishment, but instead took on a separate and autonomous life of its own: it lost its essentially territorial and patrician character, and became plutocratized, and then democratized. The quantity of honours available was greatly increased; the number of people to whom they were given out was massively enlarged; the activities recognized and rewarded were much broadened in scope; and the social background of the recipients was unprecedentedly widened. Many of the people who did the state some service – whether professional or proletarian, in high or humble capacity – deserved and earned these new awards. But some of those who had accumulated vast new fortunes acquired their titles as they acquired their houses: by paying for them. So, as the peerage was permeated and polluted by vulgar new wealth, the status of nobility was correspondingly undermined. As had happened once before, the inflation of honours was accompanied by the trade in titles, and ultimately by public scandal.

Yet to many grandees and gentry, even this was but part of a broader and even more distressing trend: the general corruption – as they saw it – of the tone and standards of British public life by the power of the purse and of the press. As the Queen had observed of Rothschild, international capitalists and speculators lacked that literal stake in the country that only the extensive ownership of land brought with it. Such rich men, in Parliament and in government, were more interested in personal gain and financial advantage than in serving the public interest. And the simultaneous entry of so many poor men into the Commons gave them only added scope for manipulation and malevolence, as such people might easily become their clients. Hence the run of major financial scandals which rocked British public life between the 1890s and the 1930s, a sure sign that the old standards were under threat. Hence, also, the growth of a new, plutocratic, and irresponsible press, which further undermined the autonomy and eroded the decency of public life. High-minded men like Salisbury and Northumberland looked on these developments with dismay. But, as with their campaign against the traffic in

titles, they achieved very little; and for every patrician who ineffectually protested against such practices, there was another who was
tainted and compromised by them.

i. The Proliferation of Titles

In the middle of Queen Victoria's reign, Ulster King of Arms, who
was himself an expert on heraldry and genealogy, noted that 'while
in continental countries, honourable decorations and medals are very
numerous, in our own country, orders, decorations and medals are
very few and very sparingly distributed, and are only bestowed by
the sovereign for eminent services.'[1] As a summary of the British
honours system in the heyday of the patrician élite, these words were
apt. There were only five major orders of knighthood; most men
held only one of them at a time; and they were given overwhelmingly to landowners, politicians, and military men. Baronetcies and
peerages were awarded sparingly; they, too, were the almost exclusive preserve of the well born and the well established; and it was
generally accepted that a landed income of at least £2,000 was
necessary to keep up the position of a baronet, and £5,000 to sustain
the dignity of a peer. Men who received baronetcies were rarely
advanced by ennoblement, and multiple promotions within the
peerage itself were rare, unless you happened to be Wellington,
which few men were. Above all, there was no alternative status
structure in existence: the honours system was essentially patrician,
landed, and limited.[2]

Yet by the First World War, it had been fundamentally transformed, both in terms of the numbers and the nature of the recipients. And this change was widely recognized at the time, not least
by members of the aristocracy themselves. In 1914, Lord Selborne,
one of the self-appointed guardians of the nation's public morality,
admitted that honours were now given essentially for 'public service', an activity that he proceeded to define very broadly, not just as
imperial or parliamentary or municipal or party endeavour, but also
as encompassing 'eminence in commerce and manufacture, eminence
in art, including . . . the stage, eminence in literature, including . . .
journalism, eminence in science, and public benevolence and
munificence.'[3] Three years later, Lord Curzon agreed that honours
had ceased to be an essentially patrician prerogative. They were now,
he noted, 'a legitimate object of public ambition', and were therefore
'widely and generously diffused.' They were no longer 'confined to
any one class or caste in the country', but were given out to those in
almost every walk of national life. There had, he concluded, been a
'democratisation of honours.'[4]

Indeed there had, and the process was to continue and even accelerate during the inter-war years. To begin with, relatively junior honours such as knighthoods were given out much more freely, as old orders were extended, and new ones were created. In 1885, there were 230 Knights Bachelor, but by 1914 there were 700. Between 1868 and 1902, the Order of St Michael and St George was more than quadrupled, at each of its three levels. In 1886, the Order of the Indian Empire was created, with three separate classes, and ten years later, the Royal Victorian Order was instituted, this time with five classes, and with no upper limit on numbers.[5] In 1902, Edward VII added the Royal Victorian Chain, and inaugurated the Order of Merit, whose membership was limited to twenty-four, and in 1904 he instituted the Imperial Service Order. And in 1917 the honours system received its last and greatest enlargement when George V set up the Order of Companions of Honour, with 65 recipients, and the Order of the British Empire, with five classes plus a separate medal, and unrestricted membership. Like his grandmother, he also toyed with the idea of creating an Order of St David, to provide for Wales an appropriate equivalent of the Garter for England, the Thistle for Scotland, and the Patrick for Ireland. But this was one case of honorific inventiveness that did not come off.[6]

Nevertheless, this increase in the number of orders made possible an even greater increase in the number of recipients. The Jubilee of 1887 was the first occasion on which honours were given out *en masse*, and from 1888 they were regularly awarded at New Year as well as on the Queen's official birthday. Between 1875 and 1884, only 448 knighthoods of all kinds were given out. But between 1915 and 1925, some 2,791 such honours were bestowed, or over five times as many. And throughout the period from 1885 to 1944, the average per decade was well over 1,500. Even Lord Salisbury was moved to remark that 'you cannot throw a stone at a dog without hitting a knight in London.'[7] And this was only the tip of the iceberg, since so many of these new honours merely provided letters after the name, but no title before. The OM and the CH were restricted by statute, but the lower levels of the Royal Victorian Order were handed out in great profusion. Within two years of its foundation, there were 22,000 members of the Order of the British Empire, and by 1938 there were 30,000. Edward VII loved to shower decorations right and left; George V hated it, and tirelessly sought to reduce the numbers of recipients. But as his secretary wearily admitted, he was 'not very successful.'[8]

What did this sudden proliferation signify? As Selborne and Curzon had recognized, it fundamentally transformed the old patrician honours system, as many people now qualified for awards who came from very different social backgrounds. The two Indian Orders, the Order of St Michael and St George, and the accolade of Knight Bachelor, were primarily given to those professionals who had done the state some service either at home or abroad. The Royal Victorian Order was bestowed on those who had rendered special service to the sovereign, especially court functionaries, personal friends, and royal physicians. The Order of Merit was intended for intellectuals and military men, and George V was astounded to discover that one of its earliest members, the naturalist Dr Alfred Wallace, 'should avow himself to be a socialist.'[9] The first Companions of Honour included people in industry, agriculture, transport, nursing, and the press. And even the older orders were not immune from changes. In 1912, George V insisted that the Garter be bestowed on Edward Grey, the first commoner to receive it since Walpole, and a decision much criticized in smart society. And in 1925, it was given to Austen Chamberlain, who was not only non-noble, but non-landed as well.[10]

This broadening in the social background of those who received high honours was yet another sign that a more diverse governing class had come into being, of which the grandees and gentry were now only one part. But even more importantly, the establishment of the Order of the British Empire signified that honours no longer went exclusively to the élite, however much that was expanding and changing. For it was deliberately instituted to be the order of chivalry of British democracy, was designed to reward total war effort, and as such was given out at all levels of society, from royal dukes and the Governor of the Bank of England to factory foremen, munitions workers, and trade-union officers.[11] Indeed, so many were the awards that one early list covered sixty quarto pages of the *London Gazette*. There was, inevitably, much criticism and ridicule in consequence: the letters OBE were rumoured to stand for Order of Britain's Everybody, or Order of the Bad Egg; it was claimed that George Robey would appear on the music-hall stage in OBE trousers; and one particularly fastidious importuner for a knighthood specified that it must be 'not of the British Empire, no nonsense of that kind, but the real thing.'[12]

As the number of honours and number of recipients increased in this way, there was a corresponding urge on the part of those at the very top of the status hierarchy to protect their position, for honours proliferating were by definition honours cheapened. In 1813, Wellington had resigned as a Knight of the Bath when appointed to the Garter, since this was regarded as a promotion, not as an additional award. As late as 1872, the Earl of Zetland handed back his Thistle when given the Garter, for essentially the same reason. But by the late nineteenth century, the aristocratic conventions of promotion and abstemiousness had been superseded by a mania for collection and accumulation. The Earl of Rosebery was given the Garter in 1892 to which was added the Thistle three years later. The Marquess of Linlithgow was already a KT when he went out to India as Viceroy, and on his return he was given the Garter as well.[13] The seventh Duke of Devonshire had been content to be a KG, but his grandson added to this both the Grand Cross of the Royal Victorian Order and that of St Michael and St George. Other magnates did even better. Lord Curzon, as Viceroy, received the two Indian orders, to which he later added the Royal Victorian Chain and the Garter. And Lord Halifax collected yet more: both Indian orders, the Garter, the GCMG, and the OM.

These men were bona fide patricians, grandees who aspired to remain ahead in the new race for honours by collecting many more letters after their names than their forebears had possessed. As if to satisfy King Edward VII, they were 'plastered' with decorations in what had previously been regarded as a very foreign way.[14] But significantly, it was not only such authentic magnificœs who garnered such a glut of gongs. Soldiers of fortune like Kitchener, Wolseley, and Roberts were given so many orders and honours that they were unable to wear all their insignia: indeed, Roberts managed the unique accumulation of the Garter, the Patrick, the Order of Merit, and the Victoria Cross. And Rufus Isaacs, a self-made Jewish outsider, was able to collect four orders of knighthood in the course of his career, as well as one for his wife. Even a lower-middle-class provincial composer like Edward Elgar was generously and progressively rewarded: from a Knight Bachelor via a KCVO to the GCVO, the OM and a baronetcy, and he was much disappointed not to obtain a peerage.[15]

As Elgar's career suggests, baronetcies were also given out in increased numbers. As with the orders of knighthood, they were no longer rare, and they no longer went primarily to landowners. During the years 1875 to 1884, only 48 were bestowed; but between 1885 and 1934 the number awarded averaged 116 a decade. From 1915 to 1924, no fewer than 322 were given out; and between January 1921 and June 1922 alone, Lloyd George accounted for 74. Of necessity, these went to a much more varied class of person than hitherto. In 1905, a herald in the Royal College of Arms complained that 'not one in six of the newly-created baronets have any arms at all.'[16] Both Queen Victoria and Edward VII gave them to their doctors. Businessmen like Guinness, Coleman, Palmer, Morris, Brunner, Lever, and Wills also received them, in most cases as a

58. Sir Edward Elgar.

stepping stone on the way to higher things. Like the Order of the British Empire, the title of baronet lost its value by being given out too freely. When Hildebrand Harmsworth was thus rewarded, ostensibly 'for public services', his baronetcy was met with cynical amusement in his family, who knew he had 'never done a stroke of work in his life.' So they sent him a telegram: 'at last a grateful nation has given you your due reward.'[17]

The trends in the creation of peers followed an identical pattern. We have already established the fundamental change in modes of recruitment to the House of Lords, as owners of great estates were supplanted by state servants, professionals, and plutocrats, thereby making the peerage increasingly non-landed, middle-class, and permeated with new and vulgar wealth. But it was not just the scope of these new creations that signified a change: it was also the *rate* of ennoblement that was much increased. Between 1837 and 1881, new peers were made – regardless of the government in power – at an average of slightly over five a year. But from 1882 until 1911, the rate was nearly double that; and between 1915 and 1944, it reached more than ten a year.[18] The change in the 1880s was as dramatic in terms of numbers as in terms of background. In his first brief ministry, lasting only seven months, Salisbury created fourteen peerages, an unparalleled number for the nineteenth century in so

59. Lord Reading by G. F.
Watts.

short a time. Gladstone retaliated by creating nine in his equally short
administration of 1886. Thereafter, the rate of creation exploded. In
their seventeen years of office between 1885 and 1905, the Conservatives bestowed 146 titles at an annual average of 8.5. During their
nine and a half years in government between 1885 and 1911, the
Liberals averaged 10.5 a year. And even this was conspicuously
surpassed by Lloyd George, who created 90 peers between 1916 and
1922.[19]

But with peerages as with knighthoods, there was not only
unprecedented proliferation, there was also unprecedented *accumulation* of titles. It was not just that the process of advancement was
dramatically foreshortened so that some men might rise from knight
to baronet to peer in one generation, when in earlier times it would
normally have taken at least three; it was also that the process of
advancement from one rank to another within the peerage was very
much speeded up. We have already met Lord Reading, who accumulated four orders of knighthood: but in addition, between 1914 and
1926, he was successively advanced from baron to viscount to earl to
marquess.[20] Considering that he had neither sat in the Commons nor

held ministerial office, Lord Iveagh did even better: a baronet in 1885, a baron in 1891, a viscount in 1905, and an earl in 1919. And politicians could advance even more speedily. Max Aitken was knighted in 1911, less than a year after he had first entered British public life; and he was made a baronet in July 1916 and a baron in January of the following year. And F. E. Smith travelled faster and further: a knighthood in 1915 when he became Solicitor-General, a baronetcy two years later, a peerage in 1919 on his appointment as Lord Chancellor, a viscountcy in 1921, an earldom in the following year, and the GCSI in 1928 on his retirement from the India Office. Even then, he was annoyed not to add the Garter to his collection of glittering prizes.[21]

But the most famous instance of this voracious acquisition of titles by a non-patrician family was provided by the Harmsworth publishing dynasty. Between 1904 and 1939 five brothers amassed four baronetcies, three baronies, and two viscountcies. Most precociously successful was Alfred: a baronet in 1904, a peer sixteen months later, and a viscount in 1918. But he was soon caught up by Harold, who obtained his baronetcy in 1910, his peerage as Lord Rothermere in 1914, his viscountcy five years later, and was much put out not to be made an earl in 1922.[22] By comparison, the three younger brothers did less well: Robert became a baronet in 1918, Hildebrand in 1922, and Cecil was created Lord Harmsworth in 1939. Indeed, so frequently were these Harmsworths honoured and promoted, that the family thought of making special arrangements to cope with the news. When Robert received his baronetcy, his youngest sister Geraldine wrote to congratulate him. 'In view of the paper shortage', he replied, 'I think the family ought to issue printed forms, viz: "Many congratulations on your being made . . . (with a blank space to be filled in according to the dignity bestowed)".'[23]

As with peerages in particular, so with honours in general, the easiest route to a title was via the House of Commons, and the astonishing proliferation of non-patrician honours in this period is well shown by looking at the 388 Unionist MPs who were returned in the 'coupon election' of 1918.[24] Eighty-three of them eventually reached the Lords, of whom only 8 succeeded to titles. A further 89 became baronets, 94 were knighted, and 23 acquired other titles such as Privy Councillor or Scottish law lord. In all, 289 out of 382 MPs, very nearly three-quarters, obtained titles, 'a performance that is hardly likely to be matched.' Not surprisingly, when Ramsay Macdonald formed his first Labour administration in 1923, George V urged that a 'firm hand' should 'be kept on the distribution of honours. With the exception of the last government', he was told, 'the bestowal has been extravagant.' Indeed it had. But although the

60. Lord Birkenhead by
O. Birley.

excesses of Lloyd George were not repeated, the rate of creation
throughout the inter-war years remained much higher than it had
been during the mid-Victorian period.[25]

Here was a mania for peerages and titles so intense as to invite
comparison with that earlier period, from the 1780s to the 1820s –
but with the significant difference that this time, the new entrants
were not so much joining the landed establishment as overwhelming
it.[26] Inevitably, with peerages as with orders of knighthood, some
grandees with venerable but inferior titles tried to stay ahead of
these vulgar upstarts by getting themselves promoted still further. In
particular, marquessates were given out to patricians on an unprecedented scale, by both Liberal and Conservative governments. In
some instances – Aberdeen, Linlithgow, Zetland – this was merely a
single step in the peerage. For others – Ripon, Crewe, Lincolnshire
– they were the last of several promotions. And in three cases – Curzon, Willingdon, and Dufferin – they came as the end point after
elevation through most steps of the peerage. Yet by deigning to
compete in this way with parvenus like Reading, Iveagh, and Birkenhead, this only emphasized still further the extent to which the

patricians' position had been undermined as the supreme status stratum. One reason why Lansdowne and Salisbury declined the promotions Queen Victoria offered them was that they preferred to be venerable marquesses than instant dukes.

Not surprisingly, the successive Prime Ministers who were ultimately responsible for this inflation of honours viewed the whole process with distaste, regret, or downright cynicism. The constant clamouring for titles was to Lord Salisbury 'a revelation of the baser side of human nature', and his idea of a latter-day inferno was a place where 'unhappy sinners should be condemned eternally to the task of distributing two honours among a hundred people so as to satisfy them all.'[27] When drawing up the Coronation honours list of 1911, Asquith described it to Arthur Balfour as 'a task, as you well know, as uncongenial and even hateful, as can fall to a man.' After the First World War, Lloyd George told the King that he would prefer the OM to an earldom, and it is easy to see why.[28] Bonar Law spoke of 'the wretched honours list', and treated the whole racket with scornful indifference. 'Make him a duke if he wishes', he remarked of one constant importuner for a baronetcy. On his retirement from public life, Ramsay Macdonald refused the Thistle; Neville Chamberlain turned down the Garter and had been most put out when his brother had earlier accepted it; and neither took the earldoms that were their due. They had seen too much of titles to have any illusions as to their value.[29]

As early as 1912, Arthur Ponsonby noted how 'the tendency in recent years' had been increasingly 'to shower broadcast knighthoods, stars, ribbons, medals and crosses', which inevitably resulted 'in making them cheap and worthless.'[30] It was, he conceded, not yet as bad as in foreign countries, but he did believe that honours 'have already become common enough in this country to have lost all sense of distinction.' The system had expanded too rapidly, was of a bewildering and incomprehensible complexity, and the criterion for award was now unclear. In theory, the qualification was no longer ancestry or territory, but merit. Yet there was the rub. For how could merit be defined? And why, in that case, did some men receive titles at all? During this period, the patrician status structure was not just undermined by the proliferation of honours; it was further tarnished because titles that had once been highly esteemed were now being awarded to those generally acknowledged to be undeserving. As *The Banker* put it in 1927, the upper house was now full of 'gross, illiterate profiteers, doubtful in their reputations.'[31] But to the extent that that was indeed the case, then how had such unworthy men ever got there?

ii. The Sale of Honours

To the cynical, the bestowal of honours is rarely free from pecuniary considerations and calculations of self-interest. But from the 1820s to the 1870s, the working of the system in Britain had been relatively decent, was carefully tied to the landed class, and was, within these limits, both rational and orderly. The necessary precondition for a United Kingdom peerage was usually a certain amount of income that was territorially generated. If this was combined with electoral influence, long service in the Commons or to the country, the possession of a Scottish or Irish peerage, or with close connection to a great family, then a peerage might reasonably be expected sooner or later. But from the 1880s onwards, the terms of trade in titles were fundamentally changed: it was no longer land that was the major prerequisite, but vast riches, mere wealth, instead. And, inevitably, it was but a short step from money as a *qualification* for a peerage to money as the means of *obtaining* it. It was not just that more people were becoming peers, nor even that most of them were no longer gentry or grandees: it was also that some of them were actually using their great wealth to buy their way into the upper house. How did this happen?

When Ramsay Macdonald refused a title, George V quite understood, and said that 'if he were one of the new rich, the last thing he would do would be to run after a peerage.' But as Curzon more acutely recognized, the demand for 'social preferment' on the part of the upstart plutocracy was in fact 'insatiable.'[32] The career of E. T. Hooley well illustrates the extremes to which such men would go in pursuit of a title, albeit in his case, unsuccessfully. Among other things, Hooley was a company promoter who bribed impoverished landowners to be ornamental directors, and who eventually went bankrupt in 1898. But he also sought to obtain an honour, and used his money unashamedly to that end. One line of attack was to establish himself as a philanthropist by presenting a gold communion service to St Paul's Cathedral – which was subsequently returned for the benefit of his creditors. The other was to woo the Tory party: by becoming a self-financing candidate for a hopeless seat; by joining the Carlton Club and donating £20,000; and by trying to buy a baronetcy for £50,000 through a party intermediary in the Jubilee honours list of 1897.[33]

Throughout this period, these methods were used by many rich men, and often with much greater success. The most decent, since in some cases it genuinely denoted a generous character, was what Lord Selborne had called 'public benevolence and munificence.' One importuner offered the Bishop of Peterborough £50,000 for his diocesan funds if he could obtain a baronetcy for the would-be donor. Another was prepared to build a sea wall round Lord Suffield's estate at Cromer in exchange for a peerage.[34] The Earl of Iveagh donated nearly one million pounds to Dublin charities and London hospitals; the Harmsworths endowed chairs at Oxford and Cambridge, and gave money to Grays Inn and Westminster Abbey; and the Wills family provided over £250,000 for Bristol University. In 1911, Lord Balcarres reported that a rich man had 'been virtually promised a peerage in return for £120,000 or more which he is prepared to pay for an extension of scientific work in South Kensington.' And in 1916, Mr Arthur du Cros, a Conservative MP who had saved the royal family from embarrassment by settling some of Lady Warwick's debts, received a baronetcy.[35]

But the most remorseless exponent of philanthropic self-advancement was the American plutocrat, William Waldorf Astor, who deployed his $170 million fortune in a massive and sustained assault on the patrician status system in the years following his arrival in England in 1890.[36] He acquired London palaces, country mansions, a seat in Parliament, and a newspaper. He became a naturalized British citizen, published an elaborate genealogy which purported to trace his descent from French and Spanish nobility, and at a fancy dress ball in London in 1911, he appeared – ever subtle – clad in peer's robes. But in addition, he spent money, and spent it with all the lavishness of self-interested altruism. He bought the flag of the US frigate Chesapeake, against American bidders, and donated it to the Royal United Services Museum; he gave $100,000 to help the national effort in the Boer War, $250,000 to the universities of Oxford, Cambridge, and London, and $275,000 to charities and hospitals; and during the First World War, he donated $200,000 to the Red Cross, $175,000 to other public organizations, and $125,000 to a fund for the benefit of officers' widows. He duly obtained a barony in 1916, and a viscountcy in the following year. To the sceptical, the link between these events seemed clear: 'there is an undisguised conviction that the grant of honours in exchange for money, though the transactions are disguised, amounts to corruption.'

A much more certain way of purchasing a peerage was by making a lavish donation to party funds. The Corrupt Practices Act of 1883 markedly limited local electoral spending, but the result was that disbursements from party headquarters went up dramatically instead. Between 1868 and 1880, Liberal party central spending averaged only £4,000 a year; but the 1880 election cost them £32,000. By the 1890s annual outlay averaged £80,000, and Conservative spending showed a parallel increase. Yet still the costs mounted.[37] Between 1899 and 1905, Herbert Gladstone, the Liberal Chief Whip, raised and disposed of £275,000; by this time, the Conservatives were spending in the region of £100,000 per year; and the two general elections of 1910 reputedly cost each party £1 million. By the 1920s, annual Conservative expenditure – aside from elections – was approximately one-quarter of a million pounds. Politics had become big business, and it needed big money to finance it.[38]

There was, in consequence, an ever growing demand by the political parties for financial assistance from rich capitalists and plutocrats, and their support took a variety of forms. It might simply mean a donation of money either annually or in a lump sum, the subsidy of a well-disposed newspaper, or an offer to contest a hopeless constituency and meet the expenses. But inevitably, the donors were inclined to expect – or to demand – a quid pro quo for such outlay. Most of the money raised by Herbert Gladstone was put up by twenty-seven people, of whom eighteen were businessmen, and seventeen ultimately received peerages or baronetcies from the Liberals. One of them, Sir John Brunner, subsidized party candidates at elections throughout the north-west from the 1880s to the 1900s, and also gave financial support to Liberal newspapers.[39] On the other side, W. W. Astor had not only spent lavishly as a philanthropist, but had also been a regular and generous subscriber to Conservative party funds from the 1890s. By the outbreak of war, this had profited him nothing, and in 1916 he mounted a further financial offensive by donating £200,000 to the coalition government, of which £40,000 was intended for charities, and the remainder was to be divided equally between the Liberal and Conservative party funds.[40] As a result, his peerage and his almost immediate promotion were finally – and very expensively – obtained.

It is neither possible nor important to establish which of the two great political parties first began to trade honours for cash by these means. But it seems clear that, from the 1880s, Chief Whips on both sides came to recognize that generous party donations merited consideration when the honours lists were drawn up. In the early 1880s, when the Tories were in opposition, Northcote actually wrote to some party benefactors, reassuring them that the claims they had 'upon the gratitude of the Conservative Party' would not be forgotten. Akers-Douglas, the Chief Whip from 1886 to 1895, was involved in some transactions so indiscreet that, over half a century later, his biographer did not feel able to refer to them directly. But he certainly received some astonishingly frank letters, such as one from a man who was 'wishful to be created a baronet', who was prepared to spend on the party, but who wanted advice as to how this might best be done.[41] Under his successor, Sir William Walrond, it became increasingly the practice to accept money from men who were giving it with the clear expectation of future recognition. The decencies were still observed, and no honours were sold directly, but it was already rumoured – and the Hooley case lent credence to this – that men like Sir William Marriott, a former Tory MP of doubtful reputation, were acting as honours touts.[42]

The Liberals seem to have operated in the same way at this time. But in the early 1890s, there was a marked slide down the slippery slope that was ultimately to lead to Lloyd George and Maundy Gregory. After the two elections of 1885 and 1886, and with another looming shortly, the party funds needed replenishing. Accordingly, in 1891, and with Mr Gladstone's apparent approval, the Chief Whip, Arnold Morley, agreed to accept large sums from two men, and explicitly undertook to obtain peerages for them in the lifetime of the Parliament when the party was next in power.[43] Neither man was landed or particularly meritorious. The one, Sydney Stern, came from a Jewish banking family, had been Liberal MP for Stowmarket since 1891, and had no established reputation either as a politician or a philanthropist. The other, James Williamson, had been an MP since 1886, and was a large-scale manufacturer, but was unknown outside Lancashire. Their claims were less deserving than those of many other Liberals, but Rosebery – suitably prompted by Gladstone – had no choice but to keep his side of the bargain. Accordingly, in July 1895, Stern became Lord Wandsworth, and Williamson was ennobled as Lord Ashton.

For the first time, there was real criticism of the way in which such honours were being given out. In May 1894, there had already been a brief Commons debate in which an unsuccessful attempt was made to insist on a public statement of the services for which honours and titles were bestowed, as was already the case with the award of the Victoria Cross.[44] But these two undeserved peerages provoked much sharper criticism. 'There is no allegation', argued *The Spectator*, 'that either Mr Stern or Mr Williamson has ever done anything worthy of reward but supply the party war-chest.' *Truth* was even more outspoken: 'It is obvious that in these cases, the transaction has been a monetary one, for politically they are mere zeroes. Such bargains are . . . in their nature corrupt.' To make matters worse, these elevations coincided with the award of a baronetcy to Captain Herbert Naylor-Leyland, a mere youth of thirty-one, under the very dubious circumstances of changing his party allegiance and resigning his parliamentary seat. 'Such an apostasy . . .', thundered *The Times*, 'ought not to be singled out for honour by the responsible advisers to the Queen.' But it was Labouchere who summarized these developments most contemptuously: 'The money brought in by this trafficking in hereditary legislatorships reeks of corruption. It stinks.'[45]

The real furore caused by these three honours – and the significant use of the word 'corruption' for the first time in this context – meant that the Liberals were more careful in the immediate future. Herbert Gladstone as Chief Whip, and Campbell-Bannerman as leader, did their best to ensure that there was no repetition of this blatant transaction. As Gladstone later explained, he never hinted 'directly or indirectly at an honour', but 'there were certain men of wealth who had freely subscribed during the twenty years of Conservative supremacy . . . who gave me money and who did receive honours.'[46] Yet while rich donors were undoubtedly rewarded in this way, there was little if any direct bargaining, they had to be beyond personal reproach, and to be genuinely deserving in other ways as well. This may only have been a difference of degree: but it was a difference, nevertheless. The case of the abortive Horniman baronetcy illustrates this contemporary Liberal practice well. As Gladstone explained to Campbell-Bannerman, early in 1905, 'he has served in two parliaments, and has given an immense sum to the public in his museum. He has supported us handsomely, and is in all ways up to the mark.' It was agreed he should be recommended when the Liberals returned to power; but in fact he died before this was possible.[47]

In general, then, the position with regard to the granting of honours up to 1905 was as follows. They were not sold openly and in public for cash, and they were not sold indiscriminately to anyone who was prepared to pay. They were given only to party supporters; such people had to be of acceptable character and deserving in other ways; the reward usually came much later, and was rarely explicitly promised; and the money went into a party fund, not to the pocket of the party leader. *Officially*, Prime Ministers and opposition leaders knew nothing of the transactions between Chief Whips and donors: they did not know where the money came from, or the connection – if any – with honours nominations. But for all this decorousness, there can be no doubt that this was merely corruption in refined guise: in practice, party leaders knew what was going on; the terms of trade were clear; great philanthropy combined with great party donations did indeed have its rewards; and as such, titles were effectively bought for cash. As Herbert Gladstone more candidly admitted, 'the ice may have been thin . . . the letter of the law has not always been observed.'[48]

Moreover, although the decencies were thus publicly observed, the real position was generally known – and derided. The suspicions about the Liberal ennoblements of July 1895 had been well founded, as they were about Balfour's resignation honours of 1905. But although Balfour's names were much criticized for the 'furious ennoblement of mere financiers', as *The Spectator* recognized, 'we cannot honestly say they differ very much from those distributed

under like conditions on previous occasions.'[49] And George Bernard
Shaw made the same point in his play, *Major Barbara*, which,
significantly, opened in November 1905. One character in it ultimately becomes Lord Saxmundham, and does so by the following
means: '[He] restored the Cathedral at Hackington. They made him
a baronet for that. He gave half a million to the funds of his party.
They made him a peer for that.' The second sum may be too big; but
the sense that honours were effectively exchanged for a combination
of philanthropic and party donations 'corresponds fairly well to the
ethics accepted at the time.'[50]

During the next ten years, even this flimsy fig-leaf of propriety
was gradually cast aside, as party warfare became more bitter, and as
the cost of politics escalated further. Among the Conservatives,
standards had clearly been slipping by the early 1900s, and a long
period in opposition, with three general elections and another expected in 1915, could only have been financed by promising peerages
more frequently and less discriminatingly than before. While Acland-
Hood was Chief Whip, between 1902 to 1912, the party fund was
built up from literally nothing to £300,000. It was, admittedly, a 'fine
performance'. But as Bonar Law discovered when he became leader,
it had been possible only because 'a year's peerages have been hypo-
thecated.'[51] A high-minded Tory patrician like Lord Selborne
naturally regarded the sale of honours as 'debasing public morality
by enhancing the value of mere wealth'. But in 1913, when he sought
to raise the matter publicly as a way of criticizing the Liberals, he was
firmly told by Law and Lansdowne that the subject would embarrass
his own party almost as much as the government.[52]

On their side, the Liberals had their own obligations to discharge
after their long period out of power; and they, too, needed money in
unprecedented amounts to fight such frequent elections. So it is
hardly surprising that this was the period when they created so many
peers and that so many of them were businessmen. Of the fifty
people identified by the *Daily Express* in 1912 as 'Radical Plutocrats',
twenty-three received peerages and thirteen were given baronetcies
between 1906 and 1914.[53] From 1910 to 1912, Alec Murray, the
Master of Elibank, was Liberal Chief Whip. He was variously
known as 'a fraudulent little cherub' and 'the Master of Oilybank',
and he certainly drove the honours system especially hard. Too
many peerages were given out; they sometimes went to men whose
only qualification was indeed 'mere wealth'; there were rumours that
a secret election fund was being built up; and high-minded party
supporters in *The Nation* condemned this policy as 'the Achilles' heel
of Liberalism', an evil contaminating public life and discrediting
the government. And they were right. In later life, Lloyd George

recalled that one of Asquith's lists was so lacking in distinction that he, Masterman, and Reading sent a telegram 'congratulating him on one of his most flagrant honours lists, "all for merit"!'[54]

Twice before the outbreak of war, the subject was raised in Parliament. In July 1907, the Liberals awarded a knighthood to James Smith of Stirling, who was not only the chairman of Campbell-Bannerman's constituency association, but also the director of a local company that had knowingly supplied a defective rudder for a British battleship. Letters were written to *The Times* in protest. The *Saturday Review* explicitly stated that such honours were bought and sold. And in the Commons, Lord Hugh Cecil read out an extract from the *Daily News*, which observed that 'Rich men pay into [party funds] and are made peers. Poor men are paid out of it, and are made slaves.'[55] Then in February 1914, and despite his own leaders' discouragement, Lord Selborne raised the matter in the Lords, proposing 'that a contribution to party funds should not be a consideration to a Minister when he recommends any name for an honour to His Majesty.' He spoke of the widespread belief that there was a traffic in honours; that they were scoffed at in the press and on the stage; that Liberals and Conservatives were equally culpable; and that the real evil was the need to raise money for large and secret party funds. But for the government, Lord Crewe was urbanely unresponsive, the debate soon fizzled out, and the *New Statesman* dismissed the whole business as 'a storm in a teacup, and an artificial one at that.'[56]

This was the unseemly background to the Prime Ministership of Lloyd George, when the sale of honours assumed such proportions that what had previously been a patrician preoccupation became for a time a real public scandal. As A. J. P. Taylor rightly noted, Lloyd George 'detested titles. This, no doubt, is why he distributed them so lavishly.' The Prime Minister himself was unrepentant: it was, after all, a far less corrupt way of raising money for political purposes than was common in the United States, where businessmen expected to purchase influence rather than status.[57] But even so, he overdid it: he gave out too many titles and ignored the royal prerogative; he honoured many men who were undeserving and inappropriate; he raised too much money, which was for his own personal use; he allowed blatant touting to be blessed with official approval; and he bestowed these baubles indiscriminately on friend and foe alike. In short, he ignored the conventions largely followed before, which required that those given honours must be both party supporters and also acceptable for other reasons. But Lloyd George did not care who they were, or what they had done, or who they supported, so long as they paid. And as a result, he offended not only the self-appointed

Lord CREWE (to Lord SELBORNE on his way to the Debate on the Sale of Honours). "I trust we shall have no stone-throwing."
Lord SELBORNE. "I'm entirely with you. Too much stained-glass about, what?"

61. 'Lord Crewe to Lord Selborne', *Punch*, 4 Mar. 1914.

patrician guardians of decency, but (much more dangerously) his political enemies as well.[58]

As Prime Minister of a coalition, with no official party endorsement, Lloyd George needed money with which to fight the general elections of 1918 and 1922. The Conservative fund was exclusively for the use of the party, and the official Liberal funds were jealously guarded by the Asquithians. Accordingly, Lloyd George resolved to create his own personal campaign fund – ultimately amounting to more than £2 million – largely by the sale of honours to those 'hard-nosed men' who had done well out of the war, and who wished to establish themselves socially in the peace. There was even a recognized tariff: £10,000 for a knighthood, £30,000 for a baronetcy, and £50,000 upwards for a peerage.[59] And the recipients were very much as *The Banker* was later to describe them. In February 1919, for instance, the Prime Minister was warned that his belated New Year's honours list was a 'grave risk', since the 'bulk of the recommendations' were for '(a) the press, (b) the trade, and (c) capitalists.' To make it slightly more acceptable, Harry Lauder was added to the list with a knighthood. But Lloyd George really did not care. By this time, he was giving out peerages at the unprecedented rate of fifteen a year. Between January 1921 and June 1922, as the next general election approached, creations reached even higher levels: 26 peerages, 74 baronetcies, and 294 knighthoods.[60]

To give out so many honours on the basis of demand rather than merit necessarily required a centralized system of brokerage. Touts had probably existed since the 1890s, working independently and in competition. But sometime in 1918, Maundy Gregory was introduced by Alec Murray to Freddie Guest, the coalition Liberal Chief Whip, and he was put in charge of the whole business.[61] He was the son of a clergyman, left Oxford without a degree, failed conspicuously as a playwright, and served ingloriously during the First World War. Thereafter, he was set up in impressive, official-looking quarters in Parliament Square, full of despatch boxes and signed photographs of royalty; he edited a bogus but plausible newspaper, the *Westminster Gazette*; and he entertained both his clients and his masters in the ostentatious surroundings of the Ambassadors Club. He affected an air of well-connected importance and worldly-wise discretion. He claimed descent from eight English kings, was connected with many esteemed charities, and even boasted contacts at Buckingham Palace. He was the perfect front man to deal with naïve but wealthy importuners, and at the height of his fame he was earning £30,000 a year.

But this free-market system inevitably meant that many people who received honours were entirely unsuitable. Richard Williamson was given the CBE 'for untiring work in connection with various charities': in fact, he was a Glasgow bookmaker with a criminal record. So many men in London (or Cardiff, the stories differ) were dubbed undeservingly that it became known as the 'city of dreadful knights.' Rowland Hodge was made a baronet in 1921, 'for public services, particularly in connection with shipbuilding.' But in April 1918, he had been convicted and fined £600 for hoarding 1,148 pounds of flour, 333 pounds of sugar, 168 lbs 6oz. of bacon and ham, 29 tins of sago, 25 tins of sardines, 10 jars of ox-tongue, and 19 tins of salmon.[62] In June 1920, John Stewart, a Dundee whisky distiller, was given a baronetcy, for unspecified 'public services'. But in 1924, he committed suicide with debts of half a million pounds, and the £50,000 with which he had apparently bought his title was returned to his creditors. As one critic put it, 'gentlemen received titles whom no decent man would allow into his home. Several of them would have been blackballed by any respectable London club.'

62. Maundy Gregory.　　63. Captain Freddy Guest.

But there was worse to come, in the famous list of July 1922, where four of the five peerages awarded were, at best, dubious.[63] One went to Sir William Vestey, who had ostensibly rendered great service to his country in war by placing his cold storage depots at the disposal of the government free of charge. In fact, the company had been paid, he had moved his meat business to Argentina to avoid paying British taxes, and English people had thus been put out of work. Another new peer, Sir Samuel Waring, was accused of having made a fortune out of wartime contracts for military equipment, yet also of having abandoned those shareholders who had lost money by investing in an earlier and unsuccessful company of his. A third, Sir Archibald Williamson, was widely thought to have traded with the enemy during the First World War. And Sir Joseph Robinson was a 'Randlord', had already purchased a baronetcy in 1908, and was a publicly convicted swindler, whose appeal had been dismissed by the Judicial Committee of the Privy Council as recently as November 1921. The only name beyond reproach was that of Sir Robert Borwick, who was merely a manufacturer of baking-custard powder.

From George V downwards, opinion was outraged.[64] The King had already complained, both frequently and ineffectually, at the way in which Lloyd George ignored the royal prerogative by cavalierly giving out peerages without even informing him. But these most recent creations caused him to protest formally against what he described as 'the excessive numbers of honours conferred; the personality of some of the recipients; and the questionable circumstances under which the honours in certain circumstances have been granted.'[65] For, as he went on to explain, there was 'growing public dissatisfaction.' In the same month, *Punch* displayed a cartoon, with this dialogue beneath:

> Hostess: It's a great secret, but I must tell you. My husband has been offered a peerage.
>
> Guest: Really! That's rather interesting. We thought of having one, but they're so expensive, and we are economising just now.

And in *The Inimitable Jeeves*, P. G. Wodehouse also had his say, in a passage where Bingo Little explains why his recently ennobled uncle, Lord Bittlesham, has cut off his allowance: 'I suppose that peerage cost the old devil the deuce of a sum. Even baronetcies have gone up frightfully nowadays, I'm told.'[66]

Much more dangerously, Lloyd George also offended the opinion of the coalition Conservatives – the very people on whose support he depended in Parliament – by allowing his touts to sell honours, not just to his own followers, but to people of any political opinion who were prepared to pay.[67] Throughout the time of the coalition, the Conservatives kept their party funds separate, and tried to replenish them in what had by now become the customary manner. But on occasions, they found that Lloyd George himself was giving honours to – and thereby obtaining money from – some of their own supporters. Sir George Younger, the coalition Conservative Chief Whip, was constantly complaining that if he turned away importuners, 'they go straight to Lloyd George's whips' office, and get what they want from him.' Sir Rowland Hodge, for instance, was a Tory stalwart, but had asked too blatantly, had been refused, and so bought his bauble from Lloyd George instead. 'There must be a stop', Younger wrote in outraged tones to Bonar Law, 'to Freddie poaching our men.'[68]

Predictably, the high-minded patricians who had been vociferous in their criticisms even before the First World War now took up the matter with renewed vigour and concern. In the spring of 1917, Lord Salisbury sent Lloyd George a letter, signed by forty like-minded men, urging the need 'to keep our public life pure and free from reproach.'[69] In August of the same year, Lord Selborne returned to the fray in the Lords, proposing that in future, a definite public statement should be provided explaining why honours were being given, and also that the Prime Minister should undertake to satisfy himself personally that no payment or expectation of payment was involved. In reply, Lord Curzon claimed that there was 'no foundation' for Selborne's claim that there was trafficking in titles. But he was magisterially rebuked by Lord Salisbury: 'Does my noble friend really expect us to believe that the leading public men in this country do not know of the corruption that exists in the administration of honours?'[70] When the debate was resumed in October 1917, Selborne came furnished with examples, and reiterated the need to prevent honours 'being bought and sold over the counter like packets of tea.' With slight modifications, his resolutions were eventually agreed to.[71]

But in practice – as Selborne must have expected – these new rules were flouted and disregarded almost at once. In March 1918, he raised the matter again, complaining that the public statements provided in the recent New Year's honours list were inadequate; that they often failed to make clear the real grounds for an award; and that they were no more than a 'technical compliance' with his resolutions.[72] In November, he returned to the attack once more, this time arguing that there had been 'great carelessness and impropriety and considerable slackness' in drawing up recent lists. When some 3,000 people were being recognized each time, he went on, it was patently impossible for the Prime Minister to satisfy himself personally that *all* the recipients were worthy – as his second resolution had required. Accordingly, he proposed the establishment of a committee of the Privy Council, both to vet the people nominated for honours, and to provide a more detailed statement as to the reasons for the award. Once more, he was strongly supported by Salisbury, who argued that the House of Lords was – or should be – 'the guardian above all other bodies in this country of all that appertains to honourable distinction.' But the proposals were not accepted.[73]

It was only the notorious list of June 1922 that actually compelled Lloyd George's government to take notice of such criticism. In the Lords, Selborne described the award of a peerage to Robinson as 'nothing less than a public scandal of the first magnitude.'[74] He pointed out that Robinson had been a Boer supporter, that his business ethics were highly suspect, and that no one in South Africa or in the British government would accept the responsibility for having recommended him for a peerage. How, then, could it be denied that there was a traffic in titles, that the honours lists were inadequately vetted, and that the Prime Minister had again flouted Selborne's own resolution? Earl Buxton, a former Governor-General of the Union, endorsed Selborne's account of Robinson's dealings and doings. Lansdowne and Long described the award of a peerage to such a person as 'deplorable'. Salisbury pressed the government to say who had recommended Robinson for it. And Northumberland actually provided the figures at which different classes of honour were currently being bought and sold. In reply, and with a fine theatrical effect, the Lord Chancellor, Birkenhead, read out a letter from Robinson that he himself had drafted for him – declining the honour.[75]

But although this got Lloyd George temporarily off the hook, the matter did not end there, since there was a great agitation in the press, and a full debate on the subject in the upper house in July.[76] Lord Salisbury, who had been actively encouraged by King George V's private secretary to take a hand, described the administration of the honours system as being like a 'rake's progress', and proposed a joint select committee to investigate the way in which honours had been given out in the past, and to make recommendations as to future practice. Lord Selborne was understandably exultant that, after eight years of denial, evasion and procrastination, the government had finally been forced to admit the truth of his charges about the trade in titles. But the bitterest speech came from the Duke of Northumberland. He gave extremely detailed evidence of the way in which titles had been bought and sold, he condemned the Prime Minister for his recklessness and dishonesty, and he concluded by accusing the government of 'inaugurating a political spoils system such as has not been seen in this country for a hundred years.'

In the Commons, Lloyd George had initially intended to brazen things out. But he was so mercilessly hounded and harried by Lord Henry Bentinck, Lords Hugh and Robert Cecil, Aubrey Herbert, Jack Seely, and Henry Page Croft, that he was compelled to concede a debate, on a motion signed by nearly 300 MPs, requesting the same joint select committee that was simultaneously being asked for in the Lords.[77] It was proposed and seconded by Locker Lampson and Sam Hoare, and many patricians spoke in the ensuing debate.[78] Page Croft regretted the falling away of 'the high traditions and the noble principles of our public life'. Lane-Fox, Seely, Herbert, and Claude Lowther waxed eloquently indignant about the corruption of public life and the undermining of the House of Lords. And Lord Robert Cecil echoed the words of his elder brother and the Duke of Northumberland: 'If it once becomes understood that subscriptions to party funds will be followed by the granting of honours, you are very far down the slope that leads to corruption.' In reply, Lloyd George made a speech so feeble and so irrelevant that Winston Churchill thought it quite the worst of his life.

But even now, the Prime Minister was able to avoid the searching inquiry that his aristocratic critics so vehemently desired.[79] On the highly tendentious grounds that the awarding of honours was a matter touching the royal prerogative, he suggested that a joint select committee was inappropriate, and offered instead a royal commission. This meant that the government would have a greater say in its

"I COULD NOT LOVE THEE, DEAR, SO MUCH,
LOVED I NOT HONOURS MORE."

64. '"I could not love thee, dear, so much, loved I not Honours more."' *Punch*, 26 July 1922.

composition, that men like Salisbury, Selborne, and Northumberland were kept off, and that there was no compulsion to accept its recommendations. In addition, by persuading the Commons that its terms of reference should be 'to advise on the procedure to be adopted in *future* to assist the Prime Minister in making recommendations of persons deserving special honour', Lloyd George was able to ensure that there was very limited inquiry into past practice. And in any case, by the time the royal commission reported, the Lloyd George coalition had fallen.[80] But its two major recommendations were accepted. A Political Honours Scrutiny Committee was immediately set up, consisting of three Privy Councillors, not in the government, to vet the names of proposed recipients. And the Honours (Prevention of Abuses) Act was eventually passed in 1925, which finally made it a criminal offence to traffic in titles.

But what in practice had all this achieved? How far did the high-minded grandees succeed in stamping out these abuses which, they felt, so debased public life, so undermined the upper house, and so corrupted the notion of aristocracy? Undeniably, the honours scandal had helped to hasten the demise of the Lloyd George ministry, and the measures that Selborne and Salisbury had asked for had to some extent been conceded. But Lloyd George himself wriggled free, and was ultimately allowed to retain control of the special fund that had been built up for him by the sale of honours.[81] And after his fall, trafficking in titles was not completely stamped out. Nor should this come as any surprise. There were still rich men wanting to buy social status and public honour, and there were still political parties needing to raise money. Even allowing for the legislation of 1925, the sale of honours was almost bound to continue, albeit in a less blatant way. In essence, all that was achieved was a return to the more discreet, but hardly less corrupt, arrangements that had prevailed before Murray, and then Lloyd George, had run the system too hard and too publicly.

Even Ramsay Macdonald, who genuinely sought to be high-minded about honours, soon got into trouble.[82] His finances had always been precarious, and in 1924, when he became Prime Minister, his friend Alexander Grant lent him a Daimler and £40,000, 'so that I may not require, whilst absorbed in public duties, to worry about income.' Most of the money was in the form of preference shares in Grant's company of McVitie and Price; it was to be returned at the end of Macdonald's time in office; and in the meantime, he was to enjoy only the dividends. But in June 1924, Grant was made a baronet, and there was an outcry that the old abuses were being resumed once more. ('Every man has his price', said the wits, 'but not every man has his McVitie and Price.')[83] In fact, Grant's philanthropic activities more than entitled him to the honour, and it seems clear that in Macdonald's mind there was no connection whatsoever between the gift and the gong. But as his biographer admits, it was 'an act of remarkable folly', made worse because the news leaked out, and because Macdonald's embarrassed innocent, unworldly, and evasive response made him seem like a second Lloyd George. At the end of the year, he returned both the car and the shares.

Where Macdonald was merely naïve, the Conservatives were more disingenuous. It was true that on becoming Prime Minister, Bonar Law told J. C. C. Davidson to 'clean up Downing Street', and that Gregory's organization was infiltrated and undermined by Davidson's agents.[84] But the Conservatives had sold honours in the coalition: what they had really resented was that Lloyd George's touts had sometimes poached their own men, and that the system had been run so indiscreetly that the result was a scandal. As Davidson later admitted, it was the '*blatant* selling of honours for party funds' that they disapproved of, not the selling itself. Indeed, while he was party treasurer, Davidson raised three million pounds for the Conservatives, and it seems clear he did it in the traditional way.[85] Two of the greatest benefactors of Ashridge, Sir Edward Brotherton and Urban Broughton, became peers; while the third, Lord Inchcape, was advanced from viscount to earl. In Baldwin's Tory party, rich men still importuned for honours, and often did so successfully. As John Ramsden rightly concludes, 'It seems clear that, apart from tidying up the worst excesses of the Lloyd George Coalition, Davidson did not materially alter his party's attitude to honours.'[86]

The real proof of this is to be found in the way in which Gregory himself was finally dealt with. Davidson's success in infiltrating Gregory's organization meant that the names of his clients were found out, steps were taken to ensure that they did not receive an honour, and Gregory was thus no longer able to deliver the goods.[87] In 1932, by which time he was pressed for money, he tried to sell a knighthood to Commander Billyard-Leake, who unfortunately for Gregory turned out to be a well-connected man of impeccable credentials. He alerted the police, Gregory was arrested under the Honours (Prevention of Abuses) Act, and was duly sent for trial. But there was a real danger that he would plead not guilty, that he would reveal the full details of his operation, and that he would divulge the names of all those who had been involved, thereby creating an even greater scandal. Eventually, he was persuaded to plead guilty; the trial was a brief and cursory affair; and he was given the lightest possible sentence of two months and a £50 fine. After his release, he lived in Dieppe on a pension of £2,000 a year, claiming to be Sir Arthur Gregory; and he died abroad in 1941.

But, as befitted his career, Gregory's silence was bought only at a price, and with a title. His pension was paid for by one Sir Julien Chan, a sporting philanthropist, who had been knighted in 1929. In 1933, Baldwin went to Macdonald with a request that Chan be given a baronetcy, essentially in return for his generosity in buying Gregory off. Macdonald initially refused: he regarded Chan as 'just the sort of man I should not dream of honouring', and had already turned away friends who had importuned on his behalf. But although he held out for six months, Baldwin was adamant: he told Macdonald that many famous names were involved, he made it clear that they came from all parties, and hinted that they included Clynes and Henderson. In the end, Macdonald had no choice, and Chan was

duly made a baronet in June 1934. 'Mr Baldwin', the Prime Minister
wearily concluded, 'involves me in a scandal by forcing me to give
an honour because a man has paid £30,000 to get Tory Headquarters
and some Tories living and dead out of a mess.'[88]

As Lord Birkenhead explained, when defending the conduct of
the Lloyd George coalition, 'honours, if wisely recommended, are
among the greatest securities of an ordered hierarchy in the state.'[89]
Since before Elizabethan times, this had been a commonplace: they
ranked and reflected the different levels of wealth and power, they
articulated and promoted the stability of the state, and they provided
recognition and reward for those who rose within the system. But in
Britain from the 1880s to the 1930s, the distribution of wealth and
power was changing, and the terms of trade in titles soon began to
change along with it. Land became less important; money became
more so. The territorial nobility declined; the plutocratic peerage
arose. All that was really different about Lloyd George was that –
pace Birkenhead – he gave out honours not wisely but too frequently.
The system was changing of its own accord: by running it too
hard, Lloyd George merely gave ammunition to his critics, especially
to those aristocrats who understandably and bitterly resented the fact
that it was changing at all.

But while some grandees and gentry regretted the devaluing of
honours into saleable commodities, and protested ineffectually
against the traffic in titles, there were others who were deeply
involved in these very activities. Many of the whips, who first began
to trade honours for cash, like Acland-Hood, Herbert Gladstone, and
Alec Murray, were authentic patricians themselves, and it was
Murray and the equally aristocratic Freddie Guest who set up
Gregory to run the system under Lloyd George. In the House of
Lords, coalition ministers such as Crewe, Curzon, and Crawford had
defended the government's conduct with artful and disingenuous
eloquence. And Gregory's net went much wider and deeper than
that. Lord Eustace Percy wrote for the *Whitehall Gazette*; the Earl of
Scarbrough was an acquaintance through the Order of St John; and
so were the Earl of Denbigh and the dowager Duchess of Norfolk
through the Order of the Holy Sepulchre. And men like Churchill,
Seely, Marlborough, Balfour, Sutherland, Spencer, and Linlithgow
were regular attenders at the Derby Dinner held at Gregory's
Ambassadors Club.[90] Knowingly or unwittingly, many members of
the landed establishment were thus conniving at the corruption of
their own order.

But in addition, there was an element of hysteria and humbug
about even the most high-minded aristocratic critics. As Lloyd
George frequently insisted, it was far less corrupting of public life for

rich men to buy up honours than for them to buy up politicians. During a period of wartime coalition government, it was hardly surprising that more titles and decorations were given out than usual. When the nation was fighting for its life, there were surely more important things to be worried about than that. Moreover, although these grandees claimed to be the high-minded guardians of public morality, there was also in their protests a strong element of snobbery and resentment: bitterness that their own social and political order was being overwhelmed so obviously and so publicly, and anger that their own previous monopoly on titles and decorations was being undermined. When Lord Salisbury and some friends wrote to *The Times* in August 1918, protesting against the irresponsible and widespread distribution of honours, they were met with this withering rebuke:

> Their indignation would have impressed me more deeply if I had been ignorant of the fact that every one of the twenty five had inherited a title or accepted one cheerfully in is own person. . . . Not one of them is less than a Privy Councillor, while Grand Crosses have been pretty liberally scattered among them.[91]

In any case, how many of these self-styled paragons were completely free from blame or responsibility? The Unionist Whip in the 1890s had been the future Lord Selborne. Between 1881 and 1911, the Tory party had been led by the Cecils. When Sir Joseph Robinson obtained his baronetcy in 1908, Lord Selborne was Governor of the Transvaal, and Lord Buxton was a member of the Liberal cabinet. As Birkenhead frequently implied, when defending the coalition's conduct in the Lords, few if any of its critics had completely clean hands in this matter. And even if they did, the same could probably not be said of their ancestors. Many of the greatest and most respectable patricians in the land were descended from families who had acquired or augmented their titles in extremely dubious circumstances in Tudor, Stuart, or Hanoverian England. They had enjoyed their share of the spoils: why should they deny them to others? As Lord Beaverbrook once put it, with a characteristic mixture of romantic exaggeration and cynical wisdom: 'I am descended from eight or ten generations of agricultural labourers. Therefore I feel quite equal to the Cecil family, with this difference, that none of my ancestors stole church funds.'[92]

iii. The Attack on 'Decency'

When Salisbury and Selborne, Lord Hugh Cecil and Lord Henry Bentinck, attacked the sale of honours by the Lloyd George coali-

65. Lord Beaverbrook by
W. R. Sickert.

tion, they were concerned with broader considerations than the mere
trade in titles. For this was but one aspect of what they regarded as
the more general undermining of the standards of British public life.
'Corruption', Lord Robert Cecil explained, 'in any form, however
slight, however seemingly innocent, is the great danger of all forms
of government, not least of a democracy.' But on this broader front,
as on the narrower, the self-appointed patrician guardians of public
decency and political probity found it an uphill struggle. Men with
new, unprecedented riches, could buy their way into the Commons,
the Lords, and even into government. Through their ownership of
the new, popular press, they might exert a powerful and totally
irresponsible influence over the nation's affairs. And by bringing
pressure to bear on poor men in Parliament, who had become
financially beholden to them, they could wield even more sinister
influence.

For members of the titled and genteel classes, this was the fundamental and most powerful objection against plutocracy: it was

neither decent nor disinterested.[93] The justification for government by a landed and leisured class was – as Gladstone had always believed – that they ruled out of a sense of duty and in the national interest. They were not men on the make: the government of the country was to be carried on, not ripped off. But financiers, capitalists, speculators, men who organized government loans and sought government contracts, were by definition not disinterested: they were in politics for what they could get out of it, rather than for what they could bring to it. Moreover, they usually possessed no territorial stake in the country, no feeling of historical association, no loyalty to a locality. Their fortunes, if based in England, were primarily held in highly liquid assets; they kept much (and sometimes most) of their wealth overseas; they moved their millions promiscuously around the world in search of higher profits; and none of them put the majority of their riches into British land. So the plutocrat was doubly dangerous: on the make in Britain, yet not even loyal to it.

But how did such men corrupt public life? One way in which they did so was through the power of the new press. From the 1880s to the 1930s, the nature of British newspapers was fundamentally changed, partly by the need to supply the new mass market brought about by the advent of an educated working class, and partly through the entrepreneurial efforts of men like Newnes and Harmsworth to cater for it.[94] As a result, the old, liberal, rational, provincial press was gradually superseded by the new, cheap, vulgar, chauvinistic, mass-circulation, London-based papers, beginning with Alfred Harmsworth's *Daily Mail* in 1896, and soon followed by the *Sketch*, the *Herald*, and the *Express*. These papers purveyed news in a much more sensationalist way; they no longer printed the speeches of major politicians in full; they sought to bribe readers by a variety of gimmicks, stunts, and offers; and their circulations were numbered in millions. They were the papers of a semi-literate democracy; and they sought to influence events as much as to report them.

Even worse, the control of these papers was now massively concentrated in the hands of a few, often dictatorial press barons.[95] By 1907, Lord Northcliffe, who was rumoured to be worth approximately £20 million, owned the *Daily Mail*, the *Evening News*, the *Weekly Despatch* and *The Observer*; and in the following year, he scored his greatest coup by acquiring *The Times*. In 1919, his younger brother, Rothermere, owned the *Daily Mirror* and the *Sunday Pictorial*, and on Northcliffe's death took over a large part of his empire. There was Lord Cowdray, who built up the Westminster Group of newspapers. There was Max Aitken, Lord Beaverbrook

– a Canadian adventurer, who acquired the *Daily Express* in 1916, founded the *Sunday Express*, and later bought up the *Evening Standard*. There were the incorrigible Astors, of whom William bought *The Observer* in 1910, and his brother John Jacob acquired *The Times* in 1922 for £1.3 million. And there were the Berry brothers, who in the inter-war years put together an empire almost rivalling the Harmsworths in their heyday, including *The Sunday Times*, *The Financial Times*, *The Daily Telegraph* and the *Daily Sketch*.

These owners were intimidating and irresponsible men. They sought to influence opinion and interfere in politics apparently out of malice and mischief. They conspicuously lacked loyalty to any particular party or principle. And they obtained their peerages either by purchase or by promises of support. Indeed, on occasions, their influence seemed to be greater than that of Parliament or the politicians. The young Max Aitken arrived in Britain in 1910, with a large fortune and a very suspect reputation as a Canadian financier. But very soon, he seemed to be making and unmaking governments, and acquiring honours in exchange for his unsavoury services.[96] He was a powerful force propelling Law to the Tory leadership in 1911; he collaborated with Northcliffe and Rothermere in helping to bring down Asquith and promote Lloyd George's palace revolution in December 1916; and he was further involved, with Rothermere, in destroying this coalition in 1922 and in pushing Law into the Prime Ministership itself. The sinister and irresponsible influence of the press could hardly be more vividly displayed. 'Lord Bunty pulls the strings' was how Beaverbrook's backstage machinations were appropriately described.[97]

Predictably, these men were hated by most high-minded patricians. The great Lord Salisbury dismissed the *Mail* as 'a paper written by office boys for office boys'. His austere children found Northcliffe himself quite distasteful – a vulgar, parvenu, syphilitic megalomaniac – and their disapproval of him was heartily reciprocated. In 1901, the young G. M. Trevelyan condemned the 'white peril' of cheap journalism, which no longer appealed to a sophisticated literate audience but to 'the uneducated mass of all classes.'[98] William Bridgeman thought Rothermere a 'cad', a 'damned scoundrel', and 'the greatest curse of this country.' And the diary of Lord Crawford is one long denunciation of such men and their medium: of Beaverbrook ('a dishonest man'), of his *Express* ('a vile newspaper'), of the *News of the World* ('infamous'), and of Rothermere (a 'scoundrel' and a 'traitor').[99] In short, to the traditional territorial aristocracy, the advent of the popular and plutocratic press was seen as 'the symbol . . . for all the corrupting forces which were at work in British society.'[100]

But this was not the only way in which it seemed that public life was being more generally corrupted by the power of new wealth. For many of these new plutocrats were able to force their way into the Commons as easily as they later bought their way into the Lords. Outsiders like Astor and Aitken, Brunner and Pearson, could use their powerful purses to overwhelm a local and underfunded constituency association, with which they had no territorial or historical connection. Some, once elected, showed barely any interest in the day-to-day work of the Commons: Aitken made no mark whatsoever, and Pearson's near-permanent absence on business was a joke in the lobbies. Yet this was, in a sense, the lesser of two evils. For others, who attended more regularly, brought the profiteering mentality of the boardroom and the dubious morality of the stock exchange to the conduct of the nation's affairs. Either way, such men conspicuously lacked what the patricians called 'character'. As William Bridgeman explained in 1916, it was 'this damned cleverness which always thinks the straightforward course too stupid to be right, which is undoing us, and the more you get so-called businessmen and pushers into politics, the more you will have of it.'[101]

This was bad enough in itself. But the threat to public decency was compounded by the fact that the advent of the new rich into the Commons coincided with the advent of the new poor – those middle-class professionals and working-class MPs who lacked adequate financial resources, and who were now to be found in unprecedented abundance. As Lord Robert Cecil explained in 1913, 'poorer men are more likely to be in Parliament in the future than in the past . . . It adds to the danger of personal corruption.'[102] And it did so because such men were often beholden to, and even dependent on, the largesse of the new plutocracy. We have already seen the difficulties Macdonald ran into by taking gifts – albeit temporarily – from Alexander Grant. Bonar Law's finances were managed by Beaverbrook, who was later to give money to Asquith, Snowden, and Hoare.[103] And F. E. Smith was even more incorrigible: he seemed too much in thrall to the brewers and publicans of Liverpool; he worked for both Lever and Northcliffe, but was not very loyal to either; and he was a great friend of Sir Robert Hudson, an unscrupulous shipping operator on the Mersey. Lord Balcarres described him, with truth, as having 'the spirit and sometimes the ethics of a freebooter.'[104]

This was the background to a series of financial scandals that rocked British public life from the 1890s, and that convinced many grandees and gentry that these new men in politics, whether rich or poor, were invariably corrupt. The most famous early example was Joseph Chamberlain, a self-made middle-class politician, around

66. Joseph Chamberlain by John Singer Sargent.

whom there gathered a dark cloud of suspicion and distrust which seemed well founded. His nonconformist background, his early radical leanings, and his business interests made him an abiding object of aristocratic disapproval. Moreover, he was a friend of Cecil Rhodes, it was generally believed that he had known about the Jameson Raid, and it was widely thought that the parliamentary select committee set up to inquire into it was a deliberate cover-up.[105] During the Boer War itself, Chamberlain and his son Austen (by then Civil Lord of the Admiralty) were accused of giving government orders to armaments firms in which they or their relatives held shares. 'The more the British Empire expands, the more the Chamberlains contract', ran the joke of the time. And Chamberlain's defence – protesting his 'middle-class commercial honour' – only confirmed the patricians' worst fears about him.[106]

Even worse was the nation-wide campaign for Tariff Reform which Joseph Chamberlain launched in 1903. It meant the abandonment of Free Trade; it was a businessman's solution to political problems; and the proposed new taxes would inevitably lead to greater corruption in government. 'Their whole way of looking at politics', observed Lord Robert Cecil, seemed 'entirely sordid and materialistic; not yet corrupt, but on the high road to corruption.' Moreover, the Tariff Reform League was well financed, with an income of £140,000 by 1904, and was both centralized in its funding and dictatorial in its operation.[107] In 1905, Hugh Cecil complained that at Greenwich, the Tariff Reformers were spending '£50 a day' to get him out; and after his defeat, they successfully kept him from finding a seat until 1910. Not surprisingly, he despised their 'grasping commercialism' and 'government by menaces', and feared general 'corruption' and the 'Americanising' of politics. Even the seventeenth Lord Derby was driven to uncharacteristic outspokenness. 'Damn these Chamberlains!' he exclaimed in 1911, 'They are the curse of our party and of the country.'[108]

The rise of Tariff Reform crystallized the Cecils' hatred of 'middle-class monsters', and heightened their fear that landowners were being 'progressively ousted by the mercantile magnates', both in the party and in Parliament. 'If the Unionist Party', Lord Robert wrote in 1907, 'were free from Tariff Reform and the middle classes – in which I include the Chamberlains, Bonar Law, Milner *et hoc genus omne* – we should get on alright.'[109] But this was wishful thinking. Early in 1911, Lord Selborne told George Wyndham that the landowners must 'make our views prevail within the party, which is the same thing as capturing the party and the party machine.' But they did not succeed: for in 1911 it was those very people enumerated by Lord Robert Cecil who took over the Tory leadership, and who kept it until 1940. And they brought their bourgeois ways with them. Austen Chamberlain's food was 'expensive, ostentatious, middle-class and uneatable'; and his politics were no better, standing as they did for 'the abandonment of principle and the disintegration of conservatism.'[110]

But the middle-class government of the Liberals was far worse: its tone and style were unprecedently self-indulgent; it gave out peerages profligately and corruptly; and it seemed in thrall to big business and the plutocracy. Men like Asquith, Lloyd George, and McKenna were all 'living in riotous luxury', well beyond their private means and public salaries. Asquith was regularly drunk in the Commons, and delighted in the more decadent parts of high society.[111] Lloyd George's house was built for him by Riddell, the newspaper pro-

67. 'The Marconi
Octopus.' *Punch*, 18 June
1913.

THE MARCONI OCTOPUS.

Liberal Party. "ANOTHER TENTACLE OR TWO AND I'M DONE!"

prietor; he received a pension of £2,000 a year from Andrew Carnegie; in 1912, he ostentatiously spent his holiday at Harold Harmsworth's villa on the French Riviera; and his son was employed by Weetman Pearson, the future Lord Cowdray.[112] To prim and high-minded aristocrats, it was all quite intolerable, as Lord Balcarres noted:

> The common talk of the lobby and the City is government corruption – personal corruption. The radicals seem to vie with one another in payment for honours, and in recoupment via public contracts. Never before have such rumours been so prevalent, nor has there been such ground for their foundation. These penniless ministers are not living at their extravagant rate upon their official salaries. Lloyd George is not building his new house out of his salary. Somebody must be financing him. Who, and above all, why?[113]

In the hope of answering these questions, the Conservatives set up the Radical Plutocrats Inquiry in October 1912, which was chaired by George Lane-Fox, and which aimed to discover and to publicize the names of the rich men who were financing – and thus manipulating – the Liberal government.[114] But even before this inquiry was fully launched, the patricians' worst forebodings about corrupt government were confirmed when the Marconi Scandal broke.[115] Four ministers were directly involved: Rufus Isaacs, the Solicitor General; Herbert Samuel, the Postmaster-General; Alec Murray, the Liberal Chief Whip; and Lloyd George himself who was Chancellor of the Exchequer. At a time when the English Marconi Company was about to be awarded a government contract, Isaacs, Murray, and Lloyd George purchased shares in the American Marconi Company, in anticipation of making a windfall profit, and with the assistance of Isaacs' brother, Godfrey. The most generous interpretation of such activity must be that it was foolish and irresponsible. But it would be more accurate to say that it was a definite abuse of public position. In fact, all three men lost money: but they should probably have lost a great deal more, besides.

Inevitably, the news of their speculations leaked out; there was a sustained press campaign against them; and as in the case of the Jameson Raid, there was a Commons Select Committee of Inquiry. Those who believed that the Liberal government was the slave of an international cabal of (mainly Jewish) financiers found what seemed to be ample and ominous supporting evidence. Samuel was Jewish, and was a member of a famous banking family. Isaacs was of similar origins, and, in the course of the inquiry, it emerged that when a young man, he had lied about his age to obtain membership of the stock exchange, and had later been 'hammered' for being unable to meet his obligations. But as with the Jameson Raid, there was a widespread feeling that the Select Committee was little more than a whitewash. Murray had by this time exchanged public life for business, was conveniently shipped off to Bogotá—to obtain oil contracts for Cowdray! – and was thus unable to give evidence.[116] The majority report gave the ministers the lightest possible censure, no one was asked to resign, and shortly afterwards, Isaacs was appointed Lord Chief Justice of England.

But to some patricians, it merely confirmed their worst fears that gentlemanly standards in public life had disappeared. On the Liberal left, C. P. Trevelyan was deeply distressed at the conduct of his own front bench. 'There is nothing dishonest', he concluded, 'but it is all not above board.'[117] And on the Tory right, Lord Robert Cecil was even more outspoken. In October 1912, at the height of the scandal, he entered an impassioned plea for decency in government: 'the life of the nation is bound up with our respect for our public men and their personal integrity. That must be preserved and, unless it is, we are done for absolutely.'[118] He was appointed a member of the Select Committee; he was almost alone in asking searching questions; he issued a minority report that censured the ministers for 'improprie-ty'; and in the final debate in the Commons, claimed that he could have made it far more damning if he had been so inclined. In early 1914, he was so distressed that 'no step is announced to check the increasing corruption of public life' that he tabled an amendment in the Commons regretting the failure of the government 'to take any steps for preventing the growing debasement of the accustomed standard of purity in public life.'[119]

After Limehouse, the People's Budget, and Marconi, many landowners would have nothing whatsoever to do with Lloyd George, and when he grasped supreme power in 1916, the style and tone of his government merely confirmed them in their belief that he was a 'windbag and a liar' (Lord Salisbury) or a 'dirty little rogue' (Lord Robert Cecil).[120] For the honours scandal was only one aspect of the widespread corruption by which his administration seemed to be characterized. To begin with, he was obsessed with the plutocrat-ic press: he relied on it in his campaign to oust Asquith; he brought men like Beaverbrook, Astor, Northcliffe, and Rothermere into his government; and he gave a disproportionate number of honours to his friends in Fleet Street. Between 1918 and 1922, he bestowed knighthoods, baronetcies, peerages, and privy councillorships on forty-nine proprietors, editors, managing directors, chairmen, and principal shareholders. One of them, Lord Riddell, was not only the owner of the *News of the World* and the man who had paid for Lloyd George's house: he was also the first divorced man to be ennobled.[121]

But in addition, this was preponderantly a middle-class govern-ment, dominated by those upstarts who had displaced the patricians, even in the Tory party itself, like Austen Chamberlain, Milner, and Bonar Law. Rufus Isaacs was loaded with honours and offices, and the dreadful F. E. Smith was translated to the upper house as Lord Birkenhead. He was always in debt and frequently drunk.[122] He had represented Isaacs and Samuel in the Marconi libel case, and was the most resourceful defender of the government's record in the Lords. He was a close friend of Maundy Gregory, by whom it was rumoured he was being blackmailed, and he may even have procured honours for some of his clients. To make ends meet, he wrote ghosted books, was later subsidized by the Tory party, and finally left politics for the City because his creditors would not wait. He hated most aristocrats, and once in the House of Lords, called Salisbury and Selborne 'the Dolly sisters', after the musical-hall act of that name. Salisbury in turn despised him for being 'disreputable', and for his 'crude attachments to the interests of wealth'. 'I do not imagine', Salisbury went on, 'he has got many political principles, and most of what he has got are wrong. Poor fellow, he will probably drink himself to death.' In the end, he did.[123]

So, for many gentry and grandees, the six years of Lloyd George government merely displayed in an exaggerated form all those most distasteful aspects of British public life that had been on the increase since the 1880s. In 1918, Lord Henry Bentinck, half-brother of the Duke of Portland, independent Conservative MP for North Norfolk, and Lord-Lieutenant of Westmorland, launched a violent attack on the politics of corruption in his book *Tory Democracy*.[124] The wartime profiteers, he argued, were on the rampage; the Golden Calf had been set up in Whitehall and Westminster; imperial financiers were lording it in government; the press was controlling opinion rather than reflecting it; honours were being too liberally distributed; and the Tory party was being 'thoroughly commercialised and vulgarised'. The longer the war – and the coalition – lasted, 'the larger the spoils, the more will plutocracy be ennobled, decorated, knighted and enriched.' 'While everything generous, self-sacrificing and noble is shedding blood on the fields of Flanders', he concluded, 'plutocracy is on the warpath at home', while the British government and empire had been turned into a 'bagman's paradise'.[125]

Although they were by now a dwindling minority group, there were several high-minded patricians in the 'hard-nosed' Commons of 1919, the survivors of the pre-war Tory Reform Group, who felt as Bentinck did, and their hatred of Lloyd George was so well developed that they began to act together. Predictably, they included such experienced MPs as Lords Hugh and Robert Cecil, Edward Wood, George Lane-Fox, Lord Winterton, Mark Sykes, Aubrey Herbert, and Lord Wolmer. And they were joined by a younger contingent including Lord Hartington, Oswald Mosley, Lord Eustace Percy and Philip Lloyd-Greame.[126] They stood for 'character' rather than 'cleverness', for religious decency instead of meretricious glitter, and for the restoration of disinterestedness in government. As Lord Hugh Cecil put it in 1921, in words strikingly reminiscent of William Bridgeman's, 'It really is a disreputable business having a Welsh wizard to control the affairs of the country. I am beginning to believe that there is nothing so dangerous as cleverness in an administrator. Give me a stupid old country gentleman.'[127]

Here was a Commons' reaction against Lloyd George that was later described as 'positively aristocratic', and it was even stronger in the Lords than in the lower house. Among active and significant

patrician politicians, it included Lord Midleton, who was so disenchanted with the government's Irish policy that he refused the Lord-
Lieutenancy in 1918, and Lord Selborne, who was so outspoken on
the subject of honours, who refused to accept either office or reward
from Lloyd George, and who fervently believed in 'the administrative prowess of an absolutely straight country gentleman.'[128] And it
also embraced a more extreme group led by the Duke of Northumberland, who shared Selborne's views about honours, but also
believed that the world was about to fall victim to an international,
Jewish-cum-Bolshevik conspiracy. These men, and their colleagues
and relatives in the Commons, gradually coalesced round Salisbury,
and his opposition to what Maurice Cowling rightly describes as
'political aggression, verbal disingenuousness, unfulfilled promises
and excessively good living.' In 1919, he revived the Association of
Unionist Peers, and within a year, was writing to *The Times*,
publicly calling for an end to the coalition.[129]

What form did this 'positively aristocratic' reaction to Lloyd
George actually take? There were two specific efforts made. The first
was inspired by Lord Robert Cecil, who sought to bring together all
decent men from the Tory and Liberal parties, to persuade Lord
Grey of Fallodon out of retirement to lead them, and to overthrow
Lloyd George, the 'spiritual "vampire"', by 'innate moral superiority'. In short, this was a self-conscious attempt to revive the notion
of patrician disinterestedness as a major force in politics. During 1921
and early 1922, Cecil exerted great and saintly efforts to this end, but
his 'high-minded intrigue never really got off the ground'.[130] The
Liberals would not fuse with the Conservatives; Asquith would not
give up the leadership to Grey; and Grey himself was far from
enthusiastic. 'The possible results', he claimed, 'of my taking an
active part in public life are being grossly overrated by my friends.'
He did indeed hate Lloyd George, believing that his government had
'let down and corrupted public life at home and destroyed our credit
abroad.' But he had had enough of politics, his health was not good,
and he preferred his rods and his birds. In the end, Cecil's high-
minded conspiracy came to nothing, and in late 1923, its instigator
returned to the Tory party.[131]

The second, and much more successful, aristocratic initiative was to
bring down the Lloyd George government from within by persuading the Conservative leadership that the party must withdraw from
the coalition and reassert its own separate identity. At one level,
Salisbury's role was especially significant: partly because he had
already provided a focus for patrician dissidents, partly because he
had issued a new die-hard manifesto just before the honours scandal
broke in June 1922, and partly because he then threatened to support

anti-coalition Tory candidates at the next election. At another, it was the junior ministers of landed background – men like Bridgeman, Winterton, Lloyd-Greame, and Wood, who had been members of the high-minded Commons group – who effectively brought about the revolt from within.[132] And it was two respectable country gentlemen, George Lane-Fox and E. G. Pretyman, who actually proposed the motion at the famous Carlton Club meeting that ended the Tory party's involvement with Lloyd George, ended the coalition, and ended his days of power for ever. Viewed in this light, the overthrow of the 'dirty little rogue' was a triumph for the forces of decency under titled and genteel leadership.[133] The patricians had finally got their own back for the People's Budget and everything that he had done to their order since.

Undeniably, this argument has a certain attractive plausibility. But too much should not be made of it. In the first place, the defeat of the coalition was brought about by much broader and more varied forces than a few disgruntled and high-minded landowners who believed in 'honesty and steadfastness' rather than 'dialectic agility' or 'powers of invective.' As Kenneth Morgan has persuasively argued, the real reason why the coalition fell was that it had lost the support of the country, and it was this feeling that communicated itself to Tory MPs and caused them to vote as they did at the Carlton Club meeting.[134] Almost as significant was the fact that the press, in the form of Northcliffe, Rothermere, Beaverbrook, and Riddell, also turned against Lloyd George. And at the level of high politics, the really powerful influences were Baldwin and Bonar Law, with the latter once more egged on by Beaverbrook. Indeed, from this perspective, one of the ironies of the decline and fall of Lloyd George is that many of the people who brought him down seemed to many notables to be almost as disreputable or unattractive as the 'Welsh attorney' himself.

But in addition, the defeat of Lloyd George was to prove a pyrrhic victory for the grandees and gentry, as the Welsh windbag was soon replaced by a quintessential 'middle-class monster', the very man whom the patricians had tried to keep out of the Conservative leadership in 1911. The Bonar Law ministry did indeed offer temporary accommodation to many of those landowners who had helped to bring Lloyd George down. But the new Prime Minister was widely supposed to be in Beaverbrook's pocket, had been criticized for his liking of 'tricky vulgarity', and had, after all, been himself a member of the Lloyd George coalition.[135] And Law was followed by Baldwin, who flirted with Protection, who brought back Birkenhead and Chamberlain into the party (despite vehement protests from Salisbury, Bridgeman, Robert Cecil, and Ormsby-

Gore), and who hated the die-hards.[136] In so far as the forces of decency did triumph in the inter-war years, they were under middle-class, not aristocratic, management. As Salisbury told Baldwin in 1931, 'You and I do not belong to the same school of Conservativ-ism.' The only unalloyed triumph for the high-minded grandees was when Lord Grey was elected as Chancellor of Oxford – the place he had been sent down from forty years before for idleness – thus keeping out Birkenhead.[137]

But as with honours in particular, so with decency in general, there was in fact no monolithic aristocratic position. Once again, many landowners were partially – or fully – involved on the other side. In the case of the Jameson Raid, Albert Grey and the titled directors of the British South Africa Company bore at least as much responsi-bility as Joseph Chamberlain, and (like Elibank at the time of Marconi) Grey was sent off to the Cape to ensure he did not appear before the parliamentary inquiry. Even more extraordinarily, one of the Randlords who did give evidence – Rutherfoord Harris – was represented by none other than Lord Robert Cecil. And it was the patrician Harcourt, the Liberal leader, who deliberately chose not to press the inquiry, who drafted the final report, and who stood by Joseph Chamberlain.[138] Likewise, over Tariff Reform, the protests against its sordid commercialism may have been made by the great grandees, but lesser squires like Bathurst, Bridgeman, Long, and Chaplin were much more sympathetic. And one of the Marconi culprits, Alec Murray was an impoverished landowner, risking reputation for money, while Balfour was as ineffectual as Harcourt had earlier been in attacking and embarrassing the government.[139]

The same division of opinion was manifest even in the case of Lloyd George himself. Although most patricians were never as well disposed to him as he was later to claim, Balfour, Churchill, Crawford, and Curzon all held office in his coalition. At the Carlton Club meeting, the majority of landed MPs may have declared against him, but there were still some who voted in his support.[140] And a lifelong Liberal like the future Lord Lothian was even more loyal. He had embraced the creed of high-capitalist imperialism in South Africa under Lord Milner; he was recruited to serve in Lloyd George's wartime secretariat; he was briefly editor of the *Daily Chronicle*, Lloyd George's party newspaper; and he later became Secretary to the Rhodes trustees and a close friend of Nancy Astor. He was not corrupt in any moral sense; but nevertheless, he was a completely plutocratized peer. Like many of his class, he knew where the money was now to be made.[141]

Men like Lothian, who were obliged to earn their living, simply could not afford to be as austere as Salisbury and his friends. In the same way, Winston Churchill needed, and earned, the largesse of the rich. He was a close friend of Beaverbrook and Birkenhead, Bracken and Baruch. He wrote articles for Hearst newspapers in America and for Lord Camrose in England. By the late 1930s, he was in such a parlous financial position that his affairs were taken over by Sir Henry Strakosch.[142] But even among the less needy and most high-minded patricians, there was once again an element of humbug, a claim to moral superiority and incorruptibility, which was ultimately both overstated and unconvincing. Ironically enough, such self-appointed capitalist haters as Wolmer and Selborne were, respectively, directors of Lloyds and of the National Provincial Bank. In 1900, when Selborne had been an Under-Secretary at the Colonial Office, his department had done business with the P & O shipping company, of which Selborne himself was a director. And in 1913, he became chairman of Natal Ammonium Limited, which was part of the Liberal and Jewish Mond empire.[143]

In any case, the contemporary corruption that such men denounced was probably less – assuming such comparisons can be usefully made – than that of the period from the 1780s to 1820s, when it had been the old aristocracy, not the new plutocracy, who had been most successfully on the make. Poor men supposedly 'enslaved' by the rich in the 1900s and 1910s were probably no more dependent than those MPs had been a century before, when they had sat for rotten boroughs but had rarely been compelled to do their aristocratic patron's bidding. Likewise, the involvement of newspapers in politics was no new thing, as the doings of Lord Palmerston himself served to show. And the influence of the new press lords was probably much overrated: Northcliffe died convinced that he had accomplished little; and Beaverbrook's reputation for mischief and wirepulling was greater than it deserved to be. But above all, it was not aristocratic disinterestedness that had won the First World War: it was Lloyd George's Celtic and corrupted magic.

iv.   Conclusion: The Impotence of Being Earnest

Throughout his lengthy political career, one of the matters of 'supreme importance' to the fourth Lord Salisbury, and to his high-minded genteel colleagues, was the need to 'keep our public life pure and free from reproach.'[144] His aim was to protect, and to perpetuate, a particular style of patrician government, administration, and public morality, which he regarded, quite understandably, as the best of all possible arrangements in the best of all possible worlds. It took for granted the fact that nobility of birth was the sole basis for legitimate social and political leadership. It drew on a nostalgic image of enlightened, disinterested aristocratic rule, which had enjoyed its transient heyday in the mid-Victorian period, when it had been purged of the excesses of early-nineteenth-century 'Old Corruption', but had not yet been challenged by the *fin de siècle* vulgarity of the new plutocracy. And it embodied a deep-rooted aristocratic prejudice against the new social and economic forces which threatened that world, its values, and the patricians' assured and unchallenged place within it.[145]

But inevitably, as the old élite declined and fell, it proved impossible to make these views prevail in the years between the 1880s and the 1930s. The proliferation (and purchase) of honours proceeded apace, as new social groups successfully asserted their claims to social recognition and political pre-eminence. When the grandees in the Lords sought to reassert their exclusive status, they appeared unacceptably snobbish and anachronistically aloof. Yet as the upper house was challenged and peopled by these new creations, the order to which they belonged only lost more prestige. If the most effective measure of any class's resilience is the degree to which it can assimilate new families of different social origins, and convert them to the style of life, system of values, and structure of honours of the social group on to which they are projected, then it is clear that by the early twentieth century, the landed establishment's power of resistance had been very greatly undermined, and during the inter-war years, it was only weakened still further.[146]

In vain but vehement protest, the patricians dismissed and disparaged these developments as scandal, as impropriety, as corruption. But words such as these were largely a bitter cry of anguished lament for the world they had lost: the world of their own exclusive and unchallenged pre-eminence. The problem for the later Cecils and their friends was that they wanted to be simultaneously high-minded and influential, in a political world where the one almost by definition precluded the other. Men who did not matter that much in public life were not in a strong position to influence or to change its tone. And men who stood for an anachronistic and essentially self-serving notion of exclusive, aristocratic decency were unlikely to wield much power in twentieth-century Britain. In Oswald Mosley's acutely unkind words, the Cecils and their friends 'buttoned up their prim little overcoats against the chill of Lloyd George's methods.' But they did so in vain. As Lloyd George said of Balfour, so he might have said of Salisbury and his brothers: their place in history would be 'just like the scent on a pocket handkerchief.'[147]

8

THE DILUTION OF SELECT SOCIETY

The sensational appearance in the London season of 1881–2 of the two
Tennant sisters . . . , the dramatic rise of presentations at Court after 1882,
and the inclusion of rich men of dubious social background in the Prince of
Wales's set, marked the end of the exclusive monopoly of larger landed
families over London 'Society'.
(L. Stone and J. C. Fawtier Stone, *An Open Elite? England 1540–1880* (1984),
p. 425.)

Since 1918, England has been full of rich people disporting in the countryside . . . . But a decreasing proportion of them have been hereditary owners of
land or sporting rights.
(R. Longrigg, *The English Squire and His Sport* (1977), p. 289.)

A greater threat to the established pattern of behaviour . . . was the alteration
in the standard of manners which opportunities for travel had brought to the
upper classes. The next generation of young aristocrats . . . were accustomed
to new habits of leisure; and were emancipated from the routine of the
London season and country-house responsibilities. The age of the motor car
and the private yacht, the weekend in Paris and the polo season in Monte
Carlo, did not breed the solid worth which the . . . previous generation had
expected.
(J. M. Lee, *Social Leaders and Public Persons: A Study of County Government in
Cheshire since 1888* (1963), p. 42.)

It was easier to be a knight-errant if one had a private income; it was not
coincidence that [Wilfrid] Scawen Blunt, [Aubrey] Herbert, and [Mark] Sykes
were all upper-class landowners . . . Knights errant tended to be drawn to
Arab countries, or to countries relatively untouched by western civilisation,
partly because they could get away on their own there, partly because they
found such traditional ways of life preferable (in short spells, at any rate) to
modern civilization.
(M. Girouard, *The Return to Camelot: Chivalry and the English Gentleman*
(1981), pp. 271–2.)

The inflation of honours and the attack on disinterested public
service were only two of the ways in which patrician status was
assailed and undermined from the last quarter of the nineteenth
century onwards. Equally threatened, and equally vulnerable, was
the general social pattern of aristocratic and genteel living. By
definition, the titled and territorial classes were also the leisured
classes. But in form and function, their leisure activities were very

carefully and consciously structured, not as irresponsible and self-indulgent recreation, but as an essential adjunct to their landed holdings and their political duties.[1] The London season brought together the great governing families of Britain, partly for pleasure and display, partly for political entertaining while parliament was in session, and partly so that marriage partners might be vetted and selected. For the remainder of the year, they returned to the country, where they superintended the administration of their estates, entertained their neighbours, patronized local sporting activities, and were unquestionably accepted as the leaders of 'the county community'. In London and in the shires, they were not just the wealth élite and the power élite: they were the social élite as well.

From the 1880s onwards, this carefully integrated and functionally significant social system began to break down. In London high society, the aristocratic monopoly was broken, as the new super-rich stormed the citadels of social exclusiveness, and flaunted their parvenu wealth with opulent and irresistible vulgarity. The number of presentations at court dramatically increased, and King Edward VII preferred the company of the 'smart' set – self-made plutocrats and Jewish adventurers – to the old-fashioned grandees, who seemed so staid and so dull by comparison. By 1914, political life and social life were becoming increasingly divorced from each other, and it was widely believed that traditional high society had effectively ceased to exist. During the inter-war years, the great town houses in Park Lane and Piccadilly were demolished, and with the conspicuous but unhappy exception of Lord and Lady Londonderry, the aristocracy all but abandoned large-scale political entertaining. A new generation of Americans took over as the leaders of society, and were much drawn to the Prince of Wales. But they counted for nothing politically, and unlike the patrician hostesses of yesteryear, they regarded social life as an end in itself.

The decay and fragmentation of London society was exactly paralleled by the decay and fragmentation of the county community. In the shires, as in the city, the new élite of money bought their way in at the very time that the old élite of birth was in decline. The agricultural depression forced many landowners to let their houses, and to give up expensive country pursuits like fox-hunting. Meanwhile, the new rich disported themselves in indulgent and ignorant opulence, with their ostentatious weekends and their sumptuous shooting parties. Instead of being a patrician preserve, the countryside was becoming a plutocratic playground. In different ways, the motor car, the shotgun, and barbed wire dealt mortal blows to the traditional style of country living, and the massive land sales in the aftermath of the First World War effectively destroyed the territorial basis of the old county community. Fox-hunting survived, but more as a middle-class pastime than as an upper-class recreation. By the 1930s, the social life of the shires was almost entirely sustained by the pleasure-seeking city-dweller rather than by the resident and dutiful landowner.

But where did the old guard go, as they withdrew from county and London society? In the age of the private railway car and the luxury liner, they spent more of their time than ever before overseas. Some holidayed on the Riviera, bought villas on the Mediterranean, wintered in Egypt, or sailed their yachts. Some went big-game hunting in the United States, in India, or in East Africa. Some went on round the world tours to prepare themselves for public life. Some were obliged to leave home because of financial embarrassment or sexual scandal. And some took refuge from the travails of modern life by going on knight-errantly quests to the Middle East. For whatever reason, the notables were in motion as they had never been before – a restless, rootless, fragmenting élite. The more they travelled, the less time they spent on their estates or in London. The more they went abroad, the less power they wielded at home. The more plutocratic they became in lifestyle, the less patrician they were in identity.

i.   The Lowering of High Society

The greatest private party of the Diamond Jubilee season was the fancy-dress ball held at Devonshire House in July 1897, 'where the elect of the British aristocracy appeared in the Court costumes of all times and countries.' They were greeted by the Duchess, 'gloriously apparelled' as Zenobia, Queen of Palmyra, and by the Duke as the Emperor Charles V, appropriately adorned with the Order of the Golden Fleece.[2] Two future English kings were present: the Prince of Wales appeared as Grand Master of the Knights of Malta, and the Duke of York as Clifford, Earl of Cumberland. Other guests included the Duchess of Sutherland as Charlotte Corday, Lady Westmorland as Maria Teresa, Lord Rosebery as Horace Walpole, and Speaker Peel as the Doge of Venice. The Duke was one of the richest and most illustrious grandees in the land, who had thrice turned down the invitation to become Prime Minister. The Duchess was one of the greatest beauties of her age, had previously been married to the Duke of Manchester, and as chatelaine of Devonshire House was a hostess of unrivalled influence and glamour. As the Duke of Portland recalled forty years later, 'it was indeed a most brilliant scene', an unforgettable display of aristocratic grandeur, political connection, and social superiority.[3]

One of the youngest guests to attend that ball was Edith, daughter of Henry Chaplin, who later, as Lady Londonderry, became in turn the greatest political hostess of her generation. Throughout the inter-war years, she mounted magnificent and much-publicized receptions at Londonderry House, especially on the eve of the parliamentary session.[4] Greeting her guests at the top of the famous staircase, in the company of the Prime Minister of the day, she was the glamorous embodiment of traditional aristocratic social power. Lord Birken-head claimed that as a result, Lord Londonderry was 'catering his way to the Cabinet'. Even more remarkable was the close friendship that developed between Lady Londonderry and the Labour leader, Ramsay Macdonald, who as Premier of the National Government turned his back on socialism, and 'took to grandeur and high life instead.' According to John Gunther, it was the social allure of the Londonderry House receptions that helped to divert him 'from nationalization of the mines to nationalization merely of the cabinet.' 'A few months ago', said the wits, Macdonald 'sang "The Red Flag." Now he whistles "The Londonderry Air." '[5]

The Devonshires' fancy-dress ball, and Lady Londonderry's sumptuous gatherings, were vivid reminders that patrician society survived from the late nineteenth century into the inter-war years. But in form and function, it was only a very pale shadow of what it had been in the time of Lady Palmerston or Lady Waldegrave. In its heyday, society was confined to 'a very definite and very limited class', which was almost exclusively aristocratic. It was a self-confident, self-perpetuating social élite, and it was extremely dif-ficult for ambitious parvenus to get in, 'until credentials had been carefully examined and discussed' by the small group of hostesses who were the arbiters in these matters.[6] In Piccadilly and Park Lane, the great town palaces of the super-rich provided the setting for unrivalled displays of conspicuous consumption, which were as much political as social in their significance. Since the wealth élite was also the power élite, high society was an essential adjunct to political life, where dinner parties might be as important as cabinet meetings. And it also functioned as a marriage market, where the system of presentation at court, and the power wielded by dowager chaperons, ensured that the choice of partner by a young patrician was effectively restricted to women of similar social background.

By the 1880s, it was becoming clear to experienced observers that this exclusive and intimate social world was beginning to break down. 'Society's chief ailment of today', noted T. H. S. Escott, 'is the want of any principle of cohesion.' It was fragmenting into many separate 'sets', which coexisted, but did not coalesce, while the Home Rule crisis meant that Unionists and Liberals were divided socially as well as politically. And there were many other signs and portents. The number of court presentations rose dramatically, the future Marquess of Ailesbury married an actress, Spencer House was 'let to a Yankee', and the appearance of the Tennant sisters in polite drawing rooms 'caused a tremendous commotion.'[7] In the same decade, *Burke's Peerage* published a *Book of Precedence*, and *The Queen* magazine began a regular column on etiquette, entitled 'Au Fait'. The old social certainties were crumbling, and newcomers needed guidance as to how to behave. As Lady Dorothy Nevill recalled, 'society in the old sense of the term may be said . . . to have come to an end in the 'eighties of the last century.' It was, agreed Lord Dunraven, unconsciously echoing the title of Lord Salisbury's famous article, the decade when 'disintegration set in.'[8]

The most significant change was that the old élite could no longer keep 'without the gates' the new international plutocracy that was clammering for admission to high society in the 'world metropolis'.[9] In the same way that they purchased pictures and peerages, the non-landed super-rich used their wealth to buy their way into society. The first step was to acquire a fashionable London address. Some 'edged their way into . . . the innermost social sanctuary of Grosvenor Square itself', such as Lord Furness and J. P. Morgan, jr. Others began by renting the town house which an indebted notable had been forced to let, and then went on to acquire a great London mansion of their own. J. B. Robinson took Dudley House, and William Waldorf Astor rented Lansdowne House, before buying his own place in St James's Square. Ernest Cassel moved from Grosvenor Square to Brook House in Park Lane, previously the residence of Lord Tweedmouth. He paid £10,000 premium for the renewal of the lease, and spent a further £20,000 on lavish redecoration, including a massive marble hall which Lady Diana Cooper called 'the giant's lavatory'. And when Barney Barnato rented Spencer House, he threw it open to journalists, boxers, racing trainers and theatre managers, a very different class of person from those accustomed to visit when the 'Red Earl' himself was in residence.[10]

By losing control of the admissions process, the aristocracy also lost control of the way society conducted itself. For the plutocrats lived far more loudly, lavishly, and luxuriously than the patricians, and it was they who increasingly set the social tone. As Lady Jeune explained, 'the list of the smartest and most magnificent entertainments are not those given by the haute noblesse of England, but by a host of people, many of whose names are foreign, and who thirty years ago would not have been heard of outside their provincial home.'[11] Anyone prepared to entertain extravagantly enough could establish themselves as a leader of society, and the profuse expenditure, the opulent vulgarity, and the 'meretricious ornamentation' of these *nouveaux riches* seemed to know no limits. Pushful hosts gloried in waste and indulgence, the newspapers recorded the details of interminable feasts and banquets, and 'society took to worshipping the almighty Dollar unabashed.'[12] When Beatrice Webb dined at Bath House, with Sir Julius Wernher, assorted financial magnates, and their hangers on, she was appalled. 'There might as well', she remembered, 'have been a Goddess of Gold erected for overt worship – the impression of worship in thought, feeling and action could hardly have been stronger.'[13]

Equally significant was the change in the numbers and the social background of the women who were being presented at court drawing rooms, either as débutantes or because their status had changed in other ways. Here again, the earlier patrician monopoly was abruptly broken, as the number of presentations more than doubled during the last twenty years of Victoria's reign, necessitating the addition of a fourth drawing room in 1880, and a fifth in 1895.[14] 'Let any person who knows London society look through the list of débutantes and ladies attending drawing rooms', thundered one disenchanted observer in 1891, 'and I wager that not half the names will be known to him or her.' It was a sign of the times that these newcomers were dismissed as 'social scum and nouveaux riches'; and many of them were certainly the daughters of self-made plutocrats from Britain, the empire and the United States. In 1841, 90 per cent of the women presented at court had been from the titled and territorial classes. Thirty years later, the percentage had dropped to 68. And by 1891 the proportion was less than half for the first time. Among débutantes, as among MPs, the titled and genteel majority had abruptly disappeared – and for ever. As one contemporary remarked, 'even trade is not debarred.'[15]

At the same time, the monarchy itself had ceased to be the champion or guarantee of exclusive society. Initially, the Prince of Wales had been drawn to such raffish members of the titled classes as Lord Charles Beresford, Lord Blandford, Lord Aylesford, and Lord Randolph Churchill. But by the 1880s, he was much more captivated by 'plutocracy, Semitic or American', and with 'the modish smartness that is its product.' He was a close friend of the Rothschilds and the Sassoons, relished the company of such tycoons as W. W. Astor, Colonel North, Lord Iveagh, J. B. Robinson, Sir Blundell Maple, and Sir Thomas Lipton, and was on especially intimate terms with Ernest Cassel and Baron Hirsch, who did much to restore his previously precarious finances.[16] In return, he secured an easy entrée for them into select society, when their birth and background might otherwise have proved a severe handicap. His accession merely 'completed the social sovereignty of wealth over every class in the realm'. In so far as he maintained friendships with such grandees as the Duke of Devonshire, it was because they were rich men, rather than because they were aristocrats. But on the whole, the 'smart society' centred on the King represented 'the revolt against the old aristocracy and excessive traditions.'[17]

In all these ways, patrician high society was being eroded by the inexorable force of 'mere wealth' which it could neither contain nor control. And from the 1880s onwards, there was a corresponding reduction in the proportion of endogamous marriages between peers, landed gentry, and their relatives, and a growth in the number of partners selected from outside the charmed circle. At the very time that society was becoming more plutocratic, the peerage was becoming more plebeian.[18] In 1876, Lord Rosebery married Hannah Rothschild, and thereafter, such links between aristocratic and banking families became much closer. During the late nineteenth and early twentieth centuries, the Baths, the Bessboroughs, the Lytteltons, the Mintos, the Shaftesburys, the Spencers, and the Sutherlands connected themselves with the Barings. Two daughters of the fifth Lord Suffield married into the Glyn and Mills families; and two brothers in the banking branch of the Grenfells married relatives of the Duke of Marlborough and Earl Grey. So pronounced was this trend by the late nineteenth century, that one quarter of the leading city bankers claimed an aristocrat for a father-in-law.[19]

Equally noteworthy was the sudden increase in the number of brides from overseas, especially from the United States of America. Between 1870 and 1914, fully 10 per cent of aristocratic marriages followed this novel pattern. Despite sensational press rumours to the contrary, the majority of these American brides were not especially rich, and many did not even come from New York. But they were, undeniably, foreign. And the growth in the number of American peeresses, from four in 1880 to more than fifty by 1914, certainly represented a significant relaxation of hitherto exclusive conventions.[20] Since they came from a country whose political culture and class structure were totally different from Britain's, many of them found the rigid hierarchy and formal entertaining intolerably stuffy. Some commentators welcomed this 'new blood' as 'fresh sap' that would 'invigorate the grand old tree of the British aristocracy.' Others believed that these women were unscrupulous adventuresses, who were pushed forward by the calculating American hostess, Lady Paget, who spoke with unrefined accents, who were probably tainted by Red Indian blood, and who 'helped to make [society] shallower, more extravagant, and more vulgar than it ever was before.'[21]

But the most sensational sign that the old status élite was failing to maintain its social tone was the 'veritable wave of marriages between the old nobility and actresses', which reached its peak in the heyday of the Gaiety and Gibson Girls in the 1900s.[22] Before 1884, only ten peers had married players during the previous hundred years. They were, after all, from a class that was deemed quite unsuitable, and many were regarded as being little better than prostitutes. But the marriage of the future Marquess of Ailesbury to Dolly Tester in that year marked the beginning of a new trend. By the First World War, there had been seventeen such marriages, including the Dukes of Leinster and of Newcastle, and bearers of such venerable names as Lords Headfort, Orkney, de Clifford, Queensberry, and Torrington. And many other patricians, like the second Duke of Westminster and the fifth Earl of Lonsdale, followed the lead of King Edward VII, and had affairs with ladies of the stage or other 'professional beauties'. Nor was this the only way in which traditional conventions relaxed: of the peers already mentioned, Newcastle, Leinster, Queensberry, and Torrington all later obtained divorces.[23] The old standards of behaviour were very definitely slipping.

How did the patricians respond to their loss of control over society, and to the decay of their own exclusive order? Was it true, as T. H. S. Escott claimed, that 'the antagonism between the aristocracy of wealth and birth' had 'long since been disappearing', and that they were blending imperceptibly and uncomplainingly into a new élite? Inevitably, reactions varied. The fact that there were so many marriages with Americans and with the daughters of bankers suggests that the younger generation were already mixing socially with a much wider section of the population than had been customary in their parents' day. Indeed, as more daughters of plutocrats were presented at court, this was almost bound to happen. At the same time, the sudden increase in the number of peers who married players was but one sign of 'the incorporation of the theatre into the estates of society'[24] By the 1890s, the aristocratic 'man about town' was a well-known phenomenon. He spent his days (and nights) in sporting clubs and near the stage door, mixed with book-keepers and racing journalists, squandered his allowance, and got into all kinds of mischief. This world of 'Pink Uns' and 'Pelicans', so memorably evoked by P. G. Wodehouse in his creation of Galahad Threepwood, was no fanciful invention. Young bloods like Lord Lonsdale, Lord Churston, and Sir Jack Astley disported themselves at least as disreputably in fact as 'Gally' did in fiction.[25]

But other notables were implacably opposed to the triumph of wealth over birth, and bitterly resented the fact that they no longer controlled the personnel or the tone of high society. Whether out of poverty or out of pique, many peers and gentry withdrew from London altogether, simultaneously abandoning both their social and their parliamentary activities. A group of high-minded, high-class wives, calling themselves the Lambeth Penitents, and including the Duchess of Leeds, Lady Tavistock, Lady Aberdeen, and Lady Stanhope, vainly urged the Princess of Wales to join them in promoting 'the moral improvement of society.'[26] Lady Dorothy Nevill resented 'the mob of plebeian wealth which surged into the drawing room.' 'Everywhere', she added, 'the doors were opened for Croesus to enter.' Birth was now of small account, while 'wealth yields an unquestioned sway.' And Arthur Ponsonby roundly condemned these new social climbers for their philistine superficiality: 'They are frightened of thought because it might plunge them into desperation, they are frightened of knowledge because it might dispel their dearest illusions.'[27]

Inevitably, many patricians sought to distance themselves from these parvenu interlopers. The Duchess of Buccleuch was 'bitterly opposed to all the vulgarity and ostentation of the smart set', took pride in the fact that she knew none of them personally, and only once entertained a Jew, as a personal favour to Edward VII. Lady Paget regretted that the King was 'always surrounded by a bevy of Jews and a ring of racing people', and had 'the same luxurious tastes as the Semites, and the same love of pleasure and comfort.'[28] Lord Salisbury accommodated the King at Hatfield only when official business required it, and even then refused to let him bring his current paramour. His high-minded brother-in-law, Lord Selborne, naturally shared these opinions. To his regret, he found himself staying at Crag Hall near Macclesfield, in August 1910, with some members of the fast set. He described them as 'a party of wives without husbands, most characteristic of that set', and felt that the atmosphere had 'a decidedly nasty taste to me'. Later in the same month, he visited more traditional company in Scotland, and he 'like[d] this lot immensely better than the smarties.'[29]

But it was not just that society was becoming increasingly divided between the smart and the staid, the plutocratic and the patrician. As politics became more bitter, and as politicians became more bourgeois, the previous close links between public life and social life were inevitably broken. At the time of Home Rule, London society was 'divided into bitterly opposed camps', and Liberal Unionists and Gladstonian loyalists no longer entertained each other, or met at the same social gatherings. By the 1900s, these divisions had healed somewhat, and men like Haldane and Asquith were welcomed in many of the great houses of London.[30] But as the Liberal legislation gathered momentum after 1906, society was once again very largely ranged in opposition to the government. There was widespread hostility to the military reforms of Esher and Fisher, and after Limehouse, Lloyd George and his friends were generally regarded as being beyond the pale. At the time of the Parliament Act crisis, and again with the controversy over Irish Home Rule and Ulster, social ostracism was widely practised. Lord Londonderry even refused an invitation to dinner to meet the King because Lord Crewe would also be there.[31]

Undeniably, the great London palaces continued to operate as centres of social-cum-political activity. Devonshire House was a focus for renegade Whigs in the aftermath of Home Rule. Lansdowne House was the favourite watering place for the Unionist leadership in the decade before the First World War. And Grosvenor House was the headquarters from which the die-hard revolt was planned in 1910–1911. But in each case, they were the homes of lost causes rather than the social centres of political power and initiative. The basic presumption of aristocratic high society, and the necessary pre-condition for its survival as an essential element in the government and parliamentary process, was that those who were politically pre-eminent were also socially pre-eminent, that high society and political society were fundamentally one and the same thing. But by the time Campbell-Bannerman became leader of the Liberals, and Bonar Law of the Conservatives, this assumption had long since ceased to be valid. In 1892, Lord Derby had already noticed the growing division 'between the social and the political world'; and early in the 1900s, T. H. S. Escott concluded that 'as a principle of social organisation, politics has been replaced by other agencies.'[32]

Even the Souls, that most self-regarding and self-assured of *fin-de-siècle* social groups, were the exception that emphatically proved the rule. Beyond any doubt, they were an aristocratic clique, dominated by members of the Charteris, Wyndham, Balfour, Lyttelton, Pembroke, Brownlow and Cowper families.[33] But as an aloof and separate set, complete with their private games, jokes, language and love affairs, they were one further sign that society was fragmenting. In the era of Home Rule, they had deliberately attempted to build friendships that crossed (and erased) the boundaries of political partisanship. But by the early 1910s, the political temperature was running so high that former Soul mates like Margot Asquith and George Curzon could no longer meet in the same house.[34] Many of the Souls were also famed for their political talents. But an aristocratic background was no longer a guarantee of success. Alfred Lyttelton and George Wyndham died before (or without) achieving the greatness that had been predicted for them, Curzon conspicuously failed to become Prime Minister, and it did Balfour's reputation no good that he succeeded. Ironically enough, the most important politician was only a Soul by marriage: the middle-class nonconformist, H. H. Asquith.

Moreover, many of the Souls were relatively poor: Alfred Lyttelton was a younger son, George Wyndham was far from rich, Arthur Balfour's finances were precarious, and Lord Elcho waited an unconscionably long time for his father to die.[35] One reason they placed so much stress on intimate friendship, on personal qualities and comradeship rather than show and display, was that most of them could not afford to live in the more ostentatious manner of the time. And even their patrician exclusiveness fails to stand up to careful scrutiny. For the two figures who did most to unify and promote the Souls were Laura and Margot Tennant, whose appearance in London society in 1881 and 1882 was regarded by many as the beginning of the end. Their father, Sir Charles Tennant, was a Glasgow chemicals manufacturer, who had only recently established himself in Peeblesshire, and who had no connections in London society. Mary Gladstone thought Margot 'rather pert and forward, . . . and somewhat lacking in good manners', and Queen Victoria considered her 'most unfit for a Cabinet minister's wife.' Long after she had married Lord Ribblesdale, her sister Charty Tennant still retained a sense of social inferiority. When visiting the Londonderrys' grand palace, she felt like 'a dirty Cinderella, all over grease spots.'[36]

By 1914, exclusive, aristocratic society had been transformed so fundamentally that it was no longer clear that it existed in its traditional sense. In the great houses of Piccadilly and Park Lane, young men and women still waltzed through the night until dawn. But these gatherings were now merely one element of London social life, and could not compete in display with the conspicuous consumption of the new plutocracy.[37] Instead of being an essential adjunct to political life, patrician society was increasingly detached from it. And even functioning as a marriage market, it was by no means as exclusive as it had been thirty years before. As one of the most important institutions through which the traditional élite had exercised power as a class, London society was effectively dead by 1914, and the First World War merely accelerated its terminal decline. The great houses closed down for the duration, and many young men, who should have set the pace and tone in the 1920s, never came back. As Lady Londonderry recalled, with only a touch of apocalyptic exaggeration: 'The *chose* that existed before the war was swept into oblivion in the holocaust that buried two generations of hapless young men, whose ideas and manners perished with them.'[38]

In the immediate aftermath of the war, most grandees decided to give up their traditional social activities. One by one, the great town palaces were sold and demolished: Devonshire House, Grosvenor House, Dorchester House, Lansdowne House and Norfolk House. Between 1919 and 1939, the Duke of Portland, the Duke of Somerset, Lord Fitzwilliam and Lord Durham left Grosvenor Square.[39] With very few exceptions, this was the death-knell of the old society. By the early 1930s, Patrick Kinross noted 'the rarity with which the great aristocratic names of old appear in the lists of hostesses.' In the decades before the First World War, he recalled, Lady Derby, Lady Shaftesbury, Lady Waldegrave, Lady Spencer, Lady Pembroke, Lady Salisbury, Lady Lansdowne, and Lady Stanhope had all been figures of importance. Among their descendants, not one was to be found. And the same was true among the dukes. Portland, Beaufort, Rutland, Devonshire, Richmond, Buccleuch, and Somerset no longer kept up any state in London, and neither Sutherland nor Westminster was particularly interested. Indeed, on the rare occasions when they mounted social events in the metropolis, they had to do so in 'improvised' accommodation.[40]

But it was not just the aristocratic houses that vanished in the inter-war years: it was also the aristocratic principle of formal entertaining. It was the era of the Bright Young Things, gossip columns, night clubs, cocktails, shorter skirts, and dancing. The Duke of Portland was appalled when he saw 'couples of all ages, solemnly performing what seemed to be flat-footed negro antics to the discordant uproar – I will not call it music – of a braying brass band.'[41] Lord Dunraven regretted that the London scene now included those who, 'before the war, would not have formed part of what the press is pleased to term society.' Members of the peerage married (and divorced) more widely, more transatlantically, and more plebeianly than ever before. The result was that hostesses no longer knew each guest personally, as they had invariably done before 1914. In 1928, Lady Ellesmere vainly tried to reassert pre-war standards of patrician exclusiveness by turning out four uninvited guests from a ball at Bridgewater House. But it later emerged that there had been *three hundred people* at her party whom she did not know personally. Without exception, public opinion was on the side of the gatecrashers.[42]

In this changed social context, the political receptions at Londonderry House were not only 'old fashioned': they were put on with 'an extravagance and panache that belonged to an earlier age', and that was widely criticized in the era of the great depression and the Jarrow hunger marches.[43] Nor did they achieve their intended political objectives. Although Lord Londonderry duly catered his way to the cabinet in 1931, he was abruptly dismissed five years later. The

Prime Minister responsible, Stanley Baldwin, told Londonderry's son that his mother's lavish entertaining of Ramsay Macdonald was widely seen as 'an act of political expediency to help your father's career.' And it did Macdonald no good, either. As Beatrice Webb remarked, such evident delight in high society on the part of a socialist argued 'a perverted taste and a vanishing faith'. It may be true, as their defenders have averred, that the minister and the Marchioness remained true to their principles, and took a genuine and compassionate delight in each other's company. But the association did them both a great deal of harm, and effectively discredited lavish, cross-party political entertaining for ever.[44]

As the old guard bowed out, they were superseded by a new generation of transatlantic social leaders, like Elsa Maxwell, Laura Corrigan, Nancy Astor, Emerald Cunard, and Henry Channon. Although they were all incorrigibly and snobbishly Anglophile, it seemed at times as if London society was 'being run by an American syndicate.' But while they presided over glittering social events, they did not entertain out of a 'sense of responsibility or duty or habit', and none of them counted for much in politics. As Henry Channon, who was MP for Southend, admitted: 'In society I am a power, . . . at the House of Commons I am a nonentity.'[45] By the inter-war years, Bonar Law, Baldwin, and Neville Chamberlain made a point of not consorting with such figures, and most cabinet ministers did not move in society at all. The frivolous world of social ambition and the pursuit of pleasure revealed in Channon's diaries is very different from the unglamorous government grind described in the journals of Tom Jones or J. C. C. Davidson. Society had ceased to be either aristocratic or political: it was, in Patrick Balfour's phrase, 'Society for society's sake', and nothing more.[46]

The only real protest against this inexorable dilution of patrician society came, not from the aristocracy, but from the new monarch. Neither King George V nor Queen Mary had any desire to be 'smart', and when they acceded in 1910, it was rightly predicted that many members of the late sovereign's 'rich and semitic entourage' would soon be disregarded, and that 'harlots and Jews' would be exchanged for 'tutors and governesses' at Sandringham and Balmoral.[47] King George V's tastes in friends ran much more towards 'landowners of ancient lineage and impeccable deportment', and included Lord Curzon, Lord Derby, the Duke of Devonshire, and the Duke of Richmond. Like the King himself, these men did not go about in the smart American society of the inter-war years. Families like the Derbys had little time for Emerald Cunard's social ambitions or cultural pretensions. And many aristocrats, who had effectively retired to what remained of their country estates, and so were much

less frequently in London than before, must have shared Lord Crawford's opinions: 'Personally, I try to keep aloof from the rich Jews
and Americans, and I don't want to be mixed up with Asiatics.'[48]

But the King's eldest son, Edward Prince of Wales, possessed a
social outlook very much more akin to his grandfather and namesake. It was later claimed that 'New York was his undoing', because
it 'modernised' and 'Americanised' him. He disliked his father's
friends on principle, and senior grandees like Lord Derby and Lord
Salisbury clearly disapproved of his lax morals and wayward habits.
He never became intimate with the younger generation of Cecils or
Cavendishes or Stanleys. He showed little interest in marrying into
the British aristocracy, as two of his brothers had done. And he
regarded genteel courtiers like Alec Hardinge and Alan Lascelles as
intolerably crusty. Instead, as Lord Winterton later explained, he
formed 'an inner circle of intimate friends bearing some similarity to
that of Edward VII'.[49] During the 1920s, he was a regular *habitué* of
the Embassy Club in Bond Street, and in the 1930s he was often
entertained by Henry Channon and Emerald Cunard. For a time,
another American, Thelma Furness, was his mistress. Then there
was Mrs Simpson from Baltimore. And during the Abdication crisis
itself, the King's cause was energetically supported by the most
mischievous British press barons: Lord Beaverbrook and Esmond
Rothermere.[50]

In short, it was not just the aristocracy that had been undermined
by two generations of social decay and plutocratic corruption: it was
the monarchy as well. This, at least, was how it seemed to many
people. In his famous post-Abdication broadcast, Archbishop Lang
described the King's entourage as 'a social circle whose standard and
way of life are alien to all the best instincts and traditions of his
people.' And Lord Crawford was even more censorious, damning
the King's American friends as 'all the touts and toadies who
revolved around Mrs Simpson, and whose influence upon society
was so corrupting.'[51] To men such as these, the accession of King
George VI and Queen Elizabeth thankfully portended the return of
old-style patrician decency. The Queen herself, as a daughter of the
Earl of Strathmore, came from 'the more decorous aristocratic
circles'. Their friends included such grandees as Lords Radnor, Stair,
Scarbrough, Harlech, Fortescue, and the Duke of Portland. And
they were happy to be served at Buckingham Palace by Lascelles and
Hardinge. As Henry Channon disapprovingly remarked, they were
'hemmed in by the territorial aristocracy.'[52]

Yet while there was some truth in this analysis, it was altogether
too simplistic. Appropriately enough, King Edward VIII had drawn
many of his friends from among the more plutocratized and disrepu-

table elements of the aristocracy: Lady Diana Cooper, Winston Churchill, the Dudleys, the Seftons, the Marlboroughs, the Sutherlands, and the Westminsters.[53] And the accession of George VI and Queen Elizabeth was a triumph, not for the old patrician society on which both Edward VII and Edward VIII had turned their backs, but for such middle-class moralists as Baldwin, Lang, and Reith of the BBC. If the Abdication affair showed anything about aristocratic society, it was merely to underscore the extent to which it had lost its identity, its coherence, its purpose. In its own way, this was a change every bit as revolutionary as the breakup of great estates, or the transformation of the peerage. As Lady Aberdeen remarked, if in 1877 it had been suggested that Grosvenor House and Devonshire House were to be demolished, and that Spencer House would become a ladies club, 'we should surely have asked ironically whether the Tower of London would be turned into a theatre or the British Museum into a circus.' Yet within her own lifetime, all this had indeed come to pass.[54]

Inevitably, it is the memoirs of the patrician (and not-so-patrician) women, rather than the men, that most discuss (and lament) the lowering of high society. Two quotations may serve by way of example and conclusion. Here is Margot Asquith (née Tennant), herself an agent of that very social disintegration she later came to deplore:

> Where today are the distinguished leaders, both in politics and in fashion, who forgathered in Devonshire House, Grosvenor House, Dorchester House, Lansdowne House and Stafford House? . . . Where are the fine manners and originality of men like the old Dukes of Westminster, Beaufort, Devonshire and Sutherland, the Lords Granville, Ribblesdale, Spencer, Pembroke and Cowper . . . ? There are several owners of beautiful houses who entertain us today, but – with a few exceptions – they do not take a conspicuous part in public affairs, or exercise a dominating influence over society.[55]

And here is Lady Londonderry, the most conspicuous and most unfortunate exception to the very same trend: 'Society as such', she wrote in 1938, 'now means nothing, and it represents nothing except wealth and advertisement . . . It does not represent what it formerly did, and it is well that this should be understood . . . . England has become Americanised.'[56]

ii.   The County Community Undermined

In his elegiac memoirs, *The Passing Years*, Lord Willoughby de Broke set out in elaborate and affectionate detail the hierarchy that had held 'undisputed and comfortable sway' in the county community during the halcyon days of his youth.[57] In descending order of importance and familiarity, it consisted of the Lord-Lieutenant, the Master of Foxhounds, the agricultural landlords, the Bishop, the chairman of quarter sessions, the Colonel of the Yeomanry, the MPs, the Dean, the Archdeacons, the Justices of the Peace, the lesser clergy, and finally the larger farmers. Although Willoughby was referring specifically to Warwickshire, this description would have held good – with appropriate modifications for Scotland and Ireland – for most parts of the British Isles in the mid-Victorian period. The county was a recognizable and autonomous unit – historically, geographically, politically, socially, and even sentimentally. And the only people who really mattered were the landowners, their relatives and their close professional associates. As the territorial class, they dominated their locality by virtue of their unrivalled wealth, their political influence, their social exclusiveness, and their unquestioned claim to leadership.

In setting out this description of the county élite (significantly, he never used the phrase 'county society'), Willoughby was very conscious that he had witnessed its virtual demise during the course of his own lifetime. By the early 1920s, when he penned these mellow reflections, it seemed to him that 'the county' as he had known, loved, and understood it no longer existed either 'geographically' or 'spiritually'. It was not talked of 'in the same tone of calm and reverent assurance that we heard when we were young', and for many people was little more than a name attached to a cricket team. Lord Winterton, who was a generation younger than Willoughby, but shared his social attitudes and also his love of fox-hunting, witnessed the whole process almost at full stretch, and had no doubt that the transformation in the shires was even greater than that in the capital itself. 'If', he recalled in 1955, surveying the previous half-century, 'the changes in London society have been marked enough, those in what is sometimes called "county society" are still more strange and curious.' So much so, indeed, that Winterton believed that 'what was true of the "county" a half century ago appears almost fantastic today.'[58]

Although the sales of country houses and the breakup of great estates were concentrated in the years immediately before and after the First World War, Willoughby was quite correct to argue that the county community began to decline during the last quarter of the nineteenth century. The changes in the franchise and in the constituencies brought about by the Third Reform Act meant that the landowners no longer dominated rural politics as of right, and the reform of local government meant the gradual but inexorable separa-

68. Lord Winterton by Sir Alfred Munnings.

tion of the social élite from the administrative élite. Even more important were the consequences of the agricultural depression. Many landowners were obliged to economize, which meant cutting or cancelling subscriptions, or letting their mansion and going to live more cheaply abroad. Inevitably, this weakened their local leadership, and lessened their local ties. In the county community, the gentry and grandees were expected to spend, and were expected to reside. But these expectations were no longer being met as fully as before. Lady Dorothy Nevill was not alone in regarding 'the modern practice of letting one's country house', as something that 'would have appalled the landed proprietors of other days, when such a thing was undreamed of.'[59]

In the counties no less than in London, the result was the same: as the patricians withdrew, the plutocrats moved in, renting, buying and building country houses with Park-Lane extravagance. William Dodge James, who was heir to two American fortunes, bought the 8,000-acre West Dean estate in Sussex, and remodelled the house in sumptuous style, with electric light, bathrooms a-plenty, and an automated laundry. But most plutocratic purchasers were more interested in a mansion than in an estate. Sir Ernest Cassel began by renting Compton Verney in Warwickshire (ironically enough from Willoughby's father), and then acquired Moulton Paddocks near Newmarket. Andrew Carnegie returned to Scotland in opulent triumph, by purchasing Skibo Castle, and lavished another £100,000 on alterations and improvements.[60] Sir Julius Wernher bought Luton Hoo in 1903, spent £30,000 a year to keep it up, and maintained a huge staff, yet rarely visited except on occasional Sunday afternoons. But the most prodigious purchaser was W. W. Astor. In 1893, he bought Cliveden from the Duke of Westminster, which prompted the *Estates Gazette* to warn that 'The American invasion of England has begun with a vengeance.' Ten years later he acquired Hever Castle in Kent, restoring and extending it at almost limitless expense, so he could live out his medieval fantasies – in Edwardian comfort.[61]

Where the international plutocrats led, the new British millionaires soon followed. Lord Iveagh bought the 15,000-acre Elveden estate in Suffolk, and converted the house into 'an appallingly luxurious mansion.' Lord Cowdray gobbled up houses and lands in Sussex and Scotland. And Lord Leverhulme bought 10,000 acres in Lancashire, as well as the islands of Lewis and Harris.[62] But most new men found a mansion and a park gave them ample scope for displays of parvenu vulgarity and self-indulgent eccentricity. The company promotor E. T. Hooley bought Papworth Hall, spent £250,000 on improvements, and filled it with furniture from Maples and other things that 'cultured people are supposed to possess.' Another speculator, Whittaker Wright, purchased Lea Park near Godalming, and installed an underwater billiard room, so that the players could look up between turns and see the fish swimming. And in 1910, Julius Drewe, the co-founder of Home and Colonial Stores, commissioned Lutyens to design Castle Drogo, a fantasy house in Devon. By comparison, Mrs Greville's purchase and renovation of Polesden Lacey in Surrey seemed almost staid – apart from the installation of a reredos from a demolished Wren church in the entrance hall.[63]

But it was not just the super-rich who were invading the shires during the late nineteenth and early twentieth centuries. On the periphery of most great cities, the prosperous middle-class businessmen and professionals were also heading for the countryside in unprecedented numbers. In Berkshire and Surrey, many small mansions were built in 'stockbroker's Tudor'. The rich men of Glasgow colonized the shores of Loch Lomond, the moguls of Manchester migrated to Cheshire, and the hardware princes of Birmingham and the Black Country established themselves in Warwickshire and the rural regions of Staffordshire.[64] Like most of the new millionaires, these lesser men did not want to establish themselves as fully-fledged landed proprietors. They regarded the country as a place for rest and repose, where money was spent, not made, and they were fully contented with the amenities of rural living – riding, hunting, shooting and entertaining. They aspired to a mansion, a park, and perhaps a home farm: but they had no interest in building up or administering a large estate. They wanted the recreational aspects of landownership without the responsibilities. They preferred houses in the country to country houses.[65] And the advent of the motor car meant that they could enjoy the best of both worlds.

More than any other technological development, the motor car spelt the end of the traditional county community. It made it easier for the new rich to work in the town and play in the country. It broke down the limited horizons and geographical immobility that had been the essential preconditions for county feeling. And it carried noise and dirt into the peace and quiet of the countryside. In 1907, *Punch* published two cartoons entitled 'The Village – Old and New Style', which vividly portrayed the chaos and filth that the motor car brought with it. As such, it was the apt symbol of irresponsible and corrosive plutocracy.[66] By definition, motorists were vulgar, selfish and inconsiderate. As they hurtled through the countryside, indifferent to tradition or locality, they seemed to epitomize what C. F. G. Masterman called 'wealth's intolerable arrogance.' They abused their privileges 'with an inconsiderate insolence' which merely served to demonstrate 'the extent to which the wealth of England, during the past half century, has passed away from the hands of gentlemen.' If the horse was the apt symbol of landed supremacy, then the car was the sure and certain sign that that supremacy was at an end.[67]

But the motor unsettled the county community still further by making possible a new and essentially subversive social custom: the 'weekend' house party from Saturday to Monday. In the mid-Victorian period, most landowners spent at least half of the year residing on their estates, attending to their local duties, and entertaining only those country neighbours living within a ten-mile radius – the maximum distance it was comfortable to travel by horse. But the motor car effectively destroyed this stable and self-sufficient mode of life, by making country houses so much more easily accessible.[68] Owners came and went more frequently, and invited guests from London rather than the locality. Houses that had once been the centres of great estates were now regarded as extensions of metropolitan drawing rooms. They were places to entertain in, rather than to live in. Many plutocratic mansions, like Luton Hoo and Polesden Lacey, were within easy driving distance of London, and were the setting for sumptuous weekends which had nothing to do with country life, but were essentially a prolonged London dinner party. As *Punch* lamented in 1914, 'the passing of the old families, and the advent of the week-end "merchant prince"' was one of the outstanding trends of the time.[69]

The result, as Lady Dorothy Nevill explained, was that 'country life, or rather, short spells of it, has now become a sort of luxury of the rich'.[70] Instead of settling down for a month or two, to discharge their rural responsibilities quietly and dutifully, they stayed for a brief interlude, indulged themselves, and then motored on somewhere else. Country houses, and especially those purchased or built by the new plutocracy, increasingly resembled luxury hotels, with their marble bathrooms, their electric lighting, their French chefs, their international guest lists, and their sumptuous entertaining. King Edward VII preferred these smart social houses of the new rich (like West Dean or Elveden) to the staid mansions of the old order (like Goodwood or Hatfield). They were better equipped, the company was more interesting, and the moral tone was less censoriously Victorian. But their owners had little interest in rural life, and little understanding of country ways or obligations: they went there to visit, rather than to live. As C. F. G. Masterman explained, 'They entertain themselves and their friends in the heart of an England for whose vanishing traditions and enthusiasms they care not at all.'[71]

These dramatic changes in country-house ownership and living were exactly paralleled by changes in the most symbolic patrician pursuit of all: fox-hunting. To be sure, some of the great magnates continued to control their hunts by hereditary right and with seemingly despotic power. The Dukes of Beaufort were dynastic huntsmen, and Badminton was the great metropolis for the horse and hound fraternity. Lord Willoughby de Broke followed his father and his grandfather as Master of the Warwickshire. When the Duke of Rutland retired from his Mastership of the Belvoir in 1896, it was described in the sporting press as a 'national calamity'. The fifth Earl Spencer was Master of the Pytchley on three successive occasions, from 1861 to 1864, 1874 to 1877, and 1890 to 1894. He was also Lord-Lieutenant of Northamptonshire and first chairman of the county council, as well as being a lifelong Liberal and member of each Gladstone administration.[72] Like Spencer, Henry Chaplin combined a political and a sporting life, and was Master of the Burton from 1865 to 1871, and of the Blankney between 1877 and 1881. By contrast, Lord Lonsdale was a full-time sportsman, playboy, and adventurer, was Master of the Quorn from 1893 to 1898, and of the Cottesmore between 1906 and 1911, and again from 1915 to 1919.[73]

But in the period of agricultural depression, even the greatest of grandees found the costs of hunting more than they could bear. The Dukes of Beaufort and Rutland were obliged to ask for subscriptions, and the latter was forced to cut back his hunting from five to four days a week in 1891. Lord Spencer had to borrow £15,000 to cover his excess hunting expenses in 1879, and refused to contemplate a fourth term as Master of the Pytchley in 1900 on account of the cost.[74] Henry Chaplin virtually bankrupted himself with the Blankney, was forced to sell his hounds in 1883, and had to part with his estate soon after. And Lord Lonsdale was obliged to resign as Master of the Quorn in 1898 because his trustees effectively ordered him to do so. Nor were these the only Masters who were hard hit and forced to withdraw. George Luttrell was a West Country gentleman, who had hunted in Somerset at his own expense: but in 1881, he simply gave up. Three years later, Lord Haldon took over the South Devon and promised to provide all the necessary funding. But in 1886, he was compelled to sell the hounds. As one historian of hunting remarked in 1902: 'Gone are the landlords of the old school, the backbone of England, the fox-hunting squires, are few and far between.'[75]

In hunting as in housing, the new men moved in as the old guard moved out. As early as the 1870s, a fashionable hunt like the Quorn had a Liverpool shipping merchant as Master, and many businessmen and manufacturers from Leicester were found in the field. In the 1890s, a Midlands sporting journalist recorded the same developments in his locality. 'Thirty years ago', he noted, 'the Warwickshire, Staffordshire and Worcestershire Hunts received little support from city men; today, hundreds of Birmingham magnates and businessmen devote a large amount of their leisure to the prince of sports.'[76] Black Country tycoons like Sir Alfred Hickman turned out with the Albrighton, while Ernest Cassel rode (somewhat unsteadily and inexpertly) with the Warwickshire when he was tenant of Compton Verney. As weekending plutocrats, city businessmen and distant strangers came to dominate the hunting field, the character of the sport inevitably changed: instead of being 'the club of the neighbourhood', it 'lost the social significance of local surroundings.' As one commentator remarked in 1908, it was no longer 'the sport of the landed interest.' Two thirds of every field were 'businessmen of sorts', and the general atmosphere was 'redolent of money.'[77]

But it was not just the men of money who threatened the landowners' pleasure and pre-eminence in the saddle. It was also their traditional allies and essential partners in the chase, the tenant farmers. For they, too, were severely hit by agricultural depression, and as their finances were squeezed, they no longer supported, or tolerated, fox-hunting as uncomplainingly as before.[78] Those who still hunted demanded an end to despotic Masterships, and insisted that the farmers should have a say in the management of the hunt. They urged Masters to restrict their numbers, and to ban those parvenu outsiders, who cared little for country ways. They sought to protect

their poultry by killing foxes: during the last quarter of the nineteenth century, there seems to have been a definite increase in
vulpicide. And they demanded compensation for trespass and for the
damage that the hunt caused to crops and to fences. In 1878, the
courts ruled that fox-hunting did not give unrestricted rights of
access, and thereafter, the demand for compensation markedly increased. At the same time, and in an effort to reduce their costs,
many farmers turned to barbed wire instead of posts and rails for
fencing. It was only one-tenth of the price of more traditional
materials. But it was anathema to huntsmen.[79]

Under these circumstances, the hunting fraternity had no alternative but to treat the farmers more gently and attentively than before.
Yet to do so required money, at the very time when hunting finances
were themselves very precarious. One of the reasons why Lord
Lonsdale spent so much as Master of the Quorn was that between
1891 and 1898, compensation for poultry claims and for damages
more than tripled. The only way that a farmer could be persuaded to
take down his barbed wire was if the hunt agreed to pay for it. But
only very rich men, like the Duke of Sutherland, who was for a time
Master of the North Staffordshire, could afford to do so. Some
Masters attempted to reduce the size of their hunting field, by
banning outsiders or demanding a minimum subscription. But this
violated the oldest tradition of the sport, that all men were welcome.
And some hunts accepted that farmers should be allowed to join the
management committee: the Worcester as early as 1873, the Quorn
in 1887, the Meynell in 1889, and the South Berkshire in 1890. But
this again was a fundamental revolution, as the traditional landed
leaders were obliged to share their power with their social
inferiors.[80]

In Ireland, the tensions between landlords and tenants were much
greater, and the consequences for hunting were much more serious.
Although the sport was greatly enjoyed by the ascendancy, there
were only twenty packs of foxhounds in the whole country, their
finances were generally precarious, and they never acquired a popular following in rural communities. At the height of the Land War,
during the winter of 1881–1882, they were subjected to a sustained
and successful campaign of violence, disruption, and sabotage.[81]
Crowds of protesters threw stones and other missiles, hounds were
poisoned, and Masters were compelled to give up the chase. By
January 1882, three-quarters of all Irish hunts had been molested, and
the sport had practically been given up. The most sensational result
was that the Marquess of Waterford resigned as Master of the
Curraghmore (which he maintained at his own expense, amounting
to £6,000 a year), broke up his establishment, and moved to

Leicestershire.[82] At least five more hunts sold their hounds, including the Wexford and the Muskerry, and many more were forced to suspend their activities for a time. In the history of the Land League, this was a brief and ephemeral episode; but it left an indelible mark on the harrassed and demoralized hunting fraternity, and widened still further the rift between landlords and tenants.

Although the concerted campaign was not renewed by the League in the autumn of 1882, hunting in Ireland thereafter was inevitably a precarious pastime. There were further sporadic disruptions, as in 1887, when the Queens County was compelled to give up hunting in the eastern part of its territory, and in 1907, when agitation by the United Irish League forced the Ormond into liquidation.[83] But it was the decline of the ascendancy, rather than the animosity of the farmers, that presented the greater threat. As the owners began to sell under successive Land Purchase Acts, the territorial basis of the sport was inevitably eroded. Between 1854 and 1913, the Westmeath had no fewer than nineteen Masters. And unlike England, there were very few plutocrats who were prepared to participate. The Tipperary Hunt was rescued by an American in 1887, and the Kilkenny in 1908, but these were rare exceptions. More typical were the experiences of the West Carbery, immortalized in the stories of Somerville and Ross. The hunt had suspended operations in the late 1870s, because of 'political troubles and bad times generally.' It was revived in 1891 by Aylmer Somerville, and he was followed as MFH by his sister Edith in 1903. But five years later, she was forced to resign for financial reasons.[84]

In Ireland, hunting was sabotaged; in Britain, it was transformed. But the end result was essentially the same: one of the greatest props to the traditional county community had been knocked away. By the 1900s, fox-hunting had ceased to be the 'national sport', and was no longer even the visible and vigorous expression of county solidarity and county identity, or of unchallenged patrician leadership.[85] In many of the shires, the MFH had ceased to be the second man in the county, and the hunt was more a middle-class pastime than an upper-class religion. And just as the motor undermined the integrity of country-house life, so it also threatened the stability of the hunt. Cars were noisy and dirty, and frightened the horses and distracted the hounds. And they made it even easier for outsiders to get to the meet and get in the way. One MFH described them as 'the invention of the evil one.' Lord Willoughby de Broke regarded them as 'a spectacle quite out of harmony with the sport of fox-hunting', and vainly tried to ban them from the Warwickshire meet.[86] In the end, the invention of the motor may have done more damage to hunting than the invention of barbed wire. But these were not the only

technological developments by which the sport was threatened: there
was also the shotgun.

In its traditional form, shooting had been an integral part of
country life. The landowner walked his estate, with a pair of
pointers, a muzzle-loading gun, and a powder flask, and thought
himself lucky if he shot ten birds in a day. But by the 1880s, 'the
whole character of the sport' was fundamentally altered, in its
technology, its scale, and its social significance. The steel-barrelled,
breech-loading shot-gun was perfected, with its single trigger and
smokeless powder, and better guns meant better shots and more
frequent firing. At the same time, the systematic rearing of tame
birds meant they could be driven towards an invited party of guns by
beaters, and slaughtered in their thousands.[87] On one estate in
Norfolk, only 39 birds were killed in 1821. Sixty years later, the
figure was 5,363. The Prince of Wales took to the new sport with
alacrity, and Sandringham soon became one of the finest shooting
estates in the country. But there were many others that provided
ample sport. Welbeck, Blenheim, Chatsworth, and Holkham were
famous for their pheasant shoots. Lords Henniker, Huntingfield, and
Albemarle provided excellent partridge in Norfolk (as did many of
the great estates in Wales). And in the north of England and on the
Scottish moors, there was grouse in plentiful abundance.[88]

Many of the greatest shots of the period were aristocrats, such as
Lord Herbert Vane Tempest, Lord Berkeley Paget, Lord de Clifford,
and Sir Harry Stonor. But it was generally reckoned that Lord de
Grey and Lord Walsingham were the best of all. De Grey shot so fast
and so accurately that on one occasion he had seven dead birds in the
air at once, and on another he killed twenty-eight pheasant in one
minute. Between 1867 and 1923, he slaughtered 250,000 pheasant,
150,000 grouse, and 100,000 partridge. Lord Walsingham held the
record for the highest number of grouse killed in a single day: 1,070
on Blubberhouse Moor in 1888. But the cost of it all was more than
his finances could bear. In 1912, he was forced to sell his Yorkshire
estates and his London property, and spent the last seven years of his
life abroad.[89] Inevitably, these big shots competed with each other,
although this was thought in certain quarters to be extremely bad
form. In retrospect it also seems an ominous foretaste of that even
greater slaughter which was soon to come, not in the butts of
Norfolk or the grouse moors of Scotland, but on the battlefields of
Flanders. And after a day's sustained shooting, it was almost impossible to avoid suffering from a violent headache.

Despite the extensive participation by landowners, both as hosts
and guns, the shooting party was a quintessentially plutocratic
affair – 'smart' society transferred from the town to the country. It

69. Lord de Grey.   70. Lord Walsingham.

was easier for middle-aged parvenus to take up than hunting, and it
could be enjoyed at such fashionable houses as Tring, Elveden, and
West Dean. Since the birds were tame and driven by beaters, there
were some who argued it was not really sport at all.[90] Hugh
Strutfield believed that shooting 'was a much more fascinating
recreation in former years, before plutocracy had laid its rapacious
paws on it and made it a toil-less pastime for the lazy and the
luxurious.' And it was also very expensive – partly because of the
cost of rearing the birds and employing the keepers and the beaters,
and partly because the house parties themselves were quite exceptionally opulent, especially if the King himself happened to be
present. As the American ambassador observed in 1913, 'you've no
idea how much time and money they spend on shooting.' Lord
Winterton was even more censorious: to him, it meant 'eating too
many big meals, meeting too many rich Jews, and shooting too
many fat pheasants.'[91]

Like deerstalking in Scotland, which was transformed and plutocratized at exactly the same time, the craze for shooting served only to
undermine the county community still further. The invited guests
stayed for a few days, indulged their 'saturnalia of slaughter', and
then moved on again, without ever really settling down in the
countryside at all.[92] And as impoverished landlords felt compelled to
let out their shooting to impersonal syndicates of London businessmen, the feeling that the old paternal connections were being undone
was only further intensified. But in addition, the rearing and preservation of so much game was a major threat to the survival of fox-
hunting. For wild foxes and tame birds did not easily cohabit in the
countryside. The big guns disliked foxes because they killed the
game; and the hunting community disliked the big guns because they
killed the foxes. It would be overstating matters to say that this
resulted in 'civil war' in the countryside. But it was certainly the case
that excessive game preservation, carried out selfishly and incon-
siderately, led to a decline in the number of foxes, and the animosity
between those who hunted and those who shot was undeniably
great.[93]

As Willoughby de Broke rightly remembered, the county community in its heyday was more than a geographical designation or an
administrative unit: it was an article of faith, a state of mind, a way of
living. But as early as the Queen's Diamond Jubilee, T. H. S. Escott
believed that the county had ceased to exist 'as an object of fetish
worship.'[94] The old élite was in decline, and the new plutocracy
could not be kept out. Fox-hunting had become middle-class, and
shooting was vulgar and competitive. As in London, so in the shires,
the political and administrative élite was no longer the social élite.
And the rise of something termed 'county society' signified an even
deeper change – the appearance of an essentially social élite who had
no territorial or historical attachment to the countryside, and who
went there for recreation rather than residence. But although the
county continued to exist in a social sense, it was not the society (or
the county) it had once been. Appropriately enough, the *Victoria
History of the Counties of England* was established in 1899. But it was
the product of metropolitan, rather than local initiative. And it
commemorated the county community whose history was essentially over.[95]

During the inter-war years, these trends were only further intensified. As the great estates were broken up, and the country houses
sold off, the social structure of the old county hierarchy effectively
collapsed. The territorial cohesion, and sense of timeless continuity,
which had been the very essence of the county community, simply
dissolved. Most of the land that came into the market in the years

immediately after 1918 was bought up by the sitting tenants. As the *Estates Gazette* rightly noted, it was 'not so much the foundations of a new aristocracy that are being laid, as the foundations of a new yeomanry.'[96] Instead of the time-honoured combination of landlord and tenant, there was a new breed of owner–occupier. But these were not the men to rejuvenate the old county community. For many of them had borrowed at high rates of interest to purchase their farms in the relatively prosperous days of 1918–21. But as agriculture collapsed yet again, they were almost all uncommonly poor by the late 1920s, and this time, there was no landlord to grant remissions and cushion the blow. There were only creditors who would not wait: by 1935, it was estimated that half of the land of Norfolk was effectively owned by the banks.[97]

Despite its depressed condition, the new rich continued to pour into the countryside. The American newspaper tycoon, William Randolph Hearst, bought St Donats Castle in Wales, ransacked Europe for art treasures to put in it, and hardly ever visited. But he was only one of many transatlantic purchasers: Lady Baillie at Leeds Castle, Ronald Tree at Ditchley, Urban Broughton at Anglesey Abbey, Henry Channon at Kelvedon, and the Elmhirsts at Dartington. And in Sussex, the weekending plutocracy continued its inexorable advance: Major Courtauld at Burton Park, Charles Bingham at Bignor Park, Lord Moyne at Bailiffscourt, and the Mountbattens at Ashdean.[98] As in the years before the First World War, very few of these interlopers were interested in setting themselves up as fully-fledged landowners. The country was a place for recreation, amusement, and entertainment, an extension of London society. Emerald Cunard hardly ever set foot there. Nancy Astor's 'Cliveden set' was merely a collection of weekending politicians, plutocrats and appeasers. And while Henry Channon liked to think of himself as the 'squire of Kelvedon', he regarded his country neighbours in Essex with scarcely concealed horror, with their 'ghastly houses smelling of gentry.'[99]

In those counties where the estate system survived most tenaciously, some grandees continued to hunt in the traditional manner, like Sir Watkin Williams-Wynn in Denbighshire, and Lord Leconfield in Sussex. At Badminton, the Dukes of Beaufort maintained their horses and hounds in traditional style, and in Yorkshire, Lord Barnard kept barbed wire out of the hunting country when he was Master of the Zetland. Lord Winterton was an energetic follower to hounds, and recorded with pride that he had hunted with thirty-eight packs during half a century.[100] But the most famous patrician hunter in the inter-war years, who combined sport and politics in a manner reminiscent of Lord Spencer and Henry Chaplin, was Ed-

71. *Three generations with the Middleton Hunt* (Lord Halifax, Lord Irwin, the Hon. Charles Wood), 1932, by Lionel Edwards.

ward Wood, Lord Halifax. In 1906 he set up his own pack of Garrowby Harriers, and even during the parliamentary session, he hunted three days a week. When he came back from being Viceroy of India, he became Master of the Middleton, and in November 1932, he turned out in the company of his father and his eldest son: three generations of the same family in the same hunting field. Despite his Christian convictions, Halifax never experienced the slightest difficulty in reconciling blood sports with religious piety. Not for nothing was he known as 'Holy Fox'.[101]

But inevitably, the sales of land and the impoverishment of the farmers 'altered the whole social basis of hunting' in many areas. Devotees of the sport rightly regarded the immediate post-war years as the most troubled in its history. The new owner–occupiers were even less sympathetic than the old tenant farmers had been, and some wanted to levy a charge when hounds and horses crossed their lands. In 1923, *The Field* claimed that the 'last remnants of the old squirearchy' could no longer afford to enjoy the sport of their ancestors. Brash newcomers poured in, who understood little of country ways, and cared even less, and Americans like Chester Beatty and the young Paul Mellon appeared in the field.[102] In 1925, William Dixon devoted an entire chapter of his book on hunting to advising them how to ride, how to dress, and how to behave. In Ireland, the demise of the ascendancy and the civil war meant that well over 'half of the country' was unhunted, and those few hunts that survived were almost entirely middle class in composition. As one observer re-marked in 1936: 'The aristocracy and squirearchy who forgathered at the meet a century ago would be surprised if they could do so today, and see the change in personnel in the field. The new rich are greatly in evidence, self-made people for the most part.'[103]

Nor did shooting recover its pre-war scale or vigour. As the older generation of big shots passed away, they left no successors, and after so much slaughter on the Somme, even the mass extermination of birds seemed somehow distasteful. In 1937, the Duke of Portland admitted to feeling 'quite ashamed' at the 'enormous number of pheasants we sometimes killed' at Welbeck in the years before 1914. When Lord Dunglass took up the sport in the early 1930s, he preferred to shoot in the more traditional style, walking a long distance, with his brother and his dog, and bagging a small number of wild birds.[104] In so far as shooting did survive in its Edwardian guise, it owned more to the King than to the aristocracy. For while George V turned his back on the 'smart' set, his passion for slaugh-tering thousands of tame birds was even more well-developed than his father's had been. When staying at Welbeck, Elveden, Holkham, or Chatsworth, he expected the game to be plentiful. And although his hosts did not share his passion, they felt obliged to comply. But many regarded the King's love of killing as anachronistic and un-balanced. As Lord Crewe once remarked, 'it is a misfortune for a public personage to have any taste so simply developed as the craze for shooting is in our beloved monarch . . . . His perspective of what is proper seems almost destroyed.'[105]

By the inter-war years, it was preservation rather than destruction that most took the aristocracy's attention in rural affairs. As a landowning élite in the process of territorial abdication, they could no longer control the countryside. But they could present themselves instead as the guardians of its beauty and its amenities. With motives that were a mixture of the snobbish and the aesthetic, they protested against ribbon development, urban blight, and 'unlovely country houses . . . savouring of urban villadom.'[106] Lord Crawford pro-moted the Council for the Preservation of Rural England, in the hope of persuading the middle classes to share that well-disposed feeling for the countryside which, he believed, had always character-ized the landowners. And G. M. Trevelyan devoted much effort to the same cause. He delivered a series of lectures alerting the public to the threat to England's natural beauty. He was chairman of the Estates Committee of the National Trust, and was a generous benefactor. And in 1930 he became the first President of the Youth Hostels Association, the purpose of which was to inculcate 'knowl-edge, care and love of the countryside' in the young.[107]

This was a far cry from the residential attachment and local leadership that had prevailed in the shires when Willoughby de Broke had been a young man.[108] As he recognized only too plainly, the 'identity of the county' had been 'blurred by the cosmopolitanism of the motor car and by quick train services to London and back.' People no longer remained in the countryside for extended periods of time, 'to steep themselves in its atmosphere.' Dinner parties in the country were virtually indistinguishable from dinner parties in London. Most of the guests had just arrived from town, or were about to go back there. There was, Willoughby felt, 'nothing bucolic' about such gatherings. But at the same time, he also noticed that the 'orbit of country people' had greatly expanded. Their grandparents might have settled for the hunt ball or the Assembly Rooms at Cheltenham. But now, there were many far-away places that beckoned alluringly.[109] It was not just that the county was plutocratized; it was also that the patricians had been internationalized.

iii.   The Allure of Far-off Places

In 1904, the Hon. Edward Wood decided to prepare himself for public life by travelling abroad with his friend Ludovick Amory. But rather than 'following the Grand Tour tradition, which had been in the early nineteenth century the normal introduction to the political stage', he decided to go 'on a trip round the world.' He began by visiting South Africa, but was almost immediately forced to return home because of an unexpected family crisis. He rejoined Amory at Port Said, and journeyed on to India, where he stayed with the Viceroy, Lord Curzon, and did 'the usual tourist round of Delhi, Agra, Benares, Cawnpore, Rawlpindi, Peshwar, [and] the Khyber'. From Bombay he proceeded via Ceylon to Australia, where he was the guest of Lord Northcote, the Governor-General, and 'met several of the principal political leaders', then travelled on to New Zealand, and finally returned home by way of a second visit to South Africa. As he later explained, it seemed wholly appropriate in the first decade of the twentieth century 'that for visits to the political and artistic countries of Europe should be substituted visits to what were still termed the Colonies.'[110]

During the forty-odd years before the outbreak of the First World War, such genteel globe trotting assumed almost epidemic proportions. In 1883, Sir Claude Champion de Crespigny made the first crossing of the North Sea in a balloon. When visiting the United States in 1873, Lord Rosebery encountered the Duke of Manchester, Lord Dunraven, Lord Skelmersdale, and Lord and Lady Alfred

Churchill. The future Lord Desborough twice swam the pool of Niagara Falls, the Hon. G. N. Curzon discovered the source of the Oxus River, and Lord Lonsdale travelled 3,000 miles in the Arctic. Lord Porchester, C. P. Trevelyan, Lord Randolph Churchill, the Hon. Edward Stanley, and Lord Spencer went on round the world tours.[111] Indeed, so widespread was this fashion for aristocratic adventuring and published reminiscence that in two successive volumes of the periodical *Nineteenth Century*, for 1892 and 1893, it was possible to read the Duke of St Albans on 'Jamaica Resurgens', Lady Galloway on 'Globe-Trotting in New Zealand', the Countess of Jersey on life in New Caledonia, Lady Grey Egerton on 'Alaska and its Glaciers', and the Earl of Meath on 'A Britisher's Impressions of America and Australasia.'[112]

By definition, the landed classes had been pre-eminently the travelling classes throughout their history. Despite, or because of, their territorial connections, their local allegiances and their national self-consciousness, they enjoyed the resources and the leisure that were necessary for lengthy journeyings abroad. From Renaissance times onwards, the Grand Tour had been an essential part of any young aristocrat's education, and during the first half of the nineteenth century, there was a growing trickle of patrician visitors to more remote parts of the globe. The Earl of Selkirk and Lady Emmeline Stuart Wortley visited the United States, while the young Lord Robert Cecil went on a two-year round-the-world tour, in successful pursuit of improved health and matured character.[113] Nevertheless, by the last quarter of the nineteenth century, it was generally recognized that more patricians were travelling more frequently, and more distantly, than ever before. Individually, their motives were the same as their forebears': the pursuit of pleasure, the search for adventure, the need to prepare for public life, the avoidance of social disgrace, and the allure of knight-errantly quests. But collectively, the consequences were much more far-reaching.

For many grandees and gentry, the greatest incentive to travel remained enjoyment; and the expansion of the German spa towns, and the development of the Riviera coast, offered unprecedented opportunities for self-indulgence (and also for recuperation). In the 1890s, it was claimed that the Riviera played host to the Tsar, the Emperor Francis Joseph, Queen Victoria, 'most of the Balkan kings, half the English peerage and the Almanac de Gotha.'[114] A. J. Balfour delighted in the casinos of Monte Carlo, Lord Spencer invariably left for Aix-les-Bains or Homburg after parliament rose, Mr Gladstone was not immune to the charms of Biarritz, and the Duke of Devonshire actually expired at the Hotel Metropole in Cannes in 1908. For those who preferred more vigorous activity, there were partridge and hares to be slaughtered on the great estates of central Europe, which were developed for shooting at exactly the same time as the cult of the gun reached its apogee in Britain. In Bohemia, Count Trautmanndorff provided an orchestra to accompany the elaborate luncheon, and on Baron Hirsch's estates in Hungary, Lord de Grey once killed seven thousand partridge during a five-week stay.[115]

By the late nineteenth century, the Continent was no longer a place to be visited once in a lifetime, as in the days of the Grand Tour: it had become a home from home for many regular and titled visitors. The most emphatic evidence of this was the proliferation of aristocratic villas in the countryside and along the coastline of France and Italy. Lord Carnarvon established himself at Portofino, while Lord Derby preferred the environs of Cannes. In 1870, Lord Salisbury bought what became the Chalet Cecil on the cliffs at Puys near Dieppe. Twenty-five years later, he sold it and, having dismissed the villas near Florence as being too reminiscent of St. John's Wood in London, built himself a new house near Monte Carlo.[116] In 1897, Lord Rosebery purchased a villa near Naples, but was so distressed by Lloyd George's attacks on aristocratic landowners that in 1909 he gave it to the Foreign Office as a summer residence for the British ambassador. Yet in the very same year, Sir George Sitwell bought Montegufoni, a vast medieval Tuscan palace, with five courtyards and over one hundred rooms, which he eagerly set about restoring.[117]

From the 1880s onwards, Egypt became the favourite destination for aristocrats in search of winter warmth, renowned for its gentle climate, its political stability, its exotic landscape, its magnificent ruins, and its palatial hotels and river steamers. Lord Randolph Churchill thought 'life on the Nile' to be 'ideal', Lord Spencer wintered there in February 1899, and the Duke and Duchess of Devonshire were also regular visitors.[118] Indeed, some patricians were sufficiently fascinated by what they saw of Egypt's ancient civilization to turn themselves into amateur archaeologists, in the tradition of Lord Brudenell and the fourth Earl of Sandwich. Lord Northampton was an early example; but the most famous was the fifth Lord Carnarvon. After a motoring accident, which severely damaged his chest, he was advised to go to Egypt each winter for his health. In 1906, he began excavations at Thebes, hiring the young Howard Carter to superintend the digging. On the eve of the First World War, he obtained a concession to begin excavating in the Valley of the Kings, and in 1922, this led to the sensational discovery of Tutankhamun's tomb, followed by his own scarcely less sensational death in the following year.[119]

72. Lord Carnarvon in Egypt.

But the most opulent new indulgence was the ownership of a seagoing yacht. Regular residents in the Mediterranean, like Lords Rosebery and Carnarvon, spent much time sailing among the islands of the Aegean. Some grandees even raced their yachts, like Lord Dunraven, who won three Queens Cups and two Kings Cups at Cowes, and twice challenged for the Americas Cup. Valkyrie II lost honourably in 1893, but Valkyrie III was defeated two years later, amid circumstances so controversial and unsporting that Dunraven was stripped of his Honorary Membership of the New York Yacht Club.[120] Even more extravagant were those steam yachts, which Arthur Ponsonby rightly called 'floating houses of luxury'. Lord Lonsdale cut a great figure at Cowes in the Verena, where he used to hob-nob with the Kaiser. The Duke of Sutherland rented out his yacht, the Catania, during the winter, but in the summer used it himself in the Mediterranean. And Lord Crawford and the Duke of Bedford steamed to far away places, like Mauritius and Tristan da Cunha, to indulge their interests in astronomy, bird watching, and collecting rare species of animals.[121]

During the inter-war years, those grandees who could afford it continued to live much of their lives for pleasure – so much so that in *Tender is the Night*, Scott Fitzgerald depicted the British aristocracy holidaying abroad in distinctly unfavourable terms as cold, effete, and repellent.[122] The most famous full-time patrician playboy was Bend Or, the second Duke of Westminster. He loved power-boat racing, motoring, and flying, and was a frequent visitor to America and Africa. He maintained one house for boar-hunting, near Biarritz, designed by Herbert Baker, and another in Normandy, close to the casinos at Le Touquet and Deauville. He regularly rented villas at Cannes and Monte Carlo, and had a suite at the Hotel Lotti in Paris permanently reserved. One of his yachts, the Flying Cloud, was fitted out to the designs of the architect Detmar Blow, in the manner of an English country house, with four poster beds and curtains of Florentine silk. The other, the Cutty Sark, was a converted destroyer, and required a crew of forty-three. 'Whose yacht is that?' Amanda asks Elyot as they look out to sea from their Mediterranean balcony in Noel Coward's *Private Lives*. 'The Duke of Westminster's, I expect', he replies. 'It always is.'[123]

More adventurous patricians were by this time able to travel far greater distances in relative comfort and safety. As Lord Ronaldshay explained, 'extraordinary facilities for travel' had 'sprung into existence . . . enabling enormous numbers of people to journey with speed and comfort over the whole of the civilised globe.'[124] The North American continent was crossed by the railroad in the late 1860s, and Asia and Africa were opened up by the end of the century. The 1880s saw the beginning of the great age of transatlantic steamships, and these were soon followed by the Royal Mail Lines to South America, the Union Castle Company to South Africa, and by P & O to India and the Antipodes. In 1873, Jules Verne wrote *Around the World in Eighty Days*; but by 1902 it was possible to complete the journey in half that time.[125] The result was unprecedented opportunities for titled and genteel travellers to see what Lord Curzon described as 'the wonders of nature' and 'the scarcely less remarkable masterpieces of man.' As Osbert Sitwell later remarked, with a characteristic mixture of insouciance and condescension: 'Whoever has the chance of seeing Angkor and doesn't is mad.'[126]

But it was not just the great sights of the world – whether natural or man made – that patricians visited in unprecedented numbers during these years. It was also that they indulged, to a degree not even possible on the great estates of Central Europe, their apparently unquenchable desire for ritualized slaughter. At home, they killed small birds; abroad, they killed large animals. As a test of courage, chivalry, endurance, and manhood, the allure of big-game hunting was irresistible for many a would-be macho magnifico.[127] Lord

Lonsdale decorated the staircase of Barleythorpe, his shooting box, with stuffed crocodiles brought back from a trip to Africa. Lord Egerton of Tatton built a vast new tenants' hall at his country house in Cheshire to display his trophies, and the Duke of Sutherland put up a museum in the grounds of Dunrobin Castle. Minor patricians, like Sir Alfred Pease and Sir Claude Champion de Crespigny spent most of their lives slaughtering animals, and produced a string of autobiographical yarns.[128] And the elephant hunter, Arthur New-mann, dedicated his book on the subject to Norman Magnus Mac-leod, twenty-sixth chief, who was a noted big-game hunter himself, and gave Newmann hospitality at Dunvegan Castle while he was writing it.

The obvious place for a titled traveller to start on a more extended foreign tour was North America. Before and during the Civil War, the United States was generally reckoned an inhospitable place, and as late as 1863, 'a trip to the States was held to be quite a serious enterprise. You made your wills before you sailed.' But as the country became more stable, as the east coast developed its own increasingly Anglophile society, as the National Parks were created out west, and as Canada grew to nationhood, it soon began to beckon alluringly. Blue-blooded visitors like the young Lord Rose-bery and C. P. Trevelyan lunched with the President, dined with the British ambassador, and stayed with the Governor-General of Canada in Ottawa. Senators, congressmen, and state governors queued up to shake their hands, while the local newspapers hung on their every word.[129] In a rather different vein, Lord Lonsdale claimed that he defeated John L. Sullivan, the heavyweight champion of the world, in a secret boxing match in New York in the early 1880s. And impoverished and déclassé grandees like the Duke of Manchester enjoyed a position in east coast society far more prominent than that to which they could possibly lay claim at home.[130]

But for many visitors, it was not the snobbish Anglophilia of the east coast social circuit that most appealed, but 'the open and the wild' of the great outdoors. From the 1870s onwards, there was a veritable procession of British notabies, who travelled out west in extravagant style, in search of scenery, excitement and adventure. In 1879, Hugh Lowther and Moreton Frewen returned to England laden with hunting trophies of bear, bison, and buffalo. Between 1869 and 1896, Lord Dunraven visited North America almost every year. He wrote with genuine feeling about the wonders of Yellow-stone, became a firm friend of Buffalo Bill, and shot moose, caribou, elk, and buffalo in Montana, Wyoming, Nova Scotia, and New-foundland. But some patricians did not fare so well.[131] In 1884, while travelling through the Rockies, W. H. Grenfell, the future Lord

Desborough, unwisely accepted a bet that he would shoot an animal
before breakfast the next morning. Within minutes of setting out, he
was lost in the wilderness, and it was two days before a solitary
trapper happened to find him. But Grenfell was lucky compared
with his friend, the Hon. Gilbert Henry Chandos Leigh, who later
on the same trip fell to his death down a precipice – 'one of the truest
and most light-hearted Englishmen who have [sic] ever been taken
by the love of nature into the Rocky Mountains.'[132]

India was more abidingly popular with titled tourists. It provided
magnificent sights, both natural and man-made. The sport was more
varied and abundant, ranging from pig-sticking to tiger shooting.
And as the raj reached the peak of its magnificence during the late
nineteenth century, ritualized hunting became an integral part of any
patrician itinerary.[133] In December 1882, the Duke of Portland set off
in the company of his friends Lord de Grey (who was the son of the
Viceroy, Lord Ripon), Lord Charles Beresford, and Lord Wenlock.
They went on a grand shoot in Nepal, accompanied by seven
hundred elephants. In six weeks, they killed fourteen tiger and eight
rhino, as well as a crocodile, which was 'good fun'. They then
moved on to another shooting party, arranged by the Maharaja of
Durbungah, at which they killed a further three tiger, twenty-eight
buffalo, and 273 pigs. Three years later, Lord Randolph Churchill
followed in their footsteps. He found the elephants 'an unfailing
source of interest and amusement', and relished the killing of his first
tiger, whose skin he thought would look well in his London home.
'This is certainly the acme of sport . . .', he exulted. 'Tiger in the zoo
give very little idea of what the wild animal is like.'[134]

At the same time that the raj reached its apogee of stylized
slaughter, the newly established British colonies in Africa began to
provide alternative attractions. Most of the game in South Africa had
been wiped out by the Boers and the early British settlers, and
Rhodesia appealed only for a brief period during the 1890s, when
Lord Randolph Churchill made his unhappy and ill-judged visit. But
Kenya and Uganda proved a much more rewarding and attractive
alternative, and from the late 1890s, big-game hunters like Lord
Cranworth, Lord Delamere, and the Cole brothers made regular
visits, breezily slaughtering elephants, lions, and giraffe.[135] In 1907,
the young Winston Churchill arrived, ostensibly to investigate the
Ugandan Railway in his capacity as junior minister at the Colonial
Office. But he, too, spent more time with his gun, and left behind a
vivid account of shooting a white rhinocerous. By the First World
War, Nairobi had become the centre of the safari industry for the
whole of the continent. Appropriately enough, it was in British East
Africa that the most bizarre aristocratic creation in all fiction spent

much of his life: John Clayton, later Lord Greystoke, better known as Tarzan.[136]

South America, by contrast, lured only the most adventurous patricians. Aristocratic scroungers like the Duke of Manchester were happy to journey through Mexico in the age of President Porfirio Diaz, and at the expense of rich Americans. But further south, they rarely ventured. The British colonial presence was minimal, and much of the terrain was inhospitable mountain or impenetrable jungle. When Lord Howard de Walden visited in the early 1900s, he bought a small mine of pale green onyx, shipped it back to England, and created a pillared staircase and gallery in his London house.[137] But the most famous blue-blooded traveller was the fictional Lord John Roxton, created by Arthur Conan Doyle in 1912 as the quintessential aristocratic adventurer. He was 'one of the greatest all-round sportsmen and athletes of the day', whose bachelor apartments in London boasted a collection of 'splendid heavy game heads . . . the best of their sort from every corner of the world.' He was a man of courage, action, and resource, a self-confessed 'South Americomaniac', had been up and down the continent from end to end, and championed the rights of the natives of Peru and Brazil against local slave drivers.[138]

By the inter-war years, these global nobles were rather less in evidence. In the United States, British aristocrats were still (if diminishingly) east coast celebrities, and liners such as the Aquitania continued to boast a 'country family sort of atmosphere'. But the great white hunters were already a thing of the past, and the account of his travels given by Lord Cottenham – with its advice on motoring and airlines, and its envenomed attack on the selfishness of the rich in their opposition to the New Deal – is very different from the zestful and buoyant innocence of Lord Dunraven's writings only a generation before.[139] By the 1920s, men like Jeffery Amherst and James Stuart were crossing the Atlantic in search of jobs on Wall Street rather than buffalo in Wyoming. In India, too, the weakening of the raj and the decline in the quantity of big game meant that the great ritualized hunts had declined in splendour and in assurance, while in East Africa, growing demands for preservation meant the camera had replaced the gun as the preferred method of shooting. Old Kenya hands like Lord Cranworth regretted the change, and yearned for the thrill of 'a bullet correctly placed.' But no doubt the animals thought otherwise.[140]

A more dutiful purpose of patrician travel was, as in the case of Edward Wood, to prepare for a career in public life, and to do so by going round the world, rather than by visiting France or Italy. At a time of raised imperial consciousness, it seemed appropriate to visit

those palms and pines over which Britannia wielded her wide
dominions, and it also offered the best way of getting to know the
most important politicians throughout the English speaking world.
When Charles Trevelyan was adopted as prospective Liberal candidate for the Elland constituency in Yorkshire, in 1898, he resolved to
use the time before the next general election to circle the globe in the
high-minded company of Sidney and Beatrice Webb. His letters
home brim with curiosity and fascination, as he describes a slaugh-
terhouse in Chicago, baseball in Portland, football in New Zealand,
and a sheep station in Australia. As well as meeting the great and
the good of three continents, he talked to farmers, teachers, factory
workers, and civil servants. And he also took pictures, which enabled
him to give magic lantern lectures to his prospective constituents,
thereby projecting a convincing image as a man of the world.[141]

Such travel was not just a training for public life at home: it was
also a preparation for proconsular responsibility abroad. Between
1877 and 1895, the young G. N. Curzon went twice round the
world, and in addition paid extended visits to Persia, central Asia,
the North West Frontier, and Afghanistan, often travelling in great
discomfort, and penetrating to regions where no white man had ever
gone before. For these adventurous wanderings, Curzon made the
most meticulous arrangements. He always took a dress suit and a
rubber bath, and on his visit to Afghanistan, wore a set of false
medals so as to obtain an audience with the Amir.[142] He wrote a
succession of massively erudite books which were prodigious syn-
theses of history, archaeology, politics, travel, and adventure. They
eloquently extolled the righteousness of Britain's imperial mission,
and established him as an expert on Asian issues. He was awarded the
Gold Medal by the Royal Geographical Society for his discovery of
the source of the Oxus River (something that he later claimed gave
him more pleasure than becoming a cabinet minister); and when
composing his own epitaph, correctly described himself not only as
an administrator and ruler of men, but also as an explorer.[143]

The young Lord Ronaldshay was also intoxicated by what he
termed 'the call of the East', and began his oriental wanderings just
after Curzon's ended. In 1898, he visited Ceylon, and was so captivated by the country and its culture that he spent the next ten years
travelling extensively in Asia, becoming in the process an expert on
the continent second only to Curzon himself. Between 1899 and
1901, he explored in Kashmir, Simla, and Persia. From 1902 to 1904,
he journeyed over land from Constantinople to Peking. And during
1906 and 1907, he visited Japan, China, and Burma.[144] The books
that resulted from these expeditions were less erudite and less mandarin than Curzon's earlier productions. But they made up in charm

what they lacked in ornateness, and showed a much more sympathetic understanding of the aspirations of Asian peoples – in Russia for southwards expansion, in Japan for great power status, and in India for constitutional reforms. Eventually, Ronaldshay became Governor of Bengal, Secretary of State for India, and Curzon's official biographer. But despite his unrivalled qualifications, and evident ambition, the viceregal throne itself eluded him.[145]

Like the aristocratic adventurers in search of spectacle and sport abroad, the young notables who prepared themselves for public life by travelling round the world were a much-diminished group by the inter-war years. This was partly because there were far fewer of them who were willing or able to take up politics, and partly because many of them now lacked the resources for a year's subsidized travel. And, since many patricians were now obliged to earn their living, they also lacked the time. But it was also that the handful who *did* go into public life, such as Oswald Mosley, Anthony Eden, and Viscount Cranborne, had already endured a much more searing rite of passage by serving in the trenches. By the time the young Lord Dunglass went on a cricketing tour of South America in the early 1930s, there was very little of the old patrician tradition left. Going round the world, and seeing the empire, was still regarded as an appropriate training for those who aspired to enter public life. But it was more likely to be undertaken by a middle-class figure like R. A. Butler than by a member of the old governing class.[146]

But while fewer patricians were travelling in anticipation of a parliamentary career, they were still leaving the country to avoid financial embarrassment or social disgrace. With rentals reduced at the time of the agricultural depression, many families were obliged to seek more economical living in Boulogne, Munich, or Dresden, or in the continental countryside. Sir Lawrence Jones, whose forebears owned 3,600 acres in East Anglia, recalled his exiled youth, 'wandering about the continent, "poor", rootless, and in the eyes of our Norfolk neighbours, distinctly peculiar.' Because he was the ninth child of an impoverished Ulster family, Alan Brooke was born and brought up in the French Pyrenees, where he learned French and German before he learned English.[147] Even for great grandees, an extended holiday was sometimes a necessary means of saving money. Lord Spencer admitted that one of the attractions of a round the world trip in 1894–5 was that 'rents are very bad', and that 'It will be a relief to shut up shop here for six months.' For the same reason, the spendthrift Lord Lonsdale was ordered abroad by his trustees in 1902, and visited India and the Far East. (He later claimed to have met Rasputin, but since he never set foot in Russia, this seems unlikely.)[148]

73. Lord Lonsdale in Arctic travelling attire, *Illustrated London News*, 11 Jan. 1890.

As Lonsdale had earlier discovered, it was also necessary on occasions to leave the country to live down scandal. His famous trip to the Arctic, in 1888–9, was billed as a serious exploratory expedition, sponsored by the so-called Scottish Naturalist Society. But the real explanation was rather less flattering: his affair with the actress Violet Cameron had become the talk of London. Her husband had brought an action for adultery, Lonsdale had admitted to fathering Violet's child, and Queen Victoria reputedly let it be known that he must go abroad. In characteristic fashion, Lonsdale later embroidered his undeniably epic adventure, claiming that he discovered the Klondyke Goldfield and even reached the North Pole. And on his return, he was greeted at Penrith by the local band playing 'See the Conquering Hero Comes'.[149] For similar reasons, Lord and Lady Tweedmouth despatched their son Dudley to America in 1895. He had fallen in love with a Gaiety Girl, and rashly promised to marry her. After private investigations by detectives, and threats of a breach of promise action, the woman was eventually bought off, and Dudley was sent abroad for penitential recovery.[150]

But some patricians had rather different sexual scandals to live down – and alternative sexual tastes to indulge. The passing of the Criminal Law Amendment Act in 1885 established new and much wider categories of homosexual misdemeanour, which made it easier for the authorities to prosecute and convict. And aristocratic lineage was no longer a guarantee of immunity. Two sons of the eighth Duke of Beaufort were exiled abroad: Lord Henry Somerset after his wife secured a judicial separation, allegedly on the grounds of his homosexual inclinations; and Lord Arthur Somerset in the aftermath of the Cleveland Street Scandal, when a warrant was actually issued for his arrest. Likewise, Lord Alfred Douglas fled the country at the time of Oscar Wilde's trial, and was later joined by his friend when he had completed his prison sentence.[151] But the most picturesque of such refugees was Lord Ronald Sutherland Gower, a roving bohemian who was a sculptor and writer, and designed the Shakespeare Monument at Stratford-on-Avon. He was the model for Lord Henry Wotton in Wilde's *Picture of Dorian Gray*, with his fine aristocratic face 'not yet brutalised by debauchery.' In 1892, Roger Fry encountered him in Venice, where he knew 'every body from the cabbies, corporals and carabinieri up to the painters, princes and philanthropic envoys.'[152]

During the inter-war years, this aristocratic exodus continued. Sir George Sitwell left Renishaw in 1925, and took up permanent residence in Montegufoni – not to avoid death, but to escape the duties associated with it. In *A Handful of Dust* (1934), Evelyn Waugh created the appropriately named Tony Last, the squire of Hetton, a dutiful, religious, and innocent landowner, who suddenly discovers that his wife has been unfaithful, and abruptly sets off for South America in the company of an eccentric explorer in search of a fabulous city supposedly built by the Incas.[153] But in real life, the most tragic titled expatriate was Earl Beauchamp. In his youth, he had been Mayor of Worcester and Governor of New South Wales, had held junior office in the pre-war Liberal governments, and had married Bend Or's sister. He was subsequently Lord-Lieutenant of Gloucestershire, Chancellor of London University, and Lord Warden of the Cinque Ports. But the Duke of Westminster, who envied Beauchamp his public reputation, his splendid offices, and his male heir, suspected him of homosexual proclivities, referred to him as his 'bugger in law', and determined to drive him into exile. In the early 1930s, Beauchamp suddenly resigned all his great public offices, ostensibly on the grounds of ill health, took up residence in France, and later died in New York.[154]

Underlying these diverse and familiar motives for travel was something more widespread and fundamental, namely a growing sense of aristocratic alienation. As Thomas Cook opened up continental Europe to the middle classes, and as railways and steamships encompassed the earth, it became progressively more difficult for the patricians to maintain their geographical distance from those inferior social groups beneath. Only by journeying to even more remote places could they hope to do so. As Lord Ronaldshay remarked, 'despite all such girding of the earth, there still remain some few secluded nooks – few and far between perhaps, and scattered over the whole world's surface – which, thanks either to natural physical features or to the accident of an anomalous political position, are still well out of the reach of the Cook's tourist ticket.'[155] Whereas in the eighteenth century, the British aristocracy had despised the despotic politics and squalid conditions of so much of abroad, some of them now saw in its remote, unspoilt recesses their last best hope – where towns and industry were non-existent, where hierarchy and paternalism prevailed, where the ancient values of chivalry and honour were still preserved, and where there was 'a feeling of escape from the furies of modern life – disillusion, doubt, democracy.'[156]

Three particular notables were attracted to distant lands by a combination of romance, chivalry, and alienation that was almost knight-errantly in its self-indulgent and quest-like intensity. The first was Wilfrid Scawen Blunt, a Sussex squire, lecherous poet and celebrated late-Victorian misfit. In 1874, he visited the Bedouin in Algeria, and was at once attracted by their 'noble pastoral life', with its chieftains and horses, its colourful traditions, and its history of heroic deeds, which contrasted so strongly with the 'ignoble squalor' of the French settler population.[157] Thereafter, Blunt and his wife went on a series of extended visits to the Arab world – to Egypt and Palestine, from Aleppo down the Euphrates to Baghdad, to the Libyan desert and the Sinai peninsular, and to the very heart of Arabia itself. In the aftermath of the British occupation, Blunt took up the cause of Egyptian nationalism, and made several unsuccessful attempts to secure election to the House of Commons. In 1881, he purchased a small estate on the outskirts of Cairo, and there, round the tomb of Sheikh Obeyd, he built himself a comfortable house. He lived simply and patriarchally, dressed as an Arab, spoke the Bedouin dialect, and arbitrated in local tribal disputes.[158]

Mark Sykes was the heir to the Sledmere estate in Yorkshire, made several early journeys to the Middle East in the company of his father, and fell completely under its spell. He hated cities and their inhabitants, greatly admired the nomadic life of the desert, and between 1897 and 1906, spent more time in the Ottoman Empire than he did in England. Although an MP from 1911, he despised politicians as 'fatuous babblers, pompous bores, polished weaklings, or self-advertising tradesmen', but regarded the great sheikhs and Kurdish chiefs as fellow aristocrats with whom he, the squire of Sledmere, might talk on equal terms.[159] His deepest wish was to protect their ancient civilization from the corrupting forces of the modern world, and to prevent what he feared would be 'the smearing of the east' with 'the slime of the west.' In 1915, he negotiated the Sykes-Picot Treaty, which divided the Middle East into British and French spheres of influence, and which he hoped would provide the framework for emergent Arab nationalism. On his memorial brass, inset into a modern Eleanor Cross at Sledmere, Sykes was depicted in full armour as a crusader knight.[160]

His closest friend was the Hon. Aubrey Herbert, a son of the fourth Earl of Carnarvon, and thus half-brother to the discoverer of Tutankhamun. He was also the model for John Buchan's Sandy Arbuthnott, who 'rode through the Yemen, which no white man ever did before', was 'blood brother to every kind of Albanian bandit', and 'used to take a hand in Turkish politics'. Like Sykes, Herbert travelled extensively in the Middle East during the 1900s, and found it hard to settle down at home. Like Sykes again, he was an MP who hated politicians, the bourgeoisie and Lloyd George, and loved 'thrones, chieftains, bandits, dangerous territories and fierce loyalty.'[161] During the early 1910s, he took up the cause of Albanian nationalism, organized a support committee in London, and was himself offered the country's throne. In the First World War, he campaigned vigorously to ensure that Albania was not ceded to Italy, and was again invited to become king. John Buchan's analysis of the Arbuthnott/Herbert personality conveys precisely the same impression as Sykes's memorial brass: 'In the old days, he would have led a crusade or discovered a new route to the Indies. Today, he merely roamed as the spirit moved him.'[162]

This particular form of patrician knight-errantry did not long survive the First World War. Sykes died in 1919, Blunt three years later, and Herbert in 1923. Neither in British nor in Arab politics had they achieved as much as they had ardently, arrogantly, and naïvely hoped, and after 1919, the Middle East no longer provided the scope for such indulgent adventures. In the same way, the countries that Bertrand Russell wrote about in *The Practice and Theory of Bolshevism* and *The Problem of China* were very different places from those which Curzon and Ronaldshay had explored around the turn of the century. By the early 1920s, Curzon admitted that the world he had known and travelled was 'quite dead', because of 'the revolution in the conditions of travel, or in the state of the peoples and lands.'[163] When Vita Sackville-West and Harold Nicolson followed an old caravan track across the Bakhtiari mountains of south-west Persia, later in the same decade, they were forced to admit that 'the globe is too small and too well mapped', and that the Anglo-Persian Company's oilfields seemed like 'an outspread town of industrial England.' And for essentially the same reason, Christopher Sykes's trips in the early thirties to Persia, India, and Afghanistan were but pale copies of his father's exploits a generation before.[164]

The patrician exception who very much proves the rule was Wilfred Thesiger, nephew of Lord Chelmsford, who was born in Abyssinia in 1910, where his father was British envoy. His exotic upbringing endowed him with 'a life-long craving for barbaric splendour, for savagery and colour and the throb of drums', a 'lasting veneration for long-established customs and ritual', a 'deep-seated resentment of western innovations in other lands', and a 'distaste for the drab uniformity of the modern world', which he indulged to the full in the years before the Second World War.[165] In 1930, following a conventional education at Eton and Oxford, he returned to Abyssinia as part of the British delegation to the corona-tion of Haile Selassie, and took the opportunity to travel into the remote Danakil country. Thereafter, he explored extensively in Abyssinia, Somaliland, the Sudan, and the French Sahara, hunted big game, felt a sense of aristocratic kinship with the tribal chiefs, and fully indulged 'the lure of the unexplored, the compulsion to go where others had not been.' He was less eccentric than Blunt, less arrogant than Sykes, and less naïve than Herbert: but he nevertheless belonged to their earlier, knight-errantly tradition.[166]

As individuals, most aristocratic travellers between the 1870s and the 1930s were, like Thesiger himself, behaving in a way that would have been recognizably familiar to their forebears. For Bath and Brighton, they had substituted Biarritz and Baden Baden. Instead of the Grand Tour of Europe, there was the world tour of empire. And the fact that Blunt, Sykes, and Herbert have been described as 'Quixotic' is yet another reminder of the venerable tradition to which they belonged.[167] Nevertheless, the greater numbers in-volved, the longer distances travelled, and the more frequent and lengthy absences abroad resulted in a new and markedly different pattern of social life, which was no longer recognizably patrician, but had become instead essentially plutocratic.[168] As Lady Dorothy Nevill explained in 1907, 'the life of a rich man of today' was 'a sort of firework! Paris, Monte Carlo, big-game shooting in Africa, fishing in Norway, dashes to Egypt, trips to Japan.' As such, it could be enjoyed by *anyone* who possessed the requisite wealth, regardless of whether he owned land in Britain. And to the extent that grandees like Westminster or Sutherland did so, there was little to distinguish their lifestyle from a Vanderbilt or an Astor or a Morgan.[169]

The real significance of this 'ample indulgence in the pleasures of plutocratic society' was that it provided one further sign of the social decay of the old landed order.[170] For these playboy patricians formed only a small part of this recently established international social élite. It was the new rich of England and the multi-millionaires of America who set the pace, the style, and the tone. It was they, rather than the landowners, who went down on the Titanic, who shot most of the tigers, and who owned most of the yachts.[171] As E. T. Hooley explained, when buying Lord Lonsdale's Verena for £5,000: 'Most newly-made millionaires buy a yacht at some time or other, and I was no exception.' In social life, as in political life, the initiative had passed elsewhere: the notables were following the fashion, not setting it. And just as some landowners resented the plutocratic assault on the honours system, so they disapproved of this new and vulgar style of life. As Sabine Baring Gould put it in his *Book of the Riviera*, 'one of the fairest spots of Europe' was now 'given over to harlots and thieves and Jew money lenders, to rogues and fools of every description.'[172]

Even more significantly, this new style of genteel leisure was no longer territorially defined. Whether as playboys or knights-errant, these globe-trotting grandees who travelled so frequently and so extensively were inevitably loosening the bonds that had bound their forebears to their estates, their local responsibilities, and their national duties. And significantly, this new development took place at exactly the same time that many of them were beginning to sell off their lands and invest in new forms of wealth that were largely bereft of local connection, and were withdrawing from their traditional involvement in local affairs and national politics. 'Incessant motion, high-speed motor cars, perpetual rush and hurry' were not the circumstances in which a stable and responsible landed class could thrive.[173] 'Settling down' was the very essence of estate ownership but 'settling down' was the last thing many of them now seemed able to do. The yacht that the Duke of Sutherland purchased from Lord Tredegar in 1927 was originally called 'Restless'. And at Mark Sykes's funeral, the wreath from his tenantry bore the telling inscription: 'He who never rested, rests.' As Curzon's father once remarked, in the old days it was considered the duty of the landlord to live on his estates, amongst his tenantry, and not go 'roving about all over the world.' But by his son's time, all this had changed.[174]

Of course, this restless travelling did not lead to total abdication of traditional activities in every case. Despite their lengthy absences abroad, Lord Spencer and Sir Charles Trevelyan were model landlords. For all their love of far-off places, Lord Desborough and Lord Ronaldshay were major figures in local life. And Curzon and Halifax

very nearly reached the top in national politics. But for many other
patricians, travel and recreation had ceased to be an interlude from or
a preparation for the more serious business of estate management,
local leadership, and national politics. Instead, they had become an
escape, an alternative, and even a substitute, as social life abroad was
inflated into a full-time activity, an end in itself, which left little time
for the performance of traditional functions at home. In 1896, the
Estates Gazette had noted that 'it is a landowner's first duty to live
upon his property.' 'If he fails to do so', it went on, 'his tenants and
ultimately himself will suffer.'[175] The next forty years amply bore
out the truth of these remarks.

iv.   Conclusion: From Leisure to Pleasure

According to Mr Gladstone, one of the reasons why 'the position of
the landed proprietor' stood so high in Britain compared with other
countries, was that 'the possession of landed property' was 'so
closely associated with definite duty.'[176] Although landowners did
not have to occupy themselves in earning a living, this did not mean
that they enjoyed endless spare time. On the contrary, they were
obliged, by tradition, by training, and by circumstance, to 'discharge
the responsibilities which great rank, birth, and vast possessions
entail.'[177] For owners of large (and lesser) estates, leisure was not an
end in itself, but rather the necessary precondition for dutiful and
worthwhile activity. But by the late nineteenth century, this stable
world of patrician activity – territorially defined, politically related,
and socially exclusive – was beginning to break down. In London
and the shires, social life became more frantic and free-floating.
Staying at home seemed less enjoyable than going abroad. Dutiful
recreation was gradually superseded by indulgent distraction. Discharging obligations counted for less than having a good time. In
many quarters the leisure class was becoming the pleasure class.

The contrasted lives of the first and second Dukes of Westminster
vividly illustrate this shift from responsibility to indulgence, stability
to restlessness, leisure to pleasure. The first duke has rightly been
depicted as the beau ideal of the Victorian gentleman.[178] He was
high-minded, morally upright, religious, abstemious. He was made
a duke by Gladstone in 1874, not just because of his Olympian
wealth, but because he seemed to possess all those admirable qualities
which ought to be associated with the highest rank of the Victorian
peerage. He believed in the sanctity and significance of home life. He
was a good and conscientious landlord. He was renowned for his
charitable endeavours and his generous philanthropy. He was MP
for Chester from 1846 until he inherited in 1869, and Master of the

Horse between 1880 and 1885. He was Lord-Lieutenant of Cheshire and also of Greater London. In his youth, he was Master of the Cheshire Hunt, and his horses won the Derby five times. At his death, in 1899, he was mourned as 'one of the finest illustrations ever beheld of what a nobleman should be', a man who 'could pass from the race course to the missionary meeting without incurring the censure of the strictest.'

How very different was the life and attitude of Bend Or, his grandson, who followed him in the dukedom. He married four times, his only son pre-deceased him, and he was morbidly preoccupied with his own death. He never stood for election to the House of Commons, and was a disaffected die-hard in politics. He instructed his third wife on no account to play 'lady bountiful' in local affairs, and was obliged to resign the Lord-Lieutenancy of Cheshire in 1920 because both he and his second wife had been divorced. (When the Prince of Wales visited the Chester Royal Show in 1893, he had stayed at Eaton; but when King George V followed suit in 1925, he preferred to stay with Lord Derby at Knowsley.) His third wife recorded that during the whole time of their marriage, they were 'only once three weeks in the same place.' He was, she concluded, afflicted with 'a sort of mental St. Vitus's dance . . . He just could not stay still.' On his death in 1953, Henry Channon offered these revealing reflections: 'His wealth was incalculable; his charm overwhelming; but he was restless, spoilt, irritable, and rather splendid in a very English way. He was fair, handsome, lavish; yet his life was an empty failure; he did few kindnesses, leaves no monument.'[179]

By virtue of their colossal riches and their distinct personalities, the first and second Dukes of Westminster illustrate in a larger-than-life way the changes in the social attitudes and social circumstances of the titled and territorial classes between the last quarter of the nineteenth century, and the outbreak of the Second World War. But in many lesser landed families, the same shift is apparent – from rootedness to restlessness, service to sport. And how, in fact, could it have been otherwise? As Isabel Colegate makes Sir Randolph Nettleby ask, in the pages of *The Shooting Party*, 'If you take away the proper functions of an aristocracy, what can it do but play games too seriously?' What, indeed? It is time to find out.[180]

PART TWO:

THE LIGHT OF COMMON DAY

The builders did not know the uses to which their work would descend; they made a new house with the stones of the old castle; year by year, generation after generation, they enriched and extended it; year by year the great harvest of timber grew to ripeness; until, in sudden frost, came the age of Hooper; the place was desolate and the work all brought to nothing; *Quomodo sedet sola civitas.* Vanity of vanities, all is vanity.
(E. Waugh, *Brideshead Revisited* (1962 edn.), pp. 330–1.)

FROM LEISURED CLASS TO LABOURING ARISTOCRACY

Individuals, prompted by the changing times, began to make their ways in fields unknown to their predecessors. Peers, often under plebeian pseudonyms, were to be found on the stage, in the cinema world, in journalism, motoring and exploration . . . . Several peers had acted as pioneers in the new techno-logical world of the twentieth century, and were well equipped to deal with their new role.

(Lord Montagu of Beaulieu, *More Equal than Others: The Changing Fortunes of the British and European Aristocracies* (1970), p. 175.)

Agricultural land by itself could no longer sustain landed society in the social role which had become traditional. So, to secure an adequate income, other strategies needed to be adopted – including the making of advantageous marriages with social outsiders, including Americans, and becoming in-volved, in unprecedented ways, in the world of business and finance.

(G. R. Searle, *Corruption in British Politics, 1895–1930* (1987), p. 14.)

By the 1930s, it was not uncommon for a local aristocrat to sit on the board of a London-based company, something quite rare fifty years earlier, but [to] have only marginal involvement in the affairs of his locality.

(J. Stevenson, *British Society, 1914–1945* (1984), p. 355.)

The landed classes as such were simply ceasing to be of national importance . . . Those who lacked the share portfolio and the guinea-pig directorships of the adaptable aristocrat disappeared from sight; as often as not to Kenya or Rhodesia, where the colour of the lower orders' faces guaranteed another two generations of undisturbed gentlemanly life. They found a few mourners, like the brilliant and quixotic novelist Evelyn Waugh, but on the whole their funeral was private.

(E. J. Hobsbawm, *Industry and Empire* (1969), p. 202.)

Between the onset of the Great Depression and the outbreak of the Second World War, the traditional British territorial classes ceased to be the wealth élite, as new, rival, and gigantic non-landed fortunes proliferated; and they also ceased to be the landed élite, as the great estates were gradually broken up and dispersed. As rental revenue declined, as broad acres were sold, and as other assets were disposed of, many notables were faced with an urgent need to find new and alternative sources of revenue. As the *Estates Gazette* explained in 1922, 'These are the days in which the greater residential properties of the country can only be owned and kept up by those whose

income is from sources apart from the property itself, and then of a
very substantial character.'[1] And if this was true of those who kept
some or all of their lands, then how much more urgent was the
need of those patricians who had sold their estates completely; of
those former Irish owners who were obliged to make a new life in
England; and of those many younger sons and more distant relatives
who could no longer expect a smooth path to a comfortable, respectable, traditional career? Instead of being dependent on revenue
generated from their estates, these men were compelled to find other
means of life support. But as they were getting out of land, what
were they getting into, instead?

As the fifth Earl of Desart explained, many were moving into
'other spheres of occupation.'[2] If the old patrician professions were
no longer so appealing, then an obvious solution was to turn to new
ones. As early as the mid-1880s, T. H. S. Escott noticed this newly
emergent trend, and set out the wide range of careers that had only
recently become acceptable for a scion of the nobility:

> Among the eligible occupations for younger sons of great noble-
> men are now recognised not only commissions in the army and
> navy, Government appointments, stipendiary magistracies and
> the like, but positions in mercantile and trading houses, sheep-
> farming, ordinary farming, plantations in the colonies, India, and
> America. When Dukes are willing to apprentice the cadets of their
> houses to merchants and stockbrokers, an example has been set
> which it is well should be widely followed.[3]

This was a predictably well-informed list, but it was by no means
comprehensive. Many patricians did not enter the alien world of the
City or the empire, but sought instead to adapt essentially traditional
remedies to the changed circumstances of the time. Some still
pursued heiresses: but now they did so across the Atlantic. Some
exploited their aristocratic connections, by selling high-quality cars
or writing their reminiscences. Some took up new careers connected
with the land, such as estate agency or engineering. And some did
none of these things, but became instead embarrassingly and publicly
déclassé.

As Escott's comments correctly implied, the titled and the genteel
were also entering the City in quite unprecedented numbers from
the last quarter of the nineteenth century. Heads of families, with
reduced rentals, sought to augment their incomes by drawing directors' fees; younger sons in search of a career hoped that finance might
be more lucrative than the church or the law. Either way, they were
forced to look for succour to those new commercial elements
they most disliked and resented: big business, finance capital, inter-

national plutocracy. For some, the experience was altogether distasteful and embarrassing: as ignorant, ornamental directors they became the dupes of unscrupulous company promoters, and were involved in public scandal and financial loss. Some, more wise or more lucky, enjoyed secure and much-valued income, which enabled them to keep up (or, if Irish, re-create) at least the façade of a landed life. And some, especially in the inter-war years, turned to business and finance as an essentially full-time occupation, which was by now thought acceptable for a gentleman.

The other new opportunities for this new breed of non-leisured notables were mainly to be found in the realm of imperial endeavour. In some cases (though never very many), the patricians pursued the same professions overseas that they had traditionally dominated at home: government administration, court service, the law, and the church. But the majority who played the imperial theme took up a new occupation: that of gentlemen emigrants. Some were possessed of a spirit of boyish and irresponsible adventure. Some were in despair at the lack of opportunity at home. Some were escaping from impoverishment or disgrace. And some were seeking to re-create an idealized world of aristocratic supremacy and genteel living which was already so conspicuously on the wane in Britain. In the short run, this meant adventure and romance, attention and notoriety. But in the long run, this attempt to transplant the territorial aristocracy from Britain to the empire did not succeed. In Canada, Australia, the United States, South Africa, and Rhodesia, the gentlemen emigrants conspicuously failed to re-create the world they had lost. Only in Kenya did they come close to success – and that was very much the exception that proved the rule.

i. New Professions and Familiar Failings

During the last quarter of the nineteenth century, two of the most illustrious chairs at the University of Cambridge were held by members of the landed aristocracy. In 1879, the third Baron Rayleigh was elected Cavendish Professor of Physics, and in 1895 the first Baron Acton was appointed Regius Professor of Modern History. In both cases, it was patrician poverty rather than scholarly ambition that had impelled them to take up paid university employment. Rayleigh's holdings in Essex had been very hard hit by agricultural depression, and he needed additional revenue to make ends meet.[4] And Acton's income from his Shropshire estates was so diminished that he had been obliged to spend much of his life abroad, he had been forced to sell both his house and his library, and he had been an unabashed importuner for courtly office in 1892.[5] By definition, these were exceptional solutions to patrician financial anxieties that could be resorted to only by quite exceptional men. But from the late nineteenth century onwards, many grandees and gentry were compelled to find new means of making money. And one obvious way for them to do so was to exploit their traditional assets of territory and title, but to do so in a new and more lucrative manner.

There were, after all, many professions connected with the land that a needy notable might decently join and expertly practise. The Hon. Edward Strutt, brother of the third Baron Rayleigh, moved into the milk supply business, with dairies at Terling and market facilities in London. 'Do you really keep shops, Lord Rayleigh?' asked one house guest, greatly daring. 'Yes', he replied, '. . . you would not be here if I didn't.'[6] In addition, he helped to set up the land agency of Strutt and Parker in 1877: it was, after all, a small step from owning land to managing it and (after 1910) to selling it. And Strutt's impeccable connections ensured he never lacked for business. In the same tradition, the Hon. George Lambton, fifth son of the second Earl of Durham, early on decided that 'my profession would be on the turf', and between the wars he was an outstandingly successful racehorse trainer for the seventeenth Earl of Derby. And Lord Marcus Beresford, fourth son of the fourth Marquess of Waterford, moved in even more exalted equine circles: in 1890 he became responsible for the stables of the Prince of Wales, and he later trained horses for King George V.[7]

The fact that cars were originally called horseless carriages is also an apt reminder of the close initial links between automobiles and aristocrats, most famously exemplified in the career of the Hon. C. S. Rolls, younger son of Lord Llangattock.[8] With an allowance of only £500 a year, Rolls needed to earn a living and, having been a motoring and racing enthusiast since his undergraduate days, he went into business in 1902, selling high-class cars to high-class people. As well as being a brilliant salesman and demonstrator, Rolls made the most of his aristocratic connections. He sold second-hand cars to his father and to Sir Oswald Mosley, and in 1903 numbered Lord Rosebery, Lord Willoughby d'Eresby, and the Duke of Suther-land among his clients. By 1905, his list of patrons included four foreign princely houses, two dukes, two earls, one viscount, seven barons, and three baronets. Initially, Rolls sold foreign cars, espec-ially Panhards, because there was no English product available of appropriate quality. But in 1904 he met Frederick Henry Royce, and two years later, Rolls Royce came into being, with Royce making the cars, and Rolls making the sales. By the time Rolls was killed in a flying accident in 1910, the Silver Ghost was already recognized as

74. The Hon. C. S. Rolls at the tiller.

'the best car in the world', and Rolls himself left £30,000.

An elder son who was drawn to the same world was John, second Lord Montagu of Beaulieu who, after Eton and Oxford, was apprenticed in the Nine Elms workshop of the L.S.W.R., where he earned eleven shillings and six pence for a forty-eight hour week, and became a skilled railway engineer and driver.[9] In the rail strike of 1919, and again in the General Strike of 1926, he drove expresses on the Waterloo to Bournemouth line. But by then, his main interest had shifted to motoring, partly through his friendship with Rolls. Between 1902 and 1916, he owned and edited *Car Illustrated*, the first major motoring magazine, and established himself as a tireless propagandist on behalf of the horseless carriage. He continued to be a prolific journalist during the 1920s, serving as *The Times* motoring and transport correspondent, and contributed regularly to *The Observer* and the *Daily Mail*. In other ways – as witness his epitaph – his life was conventionally landed. But when he inherited the title in 1905, he wrote an editorial in *Car Illustrated*, which eloquently justified his decision to stay in motoring journalism:

Some old fashioned critics may think it *infra dignitatem* for a peer to edit and work at newspapers and publishing. I am not ashamed of work or of a flourishing business reared by myself, and no change of name makes any difference. Nowadays, there is really no necessity to argue that peers should not do honest work, but remain idle drones.[10]

Other patricians disdained this dilettantish interest in the horseless carriage, and became professional engineers instead. Lord Sackville Cecil, a half-brother of the great Lord Salisbury, also trained in a railway workshop, and eventually became general manager of the Metropolitan District Railway. The seventeenth Earl of Derby remembered him as 'a very able fellow, but a bit of a crank.'[11] The eighth Earl of Mayo, who inherited the title (but not the estates, long since sold) in 1927, followed a similar career. He was articled to Fowler and Baker as a civil engineer; he was on the staff when the Forth Bridge was built; he was the resident engineer of the Manchester Ship Canal; he was a trustee and superintendent of the Bridgewater estates in Lancashire, Cheshire, and Northamptonshire; and he ran a flourishing private practice as a chartered surveyor.[12] Much more famous was Nigel Gresley, the grandson of the Revd Sir William Gresley, ninth baronet, whose family boasted one of the oldest titles in the country. In the 1890s, he trained in the railway workshops at Crewe, and later achieved international renown as the Chief Locomotive Engineer for the LNER, for whom he designed the record-breaking A4 Pacifics in the 1930s.[13]

Of all the 'new' late-nineteenth-century professions, engineering seems to have attracted the greatest interest from non-leisured notables. It was closely involved with the land, was an obvious choice for a patrician dilettante, and boasted unrivalled social prestige.[14] Sir Harley Hugh Dalrymple-Hay, grandson of the second baronet, built many underground lines in London in the early twentieth century. R. E. B. Crompton, the electrical engineer, came from a Yorkshire county family, and used his aristocratic connections to good effect in gaining contracts to install lighting systems in the 1880s. For a time, he employed Sir James Swinburne, ninth baronet, who was himself one of the leading authorities of the electrical industry, and also a pioneer of plastics before the First World War. A. A. Campbell Swinton was the son of a Berwickshire country gentleman, and became a prominent electrical contractor and consulting engineer. Like Rolls and Crompton, his patrician connections helped. He installed electric light in many country houses, and was a close friend and collaborator of the Hon. Charles Parsons, who invented the steam turbine in 1884, and was himself the youngest son of the third Earl of Rosse.[15]

Inevitably, engineering attracted younger sons and more distant relatives, rather than heads of families: its rewards could sustain a career, but they could hardly rehabilitate an impoverished estate. This required more drastic measures, of which the pursuit of an heiress was the most traditional. But instead of bankers, brewers, and merchants, this now meant the daughters of the new plutocracy and – more especially – of the American super-rich. As a transaction, the trade-off was perfect: high status and low income on the one side; high income and low status on the other. As a result, this transatlantic marriage market became well organized. In February 1901, *The Daily Telegraph* carried this advertisement, directed to the lawyers and business representatives of American heiresses:

> An English peer of very old title is desirous of marrying at once a very wealthy lady ... If among your clients you know such a lady, who is willing to purchase the rank of a peeress for £65,000 sterling, paid in cash to her future husband, and who has sufficient wealth besides to keep up the rank of a peeress, I should be pleased if you would communicate with me.[16]

And the same set of priorities was made clear in the American publication, *Titled Heiresses*, which included 'a carefully compiled list of peers who are supposed to be eager to lay their coronets, and incidentally their hearts, at the feet of the all-conquering American girl.'

Several landowners were highly successful in this quest – for money if not necessarily for happiness. One of the most famous was Lord Curzon, that great champion of landed estates and patrician government, whose ancestral acres in Derbyshire were heavily burdened, and who was subsisting in the 1890s on a miserable allowance. His unprecedentedly extravagant Indian Viceroyalty was largely financed by the Chicago-based resources of his first American wife, Mary Leiter, whom he married for her money, even if he later came to love her. And his re-entry into public life during the First World War was further facilitated by the riches of his second American wife, Grace Hinds, whom he married in 1917.[17] As Balfour explained when Curzon was passed over for the Prime Ministership in 1923, 'even if he has lost the hope of glory, he still possesses the means of grace.' Ironically, Curzon's lavish life as a grandee, not only at Carlton House Terrace and at Kedleston, but also at Tattershall and Bodiam Castles, was made possible by this large influx of American money. As such, he was unavoidably dependent on the very plutocracy he so feared and despised.[18]

Equally famous and persistent in heiress hunting were the Marlboroughs, who had been forced by accumulated debts to sell off so many of their art treasures in the 1880s. The second wife of the eighth duke was American, as were both wives of his successor. Indeed, it was the $4.2 million of railroad stock, and the guaranteed dividend income of 4 per cent brought by Consuelo Vanderbilt, that enabled the ninth duke to undertake the much-needed restoration of Blenheim in the late nineteenth and early twentieth centuries.[19] But the cost was high: the circumstances under which the marriage was arranged, in which the young and innocent Consuelo had scarcely any say, except to protest ineffectually against the venture, were peculiarly sordid and mercenary. And although she made a stunning chatelaine, she was always unhappy in what she found to be such a staid, stuffy, and snobbish atmosphere, and the marriage ended in divorce. But the Churchills were incorrigible. For Lord Randolph, being a younger son of an impoverished father, was as much in need of money to further his political career as Lord Curzon. And there can be no doubt that part of the appeal of Jennie Jerome was that she was the daughter of a New York newspaper tycoon, who was prepared to settle £3,000 a year on his new and patrician son-in-law.[20]

Even poorer, and more reckless than the Marlboroughs, were the Dukes of Manchester. Both the eighth and the ninth dukes went to the United States blatantly on the look out; both ensnared heiresses; but to little avail, either emotionally or financially. In 1876, the future eighth duke married Consuelo Yznaga, the daughter of a wealthy Cuban-American. But even so, he went through the bankruptcy courts in 1889 with debts of £100,000, the very year before he succeeded to the title. He survived only until 1892, and his successor fared little better. He brazenly and systematically searched the United States for a rich wife, claiming that he must either marry an Astor or a Vanderbilt or throw in the towel; and his vigorous but unsuccessful pursuit of Mary Goelet led to denunciations in the American press: 'England's poorest duke after our richest heiress', which put the matter precisely if unsubtly. He was unsuccessful with her, but in 1900 managed to ensnare Helen Zimmerman, the daughter of a Cincinnati railroad mogul, who also had extensive stockholdings in Standard Oil, and interests in coal and iron mining. Ironically, he, too, was declared bankrupt just before his wedding. Meanwhile, Mary Goelet, having refused not only Manchester but other impoverished landowners like Lord Shaftesbury and George Cornwallis-West, settled for the Duke of Roxburghe instead.[21]

In all, between 1870 and 1914, there were more than one hundred marriages by peers' eldest and younger sons to Americans. Of course, this amounted to only a small proportion of the aristocracy, let alone of the landed establishment as a whole.[22] But many who sought heiresses patently did not succeed. And it is the underlying attitudes and anxieties thus displayed – of an order in search of new ways of keeping going in adverse circumstances – that are most significant. Here again, plutocracy was undermining aristocracy, even as it supported it. And contemporaries noticed. In his short story 'The Noble Bachelor', Conan Doyle tells the sad tale of Lord St Simon, the second son of the Duke of Balmoral, who has 'been compelled to sell his pictures within the last few years.' St Simon becomes engaged to Hatty Doran, the only child of Aloysius Doran, the richest mine owner on the west coast of America. They do not live happily ever after. But the timing and the circumstances were perfect, and the opinions commonplace: 'One by one, the management of the noble houses of Great Britain is passing into the hands of our fair cousins from across the Atlantic.'[23]

For those impoverished notables who could neither sell cars, nor ensnare heiresses, there remained the option of writing. From Bulwer Lytton to Lord Robert Cecil, this had been a recognized way of augmenting an inadequate income earlier in the century, and in this later period, there was a very marked increase in the number of gifted – and not so gifted – patricians putting pen to paper. Among statesmen with landed links, W. E. Gladstone was reported to be earning £1,500 a year in 1890 and, according to Lord Granville, the money was 'much needed'.[24] Before he ensnared his first heiress, Curzon was a prolific writer of articles and of travel books. In a later generation, Winston Churchill, who was left virtually nothing by his father Lord Randolph, supported himself from the 1900s to the 1930s by his journalism, his histories, and his biographies. Bertrand Russell poured out philosophical pot-boilers during the inter-war years for essentially the same reason. And many others, although less prolific, followed the same path: Lord Newton wrote the official life of Lord Lansdowne, and Lord Ronaldshay commemorated Curzon in three stately volumes.[25]

Those patricians whose literary leanings ran to the fanciful rather than the factual also exercised their talents remuneratively during this period. H. Rider Haggard was the younger son of an impoverished East Anglian squire, who married the heiress to an equally depressed estate.[26] Only his string of best-selling yarns, produced between the 1880s and the 1920s, enabled him to keep up the façade of a landowner's life. Many other writers in the inter-war years turn out, on closer inspection, to be poor landowners or younger children trying to make ends meet. The three Sitwell siblings were all in straitened circumstances due to the excessive tight-fistedness of their highly eccentric father, the fourth baronet: much of their self-promotion and battle against the middle-class philistines was prompted by sheer economic need. Nancy Mitford's father, the second Lord Redesdale, was so impoverished that she was driven to earn her living by writing in the 1930s.[27] And Vita Sackville-West wrote novels and poetry so that she and her husband, Harold Nicolson, might free themselves from the limited and limiting allowance of her very eccentric mother, Lady Sackville.

Her most famous novel was *The Edwardians* and, in writing an evocation of the old, vanishing aristocratic society, she accomplished in thinly disguised fiction what many less gifted and more needy notables were doing in fact. For this period saw an unprecedented proliferation of patrician autobiographies, many ghost-written, many of indifferent quality, and many centred round the theme of the vanished splendours of yester-year. One of the earliest entrants into this field was the third Earl of Malmesbury, who had been Foreign Secretary in the two short-lived Conservative administrations of the 1850s, and who wrote his memoirs in the 1880s. These comments by the fifteenth Earl of Derby show both the necessity and the novelty of the enterprise:

> If the thing was to be done at all, he has done it in a fairly unobjectionable manner . . . . On the whole, the book is harmless and not foolish. It will give my friend no fame as an author, but it may put a few hundreds into his pocket, which I am afraid are much wanted.[28]

In fact, he made £3,000 out of it, and it may have been this that encouraged others to follow suit, especially in the years immediately before and after the First World War.[29]

Some writers, like the Duke of Portland or the Marchioness of Londonderry, did not need the money, and merely wrote to record the world that others had lost, but to which they still very largely hung on.[30] Some, like Walter Long and Lord Willoughby de Broke, write more poignantly, lamenting the demise of the lesser nobility and the landed gentry, who seemed to have disappeared in their lifetime.[31] Some, like Lords Dunraven, Midleton, and Desart, and the Countess of Fingall, were Irish nobility whose evocation of a vanished world was even more bitter-sweet.[32] And some, like the Duke of Manchester, the Earl of Rosslyn, the Earl and Countess of Warwick, and George Cornwallis-West wrote mildly salacious reminiscences in the hope of keeping their creditors at bay.[33] In one of P. G. Wodehouse's last Blandings Castle novels, much consternation is caused in Shropshire society because Lord Emsworth's younger brother, the Hon. Galahad Threepwood, is threatening to publish his memoirs of life about town in Edwardian London. As so often in Wodehouse, it was but a comic reworking of a commonplace theme.

Galahad Threepwood never became déclassé. But from the 1880s onwards, this was increasingly the fate in store for those indebted patricians who would not, or could not, make a living. Moreton Frewen was a younger son of a Sussex squire, who inherited an Irish estate in the 1890s. But his affairs were so mismanaged and so publicized that he was nicknamed 'Mortal Ruin'.[34] He spent his whole portion of £16,000 on an American cattle ranch, but by 1887 had lost the entire investment. Thereafter, he was involved in a variety of preposterous schemes, to make axle grease for locomotives, to produce ice artificially, to extract gold from refuse-ore, to separate lead from zinc, and to cut down timber in Kenya. All lost him borrowed money, and he was regularly on the brink of bankruptcy. His elder brother's Sussex estate was mortgaged and the timber cut down; his own Irish property was laden with debt; and he even persuaded his children to mortgage their life interests as soon as they came of age. When his daughter Clare married in 1910, it was from a house borrowed for the occasion; so bad was her father's reputation that her wedding dress had to be paid for in cash; and some of his many creditors gatecrashed the reception. At his death, in 1924, he left less than £50. As Kipling put it: 'He lived in every sense except what is called common sense.'[35]

The same could be said of the fifth Earl of Rosslyn, whose autobiography was published in 1928 under the ominously appropriate title, *My Gamble with Life*. On the whole, it had neither paid well nor paid off.[36] He was born in 1869, was described by a master at Eton as 'flighty and self-indulgent', and frittered his way through Oxford and the army. In 1890 he married, and the same year inherited estates in Fife and Midlothian of 3,310 acres worth £9,186, as well as further income from collieries and £50,000 in securities. On his own admission, he then 'set to work to spend it'. He bought a string of racehorses, and gambled heavily on the turf, on the stock exchange, at Cannes, and in London clubs. By 1893, the estates were mortgaged for £100,000, and Rosslyn himself had run up personal debts of £125,000. In 1893, he sold the horses; in 1896 he parted with Dysart House and its policies; and in 1897 he was declared bankrupt. For the next seven years, he acted on the London and provincial stage, using James Erskine as his *nom de théâtre*. In 1902, his bankruptcy was annulled, and he divorced his first wife; he took to gambling again, and also to drink; and in 1923 the family collieries were sold. In 1925–6, he fled abroad to avoid his creditors, but another petition for bankruptcy was served on him while he was in Madeira. Meanwhile, as an act of 'rash folly', he had remarried in 1905, only to be divorced two years later, and then married again in 1908. His third (and last) wife was known as the 'lion tamer', and tried – in vain – to get him to give up drinking and gambling.

75. Lord Rosslyn.

Becoming déclassé was not a male monopoly among *fin de siècle* patricians. Indeed, the Earl of Rosslyn's career was rivalled by that of his half-sister, Frances Evelyn Maynard, who was born in 1861 and twenty years later married the future fifth Earl of Warwick, who succeeded to the title in 1883. As heiress to the Maynard lands in Essex, she was rich in her own right, while her husband's family estates in Warwick and Somerset amounted to 10,102 acres worth £18,336 a year. By 1899 however, the family was in deep financial trouble; from 1897 there were constant sales of land, including £220,000 worth in 1919 alone; her husband became involved in Moreton Frewen's worthless speculations in Mexican gold mines, Kenyan timber, and British Columbian development; she herself was constantly in debt for sums in excess of £50,000; and in 1909–10, she appeared in court when some of her creditors sued her for non-payment of debts. Her husband died impoverished in 1924, and by then her son was in a nursing home, where he expired of drink only four years later.[37]

It was against this background that the Countess of Warwick tried to stay afloat, but became merely more déclassé in the process.[38] In

1907, she tried to start a newspaper and promote socialism; in 1911 she began a weekly column in the *Daily Express* for £300 a year; and in 1912 she went on a lecture tour to the United States, which was abandoned half way through. 'Are you an anarchist?' she was asked at one meeting. 'Not yet', she replied. There was also a string of books, including an edited version of Joseph Arch's autobiography, a history of Warwick Castle, an anthology of her (largely ghosted) journalism, and two excruciatingly bad novels. But for many years, her hopes of financial rehabilitation were pinned on writing – or, perhaps, not writing – the intimate memoirs of her youth, when she had been a lover of the Prince of Wales, from whom she had received some rather indiscreet letters. In 1914, when her own personal debts amounted to £90,000, she tried to raise money by demanding £125,000 from George V for the return of these letters, and threatened to publish them if he did not pay. But she was ultimately restrained by a court injunction, and the letters were returned and destroyed. When, finally, two volumes of ghosted autobiography duly appeared, they were, unlike her life, disappointingly bland.

The ninth Duke of Manchester provides a less spirited version of the same déclassé decline. The family estates were small in size and vulnerable in their location: 12,000 acres in County Armagh and 15,000 acres in East Anglia. The combination of the Irish troubles and severe agricultural depression meant that the ninth duke succeeded to a rent-roll of only £25,000 a year in 1892, all of which was gobbled up in jointures and interest payments on the extensive debts incurred by his two spendthrift predecessors. He himself had been kept so short of cash as a boy, with pocket money of one penny a day, that he grew up with no real sense of its value. On an allowance of £400 a year at Cambridge, he ran up debts totalling £2,000. He spent much time in America, Africa, and India, avoiding creditors, looking for a rich wife, and sponging off his friends. At different times, he worked as a journalist, an actor, and a film promoter. He was, on his own admission, 'unrepentantly addicted' to gambling; he never kept accounts or made money successfully; and he was constantly the victim of gossip columnists and confidence tricksters. His much-publicized marriage to Helena Zimmerman brought neither financial rehabilitation nor personal happiness, and they were divorced in 1931. In his artless autobiography, he candidly admitted that 'sport has appealed to me more strongly than brain work, which may be one of the reasons why I have not succeeded in making money.'[39]

Appearing in the gossip columns could be devastating evidence of a patrician family's decline and fall: but being a titled writer of them provided even more emphatic proof. During the inter-war years,

76. Lord Castlerosse (with the Prince of Wales).

such figures proliferated, and none was more fat or more famous than the sixth and last Earl of Kenmare, who inherited his titles in 1941 and died two years later, but who had been better known during the inter-war years by his courtesy title of Lord Castlerosse.[40] The family estates in Ireland were massive in acreage (118,606) but poor in yield (£34,473); the fourth earl had lived very extravagantly, and lavished £200,000 on the rebuilding of Killarney House in the early 1870s. Castlerosse was born in 1891 and, as a youth, lacked brains, looks, charm, or prospects. At university he was idle, unambitious, gluttonous, ran up many debts, and had many affairs. His war service was undistinguished, and his brief spell in the City was not a success. By then, he weighed eighteen stone, was constantly in debt to tradesmen, and depended on money-lenders for survival. He was rescued by Lord Beaverbrook, who paid him £3,000 a year plus expenses, and for whom he wrote the 'Londoner's Log' in the *Sunday Express* between 1926 and 1939, one of the earliest autographed gossip columns. Without Beaverbrook, he would never have survived; and he was, appropriately, the last of the line. As he himself correctly concluded: 'I dissipated my patrimony; I committed many sins; I wasn't important.'[41]

Individually, this was an unexceptionable judgement; but he was also illustrative of a whole segment of his class. One of Castlerosse's great rivals as a coroneted gossip columnist in the inter-war years was another indebted and indigent Irish landowner, the sixth Marquess of Donegall, Hereditary Lord High Admiral of Lough Neagh, and Governor of Carrickfergus Castle. His family had been in straitened circumstances since they had been forced to sell their lucrative Belfast lands in the first half of the nineteenth century; and the sixth marquess, who inherited in 1904 at the age of one, was obliged to earn his living. At one time or another, he wrote for the *Daily Sketch*, the *Sunday News*, and the *Sunday Graphic*; for many years he wrote the 'Almost in Confidence' column for the *Sunday Despatch*; he regularly covered the winter sports season at St Moritz; and he was one of the few journalists to travel and report on the maiden voyage of the Queen Mary.[42] Evelyn Waugh sent him up gently in *Vile Bodies*, as the fifteenth Marquess of Vanburgh, 'Hereditary Grand Falconer of the Kingdom of Connaught.' He, too, was a gossip columnist, a professional party goer, always trying to stay ahead of his great rival, the eighth Earl of Balcairn. And in this he succeeds: for Balcairn is gradually dropped from the party circuit, and eventually commits suicide.[43]

Not surprisingly, decent and responsible patricians like the Earl of Crawford and Balcarres took the greatest exception to 'the boastful record printed week by week by déclassés like Donegall and Castlerosse.'[44] But their slightly disreputable means of keeping their creditors at bay was merely a sign of the times. In the half-century from the 1880s, many patricians were obliged to earn their living somehow, as the old territorial underpinnings, which had made possible their ancestors' leisured life, were gradually but inexorably eroded. Those with brains, resource, initiative, wit, and luck were able to survive and come to terms with their new circumstances, and even to win for themselves a fame and renown that otherwise would have eluded them. But inevitably, survival on these terms was at a price. A titled racehorse trainer, or electrical engineer, or purveyor of cars to the nobility, might remain on personal, as well as professional, terms with his fellow-aristocrats. But he himself was neither landed nor leisured any more. He was a working patrician: and that, in a sense, was a contradiction in terms.

At the same time, the sad stories of the Frewens, Rosslyns, Warwicks, Manchesters, and Castlerosses, with their debts and their divorces, their gambling and their ghosted books, their palpable sense of futility and failure, show what happened to those who could not adapt. In the memoirs of these men and women, the same themes recur constantly: their inability to come to terms with their reduced inheritance; the urge to 'enjoy' themselves because there was nothing else to do; the ease and extent to which they spent money in pursuit of this unrealizable objective; and their amazing innocence when they were forced out from the protected environment of the landed estate into the much harsher world outside, like some delicate, exotic hothouse plant put into the chill blast of the open air. In her attractive and poignant memoirs, Lady Fingall tells the story of George Wyndham, the architect of the Irish Land Act of 1903, on holiday in Monte Carlo, where he met a peer in the casino who had sold his bankrupt Irish estates under the Land Act that had been named after him. The peer pointed to his chips, and greeted the former Chief Secretary with the words, 'George! George! the bonus!'[45]

Inevitably, having frittered away their money, or having had none to inherit, such people became a confidence trickster's dream. Partly through the peculiar conditions of the time in which they lived, these men and women were both innocent and irresponsible, easily beguiled into lending their names and their money to the most absurd and preposterous schemes. As such, their experience forms an integral part of the history of the British landed establishment in the years from the 1880s. And it is no coincidence that the novels of P. G. Wodehouse, which evoke the upper classes so acutely, are full of déclassé peers – gossip columnists, night-club dancers, music-hall singers, and the like – desperately trying to make ends meet.[46] More censoriously, Arthur Ponsonby summed them up exactly half way through this period: 'the aristocracy . . . are going through a transition stage . . . there are great signs of deterioration.'[47]

ii. The City: Figure-heads and Financiers

In August 1885, Lord Derby refused an invitation to become a director of the Manchester Ship Canal Company, of which Lord Egerton of Tatton, a major Cheshire landowner, was chairman. 'Great peers', Derby noted in his diary, 'and men engaged in public affairs, ought to keep out of directorates.'[48] Being a rich man, and with plenty to do, Derby could easily afford to look on such invitations and activities with disdain. But many other patricians, confronted with the urgent need to augment or replace their dwindling landed livelihood, could not afford to take such a high-minded attitude in the half-century from the 1880s. For those who found traditional means of life support either unavailable or inadequate, yet who were still determined to avoid the ultimate degradation of becoming déclassé, 'going into the City' was a new means of life support eagerly embraced. Like others, it either worked or it didn't. And, regardless of the actual outcome, it was a change in behaviour patterns and in economic circumstances so widespread as to betoken major class upheaval.

Of course, many grandees and gentry had been linked with companies during the first three-quarters of the nineteenth century, both as shareholders and as directors. But their interests were usually limited to canal and railway companies of local importance to their family holdings, as with the Marquess of Stafford's extensive investment in the Liverpool and Manchester Railway, or to enterprises directly associated with the exploitation of non-agricultural estate resources, as with the companies that the seventh Duke of Devonshire established at Buxton, Barrow, Lismore, and Eastbourne.[49] In such cases, patricians were not going 'into' business as a separate and alternative career to landownership: such commercial involvement and entrepreneurial activity was merely the logical extension of estate management and exploitation. Impoverished notables, like the Duke of Buckingham and Lord Robert Cecil, who really did go into business as the chairmen of railway companies with which they had no personal or landed connection, were very much the exceptions. Until the 1880s, as F. M. L. Thompson rightly explains, it was not at all usual for peers to become directors of public companies – and, in any case, there were not that many public companies for them to become directors of.[50]

During the last two decades of the nineteenth century, however, this changed very dramatically, as many patricians not only withdrew from their own private companies devoted to estate exploitation, but also began to involve themselves directly in the affairs of the City of London. One aspect of this – the purchase of shares in British, imperial, and foreign businesses – has already been described. And from there it was but a short step to even closer connection in the form of seats on company boards, known as 'ornamental' or 'guinea-pig' directorates. By 1896, according to *The Complete Peerage*, some 167 peers were company directors, about a quarter of the entire nobility, and by 1910 the figure was 232.[51] Some, like the Duke of Devonshire, continued to be directors of companies on their estates, although with growing reluctance and anxiety. Some, like Lords Pirrie, Armstrong, Inchcape, and Rhondda, were not bona fide patricians at all, but were members of the new plutocracy, recently created peers, without large landed estates, who were magnates in coal, shipping, and other heavy industries. But many, too, were authentic, titled landowners, 'in search of fees [and] allowing themselves to be put forward as figureheads of commercial enterprises of which they have no special knowledge and for which they have no special training.'[52]

From the City's side, this development may be easily explained.[53]

"NOBLESSE OBLIGE."

Promoter. "Um ! They cost a Lot, but I suppose they're worth it."
"Kind hearts are more than coronets and simple faith in Norman blood."—(Lady Clara Vere de Vere adapted to the occasion.)

77. '"Noblesse Oblige."' *Punch*, 13 Aug. 1898.

The company legislation passed between 1855 and 1862 gave Britain the most permissive commercial laws in Europe, which enabled seven shareholders to constitute themselves a company (either limited or unlimited), provided their object was lawful, simply by subscribing a memorandum of association. Later in the century, both Liberal and Conservative governments vainly tried to tighten up these lax laws, but they were unsuccessful, and it was not until after the Second World War that the position was effectively improved. So, in the thirty years before 1914, there was a succession of waves of company promotion, reaching peaks in 1889, 1898, and 1910, with a further and final flurry before the crash of 1929. Many of the undertakings thus promoted were entirely respectable: partnerships and family firms quietly and properly converted into public limited liability companies; new ventures in cycling, tramways, electricity, and motoring, the growth industries of the time; and large-scale mergers between companies with similar interests where rationalization seemed in order. But a great deal, too, was the direct result of fraudulent or foolhardy promotion both at home and abroad: companies set up purely for speculative purposes, or to develop land or seek for minerals in far-off and quite unsuitable places. And patricians became directors of both types of business, with the result that while some undoubtedly improved their finances, others only made them worse.

Which landowners went into the City in this way? It is worth looking at those peers who, in 1896 and in 1920, were directors of six companies and more (See Appendix D). In 1896, there were eleven: six bona fide members of the landed establishment who appear in Bateman; one landless peer, Lord Colville, who was without estates through accident of inheritance; two other non-landed peers, Guilford and Stratheden, who were descendants of nineteenth-century law lords; Lord Rothschild, the banker-cum-landowner, who was in a class by himself; and Lord Playfair, who had no connections with the titled and territorial order in terms of wealth, status, or power. Significantly, there were as yet no great plutocrats or industrial moguls. But by 1920, the picture had changed: of a total of forty-one peers, seventeen were authentic landowners (though Lord Glenconner was distinctly parvenu); four more were landless but of old creation (Selborne, Cochrane, Tenterden, and Teynham); Lord Stuart of Wortley was the grandson of the first Lord Wharncliffe; Lord St Davids was the twelfth baronet and boasted landed ancestors; and eighteen were newly ennobled plutocrats, businessmen, lawyers, and politicians. Here, simultaneously, are two significant trends revealed: as men of business were increasingly becoming peers, so peers were increasingly becoming men of business.

Of these fifty-one peers (Ribblesdale appears in both years), thirty-two were thus authentic patricians in terms of titles, lineage, and land. Nine of them were landless peers or younger sons from collateral branches, who would have had to work for a living in any age, but who, in this period, were able to find a new outlet in business. Nine owned estates in Ireland, which were small or vulnerable, and were disappearing under the Land Purchase Acts. Six held land in Scotland, again far from lucrative (although in Lord Glenconner's distinctly marginal case, the majority of his fortune was still in industry). Of the eight who remained, who were predominantly English owners, five held less than ten thousand acres, one was a Rothschild who was *sui generis*, and two were at the very bottom of the middling landowner category. In short, with the exception of Rothschild and Glenconner, all these peers with extensive City involvements were patricians whose families had never been well off, who were particularly hard hit by the agricultural depression and the Irish troubles. Not all company directors were impoverished landowners, and not all impoverished landowners were company directors. But apart from Rothschild and Glenconner, all landowners who were company directors were indeed impoverished.

And this was but the tip of a much larger iceberg. The first great promotion boom, of the 1880s, saw many poor patricians becoming company directors, especially of those firms recklessly formed to undertake mining and ranching in North America and Australia. Sir George Warrender and the Earl of Airlie were very quickly off the mark. Both needed to augment their landed incomes, Warrender because his Scottish acres were small, and Airlie because he had to retrench after a gambling spree.[54] Between them, they amassed a clutch of directorships in the late seventies and early eighties, primarily in Scottish-American enterprises.[55] But such essentially decorous directors were no guarantee of success, and one experienced and honest company promoter, William Weston, strongly criticized landowners who were prepared to prostitute their names in this irresponsible way:

> Sir George Deadbroke, Bart., Lord Arthur Pauper, Viscount Damphule . . . , and others of that ilk, are always ready to lend the charm of their great names to these enterprises and attend board meetings, for the moderate consideration of one guinea per meeting.[56]

In reality, there were many names that could easily be substituted for this fanciful list. In the early 1880s, a clutch of land and settlement companies were floated to colonize western Canada, and most were decked out with ornamental chairmen and directors, like the Duke of Manchester, the Earl of Mar and Kellie, Lord Castletown, Sir John Walrond-Walrond, and Sir John Lister-Kaye. And in the United States, sixty companies were floated at the same time to settle and farm the Midwest. One such was the Consolidated Land and Cattle Company, established in 1884, with a board including Lords Thurlow, Strathmore, Mar and Kellie, and Lovat. Other names associated with such companies included the Duke of Manchester (again), and Lords Dunraven, Tweeddale, Houghton, Dunmore, and Rosslyn.[57] By the end of the decade, most of these companies were in liquidation, as were the mining concerns that had been promoted at the same time. In 1887, for example, the Troy Gold Mines Company was floated to operate in North Carolina, with Sir Walter Barttelot-Barttelot, Bt., as chairman. No work was ever done; the company was liquidated within two years; and there were widespread complaints about 'pennyless baronets' who knew 'as much about mining as the man in the moon.'[58]

Across the other side of the world, the same picture presented itself. One such promotion during the mining boom was the Anglo-Australian Investment and Banking Company, whose English directors were Lord Camoys and the Hon. Ashley Ponsonby. But by

1891, it was in liquidation, and those who had invested or deposited recovered only three pence in the pound. Among those ruined was one John Hogan, who proceeded to prosecute the directors. Asked to tell the court whether he thought Lord Camoys was a substantial man merely because he was a lord, he replied, 'I suppose lords are blackguards, the same as everybody else.'[59] By the end of the decade, having lost his official salary, and being in need of more money than the Jerome allowance could provide, Lord Randolph Churchill was drawn into this same world. He had, Lord Derby noted, 'lately allied himself with one North, a speculator, enormously rich, but with few respectable acquaintances.' And Derby immediately saw how the transaction was mutually advantageous: 'the bargain between them being that he should give North a social position, and North help him with his money, for he is ruined.'[60]

The same tactic was used to much greater and more momentous effect by another adventurer of dubious repute, Cecil Rhodes, who went to England in 1889, at the very height of the first great promotional boom, seeking a charter for his British South Africa Company. His local directors, mainly Randlords like himself, did not inspire confidence in the mother country, and Salisbury urged Rhodes to find British directors of 'social and political standing' before applying for his charter.[61] Rhodes took the advice, and acted on it with characteristically brilliant opportunism. He approached Lord Balfour of Burleigh, a Scottish landowner of very limited acres, who already held several directorships, but he declined. More successfully, he turned to the Duke of Abercorn, who was selling off his Irish estates; to the Duke of Fife, who was systematically off-loading his lands in Moray and Banff; and to the future fourth Earl Grey, whose family estates had been encumbered since the days of his grandfather, the reforming Prime Minister, and who had himself invested extensively and wastefully in some of Moreton Frewen's more fanciful enterprises.[62]

Here, again, the trade-off was perfect. On the one hand, all three men were grateful for the money that Rhodes was able to offer them. On the other, Rhodes was grateful for the status that they could provide. Abercorn was a duke; so was Fife, as well as being the son-in-law of the Prince of Wales; and Grey was not only an ardent imperialist, but was also a man of such unexceptionable gifts that he acquired a great reputation for integrity, honesty, and straight dealing.[63] Between them, they provided Rhodes with his respectable façade, and he duly obtained his charter later in 1889. Thereafter, they did little except draw their fees. Grey was in Rhodes's pocket, and did exactly what he told him. Abercorn, who was chairman, and Fife, who was vice-chairman, did even less. The former was mildly disquieted when Rhodes assumed the Premiership of Cape Colony, but on the whole, he was mollified by his salary of £2,000 a year, and by the opportunity to purchase shares at par and sell them at a profit. As substantive figures in the company, they were thus 'worse than useless, for they gave a sheen of respectability to a company over which they had no control', and they were severely censured by the Committee of Inquiry into the Jameson Raid for 'laxity' in performance of their duties.[64]

At the end of the year that saw the climax of this first great company promotion boom, and the much-publicized antics of Cecil Rhodes, W. S. Gilbert mounted a powerful attack on patricians who behaved in this way, by creating the Duke of Plaza-Toro in *The Gondoliers*. Although ostensibly a Spanish grandee, his condition was remarkably like that of the patricians Rhodes had recruited to his board. He is 'unhappily in straitened circumstances'; his social influence, however, is 'something enormous'; he sets himself up as a limited company; he secures an 'influential directorate'; and he himself joins the board 'after allotment'. As for his activity, 'the work is light and, I may add, it's most remunerative.' In one of Gilbert's most acute and acid songs, he explains how:

> I sit by selection
> Upon the direction
> Of several companies bubble.
> As soon as they're floated
> I'm freely banknoted –
> I'm pretty well paid for my trouble

And the moral is plain:

> In short if you'd kindle
> The spark of a swindle
> Lure simpletons into your clutches,
> Or hoodwink a debtor,
> You cannot do better
> Than trot out a duke or a duchess.

Gilbert's shafts were well aimed yet, during the next promotional boom of the 1890s, more ignorant and impoverished landowners sold themselves to company promoters. The eleventh Earl of Fingall burned his fingers badly once, but then had the wit to stay clear.[65] His 9,000 acres in Meath were heavily encumbered, he wore threadbare clothes, was forced to sell his Dublin town house, often let his country seat, and declined to attend the coronation of George V because he could not afford his peer's robes. In 1894, he took a long voyage to Australia to recover from a hunting accident, and on the boat he met a financier called Myring. Together, they went to Western Australia, where they found gold; they returned triumphant to England, and set up the Londonderry Gold Mine Company, of which Fingall was a director; and there was a speculative mania as the public gobbled up the shares. But further investigation showed that there was no gold after all, and the company collapsed. 'And so', his wife ruefully recalled, 'ended our dream of wealth.' But once bitten, Fingall was twice shy. Despite other City offers, he was never tempted again. 'I upbraided him at first', his wife remembered, 'but was glad afterwards when I saw how many other fine names were tarnished by joining these dangerous companies.'

Others were less wise, and less willing to learn their lessons. The most famous instances were connected with E. T. Hooley, who promoted twenty-six companies, with a nominal capital of eighteen million pounds, between 1895 and 1898, when he went bankrupt, owing nearly half a million pounds.[66] He had loaded his companies with ornamental and titled directors, and the crash and its aftermath were a City sensation. In the course of his examination at bankruptcy proceedings, he revealed that he had paid Lords de la Warr, Winchilsea, and Albemarle some £80,000 to join the boards of Dunlop Tyres, the Horseless Carriage, and the Cycle Manufacturers Tube companies. 'What', Hooley was asked, 'was the object of paying the directors to join the board?' 'I couldn't', he replied, 'get them to join unless I did so.' 'What', he was further asked, 'was the object of having such names on the prospectus?' 'To get the company subscribed', he replied. To The Times, the moral was plain: 'Till now, the name of a peer, or a man of great family, upon the "front page" of a prospectus, has been valuable, because the public has not ceased to regard these persons as men of scrupulous honour, who would not give their names for secret "considerations." We seem to be changing all that.'[67]

De la Warr was a patrician nonentity: but the same could not be said of the Marquess of Dufferin and Ava, an impoverished and indebted Irish landowner, who in 1898 returned to the United Kingdom after a lifetime in the service of his country abroad. He agreed to become chairman of the London and Globe Finance Company – a firm heavily involved in Australian mines and run by another unscrupulous financier, Whittaker Wright – on the grounds that it offered both 'an interesting employment' and 'material remuneration'.[68] There is no evidence that Dufferin was bribed in the manner of de la Warr: on the contrary, he invested heavily himself. But there can be no doubt that his chairmanship was largely motivated by financial need, and that it greatly enhanced the standing of the company in the eyes of potential investors. Yet on his own

78. '"The Well Graced Actor."' *Punch*, 13 June 1896.

"THE WELL GRACED ACTOR."

Mr. Punch (to the Marquis of Dufferin, in last act of "Diplomacy"). "Not farewell, my Lord, but 'au revoir!' Hope soon to see you in a new Cast!"

admission, Dufferin could neither understand nor control the affairs of the company for which he was in effect responsible. Early in 1901, Wright's empire collapsed, leaving Dufferin not only 'nearly ruined' financially, but also subject to censure from *The Times* scarcely less severe than that which it had meted out de la Warr three years before.[69]

Dufferin died soon after, his end undoubtedly hastened by the Globe fiasco. But this did not deter others from treading the same dangerous path. George Cornwallis-West inherited an indebted estate at Ruthin Castle; he failed in his attempt to woo Mary Goelet; and he further increased his financial burdens by marrying the former Lady Randolph Churchill in 1900. In need of money, he sought the advice of the financier Sir Ernest Cassel. 'There are', Cassel told him, 'many young men of your class who should never go east of Temple Bar. Perhaps you are one of them.' Nevertheless,

Cassel gave him some help, and he became chairman of the Potteries Electric Traction Company, and also sat on the board of the parent firm, British Electric Traction. As such, he was unexpectedly successful; but when he went into business on his own, his luck failed. His own firm crashed shortly after the First World War began, and he was obliged to resign his other directorships as well. Cassel had been proved correct. Yet, as Cornwallis-West later recalled, the state of his finances had made it imperative that he earn some money: 'my sole motive for having gone into business, apart from having something to do, was to endeavour to make sufficient money to pay off my mortgages on my family estates.'[70]

But Cornwallis-West's misfortunes were as nothing compared with the decline and fall of the sixteenth Marquess of Winchester, who had succeeded to the august titles but limited estates of the premier English marquessate in 1899. He served as Lord-Lieutenant of Hampshire from 1904 to 1917, and was chairman of the county council from 1905 to 1909. Yet despite this highly august beginning, he soon went rapidly and irrevocably downhill.[71] During the 1890s, he had been involved in gold prospecting in Rhodesia; in 1906 he became a director of the British South Africa Company; and in the years immediately before 1914, he virtually made a full-time career for himself in the City. After wartime service, he resigned the Lord-Lieutenancy of Hampshire, sold off the remaining family estates in 1919, and resolved to earn his living entirely as a company director. In 1926, he met Clarence Hatry, a financier whose reputation was already so unsavoury that even Lord Castlerosse – on Beaverbrook's predictably astute advice – stayed clear, despite mouthwatering offers of £10,000 a year if he agreed to become a director of some of his companies.[72]

Winchester, being less well advised, and already in thrall to money-lenders, took the bait, and was soon set up as chairman of a host of Hatry enterprises: Corporation and General Securities, Drapery Trust, Oak Investment Corporation, Photomaton Patent Corporation, and Retail Trades Securities. But in the autumn of 1929, the entire Hatry empire collapsed in a scandal of Hooley-like proportions, and in the process, Winchester was completely ruined in both wealth and reputation.[73] He was obliged to resign his directorships, and was eventually declared bankrupt owing £312,000, of which £175,000 was accounted for by depreciation in the value of shares in Hatry's companies, £20,000 in debts to money-lenders, and £1,000 in debts to tradesmen. Since his assets amounted to a mere £700, he was obliged to live abroad, 'a victim', in the words of his lawyer, 'of misfortunes'. As *The Times* more censoriously noted, 'the ornamental director is fast becoming an object of alarm rather

than of awe to the average investor.' And the title of a book by Winchester, *Statesmen, Financiers and Felons*, aptly summed up his own
rake's progress.[74]

Yet this was only one side of the picture, albeit the more publicized and, on occasions, the more poignant and pathetic. For not all
needy patricians who were driven into the City in this period were
unsuccessful. Those who were lucky, or chose their companies with
care, or took a real interest in their affairs, or displayed genuine
ability, made considerable gains. Directors' fees were pure income,
and could augment and even surpass declining rental revenue. The
third Earl of Verulam was no great businessman, but he selected his
companies discerningly, and did much to revive his family's fortunes
by his directors' fees.[75] In 1896, he sat on the boards of four companies, all home based. The following year, his interests widened,
as he became a director of a Mexican and a South African Gold
Company, to which he soon added the Pacific North West Railroad
and Klondyke Consolidated. By 1913, Verulam was on the boards of
thirteen companies, most of them overseas, in mining, or both. And
it mattered: in 1897 his directors' fees and dividends amounted to
nearly one-third of his total income, and by 1913 the proportion was
even higher.

It was also possible for patricians with real business ability to do
more than merely draw directors' fees as unearned income. Lord
Balfour of Burleigh and Lord Colville were both peers of limited
territorial resources, who became chairmen of Scottish railway companies. The fifth Lord Tweeddale owned extensive but unremunera-
tive Scottish acres, and entered business so wholeheartedly that he
was a director of nineteen companies in 1896. He was Governor of
the Commercial Bank of Scotland, President of the Scottish Widows
Fund, and chairman of four telegraph companies and of the North
British Railway.[76] Likewise, the first Viscount Churchill, who sold
his family estates in Wiltshire and Oxfordshire to pay off accumulated debts, made a successful career for himself as a businessman: he
was chairman of the Great Western Railway and of the British Overseas Bank, and a director of P & O and of the British India Steamship Company. His son aptly explained how this had happened:

> In those days, in England, well-paid directorships were not too
> hard to come by if you happened to have a hereditary title, par-
> ticularly if it was thought you had some influence in politics or at
> court. My father had all three, and was alive and alert as well . . .
> Business was his real interest. Men with the social advantages of
> my father (sound financial assets in those days) used to go into
> business to the extent of lending commercial firms the pres-

tige of their names and titles, but they were usually content to pocket the directors' fees and take no active part in the business. My father's associates seemed to have found that he had ability, and that as well as his name, he himself was an asset.[77]

By the inter-war years, the experiences of Verulam and Churchill were becoming more commonplace than those of Dufferin or Cornwallis-West. There were still, as the sad end of Lord Winchester eloquently shows, occasions when naïve and impoverished land-owners allowed themselves to fall into the hands of unscrupulous speculators. But the intensive merger wave of the 1920s meant that patricians seeking 'safe' companies on whose boards they might sit as ornamental directors, or genuinely wishing to go into the City as a business career, were generally able to do so with greater security and success. And the incentive to do so was also much stronger in the aftermath of the post-war land sales and the Irish 'troubles'. Grandees and gentry alike were increasingly drawn to the City in search of lucrative directorships. Dispossessed Irish landowners had little choice but to make a new life by making a new living. And younger sons and more distant relatives increasingly came to look upon finance as a fit and proper profession for a gentleman. By this time, Lord Derby's views on the unwisdom of patrician director-ships were fully a generation out of date.

Even a ducal family as broad-acred and illustrious as the Buccleuchs had become unprecedentedly involved with the City and big business by the inter-war years.[78] The sixth duke's brother-in-law, Lord Burleigh, amassed a clutch of directorships, including the National Provincial Bank, the London and North Eastern Railway, the Firestone Tyre and Rubber Company, and the Army and Navy Stores. One of the sixth duke's sons, Lord Henry Scott, was chair-man of the Life Assurance Company of Scotland, and Deputy Governor of the Bank of Scotland. And another younger son, Lord Herbert Scott, was director of the Sun Life Assurance Society, the Tilbury Contracting and Dredging Company, the United Glass Bottle Manufacturers Company, and the Westinghouse Brake and Signal Company. He was also an appropriately patrician chairman of Rolls Royce, Vice-President of the Association of British Chambers of Commerce, a member of the council of the Corporation of Foreign Bondholders, President of the London Chamber of Com-merce from 1928 to 1931, and President of the Federation of British Industry from 1934 to 1935.

In a family as rich as the Buccleuchs, it was the younger sons who took to business: the Duke himself, and the heir to the title, remained essentially full-time landowners. But many less wealthy holders of estates could retain them only by effectively becoming full-time businessmen. This is vividly illustrated in the case of the fourth Lord Brabourne, who in 1920 was a director of thirteen companies. The family was of ancient Kentish lineage; there was a mansion and estate at Ashford; and the fourth lord's son was a county MP from 1931 to 1933. But in the early 1880s, their holdings were only 4,173 acres worth £6,000, so it is easy to see why the fourth lord sat on so many boards. More importantly, he also became managing director of Consolidated Gold Fields of British South Africa. As his *Times* obituarist noted, it 'was in the office of this company that Lord Brabourne spent his working days, finding in its varied and multifarious enterprises, and in those of other companies connected with it, full scope for the exercise of his powerful and lively critical intelligence.' As a result, he was able to keep Ashford in the family but, inevitably, 'his business occupations made it impossible for him to reside there permanently.'[79]

For some former Irish landowners, business was not a new means of keeping up an old estate, but was itself a new way of life. The ninth Earl of Bessborough had removed the pictures and furniture from his house in Kilkenny just before it was burnt down in 1923. He went into the City, and became deputy chairman of De Beers Consolidated Mines, and chairman of the Sao Paulo Railway and of the Margarine Union. With the income thus generated, he relocated himself in England, buying Stansted Park on the Hampshire border of Sussex.[80] Likewise, J. T. C. Moore-Brabazon was descended from an Anglo-Irish family in County Meath whose house, Tara Hall, had been destroyed, and whose estates had been sold under the Land Purchase Acts. He took up a career in the City in 1927, with seats on the boards of Kodak, HMV/EMI, and the Associated Equipment Company.[81] Three years later, the future seventh Earl of Drogheda, whose family left their Irish home at the time of the Troubles, found himself on the job market, having left Cambridge without a degree. He began work as a clerk for the English subsidiary of the American Smelting and Refining Company, obtained a job with *The Financial Times*, thanks to his friendship with Brendan Bracken, and was soon put on the boards of many of Bracken's companies.[82]

By this time, it was commonplace for more distantly related patricians to go into the City. Oliver Lyttelton was the younger son of a younger son, who sought to marry a daughter of the Duke of Leeds after the First World War, but who faced 'the grim problem of money and subsistence.' Through his cousin, Melville Balfour, 'a rich and successful stockbroker', he entered the banking house of Brown, Shipley and Co. Soon after, he moved to the British Metal

Corporation, and was general manager from 1922 until 1939.[83] A similar picture is revealed in the case of Colin Frederick Campbell, whose uncle owned a mere 2,100 acres in Dumbarton worth only £2,500 a year. Campbell himself made a very successful career in business and finance: as director of the National Provincial Bank from 1903 (chairman from 1933 to 1946), of London Assurance from 1897 (governor from 1914 to 1933), and of Alexander's Discount Company from 1912 (chairman from 1916 to 1950). He was also President of the British Bankers Association and chairman of the London Clearing Banks from 1938 to 1946, and was eventually ennobled as Lord Colgrain.[84]

In 1936, a random sample of 463 British companies of all sizes showed that 8 per cent of directors were titled, and that of these, probably half were entirely ornamental.[85] *They* were the direct descendants of patricians like de la Warr and Dufferin, who sought to augment their dwindling and declining resources by selling their titles for money. But whether looked at moralistically, or analytically, this blatant sale of names for directorships probably did as much to subvert the aristocratic order as it did to succour it. This was partly because the sale of status often did not pay that well: directors' fees were rarely that large, and if the company collapsed, there was not only loss of income to be endured, but also loss of reputation. But it was also because status sold was, inevitably, status undermined. If impoverished notables were prepared to sell their name and their rank so directly for cash, the patrician hierarchy of titles and honours was bound to be brought into disrepute. At the very time that it was being assailed from without, it was also being undermined from within. As the new, vulgar rich were busily engaged in buying titles, so the new, aristocratic poor were busily engaged in selling theirs.

But as the 1936 survey also shows, there was another side to this story. Some patricians were relatively passive but fortunate recipients of directors' fees from reputable and profitable companies, while others took a much more active part in business, and did rather well out of it. But inevitably, there was a price to be paid. For an aristocrat to become a full-time businessman was, as the *Estates Gazette* noted in 1928, simply a contradiction in terms:

The most obvious remedy for the threatened disintegration [of estates] would seem to be that country gentlemen should 'go into business', or qualify for more lucrative professions. In itself, this would be no bad thing, though it would mean that many landowners would be squires only in their hours of leisure, and that the personal touch between the owner and the tiller of the soil, which has been such a precious advantage to the countryside, would be seriously lessened.[86]

If 'taking boldly to trade' was the price of genteel survival, the result was a transformation so complete as to cast doubt on the very notion of survival at all. As Evelyn Waugh later put it to Nancy Mitford: 'You should have said, not that aristocracy can't make money in commerce, but that when they do, they become middle class.' Indeed, in a sense they became working class: not an aristocracy of labour, but a labouring aristocracy.[87]

iii. *Patrician Professionals Overseas*

While some needy notables turned to the new professions of late-nineteenth-century Britain or went into the City, there were others who still pursued traditionally genteel occupations, but who were increasingly obliged to do so abroad. For as the civil service, the law, and the church became either more competitive or less appealing, some patricians were forced, and others chose, to take up appointments in foreign climes, sometimes for part of their career, sometimes for the whole of their working lives. Instead of the civil service at home, there was imperial service abroad. Instead of the inns of court, there was the colonial bar. And instead of a country parish, there were episcopal appointments in the world-wide Anglican communion. In professional terms, these expatriate notables often achieved considerable successes: as governors, judges, and bishops, they were well paid, well housed, and well regarded in colonial society. But most grandees and gentry viewed such peripheral preferments in far-away places with scarcely concealed scorn. And as a result, they attracted aristocratic professionals only in relatively small numbers. On the whole, what Kipling called 'the exile's line' was not for them.

While the home civil service became increasingly competitive, bureaucratic, and professionalized from the 1870s, the administration of the British Empire remained essentially amateur and unreformed. For open competition did not come to the colonial service: recruitment was still by patronage. Yet despite the fact that the service greatly expanded in the aftermath of the Scramble for Africa, it never attracted patricians in large numbers.[88] The postings were far away from home, on the edge of events, both socially and politically. Most of the colonies were inhospitable places, justly famous for political unrest, natural catastrophe, and widespread disease. Loneliness, depression, sickness, and death were commonplace occupational hazards, as were overwork, mental breakdowns, and nervous disorders.[89]

The greatest professional proconsuls were invariably from middle-class, public-school backgrounds: Lugard in Nigeria, Milton in Southern Rhodesia, Cameron in Tanganyika, and Wingate in the Sudan. But for patricians in search of a job, the colonial service was never a very attractive proposition.

Nevertheless, as the last quarter of the nineteenth century opened, there were several proconsular postings occupied by landed-establishment professionals, who had entered the service in the mid-Victorian period, in most cases because they urgently needed to earn a living.[90] The Governor of Fiji was Sir Arthur Hamilton Gordon, the youngest son of the fourth Earl of Aberdeen, who went on to rule New Zealand and Ceylon, and eventually became Lord Stanmore.[91] The Governor of the Straits Settlements was Sir Frederick Weld, a country gentleman from Dorset, who had previously held proconsular office in Tasmania. The Governor of South Australia was Sir William Jervois, a country gentleman from the Isle of Wight, who was later promoted to New Zealand. The Governor of Bombay was Sir Philip Wodehouse, a kinsman of the Earl of Kimberley. The Governor of Victoria was the second Marquess of Normanby, who had been transferred there from New Zealand. And the Governor of Natal was Sir Henry Bulwer, a Norfolk country gentleman, who was later moved on to Cyprus. Thanks to their connections, these patricians had obtained a disproportionate share of the best postings in the Antipodes. But even then, they were only a very small minority among the total number of colonial governors.

During the years before the First World War, this pattern continued essentially unaltered, with only a trickle of new recruits from such a background. The fourteenth Viscount Gormanston was successively Governor of the Leeward Islands, British Guiana, and Tasmania. Sir Charles Cavendish Boyle, the brother of Sir Courtenay, was moved from British Guiana to Newfoundland to Mauritius.[92] Sir Lesley Probyn, the son of a minor Gloucestershire country gentleman, governed Sierra Leone, Barbados, and Jamaica. Sir George Ruthven Le Hunte, the son of a Wexford squire, progressed from New Guinea to South Australia to Trinidad. And Sir Charles Anthony King-Harman, of Longford and Roscommon, was in charge of St Lucia, Sierra Leone, and Cyprus. Like their predecessors, these men were among the most disadvantaged of the titled and the landed: they were younger sons of squires, or impoverished Irish aristocrats, or minor gentry. But unlike their aristocratic forebears in the service, they were increasingly relegated to the most insignificant and obscure appointments. They were peripheral patricians who were also peripheral proconsuls.

By the inter-war years, such notables were quite exceptionally

79. Sir Hugh Clifford and his gubernatorial entourage.

rare, and only two stand out. The Hon. Sir Charles Dundas was the
sixth son of the sixth Viscount Melville, who entered the service in
1908, and eventually became Governor of the Bahamas and Uganda.
More important was Sir Hugh Clifford, the grandson of the seventh
Lord Clifford, the only patrician who ever made a genuine reputation as one of the very greatest of colonial governors.[93] He began
his career in the Malayan Civil Service in 1883, when his relative
and patron, Sir Frederick Weld, obtained a job for him. He soon
switched to the colonial service, where he was rapidly promoted,
and in 1912 he became Governor of the Gold Coast. Thereafter, he
was successively Governor of Nigeria (1919–25), where he brilliantly sorted out the chaos and confusion left by Lugard, of Ceylon
(1925–7), and of the Straits Settlements (1927–9).[94] He possessed a
strong sense of family identity, and regarded the natives as a benevolent landowner would regard his tenantry. In the true dilettantish
tradition of government service, he also made a name for himself as
the author of many travel books, and he was a great friend of Joseph
Conrad.

But by the 1920s and 1930s, such full-time patrician professionals
were very much the exceptions: of the two hundred men who held
British colonial governorships between 1900 and 1960, scarcely a
dozen were from such a background. And nearly half of those were

not colonial service men who had reached the summit of their career, but were patronage appointments known as 'cuckoos in the nest', made by successive British governments.[95] There was the Hon. Sir E. E. Twistleton-Wykeham-Fiennes, second son of Baron Saye and Sele, who resigned as MP for the Banbury Division of Oxford, and served as Governor of the Seychelles from 1918 to 1921, and of the Leeward Islands from 1921 to 1929. There was Major-General Sir Edward Northey, a professional soldier and son of an Anglican clergyman-cum-landowner, who was Governor of Kenya from 1918 to 1922. There was Colonel Robert Peel, a kinsman of the Prime Minister, who gave up his Suffolk constituency to become Governor of St Helena from 1920 to 1924. And there was the Hon. Sir Bede Clifford, a relative of Sir Hugh, and son of the tenth baron, who left a quasi-diplomatic career to be Governor of the Bahamas, Mauritius, and Trinidad between 1932 and 1946.[96]

If the colonial service, though still recruited by patronage, was unappealing to *fin de siècle* and inter-war patricians seeking employment, then the Indian Civil Service was even less attractive. During the early 1850s, when appointment was still by nomination, over one-quarter of the new recruits were from a genteel background. But after the introduction of open competition, between 1854 and 1856, the landed element dropped away very soon and very abruptly – to a mere one-tenth by the 1860s, and to as little as 6 per cent by the 1890s. By the inter-war years, this aristocratic trickle had all but dried up completely: in 1926 and 1927, there were no recruits from such a background at all.[97] As with the home civil service, the ethos was overwhelmingly genteel: but again, this was the gentility of the public-school, Oxbridge-educated middle class. Without exception, it was from this background that the great Indian administrators like Hailey and Butler came. As Sir Penderel Moon later recalled, it was the middle class, and not the aristocracy, 'that was the mainstay of the British Raj, and was largely responsible for its character.'[98]

So, despite its excessive reputation for high quality and high status, the ICS was never an appealing career for a needy notable in search of a government job.[99] Like most of the colonial empire, India was an inhospitable place, and employment there involved long separation from family and country. The dramatic fall of the rupee in the 1870s and 1880s, and again in the aftermath of the First World War, meant that salaries (and therefore pensions) were particularly unattractive. By the inter-war years, the combination of political reform and increasing Indianization of the service meant that the future seemed ever more uncertain. Above all, the majority of the aristocracy regarded service in India in a very negative light: being shipped out to the distant obscurity of the subcontinent was essentially an admission of failure. A succession of noble Viceroys – Ripon, Dufferin, Lansdowne, and Elgin – snobbishly castigated the ICS for its lowly social origins and its general lack-lustre performance. Lord Lytton claimed that 'nineteen civilians in twenty are the most commonplace and least dignified of Englishmen', and Curzon derided and decried 'the mediocrity of my official surroundings.'[100]

Even in its pre-First World War heyday, there were fewer sons of peers in the ICS than in the colonial service (one authority rightly remarks that the number of aristocrats could be 'counted on the fingers of one hand'), and the remaining upper-class recruits came from the very margins of the landed establishment.[101] Consider the case of Sir Arthur Blennerhassett, fifth baronet. His family owned a mere 8,393 acres in County Kerry, which were worth only £2,145 a year. After graduating from Balliol, Oxford, he entered the ICS in 1895, and eventually became Chief Secretary to the Chief Commissioner of the Central Provinces. Or consider the career of Sir John Muir Mackenzie, sixth son of the second baronet. His family owned 4,241 acres of Perthshire, worth £6,419. Sir John was born in 1854, joined the ICS at twenty, remained in its employment for thirty-six years, and ended his service as Acting-Governor of Bombay. And in a later generation, had history and independence not overtaken him, the same career would no doubt have opened up for the young Humphrey Trevelyan, who joined the ICS in 1929.[102]

But as the case of Trevelyan suggests, many of the patricians who turned to the ICS between the 1880s and Indian independence did so, not because it was a new and audacious career, but because it was already a family tradition. The Stracheys of Sutton Court in Somerset were of authentically ancient and illustrious lineage, climbing slowly across the centuries to a baronetcy and eventually to a peerage. But their territorial resources were small, and successive generations were thus obliged to work for their living. Two brothers of the third baronet, Sir Richard and Sir John, both distinguished themselves in Indian affairs, the latter being Lieutenant-Governor of the North Western Provinces in the mid-1870s, and a member of the Governor-General's Council. And Sir John's second son, Sir Arthur Strachey, eventually became Chief Justice in the High Court of the same province, while other cousins in the same generation occupied more humble positions.[103] As Sir John later recalled, with understandable pride: 'There is hardly a great office of the state, from Acting-Viceroy, Lieutenant-Governor, or Member of Council downwards, which one or other of us has not held, and hardly a department of the administration with which one of us has not been intimately connected.'[104]

But even the Stracheys were surpassed, as a minor patrician dynasty in India, by the Plowdens, an ancient family of Shropshire gentry, the senior line of which held 5,934 acres worth £6,964 in 1883. The junior branch, known as the Chichele Plowdens, produced fifteen civilian administrators and five members of the Indian police force between Plassey and Independence. Although numerous, their careers have rightly been described as 'honourable rather than spectacular.' At best, they did not get far: one became Inspector-General of the Bengal Police Force, another was Resident in Mysore, and a third was Resident in Hyderabad.[105] (Indeed, the family's greatest claim to fame was that Pamela Plowden, the daughter of the Hyderabad Resident, was the first great love of Winston Churchill's life, but turned him down for the future Lord Lytton.) As such, the Plowdens were very typical of the rare and lowly patrician element in the ICS: on the whole, it was no career for the son of a gentleman or a grandee.

But while the imperial bureaucracy was no more appealing than the reformed civil service at home, the grand viceregal regimes that were established in India and the great dominions meant a proliferation of transoceanic courtly positions that attracted scions of the most illustrious names in the land. Viceroys and Governors-General were surrounded by an extensive entourage of comptrollers, secretaries, and ADCs. And since they themselves were usually aristocrats, they preferred their staff to be recruited from the same background. In securing these appointments, which invariably went to men in their twenties, personal connection was everything: the grander the name, the better the chances. A son of the sixth Earl Fitzwilliam was ADC to Lord Ripon in India during the early 1880s, and the future seventh earl was ADC to Lord Lansdowne ten years later. When the ninth Duke of Devonshire was Governor-General of Canada, his ADCs included Lords Haddington, Minto, Molyneux, and Dalkeith.[106] Indeed, Lord Richard Nevill made a lifetime's career out of such work, beginning in 1895 as ADC to the Governor of Victoria, and ending in 1921 as Comptroller to the Governor-General of Canada.

But in the main, these jobs were held for a short time, usually just for the duration of one proconsular regime. Unlike the colonial service or the ICS, they were not so much a career as a diversion. The conditions of work were pleasant, the company was congenial, and they provided an agreeable way for young notables to see something of the world after coming down from university. More positively, they were a means of acquiring experience in public life, and of establishing some useful connections, in the hope that greater things would follow. And in some cases, they did. After serving their apprenticeship as ADCs, Lords Minto and Willingdon went on to carve out their own proconsular careers. And before he became 'King of Lancashire' and a cabinet minister, the seventeenth Earl of Derby was ADC to his father when he was Governor-General of Canada, and was later private secretary to Lord Roberts in South Africa. Although Roberts was a professional soldier rather than an aristocratic proconsul, his Boer War staff was almost entirely drawn from the nobility. The high-minded Lord Balcarres did not approve at all:

> The Duke of Westminster has been sent to the base by Lord Roberts for disobedience. The Duke of Marlborough has been warned that he is in danger of being sent home. It is curious that a man like Lord Roberts should allow his wife to nominate all his ADCs. Kerry, Stanley, Downe, Gerard, two dukes, a Bruce and I don't know how many more – peers, or peers to be, all of them.[107]

While he was High Commissioner in South Africa, the self-made Lord Milner's preferences were equally patrician. Untitled young men like John Buchan and Patrick Duncan were very much the exception: his 'kindergarten' was as aristocratic as any proconsular entourage. Major William Lambton, sixth son of the second Earl of Durham, was Military Secretary. Lord Brooke, the heir to the Earl of Warwick, was an ADC. Hugh Wyndham, future fourth Earl of Leconfield, was assistant private secretary. Lord Basil Blackwood, the son of the first Marquess of Dufferin, held the same post. Philip Kerr, future eleventh Marquess of Lothian, was Assistant Secretary to the Governor of Orange River Colony. And Bend Or, the second Duke of Westminster, was ADC to Milner before joining Roberts' staff.[108] As with the full-time courtiers at Buckingham Palace, these were all patronage appointments. But unlike the royal bureaucrats at home, these courtly functionaries overseas served only for a limited period. They regarded such postings as opportunities for youthful adventure (and misbehaviour). But this was the empire as outdoor relief rather than as a patrician profession.

Like the ICS, the Colonial Bar and Indian judgeships were widely regarded as inappropriate and marginal careers by most members of the traditional titled and territorial class. But for those genteel lawyers who failed to make money at the English bar, and who had no prospect of preferment or promotion at home, they were in some ways very attractive. The Indian Chief Justiceships were worth £7,000 a year, and even Ceylon and Hong Kong paid £2,700, which compared well with the meagre £1,500 of an English county-court judge. So, despite the stigma of such appointments, there was a real attraction in exchanging 'legal life in London, with its precarious successes, its constant failures and its deferred hopes, and the sickness of heart that accompanies them', for the 'honour and comparative wealth' of a colonial judgeship. Moreover, many of these jobs were effectively in the gift of the Colonial Secretary, while a certain quota of the most sought-after legal posts in India was reserved for members of the ICS.[109]

In this regard, the case of Sir John Jardine is instructive. He joined the ICS in 1864, but spent most of his career in the law, eventually becoming Puisne Judge of the High Court of Bombay in 1885. In the very same year, Sir Ernest John Trevelyan, who had spent his earlier years practising and teaching law in India, was appointed a judge of the High Court of Calcutta. Sir Alfred George Lascelles reached a similar posting by a rather different route. He was a grandson of the third Lord Harewood, obtained a Second in history at Oxford, and was called to the Inner Temple in 1885. He went overseas, was appointed a district judge in Cyprus, became Attorney-General of Ceylon in 1902, and in 1911 was appointed Chief Justice.[110] In the same way, the Hon. Frederick Charles Moncreiff, fourth son of the first Lord Moncreiff, began his career on the north-eastern circuit, was appointed a Puisne Judge of the Supreme Court of Mauritius and was later transferred to Ceylon. And in a later generation, Kenneth James Muir Mackenzie spent the inter-war years successively as Attorney-General in Fiji and as a judge of the High Court in Tanganyika.[111]

Just as some unhappy or adventurous patricians sought to make their legal careers in the empire, so some upper-class clerics sought (or were driven to accept) preferment overseas.[112] In most cases, they went to the dominions or the Indian empire. One obviously reluctant overseas bishop was Adelbert Anson, fourth son of the first Earl of Lichfield. He was educated at Eton and Oxford, and intended to make his clerical career in the Lichfield diocese. But after serving as a curate, there was no immediate opening, and so in 1884 he was appointed first Bishop of Qu'Appelle in Canada. In a later generation, the Rt. Revd Sir Francis Cooke Caulfield Heathcote, ninth baronet, was Archdeacon of Vancouver and later Bishop of New Westminster.[113] In India, Edwin James Palmer, cousin of the second Earl of Selborne, was Bishop of Bombay, and Henry Carden, nephew of the fifth baronet, was Archdeacon of Lahore. Between 1909 and 1927, Charles Ferguson Davie, nephew of the third baronet, was Bishop of Singapore. In South Africa, Maurice Ponsonby, grandson of the second Baron de Mauley, was Dean of Johannesburg, while Neville Talbot was Bishop of Pretoria. And Harold Buxton began as Domestic Chaplain to the Bishop of Rangoon, became Archdeacon of Cyprus, and was then appointed Bishop of Gibraltar.[114]

These were remote postings, far from family, friends, and familiar surroundings. But at least they were still within the bounds of the empire and the English-speaking world. Those patrician prelates who travelled further afield could not even count on the succour and support of colonial society. The Rt. Revd Edward Francis Every was the second son of the tenth baronet. In the early 1900s, he went out to South America as Bishop of the Falklands, and from 1910 to 1937, he was Bishop of Argentina. In 1929, he published a book entitled *Twenty Five Years in South America* which, while completely lacking in self-pity, gave a vividly forlorn picture of his far-off and lonely existence. He travelled long and uncomfortable distances, from the glaciers of Tierra del Fuego to the tropical jungles of the Amazon, in his efforts to keep in touch with the sparse and scattered members of the Anglican communion. The congregations were small, their material resources were limited, and in the whole of Argentina there were, in 1922, only nineteen Anglican clergymen. As Every admitted, there were but 'a handful of churches scattered over a continent', and 'a great deal of time is occupied in achieving very little.'[115]

In most cases, these peripheral patrician professionals returned home at the end of their working lives. One or two, like Kenneth Muir Mackenzie, died on the job, and a few stayed on. Bishop Sir Francis Heathcote preferred to sell his ancestral estates in Hampshire rather than leave Canada, and Charles Ferguson Davie spent the thirty-six years of his retirement in South Africa.[116] But sooner or later, the majority came back. Sir John Jardine entered politics, and was MP for Roxburgh from 1906 to 1918. Sir Ernest John Trevelyan retired from the Calcutta High Court in 1898 and became Reader in Indian Law at Oxford. Sir Alfred Lascelles became chairman of the Malton bench. Adalbert Anson duly took up a career in the Lichfield diocese, and ended his days there as Assistant Bishop. Palmer was appointed to the same post in Gloucester; Talbot became vicar of St Mary's Nottingham; and Ponsonby and Buxton returned to country parishes. So, in the end, did Edward Every. After thirty-five years as a South American prelate, he was appointed vicar of Eggington in Derbyshire, the family living, at the age of seventy-six.

But whether at home or overseas, their patrician background and attitudes regularly emerged. Charles Ferguson Davie shot for England three times at Bisley. Ponsonby, Carden, Buxton, Pratt, and Talbot were Chaplains to the Forces during the First World War. Edward Every shot and fished, one chapter in his book on South America was a detailed account of the sport available there, while others dealt with such familiar aristocratic concerns as the servant problem and the growing materialism of the age.[117] Harold Buxton was curate at Thaxted, where he served under Conrad Noel. Edwin Palmer stayed with his cousin, Lord Selborne, when the latter was High Commissioner in South Africa. And Neville Talbot's funeral in 1943 was attended by a predictably large turn-out of Lytteltons and Talbots, by the Earl and Countess of Clarendon, and by Lords Selborne and Salisbury.[118] For Talbot, as for most of these overseas patrician professionals, it was almost as if his imperial interlude had never been. But for those members of the landed establishment who espoused overseas emigration and permanent settlement, the empire meant something very different.

iv. The Migratory Elite

It was not only as shareholders, company directors, and occasionally as professionals that gentry and grandees sought succour from the empire – sometimes successfully, sometimes not. For as the lands of the British Isles ceased to provide them with adequate financial support, many turned instead to the colonies and dominions beyond the seas, where agricultural land and mineral deposits could be found in abundance. During the first three-quarters of the nineteenth century, most imperial emigrants had been either impoverished or criminal members of the working classes: the empire had held little allure for those of higher social station. But from the late 1870s, as opportunities for gentlemen diminished at home, it became increasingly fashionable for them to look to great white dominions, the American west, and the most hospitable parts of British Africa.[119] Books and pamphlets were written, explaining how to raise the money for the ticket, how to choose between the relative merits of North America and the Antipodes, and how to make a new life in a new country thousands of miles away.[120]

So, instead of being merely a dumping ground for the lower classes, the empire increasingly became a dumping ground for those politely called 'supernumerary gentlemen' or, more often and more accurately, 'gentlemanly failures'.[121] Of course, not all of them were authentic notables: many were sons of merchants, businessmen, and professional people. But a substantial and much-discussed proportion were of landed and titled background, and most of them came from predictably straitened circumstances: younger sons, the indebted and the impoverished, those who had voluntarily sold their estates, and those in Ireland who had been forced to sell. Their motivation, too, will come as no surprise: some went to the far reaches of the empire to make a go of it for themselves and to build a new nation in the process; some went simply to have a good time away from the stern gaze of the parental eye; and some, on the brink of becoming déclassé, went to live down disgrace, and often became more unacceptable in the process. Whatever their motives, these gentlemen emigrants ranched and mined in the USA and Canada, prospected for gold in Australia and South Africa, and farmed and fornicated in Kenya.

These world-wide ramifications are well illustrated in the case of the Moncreiffes of that Ilk family.[122] The sixth baronet, Sir David, held the title from 1818 until 1830, and spent extravagantly on food, horses, hunting, gambling, and house building. The estates were heavily encumbered, and in 1883 amounted to only 4,743 acres in Perthshire worth £7,427 a year. Sir David's second son, William Aeneas, settled in Australia, where he 'fell into bad hands, trusted everybody, and was robbed on all sides', spent eighteen months alone in the bush tracking a favourite mare, at sixty-two could still ride a bucking colt, and died unmarried in Queensland at the age of eighty-one in 1906. His elder brother, Sir Thomas, became the seventh baronet, held the title from 1830 to 1879, and unwisely fathered eight sons and eight daughters. *His* third son, Thomas George Harry, became a planter in India, and died of fever in Calcutta in 1887 at the age of twenty-six. One of *his* sons, Thomas Gerald Auckland, was a keen game hunter, and cleared jungle scrub and set up a coffee plantation at Fort Ternan in Kenya in 1913. The fourth son of the seventh baronet, William, was a rancher in Wyoming from 1888 to 1923, and a friend of Buffalo Bill and Teddy Roosevelt. The fifth son, Ronald, a celebrated clubman, drinker, shot and polo player, took part in the Jameson Raid. And the sixth, Malcolm, was another Wyoming rancher. Reluctantly or eagerly, these two generations of Moncreiffes had made the world their oyster.

As their family history suggests, the first country that beckoned gentlemen emigrants in large numbers was the United States. By the 1880s, it had recovered from the traumas of the Civil War; the economy was booming; the western prairies were being opened up; and British investment was pouring in, to reach $2,625 million by 1899. During the 1880s, sixty British companies were formed, most decked out with titled and ornamental directors, to raise cattle and settle land in the Midwest. Many young patricians, like Lords Rosslyn, Dunraven, and Rodney, went out there in person, seeking fun and fortune on the prairies.[123] So did Moreton Frewen, who was extensively involved in ranching, from Texas to Wyoming. So did his friend, Hugh Lowther, the future fifth Earl of Lonsdale, who sold his contingent reversionary interest for £40,000, invested it in cattle companies, and went out to join the party. And so did the fifth Earl of Aylesford, who squandered away his family fortune by gambling, racing, and extravagance, and died in Texas at the age of thirty-six, 'one of the worst examples of the English peerage.'[124]

In a rather different category were those gentlemen emigrants who established closed, cosy, and patrician settlements, so as to preserve the amenities and outlook of upper-class life in an alien and republican nation. In the late 1870s, such communities were founded in Kansas at Victoria, in Tennessee at Rugby (by, predictably, Arnold himself), and in Iowa at Le Mars. The Iowa settlement gives a vivid impression of the aristocratic flavour of these communities. It was peopled from the outset by such sprigs of nobility as Lord Hobart, the heir to the Earl of Buckinghamshire, Captain Reynolds Moreton, the brother of the Earl of Ducie, two sons of Lord St Vincent, and Lord Harris.[125] And the tone and the style was predictably elevated. As one contemporary explained, 'you see the heir apparent to an old English earldom mowing, assisted by the two sons of a viscount; you watch the brother of an earl feeding a threshing machine.' There was a cricket club, of which Moreton was president; there was a jockey club, which even staged a local Derby; the two saloons in the town were called 'the House of Lords' and 'the House of Commons'; and the Queen's Golden Jubilee of 1887 was enthusiastically celebrated.[126]

As well as these corporate enterprises, some patricians bought property as individuals. One such was the fifth Earl of Airlie, who was a major propagandist on behalf of upper-class emigration, and acquired 2,000 acres in Colorado for his younger son, Lyulph Ogilvy, who made a successful career raising cattle and horses, and whose descendants live there to this day. Another, who operated on rather a larger scale, was John Sutherland Sinclair, who emigrated in 1875 at the age of nineteen, and in 1891 unexpectedly inherited the landless earldom of Caithness. By then, he was farming an 'enormous acreage' in North Dakota and, although he returned to take his seat in the House of Lords, he preferred to live in America, close to the source of his wealth, and finally retired, incognito, to Los Angeles.[127] But he was outdone as an emigrant territorialist by William Scully, the fifth son of a Catholic Irish landowner, who first visited the United States in 1849–50, and gradually began to accumulate land. By the end of the century, he owned 220,000 acres in Illinois, Missouri, Kansas, and Nebraska, which had cost him well over one million dollars.[128]

Mining also attracted the gentle and the titled, not only as ornamental directors, but also as hopeful prospectors. One such was Robert Moreton of Le Mars, who thought he had found coal there in 1883, and duly formed the North West Coal and Mining Company, with a capital of $500,000. But there was no coal, and he lost heavily on the venture.[129] More unusual was the story recounted by the eighth Earl of Hardwicke in the House of Lords in January 1910. By the 1880s, his family's magnificent home at Wimpole was burdened with debts of £300,000, and in 1894, the creditors foreclosed and the house was sold. Accordingly, the future earl set out to earn his living in the USA. As he explained, such experiences suggested it was untrue to claim that the peerage had no knowledge of trade or industry:

> He himself was for ten years engaged in mining engineering, and for two of those years he worked as an ordinary miner. That day thirteen years ago, he was working nightshift in a ten hundred foot level at union wages in a gold mine in Montana, in the United States of America. He was known as 'Charlie', and as 'Number 126' to the management.[130]

In Canada, most of the emigrants settled in southern Ontario and in the western provinces, which were being opened up at the same time as the prairies in the USA. Manitoba was largely given over to wheat farming, and several patricians established themselves there, like the Hon. Mountstuart Elphinstone, the younger son of the landless fifteenth earl, who arrived there in 1890 and farmed 9,000 acres at Virden. In a similar way, Edward George Everard ffoukes came from a Norfolk landed family. His uncle was the third baronet, and owned 8,000 acres; his father was a clergyman; his elder brother later inherited the title; and two other brothers went into the church and the army. Edward himself went to Haileybury, where he did not shine, and then to the Agricultural College at Guelph, Ontario. By 1883, he was farming near Portage la Prairie in Manitoba. Life was hard; there were few labourers; and he had to do most of the work himself. But he seemed to prosper, and found the local environment congenial. In the 1883 edition of *The Haileyburian*, he described local society as 'really first rate', with county families, dances, garden parties, cricket, and tennis.[131]

On the whole, however, Manitoba was more characterized by small, independent, democratically-minded wheat farmers than by communities of settlers with patrician connections. But Alberta was very different, and much more grand. Since most of the settling was initially under the auspices of the great cattle and land companies in the early 1880s, with their aristocratic chairmen and ornamental directors, the result was a ranching society with a very strong ethos of gentility. Sumptuous houses were constructed, modelled on English country mansions. There were clubs and societies, with their London periodicals and their lavish entertainments. Hunting, shooting, and fishing were readily available, and cost much less than in the old country. Hence the appearance in Alberta of men like the Hon. F. C. Lascelles, and the appearance in fiction of such characters as the Hon. Fred Ashley, late of Ashley Court in England who, in the pages of R. Connor's *The Sky Pilot*, settled in Cochrane, Alberta in the 1880s:

> At Ashley Ranch, the traditions of Ashley Court were preserved as far as possible. The Hon. Fred appeared at the wolf hunts in riding breeches and top boots, with hunting crop and English saddle, while in all the appointments of the house, the customs of the English home were observed.[132]

The most distant destination of these gentlemen emigrants who were Canada-bound was beyond the Rockies, in British Columbia. One famous purchaser was the seventh Earl of Aberdeen, who bought 500 acres in 1890 in the Okanagan Valley, where he established the Guisachan Ranch, managed by his brother-in-law the Hon. Coutts Marjoribanks. Another Governor-General of Canada, Lord Grey, owned several fruit ranches in Kootenay Valley, and once remarked that horticulture was 'a beautiful art as well as a most profitable industry'. He warmly recommended it as the natural calling of Englishmen of 'refinement, culture and distinction.'[133] And the young sixth Marquess of Anglesey, who had inherited both the title and the very large debts from his predecessor and cousin, bought lands at Walhachin in 1913, where he built for himself a large house, complete with a swimming pool and a special room for his concert piano.

Those patricians who emigrated to Canada attracted less notice in Britain than those who went to the United States. But Canadian writers were quick to spot the anecdotal possibilities of such figures. Robert Edwards, the editor of the *Calgary Eye Opener*, created a character called Albert Buzzard-Cholmondeley, late of Skookingham Hall, Leicestershire, and in 1903–4 published a series of letters home to his parents of which he was the ostensible author. They show him occupying himself as a gambler, a farmer, a newspaper proprietor, a bar tender, and a politician, in no case very successfully, and only just avoiding detention in the local prison and lunatic asylum. More affectionate was R. J. C. Stead who, in a book called *The Empire Builders*, wrote a poem in celebration of the son of Marquis Noddle:

> He is brand-new out of England and he thinks he knows it all
>   (There's a bloomin' bit o' goggle in his eye)
> The 'colonial' that crosses him is going to get a fall –

(There's a seven pound revolver in his thigh.)
He's a son of Marquis Noddle, he's the nephew of an earl,
In the social swim of England he has got 'em all awhirl,
He's as confident as Caesar and as pretty as a girl –
Oh, he's out in deadly earnest, do or die.[134]

Despite this unpromising start, he fares much better than Buzzard-
Cholmondeley, and makes a go of things in the end.

The speculative boom of the 1880s also extended as far as Australia, where the search for land and minerals attracted its share of
emigrant patricians. Many of them merely crossed the Pacific from
California to indulge in further adventures, like the Duke of Manchester, who divided his time in the 1880s between cattle and
settlement companies in Texas and Canada, and searching for gold
(he needed it) at Broken Hill.[135] Even more impoverished were
Harold and Henry Finch-Hatton, who had gone out to Australia in
the late 1870s. They were half-brothers of the very impoverished
Earl of Winchilsea, who squandered money on gambling and on two
wives, who was obliged to sell paintings and even the lead off the
roof of the family home, and who was described on his death in 1887
as 'nearly a pauper'. The two brothers worked in the Queensland
bush on a cattle station, prospected for gold in the Mount Britten
Field, and tried unsuccessfully to float a mining company. Harold
returned home in 1885, and published an account of his experiences
in a book entitled *Advance Australia!*[136]

Finch-Hatton's failure was by no means atypical: few of the
patricians who emigrated to North America or the Antipodes in the
late nineteenth century really made a go of it. The supplies of gold
and other minerals were so limited that prospecting was bound to be
a risky business, and the cattle companies were catastrophically hit
by the fall in prices and the bad winters of the mid-1880s.[137] By the
end of that decade, most of the cattlemen adventurers were back in
Britain, most of the companies were in liquidation, and the aristocratic settlements like Le Mars lingered little longer. Finch-Hatton's
Australian mine did not pay, Elphinstone's Canadian farm was not a
success, Anglesey's venture was a non-starter from the beginning,
and Rosslyn, Frewen, Lonsdale, and Manchester made nothing out
of their American ranching schemes. All too often, these genteel
emigrants were the victims of ludicrously over-optimistic propaganda, and most returned home both sadder and poorer.[138]

Their activities had also provoked great hostility in the United
States. Individuals like Scully were heavily criticized in the Midwest
and in Washington, for being 'alien landlords'. They were accused of
bringing back to America the evils of the British estate system, with

its aristocracy and tenantry, and of seeking to re-establish that very system of absentee ownership that was so criticized by Irish emigrants to America.[139] And, by attributing to individual aristocrats the properties owned collectively by the companies of which they were the directors, it was claimed that some twenty million acres of the United States were held by the titled British, who were thus in the process of reversing the defeats of the War of Independence by buying up the lands they had lost. As a result, the federal government and many Midwestern state legislatures passed Alien Land Laws between 1885 and 1895, severely restricting rights of foreign ownership. Although not retroactive, the passing of these laws, combined with the slump in the cattle trade, effectively put an end to the greatest phase of patrician emigration to North America.[140]

But there were other reasons why these sprigs and scions of nobility did not succeed. Many who emigrated were simply quite unsuitable. They had received an education entirely inappropriate for the task they were attempting, and knew next to nothing about the country that was their destination. They were neither good at manual labour nor enthusiastic about undertaking it; they wanted servants and subordinates who could not be found; and they regretted and resented the general lack of sport, amusement, and patrician leisure. Many were classic remittance men, who got their allowance from home every quarter, and then squandered it on drink and gambling.[141] Even those who remained sober and solvent could rarely resist the temptation to try to live like lords. The result, in Canada and elsewhere, was a series of 'astounding follies':

> Club houses of imposing structure sprang up in embryo prairie towns . . . Capital, that should have been invested in acres and ploughs, melted away in all kinds of riotous living . . . Pyramids of empty champagne bottles for the first and probably the last time rose upon the prairie.[142]

Moreover, the climates of the North American Midwest and the Australian outback were distinctly uncongenial, and the indigenous political culture was too egalitarian for most patricians to fit in or adapt to. They were constantly criticized and ridiculed for their superciliousness, for their determination not to adjust to colonial or republican ways, for their mistaken and patronizing attempts to treat cowboys as if they were farm labourers. 'Englishmen', one commentator remarked, 'is a synonym for inefficiency, unhandiness, inadaptability, and for an irritating, repetitious cocksureness that everything Canadian is inferior to everything English.'[143] Only if such men were 'born again', did they stand any chance, and most did not want to be. They did not like the colonials, and the colonials did not like them. With characteristic exaggeration, Lloyd George claimed that in Australia, 'they hang the scions of our upper classes to the nearest tree.' But Harold Finch-Hatton made essentially the same point: 'Too many of our own countrymen . . . seem to consider that because they are in a new country, they can behave just as they please.'[144]

From the terraces of Kimbolton or Lowther Castle to the deserts of Australia or the prairies of the Midwest was, for most patricians, too great a step. But parts of British Africa were different: the climate and terrain were good; the natives were friendly or could be made so; and with no white settlers there already, the dangers of incompatibility in an egalitarian environment were avoided. For a decade after the granting of the charter in 1889, Rhodesia was effectively ruled by the British South Africa Company, which employed buccaneering adventurers rather than sober-minded bureaucrats. And the three Administrators, who were ostensibly in charge, were distinctly unimpressive.[145] Jameson was entirely in Rhodes's pocket, and saw his job as being to pander to fortune hunters from Britain. Albert Grey was sent out to stop him giving evidence to the committee of inquiry into the Jameson Raid, and cut a ridiculous figure, with his claret, his parties, and his monogrammed bicycle. And Arthur Lawley, the younger son of the second Lord Wenlock, was generally recognized to be incompetent. Between them, they governed Rhodesia with what Lord Blake has rightly called 'a deplorable mixture of ignorance, neglect and irresponsibility.'[146]

More precisely, they administered it almost exclusively in the interests of aristocratic adventurers who, as in the United States and Canada, formed limited companies and adorned them with titled directors, to take over the available concessions in land, cattle, and minerals.[147] One such upper-class buccaneer was Sir John Willoughby, Bt., who owned a mere 2,300 acres in England, had gambled extensively, came to admire General Gordon, and set up Willoughby's Consolidated Company, which held some 600,000 acres of Rhodesia, purely as a speculation. Of the fifteen million acres in the country that were alienated between 1889 and 1899, most initially went to what Sir William Milton rightly described as 'the honourable and military elements who are rampant everywhere.' 'Jameson', he went on in 1896, 'has given nearly the whole country away to the Willoughbys and Whites and others of that class . . . It is perfectly sickening to see the way in which the country has been run for the sake of hobnobbing with the Lord This and the Hon. That.' Even Grey complained occasionally about the young nobs, like the Hon. Bobby Ward MP, son of Lord Dudley, who were 'filled with the jolly, reckless spirit of adventure, which aims at making a million

A CASE FOR CLEMENCY.

Field-Marshal Punch (addressing Lord Lansdowne, while indicating Mr. Cecil Rhodes). "Now, MY LORD, THEY 'VE REINSTATED HIM. HOW ABOUT WILLOUGHBY AND THE OTHERS!"

80. 'A Case for Clemency.'
Punch, 21 May 1898.

and a half an hour, and then clearing off to Piccadilly.' The result was the great age of fortune hunters – of Texas in Africa. Not surprisingly, the Matabele rebelled. 'The blacks', Lord Milner concluded, 'have been scandalously used.'[148]

But this was not the full extent of the patrician connection with Rhodes, for some of these gilded expatriates were prominently involved in the Jameson Raid in December 1895.[149] Indeed, many of them were the very same people who had recently been granted such lavish concessions north of the Limpopo. Among the officers in command of the raid were Raleigh Grey, a distant cousin of the future Administrator himself; the Hon. Charles Coventry, a grandson of the ninth Lord Coventry and younger brother of the tenth; and the Hon. Charles, the Hon. Harry, and the Hon. Robert White,

three of the five sons of the sixth Lord Annaly, an Irish peer. And
the commander of the expedition was none other than Sir John
Willoughby. After the ignominious collapse of the raid, they were
captured by the Boers in early 1896, and later that year they were
prosecuted in Britain, charged with 'preparing a military expedition
against a friendly state.' All were convicted: Willoughby received
fifteen months imprisonment, Robert White seven, and Harry White,
Raleigh Grey, and Charles Coventry five months apiece.

But by then, a much more attractive alternative had already
presented itself for patrician emigrants: British East Africa. Originally, like Rhodesia, in the hands of a chartered company, Kenya
was formally taken over as a protectorate by the British in 1895.
Nairobi was established in 1901; the railway from Mombasa to the
interior was completed in the same year; and in 1904 the protectorate
became a colony. It was a particularly attractive country, with no
whites already there, with relatively friendly natives, and with
beautiful, rolling hills, broad acres of grazing land, fertile soil, and
abundant game. The prospects of economic development seemed
good, and for those who yearned for home, the White Highlands
seemed strongly reminiscent of Wiltshire. Originally, in the 1890s,
the first visitors went primarily to shoot big game; but as soon as the
administration was established and the railway completed, a settlement scheme was introduced. By 1905, there were 600 emigrants,
and three years later the White Highlands were effectively reserved
for Europeans.[150] The result was that for the next thirty years, Kenya
was the scene of a unique attempt to transplant British country-
house life to the empire.

To impoverished and adventurous patricians, it presented the ideal
opportunity. Bertram Francis Gurdon, subsequently second Lord
Cranworth, first went out in 1902, drawn there by 'love of sport,
more especially big game shooting, and shortage of cash.' With
11,000 acres in Norfolk, Suffolk, and Northumberland, worth only
£8,800, the incentives were clear:

> The only means I knew of adding to an income which was pretty
> steady on the zero line, with a tendency to drop below it, was by
> farming. There were indeed far fewer opportunities of acquiring
> wealth even thirty years ago for an impoverished landowner,
> handicapped by being a peer, than there are today.[151]

He duly obtained two land grants of 15,000 acres each, grew sisal,
reared cattle, was involved with a hotel and a safari agency, and
acquired interests in coffee, ivory, and rubber in Uganda. The result
was a perfect life – aristocracy on the cheap:

81. Lord Delamere.

Never before or since have I been so rich. We had the best car in the protectorate, the best civilian house, three ponies and a goat carriage, a first class Goan cook . . . , a spacious and most beautiful garden, and domestic servants and gardeners without stint. Our total personal expenditure on these was about £1,200 a year.

It was both to advertise these delights, and to 'put a spot of money in the family till', that in 1912 he published *A Colony in the Making*, which depicted Kenya as the ideal home for patrician emigrants who were not attracted by other parts of the empire.[152]

By then, indeed, the notables were well represented among the settlers. Pre-war emigrants included Lord Cardross, a poor Scottish peer, Denys Finch-Hatton, another member of the impoverished Winchilsea clan, and the brothers Berkeley and Galbraith Cole, younger sons of the Earl of Enniskillen. But the most important pre-war patrician emigrant was the third Lord Delamere, who had succeeded to 6,000 heavily-encumbered Cheshire acres in 1887. As a boy, he was arrogant, reckless, overbearing, quick-tempered, and sarcastic, and these characteristics remained with him for the rest of his life.[153] He first went to Kenya on safari in 1898, and in 1903 obtained a land grant of 100,000 acres. In order to raise the money, he further encumbered his estate in Cheshire, so that it passed into the hands of receivers, persuaded his mother to forgo her jointure, and was severely overdrawn at the bank. With no experience of farming, and unaware of local conditions and diseases, Delamere tried sheep, wheat, and tobacco in quick succession. All failed. But he did establish himself as the spokesman of the white settler community, and was vociferous in his opposition to Joseph Chamberlain's abortive Jewish emigration scheme.[154]

The inter-war years were the golden period of patrician pre-eminence in Kenya, as the earlier settlers consolidated their dominant position in Kenya, and were joined by a new generation of post-war emigrants, many of whom were from landed backgrounds. One such was Lord Francis Scott, another of the sons of the sixth Duke of Buccleuch, who had been ADC to Lord Minto when Viceroy, married his daughter, and went out to Kenya in 1920, having been severely wounded during the First World War.[155] Another, who arrived in 1934, was Major Sir Ferdinand Cavendish-Bentinck, a kinsman of the Duke of Portland, who was ultimately to inherit the title. Together with Delamere, they dominated politics in Kenya during the inter-war years, and waged a constant battle against the British government, which they saw as putting the interests of the natives before those of the settlers. In 1923 and 1930, Delamere led deputations to London with the object of obtaining safeguards for the settlers, and in 1933 and 1936, Lord Francis Scott tried again. They were only partially successful; but for the time being, it did not really matter. In death, Delamere's statue dominated Nairobi, just as the man himself had in life. And the aristocratic settlers continued to look down on the professional administrators from the colonial service, whom they saw as mistaken in their politics, and inferior in their social position.[156]

Some of these illustrious immigrants were serious, decent, well meaning, and high-minded. But especially after the First World War, the colony also became a haven for some very unsavoury notables – men already separated from their lands, their responsibilities, their reputations (and in some cases, their wives), who went out to escape their creditors, to live down their past, or simply to indulge themselves.[157] One of the least unattractive was Gilbert Colville, the only son of Major General Sir Henry Colville of Lullington Hall, Derby. He was a small, awkward, chinless man, who was a miser and a hermit, who lived in squalor with his many dogs, and who was popularly supposed to have gone native. He was, however, relatively harmless, which was more than could be said of John Carberry. He inherited Irish lands and the title of Lord Carbery in 1898 at the age of six, served in the First World War, then departed for the USA because of his extreme dislike of England. In 1920, he was deported for alleged bootlegging, and migrated to Kenya. His first wife divorced him for cruelty in 1919; his second may well have been driven to suicide in 1928; and by 1940 he was strongly pro-Nazi.[158]

But he was by no means the only aristocratic buccaneer. There was Raymond de Trafford, descended from a Lancashire landed family, who was attractive, bibulous, and indiscreet, who was on one occasion shot by the woman he later married, and who was described by Evelyn Waugh as 'a fine desperado'. Then there was his friend, the twenty-second Earl of Erroll: of an impoverished but illustrious Scottish family, he was asked to leave Eton at seventeen, married a twice-divorced woman in 1923, and was exiled to Kenya in the following year.[159] Charming, good-looking, promiscuous, cynical, and a bully, he inherited the title in 1928, ran up very large debts, divorced his wife, and was described by a judge as a 'blackguard' in another case where he was the co-respondent. In 1930, he remarried for money; in 1935 he joined the British Union of Fascists; and his second wife took to heroin and died in 1939. And there was Sir Jock Delves Broughton, another dim and vain Etonian, with 15,000 acres in Cheshire and Staffordshire. He evaded military service in 1914 on the grounds of sunstroke, and bought the Spring Valley estate in Kenya in 1923. Like Erroll, his purpose in life was to have a good time. By 1939 he had sold much of the ancestral acres; those which remained were heavily mortgaged; and the family portraits and jewels were 'stolen', having only recently been insured.[160]

Between them, this gang of 'aristocratic fugitives' evolved an appropriately self-indulgent and escapist style of life. In their bungalow mansions, with their large verandas, magnificent gardens, and retinues of servants, filled with silver, furniture, and family portraits brought out from the ancestral home, they sought to re-create a stable, rural, hierarchical, aristocratic world, which had already disappeared in modern, industrialized, democratic Britain. It was 'a haven for those whose social self-perceptions were not matched by their economic resources.'[161] In 1924, Lord Erroll began a community in the White Highlands known as 'Happy Valley', centred on the Muthaiga Club, which was barred to Administrators, businessmen, and Jews, and was the centre of much riotous, bibulous, and promiscuous living. 'Are you married, or do you live in Kenya?' was the big joke of the time.[162] For men like Lord Francis Scott, who wanted the settlers' image to be that of toil and sacrifice, rather than of frivolity and eccentricity, it was extremely disagreeable. As

82. Members of the Muthega Club, Kenya.

Maud, Countess of Selborne once remarked: 'The best class of Englishmen don't come out to the colonies, and those who do are apt to be frightful bounders.'[163]

The most resolute defender of this decadent and déclassé regime was the young Evelyn Waugh, who took the settlers' part to the full, claimed that the 'native problem' had been dreamed up in London and Bombay, and sought to acquit the whites of the charge that they were 'a gang of rapacious adventurers.' On the contrary, he argued, they merely sought

> to transplant and perpetuate a habit of life traditional to themselves, which England has ceased to accommodate – the traditional life of the English squirearchy ... One may regard them as Quixotic in their attempt to recreate Barsetshire on the equator, but one cannot represent them as pirates and landgrabbers.[164]

Others were not so sure: Karen Blixen thought many of the people in Kenya 'dreadfully immoral'. But at a deeper level, through her lengthy affair with Denys Finch-Hatton, she realized that this was but the outward sign that they came from a decaying social order, which had lost its place and its purpose:

They did not belong to their country. Theirs was an earlier England, a world which no longer existed. In the present epoch they had no home, but had got to wander here and there . . . They believed that they were deserters, who sometimes had to pay for their wilfulness, but they were in reality exiles, who bore their role with good grace.

Or, as she put it on another occasion, they were 'a class of people who have nothing other to do than follow their own bent.'[165]

As with those seeking ornamental directorships or serious City careers, the genteel adventurers who emigrated to far-off places divide into two groups: those who worked hard and hoped to make a go of things (whether or not they succeeded); and those who wanted something for nothing, or even nothing at all. But either way, they were so divorced from their traditional environment, so thinly spread out across the world, and so escapist and resentful in their attitudes, that their transplanted aristocratic life inevitably became an irresponsible, self-indulgent parody of the original. As early as 1919, in the midst of the great post-war land sale boom, the *Estates Gazette* had made this prediction: 'Experience shows . . . that aristocracy – not necessarily a titled aristocracy – divorced from its land tends to lose its sense of public responsibility.'[166] And the story of Happy Valley certainly bore this out. Geographically uprooted, territorially dispersed, and socially fragmented, these patrician emigrants were at the ends of the world and, in some senses, at the end of the road.

v. Conclusion: Hobson Revisited

Between the 1880s and the 1930s, the economic position of many aristocrats was fundamentally transformed. And for all the qualifications that must be made, that transformation may be simply described: out of land and into business. Whether as shareholders or *rentiers*, car salesmen or train drivers, heiress hunters or novelists, ornamental directors or successful businessmen, mining prospectors or Kenyan adventurers, the trend was essentially and fundamentally the same. Of course, not all patricians in this period became estate agents, qualified as engineers, married Vanderbilts, wrote gossip columns, went into the City, or went out to the empire. And most estate agents, qualified engineers, Vanderbilt spouses, gossip columnists, City businessmen, and imperial emigrants were not drawn from among the old titled and genteel classes. Nevertheless, activities such as these, so varied and so novel, were a significant part of the aristocratic experience between the late nineteenth century and the outbreak of the Second World War. And as such, they bear eloquent witness to the changed and diminished circumstances of the landed establishment. On the one hand, they provide impressive evidence of its capacity to adapt. But on the other, they furnish emphatic proof of its irreversible fragmentation.

Nevertheless, there were significant similarities between, say, the ninth Duke of Devonshire, now drawing more income from stock-exchange dividends than from agricultural rents, and Lord Castlerosse, who was essentially dependent on the largess of Lord Beaverbrook. Both were patricians: titled, landed, aristocratic. But neither of them was primarily dependent – as their forebears had been – on revenue drawn from their landed estates or from ventures associated with their development and exploitation. Instead, they were now deriving the majority of their income from international and imperialist capitalism. And as such, they had become a part of that world described by J. A. Hobson as encompassing 'the city ground landlord, the country squire, the banker, the usurer and the financier, the brewer, the mine owner, the iron master and the ship builder'.[167] To Hobson, these were the prime agents of capitalistic imperialism, and grandees like Lord Rosebery (married to a Rothschild, Foreign Secretary and Prime Minister) and Lord Grey (descended from a Prime Minister, friend of Frewen and Rhodes, Administrator of Rhodesia, and Governor-General of Canada) were classic examples, increasingly 'living on tribute from abroad.'

As every schoolboy knows, Hobson did not get it entirely correct. On the whole, the patricians were no more the creators of the British Empire than they were of *fin de siècle* international capitalism. Nevertheless, his basic idea, in so far as it related to members of the landed establishment, was not far wrong. For they were certainly the beneficiaries, both of the new plutocracy and the new imperialism.[168] In shifting their dwindling resources from British agriculture to British business, and from British land to the British Empire, they were behaving in essentially the way Hobson described. Economically, there was something to be said for this. But in other ways, they paid a high price for this transformation. In its most blatant form, as in the case of someone like Castlerosse, it meant that they became essentially parasites on the plutocracy. And even in the case of the Duke of Devonshire, they were in reality now the clients of the bourgeoisie. As Hobson's left-wing analysis made plain, the right-wing predictions made by Mallock in the 1880s had been amply borne out by subsequent events.

10

LOST CAUSES AND DISAPPOINTED HOPES

The 'landed interest' seemed to be represented less by traditional landowners than by the quasi-collectivist National Union of Farmers.
(K. O. Morgan, *Consensus and Disunity: The Lloyd George Coalition Government, 1918–1922* (1979), p. 160.)

Between 1911 and 1928 . . . the House of Lords – the rejuvenation of which was treated at least nominally as vital by both the Liberal Government and the Conservative opposition in 1911 – was effectively relegated even by the Conservatives to an unimportant role.
(D. Close, 'The Collapse of Resistance to Democracy: Conservatives, Adult Suffrage and Second Chamber Reform, 1911–1928', *Historical Journal*, xx (1977), p. 893.)

Southern Unionism . . . tended to be Protestant, anglicised, propertied, and aristocratic . . . In an age of democracy, this narrow social basis was to prove fatal.
(P. J. Buckland, 'The Southern Irish Unionists, the Irish Question, and British Politics, 1906–14', *Irish Historical Studies*, xv (1967), pp. 234–5.)

The Cecils had somewhat receded from the heart of government since those days [of the Hotel Cecil], making do instead with the lay leadership of the Church . . . The state might have rejected the Cecils, but the Church remained in safe hands.
(A. Hastings, *A History of English Christianity, 1920–1985* (1986), p. 64.)

'From natural causes', Mr Gladstone perceptively explained to the Duke of Bedford in 1884, 'the portion of our population most associated with hereditary influences is slowly losing somewhat in relative weight.'[1] Indeed, during the next half-century, that process was to continue and markedly to accelerate. And for many of the old nobility and gentry, the political consequences were as momentous as they were unwelcome. One sign of this shift in the balance of power was the rise of adversarial politics, as the patricians became the target and victim of radical (and sometimes also conservative) attack. But the other was that the members of the landed establishment were less successful than they had been in defending the causes they held most dear. As Gladstone had predicted, the issues about which they cared most strongly, and which concerned their own circumstances most closely, were becoming increasingly marginal to modern British society as a whole. Instead of being the governing class, who set and controlled the agenda of politics, the gentry and grandees were gradually becoming the anxious but frustrated defenders of their own peripheral vested interests.

This is powerfully illustrated in the patricians' declining position as the self-appointed leaders of the rural economy. The agricultural depression, the radical political attacks on the land, the breakup of great estates, and the shift in the balance of power and population from the country to the town were challenges to which the traditional territorial classes responded ineffectually and dispiritedly. Their efforts to protect agriculture, to thwart the Liberal land campaign, and to revive the rural community under genteel leadership were singularly unsuccessful. And the ease with which the Tory party abandoned the landowners as the chief representatives of the agricultural interest, and turned instead to the National Union of Farmers and the labourers' trade unions, was only a further indication of their weakened circumstances. By the 1930s, agriculture was no longer regarded as a major or special industry; and the aristocracy and gentry had effectively given up their once pre-eminent position.

In the same way, the landowners also failed to safeguard or revive the legislative supremacy of the House of Lords. From the 1880s onwards, it was almost universally recognized that a completely hereditary second chamber was increasingly unacceptable in a democratic country, and that an overwhelmingly landed House was similarly anachronistic in a society where great wealth was no longer exclusively – or primarily – held in broad acres. And thereafter, the Parliament Act deprived the upper house of its power of veto, and a succession of honours scandals robbed it of its prestige. But it proved no easier for the patricians to revive and reform the House of Lords than to safeguard and protect agriculture. For the many subsequent attempts to restructure its composition and to claw back its powers were totally unsuccessful.

Once the upper house had capitulated, the nobles and notables became vulnerable in yet another way. For with the Lords veto abolished and unrestored, and with the rise of a new and more brutal form of agrarian nationalism in Ireland, Home Rule could no longer be prevented. Under these circumstances, there were only two alternatives for the beleaguered landowners in the south of Ireland. The majority refused to concede that the Union would ever be broken, believed that their British friends in high places would always stand by them, and opposed all change with what proved to be myopic and futile intransigence. A few sought – in a high-minded, magnanimous, and statesmanlike way – to pursue a more constructive policy of moderation and conciliation. But whatever they did, it profited them nothing. The Union was repealed; the Irish Free State was created; and the southern landowners were abandoned to their unhappy fate.

The last cause that the patricians fought and lost concerned organized religion. For many Christian gentlemen, disillusioned by the increasingly vulgar and hostile world of democratic and demagogic politics, it became more attractive to serve the church than to serve the state. Some grandees, in defiance of the social and secular trends of the time, continued to support devotional endeavours out of their own purses. Many genteel Anglicans vainly tried to prevent the disestablishment of the Welsh church. And the same men helped to bring a measure of self-government to the Church of England with the creation of the Church Assembly, which they dominated throughout the inter-war years. But for all the high hopes with which it had been greeted, the Assembly was little more than a talking shop; and in an increasingly secular age, it proved a poor exchange to trade secular power for ecclesiastical statesmanship.

But it was not just that the gentry and grandees so completely and so conspicuously failed in their specific endeavours to protect agriculture, to revive the House of Lords, to safeguard the position of the southern Unionists in Ireland, or to reinvigorate the Church of England. For underlying these particular defeats was something even more fundamental: namely the broader rejection of their historic claims to patrician leadership in each of these fields. The farmers of Britain, the politicians of Westminster, the nationalists of Ireland, and the prelates of the church were not prepared to conceed that the old aristocratic class had the right to perpetuate (or to reclaim) its once pre-eminent position of command and authority. As a result, the aristocracy and gentry were not merely being marginalized: they were well on the way to being made redundant.

i. The Land: Love's Labours Lost

In October 1899, the *Estates Gazette* made this disenchanted comment: 'This country appears to care little, if at all, for the position of the land . . . Unquestionably, politicians do mould their conduct upon the wishes of the towns rather than of the country.'[2] Despite the fact that a Conservative government was in power, and that the *Gazette* was the self-proclaimed mouthpiece of 'the landed interest', these remarks were highly apt. Throughout the whole of this period, agriculture was both the most depressed and the most marginal of the great staple industries. For much of the time, the land was the object of predatory political attack, while the great estates themselves were gradually being dismantled. And the patricians' response was hopelessly ineffectual: they did not succeed in obtaining agricultural protection; they abandoned the attempt to offer a coherent political defence of great estates; and they ceased to be accepted as the mouth-piece of the agricultural industry.

The period of most intense agricultural depression, from the late 1870s to the late 1890s, coincided with an almost unbroken era of Tory government, most of it dominated by the aristocratic cabinets of the Hotel Cecil, and characterized by an unprecedented amount of patrician support in the aftermath of Home Rule. But while the sudden fall in agricultural prices in the late 1870s led to immediate demands for Protection from grandees like Lord Bateman and the Duke of Rutland, Disraeli was far too much of a political realist to think of acceding to them.[3] He might now be Earl of Beaconsfield and a Buckinghamshire landowner, and he might have opposed repeal in his youth: but for him, politics was always the art of the possible. And he knew, at the beginning of the last quarter of the nineteenth century, that agriculture no longer determined the pros-perity of the whole nation, and that the reduced prices that were so unwelcome to the farmers and the landlords were a boon to the consumer. What the *Junkers* could achieve in Germany the land-owners could not accomplish in Britain. For Disraeli, the issue had been definitively settled in 1846. As he explained in the Lords, it was no use quoting 'rusty phrases of mine forty years ago.'[4]

Nevertheless, during the 1880s, the demand for agricultural pro-tection intensified. In 1881, the National Fair Trade League was founded, and included among its members Lord John Manners, a veteran Protectionist from 1846; patrician Tory MPs such as W. F. Tollemache, Lord Henry Thynne, Lord Claud Hamilton, and Algernon Egerton pledged their support; and at by-elections in Lincolnshire and Co. Durham, Protectionist Conservatives were victorious. In the short-lived Salisbury government of 1885, it was claimed that half the cabinet were in favour of tariffs, and at the 1886 election, sixty-nine Tory MPs declared for Protection. By this time, an impressive collection of landowners had taken up the demand, including the Duke of Rutland, Lord Dunraven, J. W. Lowther, and Henry Chaplin. And in 1887, Fair Trade resolutions were carried at the annual conference of the National Union of Conservatives, while it was rumoured that even Salisbury himself was sympathetic to the idea.[5]

But although Salisbury hedged and hovered between 1885 and 1891, he, too, was as much of a realist as Disraeli, and knew that Protection was not 'practical politics.' No party that needed the rural labourers' votes could be too overtly well disposed to the land-

HERCULES AND THE FARMER.
(Old Fable—Modern Version.)

Hercules-Salisbury *(quoting from recent Speech at Brighton).* "I AM CONSCIOUS THAT WHEN THE GOVERNMENT HAS DONE ITS BEST, EVEN IF THE GOVERNMENT WERE ABLE TO ADOPT THE ROMANTIC DREAMS OF SOME ESTEEMED FRIENDS AMONGST US, THEY WOULD ADVANCE BUT A VERY SMALL DISTANCE IN DIMINISHING THE SUFFERING WHICH THE HAND OF PROVIDENCE HAS INFLICTED —" British Farmer. "O LOR!"

83. 'Hercules and the Farmer.' *Punch*, 30 Nov. 1895.

owners; no party courting urban support could discriminate in favour of the countryside; and no party dependent on Unionist co-operation could abandon Free Trade. As Salisbury explained in 1895, there was no prospect of adopting 'the romantic dreams of some esteemed friends amongst us.'[6] The 'construction of the government' ruled it out, as did the composition of the party. When nearly half of the MPs were 'the representatives of commercial constituencies', they were naturally 'sensitive to the reproach of belonging to the stupid party and putting the clock back.' Or, as he put it even more apocalyptically, to impose a tariff would be to induce 'a state of division among the classes of this country which would differ little from civil war.'[7]

There is no more eloquent evidence of the economic and political decline of the landed interest during the last quarter of the nineteenth century than the fact that successive Conservative governments regarded Protection as being beyond the realms of practical politics. The very party to which the Whigs had fled, to which most land-owners now looked for defence of their position, and which was dominated in its higher echelons by the Salisbury clan, had effectively abandoned the landowners' agricultural interests as a lost cause. And even the composition of these new Protectionist pressure groups provided only further signs of the patricians' dwindling importance. For the Fair Trade League – like other Protectionist associations – was dominated by businessmen like Farrer Lloyd and David Maciver, who were mainly concerned to campaign for the protection of industry, and who regarded the protection of agriculture very much as an afterthought, as no more than a secondary objective.[8]

So what, if anything, did Salisbury do for the landowners as the leaders of the agricultural community? Predictably, not very much. In 1889, he established the Board of Agriculture, with Henry Chaplin as the first President. But this was a very belated and inadequate response to sustained lobbying dating back to 1874: initially, the post was not in the cabinet; the financial grant was inadequate from the beginning; there was no Parliamentary Under-Secretary; and there was not even a departmental building.[9] And the Agricultural Rating Act of 1896, which meant that such land was assessed at only half its value, brought a storm of protest, not only from the Liberals, who vilified the measure for showing 'the same spirit which inspired the Corn Laws', but also from Tories who sat for urban and industrial seats, and who objected to agriculture being singled out for preferential treatment. Thereafter, Salisbury did no more on behalf of the landed interest, and made no attempts to repeal the hated death duties.[10]

Balfour was even less sympathetic to the much-diminished agriculturalist lobby in the Commons, and his government virtually ignored them. The effect of the 1902 Education Act was so to increase local rates as to nullify the measure of 1896. The two shilling duty put on corn in 1902 was merely for revenue purposes in wartime, and was repealed in the following year, when Henry Chaplin – by now a spent and splenetic force – vainly led a deputation to Balfour protesting against this outcome.[11] Lord Onslow, the new President of the Board of Agriculture, found the Prime Minister quite 'indifferent' to the subject, and was tartly rebuffed by Balfour when he proposed a scheme of rural regeneration in 1905: 'he held the view that for good or evil, the country had at the time of the Corn Laws determined to be an industrial and urban country, and not a rural and agricultural one.' So dispirited was Onslow that in October 1905, he publicly complained of the party's indifference to agriculture, of the lack of time devoted to the subject in the Commons, of its insensitivity to the issue of rural regeneration, and of its unwillingness to lighten the burden of the rates.[12]

In opposition, the Tory agriculturalists wielded no more influence than they had when their party was in power, and by 1907–8 they had become so disenchanted with Balfour that they even toyed with the idea of forming their own separate political party. But it was uphill work, doomed to failure from the outset. Men like Turnor and Bathurst championed it ardently, but when the number of agriculturalists in the Commons had been reduced from 110 before the 1906 election to only 80 thereafter, the scheme was clearly a nonstarter. Indeed, the report of the organizing committee effectively conceded as much at the outset: 'the industry of agriculture is not represented in the legislature in the degree that its relative importance, industrially and politically, demands, and therefore it does not receive the consideration that is so freely offered to it – with such marked results – in other countries.'[13] The decline in the agricultural interest, from the pre-eminent industry of the country to a pressure group ineffectual even within the old country party, could not have been more eloquently described or more candidly admitted.

In desperation, some landowners turned to Tariff Reform, as affording the most likely prospect of successfully implementing agricultural protection. Joseph Chamberlain went out of his way to court the farming community; Henry Chaplin chaired the agricultural committee for the Tariff Reform League; and a large number of the smaller squires, like Turnor, Long, and Winterton, were enthusiastically in favour. As a result, food duties became an integral part of Chamberlain's programme, and agricultural protection was brought to the forefront of politics for the first time since demands for it had been articulated in the late 1870s.[14] But again, this was a limited accomplishment. For Chamberlain was the very embodiment of the new, thrusting, unscrupulous style of capitalist the landowners most detested. And it was a dangerous gamble to throw in their lot with a man who was more interested in taking over the Tory party for big business than in protecting agriculture for the small squires.

But much more importantly, agricultural protection remained a massive electoral liability. Even when wrapped up in the all-embracing Tariff Reform programme, it was still vulnerable to the charge of being a dole to the landowner at the expense of the labourer, and of providing support for the countryside at a high cost to the town. Not surprisingly, the Tory party did very badly in the rural constituencies in 1906; in the January 1910 election the food duties were very unpopular; and in December 1910 they were effectively abandoned.[15] Bonar Law, as a 'Whole Hogging' Tariff Reformer, initially restored the food taxes in early 1912; but within a year, he had effectively repudiated them once again. The annoyance and sense of betrayal felt by patricians like Chaplin knew no bounds. For even when the Tariff Reformers had captured the party high command, they proved to be no more attentive to agriculture than Balfour had been. Even more than he did, they knew that the party

ON HIS HOBBY.

First Agriculturist (to Second Ditto). "THAT AIN'T A REAL 'OSS! WHY, I CAN SEE HIS BOOTS!"

[Mr. Chamberlain addressed a large agricultural audience in the Riding School at Welbeck Abbey, August 4.]

84. 'On His Hobby.'
Punch, 3 Aug. 1904.

was now directed towards the urban working class, not the rural élite.

Between 1874 and 1905, successive Tory governments had effectively ignored the aristocratic leaders of the agriculturalist lobby (as had the Tory opposition thereafter). But the Liberal administrations that followed were more actively hostile. In 1906, foreseeing 'dangers ahead for the landed interest', Lord Onslow set up The Apaches, a secret organization consisting of seventy peers, who acted together in the Lords to oppose Liberal legislation. The Central Landowners' Association was formed. In the same year, the ostensible purpose was to represent all agricultural interests, but it was from the outset primarily a patricians' trade union. The inaugural meeting was held in Lord Salisbury's house in Arlington Street; the founding father was Algernon Turnor, a Lincolnshire squire; the president was Lord Onslow; and the secretary was Charles Bathurst.[16] Soon after, the 1909 Budget resulted in the establishment of the Land Defence League and the Land Union. The latter was founded by E. G. Pretyman, an obscure artillery captain who in 1899 inherited a large estate in Essex, and subsequently became Master of the Brocklesbury Hounds.[17]

But it is important to see this plethora of patrician pressure groups in proper perspective. To begin with, they did not achieve much: despite their determined opposition, the People's Budget was eventually passed. In the second place, they were not even united: Bledisloe, Onslow, and Long were much opposed to the intransigent stand of Pretyman's Land Union, which publicly pledged itself to repeal the most offensive clauses of the budget. In the third place, for all their paraphernalia of committees, secretaries, and lawyers, they were not especially efficient: Long complained of 'widespread carping and criticism' from the members of the CLA. In the fourth place, there was much apathy: the CLA claimed fewer than 700 members by 1918, and Turnor was not alone in lamenting the landowners' failure 'to take concerted action to advance the cause of agriculture.' Above all, they no longer represented the whole of the agricultural interest. Between 1908 and 1910, the National Agricultural Labourers Union and the National Union of Farmers both came into being, the latter explicitly refusing to admit landowners.[18]

Most significantly, the very need for such patrician pressure groups, and the very fact that they were divided, unrepresentative, and ultimately unsuccessful, provided yet more evidence of the decline of the landowners as an influential voice in politics. Natural ascendancy was gone, and in its place there was now only sectional interest. Organized defence was made necessary by political weakness; but political weakness made organized defence ineffectual. On the one hand, it was clearly imprudent for them to lobby in their own interest and no one else's. When, in May 1909, William Cornwallis-West urged that 'a general protest', from all landowners 'could not fail to impress the government', he was politely but firmly told that such an idea was politically naïve and potentially dangerous.[19] On the other, it was no longer possible for the patricians to present themselves as being the natural leaders of the agricultural interest. Men like Bathurst and Turnor urged their fellow-landowners to 'abandon pursuing a merely selfish policy', and to 'actively identify their interests with those of the agricultural industry.' But by the eve of the First World War, this position had been irrevocably lost.[20]

Indeed, by that time, even the Conservative party had abandoned the defence of great estates as a viable policy. For as the Liberal land campaign gathered momentum and support, it soon became clear that the only way to win back the votes of the rural labourers was to embrace a policy of widespread owner-occupation in the countryside. Between 1906 and 1910, the CLA and the Tariff Reform League both came to accept this view, as did such agricultural reformers as Turnor, Onslow, and Bledisloe, and such major political figures as Walter Long and Austen Chamberlain. Even Balfour himself was finally convinced, and found in the Irish land legislation an attractive precedent.[21] Initially, this policy was designed to bolster the position of the landowners. For the hope was that by giving as many people as possible a vested interest in rural property-ownership, the system of great estates could itself be successfully preserved. As Lord Milner explained, 'if the present social order is to endure, it is simply necessary, at whatever cost, to effect a great increase in the number of people who have a direct personal interest in the maintenance of private property.'[22]

But by 1912, with the beginning of the first great sales of land, there was every indication that 'the present social order' was not going to endure after all. On the contrary, it seemed to many that the system of great estates was finally breaking down under the combined pressure of inadequate financial returns and increased government taxation. Under these circumstances, there was no longer any point in continuing to defend the existence of great estates, and the Conservative party duly abandoned the defence of that which was politically and economically indefensible, and retreated to the next redoubt of wholesale owner-occupation. Indeed, it was none other than Walter Long who spelt this out explicitly as early as 1910, the very year in which he himself, practising what he preached, sold so much of his own estate:

> Even with all the risks, I personally am a convert to the system of small ownership, for one reason above all others. I believe it is the only way in which we can resist the march of socialism as exemplified, not by Snowden and Keir Hardie, but by the present financial policy of the government, which must undoubtedly make the ownership of land, in large quantities, impossible for anybody who has not got other very large sources of income.[23]

The significance of these concessions can scarcely be over-stressed. Here in the Conservative party, which had always been historically more fully wedded to the land than the Liberals, was an effective admission that the defence of great estates – like the protection of agriculture – was no longer practicable politics. By 1914, the Tory party had ceased to be politically committed to the maintenance of the old landed order. It was too much of an electoral liability: neither the Tariff Reformers nor Bonar Law was interested. The agriculturalists were by then even more of a minority than in the later days of Salisbury and Balfour. Their pressure groups were divided, dispirited, and ultimately ineffectual. Those who sought to rejuvenate the countryside under landed leadership lacked the influence to make their voices effectively heard, while others like Long simply took the more pragmatic view that landed society had had its day, and that the best hope – as in Ireland – was to retire with good grace and with pocket intact. By 1914, the great estates were thus abandoned by the Conservative party to the fate and the forces of the market.

The First World War completed the process whereby agriculture was relegated to the position of a subordinate industry, and the landowners forfeited their authority as its leaders. The fact that rents were deliberately held down for the duration of the conflict, while profits and wages were not, was a clear indication of where the government's sympathies lay. In 1915, Lord Bledisloe lamented 'the ever-increasing preponderance of the urban population and of urban influence in parliament'.[24] Two years later, the combined difficulties of reduced manpower in the countryside and the urgent need for more wheat forced Lloyd George to take action. He established a Ministry of Food and set up a Department of Food Production within the Ministry of Agriculture. Lord Lee was appointed Director-General of Food Production, and Agricultural Executive Committees were set up in the counties to oversee increased output.[25]

Patricians like Long, Lansdowne, and Chaplin were bitterly – but ineffectually – opposed to this government dictation to landowners of what they could do with their land, and vainly opposed Lord Lee's vigorous ploughing programme in cabinet. On the Executive Committees, too, it was the farmers not the landowners who were in charge. And the Corn Production Act gave the state even more power over the land and its owners: it established a minimum wage and a central wages board; it guaranteed minimum prices for wheat; and it empowered the government to dispossess inefficient farmers and landowners. As the *Estates Gazette* correctly noted, 'It is clear that the landed interest is even now not strong enough or real enough to make itself felt and respected.'[26] On the contrary, it was the NUF, with 80,000 members and 58 county branches by 1918, that was increasingly the authoritative voice of the landed interest, along with the 270,000 unionized workers, whose representatives also sat on the wages boards.[27]

Thereafter, Lloyd George continued to disregard the patrician element in his conduct of agricultural politics. In 1919, when setting up a Royal Commission on the Economic Prospects of Agriculture, he appointed farmers and labourers, but conspicuously excluded all landowners. In the same year, he appointed the much-disliked Lee as President of the Board of Agriculture, ignoring the claims of George Lane-Fox and Sir Robert Sanders because they were 'too wedded to the existing system of agriculture.'[28] And the Agricultural Amendment Act showed again Lloyd George's contempt for the landowners. Although the measure reserved less power to the government than the old Corn Production Act, it was still seen as 'farming from Whitehall', as a deal between the government and the farmers that deliberately by-passed the landowners. Lane-Fox claimed that 'the strongest and best and most moderate agricultural opinion was against all restrictions except "good husbandry"'; eighty-one MPs voted against the government control clauses in the report stage, including Banbury, Courthope, Lane-Fox, Mildmay, Pretyman, Stanier, and Wood; and the Lords rained amendments on the bill. Significantly, it was Lane-Fox and Pretyman who proposed the motion at the Carlton Club meeting that effectively brought down the Lloyd George coalition.[29]

Nevertheless, and despite the later repeal of the Corn Production Act, Lloyd George had effectively carried through in wartime much of the radical land campaign he had been developing in the years immediately before: the landowners were marginalized as the leaders of the agricultural interest; the farmers and the labourers were listened to more attentively; and state control had been much increased. Moreover, the disregarding of the landowners by Lloyd George coincided with the great post-war glut of land sales, which brought with it a general recognition that owner-occupation was inevitably the new mode of agricultural organization. Even the most zealous agriculturalists were now obliged to admit this. In 1929, Bledisloe and Turnor declared themselves to be 'ardent advocates of occupying ownership as the preponderant system of land tenure in Britain', conceded that 'the landlord and tenant system [had] failed', and that great estates were 'a menace alike to the principle of individual ownership and to the welfare of agriculture.' The landlord, they concluded, had either sold out, or merely 'lingers on, unable to play his allotted part, and the whole industry suffers.'[30]

Yet despite this recognition that the clock could not be put back to before 1910, there were still signs that many members of the landed establishment had not yet fully appreciated this. In 1921, Lord Selborne – himself a former President of the Board of Agriculture – addressed the CLA, and urged that 'unless they organised they would be unheard, ignored and trampled on, and it was only by standing up for themselves and their legitimate interests that they could hope to be heard.' Throughout the twenties, men like Bledisloe, Selborne, and Marlborough constantly aspired to speak for agriculture as a whole, leading deputations, urging the government to take more action, or writing to *The Times*.[31] And Turnor made one last attempt to place landowners at the head of agriculture, by arguing that they should abandon their public and political role, sell off their estates (if they had not already done so), and reduce their holdings to a manageable size, which they should then farm themselves, on as scientific and efficient a basis as possible. They should no longer be leisured *rentiers* but full-time professionals. From governing élite to professional agriculturalists was the message: great estates had gone or were going; the landowner could survive only as a working farmer.[32]

But none of this came to anything, because the governments of the twenties were not interested in agriculture, and least of all in agriculture under patrician leadership. Despite 'the imperative need of lifting agriculture out of the list of struggling industries', no government was going to attempt that operation if it meant alienating the mass of the urban population.[33] Stanley Baldwin might speak with feeling about the mystical appeal of the countryside; he might vaguely have talked of a subsidy for arable agriculture in December 1923; and the Conservatives might claim publicly that agriculture had a position 'in the national interest peculiar to itself.' But in practice, this meant nothing. Rating on agricultural land was cut again in 1923, but the white paper on policy of 1926 effectively adumbrated no policy at all, and as Colonial Secretary, Leopold Amery happily sacrificed British agriculture to the cause of imperial unity.[34] Between 1915 and 1925, there were ten ministers and seven Parliamentary Under-Secretaries of Agriculture: most were political lightweights, and this made cogency or continuity of policy impossible.[35]

Significantly, when the renewed depression of the thirties compelled governments to intervene, they did so in a ruthlessly nonromantic way, seeing agriculture, not as the supreme interest of the nation, presided over by benevolent grandees, but as yet another depressed staple industry, which needed rationalization and protection.[36] Neville Chamberlain adopted this view when he reorganized Conservative agricultural policy between 1929 and 1931: he saw it as an essentially declining industry, with inferior technology, which was subordinate to manufacturing, and which must be made as efficient and productive as possible. But it should be rationalized rather than propped up: marginal and inefficient producers should be eliminated, and there should be an increase in motor power. The Labour party took essentially the same view, and it was their Agricultural Marketing Act, passed in 1931, that opened the way for 'massive state intervention' by national governments: protection and subsidies for wheat and cattle; marketing boards for pigs, milk, and potatoes; and the creation of the British Sugar Corporation. The result was not the revival of the old paternalist system, but economic modernization – in the interests of the urban consumer.[37]

Predictably, the landowners took little part in these developments. There were only twenty-five 'agriculturalists' in the House of Commons; Christopher Turnor had to admit that, with 100,000 members, the NUF was now 'by far the strongest organised body in agriculture'; and the Estates Gazette abandoned its claim to speak for that long-vanished entity 'the landed interest'.[38] For most of the 1930s, Walter Elliot was a conspicuously non-landed Minister of Agriculture, who was in favour of intervention and integration, and who sought to carry the farmers and the labourers with him in this endeavour. Many members of the NUF became managerial figures in the new boards, and as The Times noted in 1933, 'At every turn, the Union is relied upon by the government for collaboration in the development of agricultural policy along new lines.'[39] In 1938, when several grandees wrote to The Times, urging the government to look into agriculture once more, this was the last fling of an older notion of patrician and proprietorial leadership which had long ago ceased to matter: the initiative had passed emphatically elsewhere.[40]

In 1927, the Estates Gazette had taken an unusually broad view of the matter when – unconsciously echoing both Gladstone and Balfour – it had rightly remarked that 'the polity under which we live has become permanently one-sided . . . Everything has become sacrificed to industrialism, with consequent loss of political power to those who own and till the soil.'[41] And throughout the inter-war years, that trend was only intensified. Writing in 1942, Lord Bledisloe dared to hope for a rural revival after the Second World War, just as he had looked for one after the First. But he was understandably pessimistic. As long as he had been active in politics, he recalled, agriculture had been betrayed, and the balance of life between the country and the town had become increasingly distorted. If there was to be a revival after the war, then the old culprits must be defeated: 'long-standing and persistent lack of vision on the part of our statesmen of all parties', combined with 'an easy going acquiescence in the myopic aims of a powerful urban plutocracy.'[42] The marginality of patrician agriculture could hardly have been more cogently expressed, nor more bitterly conceded.

ii.   The Lords: A Comedy of Errors

In the same way that agriculture was the most depressed sector of the economy from the 1880s to the 1930s, so the House of Lords was the most depressed part of the constitution. What had once been accepted as the great bastion of aristocratic power, the very embodiment of territorial possession and hereditary principle in government, was no longer regarded in that way. Few, from the 1880s, echoed the view of Gilbert's Lord Mountararat that 'if there is one institution in Great Britain which is not susceptible of improvement at all, it is the House of Peers.' For some, the very existence of the Lords was anathema; for some its powers were too great, for others too small; and for many, its composition was unacceptable: hereditary, one-sided, and absentee. For those who still believed in an upper house – and the majority of those who did were among its most aristocratic members – there were a variety of proposals that concerned and constructively-minded members might make. But it is one more indication of the patricians' weakened position that, from the 1880s to the 1930s, not one such reform proposal succeeded.

From the mid-1880s, when the very existence of the Lords was attacked with such sustained ferocity, many suggestions were put forward as to how the chamber might be improved.[43] The first serious proposal came from Lord Rosebery, who in June 1884 moved for a select committee to examine 'the best means of promoting the efficiency of the House.'[44] For the next thirty years, Rosebery was to be one of the foremost exponents of this subject, and in making this proposal, he sketched out arguments that he was subsequently to deploy time and again. He spoke of the unsatisfactory nature of a House composed almost entirely of hereditary landowners in an age of democracy, urged that it should represent 'a great variety of complex interests', including medicine and science, commerce and the arts, and asked that it be given more work to do. He suggested that life peerages should be instituted, and be given to a broader range of recipients, and that there should in future be joint committees of both Houses. The proposal was defeated by 77 votes to 38, with both Granville and Salisbury opposing it from their respective front benches. But, significantly, they both admitted they were personally in favour of life peerages.

Rosebery was undeterred, and in March 1888, he proposed the same motion again, this time going much further in both his criticisms and his proposals.[45] 'The weakness of the house', he declared, 'was the untempered application of the hereditary principle.' A second chamber was needed, but the present imbalance between the parties was unacceptable, and the addition of life peerages to bring in men from the arts and sciences was not enough: 'the mere zoological collection of abstract celebrities.' Instead, he proposed a much more sweeping reform scheme: peers were to elect a limited number from their own order to sit for a fixed period; municipalities and county councils were to choose their own delegates; and the colonies were to be represented by their Agents-General. Any peer not elected could stand for the Commons; life peerages were to be introduced; and there were to be joint sittings between both Houses to settle disputes. The proposal was defeated, but as Salisbury explained to the Queen, 'There was a much larger inclination to make some modification in the present system than Lord Salisbury had expected to find. A great many Conservatives went away, rather than vote against Lord Rosebery on this matter.'[46]

The other major attempt to rehabilitate the Lords during the 1880s came from a group of ambitious patrician MPs, all of whom would one day succeed to peerages, led by the young G. N. Curzon. They wanted an effective second chamber, and they wanted it created by the Tory government, partly to pre-empt any more drastic Liberal reform, and partly because their own political futures would be much brighter in an improved and strengthened upper house.[47] In 1888, Curzon severely criticized proposals Lord Salisbury had made concerning life peerages as 'paltry and peddaling measures of reform, scarcely worthy of the name', which would merely consolidate the Lords' position as 'a museum of magnificent ruins.' Instead, he offered his own scheme: hereditary peers should sit in the upper house only if qualified by public service; life peers should be nominated by the government of the day; there should be a non-hereditary category elected by the Commons for a fixed number of years; and spiritual peers should be represented as well.[48]

By these means, Curzon hoped to produce a House that was much more broadly representative of the nation as a whole, in which political careers could still be pursued and fulfilled. But since there was no likelihood of such a scheme being implemented in the foreseeable future, the only alternative was to try to stay in the Commons, even after succeeding to a peerage. So, in 1894, Curzon introduced the Peers Disabilities Removal Bill, the purpose of which was to enable an MP to keep his seat even on his accession to a peerage. It received its first reading, then languished through lack of parliamentary time. But in 1895, the chance came to force the issue when Lord Wolmer, one of Curzon's closest colleagues, succeeded to the peerage on the death of his father, the Earl of Selborne.[49] In accordance with an earlier agreement, he refused to relinquish his seat and actually took his place in the Commons, thereby provoking a debate on the matter. But it was finally resolved that no member of the House of Lords should have a choice of Houses in which to sit. Ironically, Curzon later felt he was denied the Prime Ministership because he was a peer, yet he had tried hard to prevent this happening.

So, by the end of the 1880s, the issue of rehabilitating the Lords

"GREAT CRY AND LITTLE WO(O)L-MER!"

Bathing Woman. "COME ALONG, MASTER SELBORNE, AND TAKE YOUR DIP LIKE A LITTLE NOBLEMAN!"

85. '"Great Cry and Little Wo(o)l-mer!"'
Punch, 25 May 1895.

had taken the shape it was to retain for the next half-century. In the first place, there was widespread recognition that reform was necessary: in an age of mass politics, it could no longer survive as the exclusive bastion of the aristocracy, and its social composition must be broadened. In the second place, a variety of schemes for reform were in play, which involved some or all of the following: peers electing peers, the nomination or election of other people, and the introduction of life peerages. But in the third place, it was already clear that the prospect of reform was very unlikely: the Commons were opposed to initiatives emanating from the Lords; private members' bills in the upper house seemed doomed to fail; and governments seemed decidedly unenthusiastic to take the matter up. With variations and embellishments, these remained the essential themes until the Second World War.

As Curzon had suspected, neither Salisbury nor Balfour would touch the issue, and it was only the sweeping Liberal victory of 1906 that persuaded some perceptive and anxious Tory peers to mount a pre-emptive reform attempt. In May 1907, Lord Newton, a relatively obscure back-bench Tory peer, introduced his House of Lords (Reform) Bill. He accepted that the hereditary principle was no longer defensible, and stressed that the House also suffered from 'undue numbers and scanty attendance, absence of important classes, and the excessive predominance of one political party.'[50] Instead, he proposed that membership should be limited to more strict and meritorious categories: peers possessed of certain qualifications in terms of public service; peers elected by those who were themselves no longer qualified; spiritual peers elected by the bishops; and life peers appointed by the government of the day. The remainder of the titular peerage would be eligible for election to the Commons. After extended discussion, in which Newton received enthusiastic support from the Duke of Devonshire, he withdrew his bill and the matter was referred to a select committee, chaired by Lord Rosebery.[51]

This body began by accepting that 'it was adviseable to modify in some respects the almost exclusively hereditary character of the House of Lords', and recognized that 'it is undesirable that the possession of a peerage should of itself give the right to sit and vote in the House of Lords.'[52] Here was a crucial and unprecedented distinction, between a peerage as a title of honour, and the legislative role that should be performed by those who were to sit in the upper house. But how were these newly-styled Lords of Parliament to be selected? Two hundred were to be elected by all hereditary peers (including Scottish and Irish), who could sit and vote only for the life of Parliament. In addition, there were to be 130 qualified hereditary peers, consisting of cabinet ministers and proconsuls past and present, senior civil servants and ambassadors, and those who, on succeeding to peerages, had served as MPs for ten years. Ten prelates were also included to represent the Church of England. To these were added law lords, royal peers, and life peers created at the rate of four a year.

These elaborate and detailed proposals were published in December 1908. But they were defective in several respects, and made virtually no impact. In part, this was because Rosebery had not chaired the committee well; he was out of politics and inclined to sulk; and his fellow members were enraged at the 'leisurely unconcern' of the proceedings.[53] In addition, there were several crucial issues that were conspicuously neglected: the imbalance between the parties, the representation of the colonies and the localities, and the vexed question of the relations between the two Houses. Most important of all, the report was not even discussed in the Lords, but disappeared, unread, into oblivion. Lord Dunraven's comments on the failure of reform in the 1880s applied with equal force two decades later: 'There were motions for Select Committees, Bills were introduced, and promises were made; but nothing more happened.'[54]

However, the crisis of 1909–10 placed the Lords at the forefront of political controversy, and provided a much greater incentive for peers to avert disaster by carrying their own measure of pre-emptive reform. Despite the results of the election of January 1910, which were hardly a vote of confidence in the peers' peremptory rejection of the People's Budget, the Conservative leadership was not yet eager to embrace wholeheartedly the notion of second chamber reform – partly because they did not want to be seen to panic, partly because they could not yet agree on any specific proposals, and partly because almost any scheme of reform was bound to be un-acceptable to some of their own followers since it would entail a re-duction in the overwhelming majority of Conservative peers. So, while a variety of ideas were circulating among Tory notables in the spring of 1910, neither Balfour nor Lansdowne was yet prepared to have anything to do with them.

By default, it was once more left to Rosebery to introduce proposals for second chamber reform in March 1910.[55] The House, he argued, must be reconstituted, with a much-reduced hereditary quota, and a greatly enlarged elected element. 'The alternative', he predicted, apocalyptically but presciently, 'is to cling with enfeebled grasp to privileges which have become unpopular, to powers which are verging on the obsolete.' He then put forward and carried three resolutions: 'that a strong and efficient second chamber is not merely an integral part of the British constitution, but is necessary for the well-being of the state and the balance of parliament'; 'that such a chamber can best be obtained by the reform and reconstitution of the House of Lords'; and 'that a necessary preliminary of such reform and reconstitution is the acceptance of the principle that the posses-sion of a peerage should no longer of itself give the right to sit and vote in the House of Lords.' Curzon, Salisbury, and Newton spoke in support, and even Lansdowne, although less enthusiastically, gave his approval.[56]

These vague resolutions, along with two more that Rosebery introduced in November 1910, and some very imprecise proposals put forward by Lansdowne, vanished in the confusion following the death of King Edward VII and the abortive constitutional confer-ence.[57] But before they disappeared into the dust, the Liberal leaders subjected them to merciless derision. In replying to Rosebery, Mor-ley noted the ludicrous inconsistency between the Lords' previous

PUTTING A GOOD FACE ON IT.

LORD LANSDOWNE. "SAY THIS HOUSE IS BADLY CONDUCTED, DO THEY? AND MEAN TO STOP THE LICENCE? AH, BUT THEY HAVEN'T SEEN MY COAT OF WHITEWASH YET. THAT OUGHT TO MAKE 'EM THINK TWICE."

86. 'Putting a Good Face on It.' *Punch*, 19 Apr. 1911.

claim that it was right for them to throw out the Budget, and its more recent admission that its composition was indefensible: 'you first of all commit homicide by slaying our Budget, and then proceed to commit suicide by denouncing yourselves as entirely unfit to have done the very thing you did.' And Asquith ridiculed the sudden zeal for reform that had so rapidly and so implausibly overtaken the upper house: 'What a change eleven short months have wrought! This ancient and picturesque structure has been condemned by its own inmates as unsafe ... The constitutional jerry builders are hurrying from every quarter with new plans.' Not since Dr Johnson's time had the prospect of execution concentrated the mind so wonderfully.[58]

In the light of the second general election, the outcome of which could certainly not be interpreted as a vote of confidence in the

House of Lords, the Tories had no choice but to come forward with a comprehensive scheme of reform. Inevitably, they found it exceedingly difficult to agree. But in May 1911, Lansdowne introduced his own House of Lords Reform Bill.[59] It proposed a House of three hundred and fifty Lords of Parliament, and contained few surprises. One hundred were to be elected by the peers from among their number – men who had held high political or administrative or military or proconsular office. One hundred and twenty were to be elected indirectly on a regional basis with the MPs forming electoral colleges; one hundred were to be appointed by the government in proportion to the party affiliations in the Commons; and there should be the usual smattering of prelates, law lords, and royal dukes. Lords of Parliament could sit for only twelve years, one-third retiring each four years; peers not elected to the Lords could stand for the Commons; and no more than five hereditary peers could be created each year.

Predictably, this scheme prospered no more than those that had gone before. Lansdowne's speech on the first reading was generally reckoned to have fallen very flat; the second reading was punctuated with protests from Tory die-hards like Somerset, Marlborough, and Willoughby de Broke; and the whole debate was given an air of unreality when Morley announced that the restrictions as to powers that were embodied in the Parliament Bill would apply to any reformed House as much as to the existing one. As a pre-emptive measure, the proposal was doomed; although it passed its second reading, nothing further was heard of it; and the Parliament Act itself duly passed into law. The only minor consolation was that its preamble explicitly stated that the composition of the upper house would be reformed as soon as possible: 'whereas it is intended to substitute for the House of Lords as it at present exists a second chamber, constituted on a popular instead of a hereditary basis, but such substitution cannot be immediately brought into operation.' But despite the fact that a cabinet committee considered the matter for two years, nothing had been accomplished by 1914.[60]

Thereafter, it was the desire to claw back the powers taken away by the Parliament Act that became the main impetus to further efforts at second chamber reform. In the aftermath of the many disreputable Lloyd George creations, most thoughtful patricians now conceded that a fully hereditary house could no longer be condoned. And in the post-war world of full adult suffrage, the Conservative party was no more prepared to defend a preponderantly patrician chamber than it was to justify the system of great estates. But by agreeing to jettison the hereditary principle, the would-be reformers of the inter-war years hoped that as a quid pro quo, the powers taken away from the peers by the Parliament Act might be restored. For such a restoration seemed to them increasingly necessary: in a mass democracy, where a radical or socialist or revolutionary government might be elected at any moment, it was imperative that there should be a strong and certain barrier against irresponsible legislation sent up from the lower house.[61]

So, in the aftermath of the Speaker's wartime conference on the franchise, the coalition Conservatives demanded that the upper house should be reformed (and strengthened) by the same means. The result was a conference chaired by Lord Bryce, and its findings were sent to Lloyd George in the form of a letter in April 1918.[62] It was generally recognized that the second chamber did not have powers coequal with the lower house: it should not 'oppose the people's will', it could not make or unmake ministries, and it could not control finance. On the other hand, there should be provision for disagreement between the two Houses, perhaps in the form of joint meetings, or perhaps by holding a referendum. And its composition should be reformed so as to reconcile continuity with open access. Eighty members would be chosen by and from the hereditary peers, and a further 264 would be elected by MPs in territorial units under proportional representation. They would hold office for twelve years, with one-third retiring every fourth year. And to these would be added a smattering of law lords, prelates, and royals.

But like the Rosebery committee before the war, the scheme made absolutely no impact.[63] Even Bryce's gifts of conciliation had proved inadequate, and there was no agreed report: hence the letter. The proposals as to composition were so contentious that many on the committee – like Lansdowne – thought they gave too little room to the hereditary element. And the recommendations as to powers were generally deemed to be vague, contradictory, or unworkable. Above all, the government was simply uninterested. Only in July 1918, at the prompting of Lord Crewe, were the proposals actually debated in the upper house. But Curzon claimed that there was no interest in the subject and that in wartime there were more important things to do. Haldane condemned the letter for not going far enough, while Lord Balfour of Burleigh, who had actually been a member of the conference, described the proposals concerning composition as 'the worst that could possibly be devised.' Not surprisingly, the matter was shelved, and in 1919 Curzon announced that the government did not feel itself bound to introduce any reform proposals at all.

But in 1921, in response to prodding and prompting from Selborne, Curzon admitted that a cabinet committee consisting of Churchill, Birkenhead, Austen Chamberlain, and H. A. L. Fisher was

Lord BIRKENHEAD. "DILLY-DUCKS, DILLY-DUCKS, COME AND BE KILLED."

87. 'Dilly-Ducks, Dilly-Ducks, Come and Be Killed.' *Punch*, 19 July, 1922.

considering the matter.[64] For the Conservatives, the reform of the Lords and the restoration of its powers was now official party policy, and one of the strongest reasons for remaining in the increasingly hated Lloyd George coalition was the belief that these measures could be more effectively carried by such a government than by one of a more partisan complexion. Moreover, with an extended franchise and with thrones tottering throughout Europe, the need for a strong House of Lords as a bastion against anarchy and revolution seemed to grow stronger each day. As George Younger explained in January 1922, when again expressing disappointment that nothing had happened:

> One of the chief planks of the Government's policy was their promise to reconstitute the second chamber and restore the balance of the constitution. Only a Coalition like the present could successfully deal with that vital question, and the government has

given the most specific pledges to deal with it in the coming session of parliament.[65]

Eventually, in July 1922, Lord Peel introduced the coalition government's long-awaited resolutions in favour of upper chamber reform. The new House was to consist of 350 members: there would be hereditary peers chosen by hereditary peers; there would be outsiders elected directly and indirectly; and there would be an element nominated by the crown. All members, except the few additional law lords, would serve for a limited term. The old powers of the House would not be restored, but future measures to reform the second chamber could not pass into law without its explicit consent. Once again, this package pleased no one. The proposals were so vague that it was clear the government was not seriously interested. Lansdowne derided them as 'incomplete' and 'half-baked', and Crewe called them 'a mockery', a 'fleshless skeleton'.[66] As a result, discussion of the matter was postponed until the autumn, but by then the coalition had fallen, and these proposals vanished along with it.

The fact that the Lloyd George coalition had shown itself so indifferent to House of Lords reform (in addition to the sale of honours, the neglect of agriculture, the betrayal of the southern Unionists, and the general corruption of public life) greatly increased patrician disapproval of him. But once he was out of power, they turned instead, and with renewed hope, to Bonar Law and Baldwin. Between 1920 and 1936, the Conservative party conferences passed annual resolutions in favour of House of Lords reform; in the 1922 and 1924 elections the leaders gave what seemed to be public undertakings to this effect.[67] And in the Lords itself, in December 1922, Lord Cave stated that the government would deal with both the powers and the composition of the House 'as soon as an opportunity occurs'. But it was not until 1925 that the Lord Chancellor announced the formation of a cabinet committee 'which shall fully examine the problem in all its aspects, in the hope that in the near future, possibly next year, we may be in a position to put before parliament proposals dealing with this most vital question.'[68]

There the matter rested, while the committee did its work. It found the task no easier than its predecessors, and the government soon came to regret the commitment it had given. But in July 1926, a deputation of 120 MPs and 48 peers met Baldwin, who grudgingly agreed to produce a reform scheme within the lifetime of the present Parliament.[69] Eleven months later, the Lord Chancellor duly outlined the government's proposals. The veto was to be restored – but only over bills concerning the House's own composition. There were to be 350 members, half hereditary, half selected by other means, all with a fixed term of twelve years, plus the usual smattering of prelates, princes, and judges.[70] Hard-liners like Salisbury and Northumberland supported the scheme as providing a necessary bulwark against chaos or tyranny. But the Labour Lords Parmoor and Russell ridiculed the proposal as a partisan measure, which would produce a House more Tory than ever, which could never in future be reformed except by its own consent, yet which would be quite ineffective against any government with real revolutionary intentions.[71]

Although the government comfortably survived a vote of censure against these proposals in the Commons, this was the end of House of Lords reform as official policy for the rest of the inter-war period. Baldwin, on his own admission, 'looked upon the question as one of the most difficult ones in politics, and evidently wanted to avoid it altogether', and the Commons debate gave him exactly the excuse he needed to drop it.[72] Thereafter, commitment to reform by the Tory leadership was largely academic: it was quite impossible to produce agreed proposals as to the upper house's composition; no restoration of the Lords' power could be carried through the Commons; and by the mid-1920s, it seemed clear that the fear of socialism, and thus the need for a stronger second chamber, was much exaggerated.[73] As Lord Rosebery – who wanted reform as much as anyone – had remarked in 1907, at the time of Lord Newton's abortive bill:

> I am convinced by long experience that there can be no reform of this house except when a Conservative Government is in power . . . [But] a Conservative Government, when it comes in, will find more pressing and more urgent questions to deal with than this problem, which in any hands must be a difficult and thorny one.[74]

Nevertheless, some patricians were undeterred by the government's obvious lack of enthusiasm, and refused to believe the matter was lost. In December 1928, Lord Clarendon made proposals, with a view to preventing 'the question of the reform of your lordships house being shelved'. In February 1929, at the very end of the Baldwin administration, Lord Elibank introduced a more modest proposal for reform, in the vain hope that piecemeal improvement might prevail where more grandiose schemes of reconstruction had failed.[75] And in May 1932, an unofficial reform committee was set up, under Lord Salisbury. 'The difficulties of agreement seem as great as ever', noted Lord Bayford. But in December 1933, Salisbury duly introduced his reform proposals into the Lords. They followed a familiar pattern. In the new House, 150 members were to be peers elected by peers; 150 were to be nominated or elected; there would be bishops, law lords, and royal princes; there might even be women; and those who were poor would be paid. And once a measure was vetoed by the Lords a third time, it could not be submitted again to the Commons until after a general election.[76]

There was a debate on the first reading of Salisbury's bill, and again on the second reading in May 1934.[77] But the discussions were so similar that they may be taken together. For Salisbury and his supporters, the argument was clear. Their purpose was to 'propose such a change in our constitution as may make the country safe' from 'sudden, unexpected, fundamental, subversive change', by ensuring that neither the legislature nor the electorate would be hurried into passing revolutionary measures without being given adequate time to consider them. In the light of its handling of affairs between 1929 and 1931, and bearing in mind its subsequent manifestos, Salisbury openly admitted that he wanted to create an upper house that could successfully stand against anything a future Labour government might propose. More particularly, he was seeking to get round the limitations of the Parliament Act by recovering the power of the upper house to force a general election. And, although he repeated his claims that the 'final, ultimate, conclusive authority is the people', he was determined that the Lords should stand against 'a temporary, ephemeral decision of the electors.'[78]

Despite the effort that had been lavished on this bill, it was received with scarcely any approval in the House. Some convinced reactionaries, like Lord Redesdale, opposed it on the grounds that no reform whatsoever was necessary. Many, like Lords Reading, Esher, and Lothian, thought its terms too vague, and the present power of the Lords quite adequate. Lord Arnold argued that if there was going to be a socialist revolution, then no upper house would be able stop it, however much its powers were augmented, while if there was not going to be a revolution, then no such powers were necessary.[79] But the most vehement opposition came from Lord Ponsonby, who rightly saw it as an attempt to ensure that no future Labour government could implement its legislative programme. The essence of Salisbury's argument, he insisted, was that the people were deemed to be right when voting Tory, but wrong when voting Labour. He claimed that no measure should be passed unless the will of the people had been ascertained, yet he was introducing a bill to alter the constitution, for which there was no popular mandate whatsoever. For all his talk, Ponsonby concluded, Lord Salisbury was an enemy of democracy, and wore a black shirt beneath his frock coat.[80]

In any case, the whole debate on the second reading was carried out in an atmosphere of almost total unreality. Speaking for the cabinet, Lord Hailsham made it plain that proposals for constitutional reform would receive serious consideration only if they were made by the government itself. But in the case of the composition and the powers of the Lords, the government had no intention of making any such proposals.[81] Thereafter, all speeches were made knowing that, whatever the vote, no further action would be taken. 'Is there nothing', Salisbury asked plaintively in his summing-up speech, 'that the government will do on the subject at all?' The answer was an unqualified no. The second reading was carried by 171 votes to 82. But it was a completely futile victory. Public opinion was indifferent, and the government simply ignored the result.[82] With Salisbury's effort, the last comprehensive attempt to reform the Lords in the inter-war years came to an end, and the later proposals made by Rockley, Strickland, and Ponsonby were piece-meal, unpopular – and also totally unsuccessful.[83]

Writing in 1925, Lord Rosebery described the contemporary House of Lords as 'emasculate and degraded', adding that 'I know of no operation that would put it in a better position.'[84] By then, most people felt the same way. From the 1880s onwards, it was generally accepted that the composition of the Lords was unsatisfactory, yet fifty years on, nothing substantive had been accomplished by way of reform. A succession of individual patrician initiatives had failed, while the governments of the day had never been enthusiastic. The Liberals had embarked on the subject reluctantly in 1910, but once the Parliament Act was passed, they quickly lost interest. And since there was an overwhelming Tory majority anyway, the Conserva-tives were never more than lukewarm. Moreover, no proposal to increase the power of the Lords would ever get through the Com-mons, while the Lords would accept reform in their composition only if their veto was restored. Not surprisingly, then, as Lord Peel observed in 1935, 'the Parliamentary shores are full of the wreckage of the proposals for the reform of this chamber.'[85]

But underlying this was something more fundamental, namely the increasing marginality of the patricians in the political life of the country. They could no more pressure successive governments into reforming the lords than they could persuade them to protect agri-culture. Almost without exception, the peers who took up reform of the second chamber – Rosebery, Newton, Lansdowne, Clarendon, Salisbury – were authentic grandees: they were not the new men who were flooding the House from the 1880s onwards. For them, a peerage was not just a title of honour, it was also a hereditary power position. And it was the restoration of that hereditary power position that they most ardently and vainly craved – partly because they wished to recover the influence they feared and knew they had lost, and partly so they might better defend themselves from what they believed to be the threats and dangers of twentieth-century democracy. As Austen Chamberlain perceptively put it in 1921, 'everyone in the country with something to lose must want to see a reformed second chamber in being.'[86]

iii. Ireland: The Winter's Tale

From the 1880s onwards, it was widely believed that the essential answer to the Irish question was the rapid and complete elimination of traditional landlordism and the conversion of the former tenants into owner-occupiers. On this quite revolutionary policy, politicians as varied as Davitt and Gladstone, Redmond and Salisbury, Parnell and Balfour, Wyndham and Birrell were effectively – if only tacitly – agreed.[87] But the future of the Union itself was a much more contentious matter. For the agrarian Irish nationalists, and for the British Liberal party, the policy of dismantling the landed establishment as a territorial force went hand-in-glove with the winning (or granting) of legislative independence. But most Irish landowners reluctantly accepted the liquidation of their great estates for the very *opposite* reason, namely that they were told by the Conservative leadership that it was the necessary precondition for *preserving* the Union intact. As Balfour explained as early as 1887, 'The landlords . . . must feel that the sacrifice asked of them (if sacrifice it be) is absolutely required if the Union, and all the Union means to them, is to be maintained.'[88]

Yet despite repeated assertions by politically influential peers like Londonderry that 'the maintenance of the Union (for which the Unionist Party was formed)' was 'the most important plank of our platform', the sacrifice that the landowners were called upon to make in support of this policy did not ensure its success.[89] With varying degrees of relish, reluctance, and resentment, the grandees and gentry duly sold up their estates in the ardent hope that the Union might be preserved. But despite all their enraged protests, the Union was eventually repealed, and the sacrifice of their territorial position was shown to have been utterly in vain. Caught between the strident and irresistible demands of agrarian nationalism in the south, and of Belfast big business in the north, the old patrician class surrendered the political initiative, found itself deserted by its allies in Britain, and was brutally relegated to the sidelines in Ireland. For the majority of Irish landowners, this was not just another lost cause or disappointed hope, in the manner of agricultural revival or House of Lords reform: it was a defeat so bitter, a rejection so complete, and an abandonment so total, that it amounted to nothing less than a 'great betrayal'.

In Ulster, the surviving notables at least managed to remain an integral part of the Union – albeit with their estates much diminished and as junior partners of the Belfast bourgeoisie in the government and administration of the province. And in the south, a minority zealously supported the nationalist cause, either in its constitutionalist or revolutionary manifestations. But from the time when Gladstone took up Home Rule in the mid 1880s, the majority of Irish landowners were vehemently hostile to the repeal of the Union, as they were later to be against Irish partition. And they expressed their opposition in one of two ways: many believed that outright defiance would be successful in preventing the passage of Home Rule; a few were not so sure, and argued instead for a more emollient and creative approach. Depending on the ebb and flow of events, sometimes the hard-liners were in the ascendant, and sometimes the constructive Unionists. But in the end, all southern landowners suffered the same fate: neither stubborn intransigence nor far-sighted conciliation could save them.

The most important pressure group for southern patrician intransigence was the Irish Loyal and Patriotic Union, which was established in May 1885. It was renamed the Irish Unionist Alliance in 1891, and it survived until the cause was irretrievably lost in the early 1920s.[90] From the outset, it was a closely-knit organization, exclusive and well connected in its membership, and it eventually boasted branches in every Irish county except Monaghan. It was financed and dominated by peers like Lords Longford, Castletown, de Vesci, and Meath, and by gentry such as Sir Thomas Butler, Richard Bagwell, Henry Bruen, and A. M. Kavanagh. It was well organized, adequately funded, and for nearly forty years it arranged meetings, published manifestos, and drummed up petitions in the Unionist interest, not only in Ireland, but in Great Britain as well. Its members were deeply distrustful of Home Rule, fearing it would lead to the confiscation of their estates and the end of their patrician order. And so their hostility to nationalism and their commitment to the maintenance of the Union were absolute. But from the very outset, it was clear that the fervour of their feelings was much greater than the strength of their position.

Initially, the ILPU was formed to fight the general election of 1885 under the much-extended franchise created by the Third Reform Act. But the result was a disaster: of the fifty-two (mostly patrician) candidates put up, not one was elected, and between them they obtained only 10 per cent of the total vote. The nationalists swept the board, and with the exception of Trinity College, Dublin, and Dublin South, constituency politics in the south became a waste of time and effort thereafter. In Ulster, support for the Union was broadly based: the Belfast bourgeoisie and working class were both as well disposed as the landowners. But elsewhere, the Unionist cause was emphatically an élite movement, effectively devoid of any popular appeal. Even in 1913, the IUA could claim fewer than seven hundred members.[91] This exclusive homogeneity might make organization relatively easy. But in every other way, it was to prove in the long run a fatal weakness. For once it became accepted that the will of the majority must ultimately prevail, the IUA would be easily dismissed as merely representing the vested interests of a declining, enfeebled, and marginal coterie, whose day had long since passed.[92]

Nevertheless, in the short run, the IUA could count on other, and more influential, support. From the 1880s to the 1910s, these southern patricians worked in close alliance with the Unionists in the north: they saw themselves as belonging to one party with one creed, albeit compelled to work in different ways because of their different strengths and weaknesses; and in 1907 a Joint Committee of Unionist Associations was set up, with representatives from the IUA in the south, and the Ulster Unionist Council in the north.[93] Until 1906, the leader of the Unionist Parliamentary Party was a Cavan landowner, Col. E. J. Saunderson. Although an Ulsterman, he saw himself as an Irishman first and foremost, regarded Home Rule as bad for all of the country, rejected separate terms for Ulster in 1886, felt the interests of north and south to be essentially the same, and believed that the only purpose of particularist Ulster intransigence was to prevent Home Rule throughout Ireland. Even when the parliamentary leadership of the Irish Unionists was taken over by Belfast businessmen and by Carson (who was MP for Trinity College, Dublin), this remained essentially their policy.[94]

These southern Unionists also benefited much more than their Ulster brethren from their close integration into the British political system as a whole. For what they lacked in terms of direct Commons representation, they more than made up for by virtue of their British patrician connections. To begin with, they were very strongly represented in the Lords, where over three-quarters of the 104 peers with Irish interests were from the south.[95] Until 1911, the upper house was the last redoubt for embattled Unionists, and could safely be counted on to throw out any Home Rule Bill. But in addition, southern Unionists gained admission to the Commons by sitting as MPs for English seats. In 1914, they represented only two southern Irish constituencies; but they also sat for eighteen seats in England. The Ulster Unionists, by contrast, might boast a much stronger base of local support, but they could not match this broader appeal of their southern brethren. Only a minority of peers with Irish interests were predominantly Ulstermen. And in 1914, there were sixteen

Ulster Unionist MPs sitting for the north of Ireland, while only two were returned for constituencies on the mainland. In terms of their ease of access to Parliament, the southern Unionists were well ahead.[96]

They could also count on cousinly patrician support at the very highest and most influential level. Grandees like Norfolk and Devonshire were passionately opposed to Home Rule, had abandoned their Whiggish traditions because of it, and were now to be found in Tory cabinets. From 1906 to 1910, the Irish Unionist MPs were led by Walter Long, who nearly became Conservative leader in the aftermath of Balfour, and who was generally regarded as the quintessential English country gentleman. But he was also, in Lloyd George's caustic phrase, 'an amiable Wiltshire Orangeman'.[97] Both his mother and his wife were Anglo-Irish, and in 1906, he publicly pledged himself 'to devote the rest of my political life . . . to the great cause, the maintenance of the Union.' Long was supported by the Marquess of Lansdowne, another renegade Anglo-Irish Whig, who also commanded a regular position in Conservative cabinets, and became President of the IUA. And from 1907, the Irish peers were led by the ninth Viscount Midleton, another fervent Unionist, who had previously sat as an MP for Surrey between 1880 and 1905, who had held high office under Balfour, and who later became chairman of the IUA. Between them, these men ensured that the Tory party retained its unswerving commitment to the Union until the early 1910s.[98]

This, then, was the first response by southern patrician Unionists to the threat of Home Rule: carefully orchestrated and organized defiance. They recognized their lack of popular support in Ireland itself. But they strongly believed that continuing collaboration with Ulster Unionists, the veto power of the upper house, and their powerful representation at the very hub of Tory affairs would be enough to ensure that the Union was preserved intact. The second – and even smaller – group of Irish country-house activists were not concerned to fight rearguard actions on behalf of their intransigent and self-interested fellow patricians. On the contrary, they believed that the sale of estates under successive Land Acts gave their former owners a great opportunity to re-enter Irish public life, not as a selfish and self-centred élite, still essentially parasitic on the British connection, but as the patriotic servants of the Irish people as a whole. Once the landlords had been bought out, they reasoned, class conflict would end, and class collaboration might begin. And in this more hopeful and constructive climate, the patricians would be able to fulfil the very highest aristocratic function of all – leading the nation, but for the common good.[99]

88. W. B. Yeats, Sir Hugh
Lane, J. M. Synge, and
Lady Gregory by
W. Orpen.

One form that this high-minded and essentially paternal impulse
took was cultural. In the lull after Parnell's fall, a small group of
gentry dilettanti felt that there was hope and scope for collaboration
between the different classes, races, and religions of Ireland, based on
a reawakened sense of Anglo-Irish cultural identity.[100] They were
hostile to the middle classes and to vulgar commerce. They were
interested in folklore and fairy tales, in ancient Irish sagas and
modern Irish theatre. They believed it would be possible to create an
Irish literary tradition in the English language. And they regarded
themselves as the self-appointed agents of this renaissance. Chief
among them was Lady Gregory, who lived at Coole Park in Galway.
She wrote plays, anthologized folklore, founded and funded the Irish
Literary Theatre, and was for many years Yeats' great patron. Her
neighbour, George Moore, a Mayo landlord and lapsed Catholic,
wrote novels. And his cousin, Edward Martyn, a Galway landowner, was a playwright. In turn, these patricians provided the basis
for Yeats' increasingly grandiloquent theory of aristocracy. To him,
they were 'No petty people': the very embodiment of honour,
chivalry, generosity, and service.[101]
But the major form that this patrician initiative took was, predict-

89. Sir Horace Plunkett by W. Rothenstein.   90. Lord Dunraven.

ably, political, and many of the people involved were friends or relatives of Lady Gregory herself: Sir Horace Plunkett, John Shawe-Taylor, and the fourth Earl of Dunraven. For them, as for her, there seemed scope in the 1890s for aristocratic leadership of an unparochial, cosmopolitan, constructive, and non-intransigent kind. One such initiative came from Sir Horace Plunkett, the third son of the sixteenth Lord Dunsany, who was born in 1854 and educated at Eton (where he had been a contemporary of Gerald Balfour) and Oxford. He spent the 1880s as a cattle rancher in Wyoming, returned home to manage the family estates, and in 1892 became an independent and very maverick Unionist MP for Dublin.[102] He opposed coercion, was deeply distressed at the antagonisms of landlord and tenant, and distrusted nationalist demagogues and intransigent reactionaries equally. And he believed that in a country so overwhelmingly rural, the key to national regeneration lay in agricultural regeneration. Once the pastoral economy was revived, he argued, and prosperity was restored, the old antagonisms between landlord and tenant, Protestant and Catholic, English and Irish, would simply melt away.[103]

It was this belief that underlay his advocacy of co-operative dairies and creameries. In 1878, he formed the Dunsany co-operative on the family estates, which was owned and controlled by the tenants, and which became the prototype for the national co-operative movement which he inaugurated in 1889. His prime supporters were likeminded patricians – Mary Ponsonby, his widowed sister; Alexis Roche, son of Lord Fermoy; and Lord Monteagle – and by 1914 there were 350 co-operative creameries established throughout the country.[104] In 1894, he became the president of the newly established Irish Agricultural Organization Society, another quintessentially ascendancy venture, the secretary of which was Lord Castletown's agent; and in the following year, he began the publication of the magazine *Irish Homestead*, and launched his campaign to persuade the British government to set up a Board of Agriculture for Ireland. Eventually, in 1897, they established a Department of Agriculture and Technical Instruction for Ireland, of which Plunkett was vicepresident, but emphatically in charge.[105]

Plunkett's fundamental aim was political conciliation by economic means. But some of his patrician friends preferred a more direct approach. In 1902, John Shawe-Taylor convened a conference of landowners and nationalists, in the hope of reaching agreement as to the terms for a new Land Purchase Act.[106] Initially, he invited the Duke of Abercorn, Lord Barrymore, the O'Conor Don, and E. J. Saunderson to represent the territorial interest. But as passionately committed Unionists, they were profoundly suspicious of any possible accommodation with the nationalists, and Barrymore denounced the idea as 'wholly irresponsible'. Although the Irish Landowners' Convention voted overwhelmingly against participation, a poll of the much larger body of all Irish landlords revealed more widespread support for the idea.[107] Shawe-Taylor accordingly persevered, and offered new invitations to well-known moderates – Lord Dunraven, Lord Mayo, Col. William Hutcheson Poe, and Sir Nugent Everard – to represent the landlords. They accepted, the negotiations were amicably conducted, and the results were embodied in Wyndham's Land Act of 1903.

These moderate landlords were led by the fourth Earl of Dunraven, who was also chairman of the convention itself. Like Sir Horace Plunkett, he was by Irish standards an unusually cosmopolitan patrician. He owned valuable lands in Wales and in Ireland, covered the Abyssinian campaign for *The Daily Telegraph* in 1867–8, and was a regular visitor to the United States. He was a well-known figure on the turf (where he owned horses in partnership with Lord Randolph Churchill) and was a keen sailor (who made two unsuccessful attempts to win the Americas Cup).[108] He began life as a Liberal, opposed Home Rule in 1886, held office briefly under Salisbury as Parliamentary Under-Secretary at the Colonial Office, but then resigned. He later became an active campaigner for Tariff Reform and was first President of the Fair Trade League. His talents and connections entitled him to the highest political office. But through-out his life, he lacked single-minded dedication, was a poor party man, and a born conciliator. He believed passionately in the need to preserve the unity of the empire by granting some degree of local autonomy to the colonies. He was also a cousin of George Wynd-ham, who was Irish Secretary in the early 1900s.

The success of the meetings of 1903 encouraged Dunraven in his belief that Ireland's political problems, as well as its economic difficulties, might also be solved by compromise and conciliation. Accordingly, in August 1904, his Committee of Moderate Unionist Landlords was re-established as the Irish Reform Association.[109] Besides Dunraven himself, the most influential figures were Sir Algernon Coote, Hutcheson Poe, Lindsay Talbot-Crosbie, and Nugent Everard. They immediately published a short manifesto, reaffirming their belief that the maintenance of the Union was 'essential', but urging that this was also 'compatible with the devolu-tion to Ireland of a larger measure of local government than she now possesses.' With the assistance of Sir Antony MacDonnell, the Permanent Under-Secretary at the Irish Office, Dunraven then began to work on more detailed proposals, concerning both a finan-cial council and delegated legislation. They were published in Sep-tember 1904, and their author clearly hoped that the Conservative government might entertain them sympathetically.[110]

The early 1900s thus saw the high point of these various conciliat-ory patrician initiatives in Irish affairs. But they achieved very little. Despite their best efforts, Lady Gregory and her friends conspi-cuously failed to create a broadly-based Anglo-Irish cultural tradition under their own leadership. They imposed their élitist aesthetic doctrines in a manner that was too obviously aristocratic.[111] 'Lady Gregory', one contemporary observed, 'behaved as if she were a grand duchess, and as if the people of Dublin were somehow her subjects.' From the very outset, the plays she put on at the Irish Literary Theatre were attacked for being too critical of the Irish character. And her retort – 'in art the many count less than the few' – was hardly designed to win over popular support. The impact of her own plays, and of Moore's novels, was minimal. Appropri-ately enough, Moore's greatest achievement was his three volume autobiography, *Hail and Farewell* (1911–14), which was essentially a requiem for the ascendancy. And Yeats needed much less space to convey precisely the same message. One of the last poems he wrote to Lady Gregory was correctly but candidly entitled 'To a friend whose work has come to nothing.'[112]

Nor did Plunkett's schemes for agricultural revival bring about the national regeneration he had hoped for. Indeed, his co-operative dairies never even achieved the first of these objectives, let alone the second. And although he aimed to win the broadest possible basis of support for his ideas, he was so even-handed in his criticisms of Protestant and Catholic, peasant and landowner, and so tactless and schoolmasterish in his manner, that he aroused needless antagonisms.[113] The nationalists bitterly resented what they saw as his patronizing view of the Irish character. He so enraged the Unionists by his criticisms of landlords that he lost his parliamentary seat in 1900, and he so offended the Liberals that they sacked him from the management of the Agricultural and Technical Institute in 1907. Undeterred, he turned to writing. In *Ireland in the New Century* (1904), he repeated his even-handed criticisms of all the groups whose support he needed and whose welfare he genuinely cherished. And four years later, in *Noblesse Oblige*, he held out the prospect of a revived and reinvigorated aristocracy, freed from the liabilities of its lands and debts, once again leading Ireland into a new golden age of peace, prosperity, and paternalism. But hardly anyone took any notice.[114]

Dunraven's devolution proposals fared no better. They were denounced by most Unionists as Home Rule under another name: Lord Westmeath dismissed them as 'truckling to disloyalty'; the IUA condemned them for being 'altogether contrary to the principles which have always animated the great body of Irish Unionists'; while Carson thought them 'fatuous, ridiculous, unworkable and impracticable.' MacDonnell was criticized for overstepping his position as a civil servant, and Wyndham's part was so inept and unconvincing that he was obliged to resign and his career came to an end.[115] But the consequences were more far-reaching than that. In the north, some Unionists began to question the wisdom of such a close alliance with the southern patricians, and as a direct result set up a new autonomous organization, the Ulster Unionist Council. And in the south, some gentry began to doubt the sincerity of the Conservative party's support. As Colonel O'Callaghan-Westropp later put it: 'We loath Unionist governments (with their petting and pampering of our enemies . . .) only a few degrees less than the radicals and the nationalists, from whom we expect no better.'[116]

By the time the Liberal government came into power in December 1905, these patrician initiatives were effectively spent. The collapse of the influence of Dunraven, Plunkett, and the moderate Unionists meant that 'the sound policy of moderation and conciliation' sank into the background, the extreme Unionists and Home Rulers were left to confront each other, and there was no room left for compromise.[117] In retrospect, it is clear that Plunkett and Dunraven were far- and clear-sighted men. They had realized that the landed classes could not – and would not – survive in Ireland indefinitely, and they sought to ensure a future for them inside Irish affairs, rather than outside, by preaching conciliation between landlord and tenant, and by creating a new role for the patricians as public servants. But the tragedy of their position was that it remained a minority view: Dunraven's Irish Reform Association could boast only a mere thirty supporters. Most Irish landowners wanted no concessions at all, and distrusted as disloyal those few who did. And most Irish nationalists did not want continued, or revived, genteel leadership on any terms whatsoever. However hard these men had laboured to find one, there was, in truth, no middle way.[118]

Once the Parliament Act removed the last absolute guarantee that the Union could be preserved by constitutional means, it soon became generally recognized that the cause of southern, patrician intransigence was effectively lost. The Liberal government was publicly pledged to reintroduce some measure of Home Rule, which it duly did between 1912 and 1914. Under these circumstances, the northern Unionists abandoned the united front they had previously maintained with their southern colleagues, and became firm advocates of Irish partition, as the only way of ensuring Ulster's continued existence within the United Kingdom.[119] In the aftermath of Balfour's resignation, there was also a growing recognition among the increasingly middle-class Conservative leadership that this was the only realistic policy for the party to pursue. Men like Bonar Law and F. E. Smith were strong supporters of Ulster Unionism, but did not share the class-conscious concern of Long or Lansdowne for their beleaguered cousins in the south. As Midleton sadly recalled, 'while the sympathy of Great Britain with the north had steadily increased, leading politicians in England regarded the south as a losing game.' Or, as O'Callaghan-Westropp put it more bluntly: 'Bonar Law never troubles to remember us southerns.'[120]

Nevertheless, in the short run, the southern Unionists did succeed in deterring the Conservative leadership from working wholeheartedly for a compromise on the Irish question on the basis of the exclusion of Ulster from the third Home Rule Bill. When the Liberals introduced their measure, Walter Long at once made the position emphatically clear to Bonar Law: 'As an Englishman, I cannot accept Home Rule in any form, and as one connected by the closest ties with the provinces of Leinster and Munster, I cannot sacrifice my friends there.'[121] Prominent Irish peers such as Lord Barrymore and Lord Oranmore and Browne wrote to *The Times* putting the southern Unionists' case, and urging that opposition to

Home Rule be maintained despite the passing of the Parliament Act. Deputations from the IUA waited on the Tory shadow cabinet and on Law himself, making plain their total opposition to partition, and to any separate deal for Ulster. And Long and Lansdowne exerted the greatest personal pressure on their leader not to abandon the south. The result was that although Law met Asquith for talks in late 1913, and took part in the inter-party conference of July 1914, he was not in a position to make any compromise based on the exclusion of Ulster – however much he might have wanted to do so personally – for fear of alienating the powerful southern Unionist lobby and thus effectively splitting his party.[122]

Although the Liberals eventually carried Home Rule, the outbreak of the First World War meant the measure never actually came into operation. The southern Unionists were still convinced that it never would, and even as late as 1916, they made another successful effort to defend their own interests.[123] In the aftermath of the Easter Rising, Asquith asked Lloyd George to make a renewed effort to reach a settlement based on Home Rule. By effectively ignoring the southern Unionists, by assuring Carson and the Ulster Unionists that the exclusion of their province would be permanent, and by telling Redmond and the Nationalists that it would only be temporary, he seemed on the brink of concocting a characteristically makeshift agreement. But predictably, the southern Unionists were outraged at being asked (or, rather, not even asked) 'to surrender all that was most dear to them'.[124] They bombarded the cabinet with letters of protest, and a deputation from the IUA met Asquith and Lloyd George. But their trump card was that their leaders, Long and Lansdowne, were now members of the coalition government. Both threatened resignation, Lansdowne denounced the scheme in the Lords, and the settlement was soon abandoned.[125]

But although on this occasion the southern Unionists were able to defeat Home Rule by the high political lobbying of their aristocratic friends and representatives, it was essentially a pyrrhic victory. The First World War took a severe toll of Irish patrician manhood, and the rise of Sinn Fein was an even more ominous development. Lansdowne's retirement robbed the southern Unionists of their most powerful advocate in cabinet. And the advent of Lloyd George to the Premiership was an added blow. He was no friend of the aristocracy, on either side of the Irish Sea. And as he had shown during the summer of 1916, he was quite prepared to abandon the southern Unionists to their fate, if he could thereby facilitate agreement between the Ulster Unionists and the southern nationalists. As Lord Midleton sadly admitted in September 1918, 'the Asquith cabinet,

91. Lord Midleton.

the Coalition Cabinet, and the Lloyd George Cabinet are all committed to the principle of Home Rule, and the majority of people in Great Britain regard its establishment when possible as a foregone conclusion.'[126]

Under these very changed circumstances, those patricians who had vainly advocated compromise and conciliation during the early 1900s briefly recaptured the initiative, in collaboration with the previously intransigent Lord Midleton. By 1917, it was clear to them that the maintenance of the Union was no longer a realistic possibility, and that the effective choice lay between Home Rule for the whole of Ireland, or partition on the basis of Ulster's continued adherence to the Union. Faced with these alternatives, they preferred Home Rule as the lesser of the two evils, since it was preferable for them to be a Protestant minority in a united Ireland (with strong support from Ulster and adequate safeguards for their own position) than in an independent south (where they would be effectively handed over to 'the enemy').[127] Dunraven had long been in favour of legislative devolution. Plunkett now accepted that Dominion Status was the best way of preserving Irish unity. And Midleton was prepared to work with Redmond and the moderate parliamentary nationalists to avoid partition. Thus was the stage set for the last patrician display of high-minded leadership and patriotic conciliation: the abortive Irish Convention of 1917–18.

Having failed to solve the Irish problem by personal intervention, Lloyd George decided that the Irish must be encouraged to solve it themselves. Under Plunkett's chairmanship, the Irish Convention assembled in Dublin in the summer of 1917.[128] Both the Ulster Unionists and the old Irish Parliamentary Party sent representatives, and so did the IUA, whose delegation included Midleton, Dunraven, Mayo, Desart, and Oranmore and Browne. For the first six months, very little happened beyond the settling of procedural details, and mutual expressions of goodwill. But in December, Midleton intervened decisively, proposing a comprehensive scheme that preserved the economic and financial links between Britain and Ireland, conceded a degree of Irish self-government necessary to satisfy moderate nationalist aspirations, maintained Irish unity intact, and safeguarded the position of the Protestant minority. This well-timed display of authoritative leadership and patrician high-mindedness initially commanded widespread approval, and in early 1918, the Convention seemed on the brink of agreement.[129]

But it was to no avail. Plunkett missed the opportunity by letting the delegates become bogged down again in matters of detail, and the Convention was eventually dissolved, having achieved nothing. Midleton's scheme was finally rejected by the Ulster Unionists, because it merged their province into a united and separate Ireland. And it was also rejected by most members of his own IUA, who regarded it as a 'betrayal of the cause' of Union for the defence of which their very organization existed.[130] Gentry like Richard Bagwell, Henry Macnamara, and J. M. Wilson, who were far less secure in their position than grandees like Midleton and Dunraven, were unable to share their detached, broad-minded, magnanimous, and conciliatory opinions. Even in 1918, they still believed that intransigence was the only viable policy, and that the British government would not desert them. As Bagwell explained, 'The question of the union is not susceptible to compromise: the choice is between defence and surrender.' In January 1919, Midleton was dismissed as chairman of the IUA, and was replaced by Lord Farnham, a hardline Unionist with estates in Ulster. In retaliation, Midleton and twenty-five followers formed the Unionist Anti-Partition League.[131]

So, despite the high-minded initiative of Midleton and his friends, the only lasting effect of the Irish Convention on the southern Unionists was to split them irrevocably.[132] For Lloyd George, it merely showed that it was no more profitable to encourage the Irish to solve their own problems than it had been to offer British mediation in 1916. Accordingly, he resolved to settle the matter by effectively imposing the Government of Ireland Act of 1920. From the standpoint of both of the southern Unionist organizations, this was a terrible prospect. In the first place, it embodied Home Rule (albeit with Westminster still responsible for various financial matters). In addition, it also proposed partition between the six counties of Ulster and the rest of Ireland, both parts of which would be given unicameral legislatures. And the final blow for the southern patricians was that the Ulster Unionists eagerly accepted this measure. At this point, the IUA effectively ceased to matter, since the Union was irrevocably broken, and its policy of stubborn intransigence had failed. And, ironically enough, the greatest betrayal was suffered by Farnham himself: for he held lands in Cavan – one of the Ulster counties that had been turned over to the south.[133]

By definition, the Act was no more pleasing to the UAPL, albeit for somewhat different reasons. Midleton did not so much mind Home Rule: but he was deeply saddened at the prospect of partition. Nevertheless, the moderate and conciliatory members of the UAPL were still able to exert some influence. In its original form, the bill contained no provisions for protecting the southern Unionists. But as it made its way through Parliament, Midleton and his friends in the Lords successfully inserted a series of amendments, designed to safeguard the position of the patrician minority in the south.[134] They instituted a strong Senate with real political powers; they ensured that the Irish Parliament could not impose additional taxes on income; and they established that private property was secure against confiscation without compensation. In effect, they had won back virtually all the safeguards that had been built into Midleton's abortive proposals of 1917. As such, the Act seemed to vindicate the more pragmatic and less intransigent approach of the constructive Unionists; and in recognition of his efforts, Midleton himself was made an earl in 1920.

But once more, it was a pyrrhic victory, since the civil war meant that the act was never implemented in the south. Yet again, Midleton courageously played a mediator's part in helping to bring about the truce in July 1921, and believed he had obtained assurances from the British government and from de Valera and Griffiths that the safeguards which had been inserted in the Act of 1920 would be incorporated in any new constitution for an independent Eire.[135] But Lloyd George's overriding concern was to reach an agreement with the nationalists: he had no intention of jeopardizing the negotiations by insisting on safeguards for the old and enfeebled patrician class. Having used them, he then effectively discarded them. They were rarely even consulted during the negotiations, and with Long and Lansdowne out of the cabinet, there was no one who would speak up in government on their behalf. As Midleton later, and sourly, recorded, 'none of the provisions which we had been promised over and over again . . . were inserted in the midnight treaty.' Considering the part he himself had played in bringing the opposing sides together, his feelings were understandably bitter: 'every pledge given to those who had made the conference possible was broken.'[136]

Not surprisingly, Midleton refused to move the adoption of the Treaty in the Lords. The final humiliation came in the following year, when the negotiations were completed over the Irish constitution itself. Once again, Lloyd George was determined that matters should not be delayed or jeopardized by any consideration of the southern Unionists' particular concerns, and most members of Sinn Fein were likewise disinclined to make concessions to a moribund group for whom they had no sympathy. As in 1921, they were brought into the negotiations very late, and were effectively told their terms. There was no financial settlement, nothing about the completion of land purchase, and no adequate constitutional safeguard in either the powers or the composition of the second chamber. When the Irish Free State Bill finally came to the Lords, Midleton wanted to oppose it. But he was overborne by most of his colleagues in the UAPL. The measure was passed, and the UAPL – like the IUA – lost its *raison d'être* and was wound up. Midleton himself was so disillusioned that he refused to accept a seat in the new Irish Senate, and retired altogether from Irish public affairs.[137]

So, despite their much greater insight and foresight, the constructive Unionists had in the end accomplished no more than the intransigent obstructionists. Between 1917 and 1922, they had made a series of concessions that seemed to them statesmanlike and high-minded, in the hope that this might persuade the British government and the Irish representatives to give them a place in the new Irish nation commensurate with their own estimate of their dignity and importance. But neither Lloyd George nor Sinn Fein accepted that essentially self-regarding and obsolete estimate of patrician worth. The overwhelming combination of mass agrarian nationalism, rampant Ulster sectionalism, and the Prime Minister's ruthless disregard of their concerns meant that the southern Unionists – whether UAPL or IUA – were brutally swept aside. The Union was ended; Ireland was partitioned; there were minimal safeguards in the new constitution.[138] And as country houses were plundered and burned from Clare to Cavan, the extinction of Irish landlordism seemed complete.

As many patricians watched their houses burn, or fled the country,

or stayed on in fear and poverty, all that they were left with was an
overwhelming sense of betrayal, by what J. M. Wilson called 'the
duplicity, mendacity and cowardice of our former friends.' As Lady
Alice Howard put it: 'The government have given over everything
to the rebels . . . England has cast us off, and given everything to the
murderers.'[139] For the essence of their tragedy was that the Irish
patricians had stood by the empire in its greatest time of mortal
danger, and had profligately spilled their blood and selflessly given
their lives in its defence. Yet in the darkest crisis of their own lives
and their own order, that same empire had not lifted a finger to save
them. Perhaps Midleton himself should have the last, more measured, but no less bitter word. The whole affair, he concluded, was
'one of the most deplorable desertions of their supporters of which
any ministry has ever been guilty.'[140]

iv.   The Church: Much Ado About Nothing

During the election campaign of 1885, a lengthy exchange took place
between the Earl of Selborne and Mr Gladstone in the correspondence columns of The Times, disputing the rights and wrongs of
church disestablishment in England and Wales.[141] The particular
disagreement pained both men deeply; but it was commonplace for
patricians of their generation to be publicly concerned with such
great ecclesiastical issues. Religious questions were a central element
of political life, while belief in God was for many grandees and
gentry the mainspring of their very existence. They were brought up
in Christian households; they possessed rights of patronage and
appointment; they numbered clergy and bishops among their acquaintances (and sometimes among their relatives); they placed themselves at the head of many religious organizations; and they were
interested in theology, liturgical studies, and ecclesiastical law. In
addition to Selborne and Gladstone, such men as Lord Salisbury, Sir
Michael Hicks Beach, Sir William Harcourt, Lord Halifax, the Duke
of Norfolk, the Marquess of Bute, the Duke of Westminster, and
Lord Shaftesbury, were Christian gentlemen in the fullest sense of
that phrase, and ecclesiastical statesmen of the front rank.

Among a later generation, aristocrats like Lords Salisbury, Selborne, and Halifax continued their family tradition of Christian piety
and public involvement in religious affairs. Sons of peers, such as the
Cecil brothers, Lord Wolmer, and William Ormsby-Gore – who
was married to Salisbury's daughter – were no less devout. Country
gentlemen like Alfred Cripps, Philip Wilbraham, Arthur Griffith-
Boscawen, and William Bridgeman were also firm and faithful
believers. Such patrician laymen regarded middle-class prelates like

92. Lord Selborne.   93. Lord Halifax by Logsdail.

Benson, Davidson, Henson, Lang, and Temple as co-religionists and
as personal friends. Country mansions like Hickleton and Hatfield
were visited regularly by itinerant archbishops, while Lord and Lady
Balcarres, the Lane-Foxes, and Edward Wood were among Cosmo
Lang's first house guests at Bishopthorpe in 1909.[142] And these loyal
and lordly sons of the church stated their views on politics and
theology with a directness and an assurance that sometimes fell short
of the highest ideals of Christian charity. Lord Salisbury regularly
rebuked Randall Davidson – for his stand on the Parliament Bill, on
Welsh church disestablishment, and on the Irish Treaty. Lord Halifax even tried to prevent him from consecrating Hensley Henson
Bishop of Hereford in 1919. And Cripps and Selborne were no less
astringent and assertive.[143]

But despite these continuities of belief and behaviour, the half-
century from the 1880s was as distressing and depressing a time for
the Church of England in particular (and for religion in general) as it
was for the agricultural sector of the economy, for the House of
Lords as a second chamber, and for the preservation of the Union
with Ireland.[144] It was not just that the connections between the
church and the landed establishment were being progressively and
permanently uncoupled. Religious controversies were gradually
ceasing to be at the centre of national political life. The demands for

social reform were becoming more strident and significant than those for spiritual improvement or religious equality. As Bishop Lord Arthur Hervey complained in 1885, there was 'an infidel, democratic and socialist upheaval against religion and against our Lord Christ.' Or, as Lord Halifax regretfully admitted in 1903, in an article significantly entitled 'The Crisis in the Church', 'the foundations are being shaken everywhere.'[145] How, in this increasingly secular world, did these high-minded Christian gentlemen discharge their traditional obligations to their God and to their faith? If their church was once more in danger, what did they do to defend it?

As before, some of them indulged in individual displays of ecclesiastical entrepreneurship, with a zeal that belied both the circumstances of their own order and the condition of their church. The fifteenth Duke of Norfolk was a member of Salisbury's cabinet, and a very visible and vigorous Earl Marshal, who played a more prominent part in the public life of the country than his forebears had for centuries.[146] He was widely recognized as the undisputed lay leader of the Catholic community in England, and used the massive wealth derived from his Sheffield ground rents to succour and subsidize his faith. On his own éstates, he constructed churches in Sussex and Sheffield, and rebuilt what became Arundel Cathedral, to celebrate his coming of age, in the most flamboyant Gothic style.[147] He paid for churches in Lytham St Annes and Cambridge, and was a munificent benefactor to Brompton Oratory and Westminster Cathedral. But his greatest achievement was the building of the Cathedral Church of St John Baptist in Norwich between 1884 and 1910. The town held historic associations for the Duke's family; he lavished £250,000 on the undertaking; and he himself was closely concerned with the detailed design.

Norfolk was almost matched as a crusading Catholic builder by his exact contemporary, and cousin by marriage, the third Marquess of Bute. His income from the Glamorgan coalfields meant he was fabulously rich. His Catholic zeal – unlike Norfolk's – was that of the convert: for he had been brought up a Scots Presbyterian, and had gone over to Rome in 1868. He was well read, not merely in Christianity, but also in Judaism, Islam, and Buddhism, and was a liturgist and ecclesiologist of real distinction. He was a prolific writer, who published English translations of the breviary and the orders of service for the great Catholic church festivals. And he was a compulsive restorer and builder – not only of his own palaces and castles, but of churches and monasteries as well. In Cardiff, he financed excavations into the foundations of the Grey and Blackfriars houses. In Scotland, he acquired ruined abbeys and priories, which he then restored and made available for new religious orders: Greyfriars in Elgin and Pluscarden in Moray. He built one church at Oban, which became the see of the Bishop of Argyll and the Isles, and another at Galston in Ayrshire, which was modelled on Santa Sophia in Constantinople.[148]

These pious aristocratic initiatives were not confined to church building. The second Viscount Halifax was a staunch member of the Anglo-Catholic wing of the Church of England, and for over fifty years was widely regarded as its lay leader. In 1886, he proclaimed that 'the crown and completion of the Catholic revival which has transformed the Church of England within the last fifty years is the re-union of Christendom', and for the next half-century, he single-mindedly, and almost single-handedly, devoted himself to achieving this quite impossible and unrealistic objective. His first attempt was between 1894 and 1897, when he tried to persuade the Pope to recognize the Anglican religious orders as a preliminary to closer union between Rome and Canterbury. But the only result was a papal bull condemning them.[149] Thirty years later, and quite unde-terred by this fiasco, Halifax tried again. On his own initiative, he arranged a series of meetings between Anglo Catholics and Roman Catholics known as the Conversations at Malines, which lasted from 1921 to 1926. But once again, the official leadership of both churches looked askance at these private and octogenarian pastimes, and the talks were abandoned.[150]

Although atypical in many ways, these high aspirations and un-certain achievements vividly illustrate both the attractions and the limitations of patrician ecclesiastical statesmanship during this period. To begin with, it seems clear that these men turned to religion for more than spiritual consolation: they were all in ardent and angry revolt against the modernism of the times in which they lived. The Duke of Norfolk may have drawn much of his income from the ground rents of Sheffield. But he preferred invented ceremonial and Gothic revival architecture, and built Arundel Cathedral as 'a protest against the spirit of the age.'[151] The Marquess of Bute was totally out of place in the nineteenth century, regretted any time given to his 'irksome and fatiguing' business affairs, spent a large part of each year in the Mediterranean and the Middle East, and directed that his heart be buried in the Mount of Olives. And Lord Halifax hated poachers and strikers, detested the sloppiness of the twentieth century, and clearly believed that the world had gone fundamentally and irrevocably wrong about 1885. 'Politics', he once observed, 'are a delusion, and I am quite convinced that to have a vocation to be a monk is the happiest lot in life.'[152]

Yet ironically, although these men sought refuge from the demo-cratic politics and the secular materialism of their time in spiritual devotion and pious endeavour, the fact remains that in the broader context of their own faith, they did not actually accomplish very much. Halifax's obsession with reunion combined the maximum of aristocratic stubbornness with the minimum of political realism. He spoke only for a minority wing of the Church of England, many Anglicans regarded him as a conceited, tiresome, and reactionary embarrassment, and G. G. Coulton's unflattering portrait of him as Lord Halfwayhouse in his novel *Friar's Lantern* probably expressed the majority view.[153] In the same way, Conservative and Unionist Catholics like Bute and Norfolk were very much a minority in their church, which was increasingly dominated by radical ultramontanes like Manning, who supported Home Rule and working-class demands. Even their architectural endeavours, although individually stupendous, counted for little, since most Catholic church building was plebeian and Irish in its financing, and Classical rather than Gothic in its design. As the self-appointed lay leaders of religious crusades, these three grandees never really held the ecclesiastical initiative.[154]

Nor did such men fare any better when they tried to further their religious causes or defend their religious institutions in the political arena. In their vain attempt to prevent Welsh church disestablishment, these themes of patrician disenchantment and frustrated marginality only reappear in much stronger form. For some grandees and gentry, the defence of the Welsh church was a cause that was literally more sacred than the maintenance of the Union with Ireland. Yet from the late 1880s onwards, the popular crusade for disestablishment became the strongest, most deeply rooted, and most irresistible of Welsh demands.[155] Once the alien landlords had been dethroned as local MPs, and once the nationalists and nonconformists had won control of the new county councils, the removal of the alien church, and the transfer of its endowments to the local authorities, became the next radical, nationalist objective. At the same time that the Tithe War broke out in Wales, motions were proposed in the Commons in favour of disestablishment, and the Liberal leadership was urged to embrace it as official policy. After the party's victory in the general election of 1892, some action was inevitable, and a Welsh Church Suspensory Bill, and two disestablishment measures were brought before the Commons in rapid succession.[156]

The patrician defenders of the established church formed three distinct but related groups: grandees and their relatives who regarded the support of Anglicanism as part of their traditional aristocratic duty; Unionist political leaders who were themselves of landed background; and Welsh border squires for whom the matter was of deep local concern. During the late 1880s, Lords Selborne and Salisbury were loud in their public denunciations of disestablishment proposals, even in Wales itself. In response to the Welsh Church Suspensory Bill of 1893, sixty Tory MPs formed the Church Parliamentary Committee – otherwise known as the 'Church Lads Brigade' – which became the main focus of concerted Anglican endeavour in the Commons for the next twenty years. Its Secretary was Arthur Griffith-Boscawen, the second son of a Denbighshire squire, and for many years, its chairman was Lord Cranborne.[157] At the same time, other patricians were much in evidence out of doors. Lord Halifax denounced the measure on behalf of the Anglo-Catholic English Church Union as 'robbery'; Sir Michael Hicks Beach, greatly daring, even addressed a meeting at Caernarfon; and there was a massive gathering in May 1893 at the Royal Albert Hall addressed by Lord Selborne and Col. Cornwallis-West, another Welsh squire.[158]

It was these men who also led the successful opposition to the two Disestablishment Bills that the Liberal government introduced in 1894 and 1895. In the Commons, Lord Wolmer claimed that the Welsh themselves were not in favour of the measure; Hicks Beach denounced the proposal as 'plunder and sacrilege'; and Arthur Balfour not only gave an elaborate disquisition on the subject of tithes, but also wrote a pamphlet entitled *Disestablishment Policy Exposed.*[159] At the same time, Wolmer, Cranborne, and Griffith-Boscawen also organized an extra parliamentary pressure group, known as the Central Church Committee, which was chaired by the Duke of Westminster. With the support of local Tory squires, they arranged meetings throughout the length and breadth of Wales, especially during the general election of 1895. Thereafter, the question of disestablishment virtually disappeared from public view for the next fifteen years. The Royal Commission of 1906 – of which Lord Hugh Cecil was a predictably truculent member – was largely a delaying tactic. And the bill that Asquith himself intoduced in 1909 – which was vehemently opposed by W. C. Bridgeman and Lord Robert Cecil on behalf of the Church Lads Brigade – disappeared in the aftermath of the People's Budget.[160]

As with Home Rule, the passing of the Parliament Act abruptly removed the last effective line of patrician defence. In April 1912, a fourth disestablishment measure was introduced by Reginald McKenna, to 'constant interruptions and howls of mirth' from Lords Robert and Hugh Cecil. It was vehemently opposed by the Church Parliamentary Committee, led by Alfred Lyttelton and Arthur Griffith-Boscawen, and supported by such patrician Anglicans as Cripps, Wolmer, the Cecils, Edward Wood, and William Ormsby-

Gore.[161] In the Commons, Lloyd George once more denounced the Cecils, the Cavendishes, and their friends in the language of Limehouse. How dare they oppose such a measure, he thundered, when they were themselves the descendants of men who had appropriated secularized property in the aftermath of the dissolution of the monasteries, and when their own hands were 'dripping with the fat of sacrilege'?[162] Thus provoked, the peers threw the measure out, and in 1913 it was reintroduced in the Commons. Lord Hugh Cecil made an outstandingly eloquent speech, and the Lords rejected it again. But the Commons duly passed it a third time, and in May 1914 it finally became law.[163]

Nevertheless, the war delayed its implementation, and the Cecils even hoped that the measure might be repealed altogether. This was never practical politics. But it soon became clear that the financial provisions for the newly disestablished Welsh church were going to be inadequate, and in November 1918, Lord Robert Cecil actually resigned from the coalition government on this very issue.[164] Eventually, a Treasury grant was provided to compensate the church for the loss of its endowments, and in August 1919 the Welsh Church Temporalities Bill was introduced into the Commons to tidy the matter up. For positively the last time, the patrician Tories denounced this outrageous measure. Lord Hugh Cecil claimed the government was 'carrying out robbery, knowing it to be robbery.' William Ormsby-Gore opposed it as a display of 'ecclesiastical tyranny'. Lord Robert Cecil, who regarded disendowment as a crime even more heinous than disestablishment, felt it undermined belief in private property. And Lord Salisbury added his own intransigent opinions in the upper house. But the measure was duly passed, and the Welsh church was finally disestablished in June 1920.[165]

For those aristocrats and gentry who had sought to prevent it, this represented total and complete defeat. The public meetings they organized, the pamphlets they published, their bitter protests in the Commons, their sustained intransigence in the Lords: all had been to no avail. But it was not just that this was another cause irretrievably lost: it was also that to most people, it was not even a cause worth fighting for. The final debates of 1912–14 took place in a general atmosphere of widespread indifference. By the time that the alien church had been vanquished, even the Welsh themselves had largely lost interest in the matter.[166] And Lord Robert Cecil's resignation from the Lloyd George coalition on the issue of disendowment merely reinforced the view that such people had lost all sense of proportion. On every other matter, Cecil was in agreement with the government, and he was himself playing an important part in the making of foreign policy. Yet he insisted on resigning: his decision seemed quixotic; his reasons were obscure and inadequate; the cause was very remote from the pressing concerns of the hour; and his own career never really recovered.[167]

The government and management of the Anglican church itself seemed to offer more promising scope for constructive patrician involvement in ecclesiastical affairs. Despite the attention it received at the general elections of 1880 and 1885, the disestablishment of the church in England soon ceased to be practical politics.[168] Accordingly, for most Anglicans, the major issue was no longer self-defence, but became instead self-government. On the one hand, there was a growing desire to strengthen the church's position by bringing Christian laymen more fully into its affairs: in 1885 the Convocation of Canterbury established a House of Laymen, and in 1903 the Representative Church Council was set up as a deliberative body of bishops, clergy, and laity.[169] On the other, it was becoming ever more irksome for the church to be subordinated to a legislature where the majority of MPs no longer cared about religious questions. As Lord Wolmer explained to the Archbishop of Canterbury in 1913, 'it is, under present conditions, quite impossible to carry legislation that is necessary for the full development of the Church's work'.[170]

An Anglican church increasingly eager to involve the laity in its affairs, and increasingly anxious to obtain self-governing independence from Parliament, attracted many of those notables who now felt so unhappy and uncomfortable in the world of democratic (and demagogic) politics. Men like Selborne, Salisbury, and Cripps soon became the dominant figures in the House of Laymen and the RCC, and strongly supported the view that the church should be given its autonomy from an increasingly godless and indifferent Parliament. In 1913, Cripps, Wolmer, and Halifax successfully persuaded the RCC to set up a committee to consider a system of legislative devolution for the Church of England.[171] It was chaired by Lord Selborne, and its members included the Duke of Devonshire, Lord Wolmer, Balfour, Lord Hugh Cecil, and Edward Wood. As Hensley Henson acerbically remarked, 'The atmosphere of the committee was not so much national as domestic.' Despite the outbreak of war, its deliberations continued, and it published its report in 1916. Its principal recommendation was that a suitably reformed RCC, to be known as the Church Assembly, should be given legislative powers – subject to a parliamentary veto.[172]

Because of more pressing concerns, it was not until 1919 that an Enabling Bill was brought before Parliament. The ease with which it passed owed much to the Life and Liberty Movement,

94. Lord Hugh Cecil.

which orchestrated popular support for the measure, and to the
tactical adroitness of Randall Davidson, who presented it in the
Lords as a piece of administrative reform rather than as a major
innovation. But the contribution of the 'believing aristocracy' was
also crucial.[173] On the model of the suffragettes, Lord Wolmer had
already organized the Church Self-Government Association, which
had extracted promises from candidates at the 1918 general election
that they would support such a measure. The joint honorary secretaries of the Church Enabling Bill Committee were Earl Grey and
Wolmer, who together were responsible for generating and organizing the necessary support in the lobbies.[174] In the Lords, Salisbury,
Selborne, Grey, and Parmoor (as Cripps had now become) gave
Randall Davidson very full support. In the Commons, Wolmer
lobbied Bonar Law, the Leader of the House, to provide the necessary parliamentary time, and in collaboration with Lord Robert
Cecil steered the bill through committee. The successful passing of
the Enabling Act was thus as much a tribute to Wolmer's efforts and
tactical skill as it was to Davidson's.[175]

From the very outset, these same patricians also dominated the
Assembly itself. Lord Parmoor was unanimously elected the first

chairman of the House of Laity, but resigned in 1924 when he joined the first Labour government. He was followed by Lord Selborne, who held the position until 1942. Throughout the inter-war years, the Assembly's Secretary was Sir Philip Wilbraham, an ecclesiastical lawyer and Cheshire country gentleman.[176] And the chairman of the Standing Orders Committee was Lord Hugh Cecil, who drafted the Assembly's rules in collaboration with Wilbraham, and was himself the most important – and intimidating – figure at its meetings. As Cosmo Lang later recorded, Cecil was 'the power behind the throne, ready to rebuke any lapses into irrelevant pleasantries or even into common sense.' But in addition, Cecil and his friends successfully imposed their own very narrow conception of the Assembly's functions. It was not intended, they insisted, to 'touch men's hearts', by considering great social, economic, or political questions. On the contrary, its scope was restricted to matters of business, government, and administration, and by 1930, forty such measures had successfully made their way to the statute book.[177]

By the inter-war years, these men were no longer governing the state: they were governing the church instead. And they were in control of its wealth no less than of its legislature. In 1919, Lord Selborne became chairman of the Central Board of Finance and he was followed in 1925 by his son-in-law, Earl Grey.[178] Throughout the inter-way years, Sir Arthur Griffith-Boscawen was both chairman of the Commissioners under the Welsh Church Act and in charge of the Church of England Pensions Board. A wartime committee appointed to investigate the Central Church Fund was chaired by Lord Brassey, and its other members included Beauchamp, Salisbury, Selborne, Wolmer, and Edward Wood. Its final report, presented in 1918, was a classic statement of the secular concerns and patrician priorities that these men displayed in their management of Anglican affairs. The uncertain post-war conditions, they concluded, 'require that the forces of organised religion should be utilized more than ever before for the stabilization of society, for the inspiration of the future, and the general welfare of the nation.' No wonder there were growing clerical criticisms of the power and the prejudices of these 'determined laymen'.[179]

Nevertheless, in 1927 and 1928, there was a brutal reminder of the very real limits to this patrician power. For while the Church Assembly's routine pieces of legislation were approved by Parliament with alacrity, the most important proposal – the revision of the Prayer Book – was twice crushingly rejected by the House of Commons.[180] On the first occasion, in December 1927, Bridgeman and Wolmer both spoke badly, while Hugh Cecil, who was expected to make the speech of his life, simply collapsed. He redeemed himself in June 1928, when the question was debated again, but his effort was to no avail, since the majority against was even greater. For Cecil, it was a personal humiliation and parliamentary disappointment from which he never really recovered. And for the dwindling remnants of the Church Lads Brigade, it was a disaster reminiscent of their failure over Welsh church disestablishment. Most people were no more concerned with the debates of 1927–8 than they had been with those of 1912–14: they were essentially the 'echo of dead themes'. As one Labour MP candidly but correctly put it, 'The working man is not interested in the Prayer Book, but in the rent book.'[181]

Thereafter, the aristocratic contribution to Anglican affairs was never so central or so certain again. Lord Robert Cecil was put in charge of another committee to inquire into the relations between church and state: it reported in 1935, but its verdict was equivocal, and its recommendations were effectively ignored.[182] Lord Hugh Cecil sought consolation in a variety of predictably idiosyncratic ways. He threatened to prosecute the Bishop of Liverpool for allowing a Unitarian to preach in his cathedral; he unsuccessfully attempted to persuade the Church Assembly to prohibit the use of the marriage service to all divorced persons; and he published a pamphlet entitled *The Communion Service as It Might Be*.[183] Lord Salisbury became excessively captivated with Dr Frank Buchman's pro-German Oxford Group; he helped finance its sometimes sensationalist propaganda; he lobbied the Prime Minister and the Archbishop of Canterbury on its behalf; and he even held house parties at Hatfield to further the cause. Lord Selborne served as a pallbearer at Randall Davidson's funeral, while Lord Grey busied himself with the schemes to rebuild Church House in Dean's Yard.[184]

In one way or another, all these men were ill at ease in the modern, materialist, secular, democratic twentieth century. As with Norfolk, Halifax, and Bute, religion was not only a matter of personal conviction or family tradition: it provided an escape from the world in which they had the misfortune to find themselves, and an alternative and more agreeable outlet for their increasingly frustrated political ambitions. It is not at all coincidence that Norfolk, Halifax, Selborne, and Salisbury were die-hards, as were Grey's father and Bute's son. For such men, the whole tenor of politics since the 1880s had been depressing in the extreme, and the Parliament Act had merely confirmed their worst fears. As Lord Halifax put it in 1905, 'There are few things left for a gentleman nowadays, but at least they can say "Take or leave me; but you take me on my terms, not on yours." And as far as explaining and justifying my conduct, that is a thing I will do to please nobody.'[185] For such men, the Church

Assembly and the Anglican bureaucracy were – like local government or proconsular office – infinitely preferable to the rough and
tumble of democratic politics.

To that extent, these men did indeed carve out a new role for
themselves as ecclesiastical statesmen. But this must be set in a
broader perspective. For all the time and effort they lavished on its
creation and on its deliberations, the Church Assembly never
actually accomplished very much, and by the 1930s it was widely
regarded by many churchmen with indifference or disillusionment.[186]
And for all their intimacy with prelates and bishops, it is clear that
Benson, Davidson, Lang, and Temple often found their sectional
opinions, their reactionary views and their endless, carping criticisms
extremely tiresome. 'I know well how continually I must disappoint
you', Lang wrote to Halifax in 1929. 'But you can scarcely realise
how constant are the limitations imposed by that care of all the
churches which presses upon me daily – all the churches in the
Anglican Communion.' And after visiting Lord Hugh Cecil at Eton in
1939, Hensley Henson was even more outspoken: 'I was astonished
at the obsoleteness of his opinions, the subtlety of his arguments, and
cast-iron rigidity of his mind. He is a medievalist in the methods of
his reasoning, the strength of his prejudices and the obscurantism of
his outlook.'[187]

The real difficulty for these high-minded Christian laymen was
that their diversion of effort from political to ecclesiastical statesmanship was ultimately doomed to failure and disappointment. In part,
as Henson's remarks suggest, this was because they had no more in
common with most church-goers than they did with most voters:
they could no more take a broad view of religious than of political
issues. But it was also that while the number of voters was undeniably going up, the number of church-goers was just as certainly
going down. In this sense, the 'infidel, democratic and socialist
upheaval' that Bishop Lord Arthur Hervey had feared had truly
come to pass. In shifting their ambitions from serving the state to
serving the church, these patricians had effectively exchanged increasingly democratic politics for increasingly marginalized religion,
'moving like a rudderless vessel over a rock-haunted ocean.' Once
again, they had nailed their colours to a sinking ship.[188]

v. Conclusion: All's Not Well . . .

In his warm appreciation of the part played by Lord Desart in the
Irish Convention of 1917–18, Lord Midleton remarked that 'history
takes little note of policy which has failed.'[189] The very limited
attention that historians of twentieth-century Britain have given to

such marginal issues as agricultural policy, House of Lords reform, southern-Irish Unionism, and patrician ecclesiastical statesmanship serves only to illustrate the force of his dictum. There are many great themes in modern British history: but these are emphatically not they. And, by the same token, history takes little note of people who have failed. There are many great men in twentieth-century British history: but Bledisloe and Turnor, Newton and Dunraven, Plunkett and Midleton, Grey and Wilbraham, are emphatically not they. And even men like Salisbury and Selborne, Rosebery and Halifax, are remembered – if they are remembered at all – for their activities in other fields, rather than in these.

Nevertheless, from the more limited standpoint of the recent history of the British landed establishment, these subjects were crucial and these people were significant. They boasted good connections and ease of access to those in high places. They maintained well-run organizations in the Commons and the Lords. They created extra-parliamentary pressure groups and mastered the newest techniques of publicity and propaganda. But despite their determined – if reluctant – adjustment to the new world of interest groups and political lobbying, the fact remains that in every case, they failed. They had lost control of the political agenda; they no longer held the political initiative; they were sectional groups whose sectional interests were easily defeated, ridiculed, or ignored. The issues that mattered to them no longer mattered to others. On the contrary, they seemed to most people – and especially to those who were now in charge – to be at best irrelevant and inconvenient, at worst obscurantist and anachronistic. Here, indeed, is some of the most eloquent evidence of a class in decline.

In his non-self-revealing autobiography, *Fullness of Days*, the first Earl of Halifax saluted the fourth Marquess of Salisbury for being 'a great Christian gentleman in the best and largest sense of the word.'[190] Although these two grandees had differed deeply over appeasement, they had been lifelong colleagues, and there can be no doubt that Halifax's description was sincerely meant and fully merited. But it was an epitaph much more elegiac than resounding. In his political career, Salisbury had not got far. And most of the crusades to which he had given his life had come to nought. His character, integrity, patriotism, and sense of duty were beyond reproach. But his achievements were far less enduring or significant. And he knew it. As early as 1911, he was already overwhelmed by what he called 'those festering feelings of failure and discouragement and passing time and the days that are no more.'[191] And if that was how he felt after twenty years in public life, then what must his true sentiments have been thirty years on?

11

THE POLITICS OF PARANOIA

A class unwilling to quit the stage of history could take refuge in fantasy or, more positively, hearten itself for its journey into the future by hugging rags and tatters of the past.
(V. G. Kiernan, *The Duel in European History: Honour and the Reign of Aristocracy* (1988), p. 60.)

Whiggery always bore the stamp of aristocracy . . . As politicians, the Whigs were congenitally undemocratic, and Whiggery could not flourish in a democratic constitution . . . The democratisation of the representative system . . . meant the destruction of Whiggery as a political force . . . For it was the one element in British politics so specialised that in a democratic climate it could exist only as a frail exotic.
(D. Southgate, *The Passing of the Whigs, 1832–1886* (1962), pp. xv, xvi, 322, 323.)

The Tory revolt [of 1910–14] was the last important distillation of hatred of what the social and political changes of the past sixty years had done to the power and position of the upper classes.
(R. K. Webb, *Modern England: From the Eighteenth Century to the Present* (New York, 1970), p. 470.)

In these revolutionary years, a few individuals among the Anglo-Irish did indeed turn their backs upon their own caste and, like Parnell before them, seek to identify themselves with the nationalism of their day . . . Fate was not kind to them on the whole.
(F. S. L. Lyons, *Culture and Anarchy in Ireland, 1890–1939* (1979), pp. 102–3.)

A Marxist might interpret the scattering of the Mitford children over the social target as evidence of the decline and fall of the gentry . . . Communists and Fascists, both were impelled by fear, the anxiety of being in a scrap heap instead of a social class.
(D. Pryce-Jones, *Unity Mitford: A Quest* (1976), pp. 17, 75.)

The central figure in Dennis Potter's play, *Blade on the Feather*, is Professor Jason Cavendish, 'a melancholy-looking but patrician old man in his late seventies', who lives in an 'ample English country house.' He comes from 'a normal English upper class family', which means that his two elder brothers were killed in Flanders, that his father died of cancer, and that his mother went mad. His life has been largely futile and wasted; the England that his generation 'might have thought they had inherited' has long since vanished; and he is in the process of writing his autobiography, largely out of boredom and malice. In it, he reveals that he became a Communist in the 1930s, because he could find 'nothing else' to believe in, and that while he was a don at Cambridge, he recruited Burgess, Philby, and Maclean. When asked to explain his unconventional and traitorous conduct, he offers this revealing rationalization: 'I was born into a class that loves only what it owns. But we don't quite own enough of it any more . . . Silver spoons tarnish very easily, you know. I suppose we were all riddled with disappointment.'

From the late nineteenth century onwards, many landowners and former landowners shared Cavendish's sense of anger, disappointment, frustration, and bewilderment that they were no longer lords of the earth or the makers of history. How did they respond to this powerful and pervasive sense of their own decline, disintegration, and defeat?[1] In essence, they did so by disregarding the traditions of their class and by flouting the rules of genteel political life, in the vain hope that by such drastic means, they might restore the world they feared they had lost. The pioneer patrician apostates were the Whig grandees, who abandoned their progressive traditions, turned their backs on the Liberal party, and slowly allied themselves with the Conservatives during the last quarter of the nineteenth century. In the short run, this seemed to be to their advantage, since it consolidated the landed interest in the Conservative party. But in the long run, it was ruinous: it made it easier for the Liberals to attack the lords and landlords; the Tories proved less than zealous in their defence of the landowners; and by abandoning their leadership of one of the great political parties, the patricians effectively surrendered their position as the only governing élite of the nation.

For the Tory die-hards, the next generation of aristocratic rebels, their sense of decline was more powerful, their hatred and resentment was more intense, and their defeat was correspondingly more bitter. By the 1900s, they saw the widespread decline of their own order and way of life; they contemplated with horror the twin evils of irresponsible plutocracy and proletarian democracy; they watched with scarcely concealed anger the feeble and vacillating leadership of the Conservative party; and they concluded that more drastic action was needed if the situation was to be retrieved. Accordingly, they espoused a violent, intransigent, seemingly anti-democratic credo, which skirted the very bounds of treason. They sought to arouse their lethargic and supine colleagues to the dangers of national and class decline. They attempted to defy the Liberal efforts to emasculate the House of Lords. And they were prepared to go to any lengths to prevent Home Rule and support the Ulster Loyalists. As such, their quasi-revolutionary behaviour was an almost complete rejection of the liberal, constitutionalist patrician tradition in British politics. But although the die-hards made a great deal of noise, and attracted much attention, they achieved nothing.

During the inter-war years, a later generation of disillusioned notables moved not only to the extreme right, but also to the far left. In Ireland, the disintegrating territorial class provided a handful of maverick, revolutionary nationalists, whose aspirations to leadership were no more successful than those of their more moderate forebears had been in the 1890s and 1900s. In England, some patricians joined the Labour party, not so much because they had rejected the values of their genteel upbringing, but in the vain hope that it might prove a more effective vehicle for safeguarding paternalistic decency than the declining Liberals or the plutocratic Tories. At the other end of the spectrum, many notables were so distressed by what they saw as the failure of democracy that during the thirties they flirted with extreme forms of authoritarianism. In one guise, this meant Mosley and the British Union of Fascism; in another, it meant admiration for Hitler and the Nazis. Either way, it was ineffectual. Nevertheless, the alarmism, the paranoia, and the bitterness that underlay such actions provide the most eloquent evidence of how great and how genuine many aristocrats believed the decline of their class to have been.

i.   The Passing of the Whigs

'The position of the Whigs', Arthur Balfour sardonically observed in 1880, after Lord Lansdowne had resigned from Gladstone's administration in protest against the Irish Compensation for Disturbances Bill, 'is more amusing than usual.' But this most serious, exclusive, and illustrious cousinhood, held together by birth, blood, and breeding, had never existed to provide its political opponents with comic entertainment or light relief.[2] Descended from the martyrs of the Glorious Revolution and from the first Earl Gower, and related to each other many times over across the generations, the Bedfords, Devonshires, Sutherlands, Granvilles, Westminsters, Norfolks, Carlisles, Spencers, and Egertons formed what was half-mockingly and half-admiringly known as 'the sacred circle of the Great Grand-motherhood.' The Duke of Argyll once remarked that 'some of the Whigs talked of themselves as if they were a particular breed of spaniels.' More prosaically, G. W. E. Russell agreed that 'The essence of Whiggery was relationship . . . The Whig, like the poet, is born, not made. It is as difficult to become a Whig as to become a Jew.' And, as the grandson of a Duke of Bedford, he had good cause to know.[3]

95. Lord Lansdowne by
Philip de Laszlo.

In essence, the Whigs saw themselves as 'the chosen people'. Even by aristocratic standards, most were very rich. Devonshire, Bedford, Westminster, Sutherland, Norfolk, Durham, and Fitwilliam were not just exceptionally broad-acred: their urban building estates, mineral royalties, railway shares, and holdings in the Funds meant they had also come to the most profitable terms with the industrializing economy. They were also unusually powerful. With the exception of the years 1783 to 1830, the Whigs had been governing Britain almost continually since the Glorious Revolution, and even after 1832, their prescriptive right to do so remained virtually unchallenged.[4] And they were the very embodiment of glamour and grandeur, high rank and high living. Between 1688 and 1874, dukedoms and marquessates were profligately scattered in their direction. Like Trollope's Duke of Omnium, they seemed born to be Knights of the Garter and Lord-Lieutenants of their county. And their great houses were quite unlike any other, with their black and white marble halls, their painted ceilings, their Roman busts, their magnificent libraries, and 'a certain indefinable air of distinction'. As William Makepeace

96. The Duke of Westminster by Sir John Millais.

Thackeray once put it, the Whigs are our superiors; and that's a fact.'[5]

Underlying (and justifying) all this was a deeply felt sense of historic accomplishment and of dynastic mission. For the Whigs saw themselves as the hereditary champions of civil liberty and religious freedom.[6] At the time of the Glorious Revolution, they had successfully defied royal despotism, and had safeguarded and established the liberties, not just of themselves, but of all British subjects. And in 1832, they had tamed popular agitation even as they supported it, placed the Great Reform Act on the statute book, and thereby ensured ordered change and non-revolutionary progress. Despite their calm assumption of effortless superiority, the Whigs believed that they were on the side of the people. As Lord Hartington explained in 1883, they were 'not the leaders in popular movements',

97. Lord Hartington, later eighth Duke of Devonshire, by F. C.-Gould.

but it had been their self-appointed task, 'to the great advantage of the country, to direct and guide and moderate those popular movements.' As such, the Whigs formed 'a connecting link between the advanced party and those classes which, possessing property, power and influence, are naturally averse to change', with the result that 'the great and beneficial changes, which have been made in the direction of popular reform in this country, have been made not by the shock of revolutionary agitation, but by calm and peaceful processes of constitutional acts.'[7]

In short, they appeared to enjoy the best of both worlds, as the interests of the Whigs and the interest of the nation seemed not only inseparable, but mutually reinforcing. They formed the most 'jobby and exclusive' section of the aristocracy, yet they claimed a rapport with the people denied to most patricians. And as the third quarter of the nineteenth century opened, it seemed as if nothing had yet altered. Between 1875 and 1880, the Liberals were led by the

quintessentially Whig duumvirate of Lord Hartington and Earl
Granville, the one the heir to the many-acred and multi-mansioned
Duke of Devonshire, the other related to most of the great Whig
families in the land.[8] On the eve of the 1880 general election, Lord
Hartington sent a letter of encouragement to G. W. E. Russell, who
was standing for Aylesbury, explaining that 'the names of Russell
and Cavendish have been so long associated together in the political
history of the country that I cannot help feeling something more than
a common interest in your success.'[9] And when Gladstone formed
his second ministry in 1880, the representatives of the great Whig
families once again comprised the largest single group in cabinet, just
as if the Prime Minister 'had been a Grey or a Russell'. As one
contemporary remarked, the Whigs were still very much 'the pith
and marrow of the nation.'[10]

Yet before the 1880s had ended, they had virtually disappeared –
not just from the Liberal party in particular, but in many cases from
public life altogether – as two centuries of Whig tradition was dissolved in little more than a decade, and their 'family party' came to
an abrupt, unhappy, acrimonious and much-publicized end. Quite
correctly, this dramatic development has been described as an 'earth-
quake' in British political history.[11] But it was a veritable cataclysm
in the history of the landed élite. In years to come, other disenchanted and disillusioned patricians would also renounce their
traditional allegiances. But the Whigs were the first and the most
significant apostates of them all: at once the greatest names, and the
greatest losers. As one observer noted in 1886, 'Only a few years
ago, the name [Whig] was a proud boast, a hereditary recollection,
the appanage of a great party; now it is a historical recollection,
recalling colours and cries, buff and blues, Charles James Fox and
Mrs Crewe – pictures and figures from an indistinct and fading
past.' How was it that this 'great historic party' came 'to an end', so
suddenly and so completely?[12]

The difficulty for the Whigs was that although they were the
defenders of liberty, they were not the champions of equality. They
feared democracy as much as they hated despotism. They would 'go
with the people', but 'not to extremes.' And so, as politics in late-
nineteenth-century Britain became increasingly democratic in its
tone and reformist in its preoccupations, they gradually ceased to be
the leaders of progress, and became instead its opponents. In 1866,
Earl Grosvenor and his Cave of Adullamites successfully thwarted
Gladstone's attempt to pass a reform bill, only to find themselves
betrayed by Disraeli, who passed an even more radical measure in
the following year.[13] And the Third Reform Act hit the Whig
magnates especially hard. Its passing had aroused unprecedented

popular clamour against the House of Lords. It abolished nomination boroughs like Calne, Malton, and Tavistock, on which the Whigs had relied to get their relatives into the Commons. And with the borough franchise extended to the counties, hereditary fiefdoms like Argyll and Sutherlandshire could no longer be relied upon. Not surprisingly, the result was that at the 1885 general election, a House of Commons was returned for the first time in which the titled and territorial classes were no longer in the majority.[14]

But it was not just that this portended the end of the Whig political ideal – 'government of the people, for the people, by a patrician class.' It was also that many Whigs believed the Reform Acts had destroyed the oligarchic constitution that had made it possible for them to flourish as responsible and moderate reformers. This was certainly the opinion of the first Duke of Westminster, who as Earl Grosvenor had organized the Adullamite revolt in 1866. 'The Reform Bills of 1832, of 1867, and of 1885', he informed Gladstone, 'have in the main removed the preponderance of electoral power from the aristocracy and from the middle classes, and have placed it in the hands of the masses.'[15] In the old days, the Whigs had been 'in advance of the people', leading them gently and wisely along the path of progress and reform. But now, as Lord Halifax saw it, it was 'public opinion' that would 'direct the course of public men.' And to the Duke of Somerset, it was only too clear what that portended – 'the rivalry of competing parties, seeking popular support' by putting ever more sweeping and sensational programmes before a mass electorate that was gullible and ill-informed.[16]

Inevitably, the result was a political system in which the mob manipulated the magnates, rather than the other way round. To many Whigs, who in this matter were essentially Palmerstonian in their outlook, Gladstone's view and conduct of foreign policy was a case in point. In the late 1870s, they were 'a good deal disgusted' by his populist crusades, against the Bulgarian Atrocities in particular, and 'Beaconsfieldism' in general. His moral fervour, his vulgar demagoguery, and his wilful refusal to take what Hartington called 'the magnanimous and patriotic line', seemed enough 'to drive . . . the Whigs to the side of the Government', and even threatened to 'break up the party.'[17] In January 1878, 'the disposition of many of the moderate Whigs' was 'to support the foreign policy of the government'; in February Lord Fortescue resigned in protest as chairman of the North Devon Liberal Association; and in December he voted for Disraeli over Afghanistan, supported by the Duke of Sutherland and Earl Fitzwilliam. Nor did matters improve when Gladstone returned to power. By 1884, there was widespread hostility from Whigs like Lord Stafford and Albert Grey to his 'dreadful

Egyptian policy'; and in the government, Hartington and North-brook were several times driven to the point of threatening resignation.[18]

But it was not just the security of the state that seemed increasingly threatened by the new politics of democracy: it was also the safety of the church. By definition, the Whigs were not religious enthusiasts, but they were tenaciously attached to the idea of a state church, subordinate to Parliament. Inevitably, many of them looked with misgivings on Gladstone's policy of disestablishing the Irish church, and in 1868, Cleveland, Grafton, Leinster, Somerset, Grey, Lichfield, Minto, Suffolk, and Halifax had joined with the Tories in the Lords in a vain attempt to prevent the complete confiscation of the church's revenues and resources.[19] Then, in the early 1880s, their worst forebodings seemed realized, as Chamberlain and his allies made the disestablishment of the English church a central plank of their radical programme, and campaigned vociferously for it in the general election of 1885. In November of that year, many of the most illustrious Whig peers, including Westminster, Somerset, and Devonshire among the dukes, as well as Grey, Fitzwilliam, and Halifax, felt moved to make public protest, and sent a letter to *The Times*, denouncing the radicals as 'enemies of the church.' As Lord Selborne later explained to Gladstone, 'I regard as illiberal, and not liberal, any promise to support a measure of disestablishment.'[20]

In the same way, the Whigs regarded the growing radical demand for an interventionist state as a threat to the personal liberty that they most highly prized. The Duke of Somerset regretted that 'the practice of modern ministers' was 'to revert to a system of interference tending to control and regulate the whole life and freedom of the subject.' And Lord Hartington denounced 'the interference of the state or of public bodies in the concerns of private individuals.'[21] But it was not just the threat of government intervention in private lives that alarmed the Whigs: it was the threat of government intervention in private *property*. As men who were so ostentatiously the lords of the earth, the Whigs prized property as much as they prized liberty: indeed, they very largely understood the one in terms of the other. Hence the opposition that Dundas, Grey, and Halifax mounted to Gladstone's Ground Game Bill in 1880. And hence Lord Fortescue's bitter attack on what he saw as 'a perfectly wanton little measure of claptrap confiscation', the embodiment of 'interference with local self-government, individual liberty and freedom of contract.'[22]

Underlying this was something that the Whigs regarded as even more sinister, namely the emergence of a new brand of organized, vituperative, predatory, socialistic radicalism, which began with the establishment of the National Liberal Federation in 1877, and reached its peak in the attacks on the House of Lords in 1884, and the 'Un-authorised Programme' of the following year. Men like Dilke, Labouchere, and Chamberlain dismissed the Whigs' claim to be on the side of the people as 'the selfish cant of power and wealth', and despised property as the enemy, not the guardian, of liberty. They regarded the Whigs, not as leaders to be followed, but as 'the real enemies' to be vanquished – closet conservatives and patrician fellow-travellers, who wanted to thwart reform, in the interests of their own class, not promote it, in the interests of the people.[23] They were no longer 'prepared to suit our pace to the heavy, lumbering coach of Whiggism': they wanted to be the leaders, not the lobby-fodder, of late-nineteenth-century Liberalism. And if this meant 'a complete split in the party', and even the expulsion of the Whigs, then so be it. 'I am not certain', Chamberlain noted as early as 1877, 'that this will be altogether a bad thing.' 'The future of Liberalism', he concluded, 'must come from below.'[24]

But in this radical (and, to them, revolutionary) form, Chamberlain's dream was inevitably the Whigs' nightmare. They looked down on his bourgeois origins, resented his personal attacks, were 'repelled' by the attention that Gladstone seemed to pay him during his second administration, and genuinely feared that he might soon capture the Liberal leadership in the aftermath of the Grand Old Man. Not surprisingly, Hartington twice refused to address Chamberlain's National Liberal Federation, because he resented the way it had vulgarized and Americanized British politics, and worried that it might obtain 'the chief control and direction of the Party.'[25] By 1880, the alarmist Duke of Somerset was convinced that this new 'democratic party' intended to 'pull down "the pinnacles of Burleigh and the oriels of Longleat", for the purpose of planting cabbage patches' – a reference to the current radical campaign for allotments. Five years later, even the aloof and imperturbable Lord Hartington feared that 'we are going as fast as we can in the socialist direction.' Indeed, by that time, the only subject on which the Whigs and Radicals agreed was that a split could not be long delayed. As the Duke of Argyll put it, 'The pretended unity of the Liberal Party is nothing but one great imposture.'[26]

These Whig anxieties and forebodings were only intensified when they turned to Ireland. Many of the greatest grandees, such as Lansdowne, Devonshire and Fitzwilliam, owned massive estates there, and they genuinely feared that what was happening in Ireland today was an ominous portent of what would happen in England tomorrow.[27] The Irish church had been disestablished in 1868: how long would it be before the Church of England went the same way? The Land Act of 1881 was but 'the thin end of the wedge', which would 'shatter the whole fabric of landlord-tenant relations by successive blows.' The Liberal government's Irish policy was 'to buy the support of the masses by distributing amongst them the property of their own political opponents' – which was exactly what Chamberlain wanted to do in England. So when Gladstone finally espoused Home Rule, the anger and anxiety of the Whigs knew no bounds. He was the spineless creature of a democratic electorate. Instead of restoring law and order, he had given in to violence and intimidation. Having flirted with Chamberlain, he was now in league with Parnell. If the measure was passed, the landlords would be 'completely ruined'.[28] And in proposing Home Rule, he was not only breaking the Union, but was threatening the integrity of the British Empire as a whole.

For all these reasons, the prevailing Whig feeling by the early 1880s was one of 'desolation, foreboding, apprehension and regret', which was only further intensified by the agricultural depression, the fall in rentals, and the collapse of land prices.[29] In retrospect, these fears may seem exaggerated. The three Reform Acts had not in fact brought mass democracy. The Church of England had not yet been disestablished. The working classes were not obsessed with an interventionist state. Gladstone was not really a radical, and Chamberlain's influence over him and power in the Liberal party were probably overrated. Moreover, many Whigs possessed ample sources of non-agricultural income. And their litany of grievances – national decline, too much democracy, the threat to religion, the dangers of socialism – was to be repeated *ad nauseam* by every disenchanted patrician group until the Second World War. Nevertheless, they were basically correct in their recognition that the Whig world, that 'wonderful combination of public order and personal liberty', was indeed coming to an end. And the fact that their apprehension was shared by other Liberal patricians such as Lord Selborne and the Duke of Argyll, who were Peelite rather than Whig in their antecedents, only makes the point even more emphatically.[30]

It was against this gloomy background that the secessions from the Liberal party actually took place during the last quarter of the nineteenth century. Different Whigs resigned at different times and on different issues: but the trend was both clear and cumulative. There had been a trickle of defections since the 1830s, but the first intimations of something more serious came in the late 1860s, when the Adullamite revolt over Gladstone's Reform Bill was followed by the formidable Whig protest against the terms of Irish church disestablishment. Significantly, too, Bedford, Devonshire, and Sutherland had given nothing to the Liberal election fund in 1868. In the early 1870s, there was conspicuous opposition to the Ballot Act, and between 1876 and 1878, many Whigs made plain their irritation with Gladstone's attitude to the Eastern Question.[31] Hartington several times considered resigning the Liberal leadership in the Commons, and he was not alone in fearing a split in the party. There was a widespread feeling among the Whigs that the general election of 1880 had unleashed radical forces beyond the new government's power to control, and the fact that Gladstone, rather than Hartington, eventually became Prime Minister, did not bode well for Whiggery's future prospects.[32]

Predictably, they became more anxious and more intransigent during the years 1880–5. Although numerically formidable in cabinet, the Whig ministers were easily overborne by Gladstone, and greatly resented what they saw as Chamberlain's 'audacity and want of political honour.' The old men in the Lords – the Duke of Somerset, the Marquess of Lansdowne, and Lord Halifax – were also much put out, and in the Commons, Albert Grey began to organize a group called the 'Young Whigs' in opposition to the administration's more radical proposals.[33] And when the government introduced its Irish Compensation for Disturbance Bill, 'the first visible rift in the imposing façade of the great Liberal Party' took place. In June 1880, Lord Lansdowne resigned as Under-Secretary for India, citing his 'position as an Irish landlord' as the reason, and only with difficulty was the Duke of Argyll ('I wish and long to be out') persuaded to stay.[34] In the Commons, the measure was opposed by Albert Grey, Charles and Henry Fitzwilliam, the heirs of Sutherland and Portman, and relatives of Lords Zetland and Durham. And in the upper house, the measure was thrown out by 282 votes to 51, as 60 Whigs revolted, including the Dukes of Grafton, Sutherland, and Somerset, and Lords Lansdowne, Durham, and Fortescue.[35]

By the end of the year, there was widespread talk of Whig secession, and a group of grandees, including Somerset, Bedford, and Fitzwilliam, seriously considered withdrawing their support from the government and moving to the cross-benches. In 1881, the pace quickened still further, as the Duke of Argyll finally resigned over the Irish Land Bill, and the Duke of Westminster felt unable to support the measure in its final stages in the Lords, but gave illness as his reason for non-attendance.[36] Shortly after, Lords Zetland and Listowel relinquished their appointments in the royal household, and the Duke of Bedford threatened to withdraw his wife as Mistress of the Robes. Later that year, Lord Granville was warned that 'if your future legislation follows the extreme lines of the Irish Land Bill, you will separate yourselves from names . . . which were the props of the Great Reform Bill: Somerset, Bedford, Cleveland, Grafton, Sutherland, Zetland, Fortescue, Lansdowne, Argyll, Dacre, Grey, Leicester, Suffolk.' And this prediction was born out at the North Riding by-election of January 1882, when Lord Zetland seceded from the party, and Lord Grey and the Duke of Cleveland publicly supported the Conservative candidate in what was later described, with only slight exaggeration, as 'the first great secession of the Whigs.'[37]

As John Bateman noted in his final (1883) edition of *The Great Landowners*, there were by this time 'numerous (and somewhat late) secessions of Whigs who cannot stomach recent Radical legislation', and it was widely rumoured that the Dukes of Somerset and Sutherland were now Tories in all but name. In April 1882, Lord Cowper resigned as Lord-Lieutenant of Ireland, in protest against the government's release of Irish political prisoners, and a year later, made his feelings publicly and abundantly plain. 'I am not much in favour of democracy', he wrote, 'and I particularly dislike the feeling that we are doing anything very rapidly.'[38] In December 1884, the Duke of Bedford informed Gladstone that his 'long continued . . . almost blind support' must come to an end, since he felt 'the disruption of our institutions' was proceeding 'too fast for the welfare of the country.' Early in 1885, Lords Suffolk and Monteagle refused offices in the royal household, and at the general election held later that year, the Duke of Westminster conspicuously abstained from endorsing the Liberal candidate at Chester, Lord Wenlock refused to support the party in Yorkshire because he had 'been much exercised' by 'certain of Mr Chamberlain's speeches', and at Peterborough and Rotherham, John and Henry Fitzwilliam stood as Independent Liberals – with Conservative support.[39]

In fact, most of the Whig dukes had deserted Gladstone well before he took up Home Rule: Norfolk, Sutherland, Bedford, Hamilton, Portland, Newcastle, Somerset, and Argyll. Of the two who remained, Westminster's conduct at Chester made plain the way his views were tending, and Devonshire's could be gauged from the fact that Hartington had publicly and emphatically rejected Home Rule as early as August 1885.[40] Indeed, Lord Southesk spoke for most of the Whig peerage when he told Gladstone at this time that he could not remain loyal to a party that attacked the church and the land, and that threatened to be 'the socialistic government of no distant future.' 'It is', he concluded, 'at least easier to support those who sympathies are with the landed class than those who are avowedly hostile.' So, when Gladstone espoused Home Rule itself, it merely confirmed the Whigs' worse forebodings. As Wilfrid Scawen Blunt put it, they were 'maddened with the thought of losing property in Ireland.' 'Hartington . . .', he predicted, 'will go with them, for he has great possessions.'[41] And so, indeed, he did. He would not serve in Gladstone's new government, and nor would Argyll, Selborne, Northbrook, or Derby. At the same time, the Duke of Westminster declined to be Master of the Horse, and the Duchess of St Albans refused to be Mistress of the Robes.[42]

In the spring of 1886 – when the detailed terms of the Home Rule Bill became known – there was another round of patrician defections, as Lords Cork, Methuen, Suffield, and Kenmare resigned their household appointments. On 14 April, Lords Cowper, Salisbury, and Hartington appeared together on the same platform at Her Majesty's Theatre, to speak in support of the Union, and on 10 May, Hartington himself moved the rejection of Home Rule in the Commons.[43] Truly, this was the parting of the ways. The Liberal John Brunner denounced the 'swells', the 'men of great rank, great inheritance', who opposed Home Rule because they were 'galled to the quick by the idea that they shall be governed by men of the people.' And at the general election held later that year, the Whig defectors exerted themselves mightily against what they saw as the iniquities of 'Irish separation . . . and illogical and insincere tamperings with socialist doctrine.'[44] The Duke of Westminster put his portrait of Gladstone up for sale, and threw his weight (and his wealth) firmly behind the Conservative candidate at Chester. As Gladstone noted with some asperity, in a letter published in *The Times*, 'You have interfered on this occasion, for the Tory, in a manner, and with a warmth, never I believe used by you in support of your political friends.'[45]

Although most patricians duly seceded from the Liberal party, there were some significant and – to Gladstone – very welcome exceptions. Ripon, Harcourt, and Carrington were more radical than most Whigs. Spencer believed, after his spell as Lord-Lieutenant, that there was no other solution for Ireland. And Granville – with some reluctance – stayed out of loyalty to his leader.[46] Even within the same family, different branches might take opposite views. The Duke of Bedford repudiated Gladstone, but his cousin, G. W. E. Russell did not. The Duke of Sutherland did so too, but not so his blood relation, George Leveson-Gower. The Marquess of Lansdowne crossed over, but his younger brother, Lord Edmond Fitzmaurice, stayed loyal, and was later to write Earl Granville's hagiography. Both the Duke of Devonshire and the Marquess of Hartington changed sides, but Lady Frederick Cavendish and Richard Cavendish supported Home Rule.[47] And while Albert Grey rejected his family's reforming tradition, his kinsman Edward Grey – the future Liberal Foreign Secretary – did not. As Alfred Pease later recalled, 'Families were broken up, father and sons ceased to speak to each other, and brothers were at daggers drawn.'[48] But it was usually the heads of families, with the most possessions and the most to lose, who rebelled, and younger sons and cadet branches which did not.

However wide the chasms became between the Whig apostates and the Liberals, it was not at all clear, in the short run, that these patrician renegades would find their permanent home in the Conservative party. Despite their common front on the subject of Home Rule, Whigs and Tories had been hereditary enemies for the best part of two hundred years. Lord Lyndhurst had once described Whiggery as 'a real and selfish aristocracy, under the pretence of liberty . . . an imprudent fraud.' In *Lothair*, Disraeli had mocked the moderate chic pretensions of the great Whig families: 'Liberty depended on land, and the greater the landowners, the greater the liberty of the country.'[49] And the Tory leadership of the early 1880s was not at all sympathetic. A. J. Balfour thought the Whigs were 'lukewarm and slippery' (as well as 'amusing'). Lord Randolph Churchill described them as 'political reptiles'. And Lord Salisbury had never liked them. In 1863, he had condemned them as being 'willing to sacrifice the interests of their class in order to promote the personal ambitions of those who belong to their family connections.' And in his essay 'Disintegration', he was no more enthusiastic: 'The present Whig party', he wrote, 'is a mere survival, kept alive by tradition after the true functions and significance have passed away.'[50]

Nor, initially, were the renegade Whigs eager to enter the ranks of the Tory faithful. They soon established themselves as the Liberal Unionist Party, with their own leaders, their own whips, their own organization, and their own funds, which they retained even after 1895. They held different views from the Conservatives on religion and education, the constitution and the crown, and claimed they were in being to preserve true Liberal principles.[51] In the summer of 1886, and again in the following year, Lord Hartington twice refused to be the Prime Minister of an anti-Home Rule coalition. For the rest of the decade, the Liberal Unionist peers gave only intermittent assistance to the Conservative government, and their leader, Lord Derby, was scarcely on speaking terms with Salisbury and his colleagues.[52] Only in the early nineties did the Unionist peers become more reliable supporters, and it was not until 1895 that Devonshire and Lansdowne finally consented to join the Conservative cabinet. But still the Liberal Unionists retained their separate identity. Not until 1911 were they admitted to the Carlton Club, the Tory inner sanctum – though even then, many still preferred Brooks's. And only in the following year were the two party organizations finally merged.[53]

Even as renegades and outcasts, therefore, the Whigs still retained their own well-developed sense of a special and separate identity.

One reason why Lansdowne refused office in 1886 was that he did not 'like the idea of sitting among the Conservative Peers, so strong was still the old Whig family feeling.' At the end of the decade, that 'family feeling' was in evidence again, as Spencer and Rosebery, Derby and Devonshire, collaborated in an effort to subsidize the impoverished Lord Granville and pay off the substantial debts he left behind – a remarkable post-Home Rule display of 'Whig honour and solidity'.[54] Between 1886 and 1892, there was a tacit alliance between Lords Lansdowne, Dufferin, and Northbrook on the one side, and Lord Kimberley on the other, which made possible the passing of the Indian Councils Act, a Tory measure that nevertheless embodied the classic Whig doctrine of 'timely concession.'[55] And in the early 1900s, when Joseph Chamberlain took up the cause of Tariff Reform, the Duke of Devonshire was in close touch with Earl Spencer on the question of how best to defend Free Trade. Only very slowly were the old social and dynastic links uncoupled, and reforged with the Conservatives. As Harold Macmillan later recalled, 'Whigs retained a sense of something which bound them together which they did not feel towards their Tory friends.'[56]

Nevertheless, when all these qualifications are made, the Whig apostasy was an extraordinary event in the history of the British patrician élite. Simply put, the matter came down to this: when forced to choose between their Liberalism and their landlordism, the majority of Whigs plainly opted for the second alternative.[57] By 1894, when barely forty peers could be mustered to support the second Home Rule Bill, the traditional, landowning Liberal peerage was well on the way to extinction, and support for the party in the upper house was sustained only by the plethora of plutocratic creations in the 1900s. But the full consequences of the Whigs' apostasy were more far-reaching than that. For the landowners' claim to be the governing class of Britain had ultimately depended on the fact that they led both of the major political parties. Whether Whigs or Tories were in power, the aristocracy had always ruled. But after 1886, this soon ceased to be the case. Despite the handful of loyal Whigs who stayed on, the early-twentieth-century Liberal party was overwhelmingly middle (and working) class. And this only weakened the patricians still further: for the way was open for a more virulent strain of anti-landlordism – Lloyd George, Limehouse, the People's Budget, and the Parliament Act.

Nor did the Tory party offer these Whig defectors the succour and support they might reasonably have hoped for. Although Devonshire, Norfolk, and Lansdowne eventually received comfortable billets in the Hotel Cecil, they were among the least influential members of Salisbury's last administration. In a later generation, the

Lansdowne Letter of 1917 merely confirmed the Tories in their belief that, in war or peace, the Whigs had always been 'lukewarm and slippery', while in the Conservative party of Bonar Law, Birkenhead, and Baldwin, there was little room for such obvious anachronisms as the ninth Duke of Devonshire.[58] Nor was this all. For although many patricians shared Lord Southesk's belief that the Tories' 'sympathies are with the landed class', this was not borne out by subsequent events. They may have defended the Union, but they accelerated the dismantling of the Irish landed establishment. They did not repeal death duties, did not restore protection, and by the First World War had abandoned the defence of great estates as being a political liability. In terms of policies, no less than in terms of personnel, the Whigs did not regain in the Tory party the influence they had lost when they left the Liberals. As Reginald Brett had rightly predicted in 1880: 'If the Whigs secede, they will cease to be a factor in politics.'[59]

Almost exactly two hundred years separated the beginning from the end of aristocratic Whiggism, and it had indeed been a wonderful family party while it lasted. They began, in 1688, with a protest against royal extremism; they ended, in 1886, with a protest against democratic extremism. But whereas in the late seventeenth century, the Whigs were successfully swimming with the tide of history, by the late nineteenth, they were vainly struggling against it. The libertarian rebels who had defied the Stuarts on behalf of the 'the people' had become the apprehensive conservatives who feared 'the people' were now going 'to extremes'. By the late nineteenth century, there was no room left in the British political system for moderate reform based on patrician leadership and popular support. In refusing to be hurried, the Whigs had suffered the fate of any social group that cannot adapt to changing times and changing circumstances: they became 'a little hungry, a little selfish, a little narrow', and they found themselves left behind. As Lord Hartington had divined in October 1885, there was now 'nothing for the Whigs to do but to disappear or turn Tories.' Sooner or later, most of them in fact did both.[60]

ii.   The Ditching of the Die-hards

The Whigs may have changed sides, but most stayed within bounds, observed the rules of parliamentary politics, and eventually resigned themselves to insignificance and oblivion. But the next generation of dissident and disaffected patricians were more extreme in their behaviour, and between 1910 and 1914 railed more stridently and more resentfully against their fate. For the die-hards did a great deal more than renounce their moderate traditions and embrace the party of reaction and resistance. Possessed, as Lord Salisbury put it, of 'a catastrophical theory of politics', in which everything was deemed to be getting worse, they were prepared to defy the laws and the legislature of the land, to resort to extra-parliamentary and non-constitutional means, to preach violence and to practise it if needs be, and even to support rebellion and risk civil war, in an attempt to recover their position.[61] Compared with the Whigs, the patrician die-hards were a much more varied group – young and old, rich and poor, Catholic and Protestant. And their emotions were less serene and more intemperate: greater fear, deeper rage, more bitter resentment. But although they protested more loudly, in the end, they did so no more effectively.

In terms of their public careers, most die-hards were relatively insignificant – much less important than the Whig apostates had been only one generation before.[62] Selborne, Salisbury, Norfolk, Plymouth, and Marlborough were all the bearers of famous names, and all held political office during the years of Tory hegemony at the end of the nineteenth century. But they were no more than the messenger-boys of the Hotel Cecil: Selborne at the Admiralty, Salisbury as Lord President, Norfolk as Postmaster-General, Plymouth as First Commissioner of Works, and Marlborough as Paymaster-General. There were the Dukes of Leeds and of Northumberland, whose forebears had long ago been major figures, but whose families had not been politically significant for generations at the national level. There was Earl Fitzwilliam and the Duke of Bedford, whose fathers had been Whig defectors, and who themselves played no part in national politics. Lord Stanmore was a proconsular maid of all work, holding a succession of distant posts from New Brunswick to Mauritius, from New Zealand to Ceylon. Lord Ranfurly governed New Zealand, but never governed anything else, except the Isle of Man. And while Lord Ampthill, as Governor of Madras, briefly served as Acting Viceroy, he was bitterly disappointed that no more permanent promotion came his way after 1906.[63]

These non-illustrious and non-fulfilled careers were too numerous to be explicable purely in terms of individual shortcomings and personal misfortune: they were more broadly indicative of the gradual decline and fall of the patrician ruling class. And the die-hards' awareness of their own political failure was only underscored by a growing sense of financial insecurity and unease. Undeniably, some of them were among the very richest magnates (and the very richest men) in the land: Bedford, Westminster, Norfolk, Fitz-william, and Northumberland were each enjoying incomes of

£100,000 a year or more in the 1900s. But by definition, those with the greatest possessions were also the most vulnerable in what seemed the increasingly predatory climate of the late 1900s: they were among the first to begin disposing of their landed and non-agricultural assets, and investing the proceeds more safely and securely overseas. Among the middling rich die-hards, there was an even greater sense of unease, and there were recognizable signs of patrician distress: the Hardwicke, Churchill, and Southampton estates were sold very early on indeed; Cathcart, Scarbrough and Willoughby de Broke were regularly forced to let their houses; and the Devons, Newcastles, Halifaxes, Londesboroughs, and Lovats seem to have been especially heavily indebted.[64]

Moreover, a disproportionate number of die-hards held landed estates of less than 10,000 acres (33 per cent as against 24 per cent for the peerage as a whole), and these were inevitably the most vulnerable to the economic and political trends of the time. In England, Lord Clarendon owned scarcely 2,000 acres; in Wales Lord Denbigh held less than 3,000; and in Scotland Lord Erroll possessed only 8,000. For patricians such as these, there was an ever-widening gap between their high status and their low income, and the latter inevitably threatened to undermine the former. And an even higher proportion of die-hards held land in Ireland (48 per cent compared with 30 per cent).[65] Some, like Stanhope, Harlech, Leconfield, and Fitzwilliam, owned estates in England as well. But many were primarily Irish landowners: Clanwilliam in Down, Clonbrock in Galway, Leitrim in Donegal, and so on. From the late 1870s, such Irish estates had been the most vulnerable lands in the British Isles. And by the turn of the century, many were in rapid and terminal liquidation. In the 1900s, Wicklow, Ranfurly, Massy, and Meath sold out under the Land Purchase Acts, and in the years immediately before the First World War, they were joined by Erne, Templetown, and de Freyne.

Thus described, the die-hards were essentially an amalgam of disappointed politicians and insignificant public men, the vulnerable rich and the insecure poor. But their growing sense of uncertainty and alienation went deeper than that.[66] For many of them came from the most anachronistic, obscurantist, and recessive sections of the nobility. Compared with the peerage as a whole, a disproportionately large number held titles of genuine antiquity: Erroll, Lovat, Gormanston, and Kinnoul. A disproportionately large number were active in matters of religion: pre-eminent Catholic laymen like Norfolk and Denbigh, and significant Anglo-Catholics like Halifax and Newcastle. And a disproportionately large number were relatively young: men who had been born during the last years of patrician pre-eminence during the late 1860s and early 1870s, but who had then been obliged to adjust to the less spacious age of the late nineteenth century. Fearful and anxious, bitter and resentful, these men 'trembled for the future of their beleaguered interests and positions', and looked to the past with nostalgia and the future with dread.[67]

To many die-hards, their political failings and economic anxieties were easily explained – by their loss of control of the body politic, by the inexorable advance of irresponsible democracy, and by the challenge to entrenched positions of power and wealth that inevitably resulted. Increasingly, they saw themselves as the helpless victims of a predatory, radical, all-powerful proletariat. 'The rule of the middle classes is at an end', lamented the Duke of Westminster in 1912, echoing the words of his grandfather to Gladstone in 1886. 'Democracy has arrived.'[68] The Duke of Northumberland agreed. 'Our ancestors', he noted bitterly, 'were wise enough to keep the political power of the state in the hands of those who had property. We have destroyed their systems, and placed political power in the hands of the multitude, and we must take the consequences.' And Lord Meath had absolutely no doubt as to just what these consequences would be: an all-powerful working class, 'driven to desperation and beguiled by the honeyed words of Socialists and Anarchists', would 'endeavour to improve their lot by the general destruction of society.'[69]

Inevitably, these paranoid patricians concluded that there was a close link between the decline of their class and the decay of the nation. If they were no longer in charge of affairs, was it any wonder that the 'general destruction' – of Britain and its empire – was already well advanced? From 1905, they were convinced that the Liberal governments were wilfully neglecting the nation's defences at a time of growing international tension. The Duke of Somerset was worried by 'the nations around us, armed to the teeth and jealous of our prosperity and freedom.' Lord Denbigh feared that the country might be 'reduced to the two islands on which we live and a few small, isolated colonies.'[70] And their solutions were equally drastic and simplistic. Lord Bristol wanted much larger armies and navies, 'in order that this country might wipe the floor with any nation which had the temerity unnecessarily to come into collision with it', while the Duke of Westminster believed that 'we must either unify the Empire or allow it to disintegrate.' Indeed, many die-hards – including Westminster himself, Bathurst, and Willoughby de Broke – became ardent supporters of Joseph Chamberlain's imperial designs and programme of Tariff Reform, notwithstanding its bourgeois priorities and unsavoury odour of corruption.[71]

Most of the die-hards were more directly concerned with trying to strengthen the nation's defences. In the 1900s, Lord Raglan, the Duke of Somerset, and Lord Willoughby de Broke were presidents, respectively, of the National Service, the Navy, and the Imperial Maritime Leagues. Ampthill, Westminster, Denbigh, Malmesbury, Fitzwilliam, Meath, and Ranfurly were all active in the Navy League. Lord Meath virtually invented Empire Day as an exercise in patriotic consciousness-raising.[72] And Lord Lovat sent his own Lovat Scouts to fight in the Boer War. Not surprisingly, a disproportionately large number of the die-hards had undertaken military service: 72.3 per cent, compared with 43.4 per cent of the rest of the peerage.[73] In their writing and in their speeches, they delighted in metaphors drawn from the battle or the hunting field. It was taken for granted that in a national emergency, the call of duty would not go unanswered, and unwillingness to fight was regarded as the supreme crime, deserving the ultimate punishment. When the Duke of Bedford's son, the pacifist Hastings, refused to enter the army, his father tried unsuccessfully to disinherit him, and kept him out of Woburn for twenty years.[74]

Two decades on from Gladstone's espousal of Home Rule, these gloomy grandees felt an even greater sense of anxiety and apocalypse than that experienced by the Whigs in the mid-1880s, Wherever they turned, they saw their own order in crisis, the nation's defences neglected, democracy rampant, and radicalism on the warpath. To Lord Malmesbury, the links were clear: 'Socialism, narcotic like', had 'drugged the spirit of patriotism into forced slumber', and was thus 'destroying our national defences and warping the strength of the nation.'[75] Lord Meath feared a 'single omnipotent popular assembly', which would result in 'widespread misery, or even shaking, if not destroying, the foundation of the social fabric.' In 1903, Lord Halifax thought that 'we are on the eve of great changes... There is a movement of unrest and expectation on all sides. The foundations are being shaken everywhere.' And Lord Selborne agreed. 'The social system', he contended, 'is out of joint', and it was the peers' duty 'to save the Constitution from immediate overthrow.'[76] Under these circumstances, the Liberal victory of 1906 merely reinforced their sense of gloom and doom. But this could not have been turned into active and significant opposition without an issue and a leader. The Parliament Act provided the one; Lord Willoughby de Broke provided the other.[77]

In his circumstances and in his career, Greville Verney, nineteenth Lord Willoughby de Broke, perfectly epitomized the attributes and anxieties of the die-hards, whose movement he was to create and lead in 1910. His family was the holder of one of the most ancient

98. Lord Willoughby de Broke by L. Ward.

baronies in England, and owned 18,000 acres, most of them in Warwickshire. His forebears were staunch, though not assertive Tories, who devoted their efforts to provincial, rather than metropolitan, activity, especially fox-hunting and estate management. The future nineteenth baron was born in 1869, and so grew up during the last decade of serenity that the landed establishment enjoyed, a time when, as he later recalled, there was 'peace and plenty, and the patriarchal system as it was known to my grandfather could still be carried on.' Always, thereafter, Willoughby was to look back to these golden days of patrician childhood, which he regarded nostalgically as a more simple, more spacious, and more benevolent age, when landowners presided responsibly over their great estates, when 'the bond of love between master and man' was real and abiding, when sport provided a sense of fellowship and 'a certain standard of kindliness and good conduct', and when life was ordered, static, safe, and secure.[78]

But the sudden shattering of this idyllic world, in the 1880s, when Willoughby was at his most impressionable age, scarred him for life. The agricultural depression hit the family hard, the estate became overburdened with mortgages and family charges, and Compton Verney had to be let. The Third Reform Act meant that 'parliamentary elections ceased to be a choice between a Whig and a Tory landlord; the squire was opposed by the radical . . . out to demolish the existing order.'[79] And with the extension of the franchise to the agricultural labourer, 'leaflets, pamphlets and all the other horrors of that terrible thing called propaganda were brought into full play.' Even worse, Compton Verney was too close for comfort to nearby Birmingham, a town that was the very embodiment of radicalism, democracy, industrialization, and urban sprawl – in short of those many and varied forces that were threatening to overwhelm the landed orders. And in Joseph Chamberlain, it boasted the foremost radical of his generation. In his memoirs, Willoughby was later to recall an early speech of Chamberlain's, likening the landowners to 'drones in the hive', which, he remembered, 'made for pretty reading in the *Birmingham Daily Gazette* at the family breakfast table.'[80]

These were the formative influences on Willoughby de Broke's life, to which should be added a brief spell as a Warwickshire MP from 1895 to 1900, and a passionate attachment to fox-hunting and military activity. Like all die-hards, he was convinced that the world of his youth was better than the world of his maturity; he regretted both 'class warfare' and the 'devastating worry of modern life'; and he was much concerned by the threat of mass democracy, urban growth, and agricultural depression. He hated the new, plutocratic rich, because of their lack of responsibility, and because of their non-paternal attitude to labour: they 'had not been brought up in and do not understand, the old English traditions between employers and employed.'[81] He condemned the Tory party, which under Balfour's leadership had turned away from true Tory principles, and had been corrupted by 'years of huckstering, wire-pulling and opportunism'. And he resolutely defended the ideal of hereditary landownership and feudal obligations, especially as embodied in the House of Lords itself – 'a very ancient fabric, gradually knitted together through the ages . . . I am prepared to defend the hereditary principle . . . whether that principle is applied to peers . . . or to foxhounds.'[82]

On inheriting the family estates unexpectedly early in 1902, Willoughby did not anticipate launching a political career, and looked forward to following in the family tradition of devotion to local affairs, estate management, and fox-hunting. But the mounting threats to the landed interest compelled him to take a hand. He attacked Haldane's proposals to restructure the army, and enthusiastically advocated Tariff Reform. In 1907, he spoke in the Lords against Lord Newton's scheme for reforming the upper house.[83] In the aftermath of the People's Budget, he denounced Lloyd George, and began to form a close friendship with Leo Maxse of the *National Review*. And he soon began to feel dissatisfied with Balfour's vacillating and indecisive conduct: 'If our present leaders do not take care', he noted in August 1910, 'a middle party of Tories who mean business will smash them.' 'Our only hope', he later observed, in characteristically violent and doom-laden language, 'is to fight like blazes against enemies within and without.' And it was to that end that, in October 1910, he and Henry Page Croft founded the Reveille group, 'to rouse the Unionist party without forsaking Unionist principles.'[84]

But it was only in the aftermath of the second general election of 1910 that Willoughby emerged into the national limelight, as the Conservative leadership failed to stand up to the Liberal threat to the House of Lords posed by the Parliament Bill. Even before the official line was decided on, he took preliminary steps, in mid-June 1911, to 'recruit those peers' who would 'fight to the end, even if the leadership counsel surrender.' On 12 July, thirty-one nobles met Lord Halsbury, including Somerset, Bedford, Northumberland, Sutherland, Salisbury, Amherst, Ampthill, Bateman, Raglan, and Willoughby himself, determined to urge Lansdowne not to give way, or to organize their own defiance if he did.[85] By 20 July, thanks to further lobbying by Willoughby, eighty Unionist peers met at Grosvenor House, pledged not to surrender, regardless of what their leadership decided. The next day, in the light of the Liberal threat to create sufficient peers, the party leaders decided to give way. But the patrician rebels remained unmoved. A committee was set up, with Halsbury as chairman, and with Willoughby and F. E. Smith as joint secretaries; lobbying and propaganda were put into a higher gear; and the Duke of Westminster provided a room in Grosvenor house 'to whip from'.[86]

From the die-hards, as much as for the Liberal government, the upper house thus took on a potent symbolic value. But whereas to the Liberals it was the barrier to democratic reform that must be removed at all costs, to the die-hards it was the last line of patrician defence against a mischievous, predatory, and irresponsible government, which must on no account be surrendered. Lord Bathurst believed it was 'the best possible house which could be devised by human beings as a second chamber for this country', and that any attempt to alter it was *ipso facto* wrong. According to the Duke of Northumberland, the Lords represented 'the property, the wealth of the country – that property which it is necessary to preserve, and which . . . the tendency of all democracies is to attack, and which the end of all democracies is to annihilate.' In short, the Liberal assault on the upper house was but the inevitable result of the onward march of malevolent democracy. All that lay between the nation and mob rule was the restraining hand of the Lords. And so, if the powers of the second chamber were curtailed, the result would be 'the uncontrolled autocracy of the House of Commons.'[87]

To the die-hards, therefore, it was the Liberal proposals to emasculate the upper house that were, quite literally, revolutionary. And under these circumstances, they argued, it was better to oppose them – whatever the cost – than timidly to acquiesce in their own destruction. As the Duke of Somerset put it, if the Lords gave way, the 'country now has a perfect right to say – you are a useless lot of cowards, for God's sake shut up your house and go.' Lord Stanmore was even more emphatic: 'Revolutionary attempts', he thundered, 'can only be effectively met by strong measures and strong men.' Lord Stanhope agreed. Since it was the government that wanted revolution, they must be made 'to carry that revolution by revolutionary methods, and no other.'[88] And there was a further argument. For if the Lords supinely surrendered their powers, how and when would they ever get them back? As Willoughby himself put it, 'The present powers of the House of Lords will be far more difficult to recover if they are surrendered than if they are taken away by main force.' Under these circumstances, the die-hards concluded that 'the credit of the peerage' could not be 'as much injured by the number of new peers which may be created, as it would be degraded by our failure to be faithful to our trust.'[89]

Clearly, by mid-July 1911, the die-hard peers had worked themselves into a state of great excitement, in which they genuinely believed that they were the last line of resistance against an irresponsible and revolutionary government and a feeble and incompetent opposition leadership. On 25 July, a circular was sent out to all peers, signed by Halsbury, Selborne, Salisbury, Mayo, Lovat, and Willoughby, urging implacable opposition to the Parliament Bill and demanding another general election. Further lobbying took place, organized by Ebury, Bathurst, Ampthill, Saltoun, and Rothes, who reported in turn to Willoughby. Finally, and with the outcome genuinely unknown, the Lords debated the Parliament Bill for the last time on 9–10 August. Salisbury and Ampthill were sceptical of the Liberal threat to create sufficient new peers to force the measure through; Bedford and Marlborough thought it real, but did not mind; Northumberland expressed regret that the Lords had given way in 1832, and urged that this should not be repeated. And Willoughby himself poured scorn on the notion of a popular mandate, arguing that it was in fact 'tyrannical' to use it to pass 'extraordinary legislation': 'You may claim majorities if you like in favour of the Parliament Bill at a dozen general elections, but that will not alter my view.'[90]

Eventually, the die-hards mustered the votes of 112 peers and 2 bishops. Twelve nobles who had promised support did not in the end provide it, including the Dukes of Abercorn and Sutherland; but the vote of the Duke of Norfolk was an unexpected extra. Nevertheless, the measure duly passed into law, the powers of the Lords were irrevocably diminished, the revolution that some had feared had indeed come about, and the last bastion of landed power was successfully breached. Democracy had triumphed: it was the apocalypse now. The die-hards response was predictable: bitterness at the weakness of the official Tory leadership, anger at their colleagues who had actually voted for the measure, and an enraged and disappointed sense of defeat. Lord Grey, on returning from his term as Governor-General of Canada, came 'back to this country after seven years of absence to find the constitution overthrown and Jack Cade securely established on the throne.' Lord Selborne agreed: 'There is no more a House of Commons than a House of Lords. There is nothing but the Cabinet, subject to the continuous but slight check of the crown and a violent but occasional check of the electors.'[91]

In the immediate aftermath of defeat, Willoughby's inclination was to form a new party, 'a separate organisation with its own programme.' 'Most people', he told Selborne in August 1911, 'want a new party. They simply won't work for Balfour and Lansdowne again. I won't.' And Northumberland took the same view, urging Willoughby to 'keep together men who are prepared to fight questions to the bitter end', and adding his own condemnation of Balfour and Lansdowne: 'If my leaders assent to those principles, and act upon them, I will be loyal to them; but if they won't, I have no hesitation about taking a line of my own.'[92] Eventually, Willoughby was dissuaded from so drastic a step. Selborne urged that a new party would be 'impossible to carry out successfully', and argued instead that the die-hards should try to 'capture the party and the Unionist machine, lock, stock and barrel.' And Lord Lovat urged that the 'No surrender' group should operate from within the Tory ranks, thereby strengthening 'the influence which our party could bring on the front bench.' The result was that in October 1911, the die-hards set up the Halsbury Club to formulate what Willoughby himself described as a 'militant policy'.[93]

Moreover, by this time, Willoughby had already begun to reassert the die-hard position by his collaboration in Leo Maxse's 'Balfour Must Go' campaign. This was begun by Maxse in January 1911, and in August, in the aftermath of the Parliament Act, Willoughby began to co-ordinate the drive against both Tory leaders in the upper house, on the grounds that neither Balfour nor Lansdowne 'can ever lead the party again to victory.' He himself wrote letters and articles urging that the party must return to traditional Toryism, and he championed Austen Chamberlain – largely because of his record on Tariff Reform – as the new leader. Other die-hards, like Leconfield, Bathurst, Stanhope, and Somerset, all lobbied against the leadership, and the Duke of Bedford refused to 'have anything to do' with a scheduled Liberal Unionist meeting at Bedford in October 1911, at which Lansdowne was to be the principal speaker.[94] Partly because of such patrician pressure, Balfour resigned in November. And, even though Bonar Law was not the die-hards' first choice as his successor, his more vigorous and intransigent opposition so encouraged them that they abandoned the Reveille group as a gesture of confidence in his more aggressive leadership.

But it was over Ireland that the die-hard opposition to the Liberals, and also to their own party leadership, flared up again most violently and rebelliously. For the passing of the Parliament Act removed the last certain safeguard against Home Rule being successfully carried. Once Asquith introduced the third Home Rule Bill in 1912, it soon became clear that there were only two, equally terrible alternatives: either Home Rule would be carried for the whole of Ireland, including Ulster, which must be coerced into agreement if necessary; or Ulster would be excepted, but the southern Unionists would be abandoned to their fate. For Willoughby and his friends, neither of these dreadful alternatives was acceptable, and between 1912 and 1914, he organized die-hard resistance, both inside and outside Parliament. And he did so with even less respect for the conventions of public life than he had shown in opposing the Parliament Bill. In July 1911, when that crisis was at its height, he had told Halsbury, 'we have used every weapon save personal violence. I should not be averse to using even that.'[95] Now, in this later and greater confrontation, his aversion was even less.

For the Home Rule crisis seemed to realize all the most deeply rooted fears of the paranoid patricians: the ultimate, complete, and final abandonment of the Irish landowners to their fate at the hands of the nationalists; the cowardly and supine surrender to the hostile forces of Irish nationalism; the beginning of the breakup of the British Empire; and the threat that an independent Ireland might be a strategic liability in any future war. As Willoughby summed it up in July 1913, 'we do not propose to allow on our most vulnerable flank a separate existence to a nation whose very leaders have constantly declared war upon this country.' Under these dire circumstances, violence was indeed a legitimate recourse. As early as July 1911, when it was clear that Home Rule might become a reality, Lord Farnham warned that it might 'end in plunging a part of the United Kingdom into a state of turmoil, strife and bloodshed, if not indeed an actual state of Civil War.' And in January 1913, speaking for the die-hards, he warned that 'we shall use to our utmost the time that is at our disposal in preparing for eventualities which might occur should they attempt to force this bill upon us.'[96]

Accordingly, in March 1913, Willoughby set up the British League for the Support of Ulster and the Union, 'to arm all Unionists on this side of the water who wish to fight with the Ulstermen.' It openly accepted the possibility of a recourse to illegal military force; it was supported by 100 peers and 120 MPs, including Bedford, Beaufort, Castlereagh, Lewisham, and Lord Charles Beresford; and by November 1913 it boasted 10,000 drilled volunteers.[97] The threat of violence was unmistakable. As Willoughby announced in the Lords in July 1913, he and his supporters would prefer the matter of Irish Home Rule to be subjected to the electorate before any final measure was proposed. But, he went on, 'if that means of settlement is denied to us, then we must fall back on the only other means at our disposal.' And he made it plain what those 'other means' were. He and his friends, he explained, had 'instituted a league' for the defence of Ulster and the Union, the address of which was 'curiously enough, next door to a gunmaker's shop.' The innuendo could hardly have been plainer.[98]

By this time, some landowners in Ulster were themselves very actively involved in unlawful behaviour.[99] In 1913, both Lord Leitrim and Lord Farnham ran guns from England to Donegal for the Ulster Volunteers, the latter using his own yacht, and employing his chauffeur to pick up the cargo. And although the importation of weapons was banned in December 1913, it still continued under patrician auspices. In April 1914, Lord Massereene—assisted by Lords Templeton and Dunleath – mounted a large operation to secure the landing of 11,000 rifles at Larne in South Antrim, which involved the cordoning off of the whole district. English patricians played a part, too. Lord Winterton was in favour of direct action, and advertised in the newspapers for men 'of courage and determination' to 'undertake a desperate task', namely to fight in Ireland if needs be. And in January 1914, the Duchess of Somerset wrote to Carson in these frenzied words: 'This is to assure you of our unfailing support... The day that the first shot is fired in Ireland... the Duke and I will both come over to give all the help we can.'[100]

Meanwhile, Willoughby's policy was to increase popular pressure, and to step up his campaign of parliamentary obstruction. In January 1914, he brought in Milner and Leopold Amery to revitalize the British League, to widen its basis of popular support and to give it a higher profile. Three months later, the result was an announcement, in the press, of the establishment of the British Covenant in support of Ulster, which was signed by twenty illustrious persons, including Desborough, Halifax, Lovat, and Portland. Its purpose was to obtain as much British support as possible for the campaign against Home Rule, and by the end of March, some six hundred signatures were published in the press, including eighty landowners, such as the Duke of Sutherland, and Lords Lonsdale, Manvers, Bath, and Harewood.[101] And, although they did not sign, Westminster, Salisbury, Devonshire, Bedford, Walter Long, Londonderry, and Norfolk were also active in support. By the outbreak of the First World War, some two million signatures had been obtained. As David Spring rightly notes, such patrician bellicosity in defence of Ulster can be described only as 'aristocratic resistance to duly constituted government.' At one point, it was even rumoured that Willoughby was going to lead a cavalry charge up Whitehall, burst into the Commons, and kidnap Asquith.[102]

At the same time, Willoughby also sought to delay the passage of Home Rule legislation in Parliament itself. In February 1914, in collaboration with Ampthill, Arran, and Stanhope, he circulated all peers, asking them to pledge themselves to oppose compromise on the Home Rule question, and urging that no irrevocable step should be taken until after the electorate had been consulted. The result was that the Tory leadership – much to its annoyance – felt obliged to propose amendments to the King's speech early in the session. 'Whoo-hoop!', exclaimed Stanhope. 'Really the fourth party have done pretty well for the first attempt.'[103] But it was a pyrrhic victory. In May, Asquith introduced his amending bill, allowing for the temporary exclusion of Ulster, and when it reached the Lords, the Unionist leadership allowed it to pass its second reading. Defiant to the last, Willoughby introduced an amendment, urging the rejection of the bill and opposing the exclusion of Ulster and of Home Rule in any form. But it was overwhelmingly defeated by 273 votes to 10. In effect, the die-hard revolt ended there. As Selborne later admitted to Salisbury, 'we ran away, and the government trampled on us.'[104]

Why, in defending the Lords and the Union, did the die-hards achieve so little? In part, this was because they were compelled to work in uneasy collaboration with many of those 'middle-class monsters' who, in other ways, they found quite unacceptable – men like Leo Maxse, F. E. Smith, Leopold Amery, Sir Edward Carson, and Lord Milner.[105] Indeed, it is arguable that it was with these full-time politicians, rather than the patricians, that the real power and initiative effectively lay. Maxse ran the campaign against Balfour's leadership, and Milner led the defence of the Lords and the Union, with a degree of energy and commitment that Willoughby and his titled friends could never have provided. And as these social differences suggest, there was also a real divergence of political outlook between these groups. Milner, Chamberlain, and their friends believed in government by a managerial, technocratic, middle-class élite, and were ultimately scornful of Parliament, parties, and democracy. Yet however intransigent, violent, and alienated they seemed, Willoughby and his patrician die-hards never really shared this centrist and anti-democratic outlook. Their collaboration was never more than a temporary alliance.

But in addition, Willoughby's die-hards never amounted to more than a minority of the landed establishment – one-sixth of the peerage at the very most. For all their passion and propaganda, they conspicuously failed to persuade the majority of patricians to follow their lead. And even those who were prepared to support Willoughby over one issue were not always prepared to stand with him on another. The Cecils agreed with him about the decline in religion, the threat of corruption, and the need to retain a strong House of Lords. But although they were also opposed to Home Rule, they were not prepared to countenance extreme violence, and they much resented the intrusion of such unsympathetic (and middle-class) figures as Maxse and Milner.[106] As Lord Hugh Cecil explained in 1915: 'I disagree vehemently with [their] principles...I hate nationalism, and I value personal liberty.' Put another way, the die-hards were never more than marginal figures, inhabiting the fringes of the political world while the real and important decisions were made elsewhere. And the failure of their efforts to take the centre by storm only made them more outcast still.[107].

For all their extravagant language and threats of violence, the die-hards ultimately lacked the ruthless determination, and the messianic vision, of which successful extremists are made. They were too loyal to the Tory party ever to break with it, and more eager to protect the House of Lords than to undermine the constitution. Unlike successful revolts from the right, they lacked any real creative vision: they knew what they wanted to obstruct, but it was far harder to devise a positive programme for the Reveille Group or the Halsbury Club.[108] Even Willoughby once admitted 'I don't quite know what I do want.' And for all his violent language, he himself was no would-be dictator. He was popular, even with his opponents; he was often able to poke fun at himself; and he was always, as a *Vanity Fair* cartoon had described him in 1905, 'An MFH with a sense of humour'. A man who could write these wry words was not the stuff of which tyrants are made: 'To be sent comfortably to sleep while your teeth are being pulled or your leg is being cut off is at least some compensation for the loss of the pocket boroughs.'[109]

By 1920, when the Lords debated the Government of Ireland Bill once more, only Willoughby and Lord Farnham raised the tattered banner of die-hard protest, and Curzon, no doubt remembering the years of 1910–11, took deadly and devastating revenge:

> He still remains a magnificent relic of the old guard, but the backwoods in which my noble friend ranged at the head of a formidable band some years ago are now relatively deserted, and his picturesque figure is seen stalking, consoled only by Lord Farnham, amid the scenes that were once those of his adventures and his triumphs.[110]

For there were neither adventures nor triumphs left, only sadness and humiliation. In 1921, Willoughby was obliged to sell Compton Verney to a plutocrat further tainted with a Lloyd George peerage: Joseph Watson, a soap-boiler manufacturer, who was created Lord Manton of Compton Verney three months later.[111] He began writing his elegiac autobiography, *The Passing Years*, which was less bitter than his own feelings, and which was to conclude with an appeal to the new owners of the countryside to restore the old relations he had known between masters and men. But he died in 1923 when only fifty-one, with his life story as unfinished as his life's work had been unsuccessful, having made a great deal of sound and fury, but knowing only too well that, ultimately, it had signified nothing.

iii. Labour Aristocrats

When Baron Frank Pakenham went to Buckingham Palace in 1945 on taking up his appointment as Lord-in-Waiting, the conversation with his sovereign did not flow easily. And it was not just on account of the King's stutter. 'Tell me', George VI is reputed to have asked, 'why did you . . . join them.'[112] By 'them' he meant the Labour party, of which Pakenham had been a member for more than a decade. To the King, as to most aristocrats, joining the Labour party was the supreme apostasy, the ultimate act of class treachery. For the Whigs to abandon their Liberal traditions, and for the die-hards to flirt with armed insurrection was one thing, but to become a socialist was quite another. After all, neither the Whigs nor the die-hards – so the argument ran – were seeking to undermine their class or their

99. (Left) Charles
Stewart Parnell.
(Below) Avondale,
Co. Wicklow.

country. On the contrary, they were trying to revive the one and defend the other. But socialists were pledged to destroy property and hierarchy, and their patriotism was always thought to be suspect. And patricians who embraced the cause of Irish nationalism – whether of the constitutionalist or more revolutionary variety – seemed, if anything, even more disloyal. But in both cases, their reasons for embracing these alien creeds were more complex than their detractors allowed – or than they themselves would readily admit. For while they renounced a part of their aristocratic inheritance and allegiance, they never completely abandoned either.

This was classically illustrated by the fact that the foremost champion of Irish Home Rule, Charles Stewart Parnell, never fully reconciled himself to thoroughgoing land reform.[113] After all, he was himself a Wicklow country gentlemen, with a 4,000-acre estate at Avondale. He was related to many county families, like the Howards, the Powerscourts, and the Carysforts; several of his ancestors had been elected as Wicklow MPs; he was himself a JP and served as High Sheriff in 1874–5; and in his early years, he was much involved in the hunting, shooting, and cricket of local society. He adored his ancestral acres, and sought to make them more profitable by extensive investment in mining, quarrying, and timber ventures. He was a just and popular owner, who gave generous rent abatements, and was much liked by his tenantry. And he was very strongly conscious of his ancestry and identity as one of the Protestant gentry. Yet throughout his controversial political career, he was taunted – with much justice – as 'a pariah', 'a renegade to his own class', who 'ought to be shot for stirring up the country against the landlords.'[114]

Part of the explanation for Parnell's heretical opinions on Home Rule lies in the influence of his family: his great grandfather, his grandfather, and his American mother all espoused views that were, by the standards of the time, both radical and unconventional, such as opposition to the Union and support for Catholic Emancipation.[115] But it was also true that Parnell had much less to lose than did many landowners who were more comfortably off. When he took up residence in the late 1860s, the Avondale estate was producing only £2,000 a year, of which over half was earmarked for servicing a debt of £18,500 and for paying annuities. By 1882, his finances were so precarious that he announced his intention of selling the estate altogether, and even the £37,000 subscribed in response as the National Tribute brought only temporary relief. The mining and timber ventures took more in investment than they generated in income; towards the end of his life, he was forced to begin selling off the estate to the tenants; and at his death in 1891 he left debts of

£50,000.[116] Not surprisingly, there was about Parnell an element of almost wilful self-destruction: it was relatively easy to side with the nationalists against the ascendancy when landlordism had proved so unprofitable in his own case, and when the demise of his own estate was itself only a matter of time.

Parnell was not alone in being an Irish landowner who turned his back on his class, even as he retained a lingering affection for them: we have already encountered Nugent and Esmonde, those two Catholic baronets, who also sat as nationalist MPs. But by the 1900s, several marginal patricians had repudiated both the parliamentary party and its constitutionalist methods, and had embraced a more extreme form of Irish nationalism. The most famous was Constance, Countess Markiewicz, whose father was Henry Gore-Booth of Lissadell, County Sligo. She was a classic child of the ascendancy, and counted the Scarbroughs, Dunravens, Zetlands, Carlisles, and Westminsters among her relatives.[117] But in 1903, her brother Sir Josselyn, who had by then inherited the family estates, sold off 30,000 acres to his tenants under the new Land Purchase Act. Meanwhile, Constance had married a Polish count and, after a conventional introduction to Dublin viceregal society, had begun to move sharply to the left under the influence of James Connolly, the Marxist trade-union leader. By 1909, she had founded a paramilitary movement for boys, had indulged in unsuccessful experiments in utopian self-help, and sat on the council of Sinn Fein. In 1911, she joined in the protests against the state visit of the King and Queen to Dublin, and by 1913 she was a member of the Citizen Army.[118]

Even more disloyal and unconstitutional was the Howth gun-running incident, just before the outbreak of the First World War, when a group of Anglo-Irish gentry brought arms and ammunition from Germany for the Irish Volunteers, which was later to be used in the Easter Rising of 1916.[119] The chairman of the London organizing committee was Alice Stopford-Green, a descendant of the Earls of Courtown. One of the yachts was provided by Erskine Childers, a British civil servant whose mother was a Barton of Glendalough in County Wicklow, the place where he himself had been brought up, and which he regarded as his home. And the second was provided by Conor O'Brien, the cousin of Mary Spring-Rice, who was herself a member of the crew, and the daughter of Lord Monteagle.[120] (At the very same time, her cousin, Cecil Spring-Rice, was serving his country in a very different capacity as the British Ambassador in Washington.) When Mary died in 1924, she was buried at the ancestral home in Foynes, but the IRA provided the guard of honour. And their illegal escapade furnished the exact mirror-image of Willoughby de Broke and the Ulster gun-runners: patricians in revolt against established authority, but this time from the left rather than the right.

During the First World War itself, these ascendancy renegades became even more active in the cause of revolutionary nationalism. Countess Markiewicz was second in command of the party that occupied St Stephen's Green at the time of the Easter Rising: she was caught, imprisoned, and sentenced to death, but this was commuted on grounds of her sex, and she was subsequently released. In 1918, she became the first woman elected to the British House of Commons, but she did not take her seat, partly because she was a member of Sinn Fein, and partly because she was in prison at the time. In the following year, she became Minister of Labour in de Valera's provisional government.[121] At the same time, both Erskine Childers and his cousin Robert Barton joined Sinn Fein, and they, too, became members of the Dáil (Barton, appropriately, for Wicklow) and initially supported the provisional government. But the Irish Treaty divided these patrician renegades as much as it divided the Irish people: Barton and Stopford-Green accepted it, and thereafter played almost no part in public life; Childers repudiated it, and was hunted down and shot on the orders of the Cosgrave government; and the Countess also seceded from the Dáil, dying in appropriately eccentric poverty in 1926.[122]

These patrician crusaders in the nationalist cause were very much on the edge of the ascendancy world: minor gentry, younger sons and daughters, more distant relatives of peers. Childers was possessed of an almost apocalyptic sense of class disintegration: he knew the world of Glendalough was falling apart, and seemed perversely and self-destructively determined to help it on its way. (Ironically it was at Glendalough that he was finally arrested.)[123] And the Countess, who was always too intemperate and simplistic for her own good, became almost dementedly outspoken against her class in the debates on the Irish Treaty, damning them as a 'small minority of traitors and oppressors', who did not merit representation in an Irish Senate. Not surprisingly, her brother, Sir Josselyn, had separated from her in 1917, and Lord Powerscourt was so outraged by her disloyalty that he thought she should be shot. When she was given the Freedom of Sligo by Sinn Fein, the Gore-Booths naturally stayed away, and the Countess accommodated herself in a local hotel. 'I suppose', she admitted, 'it is very embarrassing to have a relative that gets into jail and fights in revolutions that you are not in sympathy with.'[124]

But just as the Whigs failed to regain in the Tory party the influence they had lost among the Liberals, so these ascendancy

renegades, having rejected their own class, were also distrusted by
the very nationalists they so ardently (and naïvely) aspired to lead. In
an effort to identify themselves more closely with the Irish people,
Childers and Stopford-Green actually moved from London to
Dublin, but this did not bring them any closer to the nationalists.
Many suspected that Childers was a British secret agent, and during
the debates on the Irish Treaty, Griffith taunted him with being a
'damned Englishman.'[125] Nor did the Countess fare any better. Part
of her (but not all of her) desperately wanted to be accepted as an
ordinary Irish citizen of the republic. She tried (in vain) to learn
Gaelic, and became a Roman Catholic. But people like Sean O'Casey
could neither forgive nor forget the fact that she had been born at
Lissadell. She may have been loved by the poor of Dublin, but she
was never fully accepted by the Sinn Fein high command. For her, as
for the others, the fate that awaited them was the loneliness of the
déclassé and the oblivion of the self-destructive. As Professor Lyons
rightly observed, most died early and unhappily.[126]

Yet as their Irish critics noticed, they retained many of their
ascendancy attitudes to the very end. The Countess hated the
'moneyed classes', was visited by the Duchess of Bedford while
imprisoned in Aylesbury jail, and in the debates on the Irish Treaty,
stung Collins with the patrician taunt that he was a mere country boy
too fond of power.[127] And Alice Stopford-Green hated the 'piracy
and grabbing' of imperialism and the Boer War, despised Ulster
Unionism because it was too middle class and because there was no
'society' in Belfast, and when the Lloyd George coalition took
power, remarked disparagingly that 'the suburbs have surpassed
themselves.' Neither Lord Salisbury nor Lord Crawford could have
put it better. As Beatrice Webb perceptively remarked, these people
possessed both 'the good and evil qualities of aristocracy.' On the
one hand, there was the 'ready sympathy of the person who has the
leisure and the means to be considerate' towards those of a lower
social station. But on the other, they lacked the 'sincerity, persis-
tency [and] dogged faithfulness' necessary for the real revolutionary.
Nowhere was the fate of the renegade patrician more poignantly
revealed than in Ireland.[128]

In England, they were equally derided, and ultimately no more
influential. But because they were welcomed into a Labour party
conspicuously short on talent, fate dealt with them more kindly on
the whole. As with the ascendancy nationalists in Ireland, the left-
wing notables of the inter-war years traced their origins back to the
late nineteenth and early twentieth centuries. For while the Whigs
and the die-hards were moving towards the right, two very different
patricians were heading in the opposite direction. The first was

100. (Above) Wilfrid Scawen Blunt in Arabian dress, painted by his wife. (Below) Crabbet Park near Crawley.

Wilfrid Scawen Blunt. He was descended from a long line of Sussex squires, and adored obsessively the family estate of Crabbet Park, with its 4,000 acres, which he inherited in 1872. He numbered the Mayos and Wyndhams among his relatives (he was actually born at Petworth), and his wife was not only Byron's granddaughter, but also a peeress in her own right. At different times, Blunt included Gladstone, A. J. Balfour, and both Lord Randolph and Winston Churchill among his friends. He was a firm believer in the sanctity and autonomy of landed property, and he was deeply distressed that he produced no male heir: for as he once explained, 'the Crabbet estate is to me what any kingdom is to a king, a matter of duty more than any sentiment.'[129]

Yet Blunt was no ordinary patrician, but a man in passionate and notorious revolt against the creeds and conventions of his class. Twice in his life, he was branded a social outcast for making public and political use of private conversations, once with Lord Lytton at Simla, and once with Arthur Balfour at Clouds. He acquired an obsessive attachment to the middle east, learned Arabic, established an Arabian stud, and to some degree went native.[130] Even by the relatively lax standards of the time, his endless love affairs were notorious; he treated his long-suffering wife extremely badly; and he was ultimately estranged from his daughter as well. In the mid-1880s, he stood successively but unsuccessfully for Parliament as a Tory Democrat, as a Liberal Home Ruler, and finally as an Anti-Coercionist. He vehemently opposed British imperialism in Egypt, India, and Ireland, and was sent to prison for taking part in a riot in Galway in 1887. By the end of his life, he had become a supporter of Sinn Fein, and was moving rapidly in the direction of Keir Hardie, Lord Parmoor, Ramsay Macdonald, the Fabians, and the Labour movement. As he once admitted, 'I am not a party man.'

But this rebellious and rootless behaviour ultimately derived from highly commonplace patrician attitudes, namely a visceral hostility to the new and alien world of democratic politics and plutocratic finance, and a deep resentment at the consequent decline of his class.[131] His own landed resources were decidedly limited, his finances were often chaotic, he spent too extensively on houses and horses, and by the end of his life, part of the Crabbet estate had been sold. He hated the middle classes, regarded W. H. Smith and Evelyn Baring as 'grocers', Queen Victoria as 'bourgeois', and Lloyd George as a 'contemptible little dog.' He vehemently disapproved of the Jameson Raid, the Marconi Scandal, the popular press, and the very idea of party politics. And it was largely because he believed that the government's Egyptian policy was controlled by 'selfish financiers' and 'greedy Jews', and that the Irish landowners were in debt to 'the same unscrupulous gang of financiers, property holders, mortgage companies and speculators', that he supported the nationalist movements in each country. Like many landowners, his real enemy was 'the infamous capitalist system': but in Blunt's case, his exceptionally ardent and passionate nature, combined with his increasingly insecure position on the lower margin of the landed establishment, drove him to express his outraged sense of patrician decency by moving to the left rather than the right.

Whereas Blunt's unconventional behaviour and left-wing opinions provoked scorn and outrage, the socialist self-advertisement of the indebted, déclassé Countess of Warwick merely gave rise to derision and incredulity. Although a one-time friend of Cecil Rhodes, she became violently opposed to the Boer War, and thereafter moved rapidly to the left. She met H. M. Hyndman in 1904, and joined the Social Democratic Federation in the same year.[132] She campaigned vociferously for Labour in the 1906 election; she boycotted the opening of Parliament in the following year; and she appointed a socialist vicar at Thaxted in 1910. In 1912, she co-edited a book entitled Socialism and the Great State with H. G. Wells, and in 1917 she gave her support to the Bolshevik Revolution. In 1923, she contested the Warwick and Leamington seat, seeking to win for Labour the constituency she had once dominated as a chatelaine, and standing against the young Anthony Eden, the Conservative candidate to whom she was actually related. And in later life, she offered her home, Easton Lodge, to the Labour party and the TUC, in the vain hope that it might become a centre for the study of socialism.

At each stage in her radical career, Lady Warwick invariably appeared ridiculous or hypocritical or both. Many believed, not just that she was a traitor to her class, but also that she only espoused these inappropriate opinions because she was bored, spoiled, and needed new excitement. After all, she had inherited 13,000 acres in Essex, yet advocated the breakup of estates; she was a peeress of the realm, who wanted the House of Lords abolished; and she was a patron of four Essex livings, but wanted the Church of England disestablished and disendowed. Despite her left-wing views, her way of life remained essentially aristocratic, she often travelled in special trains to Labour party meetings, and in February 1905, she held an eve of session dinner at Warwick House for trade-union and socialist MPs. It was an incongruous occasion: she wore pearls; her guests were greeted by the butler; they later sang the Red Flag. Understandably, Labour leaders regarded her as a liability: she claimed she had sold all her jewels for the party, but in fact had donated only £500; the election at Warwick was a farce, not least because her husband and his relatives openly backed Eden; and neither the party nor the TUC was prepared to accept Easton.[133]

101. Lord Noel-Buxton.

But at a deeper level, it is important to remember that from the 1900s, Lady Warwick's world was in a state of chaotic collapse, with her debts, her ghosted books, and her disastrous lecture tours. In that context, her espousal of socialism was just another part of her family's much-publicized decline. She was certainly no political asset for Labour, so it was hardly surprising that in its early years, the party remained almost entirely proletarian and middle class in membership. But by the 1920s, there had been a significant influx of the landed and the titled: the second Earl Russell and his younger brother Bertrand; the two brothers Noel and C. R. Buxton; Oswald Mosley and his wife Cynthia; Lord de la Warr, Lord Parmoor, Arthur Ponsonby, and C. P. Trevelyan.[134] Unlike Lady Warwick, most of these were valuable and experienced recruits to what was still a fledgling political party: Ponsonby had been private secretary to Campbell-Bannerman; Parmoor was chairman of Buckingham County Council and a famous lawyer; Mosley was talked of as a future Prime Minister and his wife was Curzon's daughter; Bertrand Russell was one of the cleverest men of his generation; the Buxtons were high-minded members of a famous family; and Trevelyan had held government office immediately before the outbreak of the war.

Between them, they provided the respectable genteel tone to Macdonald's two inter-war administrations. Why did they do it?

102. Lord Ponsonby by William
Rothenstein.

Why did they cause their families pain and embarrassment, incur
derision as traitors to their class who had changed sides in social war,
and embrace a party whose avowed aims were totally at variance
with the most fundamental presuppositions of traditional territorial
society? The most obvious – and critical – explanation was that they
were motivated by blatant, naked opportunism. As the truncated
careers of Grey, Beauchamp, and Crewe showed, there was no
future for patricians, or for anyone else, in the Liberal party. And in a
Conservative party dominated by the middle classes, the aristocratic
element was distinctly subordinate. But Labour was short of talent,
and so the opportunities for the experienced, the able, and the well
connected were correspondingly greater. As the contemporary jibe
had it, there was more chance of promotion in a line regiment than in
the household cavalry. As Lady St Aubry remarks in Amabel
Williams-Ellis's novel *The Walls of Glass* apropos of one such upper-
class renegade, his motive was 'vanity': 'he thought there would be
less competition.'[135]

But there was probably more to it than that. For most of these
early patrician recruits to Labour came from families whose

103. Sir Charles
Trevelyan by
William
Rothenstein.

finances – like the Irish ascendancy renegades, and like Lady Warwick herself – were especially vulnerable during the half-century
from the 1880s. Lord de la Warr's father had felt compelled to take
ornamental directorships, and his reputation had been much damaged by the revelations in the Hooley bankruptcy case. The second
Earl Russell owned no land, was conspicuously unsuccessful in his
City career, was involved in expensive divorces, and died bankrupt;
while his younger brother, Bertrand, was compelled to live by his
pen and his lecture tours in the inter-war years. Lord Parmoor's
family were only recently established as fully-fledged country gentry, and the income from the small estate had to be augmented by
legal earnings. Oswald Mosley's father sold the ancestral acres at
Rolleston, leaving his son and heir completely uprooted. And Arthur
Ponsonby was a landless notable, who in 1912 had written a book
significantly entitled *The Decline of Aristocracy*.

In short, most of these patricians had inherited rather less of the
world than they might have expected: to that extent, they had more
in common with Lady Warwick than they might have cared to
admit. But unlike her, they were also genuinely decent and high-

minded. The Buxtons, Trevelyan, and Parmoor came from families renowned for religion, radicalism, or pacifism, and Bertrand Russell espoused some of the same opinions. And most of them shared the landowner's conventional concerns about the dangers of corruption and irresponsible wealth.[136] The Buxtons and Trevelyan were guilty about their own money, and critical of other people's, while Ponsonby's description of the evils of plutocracy could not have been bettered by Lord Salisbury:

> The manipulating of interests, the juggling of the money market, the mania for speculation, the creation of false money standards, the international syndicates of financial adventures to which governments have become a prey, the control of the press, the ostentatious benevolence of millionaires, and the brutalising effect of the pursuit of wealth.[137]

But how might this evil best be fought? Not from within the Liberal party, since it was already dying. Nor from among the Conservatives, since the plutocrats were already in power. Only Labour remained, both hostile to wealth and uncontaminated by it.

The process by which these notables made their way into the Labour party certainly suggests that these considerations were important. C. P. Trevelyan and the two Buxtons were radical Liberals, who fell out with the party in 1914 because of its attitude to the First World War. They soon became major figures in the pacifist Union of Democratic Control, where they were later joined by Bertrand Russell, Lord Parmoor, and Arthur Ponsonby.[138] From there to membership of the Labour party was but a short step, which all had accomplished by the early 1920s. Thereafter, they stood for a proper and pacific foreign policy not dictated by the armaments manufacturers, and for a just and benevolent domestic policy, not dictated by the plutocrats. Significantly, Trevelyan, Parmoor, Ponsonby, and the Buxtons were inter-related, were good friends, and worked closely together.[139] In a real sense, they were to the Labour party what the Salisbury clan were to the Tories: highminded, austere, prim, and slightly smug. Unlike the Cecils, they were gentry rather than grandees, and their links with middle-class evangelicals meant they were more ridden with guilt than the *habitués* of Hatfield. But the parallel is close.

It is close in another way, too: for like the later Cecils, the early genteel recruits to the Labour party leant more tone than substance to its inter-war history. They provided a respectable façade, and a guarantee of respectability. But their influence on policy and in government was decidedly limited. In terms of their political weight, they were essentially insubstantial figures. And this was even more true of those who joined slightly later. Lt. Col. Cecil L'Estrange Malone was a cousin of the Countess Markiewicz, but was himself better endowed with lineage than with land.[140] He served in naval aviation during the First World War and was elected to Parliament in 1918 as a Liberal. He visited Russia in the following year, and made such strongly pro-Soviet speeches thereafter that he was prosecuted under the Defence of the Realm Act, forfeited his seat and the OBE he had won in the war, and was sentenced to six months in prison. Thereafter, he joined the Labour party, re-entered Parliament at a by-election in 1928, and in 1931 was parliamentary private secretary to the Minister of Pensions. He was also a strong supporter of the Irish nationalists, and the Countess was very proud of him.

The Hon J. M. Kenworthy, later Lord Strabolgi, was another marginal notable who in time became a marginal socialist. The family barony dated back to 1318. But it was in abeyance from 1788 to 1916 (when his father's claim to it was established); and by then, there was no land left.[141] Kenworthy's early career was spent in the navy; he became a Fabian in 1917 and a friend of G. D. H. Cole and Sidney Webb; he supported the workers against their employers during the First World War; and he was elected as a non-coalition Liberal MP in 1918. He soon established a reputation as a pugnacious and combative 'advanced radical'; he was strongly in favour of non-intervention in Russia; and in the aftermath of the General Strike, he joined the Labour party. His autobiography – written after his defeat in 1931 and his inheritance in 1933 – was a veritable laundry list of patrician disdain: of plutocrats, big business, and war profiteers; of the Lloyd George coalition, the 1919 House of Commons, and the sale of honours. Significantly, too, he numbered among his friends such high-minded aristocrats as Lord Henry Bentinck, Lord Irwin, Lords Hugh and Robert Cecil, and Oswald Mosley.[142]

In the 1930s, the genteel defections to the left (and sometimes, now, the far left) continued. Stafford Cripps joined the Labour party at the beginning of the decade, and Frank Pakenham at the end.[143] Esmond Romilly ran away from Wellington College, dabbled with Communism, and fought in the Spanish Civil War. John Strachey became the foremost Communist writer in the thirties, and Anthony Blunt was recruited for the party at Cambridge.[144] All were marginal patricians. Cripps was a younger son of Lord Parmoor, and Pakenham was heir to the Irish earldom of Longford. Romilly's family was ancient and well connected (Churchill was a cousin), but they owned almost no land. Strachey was heir to a baronetcy and the family estate in Somerset, but was disinherited by his uncle when he took up Communism. And Blunt was a homosexual agnostic, whose second cousin was Wilfrid Scawen himself. Yet as with the Irish renegades, their aristocratic attitudes still emerged. In 1935, when John Strachey was preaching Communism on a lecture tour of the United States, he was arrested and threatened with deportation. Asked to name a relative, he grandly replied: 'My uncle is Lord Strachie, of Sutton Court, Chew Magna, Somerset, England.' The US government promptly abandoned its proceedings.[145]

In the case of Christopher Isherwood, the rejection was more complete, so much so that he refused, publicly, to acknowledge his patrician lineage until 1971, always claiming that his family were merely 'successful farmers'.[146] Yet in fact, they were classic decaying gentry. The Bradshaw-Isherwoods were a Cheshire landed family, established since the seventeenth century at Marple Hall and at Wyberslegh nearby. But by the time of Christopher's childhood, in the 1900s, the family was in irreversible decline. The suburbs of Manchester were encroaching on the estate; the family finances were precarious and chaotic; and the squire was no longer a forceful or significant figure in local affairs. Christopher's grandfather John, who was the head of the family, was incapacitated by a stroke. His own father, Frank, was killed at Ypres in 1915. His mother Kathleen possessed an altogether exaggerated sense of her own and the family's status, itself an unconscious sign of their decline. And, since his uncle Henry was homosexual, it was confidently expected that Christopher himself would ultimately inherit the estate.[147]

Against this background, Christopher took 'the Isherwood snobbery and inverted it'.[148] As a young man, he rebelled against the customs and constraints of upper-class life. In the twenties, he failed to complete his studies at Cambridge, and fared no better at medical school in London. He embraced homosexuality and agnosticism at least partly to upset and provoke his mother. In the thirties, he lived a bohemian life in Berlin where, in opposition to Fascism, he became a 'life-long, left-wing liberal'; he published a book entitled *The Memorial*, which caused great offence, because of its graphic (and ostensibly fictitious) picture of his family as textbook declining gentry; and with W. H. Auden he left Europe for America, pacifism, and safety just before the outbreak of war. In 1940, on the death of his uncle Henry, Christopher duly inherited Marple, but waived his rights in favour of his younger brother Richard. When he obtained United States citizenship in 1946, he dropped the 'Bradshaw' part of his name in an act of deliberate renunciation. And in 1959, Marple itself, which had been unoccupied by the family since John's death in 1924, was demolished, and replaced by suburban development and a grammar school. For Christopher, the result was 'wonderfully joyful . . . the lifting of a curse.'[149]

Writing in his autobiography in the 1930s, Lord Strabolgi observed that 'we have accomplished a silent revolution in England since 1914. A whole class, the landed aristocracy, has been wiped out . . . The country gentry have gone.'[150] That was, no doubt, overstating the case. But it catches well the prevailing sense of genteel disenchantment and disorientation. Like Jason Cavendish, there were many aristocrats with tarnished silver spoons, who had lost their bearings, and who deliberately rejected what they saw as a crumbling inheritance, only to embrace an equally uncertain and often equally self-destructive alternative. As such, they formed a significant section of the old élite in decline. But, among those patricians who acted out of character, this leftward lurch was not the only – nor even the majority – response. For, as Nancy Mitford has one of her characters say in *Pigeon Pie*: 'Aristocrats are inclined to prefer Nazis, while Jews prefer Bolsheviks.' And she herself had good reason to know.[151]

iv.   Extremism In Extremis

The final version of D. H. Lawrence's character, Clifford Chatterley, may well be modelled on Osbert Sitwell, that self-appointed scourge of the philistines and middle classes. Throughout his life, Sitwell hated democracy, the press, and the politicians with icy, patrician disdain. As a young man, his financial resources were regrettably meagre, his political ambitions were completely thwarted, and he was in many ways far more typical of his class than he would ever have supposed. In a brilliantly perceptive paragraph, Lawrence described Chatterley thus:

> He was at his ease in the narrow 'great world', that is, landed aristocracy society, but he was shy and nervous of all that other big world which consists of the vast hordes of the middle and lower classes and foreigners. If the truth must be told, he was just a little bit frightened of middle and lower class humanity, and of foreigners not of his own class. He was, in some paralysing way, conscious of his own defencelessness, though he had all the defence of privilege. Which is curious, but a phenomenon of our day.[152]

Whether this is Osbert Sitwell or not, it perfectly captures the anxiety and alienation that he and so many inter-war patricians undeniably felt. And their response was to be so violent that it made even the die-hards look moderate by comparison.

For if aristocratic government had been undermined by a poisonous combination of plutocratic corruption and mass democracy, and if constitutional means of defence had been tried and failed, then it clearly followed that something more drastic was required to retrieve the situation. During the war and its immediate aftermath, there were signs of aristocratic flirtation with more extreme right-wing organizations, especially on the part of the surviving die-hards. There was Henry Page Croft's National Party, supported by Lords Ampthill, Beresford, Egmont, Northesk, and Strathspey, which was opposed to Lloyd George, corruption, trade unions, socialists, profiteers, and aliens.[153] There was the Duke of Northumberland, who founded *The Patriot*, full of lurid rhetoric against the Jewish-cum-Bolshevik threat to western civilization and the British Empire. And there were the British Fascists, established in 1923, who boasted Lord Garvagh as their first president, the Earl of Glasgow and Lord Ernest Hamilton on the central committee, and Earl Temple of Stowe, Lord de Clifford, and Baroness Zouche among their members.[154] Amost without exception, these were among the most obscure and obscurantist notables, and all of them held opinions that were a bitter amalgam of paranoia and disenchantment.

But by the late 1920s and early 1930s, there had developed in Britain a more widespread disillusionment with democracy, and an enthusiasm for continental authoritarianism, which was of particular appeal to those declining and embittered landowners who hated politicians and plutocrats because they were bad for their class – and therefore bad for the country, too. When Methuen published an ostensibly light-hearted series entitled *If I Were Dictator*, the jokes turned out to be very serious indeed. Lord Raglan's volume claimed that 'the training necessary to turn a man into a front-bench politician makes him unfit to hold any executive office', and went on to argue that politicians were too busy talking to govern the country properly.[155] And many patricians genuinely believed this. In his Romanes Lecture at Oxford in 1930, Winston Churchill claimed that Parliament could no longer deal with economic problems, and that an alternative structure of executive government was needed. And younger men like Oliver Stanley, J. T. C. Moore-Brabazon, and Archibald Sinclair were equally concerned about the decay of democracy and the inadequacies of the established party leaders, and even talked of a fascist coup.[156]

Among lightweight landowners, such views were widely current at the time. Sir Henry Fairfax-Lucy was a broad-acred baronet, and a county councillor for Warwick and Roxburgh, who had twice failed to get elected as a Tory MP. In 1933, he publicly advocated a 'drastic reform in parliamentary government', which he claimed had been 'killed by universal suffrage', and argued that what was needed was a system of indirect election, which would eliminate 'the evils' of unfettered democracy. And, he concluded, 'whether we call this system Fascist or Corporative', was really neither here nor there.[157] The young Lord Knebworth was equally disenchanted with democracy and hankered after authoritarian action. What was needed was 'a man, and a drive and a policy', a 'militarist, Fascist, autocratic tyrant', who would throw out the old, discredited politicians, and get the country moving again.[158] The young Osbert Sitwell shared these feelings to the full. Alienated from his parents, forced to survive on an inadequate allowance, and disappointed and humiliated in his parliamentary ambitions, he embraced with ardent enthusiasm the ideal of the man of action, the superman, as represented by d'Annunzio, whom he had met and admired at Fiume. In a series of articles in the *Sunday Referee*, he railed against 'democratic claptrap', and overtly praised Mussolini as 'a great benefactor to his country.'[159]

For many disaffected patricians, this outward admiration of fascism was made easier because it seemed as if the regimes of such dictators were merely recreating in a national setting the benevolent paternalism of the landed estate. Viscount Lymington, another disillusioned parliamentarian, greatly admired Hitler and Mussolini for this very reason, and his description of Horthy's regime in Hungary is especially revealing: 'As a dictator, he was the nearest thing in my recollection to a larger English landlord . . . One felt instantly at home with a type of man one had always known.'[160] And the déclassé Duke of Manchester concluded his autobiography by espousing very similar sentiments. He had greatly admired Porfirio Diaz, 'the Mussolini of Mexico who built a civilised state out of anarchy'; he believed Britain was in decline because it had become 'a prey to its politicians'; he regretted the advent of democracy and the passing of great, disinterested statesmen; he urged the temporary suspension of Parliament and of petty, partisan squabbling; and he advocated the appointment of a strong man who would govern the country in the national interest and on the model of a great estate – perhaps Lord Derby, perhaps Winston Churchill.[161]

These were some of the commonplace ideas circulating among déclassé and marginal aristocrats during the twenties and thirties. And, in such a context, the nature and appeal of Mosley's Fascism are both readily understandable. As Robert Skidelsky has so brilliantly demonstrated, the key to Mosley was that 'he was an aristocrat in politics, fulfilling the old function of his family in a wider sphere and under different conditions.' His ancestors were ancient but obscure country landowners, with 4,000 acres in Staffordshire which in the 1880s yielded £10,000 a year. They had been rebuffed by the citizens of Manchester in 1846, to whom they had grudgingly sold out their market rights for £200,000, and thereafter they had retreated to their Rolleston estate, a self-contained feudal enclave, where they effectively pretended that the nineteenth century, *laissez-faire*, and the bourgeoisie did not exist. It was in this artificial world of carefully studied hierarchy, a closed and charmed circle of reciprocal rights and duties, free of class conflict or capitalistic exploitation, that the young Mosley was brought up. But in 1920, it vanished for ever, as the estate was sold, broken up, and given over to suburban development for Greater Manchester.[162]

Inevitably, Mosley found this 'a terrible uprooting, causing me much sorrow at the time', and throughout his political life, a landed estate like Rolleston was as much the model for him as it was for the Duke of Manchester or Viscount Lymington.[163] Like many from his background, he sought to re-create the world he had lost, partly to avenge a class defeat, and partly because he genuinely believed that the country would be better governed in this way. His aim was a classless, consensual society, in which people were cared for, but did what they were told. He hated liberalism, capitalism, *laissez-faire*, and the cash nexus; he despised plutocrats, press lords, corruption, and the middle class; and he had no time for democracy, for socialism, or for the mob. He loathed politicians, the caucus, and the party machine, and wanted to turn Parliament from a talking shop into a workshop. And he reserved especial disapproval for those members of his own class who had given up and given in. He spelt all this out plainly in the *Morning Post* as early as 1928:

> Feudalism worked in its crude and equitable fashion until the coming of the industrial age. Today the feudal tradition and its adherents are broken as a political power, and in most cases are ignobly lending their prestige and their abilities to the support of the predatory plutocracy which has gained complete control of the Conservative Party. In modern times, the old regime is confronted by two alternatives. The first is to serve the new world in a great attempt to bring order out of chaos and beauty out of squalor. The other alternative is to become flunkeys of the bourgeoisie. It is a matter of constant surprise and regret that many of my class have chosen the latter course.[164]

The Cecils themselves could not have put it better: here is perfectly encapsulated that sense of alienation from a triumphant plutocracy which so many patricians felt so deeply at this time. But in Mosley's case, this rootlessness in society inevitably led to rootlessness in politics: for where among the conventional parties might a man of such views and such vigour feel comfortable? He began as a high-minded Tory, and made appropriately patrician friends with men like Mark Sykes and Billy Ormsby-Gore. In the company of Lord Henry Bentinck, he withdrew his support from the Lloyd George coalition, and crossed the floor. He was much influenced in his thinking by Lord Robert Cecil, who was godfather to his first child. He moved to Labour, and deliberately contested seats in Birmingham as an attack on the vile and bourgeois Chamberlains. His memorandum on unemployment was a plea for interventionist government and national self-sufficiency: the landed estate writ large. And when it was rejected by his Labour colleagues, there were no conventional avenues left, and his disillusion with the parliamentary process was complete. Hence the New Party, the British Union of Fascists, and everything else that followed.[165]

In short, Mosley's Fascism was deeply rooted in his own rootless experiences as a landed gentlemen, and essentially articulated in more strident terms what many similar people had been thinking and saying since the early 1920s. At one time or another, there was little to distinguish his views from Lord Robert Cecil or the Duke of Manchester. The means might ultimately be extremely violent; but the ideas Mosley took up, and the policies he proposed, were very commonplace indeed. So it is hardly surprising that the BUF appealed to other marginal and alienated aristocrats. The Sitwells offered Renishaw as a venue for BUF rallies, and even considered writing a BUF anthem to be set to music by Sousa.[166] Mosley's chief of staff was Ian Hope-Dundas, whose father was twenty-sixth Chief of Dundas, an illustrious but diminished family. Lord Erroll, whom we have already met as the Casanova of Happy Valley, was the BUF's 'delegate from Kenya'. And other supporters included Lords Strathspey and Tollemache, Viscountess Downe, who had been involved in the earlier Fascist movements of the 1920s, and Lady Pearson, herself the sister of Henry Page Croft.[167]

Even if the violence and extremism of Mosley's BUF ultimately became unacceptable, the disillusionment with democracy and the allure of authoritarianism lingered long into the 1930s for many members of the old élite. In 1935, Captain George Lane-Fox Pitt-Rivers stood for North Dorset as an 'Independent Agriculturalist', on an anti-Bolshevik programme that would have gladdened the Duke of Northumberland. The Anglo-German Fellowship included many ardent and patrician pro-Germans, such as Lords Londonderry, Mount Temple, and Lothian. Londonderry was particularly besotted with Hitler, as was his wife: they both saw him as the ideal man of action who might save his country and be an example to the world.[168] And there were clearly many other aristocrats who shared these views. Here is Lady Eleanor Cecil, writing in 1936: 'Nearly all my relatives are diehards and tender to Mussolini (not so much lately) and to the Nazis, and idiotic about "Communism", which to them means everything not approved by the [Conservative] Central Office.' And here is Jessica Mitford reminiscing in *Hons and Rebels*: 'the words "that feller Hitler" on the lips of countless English squires could be expressed equally in tones of derision or admiration.'[169]

The future twelfth Duke of Bedford, then Lord Tavistock, entertained even more extreme opinions. During the 1930s, he strongly supported the BUF and the Social Credit movement; he was violently opposed to democracy and plutocracy; he hated corruption, capitalism, and big business; and he wanted peace with Germany. Of course, the head of the house of Russell was hardly a marginal aristocrat, in terms of wealth or status. But as his son's autobiography makes abundantly clear, he was indeed an embittered, alienated, and eccentric man.[170] He had quarrelled deeply and irreconcilably with his die-hard father, played only a limited part in public affairs, lived most of his life as a recluse at Woburn, and greatly resented the anti-aristocratic trends of the time. In a revealing passage, almost reminiscent of Willoughby de Broke's elegiac autobiography, he once recalled an earlier and happier time, 'when I was a boy, when parliament and the government, whatever their limitations, contained a fair percentage of members with some of the instincts and principles of gentlemen.'[171] For him, as for others, the world had long since been going to the dogs.

The varied, extreme, and ultimately self-destructive behaviour of the Mitford family illustrates this embittered patrician marginality in a particularly concentrated and poignant way. To suggest that the seven children of the second Lord Redesdale were anything other than *sui generis* may seem intrinsically rather implausible: the Mitford mythology is one of outsized characters and private language; they saw life and the world as one huge joke, 'a sort of extension of childhood naughtiness'; they were simultaneously spoiled and deprived, precocious and naïve; and they were supremely, and mistakenly, confident that they would always come through.[172] But, in fact, as Richard Griffiths has rightly pointed out, 'in their flamboyant way they reflected many of the obscure psychological and political motives which were to afflict certain sections of the British aristocracy.' For all their robust indifference, they were haunted by fear. As Diana later recalled, the burning question of their youth was 'How should we manage to keep alive when we were grown up?'[173] They found varied answers, most of them, 'choices in class abandonment.' Two of the daughters, Pamela and Debo, stayed loyal to their background. Two more, Unity and Diana, embraced Fascism, as did their brother Tom. And Nancy and Jessica moved as far in the

104. (L. to r.) Unity, Diana, and Nancy Mitford.

105. Sir Oswald Mosley.

opposite direction, the one becoming a socialist, the other a communist.

As Diana's question implies, the family background was that of textbook declining gentry. The Mitfords were of ancient lineage, and held estates in the Cotswolds, but the title was relatively recent. The first Lord Redesdale overspent and overbuilt, was frequently obliged to let his houses, wrote a string of books to bring in extra money, and died leaving large debts which could be met only by the sale of some property. The second Lord Redesdale was no more careful.[174] He built houses that he could not afford; he invested unwisely in Canadian gold mines; and he became involved in speculative ventures to make papier mâché wireless cabinets and to recover pirates' treasure, which were unsound and unprofitable. In the twenties and thirties, the land and the houses were inexorably sold off, usually at the wrong time, when the market was depressed; much of the ancestral furniture and most of the family heirlooms also disappeared; and it was often necessary to take refuge in London or abroad. By the 1930s, even Lord Redesdale's children were aware that their world was collapsing around them, and they they would have to make their way in it unaided.[175]

It was against this background – at once so claustrophobic and so

106. Diana Mitford at a 1934 Party Rally.

insecure – that the seven Mitford children reacted so variedly and so violently. Diana was born in 1910, married Bryan Guinness in 1929, but divorced him five years later. She shared the widespread hatred felt by her class for the ineffectual British politicians of the time; she deplored 'the waste of the talents of gifted, inventive and hardworking people under leaders like Macdonald and Baldwin'; and she was ardently searching for a strong, heroic man, who would be good for her and good for the country. She found him in Oswald Mosley ('he was completely sure of himself and of his ideas . . . to change the course of history'), with whom she fell in love in the early thirties, and she became a devoted supporter of his Fascist programme. She went to Germany for the first time in 1933, was a regular visitor thereafter, soon came under Hitler's spell, and thought him 'sweet' and 'beloved'. In 1938, Diana and Mosley were secretly married in Germany: the reception was held at Goebbels' house, and the Führer himself was among the guests.[176]

Diana's younger sister, Unity, espoused these right-wing causes even more flamboyantly. In many ways, she was the most naïve of the Mitfords – which is saying a great deal – and in a fundamental sense, totally unpolitical. She supported Mosley enthusiastically, and later described the notorious and violent BUF rally at Olympia as 'such heaven'. Even Diana later admitted that she 'adopted the whole creed of the National Socialists, including their anti-semitism, with uncritical enthusiasm.'[177] Nancy, less charitably, called her 'Head of bone and heart of stone.' With her great height, her blonde hair, and big blue eyes, she seemed a classic specimen of Aryan womanhood. She greeted the postmistress at Swinbrook with the Nazi salute, met Hitler over one hundred times in the thirties, wore two swastika badges which he gave her, and was rumoured – incorrectly – to be his mistress. She looked upon the Führer and the Nazis as a huge Mitford joke extended to the real world, refused to believe the stories of Nazi crimes and atrocities, and in 1935 she wrote to Der Stürmer 'as a British woman Fascist', declaring that 'I want everybody to know I am a Jew hater. England for the English! Out with the Jews! Heil Hitler!'[178]

Very different – and much more reflective – was the response of her elder sister, Nancy. She had a less naïve and more historically informed sense of aristocratic decline; she was well aware of the contemporary commonplaces about peers and plutocrats; and she poured this into the books she was compelled to write in the thirties in order or earn her living. In 1938 and 1939, she published two edited volumes, based on the family papers of her relatives, the Stanleys of Alderley, who had once been extensive landowners in Cheshire. Both books are introduced with essays of high nostalgia, which evoke and celebrate a 'dead world, past and gone': of peace and certainty, of decency and disinterestedness, when patrician men and women governed both the county and the country in the best possible way.[179] And as such, the works were simultaneously an apologia and a requiem. 'The fortunes of the Stanleys', Nancy concluded, 'continue to be typical of that kind of English family. Alderley, where they lived for five hundred years, sees them no more – the house has been pulled down, and the estate is a dormitory suburb of Manchester.'[180] The fact that a similar fate had overtaken Mosley's Rolleston should hardly need labouring.

Her novels explore these same themes more fully. They may not be great works of fiction, but they are revealing insights into her vivid sense of family and class decline. In particular, they express a hatred of plutocracy that is almost Mosleyite in its fervour. The Pursuit of Love is preoccupied with the difference between the disinterested and dutiful landed gentleman and the irresponsible and unpatriotic capitalist.[181] Uncle Matthew (based on her father) hates Jews and foreigners; he does his bit on the bench and in the Lords; his money is entirely sunk in 'sacred' English land; and if the Germans or any other invader threatens, he will stay and fight them, and never leave. By contrast, the Kroesig family epitomizes all that is worst about plutocracy. They are of foreign descent and make their money in the City; they hold most of their wealth abroad; they do so partly as a precaution in case anything happens to Britain; and they live in Surrey, which they mistakenly suppose to be the country, and where they play at being gentrified landowners. Linda Radlett, who is briefly and unhappily married to Tony Kroesig, comes to revile their 'bourgeois attitude of mind' with almost Cecilian disdain: 'Inwardly their spirit was utterly commercial, everything was seen by them in terms of money.'[182]

But in Nancy's case, regret at landed decline and hatred of the new plutocracy, drove her to the left rather than to the right. She was enraged by her sisters' flirtation with Fascism, and in *Wig on the Green* sent up Unity hilariously as Eugenia Malmains, a new recruit to the cause of Social Unionism, whose leader, 'Our Captain', is 'wise, stern and benevolent.'[183] And Eugenia's speeches brilliantly combine Nancy's feelings with Unity's Fascism: hostility to 'the deadening sway of putrescent democracy'; hatred of 'that debating society of aged and corrupt men called parliament'; concern that 'the great houses of England, one of her most envied attributes, stand empty'; and regret that 'the great families of England herd together in luxury flats and expend their patrimony in the divorce courts.' And there is an almost Wodehousian picture of dotty peers in a lunatic asylum, which again conveys Nancy's despairing sense of belonging to a class in decline. All this was almost pure Mosley. But Nancy's response was very different: she became a socialist, and in 1939 she and her husband Peter Rodd went to Perpignan to help refugees from the Spanish Civil War.[184]

In Jessica's case, the leftward reaction was more violent, and estrangement from her right-wing sisters was correspondingly greater.[185] When her closest sibling, Unity, joined the British Union of Fascists, Jessica retaliated by espousing Communism. While Unity adorned her room with swastikas, Jessica purchased hammer-and-sickle flags instead. She subscribed to the *Daily Worker*, bought Communist literature, and read voraciously. In 1934, she fell in love with another left-wing, upper-class rebel, Esmond Romilly; three years later, they ran away to Spain together and did good works on the republican side in the Civil War; and they subsequently married, despite parental protests, and the fact that Jessica was a ward of court. Eventually, they returned to England and lived in some discomfort in Rotherhithe; they worked actively for the Labour party in Bermondsey; they were self-proclaimed Communists but not yet party members; and they fought Mosley's blackshirts in the streets.[186]

In embracing such extremes of political belief, and with such naïve flamboyance, the Mitfords were indeed unusual. But as in the 1880s, so in the inter-war years, many patrician families were similarly divided in their political allegiances. The Russells produced a die-hard and a socialist, the Trevelyans a Labour minister and a Baldwinite Tory. But whatever creed they espoused, they did not reverse their class decline, and they did not regain political power. In an increasingly alien and hostile world, their own traditions seemed outmoded, but without them, they were at a loss as to what to do. Mosley in particular, whether on the right, the centre, or the left, accomplished nothing against the massive inertia of the Macdonald-Baldwin consensus. His essentially patrician vision was anachronistic and unrealizable, and it could have been achieved only by methods so brutal and so violent as to belie the very notion of feudal benevolence and aristocratic disinterestedness which he may genuinely have felt. In him, as in so many alienated, marginal, and déclassé notables, on the far right and the far left, there was a streak of self-destruction. The Cecils were probably correct: since neither extreme protest nor high-minded dissent actually prevailed, it was better to be decent than violent.

v. Conclusion: 'Traitors to their Class'

Throughout its long history as the governing class of the nation, the British landed establishment had always spawned its fair share of mavericks and rebels, dissidents and revolutionaries. Oliver Cromwell was a country squire, Charles James Fox was at the centre of aristocratic Whiggery, and the 'Young England' movement was patrician in everything except its leadership. Viewed in this perspective, the Whigs, the die-hards, the Labour aristocrats, and the Fascist notables were but the latest in a long line of titled and genteel renegades. But there the similarities end. For in each of these earlier instances, they had been in revolt against a government and a polity that was itself overwhelmingly proprietorial and aristocratic. But from the 1880s onwards, they were increasingly reacting to a political world in which the proprietorial constitution had been overturned, and in which the old territorial class was no longer the governing class. The previous generations of patrician rebels were protesting against the way aristocratic power was *used*; but these later dissidents were protesting against the fact that aristocratic power was *going*. The earlier rebels had been a sign that the aristocratic order was flourishing; but from the late nineteenth century onwards, such protests were but one more indication that the aristocratic order was in decay.

For these maverick and marginal notables were vainly struggling to recover their position, and find their bearings, in a new and increasingly hostile world. But their restless shifts of allegiance, the speed with which they moved from one party to another, from left to right or right to left across the political spectrum, were but a further sign that they had lost their way. They no longer knew where they were, who they were, what they were doing, or where they were going. Wilfrid Scawen Blunt stood for Parliament as a Conservative, as a Liberal, and as an Independent. Albert Grey started his political career as a Whig, but ended it as a die-hard. Lord Parmoor had been a Tory MP, was ennobled by the Liberals, and served as a cabinet minister under Macdonald. Oswald Mosley began as a Tory, moved to the Liberals, then to Labour, and soon moved on again. (In this context, incidentally, Winston Churchill's shifts of allegiance, from the Conservatives to the Liberals, and back to the Conservatives, seem less unusual than is often assumed.) Disoriented and disenchanted, these renegade patricians were boxing the political compass, unable to see their way clearly in a world where their aristocratic presuppositions seemed increasingly irrelevant and anachronistic.

From the standpoint of the political history of modern Britain, it is the marginality, the lack of influence, and the limited success of these renegade notables that most impresses. But from the standpoint of the patricians themselves, it is the diversity of experience, the difficulty of generalization, that is most significant. By definition, when a class is in the process of decline and fragmentation, not everyone behaves and responds in the same way. Uniformity of behaviour is much lessened. But it is not only conduct that becomes more varied: it is circumstance as well. And to this generalization, the British landed establishment in decay was no exception. For while some aristocrats vainly and violently lamented their loss of power and prestige, there were others who were enjoying a period of renewed and unprecedented social celebrity. They might no longer be the great governing families; but instead, they had become the great ornamentals.

12

THE RECONSTRUCTION OF SOCIAL PRESTIGE

It was only when aristocratic influence was a spent force that the prestige of the peerage could be exploited to further civic dignity. The Marquess [of Bute] understood his position: 'They only elected me', he wrote, 'as a kind of figurehead.'
(J. Davies, 'Aristocratic Town-Makers and the Coal Metropolis: the Marquesses of Bute and the Growth of Cardiff, 1776 to 1947', in D. Cannadine (ed.), *Patricians, Power and Politics in Nineteenth-Century Towns* (1982), p. 55.)

It gives dignity to a committee to be presided over by a lord; but in many cases, lords bring also to the task experience in public affairs and public service, both at Westminster and in the provinces.
(K. C. Wheare, *Government by Committee: An Essay on the British Constitution* (1955), p. 87.)

He acquired 'interlocking directorships' stretching across the cultural world . . . a world which had shrunk, in daily routine, to squabbling committees, museum staff obstructionism, and the giving and receiving of honorary degrees.
(J. Vincent (ed.), *The Crawford Papers: The Journals of David Lindsay, Twenty Seventh Earl of Crawford and Tenth Earl of Balcarres, 1870–1940, During the Years 1892 to 1940* (1984), pp. 472, 497.)

A rich field of sinecures lay open to them, especially overseas. 'Go out and govern New South Wales', was their abiding consolation.
(A. J. P. Taylor, *English History, 1914–1945* (1965), pp. 172–3.)

In many ways, the erosion of the British aristocracy's social prestige during the half-century from the 1880s was as marked as its economic and political decline, and inevitably so, since it was closely linked to these parallel developments. The revelations concerning 'guinea pig' directors; the proliferation of titles and the sale of honours; the financial scandals involving venerable and illustrious names; and the turn to extremist forms of political behaviour: all this classically exemplifies a social group in crisis, decay, and fragmentation. Yet patrician prestige was in some ways more robust and more durable than even its most anxious defenders supposed. Ornamental directors may have undermined the standing of the nobility, but the fact that great names did indeed encourage the unwary to invest suggests that titles still inspired confidence of a kind. And rich, self-made men may have debased the peerage by buying their way in: but it was nevertheless an honour for which they were prepared to pay.

Indeed, acute contemporary commentators had no doubt that in some ways the social prestige of the titled and genteel classes shone undimmed throughout this period. Writing in 1912, in *The Decline of Aristocracy*, Arthur Ponsonby noted that while 'their actual political power' was 'a mere ghost of what they formally enjoyed', he went on to suggest that 'in the social world, they reign supreme.' It was, he argued, an 'error' to dismiss their social dominance as 'negligible'. On the contrary, their 'social supremacy' was 'a stronger force than the positive and ostensible powers of legislation and administration.'[1] And A. L. Lowell agreed, drawing attention to 'the social lustre of the peerage', to the fact that 'rank and titles have strong attractions for almost all classes of people.' And the result was a widespread feeling that they were 'raised above the scrimmage of public life', so rich, renowned, and revered that they were 'beyond the reach of the temptations that beset the ordinary man.'[2]

In short, while the traditional notables were in some ways socially threatened during this period, they remained in others socially pre-eminent. Yet paradoxically, this was an essentially *recent* development, since the particular form of public celebrity that they now enjoyed was of a fundamentally new type, which was made both possible and necessary by broader changes occurring throughout the country as a whole. From the 1880s to the 1930s, Britain developed into a much more complex society than before: it became an almost totally urbanized nation, the agencies of government expanded rapidly, many new educational institutions and cultural organiza-tions were founded, and the empire grew in size and in formality. One major consequence was a proliferation in decorative jobs and plumage positions which the patricians were both eager and able to fill. As Lowell perceptively explained, 'All this has exalted the regard for titles and offices, and enhanced the attractiveness of those who bear them.' And the result was that 'in prestige, the titled classes have profited thereby.'[3]

So, when Ponsonby wrote that 'it is his social power to which the aristocrat still clings', he was really referring to the *reconstruction* of such prestige rather than simply to its unchanged survival.[4] During this period, many grandees and gentry suddenly emerged as major ceremonial figures in greater and lesser British towns: as the cyno-sure of public interest and adulation, and as generous and glamorous mayors. At the same time, they took on a new identity as non-political, disinterested public servants, chairing royal commissions and government inquiries, and holding a variety of formal positions in the worlds of education, the media, and the arts. And they also filled, almost exclusively, those great proconsular offices, which were being created in India and the white dominions, where their titular prestige and social graces were again much in demand. Here, as Escott noted, were 'fresh opportunities' for public service which many notables hastened to take. The best way to survive as the traditional high-prestige class was to fill these essentially new, high-prestige positions.[5]

i. The Towns: 'Ornamental Mayors'

In January 1899, the Earl of Dudley was elected first freeman of the borough from which he derived both his title and most of his revenue.[6] A large crowd assembled outside the town hall; the Mayor presented Dudley with a gold casket containing a scroll on which his name was inscribed; and, to tumultuous applause, he made a gracious speech in reply. He spoke of the 'neighbourly regard and good will' that family and borough felt for each other, and thanked them for conferring upon him the 'highest mark of honour and esteem which it is in your power as burgesses to grant.' This was followed by a nine-course civic banquet, at which Dudley and the Mayor once again outdid each other in fulsome flattery. The next morning, the local paper reflected on this 'red-letter day' in the town's history. It congratulated Lord Dudley for 'coming down into the arena of common life', and for taking 'more than his full share of municipal work', and applauded the close links between aristocracy and democracy which such ceremonials both symbolized and cemented.

From the 1890s until the Second World War, scenes such as this were commonplace in those many British towns that could claim a territorial connection with a patrician family. Yet only a decade before, it would have seemed inconceivable that men like Lord Dudley might soon find themselves the objects of such esteem and regard, and the centrepiece of such grandiose and obsequious civic ceremonial. In the 1880s, urban Britain appeared more menacing than at any time since the 1840s: there were new and ominous revelations about the conditions of town life; it was the city-dwellers who were most strident in their attacks on the House of Lords and in their demands for leasehold enfranchisement; and some newly assertive town councils cast predatory glances at the markets, docks, and urban estates of some of the greatest landowners. But this phase of suspicion, distrust, and hostility was soon replaced by a period of mutual affection and goodwill which lasted until the Second World War. And it enabled grandees like Lord Dudley to enjoy a higher social profile and a more conspicuous ceremonial role, as the old rural élite found themselves in demand as new urban celebrities.

107. 'Little Rosebery's Song.' *Punch*, 19 Jan. 1889.

The most famous example of this 'titular association of the aristocracy with the new civic democracy' was the new London County Council, where Lord Rosebery was elected first chairman in 1889–1890, and again in 1892.[7] He was followed by others of his class: Lords Welby and Monkswell in the 1900s, Viscount Peel, A. F. Buxton, and the Marquess of Crewe during the First World War, and Lord Monk Bretton (a new title but an old landowner) in 1930. And, especially in the early years, there was an influx of titled councillors and aldermen: grandees like Dudley, Norfolk, Stanhope, Malmesbury, and Carrington; heirs and younger sons like Haddo, Thynne, Percy, Bentinck, Primrose, and Legge; and a large Irish contingent, including Meath, Dunraven, Duncannon, Kerry, and Midleton. Even in 1939, members of the LCC included Lady Limerick, the Earl of Listowel, and Viscounts Curzon and Sandon.

108. The Duke of Devonshire as Mayor of Eastbourne.

But more remarkable still was the sudden upsurge of aristocratic mayors that began abruptly in 1890, when Lord Bute was elected Mayor of Cardiff, 'the first peer to hold the highest municipal office in any English or Welsh borough for several generations – certainly since the Reform Act.' The evidence for this is clear, and is gathered in Appendix E. In all types of British towns, and throughout the British Isles, landowners with local links were elected to the mayoral chair. In London, the Duke of Norfolk, the Duke of Bedford, and Earl Cadogan were, respectively, .the inaugural mayors of Westminster, Holborn, and Chelsea. In the great provincial cities, there was Shaftesbury in Belfast, Derby in Liverpool, and Norfolk in Sheffield, as well as Bute in Cardiff. In smaller industrial towns, there was Devonport at St Levans, Sutherland at Longton, Brownlow at Grantham, and Lonsdale at Whitehaven. At the seaside, there were the Devonshires at Eastbourne, the de la Warrs at Bexhill, and Lord Radnor at Folkestone. And in the country and county towns, there was Beauchamp at Worcester, Bute at Rothesay, Warwick at Warwick, Llangattock at Monmouth, Pembroke at Wilton, and Marlborough at Woodstock.

The strength, longevity, and variety of this patrician link with British towns is remarkable. In some cases, the same family provided

109. Lord Durham as
mayor of his titular town.

mayors with almost monotonous frequency: the Warwicks and the
Forsters four times each in Warwick and Wenlock, and the Brown-
lows and the Pembrokes were almost as commonplace in Grantham
and Wilton. In others, as at Liverpool, Eastbourne, Southport, and
Durham, son followed father. At Bexhill, all four noble mayors
were related.[8] Some served for more than one year, as at Dudley,
Whitehaven, Huntingdon, and Woodstock. Some towns elected
titled mayors from more than one family, as at Cardiff, Liverpool,
Sheffield, Durham, and Worcester. Some aristocrats held the same
position in several towns: the sixteenth earl of Derby at Preston and
at Liverpool, the ninth Duke of Devonshire at Buxton, Chesterfield,
and Eastbourne, and the fifteenth Duke of Norfolk at Sheffield,
Arundel, and Westminster. Indeed, if certain town councils had had
their way, the list would have been even longer: Swansea asked the
Duke of Beaufort, Rotherham wanted Earl Fitzwilliam, Cardiff
approached Lord Tredegar, and in Wigan, the Crawfords could have
had the job for the asking.[9]

The trend is clear; but why did it happen, why so suddenly, and
why then? The abrupt proliferation of titled mayors in the 1890s was
often the symbol of reconciliation after some earlier battle over
property rights or incorporation. In Cardiff, the Butes' political and

economic power was considerably weakened in the early 1880s. At Eastbourne, the town council had sought to municipalize the Duke of Devonshire's water company in 1895–6. In Whitehaven, the Lowther mayoralty actually inaugurated the new corporation, but only after the family had safeguarded its economic interests in the harbour. At Southport and Bexhill, there was a similar sense of reconciliation after an earlier period of confrontation and disagreement.[10] And when Lord Radnor became Mayor of Folkestone in 1901, it was noted that 'for years, there has been talk of conflicting interests between the Corporation and the Lord of the Manor, but as the offices of Mayor and Lord of the Manor are now combined in one, these conflicting interests will for the time being at any rate cease to exist.'[11]

But if the period is taken as a whole, it is clear that there were also broader trends at work. On the landowners' side, this willingness to play a new and more public role in municipal affairs was undoubtedly a deliberate and self-conscious attempt to project a more favourable public image in urban communities. After the battles of the 1880s, they no longer sought to impose their will on the towns by direct political intervention, nor to defend their local property rights by confrontational tactics. Instead, they sought to protect their position and their assets by cultivating an image of apolitical goodness and civic concern. By withdrawing from active political involvement in urban affairs, by distancing themselves from the day-to-day operations of their business concerns, and by simultaneously showing a greater interest in the well-being of the community, they found they were better able both to safeguard their property rights and to enhance their own personal prestige.

Throughout the British Isles, this seems a widespread development in the late nineteenth century. In Belfast, the Donegall estates passed to the Shaftesburys in 1883, and the ninth earl reoccupied the castle, opened its grounds to the public, subscribed generously to city charities, and reasserted the family's presence in the town after a long period of absenteeism. In Birmingham, the sixth Lord Calthorpe was much more tactful in dealing with the corporation than his predecessor had been, and in 1911, the Edgbaston estate withdrew from political involvement altogether as the Conservative party subscription was deleted.[12] In Southport, Charles Scarisbrick ended his family's long run of absenteeism, built himself a house close to the town, subscribed £7,000 to the local hospital, and made it plain that he was willing to undertake further municipal work. In the Potteries, the Countess of Sutherland, who was affectionately known as 'Meddlesome Millicent', concerned herself with local industrial diseases, and even contributed to a book on the subject. And in Eastbourne, the Devonshires assiduously refrained from making party-political speeches, and after 1892 ensured that their agents no longer sat on the town council.[13]

By deliberately making themselves less contentious, these land-owners could present themselves more plausibly as well-disposed, high-prestige personages, above the battle, yet occasionally prepared to descend from the mountain-top if it was in the interests of the town for them to do so. But why should the towns be interested in appointing these figures as mayor? It was, after all, in this period when Britain truly became an urban nation, when social leaders took up municipal work most enthusiastically, and when the prestige of town councils was at its peak. Yet, they were dominated by professionals and businessmen who believed in private property, and they were much concerned to proclaim the greatness and the unity of their communities by appealing to history, to pageantry, and to glamour. They built elaborate town halls rich in civic iconography; they were greatly concerned with municipal etiquette and ceremonial; and they acquired aldermanic robes, coats of arms, maces, and regalia. After the royal family, these city fathers were the greatest inventors of tradition between the 1880s and the 1930s.[14]

More especially, the office of mayor assumed particular importance at this time. He embodied the unity and the greatness of the community; he must be able to carry off the social and ceremonial side of his duties with dignity and panache; and he must have the resources to entertain lavishly, and to subscribe generously to charities, clubs, and associations. But very often, the job carried with it neither a salary nor an entertainment allowance, and it might cost the incumbent anything from £500 to £5,000 for a year's term. Even in great industrial cities, not all businessmen were prepared to serve, and in seaside resorts and smaller towns, the supply was still more limited. But in addition, the ideal mayor should be a man of ancient lineage, high social standing, and impeccable connections. Seen in this light, the election of a titled mayor was the embodiment, not the negation, of municipal pride, as aristocratic prestige was used for the furthering of civic dignity. As Lawrence Lowell correctly observed, a nobleman was appointed, essentially, 'for the lustre of his title and with a view to hospitality at his castle.'[15]

In short, patrician mayors were expected to behave heroically, especially when, as was often the case, they served in jubilee or coronation year. The Duke of Norfolk gave a magnificent ball with which to inaugurate the new town hall at Sheffield in 1897. Sir Charles Scarisbrick was Coronation Mayor of Southport, and presided over 'a year of brilliance and social functioning.' His son and successor, Sir Talbot, entertained the corporation officials, the local police, and the postmen, and put on two children's parties, and a mayoral reception and ball for nine hundred.[16] When Mayor of Eastbourne, the eighth Duke of Devonshire gave an unprecedentedly splendid inaugural banquet, a garden party at Compton Place, an old people's dinner at the town hall, and a ball at Devonshire Park. Likewise, the sixth Earl of Radnor invited the members of Folkestone Town Council to visit Longford Castle, and Lord Brassey entertained the tradesmen of Bexhill to an afternoon at Normanhurst, his nearby home.[17]

When these grand mayoralties came to an end, they were often commemorated by a gift that further served to indicate their heroic quality. Very often, it was an item of municipal regalia, which added yet more dignity and *gravitas* to civic ceremonial: a sword of state at Durham, a ceremonial mace at Sheffield, a badge for the mayoral chain at Folkestone, and the mayoral chain itself at Whitehaven and Bexhill.[18] Others were more original (or idiosyncratic) in their gifts. The Earl of Sandwich built the Montagu Club for the working men of Huntingdon, a temperance establishment that he hoped would keep them out of pubs. At Southport, Sir Charles Scarisbrick donated his mayoral salary of £500 to charity, and gave each member of the town council a pewter mug as a memento of his year of office. At Eastbourne, the eighth Duke of Devonshire gave a plot of land for the site of a proposed Technical Institute, his successor presented the town with the freehold of Motcombe Gardens, and both donated their mayoral salaries to local charities.[19]

Such glittering and glamorous episodes remained a subject of happy reminiscence for many years. But what, more substantively, did all this add up to? Were these men anything more than dignified and ornamental figure-heads? In the day-to-day business of municipalities, they did not signify. The platitudinous phrases about 'taking a deep interest', of their 'sincere concern', of never being 'a mere figurehead', ring rather hollow.[20] Their attendance at council meetings was infrequent; they were invariably ignorant of the agenda; and the real burdens of leadership and administration were usually borne by the deputy mayor. And the chairman of the LCC was even less of a directing force than the mayor of a borough, since most of the real work was done in committee.[21] As the third Marquess of Bute candidly conceded, being titled Mayor of Cardiff was really rather a sham:

> I get on pretty well with my civic government here. My official confidants are nearly all radical dissenters, but we manage in quite a friendly way. They only elected me as a kind of figurehead; and

110. Lord Bute as Mayor of
Cardiff.

although they are good enough to be glad whenever I take part in
details, I am willing to leave these in the hands of people with
more expertise than myself.[22]

Although Bute's dislike of public office was especially marked,
most aristocratic mayors were largely ornamental. When Lord Dudley
became mayor of his titular town, he pointed out that his commit-
ments to the LCC and the Board of Trade meant that he could not
expect to attend the council regularly.[23] Lord Radnor accepted the
mayoralty of Folkestone with 'great diffidence'; he had 'little knowledge of the working of municipal affairs'; and he felt that he would
'not be an efficient mayor of a borough of this size and character.' Sir
Charles Scarisbrick, despite his year as Mayor of Southport, 'was
never in the ordinary sense an intimate associate with local life' and
'did not find municipal work too congenial.'[24] And of the two
Mayors of Bexhill provided by the Brassey family, one was rightly
described as 'an exceedingly busy man, who already had his hands

full . . . , and in his seventy-second year', while the other, who spent much time in Sardinia, and preferred to hunt on Mondays than appear at the town council meetings, was, on his own admission, little more than a 'nominal mayor'.[25]

But as such, these patricians were doing exactly what was required of them, and exactly what was best for them. For as they distanced themselves from close involvement in the politics and economies of the towns, and as the corporations became more assertive, a new relationship emerged in which the previously powerful and contentious grandees were replaced by the increasingly confident and unified middle-class élites as the majority partner. While the landowners might support middle-class initiatives, respond to their requests and suggestions, and collaborate in civic and philanthropic schemes, they no longer held the initiative or dictated policy. The *Liverpool Echo's* account of the role of the sixteenth Earl of Derby in the affairs of Liverpool catches this well: 'It became almost a custom to look to him, if not for actual initiation of important movements, at least for hearty co-operation and, in some instances, perhaps, for direction.'[26] So, when the landowners participated in civic and ceremonial affairs, it was more on the councils' terms than on their own. They were enhancing the lustre of the corporation, not asserting their control over it.

Moreover, although these aristocratic mayoralties were important in the perpetuation and reconstruction of patrician prestige, they were, from the standpoint of the towns, very much minority happenings. On the Celtic fringe, they were particularly rare: in Wales, they were confined to the industrialized south and Beaumaris; in Ireland, the Shaftesbury mayoralty in Belfast was unique; and in Scotland there was only Bute at Rothesay and Munro-Ferguson at Kirkaldy. Many towns, like Leeds and Manchester, could boast no great territorial connection. And even some that could, like Birmingham and Bournemouth, preferred to appoint local businessmen rather than grandees. In municipal affairs, these were the people who really mattered, who had a large economic stake in the town, who turned up regularly to council meetings, and who served as mayor for several years: like Mander in Wolverhampton or Gurney Benham in Colchester. And many of the ornamental mayors were political or plutocratic rather than patrician, such as Ritchie at Winchelsea, Colwyn at Colwyn Bay, and Astor at Plymouth.

Thus described, these noble mayoralties were relatively rare and infrequent, and essentially non-contentious. They helped townsmen anxious for status and civic unity; and they provided a new way of perpetuating and projecting aristocratic celebrity. But there was also, within these limits, power of a kind. In those towns where the

territorial connection was especially close, or where the family was
directly involved with the local economy, it was inevitable that they
could still exert some leverage. In Southport, it was claimed that the
Hesketh agents refused to grant leases to builders with radical views,
and in Cardiff it was often asserted that no builder would ever bring
an action against the Bute estate for fear of possible future reprisals.[27]
Indeed, W. T. Lewis, who was in charge of the Bute operations
there, was reputed to be 'the best-hated man in the Principality.' He
was the contentious figure, while the Marquess kept himself distant,
Olympian, and aloof. As one contemporary remarked, 'the common
sense of the community can always distinguish between the nobleman and his lackey'. Indeed, it was precisely to deflect attacks from
themselves that the landowners so readily adopted this new
posture.[28]

Of course, the power of property ownership lasted only so long as
these assets were retained; and from the 1880s onwards, they were
gradually being dispersed. But while they endured, they remained
important. The second Earl of Dudley was told that he held his town
'and the great ring around it, in the hollow of his hand', and that
without his co-operation, 'improvements and progress could not be
carried on without great difficulty.' Likewise, it was claimed that the
sixth Earl of Dartmouth had it in his power 'to help or hinder'
municipal progress in West Bromwich.[29] They no longer had the
power to force through schemes of their own; they still had the
power to be obstructive; but on the whole, and consistent with their
new position, they preferred to help middle-class initiatives than to
thwart them. Lord Calthorpe provided land at Edgbaston for Birmingham University in 1900 and 1907; the Duke of Norfolk, the
Marquess of Bute, and the Duke of Sutherland donated parks in
Sheffield, Cardiff, and Longton; and in Bournemouth, the Tapps-
Gervis-Meyricks made over the foreshore and their rights as lords of
the manor to the town.[30]

There were other ways in which patrician mayors might be of use.
As peers of the realm, and sometimes even as cabinet ministers, they
boasted connections in London and in government that few city
councillors could match. As a result, many peers were elected mayor
at the very time when the local council was promoting a major
measure in Parliament, in the hope that their patronage and support
might be useful. The Duke of Norfolk helped the Sheffield Town
Council with bills concerning tramways and water; the Earl of
Dudley supplied useful advice on similar questions for his titular
town; the fourth Duke of Sutherland worked behind the scenes to
promote the federation of the Pottery towns; and the ninth Duke of
Devonshire became Mayor of Eastbourne at exactly the time when

the corporation was trying to secure recognition for the town as a county borough.[31] In a similar way, Lord Clarendon served as the chairman of the Watford incorporation committee, and became the town's first mayor; and the ninth Earl de la Warr, while Mayor of Bexhill, was able to persuade the council, even at the height of the depression, to spend £100,000 on what ultimately became the de la Warr Pavilion.[32]

And their social influence could be put to other uses that were to the benefit of the municipality. In resorts like Folkestone, Eastbourne, and Bexhill, each of which claimed to be more 'aristocratic' than the other, it was thought beneficial for their tourist trade to boast a peer as mayor. And if they had good connections in the court or the cabinet, they might bring illustrious people down to add even greater lustre to civic functions. In May 1897, thanks to the intercession of the Duke of Norfolk, Queen Victoria visited Sheffield, the only great provincial jaunt of her Diamond Jubilee year. She opened the new town hall, bestowed a baronetcy on the Master Cutler, a knighthood on the Deputy Mayor, and promoted the Mayor into a Lord Mayor.[33] Likewise, when Mayor of Bexhill, Lord de la Warr was also a minister in the National Government, and in successive years was able to bring, as visitors, the Chancellor, the Minister of Agriculture, the Lord Chancellor, and the Foreign Secretary. In addition, King George V and Queen Mary visited the town, and the Duke and Duchess of York opened the de la Warr Pavilion.[34]

In short, by placing their own prestige at the service of the towns, these patricians actually enhanced their own celebrity at the same time. And they were also able to exploit this in the realm of party politics. In the urban constituencies, as in the rural, the lustre of an ancient name and the allure of territorial connection could still swing the balance. In 1906 – which was, of course, a bad year for Conservatives – Lord Lewisham, the future Earl of Dartmouth, was beaten for the West Bromwich constituency. But he was described as having 'a name to conjure with' in the locality, and it was generally recognized that he performed better than any other candidate would have. And in 1910, when he won both elections, family help and influence may have been only one factor, but it was probably decisive.[35] Such illustrious connections no doubt helped the Bute MPs in Cardiff and the Derby MPs in Lancashire at the same time. Indeed, as late as 1937, when Lord Crawford was interviewing prospective candidates for his old Lancashire seat, he was urged to let his younger son James stand: 'however inexperienced he may be, he would score from association with myself.'[36]

But as with the landed establishment's ornamental functions, these latter-day political roles were essentially subordinate to middle-class initiatives. They did not represent a continuation or reassertion of aristocratic power over constituency associations. By now, these were fully in the hands of the middle class, and even urban Conservatism was a much more complex phenomenon than mere liking for lords. Here, as elsewhere, when such figures went with, and encouraged, the trend of events, they might be helpful and successful; but they could not force the initiative on their own. Indeed, in certain cases, patrician candidates even felt obliged to disavow their own background: in 1898, at Southport, Sir Herbert Naylor-Leyland advocated land reform and leasehold enfranchisement, even though he was a beneficiary of his family's building estate in the town; and in Cardiff in 1918, Lord Colum Crichton-Stuart campaigned in favour of leasehold enfranchisement and the abolition of mineral royalties.[37]

Such bizarre and unconvincing inconsistencies merely showed how difficult it was, by this period, for patricians to reconcile their roles as Olympian prestige figures above the battle, and party politicians who were by definition contentious. And, on the whole, they chose – or were forced to choose – to concentrate on the one and to abandon the other. In Cardiff, Lord Ninian Crichton-Stuart was an MP from 1910 to his death on active service in 1915. His brother, Lord Colum, unsuccessfully contested another local constituency in 1918, but despite his radical programme, was defeated. In the Black Country, Lord Lewisham was beaten in West Bromwich in 1918, and the family thereupon withdrew from active political participation.[38] In the same year, Lord Stanley was defeated for a Liverpool constituency, and another member of the Derby family was turned out of Preston in 1922. Even Lord Crawford's son was rejected at Wigan in 1923, only months after his coming of age had been effusively and affectionately celebrated. Not surprisingly, it was 'the last time a Lindsay was to take part in Wigan politics.'[39]

The limits and opportunities for involvement and initiative are most vividly illustrated in the career of the seventeenth Earl of Derby, who held the title from 1908 to 1948, and who was widely known as 'the uncrowned King of Lancashire.' We have already encountered him in an earlier chapter as a rather uninspired politician. But that was not how he seemed in the County Palatine. There, at one level, he was the quintessential grandee: he was very rich and broad-acred; he owned a string of magnificent houses, especially Knowsley, near Liverpool; and he was well known as a sportsman whose horses won the Derby three times. He was also a cabinet minister, sometime British Ambassador to France, and a close personal friend of King George V. As such, he was uniquely fitted to represent and to further Lancashire interests in London, where 'his entrée to the highest councils of the nation was of inestimable value.'

In the inter-war years, he helped to obtain Admiralty orders for Cammell Laird's shipyards, pushed hard for the Mersey Tunnel project, and joined the select committee on the Government's India policy to represent Lancashire cotton interests. And the high number of visits paid by George V, Queen Mary, and the Prince of Wales to Lancashire was very largely his doing.[40]

But at another level, he was the county's most admired and picturesque personality, whose presence adorned and enhanced any local occasion, and whose support was eagerly sought for almost any local enterprise. He was President of the Liverpool Chamber of Commerce and of the British Cotton Growers Association; he was chairman of the Liverpool Cathedral Building Fund and became Lord-Lieutenant of the county in 1928. In 1911, he followed his father as Lord Mayor of Liverpool, and was much more active than Bute had been in Cardiff: 'I am tied down here to a degree you can hardly imagine', he wrote to Bonar Law.[41] Indeed, as an ornamental figure-head, Derby worked astonishingly hard, attending bazaars and fêtes, opening swimming-pools, laying foundation stones throughout the county. On the last occasion when his horse won the Derby, he was unable to be present because of a local engagement. As he himself explained to Lord Beaverbrook, 'if I have any standing in Lancashire, it is from the fact that I have always done many things which almost come under the head of the daily round, the trivial task.' Even on into the Second World War, he still insisted on visiting every Lancastrian mayor each year in his capacity as Lord-Lieutenant.[42]

But in his third guise, Derby was also the 'lynchpin of Lancashire Toryism', an assiduous and influential party-political boss. He distributed Lancashire constituencies among his relatives as a benevolent parent might give sweets to his children. When a Stanley was defeated, as Edward was in Liverpool in 1918, another local billet was immediately found for him. But this was more than mere family promotion. In 1910, Derby was in charge of the Conservative effort in Manchester in the second general election of that year. In 1924, he was 'paying the expenses of three candidates and also subsidizing largely in five other seats.'[43] His friendship with Archibald Salvidge meant he was closely involved in the Liverpool Conservative machine; and at the end of Salvidge's time, he not only organized a testimonial fund for him, but was in charge of reconstructing the party machine after he had gone.[44]

According to Randolph Churchill, Derby was 'the last of those great territorial magnates who exercised an effective and pervasive influence based on the ownership of land and the maintenance of an historic association with it.'[45] But Derby's position, like that of many of his contemporaries, was in fact more new than old. By the end of his life, his territorial ties to Lancashire were much less than they had been at the beginning: his local prestige took on, as it were, a life of its own. And he achieved what he did because he worked with the grain of events, not against: only in a county with so overwhelmingly Conservative a political culture as Lancashire could a peer have been simultaneously as Olympian and as partisan as Derby was. Moreover, his influence on affairs was never all that great: he probably counted for less in London than his Lancashire admirers allowed; as a party-political boss, he definitely played second fiddle to Salvidge and later to Sir Thomas White; and after his appointment as Lord-Lieutenant he gradually withdrew from active participation in the Tory cause.[46] He may have been more energetic and more famous than many other patrician figure-heads; but ultimately, he, too, was more ornamental than influential.

Writing in 1896, one commentator on the landed establishment predicted that 'a merely ornamental discharge of . . . municipal functions, coupled from time to time with expressions of sympathetic interest in the masses, will not serve, and ought not to serve.'[47] Yet for the next forty years, it served extremely well. A new and ornamental public profile, which probably began as a way of defending property by niceness, gradually became a tradition of its own, so that the prestige endured even after the property had gone. And this was especially true in Lancashire, the cradle of the Industrial Revolution, yet also the last great bastion of patrician celebrity in an urbanized world. In 1935, there was a grand ceremony in Preston Town Hall to celebrate Lord Derby's seventieth birthday, and 80,000 people signed a memorial, and contributed their shillings towards a present. Ten years later, Lord Sefton was elected Lord Mayor of Liverpool to see in the allied victory. And on Lord Derby's death in 1948, the 'grand old man of Merseyside' was mourned throughout Lancashire in suitably ceremonial style: flags flew at half mast on all Liverpool buildings, the Lord Mayor attended the funeral, and a memorial service was held in the cathedral.[48]

ii. The Nation: 'The Great and the Good'

With the fall of the Lloyd George coalition in October 1922, the twenty-seventh Earl of Crawford and Balcarres found himself out of office, and contemplated his future prospects with gloom and anxiety. 'I regret the dislocation', he recorded. 'What I most fear is that what have been my relaxations will now become my occupations . . . I do not look forward to the easy-going existence which

111. Lord Crawford by Sir
James Gunn.

my few non-political avocations impose.' Yet this pessimism soon
passed, and Crawford found his time fully and agreeably occupied
until his death in 1940. He never held political office again (although
he was asked), and he resisted attempts to lure him into business
(however useful the money would have been). Instead, he consolidated and extended his 'interlocking directorships stretching across
the cultural world', and became an outstanding example of non-
political patrician public service.[49] And, from the 1880s to the
Second World War, many grandees joined the ranks of 'the great and
the good': sometimes as ornamental statesmen in the world of higher
education, sometimes as decorous and decent trustees of cultural
institutions, and sometimes as dignified and dutiful chairmen of
government committees and royal commissions.

In the realm of higher education, the thirty years before the First
World War were characterized by reform, innovation, and expansion, the result of an amalgam of civic pride, romantic aspirations,
economic calculation, nonconformist assertiveness, middle-class
ambition, and national anxiety. In England, the universities of
Oxford and Cambridge increasingly became finishing schools for the
children of businessmen; Durham was secularized and reconstructed
in 1908; London was fundamentally reorganized and reformed in the
aftermath of two royal commissions and the legislation of 1898; and

112. Lord Curzon as Chancellor of Oxford University by Philip de Laszlo.

in the 1900s, royal charters were granted to the new universities of Birmingham, Manchester, Liverpool, Leeds, Sheffield, and Bristol.[50] In Wales, university colleges were established at Aberystwyth, Cardiff, and Bangor in the 1880s, and they were brought together in a federation in 1893. In the four ancient Scottish universities, the legislation of 1889 led to changes in the curriculum, to the institution of entrance examinations, to the admission of women, and to the recognition of students' rights. And in Ireland, the Royal University was set up in 1880, which was in turn replaced by the National University and Queen's Belfast in 1908.[51]

Once again, the social prestige of the ancient, rural, patrician élite was used to enhance and adorn these new, urban, and quintessentially middle-class institutions: as dignified and ceremonial figure-heads, as grandees of high social status with good and useful connections, and as men with local territorial links who could encourage and co-operate with middle-class initiatives. As Appendix F shows, the models here were the older universities, which continued their practice of electing illustrious patricians as chancellors: Salisbury, Curzon, Grey, and Halifax at Oxford; Devonshire, Rayleigh, and Balfour at Cambridge. The ancient Scottish universities often followed suit, with two Dukes of Richmond and Lord Elgin at Aberdeen, A. J. Balfour at Edinburgh, Lord Stair and Lord Rosebery at Glasgow, and the Duke of Argyll and Lord Balfour of Burleigh at St Andrews. At London, too, there was a long line of statesmen-grandees: Granville, Kimberley, Derby, Rosebery, and Beauchamp. And once it had been reformed, Durham showed a strong preference for notables with local connections: two Dukes of Northumberland, one Marquess of Londonderry, and one titular earl.

Here were men of ancient lineage appropriately adorning universities of ancient name. And, in deliberate and striking emulation, the new, civic, redbrick universities which received their charters at the turn of the century often sought peers with territorial links as their chancellor. As with town councils, these middle-class and ostensibly assertive enterprises were also profoundly insecure and romantic in ethos: the city fathers who were so busily inventing traditions for their towns were equally energetic in inventing them for their universities. Hence the whole paraphernalia of hoods, gowns, maces, coats of arms, and degree congregations. Hence, too, the deliberately anachronistic styles of architecture – Gothic at Manchester, Italianate at Birmingham, Tudor at Sheffield, and Perpendicular at Bristol.[52] What, then, could be more appropriate than to select as Chancellor men who themselves were the embodiment of those very traditions that these new universities were trying to acquire and create: a succession of Derbys at Liverpool; two Devonshires, a Spencer, and Lord Crawford at Manchester;[53] Norfolk, Crewe, and Harewood at Sheffield; Ripon then two Devonshires at Leeds; and Shaftesbury then Londonderry at Belfast.

On the Celtic fringe, patrician involvement with universities – both new and old – was even more marked. The Royal University of Ireland was successively headed by the Duke of Abercorn, and by Lords Dufferin, Meath, and Castletown. In Wales, Lord Aberdare was President of the University Colleges of Aberystwyth and Cardiff, and became the first Chancellor of the federal university in 1895, while the fourth Lord Kenyon was later President of Bangor University College, and successively Senior Deputy Chancellor and Pro Chancellor of the university.[54] And in Scotland, patrician chancellors were joined by a sudden influx of titled lord rectors from the 1880s: Lord Huntly for nine years at Aberdeen; Lord Bute for six years at St Andrews, where Reay, Dufferin, and Aberdeen also held the office; Balfour of Burleigh, Lothian, Minto, and Dufferin (again) at Edinburgh; and Lytton and Curzon at Glasgow.[55] Indeed, some grandees collected Scottish university offices as others collected English mayoralties: Balfour was Chancellor of Edinburgh and Cambridge, and Lord Rector of Edinburgh and St Andrews, while

113. The Duke of
Devonshire as Chancellor
of Leeds University by
Philip de Laszlo.

Rosebery was not only Chancellor of London and Glasgow but also
successively Lord Rector of all four Scottish universities.

Here was a trend as novel and as pronounced as patrician involvement in municipal affairs. But what, more substantively, did it
mean? What did these titled chancellors and lord rectors actually do?
Predictably, they brought that same glamour, style, dignity, and
celebrity to university occasions that they brought, as mayors, to
civic affairs. They were hospitable, benevolent, and agreeable; they
were equally at ease with undergraduates and local worthies; and
they presided grandly and genially at degree days. The Duke of
Northumberland was especially successful at Durham; and when St
Andrews celebrated its five hundredth anniversary in 1911, Lord
Rosebery, as Lord Rector, delivered a particularly felicitous address.
And they brought down members of the royal family and important
politicians to lend added éclat to a university occasion: Edward VII
opened new buildings at Sheffield in 1905 and Leeds in 1908; and
Lord Derby brought Stanley Baldwin to Liverpool three times
between the wars.[56]

But as with aristocratic mayors, these titled chancellors could also take a more active part, provided they co-operated with middle-class initiatives in the right way. And this was especially so in the early stages of university foundation, when they needed all the well-connected help and established support they could get. At Liverpool, the fifteenth Earl of Derby chaired the first town meeting to inaugurate the University College in 1882. At Sheffield, the Duke of Norfolk subscribed £10,000; he used the coincidence of his own mayoralty and the royal visit of 1897 to launch the University College scheme; and when Sheffield failed to gain admission to the federal Victoria University, he threw his weight behind the campaign for an autonomous charter.[57] At Leeds, Lord Ripon was equally energetic: in 1887, he led a deputation to the Chancellor of the Exchequer asking for increased funds for the University College; he donated £5,000 to the appeal; and he provided firm and steady support when the university found itself unexpectedly alone with the breakup of the Victoria University federation.[58]

On the Celtic fringe, where middle-class presence and initiatives were weaker, the local patricians seem to have been even more active. At Queen's Belfast, Lord Shaftesbury provided a direct link between the university and London in the Ulster crises of 1912–14 and 1918–22.[59] In Wales, Lord Aberdare was rightly known as the 'Commander-in-Chief of the Welsh educational army': he chaired the important government inquiry into higher education there in 1880; as a former cabinet minister, his contacts at Whitehall were excellent; and he was successful in persuading the government to give grants to the Welsh colleges from the outset. In the next generation, Lord Kenyon was equally important: he led deputations to the Treasury in successful pursuit of increased grants in 1914 and 1918, and in the 1920s he was the chairman of the Court and Council, which had recently been established as the sovereign body of the university. As such, he was much more a chief executive than head of state.[60]

In Scotland, Lords Huntly and Bute also asserted themselves, albeit in rather different ways. At Aberdeen, Huntly was an unprecedentedly punctilious Lord Rector: hence his constant re-election in the 1890s. He regularly attended meetings and presided at the University Court; he chaired an important town meeting to launch the University Extension Scheme; he negotiated personally with G. J. Goschen at the Treasury about an increased grant; and he was instrumental in securing particular benefactions from the Mitchell family of Newcastle upon Tyne.[61] At St Andrews, Lord Bute's interventions were equally emphatic but less well judged, as he attempted to turn the university into his idea of a medieval place of learning. He used his residual rectorial powers to obtain a majority on the University Court; he tried to sever connections with the upstart and bourgeois college at Dundee; and he sought to re-create the original curriculum by establishing a medical and a law school, even going so far as to endow a chair of anatomy.[62]

Even in the greatest of English universities, some grandees played more than a merely decorative role. In 1907, Lord Curzon became Chancellor of Oxford, and at once resolved to be more than a nominal office holder. He invented a new and public installation ceremony, which took place in the Sheldonian; he brought down Balfour and Theodore Roosevelt as Romanes Lecturers in 1909 and 1910; he actually resided in Oxford, and was the first Chancellor to do so in centuries; and between 1909 and 1914, he delayed the setting up of a government commission, tried to persuade the university to reform itself from within, and even produced a scheme of his own.[63] In London, Lord Reay's influence was more varied and long-lasting. He was chairman of the School Board from 1897 to 1904; but his major work was for the university itself. He was elected to the council of University College in 1881, became Vice-President in 1892, and President five years later. He was an enthusiastic supporter of reform; he strongly advocated the incorporation of the college in the university in the aftermath of the 1898 legislation; and once this was accomplished, he served as chairman of the college committee from 1907 to 1922. In addition, he presided over the committee that led to the setting up of the School of Oriental Studies, and was chairman of its board from 1901 to 1918.[64]

The second area of national life where grandees and gentry assumed a more visible profile in this period was as cultural trustees. Here, in parallel with the universities, the last quarter of the nineteenth century was an era of major expansion. Between the 1880s and the 1900s, the Natural History, the Victoria and Albert, and the Science Museums all began to assume their modern form; the British Museum and the National Gallery were extended and the National Portrait Gallery was permanently housed; the Wallace Collection was left to the nation and the Tate Gallery was opened; and the National Trust and the National Art Collections Fund came into being. And in the inter-war years, this was followed by the setting up of the Royal Fine Arts Commission, the Council for the Preservation of Rural England and, most importantly, the BBC. All these institutions required boards and committees, trustees and governors, presidents and chairmen, and a large number of them were recruited from among the old patrician class.

Almost by definition, such people seemed the right men for the job. Some were still leisured enough to have time to turn up to frequent and protracted meetings. They were well connected, which might help with obtaining pictures, securing a benefaction, arranging a royal visit, or defending the institution in the House of Lords. And some were genuinely learned: perhaps because they were sensitive to their stately surroundings; perhaps because they sought to buttress their own position by disseminating aristocratic cultural values in an age of aristocratic anxiety. The ninth Earl of Carlisle was an accomplished amateur painter and a friend of Burne Jones. The seventeenth Viscount Dillon was an expert on medieval armour and devoted to his pictures at Ditchley Park. Lord Curzon's passion for houses, for history, for architecture, and for preservation were proverbial. Lord Crawford was an expert on Italian Renaissance sculpture; Lord Ilchester wrote prolifically on Holland House and his family history; and Sir Evan Charteris completed a study of John Singer Sargent.

From the 1880s onwards, such men were in great demand to sit on the boards of these new or expanding cultural institutions, and some of them acquired interlocking directorates in a manner that, during the inter-war years, Lord Crawford was to bring to an even higher level of concentration. Lord Carlisle was a trustee of the National Gallery for over twenty years, as was Lord Fitzmaurice of the National Portrait Gallery. Lord Dillon was a trustee of the British Museum and of the Wallace Collection, and was chairman of the board of the National Portrait Gallery from 1894 to 1928. In 1906, the future Lord Carmichael became the first chairman of the newly constituted National Gallery of Scotland, and later obtained seats on the boards of the National and National Portrait Galleries. Lord Curzon was appointed a trustee of the British Museum and the National Gallery on his return from India, and chaired a committee that recommended that the Tate Gallery should be established as the home of British art, with a separate administration and autonomous trustees.[65]

But it was during the inter-war years that these cultural directorships became increasingly concentrated in the hands of a few grandees. Lord Stanhope, following his uncle, his father, and his grandfather, joined the board of the National Portrait Gallery in 1930, and became the first chairman of the trustees of the National Maritime Museum three years later. With his political career abruptly ended, Lewis Harcourt consoled himself with a viscountcy, with seats on the boards of the British Museum, the National Gallery, and the Wallace Collection, and was also a founder and trustee of the London Museum. Sir Evan Charteris, the sixth son of the tenth Earl of Wemyss, was chairman of the Tate and the National Portrait Gallery boards, and was also a trustee of the Wallace Collection and the National Gallery. The sixth Earl of Ilchester was chairman of the

Royal Literary Fund and President of the Walpole Society, and sat on the boards of the British Museum and the National Portrait Gallery. And the future Earl of Harlech combined the boards of the Tate, the British Museum, and the National Gallery with the Presidency of the National Museum of Wales.

The best-documented example of this is Lord Crawford himself. We have already met him as a man who refused to be Mayor of Wigan but was happy to become Chancellor of Manchester University. His ancestors were great collectors; his father was a trustee of the British Museum; and he himself was a man of real discernment and sensibility. Even before his political fulfilment and nemesis at the hands of Lloyd George, he had begun to make his mark in the art and museum world. In the late 1890s, he was a member of a committee on the South Kensington Museum of Science and Art, whose recommendations led to the setting up of the V&A in its modern form. In 1900, he helped to pass the Ancient Monuments Preservation Act; in 1903 he became the first President of the National Art Collections Fund; and he was soon put on the boards of the National Gallery and the National Portrait Gallery.[66] While his political career prospered, in the Commons from 1895 to 1913, and in the Lords from 1916 to 1922, he had already established a reputation as a disinterested statesman in the cultural world which was to stand him in good stead when the Lloyd George coalition fell.

And so, despite his momentary gloom of October 1922, he was fully occupied in the inter-war years, as he saw in cultural entrepreneurship an important way of disseminating the brand of decency preached by Baldwin, to which he became increasingly attracted. Among his minor offices, he was President of the London Society, the Society of Antiquaries, and the Survey of London Committee. He was chairman of the Royal Commission on Historical Monuments, and a member of the Committee on the Mint and on the History of Parliament. He became a trustee of the British Museum ('The only post I ever coveted'). And he was the first chairman of the Royal Fine Arts Commission and of the Council for the Preservation of Rural England.[67] In the next generation, his son and heir followed the same path. On the eve of the Second World War, he was already a trustee of the Tate, the National Gallery, and the British Museum; and on his father's death in 1940, was to take over many of his positions as well.

From the groves of academe to the coverts of culture was a natural progression for such men; and from there to the corridors of power was only another step. Although it is true that the number of royal commissions diminished markedly in this period, this was more than outweighed by the massive proliferation of government committees and departmental advisory boards, which were largely the result of the pressures of war combined with the growth of a collectivist state. Between 1914 and 1939, the number of effective central and local advisory councils grew from none to 200.[68] In the inter-war years, the Ministry of Health set up 125 advisory committees, and the Board of Trade 76. And in the same period, the UGC, the BBC, the MRC, the National Assistance Board, and the Agricultural Research Council were all brought into being. By 1935, such boards, councils, committees, and commissions were presenting public reports to Parliament at the rate of seventy a year.

These organizations had to be staffed, and they had to be chaired: and members of the titled and genteel classes had a strong claim to be considered fit and proper material. In some matters, like agriculture or architecture, they might be genuine experts. More generally, those attributes of leisure, dignity, a broad view, and a disinterested tone, which were so appropriate in these other fields, were again just what was needed. They were less inclined to be controversial or acrimonious; they were reasonable, emollient, and fairminded; and they could temper the excessive zeal of special interest groups and departmental bureaucracy. Accordingly, many of the greatest late-nineteenth and early-twentieth-century committees and commissions were chaired by patricians: the Duke of Richmond was in charge of the Royal Commission on Agricultural Depression (1881–2); Lord Bessborough led the Committee of Inquiry into the Irish Land Act of 1870 (1881); Lord Cowper was responsible for the Royal Commission on the Irish Land Acts of 1881 and 1885 (1887); Lord Iddlesigh chaired the Royal Commission on the Depression of Trade and Industry (1886); Lord Carrington looked after the Royal Commission on Land in Wales and Monmouth (1894–6); and Lord Peel headed the Royal Commission on Licensing (1895–7).

Indeed, some patricians acquired such reputations for conscientious probity that they were in regular demand as chairmen of such committees. The ninth Earl of Elgin headed a wide variety of official inquiries: on the finance of Scottish secondary education in 1892, on Scottish prisons in 1900, on salmon fishing and on military preparedness for the Boer War in 1902, on dividing the property of the free Scottish churches in 1905, and on the finances of the Scottish universities in 1907.[69] But Elgin was far surpassed as a full-time committee man by his fellow Scot and distant relative, Lord Balfour of Burleigh. Between 1882 and 1917, he was in charge of inquiries into the educational endowments of Scotland, the water supply of London, the system of rating and local taxation, the nation's food supply in time of war, the scope for closer trade links between Canada and the West Indies, and the commercial and industrial policy to be followed

582 Light of Common Day

after the war. His abilities were well summarized by his obituarist:
'Without brilliance, he yet represented the best type of public servant
– conscientious, purposeful, and with a gift for mastering complicated details and presenting them lucidly and cogently.'[70]

In the inter-war years, these conscientious and purposeful committee men continued their labours. Some sat in the chair only once,
like Londonderry on London Squares (1927), Chelmsford on the
Miners' Welfare Fund (1931), and Stonehaven on Slow Burning Fuel
(1938).[71] But others were in demand more frequently. Lord Onslow
was Parliamentary Secretary to the Minister of Health from 1921 to
1923, and found himself in charge of several committees as a result:
on voluntary hospitals, rent restrictions, and local government. Lord
Bledisloe was an expert on agriculture, who chaired royal commissions on sugar supply and land drainage; and so was Lord Linlithgow, who was in charge of investigations into agricultural prices and
produce, and agriculture in India. Lord Desborough, by contrast,
was merely well connected: he led a wartime committee on fresh-
water fish, and was chairman of the Thames conservancy. But he
did live at Taplow and had twice swum the pool below Niagara Falls
as a young man, which may have given him some useful aquatic
experience.

Two particular patricians stand out in the inter-war years as full-
time committee men. The first was James William Lowther, who
was created Viscount Ullswater in 1921.[72] He was a great grandson
of the first, and a nephew of the third Earl of Lonsdale, and was
senior trustee of the family estates. He was elected Deputy Speaker in
1895, became Speaker ten years later, and held the job until 1921.
Before and after his retirement, he was in constant demand as a chairman. He confronted tricky constitutional questions, heading one
conference on devolution, two on electoral reform, and a Royal
Commission on Proportional Representation. He investigated established institutions with tact and firmness, as with the Royal Commission on Cambridge University and the committee of inquiry into the
BBC. He handled topics of great complexity, on which there were
many conflicting views, as with the Royal Commission on London
Government. He brought expert knowledge to bear, as when he
chaired the Agricultural Wages Board. And he dealt with sensitive
subjects, where knowledge and finesse were required, as with the
review committee on political honours in the aftermath of Lloyd
George.

The second was Edgar Vincent, sixteenth baronet, who obtained
a peerage in 1914 and a viscountcy twelve years later.[73] In the course
of a varied life, he enjoyed three separate careers: as a financier in
Turkey and Egypt in the 1880s and 1890s,[74] as a party politician in
the 1900s, and as the first Ambassador to the Republic of Germany

between 1920 and 1926. But he was also in great demand as a chairman and committee man. Wearing his hat as a businessman and financier, he chaired the Royal Commission on Imperial Trade (1912–17) and led the British economic mission to South America in 1929. His interest in the arts brought him trusteeships of the Tate and the National Gallery, and the chairmanship of the Royal Commission on National Museums and Public Galleries (1927–30). His friendship with Lloyd George resulted in the chairmanship of the Central Control Board (Liquor Traffic), from which he emerged a committed opponent of alcohol among the workers, and this led to the chairmanship of the Industrial Fatigue Research Board and the MRC. And in between, he was placed on the advisory committee of the Royal Mint, and served on the racecourse betting control board.

What was the importance of these developments, in education, in culture, and in governmental bureaucracy, as far as the notables were concerned? Of course, there had been chancellors of universities, trustees of art galleries, and chairmen of royal commissions long before the 1880s. But it was only in this period that they coalesced and interlocked, and became important and recognizable elements in the national culture. And it was only in this period, too, that members of the titled and genteel classes began to find such activities an increasing, and even a dominant, part of their life and work. Yet, as with titled mayors, it is important to keep these activities in perspective. What, in addition to lending and enhancing their own prestige, did men like Crawford actually do? On the whole, not much. Just as the history of towns in this period is normally written with only limited reference to patrician involvement, so the history of universities, of museums, and of royal commissions is usually – and rightly – written without the landed establishment playing a major role. On the whole, these institutions were more important to the patricians than they were to them.

In the case of British universities, the aristocratic contribution should certainly be recognized, but must not be overrated. Most of the initiative and funding for the big English redbricks came from local businessmen; in Scotland it was a combination of fees, government grants, and Carnegie's generosity; and in Wales it was almost entirely state aid. Indeed, in Bristol and Birmingham, the contributions of H. O. Wills and Joseph Chamberlain were so significant that patrician chancellors were initially dispensed with altogether.[75] In Scotland, too, there were outsiders like Kelvin, Carnegie, and J. M. Barrie. One Dublin university went for the Earls of Iveagh, the other for a cardinal and de Valera. Baldwin was Chancellor of Cambridge and St Andrews. Even the trend of landed lord rectors was on the wane by the 1910s, as such men were superseded by new, non-patrician politicians like Asquith, Lloyd George, Haldane, Bonar Law, Austen Chamberlain, and Birkenhead. Here, as elsewhere, the old landed élite was gradually infiltrated and undermined by the new politicians, professionals, and plutocrats.

And where they *were* involved, the patrician contribution was rarely of major significance.[76] Even as ceremonial figure-heads, they were not invariably punctilious. At Belfast, Lord Shaftesbury's residence in England 'made it difficult for him to fulfill many of the duties of the office', and when he resigned as Chancellor, 'it had been well over a year since he presided at a graduation ceremony.' His successor, Lord Londonderry, was the same: 'on formal occasions, he . . . played his part with dignity, and the office demanded little more.'[77] Sometimes, even dignity could not be relied on. When Curzon was elected as Lord Rector of Glasgow, his installation was twice postponed, once owing to ill-health, and a second time because of the House of Lords constitutional crisis. Eventually he delivered his rectorial address in January 1911, only nine months before his three-year term expired. And in Sheffield in the following year, the Duke of Norfolk was so eager to catch a train that he abruptly closed a degree congregation early, leaving some of the graduands unpresented, bewildered, and somewhat annoyed.[78]

Moreover, although they might thus represent the university to the world, such noble chancellors played little part in the internal administration, once they were successfully established. They might be useful if they co-operated with others, or helped to nudge things in the direction they were going anyway; but they themselves had little real power or initiative. Bute could obstruct and hold things up at St Andrews; but he could not do so indefinitely, and he could not carry his alternative policy instead.[79] Curzon was much more successful as President of the Royal Geographical Society, where he swam with the tide, than as Chancellor of Oxford, where he could neither persuade the university to reform itself nor keep out the royal commission indefinitely.[80] These words on the ninth Duke of Devonshire as Chancellor of Leeds make this point plainly to the well-tuned ear: 'His judgement was invariably sound and discerning; and when he took the initiative, it was always with discretion, and to the advantage of the university.'[81] Discretion, indeed, was the better part of glamour.

With the great cultural institutions, the position was essentially the same: the financial power and administrative initiative lay elsewhere; the representatives of the old titled and territorial élite were in no sense the dominant figures. As with the universities, most of the great benefactions to galleries came from rich industrialists and plutocrats, who often saw such philanthropy as a way of obtaining honours. Henry Tate gave the pictures and £80,000 to set up the gallery that bears his name, and was duly rewarded with a baronetcy. William Henry Alexander gave £80,000 of the £96,000 for the building of the National Portrait Gallery. Sam Courtauld gave £50,000 to the Tate, as well as his paintings, his house in Portman Square, and an endowment to establish the Institute that bears his name.[82] And the younger Duveen donated more than £250,000 for such purposes, including extensions to the Tate and the National Portrait Gallery, new galleries for the Elgin Marbles at the British Museum, and an endowment for a chair in art history at London University.[83] And he was duly rewarded, with a knighthood, a baronetcy, and ultimately a peerage.

But in addition, Courtauld, Lee, Duveen, and Sassoon obtained seats on the boards of the Tate, the National Gallery, the Wallace Collection, and the National Portrait Gallery, and wielded far more power than patricians like Crawford.[84] And the initiative that was not held by these plutocrats resided with the permanent staff. At the British Museum, directors like Sir Edward Thompson and Sir Frederick Kenyon were dictatorially dominant. As Lord Crawford's diaries make plain, the board did essentially what these men told it to do: great issues of policy and development were not discussed, the agenda was not circulated in advance, and the minutes had to be returned to the director. 'The fact is', Crawford concluded, 'that the trustees do not exercise adequate control.'[85] And the National Gallery was even worse: Sir Charles Holmes all but ignored the board; Kenneth Clark was more tactful but no more subservient; many of the trustees like Macdonald, Baldwin, and the Prince of Wales were not remotely interested (Crawford called them 'duds'); and Duveen could not be kept out. Even Lord Lee found the board 'the most unsatisfactory and futile and the greatest waste of time.'[86]

In the same way, most government committees were rarely at the cutting edge of political activity, but were usually set up to pacify, to buy time, to win support for policies, or to put a project to sleep.[87] Predictably, then, many of the commissions chaired by aristocrats came to little or nothing. The Richmond and Carrington inquiries into agriculture gathered information, but little more. Lord Peel's committee on licensing was so divided that he himself was in a minority, there was no action until 1908, and then the House of Lords threw the bill out. Lord Frederick Cavendish's report in 1910 on the electoral system aroused so little interest that it was not even discussed in the Commons. The Ullswater Committee on London Government was no more successful: its terms of reference were too broad, it was inadequately briefed, and there were two minority reports. Indeed, the committees that were fruitful only corroborate this view. Bledisloe on drainage and Londonderry on squares both led to legislation, but they were on trivial topics. And some of Onslow's recommendations on local government were embodied in the 1929 Act, but only because the cabinet had made up its mind it wanted legislation in any case.[88]

Moreover, whether important or not, the patricians provided only a minority of the chairmen for these committees. Of the 13 appointed by the Postmaster-General between 1921 and 1938, only 5 were led by peers. Of the 112 advisory committees set up for the Ministry of Health between 1917 and 1938, only 25 were chaired by peers, and half of these were recent, non-landed, creations.[89] For, with twentieth-century committees, as with twentieth-century government, it was expertise that ultimately mattered more than decency and dignity, character and fair-mindedness. Most of the greatest committee men in this period were academics and doctors, businessmen and lawyers, people with detailed knowledge of complex matters, who could master a brief and draft a report, like Samuel and Sankey on coal, Cunliffe on currency and exchange, Balfour on industry and trade, May on import duties. Indeed, Macmillan (a lawyer) and Colwyn (a businessman) far surpassed the labours even of D'Abernon or Ullswater: between them, they chaired or sat on more than twenty government committees, ranging from lunacy via income tax to honours.[90]

Beyond doubt, as university chancellors, cultural trustees, and committee chairmen, these public-spirited grandees regularly displayed such admirable qualities as decency, dignity, dutifulness, decorousness, and disinterestedness. And by so doing, they also renewed and enhanced their own aristocratic prestige. But once again, they were very much the junior partner, with the professionals, the plutocrats, and the middle classes wielding much more power. When they recognized that this was the case, accepted the real limits to their influence, and co-operated with those who held the initiative, then they could perform useful and decorative functions. But ultimately, they were told by others what to do. All this is well shown in the case of the BBC. As an institution, it was a unique amalgam of education and culture, bureaucracy and high-mindedness. And, during the inter-war years, four patricians were closely involved with it at crucial stages in its history: Lord Gainford, Lord Crawford, Lord Clarendon, and Lord Ullswater. But compared with the massive achievement of Sir John Reith, their importance was negligible.

Gainford was appointed first chairman of the Board of the British Broadcasting Company in 1922, and when it received its royal charter and became a corporation four years later, he became its first vice-chairman. But at the outset, he was told that his duties would 'not be arduous', he was paid only £500 a year, and having appointed John Reith as General Manager in 1922, he wielded no real influence thereafter, and in 1933 he came off the board altogether.[91] The ubiquitous Lord Crawford chaired the government committee of 1925–6 which duly recommended that the BBC be turned from a private company into a chartered public corporation. But while he lent the committee 'the desired weight of authority and gravity', it was Reith who actually dominated its deliberations; and its recommendations merely embodied in authoritative language a course of action that was already a foregone conclusion. The report may have had Crawford's name on it, but it was in reality 'a magnificent personal triumph for Reith'.[92]

The first chairman of the new corporation was Lord Clarendon, an appointment that Asa Briggs tactfully describes as 'unfortunate'. He was not very bright, lacked imagination, sympathy, and political courage, and had no great committee experience. Reith found him to be quite impossible, and after discussing the matter with Ramsay Macdonald, Clarendon was shipped off abruptly, in February 1930, to be Governor-General of South Africa.[93] Thereafter, Reith was once again able to rule unchallenged at the BBC, and his conception of its organization and its purpose was fully endorsed by the Ullswater Committee, set up to inquire into the future of the Corporation when its charter expired in 1936. Ullswater was appointed to give the inquiry appropriate 'judicial or quasi judicial status'; but he was by then already in his eightieth year, and his attitude to it was summed up as 'the shorter the better'. He wasted no time, made no waves, and said exactly what was expected. Although Reith himself was unhappy about some aspects of the report, and although he was soon to leave the BBC, he was right in his comment that 'it gives us all we want.'[94]

No doubt the BBC was an exceptional institution in many ways: it was well liked and generously treated by most politicians; it was dominated by one towering and tyrannical figure who knew exactly what he wanted to do and was able to achieve it; and it was quite astonishingly successful in its widespread dissemination of high culture and decent values. But where it was much more typical was in the limited scope it gave to aristocratic endeavour. In terms of its foundation, organization, management, and funding, the power and the initiative lay emphatically elsewhere. Grandees had their uses – provided they did what they were told. But if they did not, they were got rid of. And in terms of propaganda, the BBC was by far the most effective riposte devised in the inter-war years to plutocratic corruption and the irresponsible press. But once again, the forces of

decency were under middle-class, rather than patrician management.
Just as Baldwin accomplished more than the Cecils, so Reith was far
more significant than Crawford.

iii. The Empire: 'Great Ornamentals'

One of Hilaire Belloc's most memorable and well-judged creations is
the lachrymose Lord Lundy. He is the grandson of a duke, and a
great political career is confidently predicted for him. But his prospects are ruined because he cries too easily, and the most that he
eventually achieves is the dubious distinction of an overseas posting:

> Sir! You have disappointed us!
> We had expected you to be
> The next Prime Minister but three.
> The stocks were sold, the press was squared;
> The middle class was quite prepared.
> But as it is . . . My language fails!
> Go out and govern New South Wales![95]

In reality, many peers trod this proconsular pathway, as the proliferation of dignified jobs at home was exactly paralleled by the expansion of such decorative appointments abroad. Between the 1880s and
the 1930s, the British Empire provided secure, comfortable, well-
paid, and essentially ornamental employment opportunities in quite
unprecedented numbers. And the result was a system of outdoor
relief for the upper classes on a scale of which even John Bright had
never dreamed.

During the first three-quarters of the nineteenth century, imperial
administration was distinctly unattractive as a patrician career, except to a few impoverished aristocrats. The colonies were small,
distant, dangerous, and inhospitable; the salaries, benefits, and conditions of work were unappealing; and the top jobs usually went to
middle-class professionals who had spent a lifetime in the colonial
service. But all this changed from the 1880s, as the growth and
consolidation of the formal empire led to the creation of new and
attractive plumage positions, which were most appropriately filled
by men of high status and illustrious lineage. India acquired an
empress in 1877, and thereafter all Viceroys had to be peers. Canada
was confederated in 1867, and from the time of Dufferin, all
Governors-General were expected to be noblemen. Australia became
a federation in 1900 and needed a Governor-General to preside; New
Zealand was declared a dominion in 1907; and in 1910 the Union of
South Africa was created, the last great experiment in imperial
nation-building.

With this heightened sense of colonial self-awareness, and imperial self-satisfaction, it no longer sufficed to send a middle-class, professional, career official to represent the monarch in such places. As Joseph Chamberlain explained to the Queen when Colonial Secretary, the 'Colonies were not content unless a person of high rank and remarkable distinction was appointed.'[96] In fact, it was the title that counted for more. As one jaundiced professional noted, 'men who had served an apprenticeship in the Colonial as in every other service' were now denied the great jobs at the top of the career ladder, while 'untried and juvenile noblemen', who had been 'selected rather for their coronets they have inherited than for any distinction they have gained' were appointed in their place. Put more abruptly, this meant that proncosular posts had become 'a piece of patronage which a benevolent British government could bestow on the aristocracy.'[97]

And bestow them they did. Even among the lesser jobs, there was a marked influx of patrician personnel at the close of the nineteenth century. In New Zealand, from 1889 to 1904, the new and noble governors were, successively, Lords Onslow, Glasgow, and Ranfurly. In India, the same trend was marked among the provincial governors: Lords Reay, Harris, Sandhurst, and Northcote in Bombay; and Lords Wenlock, Connemara, and Ampthill in Madras. And it was even more pronounced in the Australian colonies: Jersey, Hampton, and Beauchamp in New South Wales; Hopetoun, Brassey, and Carmichael in Queensland; and Kintore and Tennyson in South Australia. And this new pattern remained the norm well on into the inter-war years, with Northcote, Willingdon, Lloyd, Braborne, and Lumley in Bombay; Carmichael, Zetland, Lytton, and Braborne in Bengal; and Somers, Chelmsford, Wakehurst, Gowrie, and Huntingfield in the Australian states. And these were all landed-establishment men, as were commoners like Sir Arthur Stanley (a brother of Lord Derby) in Madras, and Sir Francis Newdegate (a classic country gentleman) in Tasmania and Western Australia.

As Appendix G shows, the governors of India and the great dominions were almost invariably aristocrats from the 1880s to the 1930s: as mayors they may have been unusual, but as proconsuls they were the norm.[98] In South Africa, before 1937, those who were not landed were members of the royal family. In New Zealand, all had direct ancestors in Bateman, except Jellicoe, who had set himself up as a landed grandee thanks to the parliamentary grant that accompanied his peerage after the war. In Australia, the same was true, except for Tennyson, who was the son of the Poet Laureate, and who had authentic patrician connections, and Forster, who was a minor landowner, and who had married a daughter of Lord Montagu of Beaulieu. In Canada, all were impeccably aristocratic, except the

Duke of Connaught and the Earl of Athlone, who were royals, and John Buchan, a self-made man who had married a Grosvenor. And in India, all but one were classic patricians, even though neither Hardinge nor Chelmsford owned extensive estates.

Indeed, there were only three complete outsiders during this period, the non-genteel exceptions that essentially prove the rule. One was Rufus Isaacs, Lord Reading, a self-made lawyer-cum-politician, whom we have already encountered in the context of the Marconi Scandal, and who was later made Viceroy of India as a friendly gesture by Lloyd George. The second was his namesake, Sir Isaac Isaacs, whose appointment as the first native-born Governor-General of Australia under the new system caused George V great distress. And the third was Sir Patrick Duncan in South Africa, who was also native-born. But with these conspicuous and unusual exceptions, these jobs were virtually a patrician monopoly – so much so that when Violet Markham first proposed John Buchan for Canada in 1925, she recommended him as 'a change from the correct and conventional peer usually selected for these posts'; and when he finally landed the job ten years later, his appointment was welcomed in some quarters as 'a change from the conventional run of aristocratic fainéants.'[99]

As with titled mayors, chancellors, and committee men, the same names kept recurring with remarkable frequency, since dynastic succession and individual accumulation were once more widely practised. Many proconsuls were inter-related. Halifax's wife was Onslow's daughter; Grey was Minto's brother-in-law; one of Dufferin's daughters was married to Plunket, another to Munro-Ferguson. And there was also a high degree of family continuity, as if ancestral achievement – or lack of it – was itself somehow a recommendation. In India, Elgin followed Elgin, like the de la Warrs at Bexhill; one Lord Lytton was Viceroy while his son was Governor of Bombay; and Lord Mayo's younger brother, ennobled as Lord Connemara, was Governor of Madras. In New Zealand, three generations of the Fergusson family served as Governor-General, the first in the 1870s, the last in the 1960s. And in Australia, the Earl of Hopetoun was created Marquess of Linlithgow after serving as the first Governor-General of the Commonwealth, while his son, the second marquess, was the last peacetime Viceroy of India.

For those who established themselves as proconsular perennials, there was also a recognized ladder. Some, like Carmichael, Brabourne, and Newdegate, were moved around from state to state in Australia, or from province to province in India. Some, like Hopetoun, Tennyson and Gowrie, were promoted from junior positions to be Governors-General of Australia. Northcote, on the other hand, was imported from Bombay, whereas Chelmsford travelled in the opposite direction, from the state governorships of Queensland and New South Wales to the Viceroyalty itself. An even greater prize was to tread the golden path from Canada to India, as did Dufferin, Lansdowne, and Minto. Indeed, for those who were really lucky – or extremely good at lobbying – it was possible to spend virtually an entire lifetime on such proconsular progress. Between 1913 and 1936, Lord Willingdon moved from Bombay to Madras as Provincial Governor, then on to Canada as Governor-General, and finally back to India as Viceroy. During this period, he lived in some fifteen summer and winter residences; so it is hardly surprising that by the time he reached New Delhi, his notion of proconsular grandeur (to say nothing of his wife's) was very highly developed indeed.[100]

What sort of patricians became proconsuls? Like Lord Lundy, most were not men of great ability. *Pace* Joseph Chamberlain, they were stronger on 'high rank' than on 'remarkable distinction'. In New Zealand, Onslow, Bledisloe, and Islington were minor politicians; Plunket, Ranfurly, and Galway were not even that; Jellicoe was sent out to recover from Jutland; and Fergusson was a military man of even less renown. In Australia, Hopetoun was a bad first choice (neither Argyll nor Rosebery would do it), Tennyson was a stopgap, and the rest were uniformly undistinguished, except for Gowrie, who had won the VC in the Sudan in 1898. In South Africa, Gladstone and Buxton were superannuated politicians, and Clarendon was shipped out to get him off Reith's back at the BBC. And in Canada, the picture was essentially the same: Byng and Buchan were household names before they went out; Dufferin and Lansdowne achieved fame after they came home; the rest never really made reputations at all.

Indeed, this description of Lord Stanley may well serve for them all: 'he was fat, lethargic, honourable, not too bright, uxorious, without high seriousness, but absolutely straight.'[101] Even the Viceroyalty of India, widely regarded as 'the greatest office in the world', and as the summit of many a man's ambition, was occupied by some remarkably undistinguished people: Dufferin and Lansdowne were more charming than weighty; Elgin was a 'cautious, silent young Scottish peer', whose reputation has defeated all well-meaning attempts to revive it; Minto was 'one of those men who would probably never have risen to the high offices he held except in a country where some deference is still paid to the claims of birth and position'; Chelmsford was 'little more than a nonentity', and was serving as a captain in the Territorials when the summons to Simla came; and Halifax was actually turned down as Governor-General of South Africa by Smuts in 1920, on the grounds that he was not

114. Lord Curzon as
Viceroy of India.

distinguished enough, a view that the rest of his career in British
politics does much to endorse.[102]

Sometimes, indeed, appropriateness, experience, and expertise
seemed to be a positive disadvantage. In late 1930, urgent discussion
was begun as to who should replace Irwin in India, and the second
Marquess of Zetland seemed the obvious choice. He had the support
of the King, of Baldwin, of Macdonald, of *The Times*, and of the
Secretary of State for India. As Lord Ronaldshay, he had travelled
widely in the east; he had served on a royal commission into Indian
affairs; he had been a firm but fair Governor of Bengal; he wrote a
series of distinguished books exploring the psychology of Indian
unrest; and he produced the official, three-volume life of Curzon.
Throughout the twenties, he was talked of as a future Viceroy, and
he very much wanted to do it. But in 1930, his pre-eminent claims
were overridden by such Labour ministers as Henderson, on the
grounds that he was too staunch a Conservative to appoint. The job
was offered to several Labour people who were either inappropriate
or refused, and eventually was taken by Willingdon (once a Liberal
MP), who was thus the oldest Viceroy appointed. As Beatrice Webb
explained, it was a case of 'party first and India second.'[103]

This was but an extreme example of a general tendency, to appoint grandees with little appropriate experience or qualifications. When Beauchamp went out as an Australian state governor, he was only in his late twenties, and his knowledge of public life was limited to being Mayor of Worcester. Apart from Willingdon, none of the patrician governors of New Zealand, South Africa, or Canada had been proconsuls before: Grey had been General Administrator of Rhodesia, but that was a very different type of job, and in any case, he had not done it very well. And when Aberdeen returned from Canada, George V refused to promote him to marquess, because he had not been a success.[104] In governing India, previous Canadian experience might even have been a positive disadvantage, since the one post required an inflexible figure-head, while the other – especially in its later phases – required rather different abilities. With the exception of Curzon, Willingdon, and Linlithgow, most Viceroys knew little about India when they set foot there – and some did not know that much more when they left.

One explanation for this is that many holders of these jobs were superannuated politicians: those who believed, cynically, that the empire was a dumping ground for patricians who were disenchanted with democracy or who had failed in their careers were at least partially correct. A few of them, like Zetland, Curzon, and Halifax, actually looked forward to such appointments, partly because they genuinely believed in the white man's burden, but also because they sought release from the House of Commons. Some, like Newdegate and Willingdon, received these jobs as a reward for loyal but undistinguished service on the back-benches. Some, like Bledisloe, Stonehaven, Erskine, and Huntingfield, were disappointed politicians, who had failed to advance beyond junior rank. And there were also some larger casualties: the Liberals shipped off Pentland to Madras, and Gladstone and Buxton to South Africa, when they had outlived their usefulness in the cabinet. In short, very few genuinely gifted grandees ever took these jobs on out of choice or out of ambition.

There was also a pronounced Celtic element among these patrician proconsuls, just as there was among patrician company directors. Linlithgow, Novar, Stonehaven, Gowrie, Argyll, Aberdeen, Minto, Elgin, Glasgow, and Fergusson were all Scottish; while Mayo, Dufferin, Lansdowne, Devonshire, Bessborough, Ranfurly, and Plunket were all Irish and Anglo-Irish. The justification for this was that such men were thought to be less stiff, stuffy, and superior than Little Englanders, and so would go down better with the more informal colonists.[105] But as the possessors of estates that were particularly vulnerable in the harsh economic and political climate of the time, they were also more eager for such preferment. For in the

115. Lord Halifax as Viceroy of India.

main, it was poverty that was the great spur to proconsular office. In South Africa, Clarendon was the poor son of a poor father, and both Gladstone and Buxton were younger sons in families far from rich. In New Zealand, their resources were decidedly modest, and the same was true in Australia, with the exception of the wealthy but profligate Dudley, and of Northcote, who was a younger son, but who had married the adopted daughter of Lord Mount Stephen, the Canadian railroad magnate. And in India and Canada, only Lansdowne, Stanley, and Devonshire were among the super-rich; but there, in each case, it was more nominal than real.

Moreover, many of these proconsuls were not only of limited acres, but were often financially embarrassed and heavily encumbered as well. Almost by definition, Irish landowners like Mayo, Ranfurly, and Plunket were in deep trouble from the 1880s onwards, if not before. Robert Bourke, the younger brother of Lord Mayo, who became Lord Connemara shortly after he was made Governor of Madras, was given the job because it was 'necessary to provide for him.'[106] Among Scottish owners, the Earls of Glasgow were still living with the massive debts piled up by the profligate fifth earl; the Fergusson estates were in a precarious position; and in the inter-war years, the Linlithgows were obliged to let Hopetoun House. The Elgin estate was small, and even by the 1890s, the family had not cleared off the debts arising from the purchase of the Greek marbles

116. Lord and Lady
Willingdon.

earlier in the century. And among English owners, both the Earl of
Onslow and the Earl of Jersey had to sell their famous family
libraries in the 1880s.[107]

To aristocrats in such straitened circumstances, these proconsular
postings were quite exceptionally attractive: indeed, they were just
about the most lucrative appointments in the British government's
gift. In 1910, the Archbishop of Canterbury received £15,000 a year,
and the First Lord of the Treasury £5,000. But the Viceroy of India
earned £19,000; the Governors-General of Canada, Australia, and
South Africa each received £10,000; and the Governor-General of
New Zealand £7,500. In addition, the great Indian governorships of
Madras, Bengal, and Bombay paid £9,000 apiece, and the most
lucrative state governorships in Australia – New South Wales, Victoria, and South Australia – were each worth £5,000.[108] Moreover,
the perks were on a correspondingly viceregal scale. There was at
least one grand mansion, which was decorated and maintained free
of charge, and in most cases, there was a summer retreat as well.
There was an extensive staff of indoor and outdoor servants, which
in India ran to several hundred. Transport to, from, and within the
country was paid for, and the Viceroy was provided with a special
train of unsurpassable splendour. The salary was untaxed, and there
was also a large entertainment allowance.[109]

So, while some straitened patricians looked to the City for financial salvation, others looked to the empire, clamouring for these jobs from the 1880s with a zeal that markedly contrasted to the indifference with which they had been regarded in the previous period.[110] In 1884, the fifth Earl Spencer, whose rentals had been severely reduced, considered asking for the Viceroyalty. 'I have thought about the Indian appointment a good deal during the last few days', he wrote. 'To be away for some years just now would also be convenient financially, as in the last few years agricultural depression has hit me somewhat sharply.' Although he chose not 'to lay much stress' on this argument, it clearly counted for something.[111] Five years later, at the very same time that he was entering the financial world, it was rumoured that Lord Randolph Churchill was after the same job. 'It is odd', Salisbury noted, contradictorily, 'that he should desire it. It is said that his pecuniary position is very bad.' And until Alec Murray received Weetman Pearson's more lucrative offer in 1911, he 'thought of going to Bombay or New Zealand' as governor.[112]

During Lord Salisbury's long period of almost unbroken power, from the mid-1880s to the early 1900s, impoverished grandees importuned shamelessly for these snug and lucrative appointments. In September 1895, Lord Kintore wrote to the Prime Minister, and clearly this was not his first request:

> May I again say what a help it would be if Lord Knutsford [the Colonial Secretary] could see his way to giving me [the Governorship of] Ceylon when it becomes vacant in April? I write just after signing the cheque for my half-yearly charges and jointures.[113]

In this case, persistence brought its reward. Although denied Ceylon, Kintore was soon despatched to South Australia. By contrast, the sixth Marquess of Hertford was not so lucky. He was a major Warwickshire landowner, who did stalwart service for the Conservatives in the county between the 1870s and the 1910s. But his rentals were much depleted, and in 1895 he asked for a place in the Queen's Household, which 'might just save my having to shut up and leave Ragley.' The request was unsuccessful, and two years later his wife wrote a direct, revealing, and equally futile appeal to the Prime Minister:

> In spite of all the work that he (and I may say, I) have done for the party, he has never had any recognition of his claims; now we have let the place, and are homeless for three years. If you could appoint Lord Hertford to a colonial governorship, it would be a great help

to us. It is very disheartening to see all the best posts going to the Unionists.[114]

One such Liberal Unionist beneficiary of the system was Lord Lansdowne. In 1883, he seemed set for a golden career in British politics, but decided instead to accept the Governor-Generalship of Canada. His reasoning was simple: he needed the money. On his father's death, he had succeeded to estates burdened with debts of £300,000; there were heavy family charges; the Scottish property had passed to his mother; the Irish rental, theoretically princely, was much diminished; he was obliged to sell some pictures; and he was afraid he might have to part with Lansdowne House.[115] Under these circumstances, a period away, retrenching in Canada, was an especially attractive option. And, when his term of office there ended, he simply moved on to India. The extent to which financial considerations weighed in taking these jobs is clearly shown in this letter to his mother:

> India means saving Lansdowne House for the family. I should be able while there not only to live on my official income, but to save something every year. If I can let Lansdowne House, I might by the time I come home have materially reduced the load of debt which has been so terrible an incubus to us all, and in the meantime I shall be doing useful work for my country, instead of living in a corner of the house in England, perpetually worried by financial trouble, and perhaps increasing instead of decreasing the family liabilities.[116]

Other landowners were equally calculating and self-interested in their decisions to pursue proconsular careers abroad. Lord Lytton hoped to save £30,000 during his time as Viceroy of India. We have already met Lords Bessborough, Grey, Bledisloe, and Linlithgow, all of whom had taken up careers in the City to alleviate their financial anxieties. Before he accepted governorships in Australia and India, the future Lord Carmichael had been obliged, in the 1890s, to give up his county seat, to sell parts of his estate, and to augment his income with company directorships.[117] Lord Tennyson, while a state governor and Governor-General of Australia, intended to save enough money to educate his children, and to compensate for the decline in income from his father's royalties. And while the Duke of Devonshire was Governor-General of Canada, the major policy decision was taken to restructure his finances on a *rentier* rather than a landowning basis, by selling Devonshire House, and by investing the proceeds in stocks and shares, many of them, interestingly enough, in Canadian companies.[118]

Two of the greatest proconsuls, both with impeccable landed credentials, went even further, restructuring their finances so completely that they virtually ceased to be landowners at all. One of them, Lord Dufferin, held heavily encumbered estates in Ireland, which gave a very small disposable income, and which he began to part with from the late 1870s under successive Land Acts. As a result, he was obliged to earn his living, and it was this that turned him towards a diplomatic and proconsular career. Between 1872 and 1896, he was barely in the United Kingdom; his income from his embassies and his proconsulates was crucial for his financial survival; and most of his Irish estates were liquidated. Indeed, by the time he retired from government service, there was little land (or rental) left: hence the need to join the board of the London and Globe Company.[119] Likewise, Freeman Freeman-Thomas, later Lord Willingdon, was never more than a minor landowner in Sussex. In 1913, when he went out east as Governor of Bombay, he sold off half his Ratton estate. Thereafter, the rest of it was soon disposed of: only by his sustained proconsular progress could he continue to live in the patrician style to which he had been accustomed. Like Dufferin, as his career unfolded, his acres diminished.[120]

The real financial attraction of these proconsular jobs to many patricians should by now be clear. They lasted longer, and were more lucrative, than being mayor or chairing a royal commission; and they were more prestigious, and often less dangerous, than serving as a company director. Indeed, most poor and middling members of the landed élite were effectively – if temporarily – doubling their income, and many were also able to enjoy, at someone else's expense, a grander style of living than they themselves could afford at home. For any landowner of limited acres, or burdened with debt, or suffering from reduced rentals, or obliged to sell some or all of his lands, going out and governing New South Wales was an ideal – if temporary – solution. So it is hardly surprising that such jobs were so competed and lobbied for, in marked contrast to the earlier period, when they had often been hawked round.

Of course, governors frequently complained that they were obliged to spend more than their salary and allowance, often to the extent of £2,000 to £5,000 a year. But the economy measures of the rich are often different from those of the poor. Even expenditure of this magnitude might well be less than the annual cost of living in Britain. The country home and London house could be closed or let; many of the servants could be paid off; local subscriptions could be reduced. So, as Lansdowne had noted, taking a colonial governor-ship was a convenient and agreeable way of retrenching, while at the same time doing one's duty to one's country. Indeed, one of the most blatantly avaricious proconsuls, the Earl of Hopetoun, obtained £30,000 for eighteen months as the first Governor-General of Australia, as well as £45,000 in expenses.[121] 'Absentee landlords, unable to keep up their ancient style, and economising abroad', was a common description of many landowners in this period: it was also a perfect description of patrician proconsuls.[122]

And these were not the only financial gains that proconsuls made. For it was not just that these jobs paid well: they also opened the door to later employment in the City. On his return from Australia and India, Lord Carmichael was put on the boards of banking and insurance companies. After ruling Bengal, Lord Ronaldshay became Deputy Governor, and then Governor, of the Bank of Scotland. And for those who returned from even grander positions, directorships were almost to be had for the asking. Dufferin, of course, provides an early and spectacular example of how this might go wrong. But by the inter-war years, there was much less risk. When Novar returned from Australia, he became chairman of the North British Mercantile Assurance Company, a director of the National Bank of Scotland, and of the Railway Passengers Assurance Company.[123] When Bessborough completed his term in Canada, he resumed many of his City interests, becoming chairman of Rio Tinto, and President of the Council of Foreign Bondholders. Willingdon retired from India to the boards of the Westminster Bank and the London and Lancashire Insurance Company, and Linlithgow went straight from New Delhi to the chairmanship of the Midland Bank.[124]

Nor were the rewards – immediate and subsequent – merely financial. As the representatives of the monarch, proconsuls were obliged to wear a ribbon and a star: the Grand Cross of the Order of St Michael and St George for the white empire, or one or both of the Indian orders for the subcontinent. Most Viceroys and Canadian Governors-General were peers already, and those who were not were ennobled on their appointment, like Curzon (who took an Irish title so as to keep open the option of re-entering the Commons on his return) and Edward Wood, who was heir to the earldom of Halifax anyway, but was also created Lord Irwin in his own right. The same was true in South Africa, where Buxton and Gladstone were both given peerages before they went out. And it was only very rarely that the Governors-General of Australia and New Zealand had not inherited, or been given titles: Islington, Forster, and Stonehaven were all ennobled before they went out.

For those who did well, there was usually promotion or equiv-

alent recognition on their return. Successful state and provincial governors, like Carmichael and Northcote, were given baronies
as appropriate rewards. Munro-Ferguson, who had gone out to
Australia as a commoner, was created Viscount Novar on his return.
Bledisloe, Byng, and Chelmsford were all advanced from baron to
viscount as recognition of their labours; and Buxton, Gowrie, and
Curzon all became earls. Willingdon did even better, advancing
inexorably from baron to viscount to earl to marquess at each stage
in his proconsular progress. And even Aberdeen finally obtained the
promotion he craved. In addition, there were other honorific rewards available: Curzon (to his regret) and Willingdon both became
Lord Warden of the Cinque Ports; Clarendon was appointed Lord
Chamberlain; and several went on to join the boards of museums or
to chair royal commissions.

But what exactly did these be-ribboned representatives of their
monarch actually do? On the whole, not very much. India apart, the
Governor was expected to perform the Bagehot-like tasks of 'constitutional sovereign, guardian of imperial interests, and adviser of the
colony.' But after 1926, he was not even the chief means of com-
munication between the colony and the British government, as this
task was taken over by High Commissioners, appointed by the
colony and resident in London. Moreover, because governors came
and went more frequently than monarchs at home and colonial
politicians abroad, they could not even boast that reservoir of
accumulated experience with which both Victoria and George V
were able to advise (and intimidate) their ministers. On the contrary,
it was the politicians who knew more. This is why they were ideal
jobs for second-rate statesmen and backwoods aristocrats. As Lord
Londonderry explained, when turning down Canada in 1931, 'the
positions in which we are invited to represent your majesty are
rapidly becoming sinecures, and apart from entertaining and visiting
different parts of the area', there was almost nothing to do.[125]

They were, in short, supremely non-contentious positions, and it
was only bad luck or ill-judged behaviour that ever really threatened
this. There were, occasionally, some tricky moments, as when the
first Governor-General of Australia committed what became known
as the Hopetoun Blunder, by sending for the wrong party leader to
form the first federal administration, and later resigned in a huff over
his salary and allowances which, although princely, he regarded as
inadequate.[126] In South Africa, Gladstone faced some difficulties in
1912 when Botha resigned, and in Canada Byng got into trouble in
1926 by refusing Mackenzie King's request for a dissolution, and
then granting it to Meighten.[127] But on the whole, it was easy to stay
out of trouble, and these jobs could be safely entrusted to mediocre

men. Even in India, the Viceroyalty itself was relatively undemanding until the late 1920s. Curzon, of course, was a compulsive
worker; but Elgin, Dufferin, Lansdowne, Minto, and Chelmsford
coasted through comfortably. And although the going got rougher
later on, it was often the permanent civil service that effectively bore
the brunt of the work.[128]

In short, these proconsuls were expected to play a part aptly
described by a critic of the raj in the 1880s as 'great ornamentals.'[129]
Like titled mayors and chancellors, they were grand, genial, and
hospitable; they identified themselves closely with the affairs of the
colony; they got on well with men and women of all creeds and
classes; they placed themselves in touch with as many different
interests as possible; and they made themselves the friends of all
reasonable claims. Tactful, unaffected, approachable, sincere, sympathetic, accessible: these were the ideal proconsular attributes. Considering that most of the colonies were primary producers, it also
helped if the governor had links with agriculture. As landowners,
most did by definition; Bledisloe and Halifax had both been Secretary of Agriculture; and Bledisloe and Linlithgow had both chaired
royal commissions on the subject.[130] And it was an additional
advantage if they had reputations as good sportsmen: Willingdon
and Chelmsford were both excellent cricketers; Halifax and Dudley
were fine horsemen; most could shoot and many could fish.[131]

Thus described, the ideal proconsul was 'a high-minded Christian
gentleman', with the 'charm of a typical aristocrat of the old
country'.[132] And, in addition, he must be able, when occasion
required, to carry off the ceremonial side of the job as befitted its
viceregal function: entertaining punctiliously, providing splendid
dinners, balls, and receptions, accommodating visiting dignitaries,
and travelling in suitably magnificent style. This was especially so in
India, where the ceremonial of the court was quite extravagantly
grand, culminating in the three great durbars of 1877, 1902, and
1911. Curzon, of course, adored ceremonial, and Viceroys like
Halifax, Willingdon, and Linlithgow were men with striking physical presence. Even in the darkest days of the First and Second World
Wars, the ceremonial was kept up for the sake of appearances,
though by the early 1940s it was increasingly criticized in some
quarters as the 'laboured continuance, apparently for reasons of
prestige, of opulence that seemed unrelished.'[133]

More prosaically, these proconsuls were required to spend time in
their dominion in exactly the same way that Lord Derby spent time
in Lancashire: visiting communities, opening buildings, unveiling
memorials, laying foundation stones, and making speeches. As one
commentator explained, 'their life is one weary round of banquets,

balls, bazaars, public meetings, of visits to cattle shows, town halls, hospitals, schools, convents, races and regattas'[134]. So, within two days of their arrival in New South Wales, Lord and Lady Tennyson were subjected to a levee, a state appearance at the theatre, a reception for the YMCA at the town hall, a visit to a garden party given by the Mayor and Mayoress, an orchestral concert, and a fair for the blind: all this between Wednesday and Sunday. Of especial importance – as with being mayor – was the ability to make speeches: witty, emollient, orotund, uncontentious, extolling the merits and prospects of the locality and the greatness and unity of the country. It was, as Earl Grey put it, an exercise in 'walking on the tightrope of platitudinous generalities.'[135]

Like being a guinea-pig director or a decorative mayor, the job of ornamental proconsul was on the whole undemanding work. There was a secretariat to make the arrangements; the speeches were usually written by the staff; the colonial politicians were seen relatively infrequently; and even if the social life was in some ways demanding, it was no more arduous than the normal regime of country-house living at home.[136] For those who showed real talent, there was a lifetime's career to be made; for those who did less well, there were always the consolations of company directorships and perhaps a step in the peerage at the end. But with very rare exceptions, these were really holiday jobs: there was not even the close territorial connection of a mayoralty; they were far away from the political action in England; and the initiative in the colony lay emphatically with the local politicians. Fundamentally, they were social jobs rather than power positions. Most patricians who took them had failed as British politicians before they left home, and did not succeed when they returned.

iv. Conclusion: Schumpeter Revisited

Although Arthur Ponsonby had perceptively analysed the social prestige of the titled and genteel classes in the years before the First World War, he went on to claim that 'there is no room for a purely ornamental class in a modern state.'[137] But there, as Lowell more acutely recognized, Ponsonby erred. From the 1880s to the 1930s, the proliferation of ornamental positions, both in Britain and its empire, was quite extraordinarily widespread. Of course, many of them were often filled by people who were only part-time ornamentals: the working classes with their friendly-society and trade-union ceremonials; the lawyers and professionals who brought an informed dignity to boards and committees; the industrialists and the plutocrats who so often served as mayor of their town. In Britain, as throughout western Europe, life was becoming more ceremonial at all levels of society, so that to some extent at least, all classes were involved.

But within this broad perspective, two high-status groups assumed particular importance: at the national level, the monarchy was increasingly becoming an essentially ornamental institution; and at the local, the bureaucratic, and the imperial levels, the landed establishment was filling an essentially similar and complementary function. Some men, like the eighth Duke of Devonshire, Lord Curzon, or A. J. Balfour, regarded such jobs as agreeable distractions from the main business of life, which was politics and power. Some, like Lord Rosebery or Lewis Harcourt, took them up as a consolation. Some, like Lord Crawford or Lord Derby, deliberately chose such activities in preference to the great game in London. And some, like Lord Clarendon and Lord Willingdon, spent almost the whole of their lives being ornamental. Indeed, one reason why patrician participation in the formal political process diminished in this period may have been that these new jobs were so much more comfortable and less contentious.

For whatever reason, many grandees and gentry were increasingly able to occupy themselves with jobs that looked and sounded impressive, that took a great deal of time, that filled several columns in *Who's Who* and *Burke*, yet that, fundamentally, required them only to do what they were told, to stay out of trouble, to be beyond contention. In the towns, patrician mayoralties took place only after the landowners had withdrawn from active involvement in local government. On committees and in universities, the positions of chairman or chancellor required that those who held them should be essentially above the battle. And in the empire, the essence of proconsular office was dignity and detachment, which might only be jeopardized if the occupant had the bad luck to encounter a grave political crisis, or if (as in the case of Curzon) he pushed too hard. To that extent, the essence of these jobs lay not so much in *doing* as in *being*: in cutting a figure, setting a tone, sitting on a pedestal, rather than in making an impact on the course of events.

For those grandees who sincerely – if unrealistically – cherished more legitimate political ambitions, all this was very depressing. Lord Londonderry was a failed politician but a successful ornamental, and it is not clear which of these things he regretted more. 'All the many figurehead duties', he lamented in the aftermath of his dismissal by Baldwin, 'were very good accompaniments to the central and dominating duty, but they are uninteresting by themselves.'[138] As a chancellor of two universities, who had chaired a royal commission, served as a mayor, and turned down a Governor-

Generalship, he should have known. Yet others were quite happy to settle for this. Lord Crawford's fears when he fell with the Lloyd George coalition – that he would 'drop out', that his 'relaxations' would become his 'occupations' – were very well founded. But in his case, unlike Londonderry's, he did not mind.

For Crawford realized, as did many others, that on these changed terms, the traditional titled and territorial class could still do things, still justify its existence, still keep its prestige. But it required a real degree of self-effacement, of never taking the initiative, of not thrusting oneself forward, of encouraging and co-operating with the initiatives of others, but not instigating things oneself. When obituarists spoke of 'taking a keen interest', it was this sort of limited behaviour that they were really describing: promoting civic or dominion consciousness by speeches and ceremonial; giving their names, their prestige, and their donations to local initiatives and institutions; and exploiting their connections in the court and the cabinet to help things along, and bring people down. For those like Londonderry who aspired to do more, this was not enough. But for many others, it was quite sufficient.

Yet at the same time, the essence of these ornamental positions was that discretion had to be accompanied by ostentation. And, with the exception of the royal family itself, no group was better placed to meet this requirement than the aristocracy. Their tradition and training might make them increasingly anachronistic as far as running the country was concerned; but as far as decorating the country was concerned, it was precisely what was wanted. They could ride horses, stand to attention, make speeches. They could wear stars and orders, robes and tiaras, with assured swagger and style. They knew how to live in great houses, how to entertain, how to manage servants. As such, they met the increased demand for pomp and circumstance; they brought sparkle and romance into humdrum urban and colonial lives; men and women clamoured for invitations to the mayoral ball or a government house reception; they queued and stood for hours for a glimpse of the great, the good, and the glamorous. And the very fact that patricians were deferred to in this way was in itself a form of social power.

None of this argument would have come as any surprise to Joseph Schumpeter, the foremost commentator on the social, rather than the economic, imperatives to late-nineteenth-century imperialism. One of his concerns was to argue that, in any given social and historical situation, there are always to be found 'surviving features from earlier ages', not only as marginal anachronisms, but also as central and significant elements. So, for him, there was no paradox between the survival of the aristocracy and the drive to empire in late-nineteenth and early-twentieth-century Europe. Imperialism was an essentially atavistic impulse: not the highest stage of capitalism, but the negation of it; driven not by the pursuit of profit, but by the will to glory and to conquest, by the codes of chivalry and honour, of the old warrior and lordly class.[139] And, when looking at the aristocratic composition of the French army in the Sahara, or at the noble background of the governors of German colonies, it is easy to see why he reached the conclusions he did.

As with Hobson, so with Schumpeter, there is much in this that does not fit the British case. The tropical empire was neither made nor (with a very few exceptions) governed by patricians; they were happy to leave the administration of such inhospitable places as Ghana and Nigeria, the Sudan and the Gambia, to those very middle-class professionals in the Colonial Office whom they had driven out of the top jobs in the white dominions. But while the grandees and the gentry were not the British Empire's creators, they were indeed among its beneficiaries: they invested in colonial companies; they often became directors of them; they farmed and fornicated in Kenya; and they governed New South Wales. *Pace* Schumpeter, the connection between the British nobility and the British Empire was not that they were both hostile to capitalism, but rather that they were both well disposed to it.

But, again like Hobson, Schumpeter did notice something important. For all these fundamentally ornamental positions that proliferated so widely at this time – director of a company, mayor of a town, chancellor of a university, chairman of a committee, governor-general of a dominion – did indeed require skills and characteristics that, by tradition, training, and temperament, the old aristocratic order was best fitted to provide. As he rightly argued, 'the traditions of war, the lordly mode of life, the habit of command and of handling people', were ideal qualifications for filling these new and ornamental functions.[140] And, as Lowell had rightly observed, it was in large part by the filling of these roles that the grandees and gentry were able, not just to preserve, but actually to reconstruct their social prestige at the very time when in other ways it was being so threatened and undermined.

13

THE SECOND WORLD WAR

In Churchill, the descendant of Marlborough and historian of past glories, the oldest strain of ruling tradition had resurfaced . . . For five years, an aristocrat steeped in a romantic vision of his nation's role was the undisputed leader of an overwhelmingly working-class nation, of whose social conditions and daily concerns he was largely in ignorance.

(P. Addison, *The Road to 1945* (1975), pp. 13, 276.)

In the Second World War, the British people came of age. This was a people's war.

(A. J. P. Taylor, *English History, 1914–1945* (1965), p. 727.)

The struggle against the Nazis would merely hasten the erosion of the British aristocracy that had been slowly wearing out like wooden crosses on the graves in Flanders.

(A. Sinclair, *The Last of the Best: The Aristocracy of Europe in the Twentieth Century* (1969), p. 117.)

By the late 1930s, the British landed establishment was less British, less landed, and less of an establishment than it had been at any time since its marked disintegration first began during the 1880s. Some of its members still belonged, as individuals, to the wealth, the power, and the status élites. But collectively, the people who made up, or were descended from, or had once been part of the old territorial order were no longer conscious of themselves as God's elect. Wealth, power, and status had ceased to be either highly correlated or highly concentrated in the traditional broad-acred class. Most rich, most powerful, and most illustrious people no longer came from an authentically landed background, did not themselves become extensively landed, and on the whole had no desire to do so. On the eve of the Second World War, there may still have been an identifiable wealth élite, ruling class, and status stratum in Britain. But while some patricians qualified for inclusion as fortunate individuals, the majority collectively did not. Here was a measure of the changes that had taken place in the half-century from the 1880s.

Of course, in some cases the great territorial families had survived more successfully, more resourcefully, and more tenaciously than their enemies had hoped and their friends had feared would be the case during the late nineteenth and early twentieth centuries. And in 1939, it did indeed seem as though their fullest and finest hour had come. Beyond any doubt, the Second World War saw a triumphant 'aristocratic resurgence' in the corridors of power and on the battlefields.[1] Between 1940 and 1945, the British war effort was far more patrician in its supreme direction and high command than it had been between 1914 and 1918. In the localities, too, the old territorial classes once more appeared – in one guise as symbols of traditional authority, and in another as the agents of an increasingly intrusive central government. Moreover, despite the terrible toll exacted by the First World War, the grandees and the gentry rushed to join the colours once again. All this was noble and noteworthy. And at the same time, beneath the surface, there were many ways in which patrician life continued essentially as before, as traditional and recognizable modes of behaviour lingered on.

Yet despite the undeniable part played by the old territorial classes in the Second World War, this heroic and triumphant picture is curiously incomplete and in some ways highly misleading. For with the conspicuous – but largely accidental – exception of Churchill himself, the contribution of the patricians to the waging and the winning of the war was less significant than the contribution of other groups. In politics, most of the aristocratic figures were peripheral to the main business and fundamental decisions: their presence in Whitehall did not portend a real revival in government by the gentry and the grandees. On the contrary, in social and political terms, the most significant winners – and beneficiaries – of the war were the trade unions, the technocrats, and the businessmen, who established or consolidated their position as part of a broader and more diverse ruling class. By contrast, the patrician element in the war effort seemed at best transient and at worst almost superficial. Indeed, in some ways, a more accurate indication of the aristocracy's increasingly marginal position was the continued maverick activities of some of its members, both on the right and the left. For they were essentially tangential – and occasionally ridiculous – figures, in some cases full of sound and fury, but almost invariably signifying very little.

So, for all the Churchillian magniloquence, and aristocratic involvement, time was emphatically not on the patricians' side in 1939. Taking a broader view, it is clear that in the long run, this great conflict accelerated, more than it arrested, landed-establishment decline, decay, and disintegration. In part, this was because the surviving notables suffered the greatest deprivations: loss of income, loss of servants, loss of houses, and loss of life. But even more importantly, they lost what remained of their faith in themselves, in their class, in their purpose, and in their future. For the Second World War was almost universally seen, not as a battle to defend the old established order, but as a crusade to build a new, a better, and a very different world, a Welfare State society in which traditional aristocratic privilege was neither wanted nor admired. As the young Denis Healey brutally put it to the Labour Party Conference in May 1945, 'The upper classes in every country are selfish, depraved, dissolute and decadent.' Of course, this was not how it seemed to the grandees and the gentry who had sacrificed so much between 1939 and 1945. But for the majority of the population, the British effort to destroy Nazi tyranny and defend national honour was a peoples' war, not a patrician conflict.

i. Climacteric and Continuity

Nevertheless, when Winston Churchill succeeded Neville Chamberlain as Prime Minister in May 1940, he was the first authentically genteel Prime Minister to hold office since A. J. Balfour. As C. P. Snow has rightly described him, Churchill was 'the last aristocrat to rule – not preside over, rule – this country', and he did so with a mixture of power and panache, eloquence and magnanimity, which exemplified patrician high-mindedness at its most majestic.[2] His roots were firmly planted in the Whiggish traditions of the late-Victorian aristocracy; he was the grandson of a duke, to whose splendid titles and magnificent possessions he had once been heir; throughout his life, he regarded Blenheim Palace as his second home; he was closely related to the Londonderrys, the Airlies, and half the aristocracy of Britain; and he knew next to nothing about the ordinary lives of ordinary people. Lord Hugh Cecil had been his best man; the Hon. Freddie Guest and the second Duke of Westminster were among his oldest and closest friends; and he revered his cousin, the ninth Duke of Marlborough, as the head of his family, and as the bearer of the proudest name in the land.[3]

Predictably, Churchill surrounded himself with a ministerial entourage that was itself in many ways highly aristocratic. For most of the war, his Foreign Secretary and self-proclaimed successor was Anthony Eden, the younger son of a broad-acred north-country baronet, who was described by Beatrice Webb as 'an aristocratic country squire'. The Secretary of State for Air was another old and close friend, Sir Archibald Sinclair, fifth baronet, whose family had held estates in Caithness for generations, and who was both the MP and the Lord-Lieutenant of the county. On the home front, Churchill's closest friend and ally was another quintessential patrician, Oliver Lyttelton, whose father had sat with him in the Commons of the 1900s, and who was himself appointed President of the Board of Trade, then Minister of State in Cairo, and finally Minister of

Production. And Lord Cranborne, the eldest son of the fourth Marquess of Salisbury, was successively Dominions Secretary, Lord Privy Seal, and Lord President.[4] After having been called up to the Lords prematurely in 1941, he was chiefly responsible for the conduct of government business in the second chamber.

At a lower level, too, Churchill's administration was littered with landed luminaries. From 1941, the government chief whip was James Stuart, third son of the seventeenth Earl of Moray, who represented the local constituency of Moray and Nairn for thirty-six years.[5] J. T. C. Moore-Brabazon, an Anglo-Irish gentleman, was successively Minister of Transport and of Aircraft Production. Viscount Swinton returned to power as Minister Resident in West Africa, and subsequently became Minister of Civil Aviation. Oliver Stanley was brought back into the government as Colonial Secretary in 1942, and Lord Wolmer became Minister of Economic Warfare in the same year. The Duke of Devonshire was Parliamentary Under-Secretary of State for India and Burma, and subsequently for the Colonies. And in 1941, the premier peer in the land, the sixteenth Duke of Norfolk, became Under-Secretary of State for Agriculture.

In the Whitehall corridors of power, the patricians were equally well represented. Churchill's favourite private secretary was the young Jock Colville, closely related to many of the greatest grandees in the realm, and the grandson of Lord Crewe, who had been a Liberal colleague of the Prime Minister's in the 1900s. The tenth Earl of Drogheda was, successively, joint Director of the Ministry of Economic Warfare from 1940 until 1942, and thereafter Director General. The future last Duke of Portland, who had begun life in the diplomatic service, was Joint Secretary to the Chiefs of Staff Intelligence Committee.[6] When he was appointed Minister of Production, Oliver Lyttelton recruited two assistants: the Hon. Garrett Moore, future eleventh Earl of Drogheda, and the Hon. John Drummond, future seventeenth Earl of Perth. For most of the war, the personal assistant to Sir William Beveridge was the Hon. Frank Pakenham, brother and heir to the sixth Earl of Longford. And Harold Macmillan's wartime private secretary was the young John Wyndham, nephew of Lord Leconfield and heir to the splendid estates of Petworth.[7]

Throughout the war, the diplomatic service also retained its particularly aristocratic tone. The Permanent Under-Secretary at the Foreign Office was Sir Alexander Cadogan, the younger son of the fifth Earl Cadogan. In general, Churchill did not like the Foreign Office; but he got on well with Cadogan personally. They had moved in the same social circles all their lives and, as with Colville, there was a close family and ancestral connection: seven generations

before, the first Earl Cadogan had been the principal staff officer and
director of intelligence in ten campaigns of the first Duke of
Marlborough.[8] Even the diminished postings available overseas still
had their quota of patricians. In Washington, Lord Lothian was
replaced as Ambassador by Lord Halifax, another non-career diplomat, whom Churchill was eager to get out of the way. For similar
reasons, Lord Harlech was sent out to South Africa as High Commissioner. And in Ankara and the Vatican, the British government
was represented by such Trollopian figures as Sir Hughe Knatchbull-
Hugessen, and Sir D'Arcy Osborne, the future last Duke of Leeds.[9]

At the local level, too, the aristocracy and gentry were much in
evidence – representatives of established authority, put in ornamental positions or offices of real importance for the duration of the
conflict. In the towns, there was a noticeable resurgence in patrician
mayors: Sefton in Liverpool, Marlborough at Woodstock, Addington at Buckingham, and Hothfield at Appleby. And in many of the
most rural counties, the grandees continued at the apex of administration. In Scotland, ten of the thirty-three counties still boasted the
same notable as Lord-Lieutenant and convenor, including Home in
Berwick, Buccleuch in Roxburgh, Stair in Wigtown, and Cameron
of Lochiel in Inverness. In England, one-fifth of the chairmen of
county councils were peers or sons of peers: figures like Macclesfield
in Oxford, Heneage in Lindsey, and Brooke in Northampton. A
similar proportion were traditional country gentry: men like like Sir
W. F. S. Dugdale in Warwickshire, and Edward Hardy in Kent. And
in some counties, the same grandee was both chairman of the county
council and Lord-Lieutenant, as was Shaftesbury in Dorset and
Sandwich in Huntingdonshire. Indeed, during the early years of the
war, Lord Leconfield combined both of these positions in East
Sussex with the mastership of the foxhounds as well.

At the same time, new positions of authority were created which
in certain cases were filled by men drawn from the old élite. In the
makeshift administration of Civil Defence, some peers were
appointed Regional Commissioners: Lord Dudley for the Midlands,
Lord Rosebery for Scotland, and Lord Harlech (briefly) for north-
east England. As such, they were placed in charge of co-ordinating
local defence forces, and possessed extremely wide powers. And in
other areas, peers were appointed Deputy Regional Commissioners:
Eltisley and Cranbrook in Eastern England, de la Warr in the south-
east, and Airlie in Scotland.[10] At a lower level, many patricians
became involved with the day-to-day work of organizing the home
front, superintending nursing or first-aid work or the supply of
ambulances. The wartime committees of organizations like the Red
Cross were awash with the names of grandees and their wives. As

was appropriate for a man of his aeronautical interests and strong local connections, Lord Londonderry was the Northern Ireland Regional Commandant of the Air Training Corps, while his wife was president of the County Down and the Durham branches of the Red Cross, and also much involved with the work of the Women's Legion.[11]

But in the rural areas, the most important new local authority was the County War Agricultural Executive Committee, which was responsible for superintending and increasing the production of food at a time when overseas supplies had all but been cut off.[12] Some of these committees were chaired by local grandees: Lord Cornwallis in Kent, and Lord Cromwell in Leicestershire. Others were headed by important resident gentry: H. A. Benyon in Berkshire, Mayor J. W. Fitzherbert-Brockholes in Lancashire, and Sir Merrick Burrell in Sussex. And among the ordinary members, the patricians were well represented. There were notables like the Duke of Beaufort in Gloucestershire, the Earl of Portsmouth in Hampshire, the Duke of Grafton in West Suffolk, and the Earl of Sandwich in Huntingdonshire. And there was also a clutch of aristocratic women: the Duchess of Devonshire in Derbyshire, the Countess de la Warr in East Sussex, Lady Raglan in Monmouth, and Lady Penrhyn in Caernarfon.[13]

In many rural areas, these Agricultural Executive Committees were almost equalled in importance by the new organizations for domestic reserve forces, initially called the Local Defence Volunteers, and subsequently the Home Guard. Here, again, there was a significant – and predictable – aristocratic contribution. Even before the announcement from Whitehall, Col. the Earl of Leven and Melville had raised his own company in Nairn which was subsequently assimilated into an official unit. At the very beginning, when the LDV was set up by the War Office in May 1940, the responsibility of establishing a rudimentary organization was placed firmly on the shoulders of the Lord-Lieutenants.[14] And many appointed commanding officers with patrician–cum–military backgrounds. In Rutland, Lord Ancaster chose his brother, Lt.-Col. the Hon. C. H. D. Willoughby; in Monmouthshire, Lord Tredegar was placed in charge; in Northumberland, Col. the Viscount Allendale was Zone Commander; in Northamptonshire, Major-General Sir Hereward Wake was in command; and the South Aberdeen and Kincardine Battalion was led by Sir James Burnett of Leys, sixteenth baronet.[15]

But it was not just in the senior ranks of the Home Guard that the gentry and the grandees were to be found. Many peers joined up in more humble capacities, and cartoonists delighted in portraying aristocrats undertaking menial tasks of home defence, or wearing inappropriately splendid uniforms that dated from their earlier military or public careers.[16] In the first company of the London Battalion were to be found both the Duke of St Albans and the Earl of Clanwilliam, until they were compelled to retire on the grounds of age. In County Durham, Private Vereker, the brother of Field Marshal Lord Gort, and a former High Sheriff, joined the fifth battalion.[17] In Hertfordshire, the tenth Earl of Cavan thought he would be especially helpful, given his long military experience and expertise as an MFH. He offered his services (along with his horse) as a despatch rider, and at the same time, his chauffeur signed on with the Earl's car. In fact, the former Chief of the Imperial General Staff soon found himself appointed a mere NCO in charge of the Headquarters Communications Platoon. But later on, he was transferred to London, where he became the chairman of a board to approve officers in the Home Guard for regular commissions.[18]

It is thus clear that in some localities, individual patricians wielded much power and shouldered great responsibilities during the war years. Sir John Dunnington-Jefferson was chairman of the East Riding County Council and also of its Agricultural Committee. In the Soke of Peterborough, the Marquess of Exeter held both of these offices, and was also Lord-Lieutenant. Likewise, an untitled country gentlemanlike C. L. Chute, of The Vyne in Hampshire, was simultaneously chairman of the quarter sessions, of the county council, and of the Agricultural Committee. Lord Portsmouth, who was his colleague on the Agricultural Committee, described him (and his class) well: 'apart from his estates, his whole life was devoted to the county of his birth in a selfless voluntary capacity. Of absolute personal integrity, he typified everything that was good in the old landlord ruling class, as well as a little of its lack of imagination.'[19] Like many other notables, Chute laboured long and laborious hours, in adverse circumstances, and with no remuneration, to ensure that local administration was carried on, and that production targets in agriculture were met.

But it was, predictably, as the warrior class that the grandees and gentry made their most conspicuous contribution. Senior commanders in the RAF included the Duke of Hamilton, the Earl of Bandon, the future sixth Earl of Gosford, and Sir Archibald Philip Hope, seventeenth baronet. Of an older generation, who had already seen service during the First World War, Admiral of the Fleet the Earl of Cork and Orrery was in command of the combined expedition to Narvik in April 1940, and although he retired from active service thereafter, he so pestered the government for employment that in desperation Churchill ordered that he be despatched to oversee the

117. Lord Alexander of Tunis by John Gilroy.

defence of the Shetland Islands. Likewise, Admiral Sir Reginald Aylmer Ranfurley Plunkett-Ernle-Ernle-Drax, younger son of the seventeenth Lord Dunsany, was obliged to retire as C.-in-C. the Nore in 1941. After returning to his family estates (the inheriting of which had necessitated the adoption of his multi-hyphened surname), and after serving briefly as a private in the Home Guard, he volunteered as a Commodore of Convoys, and between 1943 and 1945, it was his proud boast that he never lost a ship.

Among the army commanders, the patrician element was even more conspicuous, as some of the greatest generals were provided – as before – by the old Anglo-Irish ascendancy. The sixth Lord Gort, who had won the Victoria Cross in the First World War, presided brilliantly over the Dunkirk evacuation, and subsequently held a succession of exacting proconsular posts in Gibraltar, Malta, and Transjordan.[20] Churchill's favourite commander, his beau ideal of the gentleman general, was Harold Rupert Leofric Alexander, the younger son of the fourth Earl of Caledon, 'an unmistakeable aristocrat, with a natural diffidence and modesty that his birth and established position provided no inducement to discard.'[21] The victor of El Alemein, General Bernard Montgomery, was descended from a long line of Ulster squires. And for most of the war, the Chief of

118. Alanbrooke, Churchill and Montgomery at the scene of the Rhineland battle, early March 1945.

the Imperial General Staff was Sir Alan Brooke, the scion of another great Ulster patrician–cum–military family, the Brookes of Colebrooke, and the uncle of Sir Basil Brooke, the Minister of Agriculture in the Northern Ireland government, who became Prime Minister of the province in 1943.[22]

At a lower level, too, the patricians were much in evidence – in some cases because they were professional soldiers already, in others because they joined up for the duration. At different periods during the conflict, Lord Gort's staff officers included Viscount Bridgeman, the Earl of Munster, the Knight of Kerry, and Captain the Hon. Guy Russell, who was later to win fame as the man who sank the Scharndhorst. Lord Lovat was a brilliant leader of Commandos in Norway, Dieppe, and Normandy.[23] The most daring raid into Yugoslavia was led by Sir Fitzroy Maclean, who came from the cadet branch of one of Scotland's oldest families and later married Lord Lovat's sister. The Hon. William Sidney won the Victoria Cross at Anzio and married Lord Gort's daughter. Men who became, in the fullness of time, the Duke of Devonshire, Lord Derby, and Lord Carrington, won the Military Cross. The two younger brothers of the Duke of Buccleuch, as well as his son and heir, were all mentioned in despatches. The heir to the Duke of Argyll was a prisoner of war for almost the whole of the conflict. The future Marquess of Bath was wounded in 1942 at El Alamein; the future Duke of St Albans served in the infantry and in military intelligence; and the future Viscount Cobham fought in France with the Worcestershire Yeomanry.

But the most poignant contribution made by the old territorial élite came from the ascendancy families of Southern Ireland. Although they had been betrayed by the Lloyd George government in the aftermath of a war in which they had shed so much blood in Britain's defence, there were many who did not hesitate to serve in this second and even greater conflict. Among the most famous figures was Sir Nugent Henry Everard, third baronet, whose grandfather had been a senator in the Irish Free State. Likewise, Peter Walker James Nugent, who became the fifth baronet in 1955, was a major in the Hampshire Regiment. While the twenty-second Knight of Kerry served on Lord Gort's staff, his son and heir was also a full-time professional British soldier. The future Earl of Granard was Air Adviser to the Minister of State in the Middle East, and the sixteenth Viscount Gormanston was a member of the British Expeditionary Force in France in 1940. Here was the last corporate endeavour by the old supra-national British landed classes, the final expression of their collective sense of identity and purpose – feelings that had outlived the social, political, and economic circumstances that had nurtured them in the first place.

At the same time that so many patricians played so conspicuous a part in the war effort, there were other ways in which aristocratic life continued in a recognizably traditional manner. They still sought grand proconsular and ambassadorial posts, or were considered for them. In January 1940, Lord Bledisloe wrote directly to the Prime Minister, bluntly asking for the Governor-Generalship of Canada on the death of John Buchan. Lord de la Warr, on the other hand, was much put out to have been offered only the governorship of Bermuda in 1941, and refused to accept it. He looked it up in an encyclopaedia, and concluded with anger that it was smaller than Bexhill, the town where he owned most of the land.[24] When the Washington embassy became vacant on the death of Lord Lothian in 1940, the names bandied around included Lords Cranborne, Willingdon, and Dudley. When a replacement had to be found for Lord Linlithgow after his unprecedentedly long spell as Viceroy of India, such prominent patricians as Eden, Lyttelton, Devonshire, Sinclair, and Cranborne were all considered. And when the Governor-Generalship of Canada fell vacant in 1945, the final short-list consisted of the Earl of Airlie, Lord Alexander, and G. M. Trevelyan.[25]

Other matters were rather less momentous: indeed, it seems almost astonishing just how much time, even in the darkest and most urgent days of the war, the supreme leadership spent on satisfying or assuaging aristocratic caprice. At the end of 1940, there was 'much discussion' as to whether the Duke of Devonshire should receive the Garter, as all his predecessors had done. Eventually, he did, because Churchill thought him 'not bad' as dukes went. Sir John Sinclair was delighted to be made a Knight of the Thistle, but Anthony Eden was not given the Garter because it was thought it would ruin his political prospects. The Duke of Sutherland was obliged to resign as Lord-Lieutenant of his titular county because of 'matrimonial delinquencies'.[26] The Duke of Westminster tried to get his friend the Prime Minister to intercede on his behalf because his latest mistress had been arrested by MI5 on entering the country. Lord Londonderry vainly badgered Churchill – his cousin – for a ministerial job in Whitehall or, at the very least, in Northern Ireland. And his Marchioness urged the Prime Minister to relax restrictions on the movement of personnel throughout the United Kingdom, so that her relatives and guests could go to Northern Ireland for a wedding.[27]

Here was a rich and familiar amalgam of aristocratic presumption and patrician hauteur, which persisted unabashed throughout the war. In December 1940, the Prime Minister bestowed a peerage on his best man and former Hughligan colleague, Lord Hugh Cecil, 'to sustain the aristocratic morale' in the upper house. The Duke of Wellington – who received an enlarged petrol allowance throughout the war simply by virtue of his styles and titles – protested vehemently to the Devonshires when they named a child Morny, thinking it was a diminutive of Mornington, a name to which he felt his family had exclusive claims. In fact, it was named after a Cavendish racehorse.[28] In 1942, the Earl of Dudley high-handedly arranged a royal visit to Birmingham in his capacity as Regional Commissioner for the Midlands, without even telling the Lord Mayor, who was understandably incensed. And when John Wyndham accompanied Harold Macmillan on a visit to General Alexander at Tunis in 1943, he revealingly described the dinner-table talk as 'like good conversation in a good country house.'[29]

Even fox-hunting survived. At the outbreak of war, the government requisitioned all hunting horses for military purposes. But some owners concealed them from the authorities (or were themselves the authorities). The Duke of Beaufort, although one of the hardiest and healthiest aristocrats in the land, was declared unfit for military service because of a duodenal ulcer. Rumour had it that this had been brought on, not by fear of fighting, but because he had worried so much that in the forces, he would not have been able to hunt. In fact, although his activities were much curtailed, he still managed to turn out on average four days a week. And he took every possible precaution. When the fears of invasion seemed most plausible, he evacuated fifty Badminton hounds to Canada so that, in the event of the ultimate catastrophe, the breed and the activity should live on.[30] Lord Leconfield shared exactly the same sense of priorities. In 1940 he was out hunting in Sussex with only his whipper–in and his heir for company. He came across a crowd, which he thought a halloa, only to find they were gathered to watch the village soccer match. 'Haven't you people got anything better to do in wartime', he bellowed at them, 'than play football?' He then continued on his way after the fox.[31]

So, for some grandees and gentry, the Second World War was an annoying interruption, and they responded to it by trying to continue their lives as if nothing untoward was happening. For many others, it was undoubtedly the most heroic and demanding time of their lives. Either way, it is possible to see this great conflict as something of a family outing for the British landed élite. Indeed, with a Britain led by the patrician Churchill, with the United States presided over by the upper-class Franklin Delano Roosevelt, and with the Free French Forces under the command of General Charles de Gaulle, it is not altogether fanciful to see the European war as the last reassertion of upper-class leadership against the upstart corporals and petty duces of the Fascist powers. In the clash between the allied patricians and the axis Pooters, it was the old established order that ultimately triumphed. As A. J. P. Taylor once remarked of Churchill, 'the British ruling classes did their best to keep him down, and he preserved them.'[32]

ii.   Marginals and Mavericks

Yet the essential truth of his observation should not obscure the fact that this is only part – and the minority part – of the overall picture. For while the Second World War did indeed witness a sudden and spectacular 'aristocratic resurgence', its deeper and more lasting effect was to accentuate those very trends towards patrician marginality that had become so pronounced during the previous half-century. The major social and political developments of the war years – the consolidation of Labour's position, the evolution of a new Welfare State consensus, the growing belief in planning, reform, and equality – largely passed the grandees and gentry by.[33] From this rather different perspective, most patricians did not know what was happening, or did not like what was happening, or could not influence what was happening. They might be the leaders of the nation in arms, but they were not setting the political agenda for the present or the future. Even Churchill himself was well aware of what this portended. As early as October 1940, he had waxed eloquent on 'the disappearance of the aristocracy from the stage . . . They were sinking noiselessly and unresisting into the background.' And that, in essence, was quite correct.[34]

In high politics, it was only the traumas of the Second World War that brought these aristocratic adventurers to the top at all. By 1939, Churchill had been out of power for ten years; without the war, he would never have held office again; and it was only the fall of Chamberlain that provided his last chance of 'winning the Derby'. Although – in unconscious fulfilment of the Duke of Manchester's prediction – Churchill did indeed become a virtual dictator, his encounter with destiny and despotism was in many ways an accident. And it was not only Churchill who was lucky in this way. Most of his aristocratic entourage were equally marginal men, fortuitously brought back – or brought in – to the centre of affairs. Eden and Cranborne had both resigned from Chamberlain's government over appeasement, and would probably never have returned to power. Swinton clawed his way back, when most people thought him finished.[35] Sinclair, as leader of the Liberals, would never have held high office at all, except in an emergency demanding a coalition. And Lyttelton was plucked by Churchill from his City career, where otherwise he would surely have stayed, and to which he soon hankered to return. In short, these were not patricians governing as of right by virtue of their class position: they were individual rebels and gatecrashers who were in power by fluke and favour.

Moreover, Churchill himself, although undeniably an aristocrat, was very much an aristocrat of his time. The fact that he had an American mother meant that, even in 1940, there were men in Whitehall who regarded him disparagingly as a 'half-breed'.[36] Despite his ducal background and his father's successful pursuit of an heiress, he was a poor man, and the books and the journalism were as much to pay the bills as they were expressions of his remarkable creativity. Like Lord Randolph, his finances were often precarious, and he needed the help of men like Baruch, Bracken, and Beaverbrook to ensure that he remained solvent. On the eve of the war, his debts were so overwhelming that he had even considered selling Chartwell. And, as Lord Crawford had noticed back in the 1900s, Churchill was one of those who yearned for luxury, and who loved taking it from those who could provide it, from Lord Beaverbrook earlier in his life to Aristotle Onassis at the end.[37] Moreover, by the

1930s, he had become almost a parody of the alienated and irrelevant die-hard: hostile to all change, sceptical of democracy, opposed to Indian constitutional progress, in favour of King Edward VIII, and much distressed by the decline of the traditional aristocratic way of life.[38]

Likewise, the other patricians whom Churchill recruited were very much men of their time – which meant that, in political terms, they were not very effective. Most of them did not count for much on the home or the overseas front. Eden at the Foreign Office did what Churchill told him: in more senses than one, he was emphatically number two. Sinclair was not particularly assertive at the Air Ministry, and stood up neither to Beaverbrook as Minister of Aircraft Production nor to the service chiefs.[39] Cranborne was never in charge of a major ministry, and leant more tone than substance to the government. And Lyttelton was wanted more for his City experience than his aristocratic background, and was a quite dreadful performer in the Commons.[40] Moreover, throughout Churchill's administration, there was a cavalcade of coroneted casualties. In May 1940, Devonshire, Dunglass, Oliver Stanley, Stanhope, and Zetland disappeared. Thereafter, Halifax was shipped off to the USA; Harlech went to South Africa; Moore-Brabazon resigned in disgrace; Swinton spent most of the war on the periphery. When the Duke of Norfolk was brought into the government, it was not so much because of his own administrative ability, but because all the other ducal candidates had ruled themselves out: Buccleuch, Westminster, Bedford, and Manchester were simply quite unsuitable.[41]

In no sense, then, did Churchill see his ministry as a way to bring back aristocratic government: on the whole, he used his patricians in the same way that Baldwin and Chamberlain had done, to provide a dignfied façade while the main work was done and the real decisions were taken elsewhere. For the majority of men in government who mattered came from very different backgrounds. Among the Prime Minister's court favourites, Beaverbrook and Bracken were self-made financiers and newspaper tycoons, and Lindemann was an émigré academic. Among other ministers, Duncan at the Board of Trade, Woolton at Food, and Leathers at Transport were businessmen who had been specially recruited. Sir John Anderson, who was first Home Secretary then Chancellor of the Exchequer, was a former civil servant. And on the home front, the Labour ministers were almost all middle or working class: Attlee, Morrison, Dalton, Bevin. Only Cripps possessed an authentically patrician background, and he was the least weighty Labour figure.[42]

Indeed, at all levels of the national effort, the war gave a much greater impetus to the businessmen, the professionals, and the trade-

union leaders than it did to the patricians. For every Colville or
Cadogan who walked the corridors of power, there were a dozen
from middle-class backgrounds: regulars like Bridges or Norman
Brook, or special recruits like Keynes, Franks, and Beveridge. In
Whitehall, it was the scientists, the technicians, and the experts who
were now needed, instead of the old-style aristocratic amateurs.
Most of the great generals were from professional, rather than landed
families like Dill, Wavell, and Auchinleck. Among the admirals,
men like Tovey and Cunningham came from service backgrounds.
And even Churchill noticed how (with slight, but not significant
exaggeration) 'none of the aristocracy chose the RAF – they left it all
to the lower middle class.'[43] At the very top, Harris, Dowding,
Park, and Portal were all non-patrician. Even the great posts in the
empire no longer went to the traditional titled ornamentals. In India,
Linlithgow (a grandee) was replaced by Wavell (a military failure). In
New Zealand, Newall was dumped for the same reason. In Canada
and Australia, members of the royal family took over. And in South
Africa, the job had already gone to a native, Sir Patrick Duncan.

The most that can thus be said of the aristocratic war effort is that
it provided some – but not the majority – of the key personnel, and
that their impact was probably greater on the battlefields abroad than
in the corridors of power at home. Despite the presence of a patrician
Prime Minister, the fact remains that, politically speaking, England
moved emphatically to the left between 1940 and 1945. This is well
shown in the case of the inquiry conducted by the coalition government into the Foreign Office. The Departmental investigation of
early 1939 may have accomplished very little, except to provoke a
restatement of traditional exclusive views. But in the changed climate of wartime opinion, a real advance was now made – ironically
enough under a patrician Foreign Secretary. In early 1943, the Eden
Committee concluded that as far as the diplomatic service was concerned, 'its members are recruited from too exclusive a social background', and recommended radical reforms in selection procedure
that would open up the service to a much broader range of talent,
which was thought essential if it was to function in what was
obviously going to be a more egalitarian world.[44] As was explained
when the recommendations were introduced to the Commons, it
was the disappearance of 'the old governing class' that meant that in
future, the Foreign Office should represent the whole nation, not just
one section of it.[45]

In short, these wartime proposals were explicitly concerned to go
much further than the earlier, piecemeal reforms, to end the old
ethos of amateur and aristocratic style, and to bring the Foreign
Office and the foreign service more rapidly into the second half of

the twentieth century. 'Democratization' was avowedly the object of the exercise. More precisely, the Eden Committee recommended the amalgamation of the foreign and diplomatic, the commercial and the consular services into one single organization that must be devoid of sectional jealousy and social divisions. It emphasized that diplomacy must in future be seen as a professional activity, and stressed the need for appropriate written examinations, and for proper training in economic and commercial affairs. It recommended the formal management and control of personnel, including the power to retire employees unsuitable for the highest posts before the age of sixty. And it proposed that more effort should be made to encourage women to join the service. Before the end of the war, most of these reforms had been implemented.[46] And it was these, combined with the passing of the Butler Education Act in 1944, that did indeed convert the foreign service from being the exclusive preserve of the notability and the products of public schools, into a career open to talents.

Likewise, in the House of Commons, the small number of new MPs elected from a genteel background were very much on the edge of events. On the premature elevation of Lord Cranborne to the upper house, Lord Hinchingbrooke was elected for South Dorset. At other wartime by-elections, the Hon. John Grimston was returned for the local seat of St Albans, James Morrison was elected for a Wiltshire constituency, and towards the very end of the war, William Sidney became MP for Chelsea. Yet despite these reinforcements, the backbench patricians achieved little. In the debate over Yalta, Lord Dunglass, William Sidney, and James Willoughby d'Eresby pleaded for Poland. It was, Henry Channon believed, 'the conscience of the gentlemen of England' on display.[47] But it was to no purpose. In the same way, Lord Winterton kept up his persistent, sniping, quarrelsome attacks on the government throughout the war, and soon became second only to Aneurin Bevan on Churchill's list of pet hates. Several times, the Prime Minister tried to tempt him away with offers of overseas postings. But he resolutely refused to go. Eventually, he was appointed chairman of the select committee to consider the reconstruction of the House of Commons and, on the elevation of Lloyd George to the peerage, he finally became the father of the House. But his substantive influence on the conduct of the war was effectively nil.[48]

Throughout the war, there were several active fringe groups, led by aristocrats, which sought to leave their mark on events, but which instead merely confirmed the peripheral position to which most patricians in politics had been driven. Within the pale of the constitution, there was the Watching Committee which old Lord

Salisbury formed in April 1940.[49] It consisted largely of dissident
peers and MPs, and met secretly at Salisbury's house in Arlington
Street; its initial purpose was to urge more immediate and more
energetic action upon the Prime Minister; and to this end Salisbury
repeatedly visited Neville Chamberlain, Lord Halifax and Winston
Churchill in person. When Churchill became Prime Minister, the
committee took upon itself the self-appointed task of rebuking and
chastising the new government with an industrious alertness and
forceful candour that few others dared employ. Again and again,
Salisbury bombarded the Prime Minister with memoranda on military and civilian, political and administrative matters, many of them
curt and some of them hurtful. But there was too much scolding of
tired and exhausted men from a politician comfortably in retirement,
and many of the problems to which he drew attention were the inevitable result of a shortage of men, time, and materials. Churchill
replied courteously. But that was all.

A younger generation of dissident Conservatives – the thirty-odd
MPs who formed the so-called Tory Reform Group – also put
themselves under landed leadership.[50] When Viscount Hinchingbrooke took his seat as the new MP for South Dorset, he at once
resolved that the Tory party must repudiate the crippling legacy of
Baldwin and Chamberlain, and eagerly take up those very policies of
social reform that were being developed on the left of the wartime
coalition. He duly became the leader of the Tory Reform Group, and
published a book entitled *Full Speed Ahead*, which set out his creed.
But for all his youth and ardour, he had nothing original to say, and
in denouncing inter-war Toryism, the enemy turned out to be that
traditional shibboleth of the landed élite, those 'individualist businessmen, financiers and speculators, ranging freely in a laissez faire
economy', who were deemed to have ruined both the country and
the party in the years since 1914. Once again, the impact was minimal. Within the Reform Group itself, it was the middle-class men
like Quintin Hogg who were much the more effective. And it was
only the defeat in the election of 1945, rather than anything Hinchingbrooke's Group did, that compelled the Tory leadership to
accept Keynes and the mixed economy of the Welfare State.

But the Conservatives did not boast a monopoly of these wartime
patrician mavericks. One of the last Liberal country gentlemen in
politics was Richard Acland, who kept up the family tradition by
being elected, in 1935, as MP for the Barnstaple constituency of
Devon.[51] A year later, he became a socialist, and in 1940 a Christian.
Thereafter, he regularly harangued the Commons with calls for
social revolution, much to the embarrassment of the Labour party.
He wrote a variety of pamphlets (in the preface to one of which J. B.

Priestley described Acland as 'intolerant, fanatical, tactless and humourless') with such unpromising titles as *How it can be Done* and *What it will be Like*, and in July 1942 he founded the Common Wealth party, which enjoyed a brief vogue.[52] But it won only the occasional by-election, and never had more than 15,000 supporters. In early 1943 he made over his estates in Devon to the National Trust, on the grounds that service to others, not private gain, must be the mainspring to all human action. But he thereby incurred renewed criticism – this time from the right – that he had abdicated his hereditary position and set his own political faith above the duty and the property he had inherited.

Patricians like Salisbury, Hinchingbrooke, and Acland were all marginal activists, ineffectively operating within the realm of established political behaviour. But there were others who skirted the very bounds of treason. In early 1940, the Duke of Buccleuch called upon Lord Dunglass, the PPS to the Prime Minister. He was a great admirer of Hitler, was thoroughly opposed to the war, and urged that peace should at once be made with Germany.[53] Even more extraordinarily, throughout that year, the newly inherited Duke of Bedford conducted his own personal peace initiatives with Germany via their embassy in Dublin, and in 1942 he actually addressed the Lords on the same subject. Many peers walked out; Lord Gainford moved that the Duke 'be no longer heard'; and the Lord Chancellor described his opinions as 'utterly irresponsible and completely pestilential.'[54] Nor were these two dukes alone in their patrician heresies. In June 1940, Churchill received from the Home Secretary the names of one hundred and fifty prominent people who had been arrested under the new Defence of the Realm Regulations. Two of the first three – Lady Mosley and George Pitt-Rivers – were in fact relatives of the Prime Minister himself.[55]

But as the example of Diana Mosley suggests, it was the Mitfords who were most marginalized by the war, which merely completed the well-developed process of family dispersal and patrician disintegration. Nancy's marriage broke up, and she eventually settled in Paris after the city was liberated. Jessica emigrated to America; her husband joined up and was killed; she married a Jewish lawyer from the Bronx; they both subsequently joined the Communist Party; and as a result her father disinherited her.[56] Diana and Oswald Mosley were both imprisoned; when they were released, Nancy and Jessica vehemently and publicly protested; and after the war they, too, went into exile in France. Unity was so distraught at the prospect of war between Britain and Germany that she shot herself in the head, was brought back home, and lingered on, an incontinent vegetable, until her death in 1949. And their brother Tom, also a Fascist sympathi-

zer, refused to fight the Germans, but joined up and was killed in the
Far East. Even their parents were caught up: they were divided as to
which side to support, and their marriage ultimately collapsed.[57]

By the end of the war, the surviving Mitfords were thus personally estranged and geographically dispersed. Only Debo, who had
married Lord Andrew Cavendish, seemed to have behaved in a conventional manner, and remained 'on speakers' with all her sisters.
But between 1939 and 1945, the Mitford belief that life was a huge
joke had turned terribly and tragically sour: the cosy childhood
world that Jessica and Nancy were later to evoke so ripely and so
mellowly had emphatically disappeared for ever. Indeed, these
words of the second Viscount Churchill – whose family fell apart in
a similar way at the same time – summarize not only his own sense
of decline, fall, and marginality, but that of the Mitfords as well:

> Before it was finished, [the war] had scattered the family and every
> material object, every record and every possession. Ancestral
> homes, heirlooms, family jewels, libraries, portraits, even trivial
> mementoes and old yellowing photographs, were dispersed for
> ever, and no one – sisters, brother, father, mother – would come
> to rest from that upheaval, until each was a stranger, and every-
> thing had disintegrated and disappeared.[58]

For the Mitfords as for many others, the war merely accentuated
and completed trends that were already well in train before it even
started. The same picture emerges in Kenya, where the murder of
Lord Erroll in January 1941 exposed to a war-weary Britain the full
frivolity, nastiness, and sheer irrelevance of patrician settler life in
Happy Valley. Sir Delves Broughton was arrested on the grounds
that he killed Erroll because the latter was having an affair with his
wife. Although he was charged with murder, and although he was
almost certainly guilty of it, he was acquitted. But retribution took
its course. He was expelled even from the Muthaiga Club for unsatisfactory conduct. In 1942, he returned to England where, impoverished, suspected of fraud, and bearing his burden of guilt, he
committed suicide in a Liverpool hotel. Even Evelyn Waugh was to
change his mind by the time he wrote *Men at Arms*. When Guy
Crouchback, who as a younger son had gone out to Kenya in the
thirties, meets Virginia for a wartime dinner at Claridges, they recall
their life in Africa—'all the forgotten scandals of the Muthaiga Club,
fights, adultery, arson, bankruptcies, card-sharping, insanity, suici-
des, even duels.' They did not miss out much.[59]

So, in the light of this more equivocal and ambiguous evidence, it
would be misconceived to see the Second World War as witnessing

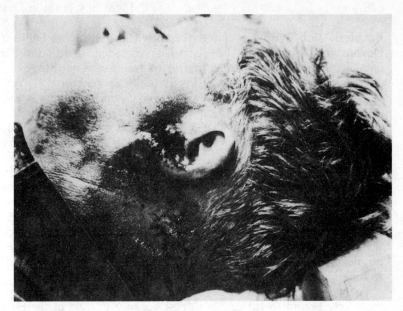

119. The murdered Lord Erroll.

the triumphant return of the aristocracy to power; or even to suggest that it was for some of them simply and safely and successfully business as usual. Clearly, the position was much more complex and ambiguous than that, as short-term celebrity and renaissance went hand-in-hand with continued and accentuated long-term decline. Even in the very cockpit of high politics, the Churchillian break-through was a freakish and in some ways surprisingly superficial phenomenon. And elsewhere on the political spectrum, the patri-cians merely became fewer in number, more ineffectual in their activities, and more eccentric in their opinions. But in addition, the grandees and the gentry were themselves the most vulnerable to the negative and destructive effects of the war itself. Ultimately, it took more away from them than it gave; it did them much more harm than good. And they knew it. As Vita Sackville-West observed despondently in January 1940, 'It is not as if we are fighting to preserve the things we care for. This war, whatever happens, will destroy them.'[60]

iii.   Death and Destruction

At the very beginning of the conflict, in September 1939, Vita Sackville-West's husband, Harold Nicolson, had lunched at the

Beefsteak Club, and sat next to the recently succeeded tenth Duke of Devonshire. 'I must say', Nicolson later recorded, 'I do admire a man like that, who must realise that all his grandeur is gone for ever, not showing the slightest sign of any gloom or apprehension.'[61] Yet, as Nicolson rightly noted, the grounds for gloom were very great, and no patrician regarded the outbreak of the Second World War with the naïve optimism that had been so prevalent in 1914. Everywhere, there was widespread recognition that, among many other things, the conflict would be a 'time of testing' for the landowner. And while in some ways these tests were triumphantly passed, in others, they were impossibly demanding. For however great was the genteel contribution to the national effort, this was emphatically not a war to make the world safe for aristocracy. As *The Times* pointed out as early as July 1940, 'the new order', which was already dimly discerned, 'cannot be based on the preservation of privilege, whether the privilege be that of a country, of a class, or of an individual.'[62]

To begin with, since so many notables did in the end join up, they were bound to suffer casualties – not on the scale of the First World War, but severe, nonetheless. The Duke of Northumberland died on active service in 1940, and the Duke of Devonshire's son and heir was killed in 1944.[63] The Earl of Suffolk was blown up by a bomb he was trying to defuse, and was posthumously awarded the George Cross. Sir Robert Peel, the sixth baronet, was killed on active service in the navy, and the senior line of the family became extinct. One of Lord Halifax's sons was killed, and another severely wounded. Among major patrician political figures, Anthony Eden, Lord Swinton, and Oliver Lyttelton each lost a son. Other grandees similarly bereaved included Lord Zetland, Lord Lytton, Lord Gort, and Lord Bessborough. The Earl of Verulam lost two sons and Lord Braybrooke two cousins. And the landed gentry fared equally badly. George Howard lost both of his brothers. And when Robert Wyndham Ketton-Cremer's brother died in 1941, the estate was left without an heir.[64]

Some families – especially those from Ireland or with very strong military traditions – suffered even worse. The Marquess of Dufferin and Ava was killed in Burma. The fact that it was near the place from which one of his titles came was a particularly unhappy coincidence. He was, in addition, the third member of his family to die in battle: one uncle had been killed in the Boer War, another in the trenches. Shane O'Neill, whose father was the first MP to die during the First World War, was himself killed in the second. Both Sir Basil and Lady Brooke, and Sir Josselyn and Lady Gore-Booth lost two sons, and the Stafford-King-Harmans lost their only son and heir.[65] Even worse in some ways was the plight of the fourth Baron Shuttle-worth. The first lord had died in 1939: but both of his sons had been killed during the First World War. The elder son's two sons (who became briefly, in succession, the second and third barons) were both killed on active service in the Second World War. The fourth lord's younger half-brother was also killed during the Second World War. And the fourth lord himself lost both his legs in battle.[66]

Then there was the destruction and severe damage of many patrician homes. High on the list were the few remaining London palaces and Thames-side mansions, now in the very front line of enemy attack. At the beginning of the war, all of the most splendid town houses were closed – in many cases, as it turned out, for good. In the autumn of 1939, 'house cooling' parties became quite the fashion. Thereafter, Portman and Holland Houses were so badly bombed that demolition was the only solution. At Dudley House, the ballroom and gallery were badly damaged; at Bridgewater House, the picture gallery was destroyed beyond restoration; and at Spencer House, the windows were blown out on the top floor, and much of the stucco was torn away. Wimborne House was occupied by the Red Cross, Derby House by Christies, and Londonderry House by troops.[67] Along the Thames, the picture was equally bleak. Osterley was in total disorder and disarray, and the Adam orangery was burned out. At Syon, the windows were smashed and the rooms boarded up. 'It is sad', Henry Channon regretfully but rightly recorded, 'that the houses of the great will never again open their hospitable doors.'[68]

But in the countryside, the mansions of the great suffered at least as much, as they were ruthlessly requisitioned for government service under the Compensation Defence Act of 1939. Very few were as lucky as Boughton, which was used to store many of the great artistic treasures from London galleries, or Badminton, where Queen Mary stayed for the duration of the war. Some, like Knebworth, Bowood, Castle Howard, Longleat, and The Vyne, were used to house evacuated schools. Some were used as military hospitals or convalescent homes, like Corsham, Hinchingbrooke, Walrond, Harewood, and Somerleyton.[69] Some were used to billet English troops, like Attingham and Wotterton. Some were used to accommodate foreign forces: the Free French at Finedon Hall, and the Americans at Sherborne Castle and Erddig. In County Fermanagh, all the country-house demesnes were requisitioned because of the flying boat bases on Lough Erne.[70] And some great houses were used for much more secret purposes: the invasion of Europe was planned from the double cube room at Wilton; the headquarters of MI5 were removed to Blenheim; at Audley End the work was so

120. Boys from Malvern School doing morning exercises outside Blenheim Palace.

The Great Hall of Blenheim as a school dormitory.

secret that even Lord Braybrooke was not allowed into his own home unescorted; while at Bletchley Park the most important work of decoding enemy messages was carried on, using the Enigma machine.[71]

From the standpoint of the war effort, the country houses made a major contribution; but from the perspective of their owners, the result was an unmitigated disaster. Very few of the temporary tenants showed any respect for their surroundings, not surprisingly, since most of them had never been inside such houses before, and had no sense of their value or importance. Everywhere, the fabric decayed, the park was ploughed up or abandoned, the railings and gates were requisitioned. At Blickling, the grounds were full of Nissen huts, and the troops who were billeted there broke the windows and forced the doors to the state rooms. At Lyme, the park was used as a lorry depot, and was cut to pieces by thousands of RAF vehicles.[72] At Compton Verney, the balustrading of the Adam bridge in the Capability Brown park was knocked off by the soldiers. At Erddig, the garden went completely to ruin. At Eggington Hall in Derbyshire, the army left the house with all the taps running, the ceilings collapsed, and the building had to be demolished. And at Tyneham in Dorset, the whole village was taken over, including the big house, from the Bond family who had held it for two hundred years. It was used for target practice throughout the war, and has yet to be given back to its owners.[73]

Like the great London palaces, the country houses of Britain were among the prime victims of the war. And their owners were powerless to protect or restore them. For even the most basic and essential maintenance was impossible due to the shortage of men and materials. Throughout the war, repairs, reconstruction, and new building were very difficult; scarce materials were available only for essential work; and from the beginning, licences for building were rigorously enforced by the local Ministry of Works offices.[74] In 1941, government regulations were extended to cover repairs as well as new construction, and owners were allowed to spend only £100 on one property within any twelve-month period, unless granted a special licence. As a result, civil building came to a virtual standstill, country-house owners were almost totally powerless, and if the regulations were infringed, the client, the architect, and the contractor could all be sent to goal. In this people's war, the patricians were not above the law, and those who flouted it to repair their great houses did so at their peril, as in 1942, when Lord Londonderry was personally fined £50 for making structural alterations to Mount Stuart without having first obtained a licence.

In addition to loss of life and loss of home, the grandees and gentry suffered further hardship, because they lost their servants. While there were well over one million of them employed in 1939, they had all but vanished within two years – either called up to active service, or moved to more essential work. At Farnley Hall, the Fawkes family lost all their staff, and had to cook their own dinner and do the washing up. At Ham, there were only two gardeners, instead of the pre-war twelve. At Petworth, there was a single housekeeper and one housemaid to look after the vast palace. At Knole, with its two hundred and fifty rooms, there was only a butler, a cook, and a housemaid – and Lord Sackville was relatively lucky.[75] At Kedleston, where Lord Curzon in his prime had thought thirty indoor servants scarcely enough, there was now merely one woman who came in for three hours each morning. And at Londonderry House, which before the Second World War had boasted twenty-eight servants in the kitchen and sixteen in the stewards room, Lord Londonderry was now obliged to answer the front door himself.[76] At best, the patricians huddled in the servants quarters, with no one to wait on them, while the rest of the house was damaged and defaced. As Lawrence Stone rightly notes, the result was that 'the whole social edifice came crashing down, for the abrupt disappearance of servants made the old style of life no longer possible, regardless of the level of affluence.'[77]

Moreover, the level of affluence was itself much reduced. For the war brought with it 'a very much altered world, with very different standards of value and existence', in which many gentry and grandees could see 'no hope for the future.'[78] In the first place, landowners were uniquely unfortunate in that they made almost nothing out of the very prosperous condition of agriculture during the war. Farmers' incomes increased more than those of any other occupational group, as they produced more food than ever before, and as agriculture received generous government support in the form of guaranteed prices and assured markets. Even the agricultural labourers obtained enhanced wages for work that was now recognized as being of the first importance. But the landowners enjoyed almost nothing of this: as in the previous conflict, rentals were ruthlessly pegged. By the end of the war, wage payments had increased by 55 per cent, and farmers' net incomes by 129 per cent. Yet landowners' gross rentals had risen by only 11 per cent, which was considerably less than the rate of inflation.[79]

But in addition, the cost of waging full-scale war meant that taxes 'reached a level hitherto undreamed of.' The first war budget, in November 1939, increased the standard rate of income tax from 5s. 6d. to 7s. 6d. in the pound. In the 1941 budget, taxation was raised to 19s. 6d. in the pound at the highest levels. For most of the war, the standard rate of tax was exactly double that of the First World War.[80] In 1944, the Duke of Wellington complained that while his gross income was £40,000, he received only £4,000 after all his taxes had been paid, 'which leaves him barely enough for wages and food.' Nor was this all. The 1940 budget removed tax relief and exemptions on private estate companies, which made death duties harder to avoid.[81] And in the same year, the rate of death duty was increased by 10 per cent, to a new peak level of 65 per cent on the greatest estates. The deaths of heirs to titles who had joined up meant that those who had tried to avoid estate duties by handing their properties on to their successor sometimes came catastrophically unstuck. For it was only on second and subsequent deaths on active service that special remissions were granted.[82]

The result of these increased demands was that the market in landed-establishment assets remained throughout the war much more active than it had been between 1914 and 1918. Of course, there was almost no sale of country houses or works of art. At home, there were simply no buyers; capital and credit were short; prices were lower than the late nineteenth century; Christies was severely bombed in 1941; and the remaining auctioneers were too involved in raising money for the war effort to be performing their usual functions.[83] Likewise, the great American collectors and galleries were not in the market for pictures that could hardly be expected to cross the Atlantic in safety. There were one or two forced sales, like the Neeld pictures from Grittleton Manor, where a Constable fetched £20,000 and a Rubens £16,800. And the newly inherited Lord Crawford was obliged to part with a Rembrandt, for death-duty payments in 1940, for £20,000. But these were minor exceptions to the general rule.[84]

Yet at the same time, there was a very active market in land – sometimes to raise money for death-duty purposes, sometimes to take advantage of the high wartime prices, sometimes because the future seemed so hopeless. Among those especially hard hit with the new, high-rate duties, was Lord Crawford who – in addition to parting with paintings and books – was compelled to sell 1,600 acres of his Haigh estate, and 2,500 acres of his Scottish property. Even the greatest grandees were hit.[85] In 1943, the new Lord Yarborough was obliged to part with some of the outlying portions of the Brocklesby estate in Lincolnshire. In the following year, the Duke of Rutland, who had succeeded in 1940, had to dispose of 4,780 acres, this being the second great sale of family estates in twenty-five years. And the death of Lord Plymouth in 1943 meant that his successor had to sell off, during the next ten years, the Hewell Grange estate in the West Midlands, and his ground rents in Barry, Penarth, and Grangetown.[86]

Others sold because of increased taxation, or because the rise in the value of agricultural land encouraged them to sell at a good price. Early in the conflict, the Duke of Norfolk completed the sale of his Littlehampton estate in Sussex, which included both the town itself and 1,100 acres of agricultural land. In 1941, major vendors included the Duke of Portland in the Dukeries, Lord Feversham in Yorkshire, Lord Leven and Melville in Fife, Major Grant in Speyside, and Earl Poulett in Somerset. But the greatest sale of all – and the biggest in the principality since the Marquess of Bute's in Cardiff in 1938 – was of 30,000 acres of the Margham estate.[87] In almost every case, the reason given was 'heavy' and 'increased' taxation. Thereafter, the pace slowed down; but for the rest of the war, there were still some famous vendors: the Duke of Wellington sold 6,000 acres in Hampshire for £197,000; Lord Rosebery parted with nearly 4,000 acres of the Mentmore estate; the Earl of Bradford disposed of £10,000 a year worth of ground rents in Walsall; 4,000 outlying acres of the Berkeley Castle estate went under the hammer; and Lord Ormathwaite offered 11,900 acres in Radnor. Here, indeed, was a much busier market in land than that which had lagged and languished throughout the First World War.[88]

As he journeyed round the country, inspecting dilapidated man-

sions with their dilapidated occupants, James Lees-Milne had no
doubt that he was witnessing an entire way of life in its death throes.
At Audley End, he met the new Lord Braybrooke, who was so
embarrassed by his inheritance that he was at his wits end. 'Who
wouldn't be?' he rightly observed. At Ham, he encountered the
Tollemaches, who were 'hopelessly defeatest, anti-government,
anti-people and anti-world.' At Tabley, he found the Leicester-
Warrens, who 'don't in the least know what to do with the place, and
who are too old to adapt themselves to a new form of life in it.'[89] But
most poignant and pathetic of all were the Newtons at Lyme Park in
Cheshire. After an unbroken family residence of six hundred years,
they knew full well that this was the end of the road. Lord Newton
did 'not know what he can do, ought to do, or wants to do', but just
threw up his hands in despair. Even more poignant, they also knew
that their own tragedy was but part of the greater tragedy of their
class:

> Both said that they would never be able to reconcile themselves to
> the new order after the war. They admitted that their day was
> done, and that life as they had known it was gone for ever. How
> right they are, poor people.[90]

Under these circumstances, when the present seemed unendurable, and the future too terrible to contemplate, many families
considered giving their homes to the National Trust. As the *Estates
Gazette* put it in July 1942, 'owners of large country houses are
becoming more and more convinced that many of them have no
future whatever as private residences.'[91] The passing of Blickling to
the Trust in 1940 on the death of Lord Lothian was a major
landmark, as was that of Packwood, with an endowment of £30,000
in the following year. Once it became clear, from 1942, that the war
was going to be won, interest in this solution became widespread. In
some cases, like Charlecote and West Wycombe, negotiations had
already been in train when the war began.[92] In others, such as
Felbrigg, Knole, and Stourhead, it was the war itself that precipitated such a decision. With houses like Althorp, Knebworth, and
Kedleston, the negotiations were begun, but eventually came to
nothing.[93] In the case like the Strachey mansion at Sutton Court,
there was insufficient architectural merit or historical distinction for
the Trust to be interested. And there were some properties, like
Audley End, where the whole matter proved to be just too complicated. But there can be absolutely no doubt of the eagerness with
which owners of once great houses sought to divest themselves of

what had now become the impossible responsibility of maintenance.[94]

Ironically, then, many of the remaining landowners were embracing the very solution that Sir Richard Acland had been so criticized for adopting: they were opting out, giving up, abdicating their responsibilities. And they were doing so because they found them unable to bear, and because they believed that in the future, their class would not be wanted to bear them anyway. Increasingly, owners of estates lacked the will or the courage to administer their own affairs. Their incomes were reduced; their houses were requisitioned; their farms were entirely under the control of the government. In 1942, the Uthwatt Report proposed increased central control over the development of agricultural land.[95] More generally, there was a widespread demand – not just from men like Acland, but from agricultural experts like Sir Daniel Hall and C. S. Orwin – that in the new world that was to come, the old structure of landownership should be abolished. In agriculture, more than ever, it was the farmers, the labourers, and the civil servants who mattered.[96] Even on the wartime county committees, it was these figures, not the old grandees and gentry, who were in the majority. As the representatives of the agricultural interest, and as the owners of the land, the old patrician class seemed on the brink of oblivion.[97]

The feebleness of the landowners' response only accentuated the weakness of their position. Early in 1943, Lord de la Warr produced an all-party manifesto on the future of agriculture, urging that the state should support the efficient landowner, not expropriate him, and that the old structure of patrician leadership of the agricultural interest should be allowed to continue. It received little attention. In the same year, Lord Portsmouth published a volume apocalyptically entitled *Alternatives to Death*, which argued eloquently – but uninfluentially – that the landowner was a live and a vigorous force in agriculture; and that such essential qualities as integrity, character, and judgement were not technical skills that could be taught at colleges of estate management, but were habits of mind that arose only from the family tradition of landownership.[98] And at the very end of the war, Lord Salisbury published a brief, dull, and austere manifesto entitled *Post-War Conservative Policy*, which urged the importance of the land, of the established church, and of a reformed and powerful House of Lords. But it sold only 3,000 copies. Compared with the best-selling Beveridge Report, no one was remotely interested – either in his musings, or in those of other would-be patrician propagandists like Acland or Hinchingbrooke.[99]

Indeed, by the very end of the war, it was becoming increasingly

121. The Marquess of
Hartington by Sir Oswald
Birley.

clear that public opinion had turned strongly against the traditional
aristocracy – however great their contribution to the war effort
might have been. One episode in particular illustrated this. In
January 1944, Colonel Hunloke, the brother-in-law of the Duke of
Devonshire, resigned as MP for West Derbyshire, the seat that had
been the bastion of Cavendish power and influence for over three
hundred years, and that the family had filled since 1885 with only a
brief interruption in 1918–23. The selection committee to choose
Hunloke's successor was chaired by the Duke of Devonshire, and after
a very brief meeting, the only name that had been considered was
formally proposed: that of his son and heir, the Marquess of Hartington. But the opposition candidate turned out to be Charles White,
the son of the man who had beaten the Cavendishes in 1918 and
1922.[100] As a result, the by-election turned into a major public event:
there was extensive press coverage; cabinet ministers went down to
speak in support of Hartington; even the Prime Minister sent an
eloquent letter, extolling the 'constancy and fidelity' of the family to
their constituency and the state. But none of it was to any avail. The
Cavendish majority of 5,500 was overturned; Charles White won by
4,500 votes; and the Marquess of Hartington departed for military
service – and death. As Loelia Westminster remarked to Henry
Channon, 'Duchess's kisses aren't what they used to be.'[101]

iv. Conclusion: Victors and Victims

Beyond any doubt, the Second World War was in some ways the 'finest hour' for the remaining members of the traditional titled and territorial élite. Many gave much, and some gave everything, to defend the land they loved – and the lands they owned. Yet on closer inspection, the glory was outweighed by the grimness. From the very beginning, there was among most gentry and grandees a deeper and more general sense that, whatever the outcome of the war, the country-house life and the patrician élite that had survived in attenuated form until 1939 would have no place in the new world that lay beyond. In 1940, G. M. Trevelyan was appointed Master of Trinity College by Winston Churchill. A year later, his brother Sir Charles made over Wallington to the National Trust. And Trevelyan himself spent the war writing his *English Social History*, an elegiac lament for the world of aristocratic decency and rural wholesomeness which he believed had vanished for ever.

This sense of patrician gloom and doom was equally evident among critical and creative writers. In 1944, Marghanita Laski published *Love on the Supertax*, a parody of Walter Greenwood's depression-ridden novel, *Love on the Dole*. In it, the daughter of a noble family crushed by the war vainly seeks the hand of a Communist proletarian, a member of the new aristocracy of munition workers. In the world of Beveridge and Butler, of planning, equality, and reform, of the Welfare State and a 'Woolworth existence', it did indeed look as though the new order that was to come had no room for the old élite, however hard they had laboured, however great had been their sacrifices, however substantial their efforts, and however glorious their deeds.[102] This, at least, was the feeling that prompted that Catholic, quixotic, and perceptive commentator on the patrician scene, Evelyn Waugh, to begin writing *Brideshead Revisited*. Convinced that 'the ancestral seats which were our chief national aristocratic achievement were doomed to decay and spoliation like the monasteries of the sixteenth century', he set out to write a novel that would be a nostalgic lament for the aristocratic style of life which he believed the war had ended for good.[103]

The truth was, as Harold Nicolson realized, that by 1945, 'class feeling and class resentment' were 'very strong', and it was the traditional landed classes – the very embodiment of Colonel Blimp – more than any other group, that were the prime victims of this resentment.[104] For all his ducal background, aristocratic instincts, and romantic inclination, Churchill himself had no doubt that the landed and titled classes were among the foremost losers of the war. And, appropriately enough, the most emphatic display of aristocratic disenchantment duly came in 1945, when Churchill himself – in his moment of supreme triumph – was dismissed by the electorate from any further conduct of their affairs. Overnight, the saviour of his country became once again what he had been in the 1930s, before his encounter with destiny: a marginal anachronism, an aristocratic antique. Four years earlier, when speaking of the ordinary people, Churchill had remarked, 'they have saved this country; they have the right to rule it.'[105] After six long years of unprecedented deprivations, how would the patricians respond, and what could they possibly hope for, when a socialist government – overwhelmingly elected in the people's name – began to exercise those rights in earnest?

14

THE END OF THE AFFAIR

Was there an upper class in post war Britain? . . . If you belong to the upper classes yourself, you may well be aware of the distinction between a true landed aristocrat and a successful industrialist; if you belong to the classes below, the distinction may not be apparent, let alone real.

(A. Marwick, *British Society Since 1945* (1982), pp. 39–40.)

Today, the coherence of the country-house world, which survived, even if under stress, up till the Second World War, has largely vanished. Many country houses have been destroyed, and many more are no longer privately owned . . . Even if a considerable number belong to families who have owned them for many generations, such families could no longer conceivably be described as a ruling class.

(M. Girouard, *Life in the English Country House: A Social and Architectural History* (1978), pp. 316–18.)

Aristocracy does not stand up well to misfortune. It is a fair weather way of life. Noblemen demonstrate a highly developed sense of class consciousness when they are on top . . . But, down trodden and oppressed, they do not seem to manifest the same class solidarity that the working class would display in similar circumstances . . . The fallen noble accepts his defeat . . . and it is rare that any other more fortunate peer would make much effort to redeem him.

(R. Lacey, *Aristocrats* (1984), p. 178.)

George VI rescued the Garter from the Prime Minister of the day, and made it 'non-political and in my gift' . . . Whom would the king, of his independent will, delight to honour? The first list of his nominations contained the obvious war leaders. There followed in 1948: the Duke of Portland, Lord Harlech, the Earl of Scarbrough, and Lord Cranworth. In 1951, there was a further batch: the Duke of Wellington, Lord Fortescue, and Lord Allendale. Who were these men? What had they done to deserve any honour, let alone the highest in the land? Did they even exist? They belonged to a world of shadows.

(A. J. P. Taylor, *Essays in English History* (1976), p. 288.)

As the victory bells rang out in 1945, the Earl of Radnor remarked to his Countess that, however much there might be a brighter dawn for the lower orders, 'now our personal problems begin.'[1] And he was quite correct. The end of the war left most surviving landowners in circumstances more reduced and distressed than they had ever known; and in the austere and egalitarian world of Welfare State socialism that followed, there was a distinct feeling that their remaining economic privileges, political influence, and social status were no longer acceptable. In fact, their most alarmist fears about the Labour government of 1945–51 proved to be exaggerated. But nevertheless, during the years since the Second World War ended, the steady and inexorable decline that had been so marked since the beginning of the twentieth century continued and even accelerated. In post-war Britain, from Attlee to Thatcher, wealth, power, and status would no longer be territorially based.

Economically, the combination of continued austerity and increased taxes meant that estates tumbled into the market in the years immediately after 1945, and that country houses, town palaces, works of art, and non-agricultural assets were destroyed or disbursed on an unprecedented scale. Some owners gave up and emigrated; some were forced to turn to the stately-homes business; the majority were obliged to earn their living. The late 1950s and early 1960s brought a brief remission, underpinned by rising land values. But the soaring costs and increased taxes levied by the end of the decade threatened to make country houses uneconomic monsters to all except the very wealthy (and therefore very lucky) few. By the 1980s, stately homes and their owners were among the most conspicuous lame ducks of Thatcherite Britain, and what remained of the old landed order had effectively ceased to be an economically definable class at all.

Politically, the post-war picture has been equally bleak, relieved only by occasional but ephemeral rays of sunshine. The Labour government of 1945 was the most radical and least landed ministry in modern British parliamentary history, and its legislation and its rhetoric emphatically reflected this. The Tory governments from 1951 to 1964 were more patrician in façade than in substance, and inept and transient Prime Ministers like Eden and Home only discredited still further the idea that the landed élite was the ruling élite. At the margins of power – in Rhodesia and in Kenya, in Northern Ireland, and in the deepest of the shires – the landowners lingered on. But even there, by the mid-1970s, their position was being fundamentally eroded. In the world of Wilson and Callaghan, Heath and Foot, public life in Britain was less aristocratic than it had been in the days of Attlee. And in the rampantly petty-bourgeois world of Thatcher, where self-made men are her ideal, the old territorial class appears – with very few exceptions – at best anachronistic and at worst plain irrelevant.

In social terms, too, the gentry and grandees have dwindled almost to invisibility. The honours system is now completely divorced from its old territorial and patrician base, and no political party – and not even a majority in the House of Lords – today defends the idea of hereditary titles. Likewise the great ornamental positions – in the empire, the nation, and the localities – have either vanished in the aftermath of decolonization, or have largely been taken over by people of every different backgrounds, who are now deemed more appropriate. The disappearance of the great London palaces, of so many of the grandest country houses, and of the once numerous servant class, means that the labour-intensive theatricality of aristocratic life has virtually come to an end. In a hostile political and economic climate, a low-profile existence seems more prudent (and more necessary) than continued conspicuous consumption. In so far as there is a glamour group in Britain today, it is an amalgam of royalty and the media: but the old landowning class barely signifies.

In short, this chapter does not so much tie up loose ends, as follow dispersing and diminishing threads as they diverge still further and in some cases disappear altogether. There is, undeniably, still much of intrinsic interest to record. But from the broader perspective of modern British history as a whole, this is necessarily the most tangential chapter. For it is a study in increasing marginality rather than in continuing class consciousness, in subordination rather than in dominance, in fragmentation rather than in solidarity. Only in one particular collective guise do today's descendants of the once rich, well born, and powerful patricians survive in the public mind: as the self-styled and self-promoting guardians of what they like to call the national heritage.

i. Plenty and Poverty

In the early 1950s, that supposed inhabitant of cloud-cuckoo-land, P. G. Wodehouse, published a rather unusual novel entitled *Ring for Jeeves*. Bertie Wooster does not appear in it, having gone to a school designed to teach the aristocracy to fend for itself (i.e. to learn to darn socks), lest 'the social revolution should set in with greater severity.' Accordingly, Jeeves has been lent out to Lord Rowcester, the owner of a magnificent but decaying stately home. The roof leaks, the farms have been sold, and the park has been leased out to the local golf club. In a lengthy speech to an American visitor amazed at the decay of the English aristocracy, Jeeves explains the facts of life as they now apply to the old territorial nobility:

> A house such as Rowcester Abbey in these days is not an asset, sir, it is a liability . . . Socialistic legislation has sadly depleted the resources of England's hereditary aristocracy. We are living now in what is known as the Welfare State, which means – broadly speaking – that every body is completely destitute.

Only by marrying a rich American widow, and by demolishing the house and rebuilding it in the United States, is Lord Rowcester enabled to live happily ever after.[2]

As this account implies, the depredations of the Second World War persisted well into the later 1940s, when many requisitioned country houses were returned to their original owners. But they were often in a ruined state that made them virtually uninhabitable, and the compensation was usually quite inadequate for any necessary restoration work.[3] Nor did conditions improve during the next five years. The ice-cold winter of 1947 made many ostensibly 'great' houses literally unliveable in. Labour was hard to obtain, fuel was in short supply, and it was almost impossible to acquire building materials. Building licences were rigorously enforced, and were only gradually phased out in the early years of Conservative rule. Earl Peel tried to embellish and extend Hyning Hall in Lancashire, to make the house a fitting residence since he had recently been appointed the new Lord-Lieutenant. But he failed to apply for a licence, was successfully prosecuted, and obliged to resign his office. And the twelfth Duke of Bedford was fined £5,000 for carrying out his illegal scheme of truncation and remodelling at Woburn.[4]

At the same time, the future financial outlook seemed bleak in the extreme. In 1950, the value of farming land remained what it had been in 1880, and this in a world where most prices had risen dramatically. Agriculture might still be booming, fostered by more generous government support, but – as in the war – it was the farmers and the labourers, not the landlords, who benefited. New legislation concerning town and country planning further eroded the landowners' remaining autonomy over their holdings.[5] Taxes on incomes were raised to unprecedented levels to pay for the big-spending government programme. There was a capital levy in 1948. Death duties were increased to 75 per cent on estates of over one million pounds. And the period that must elapse after the estate was made over before exemption was obtained was extended from three to five years in 1946. Unless avoidance was carefully managed, no patrician family could survive such exactions unscathed. The fact that the Finance Act of 1949 gave 45 per cent abatement of duty payable on agricultural land was not, at the time, much help.[6]

The result was that in this immediate post-war period, some of the greatest names fell victim to that inexorable combination of the reaper and the chancellor.[7] The second Duke of Westminster left a fortune so vast – and so vulnerable – that the Inland Revenue set up a separate department to assess and collect the duties. The death of the seventh Viscount Portman in 1948 meant that the family faced their third major call for duties in twenty years. The Bedfords were

122. *View of Harewood*, c.1960, by John Piper.

crippled by two deaths in rapid succession: the eleventh duke in 1940; and his successor in mysterious circumstances only thirteen years later. The Derbys suffered three deaths close together: Edward Stanley in 1939, the seventeenth earl in 1948, and his other son Oliver in 1950. And the Devonshires were hit at least as hard: the ninth duke in 1938; the heir to the tenth duke in 1944; and then the tenth duke himself in 1952. Had he lived four months longer, the £2.5 million duties that were levied would again have been avoided. 'What dread score', inquired Henry Channon, 'has destiny to pay off against the Devonshires? Is this the end of Chatsworth? And of Hardwick?'[8]

It was a pertinent question, and there could only be one answer. Both the Bedfords and the Devonshires were forced to make extensive sales: Chenies and Tavistock in the one case, and large tracts of Derbyshire in the other. The Portmans – even harder hit – had to give up all of their Dorset estate. Lord Bath sold in Northamptonshire, Shropshire, and parts of Wiltshire.[9] John Wyndham disposed of all the Leconfield lands in Yorkshire, Lancashire, and Dumfries, and 20,000 acres in Cumberland and 7,000 acres in Sussex. The Earl of Harewood parted with two-thirds of his Yorkshire holdings; Lord Derby sold the Fylde estate, some of the Macclesfield forest estate, and Knowsley village. The Duke of Argyll disposed of the Island of Tiree and 28,000 acres in Kintyre. The Duke of Richmond unloaded property in Banff, and the Duke of Montrose in Arran and Stirling.

Lord Dalhousie sold 10,000 acres in Angus, after an 850-year family ownership. In Wales, families like the Plymouths and the Lisburnes suffered another round of dispersals. And in Glamorgan, 30,000 acres of the Tredegar estate went under the hammer.[10]

For those who had been holding on only very precariously in the 1930s, these new exactions, combined with the generally adverse circumstances, often led to the total extinction of old territorial holdings and the complete disappearance of some patrician families. In Wales, the Pryse estates provided a rental of £7,000 a year in 1946: but all of this was swallowed up in jointures and annuities. Two rounds of death duties, levied in 1946 and 1948, obliged the trustees to sell everything to the University of Wales at Aberystwyth.[11] The Madingley estate near Cambridge, and the Harcourt lands near Oxford, were both given over for similar educational purposes. In 1947, the Nelson family abandoned completely their house – Trafalgar – and their estates in Wiltshire, and Earl St Vincent sold all his lands in Yorkshire. The descendants of John Bateman – whose ancestor had catalogued the landed establishment in its prime – sold out completely in Essex; the Sneyd family, crippled with a succession of death duties, disappeared altogether from Staffordshire; and Lord Acton sold his estate at Aldenham in Shropshire.[12]

What did this add up to? The trends were clear, and were, essentially, an intensification of those that had been so pronounced in the aftermath of the First World War. Many small and middling families gave up completely, and even the greatest grandees were obliged to sell parts of their most cherished heartland properties. By 1950, probably one-half of the farms of England and Wales were now owner occupied – the highest percentage in modern history. In 1952, in Essex, Oxfordshire, and Shropshire, only one-third of the old territorial families survived in possession of their country seats; one-quarter were listed but had sold their estates and moved to smaller properties; and the remainder had disappeared completely.[13] As the editor of *Burke's Landed Gentry* pointed out in the preface to the 1952 edition, it was 'more and more a history book rather than a record of estates'. And the same was true of the territorial nobility. As Lord Salisbury explained in a debate in the Lords in 1951: 'There still seems to be an impression in Labour circles that all the land of England is owned by a small number of immensely rich and almost medieval territorial magnates . . . But my Lords, that conception, of course, is really long out of date.' Indeed, by 1956, only one-third of the peerage possessed country estates at all.[14]

So great were the depredations, and so depressed were the conditions, that non-agricultural assets also went under the hammer in unprecedented amounts. In London, the Bedfords, Portmans, and

Cadogans were forced to realize large sections of their famous estates, and the Westminsters had to part with the whole of Pimlico to meet the duties levied on the death of the second duke. Other, less well-known London landlords who were forced to sell included the Howard de Waldens, the Calthorpes, the Tyssen-Amhersts, and the Duke of Norfolk.[15] In the provinces, the picture was exactly the same. In Lancashire, Lord Sefton sold his Kirkby Estate and Aintree racecourse, the Salisburys sold in Liverpool, and Lord Derby sold in Ormskirk. The Butes withdrew from Cardiff, the Dudleys from the Black Country, the Marquess of Anglesey from Glossop, and Lord Crawford from Haigh and Wigan. The Earl of Jersey sold in Swansea and Port Talbot, Lord Lonsdale in Whitehaven, and Lord St Germans in Lewisham. The Devonshires never returned to Compton Place at Eastbourne, where they disposed of their holdings in the Parks and Baths Company. And at Skegness, the death of the eighth Earl of Scarbrough necessitated a further round of sales.[16]

Predictably, the few remaining great town palaces were also doomed to their final disappearance. Portman House was demolished, and Holland House became a local authority park. Of those that survived the war reasonably intact, Dudley, Spencer, Bridgewater, Wimborne, and Derby Houses were soon sold for office or other institutional uses; and Apsley House was presented to the nation by the seventh Duke of Wellington to be the national museum for his illustrious ancestor. Only Londonderry House continued as a private residence for a time, and that was on a very much reduced scale. Eventually, it was sold in the early 1960s for half a million pounds, and was immediately demolished. The only great London houses remaining are lived in by members of the royal family: Marlborough House, for Queen Mary, subsequently given to the government; Clarence House for the Queen Mother; and Buckingham Palace itself.[17] But the days when the great grandees in London lived in state equal or superior to the monarch had long since gone. As Nancy Mitford rightly noted in 1955, 'aristocracy no longer keep up any state in London, where family houses hardly exist now.'[18]

This sale and destruction of town palaces were replicated on a much larger scale by the sale and destruction of country mansions. For they were too big, too uneconomical, and often damaged beyond repair, the setting for a life and for a class now generally believed to be extinct. As Lawrence Stone rightly remarked, 'in 1945, impoverished and now socialist England found itself saddled with far more great mansions than it knew what to do with.'[19] Many of them were sold to institutional purchasers, thereby perpetuating in peacetime the uses to which the houses had been put in war. Himley Hall was bought by the Coal Board from the Earl of Dudley, and Taplow and Elvetham Hall were bought by industrial concerns. Kimbolton was turned into a school, and Lumley Castle was converted into a hall of residence for Durham University. Hinchingbrooke was sold to Huntingdon County Council for 'scholastic purposes', Wentworth Woodhouse became a teacher-training college, and Welbeck an army training centre. And Aylesford Priory and Allington Castle were occupied by the Carmelite Order.

But inevitably, it was impossible to find institutional uses for many of the empty houses that remained. One or two were bought by private individuals or converted into country house hotels. But in the absence of government regulations prohibiting it, most were demolished. In some cases, demolition was only partial: at Woburn one range was destroyed; at Bowood the house was pulled down but the grand stable block retained. But in many cases, the whole house disappeared: Panshanger, Normanhurst, Lowther Castle, Rufford Abbey, and Ravensworth Castle were only the most famous victims. Between 1945 and 1955, four hundred country houses were demolished, more than at any other period of modern British history.[20] Indeed, by 1955, the peak year, they were disappearing at the rate of one every five days, and some of the greatest houses – like Eaton Hall – were yet to go. In 1951, in language much more alarmist than that which Lord Lothian had used in the 1930s, Lord Crawford lamented that 'a national tragedy, indeed a national scandal, is taking place before our eyes.' And he had good cause to know.[21]

As the great mansions were sold, demolished completely, or partially reduced in size, as some families left their ancestral homes for good, and as the great town palaces were destroyed or sold off, the result was that many aristocratic artefacts went under the hammer. The years after 1945, like those immediately before, were not a particularly good time to sell since the international art market was not yet restored: the financial system was in chaos, with widespread currency restrictions; there were fewer millionaire collectors in America willing and able to buy; and the great transatlantic museum purchasers had not yet come upon the scene. Nevertheless, during the late 1940s and early 1950s, major sellers of works of art included Ellesmere, De L'Isle, Zetland, Tollemache, Halifax, and Fitzwilliam.[22] Great libraries were also dispersed, by Howard, Crawford, Malmesbury, Bute, Derby, and Tollemache. When the Dudleys sold Himley and the Manchesters left Kimbolton, the contents of both once-great houses were auctioned. In 1951, there was a major (and very ill-advised) sale at Woburn of two hundred seventeenth-century Dutch and Flemish paintings. And in 1953, the contents of Panshanger went under the hammer, in another of the many 'demolition sales' of the time.[23]

How did the remaining members of the landed establishment respond to this unprecedentedly hostile and alien world in which they found themselves? Besides demolishing the house, selling its contents, and parting with the land, what more constructive steps could they take? Predictably, the answer was a mixture of old and new means of life-support. Ironically enough, one novel solution was to turn to the government for assistance. Even the much-hated Labour administration felt some anxiety that the mansions of the mighty had become the casualties of the Welfare State. Naturally, their concern was not so much for the fate of the occupants, as for the fate of their houses, which were seen, not as derelict machines in which the upper classes had once lived, but as part of a broader cultural phenomenon called the national heritage. Accordingly, in 1948, the Gowers Committee was set up by Sir Stafford Cripps, to consider 'what general arrangements might be made for the . . . preservation, maintenance and use of houses of outstanding historical or architectural interest, which might otherwise not be preserved.' Its major recommendation was the setting up of three Historic Buildings Councils, for England, Scotland, and Wales, which were to make grants for repairs to great houses, conditional on a certain degree of public access.[24]

Here was a new measure of aristocratic indigence: a socialist administration subsidizing patrician mansions. A second innovation of the Labour government was the setting up, in 1946, of the National Land Fund, with a capital sum of £50 million. One use to which the money could be put was to compensate the Treasury if the government decided to accept land in lieu of death-duty payments. Thereafter, these provisions were extended to cover historic houses and works of art, with the result that between 1947 and 1957 the Treasury passed on twenty-six properties to the National Trust, including houses such as Penrhyn, Saltram, and Shugborough. Some, indeed, were among the greatest mansions in the land, including Hardwick, which was accepted by the Treasury in part payment after the death of the tenth Duke of Devonshire.[25] In the same way, the magnificent pictures and splendid contents of Petworth were accepted by the Treasury after the death of Lord Leconfield. In addition, many other mansions were bequeathed directly to the National Trust in the late 1940s, 1950s, and 1960s, including Tatton Park, The Vyne, Powis Castle, and Felbrigg.

These solutions to aristocratic indigence necessarily involved the abandonment of aristocratic privacy, and the opening of the house to the public – to a lesser or greater extent. Indeed, the idea of turning the family mansion itself into a money-making venture, by opening it to a mass public, was the most significant innovation in this

123. Lord Montagu of Beaulieu.

period. The pioneer was the sixth Marquess of Bath, who inherited the dilapidated, 118-roomed mansion of Longleat, and £700,000 worth of death duties in 1946.[26] He was obliged to sell off much of the land, and in April 1949 opened the house to the public as the showplace of the West Country, the first stately home to admit visitors on a regular, paying basis. Within a year, 135,000 people had paid to come to look at Lord Bath's home and heirlooms, and by the mid-fifties, the figure was topping a quarter of a million. Soon, Longleat was open every day except Christmas, and Lord Bath was employing as large a staff as his ancestors had known in the nineteenth century – albeit for rather different purposes.

The second pioneer in the stately-homes business was Lord Montagu of Beaulieu, who succeeded to his titles in 1929, while still a minor, but who inherited the house and estates only in 1951 at the age of twenty-five.[27] Although not crippled by death duties like Bath, he, too, felt that the family mansion, Palace House, was too large to maintain as a place of residence. Accordingly, he exploited his father's early interest in the horseless carriage to turn Beaulieu into a motoring museum and, in 1952 – the first year of opening – 80,000 visitors were recorded. Shortly after, the newly inherited Duke of Bedford returned to Woburn, where he found the family facing the crippling burden of double death duties. Estates were sold in Bloomsbury and the country, and the trustees urged the new duke to abandon the struggle and give Woburn Abbey over to the National Trust. But he determined to keep the house in the family, by opening it to the public in April 1955, and promoted it with all the entrepreneurial zeal he could muster. Very soon, it was attracting 180,000 visitors a year.[28]

There were many who dismissed this idea of turning country mansions into 'a sort of funfair', as the ultimate desecration of the family home. Even in the inter-war years, there had never been anything quite like this. Occasional visitors might be tolerated out of a sense of *noblesse oblige*. But the idea of 'refloating one's fortunes on a flood of half crowns, motor-coach parties and set teas' was something altogether different. The very change in the words used signified a major transformation. A country house, sequestered and secluded, was one thing; a stately home, open to a paying public, was quite another.[29] The Duke of Bedford, in particular, was criticized for being brash, undignified, and pushy; he allowed nudists to camp in his grounds, even appeared on television, and was likened to a circus impresario. But it worked. By 1960, Woburn was visited by 431,000 people, and Beaulieu by 289,000. Blenheim, which was first opened in 1950, received its one millionth visitor six years later. And this was, for many owners, the shape of things to come: between 1950 and 1965, six hundred houses were opened, including some of the greatest in the land – Chatsworth, Houghton, Arundel, and many more.

Beyond these much-publicized innovations, the solutions resorted to by this new generation of needy notables were to do what had been done before, but to do it more intensively and more urgently. Some patricians, overwhelmed by financial difficulties, and deeply distressed by the new socialist austerity of the Welfare State, followed their forebears and emigrated, to South Africa, Kenya, and Rhodesia. Despite the murder of Lord Erroll, Happy Valley's allure remained and was, if anything, increased. One such patrician *émigré* was Lord Portsmouth.[30] He had worked hard on the Hampshire Agricultural Committee during the war, but now saw no future for his class or his country. 'All was drab, alas too drab, in England' he complained. 'The motto of the new democracy seemed to be . . . "the greatest misery to the greatest number".' In 1948, he visited Kenya, a country that he believed provided the opportunity to do something positive and constructive, and the space to re-create the old, more spacious life he had known on his family estates in his youth. Encouraged by Lord Francis Scott, he purchased 3,000 acres almost on impulse, and soon greatly extended his holdings.

Nor was Portsmouth exceptional, in attitude or action. For some of the greatest names in the land decided that their only future lay on the periphery, in the empire. The eleventh Duke of Manchester abandoned Kimbolton for Kenya. The heir to the Dukedom of Montrose settled in Rhodesia. The Marquess of Tavistock took up fruit farming in South Africa.[31] The Duke of Grafton bought 20,000 acres in Rhodesia for one of his younger sons. And when Lord Acton sold Aldenham, he, too, went to Rhodesia. There, like many an expatriate aristocrat, he combined farming with business ventures, and amassed a clutch of directorships in packaging, banking, and insurance. In 1967, he moved to Swaziland, where he became a director of the Swaziland Building Society, and in 1971 he retired to Majorca.[32]

Others were determined to sit it out in Britain, heeding the view of the Princess Royal when Harewood was hit so hard by death duties that 'whatever happens, we musn't emigrate or desert this country, however much we are tempted.'[33] But to give effect to this stiff-upper-lipped view, alternative sources of income had to be found. As from the 1880s, directorships in the City beckoned alluringly, especially in safe companies like banks and insurance. The eighteenth Earl of Derby was a director of Martins Bank and the Royal Insurance Company.[34] The premier baronet of England, Sir Edmund Bacon, was chairman of the British Sugar Corporation and a director of Lloyds Bank. Cameron of Lochiel was chairman of the Scottish Widows Insurance Company and the Royal Bank of Scotland. Sir Cennydd Traherne was a director of the Cardiff Building Society. The Norwich Union could claim Lord Townshend and Sir Hughe Knatchbull-Hugessen. The directors of the Royal Exchange included one duke, two earls, four viscounts, and two barons. How much work these patricians did remains unclear. In most cases, it seems that they emerged from the shires for monthly meetings and then went home, while subcommittees did all the work and took most of the important decisions.[35]

As before, some aristocrats took a much more active part in the City, either out of need or inclination. Lord Balfour of Burleigh was chairman of Lloyds; Lord Harlech was chairman of the Midland and the Bank of British West Africa; and Lord Pakenham was chairman of the Anglo-Irish Bank.[36] Oliver Lyttelton, during the period of Tory opposition, and after his retirement from politics in 1955, was chairman of AEI, and held a host of other directorates. But the most striking innovation was the extent to which heads of aristocratic families launched themselves into the new world of commercial television. The Earl of Antrim was the founder chairman of Ulster Television. The Marquess Townshend held the same position with Anglia, and was reputedly responsible for the company logo, of a knight on a horse. His lordship was keen on riding and chivalry, and thought that a knight in armour was an appropriate symbol for a once feudal and still rural region. And in Wales, the first holder of the commercial franchise was TWW, largely funded and controlled by Lord Derby, which was in turn superseded by Harlech Television, another coroneted communications company.[37]

Among the younger generation, few notables soiled their hands by actually working on the shop floor; but the range of careers now deemed acceptable had markedly widened. The heir to the Duke of Argyll studied electronics at McGill University in Canada, then worked for a brokerage firm on Wall Street and for Rank Xerox. The heir to the Duke of Richmond trained as a chartered accountant and worked for five years at Courtaulds in Coventry. Lord Harewood and Lord Drogheda went into the world of opera, and Lord Brabourne into films. The fifth Earl of Gosford became a wine merchant in New York. Lord Verulam was the general manager of Enfield Rolling Mills, and subsequently president of the London Chamber of Commerce. The young Lord Carrington, after demobilization and inheritance, became a trainee manager at de Havilland.[38] The Hon. Nicholas Ridley began as a civil engineering contractor. In every case, financial necessity was the imperative: even if many of these patricians kept their family mansions, their sources of income were becoming almost indistinguishable from the vast majority of the upper middle classes.

Underlying all these changes in the immediate aftermath of the Second World War was the inescapable fact of territorial decline. Between 1880 and 1976, even the greatest and most tenaciously surviving estates were diminished by 76 per cent in England and Wales, and by 69 per cent in Scotland (see Appendix H). Of course, sales had been occurring throughout much of that time, but the most extensive transfers of land probably occurred after 1945. Among the grandees in Scotland, Sutherland was down from 1.3 million acres to a mere 138,000. And of the great English magnates, Devonshire was reduced from 133,000 to 56,000, and Portland from 54,000 to 17,000.[39] Only very rare exceptions from among the old territorial nobility – like the Beauforts and the Westminsters – were able to enlarge their acreage. Significantly, the other most outstanding trend was the accumulation, post-Bateman, of massive holdings by the new plutocracy: the Levers, the Guinnesses, and the Cowdrays. But among the old aristocratic families, the once very broad-acred landowners were less great and less supra-national, while those of more limited acreage were even further diminished.

Yet during the period from the mid-1950s to the mid-1960s, this considerable truncation of patrician landownership seemed almost belied by the abrupt upturn in some territorial fortunes. Suddenly, and unexpectedly, the price of farming land began to rise, bringing to an abrupt termination the seventy-year depression in agriculture and in land prices, to which for three generations there had seemed no end. In 1871, before the beginning of the slump, farm land had been worth on average about £53 an acre, but during the worst of the inter-war depression, its selling price was at rock bottom somewhere between £23 and £28 an acre. Yet from the mid-1950s, the price began gradually and firmly to rise: to £73 an acre by 1959–60, £98 by 1961–2, and £114 by 1963–4.[40] As a result, those families who had managed to hold on to some land found themselves much better off: indeed, in terms of capital value, the loss of land through enforced sales was often more than outweighed by the increased worth of that which was left. On paper, at least, any notable with 10,000 acres was now a millionaire, while those few who had held on to greater amounts were richer than they had ever been before, notwithstanding the fact that their acres were fewer.

This dramatic increase in the capital value of agricultural land was exactly paralleled by the sudden, and quite extraordinary, increase in the worth of paintings and other *objets d'art*, as the international market was restored, and the great American galleries began to push up the prices. The most emphatic evidence of this came in 1959 when, to pay the final portion of death duties on the estate of the second duke, the Westminsters sold off some of their paintings for a record £740,000, including Rubens' *Adoration of the Magi* which alone fetched £275,000 (it had been valued at only £7,500 in 1953).[41] Thereafter, there were many noble vendors in the saleroom. In June 1960, the Berkeley Castle 168-piece silver dinner service fetched £207,000. In 1961, the Duke of Leeds sold the Goya portrait of the Duke of Wellington to the National Gallery for £140,000. Three years later, the Earl of Derby parted with Rembrandt's *Belshazzar's Feast* for £170,000, and in 1969, Lord Fitzwilliam disposed of Stubbs' *Frieze of Broodmares* for £200,000. Even for families hard hit by death duties, the sale of an old master or two was often sufficient to meet the bill.[42]

In any case, after the clutch of forced sales in the ten years after 1945, in the aftermath of the Second World War and the Labour government's legislation, the patricians again became more expert at adjusting to the new rules of death-duty avoidance. The old estate management companies – now no longer invulnerable to taxation – were rapidly wound up, and more care was taken to make over family properties in good time: the present Duke of Richmond, for instance, did so as long ago as 1969, and the Duke of Bedford in 1974. At the same time, the 1960s saw the widespread proliferation of elaborate discretionary trusts among landowning families, which were a much more effective means of tax avoidance.[43] So, in the case of the Westminsters, their affairs had been so carefully reordered in the aftermath of the death of the second duke that when the third, fourth, and fifth dukes died, the family holdings suffered hardly at all. As one adviser put it, 'the management of the estates will go on as before, and nothing is likely to cause any disintegration or fragmentation of the estates.'[44]

The result was that 'for the British aristocracy, the 1950s were a period of recovery such as nobody could have envisaged amidst the privations of World War II and its socialist aftermath.' Between the mid-1950s and mid-1960s, country houses and country-house life revived in a manner that would have never been foreseen in the grim days of post-war austerity.[45] As Evelyn Waugh rightly remarked in his introduction to the revised (1959) version of Brideshead, his first edition had proved to be 'a panegyric preached over an empty coffin'. When he wrote the book, in the dark days of the 1940s, 'it was impossible to forsee the present cult of the English country house'. 'Brideshead today', he added, 'would be open to trippers, its treasures rearranged by expert hands, and the fabric better maintained than it was by Lord Marchmain.'[46] Across the country, oil-fired central heating, labour-saving gadgets, and the installation of private bathrooms meant that some of the greatest country houses were still able to function. And everywhere, there was restoration after years of neglect, rooms were redecorated, and treasures were displayed – for the family and for the public – with a sympathy and educated discernment that was often entirely new.

At the same time, there was a revival of confidence in landowning itself. Estates like Badminton, Welbeck, and Northumberland were still administered with the old patrician and paternal style.[47] The Devonshires moved back to Chatsworth and, while they were obliged to open the house to the public, they also made it the family home for the first time since before the Second World War. The Duke even took up horse-racing again, and actually indulged in art patronage in a minor but traditional sort of way – commissioning paintings by Annigoni and Lucian Freud, and in 1970 building a new conservatory. Antiquarian squires like Wyndham Ketton-Cremer and Sir Gyles Isham kept up the tradition of local patrician scholarship.[48] More expansively, the Calthorpe family in 1958 drew up a comprehensive re-development scheme for Edgbaston, which confidently looked forward to beyond the year 2000. And in 1971, the Westminsters produced their Strategy for Mayfair and Belgravia. As the Grosvenors' senior trustee put it: 'our ability is to look far ahead. Fifty years is nothing to us, and one hundred years is normal.'[49]

Indeed, some landowners were sufficiently confident and comfortable to embark on the construction, or reconstruction, of their country houses. The early 1950s saw both the peak of demolitions and the ending of the building licence restrictions, which made it both necessary and possible for those with the resources to build again. Unlike the period from 1900 to 1940, when it was the new, non-landed rich who had predominated, some three-quarters of these country houses were put up for authentic landowning families.[50] Very few were especially large, and only the occasional one, like the new Eaton Hall for the Westminsters, was in the modern style. The majority were neo-Georgian, and designed by architects like Clough Williams-Ellis or Claud Phillimore. Two of the latter's most important commissions were Arundel Park for the Duke of Norfolk and Knowsley for Lord Derby, both of whom moved out of the big house to live in more comfortable quarters. And in an even older tradition, some landowners actually took a hand in the designing and construction, like Roger Hesketh at Meols Hall, Lord O'Neill at Shanes Castle, and Robin Leigh-Pemberton at Torry Hill.[51]

But this Indian summer, the last, silver age of the country house, was of short duration, and soon came to an end in the late 1960s and early 1970s. The combination of world inflation and higher taxation meant that by the mid-1970s, the patricians became once again an endangered species. The energy crisis, combined with soaring domestic costs, made the maintenance and upkeep of stately homes suddenly uneconomic again: oil-fired central heating became prohibitively expensive, and the cost of labour and materials spiralled with inflation and VAT. In 1965, Capital Gains Tax was introduced, and although there were opportunities for exemption and relief on agricultural land, this meant that much of the benefit from increased property values was wiped out. In 1968–9, the time that must elapse between making over and death for estate-duty avoidance was increased from five years to seven, and discretionary trusts were made liable to taxation. Then, in 1975, Capital Transfer Tax was introduced, the most elaborate attempt yet to block the loopholes in estate-duty avoidance.[52] At the same time, the National Trust found itself increasingly stretched, with too many houses on its hands that were inadequately endowed, and became very reluctant to accept any more.

As a result, many landowners found themselves burdened with historic houses that they could no longer demolish (thanks to the conservation regulations), could not sell, could not maintain, and could not give to the state. In 1974, there was a debate in the House of Lords, in which Lord Clark predicted that 'a wealth tax on the contents of English country houses large and small, would in a very short time lead to their extinction.'[53] The Historic Houses Association got up a petition, with one and a half million signatures on it, protesting against CTT. And a massive exhibition was put on at the Victoria and Albert Museum, entitled 'The Destruction of the English Country House', a heart-string-tugging exercise in nostalgia, which catalogued the unprecedented demolition of the early 1950s, and drew attention to the contemporary plight of stately homes. Even the tourists – although they enabled the owners to claim certain tax exemptions and qualify for grants from the Historic Buildings Council – did not bring in enough revenue for most of the owners to balance their books.

But significantly, this exhibition was much more a plea for help than a reassertion of patrician hubris. 'One thing . . . is quite certain', James Lees-Milne admitted. 'The country-house way of life as some of us have known it, will never be revived.'[54] The truth of that observation was soon to be borne out in the Mentmore affair. In May 1974, the sixth Earl of Rosebery died, leaving an estate of nearly £10 million, which – for unfathomable reasons – he had not given over to his heir so as to be exempt from death duties. In February 1975, the new Lord Rosebery offered Mentmore to the nation, in lieu of £4 million worth of death duties, and also asked the government to pay him £2 million. Although Lord Rosebery claimed he was offering the state a bargain, the negotiations dragged on for two years. But at a time of economic crisis and financial stringency, the government refused to make the money available, and was not even prepared to draw on the resources of the National Land Fund. Despite a massive outcry from the preservationist lobby, and attempts to put up private funds to save the house and its collection, the contents were auctioned for £6.3 million in May 1977, and the mansion itself was later sold to become a centre of transcendental meditation.[55]

This episode well illustrated the plight and problems of country-house owners in the mid-1970s: even when they wanted to give their possessions to the government, it had become almost impossible to arrange terms. The result, in 1980, was the establishment of the National Heritage Memorial Fund, with an independent endowment, and administered by its own trustees, which was free to spend and invest its money as it wished.[56] Its remit included anything ranging from the preservation of rare breeds of birds to helping to save the *Mary Rose*. But in the period since its foundation, a large amount of its budget – augmented by supplementary grants made necessary by the increased valuations in consequence of the 'Getty Factor' – has been given to salvaging great houses: Canons Ashby,

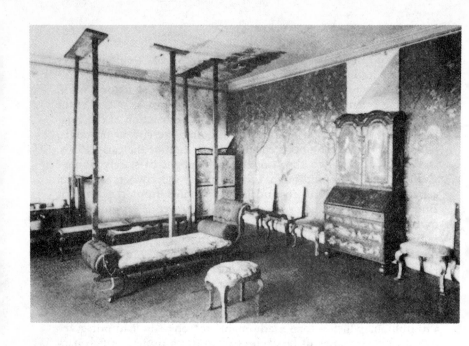

124. (Above) Erddig, the State Bedroom in 1973. (Below) The State Bedroom in 1977.

Belton, Fyvie Castle, Calke Abbey, Nostell Priory, Weston Park, and Kedleston.[57] Here, eloquently displayed, is a most illustrious list of houses, which their owners have given up, and which have been rescued by the state in the name of the national heritage. The economic weakness of the landed establishment could not be more emphatically illustrated.

Of course, some great country houses have continued to go to the National Trust because the endowments have been large enough anyway, Plas Newydd on Anglesey being a classic example.[58] In the case of Wimpole, once the magnificent residence of the Earls of Hardwicke, this was made possible because its last owner, Kipling's daughter, was able to make adequate provision from her father's royalties. In the case of Kingston Lacy, there was a massive endowment of agricultural land. But it was the example of Erddig that showed most poignantly the narrow line between poverty and riches, destruction and survival. By the 1960s, the house was in total chaos and on the brink of complete collapse. The owner was the last of the Yorkes, an eccentric recluse, who would see no one. But even in the worst times, he had bought land on the outskirts of Wrexham, and it was the sudden surge in its value that was Erddig's salvation. By selling only 60 acres for £1 million, it proved possible to endow the house and open it to the public in 1977.[59]

But these were only country mansions as relics: the National Heritage Memorial Fund and the National Trust were undertakers, embalming these once great power houses for posterity. As such, their later history forms no part of an account of the declining aristocracy, however much their disposal most emphatically does. Other families, more fortunate, have continued the recent policy of selling off the occasional work of art, to keep the tax man at bay, and in the age of the 'Getty Factor' have been able to obtain hitherto undreamed-of prices. In 1970, the Earl of Radnor parted with his Velázquez for £2.3 million to meet death duties: a predecessor had purchased it in 1811 for £151. In the same year, the Earl of Harewood sold his Titian, *Death of Actaeon*, for £1.7 million; and Lord Derby's Van Dyck, *Four Negro Heads*, realized £400,000.[60] Even more successfully, the Duke of Devonshire sold his Poussin in 1981 for £2 million to endow the Chatsworth charitable trust. Since then, he has parted with only one-twentieth of his collection of old-master prints and drawings, which, at sales held in 1984, 1985, and 1987, have realized £30 million. And the collection has 'not been trawled for the best items.'[61]

At the same time, the other trend has been – in view of the conditions governing exemption from tax and qualification for government grants – that more and more grand mansions have been

125. The cover of Woburn's 1990 promotional booklet.

opened to the public. In the mid-1970s, great families who had hitherto refused to soil their hands in the stately homes business capitulated: the Roxburghes at Floors, and the Buccleuchs at Boughton, Bowhill, and Drumlanrig. In few cases, even among the greatest stately-home tycoons, do the receipts balance the expenses: it is public relations and the tax exemptions that compel them to open their doors.[62] As a result, there has been a renewed search for gimmicks to attract a public satiated with a surfeit of stately homes. There have been rock concerts (Barry Manilow at Blenheim and Neil Diamond at Woburn), and medieval banquets even at Hatfield. The Marquess of Hertford at Ragley offers bed and breakfast at £100 a night. And the most aggressive patrician go-getters, usually in collaboration with Chipperfields' circus men, have gone in for safari parks at Longleat, Woburn, and Knowsley. To raise the necessary capital, the Earl of Derby sold his Van Dyck and his Tudor and Stuart miniatures.[63]

What, then, is the economic position of the British landed estab-

lishment today? In so far as it is possible to speak of them collectively, it must be emphasized that the old patrician class no longer forms
the wealth élite of the country. Whatever the exceptions, like the
Westminsters or the Devonshires or the Buccleuchs, the fact remains
that, compared with the new rich, their numbers and their assets pale
into relative insignificance. Only one traditional aristocrat – the
Duke of Westminster – appears among the list of the ten richest men
in Britain today, each of whom are worth in excess of £500 million.
In the 1980s, 75 per cent of all millionaires who died were businessmen, financiers, or in the great professions: only 25 per cent were
traditional landowners. Overall, it seems that wealth has not been
fundamentally redistributed in Britain since the Second World War.
But there has certainly been considerable change within the top
category of the very rich. There is much more new super-wealth;
much less old. In the era of the property tycoons of the sixties, or of
men like Vestey, Maxwell, Sainsbury, and Goldsmith in the eighties,
the traditional aristocracy is less significant than ever.[64]

Moreover, they are no longer the territorial élite either. In 1927,
after the post-war 'revolution in landholding', some 27 per cent of
the land of England was owner-occupied. After the further disruptions and sales since 1945, the figure is now thought to be nearer 65
per cent. Bearing in mind the massive increase in corporate and
institutional ownership in recent years, this means that the old
landowning class probably owns significantly less than one-quarter
of the country.[65] Of a sample of 500 landowning families studied in
1880 and again in 1980, just under half of those who had owned
10,000 acres in 1880 still owned some land. But of those who had
owned less than 10,000 acres, only 16 per cent continued as significant
owner-occupiers. And of the same sample, this time of 500 houses,
only 150 were now owned by the same family: 300 had changed
hands, and 106 had been demolished.[66] Clearly, there are local
variations: the more agricultural and less urbanized the county, the
more tenacious the old families have been. And inevitably, the great
families tend to have survived (albeit much reduced) more than the
gentry. But this is not, overall, the picture of a thriving wealth or
territorial élite.

Nevertheless, within this aggregate national picture, the economic
circumstances of individual patricians vary very markedly. A small
number of grandees remain quite extraordinarily rich – richer, in
absolute terms, than they have ever been before. In the 1970s, Lords
Fitzwilliam, Leicester, and Rosebery each left estates in the region of
£10 million.[67] For all the sales of land and of old masters, families like
the Devonshires, the Buccleuchs, the Northumberlands, and the
Westminsters remain among the richest in the country. In 1876, at

current values, the seventh Duke of Devonshire with his 133,000 acres was worth three-quarters of a million pounds. Today, his successor – less landed with only 56,000 acres – is worth £33 million in agricultural land, excluding Chatsworth and the art collections. In terms of their agricultural properties alone, the Dukes of Westminster and of Buccleuch are each worth £100 million; and if the Westminsters' urban estates are added in, then estimates begin at £400 million, and go on well beyond one billion.[68]

Although in every case, these estates are underpinned and supported by extensive stock-exchange holdings and overseas investments they remain great landed agglomerations even so. And lower down the economic scale, there are still some country gentry who survive. In England, such families as Whitbread in Bedfordshire, Legh of High Legh, Anstruther-Gough-Calthorpe of Elvetham, L'Estrange of Hunstanton, Plowden of Plowden, and Dymoke of Scrivelsby hold on to a goodly part of their ancestral estates – all of them millionaires (at present prices) provided they own over five hundred acres.[69] Some have kept their country houses, and in a few cases do not yet open them to the public. Others have sold the family mansion, but have tenaciously held on to the estate. In Scotland, such untitled Highland families as Cameron of Lochiel, Maclean of Duart, and Macleod of Macleod continue to be great owners. And in the lowlands, the same may be said of Moncriefe of that Ilk and Fletcher of Saltoun. Decayed they undeniably are, but by no means totally extinct.[70]

But among many patrician families, there has been a merging of City and landed interests to a far greater degree than even before the Second World War. Some, although they keep up their great houses, are almost entirely reliant on outside sources of income to make ends meet. Men like Lord Polwarth and the Earl of Airlie (to say nothing of his younger brother, Sir Angus Ogilvy) are virtually full-time City businessmen, with a string of company directorships and chairmanships. Similarly, when Lord Carrington resigned from the Foreign Office in 1982, he immediately resumed his business career by becoming chairman of GEC. Likewise, Robin Leigh-Pemberton, a Kent country gentleman, began his career as a barrister, then moved into the City, eventually became chairman of the National Westminster Bank, and was subsequently appointed Governor of the Bank of England.[71] Were it not for their (much diminished) estates, their coats of arms, and their titles, these men would be indistinguishable from many other upper-middle-class professionals.

This is especially true of the many expatriate Irish peers who have been obliged to make a new life and living in mainland Britain. The eighth Earl of Antrim was chairman of Ulster Television and of the

National Trust; his son, the present earl, is a director of Ulster TV, and works in the Tate Gallery. Lord Bessborough began his career as a merchant banker, and was a director of ATV from 1955 to 1963. The twelfth Lord Farnham is chairman of Brown, Shipley, and Company, and of the Avon Rubber Company. The present Earl of Longford was chairman of the Anglo-Irish Bank (as Lord Pakenham), and subsequently of Sidgwick and Jackson, the publishers. The Earl of Drogheda, in addition to being chairman of Covent Garden, was also a director of *The Economist*, and managing director, then chairman, of the *Financial Times*. Some of these notables live in the suburbs of west London; a few have country houses, but rarely an authentic estate; none are great landowners in the conventional sense. As a recent authority rightly notes, 'The majority of expatriate Irish peers maintain a way of life no different from that of the well-to-do professional and business commuters – and indeed a high proportion of them are precisely this.'[72]

Other patricians, although not so closely involved in the City, are nevertheless also very much part of the world that we would recognize as being upper middle class and professional. Some still keep up their houses and a portion of their estates, but the majority do not. Lord Brabourne makes films. Lord Lichfield is a photographer. Viscount Chilston is a film producer for the Central Office of Information. The Marquess of Queensberry is a professor of ceramics at the Royal College of Art. The Duke of Leinster runs a flying school, and his heir, the Marquess of Kildare, is a landscape gardener. The Earl of Pembroke has made a soft-porn film and was the director of 'By the Sword Divided'. Lord Dunboyne is a county-court judge. The Earl of Kintore is a mining engineer. Both Lord Gowrie and Lord Westmorland work for Sothebys. Lord Normanton has appeared in advertisements for Burberry. Lord Fermoy is a bookbinder.[73] As such, these peers are virtually indistinguishable from thousands of other members of the upper middle class. Moreover, they are not younger sons forced to earn a living: they are the heads of once great territorial families, who have now been obliged to join the salariat.

What of the expatriates? Many of their descendants have returned home, deciding that even Thatcherite Britain is preferable to the former colonies where the white man is no longer in charge: the successors of Lord Erroll, Lord Carbery, and Sir Delves Broughton have left Happy Valley, and work for their livings in England. The present Duke of Manchester, having been an alligator hunter in Australia, is a business consultant in Bedford.[74] But many are still abroad, like Lord Graham and Lord Winchester in Rhodesia, and Lady Delamere and Juanita Carberry in Kenya. Jessica Mitford still

lives in California, and Lady Mosley in France. Lord Bridport resides
in Sicily, Lord Egmont in Alberta, and the Marquess of Ormonde in
the United States. When Lord Warwick decided to sell his castle, he
himself left for New York, Paris, and the West Indies; the dowager
Countess lives in Rome; and the heir, Lord Brooke, resides in
Australia. So does the sixth Earl of Stradbroke, who is a sheep
farmer.[75] And there is also a new generation of tax exiles – men like
Lord Clifford of Chudleigh, who restored his house, passed it on to
his heir, and lives in Jersey to avoid the death duties.

The final group are those déclassés who in 1984 were christened the
nouveaux pauvres.[76] The ninth Earl of Buckinghamshire, who died in
1983, ended his career as a municipal gardener in Southend. The Earl
of Munster had to be carried to the Lords to get his attendance allowance until the day of his death, since it was his only source of income,
as he had been too poor to pay his national insurance. Earl Nelson is
a police constable. The Countess of Mar has been a saleswoman for
British Telecom. Lord Simon Conyngham is an assistant in a delica-
tessen. Lord Teviot has been a bus conductor. Lord Kingsale, the
premier baron of Ireland, is a silage-pit builder in the west country,
having previously been a bingo caller in Stourbridge, a lorry driver,
and a safari keeper at Woburn. Lord Grey—the direct descendant of
the Reform Act Prime Minister and the Governor-General of Canada—lives on a house boat and has been the director of a chain of sex
shops.

But perhaps the non-royal dukes provide the most revealing
insight into the economic condition of the aristocracy today. The
majority of them still own over 10,000 acres. Britain's richest man,
and Britain's most broad-acred man, are both dukes. But on the
other hand, Bedford, St Albans, and Montrose are all tax exiles.
Portland, St Albans, and Manchester do not own an acre of their
ancestral lands. Sutherland is no longer a force in his titular county.
Newcastle was 'the first duke ever to live in a main residence identified
by a number.' Most people do not know that the Duke of Somerset
exists at all. In the Dukeries itself, Thoresby is demolished, Leeds
is extinct, Portland is gone, and Norfolk has departed to Sussex.
Even one of the richest and the grandest, the Duke of Devonshire,
is highly pessimistic about the future: 'Two generations more I
give it. Unless matters change soon, we will see, not just the splitting
up of larger estates into smaller ones, but the total extinction of any
sizeable holdings whatsoever. The day of the big estate – even of the
fairly big estate – is nearly over.'[77]

ii. Elegant Anachronisms

One of the central characters in Jeffrey Archer's novel, *First Among Equals*, is the Hon. Charles Gurney Seymour, second son of the fourteenth Earl of Bridgewater, who owns 22,000 acres in Somerset, a Scottish castle, extensive urban property in Leeds, a magnificent collection of family paintings, and a merchant bank in the City.[78] Seymour, in turn, becomes a Conservative MP at thirty-three, holds a succession of senior posts in government, is for a time chairman of the family bank, and is seen as a strong candidate for the leadership of the party in the aftermath of Mrs Thatcher. 'His patrician background', another MP remarks, 'still counts for something with the Tories.' Here, written as recently as 1984, is a traditional view of the Tory party and of the aristocracy's special and superior place within it. Yet in the end, it all comes to nothing, as Seymour is beaten for the leadership by a middle-class provincial, thereupon renounces political ambition and parliamentary infighting, and accepts instead the dignified but detached job of Speaker of the House of Commons.

As this story suggests, to write about patrician political power in the aftermath of the Second World War is very largely to dwell on the fringes and the margins of government, as the landed and titled presence in public life has, inexorably, sunk lower and lower. By 1945, it was self-evident that broad acres by themselves no longer conferred either the right or the opportunity to wield political power. Even if they had the inclination, most gentry and grandees no longer had the leisure for public life: mere survival had itself become a full-time occupation. And the general election of that year was the most damaging for the old territorial classes since the Liberal landslide of 1906. In Anthony Sampson's words, it 'swept away shoals of squires, and brought a new catch of middle class politicians, with political expertise but without landed connections.'[79] Oliver Lyttelton, on seeing the new House of Commons, 'feared for his country.' And Ian Anstruther was equally pessimistic: 'for the first time in its history', he opined in 1947, 'the upper classes are not wanted.'[80]

In more mundane terms, this meant that the aristocratic element in the Commons was the smallest in modern times. Sir Archibald Sinclair was defeated in the family county of Caithness, the Hon. John Grimston was rejected at St Albans, Sir Richard Acland lost in Devon, and Lord Dunglass was turned out in Lanark. Of course, there were still a few patricians returned – some old hands and others new recruits. Lord Willoughby d'Eresby kept his seat for Rutland, Lord William Scott held on to Roxburgh and Selkirk, and Lord Hinchingbrooke retained South Dorset. The younger son of the Earl

of Dudley was elected for Worcester, and Derick Heathcoat-Amory
was returned for the Tiverton Division of Devon. Reginald Thomas
Guy des Voeux Paget of Sulby Hall Northamptonshire became the
Labour MP for Northampton, and Sir Richard Acland returned to
the Commons when he won the Gravesend by-election in 1947. But
in 1950, there were only thirty-odd titled MPs with close landed
links, whereas in 1935 there had been more than twice that number.
At the most generous estimate, the landed establishment formed
only 5 per cent of the total.

Predictably, the Labour government of 1945–51 was the least
aristocratic ministry to govern the country since 1660. For Attlee's
cabinet was overwhelmingly middle and working class in its social
composition. Only Sir Stafford Cripps could claim authentically
patrician antecedents. But he had long since been a renegade, and
was known as 'the red squire of Filkins.'[81] In the lower echelons of
the ministry, there were a few more such figures dotted about, like
Lords Pakenham, Lucan, and Listowel, and John Strachey. All were
rootless upper-class renegades: three were Anglo-Irish aristocrats,
who no longer owned any land across the sea; while John Strachey
had been a patrician gadfly since the days of Mosley. Moreover, they
were all political lightweights: Strachey never recovered from the
groundnuts scandal; Listowel was at the India Office; and Lucan held
no major job. Lord Pakenham, the younger son of an Irish earl, had
been ennobled by Attlee in 1945 at the tender age of thirty-nine, and
was successively Chancellor of the Duchy of Lancaster, Minister of
Civil Aviation, and First Lord of the Admiralty. But he was high-
minded, naïve, and peripheral, obsessed with religion, and always
threatening to resign – a Catholic and socialist version of Lord
Salisbury, and about as ineffectual.[82]

Not surprisingly, the Labour government looked upon the second
chamber, with its feudal connotations and its overwhelming Tory
majority, and with an average daily attendance of less than one
hundred, with 'suspicion and resentment', as 'an anachronism based
on heredity.' 'I am', Arthur Greenwood declared in 1947, 'no lover
of the House of Lords. I can see no place for hereditary peers in the
middle of the twentieth century.'[83] But significantly, there was no
repetition of the reckless, futile, and arrogant intransigence of 1906–
14. On the contrary, the Tory peers were genuinely cowed by the
size of the overwhelming government majority in the Commons,
recognized that Labour's programme had received massive endorsement from the electorate, and under the leadership of Lord Salisbury,
allowed most of the socialists' reforms through. Indeed, the peers'
major role became that of examining and revising the mass of legislation that was sent up to them, and that the Commons had not had

the time to scrutinize. Only over the nationalization of transport in 1947 and of iron and steel in 1948–9 did the Tory nobles really make any trouble; and even then, not effectively.[84]

Nevertheless, despite their good behaviour, the powers of the House of Lords were diminished yet again.[85] By 1947, the Labour government was beginning to run out of momentum, and there were real fears that, under the existing delaying provisions enshrined in the Parliament Act of 1911, the Lords would be able to thwart any further reforms during the last two years of the administration's life. Accordingly, the Labour government introduced a pre-emptive Parliament Bill in 1947, the purpose of which was effectively to reduce the upper house's powers of delay from two years to one. Naturally enough, the Lords vehemently opposed this further emasculation of their powers. But although they threw out the bill twice, there was a general lack of political and public interest, and no repetition of the over-wrought intransigence of 1909–11. In 1949, the measure became law, under the terms of the old Parliament Act. But an all-party conference, which attempted at the same time to produce an agreed reform proposal as to composition, fared no more successfully than those of the inter-war years.

The return of the Conservatives under Churchill in 1951 ushered in thirteen years that have sometimes been seen as the last 'last fling' of aristocratic government. As the number of Tory MPs increased during the elections of 1950 and 1951, a new generation of aristocrats gradually trickled into the Commons, sometimes for local constituencies with which their forebears had long maintained territorial and political links. The Derby and Salisbury families reappeared in the lower house with the election of Richard Stanley for North Fylde, and Lord Cranborne for Bournemouth. Lord Lambton was elected for Berwick-on-Tweed, and the Hon. John Grimston won back St Albans. David Ormsby-Gore became MP for the Oswestry Division of Shropshire, Richard Wood was elected for the Bridlington Division of the East Riding, and Hugh Fraser was returned for Stafford. Between the mid-1950s and the early sixties, there was a further influx of new patrician faces. Some were the sons of peers, like Lord Balniel who sat for Hertford, and the Earl of Dalkeith who represented an Edinburgh constituency. Others were authentic country gentlemen, such as Francis Pym for Cambridgeshire, William Whitelaw for Penrith, and Jasper More for Shropshire – who was following in a family tradition of representing the county which went back to the seventeenth century.

Beyond question, Churchill's administration – which brought back many of his cronies from the Second World War – was more authentically aristocratic than any since the National Governments of

126. The young Anthony Eden by Edmond Xavier Kapp.

the 1930s. Among the very senior figures, Anthony Eden was again Foreign Secretary, and undisputed heir apparent, even more closely tied to Churchill by marrying his niece, Clarissa. The Marquess of Salisbury, successively Lord Privy Seal then Lord President, was in charge of government business in the Lords. The Colonial Secretary was Oliver Lyttelton, whose father and grandfather had both held the same job; and the Secretary of State for Scotland was the Hon. James Stuart, the wartime Chief Whip. Subsequent additions to the cabinet included Lord Swinton as Secretary for Commonwealth Relations, Earl Alexander as Minister of Defence, and Derek Heathcoat-Amory at the Ministry of Agriculture and Fisheries. And junior jobs were given out to men like Lord Home, Lord de la Warr, Lord De L'Isle and Lord Carrington. Indeed, in the summer of 1953, when Churchill was incapacitated by a stroke, and Eden was in hospital, there were even rumours that Lord Salisbury should become the head of a caretaker administration.[86]

But as during the Second World War, the patricians were more the decorative than the efficient parts of the government. Eden and Alexander very largely did what Churchill told them, and the latter was 'one of the least effective Ministers of Defence on record.' Salisbury, like all Cecils, diminished his effectiveness by constantly being ill or threatening to resign, and in any case never ran a government department. Oliver Lyttelton did not fulfil his potential, partly because he never mastered the Commons, and partly because he always had an eye on the City, to which he soon returned. And Swinton and Stuart were peripheral people holding peripheral portfolios.[87] As before, the real power house in the administration were the middle-class men running the home front: Maxwell-Fyfe at the Home Office, Butler at the Exchequer, Monckton at Labour, Crookshank at Health, and Macmillan at Housing. And the other major figures were Churchill's wartime colleagues, who again were far from patrician: Woolton, Leathers, and Cherwell. Although there was criticism of the government for being too laden with peers and cousins, it was in fact less aristocratic in numbers, and in the balance of power, than the Baldwin and Chamberlain administrations of the 1930s.[88]

In strict numerical terms, Eden's government was more genteel at the outset than Churchill's had been. Alexander and Lyttelton had already gone; Swinton and de la Warr were immediately dropped; and De L'Isle followed soon after. But Amory, Salisbury, and Stuart remained, and the Earl of Home, the Earl of Selkirk, and Patrick Buchanan-Hepburn were brought in to the cabinet. But they held only relatively minor posts: at the Duchy of Lancaster or the Commonwealth Office. Again, it was the middle-class men who really mattered: Macmillan, Butler, Macleod, Monckton, and the much-promoted Selwyn Lloyd. Moreover, Eden himself did almost as much during his short administration to discredit patrician leadership as Balfour and Rosebery had done. He lacked firmness, was frequently ill, was irritable and petulant, and inclined to panic. His handling of Suez was in all ways a disaster: hysterical, maladroit, dishonest, and ultimately unsuccessful. The image of the aristocracy as the warrior class, providing firm political and military leadership, never really recovered from this miserable fiasco.

Nevertheless, it remains a widely held belief that in the aftermath of Suez, Harold Macmillan put together a new Tory team in which aristocratic cousinhood was still rampant. The Prime Minister himself was the son-in-law of a duke; he played to perfection the part of a grandee whose vocabulary was littered with phrases drawn from the hunting field; and his nephew, the Duke of Devonshire, was Minister of State at the Colonial Office. In 1958, Derick Heathcoat-Amory became Chancellor of the Exchequer; and in 1960, Lord Home was promoted to the Foreign Office. Junior jobs were held by Lords Munster, Lansdowne, Dundee, Gosford, and Carrington. Perhaps it was not altogether surprising that at this time, Hugh Thomas wrote a book on *The Establishment* which argued that 'the most sensitive institutions in England were dominated by the same anachronistic master class.'[89] And Anthony Sampson opened the first edition of his *Anatomy of Britain* with a zestful evocation of a flourishing and powerful titled group, still securely ensconced as the ruling class: 'Who would have thought', he inquired, that in 1962, so many important offices would be held by those who 'all belong, or be closely related to, the old aristocratic families?'[90]

But once again, this misleads and misrepresents. In the first place, for all his posturing as an Edwardian aristocrat, and for all his Cavendish connections, Macmillan himself was quintessentially middle class: 'a crofter's grandson, and a successful bourgeois publisher.'[91] And the authentic patricians were fewer in number, and more marginal and decorative in function, than before. Salisbury finally did resign very soon after the administration was formed, and Amory departed with evident relief in 1960. At the Foreign Office, Home was another lightweight figure, whose appointment was greeted with widespread derision and incredulity, and who basically did what Macmillan told him. Once again, the driving force in the government came from the middle classes: Butler, Brooke, Marples, Lloyd in one generation; Heath, Maudling, Boyle, and Powell in another. At the Colonial Office, it was Iain Macleod, not the Duke of Devonshire, who was in charge. In reality, the continuing decline of the aristocracy as a political force in cabinets went on unabated. More even than Haxey's accounts of the Commons in the 1930s, the attempt to depict the Macmillan government as little more than an aristocratic cousinhood mistakes genealogy for history.

In Macmillan's successor, Lord Home, the most authentically genteel Prime Minister took office since the time of Lords Rosebery and Salisbury. For unlike Churchill or Eden, he was not just a man with close aristocratic connections, but was himself the head of one of the great territorial families of the Scottish lowlands. He looked upon himself as a countryman and a Christian gentleman; he numbered the great Lord Durham among his ancestors; he was educated at Eton and Christ Church (where he obtained a Third); he had sat, as Lord Dunglass, for the local Lanark constituency from 1931 to 1945; and he was made a Knight of the Thistle in 1962.[92] At the time, many recalled Cyril Connolly's famous non-prediction in *Enemies of Promise*: 'In the eighteenth century, he would have become Prime Minister before he was twenty.'[93] Both the century and the age were incorrect; but nevertheless it happened. Among his cabinet colleagues were Christopher Soames, the son-in-law of Winston Churchill, and Lord Carrington, now promoted as the Leader of the Party in the House of Lords. And peers like Lords Newton, Bessborough, and Lothian were found in junior jobs.

127. Lord Home on the edge of events by Avigdor Arikha, 1988.

128. Lord Home of the Hirsel as the quintessential country gentleman by S. Malin.

Yet in many ways, Home was the very end of the thin purple line. His succession to the Prime Ministership was again a fluke – deliberately planned by Macmillan to do down Butler – and was met with resignations from Powell and Macleod, who regarded him as an inappropriate party leader – even for the Conservatives – in the 1960s.[94] He was much disparaged by Harold Wilson as 'the fourteenth earl', an 'elegant anachronism', with a grouse-moor image. He was able to become Prime Minister only because he could disclaim his peerage, and he was noticeably ill at ease back in the Commons. He hated television, was a poor public speaker, and did not understand economics, once admitting that he tried to solve complex problems with matchsticks. At best, he was a decent stopgap, 'charming, popular, conscientious, right-wing and undistinguished': Churchill's 'Home, sweet Home'. But at worst, he was the unacceptable face of an outdated aristocratic style which even the magic circle of the Tory party soon abandoned.[95] Significantly, too, the general tone of his ministry was much less aristocratic than Macmillan's had been.

Beyond doubt, these conservative administrations were more patrician than the Labour government that had gone before. But they need to be set in a broader historical perspective. For they were emphatically less aristocratic than the National Governments of the

1930s, and were even more markedly middle class compared with
the Baldwin administrations of the 1920s. Many of the notables
held office only because of the accident of 1940, which brought them
back or brought them in; the majority were never more than
marginal, peripheral, and decorative figures; and they were there as
individual politicians, not as members of a landed class that was also
the ruling class. Nor were the administrations to which they
belonged governing in the interests of the old territorial class: it
was finance and housing, transport and health, planning and local
government that mattered – domestic matters at which the patricians had never excelled. As Lawrence Stone explained, the appearance of aristocrats in the Tory cabinets of this period was 'a
superficial phenomena, concealing the fact that the old élite were
now the nominal political leaders of a country directed by quite other
social groups.'[96]

The same was true of the House of Lords which, despite the peers
who were dotted about in the Conservative governments of 1951–
64, had long ceased to be a chamber in which broad-acred nobles
carried on the political life of the country. Great names like Derby or
Marlborough or Bedford were now conspicuous by their absence. In
its new role as a revising chamber for complex Commons legislation, it was the professional politicians, not the patrician amateurs,
who had the most to contribute. Between 1955 and 1960, only eight
of the non-royal dukes ever spoke at all. And in the majority of cases,
their utterances had absolutely nothing to do with the great issues of
the time. The Duke of Atholl orated on salmon, the game laws, pig
meat, and leisure. The Duke of Buccleuch spoke on pests, agriculture, sugar beet, and trees. And half of the contributions of the Duke
of Sutherland were on the subject of deer. During the same period,
Lord Arran introduced two bills into the upper house, 'one on
badgers, the other on buggers.' 'On the whole', he concluded, 'I
rather think their lordships were more interested in the badgers.'[97] In
no sense could these men be regarded as members of the governing
élite: they were backwoods figures, talking on appropriately backwoods subjects.

Indeed, many patricians at the time were well aware of the way
events were going, and a few tried to make their protest. But they
were no more successful than their predecessors had been in the
inter-war years.[98] Sir Oswald Mosley attempted to stage a return in
the East End of London in the 1950s, but as before, he got nowhere.
Lord Hinchingbrooke, having failed as the leader of the Tory Reform Group, now reappeared as one of the new die-hards. He
opposed the evacuation of the Egyptian bases in 1954, and was a
vehement critic of Eden's foreign policy. But even in this new

incarnation, he barely attracted any notice. And in 1957, at almost the very beginning of Macmillan's administration, Lord Salisbury's oft-proffered resignation – this time in protest against the government's decision to free Archbishop Makarios from detention in the Seychelles – was finally accepted, to his great surprise. But it was the dampest of damp squibs, which had no effect on the government, while some party workers claimed that they had never heard of him. Most people were bewildered or indifferent, and the matter was soon forgotten.[99]

Thereafter, Salisbury joined the board of the British South Africa Company, and devoted his time and his talents to lost causes. As in the late forties and fifties, he remained (like his father) fertile in inventing elaborate schemes of upper-chamber reform. But (like his father again), they came to nothing. He continued to criticize the African policy of the Macmillan government, and in March 1961 delivered in the Lords his scathing attack on the Colonial Secretary, Iain Macleod, whom he revealingly and contemptuously dismissed as a middle-class card-sharper.[100] Although supported by Lord Graham (the Duke of Montrose), who had flown from Rhodesia especially for the occasion, Salisbury's speech was met with withering rebukes from Lord Hailsham and Lord Kilmuir. In 1965 and 1966, he sought to persuade the Conservative Party Conference to support 'our kith and kin' in Rhodesia, and when he failed to do so, he resigned as president of his local constituency association. So, at the end of his life, the aristocrat who should have been a respected elder statesman was branded 'an extremist', 'anachronism personified.'[101]

In post-war administration, as in government, the notables were very much the minority. As before, the most aristocratic part of the civil service was the Foreign Office. But even there, the patrician contingent was much reduced. There were, of course, some who had joined in the first decades of the century, whose careers now ended in a blaze of ambassadorial glory. After his arduous years as wartime Permanent Secretary, Sir Alexander Cadogan became the first British Ambassador to the United Nations. Sir Oliver Harvey, who inherited a baronetcy from his half-brother, served as Ambassador to Paris from 1948 to 1954. And the future last Duke of Portland, now released from his wartime intelligence duties, became Ambassador to Poland. Even the dynastic tradition still had some life in it: Sir Horace Rumbold, tenth baronet, followed in the footsteps of his father and his grandfather, and became Ambassador to Thailand in 1965. And there were several appointments of non-career aristocrats to the top diplomatic posts, in the tradition of Lothian and Halifax. Lord Carrington served as High Commissioner in Australia, Viscount Amory (as he had now become) was High Commissioner in Canada, and the Hon. David Ormsby-Gore became Ambassador to Washington in 1961.

Even among a later generation of professional diplomats, there were some patricians who had joined before the Eden–Bevin reforms, whose careers were steadily advancing. There was Paul Henry Gore-Booth, the nephew of Constance Markiewicz, who recalled fondly his visits to Lissadell in his autobiography, who entered the diplomatic service in 1933, and who ended his career in the 1960s as Permanent Under-Secretary at the Foreign Office.[102] There was the sixth Viscount Hood, who had joined the Foreign Office in 1942, and who was deputy Under-Secretary of State from 1963 to 1969. And there was Sir Con O'Neill, the younger son of Lord Rathcavan, who was successively Ambassador to Finland, the European Community in Brussels, and Deputy Under-Secretary at the Foreign Office. But by now, these were very much minority figures. Even the great ambassadorial posts in Europe and Washington were overwhelmingly filled by those of non-patrician background. In so far as the foreign service was criticized for exclusiveness, it was because too many of its entrants came from Oxbridge, not because their social origins were aristocratic. As Harold Nicolson wrote in 1961, 'Today, it is as difficult for an aristocrat to enter the foreign service as it would be for a camel to pass through the eye of a needle.'[103]

On the home front, the patricians were even fewer and farther between. In 1960, only 3 per cent of the top jobs in the civil service were held by those with close landed connections.[104] There was Edwin Noel Plowden, of the Shropshire family of country gentry, who worked in the Ministry of Aircraft Production during the Second World War, was later moved to the Treasury, and eventually became chairman of the Atomic Energy Commission as well as a clutch of government boards and committees. And there were those specially recruited outsiders: John Colville, who was again private secretary to Churchill; and John Wyndham, who had inherited Petworth, and who rejoined Harold Macmillan when he became Prime Minister, thereby accentuating the aristocratic tone of his administration.[105] But again, in government as in politics, these few examples were very much the exceptions that proved the rule. Even in the ostensibly halcyon Macmillan years, the most that can be said of the aristocracy as the power élite is that, at the centre, they were largely peripheral. And in so far as they were central anywhere, it was on the periphery.

In local government, too, the end of the war marked a major change, as many grandees and gentry withdrew in the years after

1945. In England, in 1950, only 3 out of 49 county councils were chaired by peers; in Scotland, there were only four coroneted convenors; in both countries, too, the numbers of chairmen who were country gentlemen had declined correspondingly. As the landowners had to spend more and more time dealing with their houses and estates, or as they ceased to be great territorial figures, the incentive even to undertake this local work much lessened. Moreover, the massive legislation of the Welfare State imposed on the localities unprecedented responsibilities concerning health, planning, and education. Between the 1930s and the 1960s, the personnel and expenditure of most county councils more than trebled. Local government thus became a fully bureaucratized profession, in which the experts – the engineers, the planners, the permanent officials – were the men who mattered, not the old patrician amateurs.[106]

So, in the localities as in Westminster and Whitehall, the trends away from aristocratic involvement intensified. But as with the House of Commons, there were residues of the older mode. In Shropshire, Sir Offley Wakeman was a most influential chairman of the county council from 1943 to 1963, since he combined this position with the chairmanship of the Education and the Finance and General Purposes Committees.[107] In Cornwall, Sir John Carew-Pole was chairman of the county council from 1952 to 1963, and was at other times High Sheriff and Lord-Lieutenant. In East Suffolk, Sir Robert Gooch was chairman from 1957 to 1967, and in the East Riding of Yorkshire Sir John Dunnington-Jefferson held the position without interruption from 1936 to 1968. In Cheshire, different members of the Bromley-Davenport family provided the Lord-Lieutenant between 1920 and 1949, the deputy chairman of the county council from 1952 to 1958, and the MP for the Knutsford division of the county from 1945 to 1970.[108] In Roxburgh, the Buccleuchs provided an MP, the Lord-Lieutenant, and the convenor of the county council. And in the East Riding of Yorkshire, different members of the Halifax family provided the Lord-Lieutenant, the Master of the Foxhounds, the chairman of the county council, and a local MP.

But of course, this apparently tenacious Trollopian world needs to be set in perspective. Only in the more rural and remote regions did these older patterns persist. Even there, local influence by landed families was no longer what it had once been. And county politics was increasingly a nationalized activity, in which the centralized party machine, rather than the old territorial forces, wielded the most influence. All this is well shown in the case of the Bromley-Davenports in Cheshire, whose apparent pre-eminence was not quite what it appears. One of them was indeed Lord-Lieutenant: but that was largely because the old and great grandees, who had traditionally held the post, were either absent or disqualified, or both. One of them was indeed deputy chairman of the county council: but no landowners in this period occupied the supreme position, which was held successively by a retail grocer, a retired engineer, the managing director of an alkali company, and a cheese factor. And one of them was a long-serving MP for Knutsford: but he was the only county MP, for the entire period after the Second World War, to be from a local landowning family. In many ways, it is clear that 1945 was as great a landmark in the decline of local patrician power as 1885 or 1888.

Significantly, it was in the most peripheral part of the United Kingdom that the traditional élite seemed to remain most completely in charge. In retrospect, it is clear that in Northern Ireland, the control of Ulster Unionism was gradually passing from the big bourgeoisie of Belfast to the more militant lower middle classes. But at Stormont, as the business element gradually declined, the old patricians briefly became something more than the decorative façade that they had provided since the foundation of Ulster in the early 1920s. When Craigavon retired as Premier, he was succeeded by Sir Basil Brooke of Fermanagh, the uncle of Churchill's wartime CIGS, and head of one of the oldest families in the province. He was an embattled, intransigent reactionary, who hated the Catholics, and held power from 1943 to 1963. On his retirement, he was followed by the more liberal, and even more aristocratic, Captain Terence O'Neill, by comparison with whom even the Brookes appeared relatively parvenu.[109] And when he was forced out of power, he was succeeded by Major James Chichester-Clark, who was closely connected with the family of the Marquess of Donegall. Here were three quintessential patricians, with their roots more deeply planted in the soil of Ulster, than among the businesses of Belfast.

Throughout the province, as the capitalist economy faltered, and as the entrepreneurs withdrew from public life, the traditional landed dynasties became more prominent. In local government, the most loyal of the six counties were still much under the influence of the old ascendancy families. In County Antrim, the Duke of Abercorn was both Lord-Lieutenant and chairman of the quarter sessions, as well as a member of the Northern Ireland Senate. In the same county, the O'Neill family provided MPs both in Westminster and in Stormont. In County Armargh, Sir Charles Norman Lockhart Stronge was MP, Lord-Lieutenant, and chairman of the county council, as well as being the Speaker of the Northern Ireland House of Commons. In County Fermanagh, Lord Belmore was chairman of the county council from 1943 until his death in 1949. He was followed as the dominant grandee by the Earl of Enniskillen who was both chairman of the county council and Lord-Lieutenant. Even in the late 1960s, the retired Prime Minister, now Viscount Brookeborough, was the Lord-Lieutenant, while his eldest son was both the chairman of the county council, and a Stormont MP. And the future fifth Duke of Westminster successfully transplanted himself across the Irish sea, and became an MP and Irish senator for Fermanagh.

Even more peripheral and more beleaguered were those expatriate patricians – Lord Salisbury's 'kith and kin' – now caught up in the final, fateful drama of decolonization and independence. In Rhodesia, the Duke of Montrose, known as Lord Graham, was Minister of Agriculture and Minister of External Affairs between 1962 and 1968. In the aftermath of UDI, he lent an aristocratic tone to the Smith regime, and until the final settlement in 1980 could have been prosecuted for treason. And in Kenya there was Ferdinand Cavendish-Bentinck, who later became the penultimate Duke of Portland.[110] He had emigrated to the colony before the Second World War, and was determined that the white settlers should not be abandoned by the British government. From 1934 until 1960, he was a member of the Legislative Council; in 1945 he became Minister of Agriculture, and in 1955 he was elected Speaker. In 1960, he resigned from the Legislative Council in protest against the Lancaster House agreement, and became leader of the right-wing Kenya Coalition, which vainly sought to obtain safeguards for the settlers.

So, in terms of power, the twenty years after the Second World War – viewed in the necessary perspective of what had happened before, and of what was happening elsewhere in British politics – saw only a further weakening of the aristocracy's position in national and local government. It is not the history of the patrician power élite but the story of particular individuals and peripheral groups. In terms of social background, the middle and working classes were by this time firmly in control. No wonder the phrase 'The Establishment' had such wide currency at this time: for it was the description of a much broader ruling group than that which had hitherto existed. And during the later 1960s and 1970s, the position of the old landed classes in the corridors of power became even more marginal, something that was emphatically portended when Edward Heath beat William Whitelaw to become the first elected leader of the Conservative party when Sir Alec Douglas-Home hastily resigned in 1965.

Harold Wilson's Labour government of 1964 was even less patrician than that of Attlee twenty years earlier. Indeed, it contained only one genuine notable: the Earl of Longford, who had previously been Lord Pakenham. But as Lord Privy Seal and (briefly) Colonial Secretary, he was a completely marginal man. His high-minded self-righteousness, his mania for publicity, his lack of interest in any substantive political issues, and his Cecilian desire to keep resigning meant that, in the cabinet of Crossman, Jenkins, Callaghan, and Castle, he appeared 'a farcical figure', a 'third eleven man'.[11] No one listened to him, no one was interested in what happened in the House of Lords, and no one wrote to him when he resigned over the relatively minor issue of raising the school leaving age. It seems clear that if he had not gone voluntarily, he would soon have been dismissed. Consoled with the Garter, he became chairman of Sidgwick and Jackson, and undertook a campaign against pornography. Thus departed from the corridors of impotence positively the last Labour grandee.[112]

Yet oddly enough, it was this government that sought to reform the House of Lords, and to do so in a constructive, rather than belligerent, spirit.[113] In early 1967 there was a preliminary discussion in the House of Lords, where Lord Harlech, on behalf of the Conservatives, admitted that hereditary membership was 'not a rational basis' for a second chamber. As a result of this encouraging response, a cabinet committee was set up in April of that year. It consisted of Lords Longford and Shackleton and Richard Crossman, and their aim was to create a strong but essentially complementary second chamber. In November, the cabinet committee was superseded by an all-party conference. There was considerable early agreement: on composition, the Conservatives conceded that the hereditary principle and the overwhelming preponderance of one party must be abandoned; and there was general acceptance that there should be delaying powers for only six or nine months.

By May 1968, the draft existed of an all-party white paper. But in June that year, the Tory peers, angry at the Labour government's successes, and frustrated at their own impotence, defied their own leaders and threw out the government's orders on Rhodesian sanctions. Almost immediately, they were reintroduced and carried. But the all-party talks on the reform of the upper house were broken off, and the government resolved instead to introduce their own unilateral legislation concerning both its powers and its composition. A new cabinet committee produced a white paper in November 1968, whose proposals owed much to the draft that had been produced by the abortive conference. The objects were to remove the hereditary element and the built-in Tory preponderance, and to ensure that the government of the day enjoyed an adequate majority. There was to be a two-tier system of voting and non-voting peers. The hereditary right to sit was to be abandoned. There was to be adequate remuneration. And the delaying powers were to be for six months only.

Significantly, the white paper was given widespread support in the

House of Lords itself. Most peers recognized that the hereditary principle was no longer defensible, and were eager to seize the opportunity for constructive reform of their chamber. But the House of Commons was far less enthused. Eventually, a Parliament Bill was introduced into the Commons, based on the white paper, and passed its second reading in February 1969. But from then until April, it became more and more bogged down in the committee of the whole House, as an unholy alliance of the far right (who wanted no reform) and the far left (who wanted abolition), led by Michael Foot and Enoch Powell, sabotaged the scheme. Eventually, to the great dismay of the Lords themselves, the reform package was abandoned. Ironically, then, the upper house voted overwhelmingly for its own reform; it was the Commons that prevented it going through. As Lord Carrington later put it, with wistful regret, 'After all, it is not your Lordships fault that you are unreformed.'[114]

Edward Heath's government, although more patrician than Wilson's (it could hardly have been less), was emphatically the most middle-class Tory administration since the war. Men like Maudling, Carr, Barber, Rippon, Joseph, Walker, and Davies represented a new-style Toryism: a compound of an abrasively professional attitude to politics and close connections with industry of a far more direct and less genteel kind than those earlier maintained by figures like Oliver Lyttelton.[115] By comparison, the few notables were largely marginal and decorative. William Whitelaw was an authentic north-country squire, married into the aristocracy: but he was Lord President. Earl Jellicoe was the son of a naval hero who had set himself up as a grandee: but he was obliged to resign through scandal. Sir Alec Douglas-Home reappeared once more as Foreign Secretary: but he did very much what Heath told him. The only really heavyweight grandee was Lord Carrington, who was Minister of Defence: but he now owned only 1,000 acres, and when in opposition had held a clutch of directorships.[116] Even allowing for junior patricians scattered about – Wood, Prior, Pym, Eden, Gowrie – the ministry was overwhelmingly middle class.

The short-lived administrations of Wilson and Callaghan in the late seventies were completely devoid of any authentic notables at cabinet level, and contained precious few in the lower echelons. And in the Thatcher governments that followed, the decline of the old order on the right in politics has been almost as complete as on the left. In cabinets peopled by Lawson, Tebbit, Baker, King, Parkinson, and Howe, and presided over by a shopkeeper's daughter from Grantham who believes in self-advancement rather than hereditary advantage, there was (and is) almost no room for the representatives of the old guard, now thought to be unacceptably wet. It is true that

Thatcher began her administration with a handful of highly placed patricians. Whitelaw was moved to the Home Office (where he was unhappy and unsuccessful); Carrington was promoted to the Foreign Office (where he was far less assertive than it was common to suppose); Francis Pym, an authentic country gentleman, took over Defence; Sir Ian Gilmour, whose mother was a Cadogan and whose wife is a Buccleuch, became Lord Privy Seal (not much to do); and Lord Soames, who was barely landed but married to Churchill's daughter, was made Lord Privy Seal (ditto).[117]

But this patrician element was almost totally removed in the ensuing years. Soames and Gilmour were sacked unceremoniously in September 1981. Carrington resigned in April 1982 in the aftermath of the Falklands.[118] Pym was moved around, from Defence to the Duchy of Lancaster, to the Lord Presidency, then to the Foreign Office, but was sacked in June 1983. And Whitelaw was elevated to decorative impotence with a viscountcy and the Lord Presidency. Within five years, all of the notables in her 1979 government had been dismissed, had resigned, or had been emasculated. Newcomers like the Earl of Gowrie did not stay the course. Today, the only authentic patrician is the Hon. Nicholas Ridley, Secretary of State for Trade and Industry, whose elder brother, Viscount Ridley, was formerly chairman of Northumberland County Council and is now Lord-Lieutenant. As *The Times* recently and rightly remarked, 'Family background is a dubious asset in the Conservative Party today. Since the early 1980s, a stream of landed squires have retired, discomforted, to the back benches, or fled to the City, because of difficulties in reconciling their conception of *noblesse oblige* with the principles instilled in the Grantham grocer's shop.'[119]

As the example of Lord Ridley suggests, some landowners have continued to play a part in local government. Other patrician chairmen of county councils in the 1970s included Lord Porchester (Hampshire), Lord Halifax (the East Riding of Yorkshire), and the Hon. Daphne Courthope (East Sussex). And there have been country gentlemen like Morris-Egerton and Swinnerton-Dyer in Shropshire and Robin Leigh-Pemberton in Kent.[120] But since the mid-1970s, with the reform of English local government, the patricians have all but disappeared. The old counties have in many cases been abolished, the disappearance of county aldermen robbed the grandees of their assured places, and the widespread custom of short-term chairman has spelt the end of any lingering personal ascendancy. In 1980, among chairmen of English county councils, there were no peers and only two baronets. In Scotland, the local government reforms were if anything even more severe, with the creation of the new Regional Councils, and signalled the departure of those lingering grandees who had still hung on. In Wales, the few patricians who had survived after the Second World War in the most Anglicized counties disappeared altogether. Even in Northern Ireland, the combination of the 'troubles' and the suspension of Stormont means that the old Ulster families have withdrawn from active politics, and have left the defence of the union to more lowly – and more militant – social groups.

In the constituencies, too, the old families no longer signify. The Devonshires have not run Derbyshire West since the Second World War, and after his brief stint in the Macmillan government, the present duke has adopted a conspicuously lower profile. In March 1982, he joined the SDP, but 'nobody took any notice.'[121] When Jasper More relinquished his Shropshire seat in 1979, he was mourned as the last real country gentleman in the Commons.[122] Today, there are only a very few patricians left: Nicholas Ridley and Charles Morrison who both sit for Wiltshire seats; Lord James Douglas-Hamilton who has represented Edinburgh West since 1974; Lord Cranborne who was returned for Dorset South in 1979; and the sixth Earl of Kilmorey, an Irish peer, who sits as Richard Needham for Wiltshire North. But on the whole, the surviving members of the landed establishment seek to avoid politics and to keep a low profile. Most hereditary peers no longer defend the House of Lords, and play a minimal part in its proceedings. And their close male relatives are too busy earning a living to have the time to stand for election to the Commons.

In the Britain of the 1990s, it is not altogether clear whether there exists anything that can be called a ruling class. In a society so complex in its structure, and so multi-national in its ramifications, it may well be that such a notion is too simplistic and too outmoded to be of any value. But even if it does still exist, it clearly cannot be identified with the old aristocratic ruling class. Whatever the qualifications, the picture here parallels very closely that painted for wealth – of continuous and accelerating decline, but this time without even the spectacular exceptions like the Duke of Westminster. For all parties, and at local as well as national levels, politics has become a full-time job: men who still proclaim the aristocratic virtues of being an amateur have no place (and no prospects) in this remorselessly professional world. And after the satire boom of the 1960s, the elegant anachronisms have had their day. If the cabinets of the 1880s and the 1980s are compared, the decline in the patrician element is overwhelmingly clear, and that is the measure of the silent revolution in the governing élite which has taken place during the last century. However the power stratum in the Britain of the 1990s is defined, the old territorial class forms only an infinitesimal part of it.

129. *The Coronation of Elizabeth II* by Terence Cuneo.

iii. *Insubstantial Pageants Fading*

Less then a decade after the end of the Second World War, and only two years after the end of Attlee's austere administration, Queen Elizabeth II was crowned in Westminster Abbey and also in front of the television cameras: her coronation thus made public for the first time the grandest tribal rituals, not just of the British monarchy, but of the British aristocracy as well. The occasion had been faultlessly and flamboyantly planned by the Duke of Norfolk, the Earl Marshal of England. The Dukes of Portland and Wellington, and Lords Allendale and Fortescue, were the four Garter knights who held the Queen's canopy at the most solemn moment in the ceremony. Lord Alexander bore the Orb, the Duke of Richmond carried the Rod with the Dove, and the Marquess of Salisbury held the Sword of State. The dowager Duchess of Devonshire was Mistress of the Robes. For months beforehand, most peers had been able to talk only of 'coaches and robes, tiaras and decorations'. As Henry Channon noted, with relish and relief, it was 'a grand day for England and for the traditional forces of the world.'[123]

Superficially, at least, this magnificent display belied in the most emphatic form the straitened condition in which the post-war aristocracy now found itself. Yet even Henry Channon was forced to admit that there was 'a Gilbert-and-Sullivan-like quality . . . something unreal about it.'[124] Like so much to do with the Coronation, this display of noble pre-eminence was in retrospect more a requiem than a renewal. For their social position has been inexorably eroded during the forty years since the Second World War. However status is defined and understood, that conclusion necessarily holds: whether it relates to changes in the formal system of titles of honour; or to the reduced opportunities for ornamental employment; or to the decline and fall of high society in the shires and the metropolis. On all these fronts, the grandees have been emphatically in retreat – unacceptably privileged in the Welfare State world of the common man; yet inadequately glittering in the age of Hollywood film stars. The Coronation notwithstanding, their bright day was done, and they have been emphatically for – and in – the dark.

Self-evidently, the advent of a Labour government, which repre-sented the vote and the voice of the ordinary citizen, which was unshakeably pledged to equality and socialism, and which was opposed to any formal hierarchy resting on inherited titles, meant an administration more hostile to the old patrician status system than any that had existed in Britain in modern memory. The 'revolution' that contemporaries feared in 1945 was not just economic and political: it was social as well. And it began at once. Although the great commanders and captains of the Second World War – Montgomery, Portal, Alexander, Mountbatten, Cunningham, Alanbrooke – were given peerages in the year of victory, they received no parliamentary grants such as had been voted to their predecessors in 1919. For it was no longer supposed that hereditary peers should be rich men, let alone great landowners. In fact, all lived out their lives in relatively modest circumstances. Indeed, one of the reasons why Alanbrooke allowed his very controversial diaries that he had kept as CIGS to be published prematurely was that he needed the money: his wartime gratuity amounted to a mere £311.[125]

There were other changes during the life of the Labour govern-ment that were of equal symbolic significance. The pension of £5,000 a year that was still paid by a grateful nation to the descendants of the victor of Trafalgar was abolished, which no doubt explains why the eighth Earl Nelson was forced to sell his Wiltshire house and estate. In 1948, the privilege whereby a peer could be tried on allegations of treason and felony only by his fellow peers in the Lords – as featured in Clouds of Witness and Kind Hearts and Coronets – was abolished.[126] Even more significant was the collapse of the system of name-changing by hyphenation on inheriting an estate. In 1945, a wife who inherited an estate conditional on altering her name successfully petitioned that she should not be obliged to do so. And in 1952, a

husband and wife petitioned that they should not have to change
their names to obtain an inheritance. The judge upheld their request,
on the grounds that such traditional patrician provisions were now
'inconsistent with the spirit of the time.'[127]

Yet the most remarkable sign that the old system of status and
honour was moribund emerges from the way in which Winston
Churchill was treated, and chose to be treated. By 1955 he was
universally acknowledged as the greatest Englishman of his time, the
saviour of his country, a national hero whose only rivals in history
were the Duke of Marlborough and the Duke of Wellington. As
such, his claims on the highest honours in the land were unassailable.
Yet Churchill's formal rewards were decidedly meagre. He was
given no parliamentary grant, and his precarious finances were
rescued only by the sensational sales of his history of the Second
World War and the generosity of a group of rich friends who bought
Chartwell but allowed him to continue to live there. Even more
significantly, the only honours that he accepted were the Order of
Merit in 1945 and the Garter from the new Queen in 1952. On his
retirement in 1955, he was indeed offered a dukedom: of Dover or of
London. But he emphatically refused it. And if the greatest man of
his time would not accept the highest honour available, then what
real validity did the system as a whole any longer possess?[128]

Ironically enough, much the greatest assault on the hereditary
system of titles of honour came from the ostensibly patrician government of Harold Macmillan, and took place at the very time of the
supposed renaissance of aristocratic government: namely the introduction of life peerages.[129] Of course, this was an idea that had been
played with on and off for over one hundred years. But in the
egalitarian world of the Welfare State, it seemed more fitting to
bestow titles of nobility on people for their life only. The debates in
both Houses were very dull and unreflective, and even Lord Salisbury was prepared to support the scheme as the only reform of the
upper house that there was likely to be. Yet despite this conspicuous
lack of interest, this measure represented a devastating attack on the
whole notion of inherited titles which was at the very heart of
aristocracy: for these honours, which were to be individually won,
were not to be passed on. As a result, the Lords had ceased to be a
hereditary chamber: and its end had come, not with a bang, with a
whimper.

The fact that this measure was introduced by the son-in-law of a
duke was much remarked upon at the time. And during the same
administration, the hereditary peerage received a further blow. The
introduction of life peerages meant that these new titles could not be
passed on. But the logical corollary was that those who inherited old

titles should now be allowed to disclaim them.[130] In this case, the
initiative came from an individual member of Parliament, Mr
Anthony Wedgwood Benn, who inherited his father's title in 1960
and became Lord Stansgate.[131] At that time, the Commons Committee of Privileges ruled that he could no longer sit in the lower
house; but at the ensuing by-election, in May 1961, he was returned
with a doubled majority. When the Election Court declared that his
opponent had been returned, it was clear that the law would have to
be altered, and in the summer of 1963 the necessary act was passed. It
was badly thought out, and frequently changed in its detailed provisions. But as a result, all hereditary peers then alive were given one
hundred days within which to disclaim their titles, and all newly
inherited peers would in future have the same option.

As with the Life Peerages Act, this was a measure at once momentous yet paradoxically quite insignificant. In a more damaging way
than the legislation of 1957, it undermined the whole notion of
aristocracy as a compact between those who were dead, those who
were living, and those who were yet unborn. It made plain the
prevailing ethos of the Welfare State that social esteem no longer had
constitutional sanction. And, in Robert Lacey's words, it 'spelt out
the political redundancy of the aristocracy.'[132] Yet ironically enough,
the most emphatic sign of this political redundancy was that so few
patricians actually availed themselves of its provisions so as to
continue their political careers. By 1981, only eleven peers had
disclaimed their titles. Some, like Home and Hailsham, did so in
connection with the struggle for the Tory leadership consequent
upon Macmillan's sudden and unexpected resignation late in 1963.
Some, like Beaverbrook and Reith, were only second generation
peers, and didn't much care anyway. And there have been a very
small number of genuine grandees disclaiming: Lords Durham,
Southampton, and Sandwich.

But the greatest threat to the patrician status system was that
between 1965 and 1983, no hereditary titles of honour were created.
Not only the Labour governments of Wilson and Callaghan, but also
the Tory administrations of Heath and (at least initially) Thatcher,
assiduously refused to give out any hereditary peerages or baronetcies. So, for the first time since 1660, the size of the hereditary
peerage has noticeably declined. The system whereby a balance was
struck to keep the numbers up, between extinctions and new creations, has broken down. The old titles have become extinct at the
rate of four to five a year, including such famous names as Leeds,
Fitzwilliam, Beauchamp, and Stamford. Nor have Mrs Thatcher's
three hereditary creations in the 1980s done much to reverse this
downwards trend. They are too few to outweigh the losses, neither

Whitelaw nor Tonypandy has a male heir to inherit the title, and since the Macmillan earldom in 1983, there have been no further new creations. For the existing hereditary peerage, this is emphatically the beginning of the end: if present trends continue, as seems highly likely, then the inherited titles will have died out completely by 2175.[133]

How have all these massive and quite unprecedented assaults on the Lords affected the social composition of the upper house in the years since the Second World War? Initially, hereditary titles were still awarded to landowners and those of patrician background who achieved distinction in the usual way. At the end of the war, peerages were given to Alexander and Alanbrooke, for their military services; to Sir John Hazlerigg, who had been so dominant in local government in Leicestershire; and to the Hon. Frank Pakenham to strengthen the Labour party in the Lords. Thereafter, patrician ministers like Sinclair, Lyttelton, Amory, and Stuart received viscountcies when they retired, as did Sir Basil Brooke, the Prime Minister of Northern Ireland. Sir Anthony Eden received the traditional reward for a former Prime Minister of an earldom. Lord Alexander was given a step in the peerage for having governed Canada, Lord Swinton was advanced from a viscount to an earl on his retirement in 1955, and Lord De L'Isle was promoted after his proconsular spell in Australia. Most recently of all, there has been the viscountcy for William Whitelaw, the squire of Penrith.

These were the traditional rewards for traditional public men. But in addition, important second-ranking public figures were still ennobled, and it is clear that a landed background helped. Oliver Harvey was given a peerage when he retired from the diplomatic service, to add to the baronetcy he had inherited from his half-brother. John Wyndham, Harold Macmillan's private secretary, was made a hereditary baron before he inherited the Leconfield title. Sir Ralph Assheton, whose family had held estates in Lancashire since Tudor times, and who was chairman of the Conservative Party Organization in the late 1940s, became Baron Clitheroe in 1955. Mr William Fletcher-Vane, a Cumberland country gentleman, who held junior office in the 1950s, became Lord Inglewood in 1964.[134] And John Morrison became Lord Margadale for traditional – almost Trollopian – reasons: he owned massive estates in Argyll and Wiltshire; he was chairman of the 1922 committee, and MP for Salisbury for twenty-one years; his heir was High Sheriff of Wiltshire and he himself was its Lord-Lieutenant; and two more sons were MPs, one for a local constituency. Here, albeit much attenuated, the old traditions of patrician and landed ennoblement lived on.

Indeed, some members of the old élite actually accepted the new life peerages – either because it was thought an appropriate reward, or because that was all that was available by the time they were deemed to be deserving. Mr Cobbold became Lord Cobbold for governing the Bank of England. Sir Bernard Fergusson became Lord Ballantrae for having governed New Zealand. Mr George Howard became Lord Howard for having been chairman of the Governors of the BBC. Among patrician mandarins, life peerages were given to Trevelyan, Gore-Booth, and Plowden. Superannuated politicians with landed connections who have been ennobled include Wood, Ward, Eden, Soames, and Pym. Both Captain Terence O'Neill and Major James Chichester-Clark were consoled with life peerages when they ceased to be Prime Minister of Northern Ireland. Even more authentic grandees who have accepted life peerages included Sir Fitzroy Maclean, the thirteenth chief of Maclean of Duart, a baronet and Lord-Lieutenant of the county. And there was also Sir Alec Douglas-Home, previously a hereditary peer, who became Lord Home of the Hirsel at the close of his political career.

But it is important to remember that these are only a very tiny minority of the total number, considering that since 1945 180 hereditary peerages and over 500 life peerages have been created and bestowed. And they have been given out to almost anyone who excels in public life, regardless of their social background.[135] In many cases – retired back-benchers, former cabinet ministers, mandarins and military, businessmen and press tycoons – they have been awarded to non-landed people who have been receiving peerages, in ever growing numbers, since the 1880s. But many others are now from very different backgrounds – academics, journalists, secretaries, raincoat manufacturers, trade-union leaders, impresarios, an accountant, a mountaineer, a West Indian cricketer, an actor, and a methodist preacher. The effect of this has been to transform the upper house yet again. By the Second World War, the Lords was still hereditary, but no longer preponderantly landed. But since the 1960s, it has ceased even to be preponderantly hereditary. The hereditary peers still outnumber the lifers quantitatively; but in terms of active personnel, the upper house is overwhelmingly a nominated second chamber. Instead of tranditional territorial grandees, or the hereditary rich and powerful, it is now essentially a chamber of nominated life senators.

The extent to which the old territorial system of titles of honour has been transformed is best shown by the changes in the personnel who now receive the Thistle and the Garter. Until the Second World War, these were bestowed almost exclusively on the great titled aristocrats. And since 1945, appointments to both orders have been taken out of the hands of the Prime Minister, and restored to the sovereign. Royal preference has clearly been for traditional grandees. George VI appointed the Duke of Portland, and Lords Cranworth, Scarbrough, and Harlech in 1947. In 1951 he added the Duke of Wellington, Lord Fortescue, and Lord Allendale.[136] Since then, politicians with a patrician background have still been among the most regular recipients, like Eden, Churchill, Home, Salisbury, Chandos, Amory, Longford, and Carrington. Some great grandees still seem to qualify almost by hereditary right: Dalhousie, Buccleuch, Airlie, and Cameron of Lochiel for the Thistle; Northumberland, Norfolk, and Grafton for the Garter. And there have been other recipients of authentically patrician background, like Lord Maclean, Lord Cobbold, Sir Edmund Bacon, and Sir Cennydd Traherne.

But there have also been great changes. Many of the old aristocratic families that once commanded automatic admission to these orders have disappeared – Argyll, Montrose, and Sutherland in Scotland; Derby, Marlborough, Devonshire, and Salisbury in England. And as the grandees have ceased to dominate public life, so the new men of power from much more humble backgrounds have forced their way in. Among military men, the majority of Garters have been bestowed on non-patricians, like Templer, Slim, Lewin, Elworthy, and Hull. Among proconsuls, it has been given to natives from the antipodes, like Lord Casey, Hasluck, and Holyoake. Among politicians, it has been accepted by middle-class figures like Butler, Shackleton, Wilson, Callaghan, and even by two authentic members of the working class, Lord Alexander and Lord Rhodes. As a result, these two orders, which were almost entirely aristocratic even down to 1945, have become unprecedentedly plebeian during the last forty years.

So much for the formal system of titles of honour: from the standpoint of the patrician element, decay and dilution are the overriding themes. And the same holds good for their activities as 'great ornamentals'. Again, there have been survivals of an earlier age, particularly in some of the proconsular appointments of successive Conservative governments. In Canada, Lord Alexander of Tunis became Governor-General immediately after the war, in preference to Lord Alanbrooke. In Australia, Lord De L'Isle held the same office between 1962 and 1967, and in New Zealand, Viscount Cobham was followed by Sir Bernard Fergusson.[137] Under Macmillan, these genteel proconsuls were briefly exported to the newly independent nations of the Commonwealth in the Third World. The Earl of Dalhousie (whose ancestor had been Governor-General of India) was Governor of the Federation of Rhodesia and Nyasaland from 1957 to 1963. Lord Listowel, formerly a member of Attlee's

Labour administration, was Governor of Ghana from 1957 to 1960. Lord Ranfurly (whose grandfather had been Governor of New Zealand) was Governor of the Bahamas between 1953 and 1956. And Lord Hailes was Governor of the Federation of the West Indies from 1957 to 1962.

In national affairs, too, members of the traditional élite continued to be recruited in the immediate post-war years to those honorific positions in the arts, the media, and the national heritage that were reserved for 'the great and the good.' The twenty-eighth Lord Crawford became as prominent a figure as his father had been in the cultural world, and served on the boards of the National Gallery, the British Museum, the Tate Gallery, and the National Gallery of Scotland, as well as being, at different times, chairman of the National Trust, of the Royal Fine Arts Commission, and of the National Art Collections Fund. When Sir Alexander Cadogan finally retired from the diplomatic service, Winston Churchill appointed him to be chairman of the Governors of the BBC – his chief qualification being that he rarely listened to the wireless and had never watched television.[138] And the fourth Lord Cottesloe was successively chairman of the Advisory Council and Reviewing Committee on the Export of Works of Art, of the Trustees of the Tate Gallery, and of the Arts Council.

Likewise, in the localities, the ornamental notables lingered on. In the smaller towns of England, such as Wenlock and Woodstock, the Forsters and the Marlboroughs continued the family traditions of providing patrician mayors. In the same way, titled chancellors were still appointed at the great redbrick universities. At Queen's Belfast, Lord Londonderry was followed by Lord Alanbrooke. At Liverpool, Lord Derby was succeeded first by Oliver Stanley and then by the Marquess of Salisbury. At Birmingham, Anthony Eden replaced Viscount Cecil. Throughout the United Kingdom, many of the Lord-Lieutenants were the bearers of historic names.[139] In England, there were grandees such as Wellington in Hampshire, Norfolk in Sussex, Stradbroke in Suffolk, and Northumberland in his titular county. In Wales, there was Williams-Bulkeley in Anglesey, Trehearne in Glamorgan, and Williams-Wynn in Denbigh. In Scotland, there was Elgin in Fife, Steel in Selkirk, and Haddington in Berwick. And in Northern Ireland, there was Rathcavan in Antrim, Kilmorey in Down, and Abercorn in Tyrone.

Even in the 1970s and 1980s, there are some grandees who have held, and still hold such ornamental offices. When Sir Bernard Fergusson returned from governing New Zealand, he became chairman of the British Council and was later installed as Chancellor of St Andrews University.[140] The fifth Baron Kenyon was President of the University College of North Wales, and a trustee of the National Portrait Gallery. The first chairman of the trustees of the Victoria and Albert Museum was Lord Carrington. The present Marquess of Anglesey is, or has been, President of the National Museum of Wales, chairman of the Historic Buildings Committee for Wales, a trustee of the National Portrait Gallery, a director of the Welsh National Opera, a trustee of the National Heritage Memorial Fund, and Lord-Lieutenant of Gwynedd. Meanwhile, his wife is, or has been, chairman of the National Federation of Women's Institutes and of the Welsh Arts Council, and a member of the boards of the British Council, the Civic Trust for Wales, and of the Pilgrim Trust.

In all these ways, the old world of patrician ornamentals lived, and lives, on. But even compared with the inter-war years, it has been much attenuated. In the case of aristocratic proconsuls, the prospect of going out and governing New South Wales virtually came to an end with the Second World War. In South Africa, no British notable was appointed after 1937. In India, Wavell was followed as Viceroy by Lord Mountbatten and then by independence. In Canada, Lord Alexander was the last non-native to be appointed, and in Australia, De L'Isle was the only authentic post-war grandee. Even in New Zealand, Freyberg and Newell were military men, and after Sir Bernard Fergusson, all subsequent Governors-General have been home-grown products. And in the newly independent nations of the former colonial empire, the early attempts to transplant traditional grandees were not repeated: Dalhousie, Listowel, Ranfurly, and Hailes were both the first and the last of the line.

The same has been true at the local level, where the further weakening of the old territorial connections and the increasingly impersonal nature of municipal government have meant that the opportunities for patrician ornamentals have very largely disappeared. After a brief resurgence during the Second World War, aristocratic mayors have virtually vanished. The majority of the new universities set up during the 1960s preferred members of the royal family or people of genuine distinction as chancellors: Strathclyde went for Lord Todd, Stirling for Lord Robbins, East Anglia for Lord Franks, and York for Lord Clark.[141] Even among the older foundations, the people who are deemed to matter now are those of international academic renown or with good government and financial connections, like Sir Alex Jarrett in Birmingham. When the Marchioness of Anglesey was recently defeated for the Chancellorship of Manchester, the redundancy of the old aristocratic tradition was emphatically pronounced.

Among the great ornamentals of the cultural world, the same anti-patrician trends have been equally in evidence. Here, too, the people deemed to matter are still those with good official connections and financial resources: but once again, they are no longer, in the main, aristocratic grandees. The recently appointed trustees of the Victoria and Albert Museum demonstrate this eloquently.[142] Some were royal chic, like Princess Michael of Kent; some were superannuated mandarins, like Lord Trend; and some were the new rich, like Lord Sainsbury and Sir Terence Conran. But the old aristocratic element was no more than negligible. Even in the counties, the same pattern has emerged. By the mid-1960s, less than half of the English Lord-Lieutenants were peers, and the reorganization of local government in 1974 saw the disappearance of many more historic names. In 1986, only 13 of the 46 English Lord-Lieutenants were hereditary peers; in Wales the figure was 1 in 7; and in Scotland it was only 12 out of 31. Never has the county lieutenancy been so plebeian.

In short, the great patrician ornamentals – in the localities, the nation, and the empire – have markedly diminished during the years since 1945.[143] Today, it is primarily as courtiers that the notables retain their decorative identity. As the Coronation eloquently demonstrated, the royal family remains overwhelmingly theatrical and spectacular in its public image, and it is aided and abetted in this by the old territorial and titled class. Since the Second World War, the Lord Chamberlains have been successively Lords Clarendon, Scarbrough, Cobbold, Maclean, and Airlie. The Queen Mother's Lord Chamberlain is Lord Dalhousie. The Mistress of the Robes is always the wife of a hereditary peer. Such offices as Earl Marshal and Master of the Horse are invariably filled by titled grandees. And minor courtly functionaries are almost invariably drawn from the same background. Here is the last patrician redoubt: as bit-part players in the Ruritanian royal family romance, where rank and precedence, honours and orders, still matter very much indeed.

What of high society, the status-conscious theatricality of upper-class life? Once again, there are residues of the older mode of conspicuous consumption. When the eighteenth Earl of Derby married in Westminster Abbey, even in the austerity-ridden year of 1948, four hundred tenants were conveyed in a special train to London. When the Marquess of Hartington came of age in 1965, there were three lavish parties at Chatsworth: for royalty, for other grandees and gentry, then for the tenantry. And when the present Duke of Westminster married in 1978, the festivities were of almost unparalleled splendour. Likewise, some grandees retain a strong sense of status identity, and marry within very limited social bounds, as in the case of the previous Duke of Northumberland. His mother was the daughter of the Duke of Richmond, his grandmother was the daughter of the Duke of Argyll, and his wife was the sister of the

Duke of Buccleuch. Moreover, one of his sisters married the Duke of Hamilton, and another married the Duke of Sutherland. In the age of Trollope, endogamy could hardly have been more exclusively practised.[144]

But again, these survivals of an older way of life need to be seen in a broader perspective. To begin with, the major precondition for the essential theatricality of upper-class living – an endless supply of cheap and menial labour – has simply vanished. As in 1914, the servants disappeared in 1939, but this time they did not come back when the conflict ended.[145] While some of the old retainers returned, the younger generation – hostile to the idea of service, and increasingly attracted by alternative, better-paid jobs in the big cities – stayed away in droves. In 1931, there were 1.3 million servants in domestic employment in Britain. But in 1951 there were only 250,000; in 1961 a mere 100,000; and the number has continued to decline ever since. At the same time, the costs of servant-keeping have mounted steeply. In 1825 a married man earning £5,000 a year could afford thirteen male and eleven female servants; by 1960 it cost over £6,000 to maintain a household of ten living in and four non-resident servants. Today, the employment of full-time, residential staff is the prerogative of the very wealthy few – the royal family, the new rich of the seventies and eighties, and the international set.

Of course, the revolution in domestic technology during the 1950s and 1960s to some extent offset this decline in the labour supply. And even today, a few of the grandees who survive as wealthy men continue to employ some personal retainers in the old way. The Marquess of Salisbury and the Duke of Norfolk each boasts his own chaplain, and at Chatsworth, there are three nightwatchmen, a silver steward, and a man who winds the clocks. But these are very much the exceptions that prove the rule. In 1939, the Marquess of Bath employed forty servants at Longleat; today, there are only two, both Spanish. One of the most compelling reasons for the demolition and rebuilding of country mansions on a smaller scale in the late 1950s and early 1960s was to take account of this sudden reduction in the number of servants. Indeed, in a sense the wheel has come full circle. Instead of employing servants, many young patricians are themselves thus occupied: 'cooks hired for the weekend, or nannies, for instance, are now more likely to be "Sloane Ranger" girls than traditional domestics'. After all, when she was Lady Diana Spencer, the Princess of Wales worked in a kindergarten.[146]

Since landed-establishment-living was essentially a labour-intensive industry, the disappearance of the thousands of low-paid servants has dealt it a mortal blow in the years since 1945. But this is not the only reason for the closing of the old theatres of country-house life. The destruction of so many great mansions, and the total disappearance of the town palaces in London, has inevitably diminished the opportunities for such lavish display. When Lord Althorp celebrated his coming of age at a party in Spencer House, the family had the use of the place only for the night, and the commercial tenants returned the following morning.[147] Moreover, even among the few patricians who remain atypically wealthy, the general rule nowadays is *inconspicuous* consumption. It is politically unwise to flaunt their remaining wealth, especially when they wish to present themselves as a harried and persecuted minority. And for the majority of notables who remain, such ostentation can no longer be afforded. Even at the time of the Coronation, many peers had to hire their costumes. The Duke of St Albans owns neither the robes nor the coronet appropriate to his high rank. The Duchess of Somerset does the cooking herself.

As a result of its economic decline, political decay, and social disintegration, the aristocracy has lost its appeal even for the gossip columnist. Names like Lord Lichfield and the Duke of Westminster occasionally appear. And there have been some famous scandals: the sacking of her butler by the dowager Lady Dufferin; the much-publicized and much-contested Ampthill peerage case; the bankruptcy and suicide of the Duke of Leinster; and the sensational disappearance of Lord Lucan.[148] But these are one-off and rare events. Since the Second World War, there has been no successor to grandees of an earlier generation like Lord Rosebery, Lord Derby, or Lord Lonsdale – rich, well-born, and influential patricians, whose every action was regarded as exciting and noteworthy. In so far as the public's appetite for glamour is satisfied today, it is more likely to be by Joan Collins than the Duchess of Westminster. It is the royal family, the international rich, and the stars of the media who now cause a stir. As two commentators recently and rightly remarked, the aristocracy 'has ceased to be either good copy for the columnist or a suitable subject for serious fiction.'[149]

Underlying these developments has been the formal end of high society. In the austere period after the Second World War, the lavish evening courts that had been postponed in 1939 were never revived. Then, in 1959, afternoon presentations of debutantes were abolished, partly in response to widespread feeling that the entire ritual now seemed ridiculous, partly as one way to modernize the monarchy and make it less remote. And the official explanation was itself revealing: 'Since the last war', noted the Court Circular, ' "Society" in the sense in which it was known even in 1939 has almost died.'[150] Undeniably, there remains a social calendar, which includes Cowes, Henley, and the Chelsea Flower Show. But the people who attend are individual *aficionados* or are enjoying the largess of corporate wealth. But such events are no longer the domestic rituals of high society. In the same way, such self-defining status groups as 'Sloane Rangers' and 'Young Fogeys', although owing something to the examples of the Prince and Princess of Wales, encompass people from a remarkably wide range of social backgrounds and occupational categories.

Likewise in the shires, there has been an almost total divergence between patrician living and county society. In the more remote regions, grandees have continued to preside over the local hunt. The last Earl Fitzwilliam was Joint Master of the Fitzwilliam Foxhounds from 1935 until his death. The Duke of Northumberland has been Master of the Percy since 1940. The second Earl of Halifax was Master of the Middleton from 1946 to 1980. During the early 1950s, the sixth Earl Winterton rode to hounds when in his seventies. The last remaining ambition of Lord Paget is to die in the saddle, like his father. But the most famous hunter since the Second World War was the tenth Duke of Beaufort. He was given a pack of hounds at the age of nine; the registration of his car was MFH I; and for most of his life he was known simply as 'Master'. For over forty years, he hunted six days a week, and he began his autobiography with the unabashed and unrepentant admission that 'Obviously, the hunting of the fox has been my chief concern.' His memorial service in 1984 was attended by almost every member of the royal family, at which he was remembered as 'The noblest master of them all.'[151]

But this is an atypical picture, as the renewed round of estate sales in the years after 1945 has further eroded the old territorial base to the sport. The growth of suburban sprawl, the building of so many motorways, the shift in agriculture from pastoral to arable, and the purchase of farms by profit-conscious investors have further threatened and undermined the activity. Many packs have thus been forced to amalgamate, like the Hertfordshire (whose territory was gobbled up by Greater London) and the South Oxford (which suffered from the building of the M4), both of which joined with the Old Berkeley to form the Vale of Aylesbury Hunt in 1974. Today, the majority of enthusiasts who go hunting are middle-class town dwellers – who may own a weekend cottage, or who just drive down to the countryside in their Range Rovers for the fun of it. But they are not county people, let alone members of the old landed class. In the case of most packs today, the continuity with the great aristocratic hunts of old is largely illusory.[152]

And what has been true for fox-hunting in particular has been equally true of county society in general. The old formal hierarchy, so carefully evoked by Trollope, and so precisely itemized by Lord

Willoughby de Broke, was already in disarray by the inter-war years, and developments since 1945 have merely speeded it on its way to oblivion. The demise of so many great estates, the professionalization of local government, and the erosion of old county loyalties mean that the Lord-Lieutenant no longer presides over a social élite of territorially based and politically active county families. Like local government, county society has largely ceased to be an extension of estate ownership. In so far as it does exist, 'county' society today is primarily middle class in composition and preponderantly recreational in purpose. Few of the people who appear in the pages of *Warwickshire Life* or who attend the Taporley Hunt Ball own any land in the area, or are involved in local government and politics. The old conflation, under aristocratic leadership, of county government, county landownership, and county society has gone, leaving the professional bureaucrats on the one side and the middle-class suburbanites on the other.[153]

Beyond any doubt, the period since the Second World War has seen the almost total disintegration of patrician high society – both as a formal and as an informal élite status group. Indeed, this sense of aristocratic social decay was already in evidence thirty years ago, when Nancy Mitford produced her celebrated piece of spoof sociology on 'U and non-U' language. In some quarters, her essay was taken as a reassertion of aristocratic panache, hauteur, and self-confidence, appropriate enough at the time of the supposed country-house revival under Harold Macmillan. But a more careful reading suggests a very different interpretation. For the central theme of the piece was that it was no longer clear precisely where the social boundaries of the upper class actually lay. On the contrary, the major social divide no longer came between the aristocracy and everyone else, but between the aristocracy and the upper middle classes on one side, and the rest on the other. As Robert Lacey rightly remarks, 'U and non-U date from the day when the U's started worrying that they might not be so superior as they had once thought they were.' And if Nancy Mitford herself was no longer clear about the existence of a high-status patrician élite, then what possible hope was there for anyone else?[154]

iv.   Conclusion: Guardians or Parasites?

In 1890, Mr Gladstone predicted that one hundred years in the future, England would still be a country dominated by great estates and also, presumably, by the grandees and gentry who lived on them. In the centenary year of that prediction, it seems clear that

Gladstone has not been proved entirely wrong. Within sight of the year 2000, Britain's richest man remains a duke, and so does the country's largest private landowner. The second chamber in the legislature still consists of a majority who have the power to make laws simply by hereditary right. And some members of the traditional aristocracy have retained their houses, their broad acres, and their sense of identity to an extent that seemed impossible in the bleak and austere days of the Second World War and its immediate aftermath. 'Living on the verge of extinction has become a way of life for the landowner which has continued since the beginning of this century. Reports of his death may yet be exaggerated.'[155]

But as with all residues from a past age that linger on into a new and in many ways alien world, this picture of aristocratic survival and continuity needs to be set in a broader perspective. For the place that the remaining patricians occupy in the Britain of the 1990 is overwhelmingly less important than that of their forebears a century ago. Economically speaking, they no longer own the majority of the land, they do not themselves constitute the wealth élite, and even the very richest of them are a minority among the contemporary super-rich. Politically, the remaining grandees and gentry do not form the governing class, and most landowners now play no part whatever in local or national politics. And socially, the honours system has ceased to be hereditary or territorially based, the great ornamental roles are usually filled by people from other social backgrounds, and neither London nor county society continues in the old sense. However much evidence can be marshalled to bear out Gladstone's prediction, the fact remains that the traditional landed class has ceased to exist as the unchallenged and supreme élite in which wealth, status, and power are highly correlated, and are underpinned by territorial pre-eminence.

Of course, there are some individual patricians who are extremely wealthy, or who are politically active, or who sometimes appear in the gossip columns. But this is the result of particular circumstances and personal inclination, rather than because of their position as members of the old aristocracy. As a rich man, the present Duke of Westminster can no longer be taken – as his illustrious nineteenth-century predecessor was – to be a larger than life epitome of all contemporary landowners. As a Member of Parliament and senior cabinet minister, the position of Nicholas Ridley does not say anything about the political functions of the landed classes as a whole. And the Princess of Wales adorns the front pages of the world's newspapers because she is married to the heir to the throne of England, not because she is the daughter of an obscure aristocrat. The result is that the remaining grandees and gentry 'seem less conscious of their own class identity' than their forebears did.[156] Their collective sense of themselves, their shared feelings of group solidarity and corporate superiority, have largely vanished. They know that they are no longer God's elect.

Even among the highest echelons of the nobility, it is low-profiled marginality that is everywhere the preferred and prudent posture. As Anthony Sampson puts it, 'with their inter-marriages, their isolated estates, and their absorption in the past, [the dukes] are becoming more and more cut off from the world around them.'[157] The Duke of Bedford is rather proud of the fact that he has not been involved in politics. The Duke of St Albans has never even taken his seat in the House of Lords. The Duke of Buccleuch, although he once served as a Tory MP, is now almost pathetically anxious to avoid public controversy. The Duke of Devonshire, having abandoned his political aspirations in the late 1960s, now finds his palaces and his racehorses 'much more interesting than the House of Lords.' And the Duke of Westminster admits that a hereditary upper house is indefensible, and that 'we are no longer a politically acceptable group.' Lord Longford still insists that a peer can get things done that lesser mortals cannot: but his essentially marginal part in the great events of his times hardly bears this out. The most that can be said of a hereditary title today is that it may be of help in booking a table at a busy and fashionable restaurant.[158]

This dramatic weakening of the landed establishment's position is best illustrated in the changed functions and circumstances of those country houses that survive in private and patrician ownership. In their heyday, and in their fully working form, these mansions existed throughout the British Isles, as bastions of power, as expressions of wealth, and as assertions of status. Each one was a citadel from which a landed family superintended its economic affairs, organized its political activities, and proclaimed its social position. As such, the country house was a going concern, from which confidence, leadership, and authority radiated outwards. But today, the balance of power and initiative is fundamentally altered. Those who hang on to their ancestral homes do so out of a backward-looking and defensive sense of family piety, rather than from feelings of confidence in their order, their purpose, or their future. Once such mansions were the springboard for assured and acceptable patrician endeavour; now it is their maintenance and retention that has become a full-time activity. The proud citadels of the old élite have become the beleaguered relics of their embattled successors. From Woburn to Chatsworth, it is the saving and the upkeep of the great house that is the all-consuming object of aristocratic existence.

It is this widespread desire to retain the family house, even when almost everything else has gone, that explains the most recent metamorphosis in the collective identity of the landed establishment, into the self-proclaimed guardians of the 'national' heritage. Today's remaining patricians are not so much the owners of private possessions, so the argument now runs, as the custodians of culture on behalf of everyone. Generation after generation, it is claimed, their forebears acquired grand works of art and nurtured and cherished their collections. Some owners were already prepared to let visitors in to look at them, and the majority no doubt intended that in the future, they might be accessible for the edification of the masses. In opening their houses to the public, today's surviving landowners are merely emulating the practice, and fulfilling the aspirations, of their forebears. As Lord Montagu put it in 1974, 'We belong to our possessions, rather than our possessions belong to us. To us, they are not wealth, but heirlooms, over which we have a sacred trust.'[159] And the moral is clear. If the guardians of the national heritage behave thus responsibly and altruistically, the government in turn has a duty to ensure that these great houses and collections should remain intact, and that their owners should be allowed to continue the residential and custodial role which fulfils their own most deeply felt desires, and realizes their forebears' most ardent and altruistic ambitions.

The difficulty with this argument is that it is historically quite unconvincing.[160] In the first place, it misleads in its fervent and adulatory portrayal of the patrician class – past and present – as public-spirited patrons of the arts. Of course, a small minority of country-house owners have always been – and still are – people of genuine refinement, sensibility, and discernment, who have taken – and still take – a real delight in collecting and displaying beautiful things. But this has never been true of the majority. Even in their heyday, most grandees and gentry were essentially philistines. They spent very little on works of art, they did not collect systematically, they did not look after their possessions with any great care, and they had no interest in displaying them for public benefit, then or in the future. In so far as there were some collectors who behaved in this way, they usually came from a more humble background, like Henry Tate or Samuel Courtauld. And in the years from the 1880s to 1940, as the diaries of Lord Crawford make plain, men like the seventeenth Earl of Derby or the second Duke of Westminster were almost completely indifferent to their family treasures. Only since 1945 have the majority of country-house owners acquired raised cultural consciousnesses, which are the necessary precondition for their new and self-appointed role as the guardians of the 'national' heritage.

But in addition, this argument misleads because it seeks to establish an illusory continuity between country-house viewing of old, and today's stately-homes business. Beyond doubt, there were always some grandees who were willing to open their doors to occasional visitors in the past. But the mass tourism of today, as it has developed since 1945, is something fundamentally different. For these owners are not concerned to display their art collections free of charge to a few discerning travellers out of a sense of *noblesse oblige*. On the contrary, they seek to exploit their treasures for their own financial and personal advantage. In part, they do this by the audacious expedient of persuading large numbers of people to pay money to look at the possessions that their forebears had acquired in earlier and more privileged days. In part they do this by obtaining tax concessions from the government which are themselves conditional on allowing such public access. And in part they do this by claiming that their 'traditional' custodial functions justify their own continued residence in their ancestral homes, in defiance of the political, social, and economic trends of the time.

Financially, politically, and socially, this recently invented identity has become the new defence of what remains of the old territorial class. Once their art collections were the almost random by-product of confident and largely indifferent patrician activity. But now their descendants' very survival as occupants of their ancestral homes has become increasingly dependent on the privileged status accorded to their art collections as part of the 'national' heritage, and thus – by extension – to themselves as its resident custodians. The resourcefulness and ingenuity that have been, and still are, lavished on the articulation of this argument and the projection of this image will come as no surprise to any one aware of the landed-establishment's powers of adaptability. But some more candid country-house owners fully admit that their motives are less elevated than this implies. 'I will not try and pretend', the Duke of Bedford wrote in his memoirs, 'that I embarked on the idea primarily out of a sense of social obligation . . . The initial drive was purely economic. I wanted to find some way of perpetuating Woburn intact. Opening it to the public seemed the only way of doing it.' Or, as George Howard more recently admitted, 'My family could not live at Castle Howard if it was not open to the public.'[161]

In practice, most country-house owners regard the stately-homes business as an unavoidable necessity that must be endured if they are to preserve what remains of their much-diminished inheritance, rather than as the fullest flowering of cultural guardianship and *noblesse oblige* for which their entire family history has been but a preparation and a preliminary. But whatever their motives, there are two major difficulties with this present arrangement. In the first place, the stately-homes business is far from agreeable. As two recent commentators candidly concede: 'to the average British aristocrat . . . a regular invasion by trippers is seldom more than a necessary evil.'[162] But in addition, it is not at all clear that the state will continue to support country-house owners indefinitely in their role as the custodians of their treasures. As Michael Heseltine brutally put it when he was Secretary of the Environment:

> I cannot see any justification for subsidising people to live in surroundings which they cannot afford . . . I do not think it is fair to the owners themselves, let alone to the taxpayer, to encourage them to go on living beyond their means.[163]

Notwithstanding the setting up of the National Heritage Fund, the Thatcher government is less worried by the plight of the remaining stately-home owners than the Attlee administration was forty years ago.

So, despite the caveats that must be made, and the qualifications that have to be entered, it is clear that Gladstone's prediction is turning out to be fundamentally more mistaken than correct. And the recent rather frenzied promotion of today's embattled and beleaguered country-house owners as the guardians of the 'national' heritage lends only added force to this view. As Robert Lacey rightly remarks, 'successful aristocracies . . . are exceptions in the age of the common man . . . While displaying remarkable staying power in the late twentieth century, aristocracy can in no sense be described as a growth industry.'[164] On the contrary, in Britain at least, it has been in continued decline for one hundred years, and is today more decayed and more marginalized than it has ever been. In April 1977, the Cambridge Union passed a motion regretting 'the passing of the aristocracy.'[165] Whether they were right to regret its passing is perhaps open to debate. But of the fact of its demise there can be little real doubt.

15

EPILOGUE: PERCEPTIONS AND
PERSPECTIVES

The supreme duty of the historian is to . . . record in one sweeping sequence
the greater events and movements that have swayed the destinies of man.
(S. Runciman, *A History of the Crusades* (3 vols., 1951–5), vol. I, *The First
Crusade and the Foundation of the Kingdom of Jerusalem*, p. xiii.)

Since World War I, in land after land, the tides of history have engulfed the
nobility.
(J. Blum, 'The Nobility and the Land', in J. Blum (ed.), *Our Forgotten Past:
Seven Centuries of Life on the Land* (1982), p. 48.)

By 1950, European states had disposed of their nobilities. In much of Eastern
Europe, the great estates had also gone, the victims either of land nationalisation or land redistribution. The surviving continental nobilities were no
more than social élites, often little more than a segment of the bourgeoisie,
distinguished only by the honorific attributes of armorial bearings and titles.
(M. L. Bush, *The English Aristocracy: A Comparative Synthesis* (1984), p. 151.)

No major European aristocracy, except perhaps the British, has voluntarily
relinquished power without a social revolution, whether violent and bloody
and brief, or commercial and casual and slow.
(A. Sinclair, *The Last of the Best: The Aristocracy of Europe in the Twentieth
Century* (1969), p. 168.)

The transience of human life and the impermanence of worldly
dominion are haunting and daunting subjects, which are, by definition, as old as civilization itself. The Book of Ecclesiastes had
much to say about them, as did the histories of Thucydides and the
writings of St Augustine. Ever since the Renaissance, the decline and
fall of individuals, of cities, of dynasties, of classes, of nations, and of
empires has been a central theme in European scholarly and creative
literature. And from Gibbon to Nietzsche, Burckhardt to Huizinga
and beyond, the study of change for the worse, of decay and de-
generation, of moral collapse and physical ruin, has given rise to
some of the most powerful historical narratives and most influential
historical writings. Providential agency and divine retribution no
longer loom large in such accounts, as once they did. But the ex-
planatory categories used today would be easily recognizable to the
Renaissance humanists and their precursors: the undeniable significance of accident and fortune; the uncertain balance between internal

and external causes of decay; and the varied importance of political, social, economic, and cultural forces.[1]

It would be absurdly parochial and unpardonably pretentious to suggest that the disintegration of the British aristocracy merits comparison with such momentous historical events and processes as the decline and fall of the Roman Empire, the waning of the Middle Ages, or the eclipse of Britain as a great power. But judged by any less exacting yardstick, it was indeed a major transformation, and it is only by approaching it as a recognizable instance of historical decline that it is possible to obtain the full measure of its significance. There was a gradual falling away from an earlier era of confidence, success, and certainty to a later time of anxiety, weakness, and woe. There was the undeniable impact of sheer bad luck, unforeseeable misfortune, and random catastrophe. There were powerful external forces that could not be resisted, and internal developments that were equally damaging. And there were signs of decay in all aspects of aristocratic life – economic, political, and social (essentially the same categories as Weber's wealth, power, and status). But what does it really mean to say that the grandees and gentry declined and fell? As with all such instances of sustained and irrevocable decay, the experience of the British patricians can be properly understood only when set in a broader context.

i. The European Perspective

The decline and fall of the British aristocracy was but a part of a much broader historical trend, namely the eclipse, extinction, and, in some cases, extermination of the titled and territorial classes throughout most of Europe. Beyond any doubt, the old regime persisted on the Continent for a longer time, and to a greater extent, than it was once fashionable to suppose.[2] And the European nobilities were much more diversely circumstanced than their British cousins in terms of wealth, status, power, numbers, and class consciousness. But even allowing for these caveats and variations, it is clear that by the late nineteenth century, the tide of history had turned definitively and irrevocably against them all. In an increasingly industrialized economy and urbanized society, the old agrarian and rural élite was bound to be superseded sooner or later. In the century of the common man, to say nothing of Communist man, patrician power was certain to be one of the prime targets and victims. And in the era of the expert professional, the amateur inevitably became outmoded and superseded. As Tocqueville noted in 1856, 'all the men of our day are driven, sometimes slowly, sometimes violently, by an unknown force – which may possibly be regulated or moderated, but cannot be overcome – toward the destruction of aristocracies.'[3]

The history of the next sixty years amply demonstrated the prescience and perceptiveness of these words, and across the Continent, 'the destruction of aristocracies' followed a recognizably similar pattern. During the late nineteenth century, the Prussian *Junkers*, Russian landowners, and Hungarian notables were as hard hit by the depression in agriculture as were their British counterparts. The extension of the franchise, the development of mass political parties, and the growth of representative institutions meant that government everywhere was shifting, as in Britain, away from the patricians towards the proletariat. From Ireland in the west, to Russia in the east, there were growing demands from a land-hungry peasantry that large estates should be broken up and redistributed.[4] The great professions ceased to be dominated by the old territorial class, and even such bastions of aristocratic exclusiveness as the Prussian army and the German diplomatic corps had effectively been surrendered to the middle classes by the time the First World War began. And the inflation of honours in Germany, in Russia, in Austria-Hungary, and in Italy merely replicated the British experience on an exaggerated scale, as state servants, military men, entrepreneurs, and financiers were awarded titles of nobility in unprecedented numbers.[5]

Not surprisingly, the continental nobilities reacted to these developments in ways that mirrored and sometimes magnified the British response. In the thirty years before the Revolution, many Russian landowners sold off part or all of their estates, and invested in stocks and shares. The French nobility rivalled the British in its search for American heiresses, and in its growing involvement in business and finance. In Germany, in Austria-Hungary, and in France, there was widespread patrician resentment against Jews and capitalists, modernity and the twentieth century, and during the inter-war years, many members of the surviving continental nobilities shared Oswald Mosley's contempt for parliamentary government.[6] Even the most pathetic victims of aristocratic decline retained a common identity: the Anglo-Irish exiles in Eastbourne lodging houses were at one in their misfortune with those Russian *émigrés* who drove taxis and worked as waiters in Paris. And this rich and varied experience of decay and disintegration stimulated continental writers of much greater power and insight than W. S. Gilbert or Evelyn Waugh: compare Tolstoy's bitter and brilliant depiction of the fading Russian nobility in *Anna Karenina*, or Proust's masterly evocation of the sadness and futility of French aristocratic life.

But while the decline and fall of the English-speaking aristocracy had much in common with the eclipse of the continental notabilities, the differences stand out at least as much as the similarities. Despite the reforms, reverses, and retreats of the late nineteenth and early twentieth centuries, it seems clear that the British patricians survived more tenaciously than some of the European aristocracies. The advent of the Third Republic in 1870 dealt the French notables a severe blow: no new titles were created once the Empire was abolished, the part they played in politics dramatically diminished after 'La Republique des Ducs', and the survivors enjoyed the dubious distinction of being the prototypical marginalized patrician élite, running around, as Nancy Mitford once put it, like a chicken without a head.[7] In Russia, the breakup of landed estates gathered momentum in the 1880s and 1890s, the nobility was completely without a corporate sense of purpose or identity, and it was further weakened by its dependence on a failing autocracy. And in Spain and Austria, it was widely believed that the aristocracy had abdicated its governing responsibilities, both in the countryside and in the capital, and was devoting itself to pleasure-loving privilege, in Madrid, in Vienna, and further afield.[8]

Compared with these feeble and failing flowers of nobility, the grandees and gentry of Britain showed substantial staying power. But elsewhere in Europe, there were resourceful, tenacious, and self-interested patricians who were far more successfully assertive than were the fainthearts of the Hotel Cecil. In Hungary, the establishment of a separate monarchy in 1867 enabled the Magyar nobles to re-claim their position as the most powerful class in the country. In the period of agricultural depression, they consolidated their estates at the expense of the poorer owners. They dominated administration, both in the capital and in the localities. And they preserved their position as the governing class by successfully restricting the franchise so that in 1914 it was still the narrowest in Europe.[9] In the new German Empire of Bismarck and Kaiser Wilhelm II, the Prussian *Junkers* were at least as powerfully entrenched. At the higher levels of authority, they still dominated the army, the bureaucracy, and the diplomatic service. They provided the majority of the personnel for local administration, and every German Chancellor between 1870 and 1914. And in 1879, they successfully pressured the government into imposing tariffs to protect agriculture, and hence bolster their rents, something that the British landowners were too divided and too weak to accomplish.[10]

During the First World War, the collective experience of the British aristocracy began to diverge even more markedly from that of the continental notables. It seems probable that the Russian,

German, and Hungarian aristocracies suffered greater casualties and even heavier fatalities than the 'lost generation' of Julian Grenfell, Raymond Horner, and Lord Feversham. In Russia, the Bolshevik Revolution of October 1917 meant the elimination of all titles of honour, the extinction of the old aristocracy, and the complete confiscation of their remaining estates, in a sweeping measure of land reform. The defeat of Germany spelt the end of the Hohenzollerns, a republican regime in which no new titles of nobility were created, and the loss of many *Junker* estates to a newly resurgent Poland. And the disintegration of Austria-Hungary brought with it the breakup of the old central European nobilities. In the new successor states of Yugoslavia, Bulgaria, Roumania, Poland, and Czechoslovakia, there was widespread land reform, in part a belated recognition that many peasants had already taken possession of great estates, in part as a measure of nationalist gratification, directed against the alien land-owners from Austria and Hungary. Even in Austria itself, titles were outlawed, entail was abolished, and many nobles were forced to sell off their remaining lands and heirlooms.[11]

In two successor states, however, the traditional landowners survived, and they retained, or even recovered, much of their old social and political influence. The land reform measures in Poland were directed against the alien, Prussian landlords to the west. But the Polish notables themselves were, on the whole, much more generously treated by the Pilsudski regime. Pilsudski was himself a minor squire, and during the inter-war years, the aristocracy played a central part in public life. The army was headed by a succession of aristocratic generals, Count Stanislaw Szeptycki, Baron Tadeusz Jordan-Rozwadowski, and Count Stanislaw Haller, and many of the front-line commanders who fell to Hilter's troops in 1939 were of traditional patrician stock.[12] But it was in Hungary that the landowning class reasserted itself with the greatest success, as the Horthy regime became the most aristocratic and Ruritanian in inter-war Europe. His two chief ministers, Count Bethlen and Count Paul Teleki, were both Transylvanian notables. The upper house was restored, land reform was thwarted and frustrated in the aftermath of the war, and in a period of renewed agricultural depression, the Magyars successfully lobbied for increased tariffs. Not surprisingly, many British visitors regarded inter-war Hungary as the last fully functioning aristocratic polity.[13]

Elsewhere in Europe, the surviving patricians were forced on the defensive, and in a world that seemed more than ever dominated by Jews, capitalism, democracy, and revolution, many of them turned to Fascism for reassurance and protection. In Austria, as in Britain (but nowhere else), the Fascist movement was actually led by a patrician: the Heimwehr was founded by Prince Starhemberg in the early 1920s. In Italy, an alliance between southern landowners and local fascisti effectively thwarted peasant demands for land in the aftermath of the First World War, and Mussolini's government was generally well disposed to great estates. Death duties were reduced, land reform was postponed, and the Duce's son-in-law, Count Ciano, provided a rallying point for aristocratic high society in Rome.[14] In Germany, the nobility held itself aloof from the Weimar Republic, but with Hindenburg as President, the *Junkers* were able to ensure that agricultural protection was retained. Indeed many of them were only too happy to see Hitler bring the much-despised republic to an end. And in Spain, where the landowners were threatened in the early 1930s with the abolition of all titles, and with sweeping land reform, the defeat of the nationalists and the establishment of the Franco regime in 1937 meant they, too, survived.[15]

But for most of these fellow-travelling Fascist patricians, the Second World War meant the end of the road. Initially, this was because their Fascist friends turned against them. In 1943, Mussolini proclaimed a socialist republic in which there was no room for his aristocratic supporters. A year later, Hitler took terrible revenge against the unsuccessful July plotters, led by Count Claus von Stauffenberg, and effectively eliminated the *Junkers* from the high command of the German army.[16] But this was as nothing compared with the retribution exacted soon after by the Russian forces advancing inexorably from the east in the autumn of 1944. In Poland and in Hungary, there was sweeping land reform, and the aristocracies that had re-emerged after 1918 came to a sudden and brutal end. And the Prussian *Junkers* suffered a fate that was authentically Wagnerian. As the Red Army pushed irresistibly forward towards Berlin, their estates were expropriated, their mansions were looted and burned, and many nobles were tortured and killed, as they vainly tried to defend their lands and their possessions. And in Italy, the defeat of the Duce and the overthrow of the monarchy meant that land reform was finally begun in the south in the early 1950s.[17]

From a patrician standpoint, the most significant result of the Second World War was that traditional aristocratic class simply ceased to exist to the east of what was once known as the Iron Curtain. Some families who have survived further west, like the Princes of Lichtenstein, still cherish the hope that they may one day regain their lost properties, but even in the era of glasnost, this seems unlikely. In France, West Germany, and Italy, there still remain a few very rich grandees, like the Prince of Thurn und Taxis, the Marquis de Grany, and the Marquis Dino Frescobaldi.[18] But like the Duke of Westminster, they are individual survivors from a class whose collective identity, power and purpose has long since vanished. In only two countries are there significant residues. One is the United Kingdom, where the House of Lords remains dominated, at least numerically, by a hereditary peerage. The other is Spain, where the slow pace of industrialization, the support of the Franco regime, and the subsequent restoration of the monarchy means that as landowners, though not as governors, the aristocracy has survived most successfully of all.[19]

Viewed in this broader European perspective, the most significant feature of the decline and fall of the British aristocracy is its essentially moderate and unviolent nature. Hereditary titles of nobility have not been discontinued, as they have in France, Germany, Austria, and Russia. There has been no land reform, even in Ireland, on the scale of that carried out in Eastern Europe in the aftermath of the First and the Second World Wars. Compared with the treatment meted out to the traditional aristocracy by Lenin, Stalin, or Hitler, even Lloyd George emerges as an almost genial and benevolent character. And the violence of the land war in Ireland or the crofters' agitation in Scotland pales into relative insignificance by the side of the peasant uprisings at the end of the First World War, or the Soviet expropriations at the close of the Second. Unlike every other major European aristocracy, the British patricians were not the victims of civil war, armed invasion, proletarian revolution, or military defeat. In appropriate conformity with their own Whiggish beliefs about the British past, the most powerful aristocracy of the mid-nineteenth century declined gradually and genteely, with neither a bang nor a whimper.

It is precisely because they went so quietly and so comfortably that the decline and fall of the British aristocracy is often seen as their last and greatest gesture of *noblesse oblige* – as a statesmanlike and far-sighted concession to the forces of progress and democracy, which ensured that Britain avoided the revolutionary upheavals so characteristic of European society.[20] No doubt there is some truth in this remark. Compared with the aristocracies of Spain, Austria, and France, the British aristocracy was, on the whole, unusually public spirited and socially responsible. And compared with the Prussian *Junkers*, it was much less inclined to pursue its own class interests at the expense of the nation as a whole. To that extent, indeed, it deserved Tocqueville's encomium as the most liberal aristocracy in the world. But it was also the most lucky aristocracy in the world.

The fact that twentieth-century Britain avoided continental convulsions had very little to do with the way in which the patricians conducted themselves. They were the benificiaries of stability more than they were its architects.

ii. The National Context

In a European perspective, the decline and fall of the British aristocracy is an epic of moderation – not because nothing happened, but because what did happen took place relatively slowly and peacefully. But within the national context, it looks – or should look – very different. As part of modern British history, the theme is – or ought to be – momentousness. Taken as a whole, and over the hundred-year span in which it occurred, the eclipse of the landed establishment amounts to nothing less than a long revolution. At the very least, there were three particular changes associated with it which were of the first magnitude in importance. The first was the virtual disappearance of the Irish grandees and gentry as the territorial, governing, and social élite of that country. It may have been a 'peaceful revolution': but it was a revolution, none the less. The second was the impact of First World War, in which a greater proportion of the aristocracy suffered violent deaths than in any conflict since the Wars of the Roses. And the third was the sales of land between 1910 and 1922, which amounted to a transfer of property on a scale rivalled in Britain this millenium only by the Norman Conquest and the Dissolution of the Monasteries.

These were hardly humdrum or insignificant developments. And they were accompanied by others that, in the century from the 1880s, were scarcely less momentous. As well as ceasing to be the territorial élite, the patricians have been toppled from their lofty eminence as the wealth élite. As the last quarter of the nineteenth century opened, the House of Commons and the House of Lords were both dominated by the landowning classes: this has long since ceased to be so. In the 1880s and the 1890s, Prime Ministers were invariably landowners, and the cabinets over which they presided were overwhelmingly patrician: by the First World War, this was no longer the case. At Westminster, the second chamber, the last redoubt of aristocratic power, was emasculated, and in the shires, the 'rural House of Lords' was also swept away. London social life dissolved into Nescafé society, and the county community disintegrated. In the era of Gladstone and Salisbury, the system of honours was still territorially related, and the standards of public life remained patrician in their probity. But by the time of Lloyd George, all this had changed. In their mid-Victorian heyday, the grandees and gentry still looked upon themselves as God's elect. By the inter-war years, this was neither possible nor realistic.

For the patricians themselves had no doubt that they belonged to a declining order. From their very different political viewpoints, both Lord Salisbury and Mr Gladstone came to share this view, and recognize this unpalatable truth. So, from even more divergent perspectives, did Lord Willoughby de Broke and Arthur Ponsonby. And so, from yet greater extremes, did Sir Oswald Mosley and Jessica Mitford. From the 1880s onwards, the public and private remarks of many grandees and gentry were redolent with the disenchanted and fatalistic language of decline. For all their partly deserved reputation for liberalism and high-mindedness, many patricians disliked Jews, disliked capitalism, disliked the middle classes, disliked modernity, disliked the twentieth century. Many were bitter, many were resentful, some were self-destructive. And in their strident and unavailing protests against corruption in public life, in their determination to return to wholesome rural values, and in their demand to purify manners and morals, they espoused policies that had been the stock in trade of every ruling group that has ever protested against its own decline, from the late Roman Empire, via twelfth-century Islam, to seventeenth-century Spain.

Why, then, has the decline and fall of the British aristocracy loomed so small in recent Brtitish history and recent British consciousness? In part, it is because much that was truly revolutionary about it has been either ignored or forgotten. The total eclipse of the Irish landed establishment was a development that most contemporary Britons regarded with equanimity or indifference, and posterity has been no more interested or concerned. The grievous losses suffered by the gentry and grandees during the First World War were submerged in the much greater numerical losses endured by the nation as a whole. And the revolution in landholding that took place between 1910 and 1922 seemed much less revolutionary than it actually was because in most cases the sitting tenants simply changed their identity and became owner-occupiers. But it is also because in many areas of British life, patrician values and traditional forms have remained unaltered, even when the substance has been radically transformed. In the great professions, the aristocratic personnel have largely disappeared, but because of the public school, the aristocratic tone lingers on. The social background of MPs and peers has altered beyond recognition, but the House of Commons and the House of Lords themselves have survived. And the honours system may have been democratized, and cut loose from its territorial base, but it has not been abolished.

But in addition, this decline has seemed less momentous because it was so gradual, and so nuanced, that for much of the time it never seemed either the foregone conclusion or undifferentiated process that in retrospect it so clearly appears to have been. As T. S. Ashton once remarked, 'no generalisations are more unsafe than those relating to social classes', and the British landed establishment was (and is) no exception to this rule.[21] A few patricians like the Duke of Westminster have managed to retain their wealth to a quite exceptionally atypical degree. Some political families, like the Salisburys, Devonshires, Derbys, and Marlboroughs, enjoyed a late nineteenth-and early twentieth-century renaissance which goes counter to the general trend of a ruling class in decline. And it is clear that in Wales and in southern Ireland, the decline of the notables was more precipitate and more complete than it was in England or in large parts of Scotland. In the areas where aristocracy was most disliked, it has disappeared most completely; in those areas where it was more generally tolerated, its decline was less controversial.

It must also be remembered that what looks like unavoidable decline from one perspective appears very much like resilient adaptation from another. When Lord Eustace Cecil told Lord Salisbury in 1880 that the patricians 'must all look about and prepare to take to some other occupation than politics', he only spoke the truth.[22] Thereafter, many landowners abandoned their highly profiled political careers, and their traditional territorials tasks and ties. Some took on uncontroversial work in local government and county administration. Some went into business or the new professions. Some became full-time domestic ornamentals. And some turned to the empire for succour and support, as globe-trotting tourists, as plumed and purpled proconsuls, as shareholders in imperial companies, as owners of colonial estates, as settlers in Happy Valley, or as patrician professionals overseas. To a far greater extent than was true in Germany or France or Belgium, the empire cushioned and concealed aristocratic decline between the 1880s and the Second World War. Much more than in the days of John Bright, it was truly a system of 'outdoor relief' for the old nobility.

By shifting their base from politics to pageantry, and from the British Isles to the British Empire, many patricians were not only adapting to changed circumstances as best they could: they were also travelling the same path that was being followed at precisely the same time by the only institution in Britain even more exclusive than they were, the monarchy itself. For there, too, the same shift in functions took place, from relatively circumscribed national concerns to the encompassment of broader imperial interests, and from political influence and individual partisanship to olympian grandeur and spectacular impartiality. As mayors of towns and Governors-

General, the adapting aristocracy was mimicking the evolving monarchy.[23] Nor can it be coincidence that from the last quarter of the nineteenth century, the monarchy and the aristocracy edged much closer together. During the early part of Queen Victoria's reign, the great magnates of the realm had despised the sovereign and her consort. But by the later stages, they were only too eager to identify themselves with the crown. And by the inter-war years, it was generally assumed that it was from the British aristocracy that the royal family now selected its marriage partners.

In the broader perspective of British history, however, aristocratic adaption was merely aristocratic decline under another name. Trading power for pomp was all very well for a popular and successful constitutional monarchy, but it did not provide an enduring base for a patrician class whose previous occupations were rapidly vanishing, and whose public standing was much more controversial. And since the Second World War, these essentially ornamental functions have largely disappeared, at both the local and the imperial level. The monarchy continues on its course to global apotheosis and soap-opera spectacular, but in the process it has left the surviving members of the aristocracy far behind. During the last twenty years or so, they have invented a new role for themselves, as the self-appointed guardians of the so-called 'national' heritage. But it is not at all clear that this is a sufficiently popular or sufficiently plausible function to carry them into the twenty-first century. And even if it is, it will only provide one more index of aristocratic decline. What would Mr Gladstone or Lord Salisbury think of an aristocracy so decayed and so demeaned that it was reduced to turning its grounds into safari parks and funfairs, and to taking money from the masses as they trip and trundle through the turnstiles?

But from the standpoint of the British past, the most significant point about the recent history of the landed establishment may well turn out to be the remarkable coincidence between the decline of the grandees and gentry as the governing class, and the simultaneous eclipse of Britain as a great power in the hundred years from the 1880s.[24] This is not to imply that if the patricians had stayed in charge, Britain would not have declined. Nor is it to assert that if Britain had remained a world power, the nobles and notables would have been more eager to go on governing. Nevertheless, it is an extraordinary coincidence that the trajectory of patrician and national decline should be so similar. And it was in the person and Prime Ministerships of Winston Churchill that these two trends most powerfully and poignantly converged. Between 1940 and 1945, and again from 1951 to 1955, his position as leader of a decaying nation mimicked his position as a member of a disintegrating class. In one guise, he was an aristocrat in an era of democracy; in another, he was the statesman in an age of decline. That does not make him the central character of this book: if anyone deserves that ambiguous accolade, it is surely Lloyd George. But it does make him a more resonant and representative figure in the history of aristocratic decline, than he is usually believed to have been.

iii. Conclusion: Lions into Unicorns

As one Victorian hymnster piously and portentously observed, 'Earth's proud empires pass away.' And so, to all intents and purposes, have Britain's once proud patricians. The families who in their heyday were the lords of the earth are now often strangers in their own land. The descendants of the makers of history are much more usually its victims. The lions of yesteryear have become the unicorns of today. To those who regret these developments, it is a heart-string-tugging threnody of unappreciated virtues, generous concessions, heroic sacrifices, uncomplaining defeats, and *noblesse oblige*. To those who view these matters rather differently, it is a triumphant tale of abuses remedied, hierarchy overturned, privilege rejected, vested interests vanquished, and oligarchy eliminated. Either way, it may well be that nothing quite became the patricians' pre-eminence like their leaving of it. However it is regarded, it is an extraordinary story, peopled by outsize characters as diverse as humanity itself, caught up in circumstances sometimes tragic, sometimes comic, which they could neither adequately control nor fully comprehend, in one guise playing melodrama, in another acting out farce. Perhaps this is what Oscar Wilde meant when he once remarked that the peerage was 'the best thing in fiction the English [sic] ever did.'

This book began by evoking one imaginary grandee: the Duke of Dorset. And in deference to Wilde's inscrutable and incisive insight, it concludes with another. Like Dorset, Lord Peter Wimsey was the proud and privileged possessor of ducal blood. He excelled at Eton and Balliol, where he must have been a near-contemporary of Julian Grenfell, took a First in Modern History, and fell hopelessly and helplessly in love. He served with distinction in the First World War, showed paternal concern for the men under his command, and was decorated with the DSO. In the 1920s, he took up detection as solace for his shell-shocked nerves, and later married a novelist. He was once described by his creator as 'an eighteenth-century Whig gentleman, born a little out of his time'; and could not conceal from himself that the aristocratic order to which he belonged was 'running down fast'.[25] In 1939, he returned to government service once more, and in his wartime diary, he attempted 'to view myself in the light of history, and acquiesce in my own decay'. It was in this mood that Wimsey composed his own epitaph, and the phrase he chose, at once self-mocking and self-revealing, may fittingly serve as the last words on the broader aristocratic experience of decline and fall, which has been imaginatively re-created in these pages:

> 'Here lies an anachronism,
> in the vague expectation of eternity'.[26]

APPENDICES

Appendix A: The Greatest British Landowners, c.1880

Family	Title	Gross Income (£)	Acres	Location E	I	S	W
Westminster	Duke	290,000	19,749	★			
Buccleuch	Duke	232,000	460,108	★		★	
Bedford	Duke	225,000	86,335	★			
Devonshire	Duke	181,000	198,572	★	★		
Northumberland	Duke	176,000	186,379	★			
Derby	Earl	163,000	68,942	★			
Bute	Marquess	151,000	116,668	★		★	★
Sutherland	Duke	142,000	1,358,545	★		★	
Hamilton	Duke	141,000	157,386	★		★	
Fitzwilliam	Earl	139,000	115,743	★	★		
Dudley	Earl	123,000	25,554	★		★	★
Ancaster	Earl	121,000	163,495	★		★	★
Anglesey	Marquess	111,000	29,737	★			★
Londonderry	Marquess	110,000	50,323	★	★		★
Portland	Duke	108,000	183,199	★		★	
Hertford	Marquess	104,000	84,596	★	★		
Portman	Viscount	100,000	33,891	★			
Rutland	Duke	97,000	70,137	★			
Cleveland	Duke	97,000	104,194	★			
Downshire	Marquess	97,000	120,189	★	★		
Overstone	Baron	93,000	51,377	★			★
Boyne	Viscount	88,000	30,205	★	★		★
Leconfield	Baron	88,000	109,935	★	★		
Brownlow	Earl	86,000	58,335	★			
Yarborough	Earl	85,000	56,893	★			
Richmond	Duke	80,000	286,411	★		★	

Seafield	Earl	78,000	305,930	★
Pembroke	Earl	78,000	44,806	★ ★
Norfolk	Duke	76,000	49,866	★

Sources: W. D. Rubinstein, *Men of Property: The Very Wealthy in Britain Since the Industrial Revolution* (1981), pp. 194–5; D. Cannadine, 'The Landowner as Millionaire: the Finances of the Dukes of Devonshire, c.1800–c.1926', *Agricultural History Review*, xxvi (1978), pp. 92–3; Bateman, *passim*.

Notes: Ancaster combines Willoughby d'Eresby and Aveland; Overstone also includes Loyd-Lindsay; Hertford also includes Wallace. Other great London and provincial ground owners should almost certainly be here.

Appendix B: Patrician Members of British Cabinets, 1880–1980

Ministry	Landowners/ Total	Aristocrats/ Total	Peers/ Total	BLE/★ Total
1880 Gladstone	na	8/14	6/14	9/14
1885 Salisbury	na	11/16	8/16	15/16
1886 Gladstone	6/15	9/15	6/15	9/15
1886 Salisbury	8/15	10/15	7/15	12/15
1892 Gladstone	6/17	9/17	5/17	8/17
1894 Rosebery	na	na	6/16	8/16
1895 Salisbury	12/19	8/19	9/19	14/19
1902 Balfour	11/19	9/19	9/19	15/20
1905 C-Bannerman	8/19	7/19	6/19	9/19
1908 Asquith	na	na	6/20	10/20
1919 Lloyd George	3/21	3/21	5/21	6/22
1922 Bonar Law	7/16	8/16	7/16	9/16
1924 Macdonald	2/19	3/19	5/19	4/19
1924 Baldwin	4/21	9/21	6/21	11/21
1929 Macdonald	2/18	2/18	4/18	3/18
1931 Macdonald	2/18	6/18	4/20	6/20
1935 Baldwin	na	9/22	6/22	9/22
1937 Chamberlain	na	8/21	6/21	9/21
1945 Churchill	na	6/16	4/16	6/16
1945 Attlee	na	0/20	4/20	1/20

1951 Churchill	na	5/16	6/16	5/16
1955 Eden	na	5/18	4/18	7/18
1957 Macmillan	na	4/18	5/18	3/18
1963 D-Home	na	5/24	3/24	3/24
1964 Wilson	na	1/23	2/23	1/23
1970 Heath	na	4/18	3/18	4/18
1974 Wilson	na	1/21	2/21	0/21
1976 Callaghan	na	1/22	2/22	0/22
1979 Thatcher	na	3/22	3/22	5/22

Sources: W. L. Guttsman, *The British Political Elite* (1965), pp. 166–7; R. C. K. Ensor, *England, 1870–1914* (1936), pp. 606–14; A. J. P. Taylor, *English History, 1914–1945* (1965), pp. 640–8; D. Butler and G. Butler, *British Political Facts, 1900–1985* (1987 edn.), pp. 31–83.

Notes: These figures relate only to initial appointments, and take no account of subsequent cabinet re-shuffles. Totals sometimes do not agree because they differ in Guttsman and the Oxford Histories.
* BLE = British landed establishment.

Appendix C: Senior Posts in the Foreign and Diplomatic Services

1. *Permanent Under-Secretaries at the Foreign Office*

Dates	Name	Remarks
1873–82	Lord Tenterden	Poor peer
1882–9	Sir J. Pauncefote	Yr. son of minor landed gentry; to US
1889–94	Sir P. Currie	Yr. son of minor landed gentry; to Turkey
1894–1906	Sir T. Sanderson	Grandson of 1st Viscount Canterbury; poor
1906–10	Sir C. Hardinge	Yr. son of poor peer; from Russia
1910–16	Sir A. Nicolson	11th Bt.; poor; Scottish; from Russia
1916–20	Lord Hardinge	Sir C. Hardinge, ennobled; to France
1920–5	Sir E. Crowe	Middle class
1925–8	Sir W. Tyrrell	Middle class
1928–30	Sir R. Lindsay	Yr. son of 26th Earl of

		Crawford; from Germany; to US
1930–8	Sir R. Vansittart	Elder son of minor landed gentry
1938–46	Sir A. Cadogan	Yr. son of 5th Earl Cadogan

2. HM Ambassadors to Austria

Dates	Name	Remarks
1877–84	Sir H. G. Elliot	Yr. son of 2nd Earl of Minto; Scots; from Turkey; son a diplomat
1884–93	Sir A. B. Paget	Grandson of 1st Earl of Uxbridge; son a diplomat; from Italy
1893–6	Sir E. Monson	Yr. son of 6th Lord Monson; to France
1896–1900	Sir H. Rumbold	8th Bt.; poor; father and son both diplomats
1900–5	Sir F. Plunkett	Yr. son of 9th Earl of Fingall; Irish; poor
1905–8	Sir W. Goschen	Middle class
1908–13	Sir F. Cartwright	Son of English landed gentry
1913–14	Sir M. de Bunsen	Middle class
1921–8	Lord Chilston	Poor peer; to Russia
1928–33	Sir E. Phipps	Gt. Nephew of 1st Marquess of Normanby; son of diplomat; to Germany
1933–7	Sir W. H. M. Selby	Eldest son of disinherited minor landed gentry

3. HM Ambassadors to France

Dates	Name	Remarks
1867–87	Lord Lyons	Poor peer
1887–91	Lord Lytton	Poor peer
1891–6	Lord Dufferin	Indebted Irish peer; non-career diplomat; from Italy
1896–1905	Sir E. Monson	Yr. son of 6th Lord Monson; from Austria
1905–18	Sir F. Bertie	Yr. son of 6th Earl of Abingdon; from Italy
1918–20	Lord Derby	Grandee; non-career diplomat
1920–2	Lord Hardinge	Yr. son of poor peer; previously Permanent Under-Secretary at FO

1922–8	Lord Crewe	Grandee; non-career diplomat
1928–34	Lord Tyrrell	Middle class
1934–7	Sir G. Clerk	Kinsman of Sir George Clerk, 8th Bt.; from Turkey
1937–9	Sir E. Phipps	Gt. nephew of 1st Marquess of Normanby; son of diplomat; from Germany
1939–40	Sir R. Campbell	Middle class

4. HM Ambassadors to Germany

Dates	Name	Remarks
1871–84	Lord Odo Russell	Yr. bro. of 9th Duke of Bedford; son a diplomat
1884–95	Sir E. Malet	4th. Bt.; poor
1895–1908	Sir F. Lascelles	Grandson of 2nd Earl of Harewood; from Russia
1908–14	Sir W. Goschen	Middle class
1920	Lord Kilmarnock	Future Lord Erroll; Scottish: poor
1921–6	Lord d'Abernon	Yr. son of 11th Bt., non-career diplomat
1926–8	Sir R. Lindsay	Yr. son of 26th Earl of Crawford; from Turkey; to FO as Permanent Under-Secretary
1928–33	Sir H. Rumbold	9th Bt.; poor; father and son both diplomats
1933–7	Sir E. Phipps	Gt. nephew of 1st Marquess of Normanby; son a diplomat; from Austria; to France
1937–9	Sir N. Henderson	Middle class; landed links

5. HM Ambassadors to Italy

Dates	Name	Remarks
1867–83	Sir A. B. Paget	Grandson of 1st Earl of Uxbridge; son a diplomat; to Austria
1883–8	Sir J. S. Lumley	Illegitimate son of 8th Earl of Scarbrough
1888–91	Lord Dufferin	Indebted Irish owner; non-career diplomat; to France
1891–3	Lord Vivian	Poor peer
1893–8	Sir C. Ford	Middle class

1898–1903	Sir P. W. Currie	Yr. son of minor landed gentry; from Turkey
1903–5	Sir F. Bertie	Yr. son of 6th Earl of Abingdon; to France
1905–8	Sir. F. Egerton	Middle class
1908–19	Sir J. R. Rodd	Grandson of landed gentry
1919–21	Sir G. Buchanan	Yr. son of 1st Bt. (diplomat); Scottish; poor; from Russia
1921–33	Sir R. Graham	Middle class
1933–9	Lord Perth	Poor Scottish peer
1939–40	Sir P. Loraine	12th Bt.; no land; wife inherits estates; from Turkey

6. HM Ambassadors to Russia

Dates	Name	Remarks
1879–81	Lord Dufferin	Indebted Irish peer; non-career diplomat; to Turkey
1881–4	Sir E. Thornton	Middle class
1884–93	Sir R. D. B. Morier	Middle class
1894–5	Sir F. C. Lascelles	Grandson of 2nd Earl of Harewood; to Germany
1895–7	Sir N. R. O'Conor	Head of minor Irish gentry family; to Turkey
1898–1904	Sir C. S. Scott	Yr. son of Irish landed gentry
1904–6	Sir C. Hardinge	Yr. son of poor peer; to FO as Permanent Under-Secretary
1906–10	Sir A. Nicolson	11th Bt.; poor; Scots; to FO as Permanent Under-Secretary
1910–17	Sir G. Buchanan	Yrs. son of 1st Bt. (diplomat); Scottish; poor; to Italy
1929–33	Sir E. Ovey	Yr. son of minor landed gentry
1933–9	Lord Chilston	Poor peer; from Austria
1939–40	Sir W. Seeds	Middle class

7. HM Ambassadors to Turkey

Dates	Name	Remarks
1881–4	Lord Dufferin	Indebted Irish peer non-career diplomat; from Russia
1884–5	Sir E. Thornton	Middle class
1886–92	Sir W. A. White	Middle class

1893–8	Sir P. W. Currie	Yr. son of minor landed gentry; previously PUS at FO; to Italy
1898–1908	Sir N. R. O'Conor	Head of minor Irish gentry family; from Russia
1908–13	Sir G. Lowther	Grandson of Ist Earl of Lonsdale
1913–14	Sir L. Mallet	Middle class
1920–4	Sir H. Rumbold	9th Bt.; poor; father and son both diplomats; to Germany
1924–6	Sir R. Lindsay	Yr. son of 26th Earl of Crawford; to Germany
1926–33	Sir G. R. Clerk	Kinsman of Sir George Clerk, 8th Bt.; to France
1933–9	Sir P. Lorraine	12th Bt.; no land; wife inherits estates; to Italy
1939–44	Sir H. Knatchbull-Hugessen	Grandson of 9th Bt.; poor

8. HM Ambassadors to the United States

Dates	Name	Remarks
1881–9	Hon. L. S. Sackville-West	Future Lord Sackville; poor peer
1889–1902	Sir J. Pauncefote	Yr. son of minor landed gentry; previously PUS at FO
1902–3	Sir M. Herbert	Grandson of 11th Earl of Pembroke
1903–7	Sir M. Durand	Middle class
1907–13	J. Bryce	Middle class; non-career diplomat
1913–18	Sir C. Spring-Rice	Great grandson of 1st Lord Monteagle; poor
1918–20	Lord Reading	Middle class; non career-diplomat
1920	Lord Grey	Country gent; non-career diplomat
1920–4	Sir A. Geddes	Middle class; non career diplomat
1924–30	Sir E. Howard	Yr. son of landed gentry
1930–9	Sir R. Lindsay	Yr. son of 26th Earl of Crawford; previously PUS at FO
1939–40	Lord Lothian	Poor peer; non-career diplomat

Appendix D: Titled Company Directors, 1896 and 1920

1. Landowning Peers with Six or more than Six Directorships in 1896

Peer	Directorships	Acreage	Income (£)	Remarks
Castletown	6	23,143	15,758	Irish
Donoughmore	11	11,950	10,424	Irish
Ebury	6	2,723	5,803	English
Ribblesdale	6	4,719	6,980	English
Rothschild	6	15;378	28,901	English; unique
Tweeddale	19	43,517	26,530	Irish
Rathmore	6	3,567	3,254	Irish; yr son (Plunket)

2. Landowning Peers with Six or more than Six Directorships in 1920

Peer	Directorships	Acreage	Income (£)	Remarks
Balfour of Burleigh	14	2,715	3,364	Scottish
Bessborough	8	35,440	22,384	Mainly Irish
Bledisloe	6	4,098	5,189	English
Brabourne	13	4,173	5,646	English
Darnley	6	34,772	37,350	Mainly Irish
Denbigh	10	3,218	6,340	Mainly Welsh
Elibank	7	6,690	10,098	Scottish
Glenconner	10	3,616	7,035	Scots; industry
Harris	6	4,609	7,201	English
Harrowby	6	12,625	20,291	English
Kinnaird	7	11,818	17,003	Scottish
Lurgan	6	15,276	20,589	Irish
Midleton	9	9,580	10,752	Mainly Irish
Ribblesdale	11	4,719	6,980	English
Russell	6	4,184	4,527	Irish
Vaux	8	4,323	2,401	Irish
Verulam	9	10,117	14,101	English

Sources: G. E. Cokayne, *The Complete Peerage* (new edn., ed. by the Hon. V. Gibbs, 13 vols., 1910–1953), v, Appendix C, pp. 780–3; Bateman, *passim*.

Appendix E: Patrician Mayors of British Towns, 1880–1945

1. Great Industrial Cities

Town	Family	Terms as Mayor	Local connection
Belfast	Shaftesbury	1907	Descendants of Donegalls
Cardiff	Bute	1891	Pre-eminent local landowner
	Windsor	1896	Second major local landowner
Liverpool	Derby	1896, 1912	'Kings of Lancs'
	Sefton	1945	Major Liverpool landower
Sheffield	Norfolk	1896–7	Great Sheffield owner
	Fitzwilliam	1910	Same
Swansea	D-Llewellyn	1891	Glamorgan owner

2. Smaller Industrial Towns

Town	Family	Terms as Mayor	Local connection
Burton on Trent	Anglesey	1912	Staffs; owner
Chesterfield	Devonshire	1912	Derby; owner
Darlington	Gainford	1890	Local owner
Devonport	St. Levans	1891–2	Local owner
Dudley	Dudley	1896–7	Major mineral owner
Grantham	Brownlow	1910, 1925, 1935	Large owner
Llanelli	Norfolk	1916	Wife's estate
Longton	Sutherland	1896	Great Staffs owner
Preston	Derby	1902	'King of Lancs'
Whitehaven*	Lonsdale	1895–6	Local owner

3. Seaside Towns

Town	Family	Terms as Mayor	Local connection
Bexhill	Brassey	1908, 1909	Lived nearby
	de la Warr	1904–5, 1933–5	Major owners
Deal	Abercorn	1910	Cptn. of Castle,

		1899–1923	
Eastbourne	Devonshire	1898, 1910	Major owners
Folkestone	Radnor	1902	Major owners
Great Yarmouth	Buxton	1897	E. Anglia owners
Poole	Wimborne	1897	Dorset owners
Southport	Hesketh	1906	Major owners
	Scarisbrick	1902, 1903	Major owners

4. Small Towns

Town	Family	Terms as Mayor or Provost	Local connection
Altrincham	Stamford	1938	8,612 a in Chesh.
Appleby	Hothfield	1896, 1938–46	17,093 a in Cumb.
Arundel★	Norfolk	1903, 1936	21,446 a in Sx.
Aylesbury	Courtown	1928	Irish: relocated
Beaumaris	W-Bulkeley	1885–7, 1893	13,362 a in Caer.
Buckingham	Addington	1933–4, 1944–6	2,756 a in Bucks.
Buxton	Devonshire	1921	89,462 a in Dby.
Chipping Norton	Brassey	1899–1902	4,275 a in Ox.
Durham	Durham	1900	14,664 a in Dur.
	Londonderry	1911, 1937	12,863 a in Dur.
Honiton	Devon	1930–3	20,049 a in Dev.
Huntingdon★	Sandwich	1897–8	3,219 a in Hunts.
King's Lynn	Fermoy	1932	Irish: relocated
	Townshend	1929	18,343 a in Norf.
Kirkcaldy	M-Ferguson	1906–14	15,022 a in Ross
Monmouth	Llangattock	1897–8, 1907–8	4,082 a in Mon.
Norwich	Buxton	1907	11,461 a in Norf.
Peterborough★	Fitzwilliam	1901	18,116 a in Nhts.
Richmond★	Zetland	1896–7	11,614 a in Yks.
Ripon★	Ripon	1896	14,668 a in Yks.
Romsey	Shaftesbury	1899–1903	3,250 a in Hants.
Rothesay	Bute	1897–9	29,279 a in Bute.
Salisbury	Burnham	1928	3,207 a in Bucks.
Stamford★	Exeter	1901	8,998 a in Rut.
Warwick★	Warwick	1895–6, 1902, 1916, 1930–1	8,262 a in Warw.
Watford	Clarendon	1923	2,298 a in Herts.
Wenlock★	Forester	1899–1900, 1910, 1922, 1937	14,891 a in Sal.
Wilton★	Pembroke	1900, 1933–4,	42,244 a in Wilt.

		1934–6	
Woodstock*	Marlborough	1908–9, 1938–42	21,944 a in Ox.
Worcester	Beauchamp	1896	10,624 a in Worc.
	Coventry	1930	13,021 a in Worc.

Source: *Whitaker's Almanack*, 1880–1945

Note: A mayor's term of office includes part of two calendar years, beginning in November. To avoid confusion, this table records the single year as reported in *Whitaker's*. A succession of years accordingly indicates more than one term of office.

An asterisk (*) indicates that the town was included in the list of proprietary boroughs given in N. Gash, *Politics in the Age of Peel: a study in the technique of parliamentary representation* (1953), pp. 438–9.

Appendix F: Chancellors of British Universities, 1880–1945

University	Chancellor	Term
Aberdeen	Duke of Richmond and Gordon	1861–1903
	Lord Strathcona & Mt. Royal	1903–14
	Earl of Elgin	1914–18
	Duke of Richmond and Gordon	1918–29
	Lord Meston	1929–45
Birmingham	Joseph Chamberlain	1900–14
	Viscount Cecil	1918–44
	Sir Anthony Eden	1945–75
Bristol	H. O. Wills	1909–11
	Viscount Haldane	1913–30
	Winston Churchill	1930–65
Cambridge	Duke of Devonshire	1861–92
	Duke of Devonshire	1892–1908
	Lord Rayleigh	1908–19
	A. J. Balfour	1919–30
	Stanley Baldwin	1930–47
Dublin	Lord Cairns	1867–85
	Earl of Rosse	1885–1908

	Earl of Iveagh	1908–27
	Earl of Iveagh	1927–63
Durham	Dean Kitchen	1909–12
	Duke of Northumberland	1913–18
	Earl of Durham	1919–28
	Duke of Northumberland	1929–30
	Marquess of Londonderry	1931–49
Edinburgh	Rt. Hon. J. Inglis	1871–90
	A. J. Balfour	1891–1930
	Sir J.M. Barrie	1931–7
	Lord Tweedsmuir	1938–40
Glasgow	Earl of Stair	1898–1905
	Lord Kelvin	1905–9
	Earl of Rosebery	1909–30
	Sir Donald MacAlister	1931–5
	Sir Daniel Stevenson	1935–45
Leeds	Lord Frederick Cavendish	1874–82
	Marquess of Ripon	1883–1909
	Duke of Devonshire	1909–38
	Duke of Devonshire	1938–50
Liverpool	Earl of Derby	1881–93
	Earl of Derby	1893–1908
	Earl of Derby	1909–48
London	Earl Granville	1870–91
	Earl of Derby	1891–3
	Lord Herschell	1893–9
	Earl of Kimberley	1900–3
	Earl of Rosebery	1903–29
	Earl Beauchamp	1929–31
	Earl of Athlone	1932–56
Manchester	Duke of Devonshire	1880–92
	Earl Spencer	1892–1907
	Duke of Devonshire	1907–8
	Viscount Morley	1908–23
	Earl of Crawford and Balcarres	1923–40

Oxford	Marquess of Salisbury	1869–1903
	Lord Goschen	1903–7
	Marquess Curzon	1907–25
	Viscount Cave	1925–8
	Viscount Grey	1928–33
	Earl of Halifax	1933–59
Queen's Belfast	Earl of Shaftesbury	1908–23
	Marquess of Londonderry	1923–49
Royal University of Ireland	Duke of Abercorn	1880–5
	Marquess of Dufferin	1887–1902
	Earl of Meath	1902–5
	Lord Castletown	1906–9
St Andrews	Duke of Argyll	1851–1901
	Andrew Carnegie	1902–4
	Lord Balfour of Burleigh	1907–21
	Earl Haig	1923–9
	Stanley Baldwin	1930–48
Sheffield	Duke of Norfolk	1897–1917
	Marquess of Crewe	1917–44
	Earl of Harewood	1944–7
Wales	Lord Aberdare	1895
	Prince of Wales (Edward VII)	1895–1901
	Prince of Wales (George V)	1901–21
	Prince of Wales (Edward VIII)	1921–36
	Duke of Kent	1937–42

Notes: the Federal Victoria University of Manchester was set up in 1880, and soon included Liverpool and Leeds University Colleges as well. It was dissolved in 1903, whereupon Manchester became a separate institution, Liverpool received its charter in the same year, and Leeds in 1904. University College Sheffield was set up in 1897, but failed to gain admission to Victoria University. In 1904, it, too, received its own charter.

Appendix G: Viceroys of India and Governors-General of British Dominions

1. India

Viceroy	Dates	Acres	Income (£)	Comments
Viscount Canning	1856–62	c.2,000	c.2,000	Poor
Lord Elgin	1862–3	2,895	5,240	Debts; Scots
Sir John Lawrence	1864–9			Poor
Lord Mayo	1869–72	7,834	7,690	Irish
Lord Northbrook	1872–6	10,059	12,710	English
Lord Lytton	1876–80	4,863	5,366	Poor
Lord Ripon	1880–4	21,770	29,126	English
Lord Dufferin	1884–8	18,238	21,043	Debts; Irish
Lord Lansdowne	1888–94	142,916	62,025	Debts; UK
Lord Elgin	1894–9	2,895	5,240	Debts; Scots
Lord Curzon	1899–1905	9,929	17,859	Debts; US money
Lord Minto	1905–10	16,071	13,056	Scots
Lord Hardinge	1910–16	c.500		Govt. service
Lord Chelmsford	1916–21			Lawyers
Lord Reading	1921–5			Self-made
Lord Irwin	1926–31	10,142	12,169	Debts
Lord Willingdon	1931–6	2,935	4,122	Part sold off
Lord Linlithgow	1936–43	42,507	39,984	Debts; Scots
Lord Wavell	1943–7			Military
Lord Mountbatten	1947–8			Royal, rich

2. Canada

Governor-General	Dates	Acres	Income (£)	Comments
Lord Monck	1867–8	14,144	10,466	Irish
Lord Lisgar	1868–72	11,413	11,458	Irish
Lord Dufferin	1872–8	18,238	21,043	Debts; Irish
Lord Lorne	1878–83	175,114	50,842	Debts; Scots
Lord Lansdowne	1883–8	142,916	62,025	Debts; Irish
Lord Stanley	1888–93	68,942	163,273	Debts; Eng.
Lord Aberdeen	1893–8	62,422	44,112	Scotts;
Lord Minto	1898–1904	16,071	13,056	Scotts;
Lord Grey	1904–11	17,599	23,724	Director; Eng.
Duke of Connaught	1911–16			Royal
Duke of Devonshire	1916–21	198,572	180,750	Debts; UK
Lord Byng	1921–6	14,994	16,349	Irish; yr. son
Lord Willingdon	1926–31	2,935	4,122	Part sold off

Lord Bessborough	1931–5	35,440	22,384	Irish; sold off
Lord Tweedsmuir	1935–40			Self-made
Lord Athlone	1940–6			Royal
Lord Alexander	1946–52	34,060	22,321	Irish; yr. son

3. New Zealand

Governor-General	Dates	Acres	Income (£)	Comments
Lord Onslow	1889–92	13,488	10,872	Debts; Eng.
Lord Glasgow	1892–7	37,825	34,588	Debts; Scots
Lord Ranfurly	1897–1904	10,153	11,237	Irish
Lord Plunket	1904–10	3,567	3,254	Poor; Irish
Lord Islington	1910–12	6,908	14,298	English
Lord Liverpool	1912–20	3,624	5,517	English
Lord Jellicoe	1920–4			Naval hero
Sir C. Fergusson	1924–30	22,630	13,334	Debts; Scots
Lord Bledisloe	1930–5	4,098	5,189	English
Lord Galway	1935–41	7,008	10,557	English
Lord Newall	1941–6			Military
Lord Freyberg	1946–52			Military
Sir C. Norrie	1952–7			Military
Lord Cobham	1957–62	6,939	10,263	English
Sir B. Fergusson	1962–7	22,630	13,334	Scotts; yr. son

4. Australia

Governor-General	Dates	Acres	Income (£)	Comments
Lord Hopetoun	1901–3	42,507	39,984	Debts; Scots
Lord Tennyson	1903–4			Poet's son
Lord Northcote	1904–8	5,663	6,000	Engl. yr. son
Lord Dudley	1908–11	25,554	123,176	UK; Debts
Lord Denman	1911–14	c.2,500	c.2,500	Lawyer
Sir R. Munro-Ferguson	1914–20	25,506	18,735	Debts; Scots
Lord Forster	1920–5			Self-made
Lord Stonehaven	1925–31	11,018	12,630	Scots
Sir I. Isaacs	1931–6			Australian
Lord Gowrie	1936–45	7,624	10,981	Irish; Scots
Duke of Gloucester	1945–7			Royal
Sir W. Mckell	1947–53			Australian
Sir W. Slim	1953–60			Military
Lord Dunrossil	1960–1			HC Speaker
Lord De L'Isle	1961–5	9,252	10,232	English

Governor-General	Dates	5. South Africa Acres	Income (£)	Comments
Lord Gladstone	1910–4	6,918	18,173	Eng. yr. son
Lord Buxton	1914–20	3,160	4,769	Eng. yr. son
Pr. Arthur of C'n'ght	1920–4			Royal
Lord Athlone	1924–31			Royal
Lord Clarendon	1931–7	2,298	3,741	Eng. poor

Note: Details of acreage and income are from Bateman, and so are accurate for the 1870s and 1880s, but increasingly approximate the further they are from these decades. When no acreage or income is given this is because there is no entry in Bateman. Tables cease at the last British proconsul.

Appendix H: Patterns of Estate Ownership, 1876–1976

Owner	1876 acreage	1976 acreage
Marquess of Ailesbury	53,362	5,500
Earl of Ancaster	67,638	22,680
Marquess of Bath	41,690	10,000
Duke of Beaufort	45,848	52,000
Duke of Bedford	87,008	11,000
Marquess of Bristol	31,974	16,000
Earl Brownlow	57,798	10,000
Earl of Carlisle	78,541	3,000
Earl of Cawdor	51,517	26,000
Earl of Derby	56,597	22,000
Duke of Devonshire	132,996	56,000
Earl of Durham	30,472	30,000
Earl of Feversham	39,312	12,500
Earl Howe	33,656	2,500
Earl of Ilchester	30,716	none*
Lord Leconfield	109,900	13,000
Earl of Leicester	43,024	27,000
Earl of Lisburne	42,666	3,230
Earl of Londesborough	52,656	none**
Earl of Lonsdale	67,457	72,000
Earl Middleton	34,701	13,500
Duke of Norfolk	40,176	25,000***
Duke of Northumberland	186,397	105,000
Earl of Pembroke	40,447	14,000
Duke of Portland	53,771	17,000

Viscount Portman	31,969	1,000
Earl of Powis	61,008	19,000
Lord Redesdale	30,247	1,000
Duke of Rutland	58,9443	18,000
Earl of Stamford	30,792	3,500****
Sir Watkin Williams-Wynn	91,021	26,000
Earl of Yarborough	55,272	30,000

Source: *The Spectator*, 1 January 1977

Notes: *relation holds estate of 15,000 acres; **estate split among relatives; ***in trust for family; ****to pass to National Trust. For both years, figures relate only to land owned in England and Wales.

NOTES

Preface

1. For the historical background to this painting, see: A. L. Rowse, *The Later Churchills* (1971), p. 290; C. Balsan, *The Glitter and the Gold* (New York, 1953), pp. 145–7; G. Jackson-Stops (ed.), *The Treasure Houses of Britain: Five Hundred Years of Private Patronage and Art Collecting* (1984), pp. 640–2.
2. For another discussion of Sargent as 'the sly deflater' of patrician pretensions, see: J. Pearson, *Façades: Edith, Osbert and Sacheverell Sitwell* (1978), pp. 39–40.
3. M. Cowling, *Religion and Public Doctrine in Modern England* (1980), p. 283; *The Times*, 2 July 1934.
4. H. Nicolson, *King George V: His Life and Reign* (1967), p. 7.

Chapter I

1. M. Beerbohm, *Zuleika Dobson* (1971 edn.), esp. pp. 27–9, 36, 45–50.
2. E. H. Carr, *What is History?* (1964), pp. 22–3.
3. H. J. Perkin, *The Structured Crowd: Essays in English Social History* (1981), pp. 168–70.
4. M. Cranston, 'Noel Coward Maligned', *Encounter*, LX (May 1978), p. 93.
5. On heritage hysteria in general, see P. Wright, *On Living in an Old Country* (1985); R. Hewitson, *The Heritage Industry: Britain in a Climate of Decline* (1987). For one outstanding example of heritage hype, see G. Jackson-Stops (ed.), *The Treasure Houses of Britain: Five Hundred Years of Private Patronage and Art Collecting* (1984). For dissenting views, see D. Cannadine, *The Pleasures of the Past* (1989), pp. 256–71; F. M. L. Thompson, 'The Long Run of the English Aristocracy', *London Review of Books*, 19 Feb. 1987. The question is discussed more fully below, chapter 14, section iv.

6. E.g. W. D. Rubinstein, *Elites and the Wealthy in Modern Britain* (1987), pp. 11–12. For a fuller discussion, see D. Cannadine, 'British History: Past, Present – and Future?' *P. & P.* no. 116 (1987), p. 183.
7. J. H. Hexter, *Reappraisals in History* (1961), pp. 194–5.
8. J. G. A. Pocock, 'The Limits and Divisions of British History: In Search of the Unknown Subject', *A.H.R.*, LXXXVII (1982), pp. 311–36.
9. M. Bloch, 'Pour une Histoire Comparée des Sociétés Européennes', in F. C. Lane and J. C. Riemersma (eds.), *Readings in Economic History* (Homewood, Illinois, 1953), p. 507.
10. E. J. Hobsbawm, 'From Social History to the History of Society', *Daedalus*, C (1971), pp. 20–45.
11. L. Stone, *The Crisis of the Aristocracy, 1558–1641* (1965), p. xvii.
12. For some indication of the proliferating secondary material, see the references cited in D. Cannadine, 'The Theory and Practice of the English Leisure Classes', *H.J.*, XXX (1978), pp. 445–8. Since then, the quantity has expanded even more.
13. The most outstanding example is P. Jalland, *Woman, Marriage and Politics, 1860–1914* (1986). Linda Colley's forthcoming study, *The Rise and Fall of Female Political Power in Britain*, will also have much to say on this subject. The biographies of patrician authors by Victoria Glendinning are also very valuable: *Elizabeth Bowen: Portrait of a Writer* (1978); *Edith Sitwell: A Unicorn Among Lions* (1981); and *Vita: The Life of V. Sackville-West* (1983). See also P. Ziegler, *Diana Cooper* (1971).
14. W. G. Runciman, *A Treatise on Social Theory* (2 vols. so far, 1983–), vol. I, *The Methodology of Social Theory*,

p. 312.

15. P. Gay, *Style in History* (1975), pp. 17, 212.

16. L. Stone, *The Causes of the English Revolution, 1529–1624* (1972), pp. 33–5.

17. J. R. Vincent, *Pollbooks: How Victorians Voted* (1967), p. 33.

18. H. H. Gerth and C. Wright Mills (eds.), *From Max Weber: Essays in Sociology* (New York, 1958), pp. 180–95; W. G. Runciman, *Social Science and Political Theory* (2nd edn., 1969), pp. 135–55; W. G. Runciman, *Sociology in its Place, and Other Essays* (1970), pp. 102–40. See also R. J. Morris, *Class and Class Consciousness in the Industrial Revolution, 1780–1850* (1979), pp. 62–6.

19. F. M. L. Thompson, *English Landed Society in the Nineteenth Century* (1963), p. 27; A. Arnold, *Free Land* (1880), pp. 1–10.

20. W. Bence Jones, 'Landowning as a Business', *19C*, xi (1882), p. 254.

21. F. M. L. Thompson, 'The Social Distribution of Landed Property in England Since the Sixteenth Century', *Ec.H.R.*, 2nd ser., xix (1966), p. 512; J. V. Beckett, 'The Pattern of Landownership in England and Wales, 1660–1880', *Ec.H.R.*, 2nd ser., (1984), p. 5.

22. M. McCahill, 'Peerage Creations and the Changing Character of the British Nobility, 1750–1830', *Eng. Hist. Rev.*, xcvi (1981), pp. 259–84.

23. J. V. Beckett, *The Aristocracy in England, 1660–1914* (1986), pp. 486–9.

24. M. L. Bush, *The English Aristocracy: A Comparative Synthesis* (1984), pp. 20–1; W. Doyle, *The Old European Order, 1660–1800* (1978), p. 86.

25. Beckett, *Aristocracy*, pp. 489–91.

26. *Burke's Landed Gentry* (1886 edn.), preface. See also G. E. Mingay, *The Gentry: The Rise and Fall of a Ruling Class* (1976), pp. 1–17.

27. L. Stone and J. C. Fawtier Stone, *An Open Elite? England, 1540–1880* (1984), pp. 74–7; G. C. Brodrick, *English Land and English Landlords* (1881), pp. 96, 99, 130–4.

28. Thompson, *English Landed Society*, pp. 15–20.

29. Bush, *Aristocracy*, p. 54.

30. D. C. Moore, 'The Landed Aristocracy', in G. E. Mingay (ed.), *The Victorian Countryside* (2 vols., London, 1981), ii, p. 372.

31. S. Lukes, *Power: A Radical View* (1974),

p. 20.

32. For two recent (and patrician) restatements of the theory of timely concession by an essentially liberal aristocracy, see: Lord Montagu of Beaulieu, *More Equal than Others: The Changing Fortunes of the British and European Aristocracies* (1970), p. 164; Sir John Colville, *Those Lambtons! A Most Unusual Family* (1988), pp. 177–83. For a more cerebral articulation of the same view, see N. Gash, *Aristocracy and People: Britain, 1815–1865* (1979), pp. 347–50.

33. J. L. Sanford and M. Townsend, *The Great Governing Families of England* (1965); J. R. Vincent, *The Formation of the Liberal Party, 1857–1868* (1966), pp. 213–14.

34. J. Powys, *Aristocracy* (1984), p. 102.

35. D. Spring, 'Landed Elites Compared', in D. Spring (ed.), *European Landed Elites in the Nineteenth Century* (1977), pp. 15–17.

36. W. H. Mallock, *The Old Order Changes* (1886), pp. 178–9.

37. Quoted in Stone and Fawtier Stone, *Open Elite*, p. 14.

38. Rubinstein, *Elites and the Wealthy*, pp. 222–33.

39. Thompson, *English Landed Society*, p. 14.

40. Thompson, *English Landed Society*, p. 50.

41. Thompson, *English Landed Society*, p. 14.

42. Montagu of Beaulieu, *More Equal*, p. 57; T. Zeldin, 'France', in Spring, *Landed Elites*, p. 127.

43. S. M. Eddie, 'The Changing Pattern of Landownership in Hungary, 1867–1914', *Ec.H.R.*, 2nd ser., xx (1967), pp. 302–4; J. K. Hoensch, *A History of Modern Hungary, 1867–1986* (1988), pp. 36–7.

44. D. Spring, 'English Landowners and Nineteenth-Century Industrialism', in J. T. Ward and R. G. Wilson (eds.), *Land and Industry* (1971), pp. 16–18.

45. Zeldin, 'France', p. 129.

46. A. J. Mayer, *The Persistence of the Old Regime: Europe to the Great War* (New York, 1981), pp. 26–8.

47. F. Stern, 'Prussia', in Spring, *Landed Elites*, p. 51; Spring, 'Landed Elites Compared', pp. 12–13; *E.G.*, 4 Jan. 1902, 8 Nov. 1902.

48. Spring, 'Landed Elites Compared', pp. 6–10.

49. Alphonse de Calonne, 'The French Aristocracy', *19C*, XLII (1987), pp. 442–4.

50. J. R. Gillis, 'Aristocracy and Bureaucracy in Nineteenth-Century Prussia', *P. & P.*, no. 41 (1968), p. 113; L. Cecil, 'The Creation of Nobles in Prussia', *A.H.R.*, LXXV (1970), pp. 757–95; J. Blum, 'Russia', in Spring, *Landed Elites*, p. 71.

51. Mayer, *Old Regime*, pp. 111, 125–6; W. O. McCragg, 'Ennoblement in Dualistic Hungary: In Explanation of Bourgeois Acceptance of Service Status in Eastern Europe', *East European Quarterly* (1971), pp. 130–6; A. L. Cardoza, 'The Enduring Power of Aristocracy: Ennoblement in Liberal Italy, 1861–1914' (unpublished paper, 1985), pp. 1–13.

52. Bush, *Aristocracy*, pp. 35, 49.

53. Spring, 'Landed Elites Compared', pp. 10–12.

54. S. Clark, 'Nobility, Bourgeoisie and the Industrial Revolution in Belgium', *P. & P.*, no. 105 (1984), pp. 162–5; Zeldin, 'France', pp. 132–5; W. E. Mosse, 'Bureaucracy and Nobility in Russia at the End of the Nineteenth Century', *H.J.*, XXIV (1981), pp. 605–28.

55. Hoensch, *Hungary*, pp. 20–2, 36–8; S. Baranowski, 'Continuity and Contingency: Agrarian Elites, Conservative Institutions and East Elbia in Modern German History', *Social History*, XII (1987), pp. 285–308; L. W. Muncy, 'The Prussian Landrate in the Last Years of the Monarchy: A Case-Study of Pomerania and the Rhineland in 1890–1918', *Central European History*, VI (1973), pp. 299–338; L. W. Muncy, *The Junkers in the Prussian Administration Under Wilhelm II, 1888–1914* (1944); H. H. Herwig, *The German Naval Officers Corps: A Social and Political History, 1890–1918* (1973).

56. Bush, *Aristocracy*, pp. 8, 188.

57. E. P. Thompson, *The Making of the English Working Class* (1963), pp. 9–10; E. J. Hobsbawm, 'Class Consciousness in History', in I. Meszaros (ed.), *Aspects of History and Class Consciousness* (1971), pp. 6–15.

58. D. Spring, 'Introduction', in J. Bateman, *The Great Landowners of Great Britain and Ireland* (4th edn., reprinted 1971), pp. 7–13.

59. W. L. Burn, *The Age of Equipoise: A Study of the Mid-Victorian Generation* (1968), p. 316.

60. B. Cracroft, 'The Analysis of the House of Commons, or Indirect Representation', in *Essays on Reform* (1867), pp. 168–9.

61. P. Laslett, *The World We Have Lost* (1965 edn.), p. 22; J. Schumpeter, *Imperialism and Social Classes* (trans. H. Norden, ed. P. M. Sweezy, New York, 1951), p. 123.

62. Bush, *Aristocracy*, p. 4.

63. Thompson, *English Landed Society*, p. 6.

64. T. Judt, 'The Rules of the Game', *H.J.*, XXIII (1980), pp. 190–1.

65. Mayer, *Persistence*, p. 126; Cardoza, 'Enduring Power', p. 3; N. Stone, *Europe Transformed, 1878–1919* (1983), p. 21.

66. Stone, *Europe*, pp. 23–6, 173, 184–5, 206–7, 234, 240.

67. E. J. Hobsbawm, *The Age of Empire, 1875–1914* (1987), pp. 36, 85–95, 115–18, 171–2.

68. Stone, *Europe*, pp. 47–51.

69. Powys, *Aristocracy*, p. 63.

70. Lord Salisbury, 'Disintegration', reprinted in P. Smith (ed.), *Lord Salisbury on Politics: A Selection from His Articles in the Quarterly Review, 1860–1883* (1972), pp. 338–76. For Salisbury's general sense of anxiety about the 1880s, see P. Marsh, *The Discipline of Popular Government: Lord Salisbury's Domestic Statecraft, 1881–1902* (1978), pp. 11–17; R. Taylor, *Lord Salisbury* (1975), pp. 68–9, 73–83; A. J. Balfour, *Chapter of Autobiography* (1930), pp. 127–8.

71. R. B. Martin, *Tennyson: The Unquiet Heart* (1980), pp. 1–16, 206–14, 373–5, 472–6, 541–50.

72. Martin, *Tennyson*, pp. 559–61; Charles Tennyson, *Alfred Tennyson* (New York, 1949), pp. 491–5; V. Pitt, *Tennyson Laureate* (1962), pp. 155–62.

73. W. E. Gladstone, 'Locksley Hall and the Jubilee', *19C*, CXIX (1887), p. 10.

74. For Mallock's early life, see W. H. Mallock, *Memoirs of Life and Literature* (1920), pp. 1–27.

75. Mallock, *Old Order*, pp. 1, 19.

76. Mallock, *Old Order*, pp. 83, 86.

77. Salisbury, 'Disintegration', in Smith, *Salisbury*, p. 344.

78. J. R. Vincent (ed.), *The Later Derby Diaries: Home Rule, Liberal Unionism and Aristocratic Life in Late Victorian England* (1981), pp. 104–5.

Chapter 2

1. J. E. Williams, 'The Liberal Party and the House of Lords, 1880–1895' (M.A. dissertation, University of Wales, 1961), pp. 58–9.
2. K. T. Hoppen, 'The Franchise and Electoral Politics in England and Ireland, 1832–1885', *History*, LXX (1985), pp. 202, 217.
3. E. J. Hobsbawm, *The Age of Empire, 1875–1914* (1987), pp. 84–9.
4. H. J. Hanham, *Elections and Party Management: Politics in the Time of Disraeli and Gladstone* (1959), pp. 17–38, 405–12; S. Hogg, 'Landed Society and the Conservative Party in the Late Nineteenth and Early Twentieth Centuries' (B.Litt. dissertation, Oxford University, 1972), p. 133.
5. D. Spring, 'Land and Politics in Edwardian England', *Agricultural History*, LVIII (1984), p. 18; T. O. Lloyd, 'Uncontested Seats in British General Elections, 1852–1910', *H.J.*, VIII (1965), pp. 262–3; T. O. Lloyd, *The General Election of 1880* (1968), pp. 50–1; D. Read, *England, 1868–1914: The Age of Urban Democracy* (1979), pp. 118, 169.
6. A. Jones, *The Politics of Reform, 1884* (1972), pp. 58–9; G. D. Phillips, *The Diehards: Aristocratic Society and Politics in Edwardian England* (1979), p. 112; Hogg, 'Landed Society and the Conservative Party', pp. 133–5, 139.
7. C. Seymour, *Electoral Reform in England and Wales: The Development and Operation of the Parliamentary Franchise, 1832–1885* (Hamden, Conn., 1970 edn.), pp. 442–51; P. Marsh, *The Discipline of Popular Government: Lord Salisbury's Domestic Statecraft, 1881–1902* (1978), p. 193.
8. Jones, *Politics of Reform*, pp. 2–4; Seymour, *Electoral Reform*, pp. 456–60.
9. Read, *England, 1868–1914*, pp. 309–14; Seymour, *Electoral Reform*, pp. 456–516.
10. J. P. D. Dunbabin, 'Parliamentary Elections in Great Britain, 1868–1900: A Psephological Note', *Eng. Hist. Rev.*, LXXXI (1966), pp. 82–99.
11. N. Blewett, 'The Franchise in the United Kingdom, 1885–1918', *P. & P.*, no. 32 (1965), pp. 27–56; H. C. G. Matthew, R. I. McKibbin and J. A. Kay, 'The Franchise Factor and the Rise of the Labour Party', *Eng. Hist. Rev.*, XCI (1976), pp. 723–35; H. Pelling,

Social Geography of British Elections, 1885–1910 (1967), pp. 6–14.
12. A. K. Russell, *Liberal Landslide* (1973), pp. 19–21; D. Tanner, 'The Parliamentary Electoral System, the "Fourth" Reform Act, and the Rise of Labour in England and Wales', *Bulletin of the Institute of Historical Research*, LVI (1983), pp. 205, 216–17; M. E. J. Chadwick, 'The Role of Redistribution in the Making of the Third Reform Act', *H.J.*, XIX (1976), pp. 665–8, 670–1, 676–7, 683; Hanham, *Elections and Party Management*, pp. xvi–xvii; Seymour, *Electoral Reform*, pp. 518, 523–5.
13. A. L. Lowell, *The Government of England* (2 vols., 1910), I, p. 214; E. H. H. Green, 'Radical Conservatism: The Electoral Genesis of Tariff Reform', *H.J.*, XXVIII (1985), pp. 674–8.
14. Jones, *Politics of Reform*, p. 18; M. Bentley, *Politics Without Democracy: Great Britain, 1815–1914* (1984), pp. 250–1; B. M. Walker, 'The Irish Electorate, 1868–1915' *Irish Historical Studies*, XVIII (1973), pp. 365–6; K. O. Morgan, *Rebirth of a Nation: Wales, 1880–1980* (1981), pp. 27–8.
15. Blewett, 'Franchise in the United Kingdom', p. 27; G. H. L. Le May, *The Victorian Constitution: Conventions, Usages and Contingencies* (1979), p. 187.
16. Read, *England, 1868–1914*, pp. 310, 317; Matthew *et al.*, 'The Franchise Factor and the Rise of the Labour Party', p. 724; C. W. Boyd (ed.), *Mr. Chamberlain's Speeches* (2 vols., 1914), I, p. 131.
17. Green, 'Radical Conservatism', p. 670, note 11; Phillips, *The Diehards*, p. 113.
18. For the high-political manœuvring, see Jones, *Politics of Reform*, *passim*; C. C. Weston, 'The Royal Mediation in 1884', *Eng. Hist. Rev.*, LXXXII (1967), pp. 296–322.
19. Williams, 'Liberal Party and the House of Lords', pp. 143–8, 152–3, 342; Chadwick, 'Role of Redistribution', p. 668.
20. E. Allyn, *Lords Versus Commons: A Century of Conflict and Compromise* (New York, 1931), pp. 117–21; Williams, 'Liberal Party and the House of Lords', pp. 144, 338–44.
21. J. M. Davidson, *The Book of Lords* (1884), p. 78; Williams, Liberal Party and the House of Lords, pp. 146, 339–42; Jones, *Politics of Reform*, pp. 163–4.
22. Williams, 'Liberal Party and the House of Lords', pp. 343–4; Jones, *Politics of*

Reform, p. 59; J. G. Delapoc, *The House of Lords* (1883), p. 3.

23. Allyn, *Lords Versus Commons*, pp. 121–2; Williams, 'Liberal Party and the House of Lords', pp. 348–9; J. Bryce, 'Do We Need a Second Chamber?', *Contemporary Review*, xlvi (1884), p. 719.

24. For a full discussion, see Le May, *Victorian Constitution*, pp. 133–45; C. C. Weston, 'Salisbury and the Lords, 1868–1895', *H.J.*, xxv (1982), pp. 103–29.

25. R. Taylor, *Lord Salisbury* (1975), pp. 34, 39, 76–7; H. J. Hanham, *The Nineteenth Century Constitution, 1815–1914* (1969), p. 173; Le May, *Victorian Constitution*, pp. 128–33.

26. Weston, 'Salisbury and the Lords', p. 106; Jones, *Politics of Reform*, pp. 58–66.

27. Weston, 'Salisbury and the Lords', p. 116; Allyn, *Lords Versus Commons*, p. 117.

28. Williams, 'Liberal Party and the House of Lords', p. 329.

29. Le May, *Victorian Constitution*, pp. 150–1; Williams, 'Liberal Party and the House of Lords', pp. 238, 350–5.

30. P. Guedalla (ed.), *The Queen and Mr. Gladstone* (2 vols., 1933), ii, pp. 446–52; P. Magnus, *Gladstone: A Biography* (1954), pp. 414–22.

31. G. E. Buckle (ed.), *Letters of Queen Victoria*, 3rd ser. (3 vols, 1930), ii, pp. 447–8; Williams, 'Liberal Party and the House of Lords', pp. 365–8.

32. Allyn, *Lords Versus Commons*, pp. 161–2; Williams, 'Liberal Party and the House of Lords', pp. 371–7.

33. Marsh, *Discipline of Popular Government*, pp. 225–7; Weston, 'Salisbury and the Lords', pp. 124–9.

34. Williams, 'Liberal Party and the House of Lords', p. 329; Marsh, *Discipline of Popular Government*, p. 247.

35. R. Jenkins, *Mr. Balfour's Poodle: An Account of the Struggle Between the House of Lords and the Government of Mr. Asquith* (1968), p. 24; N. Blewett, *The Peers, the Parties and the People: The General Elections of 1910* (1972), pp. 36–42; J. Ramsden, *The Age of Balfour and Baldwin, 1902–1940* (1978), p. 32.

36. Lord Newton, *Lord Lansdowne: A Biography* (1929), pp. 353–5; Hanham, *Nineteenth Century Constitution*, p. 192; Le May, *Victorian Constitution*, p. 190.

37. C. C. Weston, 'The Liberal Leadership

and the Lords Veto, 1907–1910', *H.J.*, xi (1968), pp. 508–35.

38. Jenkins, *Mr. Balfour's Poodle*, pp. 37–48; Allyn, *Lords Versus Commons*, p. 173; Le May, *Victorian Constitution*, p. 191.

39. Jenkins, *Mr. Balfour's Poodle*, pp. 51–4; Allyn, *Lords Versus Commons*, p. 174.

40. Blewett, *The Peers, the Parties and the People*, pp. 45–50; Jenkins, *Mr Balfour's Poodle*, pp. 60–3; Le May, *Victorian Constitution*, p. 193.

41. B. B. Gilbert, *David Lloyd George, A Political Life: The Architect of Change, 1863–1912* (1987), pp. 364–77.

42. J. Grigg, *Lloyd George: The People's Champion, 1902–1911* (1978), p. 177; Blewett, *The Peers, the Parties and the People*, pp. 68–71.

43. Jenkins, *Mr. Balfour's Poodle*, pp. 76, 88–9; Grigg, *The People's Champion*, p. 198.

44. Allyn, *Lords Versus Commons*, p. 180.

45. Le May, *Victorian Constitution*, p. 192; Blewett, *The Peers, the Parties and the People*, p. 75; J. R. Vincent (ed.), *The Crawford Papers: The Journals of David Lindsay, Twenty Seventh Earl of Crawford and Tenth Earl of Balcarres, 1871–1940, During the Years 1892–1940* (1984), pp. 136–7.

46. Gilbert, *Lloyd George*, pp. 384–7, 393–6; Grigg, *The People's Champion*, pp. 203–13.

47. Gilbert, *Lloyd George*, pp. 386, 396; Grigg, *The People's Champion*, pp. 225–6.

48. Ramsden, *Age of Balfour and Baldwin*, p. 33; Jenkins, *Mr. Balfour's Poodle*, pp. 91–106; Weston, 'Salisbury and the Lords', p. 107, note 12.

49. Allyn, *Lords Versus Commons*, pp. 183–4; Lady V. Hicks Beach, *The Life of Sir Michael Hicks Beach* (2 vols., 1932), ii, p. 259.

50. Jenkins, *Mr. Balfour's Poodle*, pp. 107–14.

51. Blewett, *The Peers, the Parties and the People*, pp. 103–7, 114–16.

52. Le May, *Victorian Constitution*, p. 197; Jenkins, *Mr. Balfour's Poodle*, pp. 115–20; Blewett, *The Peers, the Parties and the People*, pp. 130–41.

53. Allyn, *Lords Versus Commons*, pp. 192–4; Vincent, *Crawford Papers*, pp. 143–50; R. Jenkins, *Asquith* (1967 edn.), pp. 227–34.

54. Jenkins, *Mr. Balfour's Poodle*, pp. 144–5; P. Magnus, *King Edward VII* (1967), pp. 530–50, 552–7.

55. Jenkins, *Mr. Balfour's Poodle*, pp. 173–84; Blewett, *The Peers, the Parties and the People*, pp. 165–8; Le May, *Victorian Constitution*, pp. 203–12. For the (unhappy) part played by George V during the latter part of the crisis, see: H. Nicolson, *King George V: His Life and Reign* (1967 edn.), pp. 174–205; K. Rose, *King George V* (1983), pp. 112–25. For a list of possible Liberal peers, see Jenkins, *Asquith*, pp. 606–9.

56. Jenkins, *Mr. Balfour's Poodle*, pp. 187–92, 197–207; Blewett, *The Peers, the Parties and the People*, pp. 169–77, 195–201.

57. Vincent, *Crawford Papers*, pp. 190–1, 195; Jenkins, *Mr. Balfour's Poodle*, pp. 207–27; Newton, *Lord Lansdowne*, pp. 418–25.

58. Vincent, *Crawford Papers*, pp. 196–7, 200–19; D. B. Southern, 'Lord Newton, the Conservative Peers and the 1911 Parliament Act', in C. Jones and D. L. Jones (eds.), *Peers, Politics and Power: The House of Lords, 1603–1911* (1986), pp. 519–27.

59. Jenkins, *Mr. Balfour's Poodle*, pp. 251–68.

60. Ramsden, *Age of Balfour and Baldwin*, pp. 38–9.

61. Spring, 'Land and Politics in Edwardian England', pp. 33–4.

62. F. M. L. Thompson, 'Land and Politics in the Nineteenth Century', *Transactions of the Royal Historical Society*, 5th ser., xv (1965), pp. 23–44; D. Martin, 'Land Reform', in P. Hollis (ed.), *Pressure from Without in Early Victorian England* (1974), pp. 131–58.

63. A. Offer, *Property and Politics, 1871–1914* (1981), pp. 36, 152.

64. L. Stone and J. C. Fawtier Stone, *An Open Elite? England, 1540–1880* (1984), pp. 416–17.

65. D. Spring, 'Introduction', in J. Bateman, *The Great Landowners of Great Britain and Ireland* (4th edn., reprinted 1971), pp. 8–13, 16–19.

66. J. R. Fisher, 'Public Opinion and Agriculture, 1875–1900' (Ph.D. dissertation, Hull University, 1972), pp. 471–3.

67. P. H. Lindert, 'Who Owned Victorian England?' (Working Paper Series, no. 12, 1983, Agricultural History Center, University of California, Davis), Appendixes C1 and C2. See also below, Appendix A.

68. Offer, *Property and Politics*, pp. 150–2;

Fisher, 'Public Opinion and Agriculture', p. 589.

69. A systematic attempt was also made to map London's great estates by John Wood, of the Municipal Reform League. It was taken over by the LCC in 1892, but was terminated during the First World War, when nearly completed. See R. Hyde, 'Mapping London's Landlords: *The Ground Plan of London, 1892–1915*', *Guildhall Studies in London History*, i (1973), pp. 28–34.

70. D. Cannadine, *Lords and Landlords: The Aristocracy and the Towns, 1774–1967* (1980), pp. 49–50; D. Reeder, 'The Politics of Urban Leaseholds in Late Victorian England', *International Review of Social History*, vi (1961), pp. 414–20; F. Banfield, *The Great Landlords of London* (1888), pp. 53–4, 72–6, 107.

71. R. C. K. Ensor, 'Some Political and Economic Interactions in Later Victorian England', *Transactions of the Royal Historical Society*, 4th ser., xxxi (1949), pp. 17–29.

72. R. F. Foster, *Modern Ireland, 1600–1972* (1988), pp. 402–15. For a valuable survey of the extensive literature on the Land War, see L. P. Curtis, Jr., 'On Class and Class Conflict in the Land War', *Irish Economic and Social History*, viii (1981), pp. 86–94.

73. R. Douglas, *Land, People and Politics: A History of the Land Question in the United Kingdom, 1878–1952* (1976), p. 27.

74. L. P. Curtis, Jr., *Coercion and Conciliation in Ireland, 1880–1892: A Study in Constructive Unionism* (Princeton, 1963), pp. 239–58.

75. D. W. Crowley, 'The "Crofters' Party", 1885–1892', *Scottish Historical Review*, xxxv (1956), pp. 110–26; H. J. Hanham, 'The Problem of Highland Discontent, 1880–1885', *Transactions of the Royal Historical Society*, 5th ser., xix (1970), pp. 21–65; J. P. D. Dunbabin, *Rural Discontent in Nineteenth-Century Britain* (1974), pp. 181–95.

76. Douglas, *Land, People and Politics*, p. 67.

77. C. E. Dewey, 'Celtic Agrarian Legislation and the Celtic Revival: Historicist Implications of Gladstone's Irish and Scottish Land Acts, 1870–1886', *P. & P.*, no. 64 (1974), pp. 50–5; I. M. McPhail, 'Prelude to the Crofters' War, 1870–80', *Transactions of the Gaelic Society of Inverness*, xlix (1975), pp. 167–73.

78. J. Hunter, 'The Politics of Highland Land Reform', *Scottish Historical Review*, LIII (1974), p. 57; J. Hunter, 'The Gaelic Connection: The Highlands, Ireland and Nationalism, 1873–1922', *Scottish Historical Review*, LIV (1975), p. 187.

79. K. O. Morgan, *Wales in British Politics, 1868–1922* (1970), pp. 94–6.

80. P. Jones-Evans, 'Evan Pan Jones – Land Reformer', *Welsh History Review*, IV (1968), pp. 143–59.

81. Morgan, *Wales in British Politics*, pp. 84–90.

82. D. W. Howell, *Land and People in Nineteenth-Century Wales* (1977), pp. 42, 85–9.

83. F. A. Channing, *The Truth About Agricultural Depression* (1897), p. 93; H. J. Perkin, 'Land Reform and Class Conflict in Victorian Britain', in J. Butt and I. F. Clarke (eds.), *The Victorians and Social Protest* (1973), pp. 191–201.

84. Fisher, 'Public Opinion and Agriculture', pp. 179–90, 536–41; Offer, *Property and Politics*, pp. 184–6; N. H. Pollock, 'The English Game Laws in the Nineteenth Century', (Ph.D. dissertation, Johns Hopkins University, 1968), pp. 297–303; A. Peacock, 'Land Reform, 1880–1914', (M.A. dissertation, Southampton University, 1961), pp. 29–59.

85. Offer, *Property and Politics*, pp. 154–7; Reeder, 'Politics of Urban Leaseholds', pp. 420–7.

86. Cannadine, *Lords and Landlords*, pp. 49–50, 190–4.

87. P. Adelman, *Victorian Radicalism: The Middle Class Experience, 1830–1914* (1984), p. 9; J. D. Wood, 'Transatlantic Land Reform: America and the Crofters' Revolt, 1878–1888', *Scottish Historical Review*, LXIII (1984), 79–103; J. Hunter, 'The Gaelic Connection: The Highlands, Ireland and Nationalism, 1873–1922', *Scottish Historical Review*, LIV (1975), pp. 178–96.

88. W. E. Vaughan, *Landlords and Tenants in Ireland, 1848–1904* (1984), pp. 13–26; E. Richards, *A History of the Highland Clearances*, vol. I (1982), pp. 7–11, 29–32; Howell, *Land and People of Nineteenth-Century Wales*, pp. 43–5, 64–5, 68–71, 85–91; Cannadine, *Lords and Landlords*, pp. 391–412.

89. The Duke of Bedford, *A Great Agricultural Estate* (1987); J. W. Mason, 'The Duke of Argyll and the Land Question in Late Nineteenth-Century Britain', *Victorian Studies*, XXI (1978), pp. 149–70; F. M. L. Thompson, *English Landed Society in the Nineteenth Century* (1963), p. 300.

90. Read, *England, 1868–1914*, pp. 118, 314.

91. Blewett, *The Peers, the Parties and the People*, p. 5; Adelman, *Victorian Radicalism*, p. 9.

92. Marsh, *Discipline of Popular Government*, p. 80.

93. Green, 'Radical Conservatism', p. 692.

94. F. S. L. Lyons, *Ireland Since the Famine* (1971), pp. 163–5, 94; M. J. Winstanley, *Ireland and the Land Question, 1800–1922* (1984), pp. 37–8.

95. Dunbabin, *Rural Discontent*, pp. 178–80; the Duke of Argyll, 'The New Irish Land Bill', *19C*, IX (1881), p. 883.

96. Curtis, *Coercion and Conciliation*, pp. 169, 336; Lyons, *Ireland Since the Famine*, pp. 174, 181.

97. Winstanley, *Ireland and the Land Question*, pp. 39–41; Lyons, *Ireland Since the Famine*, pp. 199, 213–16.

98. Douglas, *Land, People and Politics*, p. 54; A. Warren, 'Gladstone, Land and Social Reconstruction in Ireland, 1881–1887', *Parliamentary History*, II (1983), pp. 153–73.

99. Adelman, *Victorian Radicalism*, p. 107; Allyn, *Lords Versus Commons*, p. 112.

100. Curtis, *Coercion and Conciliation*, pp. 45, 344.

101. Hogg, 'Landed Society and the Conservative Party', p. 260; Curits, *Coercion and Conciliation*, pp. 133, 217; Douglas, *Land, People and Politics*, p. 81.

102. *E.G.*, 9 March 1895, 1 Aug. 1896, 19 Dec. 1896; 10 July 1897; 2 Aug. 1902; P. Davis, 'The Liberal Unionist Party and the Irish Policy of Lord Salisbury's Government, 1886–1892', *H.J.*, XVIII (1975), p. 103.

103. Hogg, 'Landed Society and the Conservative Party', pp. 263–5; Phillips, *The Diehards*, p. 117; C. B. Shannon, 'Local Government in Ireland: The Politics and Administration' (M.A. dissertation, University College, Dublin, 1963), pp. 103–9.

104. *E.G.*, 29 Sept. 1894, 19 Jan. 1907; A. W. Hoskin, 'The Genesis and Significance of the 1886 Split in the Liberal Party' (Ph.D dissertation, Cambridge University), 1964, p. 82.

105. R. E. Prothero, 'English Land, Law and Labour', *Edinburgh Review*, CLXV (1887), p. 20.

106. Hunter, 'Politics of Highland Land Reform', p. 55.

107. J. Brown, 'Scottish and English Land Legislation, 1905–11', *Scottish Historical Review*, XLVI (1968), pp. 80–5.

108. Richards, *Highland Clearances*, pp. 493, 495.

109. Hunter, 'Politics of Highland Land Reform', p. 56; Richards, *Highland Clearances*, pp. 487, 501.

110. A. Adonis, 'Aristocracy, Ariculture and Liberalism: The Politics, Finances and Estates of the Third Lord Carrington', *H.J.*, XXXI (1988), p. 890.

111. Morgan, *Wales in British Politics*, pp. 123–9, 178.

112. Reeder, 'Politics of Urban Leaseholds', pp. 427–9.

113. Fisher, 'Public Opinion and Agriculture', pp. 578–80; Pollock, 'English Game Laws', pp. 308–15.

114. J. R. McQuiston, 'Tenant Right: Farmer Against Landlord in Victorian England', *Agricultural History*, XLVII (1973), pp. 106–13.

115. Thompson, 'Land and Politics', pp. 43–4; Douglas, *Land, People and Politics*, pp. 43–4; Offer, *Property and Politics*, pp. 352–9.

116. Adonis, 'Aristocracy, Agriculture and Liberalism', pp. 893–5; Brown, 'Scottish and English Land Legislation', pp. 73–9; Douglas, *Land, People and Politics*, pp. 122–3.

117. Adelman, *Victorian Radicalism*, pp. 129–30; A. Sykes, *Tariff Reform in British Politics, 1903–1913* (1979), p. 15.

118. Adelman, *Victorian Radicalism*, p. 142.

119. B. B. Gilbert, 'David Lloyd George: Land, the Budget and Social Reform', *A.H.R.*, LXXXI (1976), pp. 1058–66.

120. Douglas, *Land, People and Politics*, pp. 141, 155.

121. J. Grigg, *Lloyd George: From Peace to War, 1912–1916* (1985), pp. 34–42, 91–105.

122. B. B. Gilbert, 'David Lloyd George: The Reform of British Landholding and the Budget of 1914', *H.J.*, XXI (1978), pp. 117–41; H. V. Emy, 'The Land Campaign: Lloyd George as Social Reformer', in A. J. P. Taylor (ed.), *Lloyd George: Twelve Essays* (1971), pp. 35–68; R. Douglas, 'God Gave Land to the People', in A. J. A. Morris (ed.), *Ed-*

wardian Radicalism (1974), pp. 148–61.

123. Douglas, *Land, People and Politics*, pp. 160, 165; Offer, *Property and Politics*, pp. 37–8.

124. Reeder, 'Politics of Urban Leaseholds', pp. 429–30; Adelman, *Victorian Radicalism*, pp. 145–6; Offer, *Property and Politics*, pp. 385–98.

125. Thompson, *English Landed Society*, p. 334.

126. A. Lambert, *Unquiet Souls: The Indian Summer of the British Aristocracy, 1880–1918* (1984), pp. 155, 185–6.

127. C. Dakers, *The Countryside at War, 1914–18* (1987), p. 87; the Marchioness Curzon, *Reminiscences* (1955), p. 55; G. Dangerfield, *The Strange Death of Liberal England* (1970 edn.), p. 372.

128. Marchioness of Londonderry, *Retrospect* (1938), p. 148; Lionel, Lord Tennyson, *From Verse to Worse* (1933), p. 7; O. Mosley, *My Life* (1968), p. 44.

129. N. Mosley, *Julian Grenfell: His Life and the Times of His Death, 1885–1915* (1976), p. 230; Viscountess Barrington, *Through Eighty Years (1855–1935)* (1936), p. 199; Duchess of Atholl, *Working Partnership* (1958), p. 80.

130. M. Beard, *English Landed Society in the Twentieth Century* (1989), p. 30; Lady A. Gordon-Lennox (ed.), *The Diary of Lord Bertie of Thame, 1914–1918* (2 vols., 1924), I, p. 223.

131. Lord Crewe, *Lord Rosebery* (New York, 1931), p. 534; R. S. Churchill, *Lord Derby: 'King' of Lancashire* (1959), p. 184; D. Sutherland, *The Yellow Earl* (1965), pp. 181–7.

132. D. Mitchell, *Monstrous Regiment: The Story of the Women of the First World War* (New York, 1965), p. 87; D. Stuart, *Dear Duchess: Millicent, Duchess of Sutherland, 1867–1955* (1982), pp. 125–8.

133. Atholl, *Working Partnership*, pp. 81–2; Lambert, *Unquiet Souls*, p. 179.

134. D. Cannadine, 'War and Death, Grief and Mourning in Modern Britain', in J. Whaley (ed.), *Mirrors of Mortality* (1981), pp. 195–7; M. Girouard, *The Return to Camelot: Chivalry and the English Gentleman* (1981), pp. 276–83.

135. G. W. E. Russell, *The Spirit of England* (1915), pp. 93, 119; Lambert, *Unquiet Souls*, p. 162.

136. M. Bence-Jones, *Twilight of the Ascendancy* (1987), p. 168; R. Pound, *The Lost*

Generation (1964), p. 79.

137. Lambert, *Unquiet Souls*, p. 172; Girouard, *Return to Camelot*, pp. 273–4; 283; J. Stevenson, *British Society, 1914–45* (1984), p. 53.

138. Gordon-Lennox, *Diary of Lord Bertie*, I, pp. 175, 223; Pound, *Lost Generation*, pp. 125–6, 159–70, 191–5; Girouard, *Return to Camelot*, p. 287.

139. Pound, *Lost Generation*, pp. 211–19; Bence-Jones, *Twilight of the Ascendancy*, p. 170; Lambert, *Unquiet Souls*, pp. 190–1; Lady C. Asquith, *Diaries, 1915–1918* (1987 edn.), pp. 90, 97.

140. Lambert, *Unquiet Souls*, p. 194; Dakers, *Countryside at War*, p. 94; Asquith, *Diaries*, p. 182; P. Ziegler, *Lady Diana Cooper* (1981), p. 77; Girouard, *Return to Camelot*, p. 287.

141. H. M. Hyde, *The Londonderrys: A Family Portrait* (1979), p. 127; R. Pound and G. Harmsworth, *Northcliffe* (1959), p. 621.

142. Pound, *Lost Generation*, pp. 107–9.

143. Asquith, *Diaries*, p. 370; Gordon-Lennox, *Diary of Lord Bertie*, II, p. 105.

144. Tennyson, *From Verse to Worse*, p. 173; Beard, *English Landed Society in the Twentieth Century*, p. 32; Lady Diana Cooper, *The Rainbow Comes and Goes* (1958), pp. 133–5.

145. Mitchell, *Monstrous Regiment*, pp. 91–106; Stuart, *Dear Duchess*, pp. 129–31, 132–42.

146. Vincent, *Crawford Papers*, p. 349.

147. Londonderry, *Retrospect*, pp. 97–124; Hyde, *The Londonderrys*, pp. 130–1; A. Marwick, *Women at War, 1914–1918* (1977), pp. 79–81.

148. Mitchell, *Monstrous Regiment*, pp. 229–43.

149. Cooper, *Rainbow Comes and Goes*, pp. 116–18, 142–9; Ziegler, *Diana Cooper*, pp. 75–6; Lambert, *Uniquet Souls*, p. 192.

150. Newton, *Lord Lansdowne*, pp. 463–8; C. F. G. Masterman, *England After the War* (1922), p. 20.

151. Newton, *Lord Lansdowne*, pp. 469–82; Vincent, *Crawford Papers*, pp. 348, 381.

152. H. Macmillan, *Past Masters: Politics and Politicians, 1906–1939* (1975), pp. 192–3, 197; Newton, *Lord Lansdowne*, pp. 442–6; P. M. Kennedy, *The Realities Behind Diplomacy: Background Influences on British External Policy, 1865–1980* (1981), p. 161.

153. R. Skidelsky, *Oswald Mosley* (1975), p. 66; Lord Chandos, *From Peace to War: A Study in Contrasts, 1857–1918* (1968),

154. D. Fraser, *Alanbrooke* (1982), p. 81; Dakers, *Countryside at War*, p. 104; W. S. Churchill, *The World Crisis: The Aftermath* (1929), p. 19.

155. For a complete list of fatalities among peers and sons of peers, see G. E. Cokayne, *The Complete Peerage* (new edn., ed. by the Hon. V. Gibbs, 13 vols, 1910–53), VIII, Appendix F, pp. 759–826.

156. Mabel, Countess of Airlie, *Thatched with Gold* (1962), pp. 92–3, 140; S. Aster, *Anthony Eden* (1976), pp. 5–6; Bence-Jones, *Twilight of the Ascendancy*, pp. 170–1.

157. K. Rose, *The Later Cecils* (1975), pp. 119, 149, 222–3, 304; J. M. Lee, *Social Leaders and Public Persons: A Study of County Government in Cheshire Since 1888* (1963), p. 103.

158. Pound, *Lost Generation*, pp. 211–13; Crewe, *Rosebery*, p. 536; Sir A. Fitzroy, *Memoirs* (2 vols., 1925), II, p. 634.

159. Pound, *Lost Generation*, p. 118; Lord Henry Bentinck, *Tory Democracy* (1918), p. 2.

160. Curzon, *Reminiscences*, pp. 85–6; Thompson, *English Landed Society in the Nineteenth Century*, p. 331; D. Hart Davis (ed.), *End of an Era: Letters and Journals of Sir Alan Lascelles, 1887–1920* (1986), p. 258.

161. Stevenson, *British Society*, pp. 331–2; Masterman, *England After the War*, pp. 27–47; G. R. Searle, *Corruption in British Politics, 1895–1930* (1987), pp. 292–3.

162. Masterman, *England After the War*, pp. 28, 31–3.

163. Russell, *Spirit of England*, p. 258.

164. Mosley, *Julian Grenfell*, pp. 236, 239; Chandos, *From Peace to War*, pp. 163, 171, 198; N. Nicolson, *Alex: The Life of Field Marshal Earl Alexander of Tunis* (1973), p. 33.

165. R. Whol, *The Generation of 1914* (1980), pp. 113–15.

166. Beard, *English Landed Society in the Twentieth Century*, pp. 26–8.

167. Hyde, *The Londonderrys*, p. 126; Earl of Swinton, *Sixty Years of Power* (1966), pp. 223–4; A. H. Brodrick, *Near To Greatness: A Life of the Sixth Earl Winterton* (1965), pp. 163, 167.

168. R. Rhodes James, *Anthony Eden* (1986), pp. 29–58; J. Stuart, *Within the Fringe* (1967), pp. 5–32; Lord Chandos, *The*

Memoirs of Lord Chandos (1962), pp. 31–6, 81, 91, 100; Rose, Later Cecils, p. 68.

169. J. Winter, The Great War and the British People (1985), pp. 92–9; Lambert, Unquiet Souls, pp. 186–8.

170. Stevenson, British Society, pp. 94–6; Beard, English Landed Society in the Twentieth Century, p. 25; J. M. Winter, 'Upper Class Casualties', London Review of Books, 5 March 1987, pp. 4–5; N. Hamilton, Monty: The Making of a General, 1887–1942 (1981), p. 108.

171. Stuart, Dear Duchess, p. 126; Ziegler, Diana Cooper, pp. 49, 92–3; Lambert, Unquiet Souls, pp. 174, 179.

172. Spring, 'Land and Politics in Edwardian England', p. 42; Lambert, Unquiet Souls, p. 146; Girouard, Return to Camelot, pp. 291–3.

173. Gordon-Lenox, Diary of Lord Bertie, II, p. 67.

174. Searle, Corruption in British Politics, p. 301.

175. Crewe, Rosebery, p. 536; Newton, Lord Lansdowne, p. 443; Lady F. Balfour, Lord Balfour of Burleigh (1924), pp. 175–7.

176. Lambert, Unquiet Souls, p. 201; Mosley, Julian Grenfell, p. 266; Lady Desborough, Pages from a Family Journal, 1885–1915 (1916); Countess of Wemyss, A Family Record (1932); F. Horner, Time Remembered (1933); E. Waugh, Brideshead Revisited (1962 edn.), pp. 105–6.

177. Asquith, Diaries, p. 480; Bence-Jones, Twilight of the Ascendancy, p. 168.

178. Lambert, Unquiet Souls, p. 166.

179. J. Pearson, Façades: Edith, Osbert and Sacheverell Sitwell (1978), p. 88.

180. R. Lacey, Aristocrats (1984), p. 178.

181. S. Gwynn, The Letters and Friendships of Sir Cecil Spring-Rice: A Record (2 vols., 1929), II, pp. 323–4, 432–3.

Chapter 3

1. F. M. L. Thompson, English Landed Society in the Nineteenth Century (1963), pp. 332–3.

2. C. M. Gaskell, 'The Country Gentleman', 19C, XII (1882), p. 465.

3. W. E. H. Lecky, The Map of Life: Conduct and Character (1901 edn.), p. 294.

4. W. D. Rubinstein, 'Introduction', and F. C. Jaher, 'The Gilded Elite: American Multimillionaires, 1865 to the Present', in W. D. Rubinstein (ed.), Wealth and the Wealthy in the Modern World (1980), pp. 18–20, 197–200, 220–3.

5. W. D. Rubinstein, Men of Property: The Very Wealthy in Britain Since the Industrial Revolution (1981), pp. 40–3.

6. J. Camplin, The Rise of the Rich (New York, 1979), pp. 28–39.

7. Rubinstein, Men of Property, pp. 60, 74.

8. D. Spring, 'Land and Politics in Edwardian England', Agricultural History, LVII (1984), p. 23.

9. Rubinstein, Men of Property, pp. 38–9; Camplin, Rise of the Rich, p. 150.

10. P. J. Perry, 'Introduction', in P. J. Perry (ed.), British Agriculture, 1875–1914 (1973), p. xiv.

11. Anon., 'Twenty Years Movement in Agriculture', Blackwoods, CXLIV (1888), p. 865.

12. Perry, 'Introduction', p. xiv.

13. E.G., 20 June 1931.

14. Lord Egerton of Tatton, 'Agricultural Depression and its Remedies', National Review, VII (1886), p. 754.

15. For one example, the estates of Lord Harrowby, see F. M. Reid, 'Economic and Social Aspects of Landownership in the Nineteenth Century' (B.Litt dissertation, Oxford University, 1956), p. 93.

16. M. Olson and C. C. Harris, 'Free Trade in Corn: A Statistical Study of the Prices and Production of Wheat in Great Britain from 1873 to 1914', in Perry, British Agriculture, p. 170.

17. E.G., 9 Aug. 1902; B. L. Solow, The Land Question and the Irish Economy, 1870–1903 (1971), pp. 174–5; J. S. Donnelly, The Land and the People of Nineteenth-Century Cork (1975), p. 382.

18. E.G., 3 Feb. 1917.

19. The Earl of Powis reduced his rents by 20 per cent during the Great Depression, raised them by 15 per cent after the First World War, but by the early 1930s was giving renewed rebates of 10 per cent in successive years: E.G., 24 Jan. 1920, 10 Sept. 1932.

20. E.G., 9 Aug. 1890, 5 May 1917.

21. The Spectator, 20 Nov. 1880.

22. J. J. MacGregor, 'The Economic History of Two Rural Estates in Cambridgeshire, 1870–1934', Journal of the Royal Agricultural Society, XCVIII (1937), pp. 146, 151; D. Cannadine, 'The Landowner as Millionaire: The Finances of the Dukes of Devonshire, c1800 to 1926', Agricultural History Review, XXV (1977), pp. 87, 97.

23. Solow, *Land Question*, p. 146.

24. *The Economist*, 12 June 1897, pp. 839–40.

25. A. Arnold, 'The Indebtedness of the Country Gentry', *Contemporary Review*, XLVII (1885), p. 228; B. E. Supple, *The Royal Exchange Assurance: A History of British Insurance, 1720–1970* (1971), pp. 337–8.

26. D. Cannadine, 'The Aristocracy and the Towns in the Nineteenth Century: A Case Study of the Calthorpes and Birmingham, 1807–1910' (D.Phil. dissertation, Oxford University, 1975), p. 153; H. Rider Haggard, *Rural England* (2 vols., 1902), I, pp. 320–1.

27. Donnelly, *Cork*, p. 304; D. Cannadine, 'Aristocratic Indebtedness in the Nineteenth Century: The Case Re-Opened', *EC.H.R.*, 2nd ser., XXX (1977), p. 646; L. P. Curtis, 'Incumbered Wealth: Landed Indebtedness in Post-Famine Ireland', *A.H.R.*, LXXXIV (1980), p. 341.

28. Cannadine, 'Landlord as Millionaire', p. 87; Solow, *Land Question*, p. 185. For the general background to the Devonshires' Irish estates, see L. Proudfoot, 'The Management of a Great Estate: Patronage, Income and Expenditure in the Duke of Devonshire's Irish Property, c. 1816 to 1891', *Irish Economic and Social History*, XIII (1986), pp. 32–55.

29. Anon., 'Landed Incomes and Landed Estates', *Quarterly Review*, CLXVI (1888), pp. 222–6; Anon., 'Agricultural Depression and its Remedies', *Quarterly Review*, CLXXVI (1893), pp. 524–5; Anon., 'Perish Agriculture', *Quarterly Review*, CLXXX (1895), p. 422.

30. *E.G.*, 21 Apr. 1894, 8 Oct. 1904.

31. *E.G.*, 26 Oct. 1901, 22 Jan. 1938.

32. *E.G.*, 2 May 1925, 18 Feb. 1928, 22 Jan. 1938.

33. *E.G.*, 20 Aug. 1921.

34. R. S. Churchill, *Lord Derby: 'King' of Lancashire* (1959), pp. 538–9.

35. *E.G.*, 26 Jan. 1918.

36. *E.G.*, 12 Nov. 1921, 31 Oct. 1925.

37. H. Cox, 'Changes in Landownership in England', *Atlantic Monthly*, CXXIX (1922), p. 559.

38. Thompson, *English Landed Society*, p. 328; *E.G.*, 1 Nov. 1924.

39. Thompson, *English Landed Society*, p. 304.

40. H. A. Clemenson, *English Country Houses and Landed Estates* (1982), p. 136.

41. *E.G.*, 9 Aug. 1890.

42. *E.G.*, 2 Dec. 1899; R. J. Colyer, 'The Pryse Family of Gogerddan and the Decline of a Great Estate, 1800–1960', *Welsh History Review*, IX (1979), pp. 418–19.

43. *E.G.*, 4 Jan. 1890, 3 Jan. 1891; J. R. Vincent (ed.), *The Later Derby Diaries: Home Rule, Liberal Unionism and Aristocratic Life in Late Victorian England* (1981), p. 8.

44. *E.G.*, 9 June 1894; Reid, 'Landownership', pp. 86, 94.

45. S. W. Martins, *A Great Estate at Work: The Holkham Estate and its Inhabitants in the Nineteenth Century* (1980), pp. 97, 272; S. Farrant, 'The Management of Four Estates in the Lower Ouse Valley and Agricultural Change, 1840–1920', *Southern History*, I (1979), p. 160; *E.G.*, 2 Mar. 1935.

46. T. W. Beastall, *A North Country Estate: The Lumleys and Saundersons as Landowners, 1600–1900* (1975), pp. 183–200; D. Cannadine, *Lords and Landlords: The Aristocracy and the Towns, 1774–1967* (1980), pp. 66, 321–32, 422.

47. R. J. Waller, *The Dukeries Transformed: The Social and Political Development of a Twentieth-Century Coalfield* (1983), pp. 3, 12–14, 70–1.

48. J. Franklin, *The Gentleman's Country House and its Plan, 1835–1914* (1981), pp. 24–38; C. Aslet, *The Last Country Houses* (1982), pp. 309–32.

49. Aslet, *Country Houses*, p. 38.

50. *E.G.*, 14 Jan. 1921.

51. J. Pearson, *Façades: Edith, Osbert and Sacheverell Sitwell* (1978), pp. 134–6, 177–8, 205–6.

52. *E.G.*, 11 Nov. 1911.

53. C. F. Kolbert and T. O'Brien, *Land Reform in Ireland: A Legal History of the Irish Land Problem and its Settlement* (Cambridge University, Dept. of Land Economy, Occasional Papers, no. 3, 1975), pp. 33–8.

54. Donnelly, *Cork*, pp. 306, 307–1.

55. *E.G.*, 8 Aug. 1885, 16 Jan. 1886; Solow, *Land Question*, p. 185.

56. *E.G.*, 28 Aug. 1886, 6 July 1889; Curtis, 'Incumbered Wealth', pp. 357–60.

57. Solow, *Land Question*, p. 167.

58. Donnelly, *Cork*, p. 384.

59. *E.G.*, 3 Oct. 1903, 7 Nov. 1903; Curtis, 'Incumbered Wealth', p. 360; G. D. Phillips, *The Diehards: Aristocratic Society and Politics in Edwardian England* (1979), p. 49.

60. Solow, *Land Question*, p. 193; J. E. Pomfret, *The Struggle for Land in Ireland, 1800–1923* (Princeton, 1930), p. 307; L. P. Curtis, 'The Anglo-Irish Predicament', *Twentieth-Century Studies*, IV (1978), p. 45.

61. Kolbert and O'Brien, *Land Reform*, p. 45.

62. Kolbert and O'Brien, *Land Reform*, pp. 55–6, 62.

63. *E.G.*, 29 June 1929; Marquess of Lansdowne, *Glanerought and the Petty-Fitzmaurices* (1937), p. 215.

64. N. Nicolson (ed.), *Harold Nicolson: Diaries and Letters, 1939–1945* (1967), pp. 216–17.

65. *E.G.*, 3 Jan. 1891; D. W. Howell, *Land and People in Nineteenth-Century Wales* (1977), p. 24.

66. *E.G.*, 2 Jan. 1897, 11 June 1898, 15 Oct. 1898; J. Davies, 'The End of Great Estates and the Rise of Freehold Farming in Wales', *Welsh History Review*, VII (1974), pp. 189–90.

67. *E.G.*, 30 Dec. 1911, 8 June 1912, 31 Oct. 1914, 2 Jan. 1915; Davies, 'Great Estates', p. 191.

68. Howell, *Land and People*, p. 24; Davies, 'Great Estates', pp. 191–2.

69. *E.G.*, 26 Jan. 1918, 14 June 1919, 3 Jan. 1920, 1 Jan. 1921.

70. Davies, 'Great Estates', pp. 193–4.

71. *E.G.* 26 Apr. 1930, 2 July 1938, 17 Dec. 1938; Howell, *Land and People*, p. 25.

72. Davies, 'Great Estates', pp. 194, 212; K. O. Morgan, *Rebirth of a Nation: Wales, 1880–1980* (1981), pp. 186–7. For a detailed chronology of estate sales in one Welsh county, see R. J. Colyer, 'The Gentry and the County in Nineteenth-Century Cardiganshire, *Welsh History Review*, X (1981), pp. 532–4.

73. *E.G.*, 25 Aug. 1888, 23 Mar. 1889, 17 Jan. 1891, 2 Jan. 1897; J. Strawhorn and W. Boyd, *Ayrshire* (1951), p. 313.

74. *E.G.*, 1 Aug. 1887; 13 Aug. 1892, 5 Aug. 1899; H. Hamilton, *Aberdeen* (1960), p. 615; H. Hamilton, *Banff* (1961), p. 193.

75. *E.G.*, 7 May 1910, 11 June 1910.

76. *E.G.*, 10 Dec. 1910, 7 Jan. 1911, 30 Dec, 1911, 4 July 1914, 11 August 1914; Hamilton, *Aberdeen*, p. 527.

77. *E.G.*, 6 Jan. 1917.

78. *E.G.*, 14 and 28 Sept. 1918, 4 Jan. 1919, 8 Mar. 1919, 3 Jan. 1920; Sir F. Lindley, *Lord Lovat: A Biography* (1935), p. 241.

79. *E.G.*, 1 Jan. 1921, 2 July 1921, 31 Dec. 1921, 9 and 30 Sept. 1922, 30 Dec. 1922;

Hamilton, *Aberdeen*, p. 361; Strawhorn and Boyd, *Ayrshire*, p. 711; D. B. Taylor, *Perth and Kinross* (1979), p. 173.

80. Hamilton, *Aberdeen*, pp. 585, 620, 626; Hamilton, *Banff*, p. 401; R. C. Rennie and T. C. Gordon, *Stirling and Clackmannan* (1966), p. 110.

81. *E.G.*, 14 June 1930, 3 Jan. 1931, 13 Feb. 1932, 27 May 1933, 11 May 1935, 8 Feb. 1936, 13 Nov. 1937.

82. *E.G.*, 5 Jan. 1924.

83. *E.G.*, 14 Jan. 1922.

84. *The Times*, 3 Oct. 1885; Thompson, *English Landed Society*, p. 319.

85. *E.G.*, 24 Aug. 1889, 4 Jan. 1890, 3 Jan. 1891, 5 Jan. 1895, 30 Nov. 1901, 7 Jan. 1905.

86. *E.G.*, 9 July 1910.

87. *E.G.*, 15 Oct. 1910, 18 May 1912, 1 Aug. 1914; H. Durant, 'The Development of Landownership with Special Reference to Bedfordshire, 1773–1925', *Sociological Review*, XXVIII (1936), pp. 93–4.

88. *E.G.*, 28 Aug. 1915, 13 Nov. 1915, 1 Dec. 1917, 26 Jan. 1918, 3 Aug. 1918.

89. *E.G.*, 3 Jan. 1920, 1 Jan. 1921.

90. *E.G.*, 31 Dec. 1921, 30 Dec. 1922, 29 Dec. 1923.

91. *E.G.*, 26 Jan. 1929, 3 Jan. 1930, 7 Jan. 1933.

92. *E.G.*, 21 July 1934, 24 Apr. 1937, 14 May 1938, 9 July 1938.

93. Durant, 'Bedfordshire', p. 85.

94. *E.G.*, 5 Jan. 1924.

95. Quoted in Pomfret, *Struggle for Land*, p. vii.

96. W. G. Constable, *Art Collecting in the USA: An Outline of a History* (1964), pp. 96–100; B. Saarinen, *The Proud Possessors: The Lives, Times and Tastes of Some Adventurous American Art Collectors* (New York, 1958), p. 79.

97. G. Redford, *Art Sales* (1888), pp. 262–3, 270–6, 319–45; H. C. Marillier, *Christies, 1766 to 1925* (1926), pp. 51–3, 55–7, 262–3.

98. *The Times*, 9 Aug. 1886; A. L. Rowse, *The Later Churchills* (1971), pp. 237–40, 249–50, 274–7.

99. Marillier, *Christies*, pp. 66, 87, 98, 263–8, 271–2; G. Battiscombe, *The Spencers of Althorp* (1984), p. 237; P. Gordon (ed.), *The Red Earl: The Papers of the Fifth Earl Spencer, 1835–1910* (2 vols., 1981–6), II, *1885–1910*, pp. 194–206.

100. *E.G.*, 20 May 1891, 2 and 9 Dec. 1899, 15 Oct. 1904.

101. *E.G.*, 15 Apr. 1906, 1 Dec. 1910, 7 Oct. 1911; F. Herrmann, *The English as Collectors: A Documentary Chrestomathy* (1972), pp. 375–6.
102. *E.G.*, 8 July 1911; D. A. Brown, *Raphael and America* (Washington, DC, 1983), pp. 31. 79–85.
103. J. R. Vincent (ed.), *The Crawford Papers: The Journals of David Lindsay, Twenty-Seventh Earl of Crawford and Tenth Earl of Balcarres, 1871–1940, During the Years 1892 to 1940* (1984), p. 416; Constable, *Art Collecting*, p. 115; Marillier, *Christies*, p. 180.
104. *E.G.*, 25 Feb. 1928, 8 Feb. 1930, 12 Mar. 1932, 10 Sept. 1938; Brown, *Raphael*, pp. 91–2; Marillier, *Christies*, pp. 50, 284–5.
105. Vincent, *Crawford Papers*, pp. 7, 532.
106. *E.G.*, 16 Nov. 1912.
107. *E.G.*, 25 Oct. 1924; *Viscount Leverhulme*, by his son (1927), pp. 252–3, 267; F. H. W. Sheppard (ed.), *The Survey of London*, XL, *The Grosvenor Estate in Mayfair*, Part II, *The Buildings* (1980), pp. 250, 270–4.
108. Thompson, *English Landed Society*, pp. 335–6; *E.G.*, 13 Sept. 1919, 25 Feb. 1928, 17 Aug. 1929.
109. D. Pearce, *London's Mansions: The Palatial Houses of the Nobility* (1986), p. 195; Vincent, *Crawford Papers*, p. 529; *E.G.*, 22 Sept. 1928, 22 Dec. 1928.
110. *E.G.*, 30 Nov. 1929, 26 July 1930, 31 Oct. 1931, 22 Oct. 1932, 7 Apr. 1934, 3 Aug. 1935, 20 Nov. 1937.
111. *E.G.*, 30 Mar. 1929, 22 Feb. 1930; Vincent, *Crawford Papers*, p. 583; Thompson, *English Landed Society*, pp. 339–40; The Duke of Portland, *Men, Women and Things* (1937), pp. 1–3.
112. Clemenson, *Country Houses*, p. 156.
113. Thompson, *English Landed Society*, p. 333.
114. *E.G.*, 13 Dec. 1930.
115. *E.G.*, 25 Dec. 1929.
116. *E.G.*, 19 June 1926, 9 Apr. 1932, 11 June 1932, 21 Apr. 1938, 29 Apr. 1939; Clemenson, *Country Houses*, pp. 140–1; R. Nevil, *English Country-House Life* (1925), p. 3.
117. *E.G.*, 29 Aug. 1931; R. Strong, M. Binney, J. Harris et al., *The Destruction of the English Country House, 1875–1975* (1974), pp. 188–92.
118. Lansdowne, *Glanerought*, pp. 202–5; D. Fitzpatrick, *Politics and Irish Life, 1913–21* (Dublin, 1977), pp. 78–9.

119. For this paragraph, see J. R. M. Butler, *Lord Lothian, 1882–1940* (1960), pp. 144–53.
120. Clemenson, *Country Houses*, p. 169.
121. *E.G.*, 8 Sept. 1934, 8 June 1935, 29 Feb. 1936, 17 July 1937, 8 Apr. 1939.
122. A. Offer, *Property and Politics, 1870–1914: Landownership, Law, Ideology and Urban Development in England* (1981), p. 157.
123. Cannadine, *Lords and Landlords*, pp. 132–3; Phillips, *Diehards*, p. 34; *E.G.*, 3 Jan. 1903.
124. F. H. W. Sheppard (ed.), *The Survey of London*, vol. XXXVI, *The Parish of St. Paul, Covent Garden* (1970), pp. 48–52.
125. *E.G.*, 11 Apr. 1914, 3 July 1915.
126. Thompson, *English Landed Society*, p. 336; Phillips, *Diehards*, p. 34; *E.G.*, 3 Jan. 1920.
127. *E.G.*, 1 Jan. 1921, 31 Dec, 1921, 12 Sept. 1925; F. H. W. Sheppard (ed.), *The Survey of London*, vol. XXXIX, *The Grosvenor Estate in Mayfair*, Part I, *General Survey* (1977), pp. 67, 72, 76, 78.
128. Cannadine, *Lords and Landlords*, p. 421.
129. C. Stephenson, *The Ramsdens and their Estate in Huddersfield* (1972), pp. 10, 15–16. For the earlier history of the Ramsden estate, see J. Springett, 'Landowners and Urban Development: The Ramsden Estate and Nineteenth-Century Huddersfield', *Journal of Historical Geography*, VIII (1982), pp. 129–44.
130. *E.G.*, 30 May 1925, 26 Nov. 1927, 1 Apr. 1928; T. J. Raybould, *The Economic Emergence of the Black Country: A Study of the Dudley Estate* (1973), pp. 124–8.
131. *E.G.*, 1 Jan. 1927, 25 July 1931, 21 May 1938, 11 Mar. 1939, 24 June 1939.
132. Cannadine, 'Landowner as Millionaire', p. 89.
133. Thompson, *English Landed Society*, p. 264; Phillips, *Diehards*, p. 35; Raybould, *Economic Emergence*, pp. 166–7, 182, 206, 218; J. T. Ward, 'Ayrshire Landed Estates in the Nineteenth Century', *Ayrshire Collection*, 2nd ser., VIII (1969), p. 110; J. T. Ward, 'Landowners and Mining', in J. T. Ward and R. G. Wilson (eds.), *Land and Industry: The Landed Estate and the Industrial Revolution* (1971), p. 69; M. J. Daunton, 'Aristocrat and Traders: The Bute Docks, 1839–1914', *Journal of Transport History*,

new ser., III (1975), pp. 73, 76.

134. Vincent, *Crawford Papers*, pp. 530–1.

135. M. W. Kirby, *The British Coalmining Industry, 1870–1946: A Political and Economic History* (1977), pp. 160–1.

136. I am grateful to Mr Ben Fine, of Birkbeck College, London University, for this information.

137. *E.G.*, 29 Apr. 1894, 31 Dec. 1898.

138. J. T. Ward, *East Yorkshire Landed Estates in the Nineteenth Century* (East Yorkshire Local History Series, no 23, 1967), p. 41.

139. *E.G.*, 5 May 1917, 25 Oct. 1930.

140. *E.G.*, 8 Sept. 1928, 31 Mar. 1934, 12 May 1934, 18 Feb. 1939.

141. For example: S. Leighton, 'The History of a Small Estate in Wales', *National Review*, XXXVI (1900), pp. 379–80; D. Jenkins, *The Agricultural Community in South-West Wales at the Turn of the Twentieth Century* (1971), pp. 13–16.

142. *R.C. On Land In Wales and Monmouthshire* (P. P. 1896, XXXIX), p. 246.

143. Jenkins, *Agricultural Community*, pp. 13–16; R. J. Colyer, 'Nanteos: A Landed Estate in Decline, 1800–1930', *Ceredigion*, IX (1980), pp. 69–73.

144. Solow, *Land Question*, pp. 183–4.

145. Thompson, *English Landed Society*, pp. 66, 129–32, 308; P. F. Brandon, 'A Twentieth-Century Squire in His Landscape', *Southern History*, IV (1982), pp. 192–7.

146. Earl of Airlie, 'Agricultural Prospects', *Fortnightly Review*, XXVI (1879), pp. 110–11.

147. Solow, *Land Question*, p. 183; Curtis, 'Incumbered Wealth', p. 359.

148. Aslet, *Last Country Houses*, p. 58.

149. J. M. Howells, 'The Croswood Estate, 1547–1947', *Ceredigion*, III (1956), p. 81.

150. Colyer, 'Pryse Family' pp. 414, 418–21.

151. *E.G.*, 14 Sept. 1912, 23 Dec. 1933.

152. R. W. Sturgess, 'Landowners, Mining and Urban development in Nineteenth-Century Staffordshire', in Ward and Wilson, *Land and Industry*, pp. 197–200.

153. Offer, *Property and Politics*, p. 362.

154. *E.G.*, 14 Jan. 1911.

155. Spring, 'Land and Politics in Edwardian England', p. 26; Phillips, *Diehards*, pp. 51–2.

156. E. Waugh, *Brideshead Revisited* (1977 edn.), pp. 168–9, 211.

157. Vincent, *Crawford Papers*, pp. 310–13, 315–17, 321, 333.

158. Vincent, *Crawford Papers*, pp. 510, 521,

530, 547.

159. Phillips, *Diehards*, pp. 33–4; J. T. Ward, 'West Riding Landowners and Mining in the Nineteenth Century', *Yorkshire Bulletin of Economic and Social Research*, XV (1963), p. 62.

160. Loulou Harcourt Diary, 23 May 1894. I am grateful to Dr John France for this reference.

161. A. H. Hastie, 'The Estate Duty and the Road Round It', *19C*, XXXVI (1894), pp. 896–7.

162. *E.G.*, 17 and 24 Jan. 1914, 27 Sept. 1924, 4 Feb. 1928, 7 Jan. 1934; Phillips, *Diehards*, p. 46; K. Rose, *The Later Cecils* (1975), p. 102.

163. *E.G.*, 21 Apr. 1894.

164. Thompson, *English Landed Society*, p. 307; Martins, *A Great Agricultural Estate*, pp. 63–5, 267–9; E. Richards, 'An Anatomy of the Sutherland Fortune: Income, Consumption, Investments and Returns, 1780–1880', *Business History*, XXI (1979), p. 54. See also John Buchan, *Law Relating to the Taxation of Foreign Income* (1905).

165. *E.G.*, 1 Oct. 1892, 15 Oct. 1910, 11 Apr. 1911; M. Harrison, *Lord of London: A Biography of the Second Duke of Westminster* (1968), pp. 102, 157, 207–8.

166. Sheppard, *Covent Garden*, pp. 49–52; Phillips, *Diehards*, p. 43.

167. A. Offer, 'Empire and Social Reform: British Overseas Investment and Domestic Politics, 1908–1914', *H.J.*, XXVI (1983), p. 124.

168. Cannadine, 'Landowner as Millionaire', pp. 87–92.

169. F. C. Mather, *After the Canal Duke* (1970), p. 335; C. Grayling, *The Bridgewater Inheritance: The Story of the Bridgewater Estates* (1983), pp. 60–72. For a similar transformation in the income-structure of an aristocrat whose holdings had been almost entirely in agricultural land, see A. Adonis, 'Aristocracy, Agriculture and Liberalism: The Politics, Finances and Estates of the Third Lord Carrington', *H.J.*, XXXI (1988), pp. 880–9. For a fuller treatment of the financial manœuvrings of the super-rich, see R. J. Farrelly, 'The Large Landowners of England and Wales, 1870–1939: An Elite in Transition' (Ph.D. dissertation, Toronto Univ., 1980).

170. *E.G.*, 15 Oct. 1910.

171. H. Macmillan, *Winds of Change, 1919–39* (1966), pp. 188–94.

172. J. R. Vincent, *The Formation of the Liberal Party, 1857–1868* (1966), pp. 212–14.

173. Earl of Ronaldshay, *The Life of Lord Curzon* (3 vols., 1928), III, p. 374.

174. Lady Troubridge and A. Marshall, *John Lord Montagu of Beaulieu: A Memoir* (1930), p. 305.

Chapter 4

1. Lord Eustace Percy, *Some Memories* (1958), p. 12.

2. S. Hogg, 'Landed Society and the Conservative Party in the late Nineteenth and Early Twentieth Centuries' (B. Litt. dissertation, Oxford University, 1972), pp. 132–9.

3. H. J. Hanham, *Elections and Party Management: Politics in the Time of Disraeli and Gladstone* (1959), pp. xvi–xvii.

4. R. J. Olney, *Rural Society and County Government in Nineteenth-Century Lincolnshire* (1979), p. 155; J. Howarth, 'The Liberal Revival in Northamptonshire, 1880–1895: A Case Study in Late Nineteenth-Century Elections', *H.J.*, XII (1969), p. 89; K. O. Morgan, *Rebirth of a Nation: Wales, 1880–1980* (1981), p. 27.

5. For an early account of electioneering under the new system, see Clara E. L. Rayleigh, 'Canvassing Experiences in An Agricultural Constituency', *National Review*, VII (1886), pp. 176–89.

6. *V.C.H., Cheshire*, II (1979), p. 144; H. M. Pelling, *Social Geography of British Elections, 1885–1910* (1967), pp. 380–4.

7. Hogg, 'Landed Society and the Conservative Party', pp. 154–9; W. Whiteley, 'The Social Composition of the House of Commons, 1868–1885', (Ph.D. dissertation, Cornell University, 1960), pp. 564–5; Morgan, *Rebirth of a Nation*, pp. 29–30.

8. *V.C.H., Cheshire*, II, p. 141; Pelling, *Social Geography*, p. 9.

9. Pelling, *Social Geography*, pp. 426–9.

10. R. Quinault, 'Warwickshire Landowners and Parliamentary Politics, 1841–1923' (D.Phil. dissertation, Oxford University, 1975), pp. 291–4.

11. Pelling, *Social Geography*, pp. 355, 366–8, 409–10; K. O. Morgan, 'Cardiganshire Politics: The Liberal Ascendancy, 1885–1923', *Ceredigion*, V (1967), pp. 320–1.

12. Quinault, 'Warwickshire Landowners and Parliamentary Politics', pp. 314–39.

13. Howarth, 'Liberal Revival in Northamptonshire', pp. 78–118; J. Howarth, 'Politics and Society in Late Victorian Northamptonshire', *Northamptonshire Past and Present*, IV (1970–1), pp. 269–74.

14. Pelling, *Social Geography*, pp. 367–8; Morgan, 'Cardiganshire Politics', pp. 328–9.

15. Pelling, *Social Geography*, pp. 12–13, 98, 426–9.

16. Hanham, *Elections and Party Management*, p. 12; N. Blewett, *The Peers, the Parties and the People: The British General Elections of 1910* (1972), pp. 374–6, 402–5.

17. *V.C.H., Cheshire*, II, p. 146.

18. *V.C.H., Wiltshire*, V (1957), p. 313.

19. *V.C.H., Shropshire*, III (1979), pp. 347, 349, 353, 358.

20. Pelling, *Social Geography*, pp. 384, 394, 397, 409–10.

21. I. G. C. Hutchinson, *A Political History of Scotland, 1832–1914: Parties, Elections and Issues* (1986), p. 221.

22. K. O. Morgan, 'Democratic Politics in Glamorgan, 1884–1914', *Morgannwg*, IV (1960), p. 10; K. O. Morgan, 'The Liberal Unionists in Wales', *National Library of Wales Journal*, XVI (1969), pp. 165–7.

23. Morgan, 'Cardiganshire Politics', pp. 323–30.

24. D. Sheets, 'British Conservatism and the Primrose League: The Changing Character of Popular Politics, 1883–1901' (Ph.D. dissertation, Columbia University, 1986), pp. 31–2, 295–6, 306–7.

25. P. Marsh, *The Discipline of Popular Government: Lord Salisbury's Domestic Statecraft, 1881–1902* (1978), pp. 185–6.

26. Pelling, *Social Geography*, p. 11.

27. M. Carmichael, *Lord Carmichael of Skirling: A Memoir* (1929), pp. 70, 81, 87, 95, 259; J. R. Vincent (ed.), *The Crawford Papers: The Journals of David Lindsay, Twenty Seventh Earl of Crawford and Tenth Earl of Balcarres, 1871–1940, During the Years 1892 to 1940* (1984), p. 72.

28. Pelling, *Social Geography*, p. 14.

29. Quinault, 'Warwickshire Landowners and Parliamentary Politics', p. 227; Lord Redesdale, *Memories* (2 vols., 1915), II, p. 732; Lord Willoughby de Broke, *The Sport of Our Ancestors* (1921),

pp. 5–6.

30. Olney, *Rural Society and County Government*, p. 156; E. K. G. Jaggard, 'Patrons, Principles and Parties: Cornwall Politics, 1760–1910' (Ph.D. dissertation, Washington University, St Louis, 1980), p. 423.

31. *V.C.H.*, *Cheshire*, II (1979), p. 144; Quinault, 'Warwickshire Landowners and Parliamentary Politics', pp. 147, 297, 301–3; Hogg, 'Landed Society and the Conservative Party', pp. 170–3.

32. *V.C.H.*, *Shropshire*, III, p. 346.

33. Morgan, *Rebirth of a Nation*, p. 48.

34. *V.C.H.*, *Cheshire*, II, pp. 146.

35. *V.C.H.*, *Huntingdonshire*, II, (1974), p. 59; *V.C.H.*, *Leicestershire*, II (1954), pp. 137–9.

36. Quinault, 'Warwickshire Landowners and Parliamentary Politics', pp. 293–305.

37. Pelling, *Social Geography*, p. 436.

38. P. R. Shorter, 'Electoral Politics and Political Change in the East Midlands of England, 1918–1935' (Ph.D. dissertation, Cambridge University, 1975), pp. 47–9.

39. Shorter, 'Electoral Politics and Political Change', pp. 47, 50–1.

40. Shorter, 'Electoral Politics and Political Change', pp. 51, 94–7.

41. *V.C.H.*, *Shropshire*, III, p. 357.

42. Hanham, *Elections and Party Management*, pp. 164–5.

43. *V.C.H.*, *Leicestershire*, p. 140; *V.C.H.*, *Wiltshire*, p. 313.

44. *V.C.H.*, *Leicestershire*, p. 140.

45. P. J. Madgwick et al., *The Politics of Rural Wales: A Study of Cardiganshire* (1973), pp. 38–40, 46, 51, 143; Morgan, 'Cardiganshire Politics', pp. 334–8.

46. *V.C.H.*, *Cheshire*, II, pp. 144, 148.

47. *V.C.H.*, *Shropshire*, III, pp. 354–8; Shorter, 'Electoral Politics and Political Change', pp. 178–9.

48. C. M. Gaskell, 'The Country Gentleman', *19C*, XII (1882), p. 461.

49. C. H. E. Zangeril, 'The Social Composition of the County Magistracy in England and Wales, 1831–1887', *Journal of British Studies*, XI (1971), p. 115; W. C. Lubenow, 'Social Recruitment and Social Attitudes: The Buckinghamshire Magistrates, 1868–1888', *Huntingdon Library Quarterly*, XL (1977), pp. 249–51, 254, 261–2.

50. *V.C.H.*, *Shropshire*, III, p. 225; Morgan, 'Cardiganshire Politics', p. 32.

51. Zangeril, 'Social Composition of the County Magistracy', p. 124; J. R. Knipe, 'The J.P. in Yorkshire, 1820–1914' (Ph.D. dissertation, University of Wisconsin, 1970), pp. 122, 136, 139–141, 147, 153, 214–16.

52. J. M. Lee, *Social Leaders and Public Persons: A Study of County Government in Cheshire Since 1888* (1963), pp. 14, 16, 19–20, 31–4; Olney, *Rural Society and County Government*, pp. 101–3.

53. J. M. Lee, 'Parliament and the Appointment of Magistrates: The Origin of Advisory Committees', *Parliamentary Affairs*, XIII (1959–60), pp. 88–9.

54. *V.C.H.*, *Shropshire*, III, pp. 224–6; Lee, *Social Leaders*, pp. 226–227.

55. J. S. Shepherd, 'James Bryce and the Recruitment of Working-Class Magistrates in Lancashire, 1892–4', *Bulletin of the Institute of Historical Research*, LII (1979), pp. 155–8.

56. E. Moir, *The Justice of the Peace* (1969), p. 184; Morgan, *Rebirth of a Nation*, p. 53.

57. R. F. V. Heuston, *Lives of the Lord Chancellors*, *1885–1940* (1987 edn.), pp. 153–8.

58. *V.C.H.*, *Shropshire*, III, p. 225; Lee, 'Parliament and the Appointment of Magistrates', pp. 90–3.

59. See Sir W. E. Whyte, *Local Government in Scotland* (2nd edn., 1936), p. 31: 'Although the positions of Lord Lieutenant and Deputy Lieutenant are regarded as positions of high honour, the Lord Lieutenant and his deputies have now no administrative duties in regard to the local government of the county.'

60. For the contemporary debate, see: T. E. Kebbel, 'The County System', *Fortnightly Review*, XXXIII (1883), pp. 417–36; R. A. Cross, 'County Government', *Contemporary Review*, XLIII (1883), pp. 305–10; G. C. Brodrick, 'The Reform of Local Government in the Counties', *Fortnightly Review*, XXXIII (1883), pp. 691–704; W. Rathbone, 'Local Government in England and Wales', *19C*, XIII (1883), pp. 297–313, 509–28.

61. P. A. Moylan, *The Form and Reform of County Government: Kent, 1889–1914* (Leicester University Occasional Papers in Local History, 3rd ser., III, 1978), p. 9; J. P. Dunbabin, 'The Politics of the Establishment of County Councils', *H.J.*, VI (1963), pp. 238–50.

62. Marsh, *Discipline of Popular Government*, p. 162.
63. Moylan, *Form and Reform of County Government*, p. 7.
64. *The Times*, 14 Jan. 1889; J. P. Dunbabin, 'Expectations of the New County Councils, and their Realisation', *H.J.*, VIII (1965), pp. 354–5.
65. F. W. Maitland, 'The Shallows and Silences of Real Life', in H. A. L. Fisher (ed.), *The Collected Papers of F. W. Maitland* (3 vols., 1911), I, p. 472.
66. Dunbabin, 'Expectations of the New County Councils', pp. 360, 370–3. For Lord Spencer's election and activity at first chairman of the Northamptonshire County Council, see P. Gordon (ed.), *The Red Earl: The Papers of the Fifth Earl Spencer, 1835–1910* (2 vols., 1981–6), vol. II, *1885–1910*, pp. 181–93.
67. *Devon Weekly Times*, 25 Jan. 1889.
68. Moylan, *Form and Reform of County Government*, p. 31; B. J. Barber and M. W. Beresford, *The West Riding County Council, 1889–1974: Historical Studies* (1979), pp. 145, 180.
69. Lee, *Social Leaders*, pp. 57–8; S. Drummond, 'The Election of the First Durham County Council', *Public Administration*, XL (1962), p. 149; J. D. Marshall, 'The Government of Lancashire from 1889: Its Roots and Characteristics', in J. D. Marshall (ed.), *The History of Lancashire County Council, 1889 to 1974* (1977), pp. 8–12, 57–8.
70. Olney, *Rural Society and County Government*, pp. 135–9.
71. Morgan, *Rebirth of a Nation*, pp. 52–3.
72. K. O. Morgan, *Wales in British Politics, 1868–1922* (1970), p. 107; *The Times*, 25 Jan. 1889.
73. *The Times*, 26 Jan. 1889.
74. Morgan, 'Cardiganshire Politics', pp. 330–1.
75. Dunbabin, 'Expectations of the New County Councils', p. 355.
76. *The Scotsman*, 6, 7, 8 Feb. 1890.
77. *The Times*, 7 Feb. 1890.
78. *The Scotsman*, 14, 15, 18 Feb. 1890.
79. Lee, *Social Leaders*, pp. 44, 58.
80. Mrs. S. Erskine, *Memoirs of Edward, Earl of Sandwich, 1839–1916* (1919), pp. 195–9, 216–17.
81. *V.C.H., Wiltshire*, v, p. 265.
82. Moyhan, *Form and Reform of County Government*, p. 33; *V.C.H., Shropshire*, III, p. 186.
83. E. R. Davies, *A History of the First Berk-shire County Council* (1981), ch. 54.
84. *V.C.H., Wiltshire*, v, p. 265.
85. *V.C.H., Huntingdonshire*, II, p. 59; *V.C.H., Leicestershire*, II, p. 139.
86. Significantly, the fifth Earl Spencer resigned as chairman (although he remained a member) of Northamptonshire County Council when he took office in the Liberal government of 1892; See Gordon, *Red Earl*, II, p. 182.
87. Morgan, *Rebirth of a Nation*, pp. 53, 187; Morgan, *Wales in British Politics*, p. 107.
88. D. T. Denver and H. T. G. Hands, 'Politics to 1929', and Appendix 2, in Marshall, *Lancashire County Council*, pp. 61, 388–90.
89. Lee, *Social Leaders*, pp. 178–9.
90. Barber and Beresford, *West Riding County Council*, pp. 148, 182–190.
91. Moyhan, *Form and Reform of County Government*, p. 50; *V.C.H., Shropshire*, III, p. 186.
92. J. Redlich and F. W. Hirst, *Local Government in England* (2 vols., 1903), II, p. 50.
93. Lee, *Social Leaders*, pp. 72–4, 81.
94. *V.C.H., Wiltshire*, v, p. 270.
95. Moyhan, *Form and Reform of County Government*, p. 70.
96. *V.C.H., Shropshire*, III, p. 188.
97. See below, ch. 12, sections i and iii.
98. L. P. Curtis, *Coercion and Conciliation in Ireland, 1880–1892: A Study in Constructive Unionism* (Princeton, 1963), p. 344.
99. H. Gailey, 'Unionist Rhetoric and Irish Local Government Reform, 1895–9', *Irish Historical Studies*, XXIV (1984), p. 60; D. Fitzpatrick, *Politics and Irish Life, 1913–1921* (Dublin, 1977), p. 51.
100. C. C. O'Brien, *Parnell and His Party, 1880–90* (1957), pp. 13–20; B. M. Walker, 'The Land Question and Elections in Ulster, 1868–86', in S. Clark and J. Donnelly (eds.), *Irish Peasants: Violence and Political Unrest, 1780–1914* (Madison, Wisconsin, 1983), pp. 245–7.
101. P. Buckland, *Irish Unionism*, vol. I, *The Anglo-Irish and the New Ireland, 1885–1922* (Dublin, 1972), p. 5.
102. Curtis, *Coercion and Conciliation*, p. 16.
103. J. C. Beckett, *The Anglo-Irish Tradition* (1976), pp. 113–14, 117.
104. P. Bew and F. Wright, 'The Agrarian Opposition in Ulster Politics, 1848–1887', in Clark and Donnelly, *Irish Peasants*, p. 224.
105. F. S. L. Lyons, *The Irish Parliamentary*

Party, 1890–1910 (1951), pp. 169–70, 174.

106. Lyons, *Irish Parliamentary Party*, pp. 45–6, 140–57.

107. Bew and Wright, 'Agrarian Opposition in Ulster Politics', in Clark and Donnelly, *Irish Peasants*, pp. 218–25.

108. P. Buckland, *Irish Unionism*, vol. II, *Ulster Unionism and the Origins of Northern Ireland, 1886–1922* (Dublin, 1973), p. 136.

109. T. M. Bottomley, 'The North Fermanagh Elections of 1885 and 1886: Some Documentary Illustrations', *Clogher Record*, VII (1974), pp. 167–181; P. Gibbon, *The Origins of Ulster Unionism: The Formation of Popular Protestant Politics and Ideology in Nineteenth-Century Ireland* (1975), pp. 113–14.

110. Buckland, *Ulster Unionism*, pp. 23–4, 32.

111. P. Buckland, 'The Unity of Ulster Unionism, 1886–1939', *History*, LX (1975), pp. 212–15.

112. F. S. L. Lyons, *Ireland Since the Famine* (1971), pp. 288, 299; Gibbon, *Origins of Ulster Unionism*, pp. 106, 117–19, 130, 145.

113. W. L. Feingold, 'The Tenants' Movement to Capture the Irish Poor Law Boards, 1877–1886', *Albion*, VII (1975), pp. 222–4.

114. Feingold, 'Tenants Movement', pp. 218, 225, 230. For a fuller account see W. L. Feingold, 'The Irish Boards of Poor Law Guardians, 1872–1886: A Revolution in Local Government' (Ph.D. dissertation, University of Chicago, 1974).

115. For a detailed case study, see W. L. Feingold, 'Land League Power: The Tralee Poor Law Election of 1881', in Clark and Donnelly, *Irish Peasants*, pp. 286–309.

116. C. B. Shannon, 'The Ulster Liberal Unionists and Local Government Reform, 1885–98', *Irish Historical Studies*, XVIII (1973), pp. 413–18.

117. *E.G.*, 29 May 1897; E. Barker, *Ireland in the Last Fifty Years, 1886–1916* (1917), p. 22.

118. C. B. Shannon, 'Local Government in Ireland: The Politics and Administration' (MA dissertation, University College, Dublin, 1963), p. 210.

119. Shannon, 'Local Government in Ireland', p. 217.

120. *Morning Post*, 11 Apr. 1899; *The Times*, 10 Apr. 1899.

121. Shannon, 'Local Government in Ireland', pp. 225–51.

122. Shannon, 'Local Government in Ireland', pp. 255–8.

123. Fitzpatrick, *Politics and Irish Life*, pp. 55–6; E. Brynn, *Crown and Castle: British Rule in Ireland, 1800–1830* (Dublin, 1978), p. 157.

124. Lyons, *Ireland Since the Famine*, pp. 394–7, 405.

125. Buckland, *Ulster Unionism*, p. 151.

126. N. Mansergh, *The Government of Northern Ireland* (1936), pp. 169–76, 234.

127. Lyons, *Ireland Since the Famine*, pp. 682, 715.

128. P. Livingstone, *The Fermanagh Story* (1969), p. 329.

129. Lyons, *Ireland Since the Famine*, pp. 696–7.

130. Buckland, 'Unity of Ulster Unionism', pp. 216–19.

131. Lyons, *Ireland Since the Famine*, p. 708.

132. Lyons, *Ireland Since the Famine*, p. 468. For the political background to the Irish settlement and the creation of the Senate in the south, see below, ch. 10, sect. iii.

133. D. O'Sullivan, *The Irish Free State and Its Senate: A Study in Contemporary Politics* (1940), p. 90.

134. O'Sullivan, *Irish Free State and Its Senate*, pp. 103–15.

135. For one example of this, see R. B. McDowell, *Alice Stopford Green: A Passionate Historian* (Dublin, 1967), pp. 105–11.

136. Buckland, *Anglo-Irish* p. 297.

137. O'Sullivan, *Irish Free State and Its Senate*, pp. 598–602.

138. Lyons, *Ireland Since the Famine*, p. 537; O'Sullivan, *Irish Free State and Its Senate*, pp. 374, 465, 503.

139. Buckland, *Anglo-Irish*, pp. 42, 217, 298–99.

140. Buckland, *Anglo-Irish*, p. 300.

Chapter 5

1. J. Camplin, *The Rise of the Rich* (New York 1979), p. 12.

2. Chaplin, *Rise of the Rich*, p. 117.

3. F. M. L. Thompson, 'Britain', in D. Spring (ed.), *European Landed Elites in the Nineteenth Century* (1977), pp. 22–3, 42.

4. D. Dilks, 'Baldwin and Chamberlain', in Lord Butler (ed.), *The Conservatives: A History of their Origins to 1965* (1977),

p. 398.

5. J. R. Vincent, *The Formation of the Liberal Party, 1859–1868* (1966), p. 2; J. Ramsden, *The Age of Balfour and Baldwin, 1902–1940* (1978), pp. 360–1.

6. W. Whiteley, 'The Social Composition of the House of Commons, 1868–1885' (Ph.D. dissertation, Cornell University, 1960), pp. 459, 504, 550–1, 549.

7. Earl of Birkenhead, *Halifax* (1965), pp. 87–8, 91; A. H. Brodrick, *Near To Greatness: A Life of the Sixth Earl Winterton* (1965), p. 82.

8. N. Blewett, *The Peers, the Parties and the People: The British General Elections of 1910* (1972), p. 227.

9. J. M. McEwen, 'Conservative and Unionist M.P.s, 1914–1939' (Ph.D. dissertation, London University, 1959), pp. 58–61.

10. Earl of Portsmouth, *A Knot of Roots*, (1965), p. 97.

11. Earl of Lytton, *Anthony: A Record of Youth* (1935), p. 316.

12. S. Haxey, *Tory MP* (1939), p. 142.

13. *The Times*, 15 Aug. 1935; P. Williamson, *The Modernisation of Conservative Politics: The Diaries and Letters of William Bridgeman, 1904–1935* (1988), p. 1.

14. McEwen, 'Conservative and Unionist M.P.s', p. 297. For other examples, see J. Stevenson, *British Society, 1914–45* (1984), p. 354.

15. B. Harrison, 'Women in a Men's House: The Women M.P's, 1919–1945', *H.J.*, xxix (1986), pp. 623–54.

16. N. Mosley, *Rules of the Game: Sir Oswald and Lady Cynthia Mosley, 1896–1933* (1982), pp. 82, 117–18.

17. Duchess of Atholl, *Working Partnership* (1958), pp. 134–44, 219–32.

18. Haxey, *Tory MP*, p. 127.

19. Whiteley, 'Social Composition of the House of Commons', pp. 505, 551–2.

20. Whiteley, 'Social Composition of the House of Commons', p. 461.

21. *The Times*, 24 Aug. 1983.

22. Whiteley, 'Social Composition of the House of Commons', p. 503.

23. W. Long, *Memories* (1923), p. 80. See also, for a prescient warning: A.C.G. 'A Word to Country Gentlemen, by One of Themselves', *National Review*, xxviii (1885), pp. 437–43.

24. R. Blake, *The Unknown Prime Minister: The Life and Times of Andrew Bonar Law, 1858–1923* (1955), p. 96; B. Tuchman, *The Proud Tower: A Portrait of the World Before the War, 1890–1914* (New York, 1967), p. 428; J. A. Thomas, *The House of Commons, 1906–11: An Analysis of its Economic and Social Character* (1958), pp. 14, 27–8. For an analysis of the occupational background of the candidates at that election, see A. K. Russell, *Liberal Landslide: The General Election of 1906* (1973), p. 61.

25. Blewett, *Peers, Parties and People*, p. 230; Tuchman, *Proud Tower*, pp. 429–32; R. Jenkins, *Mr. Balfour's Poodle* (1954) pp. 19–20.

26. J. McEwen, 'The Coupon Election of 1918 and Unionist Members of Parliament', *Journal of Modern History*, xxxix (1962), pp. 298–9.

27. Blake, *Bonar Law*, p. 412; R. Rhodes James (ed.), *Memoirs of a Conservative: J. C. C. Davidson's Memoirs and Papers, 1910–37* (1969), p. 103. Significantly, it was the widespread awareness of the disappearance of the traditional patrician personnel from the Commons that prompted the setting up of the History of Parliament Trust. Its first report, in 1932, contained these revealing remarks: 'A wider franchise has tended to exclude from public life ... many public-spirited people, whose unwillingness any longer to take part in government was a loss to the state'. See L. J. Colley, *Namier* (1989), pp. 75–7.

28. J. P. Cornford, 'The Parliamentary Foundations of the Hotel Cecil', in R. Robson (ed.), *Ideas and Institutions of Victorian England: Essays Presented to G. Kitson Clark* (1967), pp. 277, 310.

29. Ramsden, *Age of Balfour and Baldwin*, p. 50; Cornford, 'Parliamentary Foundations of the Hotel Cecil', pp. 278–82.

30. Ramsden, *Age of Balfour and Baldwin*, pp. 98–9, 360–1; McEwen, 'Conservative and Unionist M.P.s', pp. 20–2, 82, 385, 405, 432.

31. S. Hogg, 'Landed Society and the Conservative Party in the Late Nineteenth and Early Twentieth Centuries' (B. Litt. dissertation, Oxford University, 1972), pp. 184–9.

32. McEwen, 'Conservative and Unionist M.P.s', pp. 280, 395, 483.

33. Birkenhead, *Halifax*, pp. 87–8, 91; K. Rose, *Curzon: A Most Superior Person* (1985), p. 120.

34. Lord Brabazon of Tara, *The Barbazon Story* (1956), pp. 106–7.

35. Lord Ernest Hamilton, *Forty Years On*

(n.d), pp. 203, 222–3; Cornford, 'Parliamentary Foundations of the Hotel Cecil', p. 269.

36. Birkenhead, *Halifax*, p. 93; Marquess of Zetland, *'Essayez'* (1956), pp. 58–60; H. M. Hyde, *The Londonderrys: A Family Portrait* (1979), pp. 106–8.

37. Lord Eustace Percy, *Some Memories* (1958), p. 19; Brodrick, *Earl Winterton*, (1965), pp. 86, 133; J. A. Cross, *Lord Swinton* (1982), pp. 85–6.

38. Hyde, *Londonderrys*, p. 180; Lytton, Anthony, p. 231; Portsmouth, *Knot of Roots*, pp. 107, 123.

39. Percy, *Some Memories*, p. 76.

40. R. A. Rempel, 'Lord Hugh Cecil's Political Career, 1900–1914: Promise Unfulfilled', *Journal of British Studies*, XI (1972), esp. pp. 104–6; R. Rhodes James, *Victor Cazalet: A Portrait* (1976), p. 122.

41. W. L. Guttsman, *The British Political Elite* (1965), pp. 22, 93, 227, 236–7; D. Southgate, 'Introduction', in D. Southgate (ed.), *The Conservative Leadership, 1832–1932* (1974), p. 1.

42. Ramsden, *Age of Balfour and Baldwin*, pp. 61, 93.

43. W. D. Rubinstein, *Men of Property: The Very Wealthy in Britain Since the Industrial Revolution* (1981), pp. 164–8.

44. Camplin, *Rise of the Rich*, p. 38; S. Koss, *Sir John Brunner: Radical Plutocrat, 1842–1919* (1970), p. 2.

45. Haxey, *Tory MP*, pp. 35–6.

46. Haxey, *Tory MP*, pp. 162–3.

47. Whiteley, 'Social Composition of the House of Commons', p. 516; Ramsden, *Age of Balfour and Baldwin*, p. 362.

48. McEwen, 'Conservative and Unionist M.P.s', pp. 189, 407; Haxey, *Tory MP*, p. 57.

49. A. C. Benson, *Life of Edward Benson* (2 vols., 1899), II, p. 394.

50. F. M. L. Thompson, *English Landed Society in the Nineteenth Century* (1963), pp. 51, 62–3.

51. Guttsman, *British Political Elite*, pp. 121–6.

52. R. E. Pumphrey, 'The Creation of Peerages in England, 1837–1911' (Ph.D. dissertation, Yale University, 1934), p. 104. For the full correspondence between the sovereign and her Prime Minister on the subject of honours in late 1869, see P. Guedalla (ed.), *The Queen and Mr Gladstone* (2 vols., 1933), I, pp. 195 ff.

53. Thompson, *English Landed Society*, p. 294; R. E. Pumphrey, 'The Introduction of Industrialists into the British Peerage: A Study in Adaption of a Social Institution', *A.H.R.*, LXV (1959), p. 7.

54. *Saturday Review*, 16 Dec. 1905.

55. Thompson, *English Landed Society*, pp. 35–6.

56. Pumphrey, 'Creation of Peerages', pp. 136–7; *The Times*, 14 Feb. 1907.

57. Pumphrey, 'Creation of Peerages', pp. 134, 143.

58. G. E. Buckle (ed.), *Letters of Queen Victoria*, 3rd ser. (3 vols., 1932), II, p. 85; W. D. Rubinstein, *Elites and the Wealthy in Modern British History: Essays in Social and Economic History* (1987), p. 246; Pumphrey, 'Creation of Peerages', p. 138; *The Times*, 1 Jan. 1897.

59. Rubinstein, *Elites and the Wealthy*, p. 247; Pumphrey, 'Creation of Peerages', pp. 55, 62.

60. Thompson, *English Landed Society*, pp. 293–7; Rubinstein, *Elite and the Wealthy*, p. 233; Pumphrey, 'Creation of Peerages', p. 116.

61. Pumphrey, 'Creation of Peerages', p. 120.

62. Pumphrey, 'Introduction of Industrialists into the British Peerage', pp. 9–11.

63. Thompson, *English Landed Society*, p. 293.

64. Pumphrey, 'Creation of Peerages', pp. 148–9.

65. Pumphrey, 'Creation of Peerages', pp. 149–51.

66. Guttsman, *British Political Elite*, p. 87.

67. Thompson, *English Landed Society*, pp. 297–8.

68. Thompson, *English Landed Society*, p. 299.

69. Guttsman, *British Political Elite*, p. 119.

70. K. Rose, *The Later Cecils* (1975), pp. 94, 289; N. Nicolson (ed.), *Harold Nicolson: Diaries and Letters, 1939–1945* (1967), p. 287.

71. *The Times*, 3 Sept. 1942.

72. Thompson, *English Landed Society*, pp. 340–1; P. Bromhead, *The House of Lords and Contemporary Politics, 1911–1957* (1958), pp. 20–30.

73. Guttsman, *British Political Elite*, p. 134.

74. Guttsman, *British Political Elite*, pp. 122, 126.

75. Pumphrey, 'Creation of Peerages', pp. 58–60.

76. Rubinstein, *Elites and the Wealthy*, p. 248; Bromhead, *House of Lords*, p. 28.

77. Haxey, *Tory MP*, pp. 166–7, 169–70.

78. Pumphrey, 'Creation of Peerages', p. 105.

79. Rose, *Later Cecils*, p. 70.

80. Guttsman, *British Political Elite*, p.

81. A. B. Cooke and J. R. Vincent (eds.), *Lord Carlingford's Journal: Reflections of a Cabinet Minister, 1885* (1971), pp. 26–30.

82. Tuchman, *Proud Tower*, p. 2.

83. Cornford, 'Parliamentary Foundations of the Hotel Cecil', p. 294.

84. *The Times*, 7 Oct. 1891; Thompson, 'Britain', p. 25; D. Southgate, 'The Salisbury Era, 1881–1902', in Southgate, *Conservative Leadership*, p. 135.

85. Percy, *Some Memories*, p. 16; Ramsden, *Age of Balfour and Baldwin*, p. 45.

86. Guttsman, *British Political Elite*, p. 91; Thompson, 'Britain', p. 26.

87. Tuchman, *Proud Tower*, pp. 427–8, 433, 442; Rose, *Later Cecils*, p. 150; J. R. Vincent (ed.), *The Crawford Papers: The Journals of David Lindsay, Twenty Seventh Earl of Crawford and Tenth Earl of Balcarres, 1871–1940, During the Years 1892 to 1940* (1984), p. 116.

88. R. Blake, *The Conservative Party from Peel to Churchill*, (1972), pp. 191, 196; Guttsman, *British Political Elite*, p. 213.

89. A Political Correspondent, 'The Disappearance of the Governing Classes', *Political Science Quarterly*, I (1930), p. 104.

90. D. Marquand, *Ramsay Macdonald* (1977), pp. 300–1; A. J. A. Morris, *C. P. Trevelyan, 1870–1958: Portrait of a Radical* (1977), p. 156.

91. *Punch*, 1 Nov. 1922.

92. P. Wright, *Portraits and Criticism* (1925), p. 36.

93. Haxey, *Tory M.P.*, pp. 124–9.

94. Guttsman, *British Political Elite*, pp. 28–9.

95. Guttsman, *British Political Elite*, pp. 161–3, 220.

96. Morris, *Trevelyan*, p. 13.

97. Guttsman, *British Political Elite*, pp. 201–2.

98. A. Newman, *The Stanhopes of Chevening: A Family Biography* (1969), p. 332.

99. J. Wilson, *C.B.: A Life of Sir Henry Campbell-Bannerman* (1973), pp. 234, 243.

100. Cornford, 'Parliamentary Foundations of the Hotel Cecil', pp. 268, 308–9.

101. Cooke and Vincent, *Carlingford's Journal*, pp. 13–14, 124, 144; W. O. Chadwick, *Acton and Gladstone* (1976), pp. 28–9; J. R. Vincent (ed.), *The Later Derby Diaries: Home Rule, Liberal Unionism and Aristocratic Life in Late Victorian England* (1981), pp. 92–7; Lord Newton, *Lord Lansdowne: A Biography* (1929), pp. 24–5, 51–5; P. Gordon (ed.), *The Red Earl: The Papers of the Fifth Earl Spencer, 1835–1910* (2 vols., 1981–6), vol. I, *1835–1885*, pp. 29, 72–3.

102. D. Cannadine, 'The Landowner as Millionaire: The Finances of the Dukes of Devonshire, c.1800–1926', *Agricultural History Review*, xxv (1977), pp. 88–9.

103. F. M. L. Thompson, 'Nineteenth-Century Horse Sense', *Ec.H.R.*, 2nd ser. xxix (1976), p. 69.

104. Cornford, 'Parliamentary Foundations of the Hotel Cecil', pp. 304–5.

105. K. Robbins, *Sir Edward Grey: A Biography of Lord Grey of Fallodon* (1971), p. 71.

106. Ramsden, *Age of Balfour and Baldwin*, pp. 24, 95; Vincent, *Crawford Papers*, p. 116.

107. M. Cowling, *The Impact of Labour, 1920–1924* (1971), p. 16; Wilson, *C.B.*, pp. 435, 438–41, 456.

108. Robbins, *Grey*, p. 358.

109. Vincent, *Crawford Papers*, pp. 191–2.

110. Rose, *Curzon*, p. 379; Vincent, *Crawford Papers*, p. 378.

111. Rhodes James, *Memoirs of a Conservative*, p. 116.

112. Cross, *Swinton*, p. 43.

113. Brabazon, *Brabazon Story*, pp. 161, 181.

114. Cross, *Swinton*, pp. 84–6.

115. Percy, *Some Memories*, p. 163; Morris, *Trevelyan*, pp. 174, 180, 187; Ramsden, *Age of Balfour and Baldwin*, p. 318.

116. Hyde, *Londonderrys*, pp. 92, 210, 216–17, 221, 226; Rhodes James, *Memoirs of a Conservative*, p. 405; Cross, *Swinton*, pp. 144–5, 256; Newman, *Stanhopes of Chevening*, pp. 349–53.

117. Guttsman, *British Political Elite*, p. 207.

118. Newman, *Stanhopes of Chevening*, pp. 348, 355.

119. Birkenhead, *Halifax*, pp. 147–8, 162, 323–5, 334–45, 362, 418, 420–5.

120. Guttsman, *British Political Elite*, p. 223.

121. Rose, *Later Cecils*, pp. 2, 154, 321.

122. Cowling, *Impact of Labour*, pp. 414–15.

123. Rose, *Later Cecils*, pp. 104, 136.

124. Percy, *Some Memories*, p. 16.

125. Rose, *Later Cecils*, p. 181.

126. Vincent, *Formation of the Liberal Party*, p. 212.
127. M. Barker, *Gladstone and Radicalism: The Reconstruction of the Liberal Party in Britain, 1885–1894* (1975), pp. 15, 250–1.
128. R. Taylor, *Lord Salisbury* (1975), p. 74; Rubinstein, *Men of Property*, p. 175, note 43.
129. Blake, *Conservative Party from Peel to Churchill*, p. 132; Taylor, *Salisbury*, p. 17.
130. Barker, *Gladstone and Radicalism*, pp. 13–15.
131. P. Magnus, *Gladstone: A Biography* (1954), pp. 269, 405.
132. Taylor, *Salisbury*, pp. 123, 126.
133. Rubinstein, *Men of Property*, p. 175, n.43.
134. R. Blake, *The Office of Prime Minister* (1975), p. 19.
135. R. Rhodes James, *Rosebery: A Biography of Archibald Philip, Fifth Earl of Rosebery* (1963), pp. 362–3, 369–70, 378–9.
136. Lord Winterton, *Pre-War* (1932), pp. 16–18; Ramsden, *Age of Balfour and Baldwin*, pp. 28, 42.
137. Wilson, *C.B.*, pp. 24, 32, 37–8, 46, 59.
138. Wilson, *C.B.*, pp. 236, 337.
139. Thompson, 'Britain', pp. 26–8.
140. Rose, *Later Cecils*, p. 150.
141. Ramsden, *Age of Balfour and Baldwin*, p. 136; Rose, *Later Cecils*, p. 77.
142. M. Girouard, *Life in the English Country House: A Social and Architectural History* (1978), pp. 316–18. Predictably, some aristocrats were opposed to this benefaction. In the early 1930s, Lord Lee was rebuked by the Dowager Duchess of Norfolk: 'She clearly disapproved of the whole idea, and considered that "corrupt" politicians should be kept in their place, and not encouraged to ape the aristocracy.' (A. Clark (ed.), '*A Good Innings': The Private Papers of Viscount Lee of Fareham* (1974), p. 323.)
143. Vincent, *Crawford Papers*, p. 231.
144. Blake, *Bonar Law*, pp. 17, 22, 25, 31–2, 37, 61; D. Southgate, From Disraeli to Law', in Butler, *The Conservatives*, pp. 243, 248.
145. Lord Winterton, *Orders of the Day* (1953), p. 59; Ramsden, *Age of Balfour and Baldwin*, p. 91.
146. Vincent, *Crawford Papers*, pp. 247, 248, 260.
147. K. Middlemas and A. J. L. Barnes, *Baldwin: A Biography* (1969), pp. 21–5,

43, 53, 56, 73, 260.
148. Ramsden, *Age of Balfour and Baldwin*, p. 213; Cowling, *Impact of Labour*, pp. 400, 414–15.
149. A. Marwick, *British Society Since 1945* (1982), p. 40; D. Dilks, *Neville Chamberlain*, vol. I, *Pioneering and Reform, 1869–1929* (1984), p. 327.
150. Dilks, *Chamberlain*, I, pp. 26–33, 77, 132, 307.
151. Wilson, *C.B.*, pp. 423–7, 450.
152. Blake, *Office of Prime Minister*, pp. 151–6.
153. Blake, *Bonar Law*, p. 519.
154. Rhodes James, *Memoirs of a Conservative*, pp. 156, 165. The fullest accounts of this episode are to be found in Blake, *Bonar Law*, pp. 518–27, and K. Rose, *King George V* (1983), pp. 266–73.
155. Blake, *Bonar Law*, pp. 520–1.
156. Rhodes James, *Memoirs of a Conservative*, p. 157.
157. Blake, *Bonar Law*, p. 528.
158. Vincent, *Crawford Papers*, pp. 465, 477, 482–3, 507; Blake, *Bonar Law*, pp. 520–1.
159. J. W. Wheeler-Bennett, *King George VI: His Life and Reign* (1958), pp. 440–6.
160. Birkenhead, *Halifax*, pp. 449–54.
161. Guttsman, *British Political Elite*, p. 206.
162. Duke of Bedford, *A Silver-Plated Spoon* (1959), pp. 17–19, 22–4, 29.
163. A. Ponsonby, *The Decline of Aristocracy* (1912), pp. 22–3, 141, 320.
164. Guttsman, *British Political Elite*, p. 109.

Chapter 6

1. G. Kitson Clark, *The Making of Victorian England* (1985), p. 252; J. Thirsk, 'Younger Sons in the Seventeenth Century', *History*, LIV (1969), pp. 358–77.
2. S. Hynes, *The Edwardian Turn of Mind* (Princeton, 1968), p. 389.
3. For two other examples, see K. Rose, *The Later Cecils* (1975), chs. 3–7; Sir John Colville, *Those Lambtons! A Most Unusual Family* (1988), chs. 6–7.
4. W. Fielding, 'What Shall I Do With My Son?', *19C*, XIII (1883), p. 579. For other contemporary comment, see T. H. S. Escott, *England: Its People, Polity and Pursuits* (1885 edn.), esp. pp. 555–7; W. R. Greig, 'Life at High Pressure', *Contemporary Review*, XXV (1874–5), esp. pp. 629–33; S. H. Jeys, 'Our Gentlemanly Failures', *Fortnightly Review*, LXI (1897), pp. 389–98.

5. T. R. Gourvish, 'The Rise of the Professions', in T. R. Gourvish and A. O'Day (eds.), *Later Victorian Britain, 1867–1900* (1988), pp. 18–23; P. A. Dunae, *Gentlemen Emigrants: From the British Public School to the Canadian Frontier* (1981), pp. 48–51; F. Musgrove, 'Middle-Class Education and Employment in the Nineteenth Century', *Ec.H.R.*, 2nd ser., XII (1959), pp. 99–111; H. J. Perkin, 'Middle-Class Education and Employment in the Nineteenth Century: A Critical Note', *Ec.H.R.*, 2nd ser., XIV (1961), pp. 122–30; W. J. Reader, *Professional Men: The Rise of the Professional Classes in Nineteenth-Century England* (1966), pp. 183–5.

6. P. Elliott, *The Sociology of the Professions* (1972), pp. 14, 143.

7. R. K. Kelsall, *Higher Civil Servants in Britain: From 1870 to the Present Day* (1955), pp. 205–6, note 5.

8. H. Roseveare, *The Treasury* (1969), p. 178.

9. J. Pellew, *The Home Office, 1848–1914: From Clerks to Bureaucrats* (1982), p. 30.

10. J. Hart, 'Sir Charles Trevelyan at the Treasury', *Eng. Hist. Rev.*, LXXV (1960), p. 110; J. M. Bourne, *Patronage and Society in Nineteenth-Century England* (1986), pp. 31–4; Reader, *Professional Men*, pp. 82–92.

11. Bourne, *Patronage and Society*, pp. 39–41; Roseveare, *The Treasury*, p. 177; Pellew, *The Home Office*, pp. 20–2, 35; Reader, *Professional Men*, p. 96.

12. G. Sutherland, 'Administrators in Education After 1870: Patronage, Professionalism and Expertise', in G. Sutherland (ed.), *Studies in the Growth of Nineteenth-Century Government* (1972), pp. 263, 266.

13. M. J. Daunton, *Royal Mail: The Post Office Since 1840* (1985), p. 315; *D.N.B.*, *1931–40*, pp. 637–8.

14. *D.N.B.*, *1901–11*, p. 193; Roseveare, *The Treasury*, pp. 172, 213–220; J. Morley, *The Life of William Ewart Gladstone* (3 vols., 1903), III, pp. 210–11.

15. Pellew, *The Home Office*, p. 60.

16. C. H. Dudley Ward and C. B. Spencer, *The Unconventional Civil Servant: Sir Henry H. Cunninghame* (1938), pp. 14–17, 274, 279; Pellew, *The Home Office*, pp. 208, 211.

17. *D.N.B.*, *1901–11*, pp. 205–6.

18. *D.N.B.*, *1912–21*, pp. 356–7; *D.N.B.*, *1922–30*, pp. 538–9.

19. Roseveare, *The Treasury*, p. 215.

20. *D.N.B.*, *1901–11*, pp. 581–3; *D.N.B.*, *1922–30*, pp. 696–7; Daunton, *Royal Mail*, pp. 314–15.

21. For other examples, see *D.N.B.*, *1912–21*, pp. 126–7; Sir John Craig, *The Mint* (1953), pp. 330–1.

22. Sutherland, 'Administrators in Education', p. 272.

23. Sir Almeric Fitzroy, *Memoirs* (2 vols., 1925), I, pp. ix–xvi, 72, 224, 276, 345, 357–358; II, pp. 486, 688, 808.

24. Roseveare, *The Treasury*, pp. 217–18. He wrote a biography of his former chief, *Mr Gladstone* (1893), and was also an amateur composer of some note.

25. Dudley and Spencer, *Unconventional Civil Servant*, esp. pp. 8, 10, 120; Sir A. C. Lyall, 'Sir Spencer Walpole', *Proceedings of the British Academy*, I (1907–8), pp. 373–8.

26. Daunton, *Royal Mail*, p. 316.

27. Reader, *Professional Men*, p. 193.

28. Pellew, *The Home Office*, pp. 71–2, 183–91.

29. R. Lowe, 'Bureaucracy Triumphant or Denied? The Expansion of the British Civil Service, 1919–1939', *Public Administration*, LXII (1984), pp. 291–309; Roseveare, *The Treasury*, pp. 235–8, 246–8, 252–5, 259–61.

30. Pellew, *The Home Office*, pp. 71, 92; J. R. Greenaway, 'Warren Fisher and the Transformation of the British Treasury, 1919–1939', *Journal of British Studies*, XXIII (1983), pp. 125–42.

31. Daunton, *Royal Mail*, p. 317; R. Lowe and R. Roberts, 'Sir Horace Wilson, 1900–1935: The Making of a Mandarin', *H.J.*, XXX (1987), pp. 641–62.

32. W. D. Rubinstein, 'Education and the Social Origins of British Elites, 1880–1970', *P. & P.*, no. 112 (1986), pp. 166–7, 173–4, 186, 192.

33. Pellew, *The Home Office*, p. 200; Kelsall, *Higher Civil Servants*, pp. 150–1, 185–6.

34. J. Powys, *Aristocracy* (1984), p. 63.

35. P. R. Williams, 'Public Discussion of the British Monarchy, 1837–87' (Ph.D. dissertation, Cambridge University, 1988), ch. 3.

36. H. J. Laski, 'The King's Secretary', *Fortnightly Review*, CLII (1942), pp. 389–93; J. W. Wheeler-Bennett, *King George VI: His Life and Reign* (1958), pp. 817–23.

37. D. Cannadine, 'The Context, Perform-

ance and Meaning of Ritual: The British Monarchy and the "Invention of Tradition", c.1820–1977', in E. J. Hobsbawm and T. Ranger (eds.), *Inventing Traditions in Nineteenth-Century Europe* (1983), pp. 133–8.

38. Sir John Fortescue, *Author and Curator* (1933), pp. 95, 100.

39. Sir Lionel Cust, *King Edward VII and His Circle* (1930), pp. 3, 9.

40. K. Rose, *Kings, Queens and Courtiers* (1985), pp. 141–2; H. Hardinge, *Loyal to Three Kings* (1967), pp. 17, 25, 28, 178.

41. Rose, *Kings, Queens and Courtiers*, pp. 167–9; D. Hart-Davis (ed.), *End of an Era: Letters and Journals of Sir Alan Lascelles, 1887–1920* (1986), pp. 24, 36, 41, 53–4, 69, 127, 145, 321–2, 333.

42. Rose, *Kings, Queens and Courtiers*, pp. 242–3; W. A. Lindsay, *The Royal Household, 1837–1897* (1898), pp. 49, 158–60.

43. A. Ponsonby, *Henry Ponsonby: Queen Victoria's Private Secretary* (1942), pp. 36, 64; P. H. Emden, *Behind the Throne* (1934), p. 164.

44. Rose, *Kings, Queens and Courtiers*, pp. 16–17; Mabell, Countess of Airlie, *Thatched with Gold* (1962), pp. 96–7, 127, 232, 237.

45. Rose, *Kings, Queens and Courtiers*, pp. 50–3; Lady Cynthia Colville, *Crowded Life* (1958), pp. 107–35.

46. Sir Frederick Ponsonby, *Recollections of Three Reigns* (1951), p. xi.

47. Hardinge, *Loyal to Three Kings*, pp. 40–4; Fortescue, *Author and Curator*, p. 124; Lord Ormanthwaite, *When I was at Court* (1937), p. 177.

48. Airlie, *Thatched with Gold*, pp. 169–70, 191; Fortescue, *Author and Curator*, pp. 73, 77–81.

49. Ormanthwaite, *When I was at Court*, p. 9; Hart Davis, *End of an Era*, pp. x, 141.

50. Cust, *King Edward VII*, p. 223; Rose, *Kings, Queens and Courtiers*, p. 141.

51. D. Duman, 'The Late Victorian Bar: A Prosopographical Survey', in E. W. Ives and A. H. Manchester (eds.), *Law, Litigants and the Legal Profession* (1983), pp. 144–7, 150–1; D. Duman, *The English and Colonial Bars in the Nineteenth Century* (1983), pp. 49, 186, 191–2.

52. *The Times*, 5 Jan. 1884; B. Abel-Smith and R. Stevens, *Lawyers and the Courts:*

A Social Study of the English Legal System, 1750–1965 (1967), p. 228.

53. D. Duman, *The Judicial Bench in England, 1727–1875: The Reshaping of a Professional Elite* (1982), pp. 129–30, 139.

54. R. F. V. Heuston, *Lives of the Lord Chancellors, 1885–1940* (1987 edn.), pp. 3, 31.

55. Sir E. C. Leigh, *Bar, Bat and Bit: Recollections and Experiences* (1913), pp. 21, 45, 51, 71, 105, 109, 121–2, 146–150, 154, 189.

56. A. C. Plowden, *Grain or Chaff? The Autobiography of a Police Magistrate* (1903), pp. 1–19, 26, 45–8, 54, 70, 86–90, 94, 133–7, 193, 197–200.

57. Heuston, *Lives of the Lord Chancellors*, pp. 43, 50, 59.

58. Duman, *English and Colonial Bars*, pp. 178, 182.

59. A. M. Carr-Saunders and P. A. Wilson, *The Professions* (1933), pp. 16–17, 45–9.

60. Abel-Smith and Stevens, *Lawyers and the Courts*, pp. 165, 169, 174–6, 215–18, 226; A. Harding, *A. Social History of English Law* (1966), pp. 341–4.

61. D. Duman, 'Pathway to Professionalism: The English Bar in the Eighteenth and Nineteenth Centuries', *Journal of Social History*, XIII (1980), pp. 620–3.

62. Harding, *English Law*, p. 348; Duman, *English and Colonial Bars*, p. 55; Escott, *England*, p. 556.

63. Abel-Smith and Stevens, *Lawyers and the Courts*, pp. 227–8.

64. Duman, *English and Colonial Bars*, pp. 154–5; R. Stevens, *Law and Politics: The House of Lords as a Judicial Body, 1800–1976* (1979), pp. 58–69, 107–9, 256–69.

65. Heuston, *Lord Chancellors*, p. xxii.

66. Duman, *English and Colonial Bars*, pp. 29, 50, 144–54.

67. For one patrician account of these difficulties, see Plowden, *Grain or Chaff?*, pp. 121–30.

68. Harding, *English Law*, pp. 349–50; Abel-Smith and Stevens, *Lawyers and the Courts*, pp. 165–8.

69. Duman, *English and Colonial Bars*, p. 97; Plowden, *Grain or Chaff?*, p. 174; Leigh, *Bar, Bat and Bit*, p. 157.

70. Duman, *English and Colonial Bars*, pp. 93–4; A. G. C. Liddell, *Notes from the Life of an Ordinary Mortal* (1911), pp. 2, 138–40, 244–5.

71. Harding, *English Law*, p. 349; Duman, *English and Colonial Bars*, pp. 55–71,

199–207; Duman, *Judicial Bench*, pp. 173–82.

72. M. J. D. Roberts, 'Private Patronage and the Church of England, 1800–1900', *Journal of Ecclesiastical History*, XXXII (1981), pp. 201–4; W. O. Chadwick, *The Victorian Church*, Part II (1970), pp. 207–9; B. Heeney, *A Different Kind of Gentlemen: Parish Clergy as Professional Men in Early and Mid Victorian England* (Hamden, Conn., 1976), p. 112.

73. A. D. Gilbert, 'The Church and the Land', in G. E. Mingay (ed.), *The Victorian Countryside* (2 vols., 1981), I, p. 50; D. W. R. Bahlman, 'The Queen, Mr Gladstone and Church Patronage', *Victorian Studies*, III (1960), pp. 349–80; G. Kitson Clark, *Churchmen and the Condition of England, 1832–1885* (1973), pp. 137–47, 158–68, 175–84, 198–208.

74. A. Haig, *The Victorian Clergy* (1984), pp. 254–6.

75. J. W. Leigh, *Other Days* (1921), pp. 85–6, 119, 193, 199, 222; F. D. How, *A Memoir of Bishop Sir Lovelace Tomlinson Stanmer, Bt., D.D.* (1910), pp. 2–3, 62–4, 89, 104.

76. K. Rose, *Curzon: A Most Superior Person* (1985), pp. 14–15; Rev. and Hon. E. Lyttelton, *Memories and Hopes* (1925), p. 4; Chadwick, *Victorian Church*, p. 153.

77. Bahlman, 'The Queen . . . and Church Patronage', p. 364; D. H. J. Morgan, 'The Social and Educational Background of Anglican Bishops – Continuities and Changes', *British Journal of Sociology*, XX (1969), p. 297; T. B. Lundeen, 'The Bench of Bishops: A Study of the Secular Activities of the Bishops of the Church of England and of Ireland, 1801–1871' (Ph.D. dissertation, University of Iowa, 1963), pp. 18–38.

78. F. D. How, *Archbishop Plunket: A Memoir* (1900), pp. 305–8; F. Arnold, *Our Bishops and Deans* (2 vols., 1875), II, pp. 194–5.

79. Lyttelton, *Memories and Hopes*, p. 194.

80. Rose, *Curzon*, p. 17; F. D. How, *The Rev. Thomas Mainwaring Bulkeley Bulkeley-Owen* (1914), pp. 144–9.

81. Hon. and Rev. G. T. O. Bridgeman, *History of the Church and Manor of Wigan* (4 vols., 1888–90); W. Addison, *The English Country Parson* (1947), pp. 204–14.

82. C. F. K. Brown, *A History of the English Clergy, 1800–1900* (1953), p. 117.

83. G. Stephenson, *Edward Stuart Talbot, 1844–1934* (1936), pp. 1–6, 9–17, 94, 100, 207; G. L. Prestige, *The Life of Charles Gore* (1935), pp. 1–3, 29, 532; C. A. Alington, *A Dean's Apologia: A Semi-Religious Autobiography* (1952), pp. 31–2, 49.

84. P. Colson, *Life of the Bishop of London: An Authorized Biography* (1935), pp. 15–17.

85. Prestige, *Life of Charles Gore*, pp. 168, 251; J. Bromley, *The Man of Ten Talents: A Portrait of Richard Chenevix-Trench, 1807–1886: Philologist, Poet, Theologian, Archbishop* (1959), pp. v, 228–47.

86. Stephenson, *Edward Stuart Talbot*, pp. 31–2, 40–2, 76, 186, 190.

87. Gilbert, 'The Church and the Land', p. 47.

88. Roberts, 'Private Patronage and the Church of England', pp. 214–22; Chadwick, *Victorian Church*, p. 213.

89. L. Paul, *The Deployment and Payment of the Clergy* (1964), p. 286.

90. M. J. D. Roberts, 'The Role of the Laity in the Church of England, c.1850–1885' (D.Phil. dissertation, Oxford University, 1974), pp. 78–85; K. A. Thompson, *Bureaucracy and Church Reform: The Organisational Response of the Church of England to Social Change, 1800–1965* (1970), pp. xiii–xxiii, 181–202.

91. G. F. A. Best, *Temporal Pillars: The Story of Queen Anne's Bounty* (1964), pp. 471–2; K. S. Inglis, *Churches and the Working Class in Victorian England* (1963), pp. 37–9; Gilbert, 'The Church and the Land', p. 52.

92. E. J. Evans, *The Contentious Tithe: The Tithe Problem and English Agriculture, 1750–1850* (1976), pp. 163–8; Best, *Temporal Pillars*, pp. 477–9; Chadwick, *Victorian Church*, p. 169.

93. Rose, *Later Cecils*, p. 116; Chadwick, *Victorian Church*, p. 159; R. Lloyd, *The Church of England, 1900–1965* (1966), pp. 147–9, 169–70, 342–5, 351–9.

94. Kitson Clark, *Churchmen and the Condition of England*, pp. 233–5; Haig, *Victorian Clergy*, p. 54; Bishop Lord A. C. Hervey, *Charge Delivered to the Clergy and Churchwardens of the Diocese of Bath and Wells* (1876), pp. 11–13.

95. Haig, *Victorian Clergy*, pp. 72–90.

96. Best, *Temporal Pillars*, pp. 505–11; Haig, *Victorian Clergy*, pp. 319–29; D. Macleane, 'The Church as a Profession', *National Review*, xxxiii (1899), p. 945.

97. Kitson Clark, *Churchmen and the Condition of England*, pp. 264–5; B. R. Wilson, *Religion in Secular Society* (1966), pp. 57, 74; A. D. Gilbert, *Religion and Society in Industrial England: Church, Chapel and Social Change, 1740–1914* (1976), pp. 133–4.

98. Chadwick, *Victorian Church*, p. 156, note 2; A. Hastings, *A History of English Christianity, 1920–1985* (1986), p. 56; A. Lyttelton, *Modern Poets of Faith, Doubt and Paganism, and Other Essays* (1904), pp. 8, 13.

99. Gilbert, 'The Church and the Land', p. 52; Haig, *Victorian Clergy*, pp. 29–35; A. Russell, *The Clerical Profession* (1984), pp. 40–1, 45, 167–8, 182–3, 200–2, 212–13, 234–8.

100. Gilbert, 'The Church and the Land', p. 51; Macleane, 'Church as a Profession', p. 949; Haig, *Victorian Clergy*, pp. 11–12.

101. A. C. Deane, 'The Falling Off in the Quantity and Quality of the Clergy', *19C*, xlv (1899), pp. 1026, 1029.

102. Escott, *England*, p. 563; Morgan, 'Social and Educational Background of Anglican Bishops', pp. 297–9, 308.

103. K. Thompson, 'Church of England Bishops as an Elite', in P. Stanworth and A. Giddens (eds.), *Elite and Power in British Society* (1974), pp. 198–207; D. H. J. Morgan, 'Social and Educational Backgrounds of English Diocesan Bishops, 1860–1960' (MA dissertation, Hull University, 1963), pt. 3, ch. 5, pp. 6–12.

104. Inglis, *Churches and the Working Classes*, pp. 143–6, 157–8, 258–76; E. R. Norman, *Church and Society in England, 1770–1970* (1976), pp. 143–4, 155–65, 167–85. Henry Scott Holland was the grandson of Lord Clifford. See E. Lyttelton, *The Mind and Character of Henry Scott Holland* (1926), pp. 1, 2, 29, 77–87; S. Paget, *Henry Scott Holland* (1921), pp. 3–4, 12, 70, 97, 168–73, 202–26.

105. Norman, *Church and Society in England*, pp. 221–46; A. F. Winnington-Ingram, *Fifty Years Work in London (1889–1939)* (1940), pp. 211–17.

106. Inglis, *Churches and the Working Class*, pp. 277–79, 281–3; J. Adderley, *In Slums and Society* (1916), pp. 114–18, 193–5, 209, 244, 254.

107. Hastings, *Christianity in England*, p. 173; R. Groves, *Conrad Noel and the Thaxted Movement* (1967), pp. 9, 14, 25, 30, 48, 183, 256, 307.

108. Norman, *Church and Society in England*, pp. 141–2.

109. Hastings, *Christianity in England*, p. 45; Norman, *Church and Society in England*, pp. 165, 232–4.

110. Rose, *Later Cecils*, pp. 116–17, 120–6; Norman, *Church and Society in England*, p. 221; Hastings, *Christianity in England*, p. 172.

111. Norman, *Church and Society in England*, pp. 227, 251, 333–6; A. Fox, *Dean Inge* (1960), pp. 12–13, 145–8, 199.

112. E. Morgan et al., *The Church in the Country Parishes* (1940), p. 8.

113. E. M. Spiers, *The Army and Society, 1815–1914* (1980), pp. 1–2, 10; R. Cunningham, *Conditions of Social Well-Being* (1878), p. 328; Escott, *England*, pp. 441, 445.

114. B. Bond, *The Victorian Army and the Staff College, 1854–1914* (1972), pp. 17, 20–1, 25–9; A. Bruce, *The Purchase System in the British Army, 1660–1871* (1980), pp. 65–7; H. Moyse-Bartless, 'The British Army in 1850', *Journal for the Society of Army Historical Research*, lii (1974), pp. 228–33; C. B. Otley, 'The Social Origins of British Army Officers', *Sociological Review*, xviii (1970), p. 213.

115. Sir E. R. Fremantle, *The Navy As I Have Known It, 1849–1899* (1904), p. 458.

116. Sir W. L. Clowes, *The Royal Navy: A History from the Earliest Times to the Death of Queen Victoria* (7 vols., 1897–1903), vii, pp. 85–9; M. Lewis, *The Navy in Transition, 1814–1864: A Social History* (1965), p. 22; P. Padfield, *Rule Britannia: The Victorian and Edwardian Navy* (1981), p. 55.

117. For an excellent discussion, which regrettably ends in 1901, see G. Harries-Jenkins, *The Army in Victorian Society* (1977), pp. 12–59.

118. Earl of Cork and Orrery, *My Naval Life, 1886–1941* (1942), p. 178.

119. Spiers, *Army and Society*, pp. 253, 274; Sir N. Lyttelton, *Eighty Years: Soldiering, Politics, Games* (1927), pp. 268–9, 285; V. Stuart, 'The Beloved Little Admiral': *The Life and Times of Admiral of the*

Fleet the Hon. Sir Henry Keppel, GCB, OM, DCL, 1809–1904 (1967), pp. 21, 24, 26; Lord Charles Beresford, *The Memoirs of Admiral Lord Charles Beresford* (2 vols., 1913), I, pp. xiii–xxviii.

120. K. Jeffery (ed.), *The Military Correspondence of Field Marshal Sir Henry Wilson, 1918–1922* (1985), pp. 1–2; P. Buckland, *Irish Unionism*, vol. I, *The Anglo-Irish and the New Ireland, 1885 to 1922* (Dublin, 1972), p. xv; *D.N.B., 1914–1950*, pp. 605–6.

121. R. S. Churchill, *Winston S. Churchill*, vol. I, *Youth, 1874–1900* (1966), pp. 153–5; I. F. W. Beckett, *Johnnie Gough, VC* (1989), pp. 1–5.

122. *D.N.B., 1922–1930*, pp. 114–15; E. Sherston, *Townshend of Chitral and Kut* (1928), pp. 1–2, 184.

123. Lady Wester Wemyss, *The Life and Letters of Lord Wester Wemyss* (1935), p. 12; *D.N.B., 1931–1940*, p. 896; Fremantle, *Navy as I Have Known It*, pp. 1–2; A. Parry, *The Admirals Fremantle* (1971), pp. 11–14, 137–8, 199–200, 228, 253–4.

124. Sir Sydney Robert Fremantle, *My Naval Career, 1880–1928* (1948), pp. 13–17, 351; Earl of Dundonald, *My Army Life* (1934 edn.), pp. 1–4.

125. Harries-Jenkins, *Army in Victorian Society*, p. 42; C. Barnett, *Britain and Her Army, 1509–1970: A Military, Political and Social History* (1970), pp. 314–15.

126. D. Fraser, *Alanbrooke* (1982), pp. 36–40, 45, 51, 55; C. B. Otley, 'Origins and Recruitment of the British Army Elite, 1870–1959' (Ph.D. dissertation, Hull University, 1965), pp. 22–3; N. Hamilton, *Monty*, vol. I, *The Making of a General, 1887–1942* (1984), pp. 12–17, 30–1, 42–5.

127. Spiers, *Army and Society*, p. 25.

128. Churchill, *Winston Churchill*, pp. 216, 241–2, 248, 257, 308–9, 328–9, 349, 354, 370–1; Sherston, *Townshend*, pp. 1, 65.

129. Cork and Orrery, *My Naval Life*, p. 138; Fremantle, *My Naval Career*, pp. 50, 317–18.

130. C. C. Penrose Fitzgerald, *Life of Vice-Admiral Sir George Tryon, KCB* (3rd edn., 1897), p. 73; Stuart, *Henry Keppel*, pp. 234, 237–8; Fremantle, *My Naval Career*, pp. 22–3, 40.

131. Sherston, *Townshend*, pp. 68, 81–2, 175, 198–9; Churchill, *Winston Churchill*, pp. 243, 280, 283–7, 300, 340,

386–9, 392–3; P. E. Razzell, 'Social Origins of Officers in the Indian and British Home Army', *British Journal of Sociology*, XIV (1963), p. 254.

132. Penrose Fitzgerald, *Tryon*, pp. 186, 196, 244–9.

133. G. Bennett, *Charlie B* (1968), pp. 45–7, 312.

134. Fremantle, *My Naval Career*, p. 35; Lyttelton, *Eighty Years*, pp. 270–3; J. Gooch, *The Plans of War: The General Staff and British Military Strategy, c1900–1916* (1974), pp. 68, 77–9.

135. Bennett, *Charlie B*, pp. 320–3; Sir C. Walker, *Thirty Six Years at the Admiralty* (1934), pp. 65, 79, 173; Wemyss, *Wester Wemyss*, pp. 128–9; Fremantle, *My Naval Career*, pp. 268, 367.

136. Cork and Orrery, *My Naval Life*, pp. 45–6; Fremantle, *My Naval Carer*, p. 72; Lyttelton, *Eighty Years*, pp. 26, 159.

137. Bennett, *Charlie B*, pp. 4, 19, 38, 94, 159–73, 207; Sherston, *Townshend*, pp. 122, 176, 196–7, 215, 365, 399.

138. Spiers, *Army and Society*, pp. 248–9; Lyttelton, *Eighty Years*, p. 54; E. S. Turner, *Gallant Gentlemen: A Portrait of the British Officer, 1600–1956* (1956), p. 242; Marquess of Anglesey, *A History of the British Cavalry, 1816 to 1919*, vol. IV, *1899–1913* (1986), pp. 454–5.

139. Barnett, *Britain and Her Army*, pp. 410–11; B. Bond, *British Military Policy Between the Two Wars* (1980), pp. 64–6.

140. Stuart, *Henry Keppel*, pp. 232–3; Beresford, *Memoirs*, II, pp. 524–36; Wemyss, *Wester Wemyss*, p. 35; Penrose Fitzgerald, *Tryon*, pp. 37, 120, 194, 251; Sir Charles Dundas, *An Admiral's Yarns: Stray Memories of Fifty Years* (1922), pp. 234–50.

141. Fremantle, *My Naval Career*, p. 124; Bennett, *Charlie B*, p. 283; L. Dawson, *Gone For a Sailor* (1936), pp. 131–2.

142. C. B. Otley, 'Militarism and the Social Attitudes of the British Army Elite', in J. van Doorn (ed.), *Armed Forces and Society: Sociological Essays* (The Hague, 1960), pp. 89, 100.

143. Bond, *British Military Policy*, p. 67; Otley, 'Social Origins of British Army Officers', p. 229.

144. C. B. Otley, 'Public Schools and Army', *New Society*, 17 Nov. 1966, pp. 754–7; C. B. Otley, 'The Educational Background of British Army officers', *Sociology*, VII (1973), pp. 191–209; C. B. Otley, 'Militarism and Militarization in

the Public Schools, 1900–1972', *British Journal of Sociology*, XXIX (1978), pp. 321–39; Harries-Jenkins, *Army In Victorian Society*, pp. 133–46; M. Lewis, *England's Sea Officers: The Story of the Naval Profession* (1939), p. 110.

145. Otley, 'Origins and Recruitment of the British Army Elite', p. 90.

146. Spiers, *Army and Society*, p. 187.

147. Harries-Jenkins, *Army in Victorian Society*, pp. 91–2.

148. Lewis, *England's Sea Officers*, pp. 101–2, 107–10, 114–17, 286–7; R. F. Mackay, *Fisher of Kilverstone* (1973), pp. 426–7; A. J. Marder, *From the Dreadnought to Scapa Flow: The Royal Navy in the Fisher Era, 1904–1919*, vol. I, *The Road to War, 1904–1914* (1961), pp. 28–32.

149. Barnett, *Britain and Her Army*, p. 314.

150. Anglesey, *British Cavalry*, pp. 458, 469.

151. Cork and Orrery, *My Naval Life*, p. 3; Walker, *Thirty Six Years*, pp. 22, 181–2.

152. Anglessey, *British Cavalry*, pp. 391–2; Barnett, *Britain and Her Army*, pp. 325–8, 367; B. Bond, 'Doctrine and Training in the British Cavalry, 1870–1914', in M. Howard (ed.), *The Theory and Practice of War: Essays Presented to Captain B. H. Liddell Hart* (1965), pp. 111–12.

153. Gooch, *Plans of War*, p. 78.

154. Bond, *British Military Policy*, pp. 52–5, 127–39; Barnett, *Britain and Her Army*, pp. 412–15.

155. Harries-Jenkins, *Army in Victorian Society*, p. 44; Anglesey, *British Cavalry*, p. 457; P. Mansel, *Pillars of Monarchy* (1984), p. 78.

156. Bond, *British Military Policy*, pp. 35–7, 61; Dundonald, *My Army Life*, p. 17.

157. Harries-Jenkins, *Army in Victorian Society*, pp. 258–62; R. Blake, 'Great Britain: The Crimean War to the First World War', in M. Howard (ed.), *Soldiers and Governments: Nine Studies in Civil-Military Relations* (1957), p. 36.

158. Spiers, *Army and Society*, pp. 2, 220, 227; Wemyss, *Wester Wemyss*, p. 126; Beckett, *Gough*, pp. 147–72; Harries-Jenkins, *Army in Victorian Society*, p. 271.

159. Wemyss, *Wester Wemyss*, pp. 306, 308, 423; Jeffrey, *Henry Wilson*, pp. 132–6, 148–51, 165–6, 211, 264–5, 294–7; Sir C. E. Callwell, *Field Marshal Sir Henry Wilson: His Life and Diaries* (2 vols., 1927), II, pp. 219, 231–2, 235, 252, 264, 275, 280.

160. Turner, *Gallant Gentlemen*, p. 288.

161. Blake, 'Great Britain', p. 30; Turner, *Gallant Gentlemen*, pp. 230–1.

162. Bruce, *The Purchase System*, pp. 31, 129, 139–43, 170–1.

163. Spiers, *Army and Society*, p. 229; Anglesey, *British Cavalry*, pp. 409–10; Bond, 'Doctrine and Training', pp. 114–15.

164. J. K. Dunlop, *The Development of the British Army, 1899–1914* (1938), pp. 42–52, 57–8, 272–81; G. D. Phillips, *The Diehards: Aristocratic Society and Politics in Edwardian England* (1979), pp. 87–8, 93–9; I. Beckett, 'H. O. Arnold-Forster and the Volunteers', in I. Beckett and J. Gooch (eds.), *Politicians and Defence* (1981), pp. 53–4.

165. Mackay, *Fisher*, pp. 1–3, 138–9, 231–2, 372–3, 394–5, 252, 348; Marder, *The Road to War*, pp. 14–17, 76–9, 88–93; Bennett, *Charlie B*, pp. 86, 240–1.

166. P. K. Kemp, 'The Royal Navy', in S. Nowell-Smith (ed.), *Edwardian England, 1901–1914* (1964), pp. 509–15.

167. Bond, *British Military Policy*, p. 43; Jeffrey, *Henry Wilson*, pp. 221, 322, 376.

168. Bond, *British Military Policy*, pp. 56, 70–1, 145–7, 162; R. J. Minney, *The Private Papers of Hore-Belisha* (1960), p. 18; A. Trythall, 'The Downfall of Leslie Hore-Belisha', *Journal of Contemporary History*, XVI (1981), pp. 391–412; J. R. Colville, *Man of Valour: The Life of Field Marshal the Viscount Gort* (1972), pp. 74–5, 96–9, 112, 136, 164–5.

169. Fraser, *Alanbrooke*, pp. 86–7, 92–5; Hamilton, *Monty*, pp. 177–82.

170. Airlie, *Thatched with Gold*, p. 181; Wemyss, *Wester Wemyss*, p. 471; Lyttelton, *Eighty Years*, p. 311.

171. D. C. M. Platt, *The Cinderella Service: British Consuls since 1825* (1971), pp. 240–2; Sir Hughe Knatchbull-Hugessen, *Diplomat in Peace and War* (1949), pp. 39–40.

172. G. Young, *Diplomacy Old and New* (1921), p. 31.

173. D. C. M. Platt, *Finance, Trade and Politics in British Foreign Policy, 1815–1914* (1968), p. xxvi; R. B. Mowat, *The Life of Lord Pauncefote* (1929), pp. 1–2; Lord Vansittart, *The Mist Procession* (1958), pp. 15–20.

174. Z. Steiner, *The Foreign Office and Foreign Policy, 1898–1914* (1969), pp. 4, 7, 10–23, 46–82; Sir J. Tilley and S. Gaslee, *The Foreign Office* (1933), pp. 153–66; R. A. Jones, *The Nineteenth-Century*

Foreign Office: An Administrative History (1971), pp. 111–35.

175. P. M. Kennedy, *The Realities Behind Diplomacy: Background Influences on British External Policy, 1865–1980* (1981), pp. 60–1; R. T. Nightingale, 'The Personnel of the British Foreign Office and Diplomatic Service, 1851–1929', *American Political Science Survey*, XXIV (1930), pp. 310–31; R. A. Jones, *The British Diplomatic Service, 1815–1914* (1983), pp. 139–51; Steiner, *Foreign Office*, pp. 173–85.

176. A. J. P. Taylor, *The Trouble Makers: Dissent Over British Foreign Policy, 1792–1939* (1957), p. 63. For detailed studies of two of these patrician ambassadors, see F. L. Ford, 'Three Observers in Berlin: Rumbold, Dodd and Francois-Poncet', and F. Gilbert, 'Two British Ambassadors: Perth and Henderson', in G. A. Craig and F. Gilbert (eds.), *The Diplomats, 1919–1939* (Princeton, 1953), pp. 438–67, 544–8.

177. Platt, *Finance, Trade and Politics*, pp, xxviii–xxix; Jones, *Nineteenth-Century Foreign Office*, pp. 53–60.

178. C. Gladwyn, *The Paris Embassy* (1976), p. 125; Sir G. Buchanan, *My Mission to Russia, and Other Memories* (2 vols., 1923), I, p. 1; M. Gilbert, *Sir Horace Runbold, Portrait of a Diplomatist, 1869–1941* (1973), p. 6.

179. Steiner, *Foreign Office*, pp. 41, 203–4; V. Chirol, *Cecil Spring-Rice: In Memoriam* (1919), p. 8; S. Gwynn, *The Letters and Friendships of Sir Cecil Spring-Rice: A Record* (2 vols., 1929), I, pp. 35–6; Lord Hardinge of Penshurst, *Old Diplomacy* (1947), pp. 21, 23, 55, 81, 98, 186–7.

180. Nightingale, 'Personnel of the British Foreign Office', p. 314.

181. Platt, *Finance, Trade and Politics*, p. xxvii; J. D. Gregory, *On the Edge of Diplomacy: Rambles and Reflections, 1902–1928* (1929), p. 36.

182. Hardinge, *Old Diplomacy*, p. 99.

183. *Fifth report of R.C. on the Civil Service*, P.P. 1914–16 (Cd. 7748), vol. XI, p. 14; *Fourth Report of the R.C. on Civil Establishments*, P.P. 1890 (Cd. 6172), vol. XXVII, Appendix, p. 176; Minutes of Evidence, QQ. 27025–27060.

184. Gladwyn, *Paris Embassy*, p. 241.

185. Platt, *Finance, Trade and Politics*, p. xxv; Buchanan, *My Mission to Russia*, I, pp. 170–3; Hardinge, *Old Diplomacy*, pp. 25, 81–3, 105–6; Sir A. Hardinge, *A*

Diplomatist in Europe (1927), pp. 65, 73–4, 91, 259–60; F. Wellesley, *Recollections of a Soldier Diplomat* (1941), pp. 151–2; Lord Howard of Penrith, *Theatre of Life*, vol. II, *Life Seen from the Stalls, 1905–1936* (1936), pp. 419–21.

186. W. Taffs, *Ambassador to Bismarck: Lord Odo Russell, First Baron Ampthill* (1938), pp. 3–4, 391; P. Kennedy, *The Rise of Anglo-German Antagonisms, 1860–1914* (1982), p. 135; Lord Newton, *Lord Lyons: A Record of British Diplomacy* (2 vols., 1913), I, p. 177; II, p. 214; Mowat, *Pauncefote*, pp. 276, 292, 298–9; J. Grenville, 'Great Britain and the Isthmian Canal, 1898–1901', *A.H.R.*, LXI (1955), pp. 57–7.

187. Steiner, *Foreign Office*, pp. 37, 180–1; Gladwyn, *Paris Embassy*, p. 160.

188. Hardinge, *Old Diplomacy*, pp. 56–7, 98–9, 191, 197, 278.

189. *Fourth Report of R.C. on Civil Establishments*, P. P. 1890 (Cd. 6172), vol. XXVII, Minutes of Evidence, Q. 26961.

190. Gladwyn, *Paris Embassy*, pp. 135–6; S. M. Alsop, *Lady Sackville: A Biography* (1978), p. 120.

191. Hardinge, *Old Diplomacy*, p. 7.

192. Gwynn, *Cecil Spring-Rice*, I, p. 4; II, p. 436; Chirol, *Cecil Spring-Rice*, p. 58.

193. Knatchbull-Hugessen, *Diplomat in Peace and War*, pp. 9–10.

194. Taffs, *Ambassador to Bismark*, p. x.

195. Gladwyn, *Paris Embassy*, p. 218; Jones, *British Diplomatic Service*, pp. 43–7.

196. Newton, *Lord Lyons*, I, pp. 11, 139; II, pp. 222, 417, 424.

197. B. D. Rhodes, 'Sir Ronald Lindsay and the British View from Washington, 1930–1939', in C. L. Egan and A. W. Knott (eds.), *Essays in Twentieth-Century American Diplomatic History Dedicated to Professor Dan. M. Smith* (Washington, DC, 1982), pp. 62–4; Chirol, *Cecil Spring-Rice*, pp. 16, 26; Gwynn, *Cecil Spring-Rice*, I, pp. 5, 20, 253, 345, 411; II, pp. 83–4; Lady A. Gordon-Lennox (ed.), *The Diary of Lord Bertie of Thame, 1914–1918* (2 vols., 1924), I, pp. 63, 223; II, pp. 15, 167, 193; Lord Howard of Penrith, *Theatre of Life*, vol. I, *Life Seen from the Pit, 1863–1905* (1935), pp. 13, 23, 50, 260–73.

198. Newton, *Lord Lyons*, II, pp. 213, 217, 222, 428; Gladwyn, *Paris Embassy*, pp. 150, 172, 192.

199. Gwynn, *Cecil Spring-Rice*, I, p. 217; II,

pp. 390, 402; Mowat, *Pauncefote*, pp. 154, 292; D. Reynolds, 'Lord Lothian and Anglo-American Relations, 1939–1940', *Transactions of the American Philosophical Society*, LXXIII, part ii (1980), p. 2; Howard, *Life Seen from the Pit*, p. 144; Howard, *Life Seen from the Stalls*, p. 548.

200. Hardinge, *Diplomatist in Europe*, pp. 101–3; Gilbert, *Rumbold*, pp. 74, 79, 87, 180; Kennedy, *Anglo-German Antagonisms*, pp. 137–8; Sir V. Wellesley, *Diplomacy in Fetters* (1944), p. 124.

201. Steiner, *Foreign Office*, pp. 123, 139; Hardinge, *Diplomatist in Europe*, p. 185; Hardinge, *Old Diplomacy*, p. 205; Gordon-Lennox, *Diary of Lord Bertie*, I, pp. 233–4; II, pp. 77, 302, 323, 313; Howard, *Life Seen from the Pit*, p. 144; Howard, *Life Seen from the Stalls*, p. 199.

202. Platt, *Finance, Trade and Politics*, pp. xx–xiv.

203. Rhodes, 'Sir Ronald Lindsay', p. 70; Gordon-Lennox, *Diary of Lord Bertie*, II, pp. 153, 170, 305; Howard, *Life Seen from the Pit*, pp. 169, 171, 175, 177; Gwynn, *Cecil Spring-Rice*, I, pp. 75, 107, 115, 343, 376.

204. Vansittart, *Mist Procession*, pp. 53–4, 165; Wellesley, *Diplomacy in Fetters*, pp. 20, 211; Sir J. Tilley, *London to Tokyo* (1942), p. 97.

205. Gladwyn, *Paris Embassy*, p. 160; A. Cecil, 'The Foreign Office', in Sir A. W. Ward and G. P. Gooch (eds.), *The Cambridge History of Foreign Policy, 1783–1919*, vol. III, 1866–1919 (1923), p. 619.

206. Reynolds, 'Lord Lothian', pp. 6–8; Nightingale, 'Personnel of the British Foreign Office', p. 330; A. L. Kennedy, *Diplomacy Old and New* (1922), pp. 388–9.

207. Knatchbull-Hugessen, *Diplomat in Peace and War*, p. 18; D. G. Boadle, 'The Formation of the Foreign Office Economic Relations Section, 1930–1937', *H.J.*, XX (1977), pp. 919–36.

208. Jones, *Diplomatic Service*, pp. 124–38; R. M. Warman, 'The Erosion of Foreign Office Influence in the Making of Foreign Policy, 1916–1918', *H.J.*, XV (1972), pp. 135–59; A. J. Sharp, 'The Foreign Office in Eclipse, 1919–22', *History*, LI (1976), pp. 198–218; Gilbert, *Rumbold*, pp. 214–15; Kennedy, *Diplomacy Old and New*, pp. 364–5.

209. Gordon-Lennox, *Diary of Lord Bertie*, II, p. 325; Buchan, *Misson to Russia*, II, pp. 260–1; Wellesley, *Diplomacy in Fetters*, p. 33; G. A. Craig, 'The British Foreign Office from Grey to Austen Chamberlain', in Craig and Gilbert, *The Diplomats*, pp. 15–47.

210. Taylor, *The Troublemakers*, pp. 144–5; Steiner, *Foreign Office*, pp. 167–8; J. H. Hudson, 'Labour's Greatest Menace: The Foreign Office', *Foreign Affairs*, January 1920, p. 14.

211. H. Grenfell, 'Behind the Veil in Diplomacy', *Foreign Affairs*, May 1920, pp. 5–6.

212. Steiner, *Foreign Office*, pp. 19, 218–19; D. C. Watt, *Personalities and Politics: Studies in the Formation of British Foreign Policy in the Twentieth Century* (1965), p. 41.

213. Platt, *Finance, Trade and Politics*, pp. xxvii–xxviii; Fifth *Report of R.C. on the Civil Service*, P.P. 1914–16 (Cd. 7749), pp. 38–41.

214. C. Larner, 'The Amalgamation of the Diplomatic Service with the Foreign Office', *Journal of Contemporary History*, VII (1972), pp. 107–26; Z. Steiner and M. L. Dockrill, 'The Foreign Office Reforms, 1919–21', *H.J.*, XVII (1974), pp. 131–56.

215. Wellesley, *Diplomacy in Fetters*, p. 211; Nightingale, 'Personnel of the British Foreign Office', p. 320; C. P. Snow, *The Light and the Dark* (1962 edn.), p. 108.

216. Watt, *Personalities and Politics*, pp. 187–8.

217. Stephenson, *Edward Stuart Talbot*, pp. 7–8.

218. A. Trollope, *The Vicar of Bullhampton* (1924 edn.), pp. 60–1.

219. O. Wister, 'Preface' to Leigh, *Other Days*, p. 10.

220. Nightingale, 'Personnel of the British Foreign Office', p. 326.

221. H. J. Laski, *The Danger of Being a Gentleman, and Other Essays* (1939), pp. 22, 28.

222. H. J. Perkin, *Professionalism, Property and English Society since 1880* (1980), p. 23.

Chapter 7

1. Sir I. de la Bere, *The Queen's Orders of Chivalry* (1968), pp. 15–16.

2. K. Rose, *King George V* (1983); M. De-

la-Noy, *The Honours System* (1985), p. 88; W. D. Rubinstein, *Elites and the Wealthy in Modern Britain: Essays in Social and Economic History* (1987), pp. 222–33.

3. *Hansard*, H.L., 23 Feb. 1914, col. 256.

4. *Hansard*, H.L., 7 Aug. 1917, cols. 193–4.

5. De la Bere, *Orders of Chivalry*, pp. 140, 144–5; F. M. L. Thompson, 'England', in D. Spring (ed.), *European Landed Elites in the Nineteenth Century* (1977), p. 40.

6. Rose, *King George V*, p. 259. In the aftermath of the Irish Treaty of 1921, the Order of St. Patrick went into abeyance. See E. D. Goldstein, 'Quis Separabit: The Order of St. Patrick and Anglo-Irish Relations, 1922–34', *Historical Research*, LXII (1989), pp. 70–80.

7. P. Marsh, *The Discipline of Popular Government: Lord Salisbury's Domestic Statecraft, 1881–1902* (1978), p. 126; J. Lant, *Insubstantial Pageant: Ceremony and Confusion at Queen Victoria's Court* (1979), p. 187; B. McGill, 'Glittering Prizes and Party Funds in Perspective, 1882–1931', *Bulletin of the Institute of Historical Research*, LV (1982), p. 187.

8. De la Bere, *Orders of Chivalry*, p. 158; Rose, *King George V*, p. 248.

9. De-la-Noy, *Honours System*, p. 77.

10. Rose, *King George V*, pp. 256, 259; de la Bere, *Orders of Chivalry*, p. 88.

11. De la Bere, *Orders of Chivalry*, pp. 157, 161.

12. Rose, *King George V*, pp. 257–8.

13. De la Bere, *Orders of Chivalry*, pp. 16, 96–7, 114.

14. De la Bere, *Orders of Chivalry*, pp. 145–6.

15. J. Northrop Moore, *Edward Elgar: A Creative Life* (1984), pp. 622, 770, 790.

16. De-la-Noy, *Honours System*, p. 57; H. J. Hanham, 'The Sale of Honours in Late Victorian England', *Victorian Studies*, III (1960), p. 279.

17. De-la-Noy, *Honours System*, p. 111.

18. R. E. Pumphrey, 'The Introduction of Industrialists into the British Peerage: A Study in Adaption of a Social Institution', *A.H.R.*, LXV (1959), pp. 4–18.

19. R. E. Pumphrey, 'The Creation of Peerages in England, 1837–1911' (Ph.D. dissertation, Yale University, 1934), pp. 130–1; Rose, *King George V*,

p. 248.

20. D. Judd, *Lord Reading* (1982), pp. 69, 113, 123, 140, 232.

21. J. Campbell, *F. E. Smith: First Earl of Birkenhead* (1983), p. 598; G. R. Searle, *Corruption in British Politics, 1895–1930* (1987), pp. 306–7.

22. R. Blake, *The Unknown Prime Minister: The Life and Times of Andrew Bonar Law, 1858–1923* (1955), p. 472.

23. R. Pound and G. Harmsworth, *Northcliffe* (1959), p. 642.

24. J. McEwen, 'The Coupon Election of 1918 and Unionist Members of Parliament', *Journal of Modern History*, XXXIX (1962), pp. 305–6.

25. De-la-Noy, *Honours System*, p. 123.

26. M. McCahill, 'Peerage Creations and the Changing Character of the British Nobility, 1750–1830', *Eng. Hist. Rev.*, LXXXXVI (1981), pp. 259–84.

27. De-la-Noy, *Honours System*, p. 89; R. Taylor, *Lord Salisbury* (1975), p. 147.

28. De-la-Noy, *Honours System*, p. 100; Rose, *King George V*, p. 246.

29. Blake, *Bonar Law*, pp. 346–8; D. Marquand, *Ramsay Macdonald* (1977), pp. 775–6; D. Dilks, *Neville Chamberlain*, vol. I, *Pioneering and Reform, 1869–1929* (1984), pp. 255, 445–6.

30. A. Ponsonby, *The Decline of Aristocracy* (1912), pp. 124–6.

31. De-la-Noy, *Honours System*, p. 118.

32. Rose, *King George V*, p. 245; Marquand, *Macdonald*, pp. 775–6.

33. Hanham, 'Sale of Honours', p. 280; Searle, *Corruption*, pp. 11, 88–9.

34. De-la-Noy, *Honours System*, p. 88.

35. J. R. Vincent (ed.), *The Crawford Papers: The Journals of David Lindsay, Twenty Seventh Earl of Crawford and Tenth Earl of Balcarres, 1871–1940, During the Years 1992 to 1940* (1984), p. 188; De-la-Noy, *Honours System*, p. 61.

36. D. Sinclair, *Dynasty: The Astors and their Times* (1983), pp. 252–70.

37. M. Pinto-Duschinsky, *British Political Finance, 1830–1980* (Washington, 1981), pp. 26–28, 33; H. J. Hanham, 'British Party Finance, 1868–1880', *Bulletin of the Institute of Historical Research*, XXVII (1954), p. 70; Searle, *Corruption*, p. 85.

38. J. Ramsden, *The Age of Balfour and Baldwin, 1902–1940* (1978), pp. 69, 220; N. Blewett, *The Peers, the Parties and the People: The British General Elections of 1910* (1972), p. 290; T. O. Lloyd, 'The

Whip as Paymaster: Herbert Gladstone and Party Organisation', *Eng. Hist. Rev.*, LXXXIX (1974), p. 807.

39. S. Koss, *Sir John Brunner: Radical Plutocrat, 1842–1919* (1970), pp. 131, 157, 159, 176, 185, 200.

40. Searle, *Corruption*, p. 389; Blake, *Bonar Law*, pp. 496–8; Rose, *King George V*, pp. 279–80.

41. Viscount Chilston, *Chief Whip: The Political Life of Aretas Akers-Douglas, First Viscount Chilston* (1962), pp. 196–200; Hanham, 'Sale of Honours', p. 283.

42. Searle, *Corruption*, pp. 88–9.

43. Hanham, 'Sale of Honours', pp. 284–5; Searle, *Corruption*, pp. 85–6.

44. Hanham, 'Sale of Honours', pp. 286–7; Searle, *Corruption*, p, 87.

45. De-la-Noy, *Honours System*, p. 92.

46. Lloyd, 'Whip as Paymaster', p. 789; Searle, *Corruption*, p. 145.

47. Lloyd, 'Whip as Paymaster', p. 810.

48. Searle, *Corruption*, p. 146.

49. *Saturday Review*, 16 Feb. 1905; *The Spectator*, 16 Dec. 1905.

50. Lloyd, 'Whip as Paymaster', p. 808.

51. Blake, *Bonar Law*, p. 100.

52. Searle, *Corruption*, pp. 161–5; Ramsden, *Age of Balfour and Baldwin*, pp. 80–1.

53. Lloyd, 'Whip as Paymaster', pp. 805–6; Searle, *Corruption*, pp. 144–56.

54. P. Rowland, *Lloyd George* (1975), p. 576.

55. J. Wilson, *C.B.: A Life of Sir Henry Campbell-Bannerman* (1973), p. 334.

56. *Hansard*, H.L., 23 Feb. 1914, cols. 252–96; Searle, *Corruption*, p. 171.

57. A. J. P. Taylor, *Essays in English History* (1976), p. 257; R. Rhodes James (ed.), *Memoirs of a Conservative: J. C. C. Davidson's Memoirs and Papers, 1910–37* (1969), pp. 278–9.

58. T. Cullen, *Maundy Gregory: Purveyor of Honours* (1974), p. 107.

59. Rhodes James, *Memoirs of a Conservative*, pp. 265, 281; De-la-Noy, *Honours System*, p. 102.

60. Cullen, *Maundy Gregory*, p. 104; G. Macmillan, *Honours for Sale* (1954), p. 66.

61. Cullen, *Maundy Gregory*, pp. 93–102.

62. Searle, *Corruption*, p. 354; Cullen, *Maundy Gregory*, pp. 28–9, 108–10.

63. Rose, *King George V*, pp. 249–51.

64. But cf. Rubinstein, *Elites and the Wealthy*, pp. 243–4.

65. De-lay-Noy, *Honours System* p. 116; Cullen, *Maundy Gregory*, p. 117; Rose,

King George V, p. 252.

66. P. G. Wodehouse, *The Inimitable Jeeves* (1923), p. 20; *Punch*, 12 and 26 July 1922.

67. Ramsden, *Age of Balfour and Baldwin*, pp. 222–3.

68. Cullen, *Maundy Gregory*, p. 108; Searle, *Corruption*, p. 365.

69. K. Rose, *The Later Cecils* (1975), p. 87.

70. *Hansard*, H.L., 7 Aug. 1917, cols. 172–212.

71. *Hansard*, H.L., 31 Oct. 1917, cols. 835–86.

72. *Hansard*, H.L., 20 Mar. 1918, cols. 513–33.

73. *Hansard*, H.L., 13 Nov. 1918, cols. 4–34.

74. *Hansard*, H.L., 22 June 1922, cols. 1126–40.

75. *Hansard*, H.L., 29 June 1922, cols. 103–38.

76. *Hansard*, H.L., 17 July 1922, cols. 475–512.

77. *Hansard*, H.C., 20 June 1922, col. 1038; 21 June 1922, cols. 1298–9; 22 June 1922, cols. 1496–7; 27 June 1922, cols. 1841–8; 29 June 1922, cols. 2312–14; 3 July 1922, cols. 23–4; 5 July 1922, cols. 367–70.

78. Searle, *Corruption*, pp. 363–70; *Hansard*, H.C., 17 July 1922, cols. 1745–1862.

79. Searle, *Corruption*, pp. 370–4.

80. *Hansard*, H.L., 7 March 1923, cols. 259–91.

81. Searle, *Corruption*, pp. 379–86.

82. Marquand, *Macdonald*, pp. 133, 240, 357–61, 397–9.

83. Dilks, *Chamberlain*, I, p. 394.

84. Rhodes James, *Memoirs of a Conservative*, pp. 139, 280–2, 288–90.

85. Ramsden, *Age of Balfour and Baldwin*, pp. 220–4.

86. McGill, 'Glittering Prizes and Party Funds', pp. 92–3; Searle, *Corruption*, pp. 407–9.

87. Ramsden, *Age of Balfour and Baldwin*, p. 223.

88. Marquand, *Macdonald*, pp. 745–7; Rose, *King George V*, pp. 254–5.

89. *Hansard*, H.L., 17 July 1922, col. 482.

90. Macmillan, *Honour for Sale*, pp. 36, 138, 151, 164, 218 19; Cullen, *Maundy Gregory*, pp. 138, 164, 171.

91. Rose, *Later Cecils*, p. 88; Searle, *Corruption*, p. ?13. See also Lord Lee's earlier riposte to Selborne in the Lords debate of N ember 1914: He 'retorted with considerable sarcasm about the Noble Lords of high lineage, who were them-

selves not averse to accepting the Garter and other high decorations, but who seemed shocked at the idea that humble but devoted people, who had "done their bit" to the uttermost, should receive any recognition at the hands of their sovereign.' (A. Clark (ed.), 'A Good Innings': The Private Papers of Viscount Lee of Fareham (1974), p. 184).

92. A. J. P. Taylor, Beaverbrook (1972), p. 1.

93. Searle, Corruption, pp. 4–5, 24–5.

94. A. J. Lee, The Origins of the Popular Press, 1855–1914 (1976), pp. 79, 94, 114; G. A. Cranfield, The Press and Society from Caxton to Northcliffe (1978), pp. 216–20.

95. G. Boyce, J. Curran, and P. Wingate, Newspaper History from the Seventeenth Century to the Present Day (1978), pp. 136–7.

96. Searle, Corruption, pp. 306–7, 318–23.

97. Blake, Bonar Law, pp. 299–300.

98. S. Koss, The Rise and Fall of the Political Press in Britain, vol. I, The Nineteenth Century (1981), pp. 369, 414–15; M. Cowling, The Impact of Labour, 1920–1924 (1971), pp. 45–9; G. M. Trevelyan, 'The White Peril', 19C, L (1901), pp. 1043–55.

99. Vincent, Crawford Papers, pp. 386, 477, 557; P. Williamson (ed.), The Modernisation of Conservative Politics: The Diaries and Letters of William Bridgeman, 1904–1935 (1988), pp. 242, 249.

100. Taylor, Beaverbrook, p. 135.

101. Williamson, Modernisation of Conservative Politics, p. 109.

102. Searle, Corruption, p. 109.

103. Taylor, Beaverbrook, pp. 45, 54, 236, 335, 386.

104. Campbell, F. E. Smith, pp. 97, 173–5, 285–8; Vincent, Crawford Papers, p. 319.

105. G. P. Taylor, 'Cecil Rhodes and the Second Home Rule Bill', H.J., XIV (1971), p. 771; E. Longford, Jameson's Raid (1960), pp. 306–8, 318–22; J. Butler, The Liberal Party and the Jameson Raid (1968), pp. 228, 233, 262, 270–2.

106. Searle, Corruption, pp. 52–65; Dilks, Neville Chamberlain, pp. 12, 76–7, 83–5.

107. R. A. Rempel, Unionists Divided: Arthur Balfour, Joseph Chamberlain and the Unionist Free Traders (1972), p. 109; M. J. Wiener, English Culture and the Decline of the Industrial Spirit, 1850–1980 (1981), pp. 99–100; Ramsden, Age of Balfour and Baldwin, p. 12.

108. Searle, Corruption, p. 71; N. Blewett, 'Free Fooders, Balfourites, Whole Hig-

gers: Factionalism within the Unionist Party, 1906–10', H.J., XI (1968), p. 95; Ramsden, Age of Balfour and Baldwin, p. 37.

109. Viscount Cecil of Chelwood, A Great Experiment (1941), pp. 32–4; Rose, Later Cecils, p. 138; H. P. Cecil, 'The Development of Lord Robert Cecil's Views on the Securing of a Lasting Peace, 1915–1919' (D.Phil. dissertation, Oxford University, 1971), pp. 13–16, 24–8, 406–13.

110. Ramsden, Age of Balfour and Baldwin, p. 41; Rose, Later Cecils, p. 93.

111. Searle, Corruption, pp. 124–8; Vincent, Crawford Papers, pp. 146, 149, 282, 292.

112. Taylor, Essays in English History, p. 268.

113. Vincent, Crawford Papers, p. 280.

114. Searle, Corruption, pp. 139–44.

115. For a full account of this episode, see Searle, Corruption, pp. 172–200; Judd, Lord Reading, pp. 90–107; J. Grigg, Lloyd George: From Peace to War, 1912–1916 (1985), pp. 44–66; F. Donaldson, The Marconi Scandal (1962).

116. P. Calvert, The Mexican Revolution, 1910–1914 (1968), pp. 174–77.

117. A. J. A. Morris, C. P. Trevelyan, 1870–1958: Portrait of a Radical (1977), pp. 91–2. Readers of Anthony Powell will remember that Lady Molly's first husband, the Marquess of Sleaford, actually resigned from the Liberal government over the Marconi Scandal, and thereafter devoted himself to good works. See H. Spurling, Handbook to Anthony Powell's Music of Time (1977), pp. 150–1.

118. Donaldson, Marconi Scandal, p. 34.

119. Searle, Corruption, p. 122; Donaldson, Marconi Scandal, pp. 199–204, 215–16, 268–96; Rose, Later Cecils, pp. 145–6; Cecil of Chelwood, A Great Experiment, p. 37.

120. Searle, Corruption, p. 303; Ramsden, Age of Balfour and Baldwin, p. 137.

121. Rose, King George V, pp. 249–50; Rowland, Lloyd George, pp. 575–6; Williamson, Modernisation of Conservative Politics, p. 127.

122. Judd, Lord Reading, p. 107; Vincent, Crawford Papers, p. 327.

123. Searle, Corruption, pp. 395–6; Cowling, Impact of Labour, p. ix; Campbell, F. E. Smith, pp. 334–6, 472, 625, 719–20, 804.

124. Searle, Corruption, pp. 291–2; Cowling, Impact of Labour, pp. 67–8.

125. Lord Henry Bentinck, Tory Democracy

(1918), pp. 1–3, 62–3.

126. Cowling, *Impact of Labour*, pp. 62–3, 88–90; K. O. Morgan, *Consensus and Disunity: The Lloyd George Coalition Government, 1918–1922* (1979), p. 183. For their pre-war antecedents, see: J. Ridley, 'The Unionist Social Reform Committee: Wets Before the Deluge', *H.J.*, xxx (1987), pp. 391–413.

127. Morgan, *Consensus and Disunity*, p. 207.

128. Searle, *Corruption*, p. 345; Cowling, *Impact of Labour*, pp. 75, 90.

129. Cowling, *Impact of Labour*, pp. 72–3, 243.

130. Morgan, *Consensus and Disunity*, pp. 205–12; Searle, *Corruption*, pp. 344–9; Cowling, *Impact of Labour*, pp. 65–688; K. Robbins, *Sir Edward Grey: A Biography of Lord Grey of Fallodon* (1971), pp. 355–62; M. Bentley, 'Liberal Politics and the Grey Conspiracy of 1921, *H.J.*, xx (1977), pp. 461–78.

131. K. Middlemas (ed.), *Thomas Jones: Whitehall Diary* (2 vols., 1969), ii, *1926–1930*, pp. 165–6.

132. Morgan, *Consensus and Disunity*, pp. 340–2; Williamson, *Transformation of Conservative Politics*, pp. 156–9.

133. M. Kinnear, *The Fall of the Lloyd George Coalition: The Political Crisis of 1922* (1973), pp. 77–80.

134. Williamson, *Transformation of Conservative Politics*, p. 108; Morgan, *Consensus and Disunity*, pp. 354, 373.

135. Rhodes James, *Memoirs of a Conservative*, p. 28; Williamson, *Transformation of Conservative Politics*, p. 115.

136. Searle, *Corruption*, p. 395; Williamson, *Transformation of Conservative Politics*, pp. 168–9.

137. Rose, *Later Cecils*, p. 94; Vincent, *Crawford Papers*, p. 346.

138. Longford, *Jameson's Raid*, pp. 286, 318, 329; Butler, *Liberal Party and the Jameson Raid*, pp. 187, 270, 276.

139. Searle, *Corruption*, p. 189; Ramsden, *Age of Balfour and Baldwin*, p. 14; Williamson, *Transformation of Conservative Politics*, p. 8.

140. Kinnear, *Fall of the Lloyd George Coalition*, p. 86; A. J. P. Taylor (ed.), *Lloyd George: A Diary by Frances Stevenson* (1971), p. 323.

141. J. R. M. Butler, *Lord Lothian* (1960), pp. 37, 63, 88, 126, 249; J. Turner, *Lloyd George's Secretariat* (1981), pp. 2–3, 21–3, 25–6, 186–9, 193–6.

142. W. Manchester, *The Last Lion: Winston Spencer Churchill*, vol. ii, *Alone, 1932–1940* (New York, 1988), pp. 300–4.

143. Vincent, *Crawford Papers*, p. 348; Searle, *Corruption*, pp. 47, 332.

144. Rose, *Later Cecils*, p. 87; Rose, *King George V*, p. 249.

145. Searle, *Corruption*, pp. 29, 425.

146. L. Stone, *The Crisis of the Aristocracy, 1558–1641*, (1965), p. 39.

147. Rose, *Later Cecils*, pp. 159, 321.

Chapter 8

1. G. F. A. Best, *Mid-Victorian Britain, 1851–1875* (1971), pp. 242–3; J. Manners, 'Are Rich Landowners Idle?' *National Review*, x (1888), pp. 836–40.

2. B. Holland, *The Life of Spencer Compton, Eighth Duke of Devonshire 1833–1908* (2 vols., 1911), ii, pp. 263–4.

3. E. S. Shkolnik, *Leading Ladies: A Study of Eight Late Victorian and Edwardian Political Wives* (1987), pp. 322, 375; The Duke of Portland, *Men, Women and Things* (1937), p. 159.

4. The Marchioness of Londonderry, *Retrospect* (1938), pp. 13, 25–7, 40–2, 173–5.

5. J. Gunther, *Inside Europe* (1937 edn.), p. 248; D. Marquand, *Ramsay Macdonald* (1977), pp. 415–16, 687–92; R. Rhodes James (ed.), *'Chips': The Diaries of Sir Henry Channon* (1967), p. 140; H. M. Hyde, *The Londonderrys: A Family Portrait* (1979), pp. 168, 194.

6. R. Nevill (ed.), *The Reminiscences of Lady Dorothy Nevill* (1906), p. 103; The Marchioness of Aberdeen, *More Cracks with 'We Twa'* (1929), p. 5.

7. Anon, 'English Society and Its Historians', *Quarterly Review*, clxi (1885), pp. 156–8; P. Gordon (ed.), *The Red Earl: The Papers of the Fifth Earl Spencer, 1835–1910* (2 vols., 1981–6), vol. ii, *1885–1910*, p. 163; N. W. Ellenberger, 'The Souls and London Society at the End of the Nineteenth Century', *Victorian Studies*, xxv (1982), p. 140.

8. R. Nevill (ed.), *Under Five Reigns, by Lady Dorothy Nevill* (1910), p. 151; Lord Dunraven, *Past Times and Pastimes* (2 vols., 1922), i, p. 196; L. Davidoff, *The Best Circles: Society, Etiquette and the Season* (1973), pp. 45–7.

9. Nevill, *Reminiscences*, p. 127; H. J. Perkin, *The Rise of Professional Society: England Since 1880* (1989), pp. 64–75; G. R. Searle, *Corruption in British Politics,*

1895–1930 (1987), pp. 12–30.

10. J. Camplin, *The Rise of the Rich* (New York, 1979), pp. 161–72, 182, 204; C. Aslet, *The Last Country Houses* (1982), p. 62; F. H. W. Sheppard (ed.), *The Survey of London*, vol. XXXIX, *The Grosvenor Estate in Mayfair*, Part I, *General Surrey* (1977), pp. 99–100; Gordon, *Red Earl*, II, pp. 36–7.

11. Lady Jeune, 'London Society', *North American Review*, CLIV (1892), pp. 602–7, 610–11.

12. Ouida, 'The Sins of Society', *Fortnightly Review*, LVIII (1892), pp. 780–5; N. Arling, 'The Future of "Society"', *Westminster Review*, CXL (1893), pp. 229–31; A. West, 'Some Changes in Social Life During the Queen's Reign, *19C*, XLI (1897), p. 651; H. E. M. Strutfield, 'The Higher Rascality', *National Review*, XXXI (1898), pp. 74–5.

13. B. Webb, *Our Partnership* (1948), p. 347.

14. N. W. Ellenberger, 'The Transformation of London "Society" at the End of Victoria's Reign: Evidence from the Court Presentation Records', *Albion* (forthcoming); Lady V. Greville, *The Gentleman in Society* (1892), pp. 112–14.

15. Camplin, *Rise of the Rich*, p. 247; K. Middlemas, *Pursuit of Pleasure: High Society in the 1900s* (1977), p. 247.

16. T. H. S. Escott, 'The New Reign and the New Society', *Fortnightly Review*, LXX (1901), p. 684; P. Thane, 'Financiers and the British State: The Case of Sir Ernest Cassel', *Business History*, XXVIII (1986), pp. 80–2; K. Middlemas, *The Life and Times of Edward VII* (1972), pp. 68–88, 186–99.

17. A Foreign Resident [pseud. T. H. S. Escott], *Society in the New Reign* (1904), pp. 118, 228; P. Magnus, *King Edward VII* (1964), pp. 106, 141, 144, 150, 153, 170, 217–19, 245–6, 257–60; Camplin, *Rise of the Rich*, pp. 101–5, 216–19.

18. T. H. Hollingsworth, 'The Demography of the British Peerage', supplement to *Population Studies*, XVIII (1964–5), pp. 9–10; D. Thomas, 'The Social Origins of Marriage Partners of the British Peerage in the Eighteenth and Nineteenth Centuries', *Population Studies*, XXVI (1972), pp. 99, 102–3, 106–7; D. M. Thomas, 'Marriage Patterns in the British Peerage in the Eighteenth and Nineteenth Centuries' (M.Phil. dissertation, London University, 1969), pp. 88–99; F. M. L. Thompson, *The*

Rise of Respectable Society: A Social History of Victorian Britain, 1830–1900 (1988), pp. 104–8.

19. J. Harris and P. Thane, 'British and European Bankers, 1880–1914: An Aristocratic Bourgeoisie?' in P. Thane, G. Crossick and R. C. Floud (eds.), *The Power of the Past: Essays for Eric Hobsbawn* (1984), pp. 226–8; Y. Cassis, 'Bankers in English Society in the Late Nineteenth Century', *Ec.H.R.*, 2nd ser., XXXVIII (1985), pp. 217–29; M. Lisle-Williams, 'Merchant Banking Dynasties in the English Class Structure: Ownership, Solidarity and Kinship in the City of London, 1850–1960', *British Journal of Sociology*, XXXV (1984), pp. 353–8.

20. Thompson, *Rise of Respectable Society*, p. 107; M. E. Montgomery, *Gilded Prostitution: Status, Money and Transatlantic Marriages, 1870–1914* (1989), pp. 22–3, 43, 80–1, 129–30, 137–8.

21. 'Colonial', 'Titled Colonials v. Titled Americans', *Contemporary Review*, LXXXVII (1905), pp. 861–9.

22. F. M. L. Thompson, *English Landed Society in the Nineteenth Century* (1963), pp. 301–2; C. Metcalfe, *Peeresses of the Stage* (1913), pp. 163–7, 174–5, 240–51; J. M. Bulloch, 'Peers Who Have Married Players', *Notes and Queries*, CLXIX (1935), pp. 92–4.

23. Magnus, *Edward VII*, p. 153; Hollingsworth, 'Demography of the British Peerage', pp. 23–5; M. Harrison, *Lord of London* (1966), pp. 121–8; D. Sutherland, *The Yellow Earl* (1965), pp. 81–8.

24. Foreign Resident, *Society in the New Reign*, p. 182; T. H. S. Escott, *England: Its People, Polity and Pursuits* (1885), pp. 314–15.

25. D. Cannadine, 'Another "Last Victorian"?: P. G. Wodehouse and His World', *South Atlantic Quarterly*, LXXVII (1978), pp. 481–3; F. M. Boyd, *A Pelican's Tale* (1919), pp. 131–8; Sutherland, *Yellow Earl*, pp. 74–8, 92–6.

26. Middlemas, *Edward VII*, p. 83.

27. Nevill, *Reminiscences*, pp. 103–5; Nevill, *Under Five Reigns*, p. 140; Camplin, *Rise of the Rich*, p. 246.

28. Lord Winterton, *Fifty Tumultuous Years* (1955), pp. 75–8; J. R. Vincent (ed.), *The Crawford Papers: The Journals of David Lindsay, Twenty Seventh Earl of Crawford and Tenth Earl of Balcarres, 1871–1940, During the Years 1892–1940* (1984), pp. 268–9; Middlemas, *Pursuit*

of Pleasure, p. 15.

29. K. Rose, *The Later Cecils* (1975), pp. 53–4; G. D. Phillips, *The Diehards: Aristocratic Society and Politics in Edwardian England* (1979), pp. 20–1.

30. Ellenberger, 'Souls and London Society', p. 158; Gordon, *Red Earl*, II, pp. 13–14; V. Bonham Carter, *Winston Churchill As I Knew Him* (1967), p. 137.

31. Bonham Carter, *Churchill As I Knew Him*, pp. 228, 303–4.

32. J. R. Vincent (ed.), *The Later Derby Diaries: Home Rule, Liberal Unionism and Aristocratic Life* (1981), p. 142; Foreign Resident, *Society in the New Reign*, p. 72.

33. There is a vast and varied literature on the Souls. See especially: Ellenberger, 'Souls and London Society', pp. 133–60; K. Rose, *Curzon: A Most Superior Person* (1985), pp. 176–90; A. Lambert, *Unquiet Souls: The Indian Summer of the British Aristocracy 1880–1918* (1984), pp. 3–102.

34. M. Oxford, *More Memories* (1933), pp. 181–3.

35. Ellenberger, 'Souls and London Society', pp. 155–6.

36. Shkolnik, *Leading Ladies*, pp. 463–5; Ellenberger, 'Souls and London Society', p. 153.

37. Winterton, *Fifty Tumultuous Years*, pp. 75, 78–80; Dunraven, *Past Times and Pastimes*, I, pp. 194, 196–8; Nevill, *Reminiscences*, pp. 99–100.

38. Londonderry, *Retrospect*, p. 251.

39. Portland, *Men, Women and Things*, pp. 1–2, Sheppard, *Grosvenor Estate in Mayfair*, p. 101.

40. P. Balfour, *Society Racket: A Critical Study of Modern Social Life* (1932), p. 134; Rhodes James, 'Chips', pp. 25, 190.

41. Winterton, *Fifty Tumultuous Years*, pp. 92–4; Portland, *Men, Women and Things*, p. 158; Balfour, *Society Racket*, p. 57.

42. Montgomery, *Gilded Prostitution*, pp. 3, 285–8; Hollingsworth, 'Demography of the British Peerage', pp. 9–10, 23–5; Balfour, *Society Racket*, pp. 128–32.

43. Vincent, *Crawford Papers*, p. 583; Rhodes James, 'Chips', p. 35.

44. Hyde, *The Londonderrys*, pp. 185, 220, 236; Marquand, *Macdonald*, pp. 687–92; Londonderry, *Retrospect*, pp. 233–8.

45. Winterton, *Fifty Tumultuous Years*, pp. 91–2; Balfour, *Society Racket*, pp. 126, 135–7; Rhodes James, 'Chips', p. 81.

46. R. Rhodes James (ed.), *Memoirs of a Conservative: J. C. C. Davidson's Memoirs and Papers, 1910–37* (1969); K. Middlemas (ed.), *Thomas Jones: Whitehall Diary, 1916–30* (2 vols., 1969); Balfour, *Society Racket*, pp. 48, 82, 124; Rhodes James, 'Chips', p. 194.

47. Searle, *Corruption in British Politics*, p. 28; Vincent, *Crawford Papers*, p. 153; Thane and Harris, 'British and European Bankers', p. 227.

48. K. Rose, *King George V* (1983), pp. 87, 90, 96, 236, 272, 274, 295, 321; Balfour, *Society Racket*, pp. 77–8; Vincent, *Crawford Papers*, pp. 400, 519.

49. F. Donaldson, *Edward VIII* (1974), pp. 43, 56–7, 104, 121, 124, 137; Winterton, *Fifty Tumultuous Years*, p. 77.

50. Rhodes James, 'Chips', pp. 25, 33, 50, 60, 75, 88; Donaldson, *Edward VIII*, pp. 137, 158–9, 182–3, 257, 281.

51. Vincent, *Crawford Papers*, p. 575; Donaldson, *Edward VIII*, pp. 165–6, 298.

52. P. Mortimer, *Queen Elizabeth: A Portrait of the Queen Mother* (New York, 1986), pp. 50, 93, 124, 134, 159; J. W. Wheeler-Bennett, *King George VI: His Life and Reign* (1958), pp. 260–1, 271, 759–60; Rhodes James, 'Chips', p. 130.

53. Vincent, *Crawford Papers*, p. 575; Donaldson, *Edward VIiI*, p. 173.

54. Aberdeen, '*We Twa*', pp. 8–9.

55. Oxford, *More Memories*, p. 33. See also Mary, Countess of Minto, in M. Oxford (ed.), *Myself When Young: by Famous Women of Today* (1938), p. 227.

56. Londonderry, *Retrospect*, p. 251.

57. Lord Willoughby de Broke, *The Passing Years* (1924), pp. 56–8.

58. Winterton, *Fifty Tumultuous Years*, pp. 99, 110. Significantly, he, too, had no time for the phrase 'county society', which he thought had been 'invented by urban journalists and novelists.'

59. R. Nevill (ed.), *Leaves from the Note-Books of Lady Dorothy Nevill* (1907), pp. 43–4; *E.G.*, 27 April 1901.

60. Aslet, *Last Country Houses*, pp. 16, 23, 28, 33, 66–9, 185–7.

61. F. M. L. Thompson, 'English Landed Society in the Nineteenth Century', in Thane, Crossick and Floud, *The Power of the Past*, pp. 210–11; Aslet, *Last Country Houses*, pp. 190–4; *E.G.*, 15 April 1893.

62. *E.G.*, 5 Jan. 1895; Aslet, *Last Country Houses*, p. 56; N. Nicolson, *Lord of the Isles* (1960), pp. 22, 25, 50–1, 78, 101,

121–2, 236–7; M. Beard, 'The Impact of the First World War on Agricultural Society in West Sussex (M.Litt. dissertation, Cambridge University, 1984), pp. 16, 27, 140.

63. Camplin, *Rise of the Rich*, pp. 188–9, 192, 221; Searle, *Corruption in British Politics*, p. 218.

64. *E.G.*, 9 June 1900; R. H. Trainor, 'The Gentrification of Victorian and Edwardian Industrialists', in A. L. Beier, D. Cannadine and J. M. Rosenheim (eds.), *The First Modern Society: Essays in English History in Honour of Lawrence Stone* (1989), pp. 180–5, 193.

65. Thompson, *Rise of Respectable Society*, pp. 159, 163–4, 167; J. Franklin, *The Gentleman's Country House and Its Plan, 1835–1914* (1981), pp. 4, 30–6.

66. Aslet, *Last Country Houses*, pp. 50–1; Camplin, *Rise of the Rich*, pp. 253–4.

67. Searle, *Corruption in British Politics*, p. 25; J. Kern, *The Culture of Time and Space, 1880–1918* (1983), p. 114; Thompson, *English Landed Society*, p. 1; R. Carr, *English Fox-Hunting: A History* (1976), p. 147.

68. Camplin, *Rise of the Rich*, p. 95; Kern, *Culture of Time and Space*, p. 217.

69. Aslet, *Last Country Houses*, pp. 49–55, 66–9.

70. Nevill, *Note-Books of Lady Dorothy Nevill*, p. 44.

71. Camplin, *Rise of the Rich*, p. 95; Aslet, *Last Country Houses*, pp. 17–19, 55, 58–9.

72. Carr, *Fox-Hunting*, pp. 159–60; Gordon, *Red Earl*, I, pp. 5, 13, 121, 124–5; II, 36, 161–3, 179, 237; H. Wyndham, *The Pytchley Mastership of the Fifth Earl Spencer* (1970), passim.

73. Sutherland, *Yellow Earl*, pp. 135–40, 158–9, 189, 206; Carr, *Fox-Hunting*, pp. 162–3; Marchioness of Londonderry, *Henry Chaplin: A Memoir* (1926), pp. 191–251.

74. R. Longrigg, *The English Squire and His Sport* (1977), p. 225; Gordon, *Red Earl*, II, p. 36.

75. Sutherland, *Yellow Earl*, pp. 139, 159; Carr, *Fox-Hunting*, p. 166; G. E. Collins, *History of the Brocklesby Hounds, 1700–1901* (1902), p. 10; D. Itzkowitz, *Peculiar Privilege: A Social History of Fox-Hunting, 1753–1885* (1977), pp. 157–8.

76. Carr, *Fox-Hunting*, p. 165; Thompson, *Rise of Respectable Society*, pp. 267–8; R. Longrigg, *The History of Fox-Hunting*

(1975), p. 154.

77. Camplin, *Rise of the Rich*, p. 203; Searle, *Corruption in British Politics*, p. 16; Trainor, 'Gentrification of Victorian and Edwardian Industrialists', p. 184; C. Richardson, *The Complete Fox-Hunter* (1908), pp. 56–7; G. F. Underhill, 'Fox-hunting and Agriculture', *19C*, XLIII (1898), p. 746.

78. Lord Suffolk and Berkshire, 'Fox-hunters and Farmers', *National Review*, XXIV (1894), pp. 546–56.

79. Carr, *Fox-Hunting*, pp. 218–23; Itzkowitz, *Peculiar Privilege*, pp. 154–6; Longrigg, *Fox-Hunting*, p. 152; *E.G.*, 7 Jan. 1899.

80. Itzkowitz, *Peculiar Privilege*, pp. 160–74.

81. L. P. Curtis, jr., 'Stopping the Hunt 1881–1882: An Aspect of the Irish Land War', in C. H. E. Philpin (ed.), *Nationalism and Popular Protest in Ireland* (1987), pp. 356–86.

82. J. N. P. Watson, 'Heirs to "The Wild Marquis"', *Country Life*, 3 March 1983, pp. 502–3.

83. C. A. Lewis, *Hunting in Ireland: An Historical and Geographical Analysis* (1975), p. 57.

84. Curtis, 'Stopping the Hunt', pp. 390–3; Longrigg, *Fox-Hunting*, pp. 162–4, 212–13.

85. Carr, *Fox-Hunting*, pp. 186–7.

86. Longrigg, *Fox-Hunting*, p. 153; S. A. Walker, *British Sporting Art in the Twentieth Century* (1989), p. 21.

87. Anon, 'Pampered Sport and Pheasant Rearing', *Westminster Review*, CXXX (1888), pp. 464–71; Longrigg, *English Squire and His Sport*, pp. 241–55.

88. J. G. Ruffer, *The Big Shots: Edwardian Shooting Parties* (1984 edn.), pp. 15–21, 57–69; R. J. Colyer, 'The Gentry and the County in Nineteenth-Century Cardiganshire', *Welsh History Review*, X (1981), p. 510; C. Mathieson, 'Gamebook Records of Pheasants and Partridges in Wales, *National Library of Wales Journal*, IX (1956), pp. 287–94.

89. Portland, *Men, Women and Things*, pp. 228–38; Ruffer, *Big Shots*, pp. 43–53, 135.

90. Anon., 'Dog and Gun', *Quarterly Review*, CLXXI (1890), pp. 421, 438; Anon., 'Pampered Sport', pp. 471–3.

91. Lord Winterton, *Pre-War* (1932), p. 271; Camplin, *Rise of the Rich*, p. 256; Searle, *Corruption in British Politics*, p. 17; Vin-

cent, *Crawford Papers*, pp. 316–17.

92. Thompson, *Rise of Respectable Society*, pp. 268–70; Londonderry, *Henry Chaplin*, pp. 252–81; W. Orr, *Deer Forests, Landlords and Crofters: The Western Highlands in Victorian and Edwardian Times* (1982), pp. 32–50; Ouida, 'Sins of Society', p. 783.

93. Underhill, 'Fox-hunting and Agriculture', p. 752; Carr, *Fox-Hunting*, pp. 223–6; *E.G.*, 15 Aug. 1896.

94. T. H. S. Escott, *Social Transformations of the Victorian Age* (1897), p. 90.

95. M. Pugh, 'The Structure and Aims of the Victoria History of the Counties of England', *Bulletin of the Institute of Historical Research*, XL (1967), p. 67.

96. *E.G.*, 19 Oct. 1918.

97. Thompson, *English Landed Society*, pp. 333–4.

98. Aslet, *Last Country Houses*, p. 199; Beard, 'Agricultural Society in West Sussex', pp. 146, 174–8.

99. Rhodes James, '*Chips*', pp. 23, 177.

100. Carr, *Fox-Hunting*, pp. 229; Beard, 'Agricultural Society in West Sussex', p. 34; Winterton, *Fifty Tumultuous Years*, pp. 136–59; Winterton, *Pre-War*, pp. 208–9, 268.

101. Earl of Birkenhead, *Halifax: The Life of Lord Halifax* (1966), pp. 59–60, 70, 80–1, 101, 322–3; Lord Halifax, *Fullness of Days* (New York, 1957), pp. 83–7, 318; J. G. Lockhart, *Charles Lindley, Viscount Halifax* (2 vols., 1936), II, pp. 99–100, 364–5.

102. Carr, *Fox-Hunting*, pp. 226–33; Walker, *British Sporting Art*, p. 111.

103. Lewis, *Hunting in Ireland*, pp. 57, 84; Longrigg, *Fox-Hunting*, pp. 212–13; R. Clapham, *The Book of the Fox* (1936), p. 90; W. S. Dixon, *Fox-Hunting in the Twentieth Century* (1925), pp. 19–30.

104. Portland, *Men, Women and Things*, p. 237; Ruffer, *Big Shots*, p. 133; Lord Home, *The Way the Wind Blows* (1976), pp. 40–2.

105. Rose, *George V*, pp. 39–40, 99–100, 135, 288, 293–4.

106. M. Beard, *English Landed Society in the Twentieth Century* (1989), p. 56.

107. Vincent, *Crawford Papers*, pp. 521, 541, 582; K. Thomas, *Man and the Natural World: Changing Attitudes in England, 1500–1800* (1983), pp. 13–15; K. Robbins, *The Eclipse of a Great Power: Britain, 1870–1975* (1983), p. 148.

108. J. M. Lee, *Social Leaders and Public Persons: A Study of County Government in Cheshire since 1888* (1963), pp. 39–43, 96–8.

109. Willoughby de Broke, *Passing Years*, pp. 56–8.

110. Birkenhead, *Halifax*, pp. 72–6; Halifax, *Fullness of Days*, pp. 49–52.

111. *The Times*, 27 June 1937; A. R. C. Grant (ed.), *Lord Rosebery's North American Journal, 1873* (1967), pp. 9, 12, 18, 41, 43–4, 62–3; R. F. Foster, *Lord Randolph Churchill: A Political Life* (1981), pp. 378–9; R. S. Churchill, *Lord Derby: 'King' of Lancashire* (1959), p. 25.

112. The Duke of St Albans, 'Jamaica Resurgens', *19C*, XXII (1892), pp. 97–103; Countess of Galloway, 'Globe Trotting in New Zealand', *19C*, XXII (1892), pp. 403–15; Countess of Jersey, 'A French Colony', *19C*, XXII (1892), pp. 524–35; Lady Grey Egerton, 'Alaska and its Glaciers', *19C*, XXII (1892), pp. 991–1001; Countess of Jersey, 'Three Weeks in Samoa', *19C*, XXIII (1893), pp. 52–64, 249–60; Earl of Meath, 'A Britisher's Impressions of America and Australasia', *19C*, XXIII (1893), pp. 493–514.

113. P. White (ed.), *Lord Selkirk's Diary, 1803–1804: A Journal of His Travels in British North America and the United States* (1958); Lady E. Stuart-Wortley, *Travels in the United States etc. During 1849 and 1850* (3 vols., 1851); R. Taylor, *Lord Salisbury* (1975), pp. 3–4.

114. L. Turner and J. Ash, *The Golden Hordes: International Tourism and the Pleasure Periphery* (1975), pp. 61–9.

115. Holland, *Duke of Devonshire*, II, p. 413; Gordon, *Red Earl*, II, pp. 15–16; Ruffer, *Big Shots*, pp. 70–5; J. Pemble, *The Mediterranean Passion: Victorians and Edwardians in the South* (1987), p. 101.

116. Churchill, *Lord Derby*, p. 608; Rose, *Later Cecils*, pp. 42–3; Pemble, *Mediterranean Passion*, p. 2; Sir A. Hardinge, *The Life of Henry Howard Molyneux Herbert, Fourth Earl of Carnarvon, 1831–1890* (3 vols., 1925), III, pp. 75–6.

117. Lord Crewe, *Lord Rosebery* (New York, 1931), pp. 446, 527; J. Pearson, *Facades: Edith, Osbert and Sacheverell Sitwell* (1978), pp. 42–8, 60.

118. Holland, *Duke of Devonshire*, II, p. 413; Gordon, *Red Earl*, II, p. 43; Pemble, *Mediterranean Passion*, p. 47; W. S. Churchill, *Lord Randolph Churchill* (2 vols., 1906), II, p. 438.

119. J. Black, *The British and the Grand Tour* (1985), p. 23; the Marquess of Northampton and P. E. Newberry, *Excavations at Thebes* (1908); the Earl of Carnarvon and H. Carter, *Five Years Explorations at Thebes: A Record of Work Done, 1907–1911* (1912), preface and pp. 1–2; Lady Burghclere, 'Biographical Sketch of the Late Lord Carnarvon', in H. Carter, *The Tomb of Tutankhamen* (3 vols., 1923–33), I, pp. 26–39.

120. Crewe, *Rosebery*, pp. 501, 523–4; Hardinge, *Carnarvon*, II, pp. 41–2, 46–8; Dunraven, *Past Times and Pastimes*, I, pp. 42–8; H. L. Stone, W. H. Taylor and W. W. Richardson, *The Americas Cup Races* (New York, 1970), pp. 99–127.

121. Camplin, *Rise of the Rich*, p. 263; Sutherland, *Yellow Earl*, pp. 3, 114–15; Portland, *Men, Women and Things*, pp. 286–7; E. Hofman, *The Steam Yacht: An Era of Elegance* (New York, 1970), pp. 76–7, 208–9.

122. Turner and Ash, *Golden Hordes*, pp. 72–3.

123. Hofman, *Steam Yachts*, pp. 230–1; Harrison, *Lord of London*, pp. 73–4, 104, 112, 201–4; Loelia, Duchess of Westminster, *Grace and Favour* (1961), pp. 160–3, 214–15, 219–27.

124. Lord Ronaldshay, *Sport and Politics Under an Eastern Sky* (1902), p. xvii.

125. J. M. Brinnin, *The Sway of the Grand Saloon: A Social History of the North Atlantic* (New York, 1971), pp. 265, 273–6, 282–7, 322, 362; Kern, *Culture of Time and Space*, pp. 109–10, 212–13, 230, 250–4.

126. Lord Curzon, *Tales of Travel* (1923), pp. 4–5; P. Fussell, *Abroad: British Literary Travelling Between the Wars* (1980), p. 216.

127. J. M. Mackenzie, *The Empire of Nature: Hunting, Conservation and the British Empire* (1988), pp. 29–35, 41–6, 50–1.

128. E.g., Sir A. Pease, *Hunting Reminiscences* (1898); *Travels and Sport in Africa* (1902); *The Book of the Lion* (1914); *Half a Century of Sport* (1932); Sir Claude Champion de Crespigny, *Sporting Memoirs* (1896); *Forty Years of a Sportsman's Life* (1910).

129. Brinnin, *Sway of the Grand Saloon*, p. 239; Grant, *Rosebery's North American Journal*, pp. 18, 31, 63, 145–6; C. P. Trevelyan, *Letters from North America and the Pacific, 1898* (1969), pp. xv–xvi, 14.

130. Sutherland, *Yellow Earl*, p. 57; the Duke of Manchester, *My Candid Recollections* (1932), pp. 85–94, 111–15.

131. Sutherland, *Yellow Earl*, pp. 40–3; Dunraven, *Past Times and Pastimes*, I, pp. 65–167.

132. Portland, *Men, Women and Things*, pp. 71–3, 354–61.

133. Mackenzie, *Empire of Nature*, pp. 168–93.

134. Portland, *Men, Women and Things*, pp. 256–63; Churchill, *Lord Randolph*, I, pp. 560–1; Foster, *Lord Randolph*, pp. 168–73. For a later patrician hunting extravaganza, in 1903–4, see Londonderry, *Retrospect*, pp. 47–71.

135. Mackenzie, *Empire of Nature*, pp. 94–5, 112–13, 132–8; B. Bull, *Safari: A Chronicle of Adventure* (1988), pp. 123–7, 163–5, 169–71, 188–97, 202–11; B. Roberts, *Churchills in Africa* (1970), pp. 4–81; Lord Randolph Churchill, *Men, Mines and Animals in South Africa* (1891); Lord Cranworth, *Kenya Chronicles* (1939), pp. 95–121, 251–2.

136. R. Hyam, *Elgin and Churchill at the Colonial Office, 1905–1908: The Watershed of Empire-Commonwealth* (1968), pp. 349–66; P. J. Farmer, *Tarzan Alive: A Definitive Biography of Lord Greystoke* (New York, 1972), pp. 3–5, 116.

137. Manchester, *Candid Recollections*, pp. 98–9, 105–6; Lady M. Howard de Walden, *Pages from My Life* (1965), p. 45.

138. A. Conan Doyle, *The Lost World* (1911), esp. pp. 80–3, 88–91, 98–9, 317–19.

139. Brinnin, *Sway of the Grand Saloon*, pp. 446–7; A. Nevins (ed.), *America Through British Eyes* (New York, 1948), p. 406; Lord Cottenham, *Mine Host America* (1937), *passim*.

140. Lord Stuart of Findhorn, *Within the Fringe* (1967), pp. 57, 62–8; J. Amherst, *Wandering Abroad* (1976), pp. 60, 69–78; Cranworth, *Kenya Chronicles*, p. 125; Mackenzie, *Empire of Nature*, pp. 195, 201–23, 284–9.

141. A. J. A. Morris, *C. P. Trevelyan, 1870–1958: Portrait of a Radical* (1977), pp. 20, 29–33; Trevelyan, *Letters from North America and the Pacific*, pp. 42, 109, 144, 194–97.

142. Rose, *Curzon*, pp. 78–89, 193–241, 245–51, 253–72; Curzon, *Tales of Travel*, p. 4.

143. Lord Curzon, *Russia in Central Asia* (1889); *Persia and the Persian Question*

(1892); *Problems of the Far East* (1894).

144. Lord Ronaldshay, *An Eastern Miscellany* (1911), pp. 5–19; Lord Zetland, 'Essayez' (1956), pp. 13–21, 23–7, 28–40, 41–7, 161.

145. Lord Ronaldshay, *Sport and Politics Under an Eastern Sky; On the Outskirts of Empire in Asia* (1904); *A Wandering Student in the Far East* (2 vols., 1908).

146. Home, *The Way the Wind Blows*, p. 39; Lord Butler, *The Art of the Possible* (1971), p. 20.

147. E. L. Jones, *A Victorian Boyhood* (1955), pp. 76–82, 101–50; D. Fraser, *Alanbrooke* (1982), pp. 39–42.

148. Sutherland, *Yellow Earl*, pp. 142–5, 203; Gordon, *Red Earl*, ii, p. 37.

149. J. V. Beckett, 'The Yellow Earl: Hugh Cecil Lowther, Fifth Earl of Lonsdale, 1857–1944', in S. Krech iii, *A Victorian Earl in the Arctic: The Travels and Collections of the Fifth Earl of Lonsdale, 1888–9* (1989), pp. 10–15; Sutherland, *Yellow Earl*, pp. 80–90, 201–2.

150. Shkolnik, *Leading Ladies*, pp. 451–2. Wodehouse devotees will remember that around the turn of the century, Galahad Threepwood fell in love with Dolly Henderson, who sang songs at the Tivoli, and was duly shipped off to South Africa. Cannadine, 'Another "Last Victorian?"', p. 483.

151. H. M. Hyde, *The Cleveland Street Scandal* (1976), pp. 35–6, 43–4, 95, 99, 105–6, 131, 215–6, 237–9, 246–7, 254–5; H. M. Hyde, *Lord Alfred Douglas: A Biography* (1984), pp. 47, 67, 83–128.

152. Pemble, *Mediterranean Passion*, pp. 159–61.

153. Pearson, *Facades*, p. 201; H. Carpenter, *The Brideshead Generation: Evelyn Waugh and His Friends* (Boston, 1990), pp. 252–4.

154. Harrison, *Lord of London*, 218–20; Aslet, *Last Country Houses*, pp. 252–5.

155. Thompson, *Rise of Respectable Society*, pp. 262–4; Ronaldshay, *Sport and Politics Under an Eastern Sky*, p. xvii.

156. Pemble, *Mediterranean Passion*, pp. 129–35, 150; Black, *Grand Tour*, pp. 172–86.

157. M. Girouard, *The Return to Camelot: Chivalry and the English Gentleman* (1981), p. 271.

158. E. Longford, *A Pilgrimge of Passion: The Life of Wilfrid Scawen Blunt* (1979), pp. 97–8, 114–16, 123–35, 136–51, 167–76.

159. S. Leslie, *Mark Sykes: His Life and Letters*

(1923), pp. 71, 204–7; R. Adelson, *Mark Sykes: Portrait of an Amateur* (1975), pp. 34–7, 42–4, 51, 61–2, 144.

160. Girouard, *Return to Camelot*, p. 272; Adelson, *Mark Sykes*, pp. 100–1.

161. M. Fitzherbert, *The Man Who was Greenmantle: A Biography of Aubrey Herbert* (1985), pp. 1–2, 35–45, 54–67, 73, 121–2, 188.

162. Girouard, *Return to Camelot*, p. 271.

163. A. Ryan, *Bertrand Russell: A Political Life* (1988), pp. 83–6, 93–7; Curzon, *Tales of Travel*, p. 6.

164. V. Sackville-West, *Twelve Days* (1928), pp. 27, 117–30; Fussell, *Abroad*, pp. 93–4; C. Sykes, *Four Studies in Loyalty* (1946), pp. 61, 83, 86, 124–5.

165. W. Thesiger, *The Life of My Choice* (1988), p. 56.

166. Bull, *Safari*, pp. 317–18; Thesiger, *Life of My Choice*, p. 95.

167. Girouard, *Return to Camelot*, p. 271.

168. D. Spring, 'The Role of the Aristocracy in the Late Nineteenth Century', *Victorian Studies*, iv (1960), p. 59.

169. Camplin, *Rise of the Rich*, p. 264.

170. Spring, 'Role of the Aristocracy', p. 63.

171. For the full Titanic passenger list, see W. Lord, *A Night to Remember* (1955), pp. 185–200. Only three were patricians: Sir Cosmo and Lady Duff, and the Countess of Rothesay. All survived.

172. Camplin, *Rise of the Rich*, p. 262; Turner and Ash, *Golden Hordes*, p. 67.

173. The Countess of Minto in Oxford, *Myself When Young*, p. 232.

174. Hofman, *Steam Yachts*, pp. 236–7; Adelson, *Mark Sykes*, p. 295; Rose, *Curzon*, p. 19.

175. *E.G.*, 21 Nov. 1896.

176. E. D. Steele, 'Gladstone and Ireland', *Irish Historical Studies*, xvii (1970), pp. 63–70.

177. Lady Jeune, 'London Society', p. 611.

178. *The Times*, 23 Dec. 1899; G. Huxley, *Victorian Duke* (1967), pp. x–xi; M. Girouard, *The Victorian Country House* (1979), pp. 1–2.

179. Lee, *Social Leaders and Public Persons*, pp. 96–8; Westminster, *Grace and Favour*, pp. 186, 198; Rhodes James, 'Chips', p. 477.

180. I. Colegate, *The Shooting Party* (1982 edn.), p. 26.

Chapter 9

1. *E.G.*, 10 June 1922.

2. Lady Sybil Lubbock (ed.), *A Page From*

the Past: Memoirs of the Earl of Desart (1936), p. 222.

3. T. H. S. Escott, *England: Its People, Polity and Pursuits* (1885), p. 558.

4. Robert John Strutt, Fourth Baron Rayleigh, *John William Strutt, Third Baron Rayleigh* (1924), pp. 99–102, 147–9.

5. W. O. Chadwick, *Acton and Gladstone* (1976), pp. 19–22, 24–6, 42–7; H. Tulloch, *Acton* (1988), pp. 64, 67.

6. G. D. Phillips, *The Diehards: Aristocratic Society and Politics in Edwardian England* (1979), p. 41.

7. Sir William Gavin, *Ninety Years of Farming* (1967), chs. 2, 5, 6; Hon. George Lambton, *Men and Horses I Have Known* (1924), pp. 22, 95, 98, 201, 215.

8. Lord Montagu of Beaulieu, *Rolls of Rolls Royce* (1966), *passim*; C. W. Morton, *A History of Rolls Royce Motor Cars*, vol. I, *1903–07* (1964), pp. 37–9, 45, 51–5, 73–4, 84, 98, 129, 243, 410.

9. Lord Montagu of Beaulieu, *The Motoring Montagus* (1959), pp. 3–11, 24–30, 39–58; *The Times*, 30 June 1929.

10. Montagu of Beaulieu, *Motoring Montagus*, p. 25.

11. *The Times*, 29 Jan. 1898; J. R. Vincent (ed.), *The Later Derby Diaries: Home Rule, Liberal Unionism and Aristocratic Life in Late Victorian England* (1981), pp. 14–15.

12. *E.G.*, 13 May 1939.

13. F. A. S. Brown, *Nigel Gresley: Locomotive Engineer* (1961), pp. 11–12.

14. R. A. Buchanan, 'Gentlemen Engineers: The Making of a Profession', *Victorian Studies*, XXVI (1983), pp. 407–29.

15. W. J. Reader, '"At the Head of All the Professions": The Engineer in Victorian Society', in N. McKendrick and R. B. Outhwaite (eds.), *Business Life and Public Policy: Essays in Honour of D. C. Coleman* (1986), pp. 183–4.

16. R. Brandon, *The Dollar Princesses* (1980), pp. 1, 5.

17. K. Rose, *Curzon: A Most Superior Person* (1985), pp. 280–1. But cf. N. Nicolson, *Curzon* (1977) pp. 57–9.

18. R. Blake, *The Conservative Party from Peel to Churchill* (1972), p. 213.

19. C. Balsan, *The Glitter and the Gold* (New York, 1953), chs. 3 and 4; A. L. Rowse, *The Later Churchills* (1971) pp. 280–9.

20. R. F. Foster, *Lord Randolph Churchill: A Political Life* (1981), p. 18.

21. Brandon, *Dollar Princesses*, pp. 31, 71.

22. Phillips, *Diehards*, p. 36; F. M. L. Thompson, *The Rise of Respectable Society: A Social History of Victorian Britain, 1830–1900* (1988), pp. 106–8. For a full analysis, see: M. E. Montgomery, *Gilded Prostitution: Status, Money and Transatlantic Marriages 1870–1914* (1989).

23. A. Conan Doyle, *The Adventures of Sherlock Holmes* (1974 edn.), p. 242.

24. Vincent, *Later Derby Diaries*, p. 136.

25. R. W. Clark, *The Life of Bertrand Russell* (1975), pp. 405, 428; B. Russell, *The Autobiography of Bertrand Russell*, vol. II, *1914–44* (1968), pp. 152–3; The Marquess of Zetland, '*Essayez*' (1956), pp. 167–72.

26. D. S. Higgins, *Rider Haggard: The Great Storyteller* (1981), pp. 102–4.

27. H. Acton, *Nancy Mitford: A Memoir* (1985), p. 25.

28. Vincent, *Later Derby Diaries*, p. 91.

29. Sir Edward Grey's autobiography, *Twenty Five Years*, sold 35,000 copies, and earned its author £7,000. Another book by him, *The Charm of Birds*, went through ten editions between 1927 and 1937. See K. Robbins, *Sir Edward Grey: A Biography of Lord Grey of Fallodon* (1971), pp. 366–7.

30. The Duke of Portland, *Men, Women and Things* (1937); The Marchioness of Londonderry, *Retrospect* (1939).

31. W. Long, *Memories* (1923); Lord Willoughby de Broke, *The Passing Years* (1924).

32. Earl of Dunraven, *Past Times and Pastimes* (2 vols., 1922); Earl of Midleton, *Records and Reactions, 1856–1939* (1939); Elizabeth, Countess of Fingall, *Seventy Years Young* (1937).

33. The Countess of Warwick, *Life's Ebb and Flow* (1929); *Afterthoughts* (1931); Earl of Warwick, *Memories of Sixty Years* (1917); Earl of Rosslyn, *My Gamble With Life* (1928); The Duke of Manchester, *My Candid Recollections* (1932).

34. See M. Frewen, *Melton Mowbray and Other Memories* (1924); A. Leslie, *Mr Frewen of England: A Victorian Adventurer* (1966); A. Andrews, *The Splendid Pauper* (1968).

35. Leslie, *Mr Frewen*, p. 202; Andrews, *Splendid Pauper*, p. 215.

36. Rosslyn, *My Gamble With Life*, *passim*.

37. Warwick, *Memories of Sixty Years*, pp. 151–2, 167, 178–80.

38. M. Blunden, *The Countess of Warwick*,

esp. pp. 135, 195, 201–3, 210–14, 219–24, 262–3, 281.

39. Manchester, *Candid Recollections*, pp. 47–53, 85–94, 111–15.

40. *The Times*, 21 Sept. 1943.

41. L. Mosley, *Lord Castlerosse* (1956), p. 188.

42. *The Times*, 26 May 1975.

43. E. Waugh, *Vile Bodies* (1938 edn.), p. 50.

44. Vincent, *Crawford Papers*, p. 544. It was not only aristocrats themselves who took exception to déclassé notables. On 12 January 1930, Lord Lee of Fareham – a non-patrician peer – recorded this entry in his diary: 'It is a sad sign of the times that, when lunching with Lady Rossmore the other day, I found myself sitting between two young peers; one of whom, the Marquis of Cambridge (the Queen's nephew) informed me that he was a clerk in a bank, whilst the other, Lord Rossmore, makes his living by selling jam.' (A. Clark (ed.), *'A Good Innings': The Private Papers of Viscount Lee of Fareham* (1974), p. 298.)

45. Fingall, *Seventy Years Young*, p. 282.

46. H. Montgomery-Massingberd, 'The Best Thing in Fiction: Plum's Peerage', in *Debrett's Peerage and Baronetage* (1985 edn.), pp. 22–3.

47. A. Ponsonby, *The Decline of Aristocracy* (1912), pp. 18–23.

48. Vincent, *Later Derby Diaries*, p. 117.

49. D. Cannadine, *Lords and Landlords: The Aristocracy and the Towns, 1774–1967* (1980), pp. 292–6.

50. F. B. Heath, 'Richard Grenville, third Duke of Buckingham and Chandos: A Case Study of the Nineteenth-Century "Amphibious" British Aristocrat' (Ph.D. dissertation, University of Southern California, 1959), pp. 39–72; F. B. Heath, 'The Grenvilles in the Nineteenth Century: The Emergence of Commercial Affiliations', *Huntingdon Library Quarterly*, xxv (1961), pp. 40–9; T. C. Barker, 'Lord Salisbury: Chairman of the Great Eastern Railway, 1868–72', in S. Marriner (ed.), *Business and Businessmen: Studies in Business, Economic and Accounting History Presented to F. E. Hyde* (1978), pp. 81–103; F. M. L. Thompson, *English Landed Society in the Nineteenth Century* (1963), p. 305; Vincent, *Later Derby Diaries*, p. 113.

51. G. E. Cokayne, *The Complete Peerage* (new edn., ed. Hon. V. Gibbs, 13 vols.,

1910–53), v, Appendix C, pp. 780–3. It is also noteworthy that more than half of the members of Salisbury's cabinet of 1895 held directorships in public companies: G. R. Searle, *Corruption in British Politics, 1895–1930* (1987), p. 44.

52. Thompson, *English Landed Society*, pp. 305–8; J. H. Clapham, *An Economic History of Modern Britain* (3 vols., 1926–38), iii, p. 238.

53. P. L. Cottrell, *Industrial Finance, 1830–1914: The Finance and Organisation of English Manufacturing Industry* (1980), chs. 3, 6.

54. *The Times*, 14 June 1901; Mabel, Countess of Airlie, *Thatched with Gold* (1962), pp. 45–6.

55. W. Turrentine Jackson, *The Enterprising Scot: Investors in the American West After 1873* (1968), pp. 14–15, 24, 28–30, 39, 75, 167–72, 216–18.

56. C. C. Spence, 'When the Pound Sterling Went West: British Investment and the American Mineral Frontier', *Journal of Economic History*, xvi (1956), pp. 482–5.

57. Turrentine Jackson, *Enterprising Scot*, pp. 98–9; N. Macdonald, *Canada: Immigration and Colonisation, 1841–1903* (1966), pp. 242–7; R. V. Clements, 'British Investment and American Legislative Restrictions', *Mississippi Valley Historical Review* xlii (1955–6), p. 208.

58. A. P. Tischendorf, 'North Carolina and the British Investor, 1880–1910', *North Carolina Historical Review*, xxxii (1955), pp. 512–14.

59. M. Cannon, *The Land Boomers* (Melbourne, 1967), pp. 97–9.

60. Vincent, *Later Derby Diaries*, p. 126; Foster, *Lord Randolph Churchill*, pp. 9, 16–18, 33–4, 46, 54, 62, 111, 124, 216–17, 270, 349.

61. J. G. Lockhart and C. M. Woodhouse, *Rhodes: The Colossus of South Africa* (New York, 1963), pp. 164–5.

62. J. S. Galbraith, *Crown and Charter: The Early Years of the British South Africa Company* (1974), pp. 114–16.

63. Lockhart and Woodhouse, *Rhodes*, pp. 170–1; S. Sims, *Paladin of Empire: Earl Grey and Rhodesia* (Central African Historical Association, Local Series, xxvi, Salisbury, 1970), pp. 2–8; L. H. Gann, *A History of Southern Rhodesia: Early Days to 1934* (1965), pp. 82–3; J. Marlowe, *Cecil Rhodes: The Anatomy*

of Empire (New York, 1972), pp. 122–3.

64. E. Longford, *Jameson's Raid* (1960), pp. 306–7; Galbraith, *Crown and Charter*, p. 116.
65. Fingall, *Seventy Years Young*, pp. 213–25.
66. Clapham, *Economic History of Modern Britain*, II, pp. 237–8; J. Armstrong, 'Hooley and the Bovril Company', *Business History*, XXVIII (1986), pp. 18–34.
67. *The Times*, 28 July 1898; 2, 17, and 18 Aug. 1898.
68. H. Osborne O'Hagan, *Leaves from My Life* (2 vols., 1929), II, p. 186.
69. *The Times*, 10 Jan. 1901; 13 Feb. 1902; Sir A. Lyall, *The Life of the Marquis of Dufferin and Ava* (2 vols., 1905), II, pp. 300, 304–5, 309. Two years before, E. F. Benson had written a novel that told how an impoverished Irish peer, the Marquis of Conybere, suffered similar misfortune at the hands of Frank Allington, an unscrupulous company promotor. E. F. Benson, *Mammon & Co.* (1916 edn.), pp. 7, 15, 112.
70. G. Cornwallis-West, *Edwardian Heydays* (1930), pp. 121, 137. For another impoverished peer who was a singularly unsuccessful businessman, see Earl Russell, *My Life and Adventures* (1923), pp. 42–3, 310–21.
71. *The Times*, 11 Feb. 1931.
72. *The Times*, 12 June 1965; G. M. Thompson, *Lord Castlerosse: His Life and Times* (1973), p. 120.
73. *The Times*, 11 Mar. 1931; 17 June 1931.
74. *The Times*, 25 Jan. 1930; 4 July 1930; 20 Nov. 1930; 30 June 1962; Searle, *Corruption*, p. 412.
75. Thompson, *English Landed Society*, pp. 305–8.
76. *The Times*, 27 Nov. 1911.
77. Viscount Churchill, *All My Sins Remembered* (New York, 1965), pp. 40–7. During the 1900s, the chairmen of the North Eastern Railway, the Great Eastern, and the Great Western were, respectively, Edward Grey, Lord Claud Hamilton, and Lord Cawdor.
78. S. Haxey, *Tory MP* (1939), pp. 134–5.
79. *The Times*, 16 Feb. 1933. For the earlier phase of the family's landed-cum-business history, see J. D. Rowbotham, 'Edward Knatchbull-Hugessen, First Lord Brabourne, and the British Empire, 1870–1893' (Ph.D. dissertation, University of Wales, 1982).
80. C. Aslet, *The Last Country Houses* (1982), p. 58.
81. Lord Brabazon of Tara, *The Brabazon Story* (1956), pp. 7–9, 149–53, 161.
82. The Earl of Drogheda, *Double Harness* (1978), pp. 4–10, 25, 32, 43, 46, 54, 63.
83. Lord Chandos, *The Memoirs of Lord Chandos* (1962), pp. 113–18, 122–5, 129, 144.
84. *The Times*, 4 Nov. 1954.
85. H. Samuel, *Shareholders' Money* (1933), pp. 111–18; P. S. Florence, *The Logic of British and American Industry* (1953), p. 206.
86. *E.G.*, 8 Sept. 1928.
87. N. Mitford, *Noblesse Oblige* (1956), p. 71.
88. R. Heussler, *Yesterday's Rulers: The Making of the British Colonial Service* (1963), pp. 14–26, 48–51; L. H. Gann and P. Duignan, *The Rulers of British Africa* (1978), pp. 173–5, 199–200.
89. T. H. R. Cashmore, 'Studies in District Administration in the East African Protectorate, 1895–1918' (Ph.D. dissertation, Cambridge University, 1965), pp. 36–8; I. F. Nicolson, *The Administration of Nigeria, 1900–1960: Men, Methods and Myths* (1969), pp. 23–4, 39–40, 231–2.
90. J. W. Cell, *British Colonial Administration in the Mid Nineteenth Century: The Policy Making Process* (1970), pp. 289–300.
91. Gordon's life is fully explored in J. K. Chapman, *The Career of Arthur Hamilton Gordon, First Lord Stanmore, 1829–1912* (Toronto, 1964).
92. This was an exceptionally peripheral career, but Boyle was widely regarded as being amongst the least able colonial governors of his time. See R. Hyam, 'The Colonial Office Mind, 1900–1914', *Journal of Imperial and Commonwealth History*, VIII (1979), p. 39.
93. H. A. Gailey, *Clifford: Imperial Proconsul* (1982), pp. 3–9, 16, 26, 94–6; H. A. Gailey, 'Sir Hugh Clifford (1866–1947)', in L. H. Gann and P. Duignan (eds.), *African Proconsuls: European Governors in Africa* (New York, 1978), pp. 266, 287.
94. Nicolson, *Administration of Nigeria*, pp. 217–27.
95. I. F. Nicolson and C. A. Hughes, 'A Provenance of Proconsuls: British Colonial Governors, 1900–1960', *Journal of Imperial and Commonwealth History*, IV (1975), pp. 81, 102–3; A. H. Kirk-

Greene, 'On Governorship and Governors in British Africa', in Gann and Duignan, *African Proconsuls*, p. 249.

96. See his autobiography, Sir Bede Clifford, *Proconsul* (1964).

97. J. M. Compton, 'Open Competition and the Indian Civil Service, 1854–1876', *Eng. Hist. Rev.*, LXXXIII (1968), pp. 281–3; C. J. Dewey, 'The Education of a Ruling Caste: The Indian Civil Service in the Era of Competitive Examination', *Eng. Hist. Rev.*, LXXXVIII (1973), pp. 283–4; T. H. Beaglehole, 'From Rulers to Servants: The I.C.S. and the British Dimension of Power in India', *Modern Asian Studies*, XI (1977), pp. 244–6; H. A. Ewig, 'The I.C.S., 1919–1942: Some Aspects of British Control in India' (Ph.D., Cambridge University, 1980), pp. 175–8.

98. D. C. Potter, *India's Political Administrators, 1919–1983* (1986), pp. 57–8; Sir P. Moon (ed.), *Wavell: The Viceroy's Journal* (1973), p. 46.

99. B. Spangenberg, 'The Problem of Recruitment for the Indian Civil Service During the Late Nineteenth Century', *Journal of Asian Studies*, XXX (1971), pp. 341–4, 350–7.

100. Ewig, 'The I.C.S., 1919–1942', pp. 53–4.

101. Dewey, 'The Education of a Ruling Caste', p. 283.

102. H. Trevelyan, *Public and Private* (1980), pp. 3–12.

103. C. R. Sanders, *The Strachey Family, 1588–1932: Their Writings and Literary Associations* (New York, 1968), pp. 28, 33, 40, 147–9, 182–4, 195–6, 209.

104. Sir John Strachey, *India: Its Administration and Progress* (4th edn., 1911), preface.

105. M. Bence Jones and H. Montgomery-Massingberd, *The British Aristocracy* (1979), pp. 160–1.

106. R. H. Hubbard, *Rideau Hall* (Montreal, 1977), p. 260, note 106.

107. Vincent, *Crawford Papers*, p. 62.

108. J. Adam Smith, *John Buchan* (1965), p. 113.

109. D. Duman, *The English and Colonial Bars During the Nineteenth Century* (1983), p. 127.

110. *The Times*, 30 July 1924; 11 Feb. 1952.

111. *The Times*, 5 Jan. 1929; 5 June 1931.

112. For the broader historical background, see S. Neill, *Christian Missions* (1964), pp. 322–96.

113. *The Times*, 28 May 1909; 13 Sept. 1961;

P. Dunae, *Gentlemen Emigrants: From the British Public Schools to the Canadian Frontier* (1981), p. 198.

114. *The Times*, 22 Jan. 1941; 5 Apr. 1943; 30 Mar. 1954; 19 Mar. 1976.

115. E. Every, *Twenty-Five Years in South America* (1929), pp. 95, 105.

116. *The Times*, 17 Sept. 1963.

117. Every, *Twenty Five Years*, pp. 50–2, 187–200.

118. *The Times*, 9 Apr. 1943.

119. Dunae, *Gentlemen Emigrants*, pp. 48–51, 57–60; F. Musgrove, *The Migratory Elite* (1963), p. 21.

120. T. Hughes (ed.) *Gone to Texas: Letters from our Boys* (1884), esp. p. xi; W. Stamer, *The Gentleman Emigrant: His Daily Life, Sports and Pastimes in Canada, Australia and the United States* (2 vols., 1974), I, pp. 21–31; W. Fielding, 'What Shall I Do with My Son?', *19C*, XIII (1883), pp. 578–86; W. Fielding, 'Whither Shall I Send My Son?', *19C*, XIV (1883), pp. 65–77.

121. S. H. Jeys, 'Our Gentlemanly Failures', *Fortnightly Review*, LXI (1897), pp. 387–98.

122. F. Moncreiff and W. Moncreiffe, *The Moncreiffs and the Moncreiffes: A History of the Family of Moncreiff of that Ilk and its Collateral Branches* (2 vols., 1929), II, pp. 474–504.

123. W. B. Grohman, 'Cattle Ranches in the Far West', *Fortnightly Review*, XXVIII (1880), pp. 438–57; R. Graham, 'The Investment Boom in British-Texan Cattle Companies, 1880–1885', *Business History Review*, XXXIV (1960), pp. 421–45; J. F. Rippy, 'British Investment in Texas Lands and Livestock', *Southern Historical Quarterly*, LVIII (1955), pp. 331–41. The fullest treatment of this subject is to be found in L. M. Woods, *British Gentlemen in the Wild West: The Era of the Intensely English Cowboy* (1989).

124. D. Sutherland, *The Yellow Earl: The Life of Hugh Lowther, Fifth Earl of Lonsdale, K.G., G.C.V.O., 1857–1944* (1965), pp. 40–5; Vincent, *Later Derby Diaries*, p. 103.

125. J. van der Zee, *The British in Iowa* (Iowa, 1922), pp. 145–6.

126. R. T. Berthoff, *British Immigrants in Industrial America, 1790–1850* (Cambridge, Mass., 1953), pp. 114–17; van der Zee, *British in Iowa*, pp. 173, 190, 193–4, 210.

127. Earl of Airlie, 'The United States as a

Field for Agricultural Settlers', *19C*, IX (1881), pp. 292–301; Berthoff, *British Immigrants*, pp. 116–17.

128. H. E. Socolofsky, 'The Scully Land System in Marion County', *Kansas Historical Quarterly*, XVIII (1950), pp. 337–44, 348–51, 356–61; P. W. Gates, 'Frontier Landlords and Pioneer Tenants', *Journal of the Illinois State Historical Society*, XXXVIII (1945), pp. 176–91.

129. Van der Zee, *British in Iowa*, pp. 179–86.

130. Phillips, *The Diehards*, p. 40.

131. Dunae, *Gentlemen Emigrants*, pp. 82–4, 196–7, 204.

132. Dunae, *Gentlemen Emigrants*, pp. 89–90, 102–3, 203.

133. Dunae, *Gentlemen Emigrants*, pp. 103–4, 114, 168–9.

134. Dunae, *Gentlemen Emigrants*, pp. 139, 221.

135. G. Blainey, *The Rush that Never Was: A History of Australian Mining* (3rd edn., Melbourne, 1978), pp. 149, 184.

136. Vincent, *Later Derby Diaries*, p. 108; H. Finch-Hatton, *Advance Australia! An Account of Eight Years Work, Wandering and Amusement in Queensland, New South Wales and Victoria* (1885), pp. 27–8, 209–13, 261, 341.

137. Turrentine Jackson, *Enterprising Scot*, pp. 120–30.

138. Sutherland, *Yellow Earl*, p. 45; Leslie, *Mr Frewen*, pp. 79, 86–9; Dunae, *Gentlemen Emigrants*, pp. 168–9, 204.

139. Gates, 'Frontier Landlords', pp. 195–203; R. V. Clements, 'The Farmers' Attitude Towards British Investment in American Industry', *Journal of Economic History*, XV (1955), pp. 151–2, 154–6, 158–9.

140. E. P. Crapol, *America for Americans: Economic Nationalism and Anglophobia in the Late Nineteenth Century* (1973), pp. 91–119; R. V. Clements, 'British Investment and American Legislative Restrictions in the Trans-Mississippi West, 1880–1900', *Mississippi Valley Historical Review*, XLII (1955–6), pp. 207–28; R. V. Clements, 'British Investment in the Trans-Mississippi West, 1870–1914: Its Encouragement and the Metal Mining Interests', *Pacific History Review*, XXIX (1960), pp. 35–50.

141. Fielding, 'What Shall I Do With My Son?', pp. 578–81; W. H. P. Jarvis, *The Letters of a Remittance Man to His Mother* (1908), pp. 22–49.

142. Dunae, *Gentlemen Emigrants*, pp. 139–43; Anon., 'Gentlemen Emigrants', *Macmillans Magazine*, LVIII (1888), p. 35.

143. A. Hawkes, 'The Imperial Emigrant and His Political Religion', *19C*, LXXI (1912), p. 113; R. G. Athearn, *Westward the Briton* (New York, 1953), pp. 79–87.

144. Finch-Hatton, *Advance Australia!!*, pp. 354–5; Lord Cranworth, *A Colony in the Making, or Sport and Profit in British East Africa* (1912), pp. 182–3.

145. Gann, *History of Southern Rhodesia*, pp. 58–65.

146. R. Blake, *A History of Rhodesia* (1977), pp. 114–16, 146–8.

147. D. Kennedy, *Islands of White: Settler Society and Culture in Kenya and Southern Rhodesia, 1890–1939* (Durham, NC, 1987), pp. 14–19; Blake, *History of Rhodesia*, pp. 114–16.

148. Sims, *Paladin of Empire*, pp. 55–6; T. O. Ranger, 'The Last Word on Rhodes?', *P. & P.*, no. 28 (1964), pp. 119–122; T. O. Ranger, *Revolt in Southern Rhodesia, 1896–7: A Study in African Resistance* (1967), pp. 103–4.

149. Longford, *Jameson's Raid*, pp. 56–9, 77, 118, 167–74.

150. G. Bennett, 'Settlers and Politics in Kenya, up to 1945', in V. Harlow and E. M. Chilner (eds.), *History of East Africa* (1965), pp. 174–278.

151. Lord Cranworth, *Kenya Chronicles* (1939), pp. 1–2.

152. Cranworth, *Colony in the Making*, pp. 185–6; Cranworth, *Kenya Chronicles*, pp. 37, 56.

153. J. Fox, *White Mischief* (1984), p. 12; E. Trzebinski, *Silence Will Speak: A Study of the Life of Denys Finch Hatton and His Relation With Karen Blixen* (1977), pp. 10–14, 66–9, 81, 187–8, 310; Cranworth, *Kenya Chronicles*, pp. 251–77.

154. E. Huxley, *White Man's Country: Lord Delamere and the Making of Kenya* (2 vols., 1935), I, pp. 6–8, 16, 96, 170; E. Trebinski, *The Kenya Pioneers* (1985), pp. 62, 80–2, 111.

155. *The Times*, 28 July 1952; Fox, *White Mischief*, p. 21; Cranworth, *Kenya Chronicles*, p. 325; M. G. Redley, 'The Politics of a Predicament: The White Community in Kenya, 1918–32' (Ph.D. dissertation, Cambridge University, 1976), pp. 9–12.

156. Bennett, 'Settlers and Politics in Kenya', pp. 299–318, 323–4; Huxley, *White Man's Country*, II, pp. 143, 167.

157. This is well caught in Isobel Colgate's fictional character Lord Hartlip, who shoots an estate employee in extremely dubious circumstances in 1913, and is obliged to leave the country: 'He had spent several months in East Africa, big game shooting, and had taken a particular liking to Nairobi and the White Highlands. He sold his estates in England, and bought a farm near Nanynki.' His wife 'at first horrified, soon settled down. She took up rifle shooting herself, and carried on a discreet affair with a ne'er-do-well scion of a noble family who had been sent out to Kenya to redeem himself. At least, she felt, one was out of the way of that ghastly war.' (I. Colgate, *The Shooting Party* (1982 edn.), pp. 175–6.

158. Fox, *White Mischief*, pp. 66–8, 215.
159. Fox, *White Mischief*, pp. 29–33.
160. Fox, *White Mischief*, pp. 35–48, 53–64.
161. Kennedy, *Islands of White*, pp. 46–7, 72, 92.
162. Fox, *White Mischief*, pp. 2, 4; I. Dinesen (pseud. K. Blixen), *Letters from Africa* (Chicago, 1981), pp. 240, 344, 387.
163. Fox, *White Mischief*, pp. 25–7, 32; K. Rose, *The Later Cecils* (1975), p. 301.
164. E. Waugh, *Remote People* (1931), pp. 179, 183–5.
165. Dinesen, *Letters from Africa*, pp. 67, 344; K. Blixen, *Out of Africa* (1937), pp. 205–6.
166. *E.G.*, 6 Sept. 1919.
167. J. A. Hobson, *Imperialism: A Study* (1902), pp. 142, 159, 160, 234, 261, 269.
168. For quantitative corroboration, see L. E. Davies and R. A. Huttenback, 'The Political Economy of Imperialism: Measures of Benefit and Support', *Journal of Economic History*, XLII (1982), pp. 129–30.

Chapter 10

1. J. E. Williams, 'The Liberal Party and the House of Lords, 1880–1895' (MA dissertation, University of Wales, 1961), p. 358.
2. *E.G.*, 14 Oct. 1899.
3. B. H. Brown, *The Tariff Reform Movement in Great Britain, 1881–1895* (New York, 1943), pp. 10–12, 16.
4. R. Blake, *Disraeli* (1966), p. 698.
5. Brown, *Tariff Reform*, pp. 17–19, 58–9, 62–8.
6. Brown, *Tariff Reform*, p. 82.

7. P. Marsh, *The Discipline of Popular Government: Lord Salisbury's Domestic Statecraft, 1881–1902* (1978), pp. 129–30.
8. Brown, *Tariff Reform*, pp. 17–19.
9. A. H. Matthews, *Fifty Years of Agricultural Politics: The History of the Central Chamber of Agriculture, 1865–1915* (1915), pp. 246–52.
10. A. Offer, *Property and Politics, 1870–1914: Landownership, Law, Ideology and Urban Development in England* (1981), p. 201.
11. A. Sykes, *Tariff Reform in British Politics, 1903–1913* (1979), pp. 31–5.
12. M. fforde, 'The Conservative Party and Real Property in England' (D.Phil. dissertation, Oxford University, 1984), pp. 117–25, 135–7.
13. Matthews, *Fifty Years*, p. 341.
14. Sykes, *Tariff Reform*, pp. 55, 192.
15. Sykes, *Tariff Reform*, pp. 236, 253–6, 263, 270, 273.
16. fforde, 'Conservative Party and Real Property', pp. 41–50.
17. Offer, *Property and Politics*, pp. 364–6.
18. *E.G.*, 30 May 1925; C. Turnor, *Land Problems and National Welfare* (1911), pp. 2, 271.
19. fforde, 'Conservative Party and Real Property', p. 172.
20. Turnor, *Land Problems*, pp. 2–4.
21. Offer, *Property and Politics*, p. 356; Turnor, *Land Problems*, pp. 8–9; fforde, 'Conservative Party and Real Property', pp. 192–9.
22. Offer, *Property and Politics*, p. 380.
23. Offer, *Property and Politics*, pp. 360–2.
24. E. H. Whetham, *The Agrarian History of England*, vol. VIII, *1914–39* (1978), pp. 90–1.
25. A. Clark (ed.), *'A Good Innings': The Private Papers of Lord Lee of Fareham* (1974), pp. 165–78.
26. *E.G.*, 4 Aug. 1917.
27. Whetham, *1914–39*, pp. 94–5, 113–15, 129–30.
28. K. O. Morgan, *Consensus and Disunity: The Lloyd George Coalition Government, 1918–1922* (1979), pp. 157–8.
29. A. F. Cooper, 'The Transformation of Agricultural Policy, 1912–1936: A Study in Conservative Politics' (D.Phil. dissertation, Oxford University, 1979), pp. 71–2.
30. C. Turnor, *The Land: Agriculture and the National Economy* (1929), pp. x, 34, 55–6. The foreword to this book was by

Lord Bledisloe.

31. *E.G.*, 15 Oct. 1921, 3 Dec. 1921, 26 May 1923, 27 Oct. 1923, 10 Nov. 1928, 7 July 1934, 15 Jan. 1938.

32. C. Turnor, *The Land and Its Problems* (1921), pp. 39–40, 47–9. See also Lord Bledisloe, *The Proper Functions of the Landowners in Relation to the Agricultural Industry* (1922), *passim*.

33. *E.G.*, 10 Nov. 1928.

34. Whetham, *1914–39*, pp. 165–6; Cooper, 'Transformation of Agricultural Policy', pp. 96–9, 114–16.

35. *E.G.*, 14 Nov. 1925.

36. Whetham, *1914–39*, pp. 226–38, 241–8, 255–62.

37. Cooper, 'Transformation of Agricultural Policy', pp. 122–9, 163–9.

38. *E.G.*, 8 June 1929.

39. *The Times*, 23 Jan. 1933; Cooper, 'Transformation of Agricultural Policy', pp. 203, 218–24.

40. *E.G.*, 15 Jan. 1938; *The Times*, 6 Jan. 1938.

41. *E.G.*, 9 July 1927.

42. Lord Bledisloe, *The Land and Life* (1942), pp. 6–11.

43. See, for example, the Earl of Dunraven, 'The House of Lords: Its Reform', *19C*, xv (1884), p. 200.

44. Williams, 'Liberal Party and the House of Lords', pp. 345–8; The Marquess of Crewe, *Lord Rosebery*, (2 vols., 1931), I, pp. 197–201.

45. Crewe, *Rosebery*, I, pp. 318–23.

46. Williams, 'Liberal Party and the House of Lords', pp. 345–8.

47. K. Rose, *Curzon: A Most Superior Person* (1985), pp. 139–43.

48. R. E. Pumphrey, 'The Creation of Peerages in England, 1837–1911' (Ph.D. dissertation, Yale University, 1934), p. 129; E. Allyn, *Lords Versus Commons: A Century of Conflict and Compromise, 1830–1930* (New York, 1931), pp. 146–7.

49. P. Bromhead, *The House of Lords and Contemporary Politics, 1911–1957* (1958), pp. 252–3; *The Times*, 13 May 1895.

50. Allyn, *Lords Versus Commons*, pp. 177–8; *Hansard*, H.L., 6 May 1907, col. 1206.

51. R. Jenkins, *Mr Balfour's Poodle* (1954), pp. 49–50; *Hansard*, H.L., 7 May 1907, col. 13.

52. 'Report from the S.C. on the H.L., 1908', reprinted as Appendix IV in *Parliamentary Affairs*, VII (1954), p. 141.

53. R. Rhodes James, *Rosebery: A Biography of Archibald Philip, Fifth Earl of Rosebery* (1963), pp. 461, 467.

54. Jenkins, *Mr Balfour's Poodle*, p. 138; *Hansard*, H.L., 6 May 1907, col. 1283.

55. Jenkins, *Mr Balfour's Poodle*, pp. 138–44.

56. Bromhead, *House of Lords*, pp. 260–1.

57. Jenkins, *Mr Balfour's Poodle*, p. 184; Rhodes James, *Rosebery*, p. 468.

58. Allyn, *Lords Versus Commons*, p. 191; Jenkins, *Mr Balfour's Poodle*, p. 189.

59. Jenkins, *Mr Balfour's Poodle*, pp. 197–203.

60. Parliament Act, 1911, Preamble, reprinted as Appendix VI, *Parliamentary Affairs*, VII (1954), p. 148.

61. D. Close, 'The Collapse of Resistance to Democracy: Conservatives, Adult Suffrage and Second Chamber Reform, 1911–1928', *H.J.*, xx (1977), p. 909.

62. 'Letter from Viscount Bryce to the Prime Minister, April 1918', reprinted as Appendix VII in *Parliamentary Affairs*, VII (1954), pp. 151–68.

63. Allyn, *Lords Versus Commons*, pp. 225–6.

64. Allyn, *Lords Versus Commons*, pp. 226–7.

65. Close, 'Collapse of Resistance', p. 910; J. Ramsden (ed.), *Real Old Tory Politics: The Political Diaries of Sir Robert Sanders, Lord Bayford, 1910–35* (1984), pp. 171–2.

66. *Hansard*, H.L., 18 July 1922, cols. 549, 555.

67. Close, 'Collapse of Resistance', pp. 910–11.

68. *Hansard*, H.L., 25 Mar. 1925, col. 709.

69. Close, 'Collapse of Resistance', p. 911; Ramsden, *Real Old Tory Politics*, pp. 220, 223, 225.

70. Allyn, *Lords Versus Commons*, p. 233.

71. *Hansard*, H.L., 22 June 1927, cols. 874, 883; 23 June 1927, cols. 961–3, 985.

72. Ramsden, *Real Old Tory Politics*, p. 233.

73. Close, 'Collapse of Resistance', p. 910.

74. *Hansard*, H.L., 7 May 1907, col. 27.

75. *Hansard*, H.L., 11 Dec. 1928, col. 486; *Hansard*, H.L., 28 Feb. 1929, cols. 1165–70.

76. Close, 'Collapse of Resistance', p. 913; Ramsden, *Real Old Tory Politics*, p. 247; K. Rose, *The Later Cecils* (1975), pp. 80–1; *Hansard*, H.L., 19 Dec. 1933, cols. 608–17.

77. Bromhead, *House of Lords*, pp. 263–4.

78. *Hansard*, H.L., 19 Dec. 1933, cols. 610–

11; *Hansard*, H.L., 8 May 1934, col. 70.
79. *Hansard*, H.L., 19 Dec. 1933, cols. 644–5; *Hansard*, H.L., 8 May 1934, cols. 84–8, 108–15; *Hansard*, H.L., 9 May 1934, cols. 182–5; *Hansard*, H.L., 10 May 1934, cols. 240–6.
80. *Hansard*, H.L., 10 May 1934, cols. 278–82.
81. Bromhead, *House of Lords*, pp. 263–4; *Hansard*, H.L., 8 May 1934, col. 118; *Hansard*, H.L., 10 May 1934, cols. 272–7.
82. *Hansard*, H.L., 10 May 1934, col. 291; Ramsden, *Real Old Tory Politics*, p. 250.
83. Bromhead, *House of Lords*, p. 264; *Hansard*, H.L., 4 Apr. 1935, cols. 577–85, 600–1; *Hansard*, H.L., 24 Mar. 1937, col. 793.
84. Rhodes James, *Rosebery*, p. 484.
85. *Hansard*, H.L., 4 Apr. 1935, col. 609.
86. Close, 'Collapse of Resistance' p. 910.
87. J. C. Beckett, *The Anglo-Irish Tradition* (1976), pp. 94–5.
88. C. B. Shannon, 'Local Government in Ireland: The Politics and Administration' (MA dissertation, University College Dublin, 1963), pp. 47–8.
89. J. R. Fanning, 'The Unionist Party and Ireland, 1906–1910', *Irish Historical Studies*, xv (1966), p. 150.
90. Beckett, *Anglo-Irish Tradition*, pp. 116–17; P. Buckland, *Irish Unionism*, vol. I, *The Anglo-Irish and the New Ireland, 1885–1922* (Dublin, 1972), pp. xxiii–xxvi.
91. Buckland, *Anglo-Irish*, pp. 1–3, 18–21.
92. R. B. McDowell, *The Irish Convention, 1917–1918* (1970), p. 17.
93. Beckett, *Anglo-Irish Tradition*, pp. 120–4.
94. Buckland, *Anglo-Irish*, p. 16; A. T. Q. Stewart, *The Ulster Crisis* (1967), pp. 38–40.
95. P. Buckland, 'The Southern Irish Unionists, the Irish Question, and British Politics, 1906–14', *Irish Historical Studies*, xv (1967), p. 246.
96. F. S. L. Lyons, *Ireland Since the Famine* (1971), pp. 296–7.
97. Buckland, 'Southern Irish Unionists', pp. 243–4; R. Murphy, 'Faction in the Conservative Party and the Home Rule Crisis, 1912–14', *History*, LXXI (1986), p. 222.
98. Buckland, *Anglo-Irish*, pp. xviii, 72; Buckland, 'Southern Irish Unionists', p. 231.
99. D. Fitzpatrick, *Politics and Irish Life:*

Provincial Experience of War and Revolution, 1913–21 (Dublin, 1977), p. 51.
100. F. S. L. Lyons, *Culture and Anarchy in Ireland, 1890–1939* (1979), pp. 35–48; Lyons, *Ireland Since the Famine*, pp. 224–32.
101. E. Cullingford, *Yeats, Ireland and Fascism* (1981), pp. 44–53, 68–72, 77–9, 176, 184.
102. T. West, *Horace Plunkett: Co-Operation and Politics: An Irish Biography* (1986), pp. 39–41.
103. P. L. Rempe, 'Sir Horace Plunkett and Irish Politics, 1890–1914', *Eire-Ireland*, XIII (1978), pp. 6–17.
104. Lyons, *Ireland Since the Famine*, pp. 202–6; L. Kennedy, 'Agricultural Co-Operation and Irish Rural Society, 1880–1914' (Ph.D. dissertation, York University, 1978), pp. 5–7, 13–15.
105. Lyons, *Culture and Anarchy*, pp. 52–3.
106. Lyons, *Ireland Since the Famine*, pp. 213–14.
107. *E.G.*, 20 and 27 Sept. 1902, 18 Oct. 1902; Shannon, 'Local Government in Ireland', pp. 363–4.
108. *D.N.B.*, *1922–30*, pp. 699–701; Earl of Dunraven, *Past Times and Pastimes* (2 vols., 1922), I, chs. 2 and 3; M. E. Chamberlain, 'Lord Dunraven and the British Empire', *Morgannwg*, xv (1971), pp. 50–72.
109. Shannon, 'Local Government in Ireland', pp. 395–6; Lyons, *Ireland Since the Famine*, pp. 216–18.
110. F. S. L. Lyons, 'The Irish Unionist Party and the Devolution Crisis of 1904–5', *Irish Historical Studies*, VI (1948), pp. 1–9; Dunraven, *Past Times and Pastimes*, II, pp. 25–38.
111. Lyons, *Culture and Anarchy*, p. 63; Lyons, *Ireland Since the Famine*, p. 232.
112. M. L. Kohfeldt, *Lady Gregory: The Woman Behind the Irish Renaissance* (New York, 1985), pp. 122, 177, 194, 211.
113. Lyons, *Culture and Anarchy*, p. 75.
114. For an extended discussion of *Noblesse Oblige*, see *E.G.*, 8 Feb. 1908.
115. Lyons, 'Devolution Crisis', pp. 9–22; Shannon, 'Local Goverment in Ireland', pp. 381–5; A. L. H. Gailey, 'The Unionist Governments' Policy Towards Ireland, 1895–1905' (Ph.D. dissertation, Cambridge University, 1982), pp. 212–87.
116. P. Gibbon, *The Origins of Ulster Unionism: The Formation of Popular Protestant Politics and Ideology in Nineteenth-Century*

Ireland (1975), p. 139; P. Buckland, *Irish Unionism*, vol. II, *Ulster Unionism and the Origins of Northern Ireland, 1886–1922* (Dublin, 1973), pp. 20–1; Fitzpatrick, *Politics and Irish Life*, p. 59.

117. Lord Dunraven, *The Outlook in Ireland: The Case for Devolution and Conciliation* (1907), p. 4.

118. Lyons, *Ireland Since the Famine*, pp. 218, 241–2; Fitzpatrick, *Politics and Irish Life*, p. 51.

119. Stewart, *Ulster Crisis*, pp. 55–9, M. Bence Jones, *Twilight of the Ascendancy* (1987), pp. 156–7.

120. Fitzpatrick, *Politics and Irish Life*, p. 61; Earl of Midleton, *Records and Reactions, 1856–1939* (1939), p. 226.

121. P. Jalland, *The Liberals and Ireland: The Ulster Question in British Politics to 1914* (1980), p. 93.

122. Buckland, 'Southern Irish Unionists', pp. 238–40; Murphy, 'Faction in the Conservative Party', pp. 214–34.

123. Buckland, *Anglo-Irish*, pp. 41, 224–34.

124. Earl of Midleton, *Ireland – Dupe or Heroine* (1932), p. 103.

125. McDowell, *Irish Convention*, pp. 56–76; P. Williamson (ed.), *The Modernisation of Conservative Politics: The Diaries and Letters of William Bridgeman, 1904–1935* (1988), pp. 100–7.

126. Buckland, *Anglo-Irish*, p. 85.

127. McDowell, *Irish Convention*, p. 115.

128. Buckland, *Anglo-Irish*, pp. 91–126.

129. Beckett, *Anglo-Irish*, pp. 125–9; Midleton, *Ireland – Dupe or Heroine*, pp. 113–18; Bence Jones, *Twilight of the Ascendancy*, pp. 182–3; McDowell, *Irish Convention*, pp. 127–9, 136, 143–7.

130. Buckland, *Anglo-Irish*, pp. 129–45; Midleton, *Ireland – Dupe or Heroine*, pp. 118–20; West, *Horace Plunkett*, pp. 171–5.

131. Buckland, *Anglo-Irish*, pp. 146–84.

132. McDowell, *Irish Convention*, p. 195.

133. Buckland, *Anglo-Irish*, pp. 197–201, 220–2; Buckland, *Ulster Unionism*, pp. 116–21.

134. Buckland, *Anglo-Irish*, pp. 198–200, 225–6, 230–2.

135. Bence Jones, *Twilight of the Ascendancy*, p. 213; McDowell, *Irish Convention*, p. 211; Beckett, *Anglo-Irish*, pp. 129–30.

136. Buckland, *Anglo-Irish*, pp. 244–52; Midleton, *Records and Reactions*, p. 263; Midleton, *Ireland – Dupe or Heroine*, p. 160.

137. Buckland, *Anglo-Irish*, pp. 260–71, 291–7.

138. Buckland, *Anglo-Irish*, pp. xxiv–xxvi, 282.

139. Bence Jones, *Twilight of the Ascendancy*, p. 214; Buckland, *Anglo-Irish*, p. 276.

140. Lyons, *Culture and Anarchy*, p. 102; Midleton, *Records and Reactions*, p. 264.

141. *The Times*, 14 to 24 Nov. 1885; Lord Selborne, *Memorials, Part II, Personal and Political, 1865–1895* (2 vols., 1898), II, pp. 182–7.

142. J. G. Lockhart, *Cosmo Gordon Lang* (1949), pp. 34, 49, 75, 114, 170, 217–18, 373–4; Lord Halifax, *Fullness of Days* (New York, 1957), pp. 163, 169.

143. G. K. A. Bell, *Randall Davidson: Archbishop of Canterbury* (2 vols., 1935), I, pp. 577, 602, 628–30; II, pp. 982, 1066.

144. G. I. T. Machin, *Politics and the Churches in Great Britain, 1869 to 1921* (1987), pp. 13–16, 281, 324–31; A. Hastings, *A History of English Christianity, 1920–1985* (1986), pp. 35–41.

145. Machin, *Politics and the Churches*, p. 153; A. Simon, 'Church Disestablishment as a Factor in the General Election of 1885', *H.J.*, XVIII (1975), pp. 804–5; G. D. Phillips, *The Diehards: Aristocratic Society and Politics in Edwardian England* (1979), p. 111.

146. J. M. Robinson, *The Dukes of Norfolk: A Quincentennial History* (1982), pp. 212–26.

147. F. W. Steer, *The Cathedral Church of Our Lady and St. Philip, Arundel: A Monograph to Celebrate its First Hundred Years, 1873–1973* (1973), pp. 12–22.

148. D. Hunter Blair, *John Patrick, Third Marquess of Bute, K.T., 1847–1900: A Memoir* (1921), pp. 80, 105–8, 122, 129, 153–5, 208, 215, 223.

149. Machin, *Politics and the Churches*, p. 180; E. R. Norman, *The English Catholic Church in the Nineteenth Century* (1984), pp. 216, 369–71; J. G. Lockhart, *Charles Lindley, Viscount Halifax* (2 vols., 1936), II, ch. 4.

150. Lord Halifax (ed.), *The Conversations at Malines: Official Documents* (1930); Hastings, *English Christianity*, pp. 209–12; Lockhart, *Halifax*, II, chs. 18–22.

151. Robinson, *Dukes of Norfolk*, p. 214.

152. Hunter Blair, *Marquess of Bute*, pp. 125, 144; Lockhart, *Halifax*, II, pp. 2–3, 37, 93–5, 103.

153. H. Henson, *Retrospect of an Unimportant Life* (3 vols., 1942–50), vol. II, *1920–*

1939, pp. 138, 142; Lockhart, *Halifax*, II, pp. 148–9.

154. Machin, *Politics and the Churches*, pp. 114, 124; Norman, *English Catholic Church*, pp. 77, 205, 235, 275–8.

155. K. O. Morgan, *Wales in British Politics, 1868–1922* (1970), pp. 76–84; Machin, *Politics and the Churches*, pp. 191–3.

156. Morgan, *Wales in British Politics*, pp. 90–3; P. M. H. Bell, *Disestablishment in Ireland and Wales* (1969), pp. 240–1; W. O. Chadwick, *The Victorian Church*, Part II (1970), pp. 433–6.

157. Machin, *Politics and the Churches*, p. 210; A. S. T. Griffith-Boscawen, *Fourteen Years in Parliament* (1907), p. 41; A. S. T. Griffith-Boscawen, *Memories* (1925), p. 74.

158. Morgan, *Wales in British Politics*, pp. 80, 136–9; Selborne, *Memorials*, II, p. 380.

159. Lady Victoria Hicks Beach, *The Life of Sir Michael Hicks Beach* (2 vols., 1932), II, pp. 6–8.

160. Morgan, *Wales in British Politics*, pp. 143–150, 171–3, 231–5, 238–40; Machin, *Politics and the Churches*, pp. 215–16, 224, 301–2; Griffith-Boscawen, *Fourteen Years*, p. 57; Williamson, *Modernisation of Conservative Politics*, pp. 54–5.

161. Machin, *Politics and the Churches*, p. 307; Morgan, *Wales in British Politics*, pp. 261–71; Griffith-Boscawen, *Memories*, p. 76. William Ormsby-Gore wrote a pamphlet entitled *Welsh Disestablishment and Disendowment* (1912).

162. See the ensuing correspondence between A. F. Pollard and Lord Hugh Cecil, *The Times*, 26 Apr.–1 May 1912. For Lord Robert Cecil's recollections, see Lord Robert Cecil, *All The Way* (1949), p. 120.

163. Machin, *Politics and the Churches*, pp. 307–10; Williamson, *Modernisation of Conservative Politics*, pp. 77–84.

164. Cecil, *All the Way*, p. 146; Machin, *Politics and the Churches*, pp. 314–15; Williamson, *Modernisation of Conservative Politics*, pp. 135–6.

165. Morgan, *Wales in British Politics*, pp. 286–90; Bell, *Disestablishment*, pp. 308–18.

166. Morgan, *Wales in British Politics*, pp. 271–3; Morgan, *Consensus and Disunity*, (1979), pp. 34, 160.

167. Morgan, *Wales in British Politics*, p. 282; Cecil, *All The Way*, p. 146; Rose, *Later Cecils*, p. 154.

168. Machin, *Politics and the Churches*, pp.

141–67; Chadwick, *Victorian Church*, Pt. II, pp. 436–8; W. H. Mackintosh, *Disestablishment and Liberation: The Movement for the Separation of the Anglican Church from State Control* (1972), pp. 213–14, 233, 300–2.

169. Machin, *Politics and the Churches*, pp. 231–4; K. A. Thompson, *Bureaucracy and Church Reform* (1970), pp. 93, 122, 125.

170. Bell, *Davidson*, II, p. 957; Hastings, *English Christianity*, p. 51.

171. Machin, *Politics and the Churches*, p. 317; Bell, *Davidson*, II, pp. 957–9; Lord Parmoor, *A Retrospect* (1936), pp. 87–9.

172. Hastings, *English Christianity*, pp. 63–4.

173. D. M. Thompson, 'The Politics of the Enabling Act, 1919', in D. Baker (ed.), *Studies in Church History*, XII (1975), pp. 383–91.

174. Thompson, *Bureaucracy and Church Reform*, pp. 140, 175.

175. H. Henson, *Retrospect*, I, *1863–1920*, p. 206.

176. Parmoor, *Retrospect*, pp. 90–3; Hastings, *English Christianity*, pp. 252–4; *D.N.B., 1951–60*, pp. 1054–5.

177. Rose, *Later Cecils*, pp. 272–5; Thompson, *Bureaucracy and Church Reform*, pp. 220–1; F. A. Iremonger, *William Temple, Archbishop of Canterbury: His Life and Letters* (1948), p. 281.

178. *The Times*, 3 Apr. 1963.

179. Thompson, *Bureaucracy and Church Reform*, pp. 190–2.

180. For a full account of this, see: Bell, *Davidson*, II, ch. 72; Lockhart, *Lang*, ch. 25; Henson, *Retrospect*, II, ch. 15; Hastings, *English Christianity*, pp. 204–8.

181. Rose, *Later Cecils*, pp. 276–9; Machin, *Politics and the Churches*, p. 11; A. J. P. Taylor, *English History, 1914–1945* (1965), p. 259.

182. Rose, *Later Cecils*, p. 120; Iremonger, *Temple*, p. 357.

183. Rose, *Later Cecils*, pp. 59, 270, 280–3; Henson, *Retrospect*, II, ch. 25; Iremonger, *Temple*, pp. 467–73; W. O. Chadwick, *Hensley Henson: A Study in the Friction Between Church and State* (1983), pp. 215–18.

184. Rose, *Later Cecils*, pp. 95–102; Bell, *Davidson*, II, p. 1380; *The Times*, 3 Apr. 1963.

185. Lockhart, *Halifax*, II, pp. 200–2, 225.

186. Thompson, *Bureaucracy and Church Reform*, p. 179.

187. Lockhart, *Lang*, pp. 213–14, 337; Henson, *Retrospect*, III, *1939–46*, p. 67.
188. Hastings, *English Christianity*, p. 252.
189. Lord Midleton, 'Lord Desart and the Irish Convention', in Lady S. Lubbock (ed.), *A Page from the Past: Memories of the Earl of Desart* (1936), p. 244.
190. Halifax, *Fullness of Days*, p. 154.
191. Rose, *Later Cecils*, pp. 60–1.

Chapter 11

1. R. Blake, *Disraeli* (1968), p. 171.
2. R. Douglas, *Land, People and Politics: A History of the Land Question in the United Kingdom, 1878–1952* (1876), p. 50, The Whigs always knew who they were, but historians have been less sure. For two conflicting views, see: J. R. Vincent, *The Formation of the Liberal Party, 1859–1868* (1966), pp. 3, 20–5; T. A. Jenkins, *Gladstone, Whiggery and the Liberal Party, 1874–1886* (1988), pp. 2–10.
3. D. Southgate, *The Passing of the Whigs, 1832–1886* (1962), pp. vii, 282; G. W. E. Russell, *Sketches and Snapshots* (1910), pp. 153–4; G. W. E. Russell, *Half Lengths* (1910), p. 39.
4. Russell, *Half Lengths*, pp. 46, 49.
5. Russell, *Sketches and Snapshots*, p. 154; O. F. Christie, *The Transition to Democracy, 1867–1914* (1934), p. 181; H. Macmillan, *The Past Masters: Politics and Politicians, 1906–1939* (1975), pp. 184–6.
6. Russell, *Half Lengths*, p. 45.
7. B. Holland, *The Life of Spencer Compton, Eighth Duke of Devonshire, 1833–1908* (2 vols., 1911), I, pp. 405–6.
8. For two different views of Hartington's performance as leader, see: Jenkins, *Gladstone, Whiggery and the Liberal Party*, pp. 51–101; J. P. Rossi, 'The Last Whig: Lord Hartington as Liberal Leader, 1875–80', *Canadian Journal of History*, XXI (1986), pp. 167–86.
9. Russell, *Half Lengths*, p. 39.
10. J. Morley, *The Life of William Ewart Gladstone* (3 vols., 1903), II, p. 629; H. Reeve, 'Plain Whig Principles', *Edinburgh Review*, CLI (1880), pp. 257–80.
11. Russell, *Sketches and Snapshots*, p. 46; H. J. Perkin, *The Rise of Professional Society: England Since 1880* (1989), p. 40.
12. Southgate, *Passing of the Whigs*, p. xv; Viscount Gladstone, *After Thirty Years* (1928), pp. 166–7, 175, 278, 288.

13. Russell, *Half Lengths*, p. 46; Southgate, *Passing of the Whigs*, pp. xvi, 312–17; B. Mallet, *Thomas George, Earl of Northbrook: A Memoir* (1908), pp. 32–3.
14. Southgate, *Passing of the Whigs*, p. 381; Perkin, *Rise of Professional Society*, p. 41.
15. Southgate, *Passing of the Whigs*, p. 16; G. Huxley, *Victorian Duke: The Life of Hugh Lupus Grosvenor, First Duke of Westminster* (1967), p. 164.
16. Jenkins, *Gladstone, Whiggery and the Liberal Party*, p. 9; Southgate, *Passing of the Whigs*, p. 321.
17. Christie, *Transition to Democracy*, pp. 183–4; Rossi, 'The Last Whig', pp. 172–8; Holland, *Eighth Duke of Devonshire*, I, p. 184; Lord Edmond Fitzmaurice, *The Life of Granville Leverson Gower, KG, Second Earl Granville, 1815–1891* (2 vols., 1905), II, p. 167.
18. Jenkins, *Gladstone, Whiggery and the Liberal Party*, pp. 72, 75, 174, 184, 189.
19. Southgate, *Passing of the Whigs*, pp. 218–24, 341–2.
20. Huxley, *Victorian Duke*, p. 159; Earl of Selborne, *Memorials*, Part II: *Personal and Political, 1865–1895* (2 vols., 1898), II, p. 184.
21. Southgate, *Passing of the Whigs*, p. 414; W. H. Mallock and Lady G. Ramsden (eds.), *Letters, Remains and Memoirs of Edward Adolphus Seymour, twelfth Duke of Somerset, KG* (1893), pp. 480–1.
22. Russell, *Half Lengths*, pp. 47–8; Southgate, *Passing of the Whigs*, pp. 368–9.
23. S. Gwynn and G. M. Tuckwell, *The Life of the Rt. Hon. Sir Charles W. Dilke, Bt., MP* (2 vols., 1917), II, p. 221; Southgate, *Passing of the Whigs*, pp. 360, 389.
24. Southgate, *Passing of the Whigs*, pp. 359, 418.
25. T. A. Jenkins, 'Gladstone, the Whigs and the Leadership of the Liberal Party, 1879–1880', *H.J.*, XXVII (1984), p. 348; G. L. Goodman, 'Liberal Unionism: The Revolt of the Whigs', *Victorian Studies*, II (1959), p. 175; Rossi, 'The Last Whig', p. 182; Holland, *Eighth Duke of Devonshire*, I, pp. 245–8.
26. Southgate, *Passing of the Whigs*, pp. 365, 385–9; Holland, *Eighth Duke of Devonshire*, II, p. 72; J. E. Williams, 'The Liberal Party and the House of Lords, 1880–1895', (MA dissertation, University of Wales, 1961), pp. 223–5.
27. Duchess of Argyll (ed.), *George Douglas, eighth Duke of Argyll (1823–1900): Auto-*

biography and Memoirs (2 vols., 1960), II,
pp. 380–1.

28. Southgate, Passing of the Whigs, pp. 286–
7; Goodman, 'Liberal Unionism', p.
180; Jenkins, Gladstone, Whiggery and
the Liberal Party, pp. 286–7; Sir A.
Lyall, The Life of the Marquess of Dufferin and Ava (2 vols., 1905), II, p. 139.

29. Southgate, Passing of the Whigs, p. 322;
R. C. K. Ensor, 'Some Political and
Economic Interactions in Later Victorian
England', Transactions of the Royal His-
torical Society, 4th. ser., XXXI (1949),
esp. pp. 19–20, 25–7.

30. Christie, Transition to Democracy, p. 185;
W. C. Lubenow, 'Irish Home Rule and
the Social Basis of the Great Separation
in the Liberal Party in 1886', H.J.,
XXVIII (1985), pp. 134–5.

31. Christie, Transition to Democracy, p.
183; Southgate, Passing of the Whigs,
pp. 332, 352.

32. Williams, 'Liberals and the House of
Lords', pp. 205–6; Rossi, 'The Last
Whig', pp. 175–7; Jenkins, 'Gladstone,
the Whigs and the Leadership of the
Liberal Party', pp. 347, 352–60.

33. Jenkins, Gladstone, Whiggery and the
Liberal Party, pp. 146–51, 300–4; Wil-
liams, 'Liberal Party and the House of
Lords', pp. 213–15.

34. Argyll, Autobiography and Memoirs, II,
pp. 349–54; Lord Newton, Lord Lansdowne: A Biography (1929), pp. 18–20.

35. Southgate, Passing of the Whigs, pp. 371–
3.

36. Jenkins, Gladstone, Whiggery and the Liberal Party, p. 153; Argyll, Autobiography
and Memoirs, II, pp. 363–82.

37. Williams, 'Liberal Party and the House
of Lords', pp. 197, 210; Southgate,
Passing of the Whigs, pp. 370–1; Jenkins,
Gladstone, Whiggery and the Liberal Party,
p. 163; Sir Alfred Pease, Elections and
Recollections (1932), pp. 58–61.

38. Russell, Half Lengths, p. 69; Goodman,
'Liberal Unionism', p. 177; Williams,
'Liberal Party and the House of Lords',
p. 69; J. Bateman, The Great Landowners
of Great Britain and Ireland (4th edn.,
reprinted 1971), p. 499.

39. Williams, 'Liberal Party and the House
of Lords', pp. 218–20; Jenkins, Gladstone, Whiggery and the Liberal Party,
pp. 222–3.

40. Christie, Transition to Democracy, p. 188;
Southgate, Passing of the Whigs, p. 398.
For an idiosyncratic view of the high-

political manœuvring of these years,
see A. B. Cooke and J. R. Vincent, The
Governing Passion: Cabinet Government
and Party Politics in Britain, 1885–1886
(1974).

41. Williams, 'Liberal Party and the House
of Lords', pp. 221–2; Lubenow, 'Home
Rule and the Social Basis of the Great
Separation', p. 135.

42. Williams, 'Liberal Party and the House
of Lords', pp. 229–32; Huxley, Victorian
Duke, p. 162; J. R. Vincent (ed.), The
Later Derby Diaries: Home Rule, Liberal
Unionism and Aristocratic Life in Late
Victorian England (1981), p. 61.

43. Williams, 'Liberal Party and the House
of Lords', p. 233; Southgate, Passing of
the Whigs, pp. 412–13.

44. Goodman, 'Liberal Unionists', p. 180;
Southgate, Passing of the Whigs, p. 414;
Lubenow, 'Home Rule and the Social
Basis of the Great Separation', p. 127.

45. Huxley, Victorian Duke, pp. 160–5.

46. Christie, Transition to Democracy, pp.
188–92; Russell, Sketches and Snapshots,
p. 172; Fitzmaurice, Granville, II, p. 489;
A. Adonis, 'Aristocracy, Agriculture
and Liberalism: The Politics, Finances
and Estates of the Third Lord Carrington', H.J., XXXI (1988), pp. 876–7; P.
Gordon (ed.), The Red Earl: The Papers
of the Fifth Earl Spencer, 1835–1910 (2
vols., 1981–6), vol. II, 1885–1910, pp.
5–14, 105–30.

47. Macmillan, Past Masters, p. 190; Sir
George Leveson-Gower, Years of Content, 1858–1886 (1940), pp. 223–4, 230,
246. For a glimpse of the disagreement
between G. W. E. Russell and the tenth
Duke of Bedford, see D. Spring, 'Land
and Politics in Edwardian England',
Agricultural History, LVIII (1984), pp. 19–
20.

48. Pease, Elections and Recollections, p. 137.

49. Russell, Half Lengths, p. 46; Russell,
Sketches and Snapshots, pp. 335–6.

50. Southgate, Passing of the Whigs, p. 419;
P. Fraser, 'The Liberal Unionist Alliance: Chamberlain, Hartington and
the Conservatives, 1886–1904', Eng.
Hist. Rev., LXXVII (1962), p. 65.

51. Williams, 'Liberal Party and the House
of Lords', pp. 236–7; Fraser, 'Liberal
Unionist Alliance', pp. 58–9, 66; Lord
Selborne, 'Thoughts About Party', Contemporary Review, LI (1887), p. 6.

52. Vincent, Later Derby Diaries, pp. 78–9;
G. D. Phillips, 'The Whig Lords and

Liberalism, 1886–1893', *H.J.*, XXIV (1981), pp. 167–73.

53. Macmillan, *Past Masters*, pp. 194–5; Goodman, 'Liberal Unionists', p. 189; W. C. Lubenow, 'Irish Home Rule and the Great Separation in the Liberal Party in 1886: The Dimensions of Parliamentary Liberalism', *Victorian Studies*, XXVI (1983), p. 180.

54. Holland, *Eighth Duke of Devonshire*, II, p. 183; Vincent, *Later Derby Diaries*, pp. 92–6; Gordon, *The Red Earl*, II, p. 41.

55. R. J. Moore, 'The Twilight of the Whigs and the Reform of the Indian Councils, 1886–1892', *H.J.*, X (1967), pp. 400, 403, 410, 413–14.

56. Gordon, *The Red Earl*, II, pp. 321–3, 327–9; Macmillan, *Past Masters*, p. 191.

57. R. Douglas, 'Riddle of the Whigs', *Times Higher Education Supplement*, 10 June 1988, p. 29.

58. Macmillan, *Past Masters*, pp. 192–3, 197.

59. Jenkins, *Gladstone, Whiggery and the Liberal Party*, p. 181.

60. Russell, *Half Lengths*, p. 69; Fitzmaurice, *Granville*, II, p. 464; Holland, *Eighth Duke of Devonshire*, II, p. 74.

61. G. D. Phillips, 'Lord Willoughby de Broke and the Politics of Radical Toryism, 1909–14', *Journal of British Studies*, XX (1980), p. 206.

62. G. D. Phillips, 'The "Diehards" and the Myth of the "Backwoodsmen"', *Journal of British Studies*, XVI (1977), pp. 105–20.

63. G. D. Phillips, *The Diehards: Aristocratic Society and Politics in Edwardian England* (1979), pp. 7–8.

64. Phillips, *The Diehards*, pp. 51–52.

65. Phillips, *The Diehards*, pp. 27–9.

66. Phillips, *The Diehards*, pp. 7–8, 21, 84.

67. A. J. Mayer, 'Internal Crisis and War Since 1870', in C. L. Bertrand (ed.), *Revolutionary Situations in Europe, 1917–1922* (Montreal, 1977), pp. 201, 206–11; G. R. Searle, 'The "Revolt from the Right" in Edwardian Britain,' in P. Kennedy and A. Nicholls (eds.), *Nationalist and Racialist Movements in Britain and Germany Before 1914* (1981), pp. 22–3.

68. Duke of Westminster, 'Practical Imperialism', *19C*, LXXII (1912), pp. 870–5.

69. Phillips, *The Diehards*, p. 113; Earl of Meath, '"A Thousand More Mouths Every Day"', *19C*, XXV (1889), p. 60.

70. Phillips, *The Diehards*, pp. 89, 92, 108.

71. Phillips, *The Diehards*, pp. 107, 119–22.

72. J. Springhall, 'Lord Meath, Youth and Empire', *Journal of Contemporary History*, V (1970), pp. 97–112.

73. Phillips, *The Diehards*, p. 90.

74. Hastings, Duke of Bedford, *The Years of Transition* (1949), pp. 84–5.

75. Earl of Malmesbury, *The New Order* (1908), pp. 7, 13.

76. Lord Halifax, 'The Crisis in the Church', *19C*, LII (1903), p. 553; Phillips, *The Diehards*, p. 113.

77. The following paragraphs are much indebted to Phillips, 'Lord Willoughby de Broke', pp. 205–24.

78. Lord Willoughby de Broke, *The Passing Years* (1924), pp. 2–3, 41–2, 54–5.

79. Lord Willoughby de Broke, *The Sport of Our Ancestors* (1921), pp. 5–6.

80. Willoughby de Broke, *The Passing Years*, p. 167.

81. Willoughby de Broke, *The Passing Years*, p. 111; *The Sport of Our Ancestors*, p. 35; A. Sykes, 'The Radical Right and the Crisis of Conservatism Before the First World War', *H.J.*, XXVI (1983), pp. 668–9.

82. Phillips, *The Diehards*, pp. 128–9.

83. Lord Willoughby de Broke, 'A Plea for an Unreformed House of Lords', *National Review*, XLIX (1907), p. 772.

84. Phillips, 'Willoughby de Broke', pp. 207–8.

85. R. Jenkins, *Mr Balfour's Poodle* (1954), pp. 217–18.

86. Phillips, 'Willoughby de Broke', p. 209.

87. Phillips, *The Diehards*, pp. 128–9, 138–9.

88. Phillips, *The Diehards*, pp. 138–9.

89. Jenkins, *Mr. Balfour's Poodle*, pp. 235–6; Phillips, 'Willoughby de Broke', pp. 210–11.

90. Jenkins, *Mr. Balfour's Poodle*, pp. 251–7, 265.

91. Spring, 'Land and Politics in Edwardian England', p. 34.

92. Phillips, 'Willoughby de Broke', pp. 215–16.

93. Phillips, *The Diehards*, pp. 145–6.

94. Phillips, 'Willoughby de Broke', pp. 217–18.

95. Jenkins, *Mr. Balfour's Poodle*, pp. 234–5.

96. Phillips, *The Diehards*, pp. 149–51.

97. A. T. Q. Stewart, *The Ulster Crisis* (1967), pp. 125, 132.

98. Phillips, 'Willoughby de Broke', p. 219.

99. Stewart, *Ulster Crisis*, pp. 61, 61, 70, 93–5, 134, 198–205.

100. P. Buckland, *Irish Unionism*, vol. II, *Ulster Unionism and the Origins of Northern Ireland, 1886–1922* (Dublin, 1973), p. 52.

101. Spring, 'Land and Politics in Edwardian England', p. 39; Phillips, 'Willoughby de Broke', p. 220.

102. Spring, 'Land and Politics in Edwardian England', pp. 17.

103. Phillips, 'Willoughby de Broke', pp. 222–3.

104. Spring, 'Land and Politics in Edwardian England', p. 40.

105. Searle, 'Revolt from the Right', pp. 32–5.

106. Sykes, 'Radical Right and the Crisis of Conservatism', pp. 663–5, 670; W. S. Rodner, 'Leaguers, Covenanters, Moderates: British Support for Ulster, 1913–1914', *Eire-Ireland*, XVII (1982), pp. 71–2, 78–81.

107. Phillips, 'Willoughby de Broke', p. 219; G. R. Seale, 'Critics of Edwardian Society: The Case of the Radical Right', in A. O'Day (ed.), *The Edwardian Age: Conflict and Stability, 1900–1914* (1979), pp. 94–5.

108. Searle, 'Revolt from the Right', pp. 36–7; Sykes, 'Radical Right and the Crisis of Conservatism', p. 673.

109. Willoughby de Broke, *The Passing Years*, p. 33.

110. *Hansard*, H.L., 25 Nov. 1920, col. 667.

111. F. M. L. Thompson, *English Landed Society in the Nineteenth Century* (1963), p. 333.

112. Lord Pakenham [Earl of Longford], *Born to Believe* (1953), pp. 153, 159.

113. F. S. L. Lyons, *Ireland Since the Famine* (1971), pp. 158–9.

114. R. F. Foster, *Charles Stewart Parnell: The Man and His Family* (1976), pp. xiii–xiv, 114, 121–3, 205–8.

115. Lyons, *Ireland Since the Famine*, p. 148.

116. Foster, *Parnell*, pp. 113, 130, 172, 183, 190–6.

117. B. Farrell, 'Markievicz and the Women of the Revolution', in F. X. Martin (ed.), *Leaders and Men of the Easter Rising: Dublin, 1916* (Ithaca, NY, n.d.), pp. 230–4.

118. A. Marreco, *The Rebel Countess* (1967), pp. 91, 103, 121–4, 131–5.

119. F. X. Martin (ed.), *The Howth Gun Running and the Kilcoole Gun Running, 1914* (Dublin, 1964), pp. xiv–xv, xix–xx, 27, 68, 108–9; Lyons, *Ireland Since*

120. A. Boyle, *The Riddle of Erskine Childers* (1977), pp. 26, 30, 38, 62; R. B. McDowell, *Alice Stopford Green – A Passionate Historian* (Dublin, 1967), pp. 96–7.

121. Lyons, *Ireland Since the Famine*, pp. 367, 376; Farrell, 'Markievicz and the Women of the Revolution', pp. 236–7.

122. Boyle, *Erskine Childers*, pp. 223–6, 246, 290–4.

123. Boyle, *Erskine Childers*, pp. 162–3, 299, 319.

124. J. Van Voris, *Constance de Markievicz: In the Cause of Ireland* (Amherst, Mass., 1967), pp. 236, 346; S. O'Faolain, *Constance Markievicz* (1967 edn.), p. 194.

125. Boyle, *Erskine Childers*, pp. 254, 298, 303.

126. Marreco, *Rebel Countess*, 161, 264, 260; F. S. L. Lyons, *Culture and Anarchy in Ireland, 1890–1939* (1979), pp. 102–3.

127. Van Voris, *Constance de Markievicz*, pp. 217, 304; E. Roper (ed.), *Prison Letters of Countess Markievicz* (New York, 1970 edn.), pp. 257–8.

128. MacDowell, *Passionate Historian*, pp. 62, 55–60, 102, 107.

129. E. Longford, *A Pilgrimage of Passion: The Life of Wilfrid Scawen Blunt* (1979), pp. 4, 354, 431.

130. Longford, *Pilgrimage of Passion*, pp. 153–4, 167, 210, 256.

131. Longford, *Pilgrimage of Passion*, pp. 103, 134, 230, 234, 242, 274, 311, 342, 345, 384–5, 406, 409.

132. M. Blunden, *The Countess of Warwick* (1967), pp. 148, 168, 193, 206, 219, 273, 290.

133. Blunden, *Countess of Warwick*, pp. 173, 178–9, 181–2, 292–304.

134. C. A. Clynes, *Recruits to Labour: The British Labour Party, 1914–1931* (Syracuse, NY, 1963), pp. 153–6, 167–70, 172, 176.

135. R. Skidelsky, *Oswald Mosley* (1975), p. 129.

136. V. de Bunsen, *Charles Roden Buxton: A Memoir* (1948), pp. 39–49, 78–9.

137. A. Ponsonby, *The Decline of Aristocracy* (1912), p. 314.

138. Clynes, *Recruits to Labour*, pp. 11–22.

139. De Bunsen, *Buxton*, p. 128; Lord Parmoor, *A Retrospect* (1936), pp. 134, 233.

140. *The Times*, 27 Feb. 1965; Van Voris, *Constance de Markievicz*, pp. 271, 275.

141. *The Times*, 9 Oct. 1953.

142. J. M. Kenworthy, *Sailors, Statesman and*

Others (1933), pp. 123, 137, 148, 157, 163, 169, 197.

143. C. Cooke, *The Life of R. S. Cripps* (1957), pp. 84, 96, 109; M. Craig, *Longford: A Biographical Portrait* (1978), pp. 50–4; Readers of Anthony Powell may note the apparent similarity between Viscount Erridge (a high-minded and slovenly dressed patrician socialist of the 1930s) and Lord Longford (as the Hon. Frank Pakenham eventually became). Is it just coincidence that Longford and Powell are brothers-in-law? See H. Spurling, *Handbook to Anthony Powell's Music of Time* (1977), pp. 55–7.

144. G. and E. Romilly, *Out of Bounds* (1935), pp. 141, 176, 179, 200, 205, 264; R. D. Richardson, *Comintern Army: The International Brigades and the Spanish Civil War* (Kentucky, 1982), p. 46; V. Brome, *The International Brigades: Spain, 1936–1939* (1965), pp. 51–9, 83, 98–102; H. Thomas, *John Strachey* (1973), pp. 112, 119, 123, 129, 145–6; A. Boyle, *The Climate of Treason: Five Who Spied For Russia* (1979), pp. 37, 70.

145. Thomson, *Strachey*, p. 143.

146. B. Finney, *Christopher Isherwood: A Critical Biography* (New York, 1979), pp. 15–20.

147. J. Fryer, *Isherwood: A Biography of Christopher Isherwood* (1977), pp. 7–9, 13–16.

148. C. Isherwood, *Kathleen and Frank* (New York, 1971), p. 266.

149. Finney, *Isherwood*, pp. 81, 95–6; Fryer, *Isherwood*, pp. 12, 204–5, 276.

150. Kenworthy, *Sailors, Statesman and Others*, pp. 48–9.

151. N. Mitford, *Pigeon Pie* (1976 edn.), p. 43. The book was first published in 1940.

152. J. Pearson, *Facades: Edith, Osbert and Sachaverell Sitwell* (1978), pp. 227–32.

153. W. D. Rubinstein, 'Henry Page Croft and the National Party, 1917–22', *Journal of Contemporary History*, IX (1974), pp. 129–48.

154. M. Cowling, *The Impact of Labour, 1920–1924* (1971), pp. 80–4; R. Benewick, *The Fascist Movement in Britain* (1972), pp. 32–3; R. Griffiths, *Fellow Travellers of the Right: British Enthusiasts for Nazi Germany, 1933–9* (1983), pp. 61, 85–7.

155. Lord Raglan, *If I Were Dictator* (1934), pp. 1–8.

156. Skidelsky, *Mosley*, p. 224.

157. Griffiths, *Fellow Travellers*, p. 45.

158. Earl of Lytton, *Anthony: A Record of Youth* (1935), pp. 298, 333–4.

159. Pearson, *Facades*, pp. 113–15, 129–30, 157–9, 302–3.

160. Earl of Portsmouth, *A Knot of Roots* (1965), pp. 141, 149–151.

161. The Duke of Manchester, *My Candid Recollections* (1932), pp. 98–9, 243, 254–64.

162. Skidelsky, *Mosley*, pp. 23–43, 134.

163. N. Mosley, *Rules of the Game: Sir Oswald and Lady Mosley, 1896–1933* (1982), p. 31.

164. Skidelsky, *Mosley*, pp. 45, 53, 57, 81, 134, 227.

165. Skidelsky, *Mosley*, pp. 90, 96, 111, 130–2, 205, 288–90.

166. Pearson, *Facades*, p. 284; Skidelsky, *Mosley*, pp. 263, 297.

167. Benewick, *Fascist Movement in Britain*, pp. 125–7; W. F. Mandle, 'The Leadership of the British Union of Fascists', *Australian Journal of Politics and History*, XII (1966), p. 363; C. Cross, *The Fascists in Great Britain* (1961), pp. 79, 98, 179.

168. Griffiths, *Fellow Travellers*, pp. 184–6, 218–19, 269–71, 275, 323–4; Marquess of Londonderry, *Ourselves and Germany* (1938), pp. 16–17.

169. K. Rose, *The Later Cecils* (1975), p. 179; J. Mitford, *Hons and Rebels* (1960 edn.), pp. 62–3.

170. J. L. Finlay, *Social Credit: The English Origins* (1972), pp. 132, 138, 174, 177, 222, 256; John, Duke of Bedford, *A Silver-Plated Spoon* (1959), pp. 15, 40, 50, 155–7.

171. Bedford, *Years of Transition*, pp. 146–56, 160–80, 186, 207.

172. Griffiths, *Fellow Travellers*, p. 175; Mitford, *Hons and Rebels*, p. 220.

173. D. Mosley, *A Life of Contrasts* (1984 edn.), p. 39.

174. H. Acton, *Nancy Mitford: A Memoir* (1984 edn.), pp. 21–7; J. Guinness with C. Guinness, *The House of Mitford* (1984), pp. 97–102, 114–15, 118, 240.

175. Mosley, *Life of Contrasts*, pp. 11, 19–22, 39–42, 56; Guinness and Guinness, *House of Mitford*, pp. 254–5, 271, 290–1, 296; D. Pryce Jones, *Unity Mitford: A Quest* (1976), pp. 17–19.

176. Mosley, *Life of Contrasts*, pp. 94–8, 123–5, 139.

177. Guiness and Guiness, *House of Mitford*, p. 363; Mosley, *Life of Contrasts*, p. 156.

178. Pryce Jones, *Unity Mitford*, p. 262; Guinness and Guinness, *House of Mitford*, pp. 370, 377, 411.
179. N. Mitford (ed.), *The Ladies of Alderley* (1938), p. xv.
180. N. Mitford (ed.), *The Stanleys of Alderley* (1939), p. xvi.
181. Guinness and Guinness, *House of Mitford*, pp. 471–4.
182. N. Mitford, *The Pursuit of Love* (1980 edn.), pp. 87–9. This novel was first published in 1945.
183. N. Mitford, *Wigs on the Green* (1935), pp. 16–20, 152–7.
184. Acton, *Nancy Mitford*, pp. 40–2, 47.
185. Mitford, *Hons and Rebels*, pp. 60–2, 91, 95, 100–2, 107–8, 133, 141–5.
186. P. Toynbee, *Friends Apart* (1954), pp. 98–102, 106–7.

Chapter 12

1. A. Ponsonby, *The Decline of Aristocracy* (1912), pp. 16–17.
2. A. L. Lowell, *The Government of England* (2 vols., New York, 1912), II, pp. 412–13, 420.
3. Lowell, *Government of England*, I, p. 49.
4. Ponsonby, *Decline of Aristocracy*, p. 320.
5. T. H. S. Escott, *Social Transformations of the Victorian Age* (1897), p. 113; Anon., 'The Citizenship of the British Nobility', *Quarterly Review*, CLXXXIV (1896), pp. 283–7.
6. D. Cannadine, *Lords and Landlords: The Aristocracy and the Towns, 1774–1967* (1980), pp. 53–4; *The Herald and Wednesbury Borough News*, 14 Jan. 1899.
7. Escott, *Social Transformations*, p. 113; Marquess of Crewe, *Lord Rosebery* (2 vols., 1931), I, pp. 330–8; R. Rhodes James, *Rosebery: A Biography of Archibald Philip, Fifth Earl of Rosebery* (1963), pp. 197–9.
8. Earl of Warwick, *Memories of Sixty Years* (1917), pp. 210–16; *Bexhill-On-Sea Observer*, 12 Nov. 1932.
9. Cannadine, *Lords and Landlords*, p. 51; J. R. Vincent (ed.), *The Crawford Papers: The Journals of David Lindsay, Twenty-Seventh Earl of Crawford and Tenth Earl of Balcarres, 1871–1940, During the Years 1892 to 1940* (1984), p. 360.
10. Cannadine, *Lords and Landlords*, pp. 50, 68–9, 333–9; C. F. O'Neill, 'The "Contest for Dominion": Political Conflict and the Decline of the Lowther "Interest" in Whitehaven, 1820–1900', *Northern History*, XVIII (1982), pp. 145–52.
11. *Folkestone Express*, 13 Nov. 1901.
12. Cannadine, *Lords and Landlords*, pp. 42, 194–7.
13. Cannadine, *Lords and Landlords*, pp. 44, 334; J. Liddle, 'Estate Management and Land Reform Politics: The Hesketh and Scarisbrick Families and the Making of Southport, 1842 to 1914', in D. Cannadine (ed.), *Patricians, Power and Politics in Nineteenth-Century Towns* (1982), p. 161; The Duke of Sutherland, *Looking Back: The Autobiography of the Duke of Sutherland* (1957), pp. 45–7.
14. Cannadine, *Lords and Landlords*, p. 52; A. Service, *Edwardian Architecture, 1890–1914* (1977), pp. 143–7.
15. Lowell, *Government of England*, II, p. 15.
16. Cannadine, *Lords and Landlords*, p. 73.
17. Cannadine, *Lords and Landlords*, pp. 339–41; *Bexhill-On-Sea Observer*, 15 Feb. 1908.
18. C. E. Whiting, *The University of Durham, 1832–1932* (1932), pp. 224–5.
19. Cannadine, *Lords and Landlords*, pp. 73, 342, 346; Mrs S. Erskine, *Memoirs of Edward, Earl of Sandwich, 1839–1916* (1919), pp. 216–17.
20. R. S. Churchill, *Lord Derby: 'King' of Lancashire* (1959), p. 131; E. J. D. Warrillow, *A Sociological History of Stoke-On-Trent* (1960), pp. 217, 227.
21. Lowell, *Government of England*, II, pp. 215–16.
22. D. Hunter Blair, *John Patrick, Third Marquess of Bute, K.T.* (1921), p. 174.
23. R. H. Trainor, 'Peers on an Industrial Frontier: The Earls of Dartmouth and of Dudley in the Black Country, c. 1810 to 1914', in Cannadine, *Patricians*, p. 111.
24. Cannadine, *Lords and Landlords*, p. 75; *Folkestone Express*, 13 Nov. 1901.
25. *Bexhill-On-Sea Observer*, 3 and 31 Oct. 1908, 24 Nov. 1908.
26. *Liverpool Echo*, 15 June 1908.
27. Liddle, 'Estate Management and Land Reform', p. 158.
28. M. J. Daunton, *Coal Metropolis: Cardiff, 1870–1914* (1977), pp. 198–9; J. Davies, 'Aristocratic Town-Makers and the Coal metropolis: The Marquesses of Bute and Cardiff, 1776 to 1947', in Cannadine, *Patricians*, pp. 55, 67 note 172.
29. Trainor, 'Peers on an Industrial Frontier', pp. 110–11.
30. Cannadine, *Lords and Landlords*, p. 196; Warrillow, *Stoke-On-Trent*, p. 375; H. K. Hawson, *Sheffield: The Growth of*

a City (1968), p. 187.

31. Cannadine, Lords and Landlords, p. 346; Hawson, Sheffield, p. 301; Warrillow, Stoke-On-Trent, pp. 216–17; Trainor, 'Peers on an Industrial Frontier', p. 111.

32. Bexhill-On-Sea Observer, 7 Feb. 1976.

33. Howson, Sheffield, p. 301.

34. Bexhill-On-Sea Observer, 9 Nov. 1935.

35. Trainor, 'Peers on an Industrial Frontier', pp. 99–100.

36. Vincent, Crawford Papers, p. 584.

37. Liddle, 'Estate Management and Land Reform', p. 163; Davies, 'Aristocratic Town-Makers', p. 57.

38. Trainor, 'Peers on an Industrial Frontier', pp. 116–17.

39. Vincent, Crawford Papers, p. 473.

40. Churchill, Lord Derby, p. 130; P. J. Waller, Democracy and Sectarianism: A Political and Social History of Liverpool, 1868–1939 (1981), p. 300; M. W. Dupree (ed.), Lancashire and Whitehall: The Diary of Sir Raymond Streat (2 vols., 1987), I, pp. xxvii, 58, 170, 238, 315–29, 437–41, 465–6.

41. Churchill, Lord Derby, pp. 130, 134–5, 155.

42. Churchill, Lord Derby, pp. 576, 614.

43. P. F. Clarke, Lancashire and the New Liberalism (1971), pp. 75, 219.

44. Waller, Democracy and Sectarianism, pp. 300–4, 310–13.

45. Churchill, Lord Derby, p. 75.

46. Anon., 'Citizenship of the British Nobility', p. 288.

47. Churchill, Lord Derby, pp. 130, 348, 580, 605; Waller, Democracy and Sectarianism, pp. 315, 319.

48. Churchill, Lord Derby, pp. 600–3; Liverpool Echo, 4 Feb. 1948.

49. Vincent, Crawford Papers, pp. 461, 472.

50. M. Sanderson, The Universities and British Industry, 1850–1970 (1972), p. 106; H. C. Dent, Century of Growth in English Education, 1870–1970 (1970), pp. 36–7, 41, 77–8.

51. D. E. Evans, The University of Wales: A Historical Sketch (1953), pp. 33, 41; R. D. Anderson, Education and Opportunity in Victorian Scotland (1983), p. 275; T. W. Moody, 'The Irish University Question of the Nineteenth Century', History, XLIII (1958), pp. 100–9.

52. Sanderson, Universities and British Industry, p. 81.

53. Vincent, Crawford Papers, p. 487.

54. Evans, University of Wales, pp. 79, 81, 145.

55. R. G. Cant, The University of St.

Andrews: A Short History (1970), pp. 126–7. For the background to this development, see A. J. Mill, 'The First Ornamental Rector at St Andrews University: John Stuart Mill', Scottish Historical Review, XLII (1964), pp. 131–44.

56. Cant, St Andrews, p. 135; Whiting, Durham, pp. 223–4; T. Kelley and R. F. Whelan, For Advancement of Learning: The University of Liverpool, 1881–1981 (1981), p. 214; P. H. J. H. Gosden and A. J. Taylor (eds.), Studies in the History of a University, 1874–1974, To Commemorate the Centenary of the University of Leeds (1975), p. 14; A. W. Chapman, The Story of a Modern University: A History of the University of Sheffield (1955), p. 195.

57. Kelly and Wheelan, University of Liverpool, p. 54; Chapman, University of Sheffield, pp. 99–101, 137–44, 177, 183, 191.

58. Gosden and Taylor, University of Leeds, pp. 88, 97, 208, 213.

59. T. W. Moody and J. C. Beckett, Queen's Belfast, 1845–1949: The History of a University (2 vols., 1959), II, p. 482.

60. Evans, University of Wales, pp. vii, 25, 30, 50, 76, 79, 81, 93–4, 97–8.

61. P. J. Anderson, Rectorial Addresses Delivered in the University of Aberdeen, 1835–1900 (1902), pp. 36, 391.

62. Anderson, Education and Opportunity, pp. 267–8.

63. Earl of Ronaldshay, The Life of Lord Curzon (3 vols., 1928), III, pp. 34–6, 89–115.

64. S. Maclure, One Hundred Years of London Education, 1870–1970 (1970), pp. 13, 19–20; Viscount Bryce, 'Lord Reay', Proceedings of the British Academy, x (1921–3), pp. 536–8.

65. Ronaldshay, Curzon, III, pp. 68–71; J. Rothenstein and M. Chamot, The Tate Gallery: A Brief History and Guide (1951), p. 6.

66. Vincent, Crawford Papers, pp. 2–3, 55, 58, 68, 131.

67. Vincent, Crawford Papers, pp. 472, 484–5, 489, 517.

68. W. L. Guttsman, The British Political Elite (1965), pp. 339–41.

69. Anderson, Education and Opportunity, pp. 288–9; R. Hyam, Elgin and Churchill at the Colonial Office, 1905–1908: The Watershed of Empire-Commonwealth (1968), pp. 17, 33, 35, 521; S. Checkland, The Elgins, 1766–1917: A Tale of

Aristocrats, Proconsuls and their Wives (1988), pp. 211–12, 241–4.

70. *D.N.B., 1912–21*, p. 71.

71. K. C. Wheare, *Government by Committee: An Essay on the British Constitution* (1955), pp. 87–8.

72. *D.N.B., 1941–50*, pp. 531–2.

73. *D.N.B., 1941–50*, pp. 908–10.

74. For this phase in D'Abernon's career, see R. Davenport-Hines and J. J. Van Helten, 'Edward Vincent, Viscount D'Abernon, and the Eastern Investment Company in London, Constantinople and Johannesburg', *Business History*, XXVIII (1986), pp. 35–61.

75. Anderson, *Education and Opportunity*, pp. 286–8; Sanderson, *Universities and British Industry*, pp. 62–80, 124–30.

76. Lowell, *Government of England*, II, pp. 349, 353.

77. Moody and Beckett, *Queen's Belfast*, II, pp. 482, 536.

78. Ronaldshay, *Curzon*, III, pp. 46–53; Chapman, *University of Sheffield*, p. 277.

79. Cant, *St. Andrews*, pp. 128–30.

80. Ronaldshay, *Curzon*, III, pp. 60–6, 99, 108–9; H. R. Mill, *The Record of the Royal Geographical Society, 1830–1930* (1930), pp. 178–83; S. C. Ghosh, 'The Genesis of Curzon's University Reform: 1899–1905', *Minerva*, XXVI (1988), pp. 463–92.

81. A. N. Shimmin, *The University of Leeds: The First Half Century* (1954), p. 62.

82. Rothenstein and Chamot, *Tate Gallery*, pp. 3–6; J. Minihan, *The Nationalisation of Culture: The Development of State Subsidies to the Arts in Great Britain* (New York, 1977), pp. 155–7.

83. M. Caygill, *The Story of the British Museum* (1981), p. 51.

84. Vincent, *Crawford Papers*, pp. 523, 525–6; K. Clark, *Another Part of the Wood* (1974), pp. 226–8, 265–6.

85. Vincent, *Crawford Papers*, pp. 495, 498, 517–18, 523, 533–6, 560; E. Miller, *That Noble Cabinet: A History of the British Museum* (Ohio, 1974), pp. 258–62, 321–2.

86. Clark, *Another Part of the Wood*, pp. 209–11, 225–8, 230; A. Clark (ed.), *'A Good Innings': The Private Papers of Viscount Lee of Fareham* (1974), p. 6.

87. Wheare, *Government by Committee*, pp. 89–92; H. M. Clokie and J. W. Robinson, *Royal Commissions of Inquiry* (Stanford, Calif., 1937), p. 217.

88. R. V. Vernon and N. Mansergh, *Advisory Bodies: A Study of their Uses in Relation to Central Government, 1919–1939* (1940), pp. 26–7, 34–43, 266, 269, 272, 430.

89. Vernon and Mansergh, *Advisory Bodies*, pp. 462–70, 497.

90. Wheare, *Government by Committee*, pp. 87–9.

91. A. Briggs, *The History of Broadcasting in the United Kingdom*, vol. I, *The Birth of Broadcasting* (1961), pp. 123–37, 135–8, 353–4, 384; C. Stuart (ed.), *The Reith Diaries* (1975), pp. 135–6.

92. Vincent, *Crawford Papers*, pp. 504–6, 512; Briggs, *Birth of Broadcasting*, pp. 327–48; A. Boyle, *Only the Wind Will Listen: Reith of the BBC* (1972), p. 177.

93. Briggs, *Birth of Broadcasting*, p. 354; Stuart, *Reith Diaries*, pp. 140–4, 147–51; Boyle, *Reith of the BBC*, pp. 210–11, 216–26; A. Briggs, *The History of Broadcasting in the United Kingdom*, vol. II, *The Golden Age of Wireless* (1965), pp. 425–30.

94. Briggs, *Golden Age of Wireless*, pp. 4, 476–504.

95. H. Belloc, *Complete Verses* (1970), p. 207; A. J. P. Taylor, *Essays in English History* (1976), p. 31. Belloc's poem was written in 1907.

96. G. E. Buckle (ed.), *The Letters of Queen Victoria*, 3rd. ser. (3 vols., 1930–2), vol. III, *1896–1901*, p. 327.

97. Ex-Governor, 'His Excellency the Governor', *National Review*, XV (1890), pp. 614–15.

98. For three studies that vividly capture the patrician flavour of these proconsular regimes, see: M. Bence Jones, *The Viceroys of India* (1982); R. H. Hubbard, *Rideau Hall* (Montreal, 1977); C. Cuneen, *King's Men: Australia's Governors General from Hopetoun to Isaacs* (1983);

99. J. Adam Smith, *John Buchan* (1965), pp. 249, 372.

100. *The Times*, 13 Aug. 1941.

101. J. R. Vincent (ed.), *The Later Derby Diaries: Home Rule, Liberal Unionism and Aristocratic Life in Late Victorian England* (1981), p. 10.

102. *The Times*, 11 Aug. 1898; Bence Jones, *Viceroys of India*, pp. 1, 221; Earl of Birkenhead, *Halifax* (1965), p. 130; *D.N.B, 1912–21*, p. 174.

103. P. Williamson, 'Party First and India Second: The Appointment of the Viceroy of India in 1930', *Bulletin of the Institute of Historical Research*, LVI

(1983), pp. 87–9, 95–8.

104. K. Rose, *King George V* (1983), p. 246.

105. J. W. Pickersgill and D. F. Forster (eds.), *The Mackenzie King Record*, vol. II, *1944–1945* (Toronto, 1968), pp. 435–6.

106. Vincent, *Later Derby Diaries*, p. 137. For another impoverished Irish patrician proconsul, see B. Jenkins, *Sir William Gregory of Coole: A Biography* (1986), esp. pp. 218–19.

107. *E.G.*, 14 Jan. 1922; J. Glendevon, *The Viceroy at Bay: Lord Linlithgow in India* (1971), p. 12; B. Fergusson, *Travel Warrant* (1979), pp. 21–2, 32; Hyam, *Elgin and Churchill*, pp. 12–13; 'Thormanby', *Kings of the Turf* (1898), pp. 120–32, 177–87; V. Powell, *Margaret, Countess of Jersey: A Biography* (1978), pp. 42, 54, 168.

108. L. H. Gann and P. Duignan, *The Rulers of British Africa* (1978), p. 160.

109. A. Galton, 'Government House', *National Review*, XXXVI (1900), pp. 539–40.

110. J. R. Mallory, 'The Appointment of the Governor General: Responsible Government, Autonomy and the Royal Prerogative', *Canadian Journal of Economics and Political Science*, XXVI (1960), p. 102.

111. P. Gordon (ed.), *The Red Earl: The Papers of the Fifth Earl Spencer, 1835–1910* (2 vols., 1981–6), vol. I, *1835–1885*, pp. 29, 72–3.

112. Vincent, *Crawford Papers*, p. 278.

113. S. Hogg, 'Landed Society and the Conservative Party in the Late Nineteenth and Early Twentieth Centuries' (B.Litt dissertation, Oxford University, 1972), p. 122.

114. R. Quinault, 'Warwickshire Landowners and Parliamentary Politics, 1841–1923' (D. Phil. dissertation, Oxford University, 1975), p. 293.

115. Lord Newton, *Lord Lansdowne: A Biography* (1929), pp. 24–5, 55.

116. Newton, *Lansdowne*, pp. 51, 127–9.

117. M. Carmichael, *Lord Carmichael of Skirling: A Memoir* (1926), p. 259.

118. A. Hasluck (ed.), *Audrey Tennyson's Viceregal Days* (Canberra, 1978), pp. 18, 183, 249, 291; D. Cannadine, 'The Landowner as Millionaire: The Finances of the Dukes of Devonshire, c. 1800–1926', *Agricultural History Review*, XXV (1977), pp. 90–1.

119. Sir A. Lyall, *The Life of the Marquis of Dufferin and Ava* (2 vols., 1905), I, p. 201; II, pp. 300, 304; H. Nicolson,

120. *Helen's Tower* (1937), pp. 84–6; 265–76.

120. *Eastbourne Gazette*, 2 July 1913.

121. Hasluck, *Viceregal Days*, p. 216.

122. P. A. Graham, 'The Ruin of English Agriculture', *National Review*, XX (1892), p. 181.

123. *The Times*, 31 Mar. 1934.

124. *The Times*, 13 Aug. 1941; 12 Mar. 1956.

125. H. M. Hyde, *The Londonderrys: A Family Portrait* (1979), pp. 165, 178–80.

126. J. A. Le Nauze, *Alfred Deakin: A Biography* (2 vols., 1965), I, pp. 204–10, 301–3.

127. Hubbard, *Rideau Hall*, p. 159.

128. For the later Viceroys, see a succession of unpublished studies: J. F. C. Watts, 'The Viceroyalty of Lord Irwin, 1926–1931, with special reference to the Political and Constitutional Developments' (D.Phil. dissertation, Oxford University, 1973); G. W. Bergstrom, 'Lord Willingdon and India, 1931–1936: A Study of an Imperial Administrator' (D.Phil. dissertation, Oxford University, 1978); S. A. G. Rizvi, 'British Policy and the Political Impasse in India During the Viceroyalty of Lord Linlithgow, 1936–1943' (D.Phil. dissertation, Oxford University, 1976).

129. Bence Jones, *Viceroys of India*, p. 150; P. Woodruff, *The Men Who Ruled India*, vol. II, *The Guardians* (1963 edn.), p. 77.

130. *E.G.*, 31 Oct. 1925, 7 Dec. 1929, 11 Apr. 1936.

131. *The Times*, 13 Aug. 1941; Birkenhead, *Halifax*, p. 187.

132. *D.N.B., 1951–60*, p. 74.

133. Woodruff, *The Guardians*, p. 307.

134. Galton, 'Government House', p. 541.

135. Hasluck, *Viceregal Days*, pp. 26–31, 249.

136. Ex-Governor, 'His Excellency', p. 616.

137. Ponsonby, *Decline of Aristocracy*, p. 24.

138. Hyde, *Londonderrys*, p. 260.

139. J. Schumpeter, *Imperialism and Social Classes* (trans. H. Norden and ed. P. M. Sweezy, New York, 1951), pp. 83–4, 128, 195–7, 203: W. Mommsen, *Theories of Imperialism* (New York, 1980), pp. 21–8.

140. Schumpeter, *Imperialism and Social Classes*, p. 203.

Chapter 13

1. This phrase was made famous by R. R. Palmer, *The Age of Democratic Revolu-*

tion (2 vols., 1959–64), I, pp. 22–4.

2. C. P. Snow, *Variety of Men* (1969), pp. 125, 131.

3. A. Calder, *The People's War: Britain, 1939–1945* (1971), p. 111; J. R. Colville, *The Churchillians* (1981), pp. 4, 10, 20.

4. Colville, *Churchillians*, pp. 172–6; P. Addison, *The Road to 1945* (1975), p. 210.

5. J. Stuart, *Within the Fringe: An Autobiography* (1967), pp. 69–71, 90.

6. J. R. Colville, *The Fringes of Power: 10 Downing Street Diaries, 1939–1955* (1985), pp. 102, 257, 299, 645. For a full life, see: P. Howarth, *Intelligence Chief Extraordinary: The Life of the Ninth Duke of Portland* (1986).

7. Lord Longford, *The Grain of Wheat* (1974), p. 20; Lord Egremont, *Wyndham and Children First* (1968), p. 75.

8. D. Dilks (ed.), *The Diaries of Sir Alexander Cadogan, O.M., 1938–1945* (1971), pp. 300–1.

9. Osborne's difficult relations with the Papacy and the Foreign Office are fully and fascinatingly described in W. O. Chadwick, *Britain and the Vatican During the Second World War* (1986).

10. T. H. O'Brien, *Civil Defence* (1955), pp. 675–6; H. Pelling, *Britain and the Second World War* (1970), p. 320; A. Sutcliffe and R. Smith, *Birmingham, 1939–1970* (1974), p. 21.

11. P. G. Cambray and G. G. B. Briggs, *Red Cross and St. John: The Official Record of the Humanitarian Services of the War Organisation* (1949), pp. 667–9; G.P. Insh, *The War-Time History of the Scottish Branch of the British Red Cross Society* (1952), pp. 191–202; H. M. Hyde, *The Londonderrys: A Family Portrait* (1979), pp. 255–7.

12. E.G., 9 Sept. 1939.

13. A. Hurd, *A Farmer in Whitehall: Britain's Farming Revolution, 1939–50, and Future Prospects* (1951), pp. 109–23.

14. C. Graves, *The Home Guard of Britain* (1943), pp. 15, 20, 45.

15. J. W. Ogilvy-Dalgleish, *The Rutland Home Guard of 1940–44* (1955), pp. 5, 14.

16. N. Longmate, *The Real Dad's Army: The Story of the Home Guard* (1974), p. 48.

17. Graves, *Home Guard*, pp. 59, 162.

18. Longmate, *Real Dad's Army*, p. 24.

19. Lord Portsmouth, *A Knot of Roots* (1965), pp. 197–8.

20. J. R. Colville, *Man of Valour: The Life of Field Marshal the Viscount Gort* (1972), pp. 148, 226, 230, 238, 248, 256.

21. Colville, *Churchillians*, p. 151.

22. D. Fraser, *Alanbrooke* (1983), p. 39.

23. Lord Lovat, *March Past* (1985), *passim*.

24. N. Nicolson (ed.), *Harold Nicolson: Diaries and Letters, 1939–1945* (1967), p. 182.

25. Colville, *Fringes of Power*, pp. 309, 311; R. Rhodes James (ed.), *'Chips': The Diaries of Sir Henry Channon* (1967), p. 346; J. W. Pickersgill and D. F. Forster (eds.), *The Mackenzie King Record*, II, *1944–1945* (Toronto, 1968), pp. 435–6.

26. Colville, *Fringes of Power*, pp. 67, 311, 412, 531.

27. Colville, *Fringes of Power*, pp. 290, 301; Hyde, *Londonderrys*, pp. 256, 261.

28. Colville, *Fringes of Power*, pp. 321–22; Hyde, *Londonderrys*, pp. 258–9; J. Lees-Milne, *Prophesying Peace* (1977), p. 46.

29. Sutcliffe and Smith, *Birmingham*, pp. 49, 70; Egremont, *Wyndham and Children*, p. 95.

30. C. Blackwood, *In The Pink* (1987), pp. 4, 121.

31. R. Carr, *English Fox-Hunting: A History* (1976), p. 239.

32. A. J. P. Taylor, 'The Statesman', in A. J. P. Taylor et al', *Churchill: Four Faces and the Man* (1973), p. 51.

33. This is the central theme of Addison, *Road to 1945*.

34. Colville, *Fringes of Power*, p. 278.

35. J. A. Cross, *Lord Swinton* (1982), pp. 220, 222, 244, 255.

36. Colville, *Fringes of Power*, p. 122.

37. Colville, *Churchillians*, pp. 214–15; Lord Chandos, *The Memoirs of Lord Chandos* (1962), p. 187.

38. M. Cowling, *Religion and Public Doctrine in England* (1980), pp. 283, 308–10; *The Times*, 2 July 1932.

39. Colville, *Fringes of Power*, p. 165.

40. Chandos, *Memoirs*, pp. 209, 211, 314, 316.

41. Colville, *Fringes of Power*, pp. 353, 431; Dilks, *Cadogan*, p. 353.

42. Calder, *People's War*, p. 311.

43. Colville, *Fringes of Power*, p. 278.

44. Dilks, *Cadogan*, p. 501; *The Times*, 1 and 4 Jan. 1943; D. C. M. Platt, *The Cinderella Service: British Consuls since 1825* (1971), pp. 121–3; 'Proposals for the Reform of the Foreign Service' (Cmd. 6420, 1943), p. 2.

45. *Hansard*, 5 ser., H.C., 18 Mar. 1943, cols. 1361–2.
46. D.C. Watt, *Personalities and Policies: Studies in the Formulation of British Foreign Policy in the Twentieth Century* (Wesport, Conn., 1965), pp. 188–91; Platt, *Cinderella Service*, pp. 231–8.
47. Rhodes James, *'Chips'*, p. 398.
48. Colville, *Fringes of Power*, pp. 339, 350, 396, 556, 569; Pelling, *Britain and the Second World War*, p. 312.
49. K. Rose, *The Later Cecils* (1975), pp. 103–8.
50. Addison, *Road to 1945*, p. 232.
51. Calder, *People's War*, pp. 355–6, 557, 631–3, 651, 673; Addison, *Road to 1945*, pp. 158–60.
52. Pelling, *Britain and the Second World War*, pp. 185–6; R. Acland, *How It Can Be Done* (1944), p. 11.
53. Colville, *Fringes of Power*, p. 83.
54. Colville, *Fringes of Power*, p. 428; Dilks, *Cadogan*, p. 257; The Duke of Bedford, *A Silver-Plated Spoon* (1959), pp. 157, 162.
55. Colville, *Fringes of Power*, p. 177.
56. J. Mitford, *Hons and Rebels* (1960), pp. 156, 205, 221; J. Mitford, *A Fine Old Conflict* (1978), pp. 55, 120, 123.
57. D. Mosley, *A Life of Contrasts* (1984), pp. 156–65.
58. Viscount Churchill, *All My Sins Remembered* (New York, 1965), p. 11.
59. J. Fox, *White Mischief* (1984), pp. 1, 84, 95, 99–100, 210–13, 226–33; D. Pryce Jones, *Evelyn Waugh and His World* (1973), p. 88.
60. Nicolson, *Nicolson Diaries, 1939–1945*, p. 57.
61. N. Nicolson (ed.), *Harold Nicolson: Diaries and Letters, 1930–1939* (1966), p. 418.
62. *The Times*, 1 July 1940.
63. *E.G.*, 8 June 1940.
64. Lees-Milne, *Prophesying Peace*, p. 17. For a moving account of this, see R. W. Ketton-Cremer, *Felbrigg: The Story of a House* (1976 edn.), pp. 287–91.
65. M. Bence Jones, *Twilight of the Ascendancy* (1987), p. 266.
66. J. Lees-Milne, *Caves of Ice* (1983), p. 207.
67. Rhodes James, *'Chips'*, pp. 224, 270, 303; D. Pearce, *London's Mansions: The Palatial Houses of the Nobility* (1986), pp. 102–4, 135, 185, 210, 215.
68. Lees-Milne, *Prophesying Peace*, pp. 34, 167; Rhodes James, *'Chips'*, p. 224.
69. J. Lees-Milne, *Ancestral Voices* (1975), pp. 67, 151, 187; Lees-Milne, *Caves of Ice*, pp. 13, 28, 36, 49, 249–52.
70. Bence Jones, *Twilight of the Ascendancy*, pp. 270–1; Lees-Milne, *Ancestral Voices*, pp. 14, 188, 215; Lees-Milne, *Prophesying Peace*, p. 14.
71. J. M. Robinson, *The Latest Country Houses* (1984), p. 13.
72. Lees-Milne, *Ancestral Voices*, pp. 57, 243.
73. Lees-Milne, *Prophesying Peace*, p. 203; Robinson, *Latest Country Houses*, p. 13.
74. Robinson, *Latest Country Houses*, p. 13.
75. Lees-Milne, *Prophesying Peace*, pp. 103, 171–2, 232.
76. Hyde, *Londonderrys*, p. 256.
77. L. Stone and J. C. Fawtier Stone, *An Open Elite? England 1540–1880* (1984), p. 425.
78. *E.G.*, 27 Apr. 1940.
79. J. V. Beckett, *The Aristocracy in England, 1660–1914* (1986), p. 478; K. A. H. Murray, *Agriculture* (revised edn., 1975), pp. 280, 286, 289, 290, 343, 352.
80. *E.G.*, 30 Sept. 1939, 7 Oct. 1939, 27 July 1940, 12 Apr. 1941; R. S. Sayers, *Financial Policy, 1939–1945* (1956), pp. 26, 49, 111.
81. Lees-Milne, *Prophesying Peace*, p. 10.
82. *E.G.*, 15 June 1940.
83. J. Parker, *Great Art Sales of the Century* (1975), p. 35.
84. G. Reitlinger, *The Economics of Taste: The Rise and Fall of Picture Prices, 1760–1960* (1961), pp. 219–22.
85. *E.G.*, 5 Oct. 1940, 14 June 1941, 2 Aug. 1941, 4 Oct. 1941, 15 Nov. 1941.
86. *E.G.*, 14 Aug. 1953, 22 Jan. 1944, 1 and 8 Apr. 1944, 8 Sept. 1945, 21 June 1952, 31 Jan. 1953.
87. *E.G.*, 18 May 1940, 8 Mar. 1941, 26 Apr. 1941, 26 July 1941, 16 Aug. 1941, 27 Sept. 1941.
88. *E.G.*, 25 Sept. 1943, 15 July 1944, 30 Sept. 1944, 12 Dec. 1944, 16 June 1945.
89. Lees-Milne, *Prophesying Peace*, pp. 58, 167, 230.
90. Lees-Milne, *Ancestral Voices*, p. 273.
91. *E.G.*, 18 July 1942.
92. Lees-Milne, *Ancestral Voices*, pp. 80, 91, 284; Lees-Milne, *Prophesying Peace*, p. 189.
93. Lees-Milne, *Ancestral Voices*, pp, 3, 50, 61, 111, 170; Lees-Milne, *Prophesying Peace*, pp. 194, 200.
94. Lees-Milne, *Prophesying Peace*, pp. 44, 63, 71, 138.

95. Addison, *Road to 1945*, p. 178.
96. *E.G.*, 18 Dec. 1943; Sir D. Hall, *Reconstruction on the Land* (1941), pp. 63–7, 257–9, 270–1, 277.
97. Murray, *Agriculture*, p. 339; Calder, *People's War*, pp. 489–91.
98. *E.G.*, 11 Sept. 1943.
99. Rose, *Later Cecils*, p. 109.
100. Addison, *Road to 1945*, p. 250; Calder, *People's War*, pp. 637–9.
101. Colville, *Fringes of Power*, p. 474; Rhodes James, *'Chips'*, p. 386; V. Cowles, *No Cause for Alarm* (1949), p. 34.
102. Nicolson, *Nicolson Diaries, 1939–1945*, p. 170.
103. E. Waugh, *Brideshead Re-Visited* (1962 edn.), p. 8. This revised edition was first published in 1960.
104. Nicolson, *Nicolson Diaries, 1939–1945*, p. 465.
105. Colville, *Fringes of Power*, p. 433.

Chapter 14

1. R. Strong, M. Binney, J. Harris, et al., *The Destruction of the Country House, 1875–1975* (1975), p. 172.
2. P. G. Wodehouse, *Ring for Jeeves* (1953), pp. 34, 58–9, 124.
3. J. Lees-Milne, *Caves of Ice* (1983), pp. 30, 53; M. Waterson, *The Servants Hall: A Domestic History of Erddig* (1980), p. 200.
4. J. M. Robinson, *The Latest Country Houses* (1984), pp. 14–17.
5. For detailed discussion of the post-war Labour party's attitude to great estates and agriculture, see S. F. Morser, 'The Labour Party and the Land, 1947–70' (M.Phil. dissertation, London University, 1981).
6. C. F. Kolbert, 'Limited Ownership of Land in England and Scotland: A Study of the Law of Settlements and Trusts in Rural Land' (Ph.D. dissertation, Cambridge University, 1962), p. 360.
7. W. D. Rubinstein, *Men of Property: The Very Wealthy in Britain Since the Industrial Revolution* (1981), pp. 228–9.
8. *E.G.*, 11 Nov. 1950; R. Rhodes James, *'Chips': The Diaries of Sir Henry Channon* (1967), p. 450.
9. *E.G.*, 10 August 1946, 11 Nov. 1950, 19 and 26 June 1954.
10. *E.G.*, 2 Nov. 1946, 18 Nov. 1950, 10 Feb. 1951, 21 June 1952, 6 Feb. 1954, 16 March 1957; J. J. Bagley, *The Earls of Derby* (1985), p. 235; Lord Egremont,

Wyndham and Children First (1968), p. 196.
11. R. J. Colyer, 'The Pryse Family of Gogerddan and the Demise of a Great Estate, 1800–1960', *Welsh History Review*, IX (1979), pp. 421–4.
12. *E.G.*, 31 May 1947, 18 Oct. 1947, 29 April 1948, 10 Nov. 1951.
13. J. V. Beckett, *The Aristocracy in England, 1660–1914* (1986), pp. 477–8.
14. *E.G.*, 19 Apr. 1952; D. Cannadine, *Lords and Landlords: The Aristocracy and the Towns, 1774–1967* (1980), p. 427.
15. *E.G.*, 2 Feb. 1945, 29 Sept. 1945, 28 June 1952, 28 June 1958.
16. *E.G.*, 23 Apr. 1949, 22 Oct. 1949, 16 June 1951, 9 Aug. 1952, 27 Sept. 1958; Cannadine, *Lords and Landlords*, p. 426.
17. D. Pearce, *London's Mansions: The Palatial Homes of the Nobility* (1986), pp. 135, 160–3, 177, 182, 195, 210, 215.
18. N. Mitford, *Noblesse Oblige* (1956), p. 55.
19. L. Stone and J. C. Fawtier Stone, *An Open Elite? England, 1540–1880* (1984), p. 425.
20. M. Binney and G. Jackson-Stops, 'The Last Hundred Years', in G. Jackson-Stops (ed.), *The Treasure Houses of Britain: Five Hundred Years of Private Patronage and Art Collecting* (1984), pp. 71–2.
21. *E.G.*, 20 Oct. 1951.
22. G. Reitlinger, *The Economics of Taste: The Rise and Fall of Picture Prices, 1760–1960* (1961), pp. 292, 323, 425, 432, 477.
23. *E.G.*, 18 June 1949, 13 Jan. 1951.
24. *E.G.*, 17 Mar. 1951; Binney and Jackson-Stops, 'Last Hundred Years', pp. 73–4.
25. *E.G.*, 25 Aug. 1956.
26. D. Burnett, *Longleat: The Story of an English Country House* (1978), pp. 178–81.
27. Lord Montagu of Beaulieu, *The Motoring Montagus* (1959), pp. 61–9.
28. The Duke of Bedford, *A Silver-Plated Spoon* (1959), pp. 190–7, 202, 215.
29. Robert Lacey, *Aristocrats* (1984), p. 34.
30. Lord Portsmouth, *A Knot of Roots* (1965), pp. 210–13, 216–25, 228–9.
31. Bedford, *Silver-Plated Spoon*, pp. 178–80.
32. See the comments made on such people by Evelyn Waugh, *Tourist in Africa* (Boston, 1960), pp. 140–2: 'None of his family have any sentimental yearnings for their homeland.'

33. Lees-Milne, *Caves of Ice*, pp. 249–52.
34. Bagley, *Earls of Derby*, p. 236.
35. A. Sampson, *Anatomy of Britain Today* (1965), pp. 453–5.
36. Lord Longford, *Five Lives* (1964), pp. 21–2.
37. Bagley, *Earls of Derby*, pp. 236–7.
38. P. Cosgrave, *Carrington: A Life and a Policy* (1985), p. 48.
39. Beckett, *Aristocracy in England*, p. 476.
40. Rubinstein, *Men of Property*, p. 243.
41. J. Parker, *Great Art Sales of the Century* (1975), pp. 43–9, 57.
42. G. Reitlinger, *The Economics of Taste*, vol. III, *The Art Market in the 1960s* (1970), pp. 187, 220, 299, 345, 511, 547, 695.
43. J. M. Abecassis, 'The Development of the Trust as a form of Agricultural Landownership in England' (Ph.D. dissertation, Cambridge University, 1980), p. 331.
44. Cannadine, *Lords and Landlords*, p. 427.
45. M. Bence Jones and H. Montgomery-Massingberd, *The British Aristocracy* (1979), p. 218.
46. E. Waugh, *Brideshead Re-Visited* (1962 edn.), p. 8. This revised version was first published in 1960.
47. *E.G.*, 23 July 1955, 18 Aug. 1956, 16 Aug. 1958.
48. J. Cornforth, 'The Backward Look', in Jackson-Stops, *Treasure Houses of Britain*, p. 66. Ketton-Cremer's writings, which combine family piety, county loyalty and admirable scholarship with remarkable skill, include: *Norfolk Portraits* (1944); *A Norfolk Gallery* (1948); *Norfolk Assembly* (1957); *Forty Norfolk Essays* (1961); and *Norfolk in the Civil War* (1969).
49. Cannadine, *Lords and Landlords*, p. 427.
50. Robinson, *Latest Country Houses*, pp. 6–7, 26–7.
51. Robinson, *Latest Country Houses*, pp. 92–6, 124–32, 136–42, 174–86.
52. Abecassis, 'Development of the Trust', pp. 400–4.
53. Binney and Jackson-Stops, 'The Last Hundred Years', p. 74.
54. Strong, Binney, Harris et al., *Destruction of the Country House*, p. 14.
55. The fullest account is in W. Berkman, 'The Mentmore Sale: The Dilemma of National Heritage' (B.A. dissertation, Harvard University, 1987), esp. pp. 34–62.
56. A. Jones, *Britain's Heritage: The Creation of the National Heritage Memorial Fund* (1985), pp. 203–11, 234.
57. For an account of the protracted negotiations in one case, see H. M. Colvin, *Calke Abbey, Derbyshire: A Hidden House Revealed* (1985), pp. 77–83. See also A. Waugh, 'Let Curzon Holde', *The Spectator*, 12 Jan. 1985.
58. S. Winchester, *Their Noble Lordships: The Hereditary Peerage Today* (1981), p. 149.
59. Waterson, *Erddig*, pp. 200. 209–28.
60. Parker, *Great Art Sales*, pp. 57, 85.
61. *The Guardian*, 7 July 1987.
62. Bence Jones and Montgomery Massingberd, *British Aristocracy*, pp. 225–6; J. Young, *The Country House in the 1980s* (1981), pp. 19–23.
63. Burnett, *Longleat*, p. 183; Bagley, *Earls of Derby*, p. 237.
64. Rubinstein, *Men of Property*, pp. 231–40; Anon., 'The Rich in Britain', *New Society*, 22 Aug. 1986, pp. i–viii.
65. H. Newby, *Green and Pleasant Land? A Study in Rural England* (1980), p. 39. And the sale and breakup still goes on: see M. Sayer, 'Estates in Decline', *Country Life*, 23 Feb. 1989, pp. 118–20.
66. Beckett, *Aristocracy in England*, pp. 475–9; H. Clemenson, *English Country Houses and Landed Estates* (1982), pp. 111–20.
67. A. Giddens, 'The Rich', *New Society*, 14 Oct. 1976, pp. 63–6; Rubinstein, *Men of Property*, pp. 228–9.
68. *The Guardian*, 20 Feb. 1979; Winchester, *Their Noble Lordships*, pp. 255–6.
69. Bence Jones and Montgomery-Massingberd, *British Aristocracy*, pp. 133–40.
70. Bence Jones and Montgomery-Massingberd, *British Aristocracy*, pp. 143–6.
71. Giddens, 'The Rich', p. 66.
72. Bence Jones and Montgomery-Massingberd, *British Aristocracy*, p. 126.
73. N. Monson and D. Scott, *The Nouveaux Pauvres: A Guide to Downward Nobility* (1984), pp. 26, 145, 149.
74. *The Guardian*, 5 June 1985.
75. *Woman*, 8 Feb. 1986.
76. Monson and Scott, *Nouveaux Pauvres*, pp. 22, 27–8, 136, 149.
77. Monson and Scott, *Nouveaux Pauvres*, pp. 80, 185.
78. J. Archer, *First Among Equals* (New York, 1985), pp. 7–8, 16, 28, 31–2, 200, 223, 264, 376–8, 402, 412.

79. Sampson, *Anatomy of Britain Today*, p. 66.

80. K. O. Morgan, *Labour in Power, 1945–1951* (1985), p. 287.

81. V. Cowles, *No Cause for Alarm* (1949), p. 57.

82. Longford, *Five Lives*, pp. 67, 75, 188; M. Craig, *Longford: A Biographical Portrait* (1978), pp. 70–3, 77–80, 86.

83. Morgan, *Labour in Power*, pp. 83–5.

84. P. A. Bromhead, *The House of Lords and Contemporary Politics, 1911–1957* (1958), pp. 157–76.

85. B. Crick, *The Reform of Parliament* (2nd edn., 1968), pp. 124–38.

86. J. R. Colville, *The Fringes of Power: 10 Downing Street Diaries, 1939–1955* (1985), p. 668.

87. Lord Chandos, *The Memoirs of Lord Chandos* (1962), pp. 339, 431; N. Nicolson, *Alex: The Life of Field Marshal Earl Alexander of Tunis* (1976), pp. 350–4; J. Stuart, *Within the Fringe: An Autobiography* (1967), pp. 157–9, 162; J. A. Cross, *Lord Swinton* (1982), pp. 292–6.

88. A. Seldon, *Churchill's Indian Summer: The Conservative Government, 1951–1955* (1981), pp. 30, 86–7, 93–5, 297–300, 336, 349.

89. A. Marwick, *British Society Since 1945* (1982), p. 134.

90. A. Sampson, *Anatomy of Britain* (1962), p. 4.

91. Lord Longford, *Diary of a Year* (1982), p. 136.

92. Lord Home, *The Way the Wind Blows* (1976), pp. 11, 19, 40, 46, 284–5.

93. Sampson, *Anatomy of Britain Today*, p. 73.

94. Longford, *Diary of a Year*, p. 80.

95. Sampson, *Anatomy of Britain Today*, p. 73; Home, *The Way the Wind Blows*, pp. 102, 183–7, 203, 216.

96. Stone and Fawtier Stone, *Open Elite?*, p. 425.

97. Sampson, *Anatomy of Britain*, p. 13; Winchester, *Their Noble Lordships*, p. 52.

98. J. G. Darwin, 'The Fear of Falling: British Politics and Imperial Decline Since 1900', *Transactions of the Royal Historical Society*, 5th ser. (1986), pp. 37–8.

99. Lord Kilmuir, *Political Adventure* (1964), pp. 288–93.

100. Kilmuir, *Political Adventure*, pp. 315–16; Sampson, *Anatomy of Britain*, p. 81.

101. *The Times*, 24 Feb. 1972.

102. Paul Gore-Booth, *With Great Truth and Respect* (1974), pp. 21–4.

103. Sampson, *Anatomy of Britain*, p. 304.

104. Beckett, *Aristocracy in England*, p. 473.

105. Egremont, *Wyndham and Children*, p. 161.

106. J. M. Lee, *Social Leaders and Public Persons: A Study of County Government in Cheshire since 1888* (1963), pp. 129, 134, 138, 144, 158.

107. *V.C.H.*, *Shropshire*, III (1979), p. 185.

108. Lee, *Social Leaders*, p. 98.

109. T. O'Neill, *The Autobiography of Terence O'Neill* (1972), esp. chs. 1 and 2.

110. *The Times*, 15 Dec. 1980.

111. Craig, *Longford*, pp. 136–49, 185, 209–11.

112. Longford, *Grain of Wheat*, pp. 31–6, 62, 68, 70, 77, 271–3.

113. For this, and the next two paragraphs, see J. P. Morgan, *The House of Lords and the Labour Government, 1964–1970* (1975).

114. Morgan, *House of Lords and the Labour Government*, p. 220.

115. A. Sampson, *The New Anatomy of Britain* (1971), pp. 103–7.

116. Cosgrave, *Carrington*, p. 44.

117. Cosgrave, *Carrington*, pp. 13, 112, 137, 146; Marwick, *British Society*, pp. 214–16.

118. A. Sampson, *The Changing Anatomy of Britain* (1982), pp. 236–9.

119. *The Times*, 30 July 1987.

120. E. Melling, *History of the Kent County Council, 1889–1974* (1975), p. 146; C. R. V. Bell, *A History of East Sussex County Council, 1889–1974* (1975), p. 110.

121. Lacey, *Aristocrats*, p. 216.

122. *The Independent*, 11 Nov. 1987.

123. Rhodes James, *'Chips'*, pp. 476–7.

124. Rhodes James, *'Chips'*, p. 470.

125. D. Fraser, *Alanbrooke* (1983), pp. 514–15, 546.

126. Winchester, *Their Noble Lordships*, p. 38.

127. Stone and Fawtier Stone, *Open Elite?*, p. 142; C. D. Squibb, 'The End of the Names and Arms Clause', *Law Quarterly Review*, LXIX (1935), p. 224.

128. Significantly, Churchill was offered a dukedom only because it had been ascertained beforehand that he would not accept it. Colville, *Fringes of Power*, pp. 708–9; M. Gilbert, *Winston. S. Churchill*, vol. VIII, 'Never Despair: 1945–1965' (1988), pp. 1123–4.

129. Crick, *Reform of Parliament*, pp. 131–8.

130. Crick, *Reform of Parliament*, pp. 139–46.

131. P. Bromhead, 'Mr Wedgwood Benn, the Peerage and the Constitution', *Parliamentary Affairs*, xiv (1961), pp. 493–506.

132. Lacey, *Aristocrats*, p. 215.

133. Lacey, *Aristocrats*, p. 216; Winchester, *Their Noble Lordships*, p. 123.

134. Bence Jones and Montgomery-Massingberd, *British Aristocracy*, p. 99.

135. W. D. Rubinstein, *Elites and the Wealthy in Modern Britain: Essays in Social and Economic History* (1987), pp. 249–52.

136. A. J. P. Taylor, *Essays in English History* (1965), p. 288.

137. B. Fergusson, *Travel Warrant* (1979), pp. 138–9, 150, 219.

138. D. Dilks (ed.), *The Diaries of Sir Alexander Cadogan, O.M., 1938–1945* (1971), p. 792.

139. Beckett, *Aristocracy in England*, p. 473.

140. Fergusson, *Travel Warrant*, pp. 230–5.

141. Cannadine, *Lords and Landlords*, p. 59.

142. *Harpers and Queens*, July 1987.

143. They have also vanished almost completely as chairmen of committees: see P. Hennessy, *The Great and the Good: An Inquiry Into the British Establishment* (1986), pp. 75–104, Appendix 1, Royal Commissions and Committees of Inquiry, 1945–85.

144. Winchester, *Their Noble Lordships*, pp. 286–7; Sampson, *Anatomy of Britain*, p. 8.

145. P. Horn, *The Rise and Fall of the Victorian Servant* (Dublin, 1976), pp. 179, 183.

146. Robinson, *Latest Country Houses*, pp. 33, 37; D. Cannadine, 'The Theory and Practice of the English Leisure Classes', *H.J.*, xxi (1978), pp. 450–1.

147. Pearce, *London's Mansions*, p. 215.

148. Winchester, *Their Noble Lordships*, pp. 66, 85, 160–3; H. M. Hyde, *A Tangled Web* (1986), p. 178; S. Moore, *Lucan: Not Guilty* (1987); P. Marnham, *Trail of Havoc: In the Steps of Lord Lucan* (1987).

149. Bence Jones and Montgomery-Massingberd, *British Aristocracy*, p. 233.

150. Beckett, *Aristocracy in England*, p. 474.

151. C. Blackwood, *In the Pink* (1987), pp. ix, 1–8, 39.

152. R. Carr, *English Fox-Hunting: A History* (1976), pp. 239–50.

153. Lee, *Social Leaders*, p. 102.

154. Marwick, *British Society*, p. 45; Lacey, *Aristocrats*, pp. 60–1.

155. Newby, *Green and Pleasant Land?*, p. 73.

156. Lacey, *Aristocrats*, p. 214.

157. Sampson, *Anatomy of Britain*, p. 12.

158. Bedford, *Silver-Plated Spoon*, p. 232; Winchester, *Their Noble Lordships*, pp. 27, 34, 99, 112, 180, Lacey, *Aristocrats*, p. 214.

159. Jackson-Stops and Binney, 'The Last Hundred Years', p. 74.

160. D. Cannadine, *The Pleasures of the Past* (1989), pp. 256–71; F. M. L. Thompson, 'The Long Run of the English Aristocracy', *London Review of Books*, 19 Feb. 1987.

161. Bedford, *Silver-Plated Spoon*, p. 224; Strong, Binney and Harris, *Destruction of the Country House*, p. 119.

162. Bence Jones and Montgomery-Massingberd, *British Aristocracy*, p. 226.

163. Young, *Country House in the 1980s*, p. 143. Significantly, the Hon. Nicholas Ridley, the ex-Minister for the Environment, has taken precisely the same view, despite his quintessentially patrician background: *The Times*, 23 Nov. 1988. I am grateful to Professor D. E. D. Beales for this reference.

164. Lacey, *Aristocrats*, p. 204.

165. *The Times*, 22 April 1977.

Chapter 15

1. P. Burke, 'Tradition and Experience: The Idea of Decline from Bruni to Gibbon', *Daedalus*, no. 105 (1976), pp. 137–52; R. Starn, 'Meaning-Levels in the Theme of Historical Decline', *History and Theory*, xiv (1975), pp. 1–31; J. H. Elliott, *Spain and Its World, 1500–1700* (1989), pp. 215–16, 220, 242, 247, 252–6, 261.

2. A. Mayer, *The Persistence of the Old Regime: Europe to the Great War* (1981).

3. J. Powys, *Aristocracy* (1984), pp. 81–102; J. H. Kautsky, *The Politics of Aristocratic Empires* (Chapel Hill, 1982), pp. 341–59; D. Spring, 'An Outsider's View: Alexis de Tocqueville on Aristocratic Society and Politics in Nineteenth-Century England', *Albion*, xi (1980), pp. 126–31.

4. E. J. Hobsbawm, *The Age of Empire, 1875–1914* (1987), 84–107; N. Stone, *Europe Transformed, 1878–1919* (1983), pp. 42–73.

5. L. Cecil, *The German Diplomatic Service, 1871–1914* (Princeton, 1976), pp. 73–8; K. Demeter, *The German Officer-Corps in Society and State, 1650–1945* (1965), pp.

28–32, 47–58; M. Janowitz, *The Professional Soldier* (Glencoe, Ill., 1960), pp. 93–5.

6. S. Becker, *Nobility and Privilege in Late Imperial Russia* (Dekalb, Ill., 1985), pp. 28–54; D. Higgs, *Nobles in Nineteenth-Century France: The Practice of Inegalitarianism* (1987), pp. 113, 121, 126.

7. M. Raeff, 'The Russian Nobility in the Eighteenth and Nineteenth Centuries: Some Trends and Comparisons', in I. Banac and P. Bushkovitch (eds.), *The Nobility in Russia and Eastern Europe* (New Haven, 1983), pp. 106–18; R. Gibson, 'The French Nobility in the Nineteenth Century – Particularly in the Dordogne', in J. Howorth and P. G. Cerny (eds.), *Elites in France: Origins, Reproduction and Power* (New York, 1981), pp. 26–8; Lord Montagu of Beaulieu, *More Equal Than Others: The Changing Fortunes of the British and European Aristocracies* (1970), pp. 57–60.

8. R. Carr, *Modern Spain, 1875–1980* (1980), pp. 32–3.

9. H. Schissler, 'The *Junkers*: Notes on the Social and Historical Significance of the Agrarian Elite in Prussia', in R. G. Moeller (ed.), *Peasants and Lords in Modern Germany: Recent Studies in Agricultural History* (1986), pp. 24–51; F. L. Carsten, *A History of the Prussian Junkers* (1989), pp. 115–51; L. W. Muncy, *The Junkers in the Prussian Administration Under Wilhelm II, 1888–1914* (1944).

10. A. C. Janos, *The Politics of Backwardness in Hungary, 1825–1945* (Princeton, 1982), pp. 92–118; A. C. Janos, 'The Decline of Oligarchy: Bureaucracy and Mass Politics in the Age of Dualism (1867–1918)', in A. C. Janos and W. B. Slottman (eds.), *Revolution in Perspective: Essays on the Hungarian Soviet Republic of 1919* (1971), pp. 1–60.

11. H. Franklin, 'The Peasant in the Modern World', in J. Blum (ed.), *Our Forgotten Past: Seven Centuries of Life on the Land* (1982), pp. 210–13; H. Seton-Watson, *Eastern Europe Between the Wars, 1918–1941* (1962 edn.), pp. 77–80, 84–7, 123–6; J. Tomasevich, *Peasants, Politics, and Economic Change in Yugoslavia* (1955), pp. 344–82; Montagu of Beaulieu, *More Equal Than Others*, pp. 100–1.

12. S. Andreski, 'Poland', in S. J. Woolf (ed.), *Fascism in Europe* (1981), pp. 171–5, 181.

13. J. Eros, 'Hungary', in Woolf, *Fascism in Europe*, pp. 117–21, 126–9; J. Hoensch, *A History of Modern Hungary, 1867–1986* (1988), pp. 105–18; J. Held, *The Modernization of Agriculture: Rural Transformation in Hungary, 1848–1975* (New York, 1980), pp. 18–19, 37–44.

14. J. Lopreato, *Peasants No More: Social Class and Social Change in an Undeveloped Society* (San Fransisco, 1967), pp. 27–30; F. M. Snowden, *Violence and the Great Estates in the South of Italy* (1986), pp. 177–80, 194, 202.

15. Carsten, *Prussian Junkers*, 152–89; L. W. Muncy, 'The Junkers and the Prussian Administration from 1918 to 1939', *Review of Politics*, IX (1947), pp. 482–501; E. Malefakis, *Agrarian Reform and Peasant Revolution in Spain: Origins of the Civil War* (1970); R. Carr, *Spain, 1809–1938* (1966), pp. 431–2, 612–13; P. Preston, 'Spain', in Woolf, *Fascism in Europe*, pp. 329–42, 350–1.

16. Held, *Modernization of Agriculture*, pp. 46, 51–2, 70–1, 103; A. Sinclair, *The Last of the Best: The Aristocracy of Europe in the Twentieth Century* (1969), pp. 119–25.

17. E. Wiskemann, *Italy Since 1945* (1971), pp. 18–19; Sinclair, *Last of the Best*, pp. 125–36; J. Farquharson, 'Land Reform in the British Zone, 1945–1947', *German History*, VI (1988), pp. 34–56.

18. R. Lacey, *Aristocrats* (1984), pp. 25–6, 29–30, 59–60, 126–8, 177–80, 201–2, 207–9, 211–12.

19. Montagu of Beaulieu, *More Equal Than Others*, pp. 79–81.

20. Montagu of Beaulieu, *More Equal Than Others*, pp. 164–5.

21. T. S. Ashton, *An Economic History of England: The Eighteenth Century* (1955), p. 201.

22. S. Hogg, 'Landed Society and the Conservative Party in the Late Nineteenth and Early Twentieth Centuries', (B.Litt. dissertation, Oxford University, 1972), p. 133.

23. D. Cannadine, 'The Context, Performance and Meaning of Ritual: The British Monarchy and the "Invention of Tradition", c1820–1977', in E. J. Hobsbawm and T. Ranger (eds.), *The Invention of Tradition* (1983), pp. 120–55.

24. For an inadvertently suggestive articulation of this point, see C. Barnett, *Britain and Her Army, 1509–1970: A Military, Political and Social Survey* (1970), p. 479.

25. D. L. Sayers, *Gaudy Night* (1970 edn.),

p. 271; J. Hitchman, *Such a Strange Lady: A Biography of Dorothy L. Sayers* (1975), p. 90.

26. D. Cannadine, 'The Eternal Wimsey', *New Society*, 17 Apr. 1990, pp. 115–16; *The Spectator*, 8 Dec. 1939, pp. 809–10.

INDEX

PHOTOGRAPHIC ACKNOWLEDGEMENTS

The British Library: 3, 5, 6, 8, 21, 23, 28, 107; The National Portrait Gallery, London: 4, 10, 22, 26, 27, 29, 30, 31, 32, 33, 34, 35, 36, 37, 41, 46, 47, 48, 49, 50, 51, 52, 53, 54, 55, 56, 60, 65, 66, 88, 89, 93, 95, 97, 98, 101, 102, 103, 111, 117, 126, 127; National Library of Wales: 7, 9, 14, 25, 38, 61, 64, 67, 73, 77, 78, 80, 83, 84, 85, 86, 87; National Trust Photographic Library: 19, 20; Hulton Picture Company: 43; The Elgar Foundation, Broadheath, Worcester: 58; Courtauld Institute of Art: 59, 112; The Sir Alfred Munnings Art Museum, Dedham (photograph © Christie's): 68; The Griffith Institute, Ashmolean, Oxford: 72; National Motor Museum, Beaulieu: 74, 123; Church House, Westminster: 92; The Devonshire Collection, Chatsworth, reproduced by permission of the Chatsworth Settlement and Trustees (photographs courtesy the Courtauld Institute of Art): 113, 121.